SUPPLEMENT XVI
John James Audubon to Gustaf Sobin

American Writers
A Collection of Literary Biographies

JAY PARINI
Editor in Chief

SUPPLEMENT XVI
John James Audubon to Gustaf Sobin

CHARLES SCRIBNER'S SONS

An imprint of Thomson Gale, a part of The Thomson Corporation

Detroit • New York • San Francisco • San Diego • New Haven, Conn. • Waterville, Maine • London • Munich

American Writers, Supplement XVI

Jay Parini, Editor in Chief

Project Editor
Julie Mellors, James E. Person Jr.

Copyeditors
Melissa A. Dobson, Gretchen Gordon, Robert E. Jones, Linda Sanders

Proofreaders
Susan Barnett, Patricia Onorato, Carol Page, Jane Spear

Permission Researchers
Margaret Abendroth, Tracie A. Richardson, Kim Smilay, Julie Van Pelt

Indexer
Katharyn Dunham

Compositor
Gary Leach

Publisher
Frank Menchaca

LIBRARY OF CONGRESS CATALOGING-IN-PUBLICATION DATA

American writers : a collection of literary biographies / Leonard Unger, editor in chief.
p. cm.
The 4-vol. main set consists of 97 of the pamphlets originally published as the University of Minnesota pamphlets on American writers; some have been rev. and updated. The supplements cover writers not included in the original series.
Supplement 2, has editor in chief, A. Walton Litz; Retrospective suppl. 1, c1998, was edited by A. Walton Litz & Molly Weigel; Suppl. 5-7 have as editor-in-chief, Jay Parini. Includes bibliographies and index.
Contents: v. 1. Henry Adams to T.S. Eliot — v. 2. Ralph Waldo Emerson to Carson McCullers — v. 3. Archibald MacLeish to George Santayana — v. 4. Isaac Bashevis Singer to Richard Wright — Supplement[s]: 1, pt. 1. Jane Addams to Sidney Lanier. 1, pt. 2. Vachel Lindsay to Elinor Wylie. 2, pt. 1. W.H. Auden to O. Henry. 2, pt. 2. Robinson Jeffers to Yvor Winters. — 4, pt. 1. Maya Angelou to Linda Hogan. 4, pt. 2. Susan Howe to Gore Vidal — Suppl. 5. Russell Banks to Charles Wright. — Suppl. 6. Don DeLillo to W.D.Snodgrass _ Suppl. 7. Julia Alvarez to Tobias Wolff _ Suppl. 8. T.C. Boyle to August wilson. _ Suppl. 11 Toni Cade Bambara to Richard Yares.
ISBN 0-684-19785-5 (set) — ISBN 0-684-13662-7
1. American literature—History and criticism. 2. American literature—Bio-bibliography. 3. Authors, American—Biography. I. Unger, Leonard. II. Litz, A. Walton. III. Weigel, Molly. IV. Parini, Jay. V. University of Minnesota pamphlets on American writers.

PS129 .A55
810'.9
[B]   73-001759

ISBN: 0-684-31510-6

Printed in the United States of America
10 9 8 7 6 5 4 3 2 1

Acknowledgments

Acknowledgment is gratefully made to those publishers and individuals who have permitted the use of the following material in copyright. Every effort has been made to secure permission to reprint copyrighted material.

RICK BASS Bass, Rick. From *The Watch: Stories*. Norton, 1989. Copyright © 1989 by Rick Bass. All rights reserved. Used by permission of W. W. Norton & Company, Inc./ Bass, Rick. From *The Sky, the Stars, the Wilderness*. Houghton Mifflin Company, 1997. Copyright © 1997 by Rick Bass. Reproduced by permission of Houghton Mifflin Company.

CAROL BLY Bly, Carol. From *Letters from the Country*. Harper & Row, 1981. Copyright © 1981 by Carol Bly. Reproduced by permission of the author./ Bly, Carol. From "Carol Bly (Journal Selections)," in *Ariadne's Thread: A Collection of Contemporary Women's Journals*. Edited by Lyn Lifshin. Harper & Row, 1982. Copyright © 1982 by Carol Bly. Reproduced by permission of the author./ Bly, Carol. From *Backbone: Short Stories*. Milkweed Editions, 1985. Copyright © 1984 by Carol Bly. Reproduced by permission./ Buchwald, Emilie. From *Backbone: Short Stories*. Milkweed Editions, 1985. Copyright 1984 by Carol Bly. Reproduced by permission./ Jackson, Wes. From an Introduction to *Soil and Survival: Land Stewardship and the Future of American Agriculture*. Edited by Joe Paddock, Nancy Paddock, and Carol Bly. Sierra Club Books, 1986. Copyright 1986 by Joe Paddock, Nancy Paddock, and Carol Bly. Reproduced by permission of Sierra Club Books./ Bly, Carol. From a Foreword to *Full Measure: Modern Short Stories on Aging*. Edited by Dorothy Sennett. Graywolf, 1988. Foreword Copyright © 1988 by Carol Bly. All rights reserved. Reproduced by permission of the author./ Bly, Carol. From *Breaking Hard Ground: Stories of the Minnesota Farm Advocates*. Holy Cow! Press, 1990. Copyright © Text 1990 by Dianna Hunter. Copyright © Foreword 1990 by Carol Bly. Reproduced by permission./ *The New York Times Book Review*, v. xcvi, March 31, 1991 for "80 Acres Isn't Enough Personal Space" by Louis B. Jones. Copyright © 1991 by The New York Times Company. Reproduced by permission of the author./ Bly, Carol. From *Changing the Bully Who Rules the World: Reading and Thinking about Ethics*. Milkweed Editions, 1996. Copyright © 1996 by Carol Bly. Reproduced by permission./ Bly, Carol. From *My Lord Bag of Rice: New and Selected Stories*. Milkweed Editions, 2000. Copyright © 2000 text by Carol Bly. Reproduced by permission./ Wolff, Tobias. From *My Lord Bag of Rice: New and Selected Stories*. Milkweed Editions, 2000. Copyright © 2000 text by Carol Bly. Reproduced by permission./ *Georgia Review*, v. 56, 2002. Copyright © 2002 by The University of Georgia. Reproduced by permission.

HAYDEN CARRUTH Carruth, Hayden. From *The Sleeping Beauty*. Copper Canyon Press, 1990. Copyright © 1982 by Hayden Carruth. Reproduced by permission of the publisher./ Carruth, Hayden. From *The Bloomingdale Papers, 1975*. University of Georgia Press, 1975. Copyright © 1975 by Hayden Carruth. Reproduced by permission of the author./ Carruth, Hayden. From *Sonnets*. The Press of Appletree Alley, 1989. Copyright © 1989, 1991, 1992 by Hayden Carruth. Reproduced by permission./ Carruth, Hayden. From "Sex," in *Collected Shorter Poems, 1946-1991*. Copper Canyon Press, 1992. Copyright © 1948, 1950-1966, 1968-1975, 1978, 1983-1986, 1989, 1991, 1992 by Hayden Carruth. Reproduced by permission./ Carruth, Hayden. From "Spring 1967," in *Collected Shorter Poems, 1946-1991*. Copper Canyon Press, 1992. Copyright © 1948, 1950-1966, 1968-1975, 1978, 1983-1986, 1989, 1991, 1992 by Hayden Carruth. Reproduced by permission./ Carruth, Hayden. From *If You Call This Cry a Song*. Countryman Press, 1993. Copyright © 1983, 1984, 1985 by Hayden Carruth. Reproduced by permission of the author./ Carruth, Hayden. From *Nothing for Tigers*. Macmillan, 1965. Copyright 1966, 1968-1975, 1978, 1983-1986, 1989, 1991, 1992 by Hayden Carruth. Reproduced by permission of the author./ Carruth, Hayden. From "Tell Me Again How the White Heron Rises and Flies across the Nacreous River at Twilight toward the Distant Islands," in *Collected Shorter Poems, 1946-1991*. New Directions Publishing, 1989. Copyright 1984, 1985, 1986, 1989 by Hayden Carruth Reproduced by permission of New Directions Publishing Corp./ Carruth, Hayden. From "The Crow and the Heart," in *Collected Shorter Poems, 1946-1991*. Macmillan Press, 1959. Copyright © 1959, 1961, 1964, 1965, 1967, 1978, 1982, 1985, 1992, 1994 by Hayden Carruth. Reproduced by permission of the author./ Carruth, Hayden. From *North Winter*. Prairie Press, 1964. Copyright © 1964, 1965, 1967, 1978, 1982, 1985, 1992, 1994 by Hayden Carruth. Reproduced by permission of the author./ Carruth, Hayden. From *Scrambled Eggs and Whiskey: Poems, 1991-1995*. Copper Canyon Press, 1996. Copyright 1996 by Hayden Carruth. Reproduced by permission./ Carruth, Hayden. From *Doctor Jazz*. Copper Canyon Press, 2001. Copyright © 2001 by Hayden Carruth. Reproduced by permission./ *Parnassus: Poetry in Review*, v. 11, 1983 for "The Odyssey of Hayden Carruth" by R. W. Flint. Copyright © 1983 Poetry in Review Foundation, NY. Reproduced by permission of the publisher and the author./ *The Midwest Quarterly*, v. 39, 1998. Copyright © 1998 by The Midwest Quarterly, Pittsburgh State University. Reproduced by permission.

FRANK CONROY Stevens, Wallace. From *Collected Poems of Wallace Stevens*. Faber & Faber, 1955, Alfred A. Knopf, 1981. Copyright 1923, 1931, 1935-1937, 1942-1952, 1954 by Wallace

List of Subjects

Introduction   *xi*

List of Contributors   *xiii*

JOHN JAMES AUDUBON   1
Susan Carol Hauser

RICK BASS   15
Jason Gray

CAROL BLY   31
Susan Carol Hauser

HAYDEN CARRUTH   45
Brian Henry

FRANK CONROY   63
Bert Almon

REBECCA HARDING DAVIS   79
Tina Parke-Sutherland

THEODOR SEUSS GEISEL   97
Andrew Zawacki

WILLIAM GIBSON   117
Jack Fischel

CHESTER HIMES   135
Stephen F. Soitos

EVA HOFFMAN   147
Bert Almon

GARRISON KEILLOR   165
Charles R. Baker

ANITA LOOS   181
Benjamin Ivry

LEONARD MICHAELS   201
Sanford Pinsker

JAY NEUGEBOREN   217
Sanford Pinsker

GEORGE PLIMPTON   233
Charles R. Baker

FRANCINE PROSE   249
Denise Gess

SCOTT RUSSELL SANDERS   265
Jen Hirt

GUSTAF SOBIN   281
Andrew Zawacki

Cumulative Index   299

Introduction

"He knew everything about literature except how to enjoy," wrote Joseph Heller, wryly, about one of his characters in *Catch-22*. We hope that the eighteen essays in this new supplement of *American Writers* will, in fact, help readers in their quest to enjoy what they read by providing useful information about the lives of individual authors as well as an analysis of their work. A writer, not unlike a reader, undertakes a quest of sorts: a quest for knowledge, a quest for understanding of a particular kind. This can be a challenging quest, of course; but it's also something enjoyable. Literature makes it possible for us, as readers, to make this journey in good company.

American Writers had its origin in a series of monographs that appeared between 1959 and 1972. The *Minnesota Pamphlets on American Writers* were incisively written and informative, treating ninety-seven American writers in a format and style that attracted a devoted following of readers. The series proved invaluable to a generation of students and teachers, who could depend on these reliable and interesting critiques of major figures. The idea of reprinting these essays occurred to Charles Scribner, Jr., an innovative publisher during the middle decades of the twentieth century. The series appeared in four volumes entitled *American Writers: A Collection of Literary Biographies* (1974).

Since then, fifteen supplements have appeared, treating well over two hundred American writers: poets, novelists, playwrights, essayists, and autobiographers. The idea has always been to provide clear, informative essays for the general reader, not the specialist. Although these essays often rise to a high level of craft and critical vision, they are meant to introduce a writer of considerable importance in the history of American literature, and to describe the scope and nature of the career under review. Biographical and historical context is also offered, providing a context for the work itself, and to create a sense of the author's evolving vision.

The writers of these articles are mostly teachers and scholars. Most have published books and articles in their field, and several are writers of poetry or fiction as well as critics. As anyone glancing through this volume will see, our writers are held to the highest standards of prose and sound scholarship. The essays each conclude with a select bibliography intended to direct the reading of those who want to pursue the subject further.

Supplement XVI focuses on contemporary writers of fiction, many of whom have received little sustained attention from critics. For example, Rick Bass, William Gibson, Chester Himes, Eva Hoffman, Garrison Keillor, Leonard Michaels, Jay Neugeboren, Francine Prose, and Gustav Sobin, have been written about in the review pages of newspapers and magazines, and their work has in most cases acquired a substantial following, but their careers have yet to attract significant scholarship. That will certainly follow, but the essays included here constitute a beginning. (Some of these writers included here, including Bass, Hoffman, Prose, and Sobin, cross generic boundaries, writing poetry or nonfiction in addition to novels and stories. In each case, the critic looks at the various genres, as employed by the author, and considers their place in each developing career.)

Two of our most interesting contemporary poets are looked at in detail: Carol Bly and Hayden Carruth. (Gustav Sobin, of course, has written a good deal of fine poetry as well as novels, and his poetry is closely studied here as well.) These poets have been widely anthologized, but the real work of assimilation, of discovering

their true place in the larger traditions of American poetry, has only begun. These essays might be considered a start.

We also examine the work of several important writers in the tradition of nonfiction—one of those widely used terms that never seems quite specific enough. Scott Russell Sanders is a marvelous essayist and autobiographer, with a keen sense of the natural world and fine moral edge. George Plimpton has been a shrewd critic of American popular culture, and a writer of superb memoirs as well as a founding editor of *The Paris Review*. Frank Conroy, who also wrote fiction, has written one of the finest of American autobiographies. In each case, their work is considered in some detail.

A number of classic writers are treated here as well. John James Audubon, of course, was an important naturalist and nature writer in the nineteenth century. Rebecca Harding Davis also wrote during the nineteenth century, although her career spilled over into the early twentieth century as well. She was a pioneer novelist in the tradition of American realism and an important journalist in her day, with a sharp critical edge and a zeal for reform. For various reasons, they have never before been treated in this series, and it is time we looked at them in detail. Another classic author here is Dr. Seuss: Theodor Seuss Geisel. His books for children have delighted generations, and will continue to do so. The essay on his work in this volume will delight his readers, and provide useful insights into his large and diverse career. Anita Loos is also a subject here. She was a major screenwriter, playwright, and novelist, the author of *Gentlemen Prefer Blondes* (1925). Her important career as a writer across several genres has received very little in the way of sustained critical attention, and we hope this essay bring readers back to her excellent work.

The critics writing in this collection represent a catholic range of backgrounds and critical approaches, although the baseline for inclusion was that each essay should be accessible to the non-specialist reader or beginning student. The creation of culture involves the continuous reassessment of major texts produced by its writers, and my belief is that this supplement performs a useful service here, providing substantial introductions to American writers who matter, and it will assist readers in the difficult but rewarding work of close reading.

——JAY PARINI

Contributors

Bert Almon. Professor of English and Film Studies at the University of Alberta. He is the author of *William Humphrey: Destroyer of Myths* (North Texas State University Press, 1998), *This Stubborn Self: Texas Autobiographies* (TCU Press, 2001) and eight collections of poetry. He has published essays on English, American, Canadian, and Australian poets. FRANK CONROY, EVA HOFFMAN

Charles R. Baker. Poet, essayist and short story writer, Charles Baker is a longtime contributor to *American Writers, British Writers,* and *American Writers: Classics.* He is also curator of "Mark Twain: Father of American Literature" at Bridwell Library, Southern Methodist University. He lives in Dallas, Texas and is currently working on his first novel, *Sheer Morning Gladness.* GARRISON KEILLOR, GEORGE PLIMPTON

Jack Fischel. Emeritus Professor of History at Millersville University. He is the author and editor of six books and has written hundreds of articles and book reviews for such periodicals as *Virginia Quarterly Review, The Weekly Standard, The Forward, Congress Monthly, Midstream, Philadelphia Inquirer,* and *Choice.* Dr. Fischel's specialty is American intellectual history and Jewish studies. He is the former editor of *Congress Monthly,* and is presently a Visiting Professor at Messiah College. WILLIAM GIBSON

Denise Gess. Assistant professor of creative writing at Rowan University. She is the author of two novels, *Good Deeds* and *Red Whiskey Blues,* one nonfiction book, *Firestorm At Peshtigo: A Town, Its People and The Deadliest Fire In American History,* and the forthcoming novel, *Second Love.* FRANCINE PROSE

Jason Gray. Author of two volumes of poetry, *Adam & Eve Go to the Zoo* and How to Paint

the Savior Dead). His poems and criticism have appeared in such periodicals as *Poetry, The Kenyon Review, Shenandoah, The Cincinnati Review,* and elsewhere. He holds Master's degrees from Johns Hopkins University and Ohio State University. RICK BASS

Susan Carol Hauser. Her books include *Outside after Dark: New & Selected Poems; You Can Write a Memoir; Wild Rice Cooking: History, Natural History, Harvesting & Lore* (which won a 2001 Minnesota Book Award); *Sugaring: A Maple Syrup Memoir with Instructions; Outwitting Poison Ivy; Outwitting Ticks;* and *Meant to Be Read Out Loud* (which won a 1989 Minnesota Book Award). She has a Master of Fine Arts degree in poetry from Bowling Green State University and is a Professor of English at Bemidji State University. JOHN JAMES AUDUBON, CAROL BLY

Brian Henry. Author of four books of poetry, most recently *Quarantine* (Ahsahta, 2006). He has co–edited the international journal *Verse* since 1995, and he co–edited *The Verse Book of Interviews* (Verse Press, 2005). His criticism has appeared in numerous publications around the world, including *The New York Times Book Review, Times Literary Supplement,* and *Virginia Quarterly Review.* He is Associate Professor of English and Creative Writing at the University of Richmond. HAYDEN CARRUTH

Jennifer Hirt. Nonfiction writer from Ohio. She has taught at the University of Idaho, where she earned her M.F.A., and Iowa State University, where she completed her M.A. In 2004 she was the writer-in-residence at Bernheim Arboretum in Kentucky. A recipient of a 2003 Ohioana library grant for her nonfiction work, she is currently a freelance writer and editor. SCOTT RUSSELL SANDERS

Benjamin Ivry. Author of biographies of Arthur Rimbaud (Absolute Press), Francis Poulenc (Phaidon), and Maurice Ravel (Welcome Rain), as well as a poetry collection, *Paradise for the Portuguese Queen* (Orchises). He has translated many books from the French, by such authors as André Gide, Jules Verne, and Balthus. ANITA LOOS

Tina Parke-Sutherland. She has an MFA in creative writing from the University of Alaska, Fairbanks, and a Ph.D. in literature from the University of Michigan. She is a professor of English and creative writing and Dean of Liberal Arts at Stephens College, in Columbia, Missouri. She served as Fulbright Professor of American Studies in Finland in 1998. She publishes poetry and non-fiction as well as literary scholarship. REBECCA HARDING DAVIS

Sanford Pinsker. Shadek Professor of Humanities at Franklin and Marshall College. He is the author of numerous books, articles, and reviews, including *The Schlemiel as Metaphor* and *Bearing the Bad News.* He has been named the U.S. literature editor for a revised version of the *Encyclopedia Judaica.* LEONARD MICHAELS, JAY NEUGEBOREN

Stephen F. Soitos. Author of *The Blues Detective: A Study of African–American Detective Fiction.* He has published many essays and articles on African American authors and artists including a complete survey of African American art from slavery to contemporary times. An author, artist and teacher he can be contacted at StephenSoitosyahoo.com or Soitos.com. CHESTER HIMES

Andrew Zawacki. Author of two poetry books, *Anabranch* (Wesleyan, 2004) and *By Reason of Breakings* (Georgia, 2002), as well as a chapbook, *Masquerade* (Vagabond, 2001). He is a coeditor of *Verse* and, as a fellow of the Slovenian Writers' Association, edited *Afterwards: Slovenian Writing 1945-1995* (White Pine, 1999). His criticism has appeared in *New German Critique,* the *Boston Review, Antioch Review, Times Literary Supplement, Talisman,* and elsewhere. He is a doctoral candidate in Social Thought at the University of Chicago. THEODOR SEUSS GEISEL, GUSTAF SOBIN

SUPPLEMENT XVI
John James Audubon to Gustaf Sobin

JOHN JAMES AUDUBON

(1785–1851)

Susan Carol Hauser

JOHN JAMES AUDUBON was born in Cayes, Saint Domingue, now Haiti, on April 26, 1785, to Jean Audubon and Jeanne Rabin (Rabine), French citizens who met on their passage from France to Saint Domingue in 1783. Jean Audubon, who had a wife in France, was returning to his sugar plantation in the West Indies; Rabin was traveling with a family who employed her as a chambermaid. John James was known as Jean Rabin, a Creole (a child of European parentage born in the West Indies). Being illegitimate, he was unable to take his father's name or be baptized into the Church.

John James's mother died when he was seven months old, from infection associated with the birth, and Jean Rabin was cared for by Jean Audubon's mistress of several years, Catherine "Sanitte" Bouffard, the mixed-blood daughter of another plantation owner. She lived with Audubon on his estate, serving as his *ménagère,* or housekeeper. Some early biographies and articles on Audubon portray him as a "man of color" under the mistaken idea that Bouffard was his mother. Bouffard and Jean Audubon had two daughters. The elder daughter, Marie-Madeleine Bouffard, was killed in 1792 at age sixteen during a slave insurrection on Saint Domingue. Rose Bennitte Bouffard was born in 1787, when John James was two years old.

Audubon was born into volatile times. The American Revolution (1775–1783), freeing the new country from British rule, was barely ended; the French Revolution (1789–1799), an overthrow of the reigning absolute monarchy, was brewing; and the insurrection on Saint Domingue, where slaves greatly outnumbered the French plantation families, was imminent. In 1788, with violence escalating against European landholders, Audubon sent John James to France. He was three years old, and was received in Nantes by his stepmother, Anne Moynet. In 1789 his father traveled to the United States, where he purchased land in Pennsylvania. He returned briefly to Saint Domingue, but the slave rebellion was too far advanced to resist, and in 1790 he sold his island interests and returned to France; he did not visit Saint Domingue again. In 1791 he arranged for his and Sanitte's daughter Rose to join him and her half-brother in France. Rose was fair-skinned and, to conceal her mixed-blood heritage, traveled as Rose Rabin, even though she was born two years after Jeanne Rabin died.

Anne Moynet and Jean Audubon had married in 1772. Jean Audubon began a maritime career as a cabin boy at age twelve, and eventually captained his own fishing and cargo vessels. Around 1774 he purchased the sugar plantation in Saint Domingue, and spent considerable time there. Anne Moynet was accustomed to his long absences, and was cognizant and accepting of his relations with other women in Saint Domingue. He and Anne had no children of their own, and when John James and Rose immigrated to France she heartily welcomed them into her arms. They grew up in a loving and indulgent home in Nantes and at La Gerbetière, Jean Audubon's country estate in nearby Couëron. The couple legally adopted the children in 1794, and John James was baptized Jean-Jacques Fougère Audubon.

John James's boyhood in France was idyllic. With his father absent much of the time, his stepmother allowed him to follow his will, which led him to the woods and fields of his home in western France, in the Loire River valley. In an autobiographical essay, "Myself," written in 1835 for his sons, he recollected:

My father being mostly absent on duty, my mother suffered me to do much as I pleased; it was therefore not to be wondered at that, instead of ap-

plying closely to my studies, I preferred associating with boys of my own age and disposition, who were more fond of going in search of birds' nests, fishing, or shooting, than of better studies. Thus almost every day, instead of going to school when I ought to have gone, I usually made for the fields, where I spent the day; my little basket went with me, filled with good eatables, and when I returned home, during either winter or summer, it was replenished with what I called curiosities, such as birds' nests, birds' eggs, curious lichens, flowers of all sorts, and even pebbles gathered along the shore of some rivulet. (*Writings and Drawings* 769)

Audubon's father did not approve of such extensive leisure, and when he discovered that young John James, at the age of eleven, was inept at his studies and at his music lessons, he made several efforts to convert his son to the benefits of a more rigorous lifestyle, including sending him for naval training in 1796. Although John James eventually became a good violinist and enjoyed playing music all his life, by the time he was in his middle teens it was clear that he was not fit to follow his father into maritime or military service, as he recalled in "Myself":

> During all these years there existed within me a tendency to follow Nature in her walks. Perhaps not an hour of leisure was spent elsewhere than in woods and fields, and to examine either the eggs, nest, young, or parents of any species of birds constituted my delight. It was about this period that I commenced a series of drawings of the birds of France, which I continued until I had upward of two hundred drawings, all bad enough, my dear sons, yet they were representations of birds, and I felt pleased with them. (*Writings and Drawings* 772)

By 1803, when John James was eighteen, the French general Napoleon Bonaparte was conscripting for his armies, which would eventually gain control over most of western and central Europe before Napoleon's defeat at Waterloo in 1815. Audubon's father did not want his son to serve, and John James was sent to America to manage Mill Grove, Jean Audubon's estate in Pennsylvania . His passport gave his name as John James, and he was listed as a "native of Louisiana" (*Writings and Drawings* 862), in order to conceal the circumstances of his birth.

AMERICA

In 1803, fifteen years after his father rescued him from Saint Dominique, Audubon arrived in the United States. The next year, 1804, Haiti gained independence from France. 1804 also was the year Meriwether Lewis and William Clark set out on their three-year expedition from St. Louis to the mouth of the Columbia River; the United States purchased, from France, the Louisiana Territory, which extended from the Mississippi River to the Rocky Mountains between the Gulf of Mexico and the current border between the United States and Canada; and Ohio entered the Union. It was a time of development and change for the United States and for Audubon.

His first adventure occurred almost immediately after he disembarked his ship in New York City: he contracted a life-threatening illness, possibly yellow fever, which was rampant in the city. The ship's captain arranged for him to be cared for at a Quaker boardinghouse outside Philadelphia. There he received not only excellent and successful care, but also lessons in English, which he did not speak prior to coming to America and which became his primary language. The Quaker "thee" and "thou" mannerisms he acquired at that time stayed with him throughout his life. When he was well enough to travel, he moved to the home of another Quaker family, closer to Mill Grove, and then to the home of William Thomas and his family, the Quaker tenants at Mill Grove. Audubon had at last arrived at his new home, northwest of Philadelphia and near Valley Forge on the Perkiomen River.

In his first months at Mill Grove, Audubon resumed the lifestyle of his childhood, adding adult pleasures, as he related in "Myself": "Hunting, fishing, drawing, and music occupied my every moment; cares I knew not, and cared naught about them. I purchased excellent and beautiful horses, visited all such neighbors as I found congenial spirits, and was as happy as happy could be" (*Writings and Drawings* 774). He received a small income from his tenants and had no need to work. He was congenial and gregarious, good company for socializing and

hunting, and was well-received in the neighborhood.

Audubon did not, however, find "congenial spirits" among the Bakewells, an English family who had purchased and settled in to a nearby estate, Fatland Ford, shortly after Audubon arrived at Mill Grove. The English had twice imprisoned his father during Jean Audubon's maritime career, and the youthful Audubon held a grudge against the British, even though his father cautioned him against it. When William Bakewell called at Audubon's home, Audubon did not receive him and did not return the call. "Now this gentleman was an Englishman," Audubon wrote, "and I such a foolish boy that, entertaining the greatest prejudices against all of his nationality, I did not return his visit for many weeks, which was as absurd as it was ungentlemanly and impolite" (*Writings and Drawings* 774). Early in 1804, while out hunting, Audubon encountered Bakewell, also in pursuit of game. They had a conversation, and Audubon was charmed by the polite and dignified gentleman, and "I admired the beauty of his well-trained dogs, and, apologizing for my discourtesy, finally promised to call upon him and his family" (*Writings and Drawings* 775).

When Audubon called a short time later, he was received by Lucy Bakewell, nearly seventeen years old and the Bakewells' eldest daughter. They were immediately attracted to each other and became close friends. Their friendship culminated in their lifelong marriage on April 5, 1808.

During the four years between their meeting and their nuptials, Audubon accepted the mantle of adulthood and set about to earn an income that he might wed the woman he forever called his dearest friend. Mill Grove was managed in part by an agent of Jean Audubon's, Francis Dacosta; John James and Dacosta did not get along, with John James harboring the suspicion that Dacosta was trying to gain control of the estate. In March 1805 John James traveled to France to convince his father of Dacosta's treachery. While there, he witnessed the marriage, on December 16, 1805, of his half-sister Rose Benitte to Gabriel-Loyen Du Puigaudeau. Because he was still in danger of being conscripted into Napoleon's army, he spent most of his year in France confined to his father's estate, where he practiced taxidermy and continued to draw birds. When he returned to America in May 1806, he had his father's support for dealing with Dacosta, and a new business partner, Ferdinand Rozier, the son of a family friend.

Rozier and Audubon lived in New York for some time; Audubon apprenticed at a Bakewell business establishment, returning to Mill Grove when possible to visit Lucy. A deal was struck with Dacosta for sale of portions of Mill Grove, the last of the holdings sold to him in 1810. In 1807 Rozier and Audubon moved to Louisville, Kentucky, and opened a general store. In 1808, after their marriage at Fatland Ford, Audubon and Lucy settled in Louisville. Their first child, Victor Gifford, was born there on June 12, 1809. Audubon described the halcyon nature of their days: "Our pleasures were those of young people not long married, and full of life and merriment; a single smile from our infant was, I assure you, more valued by us than all the treasures of a modern Croesus would have been" (quoted in Rhodes 70).

Commerce during these years of frontier settlement was unpredictable, and the store in Louisville eventually failed. Rozier blamed the loss on Audubon's inattention to business. Indeed, Audubon preferred to be out in the woods, observing, drawing, and harvesting birds, causing Lucy to remark that every bird was her rival. As he had at Mill Grove, Audubon collected nests, eggs, and skins, and continued to work at his drawings, though at the time his ambition to render on paper all of the birds of America had not yet taken root in his heart. Eventually he and Rozier parted ways. Rozier, who had not mastered English as Audubon had, settled in French-dominant Sainte Geneviève, Missouri. The Audubons settled in Henderson, Missouri, where Rozier and Audubon had moved the store in 1810.

The Audubons lived in Henderson for nine years. In 1811 the Bakewell family and the Audubons became business partners and for a while the firm thrived. A branch was opened in New Orleans under the supervision of Lucy's brother

Thomas. This failed in 1812, in part because of President Thomas Jefferson's 1807 embargo on imports that preceded the War of 1812.

In November 1811, the small family, Lucy, John James, and two-year-old Victor Gifford, traveled by horseback to Fatland Ford to spend the winter with Lucy's family. "Gifford rode before his Papa all the way," Lucy reported in a letter to a cousin. "Now the difficulties and fatigue are over I can scarcely realize that I have rode on horseback nearly eight hundred miles" (quoted in Rhodes 91). They passed "some cultivated farms which diversify the scene a little [but the] chief part of the road is through thick woods, where the sun scarcely ever penetrates" (quoted in Rhodes 91). The trip, though rigorous, was apparently preferable to the miserable coach ride Lucy and Audubon endured on their move to Louisville in 1908, the coach often traveling so slowly over unimproved roads that the passengers walked ahead rather than suffer the jouncing of the wheels over rocks and into ruts.

In December 1811, while they were at Fatland Ford, Audubon sought out the Scottish ornithologist Alexander Wilson, then residing in Philadelphia. They had first met in Louisville in 1810, Wilson seeking subscriptions for his collection, *American Ornithology*. Wilson had heard of Audubon's work from the Bakewells, and the artists showed their work to each other. Both were surprised to discover that Audubon's art was superior to that of Wilson's. At the time, Audubon still had no thought of producing a definitive collection of American bird portraits, nor of publishing his work. The men spent time together in the woods, observing and shooting birds.

Their second meeting, in Philadelphia, was less congenial and they did not see each other again, though Audubon appears to have referenced Wilson's work in the development of his own, and it is likely that Wilson's work inspired Audubon's eventual ambition.

In July 1812, before taking his family back to Henderson, Audubon again traveled to Philadelphia, where he was granted citizenship on July 3, a process he had begun in 1806. The Audubons then returned home to Henderson, Lucy five

months pregnant. Their second son, John Woodhouse, was born there on November 30, 1812.

In 1813, with the Henderson store doing well, the Audubons moved out of shared lodgings into their own home next to the store. For the first time since her marriage three years earlier, Lucy was able to use her own furniture, dishes, and linens, most of them from Fatland Ford. The homestead included four acres of orchard and meadow, well populated by the Audubons' many animals and pets and utilized for gardens. In December 1815 a daughter, Lucy, was born. Writing later to Victor about this period in their life, Audubon said "this place saw my best days, my happiest, my wife having blessed me with your brother Woodhouse and a sweet daughter. I calculated to live and die in comfort. Our business was good [and] of course we agreed. But I was intended to meet many events of a disagreeable nature" (quoted in Rhodes 122).

The events included the death of two-year-old Lucy in 1817, of a birth disorder, probably hydrocephalus, an abnormality of the passages in the brain. This was followed by the news of the death of John James's father, in France, in February 1818.

The success of the business waned as quickly as it rose, eroded by the vagaries of the times and the Panic of 1819, which resulted in bank failures and real estate foreclosures, and was exacerbated, at least in part, by Audubon's less than apt business instincts. In an effort to reverse his failing fortunes, Audubon borrowed heavily from friends and family, and with partners planned and built a wood and grist mill in Henderson, and invested in a steamboat. He hoped these ventures would be his salvation, but in the end they were his demise. By the summer of 1819, he was forced to sell all of his holdings, including the house and its contents. Lucy and the children were able to remain in the house, and Audubon traveled to New Orleans and to Louisville, still trying to remedy their situation. In Louisville he was arrested briefly for his debts. His release was arranged by friends and he filed for bankruptcy. This should have protected him from future actions against him, but he was

harassed for the debts as late as 1831, in Philadelphia.

Audubon was back with his family in Henderson in the fall of 1819 when their daughter Rose (Rosa) was born. Further tragedy befell them early in 1820 when both Lucy and infant Rose fell desperately ill with fever. Lucy recovered, but Rose did not, and the family grieved a second time: "How I have dwelt on her lovely features when sucking the nutritious food from her dear mother," Audubon wrote. "Yet she was torn away from us when only seven months old" (quoted in Rhodes 147). Lucy later wrote that she hoped her girls were with "their grandmother in happier regions" (quoted in DeLatte 103).

For the next six years, the Audubons lived an itinerant life, often separated and almost constantly shadowed by poverty, even though Audubon sometimes made a satisfactory living drawing portraits. In an age before photography, his work was quickly recognized as superior, but demand even in cities was limited, and he had to move from place to place to generate new commissions. For a while he worked as a taxidermist at the Western Museum in Cincinnati, but the struggling institution was not able to pay him as promised. Economic times were uncertain, and Audubon often undertook and completed major art projects for which he was never paid, his only recompense room and board for the duration of the work. It was during this time, however, that the dream of *The Birds of America* came to be.

THE BIRDS OF AMERICA (1827-1838)

Throughout their trials, the Audubons' marriage held steady. While family and friends complained that Audubon spent too much time in the woods and at his drawing, Lucy, who had always called him "La Forest," encouraged it, even though it meant she frequently provided the family's income. In "Myself," Audubon described the role the woods played in his life:

One of the most extraordinary things among all these adverse circumstances was that I never for a day gave up listening to the songs of our birds, or watching their peculiar habits, or delineating them

in the best way that I could; nay, during my deepest troubles I frequently would wrench myself from the persons around me, and retire to some secluded part of our noble forests. (*Writings and Drawings* 794).

In the spring of 1820, after the massive failure of their businesses in 1819, Lucy and John James, then in Cincinnati, made a decision that changed the course of their lives, though it would not change their economic circumstances for a long time: the art that Audubon had turned to all of his life for satisfaction and comfort, and recently for income, would be called upon to redeem the family's financial security and their deeply tainted reputation. Audubon would travel as necessary to complete his drawings of the birds of America. Lucy and the boys stayed in Cincinnati at first, but later joined Audubon in Louisiana, where he taught art, music, and dance, and where Lucy took a job as a teacher for elite plantation children, a job that gave her the economic security that she had both gained and lost in Henderson.

Although the Audubons continued to live in or near New Orleans, Audubon traveled frequently and worked on his grand project. His intent was not to merely represent the birds in a simplistic or scientific way; it was to render " *nature as it existed. . . .* My wish to impart truths has been my guide in every instance; —all the observations respecting them are my own" (*Writings and Drawings* 754, 757). Most nature art of the time was drawn from stuffed specimens and was more concerned with scientific attributes than with a larger understanding of the natural world. Audubon took pride in working directly from nature, from live birds or ones that he himself had recently taken. He recognized the value of having stuffed birds in museums: they could be used to instruct and to verify. However, "in forming works entirely with a view to distinguish the true from the false, nature *must* be seen first alive, and well studied, before attempts are made at representing it" (*Writings and Drawings* 756).

Audubon's art departed from standard practice in several ways: he drew his birds to life size, included female and immature birds as well as male, and concentrated as much on the background in the drawings as on the birds themselves. He desired to show his subjects as

they appeared in the woods and fields, in relation to their environment and to each other: "My plan was then to form sketches in my *mind's eye,* each representing, if possible, each family as if employed in their most constant and natural avocations, and to complete those family pictures as chance might bring perfect specimens" (*Writings and Drawings* 754). Nearly two hundred years later, the manifestation of this vision in his art is one of the primary reasons that *The Birds of America* is recognized as a work of genius.

Audubon was an autodidact. He had little formal education, and almost none in drawing and art, yet he improved his style dramatically as his collection grew over the years. Although he observed his subjects in nature, he needed to have them at hand for finer work and had no compunction about killing birds as necessary to his cause. He was frustrated, however, by the lifeless shapes. While still at Mill Grove, and after much trial, he devised a method for posing the birds in active positions, which he said came to him in a dream: "I not unfrequently dreamt that I had made a New discovery, and long before day one morning I leaped out of bed fully persuaded that I had obtained my object" (*Writings and Drawings* 760).

Though it was still dark, Audubon dressed and rode the five miles to Norristown to purchase wire for his project. He returned home and went out and shot a bird, then tested his method: "I pierced the body of the Fishing bird and fixed it on the board—another Wire passed above his upper Mandible was made to hold the head in a pretty fair attitude, Smaller Skewers fixed the feet according to my notions, and even common pins came to my assistance in the placing [of] the legs and feet.—the last Wire proved a delightful elevator to the Bird's Tail and at Last there Stood before me the real Mankin of a Kings Fisher!" (*Writings and Drawings* 761)

Throughout the years, Audubon worked to perfect his drawing, and when he and Lucy reviewed his collection in New Orleans in 1821, they agreed that he needed to rework the birds from the earlier period. Audubon did this, all the while adding new birds to his collection.

In March 1824 Audubon took his burgeoning portfolio to Philadelphia to solicit its publication. Philadelphia was the center of science and knowledge for the still-young United States, but Audubon's lack of formal training hindered his reception in scientific and academic circles. His presentation of birds in their habitats and family groups was sometimes interpreted as subjective and unscientific and pejoratively labeled as anthropomorphic. He did have small successes while there: he was commissioned to draw an engraving for a New Jersey bank note, he published two papers in the *Annals* of the Lyceum of Natural History, and he was elected to membership in that august organization. However, he did not receive the endorsement of the Academy of Natural Sciences, in part because of the affiliation of some of its members with Alexander Wilson and his competing *American Ornithology.* He reported in a letter to a friend that he was better received in New York, but still failed to acquire subscriptions or a publisher for his work.

Audubon returned to Louisiana in the fall of 1824 without prospects, working as a portraitist to pay his steamboat passage, and for the next two years he and Lucy worked and saved money for Audubon's trip to England where he would seek a publisher. Audubon's efforts included learning oil painting so that he could produce what he called "potboilers," oil landscapes, which were popular at the time and sold well. On May 27, 1826, he departed from New Orleans aboard the *Delos* and arrived in Liverpool, England, on July 21. He was forty-one years old and had 240 drawings in his portfolio. The completed *Birds of America* contains 435 plates representing 497 species and 1,065 figures.

THE AMERICAN WOODSMAN

Audubon was a handsome and athletic man, about five feet nine inches tall, and slender. He could sing, dance, play violin and flute, and hunt and fence. He wore his naturally wavy chestnut-brown hair at shoulder length, although that was not the prevailing style, and dressed in loose-fitting clothes of the woods. When he traveled to

England and then to France, he did not change his appearance. He knew that the people of both countries were fascinated by the wild new country across the ocean, and he became known in Europe as the American Woodsman.

Although he knowingly took advantage of this persona, it was not a false one. Audubon had often lived in the woods, hunting and foraging for food. He had an enduring constitution and did not hesitate to walk hundreds of miles from one destination to the next. He had traded his hunting skills for passage on riverboats, providing crew and passengers with meat, and was unafraid of trekking into unknown territory.

But he was also a man of culture and knew how to hold forth in the drawing room. His only weakness was in scientific training, and instead of trying to conceal his intellectual deficits, he constantly studied to improve his knowledge. When he arrived in London he carried letters of introduction from American men of letters who recognized the value of his work and who valued him as a friend. As he presented the letters and his work in artistic, scientific, and academic circles, he was quickly welcomed and accepted. He met the Scottish writer Sir Walter Scott and other prominent men, and by February 1827 he had exhibited his work at the Royal Institutions in Liverpool, Manchester, and Edinburgh. Some scientists, including Robert Jameson, Professor of Natural History, University of Edinburgh, and ornithologists William Jardine and Prideaux John Selby, even took art lessons from Audubon.

In his first six months in England, Audubon received much public attention, which bolstered his hopes and also brought him to an engraver, W. H. Lizars of Edinburgh. Lizars had engraved only ten of the prints when his workers went on strike, and he advised Audubon to seek another publisher. The work was soon taken on by the London firm R. Havel and Son. The life-size art required publication in four volumes of "double elephant" folios, about two feet in height, and took eleven years to complete, from 1827 to 1838. The work was republished in 1839 in New York in a royal octavo, reduced-size edition of seven volumes, which outsold all previous natural history books.

While the prints were engraved and the coloring processes perfected, Audubon began selling subscriptions to the series, first in England and then in France. He also continued to publish in scientific journals, and resumed painting landscapes to provide for his living expenses. In 1829 he returned to the United States to bring Lucy to England. Their three-year separation had been difficult for them, yet she refused to give up her secure teaching position to join her husband in England until she was certain that Audubon could support her. The boys still lived fairly close to Lucy, Victor Gifford doing well in business and John Woodhouse becoming a writer and artist in his own right. Both sons would eventually join the Audubon enterprise, Gifford living in England for a time to manage Audubon's affairs there and Woodhouse traveling and drawing with his father.

Audubon spent nearly a year in the United States before returning to London with Lucy in April 1830. In the interim he continued to travel and draw new birds, determined to make *The Birds of America* the definitive American ornithological collection. When the first forty-nine plates were released in America, the *American Journal of Science and Arts* called them "the most magnificent work of its kind ever executed in any country" (*Writings and Drawings* 866). Audubon was feted as he had been in England and France, he dined at the White House with President Andrew Jackson, and his income was finally secure.

ORNITHOLOGICAL BIOGRAPHY (1831-1839)

During his visits abroad, Audubon came to understand how much interest the French and English had in the minutiae of American life and he began work on a prose companion to *The Birds of America*. He called it *Ornithological Biography; or, An Account of the Habits of the Birds of the United States of America, and Interspersed with Delineations of American Scenery and Manners*. The five-volumes were published in Edinburgh and Philadelphia from 1831 to 1839.

The *Ornithological Biography* was started in Edinburgh with the aid of Lucy, who served as

copyist, and in collaboration with William MacGillivray, a Scottish naturalist and professor of comparative anatomy at Edinburgh University. Audubon wanted the *Ornithological Biography* to be scientifically sound as well as to present his firsthand knowledge of America's birds, and MacGillivray edited the manuscript for scientific accuracy and added anatomical descriptions and illustrations. Audubon approached the task with characteristic zeal:

> Writing now became the order of the day. I sat at it as soon as I awoke in the morning and continued the whole long day, and so full was my mind of birds and their habits that in my sleep I continually dreamed of birds. I found Mr. MacGillivray equally industrious, for although he did not rise so early in the morning as I did, he wrote much later at night. . . . And so the manuscripts went on increasing in bulk like the rising of a stream after abundant rains, and before three months had passed the first volume was finished. Meanwhile [Lucy] copied it all to send to America to secure the copyright there. (Quoted in Rhodes 346)

Audubon's bird biographies amply portray his excitement about nature. Of the white-headed eagle (bald eagle) he writes:

> To give you, kind reader, some idea of the nature of this bird, permit me to place you on the Mississippi, on which you may float gently along, while approaching winter brings millions of water-fowl on whistling wings, from the countries of the north, to seek a milder climate in which to sojourn for a season. The Eagle is seen perched, in an erect attitude, on the highest summit of the tallest tree by the margin of the broad stream. His glistening but stern eye looks over the vast expanse. He listens attentively to every sound that comes to his quick ear from afar, glancing now and then on the earth beneath, lest even the light tread of the fawn may pass unheard.

Audubon describes the eagle's mate, then goes on to a portrayal of his pursuit of a hapless, passing swan:

> Now is the moment to witness the display of the Eagle's powers. He glides through the air like a falling star, and, like a flash of lightning, comes upon the timorous quarry, which now, in agony and despair, seeks, by various manoeuvres, to elude the grasp of his cruel talons. It mounts, doubles, and willingly would plunge into the stream, were it not prevented by the Eagle, which, long possessed of the knowledge that by such a stratagem the Swan might escape him, forces it to remain in the air by attempting to strike it with his talons from beneath.

The eagle wins the struggle, and Audubon brings his anthropomorphic vision into full play:

> It is then, reader, that you may see the cruel spirit of this dreaded enemy of the feathered race, whilst, exulting over his prey, he for the first time breathes at ease. He presses down his powerful feet, and drives his sharp claws deeper than ever into the heart of the dying Swan. He shrieks with delight, as he feels the last convulsions of his prey. . . . The female has watched every movement of her mate; and if she did not assist him in capturing the Swan, it was not from want of will, but merely that she felt full assurance that the power and courage of her lord were quite sufficient for the deed. She now sails to the spot where he eagerly awaits her, and when she has arrived, they together turn the breast of the luckless Swan upwards, and gorge themselves with gore. (*Writings and Drawings* 239-240)

In 1851, a review in *International Magazine* by Rufus Griswold expressed admiration for the *Ornithological Biography:* "Some of his written pictures of birds, so graceful, clearly defined, and brilliantly colored, are scarcely inferior to the productions of his pencil. His powers of general description are not less remarkable. The waters seem to dance to his words as the music, and the lights and shades of his landscapes show the practiced hand of a master" (469).

The sixty "Delineations of American Scenery and Manners" referenced in the title of the *Ornithological Biography* are written with equal verve and the delight of a practiced storyteller. As history took his readers further away from Audubon's time, they became more and more in awe of his accomplishments. As noted in a 1940 commentary, Audubon

> had the advantage of being a foreigner. . . . he took nothing for granted, and in the perspective of a more mature culture, all things American struck him as fresh. He had the further advantage that he was a genius, a genius of art at that, so that to

observe, to depict what he saw, was habitual and instinctive. . . . He wrote to sell, and did sell. . . . while [James Fenimore] Cooper went to England while he wrote *The Prairie* . . . Audubon was *on* the prairies. That where [Ralph Waldo] Emerson knew his Carlyle, Audubon knew his Mississippi squatters, that while [Henry David] Thoreau was traveling around Concord, Audubon was traveling around North America. While [Francis] Parkman was writing history, Audubon was making and witnessing it" (quoted in *Audubon's America,* 3-4).

The period during which Audubon sought publication for and completed *The Birds of America,* from about 1820, when he and Lucy decided to make it his life's work, to 1839, when the publication of the *Ornithological Biography* was complete, was a relatively quiet period in U.S. history. The conflicts with the British were ended; the Civil War (1861-1865) was in the future. Transcendentalism, a literary and philosophical movement, was nascent. This movement, associated with Emerson, Thoreau, and Margaret Fuller, and others, promoted a belief that an ideal spiritual reality is available to humans through intuition, rather than through science and knowledge, as was commonly promoted by the Christian Church.

Although there is no evidence that Audubon knew of this movement, he did, perhaps, live it in spirit: he came to know America's birds through experience and firsthand study, not through reading and observation of museum samples. And from his self-gained knowledge and instinctual motivation, he drew spiritual comfort: "Many a time, at the sound of the wood-thrush's melodies have I fallen on my knees, and there prayed earnestly to our God. This never failed to bring me the most valuable of thoughts and always comfort, and, strange as it may seem to you, it was often necessary for me to exert my will, and compel myself to return to my fellow-beings" (*Writings and Drawings* 794). In this sense, Audubon was a man of his times.

Audubon's portrayals of life in the "Episodes," as he called the "Delineations," are as vivid as his visual and written depictions of the birds. In one of the most famous of the essays, "The Prairie," he presents pictures of the landscape and of some of the characters inhabiting it:

On my return from the Upper Mississippi, I found myself obliged to cross one of the wide Prairies, which, in that portion of the United States, vary the appearance of the country. The weather was fine, all around me was as fresh and blooming as if it had just issued from the bosom of nature. My napsack, my gun, and my dog, were all I had for baggage and company. But, although well moccassined, I moved slowly along, attracted by the brilliancy of the flowers, and the gambols of the fawns around their dams, to all appearance as thoughtless of danger as I felt myself.

He later finds what he believes to be refuge from the night in the cabin of a stranger, whose light he can see from the path:

I discovered by its glare that it was from the hearth of a small log cabin, and that a tall figure passed and repassed between it and me, as if busily engaged in household arrangements.

I reached the spot, and presenting myself at the door, asked the tall figure, which proved to be a woman, if I might take shelter under her roof for the night. Her voice was gruff, and her attire negligently thrown about her. She answered in the affirmative. I walked in, took a wooden stool, and quietly seated myself by the fire.

As Audubon prepared himself for bed he revealed to the woman that he had a fine watch, with which she became obsessed. He thought nothing of it, however, until after he had settled for sleep onto a pile of bear and buffalo hides:

A short time had elapsed, when some voices were heard, and from the corner of my eyes I saw two athletic youths making their entrance, bearing a dead stag on a pole. They disposed of their burden, and asking for whisky, helped themselves freely to it. . . . The mother—for she proved to be, bade them speak less loudly, made mention of my watch, and took them to a corner, where a conversation took place, the purport of which it required little shrewdness in me to guess. I tapped my dog gently. He moved his tail, and with indescribable pleasure I saw his fine eyes alternately fixed on me and raised towards the trio in the corner. I felt that he perceived danger in my situation. (*Writings and Drawings* 524-528).

Audubon is saved from assault by the sudden appearance of two more travelers who fortuitously enter the cabin and readily help overpower the "incarnate fiend" and her sons. In the morning, they administer frontier justice by burning down the shack and all of its belongings. Audubon notes that such events were unusual: "During upwards of twenty-five years, when my wanderings extended to all parts of our country, this was the only time at which my life was in danger from my fellow creatures." (*Writings and Drawings* 524-528)

A FAMILY ENTERPRISE

With the success of *The Birds of America* in the United States and abroad, John James and Lucy Audubon returned permanently to the United States in 1839 with a satisfactory income and a restored reputation. Their sons John Woodhouse and Victor Gifford were now engaged in Audubon's publishing adventures, Victor Gifford contributing as a business manager—"my Right Arm and hand in every thing connected with my Publication" (*Writings and Drawings* 867)—and John Woodhouse as an artist and writer. John Woodhouse would eventually become a collaborator of his father's, and after John James's death became a travel writer in his own right.

While *The Birds of America* was being engraved and printed in England, the Audubons returned to the United States and John James traveled through the South, and to the Florida Keys, Houston, Texas, and Labrador, finishing his drawings of birds in those areas which would be added to the collected prints. In 1831, in Charleston, South Carolina, he met John Bachman, a minister and naturalist. The two became close friends, and the families intertwined when Audubon's sons married Bachman daughters. In 1840, when Audubon conceived his next great project, published in five volumes as *The Viviparous Quadrupeds of North America* in 1845, 1846, and 1848, Bachman agreed to write the text to accompany Audubon's drawings.

Audubon entered the new project with his usual intentions, but at age fifty-five his body was not as willing as it had been to withstand the rigors of frontier travel. In his 1843 journal of an eight-month journey on the Missouri River, seeking new species to draw, he frequently commented on his aging: "Our captain just sent out four hunters this evening who are to hunt early to-morrow morning, and will meet the boat some distance above; . . . How I wish I were twenty-five years younger! I should like such a tramp greatly; but I do not think it prudent now for me to sleep on the ground when I can help it, while it is so damp" (*Selected Journals and Other Writings* 239).

The journey was the last great excursion for Audubon. His daughter-in-law Georgianna Audubon recalled that "he painted little after his return from the Yellowstone River, but as he looked at his son John's animals, he said: 'Ah, Johnny, no need for the old man to paint any more when you can work like that'" (quoted in Rhodes 424). In the end, his son drew nearly half of the 150 species represented in *The Viviparous Quadrupeds of North America*.

By 1841, the Audubons were well-supported by *The Birds of America,* mostly due to the success of the reduced-size octavo edition, which Audubon called his "salvator," or savior (quoted in Rhodes 430). They purchased fourteen acres of land in New York, with 550 feet fronting on the Hudson River, and moved onto their estate in 1842. They called it Minnie's Land, "Minnie" a Scottish affectionate term for "mother." John Woodhouse and Victor Gifford built their own houses next door, and raised families there with their second wives and thirteen children. The Bachman sisters, John Woodhouse's and Victor Gifford's first wives, had died of tuberculosis within eight months of each other. John Woodhouse was left with two small daughters. At the age of fifty-three, Lucy stepped in and raised by proxy the two daughters she had lost in their infancy. The land is the current site of 155th to 158th streets from the river to Bloomingdale Road in New York City. The buildings were razed in 1931.

In 1846 John James gave up work as his eyesight failed, but he still took pleasure in his relationship with Lucy. Rufus Griswold, a

magazine writer, visited Minnie's Land in 1846 and commented on the marriage:

> The sweet unity between his wife and himself, as they turned over the original drawings of his birds and recalled the circumstances of the drawings, some of which had been made when she was with him; her quickness of perception and their mutual enthusiasm regarding these works of his heart and hand, and the tenderness with which they unconsciously treat each other, all was impressed upon my memory. Ever since, I have been convinced that Audubon owed more to his wife than the world knew or ever would. That she was always a reliance, often a help and ever a sympathizing sister-soul to her noble husband was fully apparent to me. (Quoted in Rhodes 431-432)

In 1847 Audubon had a mild stroke. When John Bachman visited him at Minnie's Land in 1848, he found his "noble mind . . . all in ruins" (quoted in DeLatte 224). By the end of 1850, Audubon had grown weaker in body and in January 1851 he stopped eating. He died on January 27, 1851 at Minnie's Land, surrounded by his family.

OTHER WRITINGS

Audubon's published writings, in addition to the *Ornithological Biography* and the *The Viviparous Quadrupeds of North America,* include journals, essays, and letters. He kept journals from 1820 into the 1840s, commencing when he left his family in Cincinnati to complete the drawings for *The Birds of America* and concluding with the Missouri River journal in 1843.

A comprehensive record of Audubon's journals does not exist. Journals written before 1821 had been stored in a warehouse in New York while the family was in England. They were destroyed, along with correspondence, firearms, and family possessions, in an 1835 fire that destroyed six hundred buildings. After his wife, Lucy, died in 1874, twenty-four years after Audubon's death, the manuscripts of journals written after the fire, along with letters and other materials, were distributed among the grandchildren. One granddaughter, Maria Rebecca Audubon, edited and

published, in 1897, some of the manuscripts as *Audubon and His Journals.* Comparison of the text of the single journal extant today with Maria's rendition reveals that she edited them not only for grammar and spelling, but also with an eye toward Victorian standards of propriety: "Maria censored, prettified, and quietly rewrote the journals in such a way as to fit her image of Audubon as a 'refined and cultured gentleman,' immune to anger or jealousy or vanity. Having given her doctored portrait to the world, she burned most of the manuscripts" (Lindsey 51).

However, a few of the original journals survived, including the 1826 journal sanitized by Maria. It was begun on Audubon's sea voyage to England in search of a publisher for *The Birds of America.* The unexpurgated version exhibits his characteristically idiosyncratic spelling and syntax, and his passion for his work and his wife and family. He wrote at the beginning of the journey:

> When I calculate that Not Less than 4 Months, (the third of a Year) must elapse, before My Friend [wife Lucy] & Children can receive any tidings of my Arrival on the Distant Shores that now soon will divide us = when I think that many more Months must run from Life's Sand Glass allotted to my existence, and that the time of my returning to my Country, & Friends is yet an unfolded and unknown event; My body and face feels a Sudden Glow of aprehension that I neither can describe or represent = I know only the acuteness of the feelings that act through my whole frame like an Ellectric Shock, I imediately feel chilled and sullenly throw my body on My Matrass and Cast My Eyes towards the asure Canopy of Heaven scarce able to hold the Tears from flowing— (*Writings and Drawings* 159)

In Maria's version of this passage, the sentiment beginning with "I know only" and ending with "Tears from flowing" is omitted, apparently to erase the history of Audubon's emotions, which were deemed inappropriate in Maria's proper eye (Lindsey 51).

In spite of the alteration of the journals, they still present vivid pictures of life in the American wilderness. The opening entry in the Mississippi River journal (October 12, 1820 through December 30, 1821) includes a typical entry on the

day's hunting activities: "we shot Thirty Partridges—1 Wood Cock—27 Grey Squirrels—a Barn Owl—a young Turkey Buzard and anAautumnal Warbler" (*Writings and Drawings* 3). Although such wanton carnage might seem inappropriate today, "the unrestricted killing of birds and mammals in the early nineteenth century was a common pastime of American men. The supply of birds seemed inexhaustible. To be a man, to win a reputation in the community as a provider, was to have and use the motivation and the skills required to kill wild things" (Shuler 9). Audubon, of course, used many of the specimens to make his drawings, and most of the food for any expedition was acquired through daily hunts.

The Missouri River journal records Audubon's trip up the Missouri River on a cargo boat in March 1843 to November 16, 1843. The full manuscript is still intact, and the unedited text relates the mundane, unsavory, and often sad details of such travel, including questionable companions, frequent groundings of the boat, and encounters with American Indian tribes devastated by smallpox. The progress of the craft was so ponderous that at times Audubon and his traveling companions would go ashore and walk ahead, hunting as they went, and wait upstream for the boat to catch up. Fuel for the boat's boiler was obtained from wood cut along the way. Still, Audubon did not complain: his primary objective, obtaining specimens, was well met:

> June 4, Sunday . . . We are now fast for the night at an abandoned post, or fort, of the Company, where, luckily for us, a good deal of wood was found cut. We saw only one Wolf, and a few small gangs of Buffaloes. Bell shot a Bunting which resembles Henslow's, but we have not means of comparing it at present. We have collected a few plants during our landing. The steam is blowing off, and therefore our day's run is ended. When I went to bed last night it rained smartly, and Alexis did not go off, as he did wish. By the way, I forgot to say that along with the three Prairie Marmots, he brought also four Spoon-billed Ducks, which we ate at dinner today, and found delicious. Bell saw many Lazuli Finches this morning. Notwithstanding the tremendous shaking of our boat, Sprague managed to draw four figures of the legs and feet of the Wolf shot by

Bell yesterday, and my own pencil was not idle. (*Selected Journals and Other Writings* 255)

Three other important autobiographical documents were left by Audubon. "Myself," the essay quoted from earlier in this article, was first published in 1893 in *Scribner's* and later in Maria's *Audubon and His Journal*. The versions are nearly similar and the facts are consistent with information published elsewhere. Audubon is likely to be responsible for the inaccuracies at the beginning of the essay, which claims he was born in Louisiana, an attempt to erase his illegitimate birth.

A second document not included in the journals is Audubon's "Account of the Method of Drawing Birds." Originally written as a letter to a friend, it was first published in 1828 in the *Edinburgh Journal of Science*. The original letter is not known to exist. A companion document to this document, "My Style of Drawing Birds," is available in its original manuscript form and was published in facsimile in 1979. A considerably altered version appeared in Maria's *Audubon and His Journals,* 1897, but the original text was restored in later publications of Audubon's work. (*Writings and Drawings* 872-873).

Audubon was an inveterate correspondent, and many original copies of his letters are extant and have been published. Besides serving as a record in their own right, they are available to confirm or raise questions regarding information in the journals.

THE LEGACY

Income from *The Birds of America* sustained the Audubon family for a decade after John James' death, but Lucy's trials were not over. Victor Gifford died in 1860 at age fifty-one, and Woodhouse in 1862 at age forty-nine. At the age of seventy, in 1857, as the health of both of her sons declined, Lucy had returned to teaching in order to help support her grandchildren. she had once remarked, "If I can hold the mind of a child to a subject for five minutes, he will never forget what I teach him" (quoted in DeLatte 220). This philosophy served her as well in her second

career as a teacher in New York as it did in her first, in Louisiana (quoted in DeLatte 220).

In 1863 Lucy sold the original drawings for *The Birds of America* to the New York Historical Society for $2,000. She later sold Minnie's Land and spent the remainder of her days living with family and friends in New York and Kentucky. On June 18, 1874, she died of pneumonia in Shelbyville, Kentucky. John James, Lucy, Victor Gifford, and John Woodhouse Audubon are buried in Trinity Cemetery in New York, as are many other family members and neighbors and friends.

Audubon, through his elegant art and writings, released the study of America's birds from the dust of the museum and the dry tome of the scientist. The field notes in the *Ornithological Biography* influenced another passionate naturalist, Charles Darwin, who heard Audubon lecture in London in 1828. Audubon is cited in *The Origin of Species* (1859) and other of Darwin's works.

Audubon's passion inspires anew today in the form of the Audubon Society, named for him and started in 1886 by George Bird Grinnell, a student of Lucy Audubon's at Minnie's Land and a close friend of the family. Grinnell was an editor at *Forest and Stream* magazine, and was responding to the common use of feathers and even whole birds for decorating women's hats. The practice was extravagant and, coupled with the use of non-game birds for meat, threatened numerous bird species with extinction.

Although Audubon did not record any notion of such a society, he was clearly aware of the changes awaiting the world he lived in, as he stated in his conclusion to "The Prairie":

Will you believe, good-natured reader, that not many miles from the place where this adventure happened, and where fifteen years ago, no habitation belonging to civilized man was expected, and very few ever seen, large roads are now laid out, cultivation has converted the woods into fertile fields, taverns have been erected, and much of what we Americans call comfort is to be met with? (*Selected Journals and Other Writings* 387)

In an entry in his journal of 1826, he addressed Sir Walter Scott, whom he greatly admired:

Wilt though not come to my country? Wrestle with mankind and stop their increasing ravages on Nature, and describe her now for the sake of future ages. Neither this little stream, this swamp, this grand sheet of flowing water, nor these mountains will be seen in a century hence as I see them now. Nature will have been robbed of her brilliant charms. The currents will be tormented and turned astray from their primitive courses. . . .Fishes will no longer bask on the surface, the eagle scarce ever alight, and these millions of songsters will be drove away by man. (Quoted in Streshinsky 191)

Although such passages indicate that Audubon's association with the Audubon Society is clearly appropriate, it is his paintings and accompanying writings that are his greatest legacy. The sale in 2000 of a complete four-volume set of the original double-elephant folios of *The Birds of America* for $8.8 million is some measure of the esteem in which Audubon is held.

Selected Bibliography

WORKS OF JOHN JAMES AUDUBON

ORNITHOLOGICAL WORKS

The Birds of America, from Original Drawings. 4 vols. London: Privately Printed, 1827–1838. Reprint. *The Birds of America, from Drawings Made in the United States and Their Territories.* 7 vols. New York: J. J. Audubon; Philadelphia: Chevalier, 1840–1844. Reprint. *The Birds of America.* 7 vols. New York: V. G. Audubon, 1859. (Current edition of special interest: *Audubon's Birds of America: The Audubon Society Baby Elephant Folio.* Introduction by Roger Tory Peterson and Virginia Marie Peterson. Rev. ed. New York: Abbeville Press, 2004.

Ornithological Biography; or, An Account of the Habits of the Birds of the United States of America: Accompanied by Descriptions of the Objects Represented in the Work Entitled The Birds of America, *and Interspersed with Delineations of American Scenery and Manners.* 5 vols. Philadelphia: Dobson, 1831–1839; Edinburgh: Black, 1831–1839.

The Viviparous Quadrupeds of North America. With John Bachman. 3 vols. New York: J. J. Audubon, 1845–1854.; republished as *The Quadrupeds of North America.* 3 vols. New York: V. G. Audubon, 1849–1854.

JOURNALS AND CORRESPONDENCE

Audubon and His Journals. Edited by Maria Audubon 2 vols. New York: Scribners, 1897; London: Nimmo, 1898.

Audubon's Western Journal: 1849–1850. Cleveland: Arthur H. Clark, 1906.

Journal of John James Audubon Made During His Trip to New Orleans in 1820–1821. Edited by Howard Corning. Boston: Club of Odd Volumes, 1929.

Journal of John James Audubon Made While Obtaining Subscriptions to His Birds of America, *1840–1843.* Edited by Howard Corning. Boston: Club of Odd Volumes, 1929.

Letters of John James Audubon, 1826–1840. 2 vols. Edited by Howard Corning (Boston: Club of Odd Volumes, 1930).

Selected Journals and Other Writing. Edited by Ben Forkner. New York: Penguin, 1996.

OTHER WORKS

Delineations of American Scenery and Character. Edited by Francis Hobart Herrick. New York: Baker, 1926; London: Simpkin, Marshall, Hamilton, Kent, 1926.

My Style of Drawing Birds. Austin, Tex.: Overland Press, 1979.

Writings and Drawings. The Library of America, New York, 1999.

CRITICAL AND BIOGRAPHICAL STUDIES

DeLatte, Carolyn E. *Lucy Audubon: A Biography.* Baton Rouge: Louisiana State University Press, 1982.

DiSilvestro, Roger. *Audubon: Natural Priorities.* Atlanta: Turner Publishing, 1994.

Ford, Alice. *John James Audubon: A Biography.* Rev. ed. New York: Abbeville Press, 1988.

Goddu, Joseph. "The Making of Audubon's *The Birds of America.*" *Magazine Antiques* 162:112 (November 2002).

Griswold, Rufus W. "John James Audubon." *International Magazine* 2, no. 4:469–474 (March 1851).

Hart-Davis, Duff. *Audubon's Elephant: America's Greatest Naturalist and the Making of* The Birds of America. New York: Holt, 2004.

Lindsey, Alton A. *The Bicentennial of John James Audubon.* Bloomington: Indiana University Press, 1985.

Moonan, Wendy. "Rarae Aves: Audubon at Auction." *New York Times Book Review,* March 3, 2000.

Peattie, Donald Culross. *Audubon's America: The Narratives and Experiences of John James Audubon.* Boston: Houghton Mifflin, 1940.

Rhodes, Richard. *John James Audubon: The Making of an American.* New York: Knopf, 2004.

Shuler, Jay. *Had I the Wings: The Friendship of Bachman and Audubon.* Athens: University of Georgia Press, 1995.

Souder, William. *Under a Wild Sky: John James Audubon and the Making of* The Birds of America. New York: North Point Press, 2004.

Streshinsky, Shirley. *Audubon: Life and Art in the American Wilderness.* Athens: University Press of Georgia, 1998.

Weissmann, Gerald. *Darwin's Audubon: Science and the Liberal Imagination.* New York: Plenum, 1998.

RICK BASS

(1958—)

Jason Gray

RICK BASS HAS become by middle-age one of America's foremost writers of environmental literature. This results partly from his prolific production (he has written eighteen books in nineteen years), but more from his unique style and unflinching ability to dedicate himself to what he loves, the wilderness that surrounds him. Equally at home with fiction and nonfiction, Rick Bass has pursued a career that walks along a tree branch arching over a river, balancing his work between art and activism.

Many critics see him as a writer of place, and place clearly means much to him. His early works are steeped in the Texas of his youth, as well as in Utah and Mississippi, and in the Yaak Valley of Montana, where he settled in 1987. Having fled there to live a simpler life, more connected to the land, Bass often skewers American environmental policy and the values that spur that policy. However, Bass's work cannot be easily defined; he has written in different genres, and those genres have at times crossed. Bass has infused his fiction with his own brand of magical realism, and his nonfiction often highlights the magical or the spiritual qualities of nature and human life. So he has become notoriously hard to categorize, a sign that Bass has opened up a field of literature all his own.

YOUTH IN THE DEER PASTURE, AT WORK IN THE OIL FIELDS

Born on March 7, 1958, in Fort Worth, Texas, Rick Bass grew up outside Houston with his parents, C. R. Bass, who was a geologist, and Mary Lucy Robson Bass, an English teacher, and with his two younger brothers, Frank and B.J. He spent his childhood in the shadow of the center of the American oil industry, though he also paid regular visits to the zoo and the natural history museum and played in Buffalo Bayou, a tiny clip of wilderness winding through the subdivisions; there his interest in nature began. And the family's trips to the Hill Country of Texas, 250 miles away, flamed the boy's passion for wilderness.

These journeys formed what later became Bass's first book, *The Deer Pasture* (1985), a series of lively sketches of his family and their lives as hunters that reads like the work of a man discovering how much he loves his life and language. His casualness borders on folksiness at times, and can be clumsy too, using such archaic language as "it bothers me not." (61) Though at times stilted, most of the stories are well told and some quite gracefully. We can see Bass teaching himself to write in these early essays, like a first time hunter fumbling a bit but learning his dead aim. The book is even Edenic in parts: "Nothing was out of synchrony. It was a perfect Hill Country afternoon. Everything was as it should be. . . . It is a closed system, still operating—oblivious to blunder, immune to disharmony." (18) This makes a subtle association with a spiritual, or magical, world that will develop throughout Bass's career. Mystery pervades his work: oddities erupt in the reality of his fiction, as moments in the wilderness segue into some other plane of being.

Bass left Texas for the first time when he went to college, attending Utah State University in Logan. He studied biology first, then turned to geology, played football, and learned a new landscape. He also began to study writing. After receiving his bachelor's degree in 1979, he took a job as a petroleum geologist in Mississippi, searching for new oil wells and spending eight years in Jackson and surrounding oil fields. This was to serve as the next major setting for more

nonfiction and also for his first fiction. He followed *The Deer Pasture* with *Wild to the Heart* (1987), another book of short essays, this time widening his range of locales. Gone are the homey bits from the earlier book, and his voice is honed, more mature, yet retains its plainspokenness. Bass roves the bottomlands of Mississippi and takes prolonged drives to get back to the Utah mountains and to return home to Texas, now as an adult.

Wild to the Heart recounts Bass's first association with environmental organizations. In "Paying Dues" he talks about going to a Sierra Club meeting and mentions that he "had always sort of assumed in [his] mind's eye absurd and baroque stereotypes for any outdoor-oriented organization, never having been associated with one [him]self." (32) His naked honesty about his assumptions is refreshing and allows his later work to maintain honesty. Bass never postures as some kind of environmental hero. Like watching him learn to write, we are allowed to watch him learn about environmentalism. Much of his later work as an activist can be traced back to the following moment. When his date for the evening club meeting wants to dance, Bass tells her he needs to check on the car. He sits on a putting green, thinking about the talk. Bass at this point mentions that, in 1981, Defenders of Wildlife fought to protect grizzly bear habitat in the Cabinet Mountains of Montana. "I would like to have been in on the fight. Where was I and what was I doing when it was going on?" (35) he asks himself. So the next time there was a chance to take part in the fight, he did, writing letters to the governor of Louisiana, the secretary of the interior, and the president of the United States. Letter writing campaigns became the staple of Bass's fight to save the Yaak Valley in Montana, where he would eventually come to live.

Wild to the Heart was followed by his first collection of short stories, *The Watch* (1989). The stories earned him early acclaim, two of them having been reprinted in *Prize Stories 1989: The O. Henry Awards* and *Best American Short Stories, 1988*. Bass's voice in his fiction is that of an oral storyteller. One can hear it in openings like this, to "Juggernaut": "When I was seven-teen, Kirby and I had a teacher who was crazy. This happened in the last year before Houston got big and unlivable." (106) Bass often has a first-person narrator tell the reader about a character, showing that person in a typical way. For example, in "Juggernaut" the narrator says Big Ed Odom, the narrator's geometry teacher,

> moved with an awkward power: as if perhaps once he had had this very great strength that had somehow been taken away: an injury inside, to some set of nerves, which still retained the strength, but did not allow him to use it. Like a loaded pistol, or a car parked on the hill without an emergency brake—that was the impression he gave Kirby and me. (107)

Odom is a storyteller too. He lasts for about twenty minutes of geometry lecture before he breaks into story, and imaginative stories they are. He tells his students, "All female lions have a claw hidden in their tail" (107) and that the FBI records people's voices when they're born, to have on file. His stories are wild, outlandish things that the narrator and Kirby relish. Bass's work is tinged throughout like this with the fantastic.

In his essay "'The Unbelievable Thing Usually Goes to the Heart of the Story': Magic Realism in the Fiction of Rick Bass," the critic Jim Dwyer feels this story fails. Dwyer takes issue with some of the early stories, saying Bass "overrelie[s] on fantastic characters, pulling them from his authorial bag of tricks like a clumsy apprentice magician." Dwyer is correct that some of Bass's early fiction is clumsy; the author does not strike a balance between realism and what might be called magical realism to the best degree. But in this story the oversized fictions created by the teacher match the oversized emotions of the teenage protagonists. In "Juggernaut" the boys eventually realize that Odom is having an affair with a student, Laura DeCastagnola, the object of their desire. They spot her at his car:

> For the first time we saw the thing, in its immensity, and it was like coming around a bend or a trail in the woods and suddenly seeing the hugeness and emptiness of a great plowed pasture or field, when all one's life up to that point had been spent close

to but never seeing a field of that size. (121)

The story is a coming-of-age story, and they experience the large swings of emotion that teenagers often do, and so the fantasizing of the teacher seems to correspond with the wild dreaming of youth.

Other writers might begin the story here, at the teens' discovery, the day when things are different. But Bass's stories often do not work in the traditional way. The structures are loose sometimes, occasionally even maddeningly loose, but what keeps them together are the characters. Bass is at times like Sherwood Anderson. The odd structures, the small towns, the quirky characters, and comments like the one about Hollingsworth in "The Watch"—"There was a thing that was not in him anymore, and he did not know where to go find it"—could be pulled straight from *Winesburg, Ohio.* Bass wants to make his reader comfortable, enjoy the characters, like them, and to feel their discomfort at the end when the world twists on them, and then, like the characters, to be uncertain about resolution. Bass can nail down character with the force of a sledgehammer. In "Mississippi," he says of Hector, "There was triumph and victory and key elements of the Magna Charta in his voice." (127) The reader can easily hear the overbearing officiousness and pride of the character.

Bass turns back to his own character in his following book. *Oil Notes,* also published in 1989, is a collection of journal entries about his experience as a petroleum geologist, though it is more skillfully drawn than the "notes" of the title would lead one to believe. Bass attempts to explain how he finds oil—though he cannot, he readily admits—and to describe the life of an oil geologist. The paradox of the well-regarded naturalist writer having started his career drilling for oil is self-evident, although for Bass it really is not a paradox. He loves the process of discovery, and he talks about it throughout the book. That love of discovery he turned into his writing.

Bass reveals much about his writing process in the book, and it opens a good window on his work and what he thinks literature should be:

Sometimes people like what I write. The smartest readers know that I am saying nothing, but like a wild fighter, occasional punches slip through the defense: knockdown. I skate around the edges of mystic things: childhood, friendship, ponies, love-sketch them; no, *detail* their every line, so that friends and others say, Look! There it is! (158)

This is Bass's version of Franz Kafka's famous notion that art should "free the frozen sea within us," which he quotes in the book's opening paragraph. Bass's artistic statement reflects his stories well, for he is often elliptical in his storytelling, circling around character, around a situation, revealing something worth thinking about at the end, but at the same time trying to show sides, facets of the story rather than its linear progression.

THE YAAK VALLEY

Bass abandoned his career as an oil geologist and moved to the Yaak (Kootenai for "arrow"), a remote valley in northwest Montana, in 1987 with his future wife, Elizabeth Hughes, and their two dogs, Homer and Ann. Before arriving there, they tried New Mexico, Arizona, Colorado, and Utah, looking for "a place of ultimate wildness," but didn't find it until Montana. They first settled in as caretakers of a hunting lodge, the Fix Ranch, near the Canadian border. Four years later, in 1991, Bass and Hughes married; and their first daughter, Mary Katherine, was born in 1992, followed by Lowry Elizabeth in 1995.

Those first six months in Montana are captured in *Winter: Notes from Montana* (1991). Returning to the journal form of *Oil Notes,* Bass recounts his labors to prepare for the long winter ahead and his growing affection for the people of the valley—all 150 of them—and for the land itself. As to form Bass says, "I don't know how to write about this country in an orderly fashion, because I'm just finding out about it. . . . For now it is all loose events, great mystery, random lives." (12) The journal form works well for him here because in the book he has not had time to process the transformation his life has undergone. So he records impressions, observations, details,

and lets them connect in less obvious ways, working almost like poetry. The book is the journal of an innocent. The landscape is new, as is the way of life, and Bass soaks it up, learning at a ferocious pace. He has to. By the time he and Elizabeth arrived in Montana, winter was not far off, and so he had to race to cut enough firewood, while mastering the use of a chainsaw. He even had to go back down south to get his old Ford Falcon when his truck broke down, and he hauled his wood through the dangerous mountain passes in his old car. Without electricity, miles from any large population and its conveniences, life is a more serious consideration for them in the valley, and Bass relishes it.

Early on Bass says something worth noting. After mentioning the possibility of a silver mine opening below the Cabinet Mountains, he writes, "It's not as if I'm going to talk anyone into being for or against clearcutting or sloppy mine operations or dam building. . . . You're on one side or the other, the battle lines have already been drawn, and sides chosen." (28) Yet Bass would go on to spend much of his time trying to convince everyone to change their minds: no clear-cutting and no mining was the way to save the Yaak Valley. As he grew into the valley, things became less black and white for him.

Having survived their first winter, Bass concludes his book with the declaration, "I won't be leaving this valley." (162) He did stay, and it became the central focus of most of his writing to come. Five years later in *The Book of Yaak* (1996), having gotten over the highs of the new discovery, Bass had begun actively trying to save it. Though, like *Winter, The Book of Yaak* celebrates the valley, it also issues a plea for help. Containing a series of essays written for publications as diverse as *House Beautiful, Sports Afield, Audubon,* and the *Southern Review,* all revolve around the single purpose of explaining how important the valley is, how magical it is, and how the future of the American environment depends upon its survival. Bass explains in the introduction that "there is a place, a sanctuary you go to, in writing fiction, or, I suppose, poetry, that is in another world. . . . It's magic. There's no other word for it—no way known to explain

it." But, he continues, "This book is not like that. It's a sourcebook, a handbook, a weapon of the heart." (xiii) The government wants to build miles of logging roads and destroy the central woods, and Bass has set about the task of protecting it, of getting the valley declared a protected wilderness. *The Book of Yaak* is an assembly of testimony, facets of a gem, that Bass can get at only one side at a time, because the valley is too multidimensional to fit onto one page.

The initial essay, "The Value of a Place," begins to talk about a dichotomy that would take over Bass's life. He and his wife set out to be artists when they moved to Montana, but their plans changed. The environmental damage being done, the clear-cuts of the forests, made Bass unable to sit still any longer. In this book he starts trying to come to terms with the balance of art and activism in his life, a theme that dominated his nonfiction for the rest of the decade. He explains, "If your home were burning, for instance, would you grab a bucket of water to pour on it, or would you step back and write a poem about it?" (10) Bass chose the water and began a massive letter writing campaign to save his home. He would help form the Yaak Valley Forest Council in 1997. He even had a copy of *The Book of Yaak* sent to every member of Congress and to President Bill Clinton. Bass's engagement with the wilderness around his home made him struggle with how best to spend his time: creating art or saving the wild? The tone of desperation in this book would only be amplified over time. He meditates on the choice:

Art is incredibly important to me—fiction, especially. But there are thousands of fiction writers in the world, and only one Yaak. It would certainly not cause the earth to pause on its axis if I never wrote another story. . . .

On the other hand, if a thing like the wilderness of Yaak were to be lost—I do believe that would cause a hesitation on the axis. (10)

Bass's honesty about his own relevance in the art world is endearing, and a tonic for the self-importance that might come with an artist begging for support. Because of his honesty we can listen to him and know he is on the level. He is

not ready to resign himself to the attitude that nothing more can be done than make a record of how the valley *was,* because it is doomed to vanish. This shadow of a place's destruction is an unavoidable condition in modern nature writing—the writer can no longer simply celebrate the wild but must also advocate its preservation.

Bass comments further about art. In "The Fringe" he writes,

> In the way that the bears are said to be able to live in two worlds—belonging to this world as well as to the spirit world, because of their disappearance underground for up to six months of each year—I believe that art, though immeasurable, lies somewhere between the world of science, facts and math, and the world of the spirit: that it can be a transition.
>
> . . .
>
> Where art exists, the spirit of a place still exists. (38)

Bass strives to come to terms with his role in all this. Wanting to be an artist, but feeling uncomfortable sitting behind his desk writing fiction instead of letters, he is reminding himself what art can do for the environment. Bass again considers the spirit. He places high value on nature because it is more than what it appears. It is like the magic that occurs in his fiction: the world is really a little different than it appears every day. If our eyes were open to it, we could see giant pigs and men who could lift a Volkswagen with ease, as we do in his fiction.

Between *Winter* and *The Book of Yaak,* Bass published two works of fiction, *Platte River* (1994) and *In the Loyal Mountains* (1995). Bass's first collection of novellas, *Platte River* concerns men and their relationships with women. The title story involves the theme of a man hunting a woman who wants to run away, an idea that Bass picked up later in "The Myths of Bears," first published in the *Southern Review* and later reprinted in his second collection of novellas, *The Sky, The Stars, The Wilderness* (1997).

Two of the three pieces in *Platte River* contain Bass's most larger-then-life characters. The first novella, "Mahatma Joe," is the story of a preacher who comes to Montana to spread the Word and convert the sparse population of heathens, single-handedly ending their Naked Days celebration, when the entire valley would go unclothed in the warm Chinook winds. Joe and his wife Lily decide to build a garden by moonlight to feed Africans. For Joe it becomes a last chance at salvation, because his conversions have soured. After his wife drowns in the icy river, Joe takes on Leena as a new partner. Leena, a woman from the south looking for a new life, is also a kind of giantess, given to swimming naked in the frigid river, even chipping holes in the ice to do so.

"Field Events," the story of two brothers and their family, and of A.C., a strongman whom the brothers train to throw the discus, features another abnormally strong swimmer. The brothers first meet A.C. after they spot him swimming the butterfly stroke up the river, pulling a canoe behind him filled with cast-iron statues. The brothers themselves are something of a wonder: "When the excitement of the night and of their strength and youth was too much, they would pick up the [Volkswagen Beetle] from either end like porters, or pallbearers, and try to carry it around the block, for exercise." (48) The brothers', and especially A.C.'s, superhuman strength is a given in the story, but it sets the story apart from strict realism. It is often suggested that Bass, in stories like this one, works in magical realism, defined by M. H. Abrams in the sixth edition of his *Glossary of Literary Terms* as interweaving, "in an ever-shifting pattern, a sharply etched *realism* in representing ordinary events and descriptive details together with fantastic and dreamlike elements." "Field Events" and to a lesser degree "Mahatma Joe" certainly have that element of magic, with fantastic and dreamlike qualities. His realism is often skewed, so that men can throw a discus three hundred feet; a certain kind of magic exists in his created world that slips the work into the mythic or the allegorical (in the case of "Field Events" the family's last name is Iron). To Jim Dwyer, Bass is not a "traditional" magical realist, but has "expanded the genre." (Weltzien, *Literary Art*, 49) Magical realism carries on in his next book of stories.

Bass's second collection of short fiction, *In the Loyal Mountains,* followed in 1995. The strongest stories in the book, as with all of Bass's fiction,

are those that stray the furthest from the writer's own familiar territory. "The History of Rodney," "Swamp Boy," "Fires," and "In the Loyal Mountains," though they all possess settings from Bass's own life, including, in the case of the first, his wife's name for the narrator's wife, they escape from what makes some of his other fiction sound too much like his essays. They take place in the Yaak Valley, have the Mercantile and the Dirty Shame saloon, even his own dogs' names for the characters' dogs. These features make it difficult to separate fact from fiction in some of the stories, and in cases like "The Valley," the pieces are less story and more description of a place, like the essays in *The Book of Yaak,* for instance.

That said, there are things in his best stories that are wonderful. In "The History of Rodney," a Volkswagen-size pig lives under the narrator's house. He explains, "Daisy says that the pigs in Rodney are descended from Union soldiers. The townspeople marched the soldiers into the Presbyterian church one Sunday, boarded up the doors and windows, and then Daisy's mother turned them all into pigs." (5) This resembles the fantastical storytelling present in earlier work, except in this case at least the end result is true in the story: there *are* gigantic pigs. In his book *Rick Bass* (1998), O. Alan Weltzien has said that Bass in this story "successfully re-animat[es]" Southern grotesquerie. Again there is something of Sherwood Anderson here—though not a Southern writer, certainly one who used the grotesque. The world in the stories is near our world, with slight distortions. Sensing Bass's ecological criticism at hand, one might read these pigs as a nod toward possible environmental mutation.

Often at the heart of Bass's stories is paradise—paradise as a place that can be achieved, as if one lived a certain way in a certain place, one might find it. It is of course in the natural world, or in living close to the natural world, where it exists for Bass. "This place isn't on the map?" asks Elizabeth of the narrator in "Rodney." "It might as well not even exist," he responds. (7) These characters are looking for what does not exist, or what is not known to exist for most

people. They find it and guard it jealously. "Days of Heaven" is in fact about just this. A Bass-like character finds a caretaking job at a Montana lodge and lives there as if he's found heaven on earth. Although he has to defend it from the owners, who do not love the valley like he does. "I knew," the narrator says of the owner, "he would keep on taking his percentage from that newness. Taking too much." (147) This sense of paradise relates to the spiritual nature of the woods that can be found throughout Bass's nonfiction.

In the three novellas of *The Sky, The Stars, The Wilderness,* which collects his first published story, "Where the Sea Used to Be," Bass continues from earlier veins in his fiction. "The Myths of Bears" finds another man chasing after a fleeing woman, as in "Platte River." This time the theme is blown up to mythic proportions. Judith runs off only to have Trapper track her down. Judith seems almost like a bear at the end, as "she gnaws at the snare" Trapper has laid for her. (44) She in part becomes transformed into a wild animal as he hunts her, making this story feel closer to something out of Ovid's *Metamorphoses* than a contemporary American writer. During the course of the story Judith thinks, "All forests deserve one man and one woman," (43) which likens the situation to that of Adam and Eve. The novella reads like they are the only two alive in the massive wood, and they act out their unique, twisted version of that creation story. Judith tries to swim away in the river, but Trapper catches her. Bass writes, "She feels some part of her escape with the current—her other life, the mythical one." (45) If Trapper and Judith are Adam and Eve, then perhaps this other Judith is Lilith, Adam's legendary first wife.

The title novella concerns character more than plot. It is, like much of Bass's fiction, a character study—how one personality exists in the world. The story does not move from conflict to conflict like most, but from interaction to interaction with nature. In his introduction to *The Literary Art and Activism of Rick Bass,* Weltzien agrees,

By the time Bass returns to the Hill Country as the setting for his title novella "The Sky, the Stars, the Wilderness," his thinking about ecology—about self and place, and self in place—has matured a

great deal. Setting often becomes the main character, infusing every element of the ostensible protagonists.

The forty-four-year-old woman narrator recounts her early days on the family ranch and the aftermath of her mother's early death. The story concerns the mystery of nature too. In one of the most beautifully descriptive passages, the narrator thinks,

> The moths were a luminescent, feathery pale green with sweeping forked tails that made them look like angels in long robes. Some people said that, as with the lightning bugs, luna moths spent their days flying around the earth at high altitudes, descending only after the sun had set, but Grandfather and I knew that they lived under old logs back in the dark cedar thickets, because we'd found them there. They didn't come from above, but emerged from the earth below. I want there to be a heaven, an afterlife, but wonder why we look to the stars so often when thinking of it. (97)

Bass manages to capture both his love of mystery and his down-to-earthness here, by blending the realism of the character's knowing the "story" isn't true, the one that sounds magical, with a different kind of magic, a different kind of afterworld, that, while based in reality, still manages its own mystery. These stories of Bass's that proceed less like traditional stories push in a unique way the boundaries of what fiction can be. They do not always work, but when they succeed, they succeed tremendously.

"Where the Sea Used to Be," originally published in the spring 1987 *Paris Review,* is set on the Black Warrior Basin in northeastern Mississippi, the same area worked by Bass as an oil geologist, and it gives the story its title. The Gulf of Mexico once extended that far north and has made the area oil rich. The story poses a dichotomy of purity and evil: doing something for the sake of the thing itself, as does the geologist hero, Wallis; or doing it for money, as do his competitors Dudley and Dudley's two underlings, Harry and Jack. The latter are slaves to oil and to Dudley, something Wallis has a hard time contemplating: "Everyone knew, Wallis thought, that it was better to belong to yourself and have one acre in a drilling well than to belong to another man, even if that man had a hundred, a thousand wells, or the whole county." (63) Both oppose Wallis, who has a preternatural ability to find oil that the two of them do not share or understand. His is a victory of virtue, because for him, finding oil is a gift, magic, and he does it for the love of the thing. Over the course of the story, he and Sara, the "pretty girl in town," (59) fall in love, and he is able to love two things, because the first (finding oil) hadn't been sold, or corrupted, as it had been for Harry and Jack. The novella wraps up a little quickly and remains a little underdeveloped but is still one of Bass's best pieces.

So it is both cause to wonder and perfectly sensible that he then labored over it for ten years, until he transformed the story into his first novel. *Where the Sea Used to Be* (1998) takes the basic story of its predecessor, and both complicates and simplifies it. Gone are the two underlings of Dudley who oppose Wallis; they are now the single character Matthew. In the novel Wallis actually works for Dudley, though he retains most of the traits of the former Wallis. Sara is now Mel, the daughter of Dudley, drawing the characters closer together. But Mel lives in Montana, where Wallis is sent by Dudley to find the oil he and Matthew could not. Wallis does find oil, but the townspeople, who tell him, "It has more power if you leave it there," convince him not to drill, echoing the earlier story's ethos of doing it for the love of the thing.

In the novel the ancient sea of the title is more metaphoric than actual, since the novel is set entirely in a fictional version of the Yaak: the Swan Valley of Montana. The novel, a cautionary tale of greed and overconsumption, acts out Bass's art/activism theory. His characters, struggling for a place they love against its possible corruption by the oil-hungry Dudley—who has written in his journal, "*The earth was given to us to eat*"—(360) reflect Bass's own work to save the Yaak. Terrell F. Dixon, in *"Where the Sea Used to Be:"* Rick Bass and the Novel of Ecological Education, says that Bass "offers a way . . . to envision and encourage change, to blend the art of literary creation with the inculcation of activism." (Weltzien, *Literary Art,* 291) Wallis

learns to see the wider scope of things in the novel, and that he is not wasting his talent if he does not extract the oil. Oil is a part of the whole landscape, and to remove it would damage that wholeness.

Art and activism continued to dog Bass after publishing his novel. He wrote the novella *Fiber,* which appeared first in the anthology *Off the Beaten Path: Stories of Place* (North Point, 1998) and then was published as a separate volume by the University of Georgia Press. *Fiber* is a troublesome work. Though Bass labels it fiction, and it opens that way, albeit with heavy associations to Bass's real life, the piece ends as a plea. A story in four parts, it details what the narrator calls his "four lives"—part one as geologist, part two as artist, part three as activist, and part four, less easily described, as "one that is built around things more immediate than the fairy-wing days of art." (4) The narrator's life resembles Bass's, except he had trouble with the law back in Louisiana, and he currently cuts logs for a living.

Fiber is the descendent of such earlier stories as "The Valley," which leans heavily on the nonfictional situation. So Bass has created the culmination of his hybrid form, mixing fact and fiction, ax and art, to open a genre that finds its closest analogy in prose poetry, not because it reads like poetry but because it exists in a border territory. By most standards in fiction, *Fiber* fails, and by many nonfiction standards as well, but it asks to be taken as something else, though its claim as fiction hinders this. If criticized through some new, unlabeled form, it makes a case for itself. Terry Gifford opines in " *Fiber:* A Post-Pastoral Georgic" that it is a "slightly flawed masterpiece" (248) that functions in a way Virgil's *Georgics* do, insofar as they concern work (in this case logging), but that it is post-pastoral, meaning that human influence on nature is more the subject than is nature's influence on humanity.

Gifford may be right about *Fiber.* More fable than anything else, the thinly drawn story functions as a metaphor for an idea, with an exposed moral:

> We—all painters and writers—don't want to be political. We want to be pure, and *artistic.* But we all know, too, I think, that we're not up to the task.

What story, what painting, does one offer up to refute Bosnia, Somalia, the Holocaust, Chechnya, China, Afghanistan, or Washington D.C.? (40)

Storytelling, art, have become too weak to correct the world's problems. *Fiber* ends with a warbling plea: "Somebody please do this. Somebody please help." (51) The request might have prompted more wide-ranging support if Bass had not just spent several paragraphs lambasting President Clinton for protecting other wild areas of the country but not the Yaak, without offering any particular reason why the Yaak is more important than those other places, other than his own now almost violent love for the place. Whatever its faults, *Fiber* remains a significant work by Bass that made the field of environmental writers quicken their attention.

Brown Dog of the Yaak: Essays on Art and Activism (1999) continues this meditation through the lens of his favorite dog, Colter, who becomes a metaphor for Bass's activism/writing dilemma. When "looking in on that sleeping dog at night," and contemplating the next morning's writing, he would think:

> It would seem, always and again, that one of those two elements, *the dog,* was always real, and the other, *the writing,* always shadow. . . . I don't mean to dismiss the shadow-life as insignificant: far from it. But it seems a great danger to me for a writer to become lost in, or too much in love with, the shadows themselves, and his or her trafficking in them, rather than the objects themselves, which cast those shadows. (17)

Bass by this time has put a functional name on his dilemma, which has allowed him to write without being constantly worried he isn't doing enough. The idea is somewhat Platonic in that nature is likened to a true form, while his art is only a reflection of that. The book is more peaceful than *Fiber,* which is not to say Bass does not still feel desperation for his home. "One of the reasons we find magic in such thin supply these days," he writes, "is not because of excess or overaccumulation of knowledge, but because so damn few of those places still exist in which magic can find a healthy medium: where magic can prosper, and get up and move around." (37)

Bass is becoming more deeply involved in the idea of wilderness as magic. As more and more of America's wilderness disappears, it too becomes more fantastic, like magic, something humans might stop believing exists. The danger of this, to Bass, is that if humans lose touch with the magic of the wilderness, to put it in religious terms, it would be something like losing their souls.

Bass followed this with a longer study of his dog, *Colter: The True Story of the Best Dog I Ever Had,* in 2000. Leaving the struggle for activism behind, he tells the story of his dog and, to a lesser degree, of all his dogs. The book connects back to *The Deer Pasture,* with hunting again the primary focus. His writing about his hunting partner, Tim, recalls the way he spoke about his family: "Tim and I don't understand that you're not supposed to hurry up to your dog when he's on point—that you're supposed to *saunter,* calling casual words of encouragement." (43) This might be advice given to Bass and Cousin Randy by their grandfather. The book is touching, and reminds us that not all nature writing is an act of anger and desperation; what motivates Bass and other writers like him is love, love for animals, for the wild.

Bass returned to direct defense of the Yaak by editing a volume of essays, *The Roadless Yaak: Reflections and Observations about One of Our Last Great Wild Places,* published in the summer of 2002. He invited writers, naturalists, and scientists to the Yaak and asked them to share their thoughts on the valley and why it should be protected as a federal wilderness. Again he distributed copies of the book to senators and congressmen, to the president and vice-president, and to the director of the U.S. Forest Service. Bass opens the book with a preface and contributes an essay, "The Community of Glaciers." In his preface, he remarks on the essayists, "Implicit in their accepting that invitation, I think, is the understanding by these artists and scientists that each of these roadless areas is more beautiful and enduring than any one artist's book, or any one artist's oeuvre." (vii) Bass continues to impress upon his readers the need to yield to something larger than themselves. He states that the Yaak

was first designed "by a Creator," (vii) which reinforces this idea. Bass does not impose a particular religious idea on the Yaak but underscores the fact that humans did not create it, nor can they understand the complexities behind its creation, and therefore they must not thrust it easily aside.

"The Community of Glaciers" compares the struggle to save the Yaak to the formation of a glacier. At the time of its initial publication in the December 1999 issue of *Audubon* magazine, Bass had been living in the valley for nearly twelve years and fighting for it most of that time. Bass is a little resigned to what small effect his and others' efforts have had in getting the Yaak designated a "wilderness," the only status that will keep it completely safe. But he finds hope in the idea of the glacier and the fact that, once sixty feet of snow pile up, the glacier begins to move. He writes, "I have begun to think that the conceit of our lives, our hearts, as hot furious maelstroms of passion is but a romantic's fancy: that what we really are is nothing more than windblown snow, swirling, beautiful yet ephemeral when measured flake by flake." (104) Those flakes build up though, and like a glacier, once they have grown tall enough, will move, and will carve out an effect on the land. This ties to his idea that humans are subject to something larger than themselves. While at once it may seem depressing to think one's actions do not matter, hope lies in the accumulation of effect.

In the summer of 2002, Bass also published another collection of short fiction, *The Hermit's Story.* Relationships between men and women dominate the book—many of them are damaged and may or may not be repaired, and some are just blooming, as in "The Cave." This remarkable story is about two people, Russell and Sissy, on a date, a canoeing trip in North Carolina. Along their way, they find an abandoned mine, and after stripping naked to fit through the shaft, explore miles of the underground cavity. Despite an element of wonder, this story seems more realistic than earlier ones by Bass. Later in the book, the reader meets these characters again in "Eating." A less successful story, more anecdotal, the action takes place prior to the cave adventure,

and one learns that Russell had gone on an eating binge that makes him rival the fantastic A.C. from "Field Events."

"The Fireman" was the most lauded selection in *The Hermit's Story*. First published in the spring 2000 issue of the *Kenyon Review*, it subsequently appeared in *Best American Short Stories, 2001* and received a Pushcart Prize. The main character, Kirby, a fireman, and his wife, Mary Ann, have a marriage that might be "rotting," but is saved whenever a dispatcher's call comes in. "As long as the city keeps burning, they can avoid becoming weary and numb," Bass writes (51). Fire keeps their marriage alive by interrupting arguments and allowing danger to put their troubles in perspective. The story opens by telling the reader that both Kirby and Mary Ann "stand on the other side of the miracle," which turns out to be Kirby's abandoning a failing marriage for this one. (51)

"Miracle" is used in the final story, "Two Deer," to describe the narrator's rescue of a deer from an iced-over river. "Two Deer" is another story of a relationship, less troubled, though the narrator acknowledges that his attempt to rescue the deer is a danger, primarily because of his wife and young child. The successful relationships in this book seem to be owing to bravery: as the narrator says in "Two Deer," "Let's not let each other become small or weak or diminished." Risking life makes it more worth living, and that zest seems to fit into Bass's own life, considering that he and his wife leapt into the dark to go live in one of the remotest parts of the country. What Laura Ciolkowski says in her *Boston Globe* review of October 20, 2002, is apt: "The unconventional characters in Bass's narrative universe are drawn to the precarious balance between the wild and the tame and struggle to make some sense out of the perplexing relationship between humans and nature." Whether his characters live in the wild or not, they have to negotiate a balance among each other, a feat that is often wild enough.

There is much beauty in this book, as the title story makes evident. It is a Thanksgiving night, and a storm has shut down the power in town, which, the narrator tells us, would ordinarily have looked, from where he resides on a distant mountainside, like "stars sunken to the bottom of a lake." This arresting image is picked up later, with the story of Ann and Gray Owl walking under the ice along the dry lakebed. They light cattail torches that set off swamp gas, which from above would have looked much like the fallen stars. This under-ice world is strange and has the mystery of Bass's earlier fiction, which does not fill this collection as much but, when it appears, remains powerfully charged.

MEGAFAUNA

After Bass began to think of the Yaak Valley as home, he began, like anyone would, to notice what was going on around him, and one of those things was the possibility of wolves making their way down to Montana from Canada. His investigations led him to write *The Ninemile Wolves* (1992), his seminal work of nonfiction and the first of a series of books about megafauna, or large animal species. *Ninemile* is the story of wolves finding their way back into United States territory, one by one forming a pack, surviving sometimes against the odds, sometimes not. It is about nature's will to undo what humans do and to restore balance despite humanity's best efforts against it. The wolves' story begins in 1989, when a female wolf was discovered near Marion, Montana. There is a scramble of activity by both wolf preservationists and those opposed to them. Over the next three years, the female wolf and other lone wolves would be captured, released, have cubs, and in some cases, be shot.

Bass breaks some rules writing this book, a fact he readily admits: "They say not to anthropomorphize—not to think of [the wolves] as having feelings, not to think of them as being able to think. . . . I can say what I want to say. I gave up my science badge a long time ago." (3-4) Bass's honesty about how he feels, and how he is going to write this book-length essay, allows the reader to trust him. Though he stands squarely on the side of the wolves and chooses to begin his book "with the mystic-tinged edges of fate," (4) he has done his research and his fair investigating.

The book turns over all aspects of the story, from the day-to-day actions of the wolves, the landowners, the government, to the history of wolf extermination in the United States, to character studies of the people involved. Writing about Ed Bangs, a U.S. Fish and Wildlife Service employee who had written, "The decision to release [an old wolf] reasoned that any period of survival in the wild would be preferable to spending the rest of his life in captivity," Bass notes "I'm encouraged when I read these words from a federal official, a G-man." (30) Bass respects the work done by some government officials when they have the interests of nature and science at heart and not bureaucratic posturing, which he abhors: "Thank God the politicians' bellies are too large to allow them to get into the woods." (90) As evenhanded as Bass may be, he is not afraid to mock the foolishness that he sees in much of the government's dealing with the wilderness.

In ways it is a hymn to the wolves too, because Bass loves them deeply and writes beautifully about them. He repeats his admonition about not anthropomorphizing, and says he's learning not to, "but in some respects, it seems bend-over-backwards ridiculous *not* to, for if a wolf does not have a spirit, then what animal, ourselves included, can be said to have one?" (131) Bass continues with this thought:

> If humans' spirituality can be said to be grounded in our relatively oversized brain, the three pounds we lug around in our craniums, then could not the opposite be true—a spirituality entirely at odds with ours, grounded almost exclusively in an earthy, bodily contact with the world of ripping and cutting . . . ? (131)

Bass has a terrific ability to imagine a system of life that may be wholly different from ours, that of the wolves, and yet to find a startling similarity there that deserves respect.

Bass continued to write about large species in *The Lost Grizzlies: A Search for Survivors in the Wilderness of Colorado* (1995). It differs from *The Ninemile Wolves* in that, in the absence of the grizzlies, the book is about humans. As more signs of the grizzlies become evident, the narration turns toward them yet still remains about the people fighting for them. The first section of the book, "The Fall," narrates the initial trip Bass, the artist Marty Ring, and the writer Doug Peacock take to explore the San Juan Mountains for grizzly signs. "The Fall" is as much a character study of Peacock as it is about the bears. Bass describes Peacock this way:

> The first and most striking mode of behavior occurs when he's wired with an anxiety that leads to a mania reminiscent of the Bugs Bunny-Tasmanian Devil cartoons. When he's wound up tight . . . he'll invariably bolt, whether through a crowd of people or a heavy, tangled briar bush. (13-4)

Bass's knack for character description developed in his fiction appears here and allows him to provide vivid pictures of the people dedicated to this task.

This book, ostensibly a quest story, really concerns healing. It becomes important that Bass reports on his own medical condition: he experiences difficulty with vision ("electric blue bolts of light out of [his] left eye" (96)), a symptom possibly indicating multiple sclerosis. The question of his condition is never resolved, much like the question of the San Juan's health and the grizzlies' health. The idea that these bears might still be out there is a sign of healing to Bass, not for himself, but for the earth. If we still have the bears with us, and can keep them with us, we might heal the livid scar that we as a species have torn on the earth. Bass extends this question of health to the ravaged land around him:

> We take a side fork by a big yellow mined–out hill, which seems to glow with cyanide, and just around the bend from the hill we come upon the old gold mine's tailing pond, whose shores are also yellow and quicksand-murky, with a few dead-gray tree skeletons upright in the water. Miracle of miracles, trout rise from the polluted pond, making slow rolls at the late afternoon mayflies. Trout with three eyes, I think, trout with livers like small raisins and brains of solid gold. Perhaps their bones are lithified, composed also of gold, or maybe cyanide. Perhaps in the frying pan the fish would vaporize into cyanide gas and everyone in the house would fall down dead. (16)

This chilling description of the environmental degradation in the mountains provides a small warning inside a much larger alarm bell that what we do will come back to haunt us.

Sight is the crux of this book. Bass and his cohorts have come to *see* grizzlies. That would be the most direct proof of their existence in these mountains. Bass's early problems with sight are countered toward the end, when he believes he actually sees a grizzly. His sight becomes the key element: possibly diseased, despite that he sees the bear. It also makes him take the vision on faith, because his eyes are not trustworthy. He believes it is a grizzly because of "the mysticism of the event," (225) and it functions as the book's climax, leading Bass to make the fine point that "to the mountain, the bear is a sort of glorified lichen, and to God or Wakan Taka or Allah above," everything is akin to lichen, (219) something that does not register much on the grand scale. It is humbling to be lichen, and Bass believes we need that. "Would we want the appropriate management agency," he asks, "in our case, God—to sign off if our numbers . . . fell below fifty?" (206) Bass seeks a broader perspective for his readers and anyone who will listen, to have empathy with nature because we are a part of it. In "'Too Damn Close': Thresholds and Their Maintenance in Rick Bass's Work," the critic Richard Kerridge writes, "The question of whether [Bass] really met a grizzly provokes a series of questions about the reliability of his perception, as if what he has seen is incompatible with normal possibility; as if his meeting, on the mountaintop, was with God." (Weltzien, *Literary Art,* 187) That the vision has a spiritual meaning for Bass becomes clearer later when he goes so far as to refer to the woods as "church." (149) For him, it is a matter of reverence—the wilderness encompasses and houses us too and deserves to be seen from within, not as something separate.

In *The New Wolves: The Return of the Mexican Wolf to the American Southwest* (1998) Bass returns to the subject of *The Ninemile Wolves*. But these wolves are not wolves in the wild migrating from one place to another; they have been bred in captivity for thirty years and are now getting a chance at wild life thanks to the reintroduction program in the Blue Mountains region of Arizona. Like Bass's previous effort, the story is well told. It details all the players in the reintroduction story, reaching back to the slaughtering of wolves by the government in the mid-twentieth century, to government workers of today, students, ranchers, and the new wolves.

Bass begins his book with a short memory of how he and his family

> would see [the wolves]—hanging vertical from the corner post of the barbed-wire fence every Sunday, on our way to church; the freshly trapped red wolves, at the place we called Wolf Corner, on the outskirts of Houston. Sometimes there would be an assemblage of buff-colored coyotes flanking the larger red wolves, like angels aiding in the wolf's ascent. (xi)

The story serves to ground the reader in the situation, to engage the reader the way a novel would. It does not sentimentalize. He poses a question at the end: "What God, or gods, will summon [endangered species'] return, and step forward with mercy to aid not their prosperity, but their mere survival?" (xiii) The implicit answer to the question is: human beings. Again his ideas about nature are couched in religious terms.

What begins as a plea for the wolf's survival becomes a character study of those involved in the reintroduction effort. He first looks at the students who volunteer with the Round River Conservation Studies program and go to work in Arizona to lay the groundwork for the wolf release: "In the meantime the students are traveling the side canyons and backcountry tirelessly, making notes and maps, and detailing the things they find." (29) The characterization of the students and subsequently of the wolves does a wonderful job humanizing, not the wolves, but their plight. Bass says, "I cannot help but keep believing that—against whatever odds—wolves will make it back to this land because the land desires it. . . . The absence of wolves is clearly a biological wrong." (31) This mixture of science and romance that appears in *The Ninemile Wovles* and *The Lost Grizzlies* tags Bass's style.

Of the reintroduction sites proposed, Bass criticizes the actions of his home state of Texas and its ranchers the most:

> consortium of three or four neighbors could corner damn near a million acres, home to the only wild Mexican lobos in the U. S. of a. We're talking an entrepreneur's dream: movies, foundation grants, concessions—the right to sell petrified wolf shit through the mail to the yuppie wolf-lovers. (52)

Bass's approach is refreshingly unscientific, since science seems often not to convince anyone. So instead he takes an economic stance. Bass tells the story of one ranching couple, Will and Jan Holder, who are trying to produce predator-friendly beef. Bass cites that enough people have sufficient money or conscience to pay a little extra for their meat, and he extols the Holders as the New Rancher—one who is aware of more than money, aware of the land, aware of the changing times. Bass makes a case for this philosophy, this way of ranching, because he sees in it what he longs for—a balanced planet.

In *Caribou Rising: Defending the Porcupine Herd, Gwich-'in Culture, and the Arctic National Wildlife Refuge* (2004), Rick Bass explores new territory, but a continuing theme. Bass visits the Arctic Village, home of the Gwich-'in Indians, who are sustained by the porcupine caribou herd that lives there. The Arctic Village adjoins the Arctic National Wildlife Refuge (ANWR), which at the time was under intense scrutiny as a place to drill for oil. The book has, interestingly, brought Bass full circle. Once an oil geologist himself, supportive of that industry, he goes to war against it, at least against the irresponsibility of the major oil companies and the politicians who support them, Alaskan Congressman Don Young and Senator Lisa Murkowski among them.

Caribou Rising narrates a hunting trip. Bass has gone to the Arctic Village for the Gwich-'in annual caribou hunt. Divided into two sections, the first takes place while Bass and his companions wait for a motor to be fixed so they can travel upriver. Amidst the waiting, Bass gets to know the Gwich-'in people better and to understand their culture, a culture they are trying to save. He lays out the situation—that drilling in the ANWR will provide only six months worth of oil ten years from now, and in the meantime will create "a two-thousand-acre Wal-Mart," (30) and destroydestroying the calving ground for the indigenous caribou as well as continuing to degrade the culture of the indigenous humans:

> [I]t's not just the caribou that will vanish, nor the population of polar bears that winter there, but the Gwich-'in culture, and perhaps even the Gwich-'in people themselves, being snuffed out finally and quickly like tendrils of smoke rising from the tundra, where previously a bright fire has burned for the last two eons. (5)

Bass sets his hunting of one caribou against the government's potentially irreparable destruction of the species. He writes, "The oil boys, the Bush boys, don't just want the lives and the land of the last natives. . . . They want time itself." But in the same paragraph he turns it on everyone: "They—we—are mining time, not oil. . . . We don't want to grow up, nor do we want to be confronted with any notions of the sacred." (18-9) Bass's, and scientists',The argument that drilling in the ANWR will not be productive is a pointed one. It suggests that the government's plan to drill has less to do with reducing dependence on foreign oil and the price of gas, and more to do with power and profit.

In the second half of the book, Bass and the hunting party finally set out, though they will come back empty-handed, as the tribe has reported few caribou sightings. Bass goes out hunting on his own and, while roaming the woods, artfully contrasts the idea of time in the first half: "Time falls away like an old snakeskin shed, like useless anger released and then blown away by the wind. Time is not even so much scrubbed clean and bare, out on this landscape, as it just vanishes—as if it never existed." (136) While the president and the oil companies drill for time, for Bass, who hunts and strives to live a sustainable life, time becomes meaningless, and his life is more peaceful because of it.

Among the religious Gwich-'in, Bass focuses increasingly on God in this book. He goes to church in the village and hears the preacher speak of giving up things to get through the "narrow door." Bass believes he is speaking of both the kingdom of God and of America and its love of

oil; it will have to go if we are to have any future. (58-9) God is a concern to the Gwich-'in and is claimed as a concern of the president and members of his administration. To this Bass says, "I know increasingly that I seem at times not to recognize whatsoever the face or sound of Bush's, or Cheney's, god: this one they keep clamoring about; the one they claim to know and understand and speak for." (153-4). Bass finds the tribe's faith and the president's faith at odds, because one is tolerant and the other not, and he struggles with it as much as he struggles with the loss of land. Bass ends his book with a question, "Is it still like the story of Genesis—still just at the beginning—or more like a reverse kind of Noah's Ark, with more and more being told to get off the ship?" (154) Bass equates nature and mystery with God; but the men he sees as the enemies of nature also claim to speak for God, and this does not jibe with Bass. The president and his administration seem to have no sense of spirit and, instead of trying to save wildlife from disaster, are kicking it aside to make more room for a bigger couch. *Caribou Rising* thus sees Bass pushing further in two directions, both as a discussion of the spiritual and as a political attack, and in this case the two are intertwined.

CONCLUSION

Much of Rick Bass's work employs religious language. While not espousing any particular religion, Bass does use a religious lexicon, one often associated with magic. English has little else to convey the sense of holiness that this writer feels for nature. There may be a God for Bass, but certainly bears and larch trees and everything between the sky and the earth that remains not quite touchable by language is God too. It goes hand in hand with his love of place. It is reverence and respect for something greater than himself. O. Alan Weltzien and many other critics see Bass as a writer of place, and that certainly is so. However, always in that place is mystery, an idea that has shaped his work from the beginning, and though mystery is just that, mysterious, and Bass never pegs any kind of

religious philosophy down over it, the mystery functions as a religion for him in his work.

Bass is many things as a writer, one who can maneuver skillfully in diverse genres and who can create new ones. He remains, however, true to his naturalist heart. All of his writing expresses his love for the land and his ardent desire to protect the wilderness. He has, more successfully than most, made nature writing a larger part of the literary community.

Selected Bibliography

WORKS OF RICK BASS

NONFICTION

The Deer Pasture. Illustrated by Elizabeth Hughes. College Station: Texas A & M University Press, 1985.

Wild to the Heart. Illustrated by Elizabeth Hughes. Harrison, Pa.: Stackpole, 1987.

Oil Notes. Illustrated by Elizabeth Hughes. Boston: Houghton Mifflin, 1989.

Winter: Notes from Montana. Illustrated by Elizabeth Hughes. Boston: Houghton Mifflin, 1991.

The Ninemile Wolves: An Essay. Livingston, Mont.: Clark City, 1992.

The Lost Grizzlies: A Search for Survivors in the Wilderness of Colorado. Boston: Houghton Mifflin, 1995.

The Book of Yaak. Boston: Houghton Mifflin, 1996.

The New Wolves: The Return of the Mexican Wolf to the American Southwest. New York: Lyons Press, 1998.

Brown Dog of the Yaak: Essays on Art and Activism. Minneapolis: Milkweed, 1999.

Colter: The True Story of the Best Dog I Ever Had. Boston: Houghton Mifflin, 2000.

The Roadless Yaak: Reflections and Observations about One of Our Last Great Wild Places. Edited by Rick Bass. Introduction by Mike Dombeck. Guilford, Conn.: Lyons Press, 2002. (Essays by various writers, naturalists, and scientists.)

Caribou Rising: Defending the Porcupine Herd, Gwich-'in Culture, and the Arctic National Wildlife Refuge. San Francisco: Sierra Club, 2004.

NONFICTION

The Watch: Stories. New York: Norton, 1989.

Platte River. Boston: Houghton Mifflin, 1994. (Novellas.)

In the Loyal Mountains. Boston: Houghton Mifflin, 1995. (Short stories.)

The Sky, The Stars, The Wilderness. Boston: Houghton Mifflin, 1997. (Novellas.)

Where the Sea Used to Be. Boston: Houghton Mifflin, 1998. (Novel.)

Fiber. Athens: University of Georgia Press, 1998. (Novella.)

The Hermit's Story: Stories. Boston: Houghton Mifflin, 2002.

The Diezmo. Boston: Houghton Mifflin, 2005. (Novel; published after the present essay was written.)

CRITICAL AND BIOGRAPHICAL STUDIES

Ciolkowski, Laura. "Poetic Tales of the Balance Between Place and People." *Boston Globe,* October 20, 2002, p. D7. (Review of The Hermit's Story.)

Dixon, Terrell F. "Rick Bass." *American Nature Writers,* Vol. 1, *Edward Abbey to John McPhee.* Edited by John Elder. New York: Scribners, 1996.

Weltzien, O. Alan, ed. *The Literary Art and Activism of Rick Bass.* Salt Lake City: University of Utah Press, 2001. (This volume includes all of the critical works quoted in the present essay, unless otherwise noted in the text.)

————. *Rick Bass.* Boise State University Western Writers Series, no. 134. Boise, Idaho: Boise State University Press, 1998.

CAROL BLY

(1930—)

Susan Carol Hauser

CAROL BLY WAS born Carolyn McLean on April 16, 1930, in Duluth, Minnesota, where her father, C. Russell McLean, owned a hotel. Her mother, Mildred (Washburn) McLean graduated from Wellesley College in 1912 with a Bachelor of Arts degree in English; she died of tuberculosis in 1942, at age fifty-two, when Bly was twelve years old. Bly had three older brothers, Russell, John and Malcolm, who served in the military in World War II. (All survived.) During that war, her father, who had served in World War I, was head of a temporary coast guard unit on Lake Superior in Duluth, Minnesota.

As an adolescent and teenager, Bly attended Abbot Academy in Andover, Massachusetts (then a girls' boarding school, now a part of Phillips Academy in Andover). In her memoir *An Adolescent's Christmas: 1944* (2000), she describes returning home for the holiday, to a house still missing its mother, who had passed away two years before; to a town worried about its children in service to a war; and to families carrying on as best they could, making conversation in order to keep from talking about larger losses and griefs. Although Bly did not write down her observations at the time, she was, characteristically, taking in the details. She observed the surface play of "kidding" that passed as intimacy in her family and community, and she recalls yearning for a different approach: "one's inside mind longs for word of bad or sad news if there is any. One's inside mind is willing to be frighted by dreams—anything! Just any corroboration of serious news if serious news there is." (*An Adolescent's Christmas,* p. 27).

During her childhood years in Duluth, Bly learned about classist systems, from the perspective of a privileged upper-middle-class child. In the essay "My Dear Republican Mother" (collected in *Three Readings for Republicans and Democrats* [2003]), she calls her mother to account:

> My dear Republican mother, if you came back to life so we could talk, I would want this out between us, first thing: is it or is it not all right for human beings to live on nature's old pecking order, which we usually call the "class system?"

> Oh—the pecking order! In everything from hawk's-eye weeds to alpha wolves to *E. coli* bacteria to Ivy League graduates. Inherited in wild creatures' genes, inherited in human beings' capital, inherited in childhood expectations. Then, in both animals and people, taught by parents to their young as if it were a virtue.

> That is where we would have our quarrel. (p. 17.)

But in recalling her childhood, whether in her stories or as in this essay and others, Bly recognizes the complexity of influence. Her mother taught her to "step forward and shake hands firmly" and gave her children "the gift of abstract words to use in ordinary conversation—beauty, glory, nature—words my friends in Brownie Scouts heard only in Sunday school and church." (*Three Readings,* p. 18) She also taught Bly "the point of beautiful moments no matter how trivial. You said, verbatim, *Treasure up whatever lovely moment comes along.*" (p. 33)

For Bly, in her writing, the detail of the moment, no matter how mundane, is often the measure of who we are and of what our lives mean. In recalling her childhood in "My Dear Republican Mother," she remembers her mother teaching her to mend: "The warp and weft must cross over and under one another at 90 degrees.... The implication... was that one must hold the fort of superior standards against the mediocre work

of the many." (*Three Readings,* p. 25) As it is proper stitches that hold fabric and the fabric of lives together, so in Bly's writing it is the details that reveal the lives. She remembers a counterpane, for instance, a bedspread rendered "utterly white, because the maids washed them twice weekly in very hot water and bleach, to kill the TB germs." (p. 25) The counterpane is described in detail, "little alternate columns of seersucker and plain weave," (p. 25) that give form to the ideas and the people Bly has been talking about: tidy rows, each keeping to itself, whiter than sunshine: this much at least shall be in control.

At the age of nine, Bly wrote "The Adventures of Hilary Melwheel," a novel about an American Revolution hero. "My entire novel consisted of two sheets of typing paper, each folded in half, torn along the folds, then folded again into quarters. I had common-pinned the signatures together through the spine. There is no joy like that of having made a book, so I carried it up to your bedroom to show you." (*Three Readings,* p. 35) Bly's mother responded with criticism of young Carol's misspelling, reading the story out loud and pronouncing the intended "whipping" as "wiping" over and over again. In retrospect, Bly identifies this as bullying, and as an adult she explored the nature of bullies in her short stories and her essays, as well as in a 1996 compilation titled *Changing the Bully Who Rules the World: Reading and Thinking about Ethics.*

As a child, Carol Bly also knew bullying from some of the servants in the household, who were present not only because of the family's class status but also because of Mildred McLean's illness. She had contracted tuberculosis when her firstborn child was two years old. The other three children were carefully planned, but eventually the servants were the parents. Many of the household employees were kind, but one in particular levied extended and brutal spankings against her charges. When Bly told her father about the abuse, he responded by saying, "I know that wouldn't happen," (p. 31) and Bly suffered the price of adult denial.

Although she sometimes lived with relatives in North Carolina, and for a time she attended boarding school on the East Coast, it was in Du-luth, Minnesota, that Bly lived the themes that would become her writing: what we do matters; what we deny matters; bullies are bullies, and good people do not let them get away with it.

Bly says in *An Adolescent's Christmas* that "I hadn't the tiniest inkling of what it means to want *reform.* I had never met anyone who intended to change the world." (51) Yet, as she set about her adult life, changing the world is exactly what *she* intended to do.

LETTERS FROM THE COUNTRY

After graduating from Abbot Academy in 1947, Bly continued her education at Wellesley College, where she earned a Bachelor of Arts degree in English and history in 1951. She attended graduate school at the University of Minnesota in 1954–1955. In 1955 she married the poet Robert Bly, and the pair moved to rural Madison, Minnesota, where they lived for twenty-four years and raised their four children, Mary, Bridget, Noah, and Micah. Carol and Robert Bly divorced in 1979.

Living with her family on a farmstead near the southern Minnesota town of Madison, population 2,200, Bly both participated in and observed the society around her, over decades in which World War II faded into the history books and U.S. attention shifted from the Korean War (1950–1953) to the Vietnam War (1954–1979). While in Madison, in addition to bearing and raising her four children, Bly also worked in the fields, the church, and the community: she was a member of the Madison Chamber of Commerce, a cofounder of the Prairie Arts Center in Madison, a lay reader in the Episcopal church, the county chair of the Countryside Council in Marshall, Minnesota, and a board member of Episcopal Community Services in Minneapolis.

At the same time, she attended to her own intellectual life. She managed the publication of the literary magazines the *Fifties and the Sixties*—counterculture journals edited by Robert Bly and the poet William Duffy that intentionally prodded the literary community to write with new vigor—and she also managed the Sixties Press and the Seventies Press. Her translation of

work by Anders Bodelson from the Danish was published by Harper & Row in 1970, and she translated other work from German, Norwegian, and French.

By the early 1970s Bly had also come to a strong affinity with the "back to the land" philosophy that had emerged from the antiwar and hippie movements of the 1960s, a trend characterized by a turning away from post–World War II materialism and patriotism. From 1973 to 1979 she shared her experience of rural life in a column titled "Letter from the Country," which she wrote for Minnesota Public Radio's newsletter *Preview* and then its magazine, *Minnesota Monthly*. From these essays, collected as a volume titled *Letters from the Country* in 1981, we learn that her own "back to the land" experience did not represent an escape from society but rather offered a means of engagement at the crucial level of personal involvement. A social activist by nature, she worked to bring to her neighbors new ideas, new ways to be sentient. Her offerings (such as helping to found an arts center in her town) were not meant merely to make available the urban experiences of the arts, but rather to create opportunity for the human experiences of the inner mind, of emotion and the expression of emotion.

The desire to open the affective life to rural citizens was driven by Bly's understanding that one of the costs of living in a small town was the suppression of feelings: "There is restraint against enthusiasm ('real nice' is the adjective—not 'marvelous'); there is restraint in grief ('real sober' instead of 'heartbroken'); and always, always, restraint in showing your feelings, lest someone be drawn closer to you," she says in *Letters*. (p. 2) She describes leaving the movie theater after a showing of *Charlotte's Web* and overhearing mothers saying to their softly crying children, "'Oh, for the love of goodness, it was just a movie!' and 'Okay, okay, OKAY! You don't have to feel it *that* much.' " (*Letters*, p. 3) For Bly, "this is the real death in our countryside, this not approving of feeling," (*Letters*, p.3) and she is compelled to fight it; it is not just loss for the individuals, but for the country, even for life on earth. The suppression of feelings, and their

counterpart opinions, allows the status quo to continue, and puts us in danger of "succumbing to the mass state." (*Letters*, p. 15)

Often in her essays Bly first lays out a problem and then offers an antidote. In one essay, for example, she selects three ideas from the American psychologist Bruno Bettelheim to apply to conversation in Madison about President Richard Nixon and Watergate: "(1) replacing the feeling of 'business as usual' with crisis thinking, (2) forcing ourselves to have a sense of time in our lives, and (3) understanding the power of negative thinking." (*Letters*, p. 15) Bettelheim, she says, "suggests we must ask ourselves at every other moment, Is this business as usual? Is this a crisis? Is it O.K. to go on just maintaining my life today, or must I act in some political way?" (*Letters*, p. 16) In this case, she suggests, the conversation about Nixon and Watergate might then proceed in this way: "Should the President be impeached? Now is the moment of our anxiety over his crookedness: should we impeach? If not, is there something else we should be doing? Is it really O.K. to just be sitting here?" (*Letters*, p. 16)

Bly also addresses moral concerns closer to home, in the necessity, for instance, of firing a minister who is more a bully than a shepherd. This calls not just for honest conversation but for courageous action, and she outlines four steps that can be taken toward that end. Bly's frank and insistent essays about her town in themselves took courage to write, because they break the very rules of reticence that they describe. But they also affirm a proposition that she repeats throughout the collection:

> Rural people tend to think history takes place at My Lai, not here. They need to be reminded that genuine local history took place a decade and a half ago in the Utah countryside when Lewis Strauss's [Atomic] Energy Commission assured the people they had nothing to fear from underground testing. And genuine local history is taking place in Utah now. People are counting their leukemia cases. The old relaxing normalcy-loving slogan, "Oh, well— give him enough time—he'll hang himself!" won't do. It isn't itself that the AEC hanged. (*Letters*, p. 174)

In the end, the essays evolve out of a deep understanding of peace and the cost of its preservation:

> In the countryside we get the point of normalcy. We garden happily. We sit on the farm stoop in the evenings. We know some body secrets which city people likely wouldn't guess, such as that the delicious, repairing thing to drink at noon during harvest is very hot coffee, not sugared cold drinks. Or when the field work is so hot one's eyes are sour with sweat and the body so exhausted at night that you stagger gingerly to the pickup, then the good thing is not the instant hot bath so dear to urbanites, but to sit on the ground and slowly dry and stiffen. I was disconcerted when this was first shown to me. Then, in the 1960s, nutritionists explained that the sun's benefits have a chance to be absorbed if you don't bathe right away. So this sitting around dirty and fragile with tiredness was a sound instinct the whole while. Everyday virtues, everyday feelings, with no sharp changes, are our genius in the country.
>
> When crises comes, however, the personality must stagger to its feet, totter into the museum of bravery, find a suit of armor gone cold that looks as it if won't fit, and get it on, and rattle the fingers. The psychic equipment of everyday life—forbearance, patience—is no good now: we have to screw up our courage to a tougher sticking place. We have to become outspoken and decisive. (*Letters*, p. 169-170)

Admiring reviews for *Letters from the Country* appeared in the *New York Times,* the *Atlantic, Publishers Weekly, Library Journal, Newsweek,* the *New Republic,* and others. Wade Hancock, writing in the *Christian Science Monitor,* described the book as "an unusual collection of stern, perceptive, and loving" essays that "explore ... why in the midst of such prosperity our inner lives are so impoverished, the social ties to our rural communities so thin." (June 3, 1981, v 73, p 17, col 1) Noel Perrin, in the *New York Times* said that Bly "wants the farmers and small town merchants of America to live with passion, to have a sense of greatness in their lives, to take themselves as seriously as a Beethoven or a Thoreau." (May 24, 1981, v 130 s7, p 4, col 1).

In a preface to a 1999 paperback reissue of *Letters from the Country* by the University of Minnesota Press, Bly takes the opportunity to turn a critical eye to her own work. She finds the first third of the essays to be "a little cross," the other two-thirds "less rebellious and more hopeful of change" and more successful at achieving her goal, which is "informally analyzing rural life and trying to figure out some ways to live both more seriously and more happily than seemed to be the general custom." (*Letters* 1999, p. ix) She also scans the landscape for change and concludes that there is more courageous thinking in rural areas in 1998 than there was in 1973:

> We used to hear people say that if you talk about the world's sad news there will be no end to your sadness. The opposite appears to be true. As country people, like urban people, have the world's sadnesses rubbed harder and harder into their faces, they name the sadnesses more and more loudly and they more and more openly say which sad reactions they have to all the sad data. So far as I can see people are more intimate as they become more conscious and more willing to look at bad news. It's as if countryside communities were growing up, the way individuals do. However appalling the *outward* news in Minnesota, for example . . . the *inward* news is that rural people seem by and large braver. They aren't nearly so given to denying evil as they were. (*Letters* 1999, p. xvii)

BACKBONE

In the late 1970s, Bly produced poetry that appeared in *Poetry Northwest* and *Coastlines* under the pseudonyms Ann Reynolds and Joanna Campbell, and in 1979 the *New Yorker* published Bly's story "The Last of the Gold Star Mothers," the first of many short stories that drew on her engaged understanding of rural people, both in Madison and from her childhood in Duluth. In 1985, this story and four others ("The Mouse Roulette Wheel," "Talk of Heroes," "Gunnar's Sword," and "The Dignity of Life," all of which had appeared individually between 1979 and 1983 in journals or anthologies) were published as Bly's first volume of short stories, *Backbone.*

"The Last of the Gold Star Mothers" introduced Mary Graving, a young, divorced single mother, and the town of Rachel River, near Duluth. Graving and other characters manifested themes that Bly had introduced in *Letters*: what is not said matters as much that which is said; what is felt should sometimes be spoken; outside cheer does not preclude inner sadness or despair. This story and the othersin *Backbone* also render two of Bly's recurring themes: the inner yearning to be taken seriously, and the nature of bullies and those who do not speak against bullying. Some more specific earlier images from Bly's work echo here as well, such as the suit of armor, of bravery, that in *Letters* she recommends we slip into, which is rendered static in a bar scene in "The Last of the Gold Star Mothers": "The fingers [of other patrons] were numb and stiff with drink, as silvery and thick as fingers in the empty suits of armor in city museums." (*Backbone*, p. 10).

In the editor's preface to *Backbone*, Emilie Buchwald quotes Bly: "The principle of literature is devotion to the particulars of life. Chekhov, for example, is not particularly universal; he is particularly particular." The observation can be viewed as an extension of 'Bly's mother's admonition to "treasure up whatever lovely moment comes along," which Bly later interpreted as "the point of beautiful moments no matter how trivial." (*Three Readings*, p. 33) For Bly, as we have noted, the trivial detail becomes the revealing detail. Buchwald notes such details, for instance, as "Mary Graving's woodworking tools in a basement once devoted to home canning and laundry tubs, the Showing Room in Jack Canon's funeral parlor, the fair isle knitting and braided rugs in the craft room at the Jacob Lutheran Home—all a part of the rich weave of Bly's stories" and contends that reading *Backbone* is

as good as or better than eavesdropping because we get to follow people around and see whether their words accord with their thoughts—which we, but not those others, in the story, are privileged to know.

The stories remind us, in fact, words don't necessarily mirror thoughts; that we don't usually say what we mean, nor do we usually mean quite what we say. Bly focuses our attention on the gulf between what is thought and felt and what is actually said.

In *Backbone,* Bly also returns to the idea of the craving of the human soul for seriousness: "The people in these stories long for these moments when the spirit cries out and gets fed," says Buchwald. In "Gunnar's Sword," Bly depicts the intuition as primal, and spanning generations. In a memorable scene, an infant and a great-grandmother both consider their shared situation and adjust to it, physically and in spirit:

She carried Christopher to her rocking chair, and sat down. For a moment baby and great-grandmother made tiny struggles to get sorted. Harriet had to get her good foot, the left, which never gave her trouble even recently, onto the ground, to use for pushing to make the chair rock. The baby had to move his tiny shoulders as though scratching an itch, but in actuality, finding where and how this set of arms would hold him. He didn't pay much attention to what he saw out of his eyes: he saw only the dull whitish light off the snow, smeary and without warmth. What he felt in his shoulders, behind the small of his back, under his knees, was the very soul of whoever was holding him; it streamed into the baby from all those places. The baby stilled, paying attention to it, deciding, using shoulder blades, backbone, and legs to make the decision whether or not the energy entering was safe and good. Everything now told him it was, so in the next second he let each part of his body loosen into those hands, and let his feet be propped on that lap, then let his chest be lifted and pressed to that breast and shoulder.... He made a little offering of his own; he let his cheek lean on that old trustworthy cheek, and then, with a final wiggle, he gave himself up to being held. (*Backbone,* p. 109)

As readers, we know what to make of this moment: stripped of ego and fear, it is possible for us to connect in trust, perhaps the deepest level of human commitment. In *Backbone* there are many such moments, when we know the best of who we are. Bly also takes us to depths of humor, but in these scenarios we are less comfortable. We see the immediate gag, and laugh aloud or to ourselves, but are less certain that it is all right that we do so. The circumstances are usually

ludicrous, which is perhaps the source of their humor, but they are also deadly real, and thus not funny at all.

In "The Last of the Gold Star Mothers," for instance, the sheriff confronts a deputy who is renowned for his bad choices:

O.K.OK, Merle ... Labor Day you were in charge of the Gold Star Mothers' car in the parade, right? OK, the parade forms in front of the Vision Avenue Apartments where you pick up the Gold Star Mother, the only one we got left, and then everyone marches and drives to the cemetery where they have the doings. I got two complaints on you. First, you stuffed our one remaining Gold Star Mother into the car so mean she got bruised. She brought a charge. But that isn't all. They you got to the cemetery, and I suppose I ought to be grateful you didn't run down them Rachel River Saddle Club horses on the way. When you got to the cemetery, what'd you do but get out and turn off the ignition, which means the air-conditioning went off. You left the windows rolled up and you left the Gold Star Mother in there. Mrs. Lorraine Graving is not a young woman; it was a hundred and five Fahrenheit. She could have died in there. I like you to know that she is a symbol of our whole national honor. Without her we wouldn't be the kind of country we are today. Now, if we're not going to have any respect any more, it'll be the end of the Gold Star Mother program completely. (*Backbone,* p. 12)

The Gold Star Mother program and the Gold Star Mother herself are presented to the reader in a straightforward way. The humor comes, allusively, in the play of values expressed. Pageantry is serious. Never mind that the reader finds out later that Lorraine Graving, Mary's former mother-in-law, is an unsympathetic, harsh woman: she is the last standing mother of a Rachel River World War II veteran and so deserves to be honored. And never mind that the honor she represents is as tarnished and untrustworthy as the woman herself: the nation is embroiled in a disastrous and dishonest war, and the president of the country is about to be impeached. As Buchwald noted, we are privy to information that the characters are not, and perhaps we must laugh, else we must cry.

Bly's seriousness about human failings is built, however, not on despair, but on hope. Buchwald says in her preface, "The fragile spine that lets us bend also allows us to stand. Carol Bly celebrates the valor it takes to live humanely." In asking that we behave better, Bly implies that we are able to do so. In the *New York Times Book Review,* the American poet Tess Gallagher observed of *Backbone* that "one of the author's most valuable insights is that our imagination and the use to which we put it can serve as a constructive moral force."

The world of the characters in *Backbone* found a larger audience when three of the stories—"The Last of the Gold Star Mothers," "The Dignity of Life," and "Gunnar's Sword"—were developed into a 1989 PBS *American Playhouse* movie titled *Rachel River,* with a screenplay by the Minnesota author Judith Guest (*Ordinary People*) and directed by Sandy Smolan.

ACTIVISM AND ETHICAL LITERATURE

In 1979, after her separation from Robert Bly, Carol Bly had moved from Madison, Minnesota, to St. Paul. Her short stories were finding their way into publication. Around this time she also found herself at the leading edge of another wave of societal change: awareness of the need to halt the degradation of the environment and the planet. The publication of Rachel Carson's *Silent Spring* in 1962 had sounded the first alarm for the need for ecological awareness and action, but now, nearly twenty years later, few were listening to its warning. There was work to be done.

In 1978 Bly began a three-year term as a humanities consultant for the American Farm Project, sponsored by the National Endowment for the Humanities and the National Farmers Union. From 1982 to 1985 she served as humanities consultant to the Land Stewardship Project in St. Paul. In 1986, she published, with Joe Paddock and Nancy Paddock, the book *Soil and Survival: Land Stewardship and the Future of American Agriculture.* It takes a broad look at our cultural attitudes toward the soil, which stands also as a symbol for the environment and the planet. As with her other work, Bly, along

with her co-authors, approaches this agricultural crisis with a call to strengthen our inner life as a way, in part, to protect our outer life. The book is thoroughly documented and builds on insights of major writers, including John Steinbeck, Marge Piercy, Elizabeth Dodson Gray, Wendell Berry, and Aldo Leopold. Echoing Bly's method in *Letters from the Country,* it also offers practical guidelines for action.

In 1986, the same year that *Soil and Survival* was published, Bly also published a twenty-page pamphlet with the Minneapolis publisher Milkweed Editions, *Bad Government and Silly Literature,* an essay that originally published in the literary journal *Milkweed Chronicle.* Once again she turns her attention to the ethical importance of what we say, and fail to say. She suggests that the moral deficiency of "silly literature" has serious implications, and she observes that while American novelists freely express sexuality in their work, they mostly leave out "political and ethical anxiety," even at a time when our government is behaving unethically, and "Americans who are educated, and who write stories, know it." As she describes the problem, offers a cure, and presents a reason for the disorder, she is both philosophical and practical. Her advice to fiction writers is, in part, to develop characters who are as curious and worried about the behavior of their government as they are about sex, and as curious and worried about their own role in their government, and its cruelties, as they are concerned about their sexuality.

Bly's creative work continued to develop parallel to her civic work. She began to teach writing, at COMPAS (a community writing program); in a Basic Arts Program in Duluth; and at universities, including Hamline in St. Paul, the University of Minnesota, and Metropolitan State University. She lectured at the Institute on Man and Science in Renssalaerville, New York, and the Rural Institute in Marshall, Minnesota, and served as a board member for the Minnesota Independent Scholars' Forum. She served as writer in residence at the Upper Midwest Writers Conference and, with a South Dakota Council of English Teachers Certificate of Honor in 1985, she began to garner the many awards that were to come her

way including Minnesota State Arts Board grants (1980, 1990), two Bush Foundation Fellowships (1981, 1991), and an honorary doctor of humane letters from Northland College (1992).

Her story "The Dignity of Life" (later collected in *Backbone*) had appeared in the literary magazine *Ploughshares* in 1982 and from there was selected for the Houghton Mifflin anthology *Best American Short Stories 1983* (1983), edited by Anne Tyler. When her story "Gunnar's Sword" (also in *Backbone*) was anthologized in the Graywolf Press anthology *Full Measure: Modern Short Stories on Aging* (1988), Bly wrote the foreword to this collection, in which she maintains that aging "is going to take some humor—living in a skin much slept in, trying hard to keep growing up, trying to maintain what decency we have and to acquire a little more, trying to learn more gaiety for every loss—while all the time we are floating closer to a universe that is more and more laid bare to us." (p. xxii-xiii) In conclusion, she says, "Here is a book of fellow travelers," and in that simple statement reveals a frame from which she operates in her own life: we are all in the same boat. It is because of connection, more than disenfranchisement, that Bly works so hard toward the achievement of a better world.

Although Bly in the 1980s was mostly a city dweller, she found opportunity to get herself back into the fields as a laborer. In a journal entry published in *Ariadne's Thread: A Collection of Contemporary Women's Journals* (1982), edited by Lyn Lifshin, she recounts the events of May 22, 1981, planting "four strawberry types: Sparkles, Scotts, Delights and Midway."

Both Ardis and I are awfully good field hands. We have the only quality you need, really. We bestir ourselves. It takes practice not to just sit there. When there is something wrong, we have to move quickly. Jump off the planter, lower our bodies under the wheels so we can see what's in the chain, if anything, and pry it out... At the ends of the rows is the blessed shade. ...

Finally we are done—at 8 at night. We all shout and Margaret drives us out of the field in the pickup. Back at the Place, which always means the owner's house and front yard, we lie in the cold grass

ecstatically before we drive home. Bruce and Margaret's dog comes up to lick our sweaty eyes. I try to love her, although she has her whole day's ticks in her white coat. (p. 266)

She also continued to labor in the fields of literature, writing forewords to anthologies that spoke her language, articulating the psychological work that these collections offered the reader. Of *Everybody's Story: Writing by Older Minnesotans* (1987), she says:

> The job of the writer in any generation is to show the reader what is various and lovely, and what is various and bad—somehow to do it all without rhetoric or self-pity. … It means getting up your nerve and trying to interpret what life has meant, occasion by occasion. It means not being so daunted by whatever lies ahead that you can't write truthfully to the rest of us. We are all coming along the same path, looking for brave writers to trust. (p. xiii)

Breaking Hard Ground (1990) is another book grounded in Minnesota and in hope. It contains the stories of thirty-one farmers who struggled against the move to corporate farming that blitzed the United States in the 1980s. In her foreword, Bly states the situation: "The writers in this book, farmers, advocates, attorneys, all know that there are people—well-organized people out there— who want family farmers off U.S.A. soil for good." (p. xi) She goes on to give this enemy a face and to imagine what she would do if she were that enemy—how she would subvert information and public image, and blame the family farmer.

> The writers of *Breaking Hard Ground* tell us how the psychological warfare of dividing farmers who are supposedly "good borrowers" from those supposedly "bad borrowers" tends to keep farmers from organizing together. We hear how lenders even hire farmers to use their equipment to enforce the foreclosure against their neighbors. We hear how farmers who stood up to the FmHA [Farmers Home Administration] and protested got thrown out of their church councils and asked not to be ushers anymore. (p. xiii)

Bly says that if she "were an enemy to family farming, I would do everything to prevent people from finding out about the Minnesota Farm Advocates Program," which, with other support organizations, prevented 78,000 family farm foreclosures. (p. xiii) For her, *Breaking Hard Ground* is an antidote to the actions of that enemy: "This book shows you how to change from being a passive Conservative to being an advocate—a change maker." (p. xiii)

The book, by virtue of its existence, advocates for change on other levels as well. One farmer woke up to the reality of the situation when, after a farm disaster, he was called a "bad manager." "He reports," says Bly, "he is not 'just a conservative' any more," and his story woke Bly up in turn:

> I don't farm. I am a writer. As I read this book, I began asking myself some questions about *my* field: have I been passive about where American literature is going? Is there something I can do to stop American stories and poems and novels from being the trash crop which giant mass publishers assure us we all want? If Minnesota farmers have learned to be active, firm but not belligerent, and ethically awake, I can translate some of their new savvy into my own field.

> After all, what we all want is a world in which small operators who like their work can live without any insult and injustice, can live in the places which are native to them, and can consort with those they do business with without fear.(p. xiv)

The stories of the farmer's and Bly's epiphanies, hers an extension of her argument in *Silly Literature and Bad Government*, reinforce Bly's internalized understanding of what it means to live consciously in a society. When we think about the land differently, we change the way we treat the land (as in *Soil and Survival*); when we shed a cloak of guilt that someone else has laid on our shoulders, we stand straighter and become more clearly and forcefully who we are. In a foreword to a reprint of *The Life of an Ordinary Woman: Anne Ellis* (1999), a 1929 memoir by a Colorado mining wife, Bly says, "Of course this book will be read as a handbook to life in an

early Colorado mining town, but its real heft is in Ellis's grasp of what it means to take part in culture—to see and keep records and have your own ethical ideas." (xii)

CHANGING THE BULLY WHO RULES THE WORLD

Bly became aware of bullies when she was a child, and that awareness was refined as she worked through her fiction, essays, and critical writing. At the same time, she developed her sense of ethics and ethical living. These two forces come together in her landmark work *Changing the Bully Who Rules the World: Reading and Thinking about Ethics* (1996). Recipient of a 1997 Minnesota Book Award for Collected Works, the compilation reproduces excerpts from preeminent literary works and supplements them with commentary by Bly. She shows us that "We have not used our knowledge of social psychology or exploited the riches of literature as a device for reconceptualizing and understanding our lives" and she "feels that we should try to interact with the characters in literature, try to assess the long-range impact of all our decisions on the lives of others and develop coherent accounts of our own values." (*Library Journal,* July 1996, page 119)

Bly's preface to the book states her goal: "to show general readers that some of the past half-century's most important insights and strategies about ethics come not from philosophy or political science but from social psychology." (xiii) Developed outside the academy, in clinics and offices, these "amazing insights and experiences are waiting to be translated into action in our businesses, schools, civic organizations, and churches." (xiii) Her hope is that "perhaps, soon, white-collar bullying, like slavery, will no longer be acceptable." (xiii)

Bly opens the book with a discussion of the enormity of some ethical situations, and she observes how common it is for us to claim that such situations are beyond our understanding and hence we can do nothing about them. She counters the shallow, evasive response, such as "there is no way we can know why the German people allowed and followed Adolf Hitler." (p. xvi) She thinks we can know: "Not only are there several very likely explanations for why the German people followed and loved Hitler, but some of the psychologists and stage-developmentalists who have investigated Nazi personality structures have drawn psychological parallels to other group phenomenon." (p. xvi) For example, she says:

Professional psychotherapists and social workers know the commonalities among the following phenomena:

- Decent Germans who implemented deaths at Auschwitz
- Decent American high school kids who make themselves take part in gang rapes
- Decent college graduates who use their corporate standing or government power to cheat the helpless or kill innocent people or wreck our planet (p. xix)

Her book "is dedicated to beautiful literature and the beautiful theory of moral growth and … a few remarkable intervention skills." The three may not seem to belong together, she says, "but then, astronomy and mathematics looked like strange bedfellows when everybody still thought the stars were no business of either one of them." (p. xx)

The point of the book, its scope, is nearly as immense as the problem of bullying, and Bly speaks to the effort of what might seem like a hopeless proposition. She believes that the reading and writing of literature belies an enthusiasm about life that is essentially hopeful. The text is arranged in nine sections, each with a theme, such as "Good News about Leaders and Followers," "The Psychological and Moral Habitats of American Children and Adults," and "Genuine Jerks and Genuine Jerk Organizations." Each section has a selection of literary readings, including poems by Mary Oliver, Donald Hall, Denise Levertov, and Robert Bly; essays by Katha Pollitt, Wendell Berry, and Alice Walker; and short stories by Tobias Wolff and Will Weaver. But the genius of the book is Bly's commentary at the end of each section, a thorough, leisurely stroll through the readings, connecting them—by theme, by the presentation of values, by the ethics acted out in the characters, the images, the ideas—and framing them in social science and

other theories: for instance, in demonstrating the commonality between Denise Levertov's poetry and the family systems theory work of Paula Gutlove at the Center for Psychology and Social Change. "Just as Denise Levertov has been an unswerving opponent of American wars abroad," says Bly,

> the center has devoted its energy to psychological ways of peacemaking. Both poet and social scientist assure us that when human beings throw over the lies they had once accepted as national or family icons, annoying the older generation, shaking up their own, risking their colleagues' scorn—when human beings do that, there likely sets in a general, secret love of everybody.

LATER STORIES

In the 1980s and 1990s Bly taught frequently at colleges and universities in Minnesota and Wisconsin, including Northland College, Carlton College, Hamline University, and the University of Minnesota, where she was the Edelstein-Keller Author of Distinction in 1998. She taught both creative writing and ethics, a blend that was evidenced as well in her own creative work of the period. In both decades she published short stories in literary journals, magazines and anthologies, including *Triquarterly* and *Ploughshares*. As with the stories in *Backbone*, these stories carry out her recommendation in *Silly Literature and Bad Government* that writers seriously address ethical issues in their creative work.

The Tomcat's Wife and Other Stories, published by HarperCollins in 1991 and recipient that year of a Friend of American Writers Award, has eight stories (five of them previously published), described on the dust jacket as being "often about the fugitive state of sweetness and light in American today." The heroines of the stories are women eventually grappling their way to a better of state of being. In "My Lord Bag of Rice," the elderly Eleanor Grummel, liberated by her husband's death, uses her inheritance to move from her small town home to Saint Paul and opens a boarding house where she will "never, never again hear cruel language around her." This of course proves more difficult than it might have seemed, but Grummel is up to the task.

Women who rally to the task frequently occupy Bly's stories. In "The Tender Organizations," one woman, beaten for decades by her husband, withholds his pain medication while he dies of cancer. Two other women, equally strong, collude to give it to him. In the title story, "The Tomcat's Wife," one woman's good country sense is challenged by a city woman's pleasures, which include parking a car by the football field during practice, and sitting there drinking whiskey and sketching the comely, muscular butts of the high school players. "In three or four years they will mostly be idiots. Makes your heart stop to think of it," says the city woman.

Although the stories are mostly built on characters and their actions, Bly's sensibility for image and simile often carry the story to the next place, and sometimes to another plane. In "After the Baptism," a grandfather goes to extremes to bring his granddaughter into the protective realm of the church while at the same time thwarting protestors at his chemical plant. The conversation moves to an uncomfortable discussion based on one person's query, "how is flesh ever safe?" Bly wisely does not try to tie up the conversation, but instead gives us this:

> In the normal course of things, such a speech would simply bring a family celebration to an absolute stop. People would sit frozen still as crystal for a moment, and then one or another would say, in a forced, light-toned way, "My word, but it's getting late. ... Dear, we really must ..." and so forth. But the Benty family were lucky. A simple thing happened: it began to rain finally, the rain people had been wanting all summer. It fell quite swiftly right from the first. It rattled the ivy, and then they could even hear it slamming down on the sidewall. Footsteps across the avenue picked up and began to run.
>
> They all noticed that odd property of rain: if it has been very dry, the first shower drives the dust upward, so that for a second your nostrils fill with dust.
>
> Then the rain continued so strongly it cleaned the air and made the whole family and their friends feel quiet and tolerant. They felt the classic old refresh-

ment we always hope for in water. (*Lord Bag of Rice,* pp. 173-174)

Reviewers of Bly's short stories are sometimes reminded of Flannery O'Connor, sometimes of James Joyce. Writing for the *New York Times Book Review,* Louis B. Jones suggested that Bly's stories could at times be compared to Joyce's "Dubliners":

Ms. Bly's stories may wobble, sermonize or (most annoyingly) forget what had been originally at stake. But we forgive her, as we do our favorite writers their defects, or we read through the defects to see the beauty. In *The Tomcat's Wife,* everything from symbol to diction works to effect. Ms. Bly knows that a story is about its network of personal secrets and about the tug that every word, every detail, exerts to make the web tremble. And, too, as in Joyce, there is arch-carved air of religion everywhere making the silence mean. Infinite layers of hypocrisy refract and distort every remark. (March 31, 1991, p. 14)

Bly's next volume, *My Lord Bag of Rice: New and Selected Stories* (2000), reprints stories from *Backbone* and *Tomcat* along with two new stories and includes a preface by Tobias Wolff. Wolff describes what it is that he likes so much about Carol Bly's stories:

Their art, first and last, the sure way she has with this exacting form. An example: One of the hardest things to do in a short story is change point of view from one character to another without losing velocity and focus. ... Bly manages to see from the eyes of different characters without any disruption in our sense of a unified, purposeful narrative. (p. x)

Wolff also recognizes Bly's main themes and her overall intent: "At bottom, her work is about responsibility, and she does not rope off the problem of political responsibility from the personal varieties that concern most writers of fiction. ...she is manifestly determined to create art that is fully responsive to the evils done in our name and with our tacit consent." (xi) And he recognizes the author herself in the spine of the stories: these characters, he says, "see their choices and they make them, for good or ill. They have, the best of them, *backbone.* Great word,

backbone. There's a strong one running right through this book." (xi)

HEART'S TRUTH

In 1990 Bly published *The Passionate, Accurate Story: Making Your Heart's Truth into Literature,* a guide to writing fiction. It draws on the resources that Bly later turned to for *Changing the Bully Who Rules the World:* stage-development theory, techniques of social work, and psychotherapy. It is a thoroughgoing book, with attention to the conventional vocabulary of fiction and writing, such as plot, subplot, and dialogue, but it also warns against using the vocabulary of the critic to inform the writing process. Criticism, she says, is analysis: "it is breaking down an already-made thing into its components so one can see those components. It does not help makers of things to do analysis at the time they are doing the making." (18) Bly's interest is getting heart to the heart of things: "Our world needs better heart than we have given it so far." (p. 197)

She carries this agenda forward in *Beyond the Writers' Workshop: New Ways To Write Creative Nonfiction* (2001). Here she addresses the temptations of the genre: to merely report one's life. She offers means for "sticking to it" for the writer who starts with passion that flags after the first draft. Most of all, she recognizes the courage that it takes to write and to keep writing: "Bravery is the major difficulty for sensitive writers in our time. More than anyone else except research scientists, who always run the chance that all their efforts will come to nothing, we writers need to brace ourselves over and over." (xvii)

The book also is, in part, an antidote to "workshop culture," a phenomenon of the surge in master of fine arts in writing programs in the United States. In 1973 there were six such programs. In 2004 there were more than sixty. The fear of most emerging writers is that they will emerge from a writing program all writing the same thing in the same voice and style. Bly offers preemptive suggestions to prevent this, while also reminding them (says the teacher and

writer Carol Conroy, on the book's back cover) to "be passionate, be brave, and tell the truth."

In the end, says Bly, "creative nonfiction is basically about the author's wisdom." (p. xvii) She addresses tapping and recognizing such wisdom throughout the book, and especially confronts it in a chapter on "Some Issues of Aesthetics and Ethics of Writing Literature." An unusual component of the book is her consideration of the teaching of writing in various situations, including public schools and conferences, and the book includes in the copious appendices an ethics code for teaching writing to middle and high school students.

PATTERNS

In Bly's story "Gunnar's Sword," the character Harriet White has designed her own pattern for a baby sweater that she was knitting:

It was immensely satisfying, because she not only had the problem of what colors and shapes would look well in wool, but she also wanted, if possible, to make up a pattern that would incorporate the different colors in any one row at least as often as every fifth stitch. If a row were to have blue and white, for example, she made sure the blue yarn was used at least as often as once in five—or the white, conversely. This way she prevented "carrying" yarn for more than an inch in the back. (*My Lord Bag of Rice*, p. 13)

In "Knit One, Purl Two," a review of five short story collections for the *Georgia Review*, Kathleen Snodgrass chooses this passage from "Gunnar's Sword" to bring the books onto common ground:

We find this sort of ingenious pattern making in the works of each of the five writers. ... Some of the variations on the well-worn theme of identity are more audacious than others, the designs more convoluted or outrageous, yet all revolve around individuals figuring out who they are. Some are reluctant to abandon a reassuringly familiar weave of communal mores and expectations while others, like Bly's iconoclast, look for new patterns.

The analogy serves also to look at Bly's work overall. From her early writing in Madison, Min-

nesota, to her stories and essays since the 1990s, and throughout her books on writing and her autobiographical works, she finds patterns and keeps them tightly woven. Snodgrass continues, "Bly deftly sidesteps a too-easy split between individual and group thinking: whatever the degrees of rebellion, her protagonists are nonetheless part of a community, usually a small town. Bly expertly dramatizes how maverick souls— the extent of whose rebellion is often hidden from themselves—maneuver in their sometimes stultifying worlds." (p. 634)

It is the parts of our lives that are hidden from ourselves and from each other that Bly is determined to bring into the light. She urges in her stories and her direct advice that we pay attention. Things are happening: important things, even when they seem inconsequential. In another Bly story, "The Tender Organizations," the protagonist, Sally, rescues a dog and brings it home. The dog is grateful, and means to say something to her new human family: "she meant to explain ... how life always looks much more ordinary than it really is—how its dangerousness, its ecstasy, scarcely show." (p. 215, *My Lord Bag of Rice*)

Selected Bibliography

WORKS OF CAROL BLY

NONFICTION

Letters from the Country. New York: Harper & Row, 1981; reprint, with a new author's preface, Minneapolis: University of Minnesota Press, 1999.

Bad Government and Silly Literature. Minneapolis: Milkweed Editions, 1986. Essay originally published in winter 1986 as *Milkweed Chronicle*.

Soil and Survival: Land Stewardship and the Future of American Agriculture. With Joe Paddock and Nancy Paddock. San Francisco: Sierra Club Books, 1986.

The Passionate, Accurate Story: Making Your Heart's Truth into Literature. Minneapolis: Milkweed Editions, 1990.

Changing the Bully Who Rules the World: Reading and Thinking about Ethics. Minneapolis: Milkweed Editions, 1996.

An Adolescent's Christmas, 1944. Afton, Minn.: Afton Historical Society Press, 2000. Memoir.

Beyond the Writers' Workshop: New Ways to Write Creative Nonfiction. New York: Anchor Books, 2001.

Three Readings for Republicans and Democrats. With Cynthia Loveland. St. Paul, Minn.: Bly and Loveland Press, 2003.

FICTION

One Down. Translation from the Danish of a novel by Anders Bodelson. New York: Harper & Row, 1970.

Backbone: Short Stories. Minneapolis: Milkweed Editions, 1985.

The Tomcat's Wife and Other Stories. New York: Harper-Collins, 1991.

My Lord Bag of Rice: New and Selected Stories. Minneapolis: Milkweed Editions, 2000.

"At the Bottom of the United States." *Idaho Review 4,* 2002.

MISCELLANEOUS PROSE

"Carol Bly." In *Ariadne's Thread: A Collection of Contemporary Women's Journals,* edited by Lyn Lifshin. New York: Harper & row, 1982.

"Extended vs. Nuclear Families." *Mother Earth News.* January–February 1984, p. 102.

"More Gratitude Than Money." *New York Times Book Review,* September 7, 1986, p. 10. Review of *No Earthly Notion,* by Susan Dodd.

"Foreword by Carol Bly." In *Everybody's Story: Writing by Older Minnesotans,* edited by Carol Bly. St. Paul, Minn.: Compas, 1987.

"Small Towns: A Close Second Look at a Very Good Place." Iowa City, IA: Iowa Humanities Board, 1987.

"Foreword by Carol Bly." In *Full Measure: Modern Short Stories on Aging,* edited by Dorothy Sennett. St. Paul, Minn.: Graywolf, 1988.

"Carol Bly: Five Essays." In *Eight Modern Essayists,* edited by William Smart. New York: St. Martin's Press, 1990.

"Foreword by Carol Bly." In *Breaking Hard Ground: Stories of the Minnesota Farm Advocates,* by Dianna Hunter. Duluth, Minn.: Holy Cow! Press, 1990.

"The Charismatic Men's Movement." *Omni 14 ,* no. 6 (March 1992): 6.

"At the Edge of Town: Duluth, Minn." In N*north Writers II: Our Place in the Woods,* edited by John Hendriksson. Minneapolis: University of Minnesota Press, 1997.

"The Maternity Wing, Madison, Minnesota." In *Imagining Home: Writing for the Midwest,* edited by Mark Vinz and Thom Tammaro. Minneapolis: University of Minnesota Press, 1995.

"Foreword by Carol Bly." *The Life of an Ordinary Woman: Anne Ellis.* Boston: Houghton Mifflin, 1999. Reprint of a 1929 memoir.

"How Radiation Oncology Nearly Made Me a Republican." *Hotel Amerika 1 ,* no. 1 (October 2002).

"Crime." *Idaho Review* 5 (2003). essay.

"Love in a Time of Empire." *Prairie Schooner* 77, no. 2 (summer 2003): 172–183.

CRITICAL AND BIOGRAPHICAL STUDIES

BOOK REVIEWS

Gallagher, Tess. "Captives of the Common Good." *New York Times Book Review,* January 27, 1985, p. 19. Review of *Backbone.*

Hancock, Wade. "Letters From the Country." *Christian Science Monitor,* June 3, 1981, p. 17.

Jones, Louis B. "The Tomcat's Wife and Other Stories." *New York Times Book Review,* March 31, 1991, p. 14.

Perrin, Noel. "Rural Time Bomb." *New York Times,* May 24, 1981. Review of *Letters from the Country.*

Snodgrass, Kathleen. "Knit One, Purl Two." *Georgia Review* 56, no. 2 (summer 2002): 623. Review of *My Lord Bag of Rice.*

HAYDEN CARRUTH

(1921—)

Brian Henry

Hayden Carruth was born on August 3, 1921, in Waterbury, Connecticut, to Gorton Veeder Carruth and Margery Carruth. His father wrote for a local newspaper, and his paternal grandfather, Fred Hayden Carruth, was a professional comic writer; both men encouraged in him an interest in reading and writing from a young age while emphasizing the importance of "the social utility of writing" (Weiss 130). Carruth's mother was Episcopalian, but his father and grandfather were atheists as well as socialists; as a result, he attended church every Sunday but did not believe what he heard. His father's "radical rationalism" (Reluctantly 9) and his mother's devoutness produced an atmosphere of "secular and neurotic puritanism" (Reluctantly 16) in the Carruth household.

At the age of three, Carruth moved with his family to Woodbury, Connecticut, where he spent most of his childhood. He attended the University of North Carolina in Chapel Hill—he focused primarily on journalism—then served as a cryptographer in Italy during World War II. Carruth has never written about his experience in the war, which emerges as a notable gap in his poetry and various autobiographical pieces. Too shy to become a journalist, Carruth moved to Chicago after the war to attend graduate school in English literature at the University of Chicago. After publishing some poems in *Poetry* and working for the magazine as a reader, he edited the magazine from 1949 to 1950. Around this time, his first wife, Sara, moved with their three-month-old daughter, Martha, to Alabama to teach at Auburn University, later divorcing Carruth. He did not see his daughter again for four years, and has always considered his separation from Sara and Martha as "the principal and determinative fact" of his life (*Reluctantly* 154).

After a psychological breakdown in 1953, Carruth was confined to a mental institution in White Plains, New York, known as Bloomingdale, where he stayed for over a year. Diagnosed with acute and chronic anxiety psychoneurosis, he was subjected to electroshock therapy and hydrotherapy as well as manual and group therapy. Carruth's illness manifested itself as extreme shyness, acrophobia, agoraphobia, and chronic insomnia. At the time he was admitted to the hospital, he felt "unable to exist in the world" (*Reluctantly* 26). After being discharged from the hospital, he lived for five years in the attic of his parents' house in seclusion and "almost complete invalidism" (*Reluctantly* 35). He later moved to Norfolk, Connecticut, to work for James Laughlin, the publisher of New Directions, and married Rose Marie Dorn, a refugee from Eastern Europe. Their son, David, whom Carruth calls "the Bo," was born shortly thereafter.

Because he was too ill to "do what literary people normally do with their lives—work in offices or classrooms, live in a city, use public transportation, go to theaters, literary parties, etc." (*Reluctantly* 35)—Carruth moved to northern Vermont, where he lived from 1963 to 1979 in a five-room house without central heating. He spent his days performing manual labor—chopping wood, baling hay, building furniture, repairing machinery, doing electrical work, growing food, helping neighbors with their chores—or what R. W. Flint has described as "a notably arduous brand of hardscrabble farming" (17). During this time, Carruth writes in *Reluctantly,* his work "was largely, say ninety-five percent, unconnected with my poetry, and much of it was outdoors in the company of people who considered me a laborer or mechanic, never a writer" (28).

But at night, Carruth earned money by working as a freelance writer and editor, establishing a reputation as "an astute and even-handed critic" (Scheele 46). He reviewed hundreds of books for newspapers and magazines, copyedited manuscripts, wrote advertising copy, and ghostwrote, never turning down an assignment, out of fear of losing a source of future income. Because of the enormous amount of reading required by his freelancing, Carruth became extraordinarily erudite; he has written incisively about a number of subjects, including modernism, the New Criticism, existentialism, the Beat poets, the Black Mountain poets, the troubadour poets, jazz, the blues, and the philosophy of love. Since 1981, selections of his prose have appeared in six volumes: *Working Papers: Selected Essays and Reviews* (1982), *Effluences from the Sacred Caves: More Selected Essays and Reviews* (1983), *Sitting In: Selected Writings on Jazz, Blues, and Related Topics* (1986), *Suicides and Jazzers* (1992), *Selected Essays and Reviews* (1996), and *Reluctantly: Autobiographical Essays* (1998).

Unable to afford a house large enough to have an office or library, Carruth wrote in a converted cowshed—"a dusty, sooty, shabby, and extremely cramped place to work" (*Reluctantly* 33)—turning to his own poems only after he had finished his chores and assigned writing. Despite these hardships, Carruth wrote prolifically, completing more than ten books of poetry during his time in Vermont. He also started to receive national recognition for his poetry at this time, winning the 1963 Carl Sandburg Award, two fellowships from the Guggenheim Foundation, grants from the National Endowment for the Arts, and the 1978 Shelley Memorial Award from the Poetry Society of America. Perhaps more importantly, he solidified his political and ethical beliefs and slowly overcame his psychological difficulties, giving his first public poetry reading when he was nearly sixty years old. Despite the period's challenges, Carruth has written that he cherished those years in Vermont because they provided him with "an opportunity to put everything together, the land and seasons, the people, [his] family, [his] work, [his] evolving sense of

survival … in one tightly integrated imaginative structure" (*Reluctantly* 37). The result is a quintessential New England quality in Carruth; as Jeff Gundy observes, "As much as any poet since Robert Frost, … Carruth exemplifies our stereotype of the New England poet—craggy, uncompromising, carrying a peculiar blend of reticence and unsparing self-revelation, suspicious of centers both literary and urban" (143).

Carruth needed more income when his son started college, so he accepted a teaching position at Syracuse University in 1979. During his tenure as a professor, he published seven books of poetry, including a volume of selected poems. On February 24, 1988, at the age of sixty-six, Carruth "intentionally and massively overdosed" (*Reluctantly* 41) on every medication he could find in his house. He woke up later in intensive care, and remained in the hospital, having contracted "radical pneumonia" (45). He was released from intensive care into a psychiatric hospital, where he stayed for two weeks. Much to his surprise, Carruth found himself "high on life" (49) because of his sense of good luck at having survived his suicide. Prior to his suicide, he writes in *Reluctantly*, "I had never been able to identify any part of my ego that might be central to the rest" (62). This lack of consistency, he claims, has contributed to a lack of a singular style or voice in his poetry. Instead of a consistent style, he finds "a disconcerting concatenation of voices, other people's voices mimicked or faked" (62). He also expresses this belief in his poetic sequence "Paragraphs," when he asks, "What true voice? Where? Humiliated, in throes / of vacillation, roundhead to cavalier to ivy league to smartass— / never who I was" (*Collected Shorter Poems* 195–196). But in suicide he discovered "a way to unify [his] sense of self, the sense which had formerly been so refracted and broken up" (*Reluctantly* 63).

The connection that Carruth establishes between his personality and poetic style points to an important issue in his poetry: his refusal to dwell in or expand upon a single style. He has written poems in traditional forms, invented forms, free verse, and syllabic verse, and his topics have included rural life, manual labor, sexual

love, the natural world, environmental degradation, human greed, war, justice, old age and death, jazz and the blues, and family life. Fittingly, Carruth's publishing record has been diverse as well as extensive; his books have been published by large New York publishing firms such as Macmillan and Harper & Row, by major independent presses such as Copper Canyon Press and New Directions, and by small presses such as Salt-Works Press and Countryman Press. He has published volumes of selected and collected poems as well as numerous limited-edition chapbooks. Few American poets have exhibited such an array of poetic activity.

Although Carruth's poetry has garnered acclaim, awards, and a relatively large readership, scholarly interest in his work has been surprisingly scant. Matthew Miller has noted that Carruth has been "consistently omitted from the important anthologies, and so correspondingly ignored by the academy" (295). The range of Carruth's poetry has presented difficulties to scholars, who have not been able to assign him to any poetic school or movement. His formal and thematic breadth as a poet makes his poetry somewhat resistant to focused, thesis-driven critiques. Also, as Miller has noted, Carruth's "clear intentions have resisted critical analysis"; because he has "always been candid about his influences" and avoids "clever wordplay and symbolism," his poetry does not require much "scholarly input" (294). Similarly, Flint surmises that "Carruth's oscillation among roles may have confused some readers—moralist, hedonist, exquisite epicure of country scenes, … a raging enemy of illness, infirmity, lovelessness, industrial spoliation and mindless greed" (18). The lack of scholarly interest, however, has not translated into an absence of readers and admirers. Because Carruth is, in Flint's words, "a poet of the first quality, no mythmaker or trendsetter in matters of style but a writer so well endowed with character, courage, stamina, honesty, and independence as to make whatever styles he has adopted or adapted peculiarly his own" (17), his poetry has found those who need it even if it has largely eluded scholars.

Although Carruth no longer teaches, he still lives in Munnsville, New York, with his wife, Joe-Anne McLaughlin Carruth, also a poet. He suffered a heart attack in 1999, and after a lifetime of smoking, he has emphysema, which requires him to be on oxygen full-time. Despite his attempted suicide and failing health, Carruth continued to write poetry, publishing *Scrambled Eggs & Whiskey: Poems, 1991–1995* in 1996 and *Doctor Jazz* in 2001. His awards include the 1990 Ruth Lilly Poetry Prize from *Poetry*, the 1991 Lenore Marshall Poetry Prize, the 1992 National Book Critics Circle Award for *Collected Shorter Poems, 1946–1991* (1992), the 1994 Paterson Poetry Prize, a 1995 Lannan Award, and the 1996 National Book Award for *Scrambled Eggs & Whiskey*.

EARLY POETRY

Carruth's early poems, particularly those in *The Crow and the Heart* (1959), *The Norfolk Poems* (1962), and *Nothing for Tigers* (1965) demonstrate some of the qualities that characterize his poems throughout his career—formal skill and variety, a fascination with nature, and social awareness—but seem overly influenced by other poets, especially W. B. Yeats and Ezra Pound. Some poems focus on patently literary topics such as the Trojan War and great art, but are hindered by an inflexible approach to poetic form—rhyming quatrains and couplets predominate—as well as a weakness for vague abstraction and awkward diction. Carruth's early poems seem too indebted to poetic tradition; and in "Midsummer Letter," he admits that "I charm / Myself (obscurely) // With terms licked from my betters" (*Nothing for Tigers* 12). As Eric Selinger has noted, Carruth's early poems are "spit-polished, proper, allusive" as well as "impersonal" (253). Carruth himself seems unenthusiastic about his early poetry, including substantially less than half of the poems from these books in his *Collected Shorter Poems*.

Some of these poems—such as "On a Certain Engagement South of Seoul," "Adolf Eichmann," and "The Event Itself"—demonstrate a strong political consciousness, but, compared with later

poems that employ more fluid styles, fail to rise above rhetoric into fully realized art. His use of form in these poems mars rather than enhances his message. "Lines Written in an Asylum" tempers the horrors of his experience in a mental institution with rhyming couplets and iambic tetrameter, producing lines such as these: "The day I build with plotted hours / To stand apart is mine, not ours. / Its joyless business is my cure; / Stern and alone, I may endure" (13). The poem represents an early attempt to broach a difficult subject that other poems, such as "The Asylum," *The Bloomingdale Papers* (1975; written 1953), and "Ontological Episode of the Asylum," address more forcefully. The strongest poem in his first book, "The Fat Lady," succeeds because it uses relatively conversational diction and irregularly rhyming blank verse—a style that Carruth hones in later poems.

In his second collection, *The Norfolk Poems,* Carruth occasionally relaxes his allegiance to strict form, clearing the ground for a more supple poetry. He even subverts Yeats's poem "The Wild Swans at Coole" in "The Wild Swans at Norfolk": "To begin with there are / No wild swans at Norfolk" (*Collected Shorter Poems* 27). "Meadow House" narrates its own process of composition—"Impromptu, / Falling out of my precipitate brain faster / Than light dropping through a torn cloud" (*Collected Shorter Poems* 28). And "Naming for Love" consists mostly of a list of the names of stones, resembling both catalog and secular prayer. The looser styles in these poems look forward to Carruth's more improvisational poems.

Nothing for Tigers, Carruth's third collection, serves as a transitional book, offering poems in both strict forms and accomplished free verse. One of the book's most successful poems, "Spring Notes from Robin Hill," is a series of nine informal sketches in free verse. Through the poem, he details his daily life in Vermont and establishes a self-contained world: "In this cottage my history is— / and my nation" (*Collected Shorter Poems* 56). Because Carruth does not strain for deeper meaning or rely on previous models, the poem succeeds. "Essay on Marriage" explicitly mentions William Carlos Williams'

metrical invention the "variable foot," as well as the German poet Friedrich Hölderlin's discussion of "the necessity / For writing one more poem" (49), but uses the poets as backdrop for a lyrical examination of his new marriage. Even when he relies upon lofty abstractions, the poem displays more flexibility than most poems at this stage in his career: "We each had known // Many bitternesses and disloyalties, and so / Recognized the advantage that loving brought to us / After the ugly hope of solitude" (49). Carruth cleverly reintroduces Williams toward the end of the poem when he asks, "Has there ever been an invariable foot?" (50); Hölderlin also makes a reappearance when Carruth muses, "And why should I write one more poem? / Will it save the world? // Will it save Rose Marie?" His answer—"I expect to write / Hundreds, but no great good will come of them" (50–51)—reveals a skepticism about the efficacy of poetry that seems striking in the work of a poet only beginning his life's work.

Carruth's thirteen-part sequence "The Asylum," which appeared in *The Crow and the Heart,* represents his first sustained attempt to address his experience in a mental institution. Interestingly, he chooses to explore that experience through a tight structure—the "paragraph," a form of Carruth's invention. Based on the sonnet, the paragraph consists of fifteen lines, but places two rhyming couplets after the first quatrain and uses an unusual rhyme scheme: ababaaccdedefef. With the paragraph, Carruth imposes a formal structure (poetic order) on the topic of insanity (mental disorder). Relatively supple in form and diction compared with some of Carruth's other poems from the 1950s, "The Asylum" serves as a precursor to his mature style while dealing with a subject that remains essential to the poet throughout his life.

Although the poet focuses primarily on himself in the sequence, the wind becomes a dominant figure in "The Asylum," ubiquitous and shifting. With its force, the wind, like the walls of the institution, has the power to imprison; it can be harsh, insistent, idle, or curative. The wind also carries associations of World War II, as in this passage:

I hurt. Hungrier flowers try my rank ground.
Indelible, one drifts across Japan,
Routed as if its stem were wound
Into the heart of a man.
A crumpling sky, a blurted dawn—the sound
Of history burst the years and history drowned.

(*Collected Longer Poems* 6)

Because of the wind, one of the flowers ends up in Japan, where the atomic bomb threatens to destroy history. But the wind also holds everything together by keeping silence and stagnation at bay.

In the final section of the sequence, Carruth asserts, "I'm a breath, / A puff in bare bones, a dry heart, / A small particular death" (10). Although his release from the asylum seems to indicate his improved mental health, the process has destroyed something in him, so the poem ends on a note of cautious optimism and candor: "Here's darkness and rain / And a small window in broken walls, dear walls. / Here am I—drowned, living, loving, and insane" (10). By addressing this experience through poetry, and thus creating beauty out of pain, Carruth transforms suffering into art.

Although "The Asylum" is one of the first poems about his experience in a mental institution to be published, Carruth wrote a book-length poem during his stay in the asylum, giving the manuscript to a friend after his release. He then forgot about it because of amnesia triggered by electroshock therapy. *The Bloomingdale Papers* appeared for the first time in 1975, twenty years after Carruth was released from the institution. In his preface to the book, he explains that a doctor had suggested he write "something that might be helpful to him and his colleagues in their consideration of [Carruth's] case" (vii). The result is, according to Flint, "a brilliantly vivid verse diary of incarceration" (19). Lillian Feder has argued that "no one has conveyed the physical and emotional 'actuality' [of mental illness] as vividly as...Hayden Carruth in *The Bloomingdale Papers*" (112). Carruth, however, has criticized the poems' "stiffness, awkwardness, phony diction" (*The Bloomingdale Papers* ix), but he authorized the book's publication because of the encouragement of some friends and because "the

total effect is what it should be, the truth of a spirit caged and struggling" (ix). Despite the poet's aesthetic misgivings about the work, *The Bloomingdale Papers* presents an impressive array of styles and forms, and exceeds many of Carruth's early poems in imagination, attention to detail, humor, and emotional power, ultimately proving that "some events are humanly / Sharable" (*The Bloomingdale Papers* 22).

Carruth has described his and other inmates' experience as one of "privation, hopelessness, violence, tears, … terrific pain, and above all … humiliation" (ix). Being incarcerated compels the poet to turn "inward":

We never mourn the filmy world outside,
We even turn our anger from the door
That opens only for someone else's key
And from the windows and their iron bars.
Prison grows warm and *is* the real asylum.
… … … … … … … … … … .
And never in our drowsy eyes appears
For an instant any boredom but the sharp
Unwearying tedium of this great despair.
These are the fascinations of our winter.

(*Collected Shorter Poems* 123)

Because it provides refuge from the cold, the mental institution becomes another kind of asylum to the patients. Yet the poem itself emerges as the poet's true asylum. Feder claims that Carruth's "experience in the very act of writing this early poem remains fundamental to his entire development as a major contemporary American poet" (112), because writing *The Bloomingdale Papers* becomes "intrinsic to the poet's struggle to reconstitute his self" (114). Thus, as he creates the poet through poetry, he re-creates the self. The process, though simultaneous, is slow and painful. In Bloomingdale, Carruth is "under constant observation," fears the "truly mad" (124), and hopes the place burns down. At one point he baldly states, "The fact is I am here, / Having collapsed, because / I can't be anywhere else" (*Collected Shorter Poems* 128).

One of the more moving sections of *The Bloomingdale Papers* is addressed to Carruth's daughter, Martha, whom he hardly knows, his first wife having left him when Martha was a

baby. He tells her, "I remember you / When you began, a subtle soft machine; / And you remember me, no, not at all" (*Collected Shorter Poems* 139). Because of the "distance that leaves me powerless to know you," he writes, "I can address you only in my mind / Or, what's the same, in this untouching poem," which "turns so dark when I had meant it light" (140). At the end, the poem becomes a prayer:

Nothing of me goes forth
To father you, lost daughter, but a prayer.

That some small wisdom always may endure
Amidst your weariness; that lovers may
Be kind to you; that beauty may arouse
You; that the crazy house
May never, never be your home: I pray.

(140)

By ending *The Bloomingdale Papers* with such a loving gesture, Carruth focuses outside himself and temporarily overcomes the despair and terror that led to and characterized his institutionalization. This is personally and artistically significant, because, according to Feder, writing *The Bloomingdale Papers* helped Carruth attain "the conviction that only in love is self-realization possible" (120).

Prayer also occurs in Carruth's final asylum poem, "Ontological Episode of the Asylum" in *Nothing for Tigers*. In the asylum, everything—human and nonhuman—is designed to prevent suicide, and the first stanza dramatizes the tension between this purpose of the asylum and the inmates' own desires:

The boobyhatch's bars, the guards, the nurses,
The illimitable locks and keys are all arranged
To thwart the hand that continually rehearses
Its ending stroke and raise a barricade
Against destruction-seeking resolution.
Many of us in there would have given all
(But we had nothing) for one small razor blade
Or seventy grains of the comforting amytal.

(*Collected Shorter Poems* 48)

After a stanza break, the poem turns to its "ontological episode":

So I went down in the attitude of prayer,

Yes, to my knees on the cold floor of my cell,
Humped in a corner, a bird with a broken wing,
And asked and asked as fervently and well
As I could guess to do for light in the mists
Of death, until I learned God doesn't care.
Not only that, he doesn't care at all,
One way or the other. That is why he exists.

(48)

As an agnostic, Carruth feels he cannot truly pray, so he assumes "the attitude of prayer." The action, which leaves him "humped in a corner," illuminates his feeling of physical brokenness and proves to him the indifference—and, paradoxically, the existence—of God.

One of Carruth's other major topics, jazz, appears as the subject in "New Orleans" and "Billie Holiday" in *Nothing for Tigers,* but the strict rhyme and meter in the poems prohibit the improvisational quality that characterizes Carruth's best poems on jazz. However, one of the last poems in the book, "Freedom and Discipline," foreshadows Carruth's later innovations in jazz-influenced poetry. Addressed to "Saint Harmony," the poem describes Carruth's personal history with music—moving from Sergei Rachmaninoff to Coleman Hawkins, Thelonius Monk, and other jazz musicians. From jazz, he learns to move beyond being "locked / in discipline, sworn to // freedom" (*Collected Shorter Poems* 61), and realizes that "Freedom and discipline concur / only in ecstasy" (62). The ecstasy afforded by improvisation appears in many of his poems after the 1960s, and Carruth's mature style emerges after he moves past the influences of Yeats and Pound to incorporate into his poetry both natural speech and the improvisational qualities of jazz.

JAZZ AND THE BLUES

From his childhood, Carruth has exhibited a passion for jazz, claiming in *Reluctantly* that "in intonation, texture, rhythm, and all its sensuous qualities, jazz moved me viscerally from the beginning" (106). He also has referred to jazz as "a bliss for fifty years, my resource, my constancy in loneliness of loving" (*Collected Shorter Poems* 379). This love of the music appears in poems throughout his career, establishing a strong

thematic and formal undercurrent in his work. His devotion to jazz, however, also has a strong intellectual component; Carruth points out that "jazz has been both a constant accessory to and an eloquent articulation of every serious artistic, social, cultural, and philosophical happening in my lifetime" (*Reluctantly* 111). As a result, he feels a powerful obligation to incorporate the music into his poetry.

Carruth has written poems in honor of numerous jazz and blues musicians, including Sidney Bechet, Benny Goodman, Pee Wee Russell, and Ben Webster. In "What a Wonder among the Instruments Is the Walloping Trombone!" Carruth offers the jazz musician Vic Dickenson singular praise: "No other could sing as you, your blasts, burbles, and bellowings, those upward leaps, those staccato declensions, / Your smears, blurs, coughs, your tone veering from muted to stentorian, your confidences, your insults, / All made in music, musically" (*Collected Shorter Poems* 379). And he extends this praise to include all time when he writes, "Never was such range of feeling so integrated in one man or instrument" (379). Carruth's love of jazz and the "range of feeling" it makes possible also extends to the blues, an art form known for expressing outrage, sorrow, and desire. His interest in the blues serves as a reminder that music and poetry can convey not only technical skill, but strong emotions. His difficult life has provided him with an array of powerful subjects for his poems, and his skills at improvisation have enabled him to harness emotion in the service of art.

A central element of jazz, especially as it influences Carruth's poetry, is the technique of improvisation within fixed forms. For Carruth, form provides "discipline," without which, he writes in "Forever in That Year," in *The Oldest Killed Lake in North America,* "all is noise" (31). According to Carruth, improvisation "is the privilege of the master, the bane of the apprentice" (*Sitting In* 101) because improvisation requires a deep knowledge of one's medium. In an essay on jazz and Carruth's poetry, Miller connects his "mastery of multiple forms, his spontaneity, his precise lyricism" (300) to his lifelong interest in jazz. Miller also claims that

"what improvisation ultimately amounts to [in Carruth's poems] is structure becoming a function of feeling" (300), which echoes Carruth's own observation about "the self-evident verity that artistic function is equivalent to feeling" and "the more passionate the feeling, the more complex and unified the form" (*Sitting In* 176).

"How To" offers a masterful lesson in both poetry and jazz: "The main / element of technique / is verve, movement, energy, what / musicians also seek // under the rubric *attack*" (*Collected Shorter Poems* 273). The poet addresses his student readers as "Chillens" while offering useful information, teaching them how to play and write jazz while playing and writing jazz himself. The result is simultaneously instructive and delightful:

Max-

imum energy is sometimes
obtained by restraining
the inner violence of force,
though always with the swing-

ing propulsion that comes from clarity of phrasing a-
gainst the beat. What you've been told is
too easy. Listen. The

ear is more important than the
eye. Dass de trooth!
(*Collected Shorter Poems* 273–274)

With its abrupt enjambments, the invented form allows Carruth to generate "maximum energy" and "swinging propulsion" in the poem, thus embodying what he recommends.

In order to outdo his previous work, Carruth frequently presents himself with significant formal challenges in his poems in traditional and invented forms as well as in his poems in free verse—an ambition that also can be found in the work of many jazz musicians. Some of Carruth's most accomplished poems foreground jazz and blues techniques that test the poet's own virtuosity. The subject of these poems can be jazz itself, as in the thirty-two-line, single-sentence poem "An Expatiation on the Combin-

ing of Weathers at Thirty-seventh and Indiana
Where the Southern More or Less Crosses the
Dog," which begins:

Oh, Ammons rolled the octaves slow
And the piano softened like butter in his hands,
And underward Catlett caught the beat
One sixteenth before the measure with a snip-snap
   touch on the snare
And a feathery brush on the cymbal …
… … … … . .
And after a while
Berigan tested a limping figure low
In the coronet's baritone and raised it a third and then
   another
Until he was poised
On the always falling fulcrum of the blues
                    (*Collected Shorter Poems* 351)

Carruth imagines himself into the scene, coming
"achingly on" with his "clarinet's most pure /
High C-sharp" (351). The experience ends in
artistic and emotional ecstasy that depends on
community:

The old, old pattern of call and response unending,
And they felt the stir of the animal's soul in the cave,
And heard the animal's song, indefinable utterance,
And saw
A hot flowing of the eternal, many-colored, essential
   plasm
As they leaned outward together, away from place,
   from time,
In one only person, which was the blues.
                                              (351)

For Carruth, the bond generated by music in this
and other poems resembles the bond created by
love, because both jazz and love allow for
transcendence and communion with others.

   Carruth's improvisational skills also appear in
his rigorous invented form, the paragraph. With
visual displacement, uneven lines, and unusual or
missing punctuation, Carruth's twenty-eight-part
"Paragraphs" sequence demonstrates a high level
of formal mastery. Although they are all composed in the same form, no paragraph resembles
another paragraph. The final three paragraphs in
the sequence are particularly jazz-oriented in
subject matter and style. Paragraph 26 begins at
a recording session with "Albert Ammons, Lips

Page, Vic Dickenson, / Don Byas, Israel / Crosby,
and Big Sid Catlett" (*Collected Shorter Poems*
196). Carruth's presentation of the opening
number mimics the silence preceding the music:

Ammons
counted off
a-waaaaan,,, *tu!*
and went feeling

his way on the keys gently,
while Catlett summoned

27

the exact beat from—
say from the sounding depths, the universe …
                    (*Collected Shorter Poems* 196)

The unconventional punctuation and the white
space before the "*tu!*" approximate the timing of
Ammons' speech, and Carruth's arrangement of
the text further enhances the pauses and pacing
of the music. Later in the poem, the structure
bolsters both the music of the poem and the
music depicted in the poem:

When Dickenson came on it was all established,
no guessing, and he started with a blur
as usual, smears, brays—Christ
the dirtiest noise imaginable
belches, farts
curses
but it was music
music now
with Ammons trilling in counterpoise.
                                              (197)

Carruth effectively conveys the ecstasy of the
musicians in the moment of creation while pursuing a similar ecstasy through poetic composition:

And it was done
and they listened *and* heard themselves
better than they were, for they had come

28

high above themselves. Above everything, flux, ooze,
loss, need, shame, improbability/ the awfulness

of gut-wrong, sex-wrack, horse & booze

(197)

The session ends with the poet's ecstasy and the musicians' ecstasy collapsing together, possible in large part because of poetic improvisation: "I druther've bin a-settin there, supernumerary / cockroach i' th' corner, a-listenin, a-listenin,,,,,, / than be the Prazedint of the Wurrurld" (198). Carruth's formal skills allow him to transcend the requirements of the paragraph form to convey the ecstasies of improvisation, which also depend on a community joined together through artistic creation. This community is idealized in a passage in Carruth's book-length poem *The Sleeping Beauty* (1982), in which Carruth imagines heaven as an eternal "jam" of "shades of strange souls … caught together / In eternity and the blues" (*Collected Longer Poems* 175). Carruth's belief in the importance of community finds a fitting home in his interest in jazz and the blues, as jazz often requires community for its energy and the blues creates community through expressions of sorrow and injustice.

POLITICS AND THE NATURAL WORLD

Carruth's emphasis on community in his poetry stems in large part from his political beliefs, a philosophical anarchism that takes freedom as its most cherished quality. According to Carruth, this freedom can be attained through lucidity and authenticity—"the two ideal virtues toward which self-conscious humanity, personally and collectively, must strain" (*Selected Essays and Reviews* 354–355). This view permeates his writing, which evinces his opinion that "art needs life, all life" (*Working Papers* 162–163) and that writing "is first of all a way of being in the world, a functioning nub of relatedness" (*Reluctantly* 66). Therefore, his poetry seeks not an escape from life, but a meaningful connection to the world around him.

Carruth sees no difference in value between natural objects and man-made objects. In fact, his views of the natural world derive from his belief that "all things in reality are part of reality, and hence are equal; they all plunge equally into transitoriness and nonexistence" (*Reluctantly* 4); thus, "everything is equivalent, every pebble and masterpiece, every atom and thought of love: they are *precisely* the same in value" (4). In this perspective, humans are no more important than stones. "The Ravine" uses a natural scene to portray this perspective. The poem begins with a catalog of objects currently in the ravine—a moment frozen in time—then considers the ravine over time from season to season and then projects far into the "geologic" future. This passage of time within an otherwise static scene encapsulates his thinking:

These are what I see here every day,
not things but relationships of things,
quick changes and slow. These are my sorrow,
for unlike my bright admonitory friends
I see relationships, I do not see things.
These, such as they are, every day, every
unique day, the first in time and the last,
are my thoughts, the sequences of my mind.
I wonder what they mean. Every day,
day after day, I wonder what they mean.

(*Collected Shorter Poems* 84)

To Carruth, nothing exists as its own entity; everything exists in relation to everything else, including time.

Because his sense of community includes not only human beings but all things in nature, Carruth possesses an extraordinary reverence for the natural world. The poet Galway Kinnell, in his introduction to *The Selected Poetry of Hayden Carruth* (1985), has described Carruth as "one of our most clear-eyed, … sympathizing, dependably sane observers of the actual world" (x). Carruth's talents as an observer have produced poems celebrating the natural world as well as poems raging against or mourning its destruction. Few, if any, American poets have populated their work with so many animals, flowers, weeds, and trees. One of Carruth's most substantial early poems, "North Winter," is a fifty-seven-part sequence focusing on winter in Vermont. Each section resembles a snapshot, or brief reflection combining natural imagery and abstract thought. The poem, written within a few years of Carruth's move to Vermont, gives the sense of the poet learning his environment by recording it in

words, as when he writes, "The song of the gray / ninepointed buck / contains much contains / many contains all" (*Collected Longer Poems* 34). The sequence ends with the snow melting and "earth glistening / releasing the ways of the / words of earth long frozen" (50–51). The poem's exacting detail and viewpoint exude a deep respect for the natural world, counteracting what he considers "the weak, insipid, tedious, petulant, and inadequate intelligence of human beings" (*Reluctantly* 5).

Carruth's poems often demonstrate resignation, if not pessimism, about the natural world in what he describes as "the time of the finishing off of the animals" (*Collected Shorter Poems* 146). In "For Peg: A Remnant of Song Still Distantly Sounding," birds' Voices of song have sunk into the whine / Of tires on pavement" (*The Oldest Killed Lake in North America* 23). When he considers the destruction of the birds' habitat, he concludes that he lives in "desolation land," "pollution land," "demoralization land," and "desecration land" (22–23). His empathy causes him to join the birds in being "unbalanced, lost in the extraordinary climactic / Chaos of this land" (23). "Song for My Sixtieth Year" juxtaposes a strip mall with a vacant lot bursting with flowers, shrubs, and trees—"an untidy garden" in a space "not yet asphalted" (*The Oldest Killed Lake in North America* 26). In "Living in the Flatlands," he bemoans "the burden of this human world" (*The Oldest Killed Lake in North America* 43), a burden he continually feels moved to express in his poems.

The poems in *Asphalt Georgics* (1985) combine a rigorous form with Carruth's ecological and political views. The form consists of quatrains that alternate between eight and six syllables per line, with the second and fourth lines rhyming. Carruth follows the form with such exactness that he hyphenates words across line and stanza breaks in order to maintain his syllable counts and rhymes. These poems' high degree of artifice contrasts with their heavily colloquial style. Carruth wrote the poems after moving to upstate New York, using voices of people he knew or overheard, and the area around Syracuse emerges in these poems as a "barren" (15) land of strip

malls and chain stores. Near "the oldest // dead lake in North America," he writes in "Names," one can see on a clear day "the factories / and chemical plants" (9–10), which hardly creates a bucolic view generally associated with the georgic. The poem connects the decline of the landscape to the pollution that poisons the water and makes the air "slimy" (11). Another poem in the collection, "Reflections," compares "gazing over / the lights reflected on / dead water" to a "deathwatch" (23). And in "Plain Song," a major blizzard emerges as an unexpectedly positive force because it covers "all the gaudy plast- / tic of the fast food chains / and filling stations, the dete- / rioration, dirt, stains // of rust and corruption" (31).

The colloquial style of these poems has led critics such as Ben Howard to remark on Carruth's democratic use of language, claiming that his "range of diction is as expansive as it is inclusive" and that his poems "incorporate the lingoes of multiple social classes and walks of life, while also admitting literary, archaic and learned speech" (66). Carruth's populism becomes even more clear when one considers his many dramatic monologues ("Regarding Chainsaws," "Johnny Spain's White Heifer," "Lady," "Marvin McCabe," and others) narrated in the voices of his Vermont neighbors. As Roy Scheele has pointed out, Carruth "relishes his characters' semi-literate speech and their propensity to tell stories on themselves as a means of handling disappointment and hardship" (47); the poems' humor stems not only from their comic situations, but also from "the laconic and sometimes exaggerative qualities characteristic of New England speech" (47). When Carruth himself praises Vermonters' use of "a living language" in his long poem "Vermont" (*Collected Longer Poems* 112), he also refers to his own use of that language in his poetry. According to Howard, this multifaceted approach to language "reflects a generous awareness of American social pluralities" (66).

Such awareness also appears in the poet's treatment of neighborliness and labor. In a 1997 interview with Scheele, Carruth commented, "Labor was the glue that held my family together

and held the community together" (56). As a result, he has a high regard for both laborers and the act of labor itself. In "Homecoming," Carruth mourns the death of a neighbor, Mr. Washer, a "tough hardminded Yankee" (*Collected Shorter Poems* 85) who embodied everything the poet respects in a person. Washer understood the importance of both community and privacy, and he worked hard his entire life and was always willing to help others. Carruth sees him as a dying breed: "Mr. Washer is gone, and in any useful sense / his virtues are gone with him" (86). One of Carruth's most well-known poems, "Emergency Haying," concerns this attachment to the responsibilities of community. In the poem, the phrase "Marshall needs help" (*Collected Shorter Poems* 89) is the sole reason the poet spends the day working so hard mowing, raking, baling, and storing hay that his exhaustion and the painful "way / [his] body hangs from twisted shoulders" (89) remind him of Jesus Christ's suffering. But the poet does not equate his suffering with Christ's—"My hands are torn // by baling twine, not nails, and my side is pierced / by my ulcer, not a lance" (89)—and he allows the image to fade. He then meditates on work itself, particularly slave labor, which his wife and father-in-law endured in Europe. Considering his reverence for freedom, he cannot stand the thought that hands "too bloodied cannot bear // even the touch of air, even / the touch of love" (90). The poem ends with the poet resorting to high rhetoric to curse "you sons of bitches who would drive men and women / to the fields where they can only die" (90). David Weiss has written that "Emergency Haying" reveals a poet "on the side of what is lost, suppressed, obsolete, bypassed" while exhibiting "a rage at the toll taken on the human" (52).

Inevitably, this "toll" includes the violence of war. In "A Summer with Tu Fu," Carruth remarks, "We forget sometimes that a shattered person / twists and cries and dies like a dog or a woodchuck" (*Scrambled Eggs & Whiskey* 22), thus prohibiting the reader from forgetting. As Matthew Zapruder has pointed out, Carruth "is concerned with the difficult and pressing problem of how one can react honestly and humanly to ...

pain" (215). But because of his worldview, Carruth, in his considerations of war, mourns the violence inflicted not only on humans but also on animals, as in "When Howitzers Began" and "The Birds of Vietnam." With the Vietnam War as its backdrop, "Spring 1967" emerges as a particularly scathing political poem. The poet, referring to himself in the second person, has been infected by the war: "You can think of nothing / that is not rotten, see nothing / not hideous" (*Collected Shorter Poems* 109). Everything in the poet's view becomes transformed; beer cans "bloom" beside the road, the snow resembles fish scales, and a chair "wrenches its way / in hysterical inaction across the yard" (109). The poet comes to resemble the chair, as his mind "wrenches across the world, tearing the dirty / shimmer of blossom from every bough" and he kneels "in the bloody mire, in the hysteria / of inaction" (109). After this harrowing scene, the poem turns to a series of direct statements:

Everything you make is taken from you,
repainted and displayed in the national exposition,
every word is stripped from you in the national tirade,
every gesture is absorbed in the national arm,
whatever you are disposed to think is already explained
in the national advertisement, and your being,
if you let yourself be,
is rung up *ping-ping* on the national cash register.

(109–110)

With everyone on exhibit, privacy ceases to exist, and lucidity and authenticity become impossible. This highlights the necessity of art, as when he claims in another poem, "Two Silences," in *Dark World* (1974), that "in a universe / regulated by magnanimity poetry / would disappear" (10).

One of Carruth's most memorable and celebrated poems, "On Being Asked to Write a Poem against the War in Vietnam," begins with startling directness—"Well I have and in fact / more than one" (*Collected Shorter Poems* 203)—then lists the many wars against which he has written poems. His gesture of defiance quickly becomes one of resignation, as he admits that his antiwar poems have had no practical effect: "and not one / breath was restored / to one // shattered

throat / mans womans or childs / not one not // one" (204). The poem's momentum stems from it being built on a single sentence without punctuation, as if the urgency of the topic forbids the poet from pausing. Yet his trenchant observation seems to negate the relevance of poetry to world affairs, until the end of the poem, when Carruth personifies death, which occasionally glances at the poet "to make sure [he] was noticing" (204). For Carruth, the viability of political poetry lies not in its immediate practical effects, but in its very existence and its potential to be noticed. As he implies in another poem, "Spring Break-Up," in *If You Call This Cry a Song* (1983), the poet cannot allow "wrongs [to] go unremarked" (48). Wendell Berry has praised "On Being Asked to Write a Poem against the War in Vietnam" for the way it "complicates our understanding of what political protest is and means" (19). All of these poems expand readers' understanding of protest and reinforce the necessity behind his question in "California," "How can poetry be written by people who want no change?" (*Scrambled Eggs & Whiskey* 15).

LOVE POEMS

A central theme in Carruth's poetry, love emerges as a potential solution to the many problems facing the world. Carruth believes that love places people "in unity" (*The Oldest Killed Lake in North America* 48) and that this unity is essential to community and to the self; love contributes to a stronger sense of self and to a heightened awareness of the world while allowing two people to become "indistinguishable" (*The Sleeping Beauty* 76) from each other. In "Survival as Tao, Beginning at 5:00 A.M.," he claims, "Loving is to survive the unbearable through freedom bestowed / From the inside, mutually" (*Collected Shorter Poems* 354–355), compelling "our otherwise denatured sensibilities to perceive and understand the positive aspects of Being" (355). And in "Renaissance," new love changes his view of the world, which is "transformed ... / its nature made like a home again, / serious, simple, and beautiful" (*Collected Shorter Poems* 404). For Carruth, love manifests itself most powerfully as

"lovingkindness"—a term that appears throughout his love poems. "Poem Catching Up with an Idea," from the 1989 collection *Tell Me Again How the White Heron Rises and Flies across the Nacreous River at Twilight toward the Distant Islands,* presents an example of the lovingkindness that Carruth seeks:

To live here, to love here,
... ...
requires an extraordinary knowledge of freedom,
unhistorical and reinvented by us here in every
act, as when I brought to you for a love token
the plastic sack of just sprouted lilies-of-the-valley
to plant around the steps of our arched doorway.
That was phenomenon, not poetry, not symbol, the act
without a proof, freedom-in-love.

(47)

A poet who connects his writing to the world, Carruth naturally sees love as essential to his poetry as well as to his life: "love, not necessity, is the mother of invention" (*Working Papers* 129). And in "Names," he asserts, "Language / not urged and crammed with love // is nothing" (*Asphalt Georgics* 7).

Perhaps because Carruth's love poems span five decades, love itself acquires various forms in his poetry. "Essay on Love" presents love as an act of manual labor, as the poet cuts wood to keep his wife warm in the winter and realizes his motivation behind the act. In "I Could Take," he creates an image of love from the image of a torn leaf that represents "love's complexity ... / the tearing and / the unique edges," which are "imperfections that match" (*Collected Shorter Poems* 75). One of Carruth's "Sonnets" offers a similar image, this time in a kiss, which allows two people to "exist / in its intelligence, original and new" because "the kiss is one and is egoless" (*Collected Shorter Poems* 325). In another of the sonnets, he identifies love as "the center of our / compassion" (*Collected Shorter Poems* 326), and compassion becomes the basis of love for him in the poem:

we found what somewhere I had always known
exists and must exist, this fervent care,
this lust of tenderness. Two were aware
how in hot seizure, bone pressed to bone

and liquid flesh to flesh, each separate moan
was pleasure, yes, but most in the other's share.

(327)

Similarly, "The Impossible Indispensability of the Ars Poetica" identifies poems as an "act of love … deeply felt gestures, which continuously bestow upon us / What we are" (*Collected Shorter Poems* 353). The common element among these poems is that Carruth locates love as an act of giving, whether through sexual union, a token, manual labor, or writing poetry.

Some of Carruth's poems focus on love in difficult circumstances. Because of his poverty and long and arduous work schedule, he naturally worries about maintaining the love in his relationships. "If It Were Not for You" depicts love in a harsh environment—winter in northern Vermont. Because of his love, the poet refuses to be defeated by the elements; and he finds that love has transformed their "bright poverty" into a shelter—"a house in the wind and a light / on the mountain" (*Collected Shorter Poems* 79). "Concerning Necessity" also draws on the hardships of Carruth's lifestyle, which requires bestowing "our love to the hard dirt / the water and the weeds / and the difficult woods" (*Collected Shorter Poems* 82). Yet "what saves the undoubted collapse," he writes, "is my coming … // and seeing her move / in some particular way / that makes me to fall in love / all over with human beauty" (83). He continually feels astonished that this beauty lies "right here where I live" (83).

The Sleeping Beauty emerges as one of Carruth's most substantial treatments of love as well as one of his major poetic achievements. Written between 1972 and 1980, *The Sleeping Beauty* is a meditation on the Romantic tradition, the role of women in history, and sexual love, pursuing "His dream of the company / Of love, of its benevolence and openness / And lovingkindness and freedom" (45). Consisting of 124 poems in his paragraph form, the poem is a formal masterpiece. Flint has called the book "one of the decade's essential poems" (18), and Charlotte Mandel argues that *The Sleeping Beauty* "strives to acknowledge the world's debt to the feminine principle" (157).

The poem begins literally "out of nothing" (1) as "out of silence / Words gather" (2). By claiming that *The Sleeping Beauty* is "a poem made slowly by no one" (2), Carruth effaces his role as maker of the poem, and thus elevates the beloved—his wife, Rose Marie Dorn, whose name in German (*Dornröschen*) means Sleeping Beauty. A primary aim of the poem is to "make / Presence from words" (4), which he accomplishes at the end of the poem when the Sleeping Beauty awakes. Until that moment, however, Carruth ranges across Western literature, philosophy, and history, paying particular attention to human suffering—war, murder, rape, torture, and madness, which emerge as antitheses to love. In this process, Carruth invokes a number of historical and literary figures whose names begin with *H* as "those who wait / For your invention" (24); thus Homer, Helen ("too washed with the lurid / Sun-streakings of romance" to be "innocent") (7), Hector, Hermes ("uniter of commerce and art, / Possession and beauty") (62), Herod, Hesiod, Hannibal, Hamlet, Hölderlin, Hegel, Heraclitus, and Hitler, as well as Hiroshima and Hydrogen Bomb, are conjured in her dreams.

Carruth interweaves a respect for nature, its "pure loveliness" (2), throughout the poem, equating the beauty of nature with love. He identifies both nature and love as things people try to own even though no one can possess "a speck of creation" (100). The poem proposes generosity as a way to approach love and nature, praising "the kind [of love] that makes / You give and go on giving" (99). This spirit of generosity also applies to the poem itself, specifically the pleasure of composition, as when he writes, "Let the song / Sing, … this world so surely / Created in her sleep" (5). He "yearns / … to give, / To give and give: to the wounded, imprisoned, poor, / And ever to women, the captive people" (110). Carruth's sympathy for women becomes particularly clear when he broaches sexual politics and the politics of power: "We must love humanly, no debasement"; "We must sing / Our passion, as ineluctable as breath, / Without distortion" (84). Through the poem, Carruth seeks not "dominion" (20) over the beloved but "loving and lovingkindness" (9), "so

very much more / Than pleasure" (19). He paradoxically "dreams of pain, / Pain everywhere, pain forever" (41) while writing a love poem and claims that "Beauty is pain plus time" (81), connecting himself to the French troubadour tradition, in which poets sang of the painful pleasures of love.

Until the end of the poem, Carruth exists only in the third person. Because he refers to the Sleeping Beauty in the second person, this tactic can be jarring:

... do you feel him bestow
Loving on you, which is a valuing? It is your beauty
Given to you in his seeing,
Your intelligence in his thought, so that truly
You become, you are becoming, in his being,
As he in yours. For loving is how you create
Each other ...

(60)

The final section of *The Sleeping Beauty* begins, "Princess, the poem is born and you have woken" (124), which implies that the completion of the poem allows her to wake from her sleep and releases her from her dreams. She is now "pure in transcendent being, free / From history" (124), and thus from subjugation or possession. The poem's final line—"My name is Hayden and I have made this song" (124)—introduces one last *H* figure and, for the first time, the first-person voice. Only after roaming through history, literature, and philosophy can the poet free the Sleeping Beauty from her slumber and attain self-realization in the process.

POEMS OF OLD AGE

Carruth's poetry has focused on death from the beginning, which does not seem surprising given his many poems about mental illness and incarceration, war, and the destruction of the natural world. Yet his poems about old age, and thus about his own gradual extinction, have become a prominent part of his oeuvre since the 1980s. At first, the deterioration of the body fills him with curiosity and astonishment, such that he does not worry about death. In "An Excursus of Reassurance in Begonia Time," he exclaims "What is old

age if not / a shaking off of darkness / finally before the plunge" (*Collected Shorter Poems* 316). But the act of "shaking off ... the darkness" takes decades for Carruth, whose poems from the 1980s and 1990s frequently dwell on dying.

The process of dying engenders poems about senility, falling asleep during the day, and "the deep twinge of pain with every / movement, or without movement" (*Doctor Jazz* 110). In these poems, he writes that he suffers from "death-laden insomnia" (*Collected Shorter Poems* 359) and carries "the low noise / of eternity" (327) in his head, and he refers to himself as "an old cripple / dragging my mind like a clubfoot" (329). "I'm foolish and old, I think I am / vanishing" (320), he writes, complaining in another poem, "Old age is failure. Natural / Exhaustion, mind and body letting go, / Words misremembered, ideas frayed like old silk" (*Scrambled Eggs & Whiskey* 91). And in "A Summer with Tu Fu," he muses, "What was strong once and reasonably // good-looking has gone to sag and shrivel" (*Scrambled Eggs & Whiskey* 27). In "Sex," this charting of the body's slow demise intersects with the poet's attachment to love. He writes, "Aging men / suffer two kinds of impotence, the ordinary / kind that everyone makes jokes about, and then / the deeper psychic failure when they are full / of eros but it is hidden, too remote / to evoke the wonder of lust in their partners" (*Collected Shorter Poems* 400–401). His inability to generate physical lust results in him feeling his love "gathering outside him, a power / with no bodily counterpart" (401). He fears that death is not physical extinction but "the end of love" (401).

For Carruth, one of the horrors of growing old is seeing his daughter Martha die of cancer. Because Martha is "crucially vulnerable," he and his first wife find themselves "in agony, / in wordless despair" (*Scrambled Eggs & Whiskey* 30), sharing "the crisis of [their] lives" (31). In "Pittsburgh," he claims that "the falling into death of a beautiful / young woman is so much more important" (*Scrambled Eggs & Whiskey* 76) than his own demise. Distraught, he cannot sleep, sharing with Martha "the crisis of forever inadequately medicated / pain" as well as "the

love of daughter and father" (77). After Martha dies in 1997 at the age of forty-six, Carruth charts his thoughts and emotions during the first twenty-four hours of her death in "Dearest M—," the centerpiece of his last book, *Doctor Jazz*. The poem begins immediately after he hears she has died, "riddled with cancer, wracked by pneumonia, / comatose in a stupor of morphine" (37). The poem seeks to honor and mourn her while providing the poet with an occasion to meditate on his own mortality. He muses, "A strange, unnatural thing is it—to outlive one's daughter" (35), and asks "Can anything arouse / passion in an old man like the death of a young / woman?" (37). During the act of writing the poem, Carruth finds language insufficient: "The immensity of what should be said defeats me. Language / like a dismasted hulk at sea is overwhelmed and founders" (36). And he refers to the poem as "this gush of words, this surging elegy" (46).

Martha's death compels the poet to consider his own death, something for which he must plan. In "Testament," he considers the process of making a will to provide for his wife after his death. Because poetry earns "at best a pittance in our civilization" (*Scrambled Eggs & Whiskey* 35), he has little money to leave behind. What he plans to leave, however, seems far more valuable than money—love and memories of "love-makings" and "embracings" (36), animals cared for, flowers planted. The poem "Prepare" begins after his wife has asked him to write a poem that will prepare her for his death. When he considers "in desperation" how he will die, he notes, "The possibilities are endless and not at all fascinating, except that I can't stop / Thinking about them, can't stop envisioning that moment of hideous violence" (*Scrambled Eggs & Whiskey* 98). As in "Testament," he knows he can leave only memories as well as "hundreds of keepsakes, such as this scrap of a poem" (99).

Despite his poignant considerations of his own deterioration, the death of his daughter, and his impending absence from his wife's life, Carruth's most remarkable poems in old age concern love. In "Birthday Cake," he claims to be "too old to write love songs now" (*Scrambled Eggs & Whiskey* 12). Rather than proclaim his love for his wife, as he has done in many of his previous love poems, he proclaims that she loves him, "confident in [his] amazement" (12). In "Song: Now That She Is Here," he actually views old age as a boon, because he has "learned at last / What it means truly to be in love" (*Scrambled Eggs & Whiskey* 91). "I am in love now, / In it totally all the time" (91), he writes, indicating the extreme importance of this love to his daily life. And in "The Best, the Most," he rejoices that "one young woman lives with me / and is my love" and that "she loves me for / myself, or for what little is left" (*Scrambled Eggs & Whiskey* 65). In "Quality of Wine," he describes how "my sweetheart rubs my back when I'm / knotted in arthritis" (*Scrambled Eggs & Whiskey* 13), intoning "let the dying be long" (13). Carruth's ability to transform love into such a healing force in his poetry—even in the face of his own death—testifies to both the humaneness of his vision and the crucial role of "lovingkindness" in all of his poetry.

Selected Bibliography

WORKS OF HAYDEN CARRUTH

BOOKS OF POETRY

The Crow and the Heart. New York: Macmillan, 1959.

Journey to a Known Place. Norfolk, Conn.: New Directions, 1961.

The Norfolk Poems. Iowa City: Prairie Press, 1962.

North Winter. Iowa City: Prairie Press, 1964.

Nothing for Tigers. New York: Macmillan, 1965.

Contra Mortem. Johnson, Vt.: Crows Mark Press, 1967.

The Clay Hill Anthology. Iowa City: Prairie Press, 1970.

For You. New York: New Directions, 1970.

The Voice That Is Great Within Us: American Poetry of the Twentieth Century.

New York: Bantam, 1970. (Compiler.)

From Snow and Rock, from Chaos. New York: New Directions, 1973.

Dark World. Santa Cruz: Kayak, 1974.

The Bloomingdale Papers. Athens: University of Georgia Press, 1975.

Brothers, I Loved You All. New York: Sheep Meadow Press, 1978.

The Sleeping Beauty. New York: Harper and Row, 1982.

If You Call This Cry a Song. Woodstock, Vt.: Countryman Press, 1983.

Asphalt Georgics. New York: New Directions, 1985.

The Oldest Killed Lake in North America. Grenada, Miss.: Salt-Works Press, 1985.

The Selected Poetry of Hayden Carruth. New York: Macmillan, 1985.

Tell Me Again How the White Heron Rises and Flies across the Nacreous River at Twilight toward the Distant Islands. New York: New Directions, 1989.

Collected Shorter Poems, 1946–1991. Port Townsend, Wash: Copper Canyon Press, 1992.

Collected Longer Poems. Port Townsend, Wash;: Copper Canyon Press, 1993.

Scrambled Eggs & Whiskey: Poems, 1991–1995. Port Townsend, Wash.: Copper Canyon Press, 1996.

Doctor Jazz. Port Townsend, Wash.: Copper Canyon Press, 2001.

NONFICTION BOOKS

Working Papers: Selected Essays and Reviews. Edited by Judith Weissman. Athens: University of Georgia Press, 1982.

Effluences from the Sacred Caves: More Selected Essays and Reviews. Ann Arbor: University of Michigan Press, 1983.

Sitting In: Selected Writings on Jazz, Blues, and Related Topics. Iowa City: University of Iowa Press, 1986.

Suicides and Jazzers. Ann Arbor: University of Michigan Press, 1992.

Selected Essays and Reviews. Port Townsend, Wash.: Copper Canyon Press, 1996.

Reluctantly: Autobiographical Essays. Port Townsend, Wash.: Copper Canyon Press, 1998.

Beside the Shadblow Tree: A Memoir of James Laughlin. Port Townsend, Wash.: Copper Canyon Press, 1999.

Letters to Jane. Keene, N.Y.: Ausable Press, 2004.

AUDIO AND VIDEO EDITIONS

Eternity Blues. Washington, D.C.: Watershed Intermedia, 1986. (Cassette.)

Hayden Carruth. Directed by Dan Griggs. Lannan Literary Videos. Santa Fe, N.M.: Lannan Foundation, 1994. (Video.)

Hayden Carruth: A Listener's Guide. Produced by Katherin Mattern. Port Townsend, Wash.: Copper Canyon Press, 1999. (Compact disc.)

INTERVIEWS

Huff, Steven. *Five Points* 8, no. 2:44–60 (2004).

Scheele, Roy. *Verse* 14, no. 2:47–59 (1997).

Weiss, David. *Seneca Review* 20, no. 1:128–146 (1990).

CRITICAL AND BIOGRAPHICAL STUDIES

Berry, Wendell. "A Poem of Difficult Hope." In *In the Act: Essays on the Poetry of Hayden Carruth,* edited by David Weiss. Geneva, N.Y.: Hobart and William Smith Colleges Press, 1990. Pp. 16–21.

Budbill, David. "When You Use Your Head, Your Ears Fall Off: My Twenty Years of Listening to Music with the Supernumerary Cockroach." In *In the Act: Essays on the Poetry of Hayden Carruth,* edited by David Weiss. Geneva, N.Y.: Hobart and William Smith Colleges Press, 1990. Pp. 113–127.

Feder, Lillian. "Poetry from the Asylum: Hayden Carruth's *The Bloomingdale Papers.*" *Literature and Medicine* 4:112–127 (1985).

Flint, R. W. "The Odyssey of Hayden Carruth." *Parnassus: Poetry in Review* 11, no. 1:17–32 (1983).

Gardner, Geoffrey. "Homage to the One-Man Band with Incredible Ears." In *In the Act: Essays on the Poetry of Hayden Carruth,* edited by David Weiss. Geneva, N.Y.: Hobart and William Smith Colleges Press, 1990. Pp. 97–105.

Gundy, Jeff. Review of *Reluctantly. Georgia Review* 54, no. 1:142–145 (2000).

Hamill, Sam. "Listening In." In *In the Act: Essays on the Poetry of Hayden Carruth,* edited by David Weiss. Geneva, N.Y.: Hobart and William Smith Colleges Press, 1990. Pp. 83–91.

Howard, Ben. "Being Human: The Art of Hayden Carruth." *Shenandoah* 50, no. 4:64–90 (2000).

Kuusisto, Stephen. "Elegiac Locales: The Anarchy of Hayden Carruth." In *In the Act: Essays on the Poetry of Hayden Carruth,* edited by David Weiss. Geneva, N.Y.: Hobart and William Smith Colleges Press, 1990. Pp. 75–82.

Mandel, Charlotte. "Beautiful Dreamers: *Helen in Egypt* and *The Sleeping Beauty.*" *Clockwatch Review* 9, nos. 1–2:155–159 (1994–1995).

Miller, Matthew. "A Love Supreme: Jazz and the Poetry of Hayden Carruth." *Midwest Quarterly* 39, no. 1:294–308 (1997).

Rivard, David. "A Meaning of Hayden Carruth." In *In the Act: Essays on the Poetry of Hayden Carruth,* edited by David Weiss. Geneva, N.Y.: Hobart and William Smith Colleges Press, 1990. Pp. 30–46.

Scheele, Roy. "Hayden Carruth: The Gift of Self." *Poets and Writers* 24, no. 3:45–59 (May/June 1996).

Selinger, Eric Murphy. "The Importance of a Small Floy Floy." *Parnassus: Poetry in Review* 22, nos. 1–2:250–279 (1996).

Thompson, Christian. "In Measured Resistance: On Hayden Carruth's 'Contra Mortem.'" *American Poetry Review* 33, no. 4:20–23 (2004).

Weiss, David, ed. *In the Act: Essays on the Poetry of Hayden Carruth*. Geneva, N.Y.: Hobart and William Smith Colleges Press, 1990.

———. "Taking Sides." In his *In the Act: Essays on the Poetry of Hayden Carruth*. Geneva, N.Y.: Hobart and William Smith Colleges Press, 1990. Pp. 50–59.

Zapruder, Matthew. Review of *Scrambled Eggs & Whiskey*. *Verse* 13, nos. 2–3:215–221 (1996).

FRANK CONROY

(1936–2005)

Bert Almon

Frank Conroy distinguished himself with three important books: a memoir, *Stop-Time* (1967), covering his life to the age of eighteen; a collection of stories, *Midair* (1985)*; and a novel, *Body and Soul* (1993). He also published a collection of essays, *Dogs Bark, but the Caravan Rolls On* (2002), and a brief travel book, *Time and Tide* (2004), about Nantucket, where he lived part of each year. His influence on later confessional memoirists, like Tobias Wolff (*This Boy's Life*, 1989) and Mary Karr (*The Liar's Club*, 1995), has been deep, although he never enjoyed their extraordinary best-seller status. Writing in *Vogue* in 1996, David Streitfeld surveyed the rather large crop of recent memoirs by the young (more than twenty) and suggested that they were "all descendants of Conroy." Traditionally, famous people write memoirs to record their achievements, but Frank Conroy set an important precedent by becoming famous because he wrote the memoir.

Conroy attained another kind of fame as an arts administrator, first as literature director for the National Endowment for the Arts and then as director of the celebrated Iowa Writers' Workshop. When he announced his retirement from the University of Iowa in August 2004, the story was reported by the *New York Times* and the Associated Press, and consequently was reported widely in newspapers all over the United States.

Frank Conroy was born in New York City on January 15, 1936. His father, (Francis) Philip Conroy, was first a magazine editor and then a successful literary agent. Philip Conroy wanted to be a writer himself, and he often placed copies of self-published work on the shelves of bookstores. Frank Conroy's mother, Helga Lassen, called Dagmar in *Stop-Time*, was an immigrant from Denmark escaping from a bourgeois

family and dreaming of singing opera. Conroy saw little of his father, who suffered increasingly from mental illness and was mostly confined to rest homes and sanatoriums. On at least one occasion the father escaped from confinement and terrorized young Frank. Philip Conroy died of cancer when his son was twelve, leaving a modest inheritance for the support of Frank and his older sister, Alison—and a large collection of books, which his son read assiduously. He told John Rodden in an interview ("The Master's Apprentice") that he had read all of Charles Dickens and Fyodor Dostoyevsky by the time he was fifteen. His mother remarried, to a man whom Conroy called Jean Fouchet in *Stop-Time*. Conroy's first marriage was in 1958, to Patty Monro Ferguson, with whom he had two sons, Daniel and Will. The marriage was dissolved in 1970. In 1975, he married Margaret Davidson Lee, with whom he had his third son, Tim. The richest source for his life to the age of eighteen, when he entered Haverford College, is *Stop-Time*, a book that sold only seven thousand copies when it was first published but that has become a modern classic. His awards include a Rockefeller Foundation grant in 1960 for work on his first book, a Guggenheim Fellowship in 1987, a grant from the National Council for the Arts, and, in 1997, the French Legion of Honor. Oddly enough, he has also won a Grammy Award, but not for his musicianship: he wrote some of liner notes for a 1998 Frank Sinatra compilation, *The Best of the Columbia Years 1943–1952*.

STOP-TIME

Conroy liked to say, "Life happens to all of us. Art answers back." From the start life "happened" to Frank Conroy. His few encounters with his

father were disturbing, especially when Philip Conroy was in a manic state. As presented in *Stop-Time*, his mother was irresponsible and his stepfather was a narcissist who almost never worked; the two of them lived on the children's income. (For the memoir, his publisher's lawyers made Conroy take the legal precaution of changing every name except his own.) The family lived sometimes in Florida—under rather primitive conditions—and sometimes in New York. Twice in his memoir Conroy speaks of "the sloppiness of things," a paralyzing sloppiness. ("Sloppiness" is perhaps too mild a word for the emotional chaos he faced. Besides his father's illness, he was aware that his stepfather's second wife was institutionalized, and he witnessed a mental breakdown of the stepfather's brother.) During his high school years he became an obsessive reader. "I could not resist the *clarity of the world* in books, the incredible way in which life became weighty and accessible. Books were reality. I hadn't made my mind up about my own life, a vague, dreamy affair, amorphous and dimly perceived, without beginning or end" (*Stop-Time*, 143). And eventually he would write his own book, something that he thought about doing when he was in his teens: from his dysfunctional childhood, he found a way to answer back to life in a work of art that scrutinizes his unhappiness and confusion, giving him some mastery of them.

He had two inspirations for his work: *Memories of a Catholic Girlhood* (1957), a work by Mary McCarthy written with the sophistication of a novel, and *Autobiography of a Schizophrenic Girl* (first published in 1951), by "Renée," an anonymous French psychiatric patient. In the introduction to the 1994 reprint of "Renée's book," Conroy says that when he began at "the ridiculous age of twenty-six, to write my own memoirs" (Foreword from *Autobiography of a Schizophrenic Girl,* 9) he was "heartened" by the existence of Mary McCarthy's book and "Renee's." McCarthy showed that ordinary life could be the substance of a memoir. *The Autobiography of a Schizophrenic Girl* "proved that a writer could successfully recreate states of consciousness despite his failure to understand those states when they had originally occurred" (9). The troubled

young narrator of *Stop-Time* was exposed to mental illness and profligate behavior, and he did not always understand his own responses to his environment. It is, in fact, the mystery of his inner life that gives the book its power. Conroy's memoir has affinities with the bildungsroman (that is, a novel showing the process of growing up), but what is distinctive about his approach is the episodic nature of the work. Chapters are generally placed in chronological order, but there are startling leaps. The book is written with concern for scenes rather than for continuity (perhaps reflecting a debt to Conroy's beloved F. Scott Fitzgerald, whose 1925 masterpiece *The Great Gatsby* is written in a series of brilliant scenes).

The epigraph to *Stop-Time* is a passage from Wallace Stevens's poem, "Less and Less Human, O Savage Spirit":

It is the human that is the alien,
The human that has no cousin in the moon.

It is the human that demands his speech
From beasts or from the incommunicable mass.

If there must be a god in the house, let him be one
That will not hear us when we speak: a coolness,

A vermilioned nothingness, any stick of the mass
Of which we are too distantly a part.

The passage suggests that human beings are alienated from the natural world. Although Conroy does very briefly have a mystical experience that enables him to converse with a tiny nature spirit and enter into the consciousness of a dog, the more penetrating experience that he associates with his childhood rambles in the Florida wilderness was an awareness that he and his friend Tobey were "pinpoints of life in a world of dead things." When the family lives in New York, the city is just as alienating for the friendless Conroy.

Conroy unifies *Stop-Time* and conveys his theme of lives out of control through the use of three carefully placed scenes set in England and involving a wild car ride at night. *Stop-Time* opens with a prologue, a dramatic scene set when Conroy was twenty-eight years old and taking a

wild, drunken ride in a Jaguar from London to a house in the countryside. He sums up his state of mind as "a wild, escalating passion of frustration, blinded by some mysterious mixture of guilt, moroseness, and desire." He is alienated from himself as well as nature. The scene, in the prologue, is at 3 A.M. In the middle of the book, he describes the same ride, at 4 A.M. And the book ends with an epilogue set at 4:30 A.M. the same night. The three scenes create suspense, suggesting a life out of control for reasons the narrator does not clearly understand. In one of the earliest and best critiques of the book, Tony Tanner points out that most of the important scenes in *Stop-Time* end with an image of motion: "on foot, on bikes, in cars, on ships," images of patternless motion that the English critic thinks are typical of rootless American life. Certainly, Conroy's family was restless and rootless—and motion seemed to take them nowhere. When at the age of eleven the young Frank Conroy witnesses his stepfather's brother, Victor, having a seizure, he panics and runs around a palm tree into a parked car, knocking himself out briefly. On regaining consciousness, he concludes "that the world was insane. Not just people. The world" (*Stop-Time*, 33). After the birth of a third child, Conroy's half-sister Jessica, his mother, Dagmar, goes with the baby for a long visit to Denmark. Left alone and petulant at Dagmar's departure, her husband Jean begins a relationship with Miss Smith, a deeply disturbed woman. Near the end of the book, Conroy describes the nervous breakdown of his sister Alison, who had always managed to screen out the chaos of the family. Conroy says that his coping strategies were rebellion and anger, while his sister chose disengagement and calmness and became a model student. Eventually the strain became too much for her and she was hospitalized for a time.

The book's opening chapter, "Savages," reveals much about the roots of Conroy's own spiritual malaise. He begins by talking about his few early contacts with his father, who offered no role model for the son. The elder Conroy's contribution to his family was to provide a modest income and buy them an apartment on Eighty-Sixth Street in Manhattan. Then Frank Conroy describes the boarding school in Pennsylvania that he attended from the ages of nine to eleven. Here too he was let down by adults incapable of giving guidance. The school was run with no real order, and the students generally did whatever they wanted. When the boys created a fire hazard by lighting hundreds of candles on the dormitory room floor, the punishment announced was grotesque: each boy would have to plunge his hand into a pot of boiling water. The effects on the first few victims were so severe that the heat was turned off, and Conroy found the experience painless. The vacuum of responsibility at the school seems to have led the boys to set up their own court. They put an unpopular boy named Ligget on trial for racism. In a scene reminiscent of William Golding's 1954 novel *Lord of the Flies*—it is no wonder the chapter is called "Savages"—they sentenced the boy to be slugged by each of his forty fellows. Conroy himself got in a severe punch before the sentence was called off. Ligget collapsed and had to be hospitalized with a jaw broken in four places. Although Conroy concludes, "I learned almost nothing from beating up Ligget," he did learn something from his own stay in the school, that brutality happens easily.

His encounter with violence from adults (as opposed to schoolboy violence) came from a source close to home: a peculiar family friend, Donald Johnson, hit him when he was nine or ten. Johnson, who had moved from being Dagmar's piano teacher to being Dagmar's resident confidante in the New York apartment, got away with the assault and also got away with hitting Conroy's little sister, Jessica, when she was only eighteen months old: Dagmar did nothing about these vicious acts. The narrator clearly has a grudge against his mother, who is presented as cold and neglectful, like the distant mothers in Dickens. Indeed, young Conroy's view of adults in general is Dickensian: he perceives almost all of them as powerful, grotesque, and irrational. He does not suffer at the hands of his stepfather in the way that David Copperfield suffers from the rule of Mr. Murdstone, but he has emotional scars. A visit to his paternal grandmother, an eccentric old woman in Jacksonville, Florida, also

has a Dickensian flavor. The grandmother, who looks like a fierce old bird, is another narcissist like his stepfather. She asks rude questions and demands declarations of affection. Even a benign figure like the mother of his friend Tobey Rawlings is described as horrendously obese.

The culmination of Conroy's parade of grotesque figures comes in a madhouse scene that Dickens would appreciate, one that takes place in a Connecticut institution for the feeble-minded, where Jean and Dagmar work as weekend wardens one winter while the family stays in an old cabin. Conroy, aged twelve at the time, is usually left alone in the cabin for the weekend, where he is terrified by the cold and encompassing dark. After some months, he persuades his parents to take him along to the institution. He spends what turns out to be a night of greater terror, overwhelmed by the squalor, the noise, and the sheer abnormality of some of the inmates. Further, he witnesses the brutality of one of the guards who keeps order with violence. The night is so disturbing that he spends the remaining weekends alone in the cabin, where the empty winter days leave him alienated from himself: "The first fragile beginnings of a personality starting to collect in my twelve-year-old soul were immediately sucked up into the silence and the featureless winter sky" (*Stop-Time*, 61). He felt lost, dematerialized.

On the other hand, he had felt alive and happy during his family's first year in Florida, the year preceding his Connecticut ordeal. He and his friend Tobey Rawlings had lived a kind of Huckleberry Finn and Tom Sawyer existence in the wilderness, with a minimum of supervision. (Conroy has a strong affection for Mark Twain's 1876 novel *The Adventures of Tom Sawyer*: his introduction to the Modern Library Classics edition of the novel calls it a "sacred text within the body of American literature.") The family's second stay in Florida is not so idyllic. His friend had started working for his father in order to discourage the man from drinking, so Frank sees little of him. One of the saddest moments in a book that is often sad comes during that second summer in Florida, when he visits Tobey in Chula Vista and finds that his friend has become a

"thickened," acne-faced redneck with a pathologically shy fifteen-year-old girlfriend.

Suffering again from the effects of isolation, Conroy has a bizarre experience, in response to a toxic family life: "The dominating elements of life at home were anger, boredom, and disapproval." One day he hears his mother's "mezzo voice" calling him as he hides (significantly) "in the dog house." He recounts falling into a dissociated state: "Faintly dizzy, half-asleep, and beyond time, I slipped gradually from the world" (*Stop-Time*, 101). A series of hallucinations draw him further and further from reality. The influence of "Renee's" memoir of abnormal perceptions is strong in this scene. He describes going into an ecstatic trance, a kind of god-like consciousness. And he recalls a conversation with a tiny woman, five or six inches tall. In the final hallucination, he became a dog running through the woods.

Such experiences are dangerous. Nothing so overwhelming happens again in the book, but after another return to New York he starts sitting on the roof of his building, toying with suicide. And he tries running away from home when he is fifteen, trying to hitchhike to Florida. When he does go back to Florida on a school vacation the following year, he takes a job as a pinsetter at a bowling alley. His coworker points out that Conroy turns the work into a dangerous game, dodging bowling balls at the last minute. Another of his jobs requires him to change the big letters on a movie house marquee. From his place on a swaying ladder the letters spell a meaningless message: "constructing the end of a word whose beginning was lost in the distance, holding a letter larger than my head, I felt I was disappearing, drifting away through the hole of an *O*, shrinking into the perspective of an immense *X*" (*Stop-Time*, 203). The symbolism is clear: the alienated self can make no sense of experience. Life is no more than the counters in a game of tic-tac-toe played with symbols that also represent nothingness and the unknown.

The book gets its title from Conroy's repeated lapses from ordinary consciousness, although none of his experiences after the long trance in the dog house manifests the rich dream content

that marked the first escape from the mundane. The term "stop-time" is well-known in jazz, which would account for its appeal to Conroy, a self-taught jazz pianist who was good enough to play in clubs. In a stop-time, the rhythm section stops playing for some measures while the soloist continues to improvise. The musicians in the rhythm section keep track of the time and resume playing exactly where they would have been if they had not stopped. A stop-time seems to liberate the soloist—and the listener—from the constraints of time.

Conroy's quasi-mystical lapses have a restorative function, or at least a coping one, although there is a danger that he might not emerge from them. Another coping element for Conroy that becomes a motif in the work is the element of game playing. In an excellent essay titled "Games in Frank Conroy's *Stop-Time*," Timothy Dow Adams notes that many of the narrator's activities are described as games: punching the time clock in one after-school job in New York, "playing chemistry set" pranks in an electroplating laboratory. Even selling fruit on the streets is described as a game.

Games are playful, but they also offer chances for control and elegance in a sloppy life. Conroy describes, for example, the way he experienced the power of games during his second year in Florida. He and Tobey go to a carnival, where they ride in bumper cars—a kind of disorderly but safe game controlled in part by the drivers and ultimately subject to the laws of physics. He plays a ring-toss game—a much more controlled game in which skill enables the player to exploit physical principles of mass and motion. He wins the game but has no witnesses, so he is denied the prize by the sideshow operator, who responds to complaints in a way that makes him another of the Dickensian grotesques. The man seems to reach out to Conroy to shake hands. "Gently but firmly he takes my wrist, bends, and spreads his knees a fraction of an inch, and slowly rubs my palm under his balls" (*Stop-Time*, 95).

It is after this experience that Conroy has his hallucinatory journey in the literal and symbolic dog house. The book does not assert a causal relationship between events: Conroy simply presents episodes and lets the reader draw conclusions. Just as he might seem in danger of a mental breakdown, however, he is saved by his fascination with a new "game": he witnesses twins from California named "Ramos and Ricardo" promoting the sales of yo-yos by putting on an extraordinary demonstration. Conroy not only buys a yo-yo but their book as well, and he becomes tremendously proficient. He admits that the practice sessions with the yo-yo had something vaguely masturbatory about them, and the yo-yo chapter also deals with his growing sexual awareness, which takes the form of peeping into the bedroom window of two slightly older girls. One afternoon, he masters the most difficult yo-yo trick of all, "The Universe," on his first try, and also succeeds as a voyeur shortly after: "That same night, hidden in the greenery under the window, I watched a naked girl let down her long red hair" (*Stop-Time*, 129). Later, when he worked part-time in a library in New York, he carried out a more repellent act of voyeurism, spying on a young woman through a gap in a shelf of books and masturbating as he watched her. Typical of the alienated point of view throughout much of the book is the author's failure to feel any concern in this instance when he notices that the young woman is weeping.

He recounts his education at Stuyvesant High School in Manhattan, where he struggles with boredom and fails several courses; he is no more fond of learning than Tom Sawyer was. At the same time, he educates himself in literature on his own and plays the piano, learning to play jazz by listening to records. These cultural pursuits were one way of keeping sane—although his stepfather assured him that he would never be able to play for money. (Conroy's interest in jazz perhaps explains his ability in his writing to unite the formal and the spontaneous.) The birth of his little sister also kept him in the human community: here was a person he could love unconditionally. The last chapters of the book trace his gradual entry into normal human life, of which sex is a compelling part: the book is set in the 1950s, before the sexual revolution. The sex is anonymous at first, mere necking with unknown girls in the balconies of theaters, until he

finally has a full sexual encounter with a girl he picks up in movie. The experience leaves him dazzled; the girl has nothing to say, except goodbye. She does ask his name, and for the first time in the work, he uses his full name to answer her: "Frank," I said quickly, "Frank Conroy."

In the chapter that begins immediately after this initiation, he departs for Europe, to meet his Danish relatives for the first time. He attends a school he calls "Elsinore Folk High School" (although, in spite of his melancholy and introversion, he is not quite an American Hamlet). He meets students from all over the world and makes his first friends since the days when he and Tobey roamed the woods and beaches in Florida. The motif of games reappears: male students had made up a game called "hysteria," a kind of tag played on ropes and other equipment, in which the rules forbade to touch the floor. The symbolism is natural and implicit. Conway has spent his high school years sitting on high ledges, flirting with suicide. "Hysteria," however, is not actually dangerous, and it is played with others, like the French students he hangs out with. He is emerging from his isolation.

This emergence results in an ordeal, a baffling flirtation with a fellow student, Christina. The relationship goes well at first. She is a musician from a small town in northern Sweden. She is twenty-two, he is seventeen. But unaccountably Christina becomes another of the disturbed people in the protagonist's life, turning ambivalent and then obsessive about Conroy. Later in Paris, he meets up with his sister who appears to be also disturbed—on the edge of a breakdown, which does indeed come a little later. Alison's words to him are plaintive: "We're too young to be all alone," referring to their lack of a sustaining family.

In Paris, Conroy learns that he has been accepted by Haverford College; his future seems secure. He makes friends with a young English painter, John. One day John shows him a mysterious drawing. In a celebrated passage, Conroy learns that the image is a diagram of the lock on a Metro door. The motion of the lock has been caught in a static drawing, one of the paradoxes of art. "In a single moment I understood distortion in art," (Stop-Time, 276) says Conroy, whose brilliant scenes in Stop-Time have themselves captured process, in their own way. The southern novelist William Faulkner believed that one function of art is to stop motion, to capture the energy of life so that the real can be examined. Stopping motion, stopping time: the process is the same, to capture the agitations of life in a medium that can hold them for contemplation. Paradoxically, it is the sloppiness of life—so abhorrent to Conroy—that he holds steady for contemplation.

His main narrative ends with a crisis and a vista of opportunity. He returns from Europe, ready to start college and to create a blank slate, to wipe out his past, which we know has been painful and confused. But a telegram from Europe demonstrates how difficult it is, in fact, to eliminate the past: Conroy's sister, he learns, is being sent home from Europe after a nervous breakdown. Her attempts to control her life have collapsed, and she gets off the plane cursing and paranoid. She avoids the mental hospital but becomes a diminished person, desperate for affection and eager to marry the boyfriend she has been unsure of.

More promisingly, however, Conroy is entering college with a very adequate allowance from his father's estate. The money is no longer being wasted by his mother and stepfather: with a twist of the knife, Conroy tells us that Jean has started a used-car lot in Florida. Haverford College is presented as a pastoral paradise. Swans swim in the lake, and the smell of freshly cut grass is in the air. At eighteen, Frank Conroy apparently has control of his young life at last.

But we are not left with such a simple, happy ending. The last page of the narrative is an epilogue, a return to that wild drive in London that began the book and reappeared briefly in the middle. It is now 4:30 A.M., and the drunken narrator speeds into the village and loses control of his car. It appears that the skidding car will crash broadside into a concrete fountain, and the narrator's reaction is suicidal: "As the fountain grew larger, I felt myself relax. I leaned toward the door. Let it come. Let it come as hard and fast as it can. Touch the wheel, make an adjustment so that it will strike right beside me. Here it

comes! *Here it comes!*" But it does not come: the wheels catch on a low curb, the car spins around the fountain "like a baton around a cheerleader's wrist," and it bumps the side of the fountain gently, coming to rest. A man raises a window and calls out: "Here. What's all this?" To know something of the complexity of that question has taken Conroy's very formidable power as a writer, the writer of *Stop-Time*. He responds not with an answer to the man but with laughter out of a throat "burning with bile." The ending is powerful, letting us know that the narrator's inner demons have not been subdued. As Peter Bailey points out in his 1981 essay "Notes on the Novel-as-Autobiography," the conclusion is the final stop-time in the book, a "pale echo of the fixing of motion which the novel [sic] accomplishes." Life happened to Frank Conroy; out of its confusions he has made a work of art.

Peter Bailey is one of several perceptive critics who insisted that the book should be considered as much a novel as a memoir. Bailey points to an interesting question of genre, one that Conroy pondered—the writer himself told interviewer John Rodden that when his publisher wanted to know if the book should be marketed as a novel or a memoir, he replied that he did not know. Bailey's most interesting comment on *Stop-Time* formulates the theme as a conflict between Conroy's craving to extinguish consciousness (the "speeding binges in his Jaguar) and his "subjugation of his experience to the organizing, conceptualizing capacities of consciousness."

Conroy's first real critic (as opposed to reviewer) was Tony Tanner. In his 1971 study *City of Words: American Fiction 1950–1970*, Tanner juxtaposed *Stop-Time* with Exley's *A Fan's Notes* as works of "fictionalized recall." He admires the skill with which each chapter of Conroy's book is structured "without any apparent thematic manipulation of each detail of the life under recall." The concluding scene in the sports car he considers an epitome of the book: "Any art can be a way of 'stopping time,' in a way which we sense comes somewhere between the fluidity of actual experience and the absolute fixity of death."

A 1974 essay by Roger Ramsey, in "The Illusion of Fiction in Frank Conroy's *Stop-Time*," demonstrates the memoir's affinity with fiction by pointing to the suggestiveness of Conroy's prose, his use of symbolism, and his ability to deal with himself objectively as a character. In a 1986 essay, "A 'Momentary Stay against Confusion': Frank Conroy's *Stop-Time*," Timothy Dow Adams continued the practice of using fictional terms to discuss this work. He christens it a "mock-autobiography." He notes that when Conroy published chapter 6 in *Paris Review* a few months before the book appeared, the author's note said "'Please Don't Take My Sunshine Away' is an excerpt from his first novel, *Hanging On,* which will be published by Viking Press." Along with discussion of the borders of fiction and nonfiction in the book, Adams's rich essay points to the importance of the body and physical space, as well as the handling of time, in Conroy's work.

John Haegert, writing in *Modern Fiction Studies* in 1987, criticized *Stop-Time* for lacking "the conclusive fictionality of most imaginative literature, thus giving the impression of being something of a clever cheat as a completed novel." He considers the narrative dubious as autobiography for its insistence on treating real people as if they were fictional characters. Part of the story's open-endedness, it must be said in Conroy's defense, seems inevitable in a book about an author who had not quite reached life's traditional halfway mark of "three score and ten." Nevertheless, Haegert has useful insights into what he calls a "marginal or hybrid form at best." He observes some important patterns: a contrast between purity and disease; a sense of the "perpetual possibilities of new beginnings," created by Conroy's family's "chronic removals and uprootings"; and the importance of Conroy's fantasy life. He also compares Conroy's treatment of his father in the memoir with the more detailed and dramatic portrait in the short story "Mid-Air."

A 1987 essay by Thomas F. Strychacz, "Controlling the 'Sloppiness of Things' in Frank Conroy's *Stop-Time*," begins by suggesting that not enough criticism has been published on the work

because readers find "Conroy's easy crossing of the boundaries between fiction and autobiography" problematic. Strychacz points out the use of metaphors from jazz, film, and painting in *Stop-Time*, and he has good observations on the role of the "frame story": the three scenes of a wild ride through the English countryside. He also suggests that the tension between control and reckless freedom that he finds in the prologue and epilogue are subtle patterns in the book as a whole. He observes a pattern of escape attempts that end in failure. Most important is Conroy's pattern of seeking control over the chaos (the "sloppiness") of his life through games and tricks. Ultimately, Strychacz believes, Conroy achieves understanding of his agonies if not liberation from them.

The critics' concern with the hybrid nature of the book now seems outmoded, thanks to the developments in the theory of autobiography that were taking place in the mid-1980s. Paul John Eakin's *Fictions in Autobiography: Studies in the Art of Self-Invention* (1985) takes for granted that the memoirist uses the techniques of the novelist and makes a primary example of Mary McCarthy, one of Conroy's important influences. As with *Stop-Time*, McCarthy's *Memories of a Catholic Girlhood* appeared in excerpts that were not always clearly short stories or recollections. Eakin emphasizes that the self in fiction, or for the memoirist using the devices of fiction, is not a given but a creation discovered in the writing: we make ourselves up as we go along. Discussing *Stop-Time,* Eakin says that from the point of view of contemporary autobiographical theory, Conroy's book may be a hybrid but it is not a "sport," or mutant: it is at the center of a flourishing genre of memoirs that use the full panoply of fictional techniques. And after the success of books influenced by *Stop-Time*, like the memoirs of Mary Karr and Tobias Wolff, it seems archetypal rather than eccentric. (Karr has said that her first memoir, *The Liar's Club*, was meant to be *Stop-Time* for girls.)

Conroy's memoir became part of a small controversy that arose in 2002 over the bowdlerization of works used on examinations in the New York State schools. In passage from *Stop-Time* used on an examination, a passage about skinny-dipping was cut without any indication that it had been censored, and the expletive "hell" was changed to "heck." Conroy was one of a number of authors who expressed indignation at the abridgement of their work, and the New York State Board of Regents ultimately ended the practice.

An appreciative review of *Stop-Time* by Peter Shaw in the June 1968 issue of *Commentary* had ended with an anticipation of pleasure in reading more from Frank Conroy—but there would be a long wait until the publication of Conroy's next volume, the story collection *Midair*. Life in its messiness intervened—in particular, the breakup of Conroy's marriage in 1970. Difficulty in making a living was also a factor: his royalties from the first book were much smaller than the critical esteem he had garnered. He made money in the late 1960s by writing for magazines and working as a "script doctor" for Hollywood films. After he made $30,000 for an original script (never filmed), he and his first wife had bought an old barn in Nantucket in 1969 and converted it to a summer house. After the divorce, he decided to live there year-round. Jobs were hard to find in Nantucket. He found work as a jazz pianist in a club, wrote for magazines, tried scallop fishing (but was not strong enough), and eventually wound up on food stamps. He was visited by his lawyer, who advised him: "Some guys just sink. Don't."

He met his second wife, Margaret Davidson Lee, on the island: she was hitchhiking after her car broke down. (He has told the story at some length in an essay collected in *Dogs Bark, but the Caravan Rolls On.*) He worked briefly at several universities, including the University of Iowa, the Massachusetts Institute of Technology, Brandeis, and Goddard College, where Mary Karr was his student. In 1981, he became director of the literature program of the National Endowment for the Arts, a job he held until 1987, when he became head of the Iowa Writers' Workshop, the oldest and most prestigious writing program in the United States. In the same year, he received a Guggenheim Fellowship. By that time, his second book, *Midair,* had appeared, a collection

of eight stories published from 1970 to 1984, mostly in the *New Yorker*.

MIDAIR

The title story of Conroy's 1985 book gives a tone to the whole collection, as Michiko Kakutani observed in a harsh review in the *New York Times*. She says of the characters, "Many are unhappily suspended in 'midair'—caught between adolescence and middle age, selfish self-reliance and familiar responsibilities—but they remain so inured to their condition that they neither attempt to articulate their dilemmas nor try to change the parameters of their lives." Kakutani describes the characters as merely "shadow puppets, mechanically going through their appointed rounds."

Certainly there is a passivity in the characters. The psychic numbness of Sean, the protagonist in the title story, arises from a terrifying and suppressed incident in his past. It takes him more than forty years to recall the day in 1942 when his manic father escaped from a rest home and held the six-year-old Sean and his slightly older sister, Mary, hostage in their apartment. The father held his son over an open window in the high building before being seized by staff from the rest home. As a result of this trauma, Sean is uneasy about heights, and on one occasion becomes distraught at a party when he learns that he is in a house where once a baby girl upstairs had fallen from a window. (The window experience was genuinely Conroy's, who was held in "midair" by his own escaped father, but he says in *Stop-Time* that he did not remember the event very well.) The story's protagonist later experiences a kind of therapeutic catharsis, when he is placed in the position of comforting a young man when the two of them are caught in a stalled elevator. The young man, paradoxically, reminds Sean of his own son: and thus a child traumatized by his own father grows up to comfort a symbolic son who is also afraid of heights. The experience brings back the protagonist's memory of being held in midair in 1942 with preternatural clarity.

A reader who knows *Stop-Time* and Conroy's 2004 book about Nantucket, *Time and Tide*, will recognize echoes of Conroy's own life in "Midair" and several other stories. In the title story, Sean and his first wife both have trust funds; Sean's son is named Philip, the name of the writer's father; Sean publishes a memoir while still a young man; he becomes a professor in middle age; he works for an arts foundation; and, like Conroy, he is part of a softball team on Nantucket. A whole life is summed up quickly in the story, a life very much like that of the author. The same cursory approach is taken in the story "Gossip," where a university in Kansas fills in for the University of Iowa. Kakutani feels that both stories are rushed, relying on summaries and abrupt transitions. She also complains accurately enough about a reliance on "muddy, muddled generalities," an odd development in the work of a writer whose first book eschewed generalities in favor of dramatic scenes and who offers here, in the story "Gossip," a writing instructor–protagonist who is full of suspicion of the abstract and who puts emphasis on portraying the actual. The traditional "show, don't tell" formula is consistently violated in this collection of stories.

"Gossip" is in part a reflection of Conroy's discovery that he is an excellent teacher of creative writing. The story is a subtle description of the eros of teaching, with the teacher and student drawn into an intimate but not at all sexual relationship. But gossip damages the rapport, making the student avoid her teacher. Another *New York Times* reviewer, William Pritchard, observes that the story "is a carefully engineered demonstration of the unsettling power over the self of what others say about that self and its relationships." At the end, when the protagonist is discussing the effects of gossip, he comes to a conclusion abut life: "What mattered was that everyone was connected in a web, that pain was part of the web, and yet, despite it, people loved one another." Reviewing the book in *Studies in Short Fiction* in 1987, Irving Malin suggests that not only are we all in "midair," but that the web-of-pain image is the key to a book that he considers religious in its scope. "Humanity is fallen—or suspended—and only by acknowledging this fact can it truly assert itself—

and try to rise." The fall and rise—the "transit" (to use another of the story titles)—is the way we learn to love our fellow sufferers.

In another story in the collection, "The Sense of the Meeting," a writing teacher attends two of his son's basketball games at a Quaker college modeled on Haverford. The conversations that the writer, Kirby, has with his son and with two of his friends, Charley and Gus, explore life choices. Charley, who is in a midlife crisis, has pursued success and finds it empty; Gus, a distinguished scientist, has lost his father, the one person he could share his successes with. Gus's work is symbolic: as an immunologist, he contemplates the ways that "self and not-self" are distinguished by living beings. Achieving selfhood is the task that awaits Kirby's son, Alan. In a Hemingwayesque manner, the testing of Alan comes on the basketball court. His father, who loves him deeply but is ultimately a spectator, sees him in a disastrous game and then in a triumphant one. While the son must pursue his life-game in his own way, he still needs and values his father's emotional support. Conroy injects an amusing bit of self-reference in the story, when Gus says of Kirby's first book, "I read your book when it came out, and I thought, okay, he's used everything up. How's he going to write anything again? I was worried about you" (*Midair*, 129). Kirby's reply is a covert defense by Conroy, surely, a retort to critics who thought he was a one-book author: "I know a wise old poet who lives in New Hampshire. He says try to use everything up every time. Then you regenerate, he says."

Irving Malin describes *Midair* as a sandwich with the real nourishment on the outside: he likes the title story, which opens the book, and the last two stories, "Gossip" and "The Sense of the Meeting." The others he finds too insubstantial; they are, he says, dreamlike and reminiscent of Franz Kafka and Nathanael West. The weakest stories are "Transit," a fantasy story about mysterious events on public transport trains, and "The Mysterious Case of R," in which a psychiatrist who works with writers finds that he has been psychoanalyzing an angel, who taunts his obtuseness and then disappears. "Car Games"

demonstrates Conroy's great skill at describing physical action. The bumper-cars episode in *Stop-Time* gets a grown-up version in which the central character drag races a woman in a Chrysler. They perish in an accident, going over a cliff instead of hanging on the edge. Malin suggests that the episode is entirely imagined by the protagonist. "Roses" narrates a day in the life of a sex-addicted painter whose ability to seduce women is comically exaggerated. A story almost up to the outsides of the sandwich is "Celestial Games," a powerful story of grief. It ends with the central character listening to his deceased mother's headphone and getting a consoling message from her—and permission to cry.

BODY AND SOUL

Midair was a slender book, and it disappointed many of Conroy's admirers. His next work was a huge novel, a bildungsroman with overtones of Dickens and Honoré de Balzac, that was launched with a 125,000-copy first printing. Almost immediately, foreign rights to the novel were sold in ten countries; it was chosen by the Book-of-the-Month Club, and film rights were picked up by Spring Creek Productions (although as of 2005 a film had not been made). The scope of the novel is enormous: it manages to be not only a life of an artist but a social panorama of life in New York. It was described on the jacket as Dickensian, and when queried about the term by John Rodden (who invoked *David Copperfield*), Conroy said: "I don't mind anybody saying that my novel is Dickensian. That's great. The more Dickensian it could be, the happier I'd be. The book is a far cry from the work of the Master, but it's the proper word for the book." The protagonist, Claude Rawlings, is a musical genius who begins as a prodigy and winds up a great composer and pianist. He starts life in great poverty. The book opens with Rawlings as a six-year-old boy, father unknown, in a slum apartment. His mother, Emma, a grotesquely large woman who hardly speaks to him, is a cab driver who attends Communist Party meetings. She eventually gets herself in trouble with the FBI by acting as driver

for Gerhardt Eisler, a leading American Communist (a figure in real life). She was once in vaudeville and still has a piano, the deus ex machina for Claude's career. The boy teaches himself the rudiments of the piano. With the aid of an extraordinary series of benefactors, he moves steadily from success to success. As David Gates reviewing for *Newsweek* perceived immediately in a piece called "Great Expectations, No Satisfaction," the template for the book is Charles Dickens's 1861 novel *Great Expectations*, the story of Pip, a boy whose mysterious benefactor rescues him from poverty and sets him up to be a gentleman. Rawlings's first and most important benefactor is not an Australian convict, as in Dickens' work, but a music store owner, Aaron Weisfeld, who gives him lessons and arranges for him to play for a rich Hungarian conductor. The conductor's bequest provides for the boy's education, which proceeds with remarkable ease, although he will be slow to harmonize his creative and emotional lives, his body and soul. His three serious music instructors are modeled on three figures from the history of classical music. His first teacher is Professor Menti, modeled on Muzio Clementi, whose "five finger exercises" are standard for music pupils. Menti is obsessed with finger technique, so in order to learn about the emotional factors in music, Claude is sent on by his mentor Weisfeld to Herr Sturm, a passionate and bad-tempered teacher based on Ludwig van Beethoven. His deepest lessons, however, come from Mr. Fredericks, the world's greatest Mozart pianist. Fredericks is modeled on Frederic Chopin, who excelled as both a composer and a performer. He teaches the boy refinement. Chopin suffered from consumption, a disease not so common in twentieth-century New York; Mr. Fredericks has the pale sickly look of a consumptive but does not have the illness. His lover, the novelist Anson Roeg, is modeled on George Sand: like the French writer, Roeg has a male name, cross-dresses, and smokes cigars. At one point, Fredericks takes Rawlings to a concert by a pianist named Wolff. The performer behaves like a matinee idol with his hysterical audience. The episode is meant to teach Claude that such manipulation is not what art is

about. It also slyly alludes to the first such idol, Franz Lizst. In *Great Expectations*, Pip is smitten by the beautiful and aloof Estella, whose name means "star." The corresponding figure for Claude is the socially well-placed Catherine (the name means "pearl") In both novels, the union of the lovers is deferred. Estella marries the unsuitable Bentley Drummle; Catherine marries an unsuitable Harvard School of Business student. Claude Rawlings drifts into marriage with Catherine's wealthy cousin, Priscilla Powers, whose nickname, "Lady," conveys her superior social status. Like Conroy's first wife, she belongs to the Social Register and has a trust fund. The marriage breaks down, and Claude is available for an affair with Catherine when they meet by coincidence in London. Conroy gives his book a twentieth-century ending: the lovers do not marry, but they have a sizzling affair. Catherine is a feminist who wishes to become a medieval historian. By the end of the novel, Rawlings has begun to integrate his emotional and creative lives. His grief for his dead mentor and his resolution of unfinished business with Catherine have helped to mature him, to turn "body and soul" into "body-soul." Although there is nearly a consensus on the weaknesses of Conroy's novel (every important review was negative, except for one in the *New York Times* by Christopher Lehmann-Haupt), the novel does also have some strengths. It has superb descriptions of the experience of playing the piano, and it gives valuable insights into the composition of music as well, especially twelve-tone music. (The classical pianist Peter Serkin, a friend of Conroy's, contributed generous advice.) Claude plays jazz as well as classical music, which is useful for the plot, and the novelist could rely on his own knowledge of that kind of performance. In his author's note, Conroy observes that his book is in some aspects a historical novel. He introduces real people, like Aaron Copland, into the text, which some readers may find detracts from the illusion of realism. (This device was used by Conroy's friend E. L. Doctorow in the 1975 novel *Ragtime*). *Body and Soul* re-creates New York from the 1940s to the early 1970s with rich detail.

The celebrated fast-food restaurant in Times Square, the Automat, is the setting for a whole scene in which a jazz musician dies after overdosing on Benzedrine extracted from an over-the-counter inhaler. Benzedrine inhalers are staples of the fiction and memoirs of the Beat Generation. Claude's mother has an apartment on Third Avenue, and life in the shadow of the now-vanished Third Avenue el (elevated train) is described in its teeming activity. The anticommunist campaigns of the 1940s and 1950s are an important element in the plot: Claude's mother is bullied into implicating her fellow communists and is almost destroyed by the experience. American racial relations are dramatized through the relationship of Rawling's mother with a black building superintendent, Al. Most nostalgic in tone are the descriptions of the great New York movie theaters on 86th Street. In a specific historical vein, Conroy mentions the New York City ordinance that put unaccompanied children in a separate section of the theater, in an attempt to protect them from molesters. In the novel, the ordinance is the work of the hypocritical Dewman Fisk, Catherine's stepfather, who is a sentimentalist—and also a child molester. In a more general vein, Rawlings, whose mind tends toward escapist fantasy, tends to interpret his experience through the movies. In his adolescence, he also engages in heavy necking and petting with anonymous girls in the theaters, something he shares with the protagonist of *Stop-Time*. The negative criticism of *Body and Soul* deals mostly with plot and characterization. The story is heavy on coincidence: when Rawlings goes to London to premier his concerto, he winds up sitting in on a jazz club session with Lord Lightning, a light-skinned American jazz pianist who is homosexual. The reader learns (but Claude does not) that Lord Lightning is nonetheless Claude's father. Such coincidence is a staple of the nineteenth-century novels that Conroy admires, and in "The Mystery of Coincidence," an essay collected in *Dogs Bark, but the Caravan Rolls On*, he suggests that it may be a cosmic principle. The second wife he met in Nantucket turned out to have been a student in a sewing class his mother taught at Brearly School. At any rate, novelists have loved to use coincidence as a principle of plot. The chief criticism of Conroy's plot is that it offers almost no serious conflicts or difficulties for the central character. Writing in *Commonweal*, Rand Richards Cooper complained that the book is full of forced optimism, and the jazz concert with the unknown father has, he says, "the sweetness of a Hollywood product." David Ulin's review in the *Nation* complains about the ease with which Rawlings rises in the world: everything seems given to him, and except for his inability to have children, he achieves everything he wants too smoothly. Ulin observes that the book has soap-opera plot twists, as when Lady Powers turns out to be Catherine's cousin. Rawlings does suffer when his marriage breaks up, but the relationship had been atrophying for some time. In a review in *Time*, Paul Gray says that "the reader may become jaded with unalloyed success. What is the point of going on. Are there no problems in this book?" In "Wrong Notes," Stanley Kauffmann suggests that Conroy pushes coincidence so far that at times "the book is close to a satire on classical serendipity." Kauffmann too invokes Hollywood, suggesting that Claude's one emotional crisis, brought on by his divorce and by the death of his mentor, Weisfeld, is the "dip-before-the-upward finish that is a Hollywood staple." Kauffmann also thinks that the novel's characterization "comes from Movieland." The most severe comments on *Body and Soul* have been directed at the characters. David Gates in *Newsweek* called them well-worn stencils before attacking the plot, which he says has no tension. David Klinghoffer's review in *The New Criterion* asserts that the characters seem of the features page of a newspaper: on the features page there are no individual human beings, but types." He particularly dislikes the saintly Al and Aaron Weisfeld, "the Stoic Holocaust Survivor." It does stretch credibility that Aaron's secret is that he was Poland's most promising young composer before a German bomb wiped out his family and sent him fleeing in despair. Rand Richards Cooper calls the characters "secondhand types," familiar from other New York fiction.

DOGS BARK, BUT THE CARAVAN ROLLS ON

Frank Conroy's distinguished essays had appeared over the years in such outlets as the *New York Times*, *Glamour*, *Esquire*, and *Gentleman's Quarterly*. In 2002, he gathered all of the essays he wanted to keep into a volume whose title is based on a Persian or Arab proverb: *Dogs Bark, but the Caravan Rolls On* comes from a saying he liked for its "quiet stoicism," he told Robert Birnbaum in an interview. The phrase also implies some disdain for critics: it suggests that literature goes on even as reviewers and journalists bark. In the interview with Birnbaum, Conroy mentions that the book has "this covert, quiet, extremely small autobiographical side to it." The other elements include commentaries on writing and essays on music, including long profiles of Peter Serkin, Keith Jarrett, and Wynton Marsalis, not to mention the Rolling Stones. Conroy discovered when he met the Rolling Stones in 1975 that he had once played with their drummer, Charlie Watts, in a London club, the Establishment—a coincidence worthy of a Victorian novel.

The essay collection is given some cohesion by the four interspersed pieces called "Some Observations Now," "More Observations Now," "More Observations Now" (a repeated title), and "Observations Now," which put some of the essays in a perspective circa 2001. (The device was perhaps picked up from Norman Mailer's 1959 collection, *Advertisements for Myself*.) The third piece, which introduces the jazz essays, has some reflections on Conroy's own semiprofessional career in clubs and recalls the few times he had the chance to perform with the great bassist Charles Mingus.

The volume includes three autobiographical essays on fatherhood, a constant theme in his work—good fathers, bad fathers. (One piece deals with his own father, the other two with being a father himself.) Less intense but biographically significant is "Running the Table," in which he provides a brief sketch of his interest in playing pool: another game that offers mastery, like the yo-yo. He took up the game at fifteen when he should have been in Stuyvesant High School. His explanation of the appeal of the game offers

a footnote to *Stop-Time:* "I was haunted by a sense of chaos, chaos within and chaos without. Which is perhaps why the orderliness of pool, the Euclidean cleanness of it, appealed to me. The formality of pool struck me as soothing and reassuring, a sort of oasis of coolness, utterly rational and yet not without its elegant little mysteries." He includes "Think about It," a sketch of his college days, when he got to know a Supreme Court justice, William O. Douglas, and acted as a go-between in a wry legal argument between Douglas and the great jurist Learned Hand.

Some of the most interesting remarks about his life come in "Observations Now," his introduction to "Great Scott," an essay on one of the novelists he most admires, F. Scott Fitzgerald. The prefatory piece candidly discusses his own nervous breakdown after writing *Stop-Time*. The older novelist's clear prose was a major influence on Conroy, and *The Great Gatsby*, with its use of terse dramatic scenes, is a presiding spirit in *Stop-Time*. "Great Scott" is a warm homage to Fitzgerald, given emphasis by its place as the final essay in the book.

Conroy's work for the National Endowment for the Arts in the 1980s is the subject of "The House of Representatives and Me," an article in which he discusses the complications of dealing with the House Subcommittee on Appropriations in hearings on the budget for writers' grants. He expresses his disquiet at having to learn a bureaucratic language very different from his style as a writer, and he is further disquieted at the sorts of Byzantine manipulation required to get an appropriation through Congress. The lessons he learned from that experience shape observations that Conroy makes about the Bill Clinton–Monica Lewinsky affair, in which the former president made some notorious distortions of the language. Conroy wonders if it is possible now for a president to avoid the entanglements of such language.

His two pieces on learning and teaching the craft of writing are high points of the collection. In "My Teacher," he pays a left-handed tribute to the first teacher who paid attention to his work, a man at Haverford College whom he calls Profes-

sor Cipher. "Cipher" implies that the name is a code, but it also says that the man was in some way a nonentity, a zero. The essay is occasioned by the professor's memorial service, which provides the occasion for Conroy to convey what he learned from him—which was a devotion to craft and some basic techniques of fiction. We learn in passing that the professor told Conroy he should find a rich wife, which he did. We also learn that his trust fund provided him with $300 a month to live on, and that he spent four years writing a bad, unpublished novel before writing his memoir. Most of the story of Professor Cipher is melancholy, a chronicle of alcoholism and growing incompetence in the classroom. Some of the blunt scrutiny of Professor Cipher was perhaps meant as an admonition to himself.

The collection's longest piece on writing grows out of his experiences at the University of Iowa. "The Writers' Workshop" is a fine description of how fiction-writing courses work. He provides some interesting diagrams but is aware that such schemes are reductive if taken too literally. The most interesting one represents a zone of interaction between writer and reader: the simple transmission of the text from the creator to the receiver is too simple, he says, and fails to take into account the role of the reader as cocreator of the text. Conroy is not, judging from his interviews, interested in literary theory, but the cocreation idea is quite contemporary: it is what the French philosopher Roland Barthes calls the "writerly text." One of his interesting insights into the workshop process is the idea that apprentice writers must not cling to their early achievements out of fear of failure: weak efforts are part of the process, not a sign that the writer is an imposter. "Writing, sayeth the workshop, is a way of life. You either sign on or you don't."

LATE LIFE

After an operation for colon cancer in 2003, Conroy retired from the directorship of the Iowa Writers' Workshop. He planned to continue teaching and phase in his complete retirement over five years. His retirement from the administrative job was meant to permit new blood into the program—his tenure as director had been extraordinarily long—and to give him more time to write. But on April 6, 2005, Conroy died of cancer, in Iowa City, Iowa.

The last book he published before his death, *Time and Tide: A Walk in Nantucket, which appeared* in 2004, is not a weak effort nor is it a major work. It was written for a series about places published by Crown Books, an imprint of Random House. (The books are written by well-known writers and most have subtitles like *A Walk in Rome* or *A Walk at Gettysburg.*) Conroy had lived at least part-time on Nantucket Island since the late 1960s, and he had seen it become an upscale playground for the rich. Membership in the best golf club costs $350,000 a year, and population growth has put an enormous strain on the infrastructure and the fragile environment. Weaving together personal anecdotes, history, and fact in a series of brief chapters with lots of illustrations, he tells a familiar story about a beautiful place damaged by its own attractions.

The reader learns about Nantucket as a whaling center and about interesting historical characters, New England produced characters. The book also makes an interesting pendant to *Stop-Time*, revealing what happened to Conroy after the memoir was published, as he struggled to survive as a jazz pianist and a scalloper. His comic adventures with boats are recounted: he managed to lose two boats by not securing them properly. He pursued golf for a while but gave up when he realized that this was one game he could not master. He and his family organized a softball team they called "Third World Baseball" and kept it going for thirteen years. He and friends set up their own bar, the Roadhouse, which was immensely popular but failed because the owners were cheated by employees. The book has charm for anyone interested in Nantucket, and anyone interested in Frank Conroy will learn more about his habits of mind and experiences.

Frank Conroy's career began rather strangely where some careers end, with the writing of a memoir, and at the time of his death, he was still known primarily as the author of that one outstanding book. *Stop-Time* is masterly and inspiring—an original. In reflecting on Conroy's

work, one is reminded of the quotation from Goethe that Conroy used as the epigraph to *Body and Soul*: "That which thy fathers have bequeathed to thee, earn it anew if thou wouldst possess it." Conroy's comments on one of his literary fathers at the end of "Great Scott" apply to his own work as well:

Most writing is collective consciousness made manifest, tinged to some degree by the author's individuality. Great writing is a *specific* consciousness made manifest, a unique sensibility illuminating the world in a way that we've never seen before and that makes sense. Fitzgerald's prose did have this exquisite inner radiance, and he was unquestionably a great writer. (*The Caravan Moves On*, 222).

Out of his alienation and solitude, Frank Conroy created a great book. He not only earned anew what he received, he added something for later writers like Tobias Wolff and Mary Karr. Conroy's remaining works are a bonus.

Selected Bibliography

WORKS OF FRANK CONROY

Stop-Time. New York: Viking, 1967; New York; Penguin, 1977.

Midair. New York: Dutton, 1985.

Body and Soul. Boston and New York: Houghton Mifflin/ Seymour Lawrence, 1993.

Dogs Bark, but the Caravan Rolls On: Observations Then and Now. Boston: Houghton Mifflin, 2002.

Time and Tide: A Walk through Nantucket. New York: Crown, 2004.

EDITED COLLECTIONS

The Iowa Award: The Best Stories from Twenty Years. Iowa City: University of Iowa Press, 1991.

The Eleventh Draft: Craft and the Writing Life from the Iowa Writers' Workshop. New York: HarperCollins, 1999.

ESSAYS

Foreword. *Autobiography of a Schizophrenic Girl: The True Story of Renée* [by Marguerite Sechehaye]. New York: Penguin, 1994. (Essay first published in the *New York Times Book Review*, September 22, 1968, p. 2.)

"Angela's Second Boy." *New York Times*, July 5, 1998, section 7, p. 5. (Review of *A Monk Swimming*, by Malachy McCourt.)

Introduction. *The Adventures of Tom Sawyer*, by Mark Twain. New York: Modern Library Classics, 2001.

"Writers on Writing: Footprints of Greatness on Your Turf." *New York Times*, April 8, 2002, section E, p. 1. Reprinted in *Writers on Writing, Volume 2: More Collected Essays from the "New York Times."* New York: Holt, 2003.

MANUSCRIPTS

The manuscripts of *Stop-Time* and *Body and Soul* are held by the Special Collections Department of the Library of the University of Iowa. Chapters 13 and 19 from the manuscript of *Stop-Time* are available online in a digital form at http://www.uiowa.edu/~iww/conroy.htm. The library also holds the complete holograph manuscript of *Stop-Time* and extensive holograph portions of the manuscript of *Body and Soul*. as well as a photocopy of the manuscript of a short story, "My Harlem."

CRITICAL AND BIOGRAPHICAL STUDIES

Adams, Timothy Dow. "Games in Frank Conroy's *Stop-Time*." *Mosaic* 20, no. 4:49–59 (fall 1987).

———. "'A Momentary Stay against Confusion': Frank Conroy's *Stop-Time*." *Critique* 27, no. 3:153–166 (spring 1986).

Alvarez-Calleja, María Antonia. "Autobiography-as-Novel: Conroy and Kazin." *Revista canaria de estudios ingleses* 16:193–204 (1998).

Bailey, Peter. "Notes on the Novel-as-Autobiography." *Genre* 14, no. 1:79–93 (summer 1981).

Cooper, Rand Richards. "A Long-Awaited Encore." *Commonweal*, November 5, 1993, 33–34.

Eakin, Paul John. *Fictions in Autobiography: Studies in the Art of Self-Invention*. Princeton, N.J.: Princeton University Press, 1985, 229–236.

Galens, David, ed. "Body and Soul." *Novels for Students* 11. Farmington Hills, Mich.: Gale, 2002, 95–116.

Gates, David. "Great Expectations, No Satisfaction." *Newsweek*, September 27, 1993, 74. (Review of *Body and Soul*.)

Gray, Paul. "Words without Music, for Sure." *Time*, July 27, 1993, 89–90. (Review of *Body and Soul*.)

Haegert, John. "Autobiography as Fiction: The Example of *Stop-Time*." *Modern Fiction Studies* 33, no. 4:621–638 (winter 1987).

Kakutani, Michiko. "Fathers and Sons," *The New York Times*, September 7, 1985, p. 13.

Kauffmann, Stanley. "Wrong Notes." *New Republic* 209, no. 16:47–49 (October 18, 1993). (Review of *Body and Soul*.)

Klinghoffer, David. "Wunderkind." *New Criterion* 12, no. 2:8–70 (October 1993). (Review of *Body and Soul*.)

Malin, Irving. *Studies in Short Fiction* 24, no. 2:176–177 (spring 1987). (Review of *Midair*.)

Midwood, Barton. "Short Visits with Five Writers and One Friend." *Esquire*, November 1970, 152–153.

Pritchard, William H. "Reasons To Be Nervous." *New York Times Book Review*, September 22, 1985, p. 12. (Review of *Midair*.)

Ramsey, Roger. "The Illusion of Fiction in Frank Conroy's *Stop-Time*." *Modern Fiction Studies* 20, no. 3:391–399 (autumn 1974).

Shaw, Peter. "Capturing Reality." *Commentary* 45, no. 6:84–88 (June 1968).

Streitfeld, David. "Advertisements for Themselves." *Vogue*, May 1996, 160ff.

Strychacz, Thomas F. "Controlling the 'Sloppiness of Things' in Frank Conroy's *Stop-Time*." *Critique* 29, no. 1:46–56 (fall 1987).

Tanner, Tony. *City of Words: American Fiction 1950–1970*, 295–321. New York: Harper & Row, 1971.

INTERVIEWS

Birnbaum, Robert. "Frank Conroy." *identitytheory.com* (http://www.identitytheory.com/people/birnbaum44.html), May 9, 2002.

Rodden, John. "The Masters' Apprentice." In his *Performing the Literary Interview: How Writers Craft Their Public Selves*, 58–66.Lincoln: University of Nebraska Press, 2001.

Steinberg, Sibyl. Interview. *Publishers Weekly*, August 23, 1993, 44–4

REBECCA HARDING DAVIS

(1831–1910)

Tina Parke-Sutherland

Living with her parents in Wheeling, Virginia (today West Virginia), where she spent most of her growing-up years, Rebecca Harding Davis wrote a remarkable novella, *Life in the Iron Mills* (1861), an angry and bitter indictment of the soul- and body-crushing working conditions created by the new American industrial system, specifically in the iron-smelting factories in mid-century Wheeling. Harding Davis's Wheeling was a crossroads in many ways, a meeting place of the past, present, and future. There the railroad met the Ohio River. Southern cotton came through on its way to the factories of the North. Northern manufactured goods passed the cotton bales going the other way. Pioneers, some native-born and itching to get away from the city, some foreign-born and still in their European dress, headed out into "the Ohio," the western wilderness, all their belongings stowed in trunks and bundles and piled on mule-drawn wagons. Other immigrants stayed to work—and work and work—in Wheeling. The power of the river drove the textile plants. The power of Virginia coal lit the fires of the rolling mills where red ore dug out of the ground in Missouri or on Lake Superior's Iron Range by other immigrants—Finns and Italians and Germans and Welshmen—became black pig iron. Spent coke—or korl—shoveled from the smelting furnaces smoked in huge waste heaps. In Wheeling, East met West, North met South, slaves met their masters, and the United States met its industrial destiny. The powers that ruled the city—and the nation—the bankers and capitalists and politicians—leaned so far out into an imagined future of limitless wealth and development that for them the present got lost. But not for Rebecca Harding Davis. She looked out her window and saw what others could not see, refused to see, and then she wrote about it.

Her novella tells the tragic story of two Welsh immigrants, Hugh Wolfe, an iron puddler, and his cousin Deb, who works in a textile mill. Entering the hell of the utterly unregulated American factory system as children, the main characters are, by the time the story opens, only about twenty, yet they seem old—and indeed at twenty they have lived more than half the average life span for people of their class, place, and time. The story's narrator tells readers, "Their lives were like those of their class: incessant labor, sleeping in kennel-like rooms, eating rank pork and molasses, drinking—God and the distillers only know what; with an occasional night in jail, to atone for some drunken excess" (15). A life of wage slavery—six days a week, fourteen hours a day—has left Deb and Hugh utterly spent—body, mind, soul. Still, in the midst of the relentless work, the grinding poverty, the wretched living—dying—conditions, they remain human. Deb loves Hugh with touching, albeit hopeless, tenderness. Hugh, amazingly, loves his art. His brilliant though utterly untrained artistic talent surfaces in the sculptures he fashions, in his few nonworking hours, out of the waste product of the iron smelting process—the scorl, or korl. His latest piece, "the white figure of a woman … of giant proportions, crouching on the ground, her arms flung out in some wild gesture of warning" becomes the symbolic center of the novel. With her "tense, rigid muscles, the clutching hands, the wild, eager face, like that of a starving wolf's" she represents the terrible longing, the "soul-starvation," of workers like Hugh, their "living death" (32; 23). Told with unflinching bravery and unprecedented realism, the story asks, "Is that all of their lives?—of the portion given to them and these their duplicates swarming the streets to-day? nothing beneath?—all?"

(15). Like most of Harding Davis's best work, *Life in the Iron Mills* refuses to answer.

In 1861 the *Atlantic Monthly* published Harding Davis' story—to the unknown, "backwoods" author's equally strong surprise and delight. "For its realism and for introducing the industrial revolution to literature," says Elaine Showalter, *Life in the Iron Mills* became an immediate success. (Showalter ix). At the age of thirty, Harding Davis became both popular and critically admired. Twentieth- and twenty-first-century readers know Harding Davis because of this work.

HISTORICAL AND CULTURAL BACKGROUND

In 1910, fifty years after the publication of *Life in the Iron Mills*, Harding Davis's colleague Elizabeth Stuart Phelps (1844–1911) placed the novella in its precise literary and cultural location: "at the point where the intellect and moral nature meet" (quoted in Tichi 362). Nineteenth-century American literature, much more than its twentieth-century counterpart, arose from this place—this intersection of the heart and the head, the soul and the brain. In the nineteenth century, with the American Revolution steady in living memory, Americans were self-consciously busy marking themselves off from Europeans, exploring the differences between the New World and the Old. They wanted to understand themselves as a nation; they fought a civil war to maintain that understanding. Perhaps more than Americans in later centuries, they identified their personal fates—both material and moral—with the fate of the nation. Their popular and serious literature, written and read by both men and women, elaborated moral issues. For them, literature might entertain, but it must always also "uplift"—make the American reader and the American nation better. When Rebecca Harding Davis wrote *Life in the Iron Mills* that American reader had much to be concerned with.

In the first half of the nineteenth century the United States underwent its industrial revolution, shifting rapidly from an agrarian and artisan economy to a modern capitalist state. With the growth of transportation and technology, cities expanded, and the site of production—the mill, the shop, the factory—separated from the place of consumption—the home. This shift opened a gap between workers and masters who no longer lived the same lives, and class differences grew. This new industrial system transformed the very nature of labor. Some people "worked" by owning, investing capital they acquired through inheritance or some other means to build factories—places where other people, laborers, actually produced goods. Still others "oversaw," or managed, the producing workers. What had been largely a subsistence and artisan economy became a cash economy. People no longer labored to produce the goods they consumed but rather to receive the money necessary to buy the things they needed to live. The investors, owners, and capitalists made money by taking the profits of the enterprise—the difference between the cost of production and the sale price of the goods produced. Owners paid both managers and workers a wage that would, supposedly, allow them to buy the goods and services they needed to keep on working. The smaller that wage—especially the workers' wage—the greater the owners' wage or profit.

While most twenty-first-century Americans find nothing strange in this arrangement, many nineteenth-century Americans did—on a number of grounds. First of all, with no environmental protection laws in place, factories despoiled the earth—polluted the water with filthy effluents and the air with the thick choking smoke Davis describes in the opening passages of *Life in the Iron Mills*:

> The idiosyncrasy of this town is smoke. It rolls sullenly in slow folds from the great chimneys of the iron-foundries, and settles down in black, slimy pools on the muddy streets. Smoke on the wharves, smoke on the dingy boats, on the yellow river, clinging in a coating of greasy soot to the housefront, the two faded poplars, the faces of the passers-by. The long train of mules, dragging masses of pig-iron through the narrow street, have a foul vapor hanging to their reeking sides. Here, inside [where the narrator positions herself], is a little broken figure of an angel pointing upward from the mantel-shelf; but even its wings are

covered with smoke, clotted and black. Smoke everywhere! A dirty canary chirps desolately in a cage beside me. Its dream of green fields and sunshine is a very old dream,—almost worn out, I think. (11-12)

Urban industrialism fouls America's soul, that broken angel on the mantel-shelf. It dirties America's spirit along with its once boundlessly pure land—its nearly "worn out" dream. Transcendentalism, the philosophical and literary production of nineteenth-century American Romantics such as Ralph Waldo Emerson (1803–1882) and Henry David Thoreau (1817–1862), sought the divine in Nature. When industrialization fouled Nature—the air, the rivers—it fouled God's home.

The new industrial system Harding Davis despised also challenged the Puritan work ethic, the dominant American understanding of the nature of work and its essential goodness. The work of nineteenth-century factory laborers like Hugh and Deb can hardly be imagined as uplifting or character building. They lived in filthy tenements, often without access to clean water or sanitation. They ate inadequate food, suffered from a range of work-related diseases and disabilities, and died young. Like Harding Davis's characters, they sold their whole lives to factory owners for this privilege. This kind of life bore no resemblance to the American ideal. "Early to bed, early to rise" would not make these workers "healthy, wealthy, and wise" as *Poor Richard's Almanac* promised.

Owners, no matter how wealthy they became, could not help to build a strong nation either, because their wealth grew precisely out of their greed, their lack of concern for the people who made them rich. This greed was part and parcel of the emerging industrial system that, by the turn of the century, made the United States into the largest economy in the world. Still this system deeply troubled Rebecca Harding Davis, who was, like almost all Americans of her time, an absolutely serious Christian. She and much of the rest of the United States understood that the factory system's selfishness, greed, and materialism directly contradicted the generosity, self-sacrifice, and spirituality at the center of their ideal New

Testament Christianity. The resolution of this ideological conflict became the central cultural work of the nineteenth century. The question was simple: How could the nation be both rich and good? The answer got pretty complicated.

Especially during the early and middle parts of the century, the cult of domesticity or separate spheres, also known as "domestic feminism," worked to resolve the obvious ideological tensions between unrestrained capitalism and New Testament Christianity. Domestic feminism accomplished that important cultural work by carefully constructing middle-class femininity as the homebound safeguard of the family's—and thus the nation's—morality. The urban woman, no longer a co-equal in the producing-consuming partnership of farm life, became the "angel in the house." Working without pay in the new capitalist system, she produced domestic goods and services, gave birth to and sustained the labor force, and organized household consumption. At the same time, she embodied the antidote to the moral poison of rapacious dog-eat-dog capitalism. At the close of each of his profitable days, when her husband left behind his ruthless business world—the world of the owners and overseers in *Life in the Iron Mills*—and returned to her pure domestic one, her virtue restored his own. Her moral superiority and her protected status assured the well-being of his and his children's eternal souls. Thus, while her domestic and sexual work made capitalism economically feasible—she worked at home without pay—her ideological work made it palatable. As keeper of both the home fires and the faith, the middle-class American matron took the threat of spiritual corruption out of burgeoning industrial capitalism; she defanged the snake in the garden. As long as she did her ideological work, American life could be both righteous and rich.

Early in her writing—in *Life in the Iron Mills* and in her first novel, *Margret Howth* (1862)—Harding Davis bitterly and brilliantly argues that domestic feminism can perform the ideological balancing act necessary to purify American commercial life only in certain middle-class situations. The saving grace of the domestic angel in the house works only if there is an angel, and

only if there is a house. In *Life in the Iron Mills* the angel is broken and filthy, the house, "a kennel." Deb, who would fulfill the angelic role, must herself work, two jobs in fact—as a picker in a textile mill and as keeper of the meager and greasy home fires of the Wolfe family. Too busy toiling beside the other families—men, women, and children—caught up in this system of industrial wage slavery unredeemed by Christian love, Deb cannot enact the same ideological magic as her middle-class counterparts. The grinding poverties and moral degradations of factory life extend to women and children as well as to men—even to the earth itself.

As she demands the nation attend to—and change—an evil economic system beyond the reach of middle-class domestic feminism, Harding Davis enjoys some famous company. In *Uncle Tom's Cabin* (1852)—the best-selling book written in nineteenth-century America—Harriet Beecher Stowe (1811–1896) argues that the moral safeguards provided by the domestic angel do not extend into the territory of the slave states. The unrestrained power of the slave master absolutely obliterates the domestic space and its saving virtues and thus denies the moral agency of women—both slave and free. In slavery neither the mistress nor the slave woman can redeem her family's—or the nation's—soul. In both the factory and the plantation, Harding Davis and Stowe agree, moral chaos reigns and threatens to send the whole nation straight to hell.

In her stories of middle-class women and their artistic aspirations, by contrast, Harding Davis seems to embrace the doctrines of True Womanhood and domestic feminism. She treats her artistic women characters with an irony that is not always gentle, since they overrate both their own talents and the merits of the artists they admire and want to emulate. These characters always end up back at home, happy and safe in the domestic sanctuary where they belong. Perhaps Harding Davis's complex experience can explain her literary tightrope walking. By all accounts, she enjoyed a heavenly childhood with a kind and gentle angel of a mother. Once grown, she looked out her window and saw a hell.

BIOGRAPHY

Rebecca Blaine Harding was born June 24, 1831, in Washington Pennsylvania, at the home of her mother's sister, although her parents actually lived in Alabama at the time. The first child of Rachel Leet Wilson and Richard Harding, Rebecca Harding had three bothers and one sister who survived infancy. In 1836, when Rebecca was five, the family moved to Wheeling, Virginia. Her mother was a "genteel" woman whose father had fought in the Revolutionary War and whose mother danced with the Marquis de Lafayette at the home of Martha and George Washington. Rebecca's father immigrated from England to Huntsville, Alabama, and later served as the city treasurer of Wheeling and managed a large insurance firm. Even though he worked in the commercial world, Richard Harding despised it and much of American life that increasingly revolved around it. "A man of integrity and strong prejudices, stern in demeanor," he loved Shakespeare and chivalric literature and thought that the democratic experiment under way in the United States was doomed to failure (Lasseter and Harris 3).

Rebecca Harding Davis enjoyed an untroubled childhood in a comfortable, although not wealthy, household. Her mother, Rachel, had been remarkably well educated as a paying, live-in pupil of Bishop Alexander Campbell, the cofounder of the Disciples of Christ and founder of Bethany College in Virginia. Rachel tutored Rebecca and her siblings when they were small and later supervised other hired tutors. In "A Family History," Harding Davis says of her mother: "She had an eager, hungry intellect and up to the day of her death never ceased to try to learn. She was the most accurate historian and grammarian I ever have known and had enough knowledge to fit out half dozen modern college-bred women" (138). In her 1904 autobiography, *Bits of Gossip*, Harding Davis reminisces about her childhood, creating lively scenes of outdoor romps, dragon-filled chivalric battles, and even an imaginary knight, Monsieur Jean Crapeaud, who lived in a locked cabinet behind the chimney. The children threw him bits of their favorite foods—"taffy or black cake"—and breathlessly listened to his tales

of wonder, told only when Rebecca's father felt particularly cheerful and ready to translate the knight's French (28).

In one of the most charming, and telling, sections of *Bits of Gossip*, Harding Davis writes about a hideaway the children's nurse built for her and her brothers and sister in the branches of a backyard cherry tree. The young Rebecca spent happy hours in the tree house imagining below her, "in the celery pit," "tents and glittering legions of the crusaders" (37). There in the cherry tree, she also read books—one day a couple of Nathaniel Hawthorne's short stories brought together in a pirated edition, the first "cheap book," a paperback, she had ever seen (37). When she was thirty years old and the newly successful author of *Life in the Iron Mills*, Rebecca Harding wrote to Nathaniel Hawthorne to tell him of her cherry tree and how, in its boughs, she had read and reread two or three of his unsigned stories until she knew "every line in them by heart" (37). In the stories she found the subject matter for a long life of writing: "the commonplace folk and things which I saw every day took on a sudden mystery and charm, and for the first time, I found that they, too, belonged to the magic world of knights and pilgrims and fiends" (37). When Hawthorne heard her story, he sent Rebecca Harding a note, saying that he was then "at Washington, and was coming on to Harper's Ferry, where John Brown had died, and still farther to see the cherry-trees and—me" (37). Hawthorne did indeed start the trip, but the Civil War intervened, the Confederates seized the Baltimore and Ohio Railroad, and he had to turn back.

Harding Davis begins "In the Old House," the first chapter of the autobiography, with an agrarian, preindustrial nostalgia shared by other of the nineteenth century's famous writers—Hawthorne, Thoreau (who hated railroads), and Emerson:

> The world that I lived in when I was a child would seem silent and empty to this generation. There were no railways in it, no automobiles or trolleys, no telegraphs, no sky-scraping houses. Not a single man in the country was a professor of huge accumulations of money such as are so common now. There was not, from sea to sea, a trust or a labor

union. Even the names of those things had not yet been invented. (23)

In that childhood home she, like "every child was taught from his cradle that money was Mammon, the chief agent of the flesh and the devil" (23). She never rejected those childhood lessons.

In 1845, at the age of fourteen, Rebecca Harding went back to the town of her birth to attend Washington Female Academy. Her studies at the academy, where she graduated in 1848 as valedictorian, certainly did not test her abilities, but her experiences there broadened her range, brought her into contact with intellectuals, lecturers, and even radicals as they passed through the college town. There she met the abolitionist, feminist, and anticapitalist Francis LeMoyne, who had founded the female academy she attended. His radicalism, the profound challenge he made to the status quo, stayed with Harding Davis all her life. She included fictionalized versions of him in short stories and wrote him into her first full-length novel, *Margret Howth*.

Even though she graduated first in her class from the academy, Rebecca could not go on to college as her brothers did because she was a female, and only scandalous Oberlin admitted women students at the time. So she came home to Wheeling and once again took up the education directed by her mother and father. Rebecca and her oldest brother, Hugh Wilson—"Wilse"—were close friends, and on his summer holidays from college, he taught her what he had learned away at school—languages, philosophy, and literature—and loaned her his college texts to read.

When Rebecca returned from the academy at age eighteen, she did not immediately marry, as people may have expected her to do. By twenty-five she still had not married, and by thirty—far past the "critical age" where young unmarried women of that time and place became unmarriageable spinsters—instead of marrying, she had published her first work in the *Atlantic Monthly*. Tillie Olsen, in her groundbreaking biographical interpretation to *Life in the Iron Mills*, published together with the novella in the 1971 Feminist Press reprint, imagines Rebecca Harding as too smart, too direct, too plainspoken, too intellectu-

ally engaged in the world around her, too solid, too talented, and—if truth be known—too artistically ambitious to make a conventional marriage (75).

The great success of *Life In the Iron Mills*, followed by lesser successes of the novel *Margret Howth* and a number of short stories, also published in the *Atlantic*, began an amazing decade for Rebecca Harding. In it she moved from the "backwoods" obscurity of Wheeling into the centers of American literary achievement. In 1862 Annie Fields—the wife of her publisher James T. Fields and the woman who through her friendship, hospitality, and keen aesthetic judgment became the "angel in the house" of a budding American literature—arranged for Rebecca Harding to travel north. In Boston she met the Fields for the first time face-to-face. In *Bits of Gossip* she calls James Fields the "shrewdest of publishers and kindest of men" (48). In Concord she met Emerson, James Russell Lowell (1819–1891), the transcendentalist Amos Bronson Alcott (1799–1888), and Alcott's daughter Louisa May (18321888). She made a deep connection with Hawthorne. On the last afternoon of her visit, she walked with him through the cemetery at Sleepy Hollow. The morning was sunny, beautiful, the wildflowers in bloom.

> Here and there, in a shady nook, was a green hillock like a bed, as if some tired traveler had chosen a quiet place for himself and lain down to sleep.
>
> Mr. Hawthorne sat down in the deep grass and then, clasping his hands about his knees, looked up laughing.
>
> "Yes," he said, "we New Englanders begin to enjoy ourselves—when we are dead." (52)

Later in the day, when she parted from him after their only personal meeting, he said "'I am sorry you are going away. It seems as if we have known you always'" (52). Only months later Hawthorne died and found his permanent spot in the lovely little cemetery.

Harding Davis counted meeting Hawthorne as one of the "pleasantest and best" experiences of her life (52). On the other hand, she despised Bronson Alcott, who left his wife and children in poverty while he "covered miles of paper with

his inspirations" that no one would publish; he might better, she concludes, "put his poor carpentering skills to use to support" his family (40). She found Alcott "absolutely ignorant of the world, but with an obstinate faith in himself which would have befitted a pagan god" (40). Of Emerson, who disappointed her partly because he paid such close attention to Alcott, she makes a more complex appraisal. Although his "voice and look and manner were full of the most exquisite courtesy," he "studied souls" rather than engaged with fellow humans. All in all, Emerson left Harding Davis cold: "He took from each man his drop of stored honey, and after that the man counted for no more than any other robbed bee" (44-43).

On the same trip north Rebecca Harding also met for the first time in person Lemuel Clarke Davis, a man who had written her a fan letter after reading *Life in the Iron Mills*. After a week together in Philadelphia, they agreed to marry. Rebecca couldn't quite believe what was about to happen to her—marriage with a man who believed in her work. The letter she wrote to Annie Fields to tell her the news nearly bursts with an anticipation so close to disbelief that it threatens to strike dumb the passionate young woman, who tells her friend, "I never *had* such trouble to write a letter before. O Annie, my summer days are coming now" (quoted in Olsen 114).

The couple married in 1863 in a private ceremony in Wheeling, and very soon clouds darkened the "summer day." Married life proved full of practical difficulties. The couple had little money—her husband's journalism career was insecure, and he was still reading for the law. They had little privacy, living in cramped quarters in Philadelphia with Clarke's sister and her children. And no one seemed to be able to stay well—the children fell ill, then Clarke, then Rebecca's father back in Wheeling. And then she was pregnant and broken down, suffering through the "rest cure" made infamous in Charlotte Perkins Gilman's 1899 short story "The Yellow Wallpaper." Forbidden to read or write, she worsened. Much later in life but perhaps remembering this time, she wrote to her soon-to-be-famous son Richard, "I don't say like Papa, stop

writing. God forbid, I would almost as soon say stop breathing, for it is pretty much the same thing" (quoted in Olsen 149). She helped herself by taking up her old Wheeling habit of walking—she walked and walked and walked.

When she recovered her health and gave birth to her firstborn son, the need to write pressed upon her in financial as well as emotional and political ways. She began producing more conventional, less creative pieces for less prestigious, although better-paying, magazines like *Peterson's.* "The Wife's Story" came out in 1866, the last Harding Davis piece to run as a lead in the *Atlantic Monthly.* What she hoped would be a great novel about Reconstruction—*Waiting for the Verdict* (1868)—failed, and the *Atlantic* dropped her because she sold the novel to a competing, better-paying journal, *Galaxy.* She stopped reading reviews. She gave birth to a second son and then a daughter and continued to write prolifically for decades—novels, short stories, essays, and editorials. In her nonfiction she argued against war, imperialism, and "the disease of money," and for social justice for all Americans. Defying the contemporary restrictions placed on women's writing, Harding Davis continued to create stories about the working class, the underclass, poor old widows, broken-down fishermen, lonely women professionals. In her 1990 study, *Doing Literary Business: American Women Writers in the Nineteenth Century,* Susan Coultrap-McQuin borrows a phrase from a nineteenth-century literary critic to express her conclusion that Harding Davis gave up the "nameless beauty of innocence which is by nature the glory of the woman," in order to tell the truth (17). Both her sons grew up to be writers; for a brief time all three competed with each other for space in popular journals and magazines. Her firstborn, Richard Harding Davis, a novelist, playwright, and war correspondent, became a kind of early-twentieth-century cultural icon, enjoying the friendship of presidents of the United States. Her younger son, Charles Belmont Davis, became a diplomat, serving as the U.S. consul to Florence. Richard wrote to his mother almost every day of his adult life.

Still, by 1891 the once-famous *Life in the Iron Mills* had fallen so completely out of literary memory that the social historians Eleanor Marx and Edward Aveling, in their *The Working Class Movement in America,* wrote "one of these days the Uncle Tom's Cabin of Capitalism will be written" (quoted in Olsen 72). Harding Davis had, of course, written it thirty years before. Her collection of short stories, *Silhouettes of American Life,* published in 1892, made her first popular and critical success in years. Both critics and the public liked *Bits of Gossip* (1904), but by the time of her death no literary journal noted her passing. At Richard's home in Mount Kisko, New York, in 1904, she suffered a stroke. She died there on September 29, of heart failure. She was seventy-nine years old. The *New York Times* did run a story about her ("Mother of Richard Harding Davis Dies at Son's Home in St. Kisco, aged 79"), mostly because she was the mother of her famous son. The article reminded readers of Rebecca Harding Davis's great contribution to American literature:

> In 1861 she sent to *The Atlantic Monthly* a story entitled "Life in the Iron Mills," depicting the grinding life of the working people around her... . It attracted attention from all over the country... . Many thought the author must be a man. The stern but artistic realism of the picture she put alive upon paper, suggested a man, and a man of power not unlike Zola's.

LIFE IN THE IRON MILLS

Written and published on the threshold of the War between the States, Rebecca Harding Davis's best work concerns not that war but another going on underneath it all, underneath the United States's ability to produce a "modern" war machine. *Life in the Iron Mills,* along with Harriet Beecher Stowe's *Uncle Tom's Cabin* and Harriet Jacob's *Incidents in the Life of a Slave-girl* (1861), was published in the run-up to the Civil War, the volatile decade of 1851 to 1861, which cultural historians variously call the "feminine fifties"—because so many women were publishing so successfully—or the "red fifties" because the spirit of reform and revolution

was surfacing everywhere in American life. Joining the spirit of her times, but applying that spirit to a new subject, Harding Davis wrote with great passion and energy about the lives of industrial workers.

Even though the story makes a strong anti-domestic argument, *Life in the Iron Mills* begins in a domestic space. The narrator sits in the upstairs of the house where the main characters in the story lived thirty years earlier. Then a half-dozen poor families shared the house. The Wolfes—Deb, Hugh, and Hugh's father—had the basement. The narrator uses her elevated vantage point to get a wider view of the town, the situation of the story, and perhaps even the nation. The upper part of the house is empty. It is not a home. The healing wings of the domestic angel have not—will not—brush its filthy walls. Then, as the narrator follows Deb downstairs into the degraded space inhabited by the workers whose story she is telling, she bids her readers come with her:

> This is what I want you to do. I want you to hide your disgust, take no heed of your clean clothes, and come right down with me,—here, into the thickest of the fog and mud and foul effluvia. I want you to hear this story. There is a secret down here, in this nightmare fog, that has lain dumb for centuries: I want to make it a real thing to you. (13-4)

There in the occupied section of the house, the basement, we find no home either: "It was low, damp,—the earthen floor covered with a green, slimy moss,—a fetid air smothering the breath" (16).This place has never been a home. It is a "lair," a "den," a terrifying site of moral and physical and spiritual degradation, an anti-home, a place of rats and disease and despair. Domestic feminism cannot work its purifying magic here; this is a space beyond salvation. Harding Davis would have readers believe that, if the people here are damned, if no "hope" exists for them, then the nation that forged this space is damned too.

As the novella unfolds, the characters journey through a series of anti-domestic spaces, spaces beyond the saving grace or the ideological rationalization of the doctrine of separate spheres. Finding at home only Hugh's father and Janey,

the young family friend Hugh loves for her already ruined beauty, Deb packs Hugh a horrid kind of picnic—"filch" and stale ale—and sets out through a dark, cold rain to the iron mill where her beloved cousin is working the night shift. As she nears the rolling mills, "immense, tent-like roofs covering acres of ground, open on every side," the reader descends with her into a Dantean Hell:

> Beneath these roofs, Deborah looked in on a city of fires, that burned hot and fiercely in the night. Fire in every horrible form: pits of flame waving in the wind; liquid metal-flames writhing in tortuous streams through the sand; wide caldrons filled with boiling fire, over which bent ghastly wretches stirring the strange brewing; and through all, crowds of half-clad men, looking like revengeful ghosts in the red light, hurried, throwing masses of glittering fire. It was like a street in Hell. (20)

Deb curls up like a dog on the refuse pile—cultural refuse warming itself on industrial refuse—and the story's attention shifts to Wolfe. Again the narrator summons the reader to look long and hard at him, his "soul-starvation," his "slow, heavy years of constant, hot work at the mill" (25). Then we learn what makes Wolfe special:

> God put into this man's soul a fierce thirst for beauty,—to know it, to create it; to be—something, he knows not what,—other than he is. There are moments when a passing cloud, the sun glinting on the purple thistles, a kindly smile, a child's face, will rouse him to a passion of pain,—when his nature starts up with a mad cry of rage against God, man, whoever it is that has forced this vile, slimy life upon him. (25)

As Hugh works, a group of wealthy men visit the mill: the overseer, the son of the mill owner, a doctor, a journalist, a gentleman. As the hellish panorama of the mill spreads out before them, before their very eyes the spouting fires consuming the lives of those that feed and tend them, the overseer can think only of "net profits" (27).

A cynical but gentlemanly conversation goes on among the visitors, and the narrator makes clear the huge distances between the lives of the visitors and the lives of the workers. Although

Wolfe is attracted to the visitors, especially to Mitchell, the aristocrat, he "listened more and more like a dumb, hopeless animal" (30). He knows that "between them, there was a great gulf never to be passed. Never!" (30). That distance turns out to be an ironic one when, after the men discover the korl-women, their responses to it, to Wolfe, and to his amazing talent make clear their pompous, ignorant, self-serving hypocrisy. They keep on talking, and we learn that these rich, privileged, educated, self-satisfied men are not half the man, half the human, both Wolfe and Deb are. None of their grand theories can untangle the terrifying puzzle of Wolfe and his amazing statue, the shared hunger for a real life, a life that matches their potential. The narrator treats these men mercilessly, gleefully exposing the self-serving pomposity of their arguments, one after another.

Night passes and in the morning we learn that Deb has picked up a wallet of money dropped by Mitchell the night before. She gives it to Wolfe, and the inexorable logic of the story grinds to its tragic end. Wolfe wanders the town searching for some way to resist the temptation of the money. He enters a church looking for salvation there. But again, a great gulf opens between him and the middle-class parishioners. He cannot understand the preacher's words—they do not even sound like language to him. They cannot possibly save him. Next Hugh finds himself in the anti-domestic space of a jail-cell, where the justice system can offer him nothing but certain soul death, a nineteen-year prison sentence. "Half a lifetime!" the narrator says (51). And so Hugh ends his life in his cell, homeless still and at last. "It is best," he tells Deb on their last visit. "I cannot bear to be hurted any more" (57). It is a brilliant use of dialect: the reader hears his words as though they came from a child.

Even though Deb is not an angel in the house, she loves Wolfe with pure, deep, long-lasting, concerned love. But in their world, that love remains powerless to save him from the terrible danger of his life and his work—the work of the new American industrial world. He commits a hopeless suicide, cutting away at his young but broken body as he has cut away at the korl. Deb,

his would-be redeemer, listens helplessly from the next cell. The reversal of middle-class logic could not be more complete. The concept of domestic salvation has utterly failed him as it fails all industrial workers like him.

Near the end of the novella, Harding Davis does imagine a redemptive space, although she does not let her readers see it. A woman comes to the jail and promises to bury Wolfe where she lives—at the Quaker home "on the hills," away from the smoke and stench of the city, out in the free air and sunshine Deb says Hugh was born in, out in the free air and sunshine of a preindustrial United States. There, and only there, will the dead Wolfe have a home. After three years in prison, Deb herself finds that same saving home with the Quakers.

At its close, the novella comes to a final domestic space, the home of the narrator. Living there with her, but veiled from view, is Wolfe's korl woman. "Sometimes,—to-night, for instance," the narrator says,

> the curtain is accidentally drawn back, and I see a bare arm stretched out imploringly in the darkness, and an eager, wolfish face watching mine: a wan, woful [sic] face, through which the spirit of the dead korl-cutter looks out, with its thwarted life, its mighty hunger, its unfinished work. Its pale, vague lips seem to tremble with a terrible question. "Is this the End?" they say,—"nothing beyond? no more?" Why you tell me you have seen that look in the eyes of dumb brutes,—horses dying under the lash. I know. (64)

Against these terrifically forceful images of longing and despair, against these terrible questions, Harding Davis sets the imagine of the dawn: "A cool gray light suddenly touches [the korl-woman's] head like a blessing hand, and its groping arm points through the broken cloud to the far East, where, in the flickering, nebulous crimson, God has set the promise of the Dawn" (65). In all the many years since the publication of *Life in the Iron Mills*, readers have had to come to their own conclusions about the particulars of that Dawn, have had to decide for themselves if its light is any match for Hugh's korl-woman.

Since the 1971 reprint of *Life in the Iron Mills* by the Feminist Press, contemporary readers, scholars, teachers, and students have looked long and hard at that amazing korl-woman and the novella she inhabits. The novella has made its way into important anthologies and critical editions. Other reprints have followed. In 1990 the Feminist Press reprinted *Margret Howth: A Story of To-day*. In *A Rebecca Harding Davis Reader* (1995), edited by Jean Pfaelzer, the University of Pittsburgh Press reprinted *Life in the Iron Mills* along with many short stories and essays. In 1998 Bedford/St. Martin's Press published, as part of its Bedford Cultural Editions, *Life in the Iron Mills* along with a large assortment of contemporaneous documents that provide a cultural context for the novella. The novella, lost for so long, has become the subject of scholarly articles, dissertations, and book-length studies. High school students, undergraduates, and graduates read it as part of nineteenth-century literature courses as well as cultural history studies. And so *Life in the Iron Mills* lives again, precisely as Rebecca Harding Davis intended it to—as the *Uncle Tom's Cabin* of industrial labor.

MARGRET HOWTH

Soon after the publication of *Life in the Iron Mills*, Rebecca Harding—not yet Davis—sent to her publisher James Fields the three-hundred-page manuscript of her first novel, a story about textile mill workers in Indiana that she named "The Deaf and the Dumb." Written on the verge of the Civil War, the novel asks not whether the nation can survive that terrible conflict, but whether "American democracy can survive the effects of urban industrialization," says Jean Yellin in her afterword to a 1990 edition of the novel.(Yellin 271). In its original version, the novel answers that question in the negative. When James Fields rejected that original because, as he said, it "assembles the gloom too depressingly," Harding wrote to Annie Fields, James Fields's wife, that she would "try to meet Mr. Fields's wishes of being more cheerful though humor had need to be as high as God's sunshine

to glow cheerily on Virginia soil just now" (quoted in Olsen 89). The published version, serialized in the *Atlantic Monthly* as "A Story of To-Day," and later republished in novel form as *Margret Howth: A Story of To-Day*, ends more happily.

The novel expands on the terse, teeth-clenching grimness of *Life in the Iron Mills*: the thwarted artist Hugh Wolfe, his body and life ruined by his work, transforms into the character of Lois, a mulatto teenager maimed and addled by a decade of laboring in the textile mills. In Lois, as in Hugh, the "artist-sense is pure" (*Margret Howth* 110). But Lois shares neither Hugh's despair nor his fate. In Lois, Harding Davis creates an underclass angel-on-earth. Even in her poverty and deformity, Lois works to redeem all the people around her, and although she dies at the end of the novel, hers is a blessed death: "The cripple was dead; but *Lois*, free, loving, and beloved, trembled from her prison to her Master's side in the To-Morrow" (262). The debate about work, class, art, industry, and the human soul that Harding Davis works into *Life in the Iron Mills* in the talk among the night visitors to the iron foundry, she stretches out across the pages of the novel, often in the conversations among Margret's father, the radical philanthropist Dr. Knowles, and Stephen Holmes, the "new man" Margret eventually reforms and marries. The long-suffering love and devotion that belongs to the hunchback Deb in *Life in the Iron Mills*, Harding Davis gives in the novel to Margret, the important difference being that, in the end, Margret gets her man, in the flesh, not just in the promise of a heavenly eternity.

Many critics consider Harding Davis's acquiescence to her publisher's request to lighten up the novel as the end of the young woman's very short career as a serious author and the beginning of her very long career as a popular one. Since no extant version of the original manuscript exists, they cannot prove that assertion. Happier ending or not, however, *Margret Howth* glows red hot with the same hatred of injustice and spit-in-your-eye fury at middle-class complacency as does *Life in the Iron Mills*. The opening of the novel alludes to the Civil War, "the shadow of

death [that] has fallen on us," (3) and then looks away from it and calls on readers to "go down into this common, every-day drudgery, and consider if there might not be in it also a great warfare... . It has its slain. Men and women, lean-jawed, crippled in the slow, silent battle, are in your alleys"(6–7).

The Harding Davis scholar Jean Fagan Yellin points out that "by the end of the book, Lois's simple creed of Christian love has been embraced by all of the other characters and ... narrator. Public problems have been privatized, economic hunger forgotten, and spiritual hunger eradicated in the endorsement of Lois's religion" (283). Still, not even Lois's death, not even Margret's decision late in the happier version of the novel to give up Knowles's crusade, marry the repentant Holmes, and enter the domestic world of True Womanhood, can, for many readers, dim the lurid vision of "hell" created by U.S. industrial capitalism.

STORIES OF WAR AND SLAVERY

After the *Atlantic* began, in October 1861, publishing installments of "A Story of To-Day," Harding turned her attention away from her first and most enduring subject, industrial wage slavery, and focused on the much more prominent issue of chattel slavery, most notably in the short stories "John Lamar" and "Blind Tom" and the novella *John Gaunt*—all published in the *Atlantic* during 1862. *Waiting for the Verdict*, a novel of Reconstruction, followed in 1868. Jane Tompkins, an important scholar of nineteenth-century women's writing, claims that women writers could approach slavery only from their sentiments and their properly domestic space—the "'closet' of the heart" (151). Rebecca Harding Davis's slave stories and war stories, however, utterly breach the confines of the closet. Her position on the war-torn border between the slave and the free states helped her understand the tragedies both of war and of slavery. From that borderland she writes fiction that is both antiwar and antislavery. In *Bits of Gossip,* Harding Davis writes about how she found the idealization of

the war, especially by the transcendentalist guru Bronson Alcott, particularly outrageous:

> I had just come up from the border where I had seen the actual war; the filthy spewings of it; the political jobbery in Union and Confederate camps; the malignant personal hatreds wearing patriotic masks, and glutted by burning homes and outraged women; the chances in it, well improved on both sides, for brutish men to grow more brutish, and for honorable gentlemen to degenerate into thieves and sots. War may be an armed angel with a mission, but she has the personal habits of the slums. (39)

The "Civil War" chapter from *Bits of Gossip* makes clear Harding Davis's unwavering opinion that, even forty years after the war, the nation had not told itself the truth if people believed there had been anything good about that terrible conflict.

Her first story about war and slavery, "John Lamar," begins with an image of the homely spaces of agrarian life turned to the uses of war and death: "The guard-house was, in fact, nothing but a shed in the middle of a stubblefield. It had been built for a cider-press" the summer before (35). All around, the land itself has been turned by the war into "stagnation, a great death" (37). In the course of the story, blood rather than apple juice stains the cider house floor. Bodies of dead combatants and civilians—old men and little girls—litter the hedges near the guardhouse, victims of the marauding bands of mercenaries— Secession "Bush-whackers" and Union "Snake-hunters"—"both armies used in Virginia as tools for rapine and murder" (37). The Snake-hunters have captured Lamar, along with his personal slave Ben, and taken them to a plantation that until recently had been owned by Lamar's grandfather, whom the mercenaries murder by the woodpile and bury with his hands above ground. One of the Snake-hunters shows Lamar a "trophy" of their recent slaughter, "a child's golden ringlet" (38). When Lamar sees the corpse, he recognizes the dead girl, "the small face in its woolen hood, dimpled yet, though dead for days ... Jessy Birt, the ferrymen's little girl" (38). Lamar, on the whole, seems strangely untroubled by such horrors, although he does worry about what will happen to his little sister

back home, left alone and unprotected from such men as these. He seems strangely unaware of the position of his body servant as well, since, as he plans an escape that depends wholly on the slave's cooperation, Lamar says to Ben, "We will be free to-night, old boy!" (47).

The ironies double in the story as we learn that the Union officer heading up the regular army unit that holds Lamar prisoner is Lamar's lifelong friend. Ben overhears Lamar and his friend talking about the war and about slavery and learns that neither man, neither North nor South, can imagine his immediate freedom. "Crushing down and out the old parasite affection for his master," Ben plans his own escape and prepares himself for the freedom he must take rather than be given (48). Spurred on to revenge by one of the Union soldiers, a fire-breathing abolitionist preacher, Ben bludgeons his master to death and runs not north to "the quiet old dream of content" but south to do the fearsome work of the slave-no-longer: revenge. As he goes, the narrator speaks directly to the reader: "his thick blood surged with passions of which you and I know nothing: he had a lost life to avenge"—his own (51). Harding Davis makes clear what path his revenge will take as, knife in hand, he "ploughed his way" toward "the white, stately dwellings, the men that went in and out from them, quiet, dominant. It was his turn for pleasure now: he would have his fill. Their wine and their gardens and," as it turns out, his dead master's not-yet-dead little sister with her golden curls (51). The story closes with the repeated question: "Was this well done?"(52). Harding Davis never lets anyone answer that question and instead closes the story with a chilling apocalyptic reference: "'The day of the Lord is ... at hand; and who can abide it?'" (53).

The author takes up that question again, and at length, in her 1868 novel, *Waiting for the Verdict,* where, according to Tillie Olsen, Harding Davis "intended to pose what [she] considered the basic question of the time: how was the nation going to redress the wrong of slavery? Were the freed slaves to have work, education, respect, freedom? The blacks, the nation, the future, were waiting for the verdict" (129). The novel, which takes

place during rather than after the Civil War, weaves together a romance plot and a story of the struggle of a former slave to find a place in American life. In it Harding Davis assumes a border position once again. She refuses generalizations about both the North and the South, about black people as well as white people. Both regions can be, by turns, paradisical or hellish; both races devilish and angelic. Culture and history—and perhaps a bit of biology—set the limits. Here, as elsewhere, her ability to identify with the powerless—often attributed to her understandings of the gender restrictions she herself suffered—couples with her keen sense of the importance of both place and history in the construction of individual character and allows her to forge a complex story flavored with a decidedly contemporary twist of cultural relativism.

The 1862 short story "Blind Tom," brings together Harding Davis's concern for slavery with one of the central thematic anchors of her writing—artistic talent, genius, thwarted by restrictions of class, race, and gender. Relying on the reportage and exposition used in journalism rather than the techniques of scenic development common to fiction, Harding Davis in "Blind Tom" tells the true story of wild, unconscious musical talent born into the body of a blind, despised slave boy—an "idiot," a "lump of black flesh," "an unsightly baby-carcass (104; 105; 106). In her introduction to *Rebecca Harding Davis: A Reader*, Jean Pfaelzer explains that the story is based on the discovery and relentless marketing of the musical talents of "Thomas Greene Bethune, a slave who was born blind, deformed, and suffering from savant syndrome, a form of autism" (Pfaelzer xxv). Although utterly untaught, the fictional Tom, just like the real Tom, can reproduce any piano music he hears as well as compose "quaint and delicate whims of music, never the same... . Never glad: uncertain, sad minors always ... one inarticulate, unanswered question of pain in all" (106). His master—who has bought him "flesh and soul" (106) parades him in concert after concert, exposing him to grueling tests that often exhaust him to the point of "epileptic spasms" (109). His music, "broken,

wandering, yet of startling beauty and pathos" speaks for "Tom's own caged soul … bitter, hopeless" (111).

In this story, Harding Davis's racism, of course expected but for all that no easier to read or identify with, sits side-by-side in unresolved opposition with her perception that "some beautiful caged spirit … struggled for breath under that brutal form and idiotic brain" (111). She wonders "when it will be free" and then answers her own wondering: "Not in this life: the bars are too heavy"(111). At the close of the story, she makes the same sharp-tongued and passionate claim on her readers as she does in *Life in the Iron Mills* to see the humanity—and thus the potential of soul-genius—in all those around them: "in your own kitchen, in your own back-ally, there are spirits as beautiful, caged in forms as bestial, that you *could* set free, if you pleased. Don't call it bad taste in me to speak for them. You know they are more to be pitied than Tom,—for they are dumb" (111).

WOMEN'S STORIES

Twentieth- and twenty-first-century scholars make much of "The Wife's Story," published in the *Atlantic Monthly* of July 1864, seeing it as a signal that Harding Davis, newly married and suffering from a serious depression, had chosen married life over the pursuit of artistic excellence. Her biography offers some support for this theory, as does the story itself, viewed strictly through the lens of gender. Once married, Rebecca Harding Davis wrote not just to express her passionate concerns for the nation and its people but also to help support herself and her growing family. In her first published work she made her most memorable contribution to American literature, and many readers, wishing she had hit that high mark again, look to "The Wife's Tale" and other stories like "Marcia" and "Anne" to explain why she did not.

All three of these stories present women with an apparently all-or-nothing choice between a family life and an artistic life—singing, writing, or simply hobnobbing with painters and writers. "The Wife's Story" details the fall and subsequent redemption of a middle-aged woman who, when her second husband suffers a financial reversal, decides to abandon him and his young son to sing in the New York City opening of an opera she has written. Her husband, Manning, is not troubled by the reversal of fortunes and seems even to look forward to leaving the city and returning to Newport and taking up his old post as a schoolteacher. The main character, Hetty, has an opposite reaction to the news. She asks herself "What would [her] taste or talent be worth in the coarse struggle we were about to begin for bread and butter?" (181). She is Concord-born; her new family, "western" people, are beneath her—they are "the mere hands by which the manual work of the world's progress was to be accomplished" (182). She decides that she has been called, by God, to a life of music, "set apart to a mission"(193). Typical of nineteenth-century women's writing, the story records an intricate ebb and flow of feelings as Hetty vacillates between pursuing her "high purpose" and giving in to the "woman's flesh" that urges her toward human warmth and loving association with her family (198).

The story follows Hetty into New York City and onto the opera house stage where she, and her opera, fail miserably. Forlorn and confused, she wanders the city streets, homeless and despairing, until she sees a crowd gathering outside a shop, goes in, and discovers her husband, dead from the shock of seeing her "bare shoulders" on the stage. A policeman mistakes her for a prostitute—she still has on her opera costume—and she faints away in a delirium, only to wake, of course, in her own warm bed with her family gathered around her. Her brief life on stage has been only a figment of her fevered brain—literally and figuratively.

"Marcia" follows an even simpler pattern. An older woman writer receives a manuscript from a younger aspiring writer who has left her home in the country to pursue her career. Her lover follows her to the city determined to wait—for years if need be—for Marcia to change her mind. It takes her years—during which she gets thinner and thinner—to realize she has no talent as a writer, something the older woman writer has

known all along. Marcia finally leaves with her faithful lover and goes back to the country.

This story makes quite clear the often paradoxical position of established nineteenth-century women writers, a position discussed by scholars such as Elaine Showalter, Nina Baum, and Susan Coultrap-McQuin. Unless a woman writer wanted to completely upend her life—which Harding Davis did not—she was forced to live inside the confinements of nineteenth-century gender and power relations. Yet, unless gave up writing altogether, which Harding Davis did not do, she had to breach those confinements, simply in the public act of writing, even if she did the actual writing at home. Harding Davis never resolved the tension between the two roles of public figure and popular writer (a culturally authorized speaker) and the private domestic wife and mother. The tension between her roles as author and angel surface, as they do in the work of other nineteenth-century women writers, as a contradiction between the fact of her writing and the plots of the women's stories she wrote. She did not give up her artistic life, her writing, even though she created so many women characters who do.

The story "Anne" proceeds in much the same way as "The Wife's Story." An older woman, a successful peach farmer and widow living with her married children and grandchildren, suddenly and quite inexplicably one day longs to recapture her brilliant youth and her first love, a poet who has since become well known. She sneaks away from the family, takes her bonds out of the bank, and gets on a train bound for the city. On the train she overhears the conversations of three sophisticated personages: a philanthropist, a painter, and a poet. As she listens, they expose themselves as charlatans—even her old lover, the poet. He turns out to be as false, as gross, as libertine as his traveling companions. They cheapen art by turning it into a crass, money-making affair. As Anne realizes this, the train derails. Her son finds her lying in the train wreckage and takes her home, where she is once again content to be "petted" and fussed over and loved in a cozy, domestic kind of way. It turns out, furthermore, that an illness has precipitated her wandering—she has mistaken the chills of an oncoming virus for the remembered thrills of her young life.

None of the women in these stories has true artistic talent. They are not like Hugh Wolfe or Blind Tom or even Lois in *Margret Howth*. They make too much of their pampered upbringings; they overestimate their talents. They do not hunger and thirst for art; they do not choke for the lack of it. As a matter of fact, all their longing seems to run in the opposite direction. They long to do the work their culture sets out for them, to heed the call to take up the life of the True Woman rather than the false artist.

When they imagine the "bright tomorrow," however, these characters do not think in typical antebellum American terms—they do not want to be the matrons of middle-class homes, minding the children and servants while their husbands run the factory and come home for dinner. They want to be part of ongoing productive units, part of working families, and, most definitely, they want to leave the city far, far behind. These women find redemption in family life—that is true, but it is a special kind of family life. The redemptive metaphor for Harding Davis and all her characters is a rural one, a preindustrial one. Redemption belongs to a world she remembers from her own childhood and the childhood of her nation. "The Wife's Story" is clearest about the nature of redemption. Hetty and Manning are not young people. He has grown children, and she is in her middle years. Manning has lived in the country before becoming financially successful and moving to posh New York. When he loses his fortune—and his wife—for a moment and then regains them, he does so by virtue of his grown sons, who provide for him and Hetty and their new baby, a perfect little farm, their own "cozery" complete with "stable and hay, and eggs every morning, only the gray hen's trying to set, if you'll believe it … And old Mary's in the kitchen, and we've got even Tinder and our old peacock from the Hudson" (219). Restored to a greater agrarian family that even includes the beloved horse "Tinder," the two middle-aged people will have a second chance. They're "beginning all new again" (214). The end of the

story is so heartfelt, so intense, so intimately imagined that it is hard not to think that Harding Davis wishes her nation to have that second chance, that "beginning all new" again, as well as her characters. These women's stories, along with the great body of Harding Davis's work, argue that economics—the way we live and make our livings—and the far-ranging moral, physical, emotional, artistic, and spiritual consequences of that way, matter much more, in the end, than gender.

All her long life, Harding Davis took as her central concern issues of class and social justice. As her century moved on, the nation became more and more tightly wedded to what she considered a soul-numbing commercialism. Mainstream Christianity became inured to the greed and ruthless oppression of unrestrained industrial capitalism. The Gilded Age arrived, with its worship of enormous and ostentatious wealth. Little wonder she imagined an idyllic preindustrial life, a cozy farm where everyone could have a second chance. Little wonder she looked for redemption "to the distant hills."

Selected Bibliography

WORKS OF REBECCA HARDING DAVIS

PRIMARY EDITIONS

Margaret Howth: A Story of To-Day. Boston: Ticknor and Fields, 1862.

Dallas Galbraith. Philadelphia: Lippincott, 1868.

Waiting for the Verdict. New York: Sheldon, 1868.

John Andross. New York: Orange Judd, 1874.

Kitty's Choice: A Story of Berrytown. Philadelphia: Lippincott, 1874.

A Law unto Herself. Philadelphia: Lippincott, 1878.

Natasqua. New York: Cassell, 1887.

Kent Hampden. New York: Scribners, 1892.

Silhouettes of American Life. New York: Scribners, 1892. (Short stories, mostly reprints of fiction that originally appeared in periodicals.)

Doctor Warwick's Daughters. New York: Harper, 1896.

Frances Waldeaux. New York: Harper and Brothers, 1897.

Bits of Gossip. Boston and New York: Houghton, Mifflin, 1904.

MODERN EDITIONS AND COLLECTIONS

Waiting for the Verdict. Upper Saddle River, N.J.: Gregg, 1967.

Silhouettes of American Life. New York: Garrett, 1968.

Life in the Iron Mills and Other Stories. Edited and with a biographical interpretation by Tillie Olsen. Old Westbury, N.Y.: Feminist Press, 1985. (Includes "Anne" and "The Wife's Story.")

Margaret Howth: A Story of To-Day. Edited and with an afterword by Jean Fagan Yellin. New York: Feminist Press, 1990.

A Rebecca Harding Davis Reader: "Life in the Iron Mills," Selected Fiction, and Essays. Edited and with an introduction by Jean Pfaelzer. Pittsburgh, Pa.: University of Pittsburgh Press, 1995. (Includes "Blind Tom" and "John Lamar." Many samples of the periodical fiction and nonfiction cited below are made accessible to the modern reader in this volume.)

Life in the Iron Mills. Edited and with commentary, "Cultural and Historical Background," by Cecelia Tichi. New York: Bedford/St. Martin's, 1997.

Rebecca Harding Davis: Writing Cultural Autobiography. Edited by Janice Milner Lasseter and Sharon M. Harris. Nashville, Tenn.: Vanderbilt University Press, 2001. (Offers an annotated edition of *Bits of Gossip* and includes the previously unpublished "A Family History.")

SELECTED PERIODICAL FICTION

"Life in the Iron Mills." *Atlantic Monthly* 7 (1861): 430–451. (Reprinted in *Atlantic Tales: A Collection of Stories from the Atlantic Monthly.* Edited by William Ticknor and James T. Fields. Boston: Ticknor and Fields, 1866.)

"John Lamar." *Atlantic Monthly* 9 (1862): 411–423.

"Blind Tom." *Atlantic Monthly* 10 (1862): 580–585. (Reprinted in *All the Year Round* 8 (1862): 126–129.)

"David Gaunt." *Atlantic Monthly* 10 (1862): 257–271, 403–421.

"The Wife's Story." *Atlantic Monthly* 14 (1864): 1–19.

"Out of the Sea." *Atlantic Monthly* 15 (1865): 533–549.

"The Harmonists." *Atlantic Monthly* 17 (1866): 529–538.

"The Story of Christine." *Peterson's* 50 (1866): 166–174.

"The Pearl of Great Price." *Lippincott's* 2 (1868): 606–617; 3 (1869): 74–83.

"Put Out of the Way." *Peterson's* 57 (1870): 413–443.

"Two Women." *Galaxy* 9 (1870): 799–815.

"Earthen Pitchers." *Scribner's* 7 (1873): 73–81, 199–207; 8 (1874): 275–281, 490–494, 595–600, 714–721.

"A Faded Leaf of History." *Atlantic Monthly* 31 (1873): 44–52.

"The Doctor's Wife." *Scribner's* 8 (1874): 108–110.

"Dolly." *Scribner's* 9 (1874): 89–92.

"The Pepper-Pot Woman." *Scribner's* 8 (1874): 541–543.

"The Poetess of Clap City." *Scribner's* 9 (1875): 612–615.

"The Yares of the Black Mountains." *Lippincott's* 16 (1875): 35–47.

"Marcia." Harper's 53 (1876): 925–928.

"Married People." *Harper's* 43 (1877): 730–735.

"A Day with Doctor Sarah." *Harper's* 57 (1878): 611–617.

"Walhalla." *Scribner's* 29 (1880): 139–145.

"Across the Gulf." *Lippincott's* 28 (1881): 59–71.

"A Silhouette." *Harper's* 67 (1883): 622–631.

"A Wayside Episode." *Lippincott's* 31 (February 1883): 179–190.

"Mademoiselle Joan." *Atlantic Monthly* 58 (September 1886): 328–336.

"Here and There in the South." *Harper's New Monthly* 75 (July–November 1887): 235–246, 431–443, 593–606, 747–760, 914–925.

"Tirar y Soult." *Scribner's* 2 (November 1887): 563–572.

"At the Station." *Scribner's* 4 (December 1888): 687–696.

"Anne." *Harper's New Monthly* 78 (1889): 744–750.

"An Ignoble Martyr." *Harper's New Monthly* 80 (March 1890): 604–610.

"In the Gray Cabins of New England." *Century* 49 (1895): 620–623.

"An Old-Time Love Story." *Century* 77 (December 1908): 219–221.

"The Coming of Night." *Scribner's* 45 (January 1909): 58–68.

SELECTED PERIODICAL NONFICTION

"Ellen." *Peterson's* 44 (July 1863): 38–48.

"Men's Rights." *Putnam's* 3 (February 1869): 212–224.

"The Middle-Aged Woman." *Scribner's Monthly* 19 (July 1875): 612–615.

"The House on the Beach." *Lippincott's* 18 (January 1876).

"Some Testimony in the Case." *Atlantic Monthly* 56 (November 1885): 602–608.

"Low Wages for Women." *Independent* 40 (8 November 1888): 1425.

"Are Women to Blame?" *North American Review* 148 (May 1889): 622–641.

"Women in Literature." *Independent* 43 (7 May 1891): 6612.

"The Newly Discovered Woman." *Independent* 45 (30 November 1893):1601.

"Some Hobgoblins in Literature." *Book Buyer* 14 (April 1897): 229–231.

"Two Points of View." *Independent* 49 (9 September 1897): 1161- 1162.

"Two Methods with the Negro." *Independent* 50 (31 March 1898): 401–402.

"Women and Patriotism." *Harper's Bazaar* 21 (28 May 1898): 455.

"The Work before Us." *Independent* 51 (19 January 1899): 177–179.

"The Curse of Education." *North American Review* 168 (May 1899): 609–614. (Reprinted as "Education and Crime." In *Report of the Department of Interior–Education, 1899,* vol. 2. House document, vol. 31. 56th Cong., 1st sess., 1899- 1900.)

"The Mean Face of War." *Independent* 51 (20 July 1899): 1931- 1933.

"On the Jersey Coast." *Independent* 52 (15 November 1900): 2730- 2733.

"Under the Old Code." *Harper's New Monthly* 100 (February 1900): 401–412.

"Lord Kirchener's Methods." *Independent* 53 (7 February 1901): 326–338.

"The Disease of Money-Getting." *Independent* 54 (19 June 1902): 1457- 1460.

"The Black North." *Independent* 54 (6 February 1902): 338–340.

"War as the Woman Sees It." *Saturday Evening Post,* 11 June 1904, 8–9.

"A Middle-Aged Woman." *Independent* 57 (1 September 1904): 489–494.

"The Love Story of Charlotte Bronte." *Saturday Evening Post,* 13 January 1906, 4–15.

"Undistinguished Americans." *Independent* 60 (26 April 1906): 962–964.

"One Woman's Question." *Independent* 63 (July 1907): 132–133.

LETTERS

Richard Harding Davis Collection (#6109). Clifford Waller Barrett Library. Special Collections Department, University of Virginia Library.

BIBLIOGRAPHIES

Harris, Sharon M. "Rebecca Harding Davis (1831-1910): A Bibliography of Secondary Criticism, 1958-1986." *Bulletin of Bibliography* 45 (1988): 233–246.

Rose, Jane Atteridge. "A Bibliography of Fiction and Non-Fiction by Rebecca Harding Davis." *American Literary Realism* 22, no. 3 (1990): 67–86.

CRITICAL AND BIOGRAPHICAL STUDIES

Boudreau, Kristin. "'The Woman's Flesh of Me': Rebecca Harding Davis's Response to Self Reliance." *American Transcendental Quarterly* 6, no. 2 (1992): 132–140.

Buckley, J. F. "Living in the Iron Mills: A Tempering of Nineteenth-Century America's Orphic Poet." *Journal of American Culture* 16, no. 1 (spring 1993): 67–72.

Coultrap-McQuin, Susan. *Doing Literary Business: American Women Writers in the Nineteenth Century.* Chapel Hill: University of North Carolina Press, 1990.

Curnutt, Kirk. "Direct Addresses, Narrative Authority, and Gender in Rebecca Harding Davis's *Life in the Iron Mills.*" *Style* 28, no. 2 (summer 1994): 146.

Davis, Charles Belmont. *The Adventures and Letters of Richard Harding Davis.* New York: Scribners, 1917.

Fetterley, Judith. Introduction and critical commentary. *"Life in the Iron Mills, 1861."* In her *Provisions: A Reader from 19th-Century American Women,* 306–314. Bloomington: Indiana University Press, 1985.

Gilbert, Sandra, and Susan Gubar. Introduction. "Rebecca Harding Davis." In their *Norton Anthology of Literature by Women: The Tradition in English,* 903–934. New York: Norton, 1985.

Harris, Sharon M. *Rebecca Harding Davis and American Realism.* Philadelphia: University of Pennsylvania Press, 1991.

Hesford, Walter. "Literary Contexts of *Life in the Iron Mills.*" *American Literature* 49 (1971): 70–85.

Hood, Richard A. "Framing a Life in the Iron Mills." *Studies in American Fiction* 23, no. 1 (spring 1995): 73–84.

Lasseter, Janice Milner. "'Boston in the Sixties': Rebecca Harding Davis' View of Boston and Concord during the Civil War." *Concord Saunterer* 3 (fall 1995): 65–72.

———. "Hawthorne's Legacy to Rebecca Harding Davis." *Hawthorne and Women: Engendering and Expanding the Hawthorne Tradition,* edited by John Idol and Melinda Ponder. Amherst: University of Massachusetts Press, 1998.

Little, Deandra. "An Alabama Realist: The Influence of the Nineteenth-Century Idea of Womanhood in Rebecca Harding Davis's *Margret Howth.*" *Alabama English* 7 (1995): 31–37.

Malpezzi, Frances M. "Sisters in Protest: Rebecca Harding Davis and Tillie Olsen." *Artes Liberales* 12, no. 2 (spring 1986): 1–9.

Mock, Michele L. "'An Ardor That Was Human, and a Power That Was Art': Rebecca Harding Davis and the Art of the Periodical." In *"The Only Efficient Instrument": American Women Writers and the Periodical, 1837–1916,* edited by Aleta Feinsod Cane and Susan Alves, 126–146. Iowa City: University of Iowa Press, 2001.

Perkins, Barbara, and George B. Perkins, eds. "Rebecca Harding Davis (1831–1910)." In their *Kaleidoscope: Stories of the American Experience,* 249–263. New York: Oxford University Press, 1993.

Pfaelzer, Jean. "Legacy Profile: Rebecca Harding Davis (1831–1910)." *Legacy* 7 (1990): 39–45.

———."'Marcia' by Rebecca Harding Davis." *Legacy* 4 (1987): 3–10.

———. *Parlor Radical: Rebecca Harding Davis and the Origins of American Social Realism.* Pittsburgh, Pa.: University of Pittsburgh Press, 1996.

———."Rebecca Harding Davis: Domesticity, Social Order, and the Industrial Novel." *International Journal of Women's Studies 4* (1981): 234–244.

———."Subjectivity as Feminist Utopia." In *Utopian and Science Fiction by Women: Worlds of Difference,* edited by Jane L. Donawerth and Carol A. Kolmerten, 93–106. Syracuse: Syracuse University Press, 1994.

———. "The Sentimental Promise and the Utopian Myth: Rebecca Harding Davis's 'The Harmonists' and Louisa May Alcott's 'Transcendental Wild Oats.'" *American Transcendental Quarterly* 3, no. 1 (1989): 85–99.

Rose, Jane Atteridge. "The Artist Manque in the Fiction of Rebecca Harding Davis." In *Writing the Woman Artist: Essays on Poetics, Politics, and Portraiture,* edited by Suzanne W. Jones, 155–174. Philadelphia: Pennsylvania University Press, 1991.

———."Images of Self: The Example of Rebecca Harding Davis and Charlotte Perkins Gilman." *English Language Notes* 29, no. 4 (1992): 70–78.

———. "Reading *Life in the Iron Mills* Contextually: A Key to Rebecca Harding Davis's Fiction." *Conversations: Contemporary Critical Theory and the Teaching of Literature,* edited by Charles Moran and Elizabeth F. Penfield, 187–199. Urbana, Ill.: National Council of Teachers of English, 1990.

Scheiber, Andrew J. "An Unknown Infrastructure: Gender, Production, and Aesthetic Exchange in Rebecca Harding Davis's *Life in the Iron-Mills.* " *Legacy* 11 (1994): 101–117.

Schocket, Eric. "'Discovering Some New Race': Rebecca Harding Davis's *Life in the Iron Mills* and the Literary Emergence of Working-Class Whiteness." *PMLA* 115, no. 1 (2000): 46–59.

Showalter, Elaine. "Introduction." In her *Scribbling Women: Short Stories by Nineteenth-Century American Women.* New Brunswick, N.J.: Rutgers University Press, 1996.

Shurr, William H. *"Life in the Iron-Mills*: A Nineteenth-Century Conversion Narrative." *American Transcendental Quarterly* 5, no. 4 (1991): 245–257.

Tompkins, Jane. *Sensational Designs: The Cultural Work of American Fiction, 1790-1860.* New York: Oxford University Press, 1985.

Thompson, Rosemarie Garland. "Benevolent Maternalism and Physically Disabled Figures: Dilemmas of Female Embodiment in Stowe, Davis, and Phelps." *American Literature* 68, no. 3 (1996): 555–561.

Waldron, Karen E. "No Separations in the City: The Public-Private Novel and Private-Public Authorship." In *Separate Spheres No More: Gender Convergence in American Literature, 1830–1930,* edited by Monika M. Elbert, 92–113.. Tuscaloosa: University of Alabama Press, 2000.

Yellin, Jean Fagan. "The 'Feminization' of Rebecca Harding Davis." *American Literary History* 2, no. 2 (summer 1990): 203–219.

REFERENCES IN THE TEXT COME FROM THE FOLLOWING DAVIS EDITIONS:

"A Family History." *Rebecca Harding Davis : Writing Cultural Autobiography*. Eds. Janice Milner Lasseter and Sharon M. Harris 1st ed. Nashville: Vanderbilt University Press, 2001, 137–48.

"Anne." *Life in the Iron Mills and Other Stories*. Ed. Tillie Olsen. New York: Feminist Press, 1985, 223–42.

Bits of Gossip. Rebecca Harding Davis : Writing Cultural Autobiography. Eds. Janice Milner Lasseter and Sharon M. Harris 1st ed. Nashville: Vanderbilt University Press, 2001, 22–130.

"Blind Tom." *A Rebecca Harding Davis Reader*. Ed. Jean Pfaelzer. Pittsburgh: University of Pittsburgh, 1995, 104–11.

"John Lamar." *A Rebecca Harding Davis Reader*. Ed. Jean Pfaelzer. Pittsburgh: University of Pittsburgh, 1995, 35–43.

Life in the Iron Mills and Other Stories. Biographical Interpretation. Ed. Tillie Olsen. New York: Feminist, 1985.

Margaret Howth: A Story of To-Day. Ed. Jean Fagan Yellin. New York: Feminist Press, 1990.

"The Wife's Story." *Life in the Iron Mills and Other Stories*. Ed. Tillie Olsen. New York: Feminist Press, 1985, 175–222.

THEODOR SEUSS GEISEL

(1904–1991)

Andrew Zawacki

THEODOR SEUSS GEISEL , better known by three generations of children and parents as DR. SEUSS , was born on March 2, 1904, in Springfield, Massachusetts. At the turn of the century the future author and illustrator's hometown was booming with factories, railroads, boat traffic, touring vaudeville companies, museums, and a zoo, all encouraging eccentricity and innovation among professionals and hobbyists. It headquartered Smith & Wesson, makers of revolvers, while the .30-caliber, magazine-fed Springfield rifle was manufactured in the local armory. The city of sixty-two thousand was also home to G. and C. Merriam, the dictionary publishers, and to the creators of Milton Bradley games. Poised between the late nineteenth-century values of hard work and progress and the early twentieth-century belief in the middle-class American dream, Springfield boasted an infectious, progressive energy that would come to characterize its zaniest, most celebrated son.

Springfield was likewise marked by the influx of German immigrants, who protected their traditional European culture even as they aspired to assimilate. Geisel's paternal grandparents, Theodor Geisel and Christine Schmaelzle, had emigrated from Germany and taken over a small brewery in Springfield in 1876 (Morgan, *Dr. Seuss and Mr. Geisel* 4). Within fifteen years it was one of New England's largest. The brewer's son, Theodor Robert Geisel, married Henrietta ("Nettie") Seuss (pronounced "zoice"), the daughter of Bavarian immigrants who owned a bakery. Nettie's father, George J. Seuss, was founding president of the Springfield Turnverein, a social and gymnastics club that formed the center of German American culture in the city.

Young "Ted," as the son of Theodor and Nettie was then known, later recalled that his father had imposed a gentle discipline, teaching his son, "Whatever you do … do it to perfection" (Morgan 7). Dr. Seuss credited his mother, who read bedtime stories to him and his older sister, Margaretha Christine ("Marnie"), with having given him "the rhythms in which I write and the urgency with which I do it." The books Ted loved most included Peter Newell's *The Hole Book*, which had a hole punched through each page; the rhyming verses of the *Goops* books by Gelett Burgess; the multivolume *Rover Boys* series by Arthur M. Winfield; Palmer Cox's *Brownies: Their Book*; and *Max and Moritz* by Wilhelm Busch (Morgan 14, and Cott quoted in Fensch, *Of Sneetches* 110). He also liked the Krazy Kat comics of George Herriman.

While demonstrating little interest in athletics or his father's favorite pastime, marksmanship, Ted accompanied his dad to basketball games at the local YMCA, where James Naismith had invented the sport in 1891, and attended Buffalo Bill's Wild West Show. Ted noted the inventions in his father's workshop, and when his dad was appointed to the Springfield park board in 1909, he took strolls through the Springfield Zoo, producing sketches of animals with gangly, mismatched features.

Though he was not an exceptional student, Ted possessed a formidable memory, an ear for rhythm in both English and German—the language of the household—a knack for reciting the names of the books of the Old Testament in rhyme, and a tendency toward pranks and exaggeration. Often playing hooky from school to watch films at the Bijou, he worked as an usher at the Court Square Theatre. Ted contributed one-liners and cartoons for the Central High weekly, the *Recorder*, under the name "Pete the Pessimist" (Morgan 23). He authored satires as well, one of which he signed "T. S. LeSieg," a backward spelling of his name that he would later

employ; it was a pseudonym his father used when playing the numbers games. When his art teacher berated Ted for drawing pictures upside down, he transferred out of art class. In his senior year he wrote and staged a minstrel show, also serving as "grind and joke editor" for the yearbook, *Pnalka*. He was voted class artist and class wit (Morgan 24).

A young English teacher, Edwin A. "Red" Smith, encouraged Ted to apply to Dartmouth College, where Ted matriculated in 1921. Ted's father's brewery had been in financial straits since the 1919 ratification of the Eighteenth Amendment and other Prohibition legislation, but the family was able to afford Ted's tuition, thanks to an inheritance from Grandfather Geisel's real estate. The freshman proceeded to work on the college humor magazine, *Jack-O-Lantern* ("Jacko") (Morgan 27). Together with the sophomore Norman MacLean, who would go on to write the classic novel *A River Runs Through It* (1976), Ted published lines and cartoons, while he and his friend Whitney Campbell read Anatole France, Leo Tolstoy, and Gustave Flaubert.

By the next year Ted drew regularly for *Jacko* and joined the art staff; he also sampled a creative writing class devoted to marketable articles, in which he wrote a book review of the Boston & Maine Railroad timetable (Morgan 32). When MacLean became *Jacko* editor, the two often wrote its entire contents, occasionally alternating lines. In 1924, having been elected editor in chief, Ted warned his staff "not to think like Babbitts," invoking the novelist Sinclair Lewis's protagonist as a symbol of all that Ted found facile and conformist (Morgan 35). When Ted was busted in April 1925 for drinking a pint of bootleg gin, he was forbidden to continue as editor—but he persisted, seeking anonymity for the final issues in pseudonyms, including "Seuss."

Ted was unanimously voted "least likely to succeed" in a balloting among his friends in the "Casque and Gauntlet," as they called their informal society, but decided to attend Oxford University to become an English professor (Morgan 37). He did not receive the fellowship for which he applied, but having prematurely told his father that he had, and his proud father

having published the news in the Springfield newspaper, the Geisel family determined to send Ted anyhow. He spent the summer writing humorous verses for the *Springfield Union* before landing at Oxford's Lincoln College.

Ted attended lectures on Chaucer, Shakespeare, Milton, Dryden, Keats, Wordsworth, and other canonical English writers. The pages of his loose-leaf notebooks from his Oxford years, however, showcase a penciled menagerie in the margins: cows and Cupids, dogs and devils, chickens and chic women (Morgan 44–45). One of Ted's classmates, a Wellesley graduate named Helen Marion Palmer, upon looking at his notes, told him that he obviously wanted not to become a professor but rather to draw. The two began courting and were soon engaged. Ted illustrated portions of *Paradise Lost*, trying to coax humor out of its lines, but he pitched the idea to Blackwell publishers with no success (Lathem, quoted in Fensch, *Of Sneetches* 66). When one of Ted's tutors suggested that he take a year off to tour the museums of Europe, Ted began a series of travels outside England, most frequently to France, often with Helen, the pair occasionally joined by their parents.

While Helen, five years her fiancé's senior, was completing her master's degree, Ted hoped for a newspaper job in Europe. In Vienna he toyed with the idea of a thesis on German drama, and soon after alighted upon, and just as quickly abandoned, a dissertation topic for the Sorbonne on Jonathan Swift; he also attempted a novel. Helen and Ted reunited in Italy before she returned to New Jersey to find a teaching position, and Ted headed home in early 1927. The couple married in November and would remain together for four decades.

Whereas Helen had taken a post at a private girls' school, Ted was stuck in Springfield without a graduate degree, a job, or any strong professional leads (Morgan 56–59). His humor pieces and cartoons of bizarrely contorted animals did not fly with New York editors, despite the efforts of several Dartmouth classmates looking out for him in their own editorial capacities. *Life* passed on his proposed cartoon series of eminent Europeans, while the *New Yorker*, founded just

two years prior, balked at poems and illustrations depicting something called the "Hippocrass"—an awkward, lanky biped sporting wings, horns, and a grin.

"THE FLIT" AND THE FIRST FEW BOOKS

On July 16, 1927, a cartoon of tourists on camels comparing themselves to Lawrence of Arabia appeared in the *Saturday Evening Post*. It was signed "Seuss," though the editors appended a note clarifying that the artist was Theodor Seuss Geisel. The drawing earned him twenty-five dollars and convinced him to move to Manhattan, where Norman Anthony, the editor of the self-proclaimed "world's wittiest weekly," *Judge*, offered him a job as writer and artist with a salary (Morgan 59–60). Geisel's first cartoon, which depicted a marital quarrel between two unicyclists, appeared there on October 22, signed "Seuss." Soon after, he tacked on "Dr.," claiming the title as compensation for the Oxford degree he never received, and Geisel initially stuck with the pseudonym in the hope of saving his real name for the great American novel he still half-intended to write. For the *Judge* serial feature "Boids and Beasties," which borrowed from the bestiary in his Oxford notebooks, he added to the pseudonym, signing the series "Dr. Theophrastus Seuss." (Morgan 62).

Geisel admitted that his comics about Prohibition and speakeasies were not sophisticated but qualified that, given the venue, he "must dumb things up. Hence the assumed name." He was soon a major contributor and, upon receiving an autograph request from a twelve-year-old, stated, "If I can be of influence to one child in this great vice-ridden country, my life ... has not been lived in vain." Over the next decade Geisel published drawings, satires, and parodies in other high-profile magazines, from *Vanity Fair* to *Liberty*, intermittently landing on covers and increasingly experimenting with neologisms and wild rhymes.

His labor turned lucrative when he was found by the world of commercial advertising. He used the name of an actual insecticide in a *Judge* cartoon depicting a knight trying to fend off a dragon. After the Standard Oil Company president's wife convinced her husband to commission Geisel to create an advertising campaign for the company's bug spray, the caption "Quick, Henry! The Flit!" became a household refrain. Geisel enjoyed a seventeen-year stint with Flit, and as his tagline circulated in newspapers, on billboards, and over radio, the company got rich and so did he (Morgan 65). The campaign remains one of the most successful of its kind, and it facilitated other gigs. Foremost was another Standard Oil campaign, for Essolube 5-Star motor oil, which introduced a new Seussian lineup of roadside critters and catchphrases: "Foil the Moto-Raspus!" (Morgan 74).

Geisel's career in books began when an editor at Viking Press asked him to illustrate a compendium of children's sayings. Alexander Abingdon's *Schoolboy Howlers*, a best seller in England, comprised quotables from classrooms and exams. Reprinted in the United States as *Boners* (1931), the book topped the *New York Times* nonfiction list and was quickly followed by a sequel, *More Boners* (1931). Geisel's first review, in *American News*, called his drawings "inimitable" and "simply swell." (Morgan 71–72). The kudos prompted Geisel to attempt a vivaciously colored ABC book of weird animals, but he deserted the project after its rejection by Viking and other houses. It would be another thirty years before he would realize his alliterative *Dr. Seuss's ABC* (1963).

By 1936 Ted and Helen had traveled to some thirty countries in Europe, the Middle East, and Latin America (Morgan 79). Never without his sketchpad, Geisel became entranced by the engine rhythm aboard a luxury liner on a return from Europe, and he tried matching words to its unrelenting anapestic tetrameter. What he came up with was: "And that is a story that no one can beat, and to think that I saw it on Mulberry Street." Over the next six months, "A Story That No One Can Beat," as it was then called, got rejected by more than two dozen publishers as "too different" from orthodox children's books: it was fantastical, carried no ostensible message, and was composed in verse (Morgan 80–81).

However, Geisel's Dartmouth friend Mike McClintock showed it to his boss at Vanguard Press,

James Henle, who was establishing a reputation as a promoter of non-mainstream books. Under a new title, *And to Think That I Saw It on Mulberry Street* (1937) was dedicated to McClintock's wife, Helene, and featured their son Marco as its protagonist. Fifteen thousand copies of the book were printed and priced at one dollar each, and it garnered relatively positive reviews, the most important of which was a single line by Clifton Fadiman in the *New Yorker*. "They say it's for children," he wrote, "but better get a copy for yourself and marvel at the good Dr. Seuss's impossible pictures and the moral tale of the little boy who exaggerated not wisely but too well." The *New York Times* noted that the book "partakes of the better qualities of those peculiarly American institutions, the funny papers and the tall tale," while Beatrix Potter, the author of *The Tale of Peter Rabbit* (1902), admired "the natural truthful simplicity" of its "untruthfulness," how the story refused condescension toward children (Morgan 82–84).

Named after a main street in Springfield, the book delights in that city's brass-band-and-confetti parade culture. Moreover, Marco's penchant for piling one curlicued unlikelihood upon another, in order to impress his father with observations made during an otherwise uneventful walk home, is an early Seussian modus operandi. As Marco's imagination builds from the ground up into the grandiose, the illustrations become increasingly dense, bombastic, precariously perched. The idea is to outdo the ordinary by inventing the outlandish, and then to assimilate everything into its hyperbolic sweep.

Dr. Seuss's follow-up, *The 500 Hats of Bartholomew Cubbins* (1938), is a somewhat traditional fairy tale and one of only four books he wrote in prose. It had grown incrementally in length and density by cut-and-paste, a method appropriate to the story of a boy who, upon removing his hat, repeatedly finds another atop his head. Without children of his own, Geisel dedicated the book to Chrysanthemum-Pearl, an imaginary child he invented when it was discovered that he and Helen would be unable to bear any. The book was well received critically but not a big seller.

Seuss published his next pair, *The Seven Lady Godivas* (1939) and *The King's Stilts* (1939), with Random House, having been coaxed away from Vanguard by a young editor named Bennett Cerf who had helped to lift the ban on James Joyce's *Ulysses* (1922) and who had ties to Hollywood. Both books are in prose, and the latter, a tale extolling hard work and playing hard, did not do particularly well despite the public appearances Random House had lined up for Seuss. The former is a silly, revisionist account of the eleventh-century legend of Lady Godiva, complete with drawings of plump, naked ladies, and bears the double distinction of representing Seuss's only book explicitly and exclusively intended for adults and the only one that flat-out flopped.

Horton Hatches the Egg (1940), however, which Seuss wrote with hands-on help from Helen, struck an immediate success with children, parents, and even the juvenile buyer for F.A.O. Schwarz. Its anapestic tetrameter mirrors the lumbering elephant Horton's tentative ascent of a tree, where he guards the egg of a lazy bird called Mayzie when she departs for vacation. After many tribulations, Horton gives birth to an "elephant-bird," the offspring's designation as "something brand new" a defense of the author's inventive procedure. More importantly, Seuss's fourth children's book, the last he would write for seven years, is a moral tale promoting faithfulness and quietly critiquing selfishness and indifference. Hence it seems appropriate that the story would be followed by a period of explicit political involvement on Geisel's part. Alarmed by the combined threat to democracy of the Nazis and other fascist regimes, he disapproved the notion that the United States should mind its own business.

THE WORLD AT WAR

As a child, Geisel had been aware that his German heritage was potentially problematic. If his family had cherished certain customs from the old country, such as those observed at the Trinity Evangelical Lutheran Church, where services were conducted in German, they had also experi-

enced discomforts. When the German navy attacked the British liner *Lusitania* in 1915, killing 128 Americans and over a thousand others, German Americans were regarded with suspicion in the town (Morgan 15). As the United States entered World War I in April 1917, German Americans were stoned in several East Coast cities, sauerkraut became "liberty cabbage," and German books were removed from the libraries of Springfield. Ted's mother and sister knitted clothes for American soldiers, among whom numbered forty-seven from Springfield.

By 1941 Geisel was fed up with Adolf Hitler and Benito Mussolini. He and Helen, visiting Italy, had heard radio speeches by the Italian leader as early as 1926. Ten years later Geisel's mood had been heavy returning from Europe, the nascent stages of *Mulberry Street* not engrossing enough to obviate his dread regarding Germany's new dictator (Morgan 54, 80). In the off hours, in the wake of the German march on Paris, Geisel started sketching politically charged cartoons. He showed one to his friend Zinny Vanderlip Schoales, who had joined Ralph Ingersoll on the tabloid *PM*, and it ran on January 30, 1941 (Morgan 100). A slap at Virginio Gayda, editor of the fascist propaganda organ *Il Giornale d'Italia* and Seuss's "second choice" for "the world's most outstanding writer of fantasy"—Seuss reserved the pole position for himself—the cartoon was the first of more than four hundred he contributed to the magazine over two years (Minear, *Dr. Seuss Goes to War* 10–11).

An advocate of President Franklin Delano Roosevelt's New Deal politics, *PM* overtly opposed isolationism, anti-Semitism, anti-black racism and, as its manifesto stated, "people who push other people around." (Minear 13). Seuss joined a list of contributors that included James Thurber, Lillian Hellman, and Erskine Caldwell. His cartoons criticized American hesitation over entering the war and savaged a clueless, infantilized, buffoonish Hitler when few other editorial cartoonists dared. They dogged former aviator Charles A. Lindbergh, an outspoken Hitler admirer, left neither Mussolini nor Emperor Hirohito untouched, and rallied American morale after Pearl Harbor. Seuss's work eventually expanded to challenge anti-Semitism and the racism directed at American blacks. As Richard H. Minear points out in *Dr. Seuss Goes to War: The World War II Editorial Cartoons of Theodor Seuss Geisel* (1999), Seuss linked the two issues, and linked them to Hitler. However, according to Minear some cartoons also demonstrate a "blind spot" regarding the Japanese and Japanese Americans. Seuss crudely, perhaps cruelly, stereotyped the former, while neglecting to speak up when nearly 120,000 of the latter were interred in California in 1942 (Minear 24–25).

Seuss's drawings are replete with contorted contraptions, entangled personae, and gaudy creatures—whether anthropomorphized beasts or humans degraded by evil—that prefigure the more embellished menagerie, makeshift mechanisms, and labyrinthine lineups in his later work. The contemporary artist Art Spiegelman claims in his introduction to Minear's book that the drawings evidence Seuss developing "his goofily surreal vision while he delivers the ethical goods." (quoted in Minear 7). Some cartoons feature rhyme, punning, and clichés to make their funny but fiery points. Others, especially his contribution of July 20, 1942, are blunt, if not shocking: as French wartime premier Pierre Laval sings with Hitler, who sports a rope, ten bodies bearing placards that read "JEW" hang from trees in the dark behind (Minear 101). That the death camps were not general knowledge until months later renders Seuss's vision of a pogrom-lynching even more portentous (Minear 77).

Having recently moved with Helen to La Jolla, California, Geisel applied for a commission with naval intelligence but was given a place in the Signal Corps in Hollywood. He was inducted into the army in January 1943 and assigned to the Information and Education Division, based in a leased Fox film studio dubbed Fort Fox. Supervised by the film director Frank Capra, the unit included other creative types such as Irving Wallace, Paul Horgan, and Meredith Willson (Morgan 106–107). Geisel learned screenwriting and later acknowledged Capra with having taught him concision and the juxtaposition of word and image. Another tutor in the military, the illustrator Chuck Jones, instructed Geisel in the art of

animation. Over the next two years, Geisel helped create biweekly newsreels and animated cartoons, such as the *Private Snafu* series, for *Army-Navy Screen Magazine*; his work exploited humor to produce training messages for soldiers (Morgan 109).

Geisel was assigned by Capra to a longer film, *Your Job in Germany*, intended for the armed servicemen who would soon occupy that country. The script, approved by Roosevelt's cabinet, followed Roosevelt and Winston Churchill's imperative that American soldiers refrain from fraternizing with Germans. Geisel, who wrote and produced the film despite reservations regarding its conclusion of nonfraternization, was sent to Western Europe to show the film to American generals; he was trapped behind German lines for three days during the Battle of the Bulge. Once back at Fort Fox, Geisel started on an assigned film meant to assist the prevention of a third world war. But when his treatment, addressing the threat of massive explosions, prefigured the use of the atomic bomb in uncannily accurate terms, the Office of Scientific Research and Development ordered him to burn it (Morgan 110–115). Geisel departed the army in January 1946, a lieutenant colonel with the Legion of Merit. The cinematic apprenticeship he had begun in an altered Hollywood was not over, however, and would flourish after the war.

MULTIMEDIA

Geisel's work won a trio of Academy Awards. *Hitler Lives?*, a remake of *Your Job in Germany*, earned one in 1946 for best documentary on a short subject. While Geisel was given little credit, the film's success opened doors in Hollywood for him (Morgan 118). He was working for Warner Brothers when RKO proposed that he write an adaptation of *Your Job in Japan*, recently created with Capra. The result earned Geisel and Helen, with whom he collaborated, an Oscar for best feature-length documentary of 1947, but not without a price. Focusing on reeducation of the Japanese, the original version included an ethnocentric voiceover about "what we like to call the American way, or democracy, or just

plain old Golden Rule common sense." Editing heavily, RKO spliced in Sherman tanks during a sequence about sixteenth-century Japan, then retitled the movie *Design for Death*. Geisel's third Oscar, in 1951 for best cartoon, honored *Gerald McBoing-Boing*, a cartoon about a boy who cannot speak but who makes noises and hence finds success as a radio sound-effects guru.

Geisel visited Japan in 1953, less than a decade after the bombings of Hiroshima and Nagasaki, under contract with *Life* to write about how American occupation had affected the aspirations of schoolchildren. The piece appeared as "Japan's Young Dreams" but was largely rewritten (Morgan 136–137). Nonetheless, inspired by his observations in Japan, Geisel conceived *Horton Hears a Who!* (1954), in which an elephant hero discovers, on a speck of dust, a city called Whoville. Its zany, tipsy avenues and apartments vaguely reminiscent of the architecture of Antoni Gaudí or designs of M.C. Escher, the village is inhabited by miniscule folk in constant danger of being snuffed out.

Horton's pledge to stick by them—his desideratum is, "A person's a person, no matter how small"—and the book's lesson about the difference a single "yopp" makes, prompted critics in competing directions. The *Des Moines Register* called the book "a rhymed lesson in protection of minorities and their rights," and Ruth K. MacDonald, going even further, claimed that Horton "represents postwar United States in the international community of nations." (quoted in Morgan 151, and in Minear 264). Minear, on the other hand, underlines that if the moral is partly democratic and broadly humanistic, it is not without suggestions of paternalism.

Geisel would receive a Peabody Award for a television adaptation of the book in 1971, and another the same year for his adaptation of *How the Grinch Stole Christmas!* (1957), collaborating with Chuck Jones on the television version. *Grinch* was expensive and strenuous to make, but it quickly became one of the most popular TV holiday specials of all time, despite its anticommercial message that Christmas is not about receiving presents but about fellowship (Morgan 223). To some extent the success of the thirty-

minute special compensated for an earlier failure that still rankled with Geisel. In the early 1950s he had struggled to realize a feature-length fantasy with live actors called *The 5,000 Fingers of Dr. T.* Geisel was burdened throughout the production by frustrations regarding the script, dropping out several times (Morgan 132–135). Released in 1953, the movie was a bust, and Geisel was so dejected that he refused to include it in his official Random House biography.

More personal discouragement found Geisel the next year when Helen developed Guillan-Barré syndrome. Following weeks of paralysis, she was able to walk again, but not without constant pain. Despite this family worry, Geisel pursued further multimedia endeavors. He had demonstrated creative restlessness as early as 1939, when he patented an "Infantograph," which projected a child's appearance by superimposing photographs of parents' faces on the outline of a baby's face (Morgan 91). In the fifties Geisel tried (fruitlessly) to adapt *The Seven Lady Godivas* as a Broadway musical, and he became a trustee of the San Diego Fine Arts Museum. In 1954 he wrote a pamphlet in favor of a local billboard ban for the La Jolla Town Council, and this eight-page *Signs of Civilization!* lost him an advertising contract with Holly Sugar (Morgan 147).

Geisel considered authoring a textbook on writing for children. The idea emerged from a series of well-received lectures he delivered in July 1949 during a ten-day writers' conference at the University of Utah, where he joined Vladimir Nabokov, Wallace Stegner, William Carlos Williams, John Crowe Ransom, and other novelists and poets invited to discuss their respective crafts. Much to Geisel's disappointment, Random House rejected his proposal, claiming that a "semiformal" book would draw only criticism as well as hinder his creative output (Morgan 123, 125).

THE METHOD BEHIND THE MADNESS

Seuss's lecture notes from that conference are among the few documents explicitly detailing their author's "literary" tenets and tendencies.

Geisel prepared rigorously, doing extensive research on texts ranging from classical myth to the nineteenth-century novel. As Judith and Neil Morgan summarize in their excellent biography *Dr. Seuss and Mr. Geisel* (1995), he deemed the fables of Aesop overly cold, mathematical, and abstract, and while *The Odyssey* was "exciting" he considered *The Iliad* "too complicated." He admired the "great roguish tricks" in *Robin Hood*, along with the wit of Hans Christian Andersen, Mark Twain, and Robert Louis Stevenson, and claimed that *Robinson Crusoe* met "the seven needs" of children: love, security, belonging, aesthetics, change, to achieve, and to know. Seuss cited himself among the pantheon of five "nonsense" writers, next to Mother Goose, Edward Lear, Lewis Carroll, and P. L. Travers. He cautioned his students that kids must be kidded seriously. "A man with two heads is not a story," Seuss remarked. "It is a situation to be built upon logically. He must have two hats and two toothbrushes." (Morgan 123–124).

Critics have cited numerous writers as comprising Dr. Seuss's lineage. The nonsensical vision of Carroll, with its "Jabberwocky" and "Snark" and its romping, roundabout Wonderland plots, is frequently invoked when discussing Seuss, as are the weird, exhilarating rhymes of Edward Lear. The *New York Times* obituary for Seuss labels him a "modern Mother Goose," but the columnist Ellen Goodman has rejected that appellation on the grounds that Seuss was more "subversive." (quoted in Morgan 290). Readers have connected Seuss with the eerie, didactic mode of the Brothers Grimm, with the allegorical angle of Aesop, and with Mark Twain's Americanized versions of picaresque and the coming-of-age narrative. The novelist Alison Lurie claims, in a 1990 essay in the *New York Review of Books*, that Seuss's innovations spring from the genres of American popular humor and the nineteenth-century tall tale (cited in Fensch, *Of Sneetches* 157). Seuss's satirical side has been favorably compared to Swift, his anti-authoritarianism to Voltaire and Hilaire Belloc, his mischievous impulse with the Uncle Remus tales and the long tradition, across Native American and African American cultures, of the trickster-hero.

The most far-reaching, occasionally far-fetched elaboration of Seuss's literary antecedents has been put forward by Jonathan Cott in his *Pipers at the Gates of Dawn: The Wisdom of Children's Literature* (1983). Cott links Seuss's unusual animals to those of "the tao-tieh of the Chinese Bronze Age, ... the fourth-century *Physiologus*, medieval bestiaries, and Topsell's seventeenth-century *The Historie of Fourefooted Beastes*," as well as to those of Father André Thevet and the British child-author Sybil Corbet's 1897 *Animal Land Where There Are No People*. According to Cott, later Seuss books such as *Mr. Brown Can Moo! Can You?* (1970) and especially *The Cat in the Hat Songbook* (1967) evidence a connection to "the wonderful tradition of American nonsense songs." Cott notes that the anapestic tetrameter characteristic of "movement and swiftness" in Seuss's work can be detected in Sir Walter Scott's translation of Goethe's "The Erl-King," a poem that, like *Mulberry Street*, depicts a son exaggerating to his father. When asked about the poem, Seuss claimed it had not inspired his book—though he had it memorized in German. Cott proposes that Seuss, as seen in *The King's Stilts*, exemplifies Friedrich Nietzsche's statement that "in any true man hides a child who wants to play."

Seuss's midcareer work employs numerous designs for playing. *McElligot's Pool* (1947), his only book in watercolor, reintroduces Marco and his imagination for inventing "Some sort of a kind of / A THING-A-MA-JIGGER." As Marco elaborates a wild, piscine compendium to a farmer, the book reprises the parade of *Mulberry Street* by positing an aquatic route running under highways, houses, hotels, and mountains, to the sea, its narrative drift effecting Seuss's statement that he liked to approach books "with a situation or a conflict and then write myself into an impossible position so there is no way of ending." (quoted in Morgan 128–129). That method landed Seuss a Junior Literary Guild selection and his first Caldecott citation for art. Geisel possessed such a strong sense of color that his art editors at Random House, whom he often instructed to devise new shades, considered his chromatic intuition the visual equivalent of perfect pitch.

The following year another Seuss book became a Junior Literary Guild selection, *Thidwick the Big-Hearted Moose* (1948), which looks at altruism. As Thidwick accommodates an untenable burden of forest creatures on his head, the author loads rhyme upon rhyme, sometimes interrupted by a page-turn to build suspense. The book was followed by Seuss's final publication in prose, *Bartholomew and the Oobleck* (1949). Partly a warning to be careful what you wish for, the tale equally comments on its author's poetics: the sticky green oobleck "goo," like Seuss's accretive, creative impulse, causes everything to cluster: "Goats were getting stuck to ducks. Geese were getting stuck to cows." Seuss was now less inclined toward the straightforward narratives that had characterized his earlier "moral" tales and far more likely to meander, stack things up, and get carried away.

Selma G. Lanes was one of the first children's literature experts to identify and legitimize this method in Seuss's work. Her *Down the Rabbit Hole: Adventures and Misadventures in the Realm of Children's Literature* (1971) refers to Seuss's unusual modus operandi as "anxiety-filled diversion," her explanation one that Geisel found fascinating and flattering. Lanes writes:

In recognizing that children's craving for excitement, in their books as in their lives, is often merely the means for releasing pent-up anxiety, Seuss cannily manages to magnify and multiply the sense of suspense in his stories, not so much by the ingenuity of his plots as by a clever and relentless piling on of gratuitous anxiety until the child is fairly ready to cry "uncle" and settle for any resolution, however mundane, that will end his at once marvelous, exquisite and finally unbearable tension (Lanes, quoted in Fensch, *Of Sneetches* 45).

An example of this tension can be found in *If I Ran the Zoo* (1950), in which young Gerald McGrew wants more exciting animals on display. Creating aloud the "New Zoo, McGrew Zoo," he founds a hypothetical Noah's Ark of creatures meek and sleek, cute and queer, hybrid and scrawny and bombastic. By the end, nothing has happened, aside from the enumeration of an inventory, from a "wild Tick-Tack-Toe" to "a

scraggle-foot Mulligatawny." The beasts become so legion and abnormal that the verse must be equally capricious and experimental to hold them. The boy says:

And, speaking of birds, there's the Russian Palooski,
Whose headski is redski and belly is blueski.
I'll get one of *them* for my Zooski McGrewski.

Seuss often mapped his verse according to its rhythm, filling in the blank end-rhymes later.

The result here is a heap of tension, signaled overtly by the book's question about the aspiring zookeeper: "When do you suppose this young fellow will stop?" The outcome: Seuss returns us to a boy standing by the real zookeeper, having merely recounted his besting bestiary. Hence "the process" of the fiction, according to Lanes, "is not unlike the blowing up of a balloon: bigger, bigger, bigger and finally, when the bursting point is reached, Seuss simply releases his grip." (Lanes, quoted in Fensch, *Of Sneetches* 45–46). The formula is repeated in *If I Ran the Circus* (1956), when Morris McGurk creates the Circus McGurkus, while an acrobatic old man named Sneelock daredevils around the illustrations with apparent nonchalance. Less a story than a crowded apologia for originality, in which Seuss in one drawing even uses commas and question marks within the image itself, the book closes with Morris having bragged about how his circus *would* be. The hypothetical buildup diffused, Seuss provides "his young disciples with a literary release not so far removed from orgasm."

Seuss's work, however, seems less about quasi-sexual gratification than unqualified competition. Both *If I Ran the Zoo* and *If I Ran the Circus* obsess about how bewildered and wowed an audience will be at the sight of novel, improved spectacles. Other books from this period, such as *Scrambled Eggs Super!* (1953), only up the ante. Little Peter T. Hooper complains that scrambled eggs "always taste always the same" because they are always made from hen eggs. Hence his quest "to make the best scramble that's ever been made," a desire for the deluxe that sends him far afield for unheard-of fowl. "If you want to get eggs you can't buy at a store, / You have to do things never thought of before," says Peter, the

produce he comes up with including eggs that taste like the air in Swiss-cheese holes.

On Beyond Zebra! (1955) likewise probes the limits of the imagination with a competitive spirit. The protagonist explains to Conrad Cornelius o'Donald o'Dell, his "very young friend who is learning to spell," that he is dissatisfied with the normal alphabet, confiding,

In the places I go there are things that I see
That I *never* could spell if I stopped with the Z.
I'm telling you this 'cause you're one of my friends.
My alphabet starts where *your* alphabet ends!

The pages advise readers to discover new creatures and fanciful letters, to transcend the vision of "most people," who stop at the twenty-sixth letter and thereby get "stuck in a rut." Like his protagonist, for whom the old alphabet is not sufficient, Seuss had decided that children's writing was in need of an overhaul.

THE DEATH OF DICK AND JANE

The late 1950s witnessed worries in the United States centered around the Cold War, among them the space race, the nuclear arms race, and a panic that American children were not learning to read well enough. Rudolf Flesch's best-selling *Why Johnny Can't Read: And What You Can Do about It* (1955) both prompted and crystallized this last hysteria, lambasting orthodox school primers as "horrible, stupid, emasculated, pointless, tasteless" instruments, with plots limited to "totally unexciting middle-class, middle-income, middle-I.Q. children's activities." (quoted in Menand 148–149). Flesch also believed Dick and Jane primers were misguided. The correct method for teaching children to read, he believed, was not word recognition but phonics, and he ended his book with seventy-two word lists for parents to practice with their children. The conclusion of his socio-linguistic enterprise was that the failure of American public schools threatened American democracy and dreams (Menand 149–150).

A year earlier, writer John Hersey had published in *Life* a provocative article attacking the "pallid" orthodox primer as an "antiseptic little sugar-book" featuring "abnormally courteous,

unnaturally clean boys and girls." (quoted in Morgan 153–154). Hersey's invective against these "uniform, bland, idealized and terribly literal" texts closed with an appeal for reform among school primers. "Why should they not have pictures that widen rather than narrow the associative richness that children give to the words they illustrate," he asked, "drawings like those of the wonderfully imaginative geniuses among children's illustrators, Tenniel, Howard Pyle, 'Dr. Seuss,' Walt Disney?"

Flesch's and Hersey's writings exerted an influence on William Spaulding, the director of Houghton Mifflin's education division. Spaulding feared that television, comic books, and crass commercialism were sowing illiteracy. Following Hersey's suggestion, he proposed that Geisel write a children's primer, using a limited number of words approved by experts in phonetics, as antidote to the detrimental prevailing trend. Spaulding sent Seuss three lists of 220 words each from which Seuss created a new list containing 199 of these words and twenty-one of his own. Although Seuss initially balked at the whole project as "impossible and ridiculous," he persisted for nine months, experiencing enormous difficulty but eventually deciding to create the title out of the first two words from the word list that rhymed-"cat" and "hat." On top of the nomenclature and numbers game, Seuss arranged the entire story in rhymed anapestic dimeter.

The Cat in the Hat was published in March 1957 to little hullabaloo. The reviews it garnered, though, instantly signaled what the Morgans term an "innovative coup," defying and exasperating long-established educational conventions through its galloping but controlled verse, as well as via its vivid, bald reds and blues (Morgan 155). Hersey hailed the breakthrough as a "harum-scarum masterpiece"; Clifton Fadiman praised it as "probably the most influential first-grade reader since McGuffey"; and *Newsweek*, as if avenging Geisel's rejection by Blackwell thirty years earlier, called Seuss "the moppets' Milton." (quoted in Morgan 156).

Moreover, as literary critic Louis Menand relays in "Cat People: What Dr. Seuss Really Taught Us," an incisive essay published in the *New Yorker*, the book got a publicity push from Cold-War anxieties (Menand 150). Seven months after *The Cat in the Hat* came out, the Soviets launched Sputnik. The Russian satellite served both the popular and military-industrial imaginations as harbinger that the United States, with its inferior educational system, was falling behind the USSR technologically. Within weeks, Seuss's magnum opus was selling twelve thousand copies per month (Menand 150, 152). In addition the decade marked the apogee of the baby boom in the United States, with 3.9 million children born in 1952 and 4.3 million in 1957, the year of *The Cat in the Hat*. By 1960 the literary phenomenon had sold almost a million copies, and editions had begun appearing internationally (Morgan 156)

The Cat in the Hat is the story of how Sally and "I," on a cold day while their mother is away, are surprised by the advent of a top-hatted cat keen to stir "Lots of good fun that is funny!" The Cat tenuously holds an assortment of domestic objects while standing on a ball, until eventually he falls. Then he produces, from out of a box, a pair of assistants, Thing One and Thing Two, to help him engineer more games, such as flying kites in the house. The feline trickster's moral opponent during the upheaval is a nagging, naysaying goldfish, who, as Jonathan Cott writes, is "a combination superego and what Geisel calls 'my version of Cotton Mather,'" who cannot abide the Cat's presence, let alone his unruly predilections (Cott, quoted in Fensch, Of Sneetches 116). By the end, the Cat employs a convoluted machine to pick up the mess before the arrival of the mother, whose dress, leg, and upraised hand are glimpsed in several frames—although the authority figure is never viewed in her entirety.

Critics have fixated on the missing mom and the permission her absence engenders. Menand, for instance, senses behind this figure "of the *mater abscondita*" a host of hidden transgressions, hypocrisies, and "private demons and desires," as Seuss attempts to explain, through fiction, the fact that "'fun' is only a distraction from the reality of separation and abandonment." (Menand 148, 154). Lanes concurs that "what

Seuss means by fun" is actually something forbidden, the story's milieu being "just the sort of world no child's mother would put up with for one instant." Lanes continues, "The greatest pleasure in Seuss is derived from the sense of having a season pass to utter chaos with no personal responsibility for any of it." (Lanes, quoted in Fensch, *Of Sneetches* 47).

It is this drive in Seuss for allowing young readers to experience vicarious pleasure, protected by the assurance that they will not be punished, that has generated the view of Seuss as champion of children and their imaginations over adult restriction and retribution. It is not clear whether the Cat is the tale's protagonist or, on the contrary, its most antagonistic force, and this rich ambiguity is integral to Seuss's rebellious project. Moreover the tale harbors a self-conscious metalinguistic vector. Menand sees the Cat as a *bricoleur* standing in for the good doctor himself, building with what he has, his "improvisations with the *objets trouvés* in the home he has invaded" an "allegory for his creator's performance with the two hundred and twenty arbitrary words he has been assigned by his publisher." (Menand 153).

That the Cat fails to hold his *bricolage* together indexes a "semantic instability," and it is this hint of deconstructionist demolition that impels Seuss's more complicated, if less popular, sequel, *The Cat in the Hat Comes Back* (1958). As Sally and "I" shovel snow, the mother gone once again on some mysterious errand, the Cat arrives and lets himself into the house. He eats a piece of cake while taking a bath, leaving a pink ring in the tub. The story then follows the erratic itinerary of this pink stain, as the Cat pretends to try to efface it, from the tub to mother's dress, then to the wall, from there to a series of other locales—dad's shoes, a rug, the television—until eventually it is blown by a fan outside, where it taints the snow that Sally and "I" had been trying to clear. The Cat solicits the help of other, increasingly smaller cats, heretofore hidden under his hat, beginning with Little Cat A and concluding with invisible Little Cat Z.

It is precisely the question of conclusion, however, that is at stake, since the narrative is nothing other than an enactment of deferral. "*The Cat in the Hat Comes Back* is the 'Grammatology' of Dr. Seuss," writes Menand, referring to Jacques Derrida's seminal deconstructionist study, as well as to an earlier linguistic milieu defined by Noam Chomsky, Claude Lévi-Strauss, and other post-structuralist avatars. Menand observes: "These semiotic felines do exactly what a deconstructionist would predict: rather than containing the stain, they disseminate it. Everything turns pink. The chain of signification is interminable and, being interminable, indeterminate. The semantic hygiene fetishized by the children is rudely violated." (Menand 154). That the semiotic stain is both "pink" and ubiquitous reverberates with Cold-War paranoia about communism, as does the feline interloper's invasion of an unlocked house. The book traffics in further undertones of sociopolitical insecurity and sexual insurrection: children with "no time for games" because of the "work to be done"; the intruder's survey of Dad's bedroom to determine whether he has "the right kind of bed"; and the last-ditch recourse to an explosive material called "Voom" that "cleans up anything."

"Voom" is exactly what Seuss's pioneering approach to reading became to the world of children's literature. Along with Bennett Cerf's wife, Phyllis, and with Helen as a third partner, Geisel formed the publishing house Beginner Books, with Random House as distributor and eventual owner. The operation provided an outlet for children's book authors to publish fun, instructive work that conformed to guidelines. According to the Morgans, among those mandates were a list, devised by Phyllis, of 379 words, from which writers could choose 220; a rule that "the text should not describe anything ... not pictured," in order to assist debutant readers in learning the words' meanings; and a stipulation that there be only one illustration per page (Morgan 158, 160). As president, Geisel was demanding with his authors, and he and Phyllis frequently quarreled over his standards, such as when he rejected a submission from Truman Capote. By 1963, Phyllis had left Beginner Books. Five years later, Bright & Early Books, a new line of Beginner Books geared toward pre-

kindergarteners, debuted with Seuss's *The Foot Book* (1968).

Some 250 publishers had become involved in the children's book trade, but Random House was by far the largest, one-third of its revenue stemming from children's books. The majority of those earnings resulted from Seuss's solidified celebrity, as he contributed books to the Beginner Books series, such as *One Fish Two Fish Red Fish Blue Fish* (1960) and *Fox in Socks* (1965). The first is an episodic, notational roll call of animals and a rhapsody for how "funny things are everywhere." The other proliferates with linguistic permutations and tongue twisters, its provocative front cover teasing, "This is a book you READ ALOUD to find out just how smart your tongue is. The first time you read it, don't go fast! This Fox is a tricky fox. He'll try to get your tongue in trouble." There are literal "bricks and blocks" in the tale, demonstrating how words get built by letters and sentences by words, initiating readers into the pleasure of making— and unmaking—meaning.

Seuss's best-known, most beloved Beginner Book, *Green Eggs and Ham* (1960), began when Bennett Cerf bet Geisel that he could not write a story using merely fifty words. The outcome remains the fourth best-selling children's book of all time, millions of American tikes and parents having been raised on its viridian, non-vegetarian, versified diet. The book features inverted utterances, compressed phrases, vertiginous trills of rhyme, litanies repeated back in negative, and the climactic, anaphoric affirmation:

And I will eat them in the rain.
And in the dark. And on a train.
And in a car. And in a tree.
They are so good, so good, you see!

...

And I will eat them here and there.
Say! I will eat them ANYWHERE!

Green Eggs and Ham is a monosyllabic tour de force—"anywhere," appearing eight times, is its sole polysyllable—illuminating how to give in to novelty, how to do things with words. It also epitomizes why Seuss was responsible, as the columnist Anna Quindlen has written, "for the

murder of Dick and Jane, which was a mercy killing of the highest order." (quoted in Morgan 290).

ANTI-"PREACHMENTS" AND "ANTICRAZY"

There was tension in the Geisel marriage during the 1960s, spurred by increasing demands on Geisel's time and energy, and Helen suffered from depression. On October 23, 1967, she was pronounced dead after overdosing on sodium pentobarbital. In a note left for her husband, she admitted to being "enmeshed in everything you do and are," and asked him to "Sometimes, think of the fun we had all thru the years." While Helen had written four children's books and served as president of the La Jolla Art Museum, she was remembered in her obituaries as Dr. Seuss's primary critic, editor, manager, and companion. The suicide of his wife, his foremost emotional support for four decades, not to mention a buffer against a practical world he often did not understand, gutted Geisel. "I didn't know whether to kill myself," he confided to a friend, "burn the house down, or just go away and get lost." (Morgan 195–196, 198).

The fictive travails that Seuss had written about in *I Had Trouble in Getting to Solla Sollew* (1965) were suddenly real. That book documents the frustrating search, through "the Valley of Vung" that is a veil of tears, for a faraway land of "No troubles at all." The planes-trains-and-automobiles chase concludes, however, with the narrator's resolution that hardships exist, and that the best one can do is be prepared. His final gesture is to buy a bat, proclaiming, "Now my troubles are going / To have troubles with *me!*" Aggression is reprised in the first of three tales comprising *I Can Lick 30 Tigers Today! and Other Stories* (1969), as the narrator boasts of his prowess for slaying an entourage of jungle cats. Eventually he concedes and flees the danger, though, leaving readers to wonder to what degree Geisel was confessing his own fear, fragility, and failure.

In August 1968, Geisel wedded a woman eighteen years his junior, Audrey Dimond, who divorced his best friend, Grey Dimond, specifi-

cally to remarry. The newlyweds were initially unpopular with a suspicious La Jolla community that continued to adore Helen's memory. Opinions differed, though, as to whether Audrey was indirectly responsible for Helen's demise or if, on the contrary, she represented a welcome relief after the discipline that Helen had always leveled (Morgan 205). Audrey would remain with Geisel for the rest of his life.

A certain "moral" vision, however contradictory across his oeuvre, had already characterized a significant portion of Seuss's work. *Solla Sollew* is equally marked by a message, albeit one whose notion of triumphing over adversity is disconcertingly premised on a comparativist, bourgeois worldview with which the later *Did I Ever Tell You How Lucky You Are?* (1973) is likewise freighted. Two further "morality tales" had gotten slightly lost in the shuffle: *Yertle the Turtle and Other Stories* (1958) had been overshadowed by the attention given to the blockbuster *Cat* the year before, while *The Sneetches and Other Stories* (1961) had been hard to hear above the hue and cry for its predecessor, *Green Eggs and Ham.*

When the reigning Yertle decides, in the former volume, that his kingdom is too small, that he cannot see the "places beyond," he enlists other turtles upon whose shells he can sit. His rage to go higher installs a type of slavery, and soon he has piled up two hundred terrapins, sees forty miles, brags that he is taller even than the clouds, and sets his sights on heaven. But the lowliest reptile, Mack, hollers that "down at the bottom we, too, should have rights," and when he's finally fed up, he burps. The entire pillar crumbles, as Yertle is cast down into the mud. Seuss identified the megalomaniacal turtle with Hitler, and his tale demonstrates the peril and punishment of hubris, the efficacy of the little man, and the inherent political freedom of everyone.

The title story of *The Sneetches* appropriates the Holocaust more explicitly, while inverting its basic terms: the Star-Belly Sneetches consider themselves superior to the Plain-Belly Sneetches. A series of swaps ensues when the Plain-Belly Sneetches find a machine to assign them their own stars; once the Plain-Belly Sneetches are

starred, the original Star-Belly Sneetches decide to efface their symbols with a Star-Off Machine. The on-again, off-again stellar volley illustrates the arbitrary nature of insignias and the insane logic of ideologies that deploy them. While the book satirizes theories of exclusivity, it also warns against the capitalist knack for creating demand. The mercenary Sylvester McMonkey McBean peddles his star-making and star-erasing machines to both clans of Sneetches before finally driving off with all the money. It takes mutual bankruptcy to force the victims of his commercialism to embrace one another under the motto, "Sneetches are Sneetches."

Geisel worried that the story's obvious parallel to the Nazi extermination of Jews would somehow harm the book or compromise its integrity. While possessing a strong moral imperative, Geisel generally wished to avoid what he called "preachments," or overly didactic tales, not least because he felt that children's literature had a history of condescendingly lecturing kids, who ought instead to be treated as adults (quoted in Gorney, from Fensch, *Of Sneetches* 88). Nonetheless, "Every once in a while I get mad," he admitted, and this was certainly the case with *The Lorax* (1971), Seuss's most polemical book, which he "intended to be propaganda," since he had become "angry about the ecology problems." (quoted in Cott and in Frutig, from Fensch, *Of Sneetches* 118, 80). Inspired by a herd of elephants Geisel had watched cross a mountain in Kenya, the book also emanated from his view of a San Diego coastline that, once empty and beautiful, was now jammed with monotone condos and tourist traffic (Morgan 210).

Long ago, so the story goes, the Once-ler chopped down a Truffula Tree to knit a Thneed out of its tuft. Because the tree could not speak, a creature known as the Lorax emerged from the trunk to defend it. Soon, however, a factory was felling trees and producing garments, for the sheer sake of "business," and the machinery choked the entire ecosystem. When the last tree had vanished, only the Once-ler and the Lorax remained, and by the book's present tense, the latter has also disappeared. He has been literally replaced by the pile of rocks he leaves behind, a

tomb of sorts bearing the foreboding inscription "UNLESS." As the Once-ler recounts his confession, his final act is to entrust the last Truffula Seed to a boy, with instructions to plant it.

Geisel had been accustomed to writing in opposition to perceived errors and evils. What was new about *The Lorax*, intended not for already informed perusers of political editorials but, rather, for young readers, was its unapologetically invective tone and its stark, cynical vision. Behind the Once-ler's admission, "I biggered my factory. I biggered my roads. / I biggered my wagons. I biggered the loads," one cannot help but hear the elided verb "bugger." Seuss had injected real vitriol into this so-called children's book, and reviewers were consequently divided. Some applauded the book's responsible eco-social message, while others deplored its bleak outlook and lack of characteristic Seussian humor.

Liz Carpenter, the press secretary for Lady Bird Johnson, convinced Geisel to donate the manuscript and artwork to the Lyndon B. Johnson Presidential Library in Austin, Texas, and the author was happy to allow the First Lady to use the gift to further her environmental concerns (Morgan 211). It was not for another decade, however, when the environmental movement had begun claiming popular legitimacy, that *The Lorax* garnered major publicity. In 1989 it provoked controversy in the redwood-logging town of Laytonville, California, where a campaign was started to have it removed from second-grade reading lists. The proposed ban drew national media attention, and the school-board president ruled to keep the book instated. "*The Lorax* doesn't say lumbering is immoral," Geisel claimed. "It's a book about going easy on what we've got. It's antipollution and antigreed." (Morgan 278).

Geisel deployed similar rhetoric regarding the nuclear arms race, which he believed to be out of control under Ronald Reagan's presidency in the early 1980s. "I'm not antimilitary," Geisel proclaimed, "I'm just anticrazy." (Morgan 249). No longer the hawk he had been during World War II, Geisel wrote *The Butter Battle Book* (1984) in response to the arms escalation being

practiced by the United States and the USSR, admitting he had "no idea if this is an adult book for children or a children's book for adults." (Morgan 250). It not only capped the juvenile best-seller lists but also reached number one on the *New York Times Book Review* fiction list (Morgan 255). A copyeditor at Random House saw a link between the tale and an episode in Jonathan Swift's *Gulliver's Travels*—the Lilliputians' dispute over which end of an egg should be broken, which leads to war—while fellow children's book author Maurice Sendak observed, "Only a genius of the ridiculous could possibly deal with the cosmic and lethal madness of the nuclear arms race." (Morgan 252).

An exploration of impasse and the impassioned will to dominate, a hard stare at paranoia and stupidity, *The Butter Battle Book* posits the Yooks on this side of a wall and the Zooks on the other. While the Yooks eat their bread with the butter side up, the Zooks eat it butter side down. Consequently, a Yook explains to his grandson, every Zook "has kinks in his soul," and the whole lot are not to be trusted. The grandfather had served in the Zook-Watching Border Patrol as a youth. As he lists the weapons that had been devised by the Boys in the Back Room, in the classic Seussian mode of accretion and augmentation the weaponry goes from switch to triple slingshot, catapult to eight-nozzled gun. But the Zooks of course continually respond in kind, and the one-upmanship percolates until a little pink bomb is invented by the Yooks. As the chronologically zigzaggy story catches up to present tense, the grandfather is standing on the wall, about to drop the bomb, when he is met by Van-Itch of the Zooks, who has exactly the same in his arsenal. The final frame depicts the boy asking, "Who's going to drop it? / Will *you* … ? Or will *he* … ?" And the response: "'Be patient,' said Grandpa. 'We'll see. / We will see. …'"

The book's subject and its lady-or-tiger ending pitted critics against one another. Some felt the arms race was not an appropriate topic for children, others believed the tale too bleak or overly simplistic, and occasional readers found it a form of brainwashing (Morgan 253–254). The journalist Art Buchwald proposed that Seuss,

already feted with several honorary doctorates and the Laura Ingalls Wilder Award for his "lasting contributions to children's literature," receive the Nobel Prize for literature. In the spring of 1984 Geisel won the Pulitzer Prize "for his contribution over nearly half a century to the education and enjoyment of America's children and their parents." (quoted in Morgan 241, 255) On New Year's Day in 1990, the televised version of the book aired in the Soviet Union.

LAST YEARS AND LEGACY

Geisel persisted as a versatile craftsman up to the end. By 1967, the Morgans note, "he had come to consider the word lists … to be 'hogwash' because television had expanded children's vocabularies," and in the seventies his *There's a Wocket in My Pocket!* (1974), *The Cat's Quizzer* (1976), and *Oh Say Can You Say?* (1979) demonstrated a devotion to linguistic innovation, subversion, and revelry. Similarly, *Oh, the Thinks You Can Think!* (1975) and *Hunches in Bunches* (1982) furthered his larger endeavor of urging kids to think, invent, and get "ga-fluppted" for themselves. Geisel's relentless drive to find new aesthetic material had manifested itself in *The Shape of Me and Other Stuff* (1973), composed entirely in silhouette, after he saw black-and-white photos of Inuit stone-cuts (Morgan 219), while *I Can Read with My Eyes Shut!* (1978), written during a five-year struggle with glaucoma, suggested that one need not even see to explore fantastic realms. Books written by Geisel but illustrated by others were published under pseudonyms, such as Theo. LeSieg and Rosetta Stone. An exhibition of his paintings was staged at the La Jolla Museum, and in 1986 he had a retrospective at the San Diego Museum of Art. While the show garnered enormous public attention, traveling around the country before landing in Springfield, it failed to satisfy Geisel's desire to be regarded a serious painter (Morgan 266).

You're Only Old Once! (1986) epitomizes the generic and generational problem that Seuss had become in the literary world. It was marketed by the adult trade division of Random House; the Book-of-the-Month Club steered it toward "ages 95 and down"; it was reviewed in the "Mind / Body / Health" section of the *New York Times*; and it topped that publication's adult nonfiction list. Dedicated "With Affection for / and / Afflictions with" Geisel's now octogenarian, mostly deceased Dartmouth class, the book indexes the woes of visiting the hospital. Characterized by esoteric departments, secretive clinicians who compete in Internal Organs Olympics, a female doctor peering up between the legs of an elderly male patient, and a Dr. Van Ness who resembles Hitler, the "Golden Years Clinic on Century Square / for Spleen Readjustment and Muffler Repair" is less haven than hell. The place is a panopticon of entrapment, subterfuge, and surveillance, complete with unwieldy contraptions and a voice issuing instructions over a speaker. The book's mock-prayer about pills, *"This long flat one is what I take / if I should die before I wake,"* could pertain only to adults and indicates Geisel's ironic sense of his own encroaching death.

Seuss's self-conscious adieu was *Oh, the Places You'll Go!* (1990). Quickly landing on the *New York Times* adult best-seller list, where it stayed for two years (Morgan 283), still a widely distributed gift at high school and university graduations, the book begins with

Congratulations!
Today is your day.
You're off to Great Places!
You're off and away!

before tackling Bang-Ups, Hang-Ups, and Slumps. In psychedelic colors and contours, *Places* cautions that life will be filled with trouble, games "you'll play against you," and encourages the reader onward, "though your arms may get sore / and your sneakers may leak." The upshot is that one will, in the end, succeed, provided one understands that "Life's / a Great Balancing Act."

This very drive to become "the winning-est winner of all," however, is what has bothered certain critics, not least Alison Lurie. Calling the book "the yuppie dream—or nightmare—of 1990 in cartoon form," she fears that Seuss's finale

sends a sinister message and that it represents a devolution in its author's outlook:

Now happiness no longer lies in exercising one's imagination, achieving, independence from tyrants, or helping weaker creatures. ... It is equated with wealth, fame, and getting ahead of others. Moreover, anything less than absolute success is seen as failure—a well-known American delusion, and a very destructive one. There are also no human relationships except that of competition—unlike most of Seuss's earlier protagonists, the hero has no friends and no family (Lurie, in Fensch, *Of Sneetches* 160, 163).

While opposed to the majority of efforts to market offshoots of his work, and though old-fashioned in his approach to book contracts, never accepting advance payment, Geisel had often cited the advantages of competition. "One reason kids are not reading up to their potential," he told Cynthia Gorney, "is a lack of being urged—you can't urge them with a big stick, but you can urge them with competition." (quoted in Fensch, *Of Sneetches* 89). Though his books often contain anti-capitalist leanings, others are premised on competing, and Geisel's life displayed this dissonance. "Theodor Geisel has played out two contradictory roles successfully," Rita Roth observes (quoted in Fensch, *Of Sneetches* 152). "As Geisel, he is a savvy businessman who knows the rules of the establishment and operates by those rules successfully enough to turn his stories into a multi-million dollar publishing business. As Dr. Seuss, the lighthearted author of children's books, he seeks to subvert the same establishment."

If competition necessarily implies inequality, another aspect of Seuss's work that critics have lamented is its conspicuous absence of women. "Of the 42 children's books Theodor Seuss Geisel published before his death," observes Jan Benzel, " ... not one had a title character who was female." (Benzel, in Fensch, *Of Sneetches* 182) Lurie too condemns the "almost total lack of female protagonists" in Seuss (Lurie, in Fensch, *Of Sneetches* 159). According to the Morgans, Geisel was perturbed by Lurie's review, pointing out that "most of his characters are animals 'and if she can identify their sex, I'll remember her in my will.'" (Morgan 286).

It was not until *Daisy-Head Mayzie*, based on an animated television special, was posthumously published in 1995 that Seuss's collected work claimed a strong female character. What few girls had appeared previously were either inferior or irresponsible. *Mayzie* had been started in the 1960s; Geisel's widow discovered the abandoned text of *Mayzie* after her husband's death. When Mayzie McGrew sprouts a daisy from her head, her school goes bonkers with excitement, until eventually "Daisy-Head fever" becomes a "world-wide sensation." The book is billed as a cautionary tale, for Mayzie becomes so popular, so imitated, that she loses sight of herself. If the tale's moral is noble—"But what is money without friends?"—there remains an implicit underside: if a girl gets too big for her britches, she will pay for it.

Seuss continues to be lauded as an advocate of children whose stories likewise appeal to adults—the very parents those same kids are wittily incited to defy. Geisel famously deplored the world of adulthood as unimaginative and restrictive: "Grownups," he complained, "have lost their sense of humor." Furthermore, "Adults are just obsolete children, and to hell with 'em." (quoted in Renthal and in Greenleaf, respectively, in Fensch, *Of Sneetches* 38, 96). Yet it is far from clear whether Geisel maintained either a strong personal rapport with children or an unqualified commitment to the greater pedagogical goal of children's writing. "I would like to say I went into children's-book work because of my great understanding of children," he stated (quoted in Lathem, in Fensch, *Of Sneetches* 73). "I went in because it wasn't excluded by my Standard Oil contract."

Seuss is credited with having engineered a sea change in literature for children, if not in American literature and language itself. Lines from *Fox in Socks* have entered *The Oxford Companion to the English Language* (1992) under "compounds in context," while the sixteenth edition of *Bartlett's Familiar Quotations* (1992) includes phrases from *The Cat in the Hat* and *Horton Hatches the Egg* (Morgan 291–292).

Theodor Seuss Geisel died on September 24, 1991, having delighted in this compliment once offered by a young fan: "Dr. Seuss has an imagination with a long tail." (quoted in Bunzel, in Fensch, *Of Sneetches* 13).

Selected Bibliography

WORKS OF DR. SEUSS

BOOKS ILLUSTRATED

Abingdon, Albert. *Boners..* New York: Viking, 1931.

Abingdon, Albert. *More Boners..* New York: Viking, 1931.

BOOKS WRITTEN AND ILLUSTRATED AS DR. SEUSS

And to Think That I Saw It on Mulberry Street. New York: Vanguard, 1937.

The 500 Hats of Bartholomew Cubbins. New York: Vanguard, 1938.

The King's Stilts. New York: Random House, 1939.

The Seven Lady Godivas. New York: Random House, 1939.

Horton Hatches the Egg. New York: Random House, 1940. 1940.

McElligot"s Pool. New York: Random House, 1947.

Thidwick the Big-Hearted Moose. New York: Random House, 1948.

Bartholomew and the Oobleck. New York: Random House, 1949.

If I Ran the Zoo. New York: Random House, 1950.

Scrambled Eggs Super! New York: Random House, 1953.

Horton Hears a Who! New York: Random House, 1954.

On Beyond Zebra! New York: Random House, 1955.

If I Ran the Circus. New York: Random House, 1956.

How the Grinch Stole Christmas! New York: Random House, 1957.

The Cat in the Hat. New York: Beginner Books/Random House, 1957.

The Cat in the Hat Comes Back. New York: Beginner Books/ Random House, 1958.

Yertle the Turtle and Other Stories. New York: Random House, 1958.

Happy Birthday to You! New York: Random House, 1959.

Green Eggs and Ham. New York: Beginner Books/Random House, 1960.

One Fish Two Fish Red Fish Blue Fish. New York: Beginner/Random House, 1960.

The Sneetches and Other Stories. New York: Random House, 1961.

Dr. Seuss's Sleep Book. New York: Random House, 1962.

Dr. Seuss's ABC. New York: Beginner Books/Random House, 1963.

Hop on Pop. New York: Beginner Books/Random House, 1963.

Fox in Socks. New York: Beginner Books/Random House, 1965.

I Had Trouble in Getting to Solla Sollew. New York: Random House, 1965.

The Cat in the Hat Songbook. New York: Random House, 1967.

The Foot Book. New York: Bright & Early Books/Random House, 1968.

I Can Lick 30 Tigers Today! and Other Stories. New York: Random House, 1969.

My Book About Me: By Me, Myself. Illustrated by Roy McKié. New York: Beginner Books/Random House, 1969.

I Can Draw It Myself. New York: Beginner Books/Random House, 1970.

Mr. Brown Can Moo! Can You? New York: Bright & Early Books/Random House, 1970.

The Lorax. New York: Random House, 1971.

Marvin K. Mooney Will You Please Go Now! New York: Bright & Early Books/Random House, 1972.

Did I Ever Tell You How Lucky You Are? New York: Random House, 1973.

The Shape of Me and Other Stuff. New York: Bright & Early Books/Random House, 1973.

Great Day for Up! Illustrated by Quentin Blake. New York: Bright & Early Books/Random House, 1974.

There's a Wocket in My Pocket! New York: Bright & Early Books/Random House, 1974.

Oh, the Thinks You Can Think! New York: Beginner Books/ Random House, 1975.

The Cat's Quizzer. New York: Beginner Books/Random House, 1976.

I Can Read with My Eyes Shut! New York: Beginner Books/ Random House, 1978.

Oh Say Can You Say? New York: Beginner Books/Random House, 1979.

Hunches in Bunches. New York: Random House, 1982.

The Butter Battle Book. New York: Random House, 1984.

You're Only Old Once! New York: Random House, 1986.

I Am Not Going to Get Up Today! Illustrated by James Stevenson. New York: Random House, 1987.

Oh, the Places You'll Go! New York: Random House, 1990.

BOOKS WRITTEN UNDER DIFFERENT PEN NAMES

LeSieg, Theo. *Ten Apples Up on Top!* Illustrated by Roy McKié. New York: Bright & Early Books/Random House, 1961.

LeSieg, Theo. *I Wish That I Had Duck Feet.* Illustrated by B. Tobey. New York: Beginner Books/Random House, 1965.

LeSieg, Theo. *Come Over to My House.* Illustrated by Richard Erdoes. New York: Beginner Books/Random House, 1966.

LeSieg, Theo. *The Eye Book.* Illustrated by Roy McKié. New York: Bright & Early Books/Random House, 1968.

LeSieg, Theo. *I Can Write!: A Book by Me, Myself.* Illustrated by Roy McKié. New York: Bright & Early Books/Random House, 1971.

LeSieg, Theo. *In a People House.* Illustrated by Roy McKié. New York: Bright & Early Books/Random House, 1972.

LeSieg, Theo. *The Many Mice of Mr. Brice.* Illustrated by Roy McKié. New York: Bright & Early Books/Random House, 1973.

LeSieg, Theo. *Wacky Wednesday.* Illustrated by George Booth. New York: Beginner Books/Random House, 1974.

Stone, Rosetta. *Because a Little Bug Went Ka-Choo!* Illustrated by Michael Frith. New York: Beginner Books/Random House, 1975.

LeSieg, Theo. *Would You Rather Be a Bullfrog?* Illustrated by Roy McKié. New York: Bright & Early Books/Random House, 1975.

LeSieg, Theo. *Hooper Humperdink … ? Not Him!* Illustrated by Charles E. Martin. New York: Beginner Books/Random House, 1976.

LeSieg, Theo. *Please Try to Remember the First of Octember!* Illustrated by Art Cummings. New York: Beginner Books/Random House, 1977.

LeSieg, Theo. *Maybe You Should Fly a Jet! Maybe You Should Be a Vet!* Illustrated by Michael Smollin. New York: Beginner Books/Random House, 1980.

LeSieg, Theo. *The Tooth Book.* Illustrated by Roy McKié. New York: Bright & Early Books/Random House, 1981.

Posthumous Publications

Daisy-Head Mayzie. New York: Random House, 1995.

My Many Colored Days. Illustrated by Steve Johnson and Lou Fancher. New York: Knopf, 1996.

Seuss-isms: Wise and Witty Prescriptions for Living from the Good Doctor. New York: Random House, 1977.

Cartoons and Artwork

Dr. Seuss' Lost World Revisited: A Forward-Looking Backward Glance. New York: Universal Publishing, 1967. (Material published by Dr. Seuss in *Liberty* in 1932.)

Dr. Seuss from Then to Now: A Catalogue of the Retrospective Exhibition. New York: Random House, 1986. (Originally published by the San Diego Museum of Art. Includes material about his advertising career and sketches for *You're Only Old Once!*)

The Tough Coughs As He Ploughs the Dough: Early Writing and Cartoons by Dr. Seuss. Edited and introduced by Richard Marschall. New York: William Morrow/Remco Worldservice, 1987.

The Secret Art of Dr. Seuss. New York: Random House, 1995. (Reprinted artwork that Geisel never used in his books.)

Minear, Richard H. *Dr. Seuss Goes to War: The World War II Editorial Cartoons of Theodor Seuss Geisel.* New York: New Press, 1999. (Political cartoons published in *PM*, 1941–1942; includes six chapters of useful exposition, contextualization, and criticism by Minear, as well as an introduction by Art Spiegelman.)

Article by Theodore Geisel

"If at First You Don't Succeed—Quit!" *Saturday Evening Post* 8–9 (November 28, 1964).

CRITICAL AND BIOGRAPHICAL STUDIES

Bandler, Michael J. "Dr. Seuss: Still a Drawing Card." *American Way* 23–27 (December 1977).

Benzel, Jan. "Dr. Seuss Finally Transcended the Gender Barrier." *Houston Chronicle*, January 20, 1995. (Reprinted in Fensch, 1997.)

Bunzel, Peter. "The Wacky World of Dr. Seuss Delights the Child—and Adult—Readers of His Books." *Life*, April 6, 1959. (Reprinted in Fensch, 1997.)

Cahn, Robert. "The Wonderful World of Dr. Seuss." *Saturday Evening Post*, July 6, 1957, pp. 17–19, 42–46.

Cott, Jonathan. "The Good Dr. Seuss." In his *Pipers at the Gates of Dawn: The Wisdom of Children's Literature.* New York: Random House, 1983. (Reprinted in Fensch, 1997.)

Curley, Suzanne. "The Nuclear Dr. Seuss." *Newsday* 3 (March 5, 1984).

Dean, Tanya. *Theodor Geisel.* Philadelphia: Chelsea House, 2002.

Fensch, Thomas, ed. *Of Sneetches and Whos and the Good Dr. Seuss: Essays on the Writings and Life of Theodor Geisel.* Jefferson, N.C.: McFarland, 1997. (Includes an introduction by Fensch; a chronology of Geisel's life and work; an annotated bibliography of Dr. Seuss books and secondary criticism; an appendix of the all-time best-selling children's books, reprinted from a 1996 issue of *Publishers Weekly*; and twenty-six reprinted reviews and essays spanning 1959–1991.)

———. *The Man Who Was Dr. Seuss: The Life and Work of Theodor Geisel.* Woodlands, Tex.: New Century Books, 2000.

Frutig, Judith. "Dr. Seuss's Green-Eggs-and-Ham World." *Christian Science Monitor*, May 12, 1978. (Reprinted in Fensch, 1997.)

Gorney, Cynthia. "Dr. Seuss at 75: Grinch, Cat in Hat,

Wocket and Generations of Kids in His Pocket." *The Washington Post*, May 21, 1979. (Reprinted in Fensch, 1997.)

Greene, Carol. *Dr. Seuss: Writer and Artist for Children.* Chicago: Children's Press, 1993. (Juvenile biography.)

Greenleaf, Warren T. "How the Grinch Stole Reading: The Serious Nonsense of Dr. Seuss." *Principal* (May 1982). (Reprinted in Fensch, 1997.)

Kahn, Jr., E. J. "Children's Friend." *The New Yorker*, December 17, 1960. (Reprinted in Fensch, 1997.)

Lamb, J. R. "Dr. Seuss Dies." *San Diego Tribune*, September 25, 1991, p. A18.

Lanes, Selma G. "Seuss for the Goose Is Seuss for the Gander." In her *Down the Rabbit Hole: Adventures and Misadventures in the Realm of Children's Literature.* New York: Atheneum, 1971. (Reprinted in Fensch, 1997.)

Lathem, Edward Connery, ed. *Theodor Seuss Geisel: Reminiscences & Tributes.* Hanover, NH.: Dartmouth College, 1996. (Short tributes to the late Dr. Seuss by Victor H. Krulak, Jed Mattes, Judith and Neil Morgan, Herbert Cheyette, Chuck Jones, and Robert L. Bernstein, with an introductory note by Audrey S. Geisel.)

————, ed. "The Beginnings of Dr. Seuss: A Conversation with Theodor S. Geisel." *Dartmouth Alumni Magazine* (April 1976). (Reprinted in Fensch, 1997.)

————, ed. *Who's Who & What's What in the Books of Dr. Seuss.* Hanover, N.H.: Dartmouth College, 2000. (Available on the Internet at http://www.dartmouth.edu/~drseuss/whoswho.pdf.)

Lurie, Alison. "The Cabinet of Dr. Seuss." *New York Review of Books*, December 20, 1990. (Reprinted in Fensch, 1997.)

MacDonald, Ruth K. *Dr. Seuss.* Boston: Twayne, 1988.

Menand, Louis. "Cat People: What Dr. Seuss Really Taught Us." *The New Yorker*, December 23, 2002, pp. 148–154.

Mensch, Betty, and Alan Freeman. "Getting to Solla Sollew: The Existentialist Politics of Dr. Seuss." *Tikkun* 2, no. 2:30–34, 113–117 (1987).

Morgan, Judith, and Neil Morgan. *Dr. Seuss and Mr. Geisel: A Biography.* New York: Random House, 1995. (Most of the biographical information in the essay comes from this authorized biography.)

Ort, Lorrene Love. "Theodor Seuss Geisel: The Children's Dr. Seuss." *Elementary English* 32:135–142 (1995).

Renthal, Helen. "25 Years of Working Wonder with Words." *Chicago Tribune*, November 11, 1962. (Reprinted in Fensch, 1997.)

Roth, Rita. "*On Beyond Zebra* with Dr. Seuss." *New Advocate* (Fall 1989).

Sadler, Glenn Edward. "Maurice Sendak and Dr. Seuss: A Conversation." *Horn Book* (September/October 1989). (Reprinted in Fensch, 1997.)

Weidt, Maryann. *Oh, the Places He Went: A Story about Dr. Seuss—Theodor Seuss Geisel.* Minneapolis: Carolrhoda Books, 1994. (Juvenile biography.)

Wheeler, Jill C. *Dr. Seuss.* Edina, Minn.: Abdo & Daughters, 1992. (Juvenile biography.)

Wilder, Rob. "Catching Up with Dr. Seuss." *Parents Magazine*, June 1979, pp. 60–64.

Wolf, Tim. "Imagination, Rejection and Rescue: Recurrent Themes in Dr. Seuss." *Children's Literature* 23:137–164 (1995).

WILLIAM GIBSON

(1948—)

Jack Fischel

Unlike traditional science fiction, whose stories often concern space or time travel, alien visitations, cosmic warfare, far future scenarios, and the like, William Gibson's novels and short stories concern the manner in which technological innovations, such as computers, have altered the world. Gibson's fiction rests on the premise that many dramatic innovations of the future already exist in the present in embryonic form. Far from being a techie, Gibson admitted to John Marshall of the *Seattle Post-Intelligencer* in an interview published on February 6, 2003, that if he "had known more about how computers actually worked, [he] couldn't have written those books." Gibson said,

> Computer guys would come up to me and say this is all BS, that there is simply not enough bandwidth in the universe to do what I had written… . There were other writers who knew how computers worked and couldn't dream up the fiction I wrote because they were so worried about bandwidth. I wasn't interested in how computers worked, I was interested in how people related to them, and how they might change human behavior.

In his groundbreaking novel *Neuromancer* (1984), Gibson describes a humanity sharply alienated from nature, having substituted an artificial world that exists in cyberspace—the realm if the Internet, the World Wide Web, the matrix. Gibson coined the term "cyberspace" two years earlier in his short story "Burning Chrome" and described it as a virtual reality simulation with a direct neural feedback. Although cyberspace does not exist as a physical reality, "hackers" nevertheless enter it and experience an alternative reality that has become their normal everyday existence. In Gibson's early fiction cyberspace has become the natural habitat for much of humanity. Gibson

indicated one inspiration for his vision of the future in a 1988 interview with Larry McCaffery published in the *Mississippi Review*:

> Watching kids in video arcades… . I could see in the physical intensity of their postures how *rapt* these kids were… . These kids clearly *believed* in the space these games projected. Everyone who works with computers seems to develop an intuitive faith that there's some kind of *actual space* behind the screen.

Gibson's fiction depicts a bleak future, wherein humanity is subjected to the vicissitudes of technological change that is indifferent to its impact on society. The characters described in his first three novels, known as the Cyberspace or Sprawl Trilogy, are able to escape the dankness of everyday reality by "jacking" into cyberspace through silicon chips implanted in their skulls. Gibson's fictional invention of silicon chips, however, is not simply the product of a creative imagination, but his effort to anticipate where the products of bioengineering are leading mankind.

Although the characters in *Neuromancer* "jack" into cyberspace by inserting "microsofts" into their skulls, Gibson does not necessarily believe that people will eventually have such implants, if only because "the chip is likely to shortly be as quaint an object as the vacuum tube or the slide rule." In "Will We Plug Chips into Our Brains?" published in the June 19, 2000, issue of *Time* magazine, Gibson notes that "from the viewpoint of bioengineering, a silicon chip is a large and rather complex shard of glass." From the standpoint of technology, it may one day be technically feasible to implant this type of chip into the human skull; but, asks Gibson, "Why should we even want to attempt such a thing?" His answer is that "mainstream medicine and the military will both find reasons for attempting such a thing,

at least in the short run," in the case of medicine, "to counter some disability, acquired or inherited." Gibson writes, "If I were to lose my eyes, I would quite eagerly submit to some sort of surgery that promised a video link to the optic nerves." As for the military, Gibson envisions the use of chip insertions for "some ... aspect of tele-present combat, in which weapons in the field are remotely controlled by distant operators." Gibson says, "Crazier things, really, have been done in the name of king and country."

Gibson does not believe that if chip insertion technology were to become commonplace, it would last very long. He notes in the *Time* essay that "various models of biological and nanomolecular computing are looming" on the horizon, and for this reason Gibson predicts that "rather than plug a piece of hardware into our gray matter," scientists will

> extract some brain cells, plop them into a Petri dish and graft on various sorts of gelatinous computing goo. Slug it all back into the skull and watch it run on blood sugar, the way a human brain's supposed to... . (The trickier aspect here may be turning data into something brain cells can understand. If you knew how to get brain cells to manage pull-down menus, you'd probably know everything you needed to know about brain cells.)

Gibson offers yet another reason "against the need to implant computing devices," which has to do with certain differences we make between computing and reality, or, as Gibson phrases it, between "the virtual and the real." As nanomolecular computing technology becomes more sophisticated, Gibson "doubt[s] that our grandchildren will understand the distinction between that which is a computer and that which isn't." He questions in the *Time* essay whether they will distinguish between the computer "as a distinct category of object or function":

> This, I think, is the logical outcome of genuinely ubiquitous computing, of the fully wired world. The wired world will consist ... of a single unbroken interface. The idea of a device that "only" computes will perhaps be the ultimate archaism in a world in which the fridge or the toothbrush is potentially as smart as any other object, including you, a world in

which intelligent objects communicate, routinely and constantly, with one another and with us.

"In this world," predicts Gibson,

> there may be no need for the physical augmentation of the human brain... . You won't need smart goo in your brain, because your fridge and your toothbrush will be very smart indeed, enormously smart, and they will be there for you, constantly and always.

Gibson does not anticipate computers overwhelming our being, but instead humanity "crawling buglike out into the mingling light and shadow of the presence of that which we will have created, which we are creating now, and which seems to me to be in the process of re-creating us."

William Gibson's fiction is grounded in his conviction that the future of the computer-driven information highway will result in new technologies that will dramatically alter the character and quality of life for much of humanity—not for the better. Science-fiction writer and sometime Gibson collaborator Bruce Sterling wrote in his preface to *Burning Chrome* (1986) that Gibson's fiction extrapolates "with exaggerated clarity, the hidden bulk of an iceberg of social change. This iceberg now glides with sinister majesty across the surface of the late twentieth century, but its proportions are vast and dark." His prediction of the future driven by a computer-based technological society is what his early books are all about.

Gibson's novels are set in the aftermath of World War III, when the world has undergone dramatic changes due to the ascendance of multinational corporations, which through their domination of technology have designed a society that serves the interest of the few at the expense of the many. Notable in Gibson's future earthly landscape is a world divorced from any semblance of democracy or free enterprise capitalism. Instead he depicts a future in which corporations have replaced government, and a judicial system is nonexistent. Although Gibson does not write directly about politics, its absence is telling. Multinational businesses have replaced older forms of political coercion with more subtle methods that leave little room for individuality or opportunity outside the corporation. Through

their control of technology, the corporations have obliterated the past, manipulated popular culture, and they control the flow of information. With lessons of the past practically expunged from human memory, the multinationals are free to pursue their material ends regardless of the consequences for society. In *Idoru* for instance, "Chia ... had only a vague idea who Hitler might have been, and that mainly from references in songs." Although there is little formal political opposition to the rule of the corporations, escape is possible through "jacking" into cyberspace, where infinite possibilities exist to engage in virtual freedom from the squalid and oppressive existence Gibson describes in his fiction.

Gibson's Sprawl Trilogy, consisting of *Neuromancer* (1984), *Count Zero* (1986), and *Mona Lisa Overdrive* (1988), as well as some of his earlier short stories, was written at the height of Japan's technological ascendance in the 1980s. Gibson writes little about the causes and nature of the conflict that led to World War III, except to note that it lasted hardly more than three weeks and resulted in the technological dominance of Japan. Traditional governments with geographical borders have evolved into multinational corporations, paper money has been replaced by credit chips, and books have become collector's items. In the United States, California for unexplained reasons has been divided into No Cal and So Cal. *All Tomorrow's Parties* (1999) takes place in petrified neighborhoods near the San Francisco–Oakland Bay Bridge side by side with futuristic interstitial communities of the homeless, all pervaded by an omnipresent drug culture, extreme poverty, and general hopelessness among its population.

Gibson's early novels inform us that the embracing influence of technology on society has not improved material conditions for the vast majority of humanity. Instead, technological evolution of the Internet, combined with the construction of artificial intelligence, has created an alternative universe in which life and death are so conjoined that his characters question which reality is the essence of existence, a dichotomy that reminds the reader of theological views of heaven and earth. In *Mona Lisa Over-*

drive, the following dialogue is exchanged between two of Gibson's a characters:

> "The mythform is usually encountered in one of two modes. One mode assumes that the cyberspace matrix is inhabited, or perhaps visited, by entities whose characteristics correspond with the primary mythform of a 'hidden people.' The other involves assumptions of omniscience, omnipotence, and incomprehensibility on the part of the matrix itself."
>
> "That the matrix is God?"
>
> "In a manner of speaking, although it would be more accurate, in terms of the mythform, to say that the matrix *has* a God, since this being's omniscience and omnipotence are assumed to be limited to the matrix."
>
> "If it has limits, it isn't omnipotent."
>
> "Exactly. Notice that the mythform doesn't credit the being with immortality... . Cyberspace exists, insofar as it can be said to exist, by virtue of human agency."

Although organized religion is not addressed in Gibson's novels, he does confront the relationship of technology to divinity. In *Neuromancer* two forms of artificial intelligence, Neuromancer and Wintermute merge and take on godlike qualities. Subsequently these entities of virtual reality spawn a bevy of smaller gods or subprograms that take on the names and personalities of voodoo deities in the matrix. Gibson's idea of divinity, located in cyberspace, evokes images and symbols of traditional Christianity. In the matrix, for example, resurrection of the dead frequently occurs. In *Neuromancer*, Case, the novel's protagonist, is searching for his departed girlfriend in cyberspace, when he comes across a young boy who reveals to him his identity:

> "Neuromancer," the boy said... . "The lane to the land of the dead... . I call up the dead ... ," and the boy did a little dance... . "I am the dead, and their land... . Stay. If your woman is a ghost, she doesn't know it. Neither will you."

In Gibson's futuristic world where virtual reality exists side by side with actual existence, technology makes possible what religion can only promise.

In *Neuromancer*, Gibson describes cyberspace as being rooted in a

consensual hallucination experienced daily by billions of legitimate operators, in every nation, by children being taught mathematical concepts... . A graphic representation of data abstracted from the banks of every computer in the human system. Unthinkable complexity. Lines of light ranged in the nonspace of the mind, clusters and constellations of data. Like city lights, receding... .

Gibson thus depicts the matrix as a global information network that provides the landscape that makes cyberspace possible, as well as an abstract representation of the relationships between data systems. In his short story "Burning Chrome," Gibson describes the effect of the matrix when he writes, "Legitimate programmers jack into their employers' sector of the matrix and find themselves surrounded by bright geometries representing the corporate data." The matrix was first discovered in primitive video arcades, where generations of the young encountered cyberspace. As he relates in his early novels, cyberspace consists of, among other things, the sum total of data in the human system, and as one of Gibson's characters states in *Mona Lisa Overdrive*, "I'd say a good three-quarters of humanity is jacked at the moment, watching the show." The characters in Gibson's early novels traverse cyberspace, where the past and future meet as well as where the living and the dead coexist. It is also a place where life can interface with and be augmented by machines, with both residual detriments and advantages: in cyberspace life loses much of its value and meaning, but therein individuals also lose their fear of death.

Gibson depicts a future in which popular entertainment takes the form of "simstims," where by jacking into a machine one can experience the sensations and perceptions of another person, usually a famous personality, an experience enhanced by the use of mind-altering drugs. The appeal of the "stims" has dwarfed the sexual drive, as the compulsion to jack in replaces libidinal urges. As described in *Neuromancer*, Gibson's characters appear to prefer to make love to their machines rather than to each other: "I saw you stroking that Sendai" Molly says to Case; "man it was pornographic." This is not to negate the presence of sex in Gibson's fiction, but the centrality of sexual motivation and activ-

ity, so prevalent in contemporary fiction, is minimal. Gibson told the *Philadelphia Inquirer* (1988) that his inspiration for the idea of simstims, or "simulated stimulus systems," derived from his short stay in Hollywood while he was writing a screenplay for *Alien 3*: "Sitting in the Polo Lounge talking to 20-year-old movie producers with money coming out of their ears—*that's* science fiction, boy."

Gibson explains that the new technological age evolved soon after World War III, when corporations came to dominate governments, and parts of the United States and Japan became the centers of a new arms race in which the weapons were not guns but information. Multinational corporations, or *zaibatsus*, battling with one another in search of new intelligence and information, employ not armies but criminal organizations like the Yakuza to do their bidding. Power, in Gibson's fiction, is corporate power, whereby the *zaibatsus* shape the course of humanity. Gibson cautions us that if the multinationals by using criminal organizations such as the Yakuza, gain not only access to the sources of information but also its control, they can easily and freely exploit society. The dire threat to humanity comes from the control of information for immoral and unethical purposes. "Viewed as organisms, [the multinationals] had attained a kind of immortality. You couldn't kill a zaibatsu by assassinating a dozen key executives; there were others waiting to step up the ladder, assume the vacated position, access the vast banks of corporate memory," or as Fox, a character in the short story "New Rose Hotel," states, "The blood of a *zaibatsu* is information, not people. The structure is independent of the individual lives that comprise it. Corporation as life form." Wars are initiated between the multinational corporations as a result of a Darwinian competition based on the principal of survival of the fittest for access to new information-breeding technology. In Gibson's bleak vision of the future there is no linear relationship between what the technology is capable of producing and the uses to which it will be put.

Gibson notes that, viewed one way, history is the record of technological advances that have

resulted in revolutionary changes that profoundly impact humanity, but whose full effect has not been immediately apparent. In his fiction he refers to those moments of technological breakthrough, when society is dramatically affected by innovation although unaware of its consequences, as "nodal points," and nanotechnology—the engineering of microscopic machines—as the means of making these changes possible. Gibson's use of nanotechnology in his novels may owe much to the research of the American engineer Eric Drexler, who popularized the word in his book *Engines of Creation: The Coming Era of Nanotechnology* (1986). Nanotechnology is the projected ability to make things from the bottom up, to place atoms and molecules in a desired place using techniques and tools that were being developed by the end of the twentieth century. Once achieved this form of molecular engineering will result in a manufacturing revolution that will have serious economic, social, environmental, and military implications. Drexler predicted the capability to build machines the size of molecules, a few nanometers wide—motors, robot arms, entire computers smaller than a single cell. He spent the next ten years describing and analyzing such future devices, and responding to accusations that he was writing science fiction, not science. Gibson appears familiar with Drexler's vision inasmuch as he uses his terminology if not his ideas.

In *All Tomorrow's Parties*, Gibson envisions corporations rewarding those who utilize nanotechnology to anticipate the direction of the nodal points of change. Laney, the novel's hero, is one such character who understands that technological innovation will create dramatic change and alter everyone's view of the past. Laney announces that history, along with geography, is dead: "History in the older sense was an historical concept... . History was plastic, was a matter of interpretation... . History was stored data, subject to manipulation and interpretation." In *The Difference Engine*, Gibson argues that history not only accurately models change but intentionally disguises relations of domination. One of the three primary characters in the novel, Edward Mallory, a paleontologist and explorer,

observes, "History works by Catastrophe! It's the way of the world... . There is no history—there is only contingency." And what Laney discovers in *All Tomorrow's Parties* is that "history ... was [now] something very different. It was that shape comprised of every narrative, every version: it was that shape that only he (as far as he knew) could see."

Future historians, according to Gibson, are those able to anticipate nodal points of change, and from the vantage point of the past provide direction to the future. Gibson argues that it is imperative that humanity identify and adapt to the nodal points, lest innovation accelerate to the point that society is overwhelmed. Gibson cites the history of labor to show how workers were impacted by developments in technology at levels of complexity that accelerated geometrically while their ability to cope with the changes lagged behind arithmetically, thus creating instability and violence. That technological change occurs dramatically while human ability to comprehend its implications lags far behind is a phenomenon that informs much of Gibson's writing. He stated in an article in the November 30, 1998, issue of *Forbes ASAP Supplement*, "This perpetual toggling between nothing being new under the sun, and everything having very recently changed absolutely, is perhaps the central driving tension of my work."

The fictive world presented in Gibson's early writings is a dank one characterized by urban sprawl, violence, pollution, drugs, and an anarchical cyberpunk environment driven by computer high-tech. Although Gibson did not invent the term—Bruce Bethke did in his story "Cyberpunk," first published in the November 1983 issue of *Amazing Science Fiction Stories*—he is one of cyberpunk's pioneering writers. "Cyberpunk" derives from the merger of two words, "cyber," which means "of or relating to computers or computer networks," fused with the counterculture of punk rock with all of the connotations associated with the drug culture, punk rock music and its extreme expressions of alienation, and punker fashion, characterized by sharp black suits and Mohawks and other outlandish haircuts.

In the Sprawl Trilogy, Gibson fuses a counter-cultural punklike environment of urban decay with the good old-fashioned noir detective novel. Case, the main character in *Neuromancer*, for example, is a skilled computer "cowboy," reminiscent of a Raymond Chandler hard-boiled private eye. The noir quality accents the dark cyberpunk aspect of Gibson's literary vision. Like characters in a Chandler novel, Gibson's heroes live on the edge of the law, faced with danger and intrigue, typically escaping threats from either gangs or corporations. Instead of a cynical private detective at the center of his narrative, Gibson provides his futuristic counterpart, a distinctly modern freebooter, the computer hacker. Gibson has written that in the future when computers worldwide will be linked through cyberspace, the multinationals will take extreme measures to protect their information. In this environment the future outlaw will appear (if he has not already) in the form of "cowboys" who will access cyberspace by jacking in to steal data, fill bank accounts with electronic money, or meet an ignominious death when the feedback from some a security program or other destroys their minds. Gibson has written, "The street finds its own use for things—uses the manufacturer never imagined."

Bruce Sterling in his preface to *Burning Chrome* describes Gibson's "extrapolative" techniques as being consistent with the classic science fiction genre,

> but his demonstration of them is pure New Wave. Rather than the usual passionless techies and rock-ribbed Competent Men of hard SF, his characters are a pirate's crew of losers, hustlers, spin-offs, castoffs, and lunatics. We see his future from the belly up, as it is lived, not merely as dry speculation.

Referring to Gibson's earlier short stories, including "Johnny Mnemonic," "New Rose Hotel," and his first published short story, "Fragments of a Hologram Rose" (1977), Sterling notes that "the Gibson trademarks are already present: a complex synthesis of modern pop culture, high tech, and advanced literary technique." Perhaps the best way to describe Gibson's stature as the leading science fiction writer of the past two decades is that his work consistently evokes a credible future that is recognizable and drawn from modern conditions. Absent are such farfetched themes of the older science fiction as robots, spaceships, intergalactic travel, and the like. In its place Gibson creates a future based on present technology and present social and economic trends.

At the same time that Gibson constructed his dark world of the future, he also created a vision of cyberspace as a place of infinite possibilities, where dead people continue to live in electronic form and where lost or forgotten experiences and images can be electronically reproduced with accuracy and detail. Gibson's genius as a science fiction writer rests in that, like many of his characters, he writes in anticipation of the nodal points of change. His vision anticipates the great potential of cybertechnology, and he understands that we presently live on the frontier of vast technological possibilities that are almost unimaginable to any but the most visionary science fiction writers such as himself.

GIBSON'S EARLY LIFE AND CAREER

William Ford Gibson was born in Conway, South Carolina, on March 17, 1948, the only child of William Ford Gibson and Otey Williams Gibson. His father was a successful contractor, one of whose projects was, as Gibson says in the *Mississippi Review* interview, "installing flush toilets in the Oak Ridge Projects." After his father died when the boy was six or eight years old (Gibson himself is not clear on the matter), he and his mother moved to Wytheville, a small town in southwestern Virginia where both of Gibson's parents came from and where his mother's family still lived. In a brief autobiography on his Web site, Gibson says, "I'm convinced that it was this experience of feeling abruptly exiled, to what seemed like the past, that began my relationship to science fiction. I eventually became exactly the sort of introverted, hyper-bookish boy you'll find in the biographies of most American science fiction writers." In his early teens his favorites were Robert Heinlein, Ray Bradbury, and Isaac Asimov.

When he was fifteen, his mother sent him to a private boys' school in Tucson, Arizona, where he encountered the writings of William S. Burroughs, Jack Kerouac, Thomas Pynchon, and Allen Ginsberg. In his late teens he discovered a volume of *The Year's Best Science Fiction*, edited by Judith Merril, featuring a different type of science fiction, including Philip K. Dick, Alfred Bester, and Fritz Leiber. He subsequently discovered the futuristic works of J. G. Ballard. Collectively these writers describe a dark and frightening future. In an interview published in London's *Financial Times* on January 17, 2004, Gibson recalls the influence of these writers on his later work: "That was the first inkling I had that there were quite a few people in the world who felt as not a part of what was going on around them as I did. There was the intimation of other modes of existence and other ways of looking at things."

In 1967 his mother died suddenly, and traumatized by her death, he dropped out of high school. Shortly thereafter, with the escalation of the war in Vietnam, Gibson moved to Canada in 1968 to avoid being drafted. Reflecting on this period of his life, Gibson has said that the sixties marked a turning point for him. He was attracted to the youth culture of the time and especially to the hard-edged music of Lou Reed and the Velvet Underground, which Gibson counts as a major influence on his subsequent career, as is made explicit in the title of his seventh novel, *All Tomorrow's Parties*, also the name of a Velvet Underground song.

In June of 1972, Gibson married Deborah Thompson, a language instructor, and the couple moved to Vancouver, where he attended the University of British Columbia, receiving his B.A. in English in 1977. During college Gibson renewed his interest in science fiction. He took a class with the science fiction scholar and critic Susan Wood, and in lieu of writing a term paper, he wrote "Fragments of a Hologram Rose," which was published a year or so later in the summer 1977 issue of an obscure Boston science fiction magazine, *UnEarth*. The story is notable for including the mix of themes that would characterize his future writing, including the importance and fragility of memory, the nebulous

relationship between human beings and machines, distrust of the power of multinational corporations over information and individuals, and the instability of postmodern society.

Following five years of marriage, Gibson's first child, Graeme Ford Gibson, was born. Later he and his wife also gave birth to a daughter, Claire Thompson Gibson. In 1977, faced with parental responsibilities and not really focused on what he wanted to do for a career, Gibson met John Shirley, a science fiction writer and punk rock musician. Gibson's style was influenced by the punk counterculture movement of the time. As he says on his Web site, "I took Punk to be the detonation of some slow-fused projectile buried deep in society's flank a decade earlier, and I took it to be, somehow, a sign. And I began, then, to write."

By the early 1980s, Gibson had established himself in what was being called the new wave in science fiction. Having published "The Belonging Kind" (in collaboration with John Shirley) and "The Gernsback Continuum" in anthologies, Gibson's short stories attracted the attention of Ellen Datlow, the fiction editor of *Omni* magazine, an important publication for rising science fiction writers. Under Datlow's editorship, Gibson published "Johnny Mnemonic" and "Red Star, Winter Orbit" in 1981, and "Hinterlands" and "Burning Chrome" in 1982. Like Dick, Bester, and Leiber, Gibson began to draw his own bleak vision of the future. This is particularly evident in "Johnny Mnemonic," which anticipates characters he would later create in *Neuromancer*. Johnny typifies what the new punk fiction was all about, what Mikal Gilmore, in his *Rolling Stone* article accompanying his 1986 interview with Gibson, calls "high-tech lowlifes." The title character hides stolen computer data on a microchip in his brain. He is chased by the Yakuza, who seek to murder him, but he is saved by a bionic hit woman who has razors implanted under her fingernails. Gibson told Gilmore in the *Rolling Stone* interview that after the publication of his early fiction "I thought I was on this literary kamikaze mission—that is, I thought my work was so disturbing it would be dismissed and ignored by all but a few people." Quite the op-

posite transpired. On the basis of his short stories Gibson acquired a reputation as a major writer of science fiction. "Johnny Mnemonic" and "Burning Chrome" were both nominated for Nebula Awards.

Gibson's reputation as the leading practitioner of cyberpunk was unshakably established when *Neuromancer* won numerous awards and became the first novel to receive the Nebula Award from the Science Fiction Writers of America, the Hugo Award for the best novel of 1984 from the World Science Fiction Society, and the Philip K. Dick Award for best original paperback of 1984 from the Philadelphia Science Fiction Society. Gilmore says,

> With his swift, colorful dialogue and his flair for creating a believably gritty future, he has forged the most convincing blend of sci-fi and hard-boiled detective styles in American pulp history. In doing so, he has yanked science fiction down from its recent Arcadian heights and forced it to wander mean, futuristic streets where flesh is cheap and dreams are lethal.

With the success of *Neuromancer*, Gibson's name became synonymous with the artistic and political rebellion against mainstream science fiction. By the end of the eighties his literary output was recognized as illustrative of cyberpunk's aesthetics and vision. Ironically Gibson was not enamored with his identification with punk culture and in interviews claimed not to know what cyberpunk really was. Toward the end of the 1980s, however, cyberpunk was beginning to lose its appeal. Gibson retreated from writing about the future and entered into a collaborative effort with Bruce Sterling to write *The Difference Engine* (1990), a quasi-historical science fiction novel set in Victorian England. While his later fiction continues to concern the impact of technology on society, it is less involved with the distant future than with the present. Reflecting on his work Gibson observed to Mikal Gilmore,

> Technology has *already* changed us, and now we have to figure a way to stay sane within that change. If you were to put this in terms of mainstream fiction and present readers with a conventional book about postindustrial anxiety, many of them would

just push it aside. But if you put it in the context of science fiction, maybe you can get them to sit still for what you have to say.

"More recently," as is reported by Ravi Mattu in the *Financial Times* interview, Gibson has been influenced by the science fiction of the Japanese novelist Haruki Murakami. "He first read him when they had the same Japanese publisher," and Gibson continues to read and be influenced by him. Gibson is also a devotee of what J. G. Ballard has called "invisible literature," a literary genre which utilizes scientific reports, government documents, and specialized advertising, which is the subject of his novel *Pattern Recognition* (2003).

THE BODY OF HIS WORK

The body of Gibson's work falls into two categories: his early short stories, such as "Johnny Mnemonic," "Burning Chrome," and "New Rose Hotel," plus the Sprawl Trilogy. These works constitute Gibson's ethereal fiction, in which he creates a world of virtual reality located in the matrix of cyberspace. These works of fiction were followed by Gibson's turn to a different type of theme, alternative history, in *The Difference Engine*, which imaginatively recreates a nineteenth century in which the Victorian inventor Charles Babbage (1791–1871) computerizes Great Britain, a century before the fact. Gibson describes the seamy side of a nineteenth-century London calling to mind the Sprawl depicted in his earlier novels. Critics credited Gibson with creating a subgenre of cyberpunk that they called "steampunk." In his subsequent fiction, which includes *Virtual Light* (1993), *Idoru* (1996), *All Tomorrow's Parties* (1999), and *Pattern Recognition* (2003), Gibson abandons the virtual reality of cyberspace for a science fiction rooted in the real world.

In addition to novels and short stories, Gibson has written several screenplays and experimental works of fiction for film and television, including a text to accompany performance artist Robert Longo's theater piece *Dream Jumbo* (1989), a script for the movie *Alien 3*, which was not used,

and episodes for the *X Files* television series. One of his more ambitious experimental works is *Agrippa: A Book of the Dead*. Written in 1992, *Agrippa* is radically different from his other works and consists of a long poem or monologue written for what Gibson calls on his Web site "a multi-unit artwork to be designed by artist Dennis Ashbaugh," whose "design eventually included a supposedly self-devouring floppy disk intended to display the text only once, then eat itself." The text first appeared in electronic form and included two pictures, one which would fade away after being exposed to light for one hour and the other which appeared only after being exposed to light for one hour. Apparently Gibson wrote *Agrippa* to honor his deceased father. The title refers to "the name of the particular model of Eastman Kodak photograph album [in which his] father kept his snapshots."

NEUROMANCER

Filled with plots and subplots, as well as some big ideas about the danger of technology run amuck, *Neuromancer* is set in the near future of "the Sprawl," a massive urbanized and economically depressed megalopolis stretching from Boston to Atlanta to Houston. The novel centers around Case, a streetwise and washed-up computer "cowboy," who earns his livelihood as well as his reputation by linking his brain directly into computers for the purpose of stealing data by breaking through the cyberspace matrix. Case's former employers accused him of conspiring against them and retaliated by instilling in him a powerful nerve poison that prevents him from using his semipsychic ability to penetrate cyberspace. Deprived of access to cyberspace, Case is reduced to scrounging for a living on the seamy side of Japan's Chiba City, and this allows us to understand the attraction of the virtual reality of cyberspace.

The plot unfolds when a mysterious employer offers to provide Case a temporary antidote for the poison in exchange for his services, which entails hacking into the matrix. Case is promised that once the assignment is completed, he will be given a permanent antidote that will eliminate the poison and restore his ability to enter cyberspace. Having accepted the assignment, Case, with the aid of Molly Millions, a cold-blooded bionic warrior and assassin (a character who figures prominently in "Johnny Mnemonic"), travels from one strange setting in cyberspace to another. He and Molly find that they are involved in a plot to penetrate a global information corporation. Their travels lead them to a space station controlled by the wealthy Tessier-Ashpool corporation, a family of genetic clones that owns two artificial intelligences (AIs), powerful computers that have been programmed with self-awareness and free will. Case ultimately discovers that his employer is one of the computers, Wintermute, which wants him to help it control the other computer, Neuromancer, in order to combine their artificial intelligence so as to free themselves from their human creators.

When it becomes apparent that the antidote promised to Case will not be readily forthcoming, Gibson introduces a subplot that entails Case's efforts to obtain it. Case's search for the remedy for the poison allows Gibson to reveal the attraction of cyberspace for his characters. The lure of cyberspace is not unlike an addictive drug. Unable to jack in, Case has cold sweats, nightmares, and becomes at times self-destructive to the extent that he yearns to die. Cyberspace has become part of Case's identity, and without it he becomes empty and depressed. Gibson, by contrasting the freedom and self-fulfillment found in the artificial environment of the matrix with that of nature, finds the latter wanting and unattractive. When Case finally penetrates cyberspace, he meets his physically dead girlfriend there, and is even able to make love to her.

Neuromancer's most intriguing characters are the two artificial intelligences Wintermute and Neuromancer, powerful entities that may secretly run the world. Wintermute's original human creators programmed it with a capability to evolve, and it has learned to manipulate people and computer systems for its own purposes. As the novel unfolds, Wintermute eventually merges with Neuromancer to produce a vast and complete artificial intelligence. Gibson intends to evoke a

comparison between human beings and the AIs, which grow in similar developmental stages leading from infancy to adulthood. Wintermute not only behaves like its creators but, like human beings, reproduces to improve its kind. However, the AI reproduces a new and uncontrollable chain, one with no rules and no scruples. We begin to understand that the technology that created the AI has also unleashed powers beyond its control. Gibson has said that *Neuromancer*, though set in the future, is about the present, and the world inhabited by Case and Molly is fundamentally our own, representing both what we have become as well as what we are on the verge of becoming.

COUNT ZERO

Count Zero, while not a direct sequel to *Neuromancer*, is set in cyberspace and develops some of the first novel's premises. Unlike *Neuromancer*, however, which focused on Case's adventures in cyberspace, *Count Zero* follows the story of three individuals whose lives gradually come together. The story takes place seven years after Neuromancer, and like the first novel, Gibson invokes religious themes that often overshadow his complicated plot. Referring to the presence of God in the matrix, the Wig explains to the Finn, a purveyor of black-market technology,

> that his technique of mystical exploration involved projecting his consciousness into blank, unstructured sectors of the matrix and waiting. To the man's credit, the Finn said, he never actually claimed to have met God, although he did maintain that he had on several occasions sensed His presence moving upon the face of the grid.

For reasons that Gibson fails to explain, his invocation of divine imagery draws on African and Haitian spiritual belief systems as they are resurrected in cyberspace. Gibson reveals that the artificial intelligence that the reader encountered in *Neuromancer* has broken apart and fragmented into many cyberspace objects, some of which appear as voodoo gods. It would appear that Gibson uses voodoo as a metaphor to personify the power of electronic and biological technology.

The plot of *Count Zero* is complex. Gibson has remarked that his story lines are less important than the ideas and the way of life that he describes. In an article by Victoria Hamburg in *Interview* for January 1989, Gibson said that he "doesn't really start with stories" but prefers to compile images, "like making a ball out of rubber bands." *Count Zero* reflects this approach. The novel's title refers to Bobby Newmark, a New Jersey born high-tech computer cowboy who searches cyberspace for adventure and reward. While traversing cyberspace, Newmark encounters a friend who provides him with a piece of software that he says will break the most difficult security system and gives him information about a safe data bank to crack. Things turn out otherwise, inasmuch as Bobby is captured and is about to have his "brain burned out" when a mysterious female steps through cyberspace to save him. At another point Bobby falls into the clutches of Haitian voodoo worshipers who take charge of him after he has undergone a religious experience.

Another of the main characters, Marly Krushkhova, is a Paris art dealer whose career is in ruins after she has been set up to sell a fake painting by her unscrupulous lover. She is employed by Josef Virek, one of Gibson's oddest character creations, for the purpose of finding an artist who has made several mysterious "boxes" with unique power, one of which is described as a "universe, a poem, frozen on the boundaries of human experience." Virek is an enormously wealthy art collector who has been confined for over a decade to a vat. Marly, however, first meets him in the form of a computerized person, and the question remains open whether he is a computer construct or human. He tells Marly, "I imagine that a more fortunate man, or a poorer one, would have been allowed to die at last, or be coded at the core of some bit of hardware." As the self-described world's most expensive invalid, Virek is being kept alive by a technological support system. He can't see, smell, taste, hear, or touch anything, but he can generate "realities" in which he can

meet real persons under special circumstances, which Gibson makes entirely believable. Marly's assignment eventually leads her to Wigan Ludgate, a burned-out cowboy who is convinced that God resides in the world's computer Net. Behind all of the novel's action lies the artificial intelligence of the Net, which sometimes appears as the gods of the voodoo and sometimes as Wigan's God.

The third character, Turner, is not unlike Case in *Neuromancer*. He is a corporate mercenary who rounds up scientists for multinationals. Much of *Count Zero* is devoted to the theme of industrial sabotage and terrorism, in which the multinationals kidnap or kill corporate employees who can generate valuable data, such as new biotechniques. Turner is hired by the Hosaka corporation to find Christopher Mitchell, the chief of research and development at the Maas-Neotek corporation, who has defected along with the biochip he's perfected. Along the way Turner finds himself protecting Mitchell's daughter, Angie, who has a unique gift—a microchip implanted in her brain by her scientist father. The microchip permits her direct access to cyberspace, where she often becomes the voice of ghostly inhabitants. The multinational corporations are after Angie and her chip. In alternating chapters Gibson describes each character's adventures until they come together in a common fate, wherein the novel's plot is resolved by the Haitian computer gods.

In the *Rolling Stone* interview Gibson says that "*Neuromancer* was a bit hypermanic—simply from my terror at losing the reader's attention." But in *Count Zero* he "aimed for a more deliberate pace. I also tried to draw the characters in considerable detail. People have children and dead parents in *Count Zero*, and that makes for different emotional territory." Gibson realizes this intention in Bobby Newmark, who is the product of an indifferent mother and is at a loss to understand anything outside the superficial existence that evolves his "simstim." Bobby is a fully developed character who is expert in the operation of his computer but ignorant of his place in the cultural matrix of the machine he operates.

MONA LISA OVERDRIVE

Fourteen years after the action of *Neuromancer*, and seven years after *Count Zero* takes place, the interface between the real world and cyberspace has been drawn tight enough to allow human characters to die in cyberspace on a regular basis, and from there to infiltrate, plot against, or defend the real world. The cast of characters in *Mona Lisa Overdrive* includes thirteen-year-old Kumiko Yanaka, the daughter of a wealthy Japanese businessman who places her with associates in London to guard her from his corporate rivals. Her protectors, however, are shady, and we are never sure about their motives in offering to protect Kumiko. One of her guardians, Sally Shears, a bizarre character, befriends Kumiko and takes her under her wing but at the same time plots against Yanaka's business associates.

The Mona Lisa of the book's title is a small-town waif who has been caught up in the seamy side of Miami nightlife. Working as a prostitute, she dreams of escaping her lot, when a mysterious "talent scout" negotiates with her pimp to employ her as an "actress" in exchange for a large sum of cash. We are not immediately told what she must do, but we do know that Mona strikingly resembles Angie Mitchell, whom we encountered in *Count Zero*. Angie Mitchell has in the interceding seven years become a celebrity in the Sense/Net media network (simstims), but has also spent time in a detoxification clinic where doctors used chemical pliers to pry her addiction from the receptors in her brain. Once released from the clinic, she is under constant surveillance from a helicopter that hovers silently and is programmed to avoid her line of sight. Subsequently, as in *Count Zero*, she gets caught up with the voodoo god entities that inhabit cyberspace.

For the first half of the novel Gibson keeps the reader guessing about where the story is going and about what is really happening. The second half, however, brings it all together as we learn why certain sinister forces are trying to kidnap Angie, and what part Mona plays in the unfolding action involving Angie. Bobby Newmark, Count Zero of the preceding novel, returns in a comalike state, which he has accepted in ex-

change for an alternative existence in cyberspace. Although *Mona Lisa Overdrive* emphasizes character and plot more than do Gibson's previous novels, it does not neglect the themes that made him a leading writer of cyberpunk fiction. He tells us a great deal more about artificial intelligence, maneuvering in cyberspace, and most interestingly the history of the Tessier-Ashpool family corporation. He describes how the family built the first automated factories for the cartels, as well as cloning embryos of individual genetic material, a subplot that figures prominently in the novel. The novel concludes with a climatic duel between police helicopters and customized robots.

BURNING CHROME

Burning Chrome, consisting of ten short stories, was published after *Neuromancer* and *Count Zero*. Three of the short stories, all published years earlier in various magazines, had been written in collaboration with other science fiction writers: "The Belonging Kind" with John Shirley; "Red Star, Winter Orbit" with Bruce Sterling; and "Dogfight" with Michael Swanwick. Notable because these stories were written before Gibson achieved fame as the prime exemplar of cyberpunk, they introduce many of the plotlines and characters that comprise his later novels.

"Johnny Mnemonic" and "Burning Chrome" anticipate the world of computer cowboys and the alternative reality of cyberspace that shape the Sprawl Trilogy. In "Johnny Mnemonic" the characters find themselves in a cybernetic jungle, ruled by corporations which seem to coexist with, or perhaps only to tolerate, governments. No entity is more powerful than the Yakuza, a Japanese criminal organization that has evolved into a formidable corporation that specializes in advanced forms of industrial espionage. Johnny, in hiding from the Yakuza because of the microchip in his brain (like the chip implanted in Angie Mitchell, who was also being chased by a corporation), asks Molly Millions (a recurring character in the Sprawl Trilogy), "Where do you go when the world's wealthiest criminal order is feeling for you with calm, distant fingers? Where

do you hide from the Yakuza … ?" In the same exchange, Johnny explains how the Yakuza had become so powerful: "Fifty years before I was born the Yakuza had already absorbed the Triads, the Mafia, the Union Corse."

Other stories in the collection deal with the futility of uncovering the mystery of the universe as exemplified by the story of Russian astronauts returning from space ("Hinterlands"), a parody on science fiction writers who write optimistically about the future benefits of technology for mankind ("The Gernsback Continuum"), our inability to comprehend our own existence ("Fragments of a Hologram Rose"), and other themes dealing with the human moral frailty that technology will never overcome.

THE DIFFERENCE ENGINE

By the end of the 1980s the cyberpunk era was reaching its end. Gibson noted in the *Bloomsbury Review* (1988) that "It's becoming fashionable now to write 'cyberpunk is dead' articles," and he then proceeded to vacate the world of cyberspace and turn to a different type of fiction. In collaboration with Bruce Sterling he wrote his fourth novel, *The Difference Engine*, a story that is both science fiction and alternate history and that combines historical personalities with fictional characters. The novel can be read as a kind of prehistory of events in the Sprawl Trilogy, although critics have pointed out that the work owes much to Thomas Pynchon's essay "Is It O.K. to Be a Luddite?" which appeared on the front page of the October 28, 1984, issue of the *New York Times Book Review*. The plot is based on drawings by Charles Babbage, a nineteenth-century British mathematician who actually designed several mechanical computers. Gibson and Sterling imagine the consequences for the world had Babbage succeeded in computerizing England during the nineteenth century. According to this vision the Victorians would have developed airplanes, cybernauts, huge steam-powered televisions, among other inventions.

The novel begins a generation after disgruntled urban workers, led by the legendary Ned Ludd, began to destroy factory machinery. The imagina-

tive recreation of Victorian England begins when the aristocratic government of the Duke of Wellington has been defeated at the polls by the Industrial Radical Party, led by its prime minister, the poet George Gordon, Lord Byron. Under the fictional prime minister's leadership, the Luddite insurgents have been overcome, and his party has promoted major new technologies to complement the glut of difference engines, or computers, that store society's information, as well as providing the machinery's "software." The novel goes on to describe the efforts of various characters to steal a set of "cards," known as the Modus, which can function as software for the difference engines. Because information represents the nation's source of power, the plot involves efforts to prevent the Modus from falling into the hands of the thieves lest it result in great harm to England. Intrigue and murder follow as the Modus is wrestled from one character to another. As the novel concludes, one of the characters predicts that the full potential of the Modus will be realized when a more sophisticated engine is developed, envisioning the coming of the computer age and preparing us for Gibson's world of cyberspace. Implicit in the novel's thesis is that technology is neutral; what makes it a force for good or evil is who controls it.

VIRTUAL LIGHT

Gibson's fifth novel takes place in what was, at the time it was published (1993), the near future (2005) in an area adjacent to the San Francisco-Oakland Bay Bridge, which has been abandoned after a cataclysmic earthquake. In this setting Gibson depicts a community inhabited by the homeless as well as by its diverse population, which invokes postmodern America itself. The novel's colorful cast of characters includes a psycho-killer tattooed with the Last Supper, a woman who comes to San Francisco to retrieve her husband's cryogenically frozen brain so that it need not feel crowded in the afterlife, and a San Francisco bike messenger, Chevette Washington, who, making a delivery at a party, steals a pair of virtual reality glasses that allow the viewer to see virtual images. Unbeknownst to her the

glasses are programmed with industrial secrets, and the plot revolves around the efforts of a bounty hunter, employed by a sinister cartel, to retrieve the stolen lenses.

As in the Sprawl Trilogy, Gibson includes a hard-boiled cynical character and his equally tough female sidekick, a variation of the Case–Molly team in *Neuromancer* and Turner–Angie in *Count Zero*. Berry Rydell, a good cop gone bad, is employed as a chauffeur by the bounty hunter, but when Berry discovers that his employer is part of a conspiracy involving the glasses, he switches sides and helps Chevette escape with the stolen property. Subsequently, with the help of computer hackers, Chevette and Berry ultimately triumph after taking on corrupt cops and a Central American drug and information cartel.

Gibson's novel returns to a theme familiar to his readers: a world degenerated into a condition wherein high-tech products coexist alongside poverty, violence, drugs, and corporate greed, and the control of information equates to real power. Despite Gibson's bleak view of the future the novel ends on an upbeat note wherein the hackers, Berry and Chevette, join together to defeat the forces of darkness in the form of the powerful corporations seeking to control information.

IDORU

In his sixth novel Gibson turns to the world of celebrity, where the famous are at the mercy of power hungry media producers who can make or break reputations. But in the near future, Gibson informs us, the global web of data has become so dense that truly useful bits of information about the famous are almost impossible to uncover. Thus the media finds itself at the end of its rope in providing information about celebrities that will attract large audiences, except for Rez, a wealthy rock and roll megastar. The plot centers around a rumor circulating on the Internet that Rez plans to marry Rei Toei, a beautiful Japanese "Idoru" or idol-singer who exists only as a software construct, an artificial intelligence constructed by information-designers, and who

appears to Rez in the form of a hologram. As Rez observes, "Rei's only reality is the realm of ongoing serial creation… . Entirely process; infinitely more than the combined sum of her various selves." Much of the novel examines the efforts of Rez's managers, his band Lo/Rez, and his fans to dissuade him from this bizarre union.

A subplot involves fourteen-year-old Chia, a member of the Seattle chapter of the Lo/Rez fan club who is sent to investigate the Rez–Rei Toei rumor, and Colin Laney, a Net researcher for a tabloid television show with an uncanny ability to uncover vital information from vast pools of digital data, who is hired by Lo/Rez's security people to investigate the truth of the rumor and explain why Rez wants to marry the Idoru.

Gibson's meditation on the meaning of celebrity in a technological age suggests that the famous exist more in the world of the media than they do in the flesh. Given projected advances in media technology, Gibson appears to argue that the near future may well blur the distinction between what is real and what is not. Under these circumstances the power of those who control technology could create an environment wherein a demented celebrity or even the average individual may well feel more kinship with a computer-generated media creation than with a real person. Gibson's novel is a warning that if we don't deal with the issues raised by the advance of technology, an elite few will have the ability to manipulate our lives.

ALL TOMORROW'S PARTIES

Gibson's seventh novel, a sequel to *Idoru*, is set in the early twenty-first century, when major earthquakes have hit Tokyo and San Francisco, and the World Wide Web has expanded into virtual reality. The Idoru, the rock superstar, has disappeared, and Laney, through his uncanny ability to sift through data, has concluded that even more world-shattering occurrences are about to happen. Suffering from what appears to be a breakdown related to his talent, Laney retreats to a cardboard box in a Tokyo subway station. From this location he uses his ability and an Internet connection to prevent the worldwide disaster

from taking place. He also hires Berry Rydell, from *Virtual Light*, who is now a freelance security cop, to investigate a pair of murders perpetrated by someone immune to Laney's psychic predictive powers. Subsequently he enlists Rydell to find the Idoru, who is seeking to escape from her creators. What subsequently unfolds sheds additional light on Rei Toei, one of Gibson's most imaginative characters. When Rydell does locate the Idoru, Laney brings her back with him to his cardboard retreat, and there he shares with Rei Toei his gift of predictive powers: "He had shown her nodal points in that flow, and they had watched together as change had emerged from these into the physical world." Asked how she intended to "marry" Rez, she is unable to answer in "any ordinary sense": "She simply continued to emerge, to be, to be more. More present. And Laney fell in love with her, although he understood that she had been designed for him (and for the world) to fall in love with."

Laney's psychic powers represent more than a character device. His ability to predict innovation mirrors the author's concern that living in the network society will force people to cope with enormous change, and although it is impossible to foretell the future, it is imperative for us to anticipate what Gibson calls the "nodal points," the places where change is most likely to occur. In *All Tomorrow's Parties* nanotechnology is the instrument of change, but its direction remains unspecified. As one of Gibson's characters explains to Laney, "I want the advent of a degree of functional nanotechnology in a world that will remain recognizably descended from the one I woke in this morning. I want my world transfigured, yet I want my place in that world to be the equivalent to the one I now occupy." Gibson insists that locating the nodal points is vital for our survival.

PATTERN RECOGNITION

Unlike his previous novels and stories, Gibson's eighth novel is set in the present, where the father

of the novel's heroine, Cayce Pollard, has vanished on September 11, 2001, in the rubble of the World Trade Center. One of the novel's subplots relates to the fact that Cayce's father, a retired cold war security expert, may not actually have died, and the mystery deepens when we learn that he had no business even being there. His disappearance is eventually tied to the main story line. The story, however, revolves around Cayce, who is a market research consultant for an advertising firm but also has exceptional skill as a "coolhunter," someone with an intuitive feel for advertising imagery and the potential of a design's efficacy. She explains her talent as recognizing a pattern before anyone else does. When Cayce is consulted by a top advertising agency to evaluate a new design, she rejects it. Subsequently strange things begin to happen to her. Her apartment is repeatedly burglarized, people are watching her, and she discovers a trail of pornography-site access on her browser. One aspect of the story entails her efforts to discover who is behind the harassment.

The primary focus of the novel, however, concerns a string of short video clips on a Web site that she constantly visits. The site has become very popular among viewers around the world, and questions begin to arise throughout the Net about the meaning of the footage and who might be creating it. She is subsequently hired by Blue Ant, an advertising firm based in London, to find the site's creator and to learn whether the footage is part of a brilliant ad campaign for some yet unrevealed product. Hubertus Bigend, the founder of Blue Ant, is intrigued by the footage's emotional appeal because this represents to him advertising's greatest triumph, the deep penetration of the human psyche. Before the mystery is resolved, the search for the site's author leads Cayce to Tokyo, Russia, and back to London. Along the way she encounters the Russian Mafia, as well as a bevy of Gibson's typical unusual characters, including an ex-American intelligence mathematician and a group of Tokyo computer hackers.

The novel is a thriller filled with intrigue and suspenseful action sequences. As in the best of crime fiction, the heroine often finds herself in peril before the story reaches its resolution. Gibson, however, is not simply writing pulp fiction, nor is the book an exposé of the advertising industry, although he does explore the subtle manipulations of big advertising, stealth marketing, and the quest for the perfect logo. Rather Gibson identifies the world of image-making as an arena wherein the forces of good and evil struggle for dominance. He recognizes the universal reach of advertising and how its products have insinuated themselves into the global consciousness. The search for pattern recognition therefore becomes for Gibson a metaphor for social control and a form of power. As Hubertus Bigend tells Cayce, "We have no idea, now, of who or what the inhabitants of our future might be. In that sense, we have no future... . We have only risk management. The spinning of the given moment's scenarios." Bigend informs her that he wants to make the public aware of something they don't yet know that they know: "It's about transferring information, but at the same time about a certain lack of specificity." Thus the only viable strategy for an advertising agency is to create enticements from the events and raw materials of the moment. Bigend characterizes this as "pattern recognition."

SUMMARY

From "Johnny Mnemonic" to *Neuromancer* to *Pattern Recognition*, a common theme shapes William Gibson's short stories and novels: technology is neutral, and dramatic changes in society are inevitable. His novels, however, warn that despite the vast innovation that portends the future he envisions, human nature remains human nature, and it is a matter of who controls technology that will determine its potential for good or evil. His novels are cautionary tales that exhort us to confront those who would distort the positive uses of technology for the common good and direct it to their own selfish advantage. At stake is the future of freedom and the lurking possibility that those who use technology for their own nefarious ends will someday control the planet.

Selected Bibliography

WORKS OF WILLIAM GIBSON

FICTION

Neuromancer. New York: Ace Books, 1984; London: Gollancz, 1984.

Burning Chrome. Preface by Bruce Sterling. New York: Arbor House, 1986; London: Gollancz, 1986. (Ten short stories: "Johnny Mnemonic," "The Gernsback Continuum," "Fragments of a Hologram Rose," "The Belonging Kind," "Hinterlands," "Red Star, Winter Orbit," "New Rose Hotel," "The Winter Market," "Dogfight," and "Burning Chrome.")

Count Zero. New York: Arbor House, 1986; London: Gollancz, 1986.

Mona Lisa Overdrive. New York: Bantam, 1988; London: Gollancz, 1988.

The Difference Engine. Cowritten by Bruce Sterling. London: Gollancz, 1990; New York: Bantam, 1991.

Virtual Light. New York: Bantam, 1993; London: Viking, 1993.

Idoru. New York: Putnam, 1996; London: Viking, 1996.

All Tomorrow's Parties. New York: Putnam, 1999; London: Viking, 1999.

Pattern Recognition. New York: Putnam, 2003; London: Viking, 2003.

OTHER WORKS

Text to accompany Robert Longo's *Dream Jumbo*. Produced at the UCLA Center for the Performing Arts, Los Angeles, California, 1989.

"Skinner's Room." Short story in the catalog for the *Visionary San Francisco* exhibition, San Francisco Museum of Modern Art, 1990.

"Rocket Radio." *Rolling Stone*, June 15, 1989, pp. 85–87.

Agrippa: *A Book of the Dead*. Etchings by Dennis Ashbaugh. New York: Kevin Begos, 1992. (Poem.)

Johnny Mnemonic. Directed by Robert Longo. TriStar Pictures, 1995. (Screenplay.)

"The Net Is a Waste of Time." *New York Times Magazine*, July 14, 1996, p. 31.

Alien 3. Unused screenplay. Hollywood, Calif.: Script City, 1997.

"Dead Man Sings." *Forbes ASAP Supplement*, November 30, 1998, p. 177.

"The Networked Neighbourhood." *New Statesman*, November 1, 1999, p. iii.

"Will We Plug Chips into Our Brains?" *Time*, June 19, 2000, pp. 84–86.

"Blasted Dreams in Mr. Buk's Window." *National Post*, September 20, 2001.

"Kill Switch." Episode of the *X-Files* cowritten by Tom Maddox.

"First Person Shooter." Episode of the *X-Files* cowritten by Tom Maddox.

CRITICAL AND BIOGRAPHICAL STUDIES

Concannon, Kevin. "The Contemporary Space of the Border: Gloria Anzaldua's *Borderlands* and William Gibson's *Neuromancer*." *Textual Practice* 12, no. 3:429–442 (winter 1998).

Csicsery-Ronay Jr., Istvan. "The Sentimental Futurist: Cybernetics and Art in William Gibson's *Neuromancer*." *Critique: Studies in Contemporary Fiction* 33:221–240 (spring 1992).

———. "Antimancer: Cybernetics and Art in Gibson's *Count Zero*." *Science-Fiction Studies* 22, no. 1:63–86 (March 1995).

Gilmore, Mikal. "The Rise of Cyberpunk." *Rolling Stone*, December 4, 1986, pp. 77–78, 107–108. (An article constructed around an interview with Gibson.)

Goh, Robbie B. H. "Consuming Spaces: Clive Barker, William Gibson, and the Cultural Poetics of Postmodern Fantasy." *Social Semiotics* 10, no. 1:21–39 (April 2000).

Grace, Dominick M. "From *Videodrome* to *Virtual Light*: David Cronenberg and William Gibson." *Extrapolation: A Journal of Science Fiction and Fantasy* 44, no. 3:344–355 (September 2003).

Hamburg, Victoria, and Aaron Rapoport. "The King of Cyberpunk." *Interview* 19, no. 1:84–88 (January 1989).

Hantke, Steffen. "Surgical Strikes and the Prosthetic Warriors: The Soldier's Body in Contemporary Science Fiction." *Science-Fiction Studies* 25, no. 3:495–509 (November 1998).

Harper, Leanne C. "The Culture of Cyberspace." *Bloomsbury Review* September/October 1988:16–17, 30.

Kozikowski, Thomas. "Gibson, William (Ford) 1948–." *Contemporary Authors*. Edited by Susan M. Trosky. Vol. 133. Detroit: Gale Research, 1991. Pp. 146–150.

Lindberg, Kathryn V. "Prosthetic Mnemonics and Prophylactic Politics: William Gibson among the Subjectivity Mechanisms." *Boundary 2* 23, no. 2:47–83 (summer 1996).

Marshall, John. "William Gibson's New Novel Asks, Is the Truth Stranger than Science Fiction Today?" *Seattle Post-Intelligencer*, February 6, 2003. (Review of *Pattern Recognition* that involves an interview with Gibson.)

Mattu, Ravi. "The Books That Matter to William Gibson." *Financial Times* (London), January 17, 2004, p. 46.

McCaffery, Larry. "An Interview with William Gibson." *Mississippi Review* 16, nos. 2/3 (spring/summer 1988).

———, ed. *Across the Wounded Galaxies: Interviews with*

Contemporary American Science Fiction Writers. Urbana: University of Illinois Press, 1990.

Mead, David G. "Technological Transfiguration in William Gibson's Sprawl Novels: *Neuromancer, Count Zero,* and *Mona Lisa Overdrive." Extrapolation: A Journal of Science Fiction and Fantasy* 32, no. 4:350–360 (winter 1991).

Murphy, Graham. "Post/Humanity and the Interstitial: A Glorification of Possibility in Gibson's Bridge Sequence." *Science-Fiction Studies* 30, no. 1:72–91 (March 2003).

Myers, Tony. "The Postmodern Imaginary in William Gibson's *Neuromancer." Modern Fiction Studies* 47, no. 4:887–909 (winter 2001).

Olsen, Lance. "The Shadow of Spirit in William Gibson's Matrix Trilogy." *Extrapolation: A Journal of Science Fiction and Fantasy* 32, no. 3:278–289 (fall 1991).

Palmer, Christopher. "*Mona Lisa Overdrive* and the Prosthetic." *Science-Fiction Studies* 31, no. 2:227–243 (July 2004).

Punday, Daniel. "The Narrative Construction of Cyberspace: Reading *Neuromancer,* Reading Cyberspace Debates." *College English* 63, no. 2:194–213 (November 2000).

Schmitt, Ronald. "Mythology and Technology: The Novels of William Gibson." *Extrapolation: A Journal of Science Fiction and Fantasy* 34, no. 1:64–78 (spring 1993).

Schroeder, Randy. "Determinacy, Indeterminacy, and the Romantic in William Gibson." *Science-Fiction Studies* 21, no. 2:155–163 (July 1994).

Siivonen, Timo. "Cyborgs and Generic Oxymorons: The Body and Technology in William Gibson's Cyberspace Trilogy." *Science-Fiction Studies* 23, no. 2:227–244 (July 1996).

Spencer, Nicholas. "Rethinking Ambivalence: Technopolitics and the Luddites in William Gibson and Bruce Sterling's *The Difference Engine." Contemporary Literature* 40, no. 3:403–429 (fall 1999).

Sponsler, Claire. "Cyberpunk and the Dilemmas of Postmodern Narrative: The Example of William Gibson." *Contemporary Literature* 33, no. 4:625–644 (winter 1992).

Staples, Brent. "A Prince of Cyberpunk Fiction Moves into the Mainstream." *New York Times,* May 11, 2003, section 4, p. 12.

Sterling, Bruce. Preface to *Burning Chrome.* New York: Arbor House, 1986; London: Gollancz, 1986.

Taylor, Christopher. "Genderbait for the Nerds." *London Review of Books,* May 22, 2003, p. 34. (Review of *Pattern Recognition.*)

Takayuki, Tatsumi. "Comparative Metafiction: Somewhere between Ideology and Rhetoric." *Critique: Studies in Contemporary Fiction* 39, no. 1:2–17 (fall 1997).

CHESTER BOMAR HIMES

(1909–1984)

STEPHEN F. SOITOS

IN OCTOBER 1956 Chester Himes was forty-seven years old and living at the Hôtel Rachou in Paris, France, soon to become famous as the "Beat Hotel" where the American writers Allen Ginsberg, William Burroughs, and Gregory Corso lived in the 1960s. Himes arrived in Paris in April 1953 after publishing four novels in the United States: *If He Hollers Let Him Go* (1945); *Lonely Crusade* (1947); *Cast the First Stone* (1952); and *The Third Generation* (1954). These novels of protest against the African American experience of racial oppression and degradation had earned Himes little critical or financial success. Now he was broke and desperate in Paris. Marcel Duhamel, the editor of the French publisher Gallimard's Série Noire, a line of crime fiction, persuaded Himes to try his hand at a detective novel set in Harlem. The result, *For Love of Imabelle* (1957), was hailed as a masterpiece by such literary giants as Jean Cocteau and Jean Giono. Translated into French as *La Reine des pommes*, it was awarded the Grand Prix de la Littérature Policiére for 1958. This was the first time the prestigious annual prize, honoring the best crime novel published in France, was awarded to a non-French, let alone African American, author.

Himes went on to write nine more novels in the crime genre, featuring the black detectives Coffin Ed Johnson and Grave Digger Jones. A satirical exploration of racism, crime, and poverty in the Harlem ghetto, the books were a popular success in France and later in the United States.

Chester Himes came of age in the 1920s, experiencing the twilight days of the Harlem Renaissance (1920-1935), when African American artists celebrated the urbanization of black folk-culture. He associated with various artists of this period including Langston Hughes, Wallace Thurman, and Carl Van Vechten. A contemporary of Richard Wright, James Baldwin, and Ralph Ellison, Himes was in the vanguard of black writers depicting the struggle against social injustice while exploring African American sensibility and culture. His early work shows the influence of the proletarian naturalism of the 1930s and 1940s. In books such as *If He Hollers Let Him Go* and *The Third Generation*, Himes dramatically analyzed the social and natural forces that imprisoned his characters in poverty, futility, and smoldering rage brought on by endemic racism.

Between 1932 and 1979 Himes wrote twenty novels, numerous essays, sixty-one short stories, and a two-volume autobiography. Recognized today chiefly for his Harlem thrillers, two of which were made into movies, his other works deserve serious attention. Himes's writing expresses the unresolved tensions of race and class relations in the United States. A link between the Harlem Renaissance and the Black Arts movement of the 1960s, Himes re-created in his semiautobiographical novels a social history of African American society extending from the Great Depression (1929-1940) to World War II (1941-1945) and into the 1970s.

EARLY LIFE

Chester Bomar Himes was born on July 29, 1909, in Jefferson City, Missouri. That same year, the influential black intellectual W. E. B. Du Bois helped found the National Association for the Advancement of Colored People (NAACP); Du Bois served as the editor of the NAACP journal *Crisis*, which would later publish Himes's short stories and essays. The youngest of the three sons of Joseph Sandy Himes and Estelle Bomar Himes, Chester Himes passed his first sixteen years in the segregated South.

His father was a professor who taught mechanical skills and black history; his mother, a gifted musician, occasionally taught music. Estelle Himes was light complexioned and claimed a genealogy back through slavery to the American Revolution and a link to British aristocracy. She was the daughter of prosperous South Carolina Presbyterians who rose from bondage to become successful in business. Estelle Himes homeschooled her sons for most of their early education. She was against segregation but was uncomfortable in both the white and black worlds of the provincial South.

Joseph Himes Sr. was dark skinned and took pride in his African heritage. He was one of the first to teach black history in southern colleges. The growing differences between his parents became a source of tension early on in Chester Himes's life. The conflict within the African American community caused by perceived degrees of blackness was a theme Himes would explore in many of his works, and interracial relationships obsessed him all his life.

From 1913 to 1925 the family relocated frequently as Joseph senior took teaching jobs at various land-grant colleges in Mississippi, Arkansas, and Missouri. Chester and his brother Joseph junior also traveled with their mother to live for a time in South Carolina and in Georgia, where she had been offered teaching posts. The brothers received their first formal education in Georgia, where they entered the eighth grade. Race riots were common during this period in most major southern cities; one of the worst riots took place in East St. Louis, Illinois, in the summer of 1917, news of which traveled through the southern black community.

In June 1923 Himes's brother Joseph junior was blinded in an accident at school. Chester was to have assisted Joseph in a presentation of a chemistry experiment involving gunpowder. On the day of the program his mother refused to let Chester participate, because he had broken a rule at home. During the experiment, a flask exploded in Joseph's face. He was refused assistance at a nearby white hospital, and did not receive adequate medical care for the injury for several days. Chester would continue to feel guilty about his brother's blindness and to rebel against his mother's stern rules.

In 1925, motivated by unemployment, racial inequality, and the lack of improvement in Joseph junior's condition under treatment at Barnes Hospital in St. Louis, Joseph Himes moved his family to Cleveland, Ohio. The Himes family thus joined the great Northern Migration of African Americans fleeing the South in the years following World War I. In January 1926, due to a clerical error, Chester Himes graduated from high school. Due to a transcription error he received a passing grade in high school Latin, which made him eligible for admission to Ohio State University after graduation. He was already working as a bartender and gambler in Cleveland's black district. In order to earn money for college, he took a job as a busboy at Wade Park Manor Hotel. While on the job, he was seriously injured in a fall forty feet down an empty elevator shaft, suffering three broken vertebrae, a broken jaw, shattered teeth, and a broken left arm. Himes spent four months in the hospital. His medical expenses were paid by the Ohio State Industrial Commission, which for the next ten years gave him a small monthly pension as compensation. Because of the injury to his back, he was forced to wear a brace for the rest of his life.

Himes enrolled at Ohio State University, in Columbus, in September 1926. He scored high on the IQ tests but his high school course work proved inadequate preparation for the premed courses he elected to take. He encountered a segregated university life at Columbus, in which black students were not admitted to the white dormitories, student union, or dining halls. The University provided no dorms or dining halls for blacks and Himes felt uncomfortable in the predominantly white middle-class environment.

Receiving poor grades in his first semester, Himes retreated to Columbus's black ghetto to drink and gamble. During this time he was introduced to the vibrant black cultural life of Columbus, and attended road shows starring such entertainers as Josephine Baker and Ethel Waters. Forced to withdraw from Ohio State in the spring of 1927 because of his poor academic performance and objectionable activities off-campus,

Himes returned to his Cleveland home sick and psychologically exhausted. By the summer of 1928, at the age of nineteen, Himes was hustling, gambling, and committing crimes. He carried a gun. Some of the people he knew during this period would later appear in fictional form in his writing. He met his future wife Jean Johnson when they worked together at a hotel.

Himes was first arrested for stealing a case of Colt automatics to sell to black workers in the Youngstown steel mills. Soon after, he was arrested for passing bad checks in Columbus, near the Ohio State campus. Finally, in November 1928, he was arrested for armed robbery after breaking into the home of a white couple in Cleveland, and he was sentenced in December to twenty to twenty-five years of hard labor in the Ohio State Penitentiary.

PRISON AND FIRST WRITINGS

Himes was nineteen when he went to prison and twenty-six when he was released on parole. Although he devoted only a few pages in his autobiography to his prison stay, Himes was radically altered by his experience behind bars. Ohio State Penitentiary was one of the most repressive state prisons of the era. On Easter Monday 1930 the prison was partially destroyed in the infamous Ohio Penitentiary fire. Hundreds of trapped inmates perished in their cells. Himes recorded the tragedy in an early short story, "To What Red Hell" (1934), published while he was still in prison.

Himes claimed in his autobiography that he turned to writing in prison because it protected him from abuse by guards and hostile prisoners because it gave him an aura of power and protection. He read westerns and detective pulps such as *Black Mask* and mainstream magazines like *Esquire*, which inspired his first efforts. He developed a social vision that centered on the psychological consequences of violence and racism and the absurdity it engendered in its victims' lives.

Himes documented his stay in Ohio State Penitentiary in a novel as well as a number of short stories. He started publishing in 1932 in black periodicals. His first publication, "His Last Day," appeared in *Abbott's Monthly* in November of that year. "He Knew" was published in December 1933 and featured two tough black cops forced to kill two burglars, who turn out to be the sons of one of the detectives. The story was an early indication of Himes's interest in mystery stories, which he would explore later in his Harlem detective series.

More prestigious and lucrative was the publication in *Esquire* of "Crazy in the Stir" (1934) and later "The Night's for Cryin'" (1937) and "Marijuana and a Pistol" (1940). In these stories, Himes's principal figures are white and the author's race is not identified. But the narratives, of individuals caught in a world of despair and violence, have a universal quality.

Himes worked on the novel about his prison experience for a number of years after his release. The book underwent many revisions before it was published in a heavily expurgated version under the title *Cast the First Stone* (1952). After Himes's death, the original manuscript was restored and published as *Yesterday Will Make You Cry* (1998).

Cast the First Stone presents the prison experience from the first-person viewpoint of Jimmy Monroe, a young white inmate. Jimmy copes with prison life through a radical resocialization to a new society of men. Monroe rebels against the boredom, petty meanness, and loneliness of prison existence by obstinately refusing to do work assignments and by gambling. This leads to beatings, reduced rations, and solitary confinement. But it is the intrigues among the convicts that prove the most devastating and revealing.

During his later life, notably in his autobiography *The Quality of Hurt*, Himes was generally critical of homosexuality. This defensive position seems confusing, however, since both the edited and unexpurgated versions of this early novel deal explicitly and tenderly with homosexual affairs. Jimmy Monroe has a relationship with a young brown-skinned inmate named Duke Dido in *Cast the First Stone*; in *Yesterday Will Make You Cry* this character appears under the name Prince Rico. Monroe's self-destructive impulses

are illuminated by his brutal honesty as the love story unfolds. Monroe and Dido are persecuted by the other inmates, and at the end of *Cast the First Stone*, after Monroe is paroled, Duke Dido hangs himself in despair.

Both versions of the novel graphically describe the gaunt, dreary, brutal rhythms of prison life, but the original version, as rendered in *Yesterday Will Make You Cry*, employs a third-person narration, as opposed to first in *Cast the First Stone*, resulting in a more lyrical depiction of Jimmy Monroe's psychological state. The character's honest self-portrayals of a mixed-up youth, his family dynamics, and his criminal activities dovetail with Himes's own story. The original version also contains an expanded account of the prison fire, perhaps the best reportage of a prison tragedy in literature.

In *Yesterday Will Make You Cry*, the affair with Prince Rico is rendered as more honest and emotional than in the edited version. The last third of the book explores in depth the love of two men trapped in prison, combating the loneliness of their fates. This version concludes, like *Cast the First Stone*, with Jimmy Monroe's parole, but the ending of *Yesterday Will Make You Cry* is redemptive. Prince Rico does not commit suicide. Instead both characters are transformed by their experiences in surviving the institution's attempts to destroy them.

In both versions of the book Himes never explicitly acknowledges Jimmy Monroe's struggles as connected to black themes, racism is implied but not directly analyzed. But the prison system offers an analogy to American society in its power structure and abuses. Repressive systems eventually demean and corrupt everyone caught in their grasp.

Chester Himes was released into his mother's custody on April 1, 1936, after serving seven and half years of his sentence. His parents were separated and living in Cleveland. He was twenty-six years old and soon drifted back to his former life among gamblers and prostitutes in Cleveland's black slums. After his mother had him transferred into the custody of his father, Chester moved into a room in downtown Cleveland. Himes worked as a waiter and bellhop

in a country club. He resumed his relationship with Jean Johnson. He met Langston Hughes, who was working on a theater project in Cleveland. Himes married Johnson on August 13, 1937. The marriage would last fourteen years.

During this period Himes recognized poverty as both the origin and reflection of racism in every aspect of American life. Poverty engendered severe social, psychological, and sexual consequences in African American society. Himes dedicated himself to writing about the African American experience from the male viewpoint. The generally negative reception his early books received among American critics was largely due to his unflinching critique of racist American society in the period before the civil rights movement of the 1950s and 1960s.

PROTEST NOVELS

In November 1937 Himes found work in the Depression-era Works Progress Administration (WPA). His first job was digging ditches but he soon qualified as an editorial assistant. He was assigned to write an Ohio history essay and a public guide to Cleveland. He also wrote articles about the Council of Industrial Organizations (CIO), a union that proclaimed its opposition to racism and supported workers' rights.

In the fall of 1941 Chester and Jean Himes moved to Los Angeles, where Himes hoped to sell his prison novel. Instead, he found rejection and race prejudice. Race relations in Southern California were tense, as a large population of southern whites had flooded the unskilled-labor market in Los Angeles during the Depression. Himes observed that blacks as well as Filipinos, Mexicans, and Japanese Americans experienced discrimination and violence.

Himes worked in shipyards and war plants over a span of four years. His writing at this time became more racially focused and defiant. He wrote an article describing the appalling treatment of Mexican Americans who were attacked and beaten by soldiers and sailors during the Zoot Suit Riots of 1942. In another article titled "Negro Martyrs Are Needed," published in *Crisis* in May 1944, he called for a black revolution to fulfill the promises of the U.S. Constitution. It

drew the attention of the Federal Bureau of Investigation.

In 1944 Himes was awarded a Rosenwald Foundation writer's grant. He and his wife moved to New York City, and over the next three years he wrote two novels concerning his experiences in the Los Angeles shipyards. *If He Hollers Let Him Go* and *Lonely Crusade* both deal with the anger, frustration, and sense of rejection in the life of a young, educated African American male trying to survive in a brutal world where war hysteria had thrown the races into conflict. Much of Himes's time in New York was spent in Harlem, the African American community he would describe in his later detective novels. In New York at this time he met two important African American writers, Richard Wright, author of *Native Son* (1940), and Ralph Ellison, author of *Invisible Man* (1952).

Himes's first published books pay homage to the tradition of American proletarian fiction of the 1920s and 1930s, being social-realist explorations of wartime workers, in which economic and political tensions are compounded by racial division and hatred. Himes demonstrates the absurdities of both racism and capitalism based on their exploitation of the underclass.

If He Hollers Let Him Go tells the story of Bob Jones, a UCLA graduate who out of financial necessity takes a job as foreman of a black work crew in the Atlas Shipyards in Los Angeles during World War II. The novel is structured around incidents of racism that Jones encounters in a feverish four-day period. Jones's vivid nightly dreams of persecution underscore the tense atmosphere in which he is living. Racism is a brutal fact of life for the Japanese, Filipino, Mexican, and black workers of the city's factories and shipyards.

Jones is engaged to Alice Harrison, a light-skinned black woman from a wealthy family. She is repulsed by Jones's rage and resentment over the prejudice he encounters at work. She would rather have him go back to college and become more assimilated. Jones risks his life under the hazardous working conditions of ship construction and also faces personal danger through his involvement with the workers' union.

Prejudice against him from his white coworkers and bosses increases as Jones's union is threatened. The novel ends with Jones being falsely accused of raping a fellow worker, Madge, a white southern woman both repelled by and attracted to Jones. Beaten by Madge's avenging white southern coworkers, pursued by police, and finally captured, Bob is given the choice of military enlistment or going to trial. In the end Bob Jones chooses enlistment in the army and is rushed away from his life in Los Angeles to fight in World War II.

If He Hollers Let Him Go was published in November 1945. On the day of its publication Himes's publicity appointments were canceled; Himes later found out that a racist editor had sabotaged his tour and also limited production of the book. Although reviews of the book were favorable, it did not sell well and Himes's writing career sputtered. In 1946 Chester and Jean visited California, where Himes wrote the first draft of *Lonely Crusade*. They returned to New York and lived for a time on Long Island and then back in Harlem, where Chester finished *Lonely Crusade* and reworked his prison novel.

To make ends meet, Himes took various jobs, including caretaker, porter, and bellhop at hotels. He began an intense and destructive relationship with Vandi Haygood, acting director of the Rosenwald Foundation. Their relationship would later be portrayed in vivid detail in the novel he believed his best, *The Primitive*, published in 1956.

Lonely Crusade is also set against the backdrop of the California war industries. Lee Gordon is a labor man hired to unionize the black workers of Comstock Aircraft. He is married to Ruth, a successful businesswoman who earns more money than he. Frustrated at work by racial prejudice and at home by an empty marriage, Gordon lashes out at Ruth. He deserts her for Jackie Forks, a white friend who is really a Communist agent trying to sabotage his plans for the union. The affair with Jackie sends Gordon into a nightmarish downward spiral.

Gordon discovers that he is being manipulated by white union officials, by Communists, and by Foster, the clever plant owner. Foster attempts to

bribe Gordon away from the union by offering him an easy job and five thousand dollars and then brutally pistol-whip him when he refuses to be bought. He sticks with the union at the risk of losing his life.

Confronting issues of black anti-Semitism, racism among union officials, and corrupt management, the novel closes with a dramatic strike, in which workers march outside the Comstock factory. A fellow union member is beaten trying to enter the plant at the head of the mass of workers. Gordon grabs the fallen banner and leads the workers into the plant. This depiction of union solidarity and nascent black power is expressive of Himes's early social vision.

Lonely Crusade's bitter reception by critics demoralized Himes. Remaining committed to his writing, in May 1948 he installed himself at Yaddo, a writer's colony in upstate New York. The experience was not a happy one, however, as the creative isolation offered at Yaddo exacerbated in Himes anxieties and fears about his role as a black artist.

Around this time he gave an impassioned address titled "The Dilemma of the Negro Writer" at the University of Chicago. In this presentation, he described his degrading experiences as an African American. His message was uncompromising. Racism, he claimed, had created an alienated class in the United States that could never be understood by whites.

By 1952 Himes had separated from his wife and was back in Harlem, living alone in a furnished room. During this period he worked on *The Third Generation*, his most autobiographical novel. Published in 1954, the narrative concerns the fortunes of the Taylor family, a saga of disintegration closely modeled on Himes's own experience. The work covers the early years of Himes's life, when his family was under intense pressure living in the segregated South. The Taylor family is an embodiment of the complex relationships blacks have with a racist American culture and the psychological and material stresses that destroy their lives.

Lillian Taylor, a light-skinned black woman, reverences the imagined aristocracy of her ancestors and wants to rear her children in the belief that they are in large part white. The father, a darker man, wants to prepare them for being black. He is fired from his job as a teacher and suffers from an angry impotence, as he struggles against his wife's constant criticism and his difficulty earning a living.

The young and creative Charles Taylor is in conflict with his possessive mother, Lillian, who dominates the family. Charles is frustrated by endless family arguments and his mother's skirmishes with both blacks and whites. She is unable to find her place between the two cultures, and this tension creates an inevitable schism in Charles Taylor's self-image.

Charles rebelliously resorts to a life on the streets complete with petty crime, indiscriminate sex, violence, and drugs. Many of the episodes ring true to Himes's own experiences building up to his prison sentence.

The Taylor family seems stalked by an evil fate. As a representative unit of African American culture, their doomed history is linked to social and naturalistic forces that are beyond their control. The history of slavery and the living presence of prejudice both influence and mold their existence. Continuously stymied by poverty and racist segregation, they become self-destructive. Their own incapacities, weaknesses, and obsessions are magnified by the seeming inescapability of their plight.

Charles Taylor, the sensitive son with the most promise, is affected the most. His despair is increased by the divorce, and then by the death, of his parents, and by his brother's blindness as a result of a failed chemistry experiment. He questions the futility of survival in a world with no place for him. Even the black ghetto and women of the street betray him into self-destructive bouts of drinking and rage.

The tragedy of the Taylors is written as an epic journey of African American dislocation and struggle. Taking place in the early part of the twentieth century in the South, the psychological restraints that are slavery's legacy are shown to dominate American society and effect the destiny of the Taylor family as well as the national psyche.

In January 1953 Himes's father died and he had to borrow money from Vandi Haygood to return to Cleveland to attend the funeral. Shortly afterward, he received a publishing advance for *The Third Generation*. The money made it possible for Himes to seek a new life overseas.

LIFE AS AN EXPATRIATE

Himes's European adventure began during his passage on the *Ile de France* in April 1953. He met Willa Thompson, a Boston socialite and mother of four in her late thirties, who was seeking a divorce from her Luxembourgian husband. It was the beginning of an intense three-year relationship.

On April 10, 1953, Himes arrived in Paris and joined a group of African American artists, including Richard Wright and James Baldwin, who had established a presence in Europe, fleeing the racism of their home country. There was a competitive tension among the group, which had the peculiar status of being a Parisian subculture. They met and mingled at cafés throughout the city.

The following month Himes and Thompson left Paris for Arcachon in the southwest of France, where Himes spent a pleasant two months relaxing and writing. He often looked back on this idyll of companionship, swimming, sailing, and writing as one of the happiest periods of his life. Himes and Thompson also collaborated on a novel about her life in German-occupied Europe during World War II, which was published under Thompson's name years later.

In July of 1953 Himes and Thompson had moved to London. After six months they were back on the Continent, living in Majorca, Spain, where Himes worked on the novel that would become *The Primitive*. The couple was back in Paris in November 1954, when Thompson grew ill and left for the United States and Himes received a one thousand dollar advance on his novel *The Primitive* from the New American Library. Himes returned to London, where he lived in a lonely bedroom walkup and finished the final draft of *The Primitive*.

Himes lived the next twenty years of his life in restless movement between countries and cities in Europe and trips back to the United States. During those years, he was in constant financial trouble and enmeshed in a series of overlapping and emotional love affairs with white women. Himes would analyze these affairs in both his autobiography and his fiction. Many of Himes's male protagonists have a self-lacerating obsession with white women. Himes saw this pathology as a direct connection to racism's legacy grounded in unconscious sexual fears and guilt.

The setting for the *The Primitive* (1955) is a ground-floor apartment in New York City; its events take place over the course of one weekend. The novel concerns the relationship between Jesse Robinson and Kriss Cummings, a black man and white woman closely modeled after Himes and Vandi Haygood. The narrative features elements of absurdist comedy as well as passages of abject horror and degradation, a pattern that Himes would continue to develop in his Harlem crime novels.

Jesse and Kriss are codependents trapped in an intense, emotionally devastating affair. The novel is a well-plotted tragedy that ends with the murder of Kriss by Jesse in a drunken haze. Himes uses shifting viewpoints and interior flashbacks to delineate both characters' states of mind as they cling to each other in a maddening cycle of obsessive need and repulsion.

Jesse is insecure and angry over his rejection as a writer. Kriss is a divorced woman of middle age who is despondent and depressed. Her business career is on the skids and she is desperate for human contact. Their frustrating affair is fueled by alcohol and drugs. At the core of their intimacy lies an unresolved tension over interracial relationships. Jesse's compulsive need is both a fascination with white women and a fear of their power over black men. Kriss is an advocate of racial harmony but under constant pressure she retaliates against Jesse using racial slurs. He engages her in this verbal abuse, and alcohol and drugs destroy their inhibitions with fatal consequences.

The television becomes a daring surrealistic motif in *The Primitive*, providing a running commentary on modern life. The TV is chorus and oracle, emphasizing the characters' loneliness

and isolation. A talking chimpanzee comments on the news, reporting the Supreme Court's 1954 decision for school desegregation. In a bizarre moment it predicts Jesse's killing of Kriss at the end of the novel. Himes would later comment that the murder was the only event in the story that was untrue.

During a nine-month visit to New York City in 1955 during which he tried to reconnect with Willa and renew publishing contacts, Himes learned of Vandi Haygood's sudden death from a drug overdose. This tragedy, combined with his continuing financial hardships, his off-and-on relationship with Willa Thompson, and his lack of success in placing his stories in magazines drove him into intense depression. He later commented that his return to New York from Paris had been a complete mistake. He took work as a busboy in a cafeteria while he waited for reprint rights to *If He Hollers* and a payment of one thousand dollars. This experience later provided the groundwork for his novel *Run Man Run* (1966), a harrowing story of a white detective trying to kill a black worker who had witnessed the detective's gunning down of two black coworkers. The book may represent the purest critique of racism Himes wrote.

Finally receiving reprint compensation from a publisher, Himes returned to Paris in December 1955. Determined to try a different type of novel, he began work on *Pinktoes* (1961). This narrative harked back to his association with a politically active Harlem couple, Henry and Molly Moon. Henry worked for the NAACP and Molly for the Urban League. Himes conceived of the work as a satirical exploration of racial politics, both black and white, revolving around minority-empowerment organizations. *Pinktoes* is a satiric mixture of Harlem anecdotes and erotic intrigues between the races based on the race relations. Himes attended in Harlem. Employing a comic style of language featuring double entendres, sexual puns, and farcical dialogue, the story is a savage critique of human folly exacerbated by racism and well-meaning, but misguided, liberalism.

Mamie Mason is the popular hostess of Harlem social life. She and her husband, Joe, both work for prominent black political groups. Mamie is ambitious, lecherous, and a glutton, who is forever manipulating people to attain political and sexual advantage.

The novel lampoons middle-class lifestyle and the pretentious hypocrisy of powerful political figures, both black and white. Himes suggests that at the core of individuals' conniving to solve the "Negro problem" lie the purely human foibles of petty egotism and domination.

Mamie Mason tries to force the wife of the great race leader Wallace Wright to come to one of her parties. Wright is having an affair with a white woman. Mamie reveals the affair, which starts a chain reaction of ludicrous behavior. Meanwhile, the rumor that white male liberals are abandoning their wives for young black women drives a cosmetic firm marketing the skin lightener Black No More to bring out a companion product, Blackamoor, for whites. White women rush to kink their hair and dye their faces black.

The struggle for black equality gets pushed to the background, replaced by interracial affairs and bedroom farce. Publishers, artists, college and foundation presidents, actors, and clerics are parodied with bawdy satire. With its farcical overtones and folk-tale elements, *Pinktoes* is a spoof of some Harlem Renaissance themes. The book owes a debt to a little-known novel, George Schuyler's satire *Black No More* (1931), in which blacks turn themselves white using a pseudoscientific cosmetic that bleaches their skin.

Pinktoes was published in Paris and became a best seller. Himes moved to the south of France and then back to Paris. He began an affair with a young German student, Regine Fischer. Their relationship lasted three years and involved trips to Germany and Denmark. Visits to Regine's middle-class German parents proved awkward for Himes, and the emotional difficulties associated with their relationship eventually led to Regine's hospitalization for suicidal behavior.

During this period of the late 1950s, Himes continued his relations with black American artists, many of whom gathered at the Café Tournon. The cartoonist Ollie Harrington and the novelist William Gardner Smith were part of this group.

Finding material in the black expatriate experience, Himes wrote the roman à clef *Une Affair de viol* (1963), published in the United States in 1980 as *A Case of Rape* (1980). Written in 1956-57 in English, it was translated into French for its initial publication. Appearing in France at the height of the Algerian War and containing a preface by the feminist and antiwar activist Christiane Rochefort, it is Himes's only novel with a European background.

Ethnic and racist violence in France are central to this story of four black expatriates falsely accused of the rape and murder of a white woman named Elizabeth Hancock. The book is a pastiche of news reports, trial records, and memoirs. It adds up to a case study in racial pathology. Parts of the story are directly related to Himes's affair with Willa Thompson.

Himes uses aspects of himself, Ollie Harrington, William Gardner Smith, James Baldwin, and Richard Wright in the book. The expatriate narrator is a writer who investigates the case, which is based on circumstantial evidence, trying to prove that the convictions of the black men are politically motivated. In the narrative, Himes explores taboos about interracial sex and the intricacies of power and violence that are rooted in the destructive force of racism.

The book is less about an actual rape than about the mythology of racial stereotypes and the tangled web of motivations surrounding black men and white women. Everyone in the story is a victim of racism, which causes a white woman to senselessly lose her life and four black men to be wrongly condemned to prison. Himes's last line in the book is "We are all guilty."

Soon after writing the book, Himes moved to the Hotel Rachou. Plagued by debts, he sent off a flood of letters seeking help from friends and publishers. Then one day in a publisher's office, he got an unexpected offer.

DETECTIVE NOVELS

Marcel Duhamel's Serie Noir included French editions of American crime fiction by writers such as James M. Cain, Dashiell Hammett, and Raymond Chandler. Duhamel knew Himes's

work and in 1956 suggested that he write a crime novel set in Harlem. The result was *For Love of Imabelle*, later published under the title *A Rage in Harlem* (1965). The novel was written in English and translated into French by Gallimard. Since Himes did not speak or write French this was a process that continued for all of Himes's French publications. *Plan B* was the only novel not published by Gallimard.

The novel, written in France but dealing with black characters living in Harlem, launched a new career for Himes. He would write a total of ten novels in the ongoing series: *For Love of Imabelle; The Real Cool Killers* (1959); *The Crazy Kill* (1959); *The Big Gold Dream* (1960); *All Shot Up* (1960); *Cotton Comes to Harlem* (1965); *Run Man Run* (1966); *The Heat's On* (1966); *Blind Man with a Pistol* (1969); and the posthumously published *Plan B* (1993).

Himes's work was a unique contribution to the African American detective tradition that began in the early twentieth century with publication of Pauline Hopkin's *Hagar's Daughter* (1901-1902), John Edward Bruce's *The Black Sleuth* (1908) and Rudolph Fisher's *The Conjure-Man Dies* (1932). Both *Hagar's Daughter* and *The Black Sleuth* were originally published in African-American periodical literature. His novels can be seen as a bridge between this early black detective fiction and later work by John A. Williams, Ishmael Reed, Walter Mosley, Barbara Neeley, and Toni Morrison. Himes also opened the way for detective stories written by other ethnic minorities.

Himes's police novels extend the tradition of African American detective fiction with the use of double-conscious detection or African American detective traits; black vernaculars such as music, language, and food; and commentary on African American religion. Himes engages and challenges the formulas of detective fiction by looking at crimes through the lens of racism.

Himes transformed the typically white, mainstream detective novels by creating a black detective team, Coffin Ed Johnson and Grave Digger Jones. These hard-boiled police officers serve as a bridge between the white and black worlds. They battle the exploitation of Harlem residents

as law officers but they are also held accountable to their white superiors in the larger Manhattan police force. They denounce the poverty and inequality that is a direct result of racism by means of clever conversational asides and astute character analysis.

Coffin Ed and Gravedigger are manipulators of language; their commentary on social conditions is both hilarious and ironic. Their ability to both indict and entertain is reminiscent of the trickster hero of black folklore.

In these episodic and satirical novels, which illuminate the spirit, religion, and life of the African American community, Harlem is a city within a city, revealing harsh social realities as well as a comic flow of absurd characters and situations. In *For Love of Imabelle* a good-hearted black sucker named Jackson, along with his unfaithful light-skinned paramour, gets caught up in a con game with disastrous results. *All Shot Up* features slapstick macabre murders and a corrupt, courageous, and secretly homosexual Harlem political leader, Casper Holmes. *The Heat's On* weaves a plot around two drug dealers, Sister Heavenly and Uncle Saint, and three million dollars of heroin stuffed into a string of Hudson River eels. In *Cotton Comes to Harlem* a bewildering search for a bale of cotton filled with eighty-seven thousand dollars gives Himes the opportunity to satirize white supremacists, jab at black nationalist movements, and poke fun at black religion. *The Big Gold Dream* contains one of Himes's favorite themes, the crooked street preacher who tricks the desperate religious-minded poor.

Himes's ten detective novels also provide a social history of Harlem and of changing race relations after the assassination of Martin Luther King Jr. and Malcolm X in the late 1960s. The riots, civil rights, and black power struggles of the period are dealt with in the last of Himes's police narratives.

Himes reworked the violence common to the detective fiction drama and gave it a social expression. In the books, violence progresses from comic to chaotic, finally erupting into revolution. In *Blind Man with a Pistol*, three marching groups, Brotherly Love, Black Power, and Black Jesus all converge for a riot at 135th Street and Seventh Avenue. Grave Digger and Coffin Ed can do nothing to stop the insanity, nor can they bring resolution to the criminal cases they are assigned. Harlem has become an unsolvable mystery that only serves to confuse the detectives. At the book's end they take out their frustration by shooting rats swarming from a tenement under demolition.

Plan B's apocalyptic vision further shatters any attempt at peaceful resolution between the races. In this book, race wars, engineered by the revolutionary Tomsson Black, bring down the whole rotten structure of American society. Coffin Ed and Grave Digger take opposing sides and Gravedigger kills Ed. Gravedigger is then killed by Tomsson Black, signifying the total collapse of law and order. This final detective novel fantasizes the ultimate desperate demise of American society.

LATER LIFE

Himes traveled widely throughout Europe during the writing of the detective novels. In 1958 he had met Lesley Packard, a thirty-year-old Englishwoman who was working in Paris as a journalist. By 1970 they were living in Alicante, Spain; they were married in November 1978. In 1970 Chester and Lesley flew to New York for the opening of *Cotton Comes to Harlem*. The movie, directed by the black actor and playwright Ossie Davis and filmed entirely in Harlem, was a popular success. In 1974 the motion picture *Come Back, Charleston Blue*, based on *The Heat's On*, was released but failed at the box office. Himes has been credited with contributing to the changing face of the popular black hero in American motion pictures. The two films *Cotton Comes to Harlem* and *Come Back, Charleston Blue* appeared at the beginning of what later came to be know as the era of blaxploitation in the film industry. This era ushered in the idea of a virile, courageous black hero who, in the fight for justice, is equal parts black power and black rebel. Melvin Van Peebles and Spike Lee are two black film directors who have acknowledged Himes's influence on their work.

Himes suffered the first of a series of strokes in 1963 and experienced various health problems throughout his later life. He continued to write despite his failing health, publishing a collection of miscellaneous writings, *Black on Black: "Baby Sister" and Selected Writings* (1973), and a two-volume autobiography, *The Quality of Hurt* (1972) and *My Life of Absurdity* (1976). Himes died in Spain on November 13, 1984. Having struggled as a writer throughout his life, he had lived to see his novels translated into many languages and to receive the praise of critics all over the world.

Chester Himes left a written legacy of the African American male consciousness in the twentieth century. He was an uncompromising writer who spared no one, including himself, in his search for racial understanding. His work continues to inspire the contemporary audience with its frightening pictures of black protagonists consumed by self-doubt and hatred, caught in a vicious cycle of racism and poverty.

Selected Bibliography

WORKS OF CHESTER HIMES

NOVELS

If He Hollers Let Him Go. Garden City, N.Y.: Doubleday, Doran, 1945.

Lonely Crusade. New York: Knopf, 1947.

Cast the First Stone. New York: Coward-McCann, 1952. (Restored to its original version and published under the title *Yesterday Will Make You Cry.* New York: Norton, 1998.)

The Third Generation. Cleveland: World Publishers, 1954.

The Primitive. New York: New American Library, 1956.

For Love of Imabelle. Greenwich, Conn.: Fawcett World Library, 1957. (Republished under the title *A Rage in Harlem.* New York: Avon, 1965.) (French edition *La Reine des pommes.* Paris: Gallimard, 1958.)

The Real Cool Killers. New York: Avon, 1959. (French edition *Il pleut des coups durs.* Paris: Gallimard, 1958.)

The Crazy Kill. New York: Avon, 1959. (French edition *Couché dans le pain.* Paris: Gallimard, 1959.)

The Big Gold Dream. New York: Avon, 1960. (French edition *Tout pour plaire.* Paris: Gallimard, 1959.)

All Shot Up. New York: Avon, 1960. (French edition *Imbroglio négro.* Paris: Gallimard, 1960.)

Pinktoes. Paris: Olympia Press, 1961. New York: Putnam/Stein & Day, 1965.

Cotton Comes to Harlem. New York: Putnam, 1965. (French edition *Retour en Afrique.* Paris: Plon, 1964.)

The Heat's On. New York: Putnam, 1966. (French edition *Ne nous énervons pas!* Paris: Gallimard, 1961. Republished under the title *Come Back, Charleston Blue,* after the American film adaptation. New York: Berkley, 1972.

Run Man Run. New York: Putnam, 1966. (French edition *Dare-dare.* Paris: Gallimard, 1959.)

Blind Man with a Pistol. New York: Morrow, 1969. (French edition *L'Aveugle au pistolet,* Paris, Gallimard, 1970.)

Plan B. Jackson: University Press of Mississippi, 1993. (French edition *Plan B.* Paris: Lieu Gommun, 1983.)

A Case of Rape. New York: Targ, 1980. (French edition *Une Affaire de viol.* Paris: Editions Les Yeux Ouverts, 1963.)

SELECTED SHORT FICTION

"His Last Day." *Abbott's Monthly* 5:32–33, 60–63 (November 1932).

"He Knew." *Abbott's Monthly and Illustrated News* 1:15 (December 2, 1933).

"Crazy in the Stir." *Esquire* 2:28, 114–117 (August 1934).

"To What Red Hell." *Esquire* 2:100–101, 122, 127 (October 1934).

"The Night's for Cryin'." *Esquire* 7:64, 146–148 (January 1937). Reprinted in *The Negro Caravan.* Edited by Sterling A. Brown, Arthur P. Davis, and Ulysses Lee. New York: Dryden Press, 1941. Pp. 101–105.

"Marijuana and a Pistol." *Esquire* 13:58 (March 1940). Reprinted in *The Best Short Stories by Negro Writers: An Anthology from 1899 to the Present.* Edited by Langston Hughes. Boston: Little Brown, 1967. Pp. 104–106. Also in *Right On!: An Anthology of Black Literature.* Edited by Bradford Chambers and Rebecca Moon. New York: New American Library, 1970. Pp. 115–117.

COLLECTED WORKS

Black on Black: "Baby Sister" and Selected Writings. Garden City, N.Y.: Doubleday, 1973.

The Collected Stories of Chester Himes. Forward by Calvin Hernton. New York: Thunder's Mouth Press, 1991.

AUTOBIOGRAPHY

My Life of Absurdity. New York: Doubleday, 1972.

The Quality of Hurt. New York: Doubleday, 1976.

SELECTED ESSAYS

"Now Is the Time! Here Is the Place!" *Opportunity* 20:271–73, 284 (September 1942).

"Zoot Suit Riots Are Race Riots!" *Crisis* 50:200–201, 222 (July 1943).

"Negro Martyrs Are Needed." *Crisis* 51:159, 174 (May 1944).

"The Dilemma of the Negro Novelist in the United States." In *Beyond the Angry Black.* Edited by John A. Williams. New York: Cooper Square, 1966. Pp.52-58. Reprinted in *New Black Voices: An Anthology of Contemporary Afro-American Literature.* Edited by Abraham Chapman. New York: Mentor, 1972. Pp. 394-401.

"Reading Your Own: My Favorite Novel." *New York Times Book Review,* June 4, 1967, p. 4.

CRITICAL AND BIOGRAPHICAL STUDIES

Fabre, Michel, and Robert E. Skinner, eds. *Conversations with Chester Himes.* Jackson: University Press of Mississippi, 1995.

Fabre, Michel, Robert E. Skinner, and Lester Sullivan, comps. *Chester Himes: An Annotated Primary and Secondary Bibliography.* Westport, Conn.: Greenwood, 1992.

Lundquist, James. *Chester Himes.* New York: Ungar, 1976.

Margolies, Edward, and Michel Fabre. *The Several Lives of Chester Himes.* Jackson: University Press of Mississippi, 1997.

Milliken, Stephen F. *Chester Himes: A Critical Appraisal.* Columbia: University of Missouri Press, 1976.

Muller, Gilbert H. *Chester Himes.* Boston: Twayne, 1989.

Sallis, James. *Chester Himes: A Life.* New York: Walker, 2001.

Silet, Charles L.P., ed. *The Critical Response to Chester Himes.* Westport, Conn.: Greenwood, 1999.

Skinner, Robert E. *Two Guns from Harlem: The Detective Fiction of Chester Himes.* Bowling Green, Ohio: Bowling Green State University Popular Press, 1989.

Soitos, Stephen F. *The Blues Detective: A Study of African American Detective Fiction.* Amherst: University of Massachusetts Press, 1996.

EVA HOFFMAN

(1945—)

Bert Almon

Eva Hoffman's work has been shaped by her ethnic and national origins and, crucially, her emigration from Poland to North America in 1959, an event that gave her the central theme of *Lost in Translation* (1989), one of the most widely applauded memoirs of the late twentieth century. Hoffman was born on July 1, 1945, in Cracow as Ewa Wydra. Her parents, Boris and Maria Burg Wydra, were Polish Jews and Holocaust survivors from the *shtetl* (a diminutive of the Yiddish word, *shtot*, meaning a town) of Załośce near Lvov. The town was Polish until the end of World War II, when it became part of the Soviet Union. Her parents initiated the exile theme in Hoffman's life by moving to Cracow, the nearest city in the newly redefined Poland. Hoffman was born two months after the end of the war. Her sister, Alina, who figures in some of her writing, was born in 1949. An anti-Semitic campaign by the Communist government of Poland led Boris and Maria Wydra to decide to emigrate to Canada, a choice that the thirteen-year-old Ewa, who felt happy in Poland, disliked intensely.

Much of Hoffman's experience is covered by her memoir. The simple facts of her early life are easily summarized. Her family left Poland for Vancouver in April 1959. She attended Rice University in Texas from 1963 to 1967 and earned a BA in English. She undertook graduate work in music at Yale University (1967–1968), then switched to Harvard from 1968, where received a PhD in English in 1974 with a dissertation titled "The Grotesque in Modern Fiction." She married Barry Hoffman, another Harvard graduate student, in 1971 and divorced him in 1976. She taught at the University of New Hampshire (1975–1976) and at Tufts University (1976–1977). But she decided, as she puts it in *Lost in Translation*, to become a "New York intellectual" rather than an academic, and she went to work for the *New York Times* in 1980, eventually rising to an editorship with the *New York Times Book Review*, which she held until 1990. During her early years with the newspaper, she had to summarize scientific and medical papers for the "Ideas and Trends" section, useful preparation for a writer who would eventually write a rather technical science fiction novel.

She has essentially been a freelance writer since, with occasional visiting appointments at universities: East Anglia University, 1994; the University of California at Berkeley, as a fellow at the Townsend Centre, 2000; and Clare Hall, Cambridge University, 2001. Honors have come her way: in 1992 she received a Whiting Foundation Award and a Guggenheim Fellowship. She presently lives in Hampstead, a London suburb where Sigmund Freud died in exile, and she holds a biennial visiting professorship in foreign languages and literatures at the Massachusetts Institute of Technology. She considers Hampstead midway between Manhattan and Poland, which is not geographically true but rather neatly expresses her transnational perspective, a point of view that her memoir accounts for. She told an Australian interviewer, Aviva Tuffield from the *Melbourne Age*, that she has some "lines of tension with American culture," tension that "involves the degree of individualism and competitiveness in the US." According to Tuffield, Hoffman finds Britain "less competitive and ego-driven," while admitting that she has "the classic immigrant misconception" that fails to distinguish between "moderate and high achievement." Her memoir is in fact a history of a highly competitive individual who created her own version of the American dream—going to Harvard, working for the *New York Times* and becoming a New York intellectual.

LOST IN TRANSLATION

Hoffman's first book, *Lost in Translation*, which won the Jean Stein Award for nonfiction, manages to be an immigrant memoir, a study in comparative cultural experience, and an account of language acquisition. The immigrant memoir has a long history in America. Hoffman herself mentions Mary Antin's 1912 classic account, *The Promised Land*, as a precedent. Antin's family came to America from a shtetl in Russia when she was thirteen, and she adapted to her new country and language with remarkable ease. For her, the change was entirely desirable. She had never felt Russian, and her book shows no nostalgia for her birthplace.

Hoffman, on the other hand, considered herself a Pole, and the opening section of *Lost in Translation* is permeated with *tęsknota*, or nostalgia—the section is called "Paradise"—though the emotion is scrutinized, not sentimentalized. The book opens out of chronological sequence, with the moment in 1959 when her family sailed from the port of Gdynia for Canada, where she would live for four years. That was the moment when she first felt *tęsknota*. The translation theme is inaugurated when she explains that the Polish term has connotations not present in the English word "nostalgia," which often implies wistfulness. The Polish term is more intense and suggests longing and sorrow and even melancholia. Hoffman observes at one point that nostalgia has been thought of as a disease. In her fine study, *Yesterday's Self: Nostalgia and the Immigrant Identity* (2002), Andreea Deciu Ritivoi has traced the term to seventeenth-century medical theories that tried to account for fatal cases of depression among soldiers and displaced peasants. Ritivoi observes that the divided self experienced by the nostalgic immigrant leads to a sense of identity as provisional, as a process: in effect, Hoffman creates a postmodern identity in the course of her narrative.

The memories of Hoffman's childhood in Cracow are astonishingly vivid. As she notes in the book, "loss is a magical preservative." She admires Vladimir Nabokov's account of his Russian childhood and youth in *Speak, Memory* (1951), and her work is comparable to his

achievement. The little world of her parents' apartment building, with its colorful inhabitants, and the streets and parks and shops of Cracow all are evoked in sensuous imagery. Cracow escaped the devastation of houses and buildings visited on Warsaw in World War II. Hoffman is particularly good at describing friends and neighbors, some of whom were Jewish, others Christian. The breadth of the social world (very different from the shtetl life of her parents) helps explain her continuing identification with Polish society even though state-sponsored anti-Semitism drove her family to emigrate. Her parents were prosperous, as her father was an extremely resourceful player in the flourishing black market. The family could even afford a servant.

The vividness of her memories is created in part by a gift for detail. The use of the present tense is also important. In the interview with Aviva Tuffield, she said:

> On one level the book had been germinating for years but when the question of the writing itself became less problematic was when I discovered the present tense. Before that I was writing in the past tense, in a continuous narrative style that was not right and then I somehow just hit on the present tense and that absolutely freed me to start writing. It was truer to the experience in a way and to the presentness of all those memories. It freed me to do reflections on my subject—transculturation—rather than tell my story which I did not want to do.

The present tense conveys her feeling that the past is alive within her, the feeling expressed by one of William Faulkner's characters, Gavin Stevens, in *Intruder in the Dust* (1948): "The past isn't dead. It isn't even past." The present tense enables her to recreate the darkening political scene in Poland—increased repression in general, growing anti-Semitism—in the same uncertain, slightly confused way that she experienced it. She makes use of the tense again in *Exit into History* (1993), where it seems mannered rather than functional.

Happy memories dominate her recollection of her childhood, hence her desire not to leave Poland. She showed aptitude for the piano and was possibly on the route to a professional career

in a country where pianists have been national heroes. She had joyful times with Marek Ruta, a boy who declared his love for her when she was eleven. His family went to Israel, but when she met him years later in New York, he validated her memories of a blissful time on a country holiday by the fact that he still shared them. She even had a moment of mystical illumination along one of the beautiful boulevards of the city, in a scene that seems not to have caught the attention of her commentators.

Her parents might have chosen to go to Israel, but they finally decided on Canada, a country her father had heard about through a book called *Canada Fragrant with Resin*, which he had with him during his period of hiding during the war. Ewa was deeply unhappy at the prospect of leaving her friends and her flourishing musical education for a country she seen described in a magazine as a "cultural desert." Indeed, the word "Canada" sounded like "Sahara" to her. The second section of her memoir is titled "Exile," a term describing the experience of immigration that makes an interesting contrast with Mary Antin's celebrated memoir *The Promised Land*, although Hoffman would in fact see the United States, rather than Canada, as her new paradise. Her experience of entering the St. Lawrence Seaway was alienating. The Canadian literary critic Northrop Frye has suggested that a traveler arriving in Canada via the St. Lawrence feels like "a tiny Jonah entering an inconceivably large whale." On landing at Montreal, Ewa Wydra felt that she was literally nowhere. Frye has also noted the fanciful theory that the word "Canada" comes from the expression, *acá nada*, "nothing here," supposedly applied to it by an early Spanish explorer; the third section of Hoffman's book, about her life in America, is called "The New World," as if Canada had indeed been nowhere.

The Vancouver in which she spent her adolescence was a collection of suburbs, an Anglophile city rather different from the multicultural city today, which sees itself as a jewel of the Pacific Rim. Ewa was immediately disoriented by being renamed, a typical ordeal for immigrants. She became "Eva," and her sister Alina became "Elaine." She spent some years trying to understand her new social reality and her role in it as Eva. The Polish community in Vancouver offered little: the immigrants who had become rich were wrapped up in a suburban and atomized existence. Her resourceful father found that his energy and bravura did not work in the new country. The wealth of social relationships the family knew in Cracow did not exist for them in Canada. She made Canadian friends, but their social rituals (particularly dating customs) were hard for her to understand. Hoffman likes to say that all immigrants are anthropologists, and first in Canada and then the United States she struggled to understand football games (but could never see the ball) and styles of conversations (the tendency of Americans to "riff" on a theme). She describes her struggles to comprehend the new by a metaphor from geometry and surveying: triangulation. In triangulation, two points are used to construct an imaginary triangle in order to find the distance of a third point. The metaphor superbly conveys her struggle to fill in gaps, to estimate realities that are at an intellectual or emotional distance from the immigrant self.

Her most severe problems were with the new language, and one of the great successes of the book is her ability to convey what it is like to struggle to internalize a new language. The title was meant to suggest multiple meanings: to be lost while struggling to translate from one tongue to another, but also to be captured or mesmerized. And it suggests that there is inevitable slippage when trying to move from the original culture to a new one. For Hoffman, the terrible moment came when she no longer felt at home in Polish but was not yet fluent in English. She no longer had a language for her inner life. When given a diary by a Canadian friend, she decided there was no point in keeping it in Polish: "I have to write in the language of the present, even if it's not the language of the self." The more effusive Polish vocabulary not being available, the diary was, she says, abstract and impersonal. Further, she found it impossible to use the first person in writing or in speaking.

She directly experienced some of the claims of structuralist and poststructuralist thought. The structuralist insight that there is no necessary

connection between the word (sign) and what it stands for (the signifier) was something that she could easily perceive: English words failed to "hook onto anything." And the poststructuralist ideas that identity and gender are not essences but constructions came easily to the hybrid Ewa/Eva, with her double sense of self, the Polish original and the new North American person. She discovered that while she had been considered attractive in Poland, she was perceived as homely, with thick eyebrows, hair without bounce, and unfashionable clothes. A kindly Polish woman in Vancouver set out to make her feminine in the local pattern, with makeup, plucked eyebrows, shaved armpits, and high heels, a guise that she found alienating. In an insightful article, " The Insertion of the Self into a Space of Borderless Possibility," Danuta Zadworna Fjellestad claims that Hoffman's greatest exile in the book is from her body, rather than from her country and language.

One of Hoffman's insights in her second book, *Exit into History*, is that the immigrant has a spectral biography, a kind of ghost self representing what the individual might have been had she remained in the old country. The imaginary Polish self is given some dialogues with the new Eva, a brilliant way of comparing cultures as well as a means of showing how identity is a construction rather than an essence. After Hoffman falls in love with a Texan at Rice University, she carries on a dialogue about passion with her Polish alter ego, a dialogue that reveals the subtle differences between cultures where love is concerned.

When she was ready for a university education, Rice University offered her financial assistance. She arrived in Houston in 1963 as American culture was entering an agitated and fragmented time. As she observes, an immigrant to "The New World," as the final section of her book is called, would once have found a sense of national purpose and would have confronted it with a "steady, self-assured ego." Instead, she encountered a reality as multiple as her own. The "New World" section is a collage of scenes rather than a continuous narrative. In fact, it begins with a party in Manhattan in 1979 rather than

with her college days: the point is to show that she did achieve her goal of becoming a New York intellectual.

Her undergraduate career in English literature went smoothly. The New Criticism was still fashionable, with its emphasis on irony and paradox. Her complex background and her "immigrant irony" enabled her to practice such criticism very well. She suggests that it was an alienated style of reading, and only years after did she suddenly experience poetry in English from inside. She was teaching T. S. Eliot's "The Love Song of J. Alfred Prufrock" in a freshman course at the University of New Hampshire when suddenly she found herself attuned to the inner sense of the words and to their music.

After a year in the Yale University music program, she decided to go back to English. Her object at Yale had been to determine whether or not a musical career was possible. In an interview with Andrew Brown in the *Guardian*, she explained her renunciation: "There are so many peerless pianists and the repertory has been recorded at a super level 20 times over. I could have been good but I didn't think I had anything to add to that." But she told Brown that she has a Bechstein grand piano in her Hampstead apartment.

She got into Harvard for graduate English studies although she had missed the application deadline—by using, she says wryly, the last blaze of "immigrant bravura." At Harvard she met her husband, Barry Hoffman, a brilliant student who eventually went into advertising and wrote a well-received book on the profession. Near the end of her stay at Harvard she encountered two people from her past. The first, Zofia Coesin, was a friend in the Cracow Music School. She had become a successful musician, a living example of what Ewa Wydra might have become. The second encounter was more significant: her close friend and proto-boyfriend, Marek, called her from New York. Her reacquaintance with Marek reaffirmed the significance of her Polish past. He also served to remind her of her spectral biography. The encounter generates another imaginary dialogue with her Polish alter ego, one

in which the American Eva asserts that "I am as real as you now. I'm the real one."

The meetings with figures from her childhood (her "personal mythology," as she calls it) sets up the scenes in which she describes her trip back to Poland in 1977. In a series of rich vignettes, she confronts her earlier world. She sees how it has changed, a way of neutralizing nostalgia. She thinks in English now and cannot think of herself as "Ewa" any more. Further, Poland has come to her, in a way: when Poland's leader Witold Jaruzelski declared martial law starting in 1981, many Polish exiles came to Manhattan.

Near the end of *Lost in Translation*, she discusses identity. As a Polish American she considers herself an oxymoron instead of a hybrid: her literary training in reading for paradox gives her the insights she needs to see her new identity as a fusion rather than a grafting. Her preoccupation with identity is, she says, an American trait: Poles take their identity (and their gender) for granted. She went through psychoanalysis, a "talking cure," to rid herself of the alienation and trauma of her uprooting: it offers another way of "translating" from one culture to another, from one conception of self (Ewa) to a new one (Eva). Psychoanalysis has remained an important tool for her in her interpretations of culture, and her novel, *The Secret* (2001), makes heavy use of it to imagine the identity of a cloned individual. After moving to Hampstead, she even began training sessions in psychoanalysis but did not pursue a career as an analyst.

The last words of *Lost in Translation* are meant to convey and affirm a sense of identity. She describes a scene in which her American friend Miriam teaches her the names of flowers: azaleas, delphiniums. "The names are beautiful, and they fit the flowers perfectly," [p. 280] she says, a statement that goes against structuralist wisdom about the gulf between signifier and signified: the point is that she is comfortable in the English language at last and at home in the New World. She ends by saying, "I am here now." [p. 280] In her brilliant essay, "See(k)ing the Self: Mirrors and Mirroring in Bicultural Texts," Judith Oster notes that "in these four words, and their being formed together into a declarative sentence, everything in the book is contained: identity, existence, and the time *and* the place which contain them both" (65). The fused identity of Ewa/Eva Wydra/Hoffman has been achieved. Oster recalls that in her early days between languages Hoffman could not say "I." The book ends with an emphatic assertion of the first person.

EXIT INTO HISTORY

Certainly *Lost in Translation* is the foundation of Hoffman's reputation, but she has written journalism as well. In 1990, she decided to visit some of the newly independent Warsaw Pact states: Poland, Hungary, Romania, Bulgaria, and Czechoslovakia, to observe the ferment of political change. Her title is ironic. Marxism prided itself on its superior knowledge of history—the scientific laws of history—and claimed history as an inexorable process leading toward a classless Communist society. The reality was a system completely antagonistic to change. With the collapse of the Soviet hegemony, the states of Eastern Europe were thrown into a period of uncertainty and rapid change. History had begun again. In her introduction, Hoffman says (echoing William Butler Yeats's poem "Easter 1916") that all was to be changed, changed utterly, and she wanted to witness it.

She witnessed the changes twice: she made a return trip to the same countries in 1991. The return visits enabled her to gauge the progress and confusion of societies attempting to construct new orders. Of course since the book's publication in 1993 enormous changes have taken place in those countries, and *Exit into History* can hardly serve as a guide to contemporary Eastern European politics. Parties and personalities have sometimes been replaced, and the dissidents who were involved in the overthrow of the old order have sometimes shown themselves to be quite incompetent at gaining power. But the work is instructive anyway, showing examples of how societies cope with change and with the legacy of a police state. She was struck by the way that progressive elements in Eastern European countries were studying Milton Friedman's extremely

conservative economic policies, showing a surprising faith in the concept of the invisible hand of the market.

The trips also served as a chance for an author who had a somewhat idealized view of her childhood milieu to see her first world more realistically. Realism is a problematic term, of course, and Hoffman observes in her introduction that Eastern Europe has always been the exotic, shadowy "other" for the West. Talk about "the other" permeates recent thinking. Hoffman says: "Our psyches seem to be so constructed that we need and desire an imagined 'other'—either a glimmering, craved idealized other, or an other than is dark, savage, and threatening. Eastern Europe has served our needs in this respect very well." [pp. x–xi] In her succeeding nonfiction works, *Shtetl: The Life and Death of a Small Town and the World of Polish Jews* (1997) and *After Such Knowledge: Memory, History, and the Legacy of the Holocaust* (2004), she frequently uses the concept, saying, for example, that Poles and Jews in Eastern Europe saw each other as the "other," an ominous habit. Hoffman makes some humorous use of the term "postmodern": as when she reports that a Bulgarian friend described a new, ramshackle area of private shops as "fast attaining the postmodern condition" in its jumbled heterogeneous character.

An important model for *Exit into History* is Rebecca West's great book about Yugoslavia, *Black Lamb and Grey Falcon* (1941), a work mentioned near the end of Hoffman's own narrative. West visited Yugoslavia three times in the late 1930s, inquiring into recent and ancient history, interviewing intellectuals and ordinary people, describing the landscape and architecture. World War I began in the Balkans, and she felt that the danger of war with Nazi Germany required an inquiry into that part of the world. One of her points was that outsiders failed to understand the Balkans, dismissing them as primitive or as the "Ruritanian" settings of operettas. The very term "Balkanize" is unfair, West said, pointing out that most of the region's problems have been created by outside powers. West did not have the later, psychological sense of the term "other" in her lexicon, but in effect she was attempting to present the peoples of Yugoslavia without myths. She did, in fact, understand the importance to these peoples of their own myths, of the ways that a battle six hundred years in the past (the Serbian defeat at Kosovo) could define the attitudes of a people.

One of Hoffman's problems in trying to understand Eastern Europe is the tendency she encountered there for new generalizations to have replaced the old ones. She is drawn to the expressions that the people of a country use about their experiences: in Poland, the motto is, "We must get through this somehow"; in Hungary everyone says, "Nothing has changed at all"; and in Romania, the favorite phrases are "It's all chaos" and "We're not ready for this. We don't understand democracy. We're practically *Oriental*." She also notices that Hungarians like metaphors of schizophrenia and that they, like the Poles, tend to cherish their melancholy. She is not in serious danger of constructing a new, essential view of the peoples she encounters, but she is bemused by the tendency of individuals to shape their appearance to fit a stereotype, like the Romanian general who looks very much like a junta member from South America or the Philippines.

Most of the work is made up of reports on her discussions with writers and politicians, with dissidents and members of the *nomenklatura* (the managerial elite). Here and there she talks to ordinary people, like the Romanian hitchhikers she and a friend pick up in Hungary, and these are among the most interesting encounters. She is clearly fascinated by those who were important in the old regime, and she tries to understand their motivations. The newly independent countries took different attitudes toward former Communists and toward the crimes of the past. Hoffman is careful to indicate the differing attitudes toward the totalitarian past in the societies she visits. For example, in 1990, the Czechs were obsessed with the misdeed of informers, while Poles were exhorted by their first post-Communist president to "draw a thick line" between the past and present." The problem for all these countries after more than forty years of thought control, Hoffman says, is to find "a usable past," a term

she borrows from American literary critics talking about their own country's attitude toward the history.

Some of her richest pages, like Rebecca West's, are simple tourism, descriptions of landscapes or historic sites like the magnificent painted monasteries of Romania. These add some tonal variety to a book made up mostly of conversations and interviews in bars, cafés, and offices. At one point, Hoffman feels that "the world is becoming a sort of Möbius strip of interviews, in which the interviewers and the interviewed exchange places and blend into each other quite seamlessly." [p.392] The reader, too, may feel locked into a long cycle of interviews. The book is a valuable document, but its function as a document ultimately works against its readability.

The most stringent critique of *Exit into History* comes in Anne Applebaum's review in the *New Republic*, "A Gathering of Dissidents." Applebaum believes that Hoffman paid too much attention to dissidents who were well known in the West and too little attention to the cultural nationalists who have been demonized but have done considerable good in reviving their societies. The effect of Applebaum's review is not to discredit Hoffman's earnest and intelligent book but to point out just how complex the countries of Eastern Europe are, and how difficult it has been for them to exit the Soviet system into normal European life. They are indeed pursued by a past that is not always usable but is definitely inescapable. A reader of Hoffman's book should keep in mind that on May 1, 2004, Poland, the Czech Republic, the Slovak Republic, and Hungary joined the European Union, an event that would have seemed most improbable in 1991.

SHTETL

Hoffman's parents were not practicing Jews, although they observed Yom Kippur. In *Lost in Translation*, she recalls her mother telling her not to imitate her friends who crossed themselves in front of churches. And she was aware from time to time of anti-Semitism. Sometimes her parents would refer to their experiences during the Holocaust, but like many survivors they said little about it. Hence their daughter reached adolescence thinking of herself primarily as a Pole. Several commentators on *Lost in Translation*, including Mark Krupnick in his 1996 essay, "Assimilation in Recent American Jewish Autobiographies," and Petra Fachinger in her 2001 article, "Lost in Nostalgia: The Autobiographies of Eva Hoffman and Richard Rodriguez," have suggested that in her 1989 memoir Eva Hoffman is not very concerned with her Jewishness.

In later years, however, she has become more clearly concerned with issues revolving around the Holocaust and the role of Poland in it. She has given lectures and interviews on the subject, and in 1997 she published *Shtetl: The Life and Death of a Small Town and the World of Polish Jews* (1997), which won the Bronislaw Malinowski Social Science Award from the Polish Institute of Arts and Sciences. The passing of her parents, furthermore, made her acutely aware that the generation who endured the horrors of Nazi persecution is dying out, and the result was her 2004 work, *After Such Knowledge: Memory, History, and the Legacy of the Holocaust.*

Shtetl was inspired by Marian Marzynski's 1996 documentary film with the same name, which aired on the PBS *Frontline* series. The film featured Zbigniew Romaniuk, a young historian who strives to preserve the history of the Jewish community of Brańsk in Eastern Poland, and it also featured on the discussions of Romaniuk with Nathan Kaplan, a Chicagoan whose mother was from Brańsk. The director of the documentary, supplied Hoffman with written sources and pointed her toward some of his informants. Hoffman worked with two purposes, as her subtitle, *The Life and Death of a Small Town and the World of Polish Jews,* implies. She wanted to further explore the history of Brańsk; but she also wanted to place the town—where very little ever happened until the catastrophe of Nazi occupation and mass murder—in a wider context through scholarly research. Omer Bartov's balanced assessment of the book, "How Not to Forget," makes the point that Hoffman's two purposes make an uneasy synthesis, creating a book which mingles the scholarly and the

popular. Bartov also believes that her frequent attempts to absolve Poles from charges of anti-Semitism and collaboration with the Nazis are forced, a view shared by a number of other reviewers, like Susan Zuccotti and Thomas Laqueur.

In *Lost in Translation*, we are told that Hoffman's mother would sometimes repeat the frequent claim that there is an anti-Semite in every Pole. The fact that the Holocaust took place mostly on Polish soil has led to the widespread belief that the Poles were somehow responsible for, or at least were counted on by the Nazis to assist in, such massive persecution. Hoffman's concern, as expressed in her preface, is to "complicate and historicize" such views. She tends to stress evidence of understanding and dialogue over the long history of Polish-Jewish relations. She suggests that at times Poland was a genuinely multicultural society. She is also aware that in the years between the world wars, anti-Semitism grew, sponsored by the powerful fascist ONR party. However, she suggests that the mass murders took place in Poland because that was where the majority of European Jews lived.

For her explorations of the massacres in Brańsk, Hoffman's major source is a project known as the Yizkor Book ("book of memory"), created by survivors of the Holocaust all over Poland, who put down their recollections of shtetl life and the Nazi years. She supplemented this rich and highly opinionated written source with personal interviews, particularly one with Jack Rubin, who escaped the Nazis after dramatic and deeply distressing experiences and described them to her at his home in Baltimore. Rubin reveals an interesting ambivalence: he told Hoffman that there was no hatred in Brańsk, but he also said, "Oh, we always knew the Poles were anti-Semites."

Hoffman finds ambivalence and misunderstanding on both sides. Her belief that we all tend to project "otherness" on groups we do not understand is a current in *Shtetl*: "We have become skilled nowadays in analyzing the imagery of Otherness, that unconscious stratum of preconceptions, fantasies, and projections we bring to our perceptions of strangers" (9). During the period when Poland was partitioned among Russia, Austria, and Prussia, nationalists often felt that Jews would have to assimilate completely to become Polish: "Herein the source of true intolerance—of hostility toward the very existence and presence of Otherness—could be discerned." (144). Understanding helps counteract such antagonisms. The Jews of Brańsk no longer remain for cultural bridges to reach them. But she praises the commemorative efforts of the historian Zbigniew Romaniuk, who has gathered the Jewish gravestones scattered by the Nazis and created a kind of memorial with them.

Hoffman visited Brańsk with Romaniuk as her guide and talked to elderly inhabitants about the vanished Jewish community. Romaniuk estimated that informers were responsible for the death of thirty-two Jews, while some forty people in nine families attempted to aid their neighbors. Hoffman's own parents found that some gentiles in their area helped them, while others tried to betray them. The year after the publication of *Shtetl*, Hoffman was finally be able to visit her parents' village, Załośce, not all that far from Brańsk. The encounter with the home village would be a powerful experience.

In early 2000, Hoffman generated a controversy in the *New York Review of Books* with an essay titled "The Uses of Hell," a long review of Peter Novick's *The Holocaust in American Life* in which she praised the book but took issue with what she saw as Novick's position that the Holocaust was being exploited in America for ideological and political reasons. In "The Uses of Hell: An Exchange" June 15, 2000), letters from Novick, Steven T. Katz, and Tad Szulc disagreed with some of her conclusions. Novick appreciated her praise of his book but denied that he saw "misuse" of the collective memory of the Holocaust in American life. For example, he found it reasonable that the Holocaust was invoked by anti-abortionists, though he himself is Pro-Choice. His feeling is that the Holocaust will be always be interpreted through contemporary concerns and he therefore is not anxious about its alleged exploitation by special interest groups. In his retort he says that memory of the Holocaust in America is generally banal: he believes that

the collective memory of the Holocaust is important in countries where it generates debate about racism and cultural conflict, like Poland. Hoffman's *Shtetl* can in fact be seen as part of the cultural debate in Poland, where the events of World War II are still the subject of soul-searching and argument. Novick vindicates Hoffman's struggle to understand the relation of Poles to the murder of their neighbors.

Hoffman's 2001 Amnesty International lecture, "The Balm of Recognition: Rectifying Wrongs through the Generations," delivered at Oxford University and collected in a volume with other such lectures called *Human Rights, Human Wrongs* (2003), discusses not only the Holocaust but other examples of atrocities, as in South Africa, Bosnia, and Rwanda. She calls for recognition and symbolic justice for victims, as well as for dialogue between the descendents of perpetrators and descendents of victims to prevent the perpetuation of hatred in later generations. Her belief is that multicultural dialogue can help to dispel the construction of sinister "others."

On September 1, 2000, Hoffman delivered the Una Lecture, a major address for the Doreen B. Townshend Center for the Humanities at the University of California at Berkeley. In this lecture, titled "Complex Histories, Contested Memories: Some Reflections on Remembering Difficult Pasts" (available only on the Internet), she considers the position of the "post" generation, those (like herself) whose parents endured the Holocaust. For this generation, she says, the need to remember the Holocaust ("Never forget") has become a slogan, and she feels uneasy about "tragedy tourism" in our time, the school trips to former slave quarters and concentration camps. But she believes that the task of memory is a responsibility, especially for people like herself. The process of memory requires investigation, and her model is Freudian. Memory selects, constructs, and reconstructs, and the person who has received testimony from a survivor is more an analyst than a patient. She says that her task has been to understand Polish-Jewish history, and she thinks that "some of the conflicts in Polish-Jewish history can be seen in terms of majority-minority tensions, rather than in terms of strong and specific anti-Semitism."

At the time of the Una Lecture, Hoffman recorded a long and revealing interview with Harry Kreisler. Under the title, "Between Memory and History: A Writers' Voice," it is available on the Internet both as text and as video broadcast and offers an excellent introduction to her work. It covers the "anthropological" stance of the immigrant, the vocation of writing, and her parents' peril during the Nazi occupation. She makes the interesting observation that in her autobiography she tried to integrate her Polish and American parts of the self, while in *Shtetl* she sought to integrate her Polish and Jewish sides. She also quotes approvingly the expatriate poet Alexander Wat, who said that being Polish-Jewish meant that he was Polish-Polish and Jewish-Jewish.

BIRTH OF A NOVELIST: THE SECRET

Hoffman has always been concerned with ethical issues. Until the publication of *The Secret* in 2002, she expressed her concerns in nonfiction, engaging politics and social conflict in the past or present. Shortly before *The Secret* was published, she wrote an article ("Reproducing Ourselves Is All Very Well") for the London *Guardian* about the unforeseeable effects of technologies like cloning. She said our sense of the "depth and mysterious dimensions of human subjectivity" may be damaged, seen to be an illusion. She believes that genetics is "a Copernican revolution."

Her apprehensions about genetic engineering and the creation of life led her to a new, speculative form of prose, a way of imagining the consequences of cloning. The subtitle of the English edition of *The Secret* is *A Fable for Our Time*. The reviews of the book were respectful but qualified: Hoffman's brilliance as a thinker is clear, but her plotting and characterization have limitations.

The novel is set in 2025, in a society not very different from our own. In the *Washington Post*, Zofia Smardz referred to the occasional science fiction touches like "robodolls" and "Feel Goods" (superior mood-changing drugs) as "a futuristic

patina," a criticism echoed by other reviewers; Anita Desai in the *New York Review of Books* complains about "futuristic touches added like cosmetics." Neil Gordon's review in the *New York Times* suggested that such elements detract from the book's "more convincing identity as a novel of ideas." What these complaints miss is that many of the futuristic touches bear on the themes of the novel. We are told that in 2025 artists create "biomorphs," designer beings, and the protagonist, Iris Surrey, is in fact a clone. The Feel-Goods and the Mnemonic Aids which enable a person to playback the experiences of another suggest that we are headed toward a world of simulated experience, and the emotions themselves can be created artificially with a device called an Affect Simulator. At one point the protagonist visits a "virtual club" where customers can create imaginary selves and experiences for themselves by various means. Authentic subjectivity seems threatened by such innovations.

Iris Surrey grows up in a kind of "feel good" environment with her mother—hers has been a blissful, almost womblike, existence in a comfortable home in a small town near Chicago. In a rare moment of conflict, she decides that she can't fight her mother, that they are like Siamese twins. She senses a mystery about her origins and her uncanny rapport with her mother. Iris and Elizabeth create disquiet in those who see them together. Eventually her mother takes a lover but, disturbed by the uncanny resemblance of mother and daughter, he leaves them. Iris realizes that she and her mother evoke a sensation in people that she calls "the Weirdness." The one visit from her mother's sister Janey is troubling: something about mother and daughter upsets the aunt. Iris gradually becomes obsessed with finding out who her father is. Like Oedipus (and "Iris" is a faint echo of the mythical figure's name) she turns detective and at seventeen unravels the secret of her origins. unraveling the bond with her mother at the same time. "I looked at her and the vertigo returned. My mother, my twin, my mother, my mater, *material materna*, from which I was made. My mother, my self. My mother, my monstrousness" (64).

Some features of the Oedipus myth need to be summarized so that their transformation can be traced in the novel. Oedipus was the son of King Laius and Queen Jocasta of Thebes. A prophecy warned that he would bring a curse on his native city by killing his father and marrying his mother. The king decided to have the infant killed, but the shepherd who was given the task simply abandoned the baby in the wilderness, where he was found by a shepherd and brought up unaware of his origins, as the adopted child of King Polybus of Corinth. Learning from an oracle that he was destined to kill his father and marry his mother, Oedipus, not understanding who his real parents were, made his way into the world. At a crossroads near Delphi he encountered Laius and killed him in a quarrel over the right of way on the road. On the outskirts of Thebes, he solved the riddles of a monster, the Sphinx, causing it to kill itself. Freed of the monster, the people of Thebes chose him as their king and he married Jocasta. After many years, a plague descended on the city. Warned by the blind seer Tiresias that the plague was a curse of the gods for a mysterious crime, he set out to discover the criminal, who turned out to be himself. Jocasta, learning that she had married and borne children to her own son, killed herself. Oedipus put out his own eyes and became a wanderer.

The parallels between the myth and the novel are not rigid. Literature, as Northrop Frye liked to say, is "displaced mythology." Iris was not abandoned as a child but nurtured. She was the "apple of her mother's eye," the two of them being as close as the iris and the pupil. She herself is a riddle: her lover Robert calls her a sphinx. Iris calls her mother "The Delphic Oracle" at one point in the novel. The plague affecting the human community is probably loss of experience and emotion. Iris's prophet Tiresias is a psychoanalyst—an excellent twist, for psychoanalysis was founded on insights that Freud garnered from the Oedipus story. Iris kills one "mother" and tries to kill another, and she does in a sense sleep with a father, yet without incest.

Horrified that she is a laboratory product, a mere copy of her mother, she leaves home for New York in a quest for identity. The search for

identity is a cliché of fiction, as is the adolescent's quest for maturity in a sinister city: Nathaniel Hawthorne's great story "My Kinsman, Major Molineux," comes to mind. The circumstances of Hoffman's character are unique. Her disgust with her origins leaves her affectless even when she takes lovers. One way that she tries to understand herself is to visit the laboratory in which she was created. By a subterfuge, she manages to talk to the head of the firm, Dr. Park, a Korean. In her lengthy and generally favorable review of the novel, Anita Desai expresses misgivings about Dr. Park, whose characterization has touches of "those sinister yellow races out of the movies." Park refuses responsibility for her when she suggests that he is in some way her father. And he is not, any more than Polybus was the father of Oedipus. Iris will have to find a father elsewhere.

Her search for an understanding of her origins leads her to not to a prophet like Tiresias but to the Internet. She cracks the encryption of her Aunt Janey's e-mails and discovers where the parents of Elizabeth and Janey live in Florida. These are her grandparents but also, in a genetic sense, her parents. She visits them, a troubling experience for all, one that leads to the grandmother's fatal heart attack. Grotesquely, she finds herself compelled to comfort the dying woman by pretending to be her mother, Elizabeth. In this female-centered version of the Oedipus story, Iris has killed not her father but her mother. In a desperate attempt to free herself of the woman who gave birth to her, she goes to Elizabeth's house and tries to strangle her, so that the copy can replace the original. She stops short of matricide, however. Iris has an opportunity to sleep with her foster father, Steven, whom she encounters at Columbia University, where he teaches. After he learns her story, he cannot resist sleeping with his uncanny stepdaughter, an act that brings a strange kind of closure to them both.

Iris clearly has problems that require special insight. She has no blind prophet Tiresias to turn to, but she does have sessions with "The Adviser," a Freudian psychoanalyst. In an excellent interview by Brenda Webster, Hoffman stated that one of her intentions in the novel was "to stage an encounter with psychoanalysis and these new things." The analyst is sometimes insightful and sometimes obtuse: like Tiresias, he is paradoxically a blind seer, or at least a blinkered one. He occasionally applies Freudian formulas without taking into account Iris's extraordinary situation, as a being with a mother but no father. But he does understand that the old stories can be applied in new ways, a process referred to in the novel as "narrative transformation."

In an important essay, "Life Stories, East and West," published in *Yale Review* in 2000, Hoffman touches on psychoanalysis and narrative transformation. She sees Freud's original insights as a "master discourse" of our time, but she realizes that the orthodox commitment to probing the structures of early childhood is a limitation. She therefore is interested in the ways that later experiences affect the psyche, and she believes that action and choice must be taken into account.

The frequent references to "Weirdness" and "eeriness" in the novel allude to Freud's concept of the "uncanny," which the psychoanalytic pioneer thought was at the basis of the fantastic tale. Freud's 1919 essay "Das Unheimliche" ("The Uncanny") is relevant to Hoffman's novel. He illustrates the concept through an analysis of story by (appropriately enough) E. T. A. Hoffman, the German Romantic. In the story, a young man falls in love with the beautiful Olympia, who turns out to be an automaton made of wood. In the course of the story her eyes are torn out, by her reputed father. Iris, whose name is the term for a part of the eye, is a woman who fears that she is an automaton, a simulacrum of human life. Freud related the Hoffman story to the Oedipus complex. Applying the Oedipus complex to women is problematic, as Freud theorized very scantily on the subject. But clearly a neurotic mother-daughter relationship is part of the complex. Freud suggested that the feeling of the uncanny is behind the gothic motif of the double in literary works, and certainly it is the doubling aspect of Elizabeth and Iris that generates the Weirdness of the mother and daughter, an eeriness experienced by Iris's Aunt Janey, her grandparents, and her stepfather, Steven. The novel is naturally filled with images of mirrors and allusions to the myth of Narcissus. Narcis-

sism is yet another Freudian concept, the focusing of the emotional life on oneself. Elizabeth is the ultimate narcissist, having chosen to create a copy of herself. Freud cites his disciple, Otto Rank in "The Uncanny," noting that the double is, in Rank's words, "an insurance against death." One of the possible uses of cloning is to cheat death by leaving one's replica behind. The novel also has some allusions to the Jewish myth of the Golem, a monster created by magic.

Iris achieves authenticity at last in the most traditional way possible, through love. Anita Desai is troubled by this solution, finding it a cliché, part of the Romantic tradition. Desai quotes with some disapproval Iris's statement: "Reader, you must forgive me," uttered when she feels doubt about the new lover, Robert. The statement is an echo of the famous line near the end of a very Romantic novel, Charlotte Brontë's *Jane Eyre* (1847): Jane says, "Reader, I married him." The marriage comes about after Jane solves the gothic mystery of the novel, the identity of the mysterious being in the attic, which turns out to be the mad wife of the hero, Rochester.

Robert, the genuine lover, comes into Iris's life after she meets him through an Internet site dealing with the nature of consciousness. He wins her, so to speak, through a riddling e-mail exchange in which she plays the sphinx and he plays Oedipus. The mythical sphinx asked travelers a question about the nature of human beings: what walks on four legs in the morning, on two legs at noon, and on three legs at night? The answer, of course, is a man—or to put it more universally, a human being. The dialogue of Iris and Robert probes into the nature of one kind of human being, a clone. Before the twentieth-century experiments with cloning animals, the riddle of a human being with no father and a mother who was her sister was inconceivable. Science has created a whole new set of riddles.

Through her love for Robert, Iris at last achieves some assurance that she is a real person, not a mere reflection of her mother/sister. "To Know is to know Someone Else. To know that there is a Someone Else. Robert was Someone to me; but at the same time, he was, thank the forces, Not Me" (256). The use of capitals is a doubtful touch, linking the book with the sentimental excesses of romance novels.

As a novel, *The Secret* has a number of weaknesses. The reviews consistently mix respect for Hoffman's grasp of important issues with misgivings about her fiction-writing skills. Tova Reich says that the book "strains to achieve animation through basically generic detail and figures who could be composites from the 'Character Catalogue' used by a novelist lover of the protagonist." A minor complaint could be registered: Hoffman, who earned a PhD at Harvard, is self-consciously literary in her use of allusions. To list a few: a funeral home offers a "Death Be Not Proud" service, echoing John Donne's great sonnet; Iris's first lover, Piotr, is working on a book he calls *The Supreme Fiction*, a title alluding to Wallace Stevens; a Clone Supremacist group (an odd variation on Nazi Master Race theories) calls itself "The Secret Sharer," alluding to Joseph Conrad's novella of that title, in which a sea captain confronts his double.

As for the protagonist, some commentators wonder about her despair: after all, twins are "clones" and cope with being replicas of each other. Justine Burley, reviewing the book in the journal *Nature*, actually defends the possibility of cloning on the grounds that children born normally suffer from all sorts of abuse by society and parents—the arguments against cloning, she says, would also prohibit normal sexual reproduction. And she thinks that clones might in fact feel special. We are all in unknown territory, Hoffman included, in trying to imagine what a clone would feel. Her speculations can only be tested when and if genuine human clones are created. But her aim in the novel was to raise the questions and imagine some answers.

AFTER SUCH KNOWLEDGE

The title of Hoffman's fifth book, *After Such Knowledge: Memory, History, and the Legacy of the Holocaust* (2004), is another literary allusion, to T. S. Eliot's 1920 poem "Gerontion," in which the speaker says, "After such knowledge, what forgiveness?" and goes on to say that "history

has many cunning passages, contrived corridors."
It is well-known that when Eliot wrote the poem
he had recently been involved in settling financial
problems arising out of the Treaty of Versailles.
The treaty has usually been seen as one of the
chief causes of the rise of the Nazis and World
War II. One of the contentious provisions created
the Polish Corridor, an opening to the North Sea
for Poland that sundered East and West Prussia.
The narrator of Eliot's poem expresses a world
of moral and spiritual dryness in which

Neither fear nor courage saves us. Unnatural vices
Are fathered by our heroism. Virtues
Are forced upon us by our impudent crimes.

In her preface, Hoffman acknowledges that
"Gerontion" is "marred by anti-Semitic overtones," [p. xiv] but "the line, and even the verse
to which it belongs, seemed exactly appropriate
for my theme; and it may be that the inclusion of
disturbing anti-Semitic or other prejudicial elements in an otherwise beautiful and masterly
work is part of the knowledge with which we
have to contend." [p. xv] In "The Second Coming," a poem published in 1921, a year after
"Gerontion," William Butler Yeats envisioned a
world in which "the best lack all conviction,
while the worst / Are full of passionate intensity."

Hoffman's book is a long meditation on the
aftermath of the most appalling event of
twentieth-century history, the Holocaust. As a
child of parents who lived through it, she belongs
to what has been called "the second generation."
The book reveals how much her thought has
evolved over the years. In *Lost in Translation*,
she was more concerned with the conflicts
between her Polish origins and her North American identity: being Jewish was not ignored but
nor was it central. From *Shtetl* on, she has been
thinking deeply about her Jewish heritage. The
deaths of her parents naturally brought this
heritage into focus and made her consider her
responsibilities as someone who is in some ways
the repository of a tragic history. She and her
sister, Alina, eventually made a journey to the
village where her parents grew up and where
their relatives were murdered. In *Lost in Translation*, she said that having her name changed to

"Eva" had a small seismic effect. The seismic effect of visiting Załośce was tremendous.

The work is an extended set of meditations
that moves from the events of the Holocaust to
present-day issues. She has chosen an interlocking progression of chapter titles to clarify the
historical process whereby the events endured by
the original survivors have been assimilated (as
much as they can be) by children of survivors
and by the rest of the world. For example, part 1
is called "From Event to Fable," and part 2 is
titled "From Fable to Psyche." This organization
helps give pattern to a very wide set of
meditations. She looks closely at how the
memory of the Holocaust has been dealt with by
survivors, their offspring, and countries like
Poland.

In talking about both the survivors and their
children, she takes care to show the diversity of
responses: there is no typical survivor, no typical
child of a survivor. Some survivors had difficulty
as parents, their experiences having damaged
them so deeply that communicating feeling was
difficult. Others placed such a weight of feeling
on their children that the children found it hard
to cope, especially when the child was seen as a
symbolic replacement of a relative who had died.
Some survivors were obsessed with remembering
the past and demanding that their children
become guardians of the memories, while other
victims refused to talk about what had happened
to them. Eva Hoffman's parents seem to have
fallen between extremes.

Attitudes of those not involved have changed
as well. Hoffman informs her readers of the
evolution of the concept of the Holocaust. At
first, the magnitude of the deaths was not
understood, nor was it clear that Jews were the
majority of the victims. It was years until the
term Holocaust (and the Hebrew term, "Shoah,"
meaning calamity) came into use. And mental
health professionals did not pay much attention
to the aftereffects in survivors until reparations
payments were assessed and psychiatric assess-
ments were required. Studies of trauma and the
nature of post-traumatic stress syndrome are so
common now that it is startling to realize how
wide the unawareness was in these fields, in spite

of the information gathered much earlier about the effects of shell shock in World War I.

Hoffman understands the diversity in what is often called the second generation (or even, rather glibly, the 2Gs). She observes that the term has to be used cautiously: "If a 'generation' is defined by shared historical experience and certain attitudes or beliefs that follow from it, then the 'second generation' is a very tenuous instance of it." [p. 28] But she has met others in her situation and has read widely; therefore, she has a basis for concluding that the second generation "recognize one another across boundaries" and share "an overwhelming given and a life task." [p. 28]

The growth of a literature by and about the second generation has aroused serious criticism. Hoffman is aware that the children of survivors must not appropriate their parent's suffering or aggrandize themselves. A long and angry review by Ruth Franklin in the *New Republic*, "Identity Theft: True Memory, False Memory, and the Holocaust," accuses many of the second generation of appropriation and exploitation. She has some criticisms of Hoffman but does not accuse her of the vulgarities she sees in a number of other writers. Franklin appreciates Hoffman's term "significance envy," and she likes Hoffman's concluding suggestion that the world cannot be made into "our own personal Holocaust museum." David Vital in "Home Grown," a review in the *Times Literary Supplement,* is troubled by what he sees as a failure to say much about Jews and Judaism in her discussion of the aftermath of the Holocaust. Björn Krondorfer's review in *Holocaust and Genocide Studies* complained that the book had nothing to say about how the memory of the Holocaust should be passed on to the third generation.

The most powerful scenes in *After Such Knowledge* come in part 6, which contains the author's encounters with the historical sites of mass murder. The previous section dealt with Polish-Jewish relations since World War II. Each group, she says, sees the other as "the other" who can be denigrated freely but who have an intertwined fate. Such abstract ideas were made concrete by her travels in part 6.

Most personal, and most moving, are her memories of visiting her parents' village, Załośce, in 1998. Her sister, Alina, suggested the visit. Alina Wydra has been an organizer of the Gesher Project in Canada, which brings together survivors of the Holocaust with members of the second generation to talk, paint, and write about their experiences. The sisters carried with them a letter, unfinished and unsent, from their father's papers. It was meant for Hryczko, the son of a family that sheltered Hoffman's parents. In the letter was the appalling fact, never spoken of by the father, that he had had to bury his two murdered brothers himself. They did in fact find Hryczko, and they were shown where their parents hid. They also saw the place where an aunt was murdered, buried in a pit where "the earth heaved for two days afterward." [p. 217]

Hoffman has from the beginning of her career tried to keep in mind that some Poles and Ukrainians helped Jews during the Holocaust, at great personal risk, though others betrayed. The emotional balance of the trip to Załośce was toward the affirmation of human goodness. The rest of section 6 looks at the worst. On July 10, 2001, she attended a ceremony commemorating the Jedwabne Massacre in 1941, in which the Jewish population of a village was killed by their neighbors. For Hoffman, the ceremony (which was attended by the president of Poland, who made a speech of apology) condensed "all the contradictions that haunt all of us who came after." The people of Jedwabne lived together, Christian and Jew, but the model of brotherhood that prevailed was the example of Cain and Abel. The massacre was particularly troubling for an author who has refuted claims that the Poles bear collective guilt for the Holocaust. She takes the ceremony seriously, with its "attempts to enact the gestures of recognition, remorse, and forgiveness." [p. 232] She has written a play about Jedwabne: "The Ceremony—Anatomy of a Massacre." In June 2003, it was given its first dramatic reading in Prague at a European Performing Arts Forum program titled "Jewish Spaces in European Theatre." The play is set during the Jedwabne Commemoration she attended, and has a chorus of the ghosts of the Jewish dead.

The play also received a London performance on December 15, 2003, in the Soho Theatre.

These visits to Załośce and Jedwabne give emotional weight to a book that often deals abstractly with a variety of issues. Hoffman ends her work with an attempt to understand other interethnic conflicts. She opens the last section by describing her stunned reaction to the terror attacks on the United States in 2001, her first experience (albeit through television) of the effects of large-scale violence in the present rather than the past. In her view, the collision of the West with Muslim fundamentalism is another example of groups who construe others as the sinister "other." She rather daringly suggests that the time of mourning for the Holocaust of 1941–1945 is over, that it must not become an excuse for morbidity and nihilism. Her subtext is surely Freud's 1917 essay "Mourning and Melancholia," mentioned near the beginning of *After Such Knowledge*. Freud believed that it was necessary to come to terms with loss and move on.

FOUND IN TRANSLATION

The core of Eva Hoffman's work remains her special heritage as an uprooted Polish Jew who made herself into an American. (Her expatriatism to England is no contradiction: she is not the first American writer to live abroad.) In her 1999 essay, "The New Nomads," she points to migration and "diasporism" as important forces in our time. The term "diaspora" was coined to describe the statelessness of the Jews, but now scholars speak of the African diaspora, the Mexican diaspora, and the Polish diaspora. Her own exile has informed her writing: even *The Secret*, she admitted in the interview with Brenda Webster, reflects her own feelings of lost identity after her migration from Poland. In "The New Nomads" she refers to a new transnational literature, the product of writers who have left their homelands voluntarily or involuntarily. She is one of these writers. The most discernible trend in her work is toward an enhanced awareness of her Jewishness, her membership in the diaspora—she has never taken up the option of moving to Israel. We can perhaps expand Alexander Wat's formula

and say that Hoffman is Polish-Polish, Jewish-Jewish, and American-American. Changing country and language was the basis of her career. Eva Hoffman was, indeed, found, not lost, in translation.

Selected Bibliography

WORKS OF EVA HOFFMAN

EDITIONS

Lost in Translation: A Life in a New Language. New York: Dutton, 1989.

Exit into History: A Journey through the New Eastern Europe. New York: Viking, 1993.

Shtetl: The Life and Death of a Small Town and the World of Polish Jews. Boston and New York: Houghton Mifflin, 1997.

The Secret: A Fable for Our Time. London: Secker and Warburg, 2001. *The Secret: A Novel*. New York: Public Affairs, 2002.

After Such Knowledge: Memory, History, and the Legacy of the Holocaust. New York: Public Affairs, 2004.

"The Ceremony—Anatomy of a Massacre." Unpublished play, performed in Prague, June 16, 2003; performed in London, December 15, 2003.

ESSAYS AND LECTURES

"Foreword. "In *Etty Hillesum: An Interrupted Life: the Diaries, 1941–1943, and Letters from Westerbork*, ix–xiii. New York: Holt, 1996.

"Time and Again: Counting the Years to Make Sense out of Life." *New York Times*, December 26, 1999, section 4, p. 1.

"The New Nomads." In *Letters of Transit: Reflections on Exile, Identity, Language, and Loss*, edited by André Aciman, 35–63. New York: New Press, 1999.

"Life Stories, East and West." *Yale Review* 88, no. 1:1–19 (January 2000).

"The Uses of Hell." *New York Review of Books* 47, no. 4:19–23 (March 9, 2000).

"Complex Histories, Contested Memories: Some Reflections on Remembering Difficult Pasts." *Doreen B. Townsend Center for the Humanities. Occasional Papers*. Paper 23 (*http://repositories.cdlib.org/townsend/occpapers/23*), presented September 1, 2000, at the University of California at Berkeley.

"Stream of Subconsciousness." *New York Times*, December

10, 2000, section 7, p. 17. (Review of Witold Gombrowicz, *Ferdydurke*.)

"Reproducing Ourselves Is All Very Well." *Guardian* (http://www.guardian.co.uk/Archive/Article/0,4273,4246794,00.html), August 29, 2001.

"The Balm of Recognition: Rectifying Wrongs through the Generations." In *Human Rights, Human Wrongs: The Oxford Amnesty Lectures 2001,* edited by Nicholas Owen, 278–303. Oxford: Oxford University Press, 2003.

"Curiosity and Catastrophe." *New York Times*, September 22, 2002, section 7, p. 10. (Review of W. G. Sebald's *After Nature*.)

"The Mask and the Pen. "In *Lives in Translation: Bilingual Writers on Identity and Creativity,* edited by Isabelle de Courtivron. New York: Palgrave Macmillan, 2003.

CRITICAL AND BIOGRAPHICAL STUDIES

Anders, Jaroslaw. "Poles Apart." *Los Angeles Times Book Review*, October 12, 1997, p. 10.

Applebaum, Anne. "A Gathering of Dissidents." *New Republic,* December 5, 1994, pp. 46–49.

Besemeres, Mary. "Language and Self in Cross-Cultural Autobiography: Eva Hoffman's *Lost in Translation*." *Canadian Slavonic Papers* 40, nos. 3–4:327–329 (September–December 1998).

———. *Translating One's Self: Language and Selfhood in Cross-Cultural Autobiography*. Oxford: Peter Lang, 2002.

Bronski, Michael. "Eva Hoffman: Parsing the Rhetoric of Memory." *Publishers Weekly,* January 19, 2004, pp. 50–51.

Browdy de Hernandez, Jennifer. "On Home Ground: Politics, Location, and the Construction of Identity in Four Women's Autobiographies." *MELUS* 22, no. 4: 21–38 (winter 1997).

Cameron, Deborah. "Language: Difficult Subjects." *Critical Quarterly* 42, no. 4:89–94 (winter 2000).

Casteel, Sarah Phillips. "Eva Hoffman's Double Emigration: Canada as the Site of Exile in *Lost in Translation*." *Biography* 24, no. 1:288–301 (winter 2001).

Clifford, Andrew. "Teach Yourself American." *New Statesman and Society,* December 15, 1989, pp. 38–39.

Durczak, Jerzy. "Multicultural Autobiography and Language: Richard Rodriguez and Eva Hoffman." In *Crossing Borders: American Literature and Other Artistic Media,.* edited by Jadwiga Maszewska, 19–30. Lodz, Poland, and Peoria, Ill.: Polish Scientific and Spoon River, 1992. 19–30.

———. *Selves between Cultures: Contemporary American Bicultural Autobiography*. Lublin, Poland: International Scholars, 1994.

"Eva Hoffman." In *Contemporary Authors*. Vol. 132, edited by Susan M. Trosky, 181. Detroit: Gale, 1991.

"Eva Hoffman." In *Contemporary Literary Criticism*. Vol. 182, edited by Janet Witalec, 136–185. Detroit: Gale, 2004.

Fachinger, Petra. "Lost in Nostalgia: The Autobiographies of Eva Hoffman and Richard Rodriguez." *MELUS* 26, no. 2:111–125 (summer 2001).

Fanetti, Susan. "Translating Self into Liminal Space: Eva Hoffman's Acculturation in / to a Postmodern World." *Women's Studies* 34, no. 5:405-419(2001).

Fjellestad, Danuta Zadworna. "The Insertion of the Self into the Space of Borderless Possibility: Eva Hoffman's Exiled Body." *MELUS* 20, no. 2:133–147 (summer 1995).

Foster, Roy. "Introduction to Eva Hoffman." *Human Rights, Human Wrongs: The Oxford Amnesty Lectures 2001,* edited by Nicholas Owen, 274–277. Oxford: Oxford University Press, 2002.

Franklin, Ruth. "Identity Theft: True Memory, False Memory, and the Holocaust." *New Republic,* May 31 2004, 31–37.

Friedrich, Marianne. "Reconstructing Paradise: Eva Hoffman's *Lost in Translation*." *Yiddish* 11, no. 3:159–165 (1999).

Gitenstein, R. Barbara. "Eva Hoffman: Conflict and Continuities of Self." In *Something of My Very Own to Say: American Woman Writers of Polish Descent,* edited by Thomas Gladsky and Rita Holmes Gladsky, 260–285. Boulder, Colo.: East European Monographs, 1997.

Gudmundsdóttir, Gunnthórunn. "Autobiography and Journeys between Cultures: Eva Hoffman, Michael Ondaatje, Kyoko Mori." In *Borderlines: Autobiography and Fiction in Postmodern Writing,* edited by Gunnthórunn Gudmundsdóttir, 141–181. Amsterdam and New York: Rodopi, 2003.

Hayes, Peter. "At Arm's Length." *Chicago Tribune*, February 8, 2004, p. 4.

Hirsch, Marianne. "Pictures of a Displaced Girlhood." In *Displacements: Cultural Identities in Question,* edited by Angelika Bammer, 71–89. Bloomington and Indianapolis: Indiana University Press, 1994.

Ingram, Susan. "When Memory Is Cross-Cultural Translation: Eva Hoffman's Schizophrenic Autobiography." *TTR: Traduction, terminologie, rédaction: études sur le texte et ses transformations* 9, no. 2: 259–276 (1996).

Kaplan, Alice Yaeger. "On Language Memoir." In *Displacements: Cultural Identities in Question,* edited by Angelika Bammer. Bloomington and Indianapolis: Indiana University Press, 1994.

Karpinski, Eva. C. "Negotiating the Self: Eva Hoffman's *Lost in Translation* and the Question of Immigrant Autobiography." *Canadian Ethnic Studies* 28, no. 1:127–134 (1996).

Kellman, Steven G. "Lost in the Promised Land: Eva Hoffman Revises Mary Antin." *Prooftexts* 18:149–159 (1998).

———. *The Translingual Imagination*. Lincoln: University of Nebraska Press, 2000. Pp. 73–84.

Krupnick, Mark. "Assimilation in Recent American Jewish Autobiographies." *Contemporary Literature* 34, no. 3:451–474 (1996).

Leonard, John. "After Such Knowledge: Memory, History, and the Holocaust." *Harper's Magazine,* January 2004, p. 75.

Levine, Madeline. "Eva Hoffman: Forging a Postmodern Identity." In *Living in Translation: Polish Writers in America*, edited by Halina Stephan, 215–233. Amsterdam: Rodopi, 2003.

Lindenmeyer, Antje. "The Rewriting of Home: Autobiographies by Daughters of Immigrants." *Women's Studies International Forum* 24, nos. 3–4:423–432 (2001).

Novick, Peter, Tad Szulc, Steven T. Katz, and Eva Hoffman. "The Uses of Hell: An Exchange." *New York Review of Books,* June 15, 2000, 78–79.

Pavlenko, Aneta. "Language Learning Memoirs as a Gendered Genre." *Applied Linguistics* 22, no. 2:213–240 (2001).

Osbourne, Thomas. "Tales of Hoffman." *History of the Human Sciences* 11, no. 3:115–124 (August 1998).

Oster, Judith. "See(k)ing the Self: Mirrors and Mirroring in Bicultural Texts." *MELUS* 23, no. 4:59–83 (winter 1998).

Proefriedt, William. "The Education of Eva Hoffman." *Journal of Ethnic Studies* 18, no. 4:123–134 (winter 1991).

———. "The Immigrant or 'Outsider' Experience as Metaphor for Becoming an Educated Person in the Modern World: Mary Antin, Richard Wright, and Eva Hoffman." *MELUS* 16, no. 2:77–89 (summer 1989–1990).

Ritivoi, Andreea Deciu. *Yesterday's Self: Nostalgia and the Immigrant Identity.* Lanham, Md.: Rowman & Littlefield, 2002. Pp.153–162.

Savin, Ada. "Passage to America, or When East Meets West." *Caliban* 31:57–63 (1994).

Schubnell, Matthias. "Lost in Translation: Complications of Bilingualism in the Memoirs of Eva Hoffman and Richard Rodriguez." *TRANS: Internet-Zeitschrift für Kulturwissenschaften, no. 13* (http://www.inst.at/trans/13Nr/schubnell13.htm), May 2002.

Spalding, Frances. "Surviving the Shoah's Shadows in Silence." *Independent*, March 31, 2004, 12.

Zaborowska, Magdalena J. *How We Found America: Reading Gender through East-European Immigrant Narratives.* Chapel Hill: University of North Carolina Press, 1995.

BOOK REVIEWS

Bartov, Omer. "How Not to Forget." *Times Literary Supplement*, March 6, 1998, 11-12.

Berenbaum, Michael. "The 'Hinge' Generation." *Jerusalem Post*, March 11, 2004, p. 31. (Review of *After Such Knowledge*.)

Bernstein, Richard. "Updating the Jewish Image of Poles." *New York Times*, October 15, 1997, p. E9. (Review of *Shtetl*.)

Bukiet, Melvin Jules. "Out of the Abyss." *Washington Post*, February 1, 2004, p. BW12. (Review of *After Such Knowledge*.)

Burley, Justine. "Exactly the Same but Different." *Nature* 417, no. 6886:224–225 (May 16, 2002). (Review of *The Secret*.)

Conrad, Peter. "Fugitive Childhoods." *New York Times Book Review*, January 15, 1989, pp. 1–3. (Review of *Lost in Translation*.)

Desai, Anita. "Cards of Identity." *New York Review of Books* (http://www.nybooks.com/articles/article-preview?article_id=15930), December 19, 2002. (Review of *The Secret*.)

Eder, Richard. "A Gene off the Old Block: A Clone's Identity Crisis." *New York Times*, December 19, 2002, p. E15. (Review of *The Secret*.)

Gordon, Neil. "Her Mother's Daughter." *New York Times*, November 10, 2002, section 7, p. 18. (Review of *The Secret*.)

Jackson, Merilyn Oniszczuk. "Pictures in Dissolving Frames." *Belles Lettres* 9, no. 3:59 (spring 1994). (Review of *Exit into History*.)

Jaggi, Maya. "Send in the Clones." *Guardian* (http://books.guardian.co.uk/reviews/generalfiction/0,6121,559704,00.html), September 29, 2001.

Kaplan, Robert D. "The View from Mitteleuropa." *New York Times Book Review,* November 21, 1993, pp. 3–4. (Review of *Exit into History*.)

Krondorfer, Björn. Review of *After Such Knowledge. Holocaust and Genocide Studies* 18, no. 2:292–293 (fall 2004).

Laqueur, Thomas. "The Old Country." *London Review of Books* (http://www.lrb.co.uk/v20/n11/laqu01_.html), June 4, 1998. (Review of *Shtetl*.)

Linklater, Andro. "Poles Together—and Apart." *Spectator*, February 14, 1998, p. 32. (Review of *Shtetl*.)

Marsden, Philip. "Sweet Are the Uses of Adversity." *Spectator,* December 4, 1993, p. 44. (Review of *Exit into History*.)

Reich, Tova. "The Virtual vs. the Real." *New Leader,* November–December 2002, pp. 41–43. (Review of *The Secret*.)

Smardz, Zofia. "Identity Crisis." *Washington Post*, November 10, 2002, p. BW06. (Review of *The Secret*.)

Vital, David. "Home Grown." *Times Literary Supplement,* July 23, 2004, p. 24. (Review of *After Such Knowledge*.)

Young, James E. "A Prisoner of Memory." *New York Times*, January 18, 2004, section 7, p. 13. (Review of *After Such Knowledge*.)

Zuccotti, Susan. "Thy Neighbor as Thyself." *New York Times*, October 12, 1997, section 7, p. 8. (Review of *Shtetl*.)

INTERVIEWS

Brown, Andrew. "Hoffman's Tale." *Guardian* (http://www.guardian.co.uk/Archive/Article/0,4273,4176778,00.html), April 28, 2001.

Kreisler, Harry. "Conversation with Eva Hoffman, Author." Conversations with History: Institute of International Studies, University of California at Berkeley (http://globetrotter.berkeley.edu/people/Hoffman/hoffman-con0.html), October 5, 2000.

Kuprel, Diana, and Marek Kusiba. "Translating the Terrain of Memory: Diana Kuprel and Marek Kusiba Speak with Eva Hoffman." *Books in Canada* 27, no. 7:16–18 (October 1998).

Tuffield, Aviva. "A Life Lived in Observation." *Melbourne Age*, August 16, 2003, p. 3.

Webster, Brenda. "Conversation with Eva Hoffman." *Women's Studies* 32 Issue 32, No. 6: 761-769 (2003).

Zournazi, Mary. "Life in a New Language." In her *Foreign Dialogues: Memories, Translations, Conversations,* 17–26. Sydney: Pluto Press, 1998.

GARRISON KEILLOR

(1942—)

Charles R. Baker

GARY EDWARD KEILLOR was born on August 7, 1942, in Anoka, Minnesota. The third of six children, Keillor grew up with three brothers (J. Philip and twins Steven and Stanley) and two sisters (Judy and Linda). His parents were John Philip and Grace Ruth (Denham) Keillor. Keillor's paternal grandfather immigrated to Minnesota from Canada in 1880 to assume responsibility of his dying brother-in-law's family and homestead in Ramsey Township, near the town of Anoka. He later married a local schoolteacher, and the farm is still owned by members of the family. Keillor's maternal grandparents were from Glasgow, Scotland.

John Philip Keillor made his living as a clerk for the Railway Mail Service, but as his family grew it was sometimes necessary for him to supplement his income by doing carpentry work. His skills as a carpenter were such that he built the family home on a one-acre lot in Brooklyn Park, Minnesota, across the Mississippi River from Anoka. Keillor lived there from the age of five until he left for college. The area was semi-rural in those days and the Keillor children enjoyed outdoor activities in the surrounding countryside. In his fictional account of his hometown, *Lake Wobegon Days* (1985), Keillor gives this description: "The woods are red oak, maple, some spruce and pine, birch, alder, and thick brush, except where cows have been put, which is like a park. The municipal boundaries take in quite a bit of pasture and cropland, including wheat, corn, oats, and alfalfa."

The Keillors were members of a fundamentalist Protestant sect called the Plymouth Brethren, a sect that rigorously tried to set themselves apart from most of the world's temptations. In addition to the usual list of sins of the flesh that were forbidden by the brethren—smoking, drinking, and dancing—followers believed that watching television resulted in moral decay. Although Keillor enjoyed sitting with his family listening to such radio programs as *Fibber McGee and Molly*, *The Lone Ranger*, *Inner Sanctum Mysteries*, and *Gang Busters*, the lack of a television in his home made the boy feel different from his friends whose families feared the effects of neither television nor motion pictures.

Certain books and magazines were also proscribed in the Keillor household. Keillor recounts in the introduction to *Happy to Be Here* (1983) how he had to sneak copies of his favorite magazine, *The New Yorker*, into the house: "My people weren't much for literature, and they were dead set against conspicuous wealth, so a magazine in which classy paragraphs marched down the aisle between columns of diamond necklaces and French cognacs was not a magazine they welcomed into their homes." The Bible, of course, was required reading and Keillor dutifully memorized long passages in preparation for the weekly meetings of the brethren. Hymns and certain ballads and poems were permissible, and Keillor's father would regale the family by reciting poems by Longfellow in their entirety without the aid of a text.

When Keillor first began to show an interest and talent in literature and journalism, it raised some concern. The early efforts, humorous character sketches he wrote in elementary school, seemed harmless enough, but his parents were worried that their boy was becoming reclusive. Worry increased as Keillor's journalistic output increased, and when Keillor at the age of thirteen began to write poetry for publication in his junior high school literary magazine, the family was certain he was on the path to damnation.

Although Keillor loved his family and found security in the fundamentalist beliefs that set them apart from others, he decided it was time to

make a symbolic declaration of independence; he chose a pen name. After experimenting with G. E. Keillor (a tribute to his favorite *New Yorker* writers, S. J. Perelman and E. B. White), he decided to use a lengthened version of his first name and selected Garrison. He never sought to legalize the name change and is still referred to as Gary by friends and family. In an interview with Alan McConagha titled "The Making of Garrison Keillor," Keillor explained the benefits of this alias: "That's a good reason for having a name like that—you can distinguish between the person that strangers know and the person who you are, which is always a good idea."

UNIVERSITY YEARS

When Keillor graduated from Anoka High School in 1960, he was determined to become a writer but was unsure of what his next step toward that goal should be. Unlike most of his friends, he had made no preparations to enter college; his academic work was unimpressive and no scholarships were forthcoming. Additionally Keillor viewed his going to college as a societal betrayal. His family was working-class poor and only his older brother had sought education beyond the high school level. Therefore Keillor decided to enter the workforce and got a job with the Salvation Army at one of their facilities in Minneapolis, the Evangeline Hotel for Women. He gives a fictional account of his experience in Minneapolis that summer in the first chapter of *Lake Wobegon Days*, "Home":

I had no prospects there except a spare bed in the basement of my dad's old Army buddy Bob's house... .

Bob kept telling me to forget about college and he would line me up with a friend of his in the plumbers' union... .

... Bob left Air Force brochures on the breakfast table, hoping I'd read them and something would click... .

... My job at the Longfellow was washing dishes for the three hundred young women who lived there, who were the age of my older sister who used to jump up from dinner and clear the table as

we boys sat and discussed dessert. The three hundred jumped up and shoved their trays through a hole in the wall where I, in the scullery, worked liked a slave. I grabbed up plates, saucers, bowls, cups, silverware, glasses, passed them under a hot rinse, the garbage disposal grinding away, and slammed them into racks that I heaved onto the conveyor that bore them slowly, sedately, through the curtain of rubber ribbons to their bath.

Whatever romantic notions Keillor may have had about class loyalty and the nobility of blue-collar work evaporated as quickly as the steam in the scullery; he applied to and was accepted by the University of Minnesota for the fall 1960 term.

Keillor managed to pay his way through school by working as a parking lot attendant and doing odd jobs for the university's two radio stations, WMMR and KUOM. The first radio job came about almost by accident; Keillor had attended a performance of the Royal Danish Ballet at the university in 1960 and, hoping to find a way to meet some of the lovely ballerinas, he suggested to the staff of WMMR that he should interview the dancers for a radio program he would call "The Royal Danish Ballet: A Portrait in Sound." The short-handed student-run radio station immediately offered him a job broadcasting a fifteen-minute daily newscast. The frustrations of struggling to make ends meet coupled with his inability to maintain a respectable grade point average, however, aggravated his nagging feeling that college was unnecessary for a man who longed to be a writer, and he left school in 1962. He went to work for the *St. Paul Pioneer Press* newspaper, but after serving four months as an entry-level copyboy Keillor returned to the University of Minnesota.

In the fall of 1963, Keillor responded to an advertisement posted by the university's news and classical music radio station, KUOM. He was given an announcer's job at the hourly rate of $1.85. Additionally the university's literary magazine, the *Ivory Tower*, made Keillor its fiction editor. Many of his pieces written for the magazine reveal Keillor to be an angry young man ready to satirize or parody everything from Lyndon B. Johnson's war policies to the Campus Crusade for Christ. There are, however, glimpses of the writer he was to become, particularly in a

short story entitled "Frankie" that explores the feelings of inadequacy experienced by a teenage boy as he drives the family car to see his girlfriend. All of Keillor's work in the *Ivory Tower* betrays a determined effort to write in the manner of those writers he most admired, the "*New Yorker* Writers": James Thurber, E. B. White, and A. J. Liebling. So great was the influence of *The New Yorker* on Keillor that he adopted a style of language reminiscent of that found in the magazine's "Talk of the Town" articles. In an interview for a newspaper feature titled "For Garrison Keillor, Fantasy Is a Lot More Fun than Reality" by Irv Letofsky, Keillor recalled his *Ivory Tower* pieces as containing "a sort of juvenile sophistication… . I pretended I was a stranger here, that I came from New York and I was commenting on this strange, outlandish behavior of the residents."

In addition to roles as radio announcer, literary magazine editor, and writer, Keillor also cultivated the role of poet, allowing his hair and beard to grow long in the prevailing style found on college campuses in the mid-1960s. Several renowned poets were on the faculty of the University of Minnesota during Keillor's years there, and he had the benefit of being taught by and associating with Allen Tate, James Wright, and John Berryman. In 1965, Keillor was awarded honorable mention in the university's annual American Academy of Poets contest for two poems he wrote in his junior year, "On Waking to Old Debts" and "Nicodemus." The following year he won first place for "This Is a Poem, Good Afternoon" and "At the Premiere." Keillor graduated in 1966 with a B.A. in English.

A MARRIAGE, A TRIP EAST, AND A SON

Keillor married a University of Minnesota classmate, music major Mary C. Guntzel. The actual date of the marriage is questionable. Some sources list September 11, 1965, as the date, and others state it as September 1 of the same year, but what makes the search for the true date most confusing is a statement Keillor made in an October 8, 1997, e-mail interview with the *Atlantic* magazine's Katie Bolick. In that online

interview Bolick asked Keillor about a trip he took to New York immediately after graduating from college in 1966. After describing his motive in going and the adventures he encountered, Keillor stated that at the time of the trip he "was engaged to marry a girl who didn't want to move to New York." In that interview he also describes his first trip east, and key realization that came to him in New York: "I thought of myself as a Midwestern writer. The people I wanted to write for were back in Minnesota. So I went home."

In a live interview with Terry Gross broadcast September 4, 2003, on National Public Radio's *Fresh Air* program, Keillor confessed that he considers it fortunate that the magazines did not hire him; he opined that he would probably still be working for one or the other, filing copy. New York's initial rejection forced Keillor to go home and hone his emerging skills.

Another reason for returning home, and to the University of Minnesota in particular, was Keillor's need to maintain his selective service status as a full-time student. Young men of Keillor's generation were being shipped off to the war raging in Vietnam at an ever increasing rate, and for those opposed to the war, as Keillor was, student deferment was a welcome solution. From 1966 through 1968, Keillor took courses toward earning an M.A. in English, found work again at the radio station KUOM, and submitted stories and poems to *The New Yorker* and the *Atlantic Monthly*. Keillor's persistent determination to be published was rewarded when his poem "Some Matters Concerning the Occupant" was printed in the *Atlantic*'s July 1968 issue. A writer's first letter of acceptance from a widely respected periodical is often mind reeling and life changing. Another such experience came to Keillor in 1969 with the birth of his son, Jason.

WRITING, RADIO, AND RESTLESSNESS

As writers sometimes do when they are first published, Keillor decided to change his surroundings and devote more time and energy to writing poems and stories. With his wife and infant son, Keillor moved to a farm several miles south of Freeport, a rural area outside of Min-

neapolis where he imagined he would find the peace and quiet and inspiration he needed to write. The family occupied a large, brick house that rented for eighty dollars a month, and Keillor wrote in an upstairs bedroom from which he could see his mailbox at the end of a long driveway. He writes humorously about his first taste of country living in his story "Happy to Be Here": "I know of several writers who sought paradise diligently, in hopes that it held a vivid description that might form the basis for several lasting poetic masterpieces." He found a different reality: "When I moved to a farm one year ago, I didn't think much of it. I had learned from the experience of others not to expect a sudden attack of delight upon arrival, or words falling over themselves to get put on paper." He decided that first he must rid himself of a "sneaky city prose style," a style he felt was overly introspective and self-conscious.

On bed rest for two weeks with a bad cold, Keillor, the implied narrator of the story, tried to write in a "plain country prose." The examples provided within the story evoke a sense of long lonely days patiently endured by a man who feels very much out of place: "One day while driving to town I was inclined to stop by an old farmer I saw looking over his crop and say, 'That's certainly doing well,' then realized I didn't know what 'that' was. Also it looked burnt." He writes, in another example,

> August 1st and still a stranger. In the town tavern, having seen Otto do this once, I held up two fingers for a whiskey-and-a-wash and was brought two beers, of which I drank one, the bartender curiously eyeing me and at last asking didn't I want two. I said no, that I had seen Otto hold up two fingers for a whiskey-and-a-wash. He said yes but I have known Otto for thirty years and know what he wants.

At story's end, however, the narrator can claim, "Found paradise. I said I would and by God I have. Here it is, and it is just what I knew was here all along. Well, I guess that is about it. I'm happy to be here, is all."

Despite having found paradise, Keillor was not selling any stories and he returned to radio work to support his family. KSJR-FM, a public,

noncommercial radio station operated by Minnesota Educational Radio in nearby Collegeville, hired Keillor as their early-morning announcer. At this time in his life Keillor viewed radio only as a means to provide for his family, a necessary interruption of what he considered his true calling. When his shift was over and he had completed presenting the station's format of news and classical music, sometimes substituting a piece of folk music, rock and roll, or bluegrass (much to the dismay of some listeners but to the delight of others), Keillor would return to his typewriter in the second-story room of his Freeport home to write: "I'd ship a batch of two or three stories off to New York every month or so, and a week later I'd start watching the road." For the rest of his life this would be Keillor's pattern, relatively brief periods of performance work broken by his desire for solitude and the time to focus on creating something that would survive on the printed page.

"*NEW YORKER* WRITER"

In 1970 two stories Keillor had sent to *The New Yorker* were accepted for publication: "Local Family Keeps Son Happy" appeared in the magazine's September 19 issue and "Snack Firm Maps New Chip Push" followed three weeks later. In the *Atlantic* e-mail interview Keillor recalled his early relationship with *The New Yorker*:

> I'd walk out for the mail and if *The New Yorker* sent me a large gray envelope it meant a story had been rejected; a small creamy envelope meant acceptance. My editor was Roger Angell, who was terribly generous with his praise and apologetic for his criticism and who, if a month passed without submissions from me, would write the most wonderful encouraging letters… . Acceptance meant a check of a thousand bucks, give or take, and in 1970, that was real money.

Acceptance by *The New Yorker* also meant that Keillor could now consider himself a "real writer." Buoyed by this dream come true and finding himself increasingly at odds with KSJR-FM's manager over his deviations from the daily

program listings, Keillor left his job at the radio station in January 1971 and devoted himself solely to writing more pieces. Early elation soon gave way to a feeling that his good fortune could suddenly disappear:

> I felt lucky to be supporting myself writing fiction and doing nothing else. I wasn't a very good writer at all, had no idea how to construct a novel, had a poor ear for dialogue, was pretentious and arrogant in all sorts of ways, and yet I had found a knack for something that somebody was willing to pay for… . I kept warning myself not to take anything for granted, to be prepared for when *The New Yorker* dumped me overboard and I'd have to find a job. I loved those years, though it's painful now to read what I wrote then (so I don't).

"Local Family Keeps Son Happy" reads like a short human-interest story that can be found in most newspapers, the sort of thing that may have sat for a while on an editor's desk and then been used as filler when a column ran short. The flat, commonplace prose and the matter-of-fact tone of the writer serve to heighten the irony and outrageousness of the story being told. The mother and father of a sixteen-year-old boy are reported to have found a way to prevent their son from falling victim to the seductive vices that claim other young men: cigarettes, alcohol, and drugs. The couple, Mr. and Mrs. Robert Shepard, arranged for the parole of an incarcerated prostitute, twenty-four-year-old Dorothy, "a shapely brunette who could easily pass for eighteen," and hired her as a live-in companion for Robert, Jr. The arrangement proves to be successful; Mr. Shepard is pleased with his son's progress; and Mrs. Shepard is happy that her boy is spending his evenings and weekends at home. Robert, Jr. admits that he was uneasy at first but soon "got used to it and settled down." The reporter opines that perhaps the reason this sort of arrangement has not caught on with other parents of teenaged boys in the Shepards' neighborhood is the cost: Dorothy's salary is seventy-five dollars per week plus room and board. As if to assuage the sticker shock his readers may experience, the writer admits that for that price Dorothy also cooks the family breakfast, and he generously includes one of Dorothy's best recipes, "fancy eggs."

"Snack Firm Maps New Chip Push" has the same understated tone as the previous story. The writer, perhaps a director of marketing, juxtaposes the horrors of the Vietnam War and the domestic unrest experienced in America with a crass concern over how to entice rebellious American youths to buy his company's new junk food, Buffalo Chips. With these two very short pieces Keillor proved himself to be capable of producing the sort of material that the editors and readers of *The New Yorker* craved: pithy, clever parodies that attack societal flaws indirectly. Keillor's long-sought marriage to *The New Yorker* was consummated in the early 1970s by an arrangement that gave the magazine first right of refusal for all of his short pieces. Over the next ten years, before *A Prairie Home Companion* began national broadcasts in 1980, Keillor contributed twenty-seven pieces to the magazine he had had to smuggle into his childhood home.

THE GENESIS OF A PRAIRIE HOME COMPANION

Something in Keillor's temperament made the necessarily lonely and isolated life of a writer unpalatable, and despite his success with *The New Yorker*, he returned to radio after an absence of only nine months. William Kling, president of Minnesota Educational Radio, had recognized Keillor's quirky talent that had occasionally emerged on KSJR's *Morning Program*. Kling also recognized that although Keillor had alienated some of that station's longtime listeners, his offbeat style had attracted many listeners who were new to public radio; therefore he sent an offer to Keillor in Freeport that included considerable programming freedom, and in October 1971, Keillor launched *The Old Morning Program* at radio station KSJN-FM in St. Paul, Minnesota. Two months later he changed the program's name to *A Prairie Home Companion*.

Freed at KSJN from the limitations imposed upon him at KSJR, Keillor began experimenting with a unique format for his program. Having grown up listening to commercial radio, he felt his program would not be realistic without a

sponsor. But KSJN was, like KSJR, a commercial-free station. He circumvented the problem this imposed by using an imaginary sponsor he had introduced during his time at KSJR, "Jack's Auto Repair." The inspiration for this particular business name came from a shop of the same name Keillor passed on his drive back and forth from Freeport to St. Paul on Highway 10. The commercial spots Keillor wrote for his nonexistent sponsor were parodies of small business, small budget commercials that are the staple of regional radio. These good-natured lampoons of a rural businessman delighted Keillor's listeners. Some sent him photographs of Jack's Auto Repair shops they had encountered, leading Keillor to invent a location for his Jack's. In a 1982 interview with Cliff Radel, Keillor explained, "So, I came up with Lake Wobegon. Then someplace along the line I started telling stories about the people who live there."

A Prairie Home Companion developed day by day as Keillor added more fictitious sponsors, eclectic music, monologues about life in Lake Wobegon, and live studio performances by jazz musicians and folk singers to the program. In an article for the *Minneapolis Tribune*, the columnist Will Jones focused on Keillor's return to radio and the popularity of the new program. Jones asked Keillor how it felt to be described as "weird and far out." Keillor replied, "With the radio program I set out deliberately to be warm and folksy and Middle American and down to earth. It's the most down-to-earth thing I have ever done and I have to believe that people are putting me on when they say it's far out." Despite the success of his new morning program and the latitude he was allowed in its creation, Keillor left the station in November 1973 to devote more time to freelance writing.

In March 1974, *The New Yorker* sent Keillor to Nashville, Tennessee, to write an article on the Grand Ole Opry's move from Ryman Auditorium, the Opry's broadcast home for more than three decades, to the newly constructed Grand Ole Opry House. The Grand Ole Opry began broadcasting in 1925 on Nashville radio station WSM, hosted by George D. Hay who, although he was

only thirty, adopted the on-the-air persona of "the Solemn Old Judge." Hay announced and interacted with such musical acts as the Possum Hunters, the Fruit Jar Drinkers, and Roy Acuff and his Crazy Tennesseans. NBC radio began broadcasting the program nationally in 1939, creating a large number of loyal listeners across the country and an ever-expanding live audience of fans who came to Nashville to see their favorite performers in person. The Ryman Auditorium could not accommodate the overflow crowds, so the program moved to a facility that increased the seating by over two thousand.

Although he had experimented with concert hall productions earlier in the year (three performances in January of *The Minnesota Grain Show* at the Walker Art Center in Minneapolis), it was the Opry experience that inspired Keillor to attempt a similar presentation format when he returned to his morning program at KSJN in the spring of 1974. On April 7, 1974, Keillor and several invited guests recorded three ninety-minute shows in the Walker Art Center for future broadcast. In these three programs, Keillor combined all the elements of his earlier shows: eclectic music, humorous commercials for nonexistent enterprises, brief public service announcements from the town of Lake Wobegon, and unrehearsed dialogue with guests. Apparently pleased with these three efforts, which were in effect rehearsals, Keillor hosted the first live broadcast of *A Prairie Home Companion* on Saturday, July 6, 1974. Given how popular the show eventually became, it is interesting to note that after Keillor had opened with what would be one of his trademark theme songs, "Hello Love," he saw that the audience at that first performance in the concert hall of the Janet Wallace Fine Arts Center of Macalester College in St. Paul, Minnesota, amounted to no more than twelve people.

DIVORCE AND FIRST COLLECTIONS

Although more and more Minnesotans were taking notice of Keillor by 1976, he had not yet achieved celebrity status, and so it is not surprising that the end of his first marriage occurred that year with little public notice. So little is

known about what led up to the event, or anything else relating to the marriage, that the biographer Peter Scholl has nothing to add except that the couple's son, Jason, was raised primarily by Keillor after the divorce. Keillor has remained mute on the subject of his first wife.

Both Keillor's daily program and his weekly program were becoming increasingly popular, and to avoid confusion with his Saturday night broadcast, he renamed the weekday program *A Prairie Home Morning Show*. Keillor's growing fame prompted Minnesota Public Radio (MPR) to compile a collection of his writings and offer it as a premium to listeners who made a financial contribution to the network. Titled *G. K. the DJ*, the slim collection was published in 1977 in a magazine format with an illustration of Keillor on the cover. Except for the preface and two poems, all the twenty pieces collected in *G. K. the DJ* were reprints of Keillor's work that had appeared in *The New Yorker*, the *Minneapolis Tribune* and MPR's magazine, *Preview*. In 1979, MPR offered to its supporters a collection of Keillor's poetry, *The Selected Verse of Margaret Haskins Durber*.

By the end of the 1970s, Keillor was a regional phenomenon, a Minnesotan telling his tales to fellow Minnesotans. It is possible that he might have contentedly continued enjoying local notoriety, bringing his fans programs of a wide variety of music, recorded and live, interspersed with jokes, imaginary news items, monologues about the town of Lake Wobegon, all interrupted occasionally by commercials for nonexistent businesses such as Jack's Auto Repair, Art's Baits, Bob's Bank, Ralph's Pretty Good Grocery, the Chatterbox Cafe, the Sidetrack Tap, Bertha's Kitty Boutique, and what is perhaps Keillor's most famous fictional sponsor, Powdermilk Biscuits, which not only promise, "Heavens, they're tasty," but claim to have the ability to "give shy persons the strength to get up and do what needs to be done." But when MPR began in 1980 to broadcast *A Prairie Home Companion* nationally by means of the public radio satellite network, Keillor found himself quickly becoming a household name from coast to coast. That same year, initial concerns that the show's format

might be too regional to appeal to a nationwide audience were quickly dispelled by its winning the George Foster Peabody Award, broadcasting's highest honor. The award, coupled with Keillor's growing popularity, may have been instrumental in Atheneum's decision to publish Keillor's first commercial book, *Happy to Be Here*, in 1982.

HAPPY TO BE HERE AND ELSEWHERE

The first edition of *Happy to Be Here* contained twenty-eight stories; in 1983 Penguin published a revised and enlarged paperback edition that increased the number to thirty-four. All the pieces are satirical and run the gamut of styles: pulp-fiction detective stories, public interest announcements, local news journalism, and sports reporting, all containing surprisingly incongruous and therefore humorous elements. The first selection, "Jack Schmidt, Arts Administrator," sets the tone for all that follow:

> I was sitting down, jacket off, feet up, looking at the business end of an air conditioner, and a numb spot was forming around my left ear to which I was holding a telephone and listening to Bobby Jo, my secretary at the Twin Cities Arts Mall, four blocks away, reading little red numerals off a sheet of paper. We had only two days before the books snapped shut, and our administrative budget had sprung a deficit big enough to drive a car through—a car full of accountants. I could feel a dark sweat stain spreading across the back of my best blue shirt.
>
> "Listen," I sputtered, "I still got some loose bucks in the publicity budget. Let's transfer that to administration."
>
> "J. S.," she sighed, "I just got done telling you. Those loose bucks are as spent as an octogenarian after an all-night bender. Right now we're using more red ink than the funny papers, and yesterday we bounced three checks right off the bottom of the account. That budget is so unbalanced, it's liable to go out and shoot somebody."
>
> You could've knocked me over with a rock.

Keillor's mastery of oral narrative, honed on his radio programs, is evident in this story and its sequel, "Jack Schmidt on the Burning Sands." It

is easy to hear the voice of Humphrey Bogart or Edward G. Robinson as one reads.

The collection includes four stories about a fictitious Minnesota radio station, WLT: "WLT (The Edgar Era)," "The Slim Graves Show," "Friendly Neighbor," and "The Tip-Top Club." There are baseball stories, United States government stories, a hilarious parody of the writing style of sixties cult author Richard Brautigan, and semiautobiographical stories of personal foibles. A poignant father-son story, "Drowning 1954," is the last selection, and it differs from the others in a way that perhaps heralds the arrival of a new aspect of Keillor's character.

The story recalls the narrator's first fearful attempts to master the skill of swimming at the age of twelve. His cousin Roger has recently drowned, and to protect her son from such a fate the narrator's mother has enrolled the reluctant boy in twice weekly swimming lessons at the YMCA. The experience is ghastly.

After being browbeaten and humiliated by the swim instructor, the boy tries to convince his mother to let him give up the lessons. She will not hear of it, and he chooses the only course he imagines is left open to him: deception. He dutifully boards the bus on lesson days but avoids the Y and divides his time between the public library and a radio studio. Guilt haunts the boy, and the bums and winos who linger near the library and aimlessly roam the street around the radio station he sees as harbingers of his future life if he continues to live a lie: "My life was set on its tragic course by a sinful error in youth."

Despite this imagined outcome, he cannot bring himself to return to the Y: "Even as I worked at the deception, I marveled that my fear of water should be greater than my fear of Hell." The session, which lasted "for most of June and July," finally ends and the boy is relieved to become "a kid again around the big white house and garden, the green lawns and cool shady ravine of our lovely suburb." He has escaped from the sinful city to the sanctified suburbs. The following summer he is delighted to find that he had been "a swimmer all along," and he feels "restored— grateful that I would not be a bum all my life, grateful to God for letting me learn to swim."

The story ends many years later: "Now my little boy, who is seven, shows some timidity around water. Every time I see him standing in the shallows, working up the nerve to put his head under, I love him more." He understands his boy's fear and the battle he is fighting to overcome it. There is a sense in this story that Keillor sees the personal fears and foibles we all carry with us as something other than material for comedy, that drunken wanderers were once little children. A loving understanding of this will permeate his next book.

LAKE WOBEGON DAYS

Keillor left his morning radio program in April 1982 for the purpose of devoting more time to converting his growing collection of Lake Wobegon monologues into a novel, but not a novel in the traditional sense. He described the book's form in a 1985 interview with Peter Hemingson:

> It's episodic, cyclical. It begins in summertime, goes through the fall and the winter and the spring, and it returns to summer. But that's its only sense of time. I go from one thing in the fall of 1959 to something in the fall of '32, and they lie on top of each other. That's my feeling about history in a small town or among families: It has to do with the time of year. Everything, every story, comes around again. And the course of the year is always tied to the growing season or the liturgical season or a particular seasonal smell or kind of feeling.

In addition to changes in dates and seasons, Keillor employs changes in narrative voice. The book's first chapter, "Home," for instance, is initially told in the first person plural: "Left to our own devices, we Wobegonians go straight for the small potatoes. Majestic doesn't appeal to us; we like the Grand Canyon better with Clarence and Arlene parked in front of it, smiling. We feel uneasy at momentous events." Halfway through this chapter, however, Keillor switches to a personal, perhaps autobiographical first-person narration to present several vignettes of boyhood in a small community. The unnamed boy's first memory—"When I was four, I told my sister about the Creation, and she laughed in my face.

She was eight."—is followed by similar recollections of growing up: schooldays, adventures with friends, first love, and first kiss. Keillor stops short of creating a dreamy, nostalgic, pastoral Neverland by inserting such incidences as teenage drinking, severe illness, and ultimate dissatisfaction with the town's physical and intellectual narrowness. Another anomaly in this otherwise Norman Rockwell–like picture of life is revealed midway in the story when the narrator suddenly comes to life in the present:

Now I lie in bed in St. Paul and look at the moon, which reminds me of the one over Lake Wobegon.

I'm forty-three years old. I haven't lived there for twenty-five years. I've lived in a series of eleven apartments and three houses, most within a few miles of each other in St. Paul and Minneapolis.

Keillor goes into minute detail in "Home" to give geographical presence and physical size to this nonexistent hamlet. A footnote at the beginning of the story provides precise information regarding directions to the town, its altitude, population, derivation of its name, ethnicity of its inhabitants, and points of interest. The source of this information is noted as "*Minnesota*, Federal Writers' Project (2nd edition, 1939)." The following chapter, "New Albion," relates the discovery and naming of the lake by French traders (who called it Lac Malheur) in the early nineteenth century, the area's early settlement by Unitarian missionaries from Boston, and the establishment of a viable community whose population was increased by the arrival of migrating German Catholics and Norwegian Lutherans.

The remaining chapters of *Lake Wobegon Days* present characters and situations immediately recognizable by faithful *Prairie Home Companion* listeners. The town's motto, "Sumus quod sumus" ("We are what we are"), explains why Lake Wobegon does not appear on any map and attempts to explain what the citizens find special about their town and what draws the occasional visitor. After listing a couple of historical curiosities, a Viking runestone and the Statue of the Unknown Norwegian, the narrator declares that there is little else that could be termed unique about Lake Wobegon. Indeed he finds his town

lacking anything exceptional in the most common commercial areas. He also admits that Lake Wobegon is certainly not a hub of intellectual activity:

So what's special about this town is not smarts either. It counted zero when you worked for Bud on the road crew, as I did one summer. He said, "Don't get smart with me," and he meant it. One week I was wrestling with great ideas in dimly lit college classrooms, the next I was home shoveling gravel in the sun, just another worker. I'd studied the workers in humanities class, spent a whole week on the labor movement as it related to ideals of American individualism, and I thought it was pretty funny to sing "Solidarity Forever" while patching potholes, but he didn't, he told me to quit smarting off.

Ultimately Keillor finds nothing in the town to account for occasional visitors other than their desire to see someone they know or their taking a wrong exit off the highway. "What's special about here," he writes, "isn't special enough to draw a major crowd, though Flag Day—you could drive a long way on June 14 to find another like it." The patriotic observance was the idea of the town's dry-goods store operator, Herman Hochstetter, who, in June of 1945, devised a way to make use of his overstock of red, blue, and white baseball caps. Herman and his wife, Louise, gathered hundreds of townspeople, dispensed caps, and assigned places to stand. A photograph of the assembly taken from a roof revealed the highlight of the holiday, the creation of a "Living Flag." But over the years this communal festivity succumbed to indifference and infighting regarding who was allowed to climb to the roof and view the flag.

Perhaps the most curious chapter in *Lake Wobegon Days* is "News." In it Keillor juxtaposes a rambling, episodic story of the town's weekly newspaper and its owner and editor, Harold Starr (dissolving into a variety of town gossip and some autobiographical reminiscences of the narrator), with what Keillor said might be "the longest footnote in American literature." An introduction to the footnote explains that an anonymous writer who had grown up in Lake Wobegon and had returned in October 1980 to introduce his new bride to his parents had brought

with him *95 Theses 95*, a long list of grievances aimed at his parents and his hometown. During the visit the writer slipped out of the house with the intention of nailing his manifesto to the door of the Lutheran church, but his determination failed him ("his upbringing made him afraid to pound holes in a good piece of wood"), and he chose instead to slide it under the newspaper's office door with a note that read, "Probably you won't dare publish this." And indeed Mr. Starr neglected the piece, losing three pages and damaging others with coffee stains as it was shifted from one pile of papers to another. How the work came into the possession of the narrator of "News" and why he chose to append it to his piece is not explained. However, it is easy to assume that *95 Theses 95* offered Keillor an outlet for pent up anger over the personal and psychological defects he developed growing up in such a smothering atmosphere. For example, in thesis 1 the writer complains,

> You have fed me wretched food, vegetables boiled to extinction, fistfuls of white sugar, slabs of fat, mucousy casseroles made with globs of cream of mushroom, until it's amazing my heart still beats. Food was not fuel but ballast; we ate and then we sank like rocks. Every Sunday, everyone got stoned on dinner except the women who cooked it and thereby lost their appetites—the rest of us did our duty and ate ourselves into a gaseous stupor and sat around in a trance and mumbled like a bunch of beefheads.

Thesis 5 declares,

> You have taught me to feel shame and disgust about my own body, so that I am afraid to clear my throat or blow my nose. Even now I run water in the sink when I go to the bathroom. "Go to the bathroom" is a term you taught me to use.

And thesis 22 confesses, "A year ago, a friend offered to give me a backrub. I declined vociferously. You did this to me." The footnote runs the entire length of the chapter, and the reader must choose how to navigate the split text. Reading each page in its entirety is perhaps the best way; that method creates a dynamic, split-

narrative argument between nostalgia and reality that is akin to Dr. Jekyll's struggles with Mr. Hyde.

Keillor's well-established celebrity helped make *Lake Wobegon Days* an immediate commercial success. Although J. D. Reed in his review "Home, Home on the Strange," published in the September 2, 1985, issue of *Time*, says that, "Far from an ideal of Norman Rockwell hominess, Lake Wobegon reverberates with terror and finalities," most reviewers overlooked this aspect. In "Tender, Hilarious Reminiscences of Life in Mythical Lake Wobegon," published in the September 6, 1985, issue of the *Christian Science Monitor*, Ruth Doan MacDougall calls the book "a love poem to small towns." A *Christianity Today* reviewer, J. Alan Youngren, writes in the November 22, 1985, issue that the book is a "listener's dream: a Saturday night monologue that goes on and on."

A feature article in the November 4, 1985, issue of *Time* further emphasizes the dreamy, sentimental aspects of Keillor and his creation. The magazine's cover illustration presents an idealized rural-town setting floating across Keillor's glasses as he gazes into the distance. The article, "Lonesome Whistle Blowing," however, concentrates more on Keillor's radio program. The reviewer, John Skow, writes that the reader can experience the same sensations produced by Keillor on the air. Retail sales of *Lake Wobegon Days* began strong and held steady; it remained on the *New York Times* best-seller list for forty-four weeks; it was chosen as a main selection of the Book-of-the-Month Club; and in 1987 the audio version of the book, containing four cassette tapes recorded by Keillor, won the Grammy Award for best spoken-word recording.

A BRIEF ESCAPE FROM INVASIVE FAME

Lake Wobegon Days is dedicated "To Margaret, my love." The Margaret so honored is Margaret Moos, producer of *A Prairie Home Companion* and live-in companion of Keillor's for several years. That arrangement suffered a setback when, in 1985, Keillor attended the twenty-fifth reunion of his high-school class. There he renewed an

acquaintance with classmate Ulla Skærved, a Danish exchange student he had not seen in twenty-five years. A fictionalized account of their subsequent romance was the subject of a Lake Wobegon monologue that was broadcast in August 1985 and published in Keillor's 1987 collection of stories, *Leaving Home.*

The piece, "David and Agnes, a Romance," opens with a sentence that has become one of the best-known sentences in radio and literature: "It has been a quiet week in Lake Wobegon." Keillor began using that line to introduce his Lake Wobegon segments on *A Prairie Home Companion*, and it invites the reader into all but one story in *Leaving Home.* After some directionless narration regarding boys' fantasies during football tryouts and some weather observations from the farmers gathered at the Chatterbox Cafe, Keillor relates that an item in Lake Wobegon's newspaper, the *Herald-Star*, has caused concern. The item's headline reads "THANK YOU," and what follows is a note of appreciation from Florence Tollefson to her family and friends for "their prayers, visits, flowers, gifts, food, when I was recovering in the hospital." This puzzles some of the ladies of the town; they cannot remember Florence being hospitalized recently. It is discovered that the item had been sitting on the editor's desk among many other outdated pieces for the past ten years and just now made its way into print. Still, Arlene Bunsen remembers that Florence and her husband, Val, were not seen in town for a few days last month.

It was not a hospital stay that accounts for the pair's disappearance, however. It was the arrival of a trunk of papers belonging to David Tollefson, Val's father. David was a carpenter who, while working on a project for Mr. and Mrs. Hedder, fell in love with Mrs. Hedder, the Agnes of the story's title. The job was completed in two months, and late on the night of the final day David drove his Ford coupe to the Hedder home, collected Agnes, and the two of them headed west. Acting as if their spouses and their children (her two and his five) never existed, the couple married the next morning in South Dakota and settled in Mount Canaan, Washington.

Lake Wobegonians put the blame on Agnes, believing she had lured David away, and eventually the pair was forgotten. David's son, Val, however, never forgot. He was eighteen at the time of his father's departure, and in a fit of rage he had thrown away everything his father had ever given him. Now, forty years later, his father has died and a trunk of books and papers has been shipped from Mount Canaan to the Tollefsons' home. Val stashes the trunk in the basement unopened, but a week later, after trying to convince himself that there might be some important Tollefson family history inside, his curiosity forces him to take a look at its contents.

What Val finds is an assortment of religious books and magazines, a certificate of appreciation for David's years of service to a Lutheran church in Mount Canaan, a Bible, a handmade maple box containing a dozen fishing lures, photographs of David and his second wife, and a coffee can filled with his letters to her. The letters reveal the progression of David's attraction, infatuation, and, finally, undeniable love for Agnes. They explode the town story that it had been Agnes who had lured David away from his family; it had been the other way around. Val decides to burn the trunk's contents, telling Florence that he doesn't need to judge David, nor keep his memory alive. Everything goes up in flames at the city's dump, everything but the trunk itself, the box of lures Val has decided he can use, and a poem Florence surreptitiously hides away in her purse. It is a poem of such romantic yearning that it makes Florence tremble. But she realizes that these are David's words to Agnes and they do not belong to her. She donates the poem to the town's historical society without revealing its author.

It is tempting to search for autobiographical revelations in this story and others in *Leaving Home*, and perhaps Keillor used his craft to analyze his situation and to assuage the guilt he may have felt in leaving Margaret Moos. In any event, Keillor and Skærved were married in Holte, Denmark, on December 29, 1985. After their honeymoon the couple returned to St. Paul and was faced with the most annoying aspect of celebrity: the loss of privacy. Particularly inva-

sive was the *St. Paul Pioneer Press*, which went so far as to print the address, price, and property taxes of the couple's new home. Keillor found the public airing of his private life unbearable; he felt that fame's concomitant self-consciousness was destructive to his writing. As he had done many times before in his career, Keillor decide to leave radio. He announced on the Valentine's Day broadcast of *A Prairie Home Companion* in 1987 that the show would end in June of that year. "It is simply time to go," he said. "I want to resume the life of a shy person and enjoy with my affectionate family a more peaceful life." He added, "We want to live for a while in my wife's country of Denmark. I want to be a writer again."

DENMARK AND NEW YORK

"July 3, 1987. Here in a little room at the back of a flat in Copenhagen, full of boxes full of wreckage from the collapse of an American career"—such was Keillor's state of mind in Denmark as revealed in the introductory chapter to *Leaving Home*, "A Letter from Copenhagen." The couple's stay in Denmark did not last long; after four months the Keillors returned to the United States and took up residence in New York City. Keillor accepted a job with the *New Yorker*, intending to leave radio work and Lake Wobegon behind and finally to establish himself as an author.

His next book, *We Are Still Married: Stories and Letters*, published in 1989, is a collection of eleven poems and sixty-one prose pieces, most of them previously published in *The New Yorker*. The title piece is a fine example of Keillor's established formula in which the extraordinary suddenly enters the lives of the ordinary: a reporter from *People* magazine comes to Minnesota to write a story about a couple, Earl and Willa, and their terminally ill dog, Biddy. The reporter and his photographer move in with the couple, and by the time they leave Willa is convinced her marriage and her husband are repulsive. The published piece, "Earl: My Life with a Louse," propels Willa into a life of talk shows, book and movie deals, and Manhattan cocktail parties. Earl, a tour-bus driver, patiently endures the public humiliations, and when Willa finally returns to him she is accepted back unconditionally, "as if none of this ever happened."

As always happened when Keillor tried to leave radio and pursue writing, radio eventually pulled him back. Keillor's new radio program, *The American Radio Company of the Air* (later shortened to *The American Radio Company*), debuted live from the Majestic Theater of the Brooklyn Academy of Music on November 25, 1989. The format was similar to that of *A Prairie Home Companion*, but the new program initially did not attract the large listening audience of the previous show. Production costs and ticket prices were higher in New York, and that, coupled with the difficulty of finding a suitable and affordable auditorium, forced Keillor to find creative ways to keep the show financially solvent. In its second season, *The American Radio Company* went on the road and broadcast fourteen of its twenty-six live programs from cities coast to coast: Chicago, St. Paul, Memphis, San Francisco, Seattle and, on March 9, 1991, London. The following year the show was on the road for twenty-three of its twenty-nine performances.

Amid the difficulties and demands of his new radio project, Keillor once again returned to writing and produced *WLT: A Radio Romance* (1991). The novel surprised, even repelled, many of Keillor's admirers, with its dark humor and off-color explicitness. In her review of this story of two brothers, Ray and Roy Soderbjerg, who stumble through the problems of creating a radio station in 1926, Diana Postlethwaite writes, "Keillor uses 'WLT' to clear his throat with a vengeance, depositing a large gob of phlegm directly on the heads of his too-adoring fans. This is assault literature."

RETURNING HOME

Keillor's self-imposed exile from Minnesota came to an end in 1992. One catalyst was the appointment of the former *Vanity Fair* editor Tina Brown as editor in chief of *The New Yorker*. Brown's style of celebrity journalism changed the focus of the long-respected magazine, and

Keillor was only one of several writers who packed up their offices. Another reason Keillor chose to leave New York may have been the deterioration of his marriage, but, as with his first divorce, Keillor maintains a silence regarding the details of his second. Whatever disappointments and emotional hurts he may have been suffering at this time, he knew that St. Paul would comfort and succor him. Indeed, in *We Are Still Married*, published three years earlier, Keillor had written, "St. Paul was a place where I believed that if I knocked on the nearest door a woman would open it and when I said, 'I feel bad. Can I talk to you?' she'd say, Sure, come on in." But the possibility that the *St. Paul Pioneer Press* might again pry into his life initially made Keillor reluctant to knock on the city's door. To maintain some distance and, he hoped, some privacy, Keillor moved into a log cabin in the Wisconsin woods across the St. Croix River from St. Paul.

This "return to nature," coupled with the popularity of Robert Bly's masculine manifesto, *Iron John: A Book about Men* (1990), may have been the inspiration for Keillor's next book, *The Book of Guys* (1993). Coming, as it did, soon after the failure of Keillor's second marriage, it is easy to read these twenty-two short sketches as his cry in the wilderness over the indignities (real or imagined) he suffered at the hands of women. He writes in the introduction,

> Guys know that we should free ourselves from women, stake out our own turf, and stop trying to be so wonderful to them. Let women deal with their own lives and solve their own problems. Stop feeling guilty, as if we could make it up to them.
>
> Guys know that we ought to get together with other guys and drink whiskey with our arms draped around each other and sing "Old Paint," and tell our ripe rich jokes.
>
> But we keep coming back to women.

The many characters through whom Keillor presents his angst range from Lonesome Shorty, a cowboy, to Dionysus, "the god of wine and whoopee," each of them trying to discover or recover his manhood.

Never content to be away from radio very long, Keillor resumed his *American Radio Company*

broadcasts in 1992, this time from a venue that felt like home and whose production costs were much less than those of New York: the World Theater in St. Paul. Within a year both the program and the theater underwent name changes; *American Radio Company* became *A Prairie Home Companion*, and the World Theater, completely renovated (thanks in part to a money-raising campaign championed by Keillor), was renamed the Fitzgerald Theater in honor of F. Scott Fitzgerald, a native of St. Paul. In recognition of his continuous efforts to preserve the entertainment value of the medium, Keillor was inducted into the Radio Hall of Fame in 1994.

Keillor's first book written primarily for children was published in 1995. *Cat, You Better Come Home*, illustrated by Steve Johnson and Lou Fancher, tells the story of Puff, a domestic feline who, feeling underappreciated by her owner, leaves home to seek her fortune. Two more followed in 1996: *The Old Man Who Loved Cheese*, illustrated by Anne Wilsdorf, and *The Sandy Bottom Orchestra*, coauthored with Jenny Lind Nilsson, Keillor's third wife. Keillor and Nilsson, a concert violinist who performed on *A Prairie Home Companion*, have one child, a daughter named Maia Grace, who was born on December 29, 1997.

The third of Keillor's Lake Wobegon books, *Wobegon Boy*, was published in 1997. The boy is John Tollefson, one of Keillor's original Lake Wobegonians. Tollefson leaves his hometown to take a job at an upstate New York college radio station, and the usual Keillor calamities ensue as the boy tries to shed his small-town values and emerge as an East Coast sophisticated young man.

The election of Jesse "The Body" Ventura, a professional wrestler turned Independence Party politician, as the thirty-eighth governor of Minnesota in 1998 inspired Keillor to write his biting political satire, *Me: By Jimmy (Big Boy) Valente* (1999). Keillor (as the fictional Valente's amanuensis) leads the reader through Valente's life: his conception on a ten-foot oak table in a Minnesota country club, his childhood with his adoptive parents, his bodybuilding regimen, his service in Vietnam, and his education in the

wrestling business. At the height of his wrestling fame, Valente is approached by the Ethical Party of Minnesota and agrees to run for governor. Valente's naïveté and lack of political polish are just what the voters are looking for, and he wins in a landslide.

In 2001, Keillor took his readers back to Lake Wobegon with *Lake Wobegon Summer 1956*. The novel, Keillor's most autobiographical to date, is the coming-of-age story of fourteen-year-old Gary. Gary possesses all the adolescent angst one would expect from a boy growing up in a conservative Christian household in postwar America. His fears and fascinations include bodily functions, pornography, and his bullying sister. Gary suffers the throes of lovesickness; he adores his cousin Kate, who is three years older and in full possession of an affected sophistication. In bold defiance of the strictures of the family's church, the Sanctified Brethren, Kate swears, smokes, and reads *The New Yorker*. Kate, however, breaks Gary's heart when she becomes involved with the local baseball team's star pitcher.

Love Me, published in 2003, allows one of Keillor's characters finally to enjoy some success as a writer. Larry Wyler, an unpublished, unknown Minnesota writer, reaps the rewards of his best-selling first novel, *Spacious Skies*. Wyler leaves his prosaic wife, Iris, to accept a job offer at *The New Yorker* and, after a dizzying time associating with such editors and writers as William Shawn, John Updike, and J. D. Salinger, he begins a downward spiral that sends him back to his long-suffering wife and a job on the local paper as an "advice to the lovelorn" columnist. Eventually his work on the column, "Ask Mr. Blue," helps Wyler understand what went wrong in his marriage and how he might repair it. It is interesting to note that, beginning in 1998, Keillor was the author of such a column, "Mr. Blue," on Salon.com. Keillor gave up the column in 2001 when he underwent heart surgery.

CLASSIFYING KEILLOR

It is very difficult to categorize Garrison Keillor; his complex ambivalence regarding his two careers begs the question: Is Keillor a radio showman who craves the admiration of audiences, or is he a writer who desires the solitary life and longs for literary recognition? It would seem that since his return from New York he has successfully managed to combine the two into one constant whirlwind of creative activity. *A Prairie Home Companion* is broadcast every Saturday evening and is heard by over three million listeners on hundreds of public radio stations. Keillor has added an after-hours program, *The Rhubarb Show*, which his Web site describes as "a new late-night cabaret series at the Fitzgerald Theater packed with young upstarts and old veterans." Additionally Keillor broadcasts a daily five-minute program called *The Writer's Almanac* on public radio in Minnesota and in some other locations. For those outside the ranges of those stations, Keillor makes the almanac available via daily e-mails.

Keillor's literary output seems equally boundless. His contributions to the arts were recognized in 2001 when he was awarded membership in the American Academy and Institute of Arts and Letters. National celebrity and an enormous following of devoted fans virtually guarantee outstanding sales of any publication that carries his name, whether it be joke books, collections of poems, songbooks, calendars, repackaged skits of Lake Wobegon, or the many audio tapes and CDs of his works. Keillor's popularity and showmanship invite comparisons to perhaps the greatest of all American humorists and entertainers, Mark Twain. The two certainly share the ability to capture regional dialect and tell heart-warming, hilarious tales; but, whereas Twain is firmly installed in the literature sections of bookstores, Keillor's novels and story collections are found in the humor and games area, tucked between comic book anthologies and magician handbooks. It is too early to tell what place they will ultimately occupy.

Selected Bibliography

WORKS OF GARRISON KEILLOR
G.K. the DJ. St. Paul: Minnesota Public Radio, 1977.

The Selected Verse of Margaret Haskins Durber. St. Paul: Minnesota Public Radio, 1979.

Happy to Be Here. New York: Atheneum, 1982. Enl. ed. New York: Penguin, 1983.

Lake Wobegon Days. New York: Viking, 1985.

Leaving Home. New York: Viking, 1987.

We Are Still Married: Stories and Letters. New York: Viking, 1989.

WLT: A Radio Romance. New York: Viking, 1991.

The Book of Guys: Stories. New York: Viking, 1993.

Cat, You Better Come Home. Illustrated by Steve Johnson and Lou Fancher. New York: Viking, 1995. (Children's book.)

The Old Man Who Loved Cheese. Illustrated by Anne Wilsdorf. Boston: Little, Brown, 1996. (Children's book.)

The Sandy Bottom Orchestra. Cowritten by Jenny Lind Nilsson. New York: Hyperion, 1996. (Children's book.)

Wobegon Boy. New York: Viking, 1997.

Me: By Jimmy (Big Boy) Valente, Governor of Minnesota, As Told to Garrison Keillor. New York: Viking, 1999.

Lake Wobegon Summer 1956. New York: Viking, 2001.

Love Me. New York: Viking, 2003.

Homegrown Democrat: A Few Plain Thoughts from the Heart of America. New York: Viking, 2004.

CRITICAL AND BIOGRAPHICAL STUDIES

Fedo, Michael W. *The Man from Lake Wobegon.* New York: St. Martin's, 1987.

Henderson, Andrea Kovacs, ed. *Encyclopedia of World Biography: 22 Supplement.* Detroit: Gale Group, 2002.

Jones, Daniel, and John D. Jorgenson, eds. "Gary (Edward) Keillor." In *Contemporary Authors New Revision Series.* Vol. 59. Detroit: Gale Research, 1998. Pp. 206–209.

Lee, Judith Yaross. *Garrison Keillor: A Voice of America.* Jackson: University Press of Mississippi, 1991.

Marowski, Daniel G., ed. "Garrison Keillor." In *Contemporary Literary Criticism.* Vol. 40. Detroit: Gale Research, 1986. Pp. 272–277.

Scholl, Peter A. *Garrison Keillor.* New York: Twayne, 1993.

———. "Garrison Keillor." In *Dictionary of Literary Biography Yearbook: 1987.* Edited by J. M. Brook. Detroit: Gale Research, 1988. Pp. 326–338.

BOOK REVIEWS

Adams, Robert M. "Boys Will Be Boys." *New York Review of Books,* January 13, 1994, p. 19. (Review of *The Book of Guys.*)

Brennan, Geraldine. "Hung Up with the Strings." *Times Educational Supplement,* July 4, 1997, p. 7. (Review of *The Sandy Bottom Orchestra.*)

Gray, Spalding. Review of *Leaving Home. New York Times Book Review,* October 4, 1987, p. 9.

Lurie, Alison. "The Frog Prince." *New York Review of Books,* November 24, 1988, pp. 33–34. (Review of *Lake Wobegon Days, Leaving Home,* and *Happy to Be Here.*)

MacDougall, Ruth Doan. "Tender, Hilarious Reminiscences of Life in Mythical Lake Wobegon." *Christian Science Monitor,* September 6, 1985, p. B4. (Review of *Lake Wobegon Days.*)

Postlethwaite, Diana. "Is This Garrison?" *Minnesota Star Tribune,* November 17, 1991, p. 8FX. (Review of *WLT: A Radio Romance.*)

Reed, J. D. "Home, Home on the Strange." *Time,* September 2, 1985, p. 70. (Review of *Lake Wobegon Days.*)

Skow, John. "Let's Hear It for Lake Wobegon!" *Reader's Digest,* February 1986, pp. 67–71. (Review of *Lake Wobegon Days.*)

———. "Lonesome Whistle Blowing." *Time,* November 4, 1985, p. 68. (Review of *Lake Wobegon Days* and *A Prairie Home Companion.*)

Walker, Sam. "Two Authors Grade the Inner Guy." *Christian Science Monitor,* January 20, 1994, p. 14. (Review of *The Book of Guys.*)

Youngren, J. Alan. "The News from Lake Wobegon: Public Radio's Small Town Has a Spiritual Dimension." *Christianity Today,* November 22, 1985, pp. 33–36. (Review of *Lake Wobegon Days.*)

Zeidner, Lisa. "Why Is Marriage Like the Electoral College?" *New York Times Book Review,* December 12, 1993, p. 13. (Review of *The Book of Guys.*)

INTERVIEWS

Bolick, Katie. "It's Just Work." *Atlantic Unbound,* October 8, 1997. (Text available to subscribers at http://www.theatlantic.com/unbound/factfict/gkint.htm.)

Gross, Terry. *Fresh Air.* National Public Radio, September 4, 2003. (Audio available at http://www.npr.org/features/feature.php?wfid=1419921.)

Hemingson, Peter. "The Plowboy Interview: Garrison Keillor: The Voice of Lake Wobegon." *Mother Earth News,* May/June 1985, pp. 17–20, 22.

Jones, Will. "After Last Night." *Minneapolis Tribune,* October 3, 1971, p. 6D.

Letofsky, Irv. "For Garrison Keillor, Fantasy Is a Lot More Fun than Reality." *Minneapolis Tribune,* July 29, 1976, p. 9D.

McConagha, Alan. "The Making of Garrison Keillor." *Washington Times,* October 10, 1985, p. 1B.

Radel, Cliff. "Home on the Prairie." *Cincinnati Enquirer,* March 4, 1982, p. B9.

ANITA LOOS

(1888–1981)

Benjamin Ivry

Anita Loos won worldwide fame as the author of the short comic novel *Gentlemen Prefer Blondes: The Illuminating Diary of a Professional Lady* (1925); however, she was also a pioneering woman screenwriter and a playwright of accomplishment. Starting in 1912 with screenplays, some of which were filmed by the legendary motion-picture director and producer D. W. Griffith (1875–1948), Loos produced scripts for such acclaimed sound films as *San Francisco* (1936) and *The Women* (1939). The latter part of her lengthy career was devoted to delightful memoirs of her Hollywood years, the last one published in 1978 when she was ninety. For endurance and delight, few literary careers can match that of Anita Loos.

Corinne Anita Loos was born in Etna, California, on April 26, 1888, the second child of Richard Beers Loos (1860–1944), a tabloid newspaper editor, and Minerva (known as Minnie) Ellen Smith (1859–1938), a West Coast farmer's daughter. Anita, as she was always called, described her father, R. Beer Loos, as a "good-looking devil" who drank beer and performed amateur theatricals, while Minnie Loos did much of the actual work of producing a newspaper while also raising the children.

Despite R. Beer's carousing and blatant unfaithfulness, the marriage continued, and in 1887 the family had moved to Sisson in the southern part of Siskiyou County, about sixty miles from the border dividing California and Oregon, in the shadow of Mount Shasta. It attracted residents after a railroad line was extended to the town in 1886, when the city was officially named and incorporated. (Named Sisson after J. H. Sisson, a hotel owner who planned the redevelopment, the town would be renamed Mount Shasta in 1922.) The Loos family had moved to a newly developed place with a whiff of the pioneer spirit that inspired prospectors during the gold rush of the 1840s and 1850s. Anita Loos was born in Etna, rather than Sisson, because her maternal grandparents lived there.

R. Beer Loos later founded the *Sisson Mascot* newspaper and in a burst of paternal pride, he put a photo of his four-year-old daughter Anita on the paper's cover. Already intrigued by publication, at age six Anita Loos won a contest for limericks in a local children's magazine. But eternally restless, R. Beers Loos did not stay long in Sisson. In 1892, he and his wife moved their three children—Anita; her brother, H. Clifford Loos (1882–1960); and her sister, Gladys A. Loos (1891–1901)—to San Francisco. There he purchased and ran a weekly publication, *Music and Drama*, turning a staid cultural journal into a racy, joke-filled show business news sheet.

In 1893, San Francisco was a vital, rough place, with ready humor to deflate pretentiousness. The Loos family befriended an aspiring writer, Jack London (1876–1916), who later published the novels *The Call of the Wild* (1903), *The Sea-Wolf* (1904), and *White Fang* (1906). Anita Loos would later claim that London was a poet only when drunk, and unfortunately he wrote his novels when sober. Yet she did praise London in her memoir *A Girl Like I* (1966) for being "one of the first Americans to read Nietzsche and Schopenhauer," which may have influenced young Loos in her reading of philosophy. As a girl, she would scribble short stories and plays, without ever completing anything.

EARLY ACTING EXPERIENCE

To supplement the family's income, Anita and Gladys Loos performed as child actors in a local

1897 production of the biblical drama *Quo Vadis*. The play, based on a dense novel by the Nobel Prize–winning Polish author Henryk Sienkiewicz (1846–1916), dramatized the struggles between flamboyant imperial Rome and strict, secretive early Christianity. Sienkiewicz's work, published in 1895, retains power today, but its stage adaptations were mostly on the level of costumed kitsch. Anita Loos and her sister played little Christian girls crying before they were fed to the lions. They wept convincingly and were next cast in the Alcazar Stock Company's production of the Norwegian playwright Henrik Ibsen's *A Doll's House* (1879).

The heroine of *A Doll's House*, Nora, is transformed from a girlish, unserious wife at the start of the play into a decisively independent woman, culminating in a famous door slam when Nora abandons her family. In the Alcazar Stock Company's production that Anita Loos participated in, the role of Nora was played by the statuesque American actress Blanche Bates (1873–1941), who would later go on to create the title roles in John Long's play *Madame Butterfly* (1900) and David Belasco's play *The Girl of the Golden West* (1905), both later turned into operas by the Italian composer Giacomo Puccini.

Another member of the Alcazar theater company at that time was Francis W. Boggs, a pioneering film director (for Fatty Arbuckle and others) who was later credited with bringing the movie industry to Los Angeles in 1909, when he established the first permanent Los Angeles film studio for the Chicago-based Selig Polyscope Company. Although Loos would not reach Hollywood until after Boggs's untimely death (by homicide) in 1911, this early brush with an important pioneer in American film history is an intriguing coincidence.

The young Anita Loos's next appearance at the Alcazar was in a dramatization of Mrs. Henry Wood's popular 1861 novel *East Lynne*. In this melodrama, the heroine, Lady Isabel Vane, runs away from her husband and children to dally with a ruthless lover and is ruined. Loos played William, the erring heroine's son, who has a splashy death scene. The play expresses a genuine malaise with traditional women's roles in the nineteenth century.

The title role in Francis Hobson Burnett's 1888 dramatization of her own novel *Little Lord Fauntleroy* (1886) provided another star part for Loos. *Little Lord Fauntleroy* is the tale of a small working-class boy from America who softens a crusty British nobleman's heart. Sub-Dickensian in its sentimentality, the play nevertheless could be a vehicle for a winning young actor.

In other productions Loos acted with Henry Miller (1859–1926), for many years one of America's most renowned actors and theater managers (not to be confused with the American novelist of the same name). Loos was also cast by the renowned showman David Belasco (1853–1931) in a production of his 1884 play *May Blossom*, a melodrama about a Civil War soldier who returns home to find that his best friend has married his fiancée.

Loos's acting career was interrupted in 1901 when tragedy struck the family: her sister, Gladys, died suddenly of peritonitis. R. Beer Loos moved his remaining family to San Diego, where he managed a theater that also screened silent films. There, Anita Loos was a voracious reader; in 1917 she recalled in *Everybody's Magazine* that she had

> read every book in the town library. When I had read all the English books I learned French and German, so as to read the few foreign books that the library contained. It's no credit to me if I am well-read. My reading has helped me in my writing, though I read not for information nor for amusement, but as Flaubert counsels in one of his letters, "I read to live."

Her favorites included *Flower, Fruit, and Thorn Pieces* (1797), a Romantic novel by the Bavarian author Jean Paul Richter. Despite her love for books, school bored Loos. A teacher once scolded her for bad spelling, and Loos answered back, "My spelling isn't any worse than Chaucer's." After high school graduation in 1907, Loos contributed written anecdotes to a column in the *New York Morning Telegraph*, which she read in the San Diego Public Library. Although these only paid ten cents per word, they kept her focused on her writing ambitions.

At her father's suggestion, Loos dashed off a one-act play, of which only the title, "The Soul Sinners," and its heroine's name, Fiamma La Flamme, survive. "The Soul Sinners" was performed on the West Coast vaudeville circuit, and Loos received modest royalties for this, her first dramatic effort. Constantly giving money to her father, Loos later explained in *A Girl Like I*, she was "beginning to sense the thrill a girl can feel in handing money to a man." Such "opportunities for self-sacrifice" would often occur in Loos's relationships in later years.

By this time Loos's brother, Clifford, had earned a medical degree, and opened an office near San Diego's red-light district where his patients included many prostitutes. Anita Loos met some of them, and concluded in *A Girl Like I* that getting to know these prostitutes helped when she was preparing to write *Gentlemen Prefer Blondes* years later: "The real truth about [prostitutes] was not that they possessed 'hearts of gold' described in fiction but that they had heads of bone. Their traditional generosity came from stupid wastefulness, and they were, almost without exception, morons." (238).

By 1911, most theaters in which she had acted also showed one-reel silent films, which she watched repeatedly with lively interest. In 1912, at age twenty-four, Loos sold three screenplays to the Biograph company and one to the Lubin company, both early film production units for the silents. The third screenplay she sold to Biograph was for *The New York Hat,* directed by D. W. Griffith in 1912 starring Mary Pickford and Lionel Barrymore.

The scenario for *The New York Hat* was signed "A. Loos"; Loos had read that male screenwriters received higher pay than women, so she hid her gender behind a first initial. More image manipulation occurred with her age, as she found that film publicists appreciated a younger prodigy writer; her birth year was often mentioned in the press as 1896, a full eight years younger than her actual age.

Loos's synopsis of *The New York Hat* reads in part :

When Mary's mother is dying, the young minister is summoned to the bedside. There, surrounded by the leading members of the church, she gives the minister a small pasteboard box requesting that he open it in secret. The young minister, after attempting to cheer up the austere father and the shy but sincere daughter, returns to the parsonage and opens the packet. It contains a few bills and numerous coins of various denominations. The minister also finds a letter which reads: "My Beloved Pastor: My husband worked me to death, but I have managed to save a little sum. Take it and from time to time buy my daughter the bits of finery she has always been denied. Let no one know. Mary Harding."

The idea of a husband working a wife "to death" was all too familiar from Loos's father's example. In *The New York Hat*, a new hat from New York priced at ten dollars is placed in the window of the village millinery shop. Loos noted in her scenario: "Three gossips high in the affairs of the church are also attracted by the hat, but after a careful inspection inside the store, they pass to more practical conceptions in the hat line."

The heroine Mary passes the window and covets the hat, at which point the minister walks by and sees the girl admiring it. He goes into the store, much to the excitement of the "ladies of the church," and buys it. When Mary wears the hat to church, a scandal results. The church ladies tell Mary's father about seeing the minister in the store, and the father tears it to shreds. Then the minister shows the church members the dead mother's bequest, and the objections are quashed. The minister asks Mary to be his wife, her father approves, and she accepts.

The hat as erotic artifact was a powerful theme for Loos, who throughout her life was obsessed with fashion. Moreover, she was intrigued by the notion of a quasi-disgraced clergyman. Her second husband, John Emerson—whom she married in 1919—was a failed seminary student before he took up show business.

Part of the lasting appeal of *The New York Hat* is its exquisitely precise camera work by G. W. "Billy" Bitzer (1872–1944), Biograph's staff cinematographer. A quality of documentary truth, akin to the Civil War photos of Matthew Brady, makes the Bitzer-Griffith collaborations permanent treasures of Americana.

In 1913 Loos sold thirty-six scripts to film companies, and in that year Biograph made short

silent films from nineteen of her scenarios. The following year she went to Los Angeles, where she finally met Griffith, whom she found resembled an "Egyptian god." Loos told *Everyone's Magazine* in 1917: "Griffith knew my name, but when I entered he almost fell off the Christmas tree. I had my hair down my back and was dressed like the rube-child I was." When Griffith asked what she enjoyed reading, Loos "prattled on about Kant, Schopenhauer, Nietzsche and other people I barely knew anything about," while criticizing Walt Whitman, one of Griffith's favorite authors, as "hysterical." She added, "Hysteria has no place in great writing … Shakespeare is never hysterical, neither is Goethe."

Loos actually did read books by Arthur Schopenhauer (1788–1860), a German philosopher who concluded that women are "decidedly more sober in their judgments" than men and sympathize more with the suffering of others. She also read the 1761 epistolary novel *Julie; ou, La nouvelle Héloïse* (*Julie; or, The New Heloise*), by the Swiss-born philosopher Jean-Jacques Rousseau (1712–1778). Much appreciated by feminist writers of the Romantic era like the British radical Mary Wollstonecraft (1759–1797), *Julie* presents its heroine's acts of transgression as acts of ideal virtue.

Loos scribbled marginal notes in such weighty tomes and recopied them painstakingly into a leather-bound notebook. In *A Girl Like I*, Loos recounts how she discovered the writings of Baruch Spinoza and urgently noted down his "advice to the lovelorn: Intellectual love is the only eternal happiness." She was equally impressed by Immanuel Kant's *Critique of Pure Reason* (1781). The silent film actress Lillian Gish (1893–1993), a favorite of Griffith's, recalled that on the Hollywood set Loos was called "Mrs. Socrates" because of her ponderous reading habits.

Loos's reading came in handy when she was asked to contribute titles for Griffith's 1916 film *Intolerance*; Loos claimed to have paraphrased the eighteenth-century French writer Voltaire in a title that read, "When women cease to attract men, they often turn to reform as a second choice." This wisecrack caused protests from cen-

sors in Pennsylvania. Defending his title and scenario writer, Griffith told *Photoplay* magazine in 1917 that Loos was the "most brilliant young woman in the world."

Returning to San Diego, Loos rejected marriage proposals from solid, unexciting businessmen, but accepted the hand of Frank Pallma, a songwriter and musical comedy stage director. A local newspaper described it as a "Tom Thumb Wedding" since Loos's adult height was four feet, eleven inches, and she weighed less than one hundred pounds, while her bridegroom was barely an inch taller than she. Loos felt the marriage with Pallma was a "clumsy, messy business," (*A Girl Like I*, 178) and hers officially lasted six months, although they only lived together for a matter of days.

Back in Los Angeles that same year, Loos was asked to adapt Shakespeare's *Macbeth* for a silent film starring the distinguished British stage actor Sir Herbert Beerbohm Tree (1853–1917). Now lost, the 1916 film also starred as Lady Macbeth the actress Constance Collier (1878–1955), who was reportedly the model for the character of Zuleika Dobson in Max Beerbohm's eponymous 1911 novel. For this film Loos shared an official screen credit for the first time: "*Macbeth* by William Shakespeare and Anita Loos."

Loos's atypically grim script for another 1916 film, *The Little Liar,* was favorably reviewed by the poet Vachel Lindsay (1879–1931), then the film critic for the *New Republic*. *The Little Liar,* directed by Lloyd Ingraham, tells of an intelligent, creative young woman from a poor background who, while in jail for a petty crime, takes to writing down her thoughts. The prison warden gets her a job on a newspaper, but when he goes to tell her the good news, he finds that the young woman has already committed suicide in despair.

The themes of desperate poverty, incarcerated women, and prison writing in *The Little Liar* appealed to Lindsay, whom Loos later called the "first film fan of any mentality." She noted with pride, "he became my pen pal from that time on." Lindsay, an avid discoverer of writing talents such as the poet Langston Hughes, found distinction in the movies, which were generally under-

valued as an art form in his day. In 1915 Lindsay had published *The Art of the Moving Picture*, a pioneering work in film studies that declared, "The supreme photoplay will give us things that have been but half expressed in all other mediums allied to it."

To date, Loos may not have produced a "supreme photoplay," but Lindsay was delighted to meet her in New York soon after the publication of his review. The pleasure was not mutual, as Loos felt that the poet resembled Mortimer Snerd, the hayseed dummy later made famous by the ventriloquist Edgar Bergen. But Lindsay did introduce her to his literary friends, including a number of left-wing writers. Of these, Loos became closest to the journalist Max Eastman (1883–1969), since 1912 the editor of the socialist magazine the *Masses*. A literary home for radical writers like John Reed, Sherwood Anderson, Carl Sandburg, and Upton Sinclair, the *Masses* was hardly Loos's cup of tea, given her refusal to take politics seriously. She preferred to spend her time in New York discussing Spinoza with Hendrik Willem van Loon, a Dutch American historian of hugely popular, if factually unreliable, books like *The Story of Mankind*. (1921)

SCREENPLAYS FOR FAIRBANKS

Loos's next important film assignment was as screenplay writer for the adventure star Douglas Fairbanks. Biograph bought Loos's work because of the literary qualities of her scripts, many of which nevertheless remained unproduced because Griffith felt they required audiences to read too many witty printed remarks linking the filmed scenes. In *His Picture in the Papers*, a 1916 vehicle for Douglas Fairbanks, directed by her future husband John Emerson, Loos created an emblematic view of early-twentieth-century American male optimism, resourcefulness, and forthright pep. Here Fairbanks plays Pete Pringle, an heir to a family fortune from vegetarian foods, although he is himself a ravenous carnivore. He meets a girl who also loves steaks, and her father grants her hand in marriage if Pringle can become famous. His wild efforts to get his picture in the papers range from faking a car accident to at-tacking two policemen. Manically energetic, capable of climbing buildings in debonair fashion, Fairbanks as presented in *His Picture in the Papers* and other films scripted by Loos is something of a "boob," as she put it. But this affectionate derision and good-natured absurdity has worn well over the years and keeps the films fresh.

Among the other silent films that Loos scripted for Fairbanks include *The Half Breed* (1916), *American Aristocracy* (1916), *The Matrimaniac* (1916), *The Americano* (1916), and *Wild and Woolly* (1917). The writing for these films has received little sustained attention, since American silent film scripts in general are still understudied and underappreciated as literature, despite their undisputed importance to American cultural history.

During this time, Loos was particularly esteemed for her witty subtitles. In the June 1917 issue of *Everybody's Magazine,* she described her most popular subtitle, which served ironically to remind viewers that they were watching a film as it introduced the name of a new character. In another scene, Fairbanks quells a riot by telling a funny story to a violent group of workmen. Loos added the playful title: "We'd like to let you in on this, but it takes 'Doug' himself to put it over."

Speed is of the essence in these comic films, like *American Aristocracy*, set at a tropical resort where Fairbanks plays a rich young man who zooms around in fast cars, motor boats, and seaplanes. Loos was familiar with Vachel Lindsay's *The Art of the Moving Picture*, which asserts that the "keywords of the stage are passion and character; of the photoplay, splendor and speed." In his book, Lindsay divides movies into categories like the action film, the intimate film, and the "photoplay of splendor, or architecture-in-motion." Of these, the Fairbanks pictures scripted by Loos were clearly action pictures, of which Lindsay wrote: "In the action picture there is no adequate means for the development of any full-grown personal passion." Such films provoke the "ingenuity of the audience, not their passionate sympathy" and remain "impersonal and unsympathetic." Even so, they remain visually

compelling because of their "endless combinations of masses and flowing surfaces" (151-152).

Adhering to this blueprint as described by Lindsay, Loos created lastingly appealing genre films, as in *The Matrimaniac,* another fast-moving 1916 comedy in which Fairbanks is presented, as usual, as an amiable, empty-headed, and accident-prone young man. *The Matrimaniac* is essentially about Fairbanks' acrobatic efforts to elope with a young woman portrayed by Constance Talmadge.

Loos churned out nine such scripts for Fairbanks in eighteen months, most of them directed by John Emerson (1874–1956), a stage actor and playwright born Clifton Paden in Sandusky, Ohio. After an unsuccessful stint at an Ohio theological seminary, Paden had assumed the stage name of Emerson and decided to focus on show business. Many people close to Anita Loos ultimately viewed Emerson as a scam artist who exploited Loos's talent once they were married. He would commandeer her salary and grab writing credit for himself where it was not due. Yet Loos recalled in her memoirs that Emerson was never dull, which for her was an essential point.

Loos also felt a lasting sense of gratitude toward Emerson. As an established director enjoying the confidence of the magisterial filmmaker D. W. Griffith, Emerson insisted on filming Loos's screenplays without altering what she wrote. He may in fact have filmed Loos's scripts without rewriting them due to laziness, but the result was the same as if he had been motivated by respect. Loos was able to see onscreen exactly what she had written, a rare privilege for Hollywood screenwriters then as now. As Loos stated with typical modesty, even when the resulting films were bad, she could learn from her errors.

By 1918, audiences loved Fairbanks' cheery, hyperactive American boob character as scripted by Loos, but Fairbanks himself began taking himself more seriously. He chose to write his own grandiose epics with higher production values, such as *The Mark of Zorro* (1920), *The Three Musketeers* (1921), and *Robin Hood* (1922). With costly sets and costumes, these films steered clear of the self-deflating sarcasm in which Loos specialized, turning Fairbanks into a more standard swashbuckling hero.

THE EARLY 1920S

Loos next turned her talent to creating witty scripts for Marion Davies, a gifted comic actress whose lover was the newspaper publisher William Randolph Hearst. She also wrote scripts for the sisters Norma and Constance Talmadge, in which they portrayed rebellious and fun-loving "flapper" characters that prefigured the heroines of her novel *Gentlemen Prefer Blondes.* She wrote scripts for five Constance Talmadge films in sixteen months: *The Love Expert* (1920), directed by David Kirkland, begins with titles by Loos joking about a "professional" seeker of love, akin to the gold-digging Lorelei Lee in *Gentlemen Prefer Blondes.*

Loos cherished her friendships with the entire Talmadge family. Norma Talmadge was married to Joseph Schenck, an independent film producer with the kind of rapscallion charm treasured by Loos. Loos was also fond of the Talmadges' mother, Margaret, known as Peg, whom she quoted verbatim for some of the character Dorothy's japes in *Gentlemen Prefer Blondes.* With Constance Talmadge, Loos would visit the high-priced hat shop of Nathan Gibson Clark, a plump gay man who would insult his customers entertainingly. She later admitted that some of the rudest jibes by Clark—whom she described in her 1978 memoir *The Talmadge Girls* as a "robust and warm-hearted aunty"—were another source for Dorothy's zingers in *Gentlemen Prefer Blondes.*

Around this time, Emerson hired a publicist to squire Loos around Europe during vacations. The young employee, James Ashmore Creelman (1901–1941), is described as "homosexual" by Loos's biographer Gary Carey (who misidentifies him as "James Ashmore Creeland"). Creelman—who wrote his own screenplays for films like *Smilin' Through* (1922), starring Norma Talmadge; *The Most Dangerous Game* (1932); *King Kong* (1933); and *The Last Days of Pompeii* (1935)—seems to have been a distant relative of Loos's friend Sherwood Anderson (1876–1941),

the author of the influential short story collection *Winesburg, Ohio* (1919). Among the friends Loos and Creelman visited in Paris was Miguel Covarrubias (1904–1957), a Mexican-born painter and author who produced vibrant caricatures for *Vanity Fair* magazine and useful books on art and culture including *Island of Bali* (1937) and *Mexico South: The Isthmus of Tehuantepec* (1946). Loos also met Gertrude Stein (1874–1946), the American author and art collector, and although she did not share Stein's interest in avant-garde prose and art, Loos did report that Stein's companion, Alice B. Toklas, was "cute."

The well-connected travelers also stopped in Vienna, where Loos met the distinguished Austrian architect Adolf Loos (1870–1933), to whom she believed she was distantly related. Although Adolf Loos was a gifted designer and teacher, it is doubtful that Anita Loos took very seriously his stern book of essays, *Ornament and Crime* (1908), urging that decorative elements must be suppressed in buildings in order for people to control their passions. In the late 1930s, however, she did commission one of Adolf Loos's leading students, Richard Neutra, to design a house for her.

She also met the popular Hungarian playwright Ferenc Molnar (1878–1952), the author of the 1920s stage hit *Liliom* (which served as the basis for the Richard Rodgers and Oscar Hammerstein musical *Carousel* in 1945) and whose comic play *The Guardsman* would reach Broadway in 1925, starring Alfred Lunt and Lynn Fontanne. Loos and John Emerson also lunched with the Austrian playwright Arthur Schnitzler (1862–1931), whose attitude and comments Loos found "attractively cynical."

Back at work in New York, Loos focused on writing stage plays at the urging of Emerson, whose theatrical roots gave him a preference for Broadway over Hollywood. She wrote *The Whole Town's Talking*, a three-act farce that premiered in 1923, and *The Fall of Eve*, which opened on Broadway on August 31, 1925. Loos wrote four other light comedies for Broadway, none of which added permanently to her literary prestige.

While in New York, Loos socialized with a number of actresses including the Talmadge sisters, Adele Astaire, and Marilyn Miller, a group she nicknamed the "cat club" after the humorist Don Marquis's *archy and mehitabel* (1927), in which Mehitabel the cat's motto is "toujours gai" (always merry). Loos's circle adopted this motto and would tour uptown Manhattan nightclubs to relish the music and dance culture that thrived during the Harlem Renaissance.

She did not socialize with women writers, apart from the Missouri-born playwright Zoë Akins (1886–1958), who would win a Pulitzer Prize in 1935 for her dramatization of Edith Wharton's story "The Old Maid." As Loos put it in *A Girl Like I*, "The only authoresses I ever respected were women first of all, like my friend the playwright Zoë Akins. That they happened to take up writing was beside the point" (113). She confessed that part of the appeal of Akins' writing for her was that Akins' dialogue was "easily burlesqued by female impersonators."

Loos much preferred socializing with male writers, and among her favorites were the infamous H. L. Mencken (1880–1956) and a Philadelphia-born novelist named Joseph Hergesheimer (1880–1954)—the latter once famous but now justly forgotten. Mencken, a journalistic dynamo who spewed out contempt for social reformers, "boobs," and "quacks," must have attracted Loos by his intellectual verve, even if his pompous and overtly jocular prose could be heavy going at times. Mencken had founded and coedited with George Jean Nathan the influential *Smart Set* magazine from 1914 to 1923, followed by the even more renowned *American Mercury* from 1924 to 1933.

Despite his notorious flaws, Mencken cared about words—his study titled *American Language*, first published in 1919, may be his best accomplishment. Most important, he offered a kind of secure masculinity that Loos relished. Indeed, she admitted in *A Girl Like I* that she would have "relegated John Emerson to second place" had Mencken ever offered romance instead of mere comradeship. To savor the Baltimore-born Mencken's company, Loos braved the heavily German atmosphere of the haunts he favored, from Lüchow's restaurant in Manhattan to a favored speakeasy in New Jersey where

Bavarian-style beer was sold. When Mencken doted on a charming but brainless blonde, Loos was moved to write the draft of a satire during a train trip to Hollywood in March 1924, which eventually became her most famous work, *Gentlemen Prefer Blondes.*

GENTLEMEN PREFER BLONDES

On returning to Manhattan from the West Coast in early 1925, Loos rediscovered her notes for *Gentlemen Prefer Blondes* among other papers, and worked them up into a story. Loos sent the Lorelei Lee story to *Harper's Bazaar* magazine, whose editor Henry Sell suggested she continue the heroine's adventures. The final episode was published in the magazine's August 1925 issue, by which time Lorelei Lee had a devoted following. In November 1925, *Gentlemen Prefer Blondes: The Illuminating Diary of a Professional Lady* was published in New York by Boni & Liverwright, and it sold out four printings by the end of the year. The ninth edition was released by March 1926, and ten more appeared over the next three years.

Gentlemen Prefer Blondes is about a 1920s flapper and gold digger, Lorelei Lee, who manipulates male admirers to obtain diamonds and other tributes. As Lorelei describes her life philosophy, "Kissing your hand may make you feel very, very good, but a diamond and safire bracelet lasts forever." (p. 101)

After being born poor in Little Rock, Arkansas—Loos seems to have appropriated Mencken's ridicule of Arkansas for being the "Sahara of the Bozarts (Beaux Arts)"—Lorelei shot and killed a lustful employer but was acquitted of murder after she charmed the judge and jury. (This plot element may have been based on the true stories of two Chicago women, Belva Gaertner and Beulah Annan, accused of murder in 1924. The local press turned the women into celebrities by praising their beauty, and both were acquitted. The story was also used in 1926 by the *Chicago Tribune* reporter Maureen Watkins, who wrote a lightly fictionalized play about the women, *Roxie Hart*, which was later filmed, inspiring Bob Fosse's 1975 Broadway musical *Chicago.*) Lorelei acquired her name from the judge at her own trial: "He said my name ought to be Lorelei which is the name of a girl who became famous for sitting on a rock in Germany." Loos was an avid reader of poets, including Lord Byron, Alexander Pushkin, and Heinrich Heine; one of Heine's most famous lyric poems is "The Lorelei," about a lovely woman who lures sailors to their doom from a rock in the sea.

Gentlemen Prefer Blondes begins with Lorelei Lee in New York, where she explains how her sugar daddy Gus Eisman, "the Button King," will pay to send her and a sharp-tongued friend, Dorothy, to Europe in order to be educated. On board their ocean liner, Lorelei spots a lawyer who was involved in her previous murder trial, but she solves any potential problem by bewitching him, dropping him, and continuing her trip to London, Paris, and beyond. In the course of her travels, Lorelei meets many notables, including Sigmund Freud, who advises her to cultivate some inhibitions.

Lorelei's overt goal is to seduce any rich gentleman she meets, including Henry Spofford, a rich but stingy American. Spofford takes Lorelei back home to America to meet his family, who are all rich and dull. During a train trip Lorelei meets an attractive young filmmaker named Gilbertson Montrose. Lorelei decides to marry Spofford, while spending her time with Montrose in order to work on his movies.

The lasting enjoyment of *Gentlemen Prefer Blondes* is not so much in its plot—such as it is—as in its tone of derisive and irreverent japes. For example, aboard the ship, Lorelei runs into a gentleman she once knew, Mr. Ginzberg. However, she admiringly explains that since a branch of the British royal family—which included Lord Louis Mountbatten—had changed their name from Battenburg to Mountbatten during World War I in recognition of anti-German feeling, her gentleman friend had decided to follow suit: "So Mr. Ginzberg changed his name to Mr. Mountginz which he really thinks is more aristocratic."

In Lorelei's idiotically illiterate narrative style, the most serious subjects are treated risibly. For instance, Dorothy tells Lorelei that to keep a straight face at Lorelei's wedding, she had to

"concentrate her mind on the massacre of the Armenians to keep herself from laughing right out loud in everybody's face." Elsewhere, Lorelei makes reference to the postwar famine in Europe after World War I, saying that her sugar daddy Gus Eisman "had dug up all his starving relatives and he had looked them all over, and decided not to bring them to America because there was not one of his starving relatives who could travel on a railroad ticket without paying excess fare for overweight."

Even the war itself is open for kidding: Lorelei asks a Frenchman at the Tomb of the Unknown Soldier for the soldier's name, and when Dorothy objects, Lorelei insists that she meant the name of soldier's mother. Henry Spofford's mannish sister is given a fleet of trucks to look after and "has never been so happy since the battle of Verdun," when she served in the transport corps. Treating murder, mayhem, and other tragic subjects irreverently, *Gentlemen Prefer Blondes* has some parallels to Voltaire's pitiless short comic novel of 1759, *Candide*.

Apart from taking recent tragedy as grist for humor, *Gentlemen Prefer Blondes* also makes sly comments about the relations between the sexes. While traveling by train through what Lorelei calls "the Central of Europe," she and Dorothy observe out the window:

> quite a lot of girls who seemed to be putting small size hay stacks onto large size hay stacks while their husbands seemed to sit at a table under quite a shady tree and drink beer. Or else their husbands seemed to sit on a fence and smoke their pipe and watch them.

LITERARY ACCLAIM AND ITS AFTERMATH

Critics appreciated *Gentlemen Prefer Blondes* immediately. In a review in the *New York Times* on December 27, 1925, Herman Mankiewicz, who would later write the screenplay for *Citizen Kane* (1941), stated:

> *Gentlemen Prefer Blondes* seems to at least one reader—who by a coincidence is also writing this piece—a gorgeously smart and intelligent piece of work... . [T]he leading character of her creation belongs clearly in the select group of genuine Americans headed by Ring Lardner's Jack Keefe... . Miss Loos's book ... is one of the most delightful of recent publications. It is civilized, human, ironic, and never crude in its effects.

The allusion to Ring Lardner's Jack Keefe refers to *You Know Me, Al: A Busher's Letters* (1914), a novel consisting of letters supposedly written by a dense baseball pitcher to a friend. Sharp-witted in its ear for less-than-literate American speech patterns and still funny today, Lardner's book is the male counterpart for the female experiences expressed in *Gentlemen Prefer Blondes*.

Loos heard from a number of admiring readers, including Mencken and the future Nobel Prize–winning author William Faulkner, who wrote to her in February 1926: "I am still rather Victorian in my prejudices regarding the intelligence of women, despite Elinor Wylie and Willa Cather and all the balance of them. But I wish I had thought of Dorothy [in *Gentlemen Prefer Blondes*]" (308). On May 14, 1926, the British novelist Aldous Huxley also wrote, requesting a meeting with Loos because he was "enraptured by the book." The Irish writer James Joyce, who was almost blind at the time, chose to read *Gentlemen Prefer Blondes* during the scant time each day that he was able to read, as a relaxation from his labors on his work in progress, *Finnegans Wake* (1939).

More praise came from overseas in the form of private letters couched in irony, as when Edith Wharton wrote from Italy to a friend. The semi-ironic tone by Wharton also reveals the genuine excitement and enjoyment that greeted Loos's work. The Spanish-born American philosopher George Santayana adopted the same tone when he ironically—but also with real appreciation—called *Gentlemen Prefer Blondes* the "best book of American philosophy." Santayana may have been referring to its pragmatic and brass-tacks portrayal of greedy flappers as emblematic of modern-day American "thought," such as it was.

Once in book form, *Gentlemen Prefer Blondes* went around the world with impressive speed, with foreign translations (often by eminent writers in their respective languages) quickly appear-

ing: it was published in Norwegian, Swedish, and French in 1926 and was translated into Czech, German, and Spanish in 1927. An Italian version appeared in 1928, and in China, the novel was translated as a newspaper serial, in a publication edited by the distinguished author Lin Yutang, himself noted for his charming and witty books explaining Chinese culture to English-language readers. The book also generated a slew of parodies, including a 1926 London edition titled *Blondes Prefer Gentlemen*, by an anonymous author under the name "Melita Noose." The Nebraska-born playwright Colin Campbell Clements offered *They Do Not: The Letters of a Non-Professional Lady Arranged for Public Consumption,* also in 1926.

As Lorelei Lee traveled across Europe, readers around the world followed her, chortling over views of their compatriots and neighbors. British readers, with a taste for irony and taking lighthearted things seriously, delighted in Lorelei's comment:

> So it seems the gentlemen in London have quite a quaint custom of not giving a girl many presents. I mean the English girls really seem to be satisfied with a gold cigaret holder or else what they call a 'bangle' which means a bracelet in English which is only gold and does not have any stones in it which American girls would really give to their maid.

The poignant tone of this acquisitive, questing young American flapper charmed the British poet and critic William Empson (1906–1984), whose poem "Reflection from Anita Loos" pays compliment by repeating one of Lorelei's observations, "A girl can't go on laughing all the time," to express existential doubt as part of human experience:

No man is sure he does not need to climb.
It is not human to feel safely placed.
"A girl can't go on laughing all the time."
William Empson, "Reflection from Anita Loos", Collected Poems (1962)

Other British writers were also admirers of Loos: H. G. Wells and Arnold Bennett became social acquaintances. The friendship with Loos revealed

Wells's insatiable appetite for Hollywood gossip. Bennett noted approvingly in his diary that Loos achieved her literary effects not "with a large vocabulary, but only with a small and very simple one."

A visual tribute came from the Irish painter Jack Yeats, the brother of the poet William Butler Yeats. He titled a canvas *Gentlemen Prefer "Books,"* showing a man turning his back on a lovely young blond woman to browse through a used-book bin outside a shop. Flattered, Loos purchased the painting for her own collection.

One result of the worldwide fame was a crisis in Loos's marriage to John Emerson, who understandably began to feel like the inferior partner. He managed temporarily to insist that Loos retire and live off the profits from her best seller. Loos later described her guilt over the hypochondria that Emerson suffered in the wake of the novel's fame, recalling in her 1974 memoir *Kiss Hollywood Goodbye* that her success had "turned a strong-willed character I had adored into a sick man."

Returning to work, in 1928 Loos produced a follow-up to *Gentlemen Prefer Blondes* titled *But Gentlemen Marry Brunettes*. The overstated and somewhat desperate dedication of the sequel reads: "To John Emerson who discovered, developed, fostered, and trained whatever I may have if I have anything that is worthwhile." An account of the life of Lorelei's friend Dorothy, the novel is mostly a disappointment, in large part because Dorothy, raised in California's entertainment milieu by an alcoholic father, seems to be from a life too close to Loos's own experiences for the kind of cheerfully derisive tone in *Blondes*. In the sequel, the taste for dark humor that worked so appealingly in *Gentlemen Prefer Blondes* instead seems strained or gratuitous, as when Dorothy discovers an antique baby cradle carved out of wood and tells Lorelei that the old woodcarver's idea was that "if the baby cashed in, the cradle was just the right shape for the funeral." The forced humor in Lorelei's account of a Greek waiter named Tony in *But Gentlemen Marry Brunettes* likewise falls flat:

> Tony's father had become quite fed up with Tony's mother, and so he got a Turkish chum of his to ar-

range for her to be present at an atrocity. It seems that the Turkish enjoy nothing so much as an atrocity … and Tony says that when he reads about the novel kind of murders we Americans can think up, and the enjoyable times we have at all of our murder trials, we Americans remind him quite a lot of the Turkish.

Loos seems to have temporarily lost her secure touch for comedy after the tumultuous success of *Gentlemen Prefer Blondes* and the crisis in her marriage, and there are other signs of passing disturbance: Loos also gave an interview at around this time to the *Paris Herald Tribune* after a meeting with Italy's Fascist dictator Benito Mussolini, in which she declared that Mussolini was the "most forceful, the most earnest, and the most heroic personality I have ever met." She would later regret this interview. She was more astute in enjoying a new friendship with Edgar Vincent, Viscount d'Abernon, a distinguished British financier and diplomat whom she met while traveling through London. At the viscount's request, Loos offered editorial advice on his memoir, *An Ambassador of Peace* (1928), which amounted to a "more dramatic arrangement of some of the chapters." In return, d'Abernon introduced Loos to literary friends including the London hostess Lady Ottoline Morrell, who informed Loos that the biographer and essayist Lytton Strachey referred to her admiringly as "the divine A."

SURVIVING SUCCESS: SCRIPTS FOR HOLLYWOOD

Loos also added to her wide-ranging social life with new friends in America. She relished the company of the entertainingly boorish brothers Addison and Wilson Mizner, who made their living as professional gamblers; she recalled in her memoirs that she was always entertained by stories from these professional con men. (The somewhat elusive charm of the pair was appreciated later in the century by another creative artist often inspired by villains, the songwriter Stephen Sondheim, who worked for decades on a poorly received 2003 musical about the Mizner brothers titled *Bounce*.)

By the end of the 1920s, Loos seemed creatively back on track. She wrote to a friend, the British photographer and stage designer Cecil Beaton, in 1930:

I know that the only real artistic satisfaction comes from a regime of honest work. To be "professional," to win the respect of "workers" in the arts and cut out the "players" at art—is the only way to make a career that will last and get more and more important, as time goes on, to yourself and others.

The regime to which Loos held, for most of her career, was to rise around 4:30 A.M. and write for hours in bed on a yellow legal pad, sometimes using a flashlight under the covers so as not to wake her pet dogs. By breakfast time, she had already put in a full day's stint as a writer, and after errands and lunch, she would return to what she had produced that morning, which by then had been typed up by a secretary.

As Hollywood entered the sound era, Loos's lively wisecracks were remembered by film producers in search of lively dialogue. Other colleagues, like D. W. Griffith, had fallen on hard times; out of friendship Loos worked on the script of what would be Griffith's last film, *The Struggle* (1931), based on the 1924 novel *L'Assommoir* by émile Zola. Griffith rejected Loos's suggestion that the only way to save the tediously grim little film would be to cast Jimmy Durante as the hero and turn it into a comedy.

Working with the Metro Goldwyn Mayer (MGM) producer Irving Thalberg (1899–1936), in 1932 Loos produced a script titled *Red-Headed Woman* for the actress Jean Harlow (1911–1937). A wisecracking personality with down-to-earth energy, Harlow became a star thanks to Loos's brass-tacks sensibility as translated onto the screen. In the film, Harlow tells a friend, "I'm in love and I'm going to be married." Those are two separate statements, since her marriage will be to a rich old man, whose chauffeur is the one she loves. Before Loos was assigned to the film, its previous scriptwriter was F. Scott Fitzgerald (1896–1940), then in the drunken throes of his unhappy alliance with Hollywood. Loos would be assigned to later Harlow films like *Riff Raff* (1936) and *Saratoga* (1937).

Hollywood in the mid-1930s offered refuge to many intellectuals fleeing Fascist Europe. Loos attended the salon of the Polish-born screenwriter Salka Viertel (1889–1978), where she socialized with émigré writers including Thomas Mann, Bertolt Brecht, Lion Feuchtwanger, and Franz Werfel; among the British writers who frequented the same parties were Aldous Huxley and Christopher Isherwood. Loos became particularly close to Huxley, who had written her a fan letter at the time *Gentlemen Prefer Blondes* was published. Like James Joyce, Huxley had not allowed near-blindness to prevent his enjoying the book.

When MGM asked Loos to write a screenplay extolling her beloved city of San Francisco, the result was the 1936 Clark Gable film *San Francisco*, which (despite the stodgy presence of the soprano Jeanette McDonald) captures some of the spirit of that city around the time of the Great Earthquake and Fire. Unfortunately, Loos's boss Irving Thalberg died of pneumonia in 1936, followed the next year by the death of Jean Harlow, from a kidney illness. Choosing to interrupt her association with Metro Goldwyn Mayer, Loos signed a contract with the film producer Samuel Goldwyn in 1938.

In 1938, she also commissioned the Viennese architect Richard Neutra (1892–1970) to design a beachfront home for her in Santa Monica. Neutra had created many flat-surfaced, industrialized residential buildings for West Coast dwellers, and this plainness corresponded well with Loos's essentially Spartan domestic life. Home was a place for working, and she was relatively unconcerned with questions of furniture and interior decoration, preferring to obsess about clothes and fashion. In this regard, Hollywood offered a wealth of brilliant talents. In his 1957 memoir, *Shoemaker of Dreams,* the famed Italian shoe designer Salvatore Ferragammo (1898–1960) recalls that, while working in Hollywood in the 1920s, he had measured Loos for a pair of shoes and, without knowing anything about her, proclaimed that her feet were those of "someone destined for great things." The anecdote is consistent with the near-occult power that Loos accorded clothes and accessories for her entire life.

By the mid-1930s Loos's husband John Emerson had faded into a permanent state of semi-invalidism, and she was not eager to replace him, misquoting a French maxim to friends, "Qui embrasse trop, manque le train"—"Too many farewell kisses and you miss the train." (A version in correct French would be "Qui trop embrasse rate le train.") Still, she did not reject emotional commitment, and in 1937 she informally adopted an ailing baby, who grew up to be the pianist Peter Duchin, after the child's mother, a friend of Loos's, suddenly died. Recounting the story in her 1977 memoir *Cast of Thousands*, Loos concludes with a Latin tag, "Nil desperandum," meaning "Never despair."

Loos's next major project was an MGM script for the Hungarian-born director George Cukor; the resulting film, *The Women* (1939), had an all-female cast, including Norma Shearer, Joan Crawford, Paulette Goddard, and Rosalind Russell. The story, about a group of self-absorbed Manhattan society women, was adapted from a 1937 stage hit by Claire Booth Luce. The film script had been through many rewrites before Loos joined the project. F. Scott Fitzgerald had yet another unhappy experience trying to make *The Women* into a film, decrying the material; Loos later pointed out that male viewers were sometimes offended by *The Women* because they don't want "to believe that their wives and mothers and girl friends can be so catty." She insisted that the film's dialogue was "not untrue to what you overheard at Elizabeth Arden or in a fitting room at Bullock's Wilshire" (*A Girl Like I*, 298). The film was considerably more witty and allusive, and less blunt, than the play. When the censors would not allow the word "virgin" to be pronounced onscreen, Loos replaced it with the suggestive term "frozen asset."

Loos followed up the success of *The Women* with yet another film directed by Cukor, a vehicle starring Joan Crawford titled *Susan and God* (1940), which she accepted to avoid the assignment of writing the screen version of Philip Barry's play *The Philadelphia Story*, a drama about upper-crust East Coast dwellers and their domestic woes. *The Philadelphia Story* was a "synthetic, snobbish play," Loos felt, although Cukor's 1940

film version became a noted success as a vehicle for Katharine Hepburn.

Loos's last full screen credit would be for the 1942 film *I Married an Angel*, starring Jeanette MacDonald and Nelson Eddy. She wrote in her diary at this time that she felt "insulted working for cretins" like the second-level MGM producers to whom she was assigned. In 1943 MGM did not renew her contract; her Hollywood career was waning, but she would be hired to doctor scripts like that of *A Tree Grows in Brooklyn* (1945), a 20th Century Fox film directed by Elia Kazan.

BROADWAY BECKONS

Casting about for new projects, Loos offered to write a play as a vehicle for the stage actress Helen Hayes (1900–1990), who was famous for playing historical costume roles such as Queen Victoria. Loos offered to write Hayes the part as Addie Beamis, a timid Newark librarian who gets drunk in a New Jersey bar and kicks up her heels. *Happy Birthday* opened at the Broadhurst Theatre on Broadway in 1946 after many rewrites, removing an acerbic edge that Loos had initially given the heroine but that Helen Hayes's adoring audiences did not appreciate.

Loos described the character of Addie Beamis as someone who believes only in reality but gradually discovers that "one of life's great realities is illusion." In its advocacy of pipe dreams, *Happy Birthday* is in accord with another play of the time, also set in a dingy bar, Eugene O'Neill's *The Iceman Cometh* (1946). Whereas O'Neill expresses his theme with self-pity and maudlin character, Loos's approach is more buoyant, and her script places over the door to the bar in *Happy Birthday* the ironic sign: "Through these portals pass the nicest people in Newark."

Another mid-1940s assignment kept her in touch with things Parisian: she was hired to doctor the script of *The Diary of a Chambermaid* (1946), directed by Jean Renoir, an adaptation of the 1900 novel by Octave Mirbeau. Starring a Hollywood friend of Loos's, Paulette Goddard, and her then-husband, Burgess Meredith, *The Diary* was poorly received. Loos's attention was next occupied with a proposed musical adaptation of *Gentlemen Prefer Blondes,* which premiered in 1949, with songs by Jule Styne. The show's star, Carol Channing, made Loos's work known to a new generation of fans, as did the 1953 film version of the musical, starring Marilyn Monroe as Lorelei Lee. (Loos would not be invited to work on a 1974 Broadway musical adaptation also starring Carol Channing, titled *Lorelei*.) Loos's extensive stage experience had been helpful in creating comic types who are solid enough to seem to live independently outside the covers of a book, which may be one reason *Gentlemen Prefer Blondes* has spawned so many stage and screen adaptations. As Loos points out in a caption in her memoir *Cast of Thousands*, "Lorelei has been harder to kill than Rasputin."

By 1950, a certain nostalgia for the 1920s was in the air, but Loos quickly dismissed questions from interviewers who asked whether she had been a flapper: "The only thing I ever flapped was the pages of a legal pad," she would reply. In 1951 she published a new humorous novel, *A Mouse Is Born*, in which the fictional protagonist, Effie Huntriss, a famous Hollywood film star, explains sex and pregnancy to the reader. The mouse in the title is the pregnant star's future child, whom she is addressing in the narrative. Only mildly amusing, *A Mouse Is Born* received mostly poor reviews.

More significant was Loos's next project, a stage adaptation of Sidonie-Cabrielle Colette's 1945 novella, *Gigi*. When Loos traveled to Paris to talk about the project with Colette, the French author was more intrigued with discussing Loos's shoes and dresses than with the literary details of the project at hand. The subsequent play helped launch the career of Audrey Hepburn in the title role on Broadway in 1951, although the 1956 London production, starring Leslie Caron (who would also perform in the 1958 MGM musical *Gigi* based on the play), was a distinct improvement on the New York production. Colette and Loos shared some experiences in common: Colette was married to Henri Gauthier-Villars, known as Willy, who was fifteen years older than she; Colette's husband signed his name to the

works she wrote and spent her money. Loos's implicit understanding of the emotional underpinnings for Colette's works no doubt helped to make *Gigi* a stage success.

Loos also possessed the chic and fizzy high spirits required for working with French material. The Parisian team of playwrights Pierre Barillet (b. 1923) and Jean-Pierre Grédy (b. 1920) specialized in bedroom farces like their later hit *Cactus Flower* (1965). Their first collaboration, from 1950, was *Le Don d'Adèle*, which Loos translated as *The Amazing Adele,* about a young woman who is psychic up to the point where she loses her virginity. She also translated the same duo's hit play *Ami-Ami* as *Darling-Darling.* Casting a shadow over these happy projects was the news that John Emerson had finally died in 1956, after many years of estrangement.

In 1958 Loos was asked to adapt two short novels by Colette, *Chéri* (1920) and *La Fin de Chéri* (1951), about a young gigolo and his sad ending. *Chéri* was produced on Broadway in 1959 starring the German actor Horst Buchholz in the title role, with Kim Stanley as his aging lover Léa. The play was not a lasting success, despite the familiarity for Loos of its theme, of a man supported by a woman in love with him. The seventy-year-old Loos perhaps was falling out of step with current trends on Broadway. She repeatedly expressed her dislike for the plays of Arthur Miller or Tennessee Williams as well as musicals, whether by Rodgers and Hammerstein or, in later years, Stephen Sondheim.

MEMOIRS AND LEGACY

By the 1950s Loos had moved permanently to a rent-controlled apartment on Fifty-seventh Street in New York City, across the street from Carnegie Hall, which was somewhat ironic given her often-stated loathing of classical music. Indeed, her favorite tunes were barroom ballads like "Melancholy Baby." Still, there she remained with her maid and companion Gladys Turner (1903–2001), who played an increasingly important role in Loos's life as she grew older. For a time, the two raised a young African American girl, Gladys Moore, whom Loos nicknamed Miss

Moore to distinguish her from her adult companion and general factotum, also named Gladys. Among other friends, Loos was in constant touch with a group of gay men involved in the arts, including the *Vogue* editor Leo Lerman and the actor Cris Alexander, a friend of Patrick Dennis, the author of the 1955 best-selling novel *Auntie Mame.*

In 1960 she rewrote a novel that was originally serialized in *Cosmopolitan* in 1930 as "The Better Things in Life" but had never appeared in book form. At the time, Edmund Wilson had praised the work as "intrepid satire ... the novel about Hollywood with the most teeth in it." Since then, of course, other more violent Hollywood satires had appeared, among them Nathaniel West's *Day of the Locust* (1939) and Evelyn Waugh's *The Loved One* (1948). Renamed *No Mother to Guide Her*, Loos's 1961 novel lampoons a dim hero reminiscent of the character of Douglas Fairbanks (as created on film by Loos) who gets a job writing inspiring postcard mottos. The novel gently skewers the world of 1920s Hollywood, with all its artifice and excess, bad architecture and fashions, religious cults, and scandals about sex and murder.

The writing process was interrupted by the news of her brother Clifford's death in August 1960. H. Clifford Loos had cofounded the Ross-Loos Medical Group in 1929, America's first health maintenance organization (or HMO), which offered publicly funded health care to thousands of families. Anita Loos was intensely proud of her brother's achievement.

In 1961, Loos's newest play, *The King's Mare*, her adaptation and translation of a work by Jean Canolle about the unhappy marriage of King Henry VIII with Anne of Cleves, opened at the Bristol Old Vic in England for a short run. In 1962, while awaiting a New York production, Loos attended a Greenwich Village birthday party for W. H. Auden in the company of Christopher Isherwood, and noted in her diary: "An incredible assortment of intellectual queens, of which I am the Queen of queens."

In 1966, Loos published a memoir, *A Girl Like I*, to critical acclaim. In a social whirl, Loos attended Truman Capote's 1966 Black and White

Ball, a much-publicized social event where she hobnobbed with other survivors of the 1920s arts scene including the novelist Glenway Wescott, the composer and critic Virgil Thomson, and the journalist Janet Flanner.

In 1974 Loos published a second memoir, *Kiss Hollywood Good-by*, full of admiring anecdotes about Wilson Mizner and other entertaining scoundrels she had known. In one story, Mizner hires a man who looks like then–Supreme Court Chief Justice William Howard Taft to sit in the parlor of an illegal Long Island gambling house and read the *New York Times*, in order to lend the place respectability:

> But the fake William Howard Taft found his job tedious. In the first place, he had never learned to read ... so one evening, fed up with the Times, he got tight, made overtures to a bus boy and, on being repulsed, stabbed him with a steak knife.
>
> The wound was a mere scratch and its perpetrator quickly hustled out of sight, but there had been enough witnesses to start a rumor that the Chief Justice of the U.S. Supreme Court was overly fond of little boys. News filtered through to Washington that a Taft look-alike was being used as a shill for a gambling house and a federal indictment closed Wilson's establishment down (202).

Despite such raucous episodes, Loos presents herself as characteristically intellectual and literary in *Kiss Hollywood Good-by*. She describes an extended conversation with the Italian author Giovanni Papini (1881–1956) at an Italian spa. Papini, author of *The Life of Christ* (1921) and other historical works, reminded Loos of Wilson Mizner, because "people who can laugh off misfortunes as a robust joke are pretty scarce." A chapter is dedicated to Papini "dredging forth" details about Loos's marriage with John Emerson, when she "had been a widow for several years." This is an intriguing slip, as Emerson and Papini died in the same year, 1956. By casting a detailed analysis of her marriage as a dialogue with an eminent European critic, poet, and novelist, however, she lent the subject intellectual glamour and dignity. Papini finally advises her to take final revenge by writing up the relationship with Emerson and selling it to a publisher— which indeed she does in *Kiss Hollywood Good-by*. Papini concludes, in an ironic twist on the philosophy of Dr. Pangloss in Voltaire's *Candide,* that "everything always turns out for the best in this worst of all possible worlds."

She immediately launched into work on another book. A study of New York written by Loos, but presented as coauthored by her old friend Helen Hayes, *Twice over Lightly: New York Then and Now,* appeared in 1972. Loos explained that, while she preferred to stay at home "in company with some honest old cynic like Anthony Trollope," New York was an inexhaustibly lively place. In 1970, when she and Paulette Goddard were lunching in the Palm Court of the Plaza Hotel, they witnessed an assassination attempt upon the Chinese politician Chiang Ching-kuo, the son of Chiang Kai-shek. Loos concludes that to "go through twenty-four hours in New York and still be breathing is a triumph that makes the risk well worth while." A zesty ode to survival, with lots of ogling of "virile males" by Loos, as well as brushes with drug dealers, boy prostitutes, and pornographic film theaters, *Twice over Lightly* is an underrated book that is still good reading. Loos concludes that she remains an optimist, and she paraphrases again the words she previously attributed to Papini, that "everything is for the best in this worst of possible worlds."

The profusely illustrated overview of her life, *A Cast of Thousands*, was her next project, drawing heavily on her other memoirs, with some up-to-date references to Richard Nixon's "astounding moral turpitude" and the "one-dimensional content" in plays by Edward Albee and Harold Pinter. Although mostly a cut-and-paste job, *A Cast of Thousands* does contain some original material, notably a signed photo from the transvestite performer Charles Pierce (1926–1999), a mainstay of Greenwich Village nightclubs with his impersonations of Hollywood stars like Bette Davis and Katharine Hepburn, with Loos's caption: "The prettiest girl I know is Charlie Pierce." Among the other images and letters reproduced in facsimile is the typed suicide note written by Ralph Barton (1891–1931), the tormented artist who wittily illustrated the original edition of *Gentlemen Prefer Blondes*.

Loos's final memoir, *The Talmadge Girls* (1978), reminisces about her friendship with the actresses Norma and Constance Talmadge, and especially their wisecracking mother, Peg. Loos notes that Peg "raised her girls, through sheer force of derision, to be virgins. In the Talmadge family sex was treated like a joke, though not a very funny one." Loos recounts stories about Talmadge cronies like William "Bill" Haines, an openly gay silent film star who was forced by his studio employers to choose between his boyfriend and his MGM contract. Haines chose his boyfriend and launched a thriving career as an interior decorator. Loos concludes: "As a love-and-success story, Bill's legend was far more thrilling than any he ever filmed for L. B. Mayer."

Loos's old age was somewhat disorganized because her companion Gladys, herself growing old, began having difficulty assuming all of the responsibilities Loos was accustomed to giving her, which extended from house duties to business and financial matters. Relying on the prescription drug Ativan to calm her nerves, Loos nonetheless remained in her nineties a paragon of chic. In *Anita Loos Rediscovered* (2003), her niece Mary Anita Loos recalls seeing her aunt during a West Coast visit in 1979:

> Anita was incredibly feminine; I remember after having her coffee and putting away the notebook she still wrote in every morning, she sat at the dressing table in a negligee tying a ribbon at the nape of her neck. Her hair was longer now, so she could pin it into a neat bun; her shapely legs were crossed, and tiny marabou slippers covered her toes. She pouted slightly putting on her lipstick; she was ageless (viii).

Loos's recipe for constant work kept her old age productive; in *A Girl Like I* she praised Winston Churchill's approach to old age as ideal, with his "interest in life as an unfrightening miracle ... one can easily dodge the mounting loneliness most people fear by being outrageously entertaining."

Citing examples of entertaining old friends like Elsie Mendel, George Bernard Shaw, and Mae Murray, Loos followed their precedent and left many happy memories behind her. At a memorial service for Loos, the producer Morton Gottlieb recalled Loos saying that life was "an upward climb, that life can get better and if there's anything wrong that happens through the day, well, face everyone head-on, anyway." The classicist Edith Hamilton—the author of *The Greek Way* (1930) and *Mythology* (1942)—left a posthumous book of essays, *The Ever-Present Past* (1964), in which she offers more formal praise of Loos's legacy:

> In that book of balance and proportion, *Gentlemen Prefer Blondes*, Miss Anita Loos does not bring an indictment against the universe in the person of Lorelei. She knows how to laugh, and that knowledge is the very best preservative there is against losing the true perspective… . Without a sense of humor one must keep hands off the universe unless one is prepared to be, oneself, an unconscious addition to the sum of the ridiculous (189).

Anita Loos, who died on August 18, 1981, surely added to the laughter, rather than the ridiculousness, of the world. She will without doubt continue to be remembered chiefly for *Gentlemen Prefer Blondes*. Nevertheless, her memoirs *A Girl Like I*, *Kiss Hollywood Good-by*, and *The Talmadge Girls* remain charming and informative about life in Hollywood during the silent and early sound eras. Finally, *Twice over Lightly: New York Then and Now* is a characterful and humane Valentine to the city where Loos chose to spend most of her adult life. The basic themes of optimism, wit, and hard work that made Anita Loos's achievement possible shine through these books, making them permanently enjoyable.

Selected Bibliography

WORKS OF ANITA LOOS

BOOKS

How To Write Photoplays. With John Emerson. New York: McCann, 1920.

Breaking into the Movies. With John Emerson. New York: McCann, 1921.

Gentlemen Prefer Blondes: The Illuminating Diary of a Professional Lady. New York: Boni & Liveright, 1925.

The Whole Town's Talking: A Farce in Three Acts. With John Emerson. New York: Longmans, Green, 1925.

But Gentlemen Marry Brunettes. Illustrated by Ralph Barton. New York: Boni & Liveright, 1928.

Happy Birthday: A Play in Two Acts. New York: Samuel French, 1948.

A Mouse Is Born. Garden City, N.Y.: Doubleday, 1951.

Gigi. New York: Random House, 1952. (Dramatized by Loos from the novel by Colette; Broadway premier in 1951.)

No Mother To Guide Her. New York: McGraw-Hill, 1961.

A Girl Like I. New York: Viking, 1966.

The King's Mare: A Play in Three Acts. With Jean Canolle. London: Evans Brothers, 1967. (Adaptation and translation by Loos.)

Twice over Lightly: New York Then and Now. With Helen Hayes. New York: Harcourt Brace Jovanovich, 1972.

Kiss Hollywood Good-by. New York: Viking, 1974.

Cast of Thousands. New York: Grosset and Dunlap, 1977.

The Talmadge Girls: A Memoir. New York: Viking, 1978.

San Francisco: A Screen Play. Edited by Matthew J. Bruccoli. Carbondale: Southern Illinois University Press, 1979.

Fate Keeps on Happening: Adventures of Lorelei Lee and Other Writings. Edited by Ray Pierre Corsini. New York: Dodd, Mead, 1984.

Anita Loos Rediscovered: Film Treatments and Fiction. Edited and annotated by Cari Beauchamp and Mary Anita Loos. Berkeley: University of California Press, 2003.

SCREENPLAYS

The Musketeers of Pig Alley (1912)

My Baby (1912)

The New York Hat (1912)

Binks' Vacation (1913)

A Cure for Suffragettes (1913)

A Fallen Hero (1913)

The Hicksville Epicure (1913)

Highbrow Love (1913)

His Hoodoo (1913)

A Horse on Bill (1913)

How the Day Was Saved (1913)

The Lady in Black (1913)

The Mistake (1913)

Pa Says (1913)

The Power of the Camera (1913)

The Telephone Girl and the Lady (1913)

The Wedding Gown (1913)

The Widow's Kids (1913)

Billy's Rival (1914)

A Bunch of Flowers (1914)

A Corner in Hats (1914)

The Deceiver (1914)

For Her Father's Sins (1914)

The Gangsters of New York (1914)

The Hunchback (1914)

Nearly a Burglar's Bride (1914)

When the Road Parts (1914)

The White Slave Catchers (1914)

The Deacon's Whiskers (1915)

The Fatal Finger Prints (1915)

Mixed Values (1915)

American Aristocracy (1916)

The Americano (1916)

A Calico Vampire (1916)

The Children Pay (1916)

A Corner in Cotton (1916)

The French Milliner (1916)

The Half-Breed (1916)

His Picture in the Papers (1916)

Intolerance: Love's Struggle through the Ages (1916)

Laundry Liz (1916

The Little Liar (1916)

Macbeth (1916)

The Matrimaniac (1916)

The Mystery of the Leaping Fish (1916)

The Social Secretary (1916)

Stranded (1916/I)

The Wharf Rat (1916)

A Wild Girl of the Sierras (1916)

A Daughter of the Poor (1917)

Down to Earth (1917)

In Again, Out Again (1917)

Reaching for the Moon (1917)

Wild and Woolly (1917)

Come On In (1918)

Good-Bye, Bill (1918)

Hit-the-Trail Holliday (1918)

Let's Get a Divorce (1918)

Getting Mary Married (1919)

The Isle of Conquest (1919)

Oh, You Women! (1919)

A Temperamental Wife (1919)

Under the Top (1919)

A Virtuous Vamp (1919)

The Branded Woman (1920)

Dangerous Business (1920)

In Search of a Sinner (1920)

The Love Expert (1920)

The Perfect Woman (1920)

Two Weeks (1920)

Mama's Affair (1921)

Woman's Place (1921) (story)

Red Hot Romance (1922)

Polly of the Follies (1922)

Dulcy (1923)

Three Miles Out (1924)

Learning to Love (1925)

The Whole Town's Talking (1926)

Stranded (1927)

Gentlemen Prefer Blondes (1928)

The Fall of Eve (1929) (story)

The Struggle (1931)

Blondie of the Follies (1932)

Red-Headed Woman (1932)

The Barbarian (1933)

Hold Your Man (1933)

Midnight Mary (1933)

The Cat and the Fiddle (1934) (uncredited)

The Girl from Missouri (1934)

The Social Register (1934) (story)

Biography of a Bachelor Girl (1935)

Riff Raff (1936)

San Francisco (1936)

Mama Steps Out (1937)

Saratoga (1937)

The Cowboy and the Lady (1938) (uncredited)

Another Thin Man (1939) (uncredited)

Babes in Arms (1939) (uncredited)

The Women (1939)

Strange Cargo (1940) (uncredited)

Susan and God (1940)

Blossoms In the Dust (1941)

They Met in Bombay (1941)

When Ladies Meet (1941)

I Married an Angel (1942)

A Tree Grows in Brooklyn (1945) (uncredited)

MANUSCRIPTS

A collection of Anita Loos's papers, consisting of scripts, essays, and articles from her career as a screenwriter and novelist, is housed in the Lincoln Center Library of the Performing Arts, New York City. The bulk of the collection dates from 1917- 1969. Included are adaptations of her works, unfinished scripts and research notes.

The Beinecke Library, Yale University, owns a collection of Anita Loos's letters to the Austrian-born architect Michael Rosenauer (1884- 1971) dated from 1928- 1932.

The Library of Congress houses the papers of the actress Ruth Gordon (1896- 1985), dating from 1924- 1969, including letters from Anita Loos.

CRITICAL AND BIOGRAPHICAL STUDIES

Affron, Charles. *Lillian Gish: Her Legend, Her Life*. New York: Scribner, 2001.

Barrow, Kenneth. *Helen Hayes, First Lady of the American Theater*. Garden City, N.Y.: Doubleday, 1985.

Bauer, Dale M. *Edith Wharton's Brave New Politics*. Madison: University of Wisconsin Press, 1994.

Bedford, Sybille. *Aldous Huxley: A Biography*. London: Chatto & Windus, 1974.

Bennett, Arnold. *The Journals*. Edited by Frank Swinnerton. Harmondsworth, U.K.: Penguin, 1971.

Bitzer, G. W. *Billy Bitzer: His Story*. New York: Farrar, Straus and Giroux, 1973.

Bode, Carl. *Mencken*. Carbondale: Southern Illinois University Press, 1969.

Carey, Gary. *Anita Loos: A Biography*. New York: Knopf, 1988.

————. *Doug & Mary: A Biography of Douglas Fairbanks and Mary Pickford*. New York: Dutton, 1977.

Channing, Carol. *Just Lucky I Guess: A Memoir of Sorts*. New York: Simon & Schuster, 2002.

Cooke, Alistair. *Douglas Fairbanks: The Making of a Screen Character*. New York: Museum of Modern Art, 1940.

Duchin, Peter. *Ghost of a Chance: A Memoir*. New York: Random House, 1996.

Dunaway, David King. *Aldous Huxley Recollected: An Oral History*. New York: Carroll & Graf, 1995.

————. *Huxley in Hollywood*. London: Bloomsbury, 1989.

Eells, George. *Hedda and Louella*. New York: Putnam, 1972.

Faulkner, William. *Selected Letters of William Faulkner*. Edited by Joseph Blotner. New York: Random House, 1977.

Flamini, Roland. *Thalberg: The Last Tycoon and the World of M-G-M*. New York: Crown, 1994.

Foot, Michael. *H. G.: The History of Mr. Wells*. Washington, D.C.: Counterpoint, 1995.

Gish, Lillian. *The Movies, Mr. Griffith, and Me*. Englewood Cliffs, N.J.: Prentice-Hall, 1969.

Golden, Eve. *Platinum Girl: The Life and Legends of Jean Harlow*. New York: Abbeville Press, 1991.

Graham, Cooper C., et al. *D. W. Griffith and the Biograph Company*. Metuchen, N.J.: Scarecrow, 1985.

Hamilton, Edith. *The Ever-Present Past*. New York: Norton, 1964.

Hayes, Helen. *My Life in Three Acts*. San Diego: Harcourt Brace Jovanovich, 1990.

———. *On Reflection: An Autobiography*. New York: M. Evans, 1968.

Henderson, Robert M. *D. W. Griffith: The Years at Biograph*. New York: Farrar, Straus and Giroux, 1970.

Huxley, Aldous. *Letters of Aldous Huxley*. Edited by Grover Smith. London: Chatto & Windus, 1969.

Johnson, Gaynor. *The Berlin Embassy of Lord D'Abernon, 1920–1926*. New York: Palgrave Macmillan, 2002.

Johnston, Alva. *The Legendary Mizners*. New York: Farrar, Straus and Young, 1953.

Jones, Llewellyn. *Joseph Hergesheimer, the Man and His Books*. New York: Knopf, 1920.

Kershaw, Alex. *Jack London: A Life*. London: HarperCollins, 1997.

Kreizenbeck, Alan. *Zoë Akins: Broadway Playwright*. Westport, Conn.: Praeger, 2004.

Lambert, Gavin. *On Cukor*. New York: Putnam, 1972. (Interviews.)

Levy, Emanuel. *George Cukor, Master of Elegance: Hollywood's Legendary Director and His Stars*. New York: Morrow, 1994.

Lindsay, Vachel. *The Art of the Moving Picture*. 1915. Rev. ed. New York: Macmillan, 1922.

Lindsay, Vachel. *Letters of Vachel Lindsay*. Edited by Marc Chénetier. New York: B. Franklin, 1978.

———. *The Progress and Poetry of the Movies: A Second Book of Film Criticism*. Edited by Myron Lounsbury. Lanham, Md.: Scarecrow, 1995.

Mann, William J. *Wisecracker: The Life and Times of William Haines, Hollywood's First Openly Gay Star*. New York: Viking, 1998.

McGilligan, Patrick. *George Cukor, a Double Life: A Biography of the Gentleman Director*. New York: St. Martin's, 1991.

Morella, Joe, and Edward Epstein. *Paulette: The Adventurous Life of Paulette Goddard*. New York: St. Martin's, 1985.

Murphy, Donn B., and Stephen Moore. *Helen Hayes: A Biobibliography*. Westport, Conn.: Greenwood Press, 1993.

Niver, Kemp R. *D. W. Griffith: His Biograph Films in Perspective*. Edited by Bebe Bergsten. Los Angeles: Niver, 1974.

O'Connor, Richard. *Rogue's Progress: The Fabulous Adventures of Wilson Mizner*. New York: Putnam, 1975.

Oderman, Stuart. *Lillian Gish: A Life on Stage and Screen*. Jefferson, N.C.: McFarland, 2000.

Pearson, Roberta E. *Eloquent Gestures: The Transformation of Performance Style in the Griffith Biograph Films*. Berkeley: University of California Press, 1992.

Pitman, Joanna. *On Blondes*. London: Bloomsbury, 2003.

Rosen, Marjorie. *Popcorn Venus: Women, Movies & the American Dream*. New York: Coward, McCann & Geoghegan, 1973.

Schickel, Richard. *D. W. Griffith: An American life*. New York: Simon & Schuster, 1984.

———. *His Picture in the Papers: A Speculation on Celebrity in America Based on the Life of Douglas Fairbanks, Sr.* New York: Charterhouse, 1974.

Stenn, David. *Bombshell: The Life and Death of Jean Harlow*. New York: Doubleday, 1993.

Sullivan, Edward Dean. *The Fabulous Wilson Mizner*. New York: Henkle, 1935.

Talmadge, Margaret L. *The Talmadge Sisters, Norma, Constance, Natalie: An Intimate Story of the World's Most Famous Screen Family, by Their Mother, Margaret L. Talmadge*. Philadelphia and London: Lippincott, 1924.

Thomas, Bob. *Thalberg: Life and Legend*. Garden City, N.Y.: Doubleday, 1969.

Tibbetts, John C. *His Majesty the American: The Cinema of Douglas Fairbanks, Sr.* South Brunswick, N.J.: Barnes, 1977.

Vickers, Hugo. Introduction. In *Gentlemen Prefer Blondes: The Illuminating Diary of a Professional Lady*, by Anita Loos. London: Folio Society, 1985.

Wells, H. G. *The Correspondence of H. G. Wells*. London and Brookfield, Vt.: Pickering & Chatto, 1998.

Wolfe, Glenn Joseph, *Vachel Lindsay: The Poet As Film Theorist*. New York: Arno Press, 1973.

CONTEMPORARY ARTICLES

Davis, Rosalind. "John and Anita Return Home." *National Magazine*, October 1920.

Durling, E. V. "Anita Loos Sues for Divorce." *New York Telegraph*, May 19, 1918.

Emerson, John. "John Interviews Anita and Anita interviews John." *Photoplay*, June 1921.

"The Emerson-Loos Way." *New York Times*, February 29, 1920.

Mankiewicz, Herman. "Gentlemen Prefer Blondes." *New York Times Book Review*, December 27, 1925, p. 21.

Mayer, Jimmie. "Closeup on Scenario Peers." *National Magazine*, May–June 1920.

Montanye, Lillian. "The Play's the Thing!" *Motion Picture*, April 1918.

Parsons, Louella. "Anita in Harness Again." *New York Telegraph*, June 15, 1919.

———. "To Whom Hath Shall Be Given." *New York Telegraph*, March 16, 1919.

Schmidt, Karl. "The Handwriting on the Screen." *Everybody's Magazine*, June 1917.

LEONARD MICHAELS

(1933–2003)

Sanford Pinsker

During a 2001 symposium on memoir sponsored by the *Partisan Review*, Leonard Michaels began his paper, "The Personal and the Individual," by insisting that "a great problem for me, in writing about myself, is how to not write merely about myself."(*Partisan Review*, Vol. 68, No. 1: 2001) The consciously chosen, delimiting word "merely" not only marks the difference between serious writers of memoir and their often-indulgent counterparts but also between fiction writers who draw too heavily on their lives as opposed to those who put autobiographical material to the service of a disinterested art.

The old maxim that urges fictionists to "write about themselves," to write about "what they know," is only partially true because writing is also about discovering what one *did not* know. Michaels, especially in his remarkable short stories, creates personae who take the life of Leonard Michaels to another level—whether it be that of his imaginative counterpart Phillip Liebowtiz or any of the other spokespersons who reflect certain Michaels attitudes without being exclusively Michaels. They are more than that, and it is the "more" that makes his stories, well, stories.

At a time when publishers were being flooded by "confessions" of every stripe, Michaels felt an obligation to comment on the widespread notion that "writing about oneself" is all that is required of the fledgling memoirist. Not entirely so, he argued, going on to cite a handful of examples from Shakespeare and Spinoza to Miles Davis— all by way of illustrating his point about local details and their wider resonance.

"The Personal and the Individual" is not only an insightful rumination about the many things that can go wrong when one sets out to write a memoir, it is also a set of principles that can be applied to Michaels's own work. He has always been interested in how a precisely rendered detail can resonate into an eerie significance, and there has always been a sense about his work that the line separating fiction from nonfiction, what he actually experienced from what was invented, is often blurred. In other, less capable hands, this benchmark might well have led to disastrous consequences—either works in which the movement from quotidian detail to hallucinatory moments is either slow to the point of creakiness or done with such blazing speed as to be unintelligible. Among the things that Michaels has down pat is timing, a sense of rhythm that is akin to what a poet's ear recognizes as the moment for a line break.

From his first story collection, *Going Places* (1969), onward, Michaels has explored what would happen if you put ordinary people into extraordinary situations and, furthermore, how writers such as Jorge Luis Borges and most especially Franz Kafka might help him create the atmospherics each story requires. "He worked at the sentence level," Wendy Lesser, the editor of *Threepenny Review*, said when asked to comment about Michaels for his *New York Times* obituary, "like a poet."

Michaels surely cared about language, and that care was made all the more impressive by the way he used other works of literature to create an allusive tissue far more intricate and revealing than most writers who simply drop a name or book title and let the matter go at that. From the beginning of Michaels's career, important reviewers such as Susan Sontag were not shy about using the word "breathtaking" to describe his prose—the curious blending of the horrific and the humorous, and the various ways in which New York City functions as both backdrop and ostensible "character" in his work. Michaels's early stories promised a new note in American

fiction, and to a large extent that is what his slim body of work accomplished.

Leonard Michaels, the son of Polish Jewish immigrants, was born on New York City's Lower East Side on January 2, 1933. Until he was five or six he spoke only Yiddish, the language of the Michaels household. In many respects his situation was similar to that of many other Jewish immigrant children, but with an important exception—somewhere during his early childhood, probably when he was around the age of six, his mother bought a complete set of Charles Dickens. As he told Curt Suplee for a profile that appeared in the pages of the *Washington Post*, "If you can imagine a little boy … listening to his mother, who can hardly speak English, reading Dickens hour after hour in the most extraordinary accent, it might help to account for my peculiar ear." It is hard to know how much of Michaels's memory is factual, how much the result of self-mythologizing, in his recollection of encountering such disparate languages at an early age, but the consequence was clearly important. Paradoxically, Dickens does not rate a mention in the writers an adult Michaels ticked off as influences: poets such as Lord Byron or Wallace Stevens are those he acknowledged, once again reinforcing the sense that Michaels came to his paragraphs as a poet comes to a stanza.

Two sociocultural facts had much to do with the formation of Michaels's sensibility. The first is a Depression-era childhood; to be born in 1933 was to enter a world in which economic despair was the resounding note, one that lasted until the beginning of World War II in 1939. The other was the cultural grip exerted by "the tradition" as defined by the influential poet and critic T. S. Eliot and those who gathered under the banner of the (formalist) New Criticism. Michaels may have felt an inclination toward literature as early as his high school years, but he also felt that his Russian Jewish heritage had placed him outside the pale of contemporary literary culture. So he studied painting instead and entered New York University as a premed student. Michaels would remain something of a gypsy scholar, flitting from one interest to another and, later, from one failed attempt at graduate school in English to another.

It was not until the early 1960s that he began writing the short stories that would become his trademark.

Ticking off the relevant dates in Michaels's unsteady academic career does not, however, convey just how difficult and how complicated the long, frustrating journey to his first attention-getting collection of short stories in fact was. Michaels entered graduate school as a student of English literature after earning a BA from New York University in 1953. But his brief stay at New York University's graduate school suggests that, from his perspective, he was deeply unhappy, while, from the school's perspective, he was probably regarded—that is, if he were "regarded" at all—as temperamentally unsuited to graduate work. Later, he tried his luck at the University of Michigan at Ann Arbor, where he received an MA in 1956 and then entered the school's PhD program in English literature. Once again, however, Michaels dropped out, unhappy with the heavy atmosphere of literary study, as he would a short time later drop out of a graduate program at the University of California at Berkeley.

At this point, in or about 1959, Michaels reversed Horace Greeley's advice, going east rather than west. He settled in Manhattan, where he became immersed in two things: the short story form and marriage. The former love affair lasted all his life, but the latter—to Sylvia Bloch—was effectively over in the mid-1960s when they separated. Their years together were simultaneously productive and painful: to scratch together a living Michaels taught English classes at Patterson State College (in Wayne, New Jersey) by day and worked on his short stories at night. Hints about his first marriage are dotted throughout his fiction, but in a piece titled "Sylvia," he directly confronts his painful memories of his first wife, who committed suicide at the age of twenty-four. Initially "Sylvia" was part of a longer, convoluted work called *Shuffle* (1990), arguably the one sustained piece of Michaels's writing that disappointed many of his critics, but two years later *Sylvia* appeared as a stand-alone work with the subtitle *A Fictional Memoir*. Most critics, however, did not

buy into Michaels's playful oxymoron: "fiction" and "memoir" do not properly belong in the same construction, because the genres are out to do very different things. With *Shuffle*, many found the book's structure more indulgent than genuinely experimental; as for the "Sylvia" section, it simply embarrassed. But Michaels could not give up the ghost, and it is clear that she haunted him throughout his life.

Michaels finally received a PhD, in English Romantic literature, from the University of Michigan in 1967—and even placed an article on Lord Byron plucked from his dissertation in the January 1969 issue of the prestigious academic journal *PMLA*. "Byron's Cain" ought to have launched Michaels's academic career, but it did not. What readers will find, in later work, of his scholarly interests are scattered references to Byron's life and letters, along with the title phrase, from Byron, of Michaels's second short story collection, *I Would Have Saved Them If I Could* (1975).

Michaels was much married during his lifetime—first to Sylvia Bloch, and then, in 1966, to Priscilla Older, then to the poet Brenda Lynn Hillman in 1976, and finally, in 1977, to Katharine Ogden. Moreover, with his dashing good looks and oversized libido, Michaels was widely known as a man about the Berkeley campus, and some have even suggested that he might have produced more writing if he had done less skirt chasing. Perhaps it is best to simply say that the man had his demons, but he dealt with most of them in the pitiless honesty of his art.

GOING PLACES

The thirteen stories collected in 1969 as *Going Places* originally appeared in such prestigious journals as the *Massachusetts Review*, *New American Review*, *Paris Review*, *Partisan Review*, and *Transatlantic Review*. Michaels may have been a virtual unknown when he first sent the manuscripts of these stories off to prospective editors, but he was no longer a novice when they were published. Certainly one of the major reasons accounting for Michaels's extraordinary critical success is the way he turned New York City into what Stephan Taylor, writing in the pages of the *Village Voice*, called a "laboratory" in which "human beings are the only remaining manifestations of nature." Taylor went on to explain that "while we've controlled natural disasters like plague and drought and famine in our cities, we may simply have freed people to perpetrate personal disasters that are just as harrowing."

Consider the collection's title story. In "Going Places," Beckman, a down-on-his-luck cabbie, is beaten senseless by a couple of fares. In the story's paragraph-long opening sentence, "going places" refers to the cityscape through which Beckman had once aimlessly driven and the brutally ugly life it had created:

> a life made wretched by rattling kidneys, the stench of gasoline, of cigarettes, of perfume and alcohol and vomit, the end of surly toughs, drunken women, whoring soldiers, vagrant blacks and whites, all the streaming, fearsome, pathetic riffraff refuse of the city's dark going places, though places in hell, while he, Beckman, driver of the cab, went merely everyplace, anyplace, until the sun returned the day and he stopped ... debauched by the night's long, winding, resonant passage and the abuse of a thousand streets. (182)

This large chunk of the story's opening paragraph (which runs some 270 words) illustrates just how hypnotic, how downright eerie, Michaels's sentences can be. If his attraction to violence suggests an affinity to a tighter-lipped Ernest Hemingway, his tongue-in-cheek sense of the darkly comic (as opposed to the merely funny) gives his work a cutting-edge middle-1960s flavoring.

As Lore Segal points out in her *New Republic* review, *Going Places* "makes these horrors" (which she earlier defines as "orgies, rapes, mayhem and suicide") "horrible again and funny." Take, for example, "City Boy," a story that begins with a presumably reluctant girlfriend uttering—and then repeating—the words "Phillip, this is crazy" (p. 17) as the two make violent love in the girl's family apartment:

> We were on the living room floor and she repeated, "Phillip, this is crazy." Her crinoline broke under us

like cinders .... She was underneath me and warm. The rug was warm, soft as mud, deep. Her crinoline cracked like sticks. Our naked bodies clapped together. Air fired out, like farts.(17)

In much the same way that the eighteenth-century critic Dr. Samuel Johnson objected to Metaphysical poets such as John Donne or Andrew Marvell because, in his words, they yoked "heterogeneous elements by violence," Michaels describes a turbulent love scene in the imagery of crinoline breaking under the lovers like "cinders" or the physical reaction of air being "fired out like farts." (17) The unlikely yoking is simultaneously unexpected—and therefore, comic—as well as existentially revealing—for this, at least in Michaels's world, is what love has devolved to in the city. In *The Waste Land* (1922), the modernist poet T. S. Eliot also wove a tapestry that contrasted classical love with the debased modern condition he associated with the figures of the bored (urban) typist and her decidedly unheroic suitor, the "young man carbuncular."

But in Michaels's postmodern world, love is less important than acting every inch the "city boy": Phillip boasts that he is "a city boy. No innocent shitkicker from Jersey. I was the A train, the Fifth Avenue bus. I could be a cop. My name was Phillip, my style New York City" (23).

Phillip, of course, is protesting far too much, and as the story's plot plays itself out, we learn that Phillip has left the apartment without enough money for the subway or, literally, a shirt to cover his back. He is naked—that is, until Veronica brings him his clothes, and Phillip learns that her father has had a heart attack.

In another, more conventional story, the star-crossed lovers would react quite differently, but this is, after all, a Leonard Michaels tale, one that dances on the cutting edge separating the gruesome and the sidesplitting, the banal from the bizarre. Phillip, who once "had been a man of feeling"(18), reverts to an earlier sense of self and yells "Oh God, no" (30), while Veronica— also changing roles—insists that they go back to the apartment and have coffee. Her mother has made arrangements to stay by her husband's side—which means that the young couple can resume their former lovemaking without the fear

of parental interruption. That, at least, is how Veronica sees it: "Let's just go upstairs and not say anything" (31).

Phillip, however, finds that proposition impossible: "Not say anything. Like moral imbeciles go slurp coffee and not say anything? What are we, nihilists or something? Assassins? Monsters?" (31). In this kaleidoscope of a story, the reader may turn the glass prism one way and the protagonists are (a) all of the above or (b) none of the above or (c) a comic response to much of the inflated, which is to say pretentious, seriousness of that cultural moment. Susan Sontag, who so admired the stories in *Going Places*, would later argue for "camp" as an aesthetics of destabilization. In a sense, "City Boy" is camp drained of the excess that tips its hand too easily and too forcefully; rather, this Michaels story sneaks up on readers who can never be quite sure about how and where they are to be grounded. In the process, the truth about the contemporary world gradually ekes out, with its grimace hidden just inside a guffaw.

Phillip Liebowitz, the protagonist of "City Boy," is at once Michaels's sly antiheroic invention (Liebowitz is best characterized by his outrageous stunts, many of which land him flat on his face) and his shadow self. In "Making Changes," for example, an orgy lies at the story's center, and the "changes" that resonate in the story's title suggest both what is gained and lost in anonymous sexual encounters and how "Cosmo" (Liebowitz's moniker at the beginning of the story) becomes Phillip. In "A Green Thought"— the line is taken from Andrew Marvell's seventeenth-century poem "The Garden": "A green thought in a green shade"—Liebowitz is shocked to discover that his girlfriend (of the hour) has a "vatchinol infection" (113). She takes green medicine, presumably to clear the problem up. Meanwhile, the color "green" threads its way through the story, leading to Liebowitz's characteristic brand of "green thoughts in a green (subway) shade":

She [Cecily] struggled, naked, shameless. I was cool. She pulled out a dollar. Green. I was sick, getting sicker. Rocking, banging rocking, banging. But this was the last time. I sang it to the mambo

of the wheels: "The last time, the last time. Chunga cha-chungo. Green Green." (214-15)

Despite his braggadocio and purported "coolness" in these two stories, Liebowitz clearly is a man out of his element at orgies and certainly thrown off balance by the mere thought of the green medicine Cecily is taking.

"Sticks and Stones," however, is the Phillip Liebowitz story that packs the most stylistic wallop in this collection. It begins with the hapless Phillip on a blind date. His first impressions are hardly promising: Marjorie limps from an industrial accident and stutters in the bargain. After they make their way through a bottle of top-shelf bourbon and are suitably positioned on the couch, she begins to spin out her life story. Phillip, meanwhile, staggers from the couch, makes his way to the glass window, and hurls himself out— only to discover, when his fainting spell subsides, that he is on the porch just beneath the window, surrounded by broken glass. It is hardly a heroic portrait, and Michaels cannot resist adding insult to Phillip's injury: as he gradually returns to consciousness, "he heard her voice repeating consonants, going on with the story of her life—a bad man, accident, disease. Broken glass lay about me like stars" (46).

Later in the story, a romantic triangle develops in which Phillip and his friend Henry each vie for the stuttering Marjorie. At one point Henry takes Marjorie to see an art film, an event that occasions this strained effort at dialoque:

"What do you think of the m-m-movie, Hen Hen??" His glance became fine, blue as the filament of smoke sliding upward and swaying to breezes no longer visible, and vastly less subtle, than the myriad, shifting discriminations that gave sense and value to his answer. "A movie is a complex thing. Images. Actors. I can't quite say." He stared at her without a word. She choked helplessly. All was light between them. It rose out of warmth. They kissed. (54)

Phillip Liebowitz's comic misadventures continue in Michaels's second collection of short fiction, *I Would Have Saved Them If I Could* (1975), with "Getting Lucky," but alas he did not get around to creating a full-length novel for what is argu-

ably his best character, as John Updike did for Henry Bech or Allegra Goodman for the Markowitz family. This is too bad, because Liebowitz is high energy, and his very presence helps Michaels to write at his freest, his most imaginative.

Consider the passage quoted in the previous paragraph, but this time in juxtaposition with what Michaels had to say about style from an essay included in his prose collection, *To Feel These Things* (1993). To talk about "style," Michaels freely admits, is a bit like trying to hold water in the cup of one's hands. Both literary style and water have a habit of slipping through the best-intentioned of grids. So, rather than offering conventional stylistic analysis, Michaels demonstrates the nature of "style" by looking to diverse sources, such as examples from sports: a particularly graceful move by the always graceful basketball player Walt Frazier ("Frazier doesn't look fast, but that's because he's so smooth" &lsqu;129]) or Joe DiMaggio effortlessly loping his way toward a long fly ball. Each is an example of the old maxim that artists make the difficult look easy and the easy look difficult.

When Michaels brings Ernest Hemingway into the discussion, one sees the subtle ways in which he is describing his own work as well as that of Hemingway. In a passage from *Death in the Afternoon* (1932), Hemingway's controversial book about bullfighting, he talks about witnessing a bullfight in which a matador was gored, his leg torn open and the bone exposed. Later, Hemingway has a sleepless night, not because he was shocked by what he had witnessed but, rather, because he couldn't write about it. It was, in Hemingway's word, a problem in "depiction." Michaels ruminates about the moment, and in the process comes as close as anyone has to describing what a literary style meant to Hemingway— and what it means to Michaels himself:

Sleepless, agonizing over the problem, Hemingway asked himself what—exactly what—had he seen. As for the poor bullfighter, that man was a coward and a showoff, a disgrace to the art. He had no style. Hemingway felt sorrier for the bull than the bullfighter. Finally, it comes to him. Hemingway recalls the moment when the bullfighter was gored.

He sees it again and writes exactly what he has seen: the bullfighter's soiled underwear and the "clean, clean, unbearably clean whiteness of his thigh bone." In his determination to remember, to see again—without pity—exactly what he had seen, Hemingway conquers resistance to memory in himself and achieves the great clarity of style. (121)

To the large influences of Borges and Kafka, one must add that of Hemingway, always hastening to add that Michaels worked as much against influence as he did with it. Still, Michaels's work reflects not only the sort of literary understanding that a PhD in literature necessarily brings to a Hemingway text but also the deep personal investments packed into his emphasis on writing "without pity." If it is true that Michaels can construct sentences strung together by alliteration and poetical imagery, it is also true that he is no stranger to the short punchy sentence with all the fat burned off its soul. Writing in the pages of *Partisan Review*, Larry Woiwode argues that Hemingway—rather than, say, contemporary writers such as Philip Roth and Donald Barthelme—hovers just around the edges of

Michaels's fascination with violence, suicide, and death (which has "eat" at its center) and perhaps a bit of patriarchal scourge, being anti-intellectual, a tyrant in most matters, and a fellow practitioner of the short sentence with the kick-back of a pistol shot.

Michaels's short stories were, from the very beginning, occasions for widespread adulation. There would also be life changes on other fronts. After completing his PhD in 1966, he married Priscilla Older in June of the same year. The newlyweds moved to northern California, where Michaels had accepted a teaching position at the University of California at Davis.

Three years later, with the publication of *Going Places* (which proved to be a prophetic title) virtually everything changed. Not only did the collection collect rave reviews by the dozens (the influential critic and essayist Susan Sontag declared Michaels the "most impressive new American writer to appear in years") but it also caught the eye of the major writer and literary scholar Mark Schorer, who made it his business to spread the word about Michaels's talent to his colleagues at the prestigious University of California campus at Berkeley. Soon Michaels received a job offer from the very school in which he had been an unsuccessful graduate student and, according to one student evaluation, a "shabby" teaching assistant. No matter, Michaels was a "hot" literary property, and the Berkeley English department wanted to grab him when they could. Michaels taught at UC-Berkeley from 1970 until his untimely death from bowel surgery in 2003.

I WOULD HAVE SAVED THEM IF I COULD

The 1975 publication of Michaels's second collection of short stories, *I Would Have Saved Them If I Could*, put to rest any doubts about Michaels's talent. The second collection solidly established him as a writer of the first rank. The truth, however, is that not every piece of typewriter paper that Michaels touched automatically turned to gold. While he was still at the University of Michigan pecking away at his dissertation about Lord Byron, he also drafted two novels, both of which were never published. The first was burned, literally chucked into the incinerator, while the second was reshaped into the stories of his second collection. Michaels told Mona Simpson, a contributor to *Threepenny Review*, that the first novel "was absolutely horrible. I wrote it ... to show I could write a novel any time I wanted to, even in two weeks." But boast though he did, Michaels essentially knew that he could not produce a worthy novel—not in two weeks or for that matter, two years. He told Simpson that "I was more interested in forms of writing that seemed to me closer to the high ideals of art." Even the most cursory glance at Michaels's career makes it clear that the short story was the form he had in mind. Granted, he would later write *The Men's Club* (1981), a novel that seems more novella than novel and, more important, that includes many of the same alternations between realism and hallucinatory fantasy, the same deep preoccupation with mayhem and mass destruction, that had marked his earlier work. The more Michaels one reads the more one can

feel his thumbprint on every sentence, every thickly layered paragraph—and this thumbprint, indeed, is the surefire test of a stylist. (Likewise, John Updike, another first-rate stylist, has claimed it is impossible for him to escape the essential thumbprint in his paragraphs.)

I Would Have Saved Them If I Could contains thirteen short stories previously published in such journals as *American Review*, *Atlantic*, *Esquire*, *Fiction*, *New American Review*, *Occident*, and *Partisan Review*. In these stories Michaels continues to explore Phillip Liebowitz's darkly comic coming of age. Thomas R. Edwards praised the collection in the pages of the *New York Review of Books* as "an important literary event" and used the occasion to say kind words about the short story form. For Edwards, *I Would Have Saved Them If I Could* serves as a "useful reminder that the rich complexity of a successful novel can, in the hands of a master, be achieved within the limitations of smaller forms."

Although literary critics keep their collective eye out for the Great American Novel, a construct that cannot entirely escape the sneer quotes that often surround terms once taken very seriously indeed, a short story writer such as Leonard Michaels reminds us that severely constricted space forces a writer to weigh every nuance. Moreover, as with, say, a play by Harold Pinter, moments of silence, of blank space, as it were, often speak more eloquently than do the fully fleshed out descriptive swatches we associate with the novel. This is particularly true for an artist like Michaels, whose sensibility leans toward the weirdly horrific.

Nonetheless, not all of Michaels's stories are so weighty. In "Some Laughed," an academic story that fellow professors are likely to relish far more than nonacademics, we meet the struggling T. T. Mandell, who is every bit as much the loser as is his friend Phillip Liebowitz. Not since T. S. Eliot dubbed one of his overly self-conscious characters J. Alfred Prufrock has there been such a preposterous moniker. Mandell teaches at Bronx Community State Extension, and he badly needs to publish a scholarly book if he is to win a tenured slot. But no matter how many times he has the department secretary retype *The Endur-*

ing Southey and send it off to a publisher, each time the manuscript is returned. Therein lies the rub of Michaels's droll academic tale, a tale of the publish-or-perish syndrome that in fact is more likely to be found at a university such as UC-Berkeley than at Bronx Community. How could one help but laugh, as one press after another turns the manuscript down, given excerpts from rejection letters that Michaels provides: "The introductory chapter, where Mandell says he approaches Southey from the inside, is bad. The rest of the manuscript falls below its level." (152).

The story's final snapper comes when Mandell finally gets a German press to publish his book—as *Der Andauernde Southey*. Fortunately, the nasty reviews the book receives are in German and do not affect his career. Soon Mandell receives requests to evaluate manuscripts, and he does so "with uncompromising and incisive hatred." The result is as deliciously satiric as any Michaels story, one that is as deliciously satiric as it is wickedly mean-spirited.

Many of the stories in Michaels's second collection revolve around Phillip Liebowitz's social-sexual development as an immigrant Jewish child during the 1950s. In "Murderers," for example, the adolescent Phillip and a group of his cronies climb a water tower to have an unobstructed view of a young rabbi having afternoon sex with his voluptuous wife. The story would be merely conventional if it were only about the voyeurism of highly impressionable, horny youngsters; but Michaels makes sure that we see, from the title onward, that more is at stake. "Murderers" begins with this line: "When my uncle Moe dropped dead of a heart attack I became expert in the subway system." As one journey—namely, Uncle Moe's—ends, another begins. This journey, namely Phillip's, is death-haunted, albeit with salient details rattled off with narrative brio:

I wanted proximity to darkness, strangeness. Who doesn't? The poor in spirit, the ignorant and frightened. My family came from Poland, then never went any place until they had heart attacks. The consummation of years in one neighborhood: a black Cadillac, corpse inside. We should have buried Uncle Moe where he shuffled away his life,

in the kitchen or toilet, under the linoleum, near the coffee pot. (3)

Phillip's larky spirit reminds one of Saul Bellow's Augie March, who in turn reminds one of Mark Twain's Huckleberry Finn. Unlike the members of an older generation trapped inside their experiences and fears, Phillip craves freedom. His comes via the subway (it can whisk him to Harlem or to the Polo Grounds) in roughly the same way that Huck finds his surrogate father, Jim the slave, by rafting down the Mississippi.

In this story, however, the action proper begins when Phillip learns that "the rabbi is home" (4), a veiled signal that a sexual romp is close at hand, and from the right vantage point, the boys might be able to see *everything*. With this expectation, they scramble up the water tower. What gives the story weight, its dimension, is the luxuriant language Michaels weaves around the adolescent Liebowitz:

> Our view of the holy man and his wife, on their living-room couch and floor, on the bed in their bedroom, could not have been improved. … For a while I watched them. Then I gazed beyond into shimmering nullity, gray, blue, and green murmuring over rooftops and towers. I had watched them before. I could tantalize myself with this brief ocular perversion, the general cleansing nihil of a view. (5)

Such passages abound in the Liebowitz stories—at once earnestly playful and playfully earnest. Michaels's word choices, including the way that "tantalize" absorbs its classical reference, are studies in excess: "This was the beginning of philosophy," the voice-over solemnly declares.

Meanwhile, the story's plotline proceeds on a level a good deal lower than the angels. The neighborhood boys are fascinated by the sheer splendor (if that is the right word) of the rabbi's wife: "After all. how many times had we dissolved stickball games when the rabbi came home (6)?" As a married, Orthodox woman, the rabbi's wife has shorn her locks, but that does not mean she is any the less alluring:

> Today she was a blonde. Bald didn't mean no wigs. She had ten wigs, ten colors, fifty styles. She looked

different, the same, and very good. A human theme in which nothing begat anything and was gorgeous. To me she was the world's lesson. (6)

Unfortunately, the "world's lesson" includes more than the adrenaline rush of the illicit and the lovely. The lesson is more even than sexuality, because the voyeurism leads to a death. One of the boys slips from the tower and falls to the pavement below.

The story could be viewed as sharing much with Hemingway's "Indian Camp," despite the obvious differences in setting. Hemingway's story revolves around a very young Nick Adams (he is seven or eight years old), who joins his father, Dr. Adams, as the physician is ministering to an Indian woman having a difficult time in childbirth. The scene is set in northern Michigan, a place Hemingway uses to represent "nature" in all its furious, unflinching beauty. Nick's father tends to the Indian woman who is lying on the bottom bunk by performing a successful caesarian surgery under primitive circumstances. He makes no effort to disguise how proud he is of his fishing-line sutures, and he even suggests that the whole business might be written up for a medical journal. Later he discovers, to his shock, that the woman's husband has committed suicide (cutting his throat with an ax) on the upper bunk. The impressionable Nick should have been spared such a sight, but that is not the way of the Hemingway world. Life and death exist as parallels in much the same way as the bunk beds signify a new birth and what happens when a husband cannot stand his wife's screams.

"Murderers" works on a similar structure, one that couples sex with death and exhilaration with suffering. The rabbi utters the fateful word, "Murderers," as a boy falls, like Icarus, to his death. Thus "interrupted" (on many levels), the rabbi "used his connections" (9) to have the remaining boys sent to a camp in New Jersey. There, the camp counselors were World War II veterans, "introspective men," some of whom had metal plates in their heads. Phillip Liebowitz, the story's protagonist, has the last poetic words, sentiments that suggest just how scary and life-altering the arc of his experience has been: "At night, lying in the bunkhouse, I listened

to owls. I'd never before heard that sound, the sound of darkness, blooming, opening inside you like a mouth" (9).

In "Getting Lucky," Phillip is a highly self-conscious adult, one whose mental exercises are occasions for his continuing hapless schlemielhood. Here, for example, is how he describes "the flow of his internal life":

> [It] forked into dialogue between himself—standing man who lived too much blind from the chest down—and the other, a soft inquisitive spider pinching the tongue of his zipper, dragging it toward the iron floor that boomed in the bones of his rooted feet, boomed in his legs and boomed through his unzipped fly. (42)

As with other Michaels stories, the New York subway system becomes a "character" in its own right; and it is on a subway ride that the sexual dimension of the title takes its grotesquely, sadly comic form:

> After so many years in the subway without feeling, or feeling he wasn't feeling, he felt. ... He believed he had done nothing to account for it, which was the way it had to be if the experience was miraculous, beautiful, warm and good. ... The emblem and foundation of his ethical domain—wife, child, responsibility of feeding them, the "Mr." on his tax forms—and yet, had someone said, "Who belongs to this hard-on?" Liebowitz himself would have led the search. Despite denials and scruples, Liebowitz had a general, friendly hard-on. Even without an object, his sensations were like love.
>
> He came. (43-44)

By contrast, the twenty-four vignettes of "Eating Out" take Liebowitz from adolescence to adulthood and, stylistically, from clear-eyed realism to fantastic scenarios. Here, for example, are the opening lines of "Basketball Player":

> I was the most dedicated basketball player. I don't say the best. In my mind I was terrifically good. In fact I was simply the most dedicated basketball player in the world. I say this because I played continuously, from the time I discovered the meaning of the game at the age of ten, until my mid-twenties. I played outdoors on cement, indoors on wood. I played in heat, wind, and rain. I played in

chilly gymnasiums. Walking home I played some more. I played during dinner. ... (13)

The poet Walt Whitman would have admired the litany—"I played ..."—that punctuates the nameless protagonist's opening paragraph (one suspects that he is none other than Liebowitz), just as those who admire the riffs Michaels's extended fantasy-hallucination will admire these lines about the movie that the Liebowitz-like narrator, aged ten, sees with his mother:

> A girl is struck by a speeding car. A beautiful girl who speaks first-class English—but she is struck down. Blinded, broken, paralyzed. The driver of the care is a handsome doctor. My mother whispers, "Na", the Polish word that stimulates free-associational capacities in children. Mind-spring, this to that. (15)

Mind-spring is a significant part of Michaels's stylistic landscape; and in the collection's title story, Michaels, who had earlier speculated about creativity and the specter of Kafka, about the relationship of sexuality to writing (nearly always filtered through comic prisms), raises the ante considerably by yoking the personal history of his narrator with the history of modern European Jewry. As with "Eating Out," the story is told through a series of short bursts, each vignette moving toward the question of individual responsibility in an absurd world. In the first vignette, the narrator (again, Phillip?) tells the story of a cousin who refused to be a bar mitzvah. His father and mother can only conclude that he has gone crazy and that an enormous amount of money will be lost if they have to cancel the banquet hall, the caterers, and the rabbi. Thus far what we have is a thrice-told tale; what Michaels does, however, is energize the conventional with the bizarre. During the argument, the cousin opens up his shirt to reveal that "green, iridescent Stars of David had grown from his nipple (119)," and after all the telegrams of cancellation have been sent, the father pulls his son's "five-hundred dollar racing bike into the driveway, mangled the handlebars, kicked out the spokes, and left it for the neighborhood to notice" (199).

The violent images are a Michaels trademark that continues as the story picks up speed and

emotional power. Two vignettes later, the narrator describes his grandfather, a Polish Jew not lucky enough to escape Poland before the Nazis arrived. As the narrator puts it, in a tight-lipped understated way that is again reminiscent of Hemingway:

> The Nazis came with the meaning of history—which flings you into a cellar, saves you for bullets. I don't say, in the historical dialectic, individual life reduces to hideous idiocy. I'm talking about my grandfather, my grandmother, and my aunt. It seems to me, in the dialectic, individual life reduces not even to hideous idiocy. (122)

Writing in the pages of the *New York Times*, Christopher Lehmann-Haupt argues that the story raises this shivery question, "By what right do we go on living and creating when our forefathers have been slaughtered?" Two quotations, the first from the poet Wallace Stevens, the second from Lord Byron, frame Phillip's aesthetic credo. From Stevens's "Sunday Morning," he chooses the line "Death is the mother of beauty" and from Lord Bryon, an extract from a letter in which he describes the executions of three robbers in Rome. After the first had been decapitated, Byron admits that the horror surrounding the other two failed to move him: "The second and third (which shows how dreadfully soon things grow indifferent), I am ashamed to say, had no effect on me as a horror, though I would have saved them if I could" (134).

Lehmann-Haupt glosses Bryon's lines and Michaels's use of them this way: "I would have saved them if I could. But I couldn't , so I rescued art from them." This, for Lehmann-Haupt, is Michaels's achievement: "He has rescued art from horror." Critics of a like mind talk about the redemptive quality of Michaels's work, the way in which life's horrors do not get the final word. Perhaps, but certainly not if one pays close attention to the concluding words of "I Would Have Saved Them":

> Long before ruling class, ideological superstructures, there were myths describing ecstasies. … Nymphs and beautiful boys, fleeing murderous gods, were always sublimating into flowers, trees, rivers, heavenly constellations, etc. The earliest stories, then, already convey an exhilarating apprehension of the world as incessantly created on incessant death. Nothing changes. Stories, myths, ideologies, flowers, rivers, heavenly constellations are the phonemes of a mysterious logos; and the light of our cultural memory. as upon the surface of black primeval water, flicker and slide into innumerable qualifications. But Jaromir Hladik [suspected of being a Jew and later executed by the Gestapo, he become the subject of a story by Jorge Luis Borges], among substantial millions, is dead. From a certain point of view, none of this shit matters any more. (138)

In strictly poetical terms, death may be the mother of beauty but in less rarified situations, death is simply death. In the passage quoted above, Phillip speaks rather than Michaels, although the connection between persona and creator is always a tenuous one. The line blurs more often than it stays firm. At bottom, one cannot pin Michaels down or fit him into a predetermined box.

Michaels's short stories introduced a new note into American letters. For many, he was master at giving dread and desire a vocabulary of their own. If Lehmann-Haupt is right that, in the final analysis, Michaels's stories rescue art from horror, this difficult work must necessarily begin by rescuing language itself from the bromides of editorials and the predictable, often sloppy thinking of ideologies. At its most engrossing, Michaels's style is as precise as it is spooky. Michaels writes as if he has never been quite comfortable with America, however much he has a sharp eye for revealing, American details and an ear for the rhythms of American speech. But he brought to both endeavors—to "see" the landscape as well as to "hear" it—an outsider's perspective. Those impatient to know what his stories "mean," or what messages they contain, are bound to be disappointed. Serious fiction simply does not operate so reductively.

THE MEN'S CLUB

For better or worse, Michaels is best known as the author of the controversial 1981 novel *The Men's Club*. One of the important differences

between most of Michaels's short stories and *The Men's Club* is setting; for the former, it is mostly New York City, for the latter it is Berkeley, California. As a member of UC—Berkeley's distinguished English department, Michaels was immersed in the ambiance of the women's liberation movement and all that the concerted push for equal opportunity, equal pay, and equal rights implied. Long before the term "political correctness" enjoyed wide recognition, Berkeley was a politically correct world. Small wonder that all manner of women's clubs sprang up there, each devoted to some aspect of consciousness-raising.

Michaels does not spend time laying out feminism's intellectual framework, partly because he is a novelist rather than a cultural analyst and partly because he wants to avoid the polemical debates that raged through America in the 1960s and 1970s. Suffice it that the novel's protagonist, Paul, in the opening lines tells us that "women wanted to talk about anger, identity, politics, etc. I saw posters in Berkeley urging them to join groups, I saw their leaders on TV" (3). When his friend Cavanaugh, a six-foot-nine-inch former basketball star, invites him to join a fledgling "men's club," Paul can only laugh. But Cavanaugh insists that this club will be a masculine version of women's clubs and that it would provide "a regular social possibility outside of our jobs and marriages" (3). Of the group, one is a tax accountant, another a lawyer. There are two schoolteachers and two psychotherapists. As Paul thinks at the time, "Solid types. I supposed that there could be virtues in a men's club, a regular social possibility.

But something about the proposed men's club rather puts Paul off: "To be wretchedly truthful, any social possibility unrelated to wife, kids, house, and work felt like a form of adultery. Not criminal, Not legitimate" (4). He nonetheless joins the group of men who assemble in the Berkeley home of a psychotherapist. The "consciousness raising" that was to be the club's purpose quickly evolves into the telling of locker-room stories that nearly always turn confessional. Beneath the initial forays of boast and brag, many of which feature the by-now familiar terrain of

the fantastic, lie large pockets of vulnerability, weakness, and shame.

With a well-sharpened eye for social satire, Michaels captures the cultural atmosphere of the late 1970s and early 1980s in his portrayal of a group of men swapping confessional tales—stories of sexual conquest, sexual dysfunction, and insatiable sexual appetites—in an era when baring one's soul was as fashionable as rigid codes of conformity had been endemic in the 1950s. At first glance—nothing seems more antifeminist than the very idea of a *men's* club. For many, to know the book's title was to know—and to hate—a book many detractors felt they need not bother to read. Others took the opposite view—that *The Men's Club* made the failings of its self-absorbed male characters abundantly clear, and in that sense, it was a novel much in the feminist tradition. Ultimately, because *The Men's Club* has a depth of vision, it resists easy generalizations at the same time that it contains enough fodder to support feminist readings, antifeminist readings, and those somewhere in between.

Robert Towers, writing in the *New Yorker*, admitted that "*The Men's Club* might at first seem to be a book that draws its "energies from male fantasies of revenge against the whole monstrous regiment of women." Viewed this way, Michaels's novel is simply the flip side of feminist tracts calling for the overthrow of the patriarchal hegemony and all those (males) who are necessarily part of its oppressive machinery. In *The Men's Club,* it is women who are tarred with the wide brush of monstrosity. Women, after all, have no monopoly either on consciousness raising or the (dubious) benefits of victimhood, As Towers puts it, the novel is an "ostensible *cri de coeur* from a small herd of male chauvinist pigs," one that "will thrive upon the outrage it provokes and the rueful yearning it indulges."

If an examination of *The Men's Club* stopped there, one might view Michaels's novel as falling into the category of cheap bids for talk-show attention and brisk sales. But Towers goes on to point out what happens during a first, and then a second, careful reading. Reductionist certainties on either side of the political divide soon disap-

pear, replaced by the mysteries—sometimes beautiful, sometimes ugly—of the human condition.

The Men's Club differs sharply from Michaels's earlier fiction in the sense that, this time, he assembles a cadre of characters (rather than concentrating on, say, Phillip Liebowitz alone) and gives the lion's share of space to dialogue. Unfortunately, the cast of male sufferers is hard to keep straight, and at least some of their stories strain too hard for significance. Their complaints seem to be sounded on a single string, ever more loudly plucked. As Towers puts it, the men in the novel add up to "one married misogynist split seven ways."

The *Newsweek* reviewer Peter S. Prescott observes that since the men unwittingly reveal themselves to be at fault in their series of failed relationships, the book takes on what he calls "a distinctly feminist cast that is far more appealing than what we find in most novels written by angry women today." Michaels, in discussing his novel, avoided any discussions about feminism, antifeminism, and which side of the coin his sympathies were on. As he told one interviewer, *The Men's Club* "is not in any sense propaganda, pro or con feminism, pro or con male sensibility. ... It is, I hope, believe it or not, a description of reality." The ambiance of his short fiction is helpful in understanding what Michaels means by "descriptions of reality" and the darkly weird shapes it can take.

Carol Rumens, writing in the pages of the *Times Literary Supplement*, characterizes the novel this way: "It is a little as if Golding's *Lord of the Flies* had been transposed to middle-class, middle-aging California." In a *National Review* article about the book, David Evanier agrees: "Here is middle-aged predatory Berkeley inferno of loss and chaos." Both are right insofar as the novel's dark atmospherics are concerned.

During the long, physically and psychologically exhausting first meeting of the men's club, fisticuffs break out; the men throw knives, destroy furniture, and howl together in unison. It is an orgy of the unrestrained id, what Joseph Conrad had in mind in "Heart of Darkness" (1899) when he describes what happens when a civilized person such as Kurtz finds himself in darkest Africa. The cultural restraints of the super-ego—parents, teachers, preachers, and cops—no longer wag their disapproving fingers, and a man can revert to his primordial, violent self:

> When I howled I felt the vibrations in my head, way up around the sinuses, ... The howling was liquid, long, and thick in the red room, heart of Kramer's house. ... We sounded lost, but I thought we'd found ourselves. ... I felt more and more separated from myself, closer to the others, rising again and again, taking us up even as we sank toward primal dissolution. ... (161)

Male conscious-raising groups once touted the benefits of men sitting around a campfire, telling stories, and howling at the moon. The poet Robert Bly attracted a certain measure of notoriety as a spokesperson for such dubious activities. By contrast, the men in Michaels's club are even more suspect, not only because their stories simultaneously demean women as well as themselves, but because they are no more decisive no more "manly," if you will, at the end of a very long evening than they were when each arrived. Some club members decide to go out for breakfast, but nobody knows quite where to go. Thus, to the long tradition of men driving aimlessly over the next hill one can add Leonard Michaels's notorious contribution, *The Men's Club*.

A MICHAELS POTPOURRI

In 1985, Michaels worked with the director Edward M. Cohen to cobble together several stories about Phillip Liebowitz into a play, *City Boy*, that had a disappointing run at the Jewish Repertory Theater in New York City in February 1985. It may be that Phillip's internal whining is better suited to the printed page and that a collection of the Liebowitz stories between hard covers would prove more successful. About *City Boy*, Michaels made only a few stray remarks for the New York newspapers—writing for the stage, he said, was "wrenching," "frightening," and, yes, "exhilarating"—but about a 1986 film version of *The Men's Club* he had much more to say:

Six or seven months after I signed the contract, a lot of the novel was cut away, and the action was "opened out" for the sake of a movie. Howard [Gottfried] said, "This is it. I can feel it in my kishkas, a great movie." (Kishkas is Yiddish for intestines.)

Lights go down and sensations of intestinal goodness begin. When the movie ends, it's like being ripped untimely from the womb. You're disoriented, adrift, homeless, burdened by regret, as if something could have been other than it is for you.
—from "Movie Eyes" included in *To Feel These Things*

Writing a novel, any novel, is essentially a solitary business. It is the battle between an individual writer and a blank piece of paper. Writing a screenplay from a novel, even if the novel happens to be your own, is a struggle of a different sort, one that involves the assets and liabilities of collaboration and compromise. Thus it is that Michaels stood helplessly by as his novel was cut by something like half and a new ending was added, one that involved his motley crew visiting a whorehouse rather than eating breakfast at a diner. The film version of *The Men's Club* was disappointing, not only in terms of ticket sales and talk but also as something that might have taken Michaels's career to another level. Commenting on the lengthy whorehouse section added to the film version, Janet Maslin's *New York Times* review points out that it "wasn't in Mr. Michaels's book" and that "it "didn't need to be." Another reviewer, writing in the *Los Angles Times*, felt that the film's long pornographic sequence is "doubly unfortunate" and the film, as a whole, fails to deliver on the potential promised in the "stinging, smart, abrasive dialogue from scenarist Leonard Michaels."

Michaels's next two works rekindled discussions about how much of his writing was fiction, how much autobiography. *Shuffle* (1990) was a mishmash that signaled Michaels's grasp of his material had become tenuous. Self-described as "autobiographical fiction," *Shuffle* contains a "Journal" that can best be described as self-indulgent; the narrative piece titled "Sylvia" that describes his disastrous first marriage without the slightest hint of aesthetic distance; and five pieces—one would be hard-pressed to say exactly whether they should be called sketches, essays,

short stories—that later appeared in *To Feel These Things*.

By the time he published *Shuffle,* Michaels had a well-earned and strong reputation. That is why his 1990 book was so perplexing. As Anatole Broyard flatly puts it in the *New York Review of Books,* "*Shuffle* is a shockingly bad book for a man of Mr. Michaels's stature." Reviewers had more positive words for *Sylvia: A Fictional Memoir* (1992), Michaels's effort to revisit, and rewrite, the "Sylvia" section of *Shuffle.* Despite the fact that Michaels's first wife died of an overdose (she took forty-seven Seconal pills) and therefore cannot offer up her point of view about their calamitous marriage, readers experienced Michaels's account of his first marriage as gripping and truthful—with all the anger, bitterness, and blame presumably burned away—while others found the prose compelling for the way it limned the countercultural atmosphere of New York's Greenwich Village in the 1960s.

When writing gets as close to the bone as Michaels's did near the end of his career, what some find self-indulgent, others proclaim as praiseworthy. In this sense Broyard is speaking about more than *Shuffle* when he says that "all the wryness" (evident in Michaels's earlier books) "had dried up and left him with a bad taste in his mouth." Indeed, many of the "bad tastes"—eating standing up and utterly alone after his third marriage dissolved— are mentioned in his "Journal." It may be that a life increasingly given over to booze and cigarettes, one-night stands, and anomie finally took its toll, even to the point of wreaking havoc on Michaels's once-remarkable style.

TO FEEL THESE THINGS: ESSAYS

The fifteen essays collected in *To Feel These Things* (1993) make us keenly regret that there will not be more, because, at the top of his game, Michaels was a first-rate stylist. Many of these essays originally appeared in journals where Michaels had been a longstanding contributor (*Threepenny Review*, for example). Five were part of a previous collection (*Shuffle*), and others were new venues such as *Playboy, Congregation,*

and *Tikkun*. Some essays pack more emotional power than others; the essays about his parents—"My Father" and "To Feel These Things"—are extraordinary efforts that deserved a better context than *Shuffle* had provided.

In "My Father," Michaels recounts a defining moment in what was a no-nonsense, no heart-to-heart-talks relationship. At fifteen, he had been dating a blond-haired, non-Jewish girl. One morning, his father says, "Let's take a walk" (59). And so they do, block after block, with "the silence so dense it felt like one infinitely heavy immobilized minute":

> Then, as if he'd rehearsed a speech and dismissed it, he sighed. "I'll dance at your wedding."
>
> Thus we spent a minute together, father and son, and he said a memorable thing. It is concise, its burden huge. If witty, it is so in the manner of Hieronymous Bosch, making a picture of demonic gaiety. My wedding takes place in the middle of the night. My father is a small figure among dancing Jews, frenzied with joy. (59)

And here is a heart-stopping passage from "To Feel These Things":

> Even as a child, I thought Jews were obsessed with meaning. We didn't just eat, sleep, work, study, and play, but needed the meaning of these things and everything… . We sought it with brain fingers, loved how it feels in the elaboration of talk. At the heart of all meaning was religion. … but I knew that beneath all meaning was the general complicity with murder. In the sidewalks, the grass, the weather, and the human heart: the need to murder. (69)

There are other moments that shine especially brightly in this collection: Michaels's riveting analysis of the Rita Hayworth film *Gilda* (in "The Zipper") or his evocation of graduate school days at the University of Michigan ("The Abandoned House") or a one-and-a-half page poetic rumination on the now-out-of-fashion "Cigarette":

> True, it's very like but morally superior to masturbation; and you look better, more dignified, We need this pleasing gas. Some of us can claim no possession the way a cigarette is claimed. What wonderful exclusiveness. In company a cigarette

strikes the individual note. If it's also a public suicide, it's yours. (95-96).

Taken together, what these essays do is make good on the Ramon Fernandez epigraph that hangs over the volume like an abiding angel: "So we find ourselves descending, when we write, into the mad fray of subjects, objects, verbs, etc., and the result is no more predictable than cloud formations." To write as well as Michaels did is to believe, despite the evidence before one's eyes, that the transient and ephemeral, the willy-nilly and evasive, can be rescued and ultimately redeemed in art. The Michaels oeuvre may be small, but it is indisputably distinguished. During his career, he won two Quill Awards from the *Massachusetts Review*, an O. Henry Award, and nominations for a National Book Award, an American Book Award, and a National Book Critics Circle Award, among other honors.

Selected Bibliography

WORKS OF LEONARD MICHAELS

Going Places. New York: Farrar, Straus and Giroux, 1969.

I Would Have Saved Them If I Could. New York: Farrar, Straus and Giroux, 1975.

The Men's Club. New York: Farrar, Straus and Giroux, 1981.

City Boy. Play adapted from short stories in *Going Places* and *I Would Have Saved Them If I Could*, produced in New York City at the Jewish Repertory Theater, 1985.

Shuffle. New York: Farrar, Straus and Giroux, 1990.

Sylvia: A Fictional Memoir. San Francisco: Mercury House, 1992.

To Feel These Things: Essays. San Francisco: Mercury House, 1993.

Time out of Mind: The Diaries of Leonard Michaels, 1961-1995. New York: Riverhead Books, 1999.

A Girl with a Monkey: New and Selected Stories. San Francisco: Mercury House, 2000.

VOLUMES EDITED

The State of the Language. Edited by Leonard Michaels and Christopher Ricks. Berkeley: University of California Press, 1980.

West of the West. Edited by Leonard Michaels, David Reid, and Raquel Scherr. San Francisco: North Point Press, 1989.

CRITICAL AND BIOGRAPHICAL STUDIES

DeCurtis, Anthony. "Self under Siege: The Stories of Leonard Michaels." *Critique* 21, no. 2 (1979): 101–11.

Ditsky, John. "A Men's Club: The Fiction of Leonard Michaels." *Hollins Critic* 28, no. 5 (December 1991): 1–11.

King, Noel. "'I Knew He Doesn't Really Love Her': Movie-Going and Memory: An Introduction to 'The Zipper.'" *Senses of Cinema: An Online Film Journal* 2, no. 22 (http://www.sensesofcinema.com/contents/02/22/zipper.html), September–October 2002.

Lyons, Bonnie, and Bill Oliver. "The Lyric Impulse." In their *Passion and Craft: Conversations with Notable Writers*, 85–98. Urbana: University of Illinois Press, 1998.

Martin, Douglas. "Leonard Michaels, Writer, Dies at 70." *New York Times*, May 13, 2003. (Obituary.)

Robinson, Sally. "Men's Liberation, Men's Wounds: Emotion, Sexuality and the Reconstruction of Masculinity in the 1970s." In *Boys Don't Cry?: Rethinking Narratives of Masculinity and Emotion in the U.S.,* edited by Milette Shamir and Jennifer Travis, 205–229. New York: Columbia University Press, 2002.

JAY NEUGEBOREN

(1938—)

Sanford Pinsker

Jay (Michael) Neugeboren (pronounced NEW-ge-born) was aware that he wanted to become to become a writer—that is, if he couldn't become a professional baseball player—from a very tender age. He had just written what, as an eight-year-old, he regarded as his first "novel." The story, outlined in *Parentheses: An Autobiographical Journey* (1970), Neugeboren's coming-of-age memoir, focuses on the two activities that were to define his life: sports (especially baseball and basketball), played outside his cramped apartment, impressing on him early both the need for boundaries (call them "rules") and a sense of honor shared by his fellow athletes; the other activity was stories, which, for Neugeboren, became a way of escaping everything that nostalgic portraits of growing up in Brooklyn conspicuously leave out—living in a cramped apartment and enduring the stinging sense of near poverty as his father failed in one business venture after another.

Later, in *Open Heart: A Patient's Story of Life-Saving Medicine and Life-Giving Friendship* (2003), Neugeboren's account of how a group of buddies from this old neighborhood correctly diagnosed his heart condition and thus saved his life in the nick of time, he speculates about what they shared as children of immigrants:

> Sometimes, when I review our conversations and reflect on the world the five of us came from, I wonder how much of our resistance to seeing technological procedures displace human interactions between doctor and patient derives from values present in the lower-middle-class, Brooklyn Jewish world in which we grew up. Is our concern for the well-being of others, especially those dispossessed of the essentials of life, merely a consequence of having been nurtured by a generation of Jewish immigrants and first-generation Jewish Americans, and by those habits and values specific to our parents' generation—by those socialist views and rabbinic teachings that formed and informed our parents' lives and our coming of age? (p. 45)

To dream about a world more attractive came with the immigrant Jewish territory, and it is this dimension of Neugeboren's work that most essentially matters. It might be viewed as bad timing that Neugeboren was a "Jewish writer" whose fiction appeared in years following the hugely successful careers of Saul Bellow, Philip Roth, and Bernard Malamud—despite the fact that Bellow wrote about Chicago streets and Roth about Newark's Jewish ghetto. Only Malamud wrote about Brooklyn, in fable-like tales of immigrant Jewish sufferers. Nonetheless, many reviewers chose to lump these writers together and concentrate on the Jewish ethnicity of Neugeboren's fiction, which they regarded as a used-up subject, rather than on the preoccupations that most identify Neugeboren's vision: the battle of purity against corruption; a plea for social justice whether it be for blacks, Hispanics, or others unfairly put upon; and a sense of the sheer joy (and freedom) that can be found when going up for a rebound or rounding third base. Even hostile reviewers never seriously doubted Neugeboren's talent, but Seymour Krim spoke for many of them when he said, in a dismissive *New York Times Book Review*: "through no fault of his own, the poor man [namely, Neugeboren] works in the shadow of older American Jewish novelists who have just about surfeited the public with once fresh Jewish material over the last three decades." For reviewers of this school, there was simply nothing new to be said about a Brooklyn Jewish American childhood. Fortunately, Neugeboren persisted, despite a mountain of rejection slips and reviewers longer on qualifications than praise.

JAY NEUGEBOREN

Jay Neugeboren was born and raised in Brooklyn, New York, in a neighborhood that was roughly divided between Italian Catholics and immigrant Jews. He attended racially integrated schools and early understood that America is a melting pot of various ethnicities. He also came to evaluate his classmates in terms of how high they could leap for a rebound or how well they could judge the arc of a fly ball. In that world, sports meant everything, or nearly everything. Born on May 30, 1938, Jacob Mordecai Neugeboren soon came to be called by the more American-sounding name, Jay Michael Neugeboren. But the last name—Neugeboren, which means "newly born,"—remained, with its hints of Yiddish and the Old World. It is a surname both appropriate and suggestive, in that each of Neugeboren's novels seems quite remote from those that have gone before, almost as if he is reborn, or perhaps newly born, as a writer with each new book.

Neugeboren's father, David Neugeboren, worked as a printing jobber and in a variety of business ventures that went bust. Anne Nassofer Neugeboren, his mother, was a registered nurse. The young Jay Neugeboren attended a local yeshiva for a few months before his father, who wanted him to be a full-fledged American above all else, transferred him to a Brooklyn public school. Neugeboren tells the story in *Parentheses*, an autobiographical rumination that puts the tensions between his immigrant parents' roots and their—and his—attraction to all things "American" into bold relief.

ROOTS AND BEGINNINGS

Neugeboren's fiction explores the ways in which the rhythms of traditional Jewish life continue to press upon the fabric of contemporary, secular life, just as Neugeboren's early love of sports finds a prominent position in many of his novels. Add urban landscapes and the vivid characters who inhabit them, and the result is the raw materials of Neugeboren's fictive world.

Neugeboren worked as an elevator operator, a busboy, and at other jobs during the time he attended Brooklyn's Erasmus Hall High School.

Then as now, Erasmus High was noted for its first-rate basketball players. Indeed, many of those consigned to the second team were nonetheless given college scholarships when they graduated. At five-feet-seven-inches tall, Neugeboren did not even dream of landing a spot on such a squad, although he did play on a number of less competitive league teams during high school and beyond.

Neugeboren entered Columbia University in 1955, during the days when fellow English majors collected gossip about famous former students such as Jack Kerouac and Allan Ginsberg and where he became devoted to the great books and high cultural ideals that were part of the university's required humanities sequence. Although sports continued to be an important part of his life (he was a member of Columbia's freshman wrestling team and varsity lightweight football team), a growing sense of himself as a novelist began to crowd out earlier interests in advertising, television, and architectural engineering. During the period between his sophomore and junior year he wrote a novel, his first if one omits the forty-page effort penned during fourth grade. His teacher Charles Van Doren (whose name would later be sullied by the era's famous quiz show scandals) was much impressed by Neugeboren's book and sent it to several publishers, but it found no takers. Neugeboren was left with a professor's praise and a handful of rejection slips.

Neugeboren may have been discouraged but he was not defeated. He continued to write and during his senior year completed another novel. This time it was the Columbia professor Richard Chase who was impressed by Neugeboren's talent. Chase wrote a letter to his own publisher, bringing Neugeboren's latest novel to the attention of those in a position to have the book published. As with the earlier novel, this one was also rejected. Neugeboren nonetheless maintained a deep-seated belief, despite the evidence thus far, that the die was cast, that he was destined to be a novelist, and that writing novels was the only thing that "mattered." The year was 1959. Neugeboren had a BA degree from Columbia but little else that would suggest he was on an arc

toward a career of writing fiction. Indeed, it would be seven years before *Big Man* (1966) became his first published novel. For the next several years his manuscript pages, nine novels' worth of them, were doomed to collect scores of rejection slips and then to molder away in a trunk.

To put some distance between himself and Brooklyn, and to support himself while he continued to write, in 1960 Neugeboren became an executive trainee at General Motors—this after a year-long stint as a graduate fellow at Indiana University. As he puts it in *Parentheses,* he got a job that would "be separate in all ways from my writing, a means to an end only, something that would give me the time, money, and freedom to write."

At Columbia, Neugeboren had been relatively unaware of the university's involvement in the military-industrial complex. During the mid-1950s there were many other Columbia English majors who were similarly naive about politics; but his experiences in Indiana quickly changed many of Neugeboren's attitudes. Corporate life taught him lessons about the relationship between automation and dehumanization, and added generous doses of racism into the bargain. In his Brooklyn neighborhood, various ethnic groups shared a crowded space and learned how to get along. On schoolyard basketball courts, there were understood, if not spelled out, codes about how one used elbows under the basket or what hand-checking was permitted and what slashing moves were not. But at the General Motors Company, what Neugeboren saw, probably for the first time, was how cruelly racist middle America could be. The experiences radicalized him.

Neugeboren received his MA from Indiana University in 1963. His stay in graduate school afforded him the time both to read and write—and increasingly Neugeboren's reading was in radical political writings. He came to see, as he put it later, the "black man's point of view," not merely as he had seen black people during his Brooklyn childhood but as he saw them now, discriminated against and systematically exploited. There were as many advantages as there were disadvantages to Neugeboren's new

political enthusiasms. On one hand, they put him in touch with a variety of "voices" that he had overheard in his childhood but had not yet internalized, while, on the other hand, his fiction ran the risk of writing, as the southern writer Flannery O'Connor once put it, "editorials with characters running through them".

In the middle 1960s, Neugeboren's letters were widely printed in left-leaning newspapers at the same time that he kept collecting rejection slips from mainstream publishers for his first four novels. In 1962, he got his first formal acceptance slip (from *Fellowship*, a peace magazine) for "A Modest Proposal with Feline Feeling," a piece Neugeboren later described as "a satirical protest against bomb shelters written in the form of a letter from John F. Kennedy's cat." Had Neugeboren been a writer with less stomach for rejection than he had, we might know him today, if at all, as a clever fellow on the order of the political satirist Al Franken. But Neugeboren was hardy content with the "exposure" his paragraphs could earn when mimeographed and distributed at protest rallies. In 1962, "ban the bomb" rallies still defined the Left; in a few years, however, college campuses—and then the nation itself—would be divided by a prolonged war in Vietnam.

In retrospect, however, 1962, looks like a relatively stable time, one not very far removed from what many, quite wrongly, regarded as the placid 1950s. In that year, Neugeboren, then twenty-seven years old, had written (but not published) seven novels and a dozen short stories. In a word, Neugeboren's prospects for a literary career did not look promising.

Two years later, things began slowly to improve. "Hoadley's Test Case in Indiana," a piece about the 1960s, one of his "political successes in Indiana," as Neugeboren put it, was published in the September 1963 *New Republic*, and one of his short stories ("The Application") appeared in the autumn 1964 issue of *Transatlantic Review*. On the domestic front, in 1964 he married a painter named Betsey Bendorf. (They were divorced in 1983; in 1985 Neugeboren began what would become a two-year marriage to Judy Karasik. Neugeboren's three children—Miriam, Aaron, and Eli are from his first

marriage.) No doubt the responsibilities of being newly married made Neugeboren seriously question how long he could continue to collect rejection slips by the handful. "The Application" had been turned down no fewer than thirty times before it was picked up by a quality quarterly, which said more about the magazines that had previously rejected the story than it did about Neugeboren's story. Still, he made a vow that he would abandon the novel if he could not place one of his bulky manuscripts by the time he was thirty.

He beat his "deadline" by two years.

BIG MAN

Big Man (1966) focuses on a college basketball player, but one very unlike Neugeboren himself: Mack Davis is black, six-foot-five-inches tall, and a former college basketball star who had been caught up in a point-shaving scandal. We meet him several years later, as he tries to deal with the professional basketball career he never had and the disgrace that continues to haunt him. *Big Man* is, in effect, the story of his redemption

There are hundreds of ways for a white writer to get a novel about blacks and basketball wrong. Neugeboren, to his credit, avoids all of them, setting his novel in a neighborhood not markedly different from the one he grew up in. Moreover, Davis comes from a literate family, able to allude to—and make quips about—Jane Austen novels. Even more important, in writing about Davis, Neugeboren is, in effect, also writing about himself, because, as the savvy reviewer for *Time* magazine points out, the essential question on both the author and protagonist's mind is none other than "What happens when you can't do the thing you love?" Certainly Neugeboren was pondering very much the same question as he wrote the paragraphs about Mack Davis.

Other reviewers were content to focus on the ways in which Neugeboren caught the essential rhythms, indeed the very feel, of a basketball game. The *Kansas City Star* called *Big Man* "the finest novel yet written about basketball," while the reviewer for the *Newark News* called the book "an essential addition to the library of every basketball fan." Other reviewers raised the ante: Robert Lipsyte hailed *Big Man* as the "best sports book ever written" and James Michener called it "the best novel ever written about basketball." Given this much positive attention, one might imagine that *Big Man* would have found its way to the best-seller list and later to the movie screen. Unfortunately, neither happened, and while Neugeboren's next novels were dutifully—and often positively—reviewed, he did not become a household name. *Big Man* remains the same powerful book about basketball and the same penetrating portrait of a former basketball player that critics raved about, but it seems to have been permanently eclipsed by novels such as John Updike's *Rabbit, Run* (1971), the tale of a high school basketball star who cannot adjust to the mediocrity of his job and wife, or Jeremy Larner's *Drive, He Said* (1971), about a college basketball star who shrugs off his coach's pep talk, preferring the excitement of chasing professors' wives.

LISTEN, RUBEN FONTANEZ

Neugeboren's next novel, *Listen, Ruben Fontanez (1968)*, chronicles the relationship between an aging Jewish teacher and his Puerto Rican student. Again, Neugeboren ran into the been-there-done-that argument from those who heard echoes in his novel of Bernard Malamud's *The Assistant* (1957), about an aging, just-hanging-on Jewish grocer and the desperate young man who robs him and then just as desperately seeks forgiveness, or Edward Lewis Wallant's *The Pawnbroker* (1961), this time about an aging Jewish pawnbroker and the Puerto Rican boy who works as his assistant. The similarities may well be there, but what gives Neugeboren's work its own distinction is the way he limns a wary friendship on both sides of the relationship.

Neugeboren prides himself on writing a radically "new" novel every time he sits down at the keyboard, and Ruben Fontanez is surely not Mack Davis—however much one might argue that both signify Neugeboren's interest in the Other and, at bottom, his abiding interest in himself. Dan Wakefield observes that both

characters are members of minorities, and that the "prejudice of each ... against the other is part of fabric of the story and the action."

In an extended review article for *Columbia* that is longer on enthusiasm than measured judgment, the editor Peter Spackman states that *Listen, Ruben Fontanez* was the novel by Neugeboren that "subtly shifted my view of him from my-friend-the-writer to the writer-my-friend." Unfortunately, Spackman goes on to make wildly inflated claims about Neugeboren's superiority as a writer, claiming that he is "a better writer than Roth" and "more solid than Bellow." Spackman may come across as an enthusiast rather than a sober critic, but as he unrolls everything that the publishing racket stacks against a writer like Neugeboren, one can see how the paragraphs dripping with praise came to be written.

SAM'S LEGACY AND *AN ORPHAN'S TALE*

Between the publications of *Listen, Ruben Fontanez* in 1968 and *Sam's Legacy* in 1974, Neugeboren, who had been a visiting writer at Stanford in 1966–1967, a full-time freelance writer in France from 1967 until 1969, and an assistant professor at the State University of New York at Old Westbury in 1969–1970, joined the faculty at the University of Massachusetts at Amherst as writer in residence and later as the director of the graduate creative writing program. Neugeboren remained at Amherst for the rest of his career, retiring in 2002. He readily admits that he possesses a certain quotient of "social skills," which no doubt helped him both as a teacher and an administrator. One can speculate that the distinguished and stable job at Amherst provided an exciting environment and was a fortunate appointment in making his ongoing career as a writer possible.

If *Big Man* was, in effect, Neugeboren's basketball book, *Sam's Legacy* (1974) can be thought of as his baseball novel, at least in terms of the three-chapter (tall?) tale that Mason Tidewater hands down to Sam Berman as his legacy. Berman is a small-time gambler who continues to eke out a life in Brooklyn long after

his high school classmates have departed for Long Island and New Jersey.

Mason Tidewater is the janitor of the rent-controlled building in which Sam spends his days waiting for his luck—and then his address—to change. Ultimately, it does, through the magical intervention of a girl named Stella who gives Sam the ability to cut to the queen four times in a row. With enough money to pay off his former gambling debts, Sam returns to Flatbush a richer, though perhaps not wiser, man than when he left. His real "legacy" is Tidewater's manuscript, "My Life and Death in the Negro League: A Slave Narrative." Neugeboren wrote these chapters at a time when most Americans had never heard of the Negro League, and his fascinating depiction of the black alternative to "white" baseball—coupled with Neugeboren's reputation as a novelist who could write convincingly about the world of sports—should seemingly have ensured success. But, according to Spackman, the novel was "killed by a single review in the *New York Times*." The reviewer, J. D. O'Hara, complained that *Sam's Legacy* contained too much Brooklyn for its own good: "A little Flatbush goes a long way, for the non-tourist, especially as perceived and inhabited by a consciousness like Sam Berman's." At this point O'Hara ticks off problems, everything from a plot too complicated to cohere to the annoying truth that Sam is none too bright ("his wisdom consists of Earl Wilsonish jingles—'If you bluff, it gets rough' or 'play the cards, watch your odds.'").

O'Hara may be unduly harsh about a novel that remains worth reading—and for more than Tidewater's intriguing narrative—but some of his observations were right on the money. For example, the theme of escaping versus accepting one's legacy or, for that matter, one's fate that is central to *Parentheses* is very much in evidence in the world Neugeboren imaginatively constructs for Sam Berman. Moreover, the story-within-a-story would become part of his drift toward postmodernist storytelling, however much Neugeboren insists that he does not know what "postmodernism" is and denies that he is a postmodernist storyteller. One need not be a literary theorist to account for the growing complexity of

Neugeboren's narratives. Stories had always been part of his earliest imaginative life, and it is no secret that the "secrets" inside the most interesting, most important stories are clustered just beneath the surfaces they comment on. That is certainly the case with *An Orphan's Tale* (1976), a story about finding one's true home—and in the case of Neugeboren, of finding that home in fiction. In *An Orphan's Tale*, there are, once again, stories—or perhaps hints of stories—within the central story. Set off in boxes surrounded by Jewish stars, we read "'THE STORY OF NEW ZION,' A STORY BY DANIEL GINSBERG" (p. 208). Later we are told, rather like the "notice" that warns off those seeking a plot in Mark Twain's *Adventures of Huckleberry Finn* (1884), "All sentences within this box are false." (p. 221)

At a time when a number of writers (one thinks, for example, of John Barth or Robert Coover) alternated between the playfully serious and the seriously playful, Neugeboren used the quests and journey as a springboard to wildly narrative inventions. "Every year, just before the World Series began, Sol would leave his apartment in Brooklyn and go around the country by train to visit his old boys." (p. 3) Hooked by that intriguing lead, readers set off with Sol and the rest is the novel's curious combination of history and tale-telling.

Sam's Legacy fell onto literary fields like a stone. Did the carping *New York Times* review "kill it," as Spackman insists, or are there other ways to account for why one novel succeeds and another one, equally worthy, never finds an audience? Certainly a less-than-enthusiastic *New York Times* review will not help, but the grimmer fact is that Neugeboren had, by then, become a writer's writer, meaning that he was more admired by fellow writers than by general readers, and it became harder and harder for him to crawl out of that hole.

THE STOLEN JEW

If a single Neugeboren work should have been able to change his reputation, it was *The Stolen Jew* (1981), a novel that won the Kenneth B. Smilen–*Present Tense* award but that had considerable difficulties getting into print. Neugeboren's publisher, Holt, at first turned it down, and so did the next sixteen places that saw the manuscript. Never one to be discouraged, Neugeboren reworked sections of the novel into short stories, eighteen of which were snapped up by large-circulation literary magazines. As Stella Dong reported in *Publisher's Weekly*, "During the process of storifying, *The Stolen Jew*, Neugeboren saw 'an overarching story line' that led him to restructure the novel." Dong goes on to report that, ironically enough, the first editor who had returned *The Stolen Jew* was so pleased with the new version that he not only accepted it but also promoted it as Neugeboren's "major novel."

"Major" is a good word to describe *The Stolen Jew*. Others might include "ambitious," "human," and "important." While some reviewers continued to worry that the novel was too ethnic, which meant bounded by Brooklyn and too populated with Jewish characters, others had a keener eye about what made the novel noteworthy. Writing in the pages of *America* magazine, Vincent D. Balitas regarded *The Stolen Jew* as a "tightly constructed novel in which action is more mental than physical." If the plot's dropped threads and loose ends had plagued some readers of *Sam's Legacy*, that was not the case with the better-made *The Stolen Jew*. Even more important, Jewishness no longer functions as backdrop or incidental flavoring but as an intertwined system that includes history, theology, and religious practice.

The novel's protagonist and narrator is Nathan Malkin, a man in middle age who achieved fame for a novel written when he was young. The novel is *The Stolen Jew*, and it is a book he is revising as the complicated story of stories-within-stories moves both backward to Malkin's past and forward to the future of Russian Jewry. As Malkin reimagines his book, he changes not only his own history but also that of the people he was closest to: a dead brother and his widow; what happened, or did not happen, in the Russia of their childhood; and the decision of whether or not he should accompany his nephew Michael,

a doctor who was once a star basketball player, back to the Soviet Union.

Malkin's original novel has continued to echo in his life, and to haunt it, long after its first publication. As their visit to the Soviet Union is ending, Michael changes places with an imprisoned Russian Jew, allowing the Jew to escape to America with Nathan. The scene reduplicates the major plot element of Nathan's novel, in which a wealthy Jew kidnaps a boy to serve in place of his own son who had been drafted and would have perished if spirited away. As the novel's multiple stories unfold, responsibility acquires a human face and fiction making gets a new lease on life. As Balitas eloquently puts it, "[Nathan's] destruction and reconstruction of his past can be seen as a metaphor of how we all forge and invent identities."

For Neugeboren, invention is at the very heart of storytelling. As Danny, the orphan, explains in the final pages of *An Orphan's Tale*: "All orphans are liars." (p. 258) So too are writers, people whose small-l "lies" are a way of getting to a capital-T Truth. Consider the following excerpt in which Nathan thinks about Willa Cather's *My Antonia* (1918)—as it so happens, one of Neugeboren's favorite books—and the way in which memories, and especially fictional memories, become superior to anything imaginable in the future:

> Later, she [Ruth] had given him a copy of *My Antonia*, which she said was her favorite book. Nathan nodded. The scene he had been remembering—of the snowstorm—had come from one of Willa Cather's books. He had never read anything by Willa Cather before he met Ruth. She had wanted him to understand about all these things she had a hard time talking about. She was not, she told him, a word-clever woman. Nathan had read the books, and had loved them—their sparseness, their simplicity, their severity. *Some memories are realities, and are better than anything that can ever happen to one again.* The line came from *My Antonia*, and Nathan had, through the years, often repeated it to himself. (p. 67)

As writers, Malkin and Neugeboren are secret-sharers, mirror images of the other at least in terms of working habits. At one point Malkin thinks about revising or rewriting each chapter of *The Stolen Jew* in a separate room, which is akin to the way in which Neugeboren once planned to divide his projects-in-projects among the rooms of his house. But the similarities go beyond certain peccadilloes that come with the strange business of being a creative writer; in Malkin's obsession with his brother lies hints of Neugeboren's intimate entwining with his brilliant younger brother Robert, who has been in the grip of mental disease through much of his adult life (in 1997 Neugeboren published a nonfiction account of their relationship). In addition, *The Stolen Jew* contains the evocation of a Jewish sensibility that goes well beyond ethnic seasoning. When a character points out, "So many Hamans, only one Purim," the bittersweet quip about an ancient enemy of the Jews named Haman who was defeated on the festival of Purim, packs layers of Jewish history into an observation that might be a joke if its point weren't so tragically true.

The Stolen Jew ultimately becomes an extended rumination on memory, just as it is a demonstration of the human heart's capacity to love despite loss and to feel regardless of how much of twentieth-century life desensitized all of us. Nathan Malkin abandoned writing fiction for making money—this after the phenomenal success of his early book, *The Stolen Jew*. Neugeboren's novel-within-a-novel gives us four chapters of Malkin's original work, but, to thicken an already thick plot, these are not the chapters as originally published. Instead, they are "revisions" that Malkin means to sell as original manuscripts. Somewhere in the layer upon layer of onion skins lies not verisimilitude, but truth—or at least as much "truth" as only fiction can provide.

From the beginning the subject of Neugeboren's novels is literature itself. The resulting novels are fictions about their making—self-conscious, reflexive, and altogether fixated on the process by which the "lies" one invents take living, breathing human characteristics and reveal more about their living counterparts than the drier disciplines of history, philosophy, and sociology. This is a very old argument, one made by the

renaissance poet Sir Philip Sydney, who tried to demonstrate the superiority of verse making. Neugeboren's contemporary version of these well-traveled arguments about imaginative power no doubt have something to do with the workshops he conducts in fiction writing: *The Stolen Jew* is an empirical demonstration of how stories are written and then revised, reshaped, and reconstituted from what seems like whole cloth. It is an ambitious novel not only about twentieth-century Jewish life but also about those writers who have given form and meaning to what might otherwise seem overwhelmingly random.

BEFORE MY LIFE BEGAN

Before My Life Began (1985) is another installment in Neugeboren's continuing effort to combine aspects of traditional fiction (character, plot, naturalistic surface) with experimentation. Like other contemporary fictionists, Neugeboren feels that it is important to raise questions about the relation of art to life—indeed, to raise destabilizing questions about fiction itself—but he wants to do this without losing the things he has always loved: character, history, and especially story. In *The Stolen Jew*, the result was as compelling as it was densely textured. Neugeboren's stories-within-stories could have become merely an affectation and then an annoyance, but they did not. In *Before My Life Began*, however, Neugeboren's large ambitions insist too much on their significance. This is a case where "less" might have been *more*. For an author who can capture speech rhythms with a deadly accuracy and who can so vividly sketch the streets where David Voloshin, the novel's protagonist, grew up, the novel's airy flights into abstraction are at best problematic, as in the following dialogue:

Oh you are so "good" inside, David, don't you know that? You're a truly good "and" strong person, and there aren't many of your kind left. It's just so hard for me to watch you walking through the world, pulled on from so many sides, without my being able to help. I keep wanting to run out in front of you—the court jester, yes?—to steer you away from Evil and Anger and Hate and Cruelty and all the forces of Darkness—so I can point you

to the true path—to righteousness and to light and to happiness. (p. 240)

But Neugeboren is swinging for the fences: given such ambition, one life is not enough. *Before My Life Began* is the story of a man forced by circumstances to live "two" lives: one as the David Voloshin who grew up in Brooklyn during World War II and the other as Aaron Levin, a civil-rights activist during the mid-1960s. As Voloshin/Levin puts it in an extended bout of narrative reflection:

It was ten years ago during the tumultuous celebration of V-J day, I was living my first life and thought there would be times in the years to come—more than I'd care to count—when I'd yearn to go back, when I would have traded all the happiness of my second life merely to have stood for a few seconds in the place where my mother and I stood on that warm summer night so long ago, what I wanted more than anything in the world in the moment itself was for my life to fade, to disappear, to be blacked out. And yet it seemed to me, then, impossible that the moment would ever end. (p. 10)

The sweep of David Voloshin's "life" seems American to its bones (he draws elaborate pencil sketches with one hand; plays basketball with the other), but his peculiar destiny is linked to a Jewish gangster uncle, and to the larger (Jewish) rhythms that make up David's Brooklyn world:

In front of our building two men stepped out from behind a parked car. One of them was a thin black man wearing sunglasses and a flowered yellow shirt. The other man was fat and wore a dark double-breasted wool suit.

"Mr. Voloshin?" the fat man asked. "Mr. Solomon Voloshin?"

"That's my name."

"And this is your son David, yes?"

"He's a nice-looking boy. Looks a bit like his uncle, wouldn't you say? You must care a lot about him, Mr. Voloshin. I got sons too. Three boys. So believe me when I tell you that you yourself don't got a thing to worry about. I ain't here to make trouble. I'm only here to say that if you get a word from your brother-in-law you tell him that maybe he shouldn't come home. That maybe he should consider settling in California." He laughed. "They

got no winters in California, I hear, so it should be much better for his health out there. Okay, Mr. Voloshin? I can count on you to deliver this message?" (pp. 66-7)

Such is the language in which "threat" comes neatly wrapped, along with the teasing suggestion—never quite confirmed—that David's real father might well be the infamous Uncle Abe.

As it turns out, the truth about his father matters less than that taint of point-shaving that shadows David's basketball career (an echo of *Big Man*, but in this case the sin of the uncle is visited upon his wide-eyed, innocent nephew), and a brutal murder seals his fate as a wanderer with a new identity.

As the plot thickens, however, David *as a character* seems to get lost in the process; despite the novel's richly textured and lyrical prose, there ultimately seems to be no "David" to grab hold of. He reappears as Aaron Levin, Freedom School teacher and civil rights activist out to do good—and dangerous—work in the Deep South of the 1960s. Although Levin's political passions cannot help but look like psychological projections of the Neugeboren who cheered the movement on from the relative safety of the North, this biographical fact would not matter if Neugeboren had been better able to make Levin convincing. Too often, however, his effort to make sense of his successive lives sounds forced and not a little wooden: "Sometimes, as now, he feels that his second life—all the years that have passed since he left Brooklyn, along with all the years to come—will only prove to be a rumination of his first life." (p. 322)

Before My Life Began is best at those moments when past and present are inextricably connected and when David Voloshin peeps through the folds of the less-interesting Aaron Levin. Although Neugeboren won an Edward Lewis Wallant award for *Before My Life Began*, most critics and readers preferred the larger ambitions and wider canvas of *The Stolen Jew*. The prizes certainly did not hurt Neugeboren's cause, but it would also be fair to say that they did not help push him into the upper ranks of contemporary American fictionists.

THE SHORT STORIES

Neugeboren had been winning prizes for his short stories long before his novels were similarly honored. He won a fellowship to the prestigious Bread Loaf Writers' Conference in 1960, a Novella Award from *Transatlantic Review* in 1967 for "Corky's Brother," and fellowships from the National Endowment for the Arts and the Guggenheim Foundation.

Neugeboren's first collection of stories was *Corky's Brother* (1969). It received warm reviews but more important, it marked the first time that Neugeboren's stories (and a novella) appeared between hard covers. In much the same way that Neugeboren takes a measure of pride in never repeating himself in novel after novel, the stories collected in *Corky's Brother* cover a wide range of subjects, settings, and characters; what binds them together is Neugeboren's ongoing fascination with sibling relationships. Neugeboren's deranged younger brother seems to haunt some of the stories, which seem in turn to foreshadow the nonfictional 1997 memoir, *Imagining Robert*. One story in particular, "The Pass," concerns a deranged boy confined to a mental institution.

Neugeboren's curious publishing history is inextricably connected to his shorter fiction: in 1965, Martha Foley, the editor of Houghton Mifflin's annual *Best American Short Stories* anthology, selected "The Application" for inclusion in that year's volume. Impressed with the story, an editor at Houghton Mifflin solicited a book-length manuscript from Neugeboren, and he submitted his just-completed eighth novel, *Big Man*, which was published in 1966. Thus it was that a short story made Neugeboren's subsequent career as a novelist possible.

Neugeboren's short stories are as sharply etched as they are inventive—this from a writer who complains that he never thinks of himself as "having an imagination." If Neugeboren is not out to pull an interviewer's leg with such a statement, he may well be pointing to the ways in which the unconscious works for many writers including himself, He perhaps does not think of himself as having an imagination because an imagination is, by definition, part of the unconscious, and that is where it remains. A writer can

work "from the eyebrows up" when revising his or her drafts, but the drafts themselves originate from the eyebrows down. Neugeboren surely "knows" that he has an imagination, and moreover, that its machinations can drive a novel or story toward the truth of human experience, but one may speculate that he does not want to spook the muse by being too self-conscious about what ought to remain somewhat mysterious.

Readers of the fifteen stories collected in 1997 as *Don't Worry about the Kids* will come to understand something of how Neugeboren's elusive imagination works. In this volume, he is at the top of his imaginative game, and the sheer range of his subjects—and narrative voices—includes everything from a protagonist going through the pains of an ugly divorce and the specter of a protracted custody fight to a young black basketballer explaining (as only he can) the social power of the dunk. Add frequent nods to a mentally retarded brother and allusions to literary figures such as Henry James and Leo Tolstoy, and what emerges is a multifaceted imaginative universe.

Here, for example, is Michael, the protagonist of the title story—a doctor who unpacks his heart to a well-seasoned court-appointed investigator:

> I take it you're going to recommend that my ex-wife get primary custody of the children and I assume nothing I say now will change your mind. But tell me, Mr. Langiello—is a good parent one who lies to her children about the other parent? Is a good parent one who threatens to put her children in a foster home when they don't do what she wants? Does a good parent deny counseling for her children? Does she threaten to kill them and maim them? Does she encourage her children to lie for her, to spy on their father, to steal things for her, to join in her war against him? (p. 18)

We feel for Michael's pain, but Langiello has heard all this, and more. Thus, Michael's heartfelt questions prompt one of his own: "Wouldn't you tell lies to protect your kid? ... I mean, who knows what a good parent is, Mike? Who really knows?" The story gains added depth from our knowledge that Neugeboren himself has gone through a painful divorces and that he often seeks respite from

his troubles in his complicated, life-affirming relationship with his mentally sick younger brother.

Other stories, such as "Leaving Brooklyn," return us to the environs that shaped his literary imagination. Revisiting a line from Willa Cather's *My Antonia*——*"Some memories are realities, and are better than anything that happen to one again"*—(p. 58) Neugeboren, in effect, announces his own manifesto. "The Year Between" is a tale set in academe, filled with references—and delightful twists—on the premise of what may, or may not, be a Jamesian tale (a husband and wife agree to live apart for a year). Mark Goldman, the story's protagonist, finds himself inexorably moving from an "idea for a short story to actually living out its implications"—that is, "a couple renewing themselves by inventing a ghost, by infusing their lives with the mystery it lacks."

The stories collected in *Don't Worry about the Kids* suggest that there may be plenty to worry about with regard to custody battles, but little to worry about in terms of Neugeboren's imagination. Moreover, the stories demonstrate that Neugeboren is as sure about technique as he is generous of spirit.

NONFICTION

Parentheses, a 1970 memoir of how Neugeboren struggled to become a writer, remains of interest to Neugeboren followers as well as to those who welcome an insider's account of the tensions between family expectations and a would-be writer's dreams or the tug of political activism and the less raucous life of shaping paragraphs—but the book is perhaps most noteworthy as a demonstration of Neugeboren's considerable ability as a nonfiction writer. The 1997 memoir *Imagining Robert: My Brother, Madness, and Survival* has its affinities with *Parentheses* but is ultimately a more difficult, more gut-wrenching book, and the one that sold more copies than any of his novels or, for that matter, any two or three of them combined. *Imagining Robert* is at least as much about Neugeboren as it is about the younger brother who went mad in his late teens

and has been institutionalized with chronic mental disease throughout most of his adult life.

In an interview for the journal *New York Stories*, the fiction writer Nicholas Montemarano asked Neugeboren if the experience of writing fiction was different than that of writing nonfiction. Neugeboren responded this way:

> The preparation that goes into the writing of a nonfiction book is different. The difficult part in writing *Imagining Robert* and *Transforming Madness* was knowing how much I needed to know before I began writing. And since both books relate to the actual world, and not the world of my imagination, I felt more of a need to make sure I was well-versed in what I was going to write about. I often think that with nonfiction I have to make things seem, on the page, as real as if they had never happened. People have said to me, "Oh, it must have been very cathartic for you, it must have been very painful for you to write about these personal things." And my answer has been, "No, not at all." Once I began writing, it was no different from writing a novel. My major concern was simply to be as clear and vivid and exact as I could be. Period. And to be as true as I could be to the subject as I sensed it, because part of the writing was discovering what I really wanted to understand. Every once in a while I would be moved or would become a bit more emotional because what I was writing related to certain memories of my family, but that also happens to me when I write fiction, when I make things up, when characters do things that surprise m, or things that seem inevitable—that moves me the same way. So I've found almost no difference in the actual writing of fiction and nonfiction.

Still, there were certain crucial differences: a novelist does not worry that members of a character's family will object to a writer including this or that sensitive scene, much less worrying that others in the family may remember a moment from the past—say, a sixth birthday party—quite differently than the writer does. Fictional characters, after all, have only such families as an author gives them. Nonfiction writing, by contrast, is—indeed, can *only* be—an account of what a writer saw or felt at a given moment, then , and how he or she remembers it, now. Moreover, Neugeboren's case was compli-

cated by the fact that he did not want to knowingly upset his delicately balanced brother.

The close relationship of Jay and Robert Neugeboren was no doubt formed in infancy, but the story Neugeboren focuses on in *Imagining Robert* begins with his younger brother's first mental breakdown at the age of nineteen. In retrospect, Neugeboren feels that there were possibly signs of impending doom that he and others in the family missed, but they were moments that, as Neugeboren puts it, "any of us might find in ourselves." By contrast, in his late teens Robert become so uncontrollable, so violent, that the family had no choice but to take him to the emergency psychiatric ward at Elmhurst Hospital. Robert later went, voluntarily, to Hillside Hospital. The memoir from there documents Neugeboren's unflagging efforts on behalf of his sick brother but also his guilts: Is he writing this book for Robert, or for himself? Isn't nonfiction always more about the writer than his or her ostensible subject?

Granted, it is impossible for anyone—not just Neugeboren but also Robert's doctors—to *know* him, which is to say, to know what is in his tortured, highly excitable mind, but Neugeboren can "imagine" his brother, and that is what he does. In the process, Neugeboren also relates a good deal about how mental patients are treated, and often mistreated. What mental health professionals do not do, or do far too seldom, he suggests, is *listen*. Many prefer to simply medicate the potentially unruly into a drugged submission.

> The people who have worked with Robert are sometimes caring and sometimes competent, but they have rarely provided him with what he needs most of all in this world: constancy and continuity. In a life filled with so much *in*constancy, one of the great needs in Robert's life has been for some professional or professionals who knew him and his history, who would stick by him, and to whom he could turn, in good times and bad, no matter where he was. (p. 53)

Whatever guilt clustered around Neugeboren as he tried to juggle a wide range of demanding family responsibilities, that guilt surely cannot include a concern that he had somehow failed to "stick by" his brother. Through it all, Neuge-

boren was there, laughing at his brother's witticisms, being patient when he lost his temper and raged against the darkness deep inside him. In Neugeboren's account of his relentless effort to find the best treatment for Robert's condition, we learn about the spectrum of treatments that have been tried on his bright, sometimes charming, sometimes deeply disturbed brother:

> Robert's diagnosis has changed frequently in the past thirty years, depending largely upon which drugs have been successful in keeping him calm, stable, and/or compliant. He was schizophrenic when enormous doses of Thoirazine and Stelazine calmed him; he was manic-depressive (bipolar) when lithium worked; he was manic-depressive-with-psychotic-symptoms, or hypomanic, when Tegretol or Depakote (anticonvulsants), or some new antipsychotic or antidepressant—Trilafon, Adopin, Mellaril, Haldol, Klonopin, Risperidone—showed promise of making him cooperative; and he was schizophrenic (again) when various doctors promised cures through insulin-coma therapy or megadose-vitamin therapy or Marxist therapy or gas therapy. At the same time, often in an attempt to minimize side effects, other drugs were poured into him: Artane, Benadryl, Congentin, Kemadrin, Symmetrel, Prolixin, Pamelor, Navane. (p. 4)

At times Robert's story threatens to drown in the names of medicines and psychiatric jargon, but Neugeboren makes sure to keep his emphasis on the human drama, and to write about "survival"—both his and Robert's—without underplaying either the ongoing mysteries or the collective pains of mental illness.

Exhaustion is one of the grim realities that Neugeboren does not skirt. During many of the years in which Robert was passed from one mental institution to another, from one promising set of treatment to yet another set of even more promising treatments, Neugeboren was caring for his three children (this after a divorce that left them in his custody), was concerned about his mother (who had moved to Florida at a point in her life when she could no longer deal with Robert's condition), and was teaching students at the University of Massachusetts at Amherst, all the while continuing to work on his own manuscripts. During those years he lived on the telephone, and on the run.

Imagining Robert is, finally, a love story, one that ultimately merges the two brothers into a single entity and demonstrates just how powerful human attention can be. Largely thanks to Neugeboren, Robert was not left to suffer his demons alone or to be at the mercy of any doctor with powerful drugs and a conviction. Neugeboren never abandons the graceful, bright child that Robert once was, and sometimes is. At one point in the last section of the book, Neugeboren asks his brother how, long ago, they lived in one small room. Robert's answer is as haunting as it is wonderfully perceptive: "Maybe … we were the same person." (p. 96)

Small wonder, then, that Neugeboren limns his brother with such a lyrical touch:

> When we leave the restaurant, the heat—it is 101 degrees outside—is brutal. Robert walks me across the street, to my bus stop. I will head south, for the ferry, and Robert will take a bus in the opposite direction, to return to his home on Hylan Boulevard. A few minutes after we cross the street, however, he sees his bus coming. He kisses me good-bye, and heads back across the boulevard—across six lanes of traffic—his satchel swinging at his side. The satchel is loaded with cigarettes, with shirts he bought at the thrift shop, with empty soda cans he will redeem, and as he hurries across the street, he seems, despite the heat and despite his age and despite the years—despite his life!—as light and graceful as he has ever been. He turns quickly between cars, dancing across a road that shimmers from the intense summer heat, racing to catch his bus before it leaves, and while he runs—he stops at the island in the middle of the streets, turns and waves to me—I see the graceful boy he once was, alive still within the body of this forty-eight-year-old man who is my brother. (p. 294)

Like all serious writers, Neugeboren hopes he will write his way to knowledge, to the truth. In *Imagining Robert*, he comes very close—especially in the final moments of the book, when Neugeboren realizes that he was "just beginning to understand—beginning, only beginning—the mysterious and unnamable ways in which, no matter the joy or sadness of our lives, knowledge and love often prove to be one." The book has earned its last line, just as Neugeboren and his brother have learned how to survive their respec-

tive struggles. At that point, Neugeboren strongly implies, one can only pray toward the ultimate Truth.

Writing in the pages of the *Washington Post*, Peter D. Kramer, the author of the 1993 best seller *Listening to Prozac*, argues that Neugeboren's effort to understand his brother's madness is more remarkable for the questions it raises than for the answers it doles out. He discusses the emergence of "meditation on identity and epistemology. How autonomous are we, and how inevitably connected? How is it that an unloved child matures while the favored sibling becomes his blighted double? How do we ever come to know a person we care about—beyond the constant production and revision of stories about an imagined other?" Neugeboren asks for no special credit for doing what he imagines any decent person in similar circumstances would do; but *Imagining Robert* makes it clear that a strong moral compass is at work inside and that his life as a fiction writer has prepared him well for the daunting task of the nonfiction book that chose him every bit as much as he chose it.

In *Transforming Madness: New Lives for People Living with Mental Illness* (1999) Neugeboren continues the investigation into madness and how it is currently being treated that he began with *Imagining Robert*. At points in the earlier book, when the tale of two brothers, one suffering from chronic mental illness and the other desperately trying to understand and to help him, was especially harrowing, Neugeboren could not entirely stave off suicidal thoughts. *Transforming Madness* is more overview than personal chronicle. It is out to take a measure of the wider mental health care system and talk about its failures and successes without flinching. The book engages both professionals and general readers alike, partly because Neugeboren assembles a wide array of research and partly because he brings unclouded eyes to everything he observes.

Neugeboren is surely critical of the mental health care system—that much is obvious from the ways he detailed the failed treatments and inadequate ideas that made his brother's condition worse rather than better. But Neugeboren is even more drawn to the hopeful, to those advances in treatment and care that show promise. Among these are advances in psychiatric and psychological approaches, psychopharmacology, and others. Taking these together, Neugeboren argues that the lives of millions of people suffering from mental disease are being helped.

Madness, Neugeboren feels, can be transformed; indeed, it must be transformed—not only because Neugeboren writes this book with the long shadow of his sick brother falling across his pages (this is true even when Neugeboren's skill as a storyteller is fastened to a wide variety of other patients), but also because the agony he went through to write *Imagining Robert* became a large deposit in the bank of research and rumination that he draws from in *Transforming Madness*. People who have suffered from mental disease—and who had little hope of ever rejoining the world—are now able to live meaningful lives.

In the final analysis, Neugeboren writes as a humanist rather than as a trained scientist. Certainly he has done his homework in the medical journals, and he has made it a habit to pick the best scientific minds he can, but because he is, first and foremost, a writer, his arguments pack a large amount of elegance into their making, along with the sanity, the *clarity*, that has always been part of Neugeboren's search for the exact word.

OPEN HEART

Open Heart: A Patient's Story of Life-Saving Medicine and Life-Saving Friendship (2003) is an intertwined story of friendship and the healing arts. At age sixty, Jay Neugeboren was what is commonly known as a picture of health. His cholesterol was low; his blood pressure and heart rates normal and steady. He had never smoked. He was a person who eats healthy foods, and in moderation. He had no history of heart disease in his family; he does not suffer from diabetes; and he weighed a scant five pounds more than he did as a high school senior. Perhaps most telling of all, he continued to engage in daily, and strenuous, exercise: half- (and sometimes, full-) court

basketball games with teenagers and *young men in their twenties,* as well as mile-long swims at the gym nearly every day. Neugeboren hardly looked like a candidate for serious heart disease,

But he was—so much so that if a small group of his high school buddies (now cardiac specialists) had not insisted that he check into a hospital, he would not have lived to write this book. Open-heart surgeries are now successfully performed with such regularity that they seem commonplace, but Neugeboren's description of the actual procedure is nothing short of scary. When he talks about a heart taken out of the chest and then iced down, in order that new arteries (in his case, five of them) may be connected to the heart where the original clogged ones had been, the procedure sounds like the miracle that it, in fact, is. Thirty years ago doctors would have told Neugeboren to go home, put his papers in order, and prepare to die. Now Neugeboren becomes his name: newly born. Recalling a quote from the rabbis, he quips that people who don't believe in miracles aren't realists.

Open Heart, however, is more than an account of a live-saving operation. That could—and has—been done by other writers as personal essays (one thinks of Joseph Epstein's "Taking the Bypass" in his 1999 collection *Narcissus Leaves the Pool*), but Neugeboren requires a book's length not only for the portraits of his boyhood friends but also to thoroughly explore the entire experience of heart disease. Like too many mental health professionals, too many doctors do not listen, *really* listen, to their patients. Machines have replaced hands-on examinations and chats about how a patient hears his or her body. In Neugeboren's case, he noticed that he began to tire after seven or eight laps in the pool, well short of the mile he usually swam. Something was wrong, very wrong. One doctor had dismissively diagnosed his condition as "viral," but during a long-distance phone call Neugeboren's old friend Rich, now a top-level cardiologist, insisted, in his rough, no-nonsense way, *It's not viral, goddamnit!"* (p. 8) Rich had listened carefully to the symptoms Neugeboren described; other doctors had simply counted up the risk factors that

he did *not* have and concluded that his problem could not be heart disease.

Doctors, Neugeboren learns, need to acknowledge what they do *not* know. The idea is at least as old as Socrates who maintained that the beginning of learning occurred when you knew that you did not know. This was a hard sell in Socrates's time (he was put to death by the state for corrupting the young into believing this foolishness), and it is still a hard sell among physicians who think it important to have patients believe that they know much more than they actually do. The truth is that contemporary doctors are very good plumbers (that is why Neugeboren is alive), but they are essentially clueless about why a person such as Neugeboren—with no risk factors whatsoever—gets heart disease.

Open Heart takes us from the doctor's office to the operating room and then to his chronicle of recovery:

> As the weeks and months pass, I continue to feel stronger and, after a while, less fatigued in the mornings. My stamina, when swimming and playing tennis is better than it's been in years; my weight stays steady at about 150; my body fat constant at about 12 percent; my cholesterol scores are ideal, my blood pressure within normal parameters, and my heart, at rest, now pulses consistently at about fifty beats a minute. (For the first several months following surgery, however, it beats at a rate that is, for me, unusually high: between seventy-five and ninety beats per minute; Rich tells me higher pulse rates are a common postsurgical event, and are of no concern.) Nor have I suffered any of the side effects, memory and cognitive losses in particular, that many people who have been through bypass surgery experience. (p. 127)

What comes through in this account of open-heart surgery is how much "heart" Neugeboren has, and how much of it he puts into his writing. As the nonfiction writer Philip Lopate put it: "Jay Neugeboren is a truly open witness, which enables him to convey so well the vulnerability that is common to us all." Neugeboren makes his four childhood friends memorable, just as he makes the process of open-heart surgery unforgettable, but most of all, the book is an intelligent weaving of the personal and the investigative as

Neugeboren seeks to find out what happened to him—and to thousands of other heart patients—and why.

Selected Bibliography

WORKS OF JAY NEUGEBOREN

NOVELS

Big Man. Boston: Houghton Mifflin, 1966.

Listen, Ruben Fontanez. Boston: Houghton Mifflin, 1968.

Sam's Legacy. New York: Holt, Rinehart, and Winston, 1974.

An Orphan's Tale. New York: Holt, Rinehart, and Winston, 1976.

The Stolen Jew. New York: Holt, Rinehart, and Winston, 1981.

Before My Life Began. New York: Simon & Schuster, 1985.

Poli: A Mexican Boy in Early Texas. San Antonio, Tex.: Corona, 1989.

COLLECTED SHORT STORIES

Corky's Brother. New York: Farrar, Straus, and Giroux, 1969.

Don't Worry about the Kids. Amherst: University of Massachusetts Press, 1997.

News from the New American Diaspora and Other Tales of Exile. Austen: University of Texas Press, 2005.

BOOK-LENGTH NONFICTION

Parentheses: An Autobiographical Journey. New York: Dutton, 1970.

Imagining Robert: My Brother, Madness, and Survival. New York: Morrow, 1997.

Transforming Madness: New Lives for People Living with Mental Illness. New York: Morrow, 1999.

Open Heart: A Patient's Story of Life-Saving Medicine and Life-Giving Friendship. Boston: Houghton Mifflin, 2003.

SELECTED UNCOLLECTED SHORT FICTION

"My Son, the Freedom Rider." *Colorado Quarterly* 13 (summer 1964): 71–76.

"The Application." *Transatlantic Review* 17 (autumn 1964): 52–58.

"Something Is Rotten in the Borough of Brooklyn." *Ararat* 8 (autumn 1967): 27–35.

"Connorsville, Virginia." *Transatlantic Review* 31 (winter 1969): 11–23.

"The Place-Kicking Specialist." *Transatlantic Review* 50 (fall–winter 1974): 111–126.

"His Violin." *Atlantic*, November 1978, pp. 48–50.

"Star of David." *TriQuarterly* 45 (spring 1979): 5–15.

"The St. Dominick's Game." *Atlantic,* December 1979, pp. 54–58.

"Visiting Hour." *Shenandoah* 31 (fall 1980): 23–29.

"Poppa's Books." *Atlantic*, July 1980, pp. 59–63.

"Bonus Baby." *John O'Hara Journal* 3 (fall–winter 1980): 10–21.

SELECTED UNCOLLECTED NONFICTION

"A Modest Protest with Feline Feeling." *Fellowship* 28 (May 1962): 27–28.

"Hoadley's Test Case in Indiana." *New Republic*, September 21, 1963, p. 14.

"They Didn't Have to Tell the Truth." *NEA Journal* 53 (November 1964): 21–22.

"Writing a First Novel." *Writer,* January 1967, p. 17.

"Humphrey and the Now Generation." *New Republic*, March 18, 1967, pp. 32–35.

"Disobedience Now!" *Commonweal,* June 16, 1967, pp. 367–369.

"Your Suburban Alternative." *Esquire*, September 1970, p. 113.

"Mall Mania." *Mother Jones*, May 1979, pp. 21–31.

"The Diamond Jubilee." *Present Tense* 8 (winter 1981): 15–18.

CRITICAL AND BIOGRAPHICAL STUDIES

Candelaria, Cordelia. "Jay Neugeboren." In *Dictionary of Literary Biography.* Vol. 28, *Twentieth-Century American Jewish Fiction Writers*, edited by Daniel Walden, 181–188. Detroit: Gale, 1984.

Montemarano, Nicholas. "Interview: Jay Neugeboren." *New York Stories* 2 (winter 2001): 8–12.

Spackman, Peter. "Wonderful Lies That Tell the Truth: Neugeboren Reviewed." *Columbia* (November 1981): 15–18.

PAPERS AND MANUSCRIPTS

Neugeboren's papers and manuscripts are housed at the University of Indiana and the Harry Ransom Humanities Center at the University of Texas, Austin.

GEORGE PLIMPTON

(1927–2003)

Charles R. Baker

One of the last things Ernest Hemingway ever wrote was a dust-jacket blurb for George Plimpton's 1961 book about baseball, *Out of My League*. Hemingway, an avid baseball fan himself, admired the work, an expanded version of a piece first published in *Sports Illustrated*, calling it "beautifully observed and incredibly conceived, his account of a self-imposed ordeal that has the chilling quality of a true nightmare. It is the dark side of the moon of Walter Mitty." Hemingway's analogy stuck, and for the rest of Plimpton's adventurous life, critics were quick to compare him to James Thurber's daydreaming Mitty. But any comparison of Plimpton to Mitty, who was introduced to the reading public in a 2,100-word short story, "The Secret Life of Walter Mitty," published in the *New Yorker* in 1939, must be tempered with Hemingway's observation that it is the "dark side of the moon of Walter Mitty" with which we are dealing. Mitty's name has become synonymous with a certain type of man: a meek timid soul forever hounded by an overbearing wife, who secretly imagines himself to be the hero of improbable adventures. Whether piloting his men through violent weather aboard a navy seaplane, performing emergency surgery on a millionaire banker, or destroying an ammunition dump single-handedly, Mitty reaches the brink of success, reward, and adoration only to be pulled back by the demands of his real life. Plimpton's real life, however, *was* one of improbable adventures with nothing to hinder or interrupt his quest other than the limits of his physical abilities. What Hemingway meant by calling *Out of My League* the "dark side of the moon of Walter Mitty," was that, despite Plimpton's most fervent efforts, triumph eluded him.

EARLY LIFE AND EDUCATION

George Ames Plimpton was born in New York City on March 18, 1927, to Francis Taylor Pearsons Plimpton and Pauline Ames Plimpton. Born in 1900, Francis Plimpton was a highly successful lawyer, public servant, and diplomat. He graduated magna cum laude from Amherst College in 1922 and earned his JD from Harvard University in 1925. The following year he married Pauline Ames, was admitted to the New York Bar, and joined the New York City law firm of Root, Clark, Buckner, and Ballantine. From 1930 through 1931, he was in charge of the firm's Paris office. He left the firm in 1932 and was a general solicitor in Washington, D.C., until he joined in partnership with his former Harvard classmate, Whitney Debevoise, to form the prestigious New York law firm Debevoise & Plimpton in 1933. For the next fifty years, Francis Plimpton was the recipient of numerous national and international awards and honors: the Legion of Honor from France; the Order of Merit from Italy; the Order of Law, Culture, and Peace from Mexico; the Order of St. John of Jerusalem; and the Distinguished Public Service Award from the New England Society of New York. He served as chairman of the New York City Board of Ethics, he was on the mayor's New York City Committee on Distinguished Guests, and, in 1961, he was appointed by the John F. Kennedy administration to be the United States ambassador to the United Nations. Francis Plimpton's children, George, Francis, Oakes, and Sarah, grew up in a household that was wealthy, culturally polished, and socially prominent; their father's example, however, tempered privilege with a willingness to serve others.

George Plimpton received the sort of education that was deemed suitable for a young man of his

background; he attended St. Bernard's School and Philips Exeter Academy. At Exeter, Plimpton proved himself to be an indifferent student and an incurable prankster. In a speech titled "How Failing at Exeter Made a Success Out of George Plimpton," given at the Exeter Association of Greater New York on December 5, 2001, and later collected in his posthumous book, *The Man in the Flying Lawn Chair and Other Excursions and Observations* (2004), Plimpton confessed,

> My marks were terrible. I had the strange idea that in class, even if I were daydreaming of something else, my brain was still absorbing all the material like a kind of specialized sponge, and the next day at the exam I could scratch around in the appropriate corner, in the detritus, and there would be the appropriate answers. Of course it didn't work that way, and my marks, the Cs, the Ds, the occasional E—the latter always in math—showed it. (p. 27)

Not that Plimpton had no interest in learning, he simply preferred Zane Grey to Tacitus.

> I had been hooked on Zane Grey ever since reading *Riders of the Purple Sage*. From the public library on Front Street, as I recall, I took out dozens of such volumes, when I should have been reading the books I'd been assigned for class. Why wasn't there an exam on *Riders of the Purple Sage*? Instead it was Tacitus, the Roman historian. What were his views on Vespasian? (p. 28)

Additionally, Plimpton preferred "funning it up" to studying, spending hours perfecting his drop-kicked fields goals with a friend on the football field late at night or learning the fine art of cigarette smoking in the butt rooms or discovering how to drive up the temperature on a thermometer in order to escape an exam by being confined in the infirmary. "But what really got me into trouble were the little things I thought were funny—like sneaking in at night and turning all the benches around in the Assembly Hall because I thought it would be funny to have my classmates sitting backwards when they came in for assembly." (p. 30) He recalls an attempt to remove a stuffed rhino head from Phillips Hall and place it in a more amusing location.

> I was, of course, caught with the rhino head. *Mortification*. What do you say if you're caught with such a thing? Afterward, but too late, the thought occurred to me that I should have said, "I'm bringing it back." ... I was caught all the time. It was as if I were attached to an invisible leash at the other end of which was an authority of some kind. (pp. 30–31)

Plimpton received weekly letters from his father reprimanding him and exhorting him to apply himself to his studies. He was reminded that the Plimptons had a long history of outstanding achievement at Exeter; indeed, the very playing fields where young Plimpton wasted so much time kicking a football when he should have been studying had been a donation to the school by his ancestor George Arthur Plimpton, class of 1873. Plimpton promised his family he would try harder and he threw himself into more promising activities: writing for the school paper, playing varsity sports, participating in theatrical productions and taking music lessons. Ultimately, however, Plimpton failed Exeter.

> In fact, I was a complete failure. I was asked to leave three months shy of graduation because of a multitude of sins, both academic and secular. My teachers couldn't take it anymore and I was sent away, down to my grandparents in Ormond Beach, Florida. I spent those three months at the Daytona Beach High School, so I could get a diploma and move on to Harvard, where I had already been accepted. (p. 25)

However humiliating this may have been to Plimpton, he wonders in this speech if his failure had laid the groundwork for his determined efforts to vindicate himself. "Could it have been that, having failed in all departments at Exeter, I was driven in later life to compensate, to try once again to succeed where I hadn't?" (p. 37)

In 1944 Plimpton, like generations of Plimptons before him, matriculated Harvard University, where he became the lifelong friend of his fellow classmate Robert Kennedy. In fact, Plimpton was to be a close friend to all the Kennedys, contributing to and working for their various political campaigns. Plimpton was walking ahead of Robert Kennedy at the Ambassador Hotel in Los Angeles on June 5, 1968, when Sirhan Sirhan

fired the shots that killed the presidential candidate. It was Plimpton and the Olympic athlete Rafer Johnson who wrestled the assassin to the floor.

The United States's entry into World War II interrupted Plimpton's studies in his freshman year, and from 1945 until 1948 he served as a tank driver in Italy, earning the rank of second lieutenant. Plimpton told the interviewer Andrew Anthony:

> I went to Italy and trained as a demolition specialist. I picked up mines, which is probably the seat of my love of fireworks. Then, they were very clever and decided to let the Italians and Germans pick up the mines they'd put down and they put me into tanks, which was even more dangerous.

He returned to Harvard and took on the editorship of the nation's oldest humor magazine, the *Harvard Lampoon*. The magazine was conceived by seven Harvard undergraduates in 1876 who, using the satirical British magazine *Punch* as their model, published cartoons, jokes, and essays that poked fun at Harvard campus life. Such notables as William Randolph Hearst, Robert Benchley, Owen Wister, and George Santyana made contributions to the magazine during their years at the university. By the time of Plimpton's editorship, the *Harvard Lampoon* had shifted its focus from campus concerns to global issues.

Plimpton graduated from Harvard with an AB in English in 1950. After Harvard, Plimpton attended Kings College, Cambridge, where he earned an additional undergraduate degree (1952) and a MA (1954).

THE PARIS REVIEW

In Paris in the summer of 1953, one of Plimpton's childhood friends, the novelist Peter Matthiessen, together with fellow novelist Harold L. Humes, were toying with the idea of producing a literary magazine. Although there was at that time a glut of such periodicals, the two writers were dissatisfied with the prevailing emphasis on criticism and politics. It was their intention to publish a new review that would showcase original works of fiction and poetry by not only established writ-

ers but talented newcomers as well. Matthiessen and Humes asked Plimpton to meet them at Matthiessen's Paris atelier to discuss the project. It was decided that Matthessian would be the fiction editor and Plimpton, because of his vast social connections and unbounded enthusiasm, would serve as the review's editor in chief. Humes, who felt his connections were just as impressive as Plimpton's, apparently took offense at being passed over for the review's prime position, returned to the United States, and refused to perform his duties as managing editor. John Train quickly filled that position. Plimpton's schoolmate from Phillips Exeter, the poet Donald Hall, was recruited to serve as the poetry editor and William Pene du Bois was the review's first art director.

After rejecting the idea of printing the review on birch bark and calling it the *Druid's Home Companion*, Plimpton and his growing number of contributing editors chose to call their enterprise the *Paris Review*. It was left to one of those contributing editors, William Styron, to write a letter of introduction to the review's readers that presented the review's purpose and editorial policy. Styron's letter, published in the review's first number, is a brilliant tongue-in-cheek response to the editor's suggestions: "The preface which you all wanted me to write, and which I wanted to write, and finally wrote, came back to me from Paris today so marvelously changed and reworded that it seemed hardly mine." He continues,

> Literally speaking, we live in what has been described as the Age of Criticism. Full of articles on Kafka and James, on Melville, or whatever writer is in momentary ascendancy; laden with terms like "architectonic," "Zeitgeist," and "dichotomous," the literary magazines seem today on the verge of doing away with literature, not with any philistine bludgeon but by smothering it under the weight of learned chatter.

Styron suggests that it should be made clear to any prospective reader or contributor that

> *The Paris Review* hopes to emphasize creative work—fiction and poetry—not to the exclusion of criticism, but with the aim in mind of merely

removing criticism from the dominating place it holds in most literary magazines and putting it pretty much where it belongs, i.e., somewhere near the back of the book.

He is quick to point out, however, that although the review will not be as controversial or confrontational as other popular literary periodicals, this editorial attitude should not be misconstrued:

> This attitude does not necessarily make us—as some of the Older Boys have called us—the Silent Generation (the fact of *The Paris Review* belies that), or the Scared Generation, either, content to lie around in one palsied, unprotesting mass. It's not so much a matter of protest now, but of waiting; perhaps, if we have to be categorized at all, we might be called the Waiting Generation—people who feel and write and observe, and wait and wait and wait. And go on writing. I think *The Paris Review* should welcome these people into its pages—the good writers and good poets, the non-drumbeaters and non-ax-grinders. So long as they're good.

But no preface could give the curious reader a clearer idea of the review's purpose than the table of contents of the first issue (dated summer 1953). There are five feature stories, including Styron's "Letter to an Editor"; four pieces of fiction, by Antoine Blondin, Peter Matthiessen, Terry Southern, and Eugene Walter; five poems, by Robert Bly, Donald Hall, and George Steiner; and a portfolio of artwork by Tom Keogh. But what set the review apart from other periodicals with similar contents was the inclusion of an interview with E. M. Forster.

It had occurred to Plimpton that the review would better serve its readers by publishing lengthy and probing interviews with prominent authors and poets, thereby creating a forum wherein writers could explain themselves and their works rather than have their life and works explained by others. Plimpton returned to Cambridge and persuaded Forster, who was a don at Kings College, to answer such questions as: "What led you to make the remark quoted by Lionel Trilling, that the older you got the less it seemed to you to matter that an artist should 'develop'?" The seventy-four-year-old author, who had not published anything in nearly thirty years, answered: "I am more interested in achievement than advance on it and decline from it. And I am more interested in works than in authors. The paternal wish of critics to show how a writer dropped off or picked up as he went along seems to me misplaced. I am only interested in myself as a producer." In its first decade of publication, the review featured interviews titled "The Art of Fiction" (the spring–summer 1959 issue offered "The Art of Poetry," an interview with T. S. Eliot) that showcased such literary notables as François Sagan, Graham Greene, Dorothy Parker, Georges Simenon, Truman Capote, and William Faulkner. From the very beginning, the tone of the *Paris Review* interview was such that it created an intimacy between author and reader; it asked the sorts of questions that appealed to the general public as well as the scholar. To further this sense of intimacy, the review has always printed an example of the interviewee's writing in manuscript complete with cross outs and corrections.

It is a tribute to Plimpton's power of persuasion that he managed to bring the private and personal side of some of the most inaccessible writers to his readers. Perhaps his most unimaginable coup occurred when Ernest Hemingway granted him an interview. Plimpton delighted in telling how that came about: while standing in the Ritz Paris in 1953, Plimpton saw Hemingway peruse and subsequently purchase the second issue of the *Paris Review* at the hotel's bookshop. (Plimpton added in later interviews that it was the only time in the review's fifty years of publication that he had ever seen anyone actually buy it.) Later that same day, a mutual friend introduced Plimpton to Hemingway, who, although he had refused all other similar requests (aside from the interview he gave to his high school newspaper soon after returning home from World War I), agreed to answer questions submitted to him in writing. Different sources tell different stories, but it hardly matters whether the interview was conducted face to face or through the mail or a combination of both; the end result was an astonishing portrait of America's most public as well as most private author.

The interview, which appeared in the spring 1958 issue, is introduced by Plimpton, who states, "Ernest Hemingway writes in the bedroom of his home in the Havana suburb of San Francisco de Paula. He has a special workroom prepared for him in a square tower at the southwest corner of the house, but prefers to work in his bedroom, climbing to the tower room only when 'characters' drive him up there." Other revelations regarding Hemingway's writing process include the observation that the author prefers to write standing up in oversized loafers. His writing surface is a reading board that sits atop a chest-high bookcase; he writes in pencil on onionskin typing paper. When he finishes a page, he places it face down on a clipboard next to a typewriter. On a piece of a cardboard box affixed to a wall, he keeps track of his daily word output. It was Plimpton who settled once and for all the idea that Hemingway was so obsessive-compulsive that he had to sharpen a certain number of pencils each day before he could start writing: "Thornton Wilder speaks of mnemonic devices that get the writer going on his day's work. He says you once told him you sharpened twenty pencils." Hemingway answered, "I don't think I ever owned twenty pencils at one time. Wearing down seven number two pencils is a good day's work."

Plimpton managed to draw from Hemingway that he was uncomfortable talking about certain aspects of his creative process, that he had some superstitions, "but he prefers not to talk about them, feeling that whatever value they may have can be talked away":

> He has much the same attitude about writing. Many times during the making of this interview he stressed that the craft of writing should not be tampered with by excess of scrutiny—"that though there is one part of writing that is solid and you do it no harm by talking about it, the other is fragile, and if you talk about it, the structure cracks and you have nothing."

In addition, the interview produced this often-quoted gem of advice from a great author to those who would wish to follow in his footsteps: "The most essential gift for a good writer is a built-in, shock-proof shit detector."

The extended, probing and entertaining literary interviews with well established authors certainly attracted readers to the review, but perhaps Plimpton's greatest gift to the reading public was the inclusion of works by lesser-known but tremendously talented writers. Several poets, novelists, short story writers, and dramatists whose names and works are widely known and appreciated today were first seen in the pages of the *Paris Review*: Jack Kerouac, Philip Roth, T. Coraghessan Boyle, George Steiner, V. S. Naipaul, Mona Simpson. Portions of works in progress were introduced as well; a short story titled "Sundays" published in the summer 1966 issue of the review is a chapter from James Salter's erotic masterpiece, *A Sport and a Pastime*, a novel championed by Plimpton, who arranged to have it published by Doubleday in 1967. Salter, now recognized as a literary genius, would continue his association with the review for some forty years; in 2005 he was still contributing stories regularly.

As with all new ventures, finances played a significant role. Plimpton's parents contributed $500 to the review's initial bankroll of $1,500, hardly enough to sustain a magazine for very long even if sales were brisk. It was Plimpton's uncanny ability to be in the right place at the right time that secured financial stability for his literary enterprise. While in Spain for the Festival of Saint Fermin in 1954, Plimpton found himself running with the bulls through the streets of Pamplona alongside his Harvard roommate, the multimillionaire Prince Sadruddin Aga Khan. Somehow able to ignore the danger presented by the frantic bulls at their heels, Plimpton and Khan reached an agreement: Khan became the review's first publisher (and remained so until 1975). Kahn was followed by Ron Dante, Bernard F. Conners, Deborah S. Pease, and the current publisher (as of 2005), Drue Heinz.

SPORTS ILLUSTRATED

Plimpton returned to the United States in 1956, bringing the *Paris Review* with him to New York City. He set up offices for the review on the ground floor of his townhouse at 541 East

Seventy-Second Street in uptown Manhattan. The site soon became a mecca for aspiring writers as well as the firmly established and a gathering place for the best and brightest in all areas of human endeavor. An invitation to a party at Plimpton's was highly sought after for nearly fifty years.

Plimpton worked as a teacher at Barnard College from 1956 to 1958. During this time, a chance encounter with an old friend lead to a change in Plimpton's career goals. The friend, Whitney Tower, had been a sports reporter for the *Cincinnati Enquirer* but had left the paper after six years to join the staff of a new magazine, *Sports Illustrated*, in 1954. Tower asked Plimpton if he could use his ties to Harvard to get an interview with another Harvard alumnus, Harold S. Vanderbilt, who had been reluctant to speak to reporters from the fledgling endeavor. Vanderbilt, a champion yachtsman who, with a crew that included his wife, Gertrude, successfully defended the America's Cup in 1930, 1934, and 1937 accepted Plimpton's request. Plimpton found the work involved in producing the Vanderbilt story, which ran for four issues, to be quite satisfying, and he decided to quit teaching and divide his time between editing the *Paris Review* and writing occasional pieces for *Sports Illustrated*.

In its April 10, 1961, issue, *Sports Illustrated* published Plimpton's first foray into what he called participatory journalism. The idea for such an approach to reporting came to Plimpton when he chanced to read Paul Gallico's 1938 book, *Farewell to Sport*. Gallico, who is now remembered for his novels such as *The Poseidon Adventure* (1969) and for his short story "The Snow Goose" (which appeared in the *Saturday Evening Post* in 1940), first gained notoriety in the 1920s as a sportswriter, sports columnist, and sports editor for the *New York Daily News*. Never content to be an armchair athlete, Gallico took every opportunity to get an insider's experience. He concluded an interview with Jack Dempsey by asking the heavyweight boxing champion to join him in the boxing ring for a little sparring practice; Gallico was quickly knocked off his feet, but he gained a firsthand knowledge that he

could relate to his readers. Gallico wrote about and played with the best in their field: baseball with Herb Pennock, tennis with Vinnie Richards, golf with Bobby Jones, race car driving with Cliff Bergere. Plimpton wrote of *Farewell to Sport* in *The Best of Plimpton* (1990),

> I read this with envy—what a lucky writer Gallico was to have experienced all this. Then I began to wonder if it wouldn't be possible to undertake the same kind of research myself and expand it somewhat—to find out not only about athletic skills at their beat, but also something about the society of athletes, to join a team as a kind of "amateur professional." I had an enormous advantage, of course, writing for *Sports Illustrated*, whose editors agreed that the exercise was interesting and who were helpful in setting up the confrontations. (pp. 3–4)

The first of these "confrontations" occurred during a 1960 postseason matchup at Yankee Stadium between the stars of baseball's National and American leagues. *Sports Illustrated* editors had arranged to have Plimpton pitch to the starting lineups of both teams in what amounted to a pregame warm-up. The team that scored the most runs would split the magazine's $1,000 prize. The story of that event, "Dreams of Glory on the Mound," published in the April 10, 1961, issue of *Sports Illustrated*, is the story of a young man who has been an avid baseball fan since childhood being given the chance of a lifetime, pitching to legends such as Willie Mays, Mickey Mantel, Billy Martin, Gil Hodges, and Ernie Banks: a dream opportunity that ended in public humiliation. Plimpton evokes the loneliness he felt on the pitcher's mound after the team huddle broke up and the players took their positions on the ball field:

> When they headed for their positions, leaving me standing alone, it was like being unveiled—and one sensed the slow massive attention of the spectators—by then almost twenty thousand of them—wheel and concentrate, and almost physically I felt the weight of it. My palms were slick with sweat. I walked around the pitcher's mound to find the resin bag. There wasn't one. (*Best of Plimpton*, p. 9)

Plimpton finds himself surprised by the enormity of the playing field:

> Out beyond the base paths, the outfielders had reached their positions. They were so far away I didn't feel we were identified with the same project. The spaces between them were vast. Everything seemed very peaceful and quiet out there. Deep back in the bleachers I could see a man, sitting up there alone, removing his coat to enjoy the afternoon sun. (pp. 9–10)

After throwing a few warm-up pitches to his catcher, the New York Yankee great Elston Howard, Plimpton felt the crowd and its noise fade:

> Mostly you hear your own voice—chattering away, keeping you company in the loneliness, cajoling and threatening if things begin to go badly, heavy in praise at times, much of everything being said half aloud, the lips moving, because although you know you're being watched, no one can hear you, and the sound of your voice is truly a steady influ-ence—the one familiar verity in those strange circumstances. (p. 10)

After achieving some success with his first two batters (he managed to retire Willy Mays, who popped out to the shortstop after three pitches) it occurs to Plimpton that the pitcher's sense of pride is short-lived. Mays was followed by the powerhouse hitter Frank Robinson. "I knew," Plimpton says, "that the pitcher's pleasure is a fragmentary thing, that the dugouts, like sausage machines, eject an unending succession of hitters to destroy any momentary complacency a pitcher may feel during an afternoon of work." (p. 13) The "afternoon of work" began to wear Plimpton down much sooner than anyone expected; as his pitch count increased, with some batters taking as many as fifteen throws, Plimpton's fatigue became obvious. Plimpton finally admits to himself "that the energy was draining from me like meal from a punctured burlap sack." (p. 26) He was ready to quit, but he had only faced eight National League batters and the American League had yet to take its turn at the plate. Nevertheless, Plimpton continued to pitch to batter number nine, Bill Mazeroski, until the Yankee coach, Ralph Houk, took over on the mound. "I walked

slowly toward the first-base dugout. Most of the players in the dugout were standing up, watching me come in, and many of them were grinning. "(*Best of Plimpton*, p. 29) Harper published an expanded version of this misadventure, *Out of My League*, in 1961. With its accurate, often unflattering, insights into America's favorite pastime and its players, it remains one of the most popular baseball books ever written.

Readers of *The Best of Plimpton* are led to believe that what followed next in Plimpton's insider's accounts was a story of his boxing match with the light-heavyweight Archie Moore. Plimpton writes in the introduction to that tale, "After the baseball stint, the *Sports Illustrated* editors suggested, why not boxing? I wrote a polite letter to the light-heavyweight champion of the world, Archie Moore, known in the fight game as 'the Mongoose.'" (*Best of Plimpton*, p. 33) Actually, the match occurred some two years previous to the 1961 baseball game. Stillman's Gym was the location of the meeting between Moore and Plimpton; the gym's manager, Lou Ingber, agreed to let *Sports Illustrated* use the facility "for an hour or so" (*Best of Plimpton*, p. 35) for a small sum. After choosing his corner men, who included a professional trainer and friend of Ernest Hemingway's, George Brown, Plimpton, with some misgivings, threw himself into the experience. "On the morning of the fight, to get a flavor of what the boxer goes through on the day of his bout, I turned up at the offices of the Boxing Commission, just uptown from Madison Square Garden, to get weighed in with the rest of the boxers scheduled to fight on vari-ous cards that evening around the city." (p. 37) The self-deprecating style seen in the baseball piece continues as Plimpton describes the weigh-in ordeal: the other fighters came ready to disrobe quickly whereas Plimpton raises a few eyebrows by showing up dressed in an overcoat, Brooks Brothers suit, waistcoat, button-down shirt, regimental tie, over-the-calf socks, and shoes.

Plimpton met his corner men for lunch at the Racquet Club and sought to quiet his nerves by ordering a rather large meal: eggs Benedict, steak Diane, and a chocolate ice cream compote. "The

elegance of the place, and the food, arriving at the table in silver serving dishes, helped me forget where I was going to be at five that afternoon." (*Best of Plimpton*, p. 38) Meanwhile, Archie Moore was having lunch with a friend of Plimpton's, the journalist Peter Maas. In response to Moore's question as to who the fellow was that he had agreed to go three rounds with that day, Maas concocted a story that Plimpton was an ambitious intercollegiate boxing champion who was out to humiliate Moore in front of a large audience of friends and the press. Moore became agitated: "If that guy lays a hand on me I'm going to coldcock him." (*Best of Plimpton*, p. 39) Maas sought, unsuccessfully, to assure Moore that he was only kidding but this made Moore suspicious of his opponent.

That evening, after being introduced to the crowd by the referee Ezra Bowen, a *Sports Illustrated* editor, Moore and Plimpton advanced on each other to the center of the ring. Plimpton recalls that Moore made a strange humming sound as he moved around his opponent, a hum that would rise abruptly just before Moore landed a punch. For his part, Moore could not really grasp why he was there and what he was supposed to do. The match began well, just some friendly sparring; then Moore somehow lost his footing and the crowd taunted him. Moore's anger at this resulted in the first serious punch being thrown. "Laughter rose out of the seats, and almost as if in retribution he jabbed and followed with a long lazy left hook that fetched up against my nose and collapsed it slightly. It began to bleed." The sight of Plimpton's blood calmed Moore and he eased up on his opponent, whom he knew now was no match for him. The punch, however, alarmed some of Plimpton's corner men; they knew something about Moore's unpredictable nature and suspected that the champ would become more aggressive if the fight went much longer. One of them surreptitiously advanced the time clock, and when the bell rang to end round three, the referee drew both fighters to the center of the ring and raised each one's hand to signal the match was declared a draw.

Numerous sporting events followed. *Sports Illustrated* somehow convinced the owners of the Boston Bruins to allow Plimpton to train with them and serve as goaltender for five minutes during a match against the Philadelphia Flyers although, says Plimpton, "I am very poor on skates. I have weak ankles. Friends joke that I am the same height on the ice as I am off." (*Best of Plimpton*, p. 55) Despite this, Plimpton managed to hold his own against seasoned professionals and their loud and loyal fans. Plimpton had been warned that the Bruins were very unpopular in Philadelphia, and when he skated out onto the Flyers's home ice in the Spectrum with his teammates he found that to be the truth. "The great banks of spectators rose up from [the tunnel to the rink] in a bordering mass out of which cascaded a thunderous assault of boos and catcalls." (*Best of Plimpton*, p. 56) The Bruins kept the action on the Flyers's half of the rink for the first two minutes, and Plimpton, at his leisure, reflected on the loneliness of the hockey goaltender. "There can be nothing easier in sport than being a hockey goalie when the puck is at the opposite end. Nonchalance is the proper attitude. One can do a little housekeeping, sliding the ice shavings off to one side with the big stick." (p. 58) But this idyllic calm could not last forever; the Flyers recovered the puck and sped toward Plimpton. He braced himself and tried to remember what he had been told to do in this situation, but "the first shot the Flyers took went in. I had only the briefest peek at the puck." (p. 60) Nevertheless, for the next three minutes Plimpton managed to block numerous shots at his net, mostly by the stratagem of falling down at just the right time and in just the right spot. "Actually, my most spectacular save was made when I was prostrate on the ice … the puck appearing under my nose, quite inexplicably, and I was able to clap my glove over it." (p. 61) The final seconds of Plimpton's five minutes as the Bruin's goalie ticked by, and he thought for a moment he would leave the ice with his head held high. But whether by design or accident, a Bruin player committed a foul that gave the Flyers a penalty shot. The Flyers player, Reggie "the Rifle" Leach, sped toward the goal with the puck. At the last moment, Plimpton flung himself sideways ("someone said later that it looked like

the collapse of an ancient sofa") (p. 63) and Leach's shot caromed off the edge of one of Plimpton's skates and skidded wide of the net. Plimpton was surprised by the hometown crowd's reaction but then realized that they were in some ways experiencing what he had come to the arena to experience. "A very decent roar of surprise and pleasure exploded from the stands. By this time, I think, the Philadelphia fans thought of me less as a despised Bruin than a surrogate member of their own kind. I represented a manifestation of their own curiosity if they happened to find themselves down there on the ice." (pp. 63–64) But, as usual, Plimpton's moment of triumph was short-lived. After the boisterous congratulations from his teammates, the stories of how many saves he had made, the prediction that Leach was now finished as a professional after being humiliated, Plimpton skated off of the ice and the game resumed. "I looked up and down the bench for more recognition. I wanted to hear more. I wanted to tell them what it had been like. Their faces were turned away now." The story appeared as "Bozo the Bruin" in the January 30, 1978, issue of *Sports Illustrated* and was expanded upon in Plimpton's 1985 book, *Open Net*.

Sports Illustrated arranged events that ran the gamut of professional games. For one month, Plimpton toured with the Professional Golfers Association and played in three West Coast tournaments: the Bing Crosby, San Francisco's Lucky International, and the Bob Hope Desert Classic. His adventures and mishaps while playing with golfing legends such as Arnold Palmer, Gary Player, Jack Nicholas, Dow Finsterwald, and Walter Hagan, interacting with the army of fans, and his relationship with his diminutive caddy, Abe, are recollected in his 1968 book, *The Bogey Man*.

Plimpton played tennis with Pancho Gonzales, swam with four-time Olympic gold medal winner Don Schollander, appeared in a Boston Celtics basketball game, and pitched horseshoes with president-elect George Bush and his son, George W. Bush, at the Naval Observatory. The long piece on the Bushes, "A Sportsman Born And Bred," published in the December 26, 1988, issue of *Sports Illustrated*, portrayed the elder Bush

as the greatest sports enthusiast ever to call the White House home; a man who had enjoyed fishing, hunting, wrestling, soccer, tennis, golf, baseball, and bicycling all his life. The horseshoe match ended in defeat for Plimpton. It was a defeat that relieved Plimpton of some concern. Although he had not played this sport in some time, Plimpton made a good showing. But when he found himself about to defeat the elder Bush,

I began to worry about winning. What would it do to the president-elect's confidence to lose to someone who hadn't thrown a horseshoe in thirty years? Would he brood? Suddenly slam the heel of his hand against his forehead at cabinet meetings? Stumble into the bushes in the Rose Garden? Talk out loud to himself at state dinners? Snap at Sununu? (*Best of Plimpton*, p. 69)

Plimpton planned to play down his certain win and blame the president-elect's loss on the possibility that his cowboy hat restricted his view of the stake. Bush rose to the challenge, however, and won. A rematch was scheduled to be played at Camp David, and, in his hope to avoid another humiliation, Plimpton sought advice on what ingredient he was lacking, the essential ingredient that separates winners from losers.

Everyone must wonder wistfully if there isn't something other than what they actually practice in their lives (playing in a yacht-club tennis tournament) at which they would be incredibly adept if they could only find out what it was. … If an idiot savant could sit down at a piano and suddenly bat out a Chopin etude, wasn't the same sort of potential locked up somewhere in all of us? (*The Man in the Flying Lawn Chair*, 177).

His quest took him to the locker rooms of sports greats such as Bill Russell and Billie Jean King, boardrooms of successful businessmen, and the United States Olympic Training Center in Colorado. He compiled his findings in his 1990 book, *The X Factor: A Quest for Excellence*.

FOOTBALL AND APRIL FOOL'S

Perhaps Plimpton's best-known sports experience and the book that recounts the event is his at-

tempt to play quarterback for the Detroit Lions. Plimpton wrote to six teams in the National Football League asking them to put him through training and allow him to run a few plays. The Detroit Lions accepted, and Plimpton arrived at training camp in Pontiac, Michigan, in the summer of 1963. In Plimpton's account of his first professional football adventure, *Paper Lion: Confessions of a Last-String Quarterback* (1966), he relates how, after three week's training on the Lions's practice field and in their classrooms, equipped with the football team's ultimate symbol of acceptance, the playbook, and a repertoire of five plays, he felt he was ready for the professional gridiron.

As in his previous participation in sporting events, Plimpton writes of himself as Everyman, the ultimate fan who, instead of cheering from the stands and perhaps wearing the jersey of his or her favorite player, is in the thick of the action on the playing field. On the night of the preseason scrimmage, Plimpton, wearing a large zero on his jersey, heard the announcer explain the situation to the crowd:

> I could hear a voice over the loudspeaker system, a dim murmur telling the crowd what was going on, telling them that number zero, coming out across the sidelines was not actually a rookie, but an amateur, a writer who had been training with the team for three weeks and had learned five plays, which he was now going to run against the first-string Detroit defense. It was like a nightmare come true, he told them, as if one of *them*, rocking a beer around in a paper cup, with a pretty girl leaning past him to ask the hot-dog vendor in the aisle for mustard, were suddenly carried down underneath the stands by a sinister clutch of ushers. (*Best of Plimpton*, p. 47)

Plimpton entered the game confidently, announced the play to his teammates in the huddle, and then lined up behind his center.

> Everything fine about being a quarterback—the embodiment of his power—was encompassed in those dozen seconds or so: giving the instructions to ten attentive men, breaking out of the huddle, walking for the line, and then pausing behind the center, dawdling amid men poised and waiting under the trigger of his voice, cataleptic, until the

deliverance of himself and them to the future. (*Best of Plimpton*, p. 48)

In his first play from scrimmage, Plimpton had trouble handling the ball exchange, and in the split second it took him to gain control he found himself out of position and on a collision course with an offensive lineman. The ball was jarred loose, and Plimpton had to scramble backward to recover it, losing five yards. He called a pass play next but as he dropped back to throw, he lost his balance and fell to the ground without being touched. Next he attempted a running play but the professionals were so fast in their execution that he was late handing off to his running back and kept the ball himself. He was stopped by the defensive linesman Roger Brown. "He tackled me high, and straightened me with his power, so that I churned against his three-hundred-pound girth like a comic bicyclist." (*Best of Plimpton*, p. 51) Brown stripped the ball from Plimpton and ran it in for an apparent touchdown, but the referee had whistled the play dead during the struggle. Plimpton had lost thirty yards in three attempts; he had one last play to regain yardage and avoid another public humiliation. He tried a lateral, but again the defense saw what he had in mind, and although Plimpton was successful in getting the ball to the right player that player was tackled behind the line of scrimmage at the one-yard line: a loss for Plimpton of thirty-nine yards in four plays. As Plimpton jogged to the sideline bench he was startled to hear applause for his miserable performance.

> Some of it was, perhaps, in appreciation of the lunacy of my participation and for the fortitude it took to do it; but most of it, even if subconscious, I decided was in *relief* that I had done as badly as I had: it verified the assumption that the average fan would have about an amateur blundering into the brutal world of professional football. He would get slaughtered.

Paper Lion remained on the *New York Times* best-seller list for twenty-four weeks. Such was its popularity that United Artists, with the producer Stuart Miller and the director Alan March, brought the story to the motion picture screen. Alan Alda portrayed Plimpton and mem-

bers of the Detroit Lions—Alex Karras, John Gordy, Roger Brown, Lou Garney—played themselves. Plimpton himself made a cameo appearance as the Lions owner William Clay Ford. (Plimpton was not new to the screen: previously he had portrayed a Bedouin in the 1962 film *Lawrence of Arabia*, and he had been an extra in the 1968 Frank Sinatra movie, *The Detective*.) The 1968 movie version of *Paper Lion* won a Golden Globe award for Alda in the New Star of the Year category.

Plimpton returned to the football field in 1971 with the defending world champion Baltimore Colts. The arrangement was the same; Plimpton would play quarterback for the Colts during halftime of an exhibition game against the Detroit Lions. This time, however, the event, from training camp through the exhibition game, was filmed for a 1971 television special called *Plimpton! The Great Quarterback Sneak*. His center for the series of plays was the football legend Bill Curry. Curry, in a piece written for ESPN.com in 2003, remembers Plimpton arriving at training camp: "Now, several things were clear from the outset. George was cultured, brilliant, and sincere. He was also tall, awkward, and knew virtually nothing about football. He was a man of refinement and distinction slipping into our warrior world, and players' reactions ranged from amusement to hostility." On his first play at camp, Plimpton was driven head first into the field and his right thumb was dislocated. Curry writes, "We all assumed our little television experiment was over. We did not know George Plimpton." Plimpton returned to the drills in the afternoon with a heavily taped right hand and survived the strenuous workouts. "Who would have thought a 44-year-old author could match us gut-check for gut-check?" Curry recalls. "We were impressed despite ourselves. George lasted the entire training camp and we became hooked on and inspired by his project."

The exhibition game in Ann Arbor, Michigan, held what was the largest crowd ever to see a National Football League game. Curry remembers,

On his four plays, George did a fine job of handling the ball and almost completing a pass on a slant route. When we walked in, he was disconsolate. Thinking he was disappointed in his performance I said, "Come on George, you did well. Cheer up." I will never forget the expression when he looked back at me and exclaimed, "That was the damned most disgusting experience of my life! You guys are sick! The hatred out there was palpable! You are all degraded!" Apparently, his ol' Lion buddies had talked a little trash and he was offended. I responded, "George, that was not hatred. That was intensity. We are all competitors, and we leave that stuff on the field when the game is over." But he was inconsolable, and refused to discuss it any more that day.

Despite his disappointment, Plimpton was later to write, "As the Baltimore quarterback darned if we didn't make eighteen yards in four downs—fifteen of them, I must admit, on a roughing-the-passer penalty!"

Plimpton included his diary of his time with the Baltimore Colts in the early editions (it was removed for the 1993 revision) of his second football book, published in 1973, *Mad Ducks and Bears: Football Revisited*. The idea for the book came from the "Mad Duck" and "Bear" of the title: the Lions's defensive lineman, Alex Karras, and offensive guard, John Gordy, who wanted to produce a how-to book for the most uncelebrated members of a football team, the linesmen. The finished product, however, is a humorous and reflective account of the careers of two of the game's best players. Plimpton collaborated with another of his Colts teammates on *One More July: A Football Dialogue with Bill Curry*. The 1977 book was not Plimpton at his best; instead of giving his readers a multifaceted, insider's view, he focuses on the reminiscences of Curry during a long car trip the two took from Lexington, Kentucky, to Green Bay, Wisconsin.

Plimpton's biggest deviation from his popular formula came six years later: "In midwinter 1983, the editors of *Sports Illustrated* called me in for a conference on an issue coming up that was dated April 1. Perhaps they thought my background as a onetime editor of the *Harvard Lampoon* might be appropriate. The first idea was for me to do a straightforward report on practical jokes in sport." (*Best of Plimpton*, p. 323) What resulted was a practical joke titled "The Curious

Case of Sidd Finch." Plimpton reported as fact to readers that the New York Mets had acquired a pitching phenomenon named Hayden (Sidd) Finch. "The secret cannot be kept much longer. Questions are being asked, and sooner rather than later the New York Mets management will have to produce a statement." (*Best of Plimpton*, p. 326) The Mets management and team members cooperated with the spoof, providing vague answers to the press and allowing the model for Sidd Finch (a high-school teacher and friend of a *Sports Illustrated* photographer) to pose with the Mets's pitching coach Mel Stottlemyre and catcher Ronn Reynolds.

Plimpton's fictitious biography of Finch included such "facts" as "he has had no baseball career. Most of his life has been spent abroad, except for a short period at Harvard University." Finch's roommate cannot give any clues to the reason he left, only that he received a letter from him stating he was in Egypt and on his way to Tibet to study. Years later, Finch showed up at the Mets' AAA farm club, the Tidewater Tides, and announced to the manager, "I have learned the art of the pitch." (*Best of Plimpton*, p. 330) After amazing the manager with his skill ("My God, that kid's thrown the ball about a hundred and fifty m.p.h."), Sidd (short for Siddhartha) agrees to appear at the Mets's training camp if they will respect five conditions concerning his privacy and reluctance to make a contractual commitment. Even when all his conditions are met, Sidd is still not sure he should use his ability in a sport that would lead him away from his pursuit of Nirvana. Then there is the bigger question, posed by Plimpton, of what such a pitcher would do to the sport itself: what would happen if one team in major league baseball could not be beaten? The *Sports Illustrated* story ends with the baseball commissioner Peter Ueberroth delaying any decision regarding Sidd and the effect he would have on the game: "I'll have to see it to believe it!" (*Best of Plimpton*, p. 338)

Readers of *Sports Illustrated did* believe it. Plimpton wrote, "The reaction to the article were extraordinary. Over a thousand letters were received. Many readers described how badly they had been duped. Others were furious that a magazine so devoted to accuracy should stoop to such a trick." (*Best of Plimpton*, p. 325) The number of letters ultimately received was closer to 2,500, the most for any story in the magazine before or since. Plimpton's interest in the possibility of a perfect pitcher entering the game led him to write an expanded version of the joke. The 1987 novel, his first and only except for a children's book, *The Rabbit's Umbrella*, which he wrote in Paris in 1955, kept the title of the article, added a love interest in the person of blond surfer and college dropout, Debbie Sue, and penetrated more deeply the world of professional baseball. In the end, Sidd realizes that his perfection is ruining the game and walks away, never to be seen or heard from again.

FIREWORKS: CELEBRATORY AND LITERARY

Plimpton was every bit as active in the literary and cultural world as he was in sports, and it is hard to imagine where he found the time to be a husband and father. Nevertheless, he married Freddy Medora Espy in 1968 and the couple produced two children, Medora Ames and Taylor Ames. That marriage ended in divorce in 1988, and in 1991 Plimpton married Sarah Whitehead Dudley and, at the age of sixty-seven, fathered twin girls in 1994, Olivia Hartley and Laura Dudley.

It seems remarkable that after facing the dangers found in professional sports—the likelihood of suffering injuries both physical and psychological from hulking brutes who might resent an amateur infiltrating their ranks—that Plimpton stated in an address at a New York Philharmonic lunch that the most frightening experience he faced as a participatory journalist was when he played percussion instruments, primarily the triangle, with the New York Philharmonic conducted by Leonard Bernstein. "One reason it was terrifying was that in music you cannot make a mistake ... It is not part of the zeitgeist. If you make a mistake, a big one, you destroy a work of art." (*The Best of Plimpton*, p. 74).

Another of Plimpton's passions where a mistake would prove costly, if not deadly, was

the production of fireworks extravaganzas. His lifelong fascination with fireworks, and his insistence that the city of New York produce more displays, resulted in his being named honorary commissioner of fireworks in 1973 by Mayor John Lindsay. In 1984, Doubleday published Plimpton's paean to pyrotechnics, *Fireworks: A History and Celebration.*

Plimpton seemed to know everyone who was anyone. The range of his social connections and friendships is reflected in the three oral history biographical studies he edited. The first was *American Journey: The Times of Robert F. Kennedy* published in 1970. Working with the interviewer Jean Stein, Plimpton compiled 347 interviews to present a life of his friend and Harvard classmate. The recollections included not only those of Kennedy's friends, family, and associates but also those of mourners who rode in Kennedy's funeral train and those who stood by the tracks and paid their respects as the train traveled from New York to Washington, D.C.

Ten years later, Plimpton worked on another oral history project with Jean Stein, *Edie: An American Biography* (1982). Like Robert Kennedy, Edie Sedgwick was a child of privilege born into a prominent Massachusetts family. Sedgwick, with her beauty, vivaciousness, and wealth grew to epitomize the "swinging" lifestyle of the 1960s. She was highly sought after by the most interesting men of her era: Bob Neuwirth, Andy Warhol, and Bob Dylan. Plimpton himself confessed in a 2003 interview with Andrew Anthony in the *Observer* to being "half in love with her, you couldn't help it. Something about the frailty and the fragility and the beauty of her was astonishing." Tall, willowy and blonde, Sedgwick was a fashion icon of the 1960s, gracing the pages of *Vogue* and *Life* magazines. As happened to so many of her generation, the easy availability and cachet of drugs proved her downfall, and she died at the age of twenty-eight in 1971. The coroner's report listed the cause of death as an accident/suicide due to barbiturate overdose.

Another tortured soul was the subject of Plimpton's next oral history. In *Truman Capote: In Which Various Friends, Enemies, Acquaintances, and Detractors Recall His Turbulent Career* (1997), Plimpton presents a series of sketches that chronicle the meteoric rise and tragic descent of one of literature's true geniuses. Most who were asked to contribute to the book were eager to participate; only the photographer Richard Avedon, the novelist and Capote's childhood friend Harper Lee, and the socialite Amanda Burdon (the daughter of Capote's best friend turned most bitter enemy, Babe Paley) refused. Plimpton's own relationship with Capote was curious. Capote had allowed himself to be interviewed by Plimpton for issue number sixteen of the *Paris Review*, and he was a fixture at Plimpton's gatherings. It is safe to assume that the two men respected each other, but that assumption makes it difficult to understand why Plimpton chose to write a piece for the November 1979 issue of *Harper's* magazine that swiftly and bitterly ended their relationship. The piece, titled "The Snows of Studiofiftyfour," was a broad parody of Hemingway's "The Snows of Kilimanjaro"—and Studio 54 was the exclusive discotheque frequented by Capote, where cocaine, or "snow," was the recreational drug of choice. There was a rumor circulating among the New York literary set that Capote was suffering from writer's block midway through his anxiously awaited *Answered Prayers*: a scathing attack (published posthumously in 1987) on some of his high-society friends, portions of which had reached the curious by means of excerpts published in *Esquire* magazine. Plimpton imagined Capote trying another writer's style, in this case Hemingway's, to resolve his problem. The story begins with a man, obviously Capote, waiting to board a flight to New York. He is returning from a stay at a California "fat farm," where he has had some cosmetic surgery and the bandages are causing him discomfort. Like the protagonist in Hemingway's story, Plimpton's character lapses into memories of former days: "He thought about being alone in the motel room in Akron with the big table lamps, having quarreled in Memphis, and he had started his enemies list, and how long it was, and he had used the Dewey decimal system to arrange it in the green calfskin notebooks." (*Best of Plimpton*, p. 319) Nearing

his destination he looks down to see "the great, high, shadow-pocked cathedral of Studiofiftyfour. ... And then he knew that this was where he was going. He thought about the smooth leather of the banquettes under his rear end and how he would look out and think about his enemies. *We will have some good destruction*, he thought." (*Best of Plimpton*, p. 322) Capote was not amused; he never spoke to Plimpton again.

THE PARTY ENDS

Plimpton lived his life to the fullest, constantly seeking new challenges and adventures. One is reminded of Hemingway and his restless drive to fill the empty space when his writing was put aside for the day. But one wonders if even Hemingway would have had the stamina to keep up with Plimpton. Many people would be content with the achievement of editing a prestigious literary review for fifty years, and, to be sure, Plimpton saw that as his greatest contribution to the arts. Andrew Anthony remembered Plimpton saying during an interview, "I'm terribly proud of the *Paris Review*. If one lives a life and you're supposed to leave something behind, then the *Review* is pretty impressive." Indeed, earlier in the interview Plimpton admitted that all of his activities had one purpose in mind: "All this I need hardly add was to supplement the *Paris Review*." The "all this" Plimpton referred to included roles in several motion pictures, among them *Beyond the Law* (1968), *Reds* (1981), *Volunteers* (1985), *Nixon* (1995), and *Good Will Hunting* (1997). In *Rio Lobo* (1970), Plimpton gained the dubious honor of portraying an outlaw who is shot by the legendary John Wayne. In addition to countless cameo appearances on television programs (including an episode of *The Simpsons* in which he portrayed himself as a judge at a crooked spelling bee) and commercials, Plimpton hosted the Disney Channel's *Mouseterpiece Theatre*, a gentle parody of the BBC's *Masterpiece Theatre* hosted by Alistair Cooke.

One activity, however, may have been accepted for the sheer male fantasy appeal of it: an invitation to submit a portfolio of photographs to *Playboy* magazine. In "My Life with *Playboy*,"

Plimpton recalled that he and Hugh Hefner "founded our magazines at the same time, fifty years ago in the summer of 1953. Both got going on a shoestring." Sometime in the mid-1970s, *Playboy*'s photo editor suggested to Plimpton that he "try my hand at taking photographs of potential Playmates for the magazine's famous Centerfold" (The Man in the Flying Lawn Chair, p. 43, 48). After a year of working on his own with women he managed to convince to pose for him, Plimpton, who disguised his identity by adopting the name "Henri Derrière," presented his slides for consideration: "my portfolio was considered inadequate, vastly so, and the photo editor took me aside afterward and said we'd start afresh with a Playboy model who knew what she was doing." The model was Kevyn Taylor. "She was perfectly suited to the scene I had in mind for the photograph, one of a young, unclothed woman standing in a field, having just slipped off a horse." This time Plimpton's abilities behind the camera, even though judged not good enough for the centerfold position, were acknowledged by having two of his shots of Taylor published in the January 1974 issue.

David Remnick, writing in the October 10, 2003, issue of the *New Yorker*, described Plimpton as "a serious man of serious accomplishments who just happened to have more fun than a van full of jugglers and clowns." Plimpton's wife Sarah told the *New York Times*'s Warren St. John that "George saw his home as a place for everybody. He loved the lights blazing, piano playing, glasses clattering, and the more oddballs the better. He loved people so much that he felt something was missing if this house wasn't full." St. John added, "Few in Manhattan have ever entertained as aggressively and with as much zeal as Mr. Plimpton did, and in literary and artistic circles, the competition isn't even close. For more than 45 years, he was host to hundreds of parties for thousands of guests, sometimes at a rate of one a week." It came as a shock that a man with such an artistic gift for living would do something as prosaic as die, and yet on September 25, 2003, in the very home that had held so much life, Plimpton passed away

in his sleep; his agent Timothy Seldes told the press that it was "most likely a heart attack."

Soon after Plimpton's death, there arose questions regarding the future of the *Paris Review*. A headline in the *Village Voice* read "Is George Plimpton Irreplaceable?" Another in the *New York Times* asked, "Does the *Paris Review* Get a Second Act?" There was a scramble to find someone who could maintain the editorial integrity of a review that had survived for fifty years thanks to the ebullient personality and sheer determined hard work of its late founder. The review's board appointed the longtime associate editor Brigid Hughes to fill the position in January 2004. A year later, the board announced that Hughes would be leaving the review for unspecified reasons, and the search for a replacement resumed. But whatever happens to the *Paris Review*, it, and indeed the entire New York literary scene, will never be the same. It is as if Plimpton were the glue that held it all together and without him the whole has broken into many separate pieces. As the novelist and short story writer James Salter wrote of Plimpton's death, "Well, the party is over. Everyone has to find their own way home."

Selected Bibliography

WORKS OF GEORGE PLIMPTON

The Rabbit's Umbrella. New York: Viking, 1955.

Out of My League. New York: Harper, 1961.

Paper Lion: Confessions of a Last-String Quarterback. New York: Harper & Row, 1966.

The Bogey Man: A Month on the PGA Tour. New York: Harper & Row, 1968.

Mad Ducks and Bears: Football Revisited. New York: Random House, 1973.

One for the Record: The Inside Story of Hank Aaron's Chase for the Home-Run Record. New York: Harper & Row, 1974.

One More July: A Football Dialogue with Bill Curry. New York: Harper & Row, 1977.

Shadow Box: An Amateur in the Ring. New York: Putnam, 1977.

Sports! With photographs by Neil Leifer. New York: Abrams, 1978.

A Sports Bestiary. With drawings by Arnold Roth. New York: McGraw-Hill, 1982.

Fireworks: A History and Celebration. Garden City, N.Y.: Doubleday, 1984.

Open Net. New York: Norton, 1985.

The Curious Case of Sidd Finch. New York: Macmillan, 1987.

The Official Olympics Triplecast Viewer's Guide. New York: Pindar, 1992.

The X Factor: A Quest for Excellence. Knoxville, Tenn.: Whittle Direct, 1990. Rev. ed. New York: Norton, 1995.

Truman Capote: In Which Various Friends, Enemies, Acquaintances, and Detractors Recall His Turbulent Career. New York: Nan A. Talese, Doubleday, 1997.

Pet Peeves; or, Whatever Happened to Dr. Rawff? New York: Atlantic Monthly Press, 2000.

COLLECTIONS

The Best of Plimpton. New York: Atlantic Monthly Press, 1990.

George Plimpton on Sports. Guilford, Conn.: Lyons Press, 2003.

The Man in the Flying Lawn Chair and Other Excursions and Observations. New York: Random House, 2004.

WORKS EDITED

Writers at Work: The Paris Review Interviews. 9 vols. New York: Viking, 1958--1992.

The American Literary Anthology. Nos. 1–2. Edited with Peter Ardery. New York: Random House, 1968, 1969, 1970.

American Journey: The Times of Robert F. Kennedy. With interviews by Jean Stein. New York: Harcourt Brace Jovanovich, 1970.

Pierre's Book: The Game of Court Tennis, by Pierre Etchebaster. Barre, Mass.: Barre, 1971.

Edie: An American Biography, by Jean Stein. New York: Knopf, 1982.

D. V., by Diana Vreeland. Edited with Christopher Hemphill. New York: Knopf, 1984.

Poets at Work: The Paris Review Interviews. New York: Viking, 1989.

Women Writers at Work: The Paris Review Interviews. New York: Viking, 1989.

The Best of Bad Hemingway: Choice Entries from the Harry's Bar & American Grill Imitation Hemingway Competition. 2 vols. San Diego: Harcourt Brace Jovanovich, 1989, 1991.

The Paris Review Anthology. New York: Norton, 1990.

The Writer's Chapbook: A Compendium of Fact, Opinion,

Wit, and Advice from the Twentieth Century's Preeminent Writers. New York: Viking, 1990.

The Norton Book of Sports. New York: Norton, 1992.

Best American Sports Writing, 1997. Boston: Houghton Mifflin, 1997.

Best American Movie Writing, 1998. New York: St. Martin's, 1998.

Home Run: The Best Writing about Baseball's Most Exciting Moment. San Diego: Harcourt, 2000.

Playwrights at Work: The Paris Review Interviews. New York: Modern Library, 2000.

Latin American Writers at Work: The Paris Review Interviews. New York: Modern Library, 2003.

As Told at the Explorer's Club: More Than Fifty Gripping Tales of Adventure. Guilford, Conn.: Lyons Press, 2003.

CRITICAL AND BIOGRAPHICAL STUDIES

"All Yesterday's Parties," *New Yorker*, June 27–July 4, 1994, p. 44.

Anthony, Andrew. "Been There, Done That." *Observer*, October 5, 2003, section 2, p. 1.

Blythe, Will. "The Man in the Flying Lawn Chair: The Raconteur." *New York Times*, January 2, 2005, section 7, p. 17.

Curry, Bill. "George Plimpton, Participatory Friend" (http://sports.espn.go.com).

Ferretti, Fred. "The Bombs Bursting in Air." *New York Times Book Review*, September 23, 1984, p. 13.

Flaherty, Joe. "Muhammed Ali Meets Ernest Hemingway." *New York Times Book Review*, November 6, 1977, pp. 9, 44.

"Focus on George Plimpton." *Harper's Bazaar*, November 1973, pp. 103, 134–135, 142.

Harris, Mark. "On the Mound Was Mr. Everybody." *New York Times Book Review*, April 23, 1961, p. 3.

Harrison, Barbara Grizzuti. "Football People." *New York Times Book Review*, January 6, 1974, pp. 24–25.

Jones, Malcolm, Jr. "Major-League Man of Letters." *Newsweek*, January 14, 1991, p. 22.

Ledbetter, James. "Paper Literary Lions: The *Paris Review* Gets in Step." *Village Voice*, June 11, 1991, p. 30.

McGrath, Charles. "Does the *Paris Review* Get a Second Act?" *New York Times*, February 6, 2005, section 4, p. 14.

Miller, Laura. "Keep Talking." *New York Times*, December 12, 2004, section 7, p. 14.

Orodenker, Richard. *Dictionary of Literary Biography.* Vol. 241, *American Sportswriters and Writers on Sport,* edited by Richard Orodenker, 205–216. Detroit: Gale, 2001.

Remnick, David. "George Plimpton." *New Yorker*, October 6, 2003, p. 46.

Richler, Mordecai. "The *Paris Review* Is a Movable Feast." *Gentlemen's Quarterly*, October 1989, pp. 183, 186.

Riley, Sam G. *Dictionary of Literary Biography.* Vol. 185, *American Literary Journalists, 1945–1995, First Series,* edited by Arthur J. Kaul, 217–232. Detroit: Gale, 1997.

St. John, Warren. "The Five-Decade Party and Its Tireless Host." *New York Times*, October 5, 2003, section 9, p. 1.

Salter, James. Letter to Charles R. Baker, October 5, 2003.

Schapp, Dick. "George Plimpton off His Game." *New York Times Book Review*, November 10, 1968, p. 8.

Stokes, John. "Raffishness Rampant." *Times Literary Supplement*, September 29, 2000, p. 21.

Styron, William. "Letter to an Editor," *Paris Review* (spring, 1953): 9-13.

Talese, Gay. *The Overreachers.* New York: Harper, 1965.

"The Art of Fiction," *Paris Review* (Spring, 1953): 29-41. [An interview with E. M. Forster conducted by P. N. Furbank and F. J. H. Haskell.]

Weber, Bruce. "Spurious George." *Esquire*, November 1985, p. 243.

Whelton, Clark. "Paper Plimpton." *Esquire*, January 1976, pp. 115–117, 142, 144, 146.

Wyatt, Edward. "Plimpton's Big Shoes Are Vacant Again." *New York Times*, January 20, 2005, section E, p. 1.

FRANCINE PROSE

(1947—)

Denise Gess

FRANCINE PROSE PROBABLY would never use the word "blossom" unless she cut it with satire. However, Prose—the author of a dozen critically acclaimed novels, two novellas, numerous short stories, a book-length travel memoir, five children's books, biographies, young adult fiction, cultural and literary criticism, and more than five hundred magazine articles—has indeed blossomed from a girl who began reading avidly at age four into a writer who cannot be ignored. Over the course of her thirty-two-year career, the author who made her debut with the novel *Judah the Pious* (1973) has achieved stature and accessibility in American letters. She has garnered a Guggenheim Fellowship, a Fulbright Fellowship to Yugoslavia, two National Endowment for the Arts Fellowships, and a coveted Director's Fellowship at the Center for Scholars and Writers at the New York Public Library, and she was a finalist for the National Book Award for her novel *Blue Angel* (2000).

In academic circles, Francine Prose has taught creative writing at Harvard University, Sarah Lawrence College, the Iowa Writers' Workshop, Warren Wilson College, and Johns Hopkins University, and she has made appearances at some of the country's most influential writers' conferences and residencies. Not only has Prose written acerbic, tantalizing, unforgettable fiction, but her other subjects range from a simple short piece on the use of knives and forks, meditations on the erotic spirit, a poignant memoir of her late friend Spalding Gray, to a near diatribe on contemporary ills in literature and the media. Displaying a range as impressive as that of a virtuoso singer, Prose's literary productivity proves that versatility could very well be her middle name.

Equally impressive is Prose's modesty about her prodigious multifaceted output and her dedicated work ethic. "I try to write every day," she said in a March 1998 interview for *Atlantic Online*. "It's a challenge to stay focused and organized . . . on an ideal day I would work on fiction in the morning when I'm really fresh, and then on reviews and journalism in the afternoon." Two years later, when questioned about her role as a social gadfly whose nonfiction pieces for *Harper's* magazine sparked no less than incendiary debates, Prose told Sandy Asirvatham of *Poets & Writers* magazine in an interview for the May/June 2000 issue: "I just feel compelled to say the things that everybody knows, that nobody's saying." It is safe to say that contrary to Prose's self-effacing estimation of her literary voice, everybody doesn't know what she knows, nor can they express as eloquently and trenchantly. Her breadth of knowledge—of history, art, photography, women's studies, folklore, and religion—and inexhaustible curiosity are only two of the qualities that have made Prose, who acknowledges in her *Atlantic Online* interview a manic devotion to rewriting a sentence "a zillion times," highly visible and laudable among fellow writers and readers. Her career can be effectively viewed as an ascending arc in four parts. Any indication of an impending denouement resides, if at all, decades away.

BEGINNINGS: THE YOUNG FABULIST

Francine Prose was born on April Fools' Day 1947, the perfect birth date for one who plans to enter the fray of the writing life, a career that succeeds or fails on a combination of innate talent, strenuous work, and good timing. Born to two physicians, Philip Prose and Jessie Rubin Prose, Francine was raised in Brooklyn and spent weekends traveling into Manhattan, where she

absorbed the pulse of city life that would make her a keen satirical observer and recorder of human nature. Her father's work as a pathologist at Bellevue Hospital made her privy to "the most notorious cases," as she recounts in "The Old Morgue," a personal essay published in the fall 1997 issue of the *Threepenny Review*. Her mother—who balanced home and professional life gracefully—provided convincing proof that women could become whatever they chose. Not until 1968, when she was an undergraduate at Radcliffe College, did Prose become aware that many women her age had grown up with imposed limitations. Years later in her book *The Lives of the Muses: Nine Women and the Artists They Inspired* (2002), Prose writes that the muse Lou Andreas-Salomé "behaved as if she had never heard anyone suggest that a woman couldn't do entirely as she pleased." That description could just as easily apply to Francine Prose.

Prose graduated summa cum laude with a BA in English then entered Harvard University, where she received her master's degree, also in English. Unlike many writers armed with such enviable credentials, she chose not to follow the prescribed route toward a tenured university position; instead she devoted herself to writing while teaching part-time, because, as she has been known to lament, she did not believe herself to be a natural teacher.

Two years after completing her MA, Prose was still living in Cambridge, Massachusetts, and working without much success on exactly the kind of first novel she had wanted to avoid: autobiographical. Bored by her lack of imagination, she fled to India for a year. Living in Bombay gave Prose the chance to inhabit a culture radically different from her own and to observe foreign customs and mores. As Prose advises her writing students, she began listening to the ways people tell their stories. She also began reading Isak Dinesen's stories. Influenced by the Danish writer's talent for oral storytelling, reportedly as captivating to listeners as her written work was to readers, Prose sought to imitate Dinesen's gothic flourishes and blend them with the Hasidic folklore she already knew well. She tossed out her first novel and began drafting another.

The result was something altogether fresh, set in the seventeenth-century Polish court of King Casimir, a far remove from either the prosaic Brooklyn or the brainy Cambridge that had been Prose's formative stomping ground. Upon her return to the United States, Prose began shopping the new novel, and in 1973, *Judah the Pious* was published to glowing reviews; the novel also received the Jewish Book Council Award. At only twenty-five years old, Francine Prose was already being compared to Geoffrey Chaucer.

Judah the Pious is the story of an old Jewish mountebank, Rabbi Eliezer of Rimanov, who comes to Cracow fueled by fear of a pogrom against the Jews. Eliezer plans to persuade the young king to reinstate the banned Jewish burial rites. In a reversal that is comic and common to this type of tale, Rabbi Eliezer quickly takes over the king's throne while the king, barely aware that he's been cast in a secondary position, becomes Eliezer's avid listener. The ensuing narrative is a series of tales within a tale filled with the ordinary (unknown fathers) and the supernatural (an immaculate conception). Prose deftly alternates the real with the imagined, keeping the reader precariously balanced until Eliezer wins his argument. God hovers over the narrative, but instead of an Old Testament God characterized by thundering omnipotence, Prose's God deploys with a wink mysterious methods of grace and revelation.

In the February 17, 1973, issue of the *New York Times*, Thomas Lask attributes Prose's success with *Judah the Pious* partly to "her tone, which suggests the narrative exposition of a Jewish sage—a tone that never falters and that is half the fun." A few weeks later in the *New York Times Book Review*, D. Keith Mano took the praise a step further, concluding that Prose "may well be a prophet" who "appears to perceive more than a writer of [her] age decently should." *Judah the Pious* would prove prophetic in more ways than one, for it predicted a successful form of narrative that would suit Prose in her next three novels. The young writer had discovered a pattern for storytelling that saved her from the more pedestrian navel-gazing novels of many of her contemporaries and instead immersed her in folk-

tale and travel as she mined the past and the exotic for her settings and characters.

Over the next five years Prose published *The Glorious Ones* (1974), *Marie Laveau* (1977), *Animal Magnetism* (1978), and a book of morality tales for children, *Stories from Our Living Past* (1974). Like *Judah the Pious, The Glorious Ones* is set in another century. This time Prose chose sixteenth-century Italy in which to set the story of a troupe of traveling commedia dell'arte actors. Rendered in seven chapters, each character tells a single story from his or her typecast role as the Lover, the Clown, the Miser until the "truth" is indistinguishable from fantasy. Obviously Prose intended to say something original on the subject of imagination and reality and the thin line between the actor and the role, but *The Glorious Ones* calls more attention to its construction and Prose's desire to eschew the autobiographical. Nevertheless, her second novel, while not as enthusiastically received as her first, survived the dreaded sophomore curse. Writing for the *Hudson Review* (summer 1974), Patricia Spacks concluded that "it's a book more satisfying to think about than to read." *The Glorious Ones* did not catapult Prose into commercial or critical success, but it did begin to solidify her reputation as an inventive narrative razzle-dazzler.

Although Prose continued to rely on the proven formula of legend combined with quirky plots and characters in her work, by 1976 she had made traditional choices in her life. She married the painter and sculptor Howard "Howie" Michels on September 24, 1977. By the following year she and Michels had left their Manhattan home, and for the second time Prose visited India. In the meantime *Marie Laveau* was published to a positive reception. It wasn't much of a departure from her previous novels; the signature Gothic strokes are present in the fictional retelling of the life of the real Marie Laveau, a nineteenth-century New Orleans native who was born with the caul—that is, a remnant of the amniotic sac, which folkloric tradition regards as representative of prophetic or magical power. In Prose's hands the birth-to-death story of the legendary figure who performed magic, healed bodies and spirits,

and influenced the politics of the time erupts into a spooky, compelling narrative about a mysterious and enchanting voodoo queen.

Before the decade was over Prose received a *Mademoiselle* magazine Mlle Award and published her fourth novel. *Animal Magnetism* (1978) takes place in nineteenth-century New England just before the advent of Spiritualism and is based on the lecture-circuit fad of self-hypnosis. The hero is a Frenchman, Charles Jordan, who arrives in Lowell, Massachusetts, seeking a willing subject for his experiments. He finds the young Zinnia Turner, who suffers from various illnesses, real and imagined. The practice of animal magnetism is coupled with the belief that people and animals share a universal fluid and that "magnetist" and subject can share one nervous system. Charles's experimentation with Zinnia is so successful he takes the magnetism cure on the road. Things begin to go awry when the Chiron-like Charles contracts Zinnia's ills. The transfer of their nervous energy is so complete that he is saddled even with Zinnia's female troubles and remains unable to cure himself. The novel is a savvy skewering of the late Victorian zeal for magic potions and occult cures for healing all manners of ailments, from hair loss to broken hearts. Critical responses to Prose's novel were again almost uniformly positive. *Animal Magnetism* is filled with the droll social portraiture that was becoming the signature of her writing.

At this time Prose was ready for another move. She and Michels pulled up stakes and went to a farmhouse near Woodstock, New York, where Prose gave birth to their first son, Bruno, in 1978. With four adult novels and one children's book to her credit, her body of work and her personal life flourished. In 1979, Prose received her first National Endowment for the Arts grant. The literary world at least was taking notice. The next decade would usher in a new phase in the trajectory of Prose's career, one in which she would release her storytelling gifts into a new landscape and begin to explore characters closer to home.

SAINTS, HEARTS, BIGFOOT, AND WOMEN

The world with its weight of sorrow and inequity was very much with Francine Prose from the

beginning of the Reagan decade. Increasingly dissatisfied with scouring history Prose finally began rooting her characters firmly in the twentieth century, but American life in the modern world proved problematic for the novelist whose view was bracing yet deeply optimistic. As she told *Poets & writers*, "the eighties really finally got to me. i mean what was i thinking? what society did i imagine i was living in?" the maturing prose soon discovered the culture she was living in to be far less forgiving, magnanimous, or hopeful than she initially believed.

prose's thematic concerns began to turn from the idealistic mystical musings and the determined faithful optimism of her early work to a sharper-edged yet cooler take on contemporary life. this shift from the believer in miracles and a winking benevolent god to the eyebrow-raising skeptic wasn't sudden. rather, just as the photos of the dreamy, earthy, winsome bohemian in peasant dresses and long hair evolved subtly over time to photos of an intense and sophisticated writer in tailored shirts, so too did prose's writing undergo reconstruction. in fact, a whole generation of readers has never read the other francine prose and remains unaware of her first four books with their penchant for the supernatural, the magical, and the historic. however, for readers and critics who had been following prose, her next group of novels signaled that exciting moment the literati call "the breakthrough." no longer a writer's writer, francine prose was on her way to becoming a reader's writer.

the novel that marks this emergence is the irresistible *household saints* (1981). funny, strange to those unfamiliar with the old-world superstitions of italian culture, and accurate in depicting the nuances of speech and belief indigenous to italian americans in 1949, *household saints* demonstrates that prose had absorbed every detail of her brooklyn childhood then poured that stored up knowledge into the story of joseph santangelo, the sausage maker, and his wife, catherine falconetti. we know immediately that prose is up to wonderful tricks. within the first few pages she describes a september heat wave so relentless that "children three and four to a bed squirmed to escape each other's sweaty skin until . . . they

dozed off only to wake, moments later, stuck together like jelly apples." the heat also drives the pinochle players in the back room of santangelo's sausage shop a little mad. what else besides the relentless heat can explain lino falconetti's betting his daughter catherine in a card game played on the feast day of san gennaro? joseph santangelo wins her. for the residents of new york's painstakingly depicted little italy, joseph's winning hand is believed to be a fateful sign from god. joseph and catherine marry despite joseph's meddling widowed mother with her conviction that the evil eye is on him and his new wife. the elder mrs. santangelo finds miracles in all the wrong places. when a flower blooms she's sure the hand of god did it instead of daily watering. likewise she fails to see the truly miraculous springing from the implausible: her son's genuine love for a woman he won in a card game.

prose's exploration of perception versus reality, of faith versus reason is examined from every possible angle. when joseph and catherine give birth to theresa, household saints kicks into even higher gear. obsessed with tales of st. therese of the little flower, theresa santangelo begins mimicking her namesake's mystic devotion to god. the end result is theresa's untimely death. the question *was theresa a saint or merely psychotic*? hovers wherever the lines between the unexplainable and the prosaic converge as they do in this novel. more than in her earlier books, the ghosts of prose's literary influences—turgenev, gogol, pushkin, chekhov—are palpable. one feels prose debating the virtue of blind belief in favor of hardened realism as the story of joseph, catherine, and their obsessed daughter unfolds, but the author wisely leaves the verdict up to her readers. in *household saints* we get a glimpse of the postmodern battle between connectedness and randomness, a battle prose explores more fiercely and thoroughly in later work.

reviewing the novel for the july 12, 1981, issue of the *new york times*, randolph hogan says, "it's hard to convey the richness and the engaging complexity of this deceptively simple novel," which "deserves the widest possible audience,"

and he concludes that "francine prose is a splendid writer." hogan accurately sensed that prose's fifth novel would in fact introduce her fiction to a wider audience. *household saints* was optioned for film, and while it would be nearly ten years before it was produced, this cast a potentially lucrative halo around prose's work. for any solidly literary writer, breaking through the scrim that separates her from a large audience is as rare an occurrence as some of the extraordinary events in prose's own work. at a certain point, usually after producing a body of critically acclaimed fiction, most writers—even the most doubting—begin looking for a sign, evidence of good fortune intervening in their fate. breakthroughs usually happen in one of two ways: either through word of mouth, which then transforms a terrific book like prose's, and sometimes even a mediocre book, into a best seller; or through movie deals, which then send filmgoers flocking to the bookstores.

During this phase Prose was living the gypsy scholar life. With her family in tow, she was accepting one-year and one-semester visiting professorships all across the country. In 1982 she gave birth a second son, Leon, and by 1983 had published her sixth novel, *Hungry Hearts*. Prose then received her second NEA grant in 1985 and published the last of that decade's novels, *Bigfoot Dreams* (1986). In both *Hungry Hearts* and *Bigfoot Dreams*, Prose's trademark optimism and metaphysical musings still limn her fiction, but, especially in the latter, a new strain of realism heightens the tension. Weekly tabloid reporter Vera Perl is very much a contemporary woman in search of justification for the kinds of sleazy stories her publisher demands that she write. Clearly Vera sits in an uncomfortable driver's seat, both a purveyor and a victim of a culture easily seduced and addicted to hyperbolic headlines: UFO sightings, miraculous cancer cures, dubious resurrections, the capture of Bigfoot— the zanier, the better.

Vera never suspects that any of her made-up stories stand a chance of becoming real; she's merely doing her job while trying to balance the disappointments that loom large in her personal life. She writes to pacify her soulless publisher, to keep the supermarket tabloid *This Week* in the black, and to prevent her strained life with an uncommunicative spouse and daughter from falling apart. How could anything she writes for such a vapid market turn out to be true? But that's exactly what happens: fact becomes stranger than fiction, and Vera is forced to confront the power of her own inventiveness. The novel spins off the old adage "be careful what you wish for, you just might get it." On the one hand Prose lacerates a public bloated from a diet of pop culture and impossible stories, while on the other she applauds the power of imagination and the written word. The contrast between the facile, easily digestible tales that Vera invents and the tricks with which she makes her readers suspend disbelief ratchets up the high-wire tension in this novel.

Although Vera is threatened with a lawsuit by real people who coincidentally resemble ones whom she is perfectly aware she invented for the sake of a good story, she gleans some satisfaction from knowing she has been so seductive that readers believe the unfathomable: that a fountain of youth flows in Brooklyn from the home of Dr. Martin Green. Vera loses everything. She despairs over her losses, but like the cryptobiologists she meets who refuse to abandon their beliefs in strange occurrences, Vera ultimately decides that being a seeker—even when the object of pursuit is slippery and mythical at best—is still preferable to a limited faith in the visible, tangible, and verifiable.

Writing about a writer is always a risky proposition for a novelist; among readers and critics alike lurks the suspicion that the novelist is making a case for her own talents. That Prose is able to avoid this caveat and make Vera an authentic and fully realized writer in her own right is part of the novel's triumph. Sadly, artistic triumph was trumped by real-life sorrow. The year *Bigfoot Dreams* was published, Prose's father died. At the same time, a society that was being nursed on greed as it inched toward a massive savings and loan scandal, a society that would before the decade's close witness both the tearing down of the Berlin Wall and the collapse of the San Francisco-Oakland Bay Bridge, gave

Prose pause. But it was her father's death that made her turn inward and begin to question her depictions of a benign universe where miracles were plausible. Metaphysics as she penned it lost some of its allure. She framed it as a rhetorical question to *Poets & Writers*: "What's the point of playing with it when it's so irrelevant at the time you need it?"

This retreat from the metaphysical might in some ways account for Prose's rise in journalism, for she had also begun writing her *New York Times* column "Hers" in addition to a variety of nuts-and-bolts articles on child rearing for parenting magazines and accessible pieces for mainstream slick magazines such as *Redbook*. Fact-based and literal, Prose's early journalism is tinted with her trademark humor, but the articles and essays are tamer by virtue of their audience-specific guidelines. There are no leaps to the supernatural; instead Prose delivers solid writing in elegant prose. She also took a break from novel writing, from the burden of creating whole worlds, and turned her talents to the exacting task of illuminating life-altering moments with her short fiction.

Her last book of the 1980s was the short story collection *Women and Children First: Stories* (1988). Disarming, mournful, funny, incisive, the collection demonstrates that Prose may choose any form—novel, journalism, personal essay, short fiction—and possess it, much the same way the dybbuks (a Yiddish word for wandering spirits that inhabit living persons) possessed the characters in her earliest novels. Whereas Prose left Vera Perl seeking comfort atop a canyon ridge in *Bigfoot Dreams*, her first short story collection picks up where we left Vera. Nearly every character in the twelve stories that comprise this stunning collection is searching—for reason, for connection, for a faith that isn't a sham or a convenient panacea in troubled times. The stories ask questions rather than confirm beliefs. For instance: What does it mean to be granted an audience with the Dalai Lama? How will it change one's life? How will "spiritual homework" enrich one's life? What news of the world should a son bring to his dying father that will assuage the emotional aridity between them? The

questions raised in each of the stories suggest Prose's surfacing doubts about maintaining a naive faith in the modern world.

This thematic and technical change in Prose's narratives, her confidence in showing her characters' unease or allowing them to unravel without rushing in to rescue them with a miracle or an answer defined her port of entry to the status of a mature, wise writer. The fantastic barely intervenes in these stories. In fact Prose herself, apparently more secure in her writing skills if not her beliefs, remains pleasantly mute in this fiction. Situations and characters take center stage while their author is content to shepherd them along from the sidelines. For example, in the title story "Women and Children First," Janet is surprised to discover how much the possibility of an extrasensory connection with her son Kevin means to her. At her business partner Gordie's suggestion, she takes Kevin to doctors studying ESP. In the process Janet becomes shocked at her ex-husband Will's jealousy of the mother-child bond. "I guess everybody wants everything," she says. Janet does not seem aware of her own insensitivity to Will nor of the truth of her casually delivered comment, but Prose trusts the reader to get it.

The poignancy, humor, and biting wit that once called more attention to the author now rises from within the characters themselves. Prose is content to let her observations, idiosyncratic vision, and humor emanate from the story and work its powerful magic. Her choice of present tense for many of the stories strengthens the reader's perception that these characters are flesh-and-blood people whom one might encounter on the street, in the supermarket, or at a PTA meeting. These characters are us: mothers, teachers, sons, wives. With the exception of Joseph and Catherine in *Household Saints*, Prose's previous characters, however endearing and compelling, inhabited foreign kingdoms, other centuries, marginal occupations, and more often than not they were portrayed as larger than life. Readers were aware of the artifice, aware that they were reading legends.

Many of the stories in the collection open with a character's decision to seek relief or affirmation

from some external source, but they end with a bittersweet moment of self-recognition rather than a finite solution. Ceci, a kindergarten teacher in "Tibetan Time," is seeking relief from nights alone wasted crying over the end of her marriage. She hopes a mountaintop Buddhist retreat she visits will be the antidote to her loneliness, but by the conclusion of the story, while practicing a breathing meditation the Lama recommends, "It began to seem to her that her problems were, when one took the larger view, really very manageable, and rather small." After a decade of offering miracles to her characters, Prose leaves the protagonists of this collection in charge of their own fates.

In 1989, Prose received a Guggenheim Foundation grant for her body of published work and the proposed work to come. The award made both a fitting capstone and a threshold—a good indication of a writer poised on the cusp of great change.

PROSE EVERYWHERE

Throughout the 1990s it seemed the name Francine Prose was everywhere. One might pick up the latest copy of a literary magazine such as *Ploughshares* and find her name listed in the table of contents, or open the Sunday *New York Times* and find her byline on a travel article, or purchase a copy of *Harper's* magazine and read her cultural criticism. Prose was unstoppable, the full flower of her talents scenting everything from fiction to journalism. The conscious decision to accept commissioned writing served her well. As a critic she let her more excoriating opinions fly freely, no longer needing to temper or camouflage them in her fiction. The result was fiction deeply rooted in characterization, meticulously rendered settings, and nonfiction so forthright that readers began looking forward to savoring Prose's insights. In addition to her newfound visibility in journalism, she would also publish two books for children during this time. She couldn't have made a wiser decision. Children's literature provided the perfect receptacle for retelling legends, dispensing morality tales, and conjuring dybbuks;

her children's books are the natural reservoir for her love of the magical and mystical.

In the meantime Prose published to rave reviews *Primitive People* (1992), her first novel since *Bigfoot Dreams* six years earlier. The novel scathingly indicts cultural narcissism as seen through the eyes of one of Prose's most loveable and fully realized characters, the Haitian au pair, Simone. Set in the Hudson River Valley outside New York City, Simone (another betrayed and brokenhearted heroine) has fled her native country to soothe her damaged ego after her painter boyfriend Joseph (whose career hits the wall in Haiti's decline) runs off with her friend Inez.

In Port-au-Prince, Simone was chief assistant to the United States Cultural Attaché; on weekends she assisted Joseph in his gallery, encouraging patrons to buy his art. Prose writes, "Even so, even with the daily riots and killings and strikes, Simone might have stayed in Haiti. . . . Inertia would have reconciled her to remaining where she was, insofar as you could be reconciled to gunfire rattling all night and the smoke of burning cars hanging over the morning." Little does Simone know that the life she's about to embark on as caregiver to Rosemary Porter's two sullen children, George and Maisie, will sometimes feel as savage as the country she left. Simone's interaction with the Porters teaches her a bracing lesson about the ugly Americans and their shameless ignorance of other cultures and of themselves.

But that's only the surface appeal of this terrific novel; the universality of betrayal and its consequences is the novel's real subject. Prose's conceit—the native of an impoverished, strife-torn country of primitives meets the true primitives in an American mansion on the Hudson—couldn't be more appropriate, giving the writer ample room to display her storytelling gifts and her talent for crafting perfect sentences. Throughout the novel Prose modulates outright hilarity and expertly dispensed sympathy; her observations on men and women, family savagery, and self-serving friendships are dead-on.

Rosemary Porter, a mouton-wearing sculptress who often forgets she's a mother, is also capable

of slaying the reader with bits of truth: "One advantage of having money and talent is that one can get away with looking as if one slept in one's clothes." What Rosemary Porter doesn't need to say is that another advantage of wealth and talent is that it excuses all manner of disregard: self-absorption, failure to pay Simone for her duties, and at its worst, her darkly comic yet wrenching capriciousness when it comes to George and Maisie's needs for a mother they can count on.

In this chronicle of betrayal and heartbreak, no one and nothing escapes Prose's satiric assessment, not even the state roads. "Connecticut and Virginia . . . the most fascist states in the nation. What I hate is how suddenly the side of the road gets so *coiffed*," the hairdresser Kenny tells Simone. Prose is wicked, no doubt about it, but what makes the novel special is that she also is often tender: "Sometimes in Haiti embassy people semi-adopted streetchildren, whom they gently returned to the street at the end of their tours of duty. For the first time Simone understood how this love could have been a real love. How gratifying, how heady it was to hold a child's interest and attention."

Kirkus gave Prose a starred review, and top book reviewers across the country hailed her accomplishment. It appeared that there was nothing she couldn't write well. In 1993 the film version of *Household Saints*, starring Tracey Ullman, hit the screen, and that year Prose also published another short story collection, *The Peaceable Kingdom* (1993). As the title suggests, these eleven stories are perhaps Prose's quietest and most elegant; certainly they are among her best. "Rubber Life" had been awarded a Pushcart Prize in 1992, and "Dog Stories" had been included in *The Best American Short Stories*, 1991. Following the intense breakneck pace of *Primitive People*, these stories unfurl slowly, focus on domestic scenes, and are laced with a kinder sensibility. An eerie sense of loss permeates the collection; apparitions show up in the form of a talking dog. The most significant change in Prose's fiction is her surprising remedy for domestic disturbance and loss. Ironically the elixir isn't at all new: time.

It is shocking to receive such a simple, nearly platitudinous cure from the same author who once depended upon voodoo, miracles, magnetists, and ghosts. The narrative control Prose exerts over these stories is nothing less than perfect. Though rarely cited by critics, the final story in the collection, "Hansel and Gretel," is the kingpin, the best example of the complex use of temporal distance that marks each of the narratives in the collection. "This was twenty years ago," the heroine Polly tells the reader, "but I can still recall the weariness that came over me as I looked at Lucia's photos."

Initially the authorial distance seems simple. Polly will tell a story from her past. And she does tell the story of her ill-fated marriage to Nelson and the numbing weekend they spent visiting his old girlfriend's mother Lucia in Vermont. The reader winces at Nelson's callous dismissals and betrayals. Our hearts break as Nelson and Lucia, an artist working on a series of photographs of herself having sex with her cat, reminisce about her daughter, Marianna. We feel Polly's mortification when Nelson asks her to sit in the backseat of Lucia's car and Polly's shock when he turns away from her in bed. Like Grimm's Hansel and Gretel, Polly is lost in the woods at the mercy of a witchy artist, but in Prose's story Nelson does not fit the role of Gretel's comforting brother, nor is he a loving husband to Polly. Prose carefully lays a soundtrack into the story. The piece is from Mozart's opera *Così fan tutte*, a mournful song that hinges on a painful joke. Three women mourn the departure of their lovers. The women's voices are suffused in sadness, but the leave-taking is a hoax, a test. The men disguise themselves as Albanians and come back to see if they are missed and their women are remaining true to them. Lucia plays the recording over and over as "one of [her] projects." Her idea is to play it "until the audience cannot stand it and runs screaming out of the room," because even "the most fantastic Mozart becomes unbearable after a while."

How will Polly's story end? In a stroke of narrative genius, Prose leaps ahead twenty years. Polly is in Vermont again with her second

husband and their children, visiting friends who mention Lucia. Polly says, "What shocked me was that my friends had known someone who seemed to belong to a whole other existence." She wonders "how often the future waits on the other side of the wall, knocking . . . too politely for us to hear." Now that Polly knows her story ends happily even though it took twenty years, she longs to reach back into the narrative to tell her former self that "her sorrows would end," that "What would rescue her was time itself and, above all, its inexorability, the utter impossibility of anything ever staying the same." Polly understands the limits of narrative, the necessity of waiting, our lack of control over our stories. Trying to warn her former self would have been much like interrupting the Mozart song to tell the grieving women, "Don't worry … there is nothing to fear but your own true love, disguised as an Albanian." The women would not have listened; they are obliged by their own desire and the limits of the song to make the discovery at the right time.

This is writing of the highest order—coincidence, fairy tale, realism, and narrative control synthesized into a seamless whole. Every story in *The Peaceable Kingdom* moves in similar temporal dimensions and shows Prose's seemingly effortless skill—and her heart. The same heart and sophistication are lacking in her next novel, *Hunters and Gatherers* (1995), which satirizes the New Age goddess movement. Martha, a heroine dissatisfied with her job as a fact checker at a trendy New York magazine, has been left by her boyfriend, Dennis. During a weekend visit to Fire Island she stumbles upon the goddess group in midritual and jumps into the ocean to save its leader, Isis Moonwagon. Before she can protest, Martha is co-opted into the group. Later, during a sojourn out West, she discovers that life with the New Age goddesses can be as rife with pettiness, jealousy, carping, and irritation as any relationship with a man. Repetitive and chatty, all too soon the machinations of the goddess group begin to sound more like a pajama party gone haywire, with all the women in premenstrual syndrome, than a fully realized story about women one wants to spend time with.

If that is the point Prose intended to make it's a one-note complaint, not comparable to the novelistic talents on display in *Primitive People* or the profound and resonant *Peaceable Kingdom*.

In 1996, Prose and her family returned to life in Manhattan, and a year later she tried her hand at yet another narrative form: the novella. "Guided Tours of Hell" and "Three Pigs in Five Days," published together in *Guided Tours of Hell* (1997), are set in contemporary Prague and Paris, respectively, where the protagonists, like many of Prose's protagonists, are seeking rescue from their own tortured minds and souls. In the title novella, Landau, a Jewish, New York college professor, hopes that during the four days he's attending the First International Kafka Congress he will be able to slough off his outrage and hurt at seeing listeners dozing during his reading. He's also determined to find something good to say about the star conferee, Jiri Krakauer, and to relieve himself of his pernicious and insane jealousy of Jiri's having survived the Holocaust. Jiri has written memoirs and poems of surviving the death camp. Landau inappropriately worries that his play, based on the letters of Felice, Kafka's badly treated lover, is simply small potatoes, not worth the time or paper it's written on. Of course the real cause of Landau's envy is not Jiri's work or even his survival from something too hideous to contemplate.

When the group takes a package tour of the camp where Jiri was imprisoned as a child, the reader discovers that Landau resents both Jiri's proprietary knowledge of the camp and his attractiveness, popularity, and annoying (to Landau) good cheer despite his authentic hardships. Jiri regales the group with stories of how he tricked the commandant, stole his torturer's girlfriend, and managed to escape through a tunnel. Each time Jiri speaks, Landau's envy solidifies in his heart like rock candy. Landau wants to believe Jiri is a fake, even a thief, who stole Primo Levi's stories of survival and passes them off as his own recollections in order to garner more sympathy and admiration than Landau thinks even a Holocaust survivor deserves. Yet Landau's mental gymnastics cannot save him. Jiri possesses the

qualities that the narcissistic, self-defeating, venal Landau lacks and may never have. As the group tours the camp-cum-ghoulish-theme-park where the former gas-dispensing showers have been turned into a movie theater showing documentaries, Landau cannot manage empathy. He wants to feel the horror, but he is missing the quality central to being human—a heart. The only perspective he can understand, and that one just barely, is his own.

Prose's choice to situate the reader inside Landau's head creates the claustrophobic sensation of merciless self-imposed emotional and mental imprisonment. She exquisitely suggests that Jiri's spirit, his soul, his faith in himself is the real reason he survived the unbearable. The novella ends on a dark note of self-loathing: "Jiri is right: Landau would feel better, he would have been better off if something or someone had picked him up and thrown him into the abyss."

Nina, the travel-writer heroine of the second novella, *Three Pigs in Five Days*, suffers from a similar emotional imprisonment, but of an entirely different nature. Her twin nemeses are lack of trust and an emotional neediness that borders on juvenile idolatry. Her lover, Leo, is also her boss, and until this particular travel-writing trip, they have always come to Paris together. What triggers Nina's maelstrom of anxiety and paranoia begins before she ever steps onto Parisian soil. This time Leo has bought only one plane ticket. Although they've been lovers for quite some time, Nina is too shocked, wounded, and afraid to ask Leo directly if he'll be joining her in Paris. This is the first hint that the man she has anointed the love of her life is far less emotionally available to her than she thinks. Slowly, as readers inhabit Nina's bones and thought processes, they discover in bits and pieces all the clues Nina has been denying. Leo is fairly easy to spot as a seducer, a player, a nonbeliever in deep and abiding love whom Nina has knighted a prince.

That the reader understands this before Nina does is a narrative risk with a fifty-fifty chance of succeeding. Nina's doubts and twisted paranoid thoughts about love, her incessant yearning, and her doubt about Leo's intentions run a chance of tiring readers or—worse—boring them. Fortunately the inner workings of Nina's mind induce sympathy and, surprisingly, anger. Like a stealth missile we don't even detect, protective feelings for Nina explode as if we are her best friends trying to save her from more heartache at the hands of this snake in the grass.

By the time Leo arrives in Paris, Nina's fear that their relationship is unraveling and the anxiety this fear has cost her begin to shed new light on the man she adores. Over the course of several days, the chinks in his armor become visible to Nina as well. Finally during a tour of the Conciergerie, the thirteenth-century Revolutionary Prison, when Leo strikes up a conversation with Susanna Rose and her daughter Isadora, ignoring Nina in much the same way Nelson slights Polly in "Hansel and Gretel," Nina hopes for a soothing message from ghosts of prisoners past. When it becomes clear that the tragedies of the past can't save her, Nina breaks loose from her mental prison. "Then Nina was outside herself. Absent. Visiting Cathedrals."

In a stunning denouement, the least likely messenger of hope is the too real Susanna Rose, who tells Nina the story of Georges-Jacques Danton, whose wife died suddenly while he was away in the Revolution. Susanna reports that Danton's grief was so unbearable he dug up his wife's grave and sobbed as he held her corpse in his arms. As Nina and Leo leave the prison, Leo tells Nina that Susanna forgot to mention that Danton married a young woman a year after his great display of grief. But amazingly Leo's former power to dissuade Nina from her beliefs, to keep her off balance about his feelings for her, no longer works. Nina's story ends with her reaffirmed belief in "the existence of love beyond reason" and the knowledge that Leo was never, and will never become, that love.

Reviews of Prose's novellas were mixed, caroming between raves and low-key though not faint appreciation. However, the busy Francine Prose was already happily engaged in other projects. She gave up full-time teaching and indulged her journalistic side, writing essays for *Harper's* magazine that sparked incredible controversy. The writer who had staked her claim

on skewering the culture took high school teachers to task in an unsparing essay titled "I Know
Why the Caged Bird Cannot Read." Prose tore
into the revered canon of high school reading
lists, toppling the golden calf *To Kill a Mockingbird*, mocking Maya Angelou's *I Know Why the
Caged Bird Sings*, and pretty much decimating
the books considered to be cornerstones of
American high school literature classes. As if
that weren't enough, she turned her withering
judgment on teachers as well, suggesting that
laziness prevented them from revising the list or
engaging their students in precise line-by-line
reading. Is it any wonder, her essay asks, our
high school students can neither read nor write as
well as they should? The essay, which fails to
provide a solution in the form of a new and
improved list, sparked fury among educators and
writers alike. Letters to the editor poured in,
admonishing Prose for criticizing the sacred, for
being elitist, and in some cases for not knowing
what she was talking about.

Despite criticism from readers and shock from
fellow writers, Prose remained unflappable. Right
or wrong is beside the point; she made people
think about their choices in ways they had not
thought of them before. She may have ruffled
feathers, but none of the birds boycotted her
work. Instead quite the opposite happened. Prose
penned "Scent of a Woman's Ink" for *Harper's*
and reopened the argument that women writers
do not receive the same acclaim, respect, or
awards as their male counterparts. Norman Mailer
was one of Prose's easy targets. More times than
anyone cares to acknowledge Mailer has made
his disdain for female authors abundantly clear,
criticizing Virginia Woolf among others.

In 1999, Prose shared her wealth of writing
expertise in a book titled *Writers on Writing*.
Along with other luminaries in her field, Prose
discusses her own work, its strengths and weaknesses, and dispenses advice on writing well.
Meanwhile she was spending at least four days a
week in the New York Public Library as the
recipient of the Director's Fellowship. Recipients
receive a fifty-thousand-dollar stipend, propose a
project, and then use the library setting and
sources to complete it. With her next novel slated

for publication in 2000, Prose decided her next
work would be nonfiction.

THE ARC EXTENDS: THE FULL MEASURE OF HER POWERS

Washed-up creative writing professors seemed to
capture the public imagination in the year 2000.
Michael Chabon's *Wonder Boys*, a novel about a
Pittsburgh writer whose career and personal life
are in shambles, became a major motion picture.
And Francine Prose offered up her story of Ted
Swenson, a creative writing professor at Euston
College in rural Vermont. When *Blue Angel* opens
the reader discovers that, similar to Chabon's
hero, Prose's Ted Swenson is a likable if disenchanted novelist, a one-time literary luminary
who hasn't published another novel in ten years.
In twenty-one years of marriage he's never
cheated on his wife, Sherrie, who works as the
school nurse, and in fact he still feels lust for her.
And Ted's a decent if cloddish father to his
daughter, Ruby, who isn't speaking to him
because he broke up her relationship with Euston's bad boy, Matt McIlwaine, a move that
returns to haunt him.

Far from scintillating, Swenson's life coasts
pleasantly enough on cruise control. At least he's
in better shape than the art history professor at
the neighboring state university who has been
fired from his job for murmuring *yum* while
showing slides of Greek sculptures of female
torsos. A collegiate atmosphere where even a
benign comment sounds like sexual harassment
catches Ted Swenson between wariness and finding intelligent inoffensive ways to discuss his
students' short stories. How to parse a story in
which people have sex with animals and, in one
of them, sex with a roasted chicken out of the
fridge? Is delicacy even possible? Swenson's
only talented student is Angela Argo, a green-
haired, leather-clad, pierced wonder girl who
enlists him to read, chapter by chapter, her novel.

Since creativity and seduction often make
natural bedfellows, how many choices are there
for a middle-aged male writer and an odd but
gifted co-ed in the frosty climate of political correctness? They are not Heloise and Abelard, after

all. And with a title taken directly from the Marlene Dietrich film, an affair between Swenson and Argo is a fait accompli. But Prose, forever full of surprises, turns *Blue Angel* into that compelling thing, a solidly good novel. Her insight, dark humor, inside knowledge of university life with its Byzantine protocols and foibles, combined with flawless sentences, manage to make Swenson "the kind of guy who can have no idea what's going on until after it's happened." Readers of Prose have seen sympathetic portraits of her male characters in the past. Rather than paint men bad and women good, Prose is judicious and fair when it comes to gender. *Blue Angel* makes the point—that men are more often stupid than they are merciless cads, and that when it comes to writing, ambition knows no gender—in the same way Chekhov may have made it: compassionately.

In this book Prose carves biting comedy (everyone in the novel seems to be reading *Jane Eyre* at the same time; the characters' reactions to it run through the book as a unifying trope and recurring joke) from the tension within Swenson's intellectually defined but emotionally untested moral code. Unfortunately Swenson is careful about the wrong things and pays little attention to the trail of crumbs he leaves in the wake of his relationship with Argo. True to form, Prose makes us question our judgments about these all-too-human characters. Often the reader is as mystified by Argo as Swenson is. Is Argo truly the wounded baby bird or a calculating opportunist who knows that one of the ways to the failed novelist's brain is through his ego and his pants? At other times the reader wonders about Ted. Is he a garden-variety cad or as clueless about Angela Argo as he seems? Amazingly, given the ordinariness of the situation, what happens to Ted and Angela is anything but hackneyed. Ted Swenson is undone, not by his flaws but by his integrity. Prose emerges as a novelist in full possession of her characters, her themes, and her vision. Swenson may be the first of her protagonists who takes an unpopular stand despite what it will cost him—and feels at peace with himself. Prose's *Blue Angel* met with rave

responses and earned a nomination for the National Book Award.

Never one to rest on her accomplishments, Prose's *Lives of the Muses* was published in 2002. Critics asked, Why muses? Francine Prose? With her searing sensibility, her satirical tongue? The answer is, Who other than Francine Prose? The subject matter is fitting Prose territory. Writing it demanded all of her skills: scholarship, love of history, journalistic precision, and empathy. Its title is not a far stretch from the book Prose read and admired as a girl: *The Lives of the Saints*. Considering that in her youth Prose interpreted the stories of the saints' lives as fairy tales, it makes sense that the novelist who built her career combining the supernatural, the unexplainable, faith, and love should write about Gala Dalí, Hester Thrale, Lou Andreas-Salomé, Lee Miller, Suzanne Farrell, Elizabeth Siddal, Alice Liddell, Charis Weston, and Yoko Ono. In *The Lives of the Muses* Prose scours her vast trove of knowledge to create nine sparkling essays, employing a sharp biographer's eye and a passionate novelist's vision.

Prose's entry on serial muse Lou Andreas-Salomé, who appeared to cast a spell over three of the greatest minds of the twentieth century—Friedrich Nietzsche, Rainer Maria Rilke, and Sigmund Freud—is like revisiting the mysterious Marie Laveau. In thrall to Lou's intelligence, wounded by her capricious sexuality yet transfixed nonetheless, each man wrote his best work after Lou had worked her magic on him. And like Prose's voodoo queen who managed to influence politicians, Lou casts a wide shadow over philosophy, poetry, and psychology.

The quirky experimentation of *Animal Magnetism* is recalled in the essay on Lee Miller, whose casual flicking of a light switch led Man Ray to the photographic process of solarization. Man Ray would never be free of Miller, Prose writes. In fact the gifted Ray was jealous of Miller, who modeled for *Vogue* and had been her father's photographic muse long before meeting Ray. Ray was at once admiring and possessive of the woman he could never possess. The magnetism between Miller and Man Ray was intense. After she left him, Miller enjoyed fame as a photogra-

pher for *Vogue*, a muse who gave the world some of the most unforgettable pictures of World War II.

As for similarities to slavish devotion and subservience that Prose depicted in *Household Saints*, one need look no further than Lizzie Siddal, Dante Gabriel Rossetti's muse, who in her devotion to him became ill posing for his painting of Ophelia's drowning. Lizzie lay in a cold bath while Rossetti painted, never complaining of the discomfort. Half of Lizzie's life was spent in an opium haze, yet she willingly cast aside her own painting and offered herself as Rossetti's version of Dante's Beatrice, albeit a drug-addicted and suicidal one.

The usual suspects, Zelda Fitzgerald and Rodin's protégé and muse, Camille Claudel, are missing. Perhaps since Prose devoted a section of *Guided Tours of Hell* to Rodin, she didn't want to cover that territory again. But the book is rich enough without them. Prose's muses make excellent subjects and provide plenty of room to explore their roles in their artists' lives. One of the questions Prose's book raises is: Can a man be a muse?

Mutual museship certainly applies to the relationship between the great choreographer George Balanchine and prima ballerina Suzanne Farrell. There is only a blank space without a dancer to fill it, and little left to the ballerina without a choreographer. In the case of Balanchine and Farrell, Prose suggests that it may have been Farrell's unavailability—similar to Alice Liddell's unavailability to Charles Dodgsen— that fanned the flames of ardor and achievement for the artist. As Prose points out, Balanchine had married each of his former muses; Farrell always floated somewhere out of his reach. In a sense she is the closest to the original Greek concept of the muse: goddess, ethereal, present but untouchable. In fact the ballet world is predicated on such relationships, a point Prose could have brought more into focus. It's no accident that the phrase "he made that ballet on her" requires a muse. There's no greater compliment to a dancer's artistry and no better feather in a choreographer's cap than to discover and love the inspirational body—not person—that can perform his most taxing and imaginative ballets.

Of the nine women Prose presents, Suzanne Farrell and Alice Liddell (the girl who inspired *Alice's Adventures in Wonderland*) most embody her observation that the artists "rarely create *for* the muse, to win or keep the muse's love and admiration, but rather for themselves, for the world, and for the more inchoate and unquantifiable imperatives of art itself." In the case of Alice Liddell, Charles Dodgsen could hardly hope to win the love of his "child-guest." Farrell and Liddell's relationships with their artists are the purest examples of muse life.

Prose artfully depicts the artists' disinterested interest throughout the book. Nowhere is this more apparent than in her essay on Charis Weston, photographer Edward Weston's muse. The relationship was intensely sexual at its beginning, and Charis inspired many of Weston's most brilliant photographs, but by the late 1940s as Weston's work changed, neither Charis's beauty nor her wifely status interfered with Weston's intentions. Prose makes the chilling point that, when it comes to being a muse, the only way forward seems a rude step off the artist's pedestal.

The collection is meticulously researched, but Prose's advantage over many historians is her narrative gift. Each muse springs to life on the page. Prose's beautiful sentences, especially in the absence of a photograph, re-create them in words. Of a Lee Miller photograph, Prose writes, "The grainy, slightly blurred focus emphasizes the alien otherworldliness of the wrapped-up mummy whose white pillow and bandages cut diagonally across the image. His hands are swathed so thickly they look like boxing mitts." *Muses* may have been an exercise in an untried genre, yet just as Prose concludes that "all these muses loved and were loved by their artists," clearly she has loved them as well, which makes the book another triumph for the author.

In March 2005 the triumph could not be sweeter, when *A Changed Man* became her best work to date. Throughout her foregoing career Prose exhibited nearly magical shape-shifting

powers. In *A Changed Man* she offers a protagonist least likely to be liked and least likely to change: thirty-two-year-old Vincent Nolan, a tattooed neo-Nazi whose conversion impulse is triggered under suspicious circumstances at a rave while he is under the influence of Ecstasy. Meyer Maslow, a Holocaust survivor and the charismatic leader of World Brotherhood Watch, an organization devoted to peace and goodwill, and Meyer's assistant Bonnie Kalen, a divorced mother of two boys, become Vincent's mentors in conversion.

The story tests ideologies and moralities. Can a Jew who's survived a concentration camp even speak with a skinhead? Should Maslow (cagily named after the psychologist, Abraham Maslow, the father of the fifteen steps toward self-actualization) consider trusting Vincent? Given Maslow's fervent beliefs, he'd be a hypocrite not to. And when Meyer asks Bonnie to take in Vincent, what choice does she, a disciple of Maslow-think, have but to oblige? "Relax. It's only the footsteps of the Nazi moving in," Bonnie's son Danny thinks. It's an image, a sound that simultaneously stops the reader cold and fascinates. On every page Prose delivers images of equal power.

How seriously are we to consider Vincent's desire to change if his initial explanation for involvement in the Aryan Resistance Movement (ARM), a Nazi organization, is, "I was having a hard time." That's it? He becomes a card-carrying white supremacist because life wasn't so good? Yet Prose manages to convince that having a hard time is often the paltry reason du jour for guys like Vincent Nolan to shuck off their humanity in favor of intolerance and hatred. The novel satirically chronicles American society's worst political, social, and personal moments: Columbine, Waco, talk shows, neglect, abuse, the terrorist Timothy McVeigh's televised execution vigil. No one escapes the author's searing observations. Prose's point? Morality cannot be built on the broken backs of racism, greed, self-interest, intolerance, and exclusion. It's an all-or-nothing proposition. Either you believe and live kindness and peace, as Meyer Maslow espouses, or you don't. Halfway doesn't cut it. The human desire to do good is tenuous at best, especially when incentives for doing harm seem to offer more reward.

At the start of her career, in *Judah the Pious*, Prose gave us a rabbi on a mission. Eliezer wanted to convince the Polish king that denying the Jews their burial rites was the first step toward dehumanizing a race, that the rites should be reinstated. In that novel Prose relied on Hasidic legend and told a story at a far remove from contemporary life. *Judah* does not directly touch us. *A Changed Man* directly responds to and reflects our world, a brilliant reversal and an extraordinary conversion story for both Prose and her characters. This time the sage is not a rabbi. Instead the sage is Vincent Nolan come to persuade the Jewish charismatic leader to consider admitting him to World Brotherhood Watch, to believe that a Jew-hater can indeed transform himself—without miracles or apparitions from the supernatural—into "the messenger who has come to offer them a vision of the meaningful life before them."

Prose's guises always shift. No one can predict what she'll write next, only that it will be quintessential Prose—disarming, beautifully crafted, richly imagined. No one can predict what form it will take—novel, short story, memoir, journalism. But her message? Like Vincent Nolan's message, Prose's has always been the same: "Do good. *Be* good. Love your fellow humans. Be conscious. Change one heart at a time."

Selected Bibliography

WORKS OF FRANCINE PROSE

NOVELS

Judah the Pious. New York: Atheneum, 1973.
The Glorious Ones. New York: Atheneum, 1974.
Marie Laveau. New York: Berkley, 1977.
Animal Magnetism. New York: Putnam, 1978.
Household Saints. New York: St. Martin's, 1981.
Hungry Hearts. New York: Pantheon, 1983.

Bigfoot Dreams. New York: Pantheon, 1986.

Primitive People. New York: Farrar, Straus and Giroux, 1992.

Hunters and Gatherers. New York: Farrar, Straus and Giroux, 1995.

Blue Angel. New York: HarperCollins, 2000.

After. New York: HarperCollins, 2003. (Juvenile novel.)

A Changed Man. New York: HarperCollins, 2005.

NOVELLAS AND SHORT STORIES

Women and Children First: Stories. New York: Pantheon, 1988.

The Peaceable Kingdom: Stories. New York: Farrar, Straus and Giroux, 1993.

Guided Tours of Hell: Novellas. New York: Metropolitan/Henry Holt, 1997.

CHILDREN'S BOOKS

Stories from Our Living Past. New York: Behrman, 1974.

Dybbuk: A Story Made in Heaven. Illustrated by Mark Podwal. New York: Greenwillow, 1996.

The Angel's Mistake: Stories of Chelm. Illustrated by Mark Podwal. New York: Greenwillow, 1997.

You Never Know: A Legend of the Lamed-Vavniks. Illustrated by Mark Podwal. New York: Greenwillow, 1998.

The Demons' Mistake: A Story from Chelm. Illustrated by Mark Podwal. New York: Greenwillow, 2000.

NONFICTION

The Lives of the Muses: Nine Women and the Artists They Inspired. New York: HarperCollins, 2002.

Sicilian Odyssey. Washington, D.C.: National Geographic Society, 2003.

Gluttony: The Seven Deadly Sins. New York: Oxford University Press, 2003.

OTHER WORKS

"The Arrival of Eve." In *Gates to the New City: A Treasury of Modern Jewish Tales*. Edited by Howard Schwartz. New York: Avon, 1983.

"The Seven Month Home." In *A Place Called Home: Twenty Writing Women Remember*. Edited by Mickey Pearlman. New York: St. Martin's, 1996.

Introduction to *Master Breasts: Objectified, Aestheticized, Fantasized, Eroticized, Feminized by Photography's Most Titillating Masters*. Edited by Melissa Harris. New York: Aperture, 1998.

Janis. Screenplay by Francine Prose. Directed by Nancy Savoca. Redeemable Features, 1999. (Produced screenplay.)

"What Makes a Short Story?" In *On Writing Short Stories*. Edited by Tom Bailey. New York: Oxford University Press, 2000.

"Learning from Chekhov." *Western Humanities Review* 41:1–14 (spring 1987).

"Good Guy, Bad Guy." *Antioch Review* 49:538–550 (fall 1991). (Short story.)

"Small Miracles." *Redbook*, December 1992, p. 70.

"She and I … and Someone Else." *Antaeus* 73/74:51–53 (spring 1994).

"In the Back Seat for Seven Years." *New York Times*, March 12, 1995, pp. 41–42. (Travel piece about driving with family to temporary appointments at universities around the U.S.)

"Outer City Blues." *New York Times Magazine*, April 21, 1996, p. 68.

"The Old Morgue." *Threepenny Review* 71 (fall 1997).

"The Lunatic, the Lover, and the Poet." *Atlantic Monthly*, March 1998, pp. 64–80. (Short story.)

"Hawks and Sparrows." *GQ: Gentleman's Quarterly*, April 1998, pp. 152–160.

"Scent of a Woman's Ink: Are Women Writers Really Inferior?" *Harper's*, June 1998, pp. 61–70.

"I Know Why the Caged Bird Cannot Read." *Harper's*, September 1999, pp. 76–84.

"A Wasteland of One's Own." *New York Times Magazine*, February 13, 2000. (Cultural criticism of Web sites aimed at women.)

"Trieste, Where Vienna Meets Venice." In *Italy: The Best Travel Writing from the New York Times*. New York: Abrams, 2005.

CRITICAL AND BIOGRAPHICAL STUDIES

Aarons, Victoria. "Responding to an Old Story: Susan Fromberg Schaeffer, Lesléa Newman, and Francine Prose." In *Daughters of Valor: Contemporary Jewish American Women Writers*. Edited by Jay L. Halio and Ben Siegel. Newark: University of Delaware Press, 1997.

Anastas, Benjamin. "A Brief and Risky Business: Nine Who Nurtured Artists." *New York Observer*, October 28, 2002. (Review of *The Lives of the Muses*.)

Asirvatham, Sandy. "Tipping Sacred Cows: The Enlightenment of Francine Prose." *Poets & Writers* 28:28–32 (May/June 2000).

Baker, John F. "Francine Prose." *Publishers Weekly*, April 13, 1992, pp. 38–39.

Bell, Pearl K. "The Artist as Hero." *New Leader* 57:17–18 (March 4, 1974). (Review of *The Glorious Ones*.)

Cruttwell, Patrick, and Faith Westburg. "Fiction Chronicle." *Hudson Review* 26:415–423 (summer 1973). (Includes a one-paragraph review of *Judah the Pious* on p. 421.)

Dear, Pamela S., ed. "Francine Prose." *Contemporary*

Authors. New Revision Series, vol. 46. Detroit: Gale, 1995. Pp. 305–308.

Graves, Laurie Meunier. "The Uncleanness of Desire." *Wolf Moon Press Journal*, September 23, 2004. (Review of *Gluttony*.)

Harlan, Megan. "Guided Tours of Hell." Salon.com (http://www.salon.com/sneaks/sneakpeeks961223.html).

Hertzel, Ellen Emry. "A story of nine women who found their destiny with celebrity." *USA Today* (http://www.usatoday.com/life/books/reviews/2002-09-18-muses_x.htm), September 18, 2002. (Review of *Lives of the Muses*.)

Hogan, Randolph. "The Butcher Won a Wife." *New York Times Book Review*, July 12, 1981, pp. 12, 37. (Review of *Household Saints*.)

Jones, Malcolm. "Smart Book, Dumb Guy: Updating *Blue Angel*." *Newsweek*, April 3, 2000, p. 81.

Kakutani, Michiko. "Stranger Than Fiction." *New York Times*, April 12, 1986, p. 12. (Review of *Bigfoot Dreams*.)

Lask, Thomas. "The Sage and the Gentleman." *New York Times*, February 17, 1973, p. 29. (Review of *Judah the Pious*.)

Lehmann-Haupt, Christopher. "The Professor's Still a Prof, but the Showgirl's a Student." *New York Times on the Web* (http://query.nytimes.com/gst/fullpage.html?res=9504E1D9163DF930A15750C0A9669C8B63), March 23, 2000. (Review of *Blue Angel*.)

Lodge, David. "Excess Baggage." *New York Times on the Web* (http://partners.nytimes.com/books/00/04/16/specials/prose-tours.html), January 12, 1997. (Review of *Guided Tours of Hell*.)

Mano, D. Keith. "Judah the Pious." *New York Times Book Review*, February 25, 1973, pp. 2–3.

Marowski, Daniel G., and Roger Matuz, eds. "Francine Prose." In *Contemporary Literary Criticism*, vol. 45. Detroit: Gale, 1987. Pp. 322–328.

May, Hal, ed. "Francine Prose." In *Contemporary Authors*, vol. 109. Detroit: Gale, 1983. P. 380.

Miller, Laura. "Are Men Better Writers Than Women?" Salon.com (http://www.salon.com/media/1998/06/03media.html), June 3, 1998. (Response to "Scent of a Woman's Ink.")

Orecklin, Michele. "A Teacher's Pet with Fangs." *Time*, April 10, 2000. (Review of *Blue Angel*.)

Potok, Rena. "Francine Prose." In *Jewish American Women Writers: A Bio-Bibliographical and Critical Sourcebook*. Edited by Ann R. Shapiro. Westport, Conn.: Greenwood Press, 1994.

Sage, Lorna. "Pictures from a Politically Correct Institution." *New York Times Book Review*, April 16, 2000, p. 2. (Review of *Blue Angel*.)

Spacks, Patricia Meyer. "Fiction Chronicle." *Hudson Review* 27:293–294 (summer 1974). (Includes a short review of *The Glorious Ones*.)

INTERVIEWS

Bolick, Katie. "As the World Thrums: A Conversation with Francine Prose." *Atlantic Online* (http://www.theatlantic.com/unbound/factfict/ff9803.htm), March 1998.

Eisenberg, Deborah. "Francine Prose." *Bomb* 45 (fall 1993).

Pearlman, Mickey. "Francine Prose." In *Inter/View: Talks with America's Writing Women*. Edited by Mickey Pearlman and Katherine Usher Henderson. Lexington: University Press of Kentucky, 1990.

SCOTT RUSSELL SANDERS

(1945—)

Jen Hirt

The repertory of praise given Scott Russell Sanders defines him as one of America's most astute and masterful writers. Spiritual, candid, elegant, luminous—such words routinely grace the back covers of his essay collections. Although he was regaled with academic scholarships and university trained as a physicist and literary critic, his language inhabits the sphere of the common. Sanders is a complex thinker who nonetheless conveys his observations with a clarity and honesty that have become his trademark. As a result, the audience for his books cuts like a cross section through the strata of society. In the introduction to his award-winning collection of essays, *The Paradise of Bombs* (1987), Sanders reveals how he approaches his task:

> For me the writing of a personal essay is like finding my way through a forest without being quite sure what game I am chasing, what landmark I am seeking. I sniff down one path until some heady smell tugs me in a new direction, and then off I go, dodging and circling, lured on by the calls of unfamiliar birds, puzzled by the tracks of strange beasts, leaping from stone to stone across rivers, barking up one tree after another. The pleasure in writing an essay—and, when the writing is any good, the pleasure in reading it—comes from this dodging and leaping, this movement of the mind. (xiii)

One reason that the movement of Sanders' mind has proven so interesting to readers is his perspective as an amateur jack-of-all-trades. Believing that society is plagued with trouble partly because individuals put too much weight on the words of experts and show so little faith in the commoner, Sanders sets out, in each essay, to demonstrate that he's a curious, thinking human being first and a writer and scholar second. His essays never lapse into academic lingo or postmodern fits of experiment. Such an even-handed approach has prompted a handful of dubious critics to label Sanders quaint and old-fashioned, a dreamy subscriber to the old-line activist notion that clarity, patience, and reason will always succeed. Reviewer Jeff Gundy concluded in 1994 that some readers will also be turned off by Sanders' perennial themes of family values and community conservation. But, opined Gundy, "I doubt that he would resist such a charge" (399).

Scott Russell Sanders has made a career out of steadfastly embracing midwestern family life and the wholesome vitality of the seemingly dull region of southern Indiana. "Home-centered but not homespun," Edward Lueders summarized in 1992. Others certainly agree. Sanders has won a Guggenheim Fellowship, a National Endowment for the Arts fellowship, and the Lannan Literary Award, among numerous other distinctions. In 2005 he was a professor of English at Indiana University, where he had been teaching since 1971. With a reputation as a master teacher, and as the author of a slew of widely anthologized essays, Sanders has been a highly sought-after speaker and instructor.

FAMILY, CHILDHOOD, AND EDUCATION

Sanders' childhood was characterized by uprooting, as his alcoholic father shifted from job to job across the South and Midwest. Each locale's opportunities had an impact on the young Sanders, such as watching inmates of a Tennessee prison work in farm fields, or roaming the backwoods of an Ohio arsenal. His early adulthood was also one of travel—both coasts, England, and Europe. The chronology of his life

265

is well documented in his essays because Sanders so often reaches into his past to understand his present.

Sanders' mother, Eva Mary Solomon, married Greeley Ray Sanders in 1939 in Chicago, Solomon's hometown. After the birth of a daughter, Sandra, in 1942, the family moved south to Mississippi. Greeley Sanders secured a wartime job loading shells at the Gulf Ordnance Plant. Eva Sanders found work as a medical researcher. Three years later, the family moved to Memphis, Tennessee, where Greeley Sanders made tires at Firestone. Scott Russell Sanders was born in Memphis on October 26, 1945. In his essay "Letter to a Reader" from his 1995 collection, *Writing from the Center,* Sanders says of his first home that it was "close enough to the Mississippi to give me an abiding love for rivers, far enough south to give me an abiding guilt over racism" (170). He read Mark Twain at the age of eight and his interest in books never waned.

In 1951 Greeley Sanders changed jobs again, heading north to the Ravenna Arsenal in Portage County, Ohio. The Sanders family, joined by a third child, Glen, in 1954, made the arsenal their home until 1956. Proximity to the munitions industry had a far-reaching impact on Sanders—references to the arsenal as a starting point for a dire future appear often in his writing. In "Letter to a Reader," Sanders confesses that the move "opened a fissure in me that I have tried to bridge, time and again, with words" (171). The next relocation was not so drastic; the family moved to a nearby farm on Esworthy Road in Charlestown Township. Sanders' teen years were defined by a lower-middle-class rural life and repressed frustration over his father's alcoholism, which was a family secret. Sanders graduated from Southeast High School in 1963. That year, the family returned south to Lake Charles, Louisiana, but Sanders headed east to Brown University in Rhode Island.

Physics held Sanders' attention until his senior year of college. He switched to English, had his first essay, "Nuclear Arms and Morality," published in the March 1966 issue of Brown's *Res Publica,* and graduated valedictorian in 1967. That year he was accepted into graduate school in England at Cambridge University. From 1967 to 1971 he pursued a Ph.D. in literature as a Marshall Scholar, a Danforth Fellow, and a Woodrow Wilson Fellow. His dissertation on D. H. Lawrence was well received and would be published two years later. Sanders wrote literary reviews for the *Cambridge Review* and served as editor, but he also had success publishing short stories. His first published fiction was "The Operation," a one-page story that appeared in the February 16, 1968, issue of the *Cambridge Review.* In much the same way that literature eclipsed his interest in physics, creative writing was becoming more appealing than literary criticism, but at the time, creative writing was not offered as a major.

Despite being offered teaching jobs in England, and despite the temptation of embracing the literary expatriate life, Sanders and his wife of four years, Ruth, returned to the United States in 1971. Both accepted teaching jobs at Indiana University in Bloomington—Scott in literature and Ruth in the sciences. The decision was fortuitous, as the location allowed Sanders to reconnect with strong roots. In "Letter to a Reader," Sanders explains his decision to inhabit the "unfashionable" Midwest: "Some editors and fellow writers have asked me, directly or indirectly, how I can bear to live in a backwater. I tell them there are no backwaters. There is only one river, and we are all in it" (*Writing from the Center*, p. 179). Over the next thirty years, Sanders would write and publish nine nonfiction books, seven works of fiction, and eight storybooks for children, in addition to hundreds of small-press publications ranging from science fiction to reporting to interviews. Taken altogether, his resume includes over 350 publications. His personal essays, for which he is most well known, have been anthologized in over fifty publications, such as *The Best American Essays* series and the cornerstone of nonfiction anthologies, *The Art of the Personal Essay.*

EARLY PUBLICATIONS: FICTION AND CRITICISM

Before his success as an essayist, Sanders was considered a novelist and literary critic. He was

also a young writer enduring the difficulties of finding his place and emerging into the publishing world. One of the most telling details of Sanders' early career is that he worked on multiple projects simultaneously, juggling short stories with novels with criticism without any guarantee of publication. While this multitasking would continue to define him, it became less evident as he matured as a writer. For example, from 1967 to 1984 Sanders worked on ten different projects in a mix of genres. The order in which these writings were published does not reflect the sequence in which Sanders focused on them. In some cases, by the time a book was published, Sanders had long since set aside his interest in that topic or genre and was on to different projects. By the late 1980s and early 1990s, Sanders was recognized as an established writer, so lag times between writing and publication shortened considerably. It is instructive to look at the early publications in terms of thematic connections rather than publication dates, and to study the nonfiction publications in terms of their chronological development.

Sanders' first scholarly task upon his return to the Midwest was to revise his dissertation on D. H. Lawrence and find a publisher. *D. H. Lawrence: The World of the Major Novels,* was published in 1973 in London, followed by a stateside printing in 1974. It was Sanders' first and only book-length work of criticism. The British writer David Herbert Lawrence (1885–1930) is perhaps best known for his novel *Lady Chatterley's Lover,* published in 1928. Sanders critiqued how Lawrence's fiction was a response to historical developments by analyzing each novel in terms of what it said about culture and nature. As Sanders explains in "Letter to a Reader," he chose to write about Lawrence because he felt they shared similar backgrounds—both had alcoholic fathers, both grew up in rural places, both received privileged educations through scholarships. "Whatever [the dissertation] may reveal about Lawrence, it says a great deal about me" (*Writing from the Center* 176).

In 1973 Sanders' life changed with the birth of his daughter, Eva, and he siphoned time from the academically esteemed realm of literary criticism to begin work on a novel. Despite these creative and domestic demands, Sanders served as the 1974–1975 writer in residence at Phillips Exeter Academy in Exeter, New Hampshire. Financial support came in the form of a Bennett Fellowship. During this time he not only finished the manuscript of his novel, titled "Warchild," but also returned to the study of short fiction. Recognition, however, remained elusive. Excerpts from the novel appeared in the spring 1974 issue of the *Berkeley Samisdat Review* and the July 1978 issue of *Center,* but Sanders was unsuccessful in publishing "Warchild" in book form. Sanders concedes in "Letter to a Reader" that the novel's zealous attempt to chronicle the "decline of industrial civilization and the death of nature" resulted in a "botched" project that was "better off ... in a box on my shelf" (*Writing from the Center* 180). The short stories he wrote in Cambridge and the new fiction he was writing in Exeter would not be published for nearly a decade. At the end of his residency, he returned to Indiana with various manuscripts but no publishers.

In 1977 his son, Jesse, was born, and from 1978 to 1979 the entire family followed Sanders to Eugene, Oregon, for a sabbatical. Taking full advantage of time off from teaching, Sanders worked on a series of short stories about the settlement of America; finished a second novel; began a science fiction novel; and finally began writing the personal essays that would earn him widespread praise. During this time, the small presses were quick to accept Sanders' reviews, short stories, and criticism. Between 1976 and 1980 he added sixty-five publication credits to his resume. By 1982 he had finished his first science fiction narrative, but his second novel was still waiting for acceptance. Major publication remained out of reach.

Persistence and simple stubbornness paid off. Before the year's end, the publishing house of William Morrow accepted the short story collection, titled *Wilderness Plots,* heralding the historical fiction phase of Sanders' writing. Subtitled *Tales about the Settlement of the American Land,* the collection was released in 1983, illustrated with pencil sketches by the artist Dennis B.

Meehan. Sanders had started writing the stories nine years before while in New Hampshire, finishing the collection during the Oregon sabbatical, which is an interesting feat, considering the historical and regional nature of the stories. The fifty vignettes—most no longer than two pages—capture the successes and failures of settlers in the Ohio River Valley from 1778 until 1861.

Sanders purposefully avoided retelling traditional folklore. In the foreword, he explained, "I have written about the unmemorialized common folk, the carpenters and farmers, the fierce parents and moonstruck lovers, the sort of people who, in all ages, have actually made human history" (7). The common folk he sought to memorialize were also real people, and the events that are narrated actually happened, while the emotional reactions of the characters and the descriptions of the landscape were reimagined by Sanders. He culled the plots from historical research, noting in his foreword that "often I had no more than a sentence to work from, rarely more than a paragraph" (7). The vignettes are narrative summaries, in which a period of years might be covered in one sentence. Although traditional in tone and structure, one vignette, "The Philosophical Cobbler," was selected for an edition of *Flash Fiction: Seventy-two Very Short Stories*—an anthology usually reserved for experimental fiction.

Shelved as fiction, *Wilderness Plots* is a mix of nonfiction and fiction. The vignette "The Naming of Names," for example, is a lyrical meditation on how parts of Ohio were known by Indian names, then renamed by white settlers, even though many rivers retained their Indian monikers. There is no main character, only a broad conflict, and Sanders' sympathies are evident in his critical tone toward the white settlers' place names. At the other end of the spectrum, Sanders writes detailed dialogue between characters in "The Multiplication of Wool." Such dialogue is clearly a fictional device. In general, he leaned toward nonfiction when writing about national conflicts faced by the settlers, and toward fiction when trying to capture precise, interpersonal drama.

Bad Man Ballad (1986), Sanders' second attempt at a novel after "Warchild," finally found a publisher in 1986, after being completed in New Hampshire in 1974. Brimming with more details of the Ohio River Valley in the nineteenth century, the narrative stands with *Wilderness Plots* as Sanders' foray into historical fiction.

Sanders used news articles about a legendary Midwest giant, a historical figure known as the Pennsylvania Ironman, as the foundation for the plot of *Bad Man Ballad*. Set during the War of 1812, the novel is part murder mystery, part journey narrative, and part meditation on law and justice. When a forest-smart teenager stumbles upon a freakish murder scene ringed with the footprints of a giant, he hooks up with a good-hearted yet naive lawyer to bring the giant, the presumed murderer, to justice. The two set out on an enlightening Ohio journey as they track the unusual man. The evenhanded teenager wants to learn about the giant, but the lawyer wants to use the opportunity to prosecute the giant. The conflicts of human versus human and human versus the unknown unfold as the teen and the lawyer find the giant and solve the mystery behind the murder, which complicates the court proceedings. The giant is executed, and the disillusioned teen heads west "toward the unpeopled lands" (241).

In "Letter to a Reader," Sanders explains his intentions behind *Bad Man Ballad*. After he read the news articles about the life and death of the real Pennsylvania Ironman, Sanders ruminated that "the conjunction of war and wilderness, a fearful village and a mysterious fugitive, set me thinking. ... The concerns of the book are not so different from those of *Warchild*, for I was still trying to figure out how we had become so violent" (*Writing from the Center* 180).

Sanders rounded out his interest in historical creative writing with three books for children. *Hear the Wind Blow* was written in 1984 and published in 1985. The book posits the lyrics from American folk songs, such as "Yankee Doodle," as starting points for stories. *Hear the Wind Blow* was an American Library Association Booklist Editors' Choice for 1985. That success led to two picture books, *Aurora Means Dawn*

(1989) and *Warm as Wool* (1992). Both books were adapted from *Wilderness Plots.* Sanders has continued to write nonhistorical children's books, publishing *Here Comes the Mystery Man* (1994); *The Floating House* (1995); *A Place Called Freedom* and *Meeting Trees* (both 1997); and *Crawdad Creek* (1999).

Sanders' next major phase would be a focus on science fiction, but three more publications (which are not easily grouped) need mentioning. Those publications are the short story collection *Fetching the Dead* (1984), and two projects he edited concerning the French American naturalist and ornithologist John James Audubon (1785–1851).

Fetching the Dead is a collection of autobiographical short stories that Sanders wrote while in Cambridge. The collection is worth mentioning because Sanders was starting to develop his nonfiction themes. Two stories involve young American couples learning about each other as they travel in England and Europe—Sanders was in his twenties and newly married when he did the same. A conflicted man resists the draft in "Time and Again," which mirrors Sanders' experience. Three of the stories are set around the Roma Arsenal, a clear nod to the Ravenna Arsenal. *Fetching the Dead* earned little critical acclaim. It closes the chapter on Sanders' historical and autobiographical fiction phase, yet serves as a necessary stepping stone to his nonfiction success. Sanders had a dozen additional short story publications in magazines and journals from 1984 until as late as 1994, and even won a PEN Syndicated Fiction Award in 1988, but those stories remain uncollected.

One of Sanders' major projects was serving as the editor for *The Audubon Reader: The Best Writings of John James Audubon.* The reader, published in 1986, contains transcriptions of Audubon's prolific journal writing. The journals had been collected and published earlier by Audubon's granddaughter, who imposed major changes that Sanders felt were inconsistent with Audubon's style and intentions. Audubon, who did not speak English until he was eighteen but nonetheless wrote in English, was a phonetic speller, a grand ignorer of punctuation, and was described by Sanders as impulsively "launching himself into sentences before he had any clear notion of how to exit from them" (2). When the granddaughter published the journals, she cleaned up the spelling and punctuation, but also cut or softened parts that she felt showed Audubon's crassness and lack of proper schooling. Sanders claims that these "prim and ruthless" edits were so pervasive that the end result more accurately reflected the granddaughter's self-consciousness than Audubon's true writings (189). Sanders therefore exerted his editorial power, noting that such famous Americans as Thomas Jefferson were phonetic spellers and that schooling was not a precursor for intelligence. Other than modernizing certain spellings, Sanders made no changes to the original writings. "The grammar and punctuation I have left alone, for their eccentricity is one of the pleasures of reading Audubon" (189).

Sanders had attempted a fictionalized account of Audubon's life prior to completing the reader. He outlined an encompassing narrative, but fleshed out only Audubon's childhood years in historical fiction form. The novella was titled *Wonders Hidden,* and it was published with a narrative by Ursula K. Le Guin in a limited run in 1984. In "Letter to a Reader," Sanders implied that his taking on the project of a fictionalized account of Audubon's entire life was still a distant possibility.

THE MIDDLE YEARS: SCIENCE FICTION

A world away from the Americana of the folklore stories and the editorial responsibilities of the Audubon projects was a series of science fiction novels, or "speculative fiction," as Sanders called them. Compared with his earlier works, the science fiction novels are far more political, rife with Sanders' concern for and criticism of the excesses of hedonistic America. The utopia/dystopia settings of these novels question the supposed "progress" of humankind; they were clearly intended to make contemporary readers consider the consequences of their actions. It is no accident that the main character in each of the science fiction novels serves as an example of

how the everyday citizen can rise above the system, attaining a spiritually sound existence.

Sanders began writing *Terrarium* during the Oregon sabbatical in 1978–1979 and finished it in 1982. The book was published in 1985 and reissued in 1995 with an afterword written by Sanders. Set in the fictional Oregon City around 2050, the novel supposes that by this time, humans have so poisoned and mishandled the land that the human population must live in domed oceanic cities in order to free themselves from Terra, the land outside the domes. The main character, a passive young weatherman named Phoenix, is mostly content with his "Enclosure" life until he meets a young woman, Teeg, a mischievous dissident. Teeg's complicated familial connections to the designers of Oregon City and to the "wildergoer" resistors back on Terra provide the conflict and tension in the novel. With Teeg's urging, Phoenix agrees to escape Oregon City with a group of radicals. The trials that the hopeful group face back on Terra test their intelligence and resolve, and provide a glimmer of hope that humans can relearn how to live in harmony with their environment.

Terrarium is one in a long line of science fiction novels that shared certain characteristics—depictions of a dark future full of misjudgments, societal control run amok, and bands of rebels clinging to restorative ideals. Sanders acknowledged his science fiction predecessors in his 1995 afterword, noting that he purposefully completed the novel in 1984, as a nod to George Orwell's futuristic *1984* (1949).

But the novel was not merely genre fiction. It also represented the embryonic stage of many of Sanders' nonfiction themes. In the 1995 afterword, Sanders commented, "When I pluck at any line in *Terrarium,* I am liable to find it connected through memory to the whole of my life" (280). The characters in *Terrarium* grapple with the same philosophical dilemmas Sanders would expound upon in his nonfiction.

In the 1995 afterword, Sanders made a point of explaining how *Terrarium* continued to be relevant, especially considering the advent of two American projects that he felt were the precursors to a real Oregon City. Sanders shows that

"our impulse to create an enclave where nothing can harm us, an infantile paradise where we need only eat and play, has achieved an apotheosis of sorts in the Mall of America" (282). Sanders also cites the failed Biosphere 2 project in Arizona as an ominous practice-run for Oregon City. In the end, Sanders asserts that *Terrarium* was ultimately about maintaining hope (another nonfiction theme soon to appear in his essays). "Like the colonists gathered on the Oregon shore, we may use the wealth of human knowledge to build communities that are materially simple and spiritually complex, respectful of our places and of the creatures who share them with us" (283).

Sanders' second science fiction novel was *The Engineer of Beasts,* written during the 1986–1987 school year when Sanders was a visiting scholar at the Massachusetts Institute of Technology (MIT) on a Lilly Endowment Fellowship. It was published in 1988 and marketed toward young adults.

The influence of the MIT community is apparent. The main character is a genetically engineered preteen named Emitty Harvard Tufts, whose name is the clue to her past. She was created from an egg from an MIT (em-i-tee) professor and the sperm from a Harvard professor. The girl is deemed a "failed experiment" when her demeanor leans toward the difficult and her red hair and freckles are considered ugly. Years of neglect in an orphanage prompt her escape. She ends up at a "disney," which is what Sanders calls amusement parks of the future. There, her engineering skills earn her a job fixing robotic animals, which are a prime attraction at a disney of the future. Ever the dissident, and rather like Teeg from *Terrarium,* Emitty secretly engineers the animals to break out of the domed enclosure and run for the hills. Emitty survives a series of trials in the wilderness and bonds with a bear. Appropriately termed a coming-of-age narrative, *The Engineer of Beasts* was roundly but briefly praised for its disturbing yet thoughtful questioning of genetic engineering.

The Invisible Company was Sanders' final science fiction novel. Written at the same time as *The Engineer of Beasts,* it was published in 1989. In the same way that *Terrarium* employed well-

worn strategies of science fiction, *The Invisible Company* was a riff on the age-old dilemma of perception—How do we know that what we are seeing is real? At the time of its publication, Sanders' nonfiction essays were winning awards, and *The Invisible Company* fell by the wayside. In the early twenty-first century, renewed interest in the novel might be based on the real-world phenomenon of reality TV shows, a "futuristic" development in *The Invisible Company*.

In the novel, the Invisible Company is a hive of fully functioning human brains suspended in nutrient solution. They live vicariously by experiencing the plots of famous novels played out by unsuspecting vacationers in the domed Paradise Island resort. The resort is like a modern Las Vegas, without the gambling—its buildings mimic famous locations. The vacationers think they are on vacation. However, actors hired by the Invisible Company guide the visitors through scripted drama, the events of which are then transmitted back to the brains. The brains thrive on constant entertainment, serving as both audience and directors as they switch between eighty-one "channels" that are really the brainwaves of vacationers. The brains do not realize they are just brains—each thinks it is a full human body in a dark theater inhabited by other humans.

The main character, Leon Ash, a physicist haunted by his research, which unexpectedly led to weapons development, is obligated to vacation at Paradise Island after the Invisible Company saves him from a near-fatal car accident. By earning the trust of a doubtful female actor and a few other subversives, Leon seeks to uncover the mystery of Paradise Island and the Invisible Company, eventually discovering the hive of brains and putting a spectacular end to the charade.

Intriguing thematic connections can be made to popular movies not conceived until years after *The Invisible Company* was published, such as *The Truman Show* (1998) and *The Matrix* trilogy (1999–2003), films that demonstrate, as does Sanders' novel, a keen eye for the disturbing link between surveillance and entertainment. But the critical reception to Sanders' work in the science fiction genre has been mixed. Ellen Datlow, the editor of the acclaimed science fiction journal *Omni,* routinely published his short stories and cut Sanders substantial paychecks for his work. However, the monolithic authors in science fiction history are difficult to outshine, and Sanders never achieved prominence. Sanders read other science fiction, and often wrote reviews or critical analyses about the state of the genre. His stories found regular homes in the pages of *Isaac Asimov's Science Fiction Magazine*. But what brief reviews the books received were mostly summaries, with little critical reaction or noteworthy praise.

FINDING A VOICE: THE PERSONAL ESSAYS

Sanders' interest in how humans build and maintain communities was apparent in his science fiction, and it was a relevant interest given the state of American culture in the 1980s. This concern found an even stronger outlet in his nonfiction. Starting in the 1980s, Sanders focused on the nonfiction subgenre known as the personal essay; by the 1990s, he was a well-known essayist.

His first nonfiction book, *Stone Country,* was published in 1985 by Indiana University Press. Sanders wrote the book with the help of a National Endowment for the Arts fellowship, which he received for the 1983–1984 academic year. The twelve essays by Sanders and black-and-white photos by Jeffrey A. Wolin document the limestone industry community in southern Indiana, famous for its outcrop of Salem limestone. The walls of the Pentagon, Grand Central Station, and fourteen state capitols, among other major buildings, are made from Salem limestone. Sanders, however, was after the human story behind the white stone, not the objective history. In fact, he calls the book a "documentary narrative." Written in the first person, the essay-to-essay narrative reads like a scavenger hunt of regional oddities, a limestone grotesque in the literary tradition of the southern grotesque. "Bones and Shells" finds Sanders and Wolin at a cemetery, searching for limestone grave markers. They find one, but also must contend with the gun-toting caretaker, who warns

Sanders that a teenage convict is a fugitive in the nearby quarries. In "Digging," Sanders tells of the geology of limestone and the history of the region while simultaneously weaving in a narrative about him and Wolin successfully finding, deep in the woods, the ruins of the first quarry. Sanders also interviews old-timers in the region, including the last full-time carver in a once thriving industry. Sanders comes away with a new-found respect for the limestone culture, whose cutters and carvers possess such unique, specialized knowledge, yet have no apprentices to keep the tradition alive. But his critical eye never shuts—anecdotes remind the reader that quarrying is not sustainable, the work is dangerous, and many of the quarries became toxic dumps.

The less-polluted quarry lakes attract the heedless and incautious, another problem that Sanders unexpectedly encounters as he hikes. In "Doorways into the Depths," Sanders recounts how one afternoon, in order to escape the heat, he settled into an overhang in a quarry. Three youths arrived and, not seeing Sanders, began to fire revolvers at the quarry walls. Concerned that they could shoot him by accident, and paralyzed with dread that they might shoot him on purpose, Sanders cowers in the crevice long after the troublemakers leave. How Sanders writes about the incident shows his talent for suspense and insight: "It would have seemed more in keeping with their helter-skelter mayhem to have shot me than not to, and nobody could ever have known. ... I kept well hidden. A quarry in a quarry. Except for their laughter, not a sound emerged from their throats. They spoke only in bullets" (54). Such moments helped *Stone Country* win the 1986 Penrod Award for creative nonfiction.

The fine writing in *Stone Country* is complemented by Wolin's photographs and the text's artistic design. Printed as an oversize coffee-table book to accommodate the eight-by-ten-inch photos, the edition is long out of print. A text-only paperback version was published under the title *In Limestone Country* in 1991.

Sanders' next collection was 1987's *The Paradise of Bombs*. Sanders wrote the earliest essays during his sabbatical in Oregon, but put the most effort into the book in 1985. The collection's eleven essays, which arc like pendulums through a gamut of topics, showcasing Sanders' narrative control, remains one of his most praised accomplishments.

The Paradise of Bombs marks Sanders' entry into the subgenre of nonfiction at which he most excels, personal essays, which differ from memoirs and autobiographies. Memoir writing is usually chronological and scene based, relying on reconstructed crises and conflict resolution. Traditional memoirs document an important period of time, often a coming-of-age phase. Autobiographies generally recount an entire life. Personal essays, in contrast, do not follow a chronological timeline—instead, their "plot" is based on thematically similar anecdotes, relevant research, or literary journalism, and an awareness that the writer is writing and thinking, looking back in order to gain insight. As Sanders explains in the introduction, "These essays are personal without being, except incidentally, autobiographical. I write of my own life only when it seems to have a larger bearing on the lives of others" (xv).

Assigning an overarching theme to *The Paradise of Bombs* is difficult, but Sanders states, in the introduction, that the essays are about aspects of violence. The opening essay, "At Play in the Paradise of Bombs," sets the stage. On one level, the essay is about Sanders' childhood at the Ravenna Arsenal. The essay is pocked with anecdotes about the games of boys in a place thrumming with the war games of men. But on another level, the essay is about the limitations of war. Sanders' unease is conveyed through repeated images of confines; the arsenal is circled by an intimidating chain-link fence topped with barbed wire. Meditations on the implications of this fence surface throughout the narrative. The essay begins with a straightforward description of it. In the middle of the essay, Sanders uses the fence and a herd of deer as a metaphor for the paradox humans mire themselves in over war. The fence protects the deer, making the arsenal a haven, but the fence is also their undoing—guided hunts end with the deer cornered and slaughtered. The deer/fence theme reaches a sobering climax when, not long after the Cuban

missile crisis, a visiting general shoots a legendary pair of albino deer. At the end of the essay, Sanders ruminates on how even though he left the arsenal decades ago, a haunting worry nags him. The concluding sentences allow the fence metaphor to resonate: "The fences of the Arsenal have stretched outward until they circle the entire planet. I feel, now, I can never move outside" (19). Again, the theme of enclosures—which first emerged in his science fiction—provides a profound basis for a narrative.

The Paradise of Bombs contains Sanders' most-reprinted pieces, two essays that each appear in at least thirteen different anthologies. "The Men We Carry in Our Minds" and "The Inheritance of Tools" are the essays most readers think of when they think of Scott Russell Sanders.

For all the attention it has received, "The Men We Carry in Our Minds" is a surprisingly short essay—in six pages, Sanders eloquently questions certain aspects of the feminist movement and takes a compelling stand against the idea that the male life is one of privilege. The essay begins in dialogue, as Sanders and a female friend discuss who has it worse—men or women? The friend argues that while women are aided by the invigoration of the feminist movement, "men feel they're in the wrong. Men are the ones who've been discredited, who have to search their souls" (112). With respect, Sanders takes the friend's observation as his thesis, and the essay unfolds from there. Sanders describes the difficult lives of the working-class men he has known, leading up to his own entrance into college, where he was "baffled when the women at college accused me and my sex of having cornered the world's pleasures" (116). He concludes by wondering if the women then (and now) realize that he is their friend and ally, not their enemy.

The essay employs a trio of noteworthy craft techniques. Its use of dialogue acknowledges that the gender debate is an ongoing discussion too often derailed by fervent politics. Its ending question, leaving the reader to supply an answer, elicits an intelligent rebuke to the status quo. Finally, the plural (and gender-neutral) pronouns in the title—"we" and "our" instead of "I" and "my"—reach out to men and women, to be inclusive rather than exclusive, to set an example.

This volume's other frequently anthologized essay, "The Inheritance of Tools," begins with a coincidence: "At just about the hour when my father died, soon after dawn one February morning when ice coated the windows like cataracts, I banged my thumb with a hammer" (102). Readers find out that Sanders is the third-generation owner of the hammer. Knowledge of tools and woodworking is cherished among the men in his family, and Sanders describes a bevy of tool trivia. The essay is organized around a series of thematically related metaphors. The technique for pounding a nail serves as a metaphor for learning to focus; the scar on Sanders' thumbnail slowly heals and fades, paralleling Sanders' mourning of his father. Other metaphors, about right angles, levels, mistakes, and corrections, guide the essay to its conclusion, in which Sanders resolutely finishes the wall he was building when he heard the news of his father's death.

The critical attention *The Paradise of Bombs* has received reflects its strength as a literary work. It was the winner of the Associated Writing Programs Award for Creative Nonfiction, a prestigious award known for launching careers. "The Inheritance of Tools" was reprinted in *The Best American Essays for College Students* and *The Best American Essays 1987.* Nine of the eleven essays appeared first in the *North American Review,* under the editorship of Robley Wilson Jr. (The other two essays had appeared in *Stone Country.*)

Sanders' next book was *Secrets of the Universe.* Published in 1991, it contained personal essays that he started during his year at MIT and finished in 1990. It is his only collection organized into distinct parts—"People," "Places," and the final section, "Purposes and Powers." Sanders describes his process in the book's preface:

What I love binds me in cords that stretch to infinity. In these essays I begin with the fierce, tangled relationships between parent and child, between man and woman. From the family I move to the larger loyalties of neighborhood, community, and region. Then I speak of belonging to nature, this order that sustains us, and of inhabiting the

earth. Finally, warily, I reflect on that encompassing mystery we call the universe. The movement outward to greater and greater circles is also a movement inward, ever closer to the center from which creation springs. (ix–x)

Appropriately, the collection is subtitled *Scenes from the Journey Home.* The essays are both exploration and justification, and they showcase Sanders' talent for twining observations, facts, questions, and conclusions.

The book opens with his third most anthologized essay, "Under the Influence," a wrenching meditation on his father's alcoholism. Sanders admits to not yet fully coming to terms with having an alcoholic father, despite Greeley Sanders' death in 1981. In a tone best described as raw, Sanders portrays himself as a typical child of an alcoholic. He blamed himself and tried to compensate by excelling at school and sports, devoting his energy to a diligent pursuit of achievement. "If my father was unstable, I would be a rock," he writes (21). The essay draws to an unsettling conclusion when Sanders concedes that his obsessive hard work is "endless and futile," because he still overreacts to anger (remembering drunken rages) and blames himself for the unhappiness of others. He laments that "guilt burns like acid in my veins" (22).

In a 1992 review, Susan Smith Nash noted that in *Secrets of the Universe,* Sanders "constantly questioned the relation between surface appearance and underlying reality" (797), a questioning that germinated from life with an alcoholic father. Sanders intends the questions to spark dialogue, not precede a single answer. For example, in "Reasons of the Body," Sanders wonders if it is possible to raise his son and daughter without subjecting them to preconceived notions of gender. The essay "Looking at Women" simply asks, "How should a man look at a woman?" Through such questioning—basic in tone but expertly crafted—Sanders relates his thinking on various topics. The tight spiral of metaphysical questions spurred Nash to remark that Sanders' "profound existential doubt" sometimes mires the essays in a slough of nonnarrative (797). In comparison with his two previous nonfiction collections, *Secrets of the Universe* is noticeably

less action-driven—what happens in each essay is what happened in Sanders' head as he thought about an abstract concept.

One essay in the collection represents another turning point in Sanders' self-image as a writer. In "The Singular First Person," Sanders steps away from the topics of family and nature and writes about the art form of the essay. Writing about truth is a risky pursuit for many reasons, and Sanders explores a few of these reasons, offering his justification for why he believes the personal essay is a worthwhile genre. He also chastises critics for judging nonfiction against fiction, as if fiction is more esteemed and nonfiction has to prove itself worthy. The origin of that debate comes from the fact that Sanders' "At Play in the Paradise of Bombs" was once mistaken for a short story. Sanders defends nonfiction from critics who believe that drama, poetry, and fiction are more respectable.

One characteristic of Sanders' writing that does not change no matter what genre he's writing in is the fact that he consistently builds upon his previous projects, never shelving a topic as "done" merely because he's published a book or two on the topic. For example, *Secrets of the Universe* was subtitled *Scenes from the Journey Home,* implying that another book will be about the homecoming. In Sanders' fourth nonfiction book, *Staying Put: Making a Home in a Restless World* (1993), finished with the aid of a Guggenheim Fellowship, he has arrived home. The thoughts he began in *Secrets of the Universe* extend to *Staying Put.*

Sanders' writing literally and metaphorically covers the same fertile ground, even when circumstances relegate the terrain to Sanders' memory. This is the compelling topic of the first essay in *Staying Put,* ominously titled "After the Flood." In that essay, the adult Sanders views, for the first time, the West Branch Reservoir, which flooded Ohio's Mahoney Valley near his childhood home. The "muddy expanse of annihilating water" prompts him to cycle through other memories of lost stomping grounds (6). He concludes that "I am all the more committed to know and care for the place I have come to as an adult because I have lost irretrievably the child-

hood landscapes that gave shape to my love of the earth" (12). This impassioned commitment fuels the other essays in the collection. Jeff Gundy summarized that "all the essays here are driven by this myth of the lost home, and by the yearning to reclaim a sense of groundedness, of feeling at one with the world" (399).

The most recognized essay in *Staying Put* is "Wayland," selected for *The Best American Essays 1993*. Wayland is the name of a crossroads in Northeast Ohio. The essay is about what Sanders realizes he's forgotten when he visits Wayland after a twenty-five year absence. He organizes the recollection of the homecoming into a description of seven mysteries he learned about as a child and how those mysteries were all dependent on a place. The mysteries are of death, life, animals, food, mind, sex, and God, but Sanders concedes that, "if you have been keeping count, you may have toted up seven mysteries, or maybe seven times seven, or maybe seven to the seventh power. My hunch is that, however we count, there is only one mystery" (193). The larger mystery Sanders is concerned with is "how can one speak or even think about the whole of things? Language is of only modest help" (193). The sublime abstraction of such thoughts is balanced by rich sensory descriptions—of apple pressing, church pews, ponies, and a kiss with a girl high in a tree. Gundy echoes what many critics have observed about Sanders: "He can effortlessly enclose the personal and the universal, the abstract and the concrete, the figurative and the referential, in a single paragraph" (398).

At work behind each paragraph in the collection is a plethora of resources and research. To write *Staying Put,* Sanders referenced many sources, from American humorist Mark Twain to Zen master Thich Nhat Hanh. The collection ends with 169 entries of endnotes, giving credit where credit is due to the thinkers whom Sanders drew upon for witticisms, lines of poetry, or profound observations. In defense of the endnotes, Sanders explained that merely supplying a traditional bibliography "would have given a false appearance of expertise; but I do want to acknowledge some of my elders, the books that are my grandparents" (195). It was the first of Sanders'

books to cite extensive thematic research, and all his later books would include such references.

THE ESTABLISHED WRITER: LATER ESSAYS

Staying Put makes the case for fully inhabiting a region; Sanders' next collection, *Writing from the Center* (1995), explores foremost how imagination is influenced by connection to place, and it has a secondary purpose of championing the marginalized Midwest. "This book is about glimpsing and seeking and longing for that center, that condition of wholeness," Sanders writes in the preface (ix). The concept of "center" also refers to the geographical center of America. The collection has a third purpose of simply being about writing, specifically as a retrospective account of how Sanders approached his many books. It includes the essay "Letter to a Reader," which was cited earlier in this article.

Sanders chose to defend the peculiarities of the Midwest at a time when American homogenization threatened totality, and he acknowledges this dilemma in "Beneath the Smooth Skin of America." In lamenting the taunting he faced as a teenage Ohioan arriving wide-eyed at Brown University in Rhode Island, he adds that today's college-bound midwesterners won't face such teasing, because "vivid regional differences ... have been erased" (11). One might expect the essay to plow ahead with the usual regret over this loss, but Sanders spins the piece around and proffers that "the blurring of regional boundaries may be liberating, if it makes us less eager to judge one another in light of birthplaces or mailing addresses" (15). The statement is a classic example of Sanders' ability to remain evenhanded and open-minded in times of frustration, which, by the time *Writing from the Center* was published, was central to his signature style.

The collection was calling for a "richer vocabulary of place" (18), not as a means of immediately ending stereotypes and homogenization, but as a tool for showing the limitations of regional labels. "Imagining the Midwest" expounds upon the dire need for the writing world to rethink regional labels, especially the presumptions that have shadowed Midwest writers for

over a century. Trenchant in tone, "Imagining the Midwest" reads like a theme paper on popular topics and successful authors in Midwest literature. However, it is also a jeremiad about one commonality among Midwest writers:

> We have had just over a century's worth of serious writing about the Midwest, most of it composed from a distance by men and women who grew up in the region and who then moved to places more stimulating, more fashionable, more hospitable to art. …
>
> Why this pattern of exile among our best writers? … Midwestern writers have not been so much lured elsewhere, I suspect, as driven out, by a combination of puritanical religion, utilitarian economics, and anti-intellectualism. (24–25)

As mentioned earlier, Sanders was an intellectual who felt driven out of the Midwest, but he always migrated back. He posits his restlessness against that of other Midwest writers. To highlight the long list: Mark Twain wrote about the Mississippi from Connecticut; Willa Cather wrote about Nebraska but lived on the East Coast; Toni Morrison has written about her home state of Ohio, but resides in New Jersey (24–25). The conclusion is predictable yet still lyrical. "I have no desire to add to the literature of exile. I believe that we need a literature—as we need a culture—of inhabitation" (50).

Sanders' defense of long-term habitation is coupled with his defense of centered writing. Sanders claims that higher-ups in the publishing business presume that writers who live on the edge—be it by drug abuse, trauma, or physical location (the coastal edges of America)—are more authentic and interesting than writers who are stable, centered, and don't capitalize on dramatic vices. Sanders notes, "We have expected the writer to be a misfit, an outsider, a stranger in strange lands, uprooted, lonely and lorn" (150). His thesis is that while some important literature does originate at an edge, decenteredness is not a prerequisite. "In our infatuation with edges, we have scorned the center," he warns (163). The essay makes a strong case for examining the centered life. Appropriately, it won the 1996 Great Lakes Book Award for books that deal with issues that define the Midwest.

The story behind how Sanders' next book, *Hunting for Hope: A Father's Journeys* (1998), came to be is often summarized in reviews and brought up in interviews because it is about a provocative incident in Sanders' life, an incident that illustrates how far Sanders will go to explore one idea. It is also the basis of the lynchpin essay of the book, "Mountain Music I," the first part of a four-part essay. In 1995 Sanders hiked in the Rockies with his teenage son, Jesse, in an attempt to placate tense father-son relations. The trip backfired—the two antagonized each other until Jesse revealed his discontent. He was angry that his father's outlook on the world was always so dreary. "There's no room for hope," Sanders quotes his son as saying. "Maybe you can get by without hope, but I can't" (9). Sanders was startled by this unintended pall he'd cast over his son. He took a hard look at himself, and his previous essays, and asked, "Had I really deprived my son of hope?" (9). It was a question important enough to shepherd the book to completion.

Hunting for Hope delivers exactly what its title promises. In fifteen accomplished and connected essays, Sanders delves into his conceptions of where one can find hope in a troubled world. The essay titles hint at the guideposts for finding hope: "Wildness," "Body Bright," "Family," and "Simplicity" are just a few. Sanders has covered these perennial topics before, but never through the specific lens of hope. The essays are linked by the four "Mountain Music" essays, which are more accurately described as a sustained narrative rather than traditional personal essays. Part I introduces the aforementioned conflict on the backpacking trip. Part II is the day after the fight. Sanders makes up his mind to show his son—and his readers—that there is hope in the world, and he chronicles the on-the-trail observations that will lead to the other essays in the book. Part III recounts the third day of the backpacking trip, where Sanders continues to note small events that strike him as hopeful. Part IV is about another backpacking trip one year later. Camping in the wet Smoky Mountains, father and son finally bond when they must cooperate to build a

campfire in the rain—the fire a metaphor for hope in a gloomy night.

Critics have praised the "Mountain Music" essays because of the way they serve as a scaffold for the rest of the book. *Hunting for Hope* is, in fact, an unusual nonfiction book—part personal essay suffused with intellect and research, part action-driven memoir, all under the umbrella of the theme of hope. The commentator David Wheeler called the book a "cohesive series of chapters" (B2). Another reviewer, Robert Taylor, deemed it "a notable example of craft" (E8). The book is a study in how the ever-evolving genre of nonfiction lends itself to a variety of organizations. In addition, the sumptuous descriptions in "Beauty," in part about the wedding of Sanders' daughter, earned that essay a place in the *Best American Essays 1999*.

With hardly a pause to savor the success of *Hunting for Hope*, Sanders published the book-length essay *The Country of Language* in 1999. The book includes a biography of Sanders written by Scott Slovic, as well as a bibliography of Sanders' work. The bibliography includes notable articles about Sanders and interviews with Sanders.

The Country of Language is part of the Credo Series published by Milkweed Editions. A nonprofit group started in 1979, Milkweed Editions publishes nonfiction, fiction, and poetry to create a forum for writers and readers who are concerned about community, nature, and harmony. To date, ten other authors have taken part in the Credo Series, such as Rick Bass, William Kittridge, Robert Michael Pyle, and Pattiann Rogers.

The Country of Language is subdivided into seventeen vignettes with topical titles such as "Looking," "Freshman," and "Writer." Mostly chronological, the vignettes allow Sanders to trace his development as a writer—his earliest understanding of language or his rigorous submersion in literature while in Cambridge, for example. The final vignette, "Writer," is a modest retrospective on how that label fit (or didn't fit) Sanders. "For a long while, nobody except my family knew that I was writing, and for an even longer while hardly anybody else cared, and

for good reasons," he writes (86). The general theme of the book is that Sanders did not set out to become a writer—he did not take a creative writing class until he taught his first one at Indiana University, and was never a student in the popular writing workshops that saturate the academy today. Nonetheless, his simple fascination with language served him well in life, and he came to realize that "my impulse to write is bound up with my desire to salvage worthy moments from the river of time" (85).

Avid readers have enjoyed *The Country of Language* because it fills in a few gray areas of Sanders' life. From his previous books, readers know that he resisted his Vietnam draft orders; the vignette "War and Peace" finally reveals how he was assigned F-4 status. "Pony" offers one more arsenal story as powerful as "At Play in the Paradise of Bombs." Other essays highlight important moments from his little-mentioned high school days, and "Father" adds another chapter to "Under the Influence," the essay about his father's alcoholism. As a bonus, black-and-white family photos are interspersed throughout the book.

Scott Slovic's biography, and the extensive bibliography, are a valuable resource for academics. Slovic founded the Association for the Study of Literature and Environment, and he has authored or edited numerous books on the environment, so his interest in Sanders is obvious. His biography applauds Sanders for pointing "to the small beauties of the world and to the achievable transformations of lifestyle that might offer us solace and some chance of sustainability" (106). The biography is brief but accurate regarding Sanders' life, focusing on the themes and issues in his work, especially in terms of environmental responsibility. *The Country of Language* is an essential source for anyone studying the life and works of Sanders.

In *The Force of Spirit* (2000), Sanders returns to the personal-essay mode to deliver fourteen more commentaries on life. The focus this time, however, is on spirituality, which became more important to Sanders as he headed into his mid-fifties at the end of the twentieth century. "The deeper I go into my days," he says in the

introduction, "the more I am convinced that living itself is an experiment. Life keeps confronting me with puzzles that I can neither ignore nor easily solve. I am moved to write essays not because I understand so much but because I understand so little" (2).

What sets the essays in *The Force of Spirit* apart from any of Sanders' earlier essays is that they are more overtly religious while remaining nondenominational. The essays are far from dogmatic, yet they show that Sanders is coming to some conclusions about Christianity, and he now has the wisdom to share those observations. Clear events in his life trigger this spiritual contemplation; the title essay is about a visit to his father-in-law in a nursing home; two essays are letters to his son and daughter on their wedding days; two more are about how Sanders is gaining new understanding about his father. The essays are full of quotes from people Sanders regards as wise—the essayist Wendell Berry, the biologist Edward O. Wilson, and the Quaker founder George Fox, for example. But sharing equal (if not more) time on the page are numerous biblical verses. Other than a few brief moments in *Hunting for Hope,* none of Sanders' collections have foregrounded biblical verses and stories in this way.

Aware that readers will notice the development, Sanders takes two steps to explain his intentions. First, in the introduction, he notes that "the word *religion* comes from *re-* plus *ligare,* meaning to bind back together, as if things have been scattered and now must be gathered again" (3). He also explains that he prefers the word *spirit* to *God* because *God* (and the many synonyms for that figure) is "freighted with a long, compromising history" (3).

The second step was including the essay "Silence," which is about Sanders' attending of a Quaker meeting. The final essay in the book, it is an explanation of why Sanders is drawn to the Quakers above all other religions and how the Friends (as Quakers are also known) use silence to approach spirituality. "They recite no creed, and they have little use for theology, but they do believe that every person may experience direct contact with God. They also believe we are most

likely to achieve that contact in stillness," he explains (155). Given the low-key nature of the Quakers, the intimate account of their meetings is unusual and instructive without being preachy.

In the tradition of recovering favorite paths, Sanders includes three more essays about writing. "The Power of Stories" is a ten-point defense of storytelling. "Witnessing to a Shared World" discusses key differences between nonfiction and fiction: "Fidelity to life outside the page does not make nonfiction more virtuous than fiction, nor more important, nor more true. It merely enforces on the writer the stringent discipline of bearing witness" (108). The final essay about writing, "Who Speaks on the Page?" is about how teachers stifled or encouraged Sanders' impulse to write, and how he changed his teaching habits to accommodate a more personal style of academic writing.

LOOKING FORWARD

After a brief hiatus to oversee the Wells Scholar program at Indiana University, Sanders returned to teaching in the fall of 2004 as a distinguished professor of English.

In 2005 Sanders was finishing what he has called a "spiritual autobiography," *A Private History of Awe.* "Since the age of twelve, I've been suspicious of people who claim to know God's thoughts," he wrote in an e-mail response. "Lately, I've been more suspicious than ever. … The current administration in Washington, together with the religious ideologues who've seized control of politics … have made me more determined than ever not to abandon the language of morality to the bigots." In addition to this commentary, the new book will include "narratives of my mother's agonizing departure from life and my granddaughter's marvelous entrance."

He was also finishing the introduction to *Wild and Scenic Indiana,* a book of photographs, and was active in the Orion Society as well as a contributing editor to the magazine *Orion.* He had three future projects in mind: *Common Wealth,* slated to be a collection of essays; a "small book" of essays on the writing process; and, as always, "maybe a novel."

Selected Bibliography

WORKS OF SCOTT RUSSELL SANDERS

NONFICTION ESSAY COLLECTIONS

Stone Country. Bloomington: Indiana University Press, 1985. (With photographs by Jeffrey A. Wolin. Text-only version published under the title *In Limestone Country.* Boston: Beacon Press, 1991.)

The Paradise of Bombs. Athens: University of Georgia Press, 1987. *Secrets of the Universe: Scenes from the Journey Home.* Boston: Beacon Press, 1991.

Staying Put: Making a Home in a Restless World. Boston: Beacon Press, 1993.

Writing from the Center. Bloomington: Indiana University Press, 1995.

Hunting for Hope: A Father's Journeys. Boston: Beacon Press, 1998.

Travels in the Country of Language. Tuscaloosa, Ala.: Wing and the Wheel Press, 1998. (Chapbook; edition of 200 copies)

The Country of Language. Minneapolis: Milkweed Editions, 1999. (Part of the Credo Series, this book has a bibliography of Sanders' work, a bibliography of work about Sanders, and a biography of Sanders written by Scott Slovic.)

The Force of Spirit. Boston: Beacon Press, 2000.

SELECTED ANTHOLOGIZED ESSAYS AND STORIES

"Beauty." *The Best American Essays 1999*, edited by Edward Hoagland and Robert Atwan. Boston: Houghton Mifflin, 1999.

"The Inheritance of Tools." *The Best American Essays for College Students*, edited by Robert Atwan. Boston: Houghton Mifflin, 1994.

"The Inheritance of Tools." *The Best American Essays 1987*, edited by Gay Talese and Robert Atwan. New York: Ticknor & Fields, 1987.

"Under the Influence." *The Art of the Personal Essay: An Anthology from the Classical Era to the Present.* Compiled by Phillip Lopate. New York: Anchor Books, 1994.

"The Philosophical Cobbler." In *Flash Fiction: seventy-two very short stories*, edited by James Thomas et al. New York: Norton, 1992.

"Wayland." *The Best American Essays 1993*, edited by Joseph Epstein. New York: Ticknor & Fields, 1993.

FICTION AND SCIENCE FICTION

"Warchild." *Berkeley Samisdat Review* Vol. II, no. 1, pp. 41-50. (spring 1974). *Center* No. II, pp. 2-12. Albuquerque, NM, (July 1978). (Excerpts of unpublished novel).

Wilderness Plots: Tales about the Settlement of the American Land. New York: Morrow, 1983. *Wonders Hidden: Audubon's Early Years.* Santa Barbara, Calif.: Capra Press, 1984. (Published with *The Visionary: The Life Story of Flicker of the Serpentine,* by Ursula K. Le Guin.)

Fetching the Dead: Stories. Urbana: University of Illinois Press, 1984.

Terrarium. New York: Tor Books, 1985. (Reprinted with an afterword by Sanders.. Bloomington: Indiana University Press, 1995.)

Bad Man Ballad. New York: Bradbury/Macmillan, 1986.

The Engineer of Beasts. New York: Orchard Books/Franklin Watts, 1988.

The Invisible Company. New York: Tor Books, 1989.

CHILDREN'S BOOKS

Hear the Wind Blow: American Folk Songs Retold. New York: Bradbury/Macmillan, 1985.

Aurora Means Dawn. New York: Bradbury/Macmillan, 1989. *Warm as Wool.* New York: Bradbury/Macmillan, 1992.

Here Comes the Mystery Man. New York: Bradbury/Macmillan, 1994.

The Floating House. New York: Macmillan, 1995.

A Place Called Freedom. New York: Atheneum, 1997.

Meeting Trees. Washington, D.C.: National Geographic Society, 1997.

Crawdad Creek. Washington, D.C.: National Geographic Society, 1999.

SELECTED OTHER WORKS

D. H. Lawrence: The World of the Major Novels. London: Vision Press, 1973. Reprinted under the title *D. H. Lawrence: The World of the Five Major Novels.* New York: Viking, 1974.

Audubon Reader: The Best Writings of John James Audubon. Editor. Bloomington: Indiana University Press, 1986.

In a Word: A Harper's Magazine Dictionary of Words That Don't Exist, but Ought To. Edited by Jack Hitt. New York: Dell, 1992. (Sanders' contributions appear on pp. 11, 19, 42, 51, 120, 121, 130, 163, 177.)

CRITICAL AND BIOGRAPHICAL STUDIES AND BOOK REVIEWS

Gundy, Jeff. "How Others Have Lived Here." *Georgia Review* 48, no. 2:391–400 (summer 1994). (Review of *Staying Put* and three other books by other authors.)

Lueders, Edward. "Considering the Protean West." *Southern Review* 28, no. 2:412–420 (spring 1992). (Review of *Secrets of the Universe*, among other works by other authors.)

Nash, Susan Smith. "The Courage to Fall." *Georgia Review* 46, no. 4:794–798 (winter 1992). (Review of *Secrets of the Universe.*)

Nichols, William. "Environmentalism and the Legitimacy of Hope." *Kenyon Review* 18, no 3/4:206–214 (summer/fall 1996). (Review of *Writing from the Center.*)

———. "Scott Russell Sanders." *American Nature Writers.* Vol. 2. Edited by John Elder. New York: Scribners, 1996.

Ryden, Kent C. *Mapping the Invisible Landscape: Folklore, Writing, and the Sense of Place.* Iowa City: University of Iowa Press, 1993.

Taylor, Robert. "For Sanders, Hope Springs from Reason." *Boston Globe,* October 6, 1998, p. E8. (Review of *Hunting for Hope.*)

Wheeler, David L. "A Quarrel with His Son Prompts a Writer to Meditate on Hope." *Chronicle of Higher Education.* October 2, 1998 p. B2. (Review of *Hunting for Hope.*)

INTERVIEWS

Borish, Barrie Jean, and Pam Loern. "An Interview with Scott Russell Sanders." *Water-Stone* 3, no. 1:108–121 (fall 2000).

Hirt, Jen. "An Interview with Scott Russell Sanders." *Fugue* (Moscow, Idaho) 25:163–175 (summer 2003).

Lee, Jeff. "Honoring the Given World: An Interview with Scott Russell Sanders." *Stone Crop: A Natural History Book Catalogue* (Denver), pp. 27–31 (summer 1997).

Lertzman, Renée. "In a Broken World: Scott Russell Sanders on Resisting Despair." *Sun* 290:4–9 (February 2000).

Nolting, Leandra. "An Interview with Scott Russell Sanders." *Evansville Review* 12:52–57 (2002).

Perry, Carolyn, and Wayne Zade. "Something Durable and Whole: An Interview with Scott Russell Sanders." *Kenyon Review* 22, no. 1:10–25 (fall 1999).

Philippon, Daniel J. "A More Decent Way of Life: An Interview with Scott Russell Sanders." *Ruminator Review* (Minneapolis) 14:34–35, 40, 63 (summer 2003).

Root, Robert. "An Interview with Scott Russell Sanders." *Fourth Genre* 1, no. 1:119–132 (spring 1999).

Tydeman, Bill. "New Directions: An Interview with Scott Russell Sanders." *Iron Horse Literary Review* (Lubbock, Tex.) 3, no. 2:98–109 (spring 2002).

Vaillancourt, Renée J. "The Country of Language: An Interview with Scott Russell Sanders." *Public Libraries* 39, no. 4:200–201 (July/August 2000).

Zirker, Joan McTigue. "A Meeting of Midwestern Minds." Joint interview with Frank Popoff. *College* 19, no. 2:4–9 (spring 1996).

GUSTAF SOBIN

(1935–2005)

Andrew Zawacki

The American poet, novelist, and essayist GUSTAF SOBIN lived in southern France for more than forty years. This may, in part, account for why, until the mid-1990s, he was very much a "poet's poet," with a small, albeit prominent, group of admirers and apologists but lacking a wider public. Amid a literary generation that includes, among others, Ted Berrigan, Susan Howe, Michael McClure, Jerome Rothenberg, Armand Schwerner, Charles Simic, Mark Strand, Keith Waldrop, Rosmarie Waldrop, and Charles Wright, Sobin received fewer overt accolades than these fellow artists. If his writing is unusually attentive to the world, to language, and to the mysteries underlying both, it is also a form of communication that—growing out of silence and longing to return there—refuses to beg for attention, demanding instead the patient, voluntary openness of the other. This is an exigency not easily heard, let alone answered, by participants in an increasingly careerist American literary milieu, where prizes, pedigree, university posts, and divisive politico-aesthetic loyalties have come to dominate the would-be poetic discourse.

He was far from feeling alienated, however, from a culture inimical to the very notion of reception: "It's almost an advantage," Sobin claimed in an interview with Edward Foster for the poetry journal *Talisman*, "living at a distance in which one's own language is used—almost exclusively—for writing. The words take on a kind of buoyancy, a kind of freshness. They're free of so much exhausted usage" and "day-to-day attrition" (Foster, "An Interview with Gustaf Sobin," *Talisman* 10 [Spring 1993], p. 36). While acknowledging the risk entailed in such self-imposed exile, of "losing one's sense of the colloquial," Sobin made a virtue and avowal of this potential vice. "My entire work," he told Tedi López Mills, "might be seen as a transcript of

sorts, celebrating margins" (*Matrices de Viento y de Sombra*, p. 7). Sobin's meditative focus, honed at a great remove from what others might call home, resulted in an opus best conceived in terms of music, as plainsong or passacaglia. Reviewing Sobin's selected poems, *By the Bias of Sound* (1995), Fred Muratori rightly claims that across several decades the author's "themes, even his technique, have remained remarkably consistent," such that "reading his collection is like reading one continuous poem, following the oscillation of a wave, or tracking a cyclical history of erosion and recombination" (*American Book Review*, p. 21).

LIFE AND BACKGROUND

Gustaf Peter Sobin was born on November 15, 1935, in Boston, Massachusetts. His father, Newton Sobin, born in Odessa, Russia, in 1897, worked as a dyestuff manufacturer and tradesman, while his mother, Rena Pearl Sobin, hailed from Worcester, Massachusetts. The young Gustaf entered the Fessenden School in West Newton in 1946, as a boarder. The family owned a second residence in Palm Beach, and in vacationing there, three times a year for several years in his early teens, Sobin developed an affinity with the sea, tropical vegetation, and Latin American culture. He attended the Rivers Country Day School in Chestnut Hill from 1949 to 1951, before matriculating at the Choate School in Wallingford, Connecticut. Gustaf spent consecutive summers in France and Italy.

In 1952 he made the first of three visits to Ernest Hemingway in Cuba. At once entirely American and "consummately expatriate," Hemingway was, according to Sobin, "the bridge" between two continents, the "gateway out"

(Foster, p. 37). Resolved to flee "an ultra-conservative Cold War aesthetics" and "the rigid provincialism" of his generation, Sobin continued traveling frequently to Europe while attending Brown University (cf. Mills). Already writing poetry and prose, upon graduating in 1958 Sobin undertook a year of military service, stationed with U.S. Artillery at Forts Dix and Chaffee. Thereafter he worked for his father in the dyestuff trade, writing intensively in the off hours.

After discovering, in 1962, the work of the French poet René Char, Sobin departed for Paris. It was "that very volume," Sobin asserted—a Random House translation edited by Jackson Matthews, with a blurb from William Carlos Williams—"that brought me to France, to Provence" (Foster, p. 32). Through the intermediary of Guy Levis Mano, Sobin met the French master, who encouraged the aspiring writer to visit the site of the poems he admired. Char was Sobin's host in Provence several weeks later. After having returned to the United States to sell his belongings, resolved to live in France for as long as possible, Sobin arrived in Provence in February 1963. He lodged in hotels and rented houses until 1965, when he purchased an abandoned silk co-coonery in Goult, a village in the Vaucluse, for $800. He lived in that small stone cottage until his death, on July 7, 2005, of pancreatic cancer. "I learnt how to read the landscape as one might read a text," Sobin recollected of his adopted countryside, "a *textus*, a woven fabric" (Foster, p. 27).

The period from 1963 to 1972 marked a fierce apprenticeship. While translating Char's *Retour amont* (1966) and *L'âge cassant* (1967), the newly self-exiled American persisted with his own reading and writing. What had drawn him to Char, he recalled, was "a level of urgency, necessity in his verse such as I'd never seen elsewhere, a seriousness in regard to the art of poetry that struck me as utterly devotional" (cf. Mills). The other French writer who exerted an influence on the barely thirty-something Sobin was Stéphane Mallarmé, whose attention to existential absence, the blank page's whiteness, the art of leaving things out, and the way one word generates another, have been brought to bear on Sobin's

œuvre. Early on, Mallarmé provided a "rush // of crushed / shadow," as Sobin writes in his 1988 volume *Voyaging Portraits* (p. 62).

That book's uncharacteristically autobiographical, central section, "A Portrait of the Self as Instrument of Its Syllables," details its author's genealogy and difficult aesthetic genesis. "[F]or / ten / years, the / breath went, dis- / membered," he recounts, "erred bone, erred / measure. through the *nomen* (in its cell- / ulated / wastes) the poem moved, dis- / assembled, un- / spoken" (Sobin, *Voyaging*, pp. 55–56). During that decade, Sobin read classical writers such as Sappho, Pindar, Anacreon, and Catullus, along with biblical authors and the pre-Socratics. Moreover, the poem figures them all as having engendered not only Sobin the poet, but also—in the manner of God's inaugural fiat—his very world: "out of / Isaiah, sprang summer; Parmenides, night. / from ... Ibn' / Arabî, those / suspended, / reciprocal // stars" (Sobin, *Voyaging*, p. 63).

Referring to Blake and Char as "my // first masters," Sobin indicates that English poetry played an equally significant role in his development. Gerard Manley Hopkins gave him "the / bow," William Wordsworth "the / quiver" (Sobin, *Voyaging*, pp. 62–64). Sobin credits Thomas Traherne with having shown him "the psalm, burnt / to a glass / whisper," arguing that this undervalued writer is "the most luminous—the most weightless—of the metaphysical poets." Indeed, Sobin shares with his seventeenth-century Anglican predecessor an obsession with origins, a phenomenological bent, and a tendency toward hymns of celebration (Foster, p. 30).

Sobin's roots in American literature were no less formative. As an undergraduate he had already, by perusing the Gertrude Stein collection at Yale, found the works of T. S. Eliot and Ezra Pound. The former, in turn, led him to the French symbolists, while the latter directed him toward the French troubadours, poets from the T'ang and Sung dynasties, and other modernists like James Joyce and Djuna Barnes. Nor did Sobin neglect the current American poetry, especially writers following in Williams's line. He claimed Robert Duncan and George Oppen as his primary American exemplars. Duncan provided Sobin

with a notion of language as Orphic "source of all being" and of "the poem itself as a virtual act of reverence," while Oppen valorized a "focused intensity" toward "investing the particular with its all-too-lost significance" (Foster, p. 29). In addition, Robert Creeley impressed Sobin with his quiet, "profound exploration—in often nothing more than monosyllables—of the human heart," indicating also the formal "cadence of disclosure": measures of breathing and breaking a line, enjambment, the idea of the poem as a "vertical gesture" cascading naturally down the page rather than spanning horizontally (Foster, p. 31). Sobin was conscious of Black Mountain writers like Gary Snyder and of the Objectivists, whom he considered "scrupulously mindful of particulars, discreet if not downright self-effacing in regard to the personal self, and charged with an innate faith in the power of language as a vehicle of revaluations" (cf. Mills). The poetry that exerted the most profound effect on him, in the period immediately preceding his debut volume, was McClure's, "conjuring, creating as it went, whole, unexplored areas—worlds—of potential experience."

The scope of Sobin's study extended to philosophy and linguistic anthropology. Through Char he met Martin Heidegger several times in the mid-1960s. Sobin remembers how, on one such occasion, the German thinker had "e- // lucidated the / verb, alone: its clipped, arrested movement" (Sobin, *Voyaging*, p. 68), and Heidegger can be seen as articulating many of the issues that became crucial to Sobin: the relation between Being and beings; the insistence on language as ontologically central; the fraught quest for authenticity in the face of fear and forgetting; the fourfold gathering of earth, sky, mortals, and gods; concern with the encroaching dangers of technology; the doctrine of care; and a belief in the primacy of Greek thought. Finally, linguists such as Benjamin Lee Whorf and Edward Sapir showed Sobin "how the / least / shift in syntax, tense- / perception, would / re- // set the / heavens" (Sobin, *Voyaging*, p. 65). Of particular import to the growing poet was Whorf's revelation that, because the Hopi language possessed no past tense, origin in that culture could only be expressed by way of imminence.

Sobin married Susannah Estelle Bott, an English painter, in 1968. They had a daughter, Esther Renée, that same year, and in 1971 a son, Gabriel Olivier, was born. These births paralleled yet another: Sobin's own emergence as a poet. The early 1970s constituted a "highly generative moment," he remembers, "in which everything I wrote could well come under the title: 'becoming'" (Foster, p. 30). In December 1972, after ten years of frustrating incubation, at age thirty-seven, Sobin wrote what he considered his first poem.

CRYSTAL AND CHRYSALID: EARLIEST POEMS

Sobin's first poem included "a term of omission," by which he knew he'd gotten under way. That word, "crystal," wielded a sort of talismanic power for the young poet. "'Crystal,' for me, is something both palpable and impalpable, solid yet transparent," he recounted (Foster, p. 30). "Neutral in itself, it nonetheless shatters light. The word alone, at that time, possessed for me an essential ambivalence. It shimmered, it seemed, between the *was* and the *wasn't*. And doing so gave me the kind of license I needed."

The paradoxical notion of something at once essential and ambivalent, both there and not there, is inscribed throughout Sobin's first book, *Wind Chrysalid's Rattle* (1980): "the absence that is," "what isn't … is breath," "It's by what we didn't see that we'll recognize ourselves." Divided into the halves "Wind Chrysalid's Rattle" (1973) and "Mirrorhead" (1975), and anchored by seven interspersed poems titled "Helix," the book is loosely split between relatively short, staccato, enigmatic lyrics that stagger down the page and slightly longer, more expansive and explanatory poems whose syntax is based in the epigram or aphorism. The volume already contains many of the predominant themes and formal structures of Sobin's mature work. Foremost among his fervent assertions is that the earth, because aboriginal, is irreducible, even sacred, and that the poet, far from ordering it, instead serves as its custodian. "We're earless," he writes in "Eototo," "It's the earth / that hears," and in

GUSTAF SOBIN

"All Octaves Simultaneous" he speaks of "Wind, whose iris we are. Whose stutter," concluding that "Pollen is its own godhead."

Insofar as a natural, if not supernatural force is responsible for all being—"Nothing I say, but that I'm said" —the agency and identity of the self is likewise at issue. In the "vast cellular weave" of the universe, humanity and the organic world mirror and move one another, each receiving its orientation from its "counterweight." Poetic utterance becomes nothing less than hearing elemental sound, by "unnaming myself" and echoing "the silage of the ecstatic presence." It's not strange, then, that *ars poetica* joins *de rerum natura* in "That the Universe Is Chrysalid," elaborating Sobin's conviction that "all things that are, are continuous emanations," and that "in creating we extend the very energy that creates us."

Enacting a principle of energy on the level of the individual phoneme, nouns or adjectives become, in Sobin's recasting, verbs: "iridesce," "aureole," "diamond," "star," "icon," and "transluce" all get put to active use. Moreover, the generative process is often figured erotically—the poems abound with intertwined bodies, seeds, germination, liquid, spasms, blowing, swallowing—as the "tongue-cast anatomy of the other: the errant twin" constitutes both the self's stability and its very "risk." This essential ambivalence is maintained through the book's final, appropriately interrogative passage:

who are you,
who are you   who's breathing through me?
     whose hair   braids itself   in my breath?
who still   wordless
is waiting in   shimmers
     for your name to name me. ...

Completed in 1975, the volume appeared five years later from the Montemora Foundation, as a supplement to *Montemora*, a magazine of international poetry and poetics in which Sobin had been publishing. He became a regular contributor to further small journals, such as *Kayak*, *Text*, *Ironwood*, and *Sulfur*, and he also published several chapbooks with Shearsman in England (a small, independent press that published titles by Tomas Tranströmer, Christopher Middleton, Gunnar Har-

ding, and others). The art critic, novelist, and fellow expatriate John Berger was an early champion of Sobin's poetry, introducing it to the poet Charles Tomlinson, who, in turn, recommended it to James Laughlin, the founder and editor of the New York publishing house New Directions. Starting in 1976, Laughlin ran Sobin's poems, over many years, in numerous numbers of the annual *New Directions Anthology in Prose and Poetry*. Another advocate of Sobin's earliest poetry was Eliot Weinberger, whom Sobin met in New York in 1976.

In 1974 Sobin had begun teaching at the Lacoste School of the Arts, initially affiliated with Sarah Lawrence College and later with Bard, a post he would hold for nearly twenty-five years. He visited New York frequently in the late 1970s and early 1980s and also began receiving literary visitors at his home in France, among them Michael Palmer, Clayton Eshleman, Rachel Blau DuPlessis, Susan Howe, James Laughlin, Charles Tomlinson, and Eliot Weinberger, as well as younger writers.

Celebration of the Sound Through (1982), also from Montemora, elaborates Sobin's celebratory dramas of union and division, from its Heraclitean rapport between one and many, sameness and difference, to its juxtaposition of eternity and the ephemeral. Sobin also engages the sexual fusion of bodies, the metaphysical blending and disjoining of selves, and the tenuous relation of one's voice to one's existence. The very manner in which the book's sequences, lines, and even syllables are broken apart and partially reconstituted—"puz- / ling thunder. o- / pen // vocable"—also enacts flux, flight, the dynamics of a late, latent "earth-the-word" in the act of being renewed. Many lines lack a subject, beginning instead with a verb, to indicate how the world worlds itself.

The volume's spiritual as well as its formal arc, announced in the opening sequence "Caesurae: Midsummer," is of "outwards" and "return," of "letting the words take you," as "Way" ventures, "towards wherever they'd come from." Many of those words are characteristically transitive, but poems like "Ash," "Ode," "Who," and "The Hut" feel equally inflected by Paul Celan's

dense, nominal constructions: "voice-bone" and "voice-net," "wind-tombs" and the "where-cage," "mud- / hovels" and "voice-hovel," "heart- // stops," "the no- // body's name," "breath-prints," "breath- / combs," "breath- / holes." In his "A Few Stray Comments on the Cultivation of the Lyric," printed in a 1993 issue of *Talisman* devoted to his work, Sobin advises, "the poem is verbal, rather than nounal," and that the poem should render nouns "light and evocative," should "verbalize" them (Sobin, *Talisman*, p. 43). If, like Ralph Waldo Emerson, Sobin privileges movement and transition over stasis, seeking a "discourse of continuous becoming, unobstructed by the nounal," it does not follow that he eschews tangible objects or rejects words that, in their tactility, slow or stagger a poem's linguistic rush (Foster, p. 34). There is as much "against" in Sobin's work as "toward," as much bunching, clotting, and interruption as "unto." This oscillating, "catch- / flow" duality is in keeping with his recurrent tropes of respiration, mirroring, love-making, kinesis.

Split into halves, "Wave's Scaffolds" (1977) and "Nenuphar" (1980), the book reaches outward to "the / real, un- / remittent grace of the impossible," acknowledging no contradiction between reality and impossibility and even wondering whether such mutuality, however counterintuitive, might not itself be the meaning of grace. "[T]he poem moves // through the death of its making," the last of the "Shadow Rattles" triptych asserts. Appropriating the Hegelian concept of negativity as death put to work, Sobin affirms that none other than "death, / its crushed vapors," is what keeps the poem "alive." The book concludes—precisely without concluding—on the phrase, "*was, / wasn't, // world / blew through*," as if a poem could only be considered present, here and now, when "we send it across … instead of us." As though *Celebration of the Sound Through* were not so much a volume as a volute.

BEING: PORTRAITURE AND PASSAGE

The idea of the poem as passage achieves its most exhaustive enunciation in the title sequence of *The Earth as Air* (1984), the first of a trio of Sobin's books to appear from New Directions. Subtitled "An Ars Poetica," the series begins with an epigraph from Mallarmé and proceeds to affirm his method of working "by elimination," which implies, Sobin says, "a translation of intensities: an *othering*," so that "we articulate *away* from ourselves in a continuous elision *towards*" (Sobin, *The Earth as Air*, p. 89). Eliciting Mallarmé's observation that the word "rose," in replacing the real object, signals the flower's actual absence while maintaining its presence in language, Sobin avers that the poem comes into existence via the dissolution of the self who speaks, and that the poem's utterance and envoy, in turn, likewise coincide with its own disappearance. Vanishing presides over both poet and poem, the former "expelled," the latter "a quit body: a quittance. // a locution-in-displacement, in ritual flight towards its own reception" (Sobin, *Earth*, pp. 98, 90). The self and the poem alike, then, are means to an end, each "being nothing, in itself: an otherwise-isn't, except for the syllables, either side, that channel, sluice, project it forth" (Sobin, *Earth*, p. 88). By this "as if sacrificial" procedure, the word inaugurates "a dimension that we've metrically fashioned, projected past us, and assembled forever *to our own exclusion*" (Sobin, *Earth*, pp. 98, 92).

In this domain, where the poet can no longer follow his poem, and where the poem too will dissolve, the "created" is "syncretic with creation," and "each / thing, unto its sign- / auspicious, is / rendered" (Sobin, *Earth*, pp. 97–98). Yet that marriage of world and word, whereby the rose is "*one // with its / absence*," is not a straightforwardly Orphic gesture or an Adamic imperative to name (Sobin, *Earth*, p. 94). The lyric act, in Sobin's estimation, indeed shuns the traditional aims of representation, reflection, repetition, but his *ars poetica* also heralds, if not the death of the author—which was then gaining prominence in American literary culture, thanks to Jacques Derrida, Michel Foucault, Roland Barthes, and others—then a suspension of the authorial. In writing, Sobin offers, the writer, a "pre- / fix for setting / sub- / stance to // syl-

lable," becomes "neither living nor dead, now, but extravagated, an *ex-vita*" (Sobin, *Earth*, pp. 59, 91). Not yet deceased, but no longer vital: the author is touched by the "null," the "no-breath," that the poem carries "within." This interior "death," endemic to writing, pushes both writer and written outside themselves, but it is different from the mere extinction of life. Instead, it is a "death continuously discharged, expelled, projected"—a death, Sobin proposes, appealing again to Hegelian negativity, "*kept alive.*"

That the poet is finally exempted from the poem hints at a transposed theology, and *The Earth as Air* flirts with paradigms of divinity: with what, speaking of the late painter Ambrogio Magnaghi, Sobin calls a "lingering religiosity" (Sobin, *Ambrogio Magnaghi*, p. 11). In associating "the // wrought heavens" with "our blanched / reflectives," Sobin suggests a Platonic hierarchy of forms (Sobin, *Earth*, p. 8). The colon that separates—and also joins—these two phrases, however, does not specify the nature of the association between celestial and earthly perfection, between "the rose- / iconic" and "the rose- // votive," unless the first be vanishing point to the second through the transformative properties of the poem (Sobin, *Earth*, p. 94). Elsewhere Sobin regrets, however, that there is "no / heaven" whatsoever "and / scarce- // ly an / earth," evoking what is "neither this world's, nor / another's" (Sobin, *Earth*, pp. 25, 20). It would seem that each human has been thrown into a situation that, through "sleights- / of- / life," she alone is responsible for making habitable (Sobin, *Earth*, p. 19). Yet despite living "ever in default of a face"—in an era that has forgotten God, or in which the gods have turned away—Sobin discovers an overwhelmingly redemptive quality to "the wind- / light we live in" (Sobin, *Earth*, p. 42, 22). The trees, he sings, are "conjugates" of some mysterious grammar, and our first and final impulse is to "dwell, had said. / dwell, would / dwell" (Sobin, *Earth*, p. 65, 67).

It may be only "through the words / we'd // enter," but Sobin also establishes the singularity of poetic expression syntactically (Sobin, *Earth*, p. 65). Eccentric punctuation, indentation, line breaks, and interpolated blank space render major portions of his poems resistant to being cited—or cited accurately—within expository prose. Throughout Sobin's poetry extra space is sometimes inserted between words, which though possible to signal in offset quotations is awkward when citing within an essay. Similarly, his poems often begin or end with ellipses, and some even feature long strings of dots, spanning several lines. The reader of an essay citing such passages can never be certain whether ellipses within quotation marks are the commentator's or the poem's. In addition, many of Sobin's lines are half stepped, testing the critic's ingenuity: if she decides in favor of the standard symbol "/" she risks denoting a full line break, yet otherwise she ignores the shift altogether, or else is forced to devise a new mark. There are other features of Sobin's syntax that are difficult to intimate when reprinting: left margins shift; page breaks fail to indicate if a stanza continues or ends; and sentences frequently begin without capital letters, which would "set up a tiny, typographical hierarchy," Sobin avers, "that I've always considered slightly imperious" (cf. Mills). Asserting the irreducibility of poetry, Sobin constantly frustrates the capacity of orthodox prose to assimilate or reproduce the poetic utterance—let alone to accommodate the experience.

That is not to say, however, that Sobin's poems do not intermittently behave like essays. "He either writes skinny poems," William Corbett observes bluntly of Sobin in the *Boston Phoenix*, "or spreads his lines over the whole page, leaving a lot of white space." Sobin has argued that his poetry moves "from statement to implication," that the "vertical tracking" and "gravitational pull" of his poems downward is "natural" and "innate" rather than "intellectually acquired," and that breaking with linear prosody, as he often does, means breaking with linear thought (Foster, pp. 28, 31). With the publication of three "Carnets," however, initially as a chapbook (1984) and subsequently as an integral part of *The Earth as Air*, Sobin inaugurated a new tendency in his verse. Oriented horizontally and conceptually less oblique, "Carnets: 1979" is the first in a mostly contiguous string (there are none for the second half of the 1980s) of annual poetic

sequences that seek not, as in his other lyrics, to move organically "from a place, a locus, a set of material circumstances, to a proposition," but rather to consciously recycle the season's left-overs (Foster, p. 26). "Each year, at the end of the year or the beginning of the next," Sobin explains,

I draw—from so many disparate passages—a sense. A sequence. What I call an itinerary, a transparent itinerary ... Here, indeed, I create a mosaic out of so many given pieces, a collage of sorts. I type up whatever passages might be potentially useful, then, cutting each into a separate strip of paper, lay them out over the bedspread. There, keeping an eye on the *ensemble*, I begin making a sequential arrange- ment, adding passages as I need them, while eliminating others as I go. Bit by bit, they begin describing a direction, a thematic itinerary, taking me somewhere that I've never been before (Foster, p. 35).

If this procedure departs from Sobin's less-methodical usual method, "the result," he claims, "is identical: extending sense past oneself, and reaching into the revelatory." Indeed, in explicat-ing the process he uses the word "passage" no fewer than three times.

The serial poem has a notable twentieth-century American lineage, and Sobin's hail in part from Louis Zukofsky's *"A"* (written between 1928 and 1974), Duncan's "The Structure of Rime," and "Passages" (written and published mainly in the 1960s), and Charles Olson's "Maxi-mus" poems (published in three volumes: 1960, 1968, and 1975). No sooner does "Carnets: 1979" begin with ellipses, "air," and "things the / breath / first fluted"—in a spirit of openness, and as if continuing some conversation already ongoing— than it swerves, gets lost among detours, makes the parenthetical its priority. The "Carnets" refer to themselves languorously as "waves, chasing the scooped and wobbling heart of their own craters" and as "the length of some taut, indis-soluble rhythm," but other characterizations demonstrate that Sobin will not entirely relinquish his instinct to stagger: "these / sudden // ver- / tebrae / of // breath," "ledge of / the // hesitant / in its throe // forwards" (41, 36, 38, 30).

Beginning in *Voyaging Portraits*, Sobin's an-nual series assumes the title "Transparent Itinerar-ies," a phrase that had appeared on the back of the 1984 *Carnets* chapbook. "Essentially ephem-eral in nature," the description runs, "each pas-sage lasts exactly the length of its implication: its 'sign.' In each of the poem's four sequences, or itineraries, these signs indicate more than they reveal: they suggest, rather than disclose. One elicits another, each linking—transparently—with the next, as the poem moves across the broken landscapes of the experiential." Aside from continued emphasis on passages, that text points explicitly to the Heraclitean propositions that the world loves to hide and that, like an oracle, it neither reveals nor conceals things but offers signs to be deciphered. The world might mask itself, according to "Transparent Itineraries: 1983," phenomenologically, one object resem-bling or standing behind a second, as "each thing discloses another in an uninterrupted game of spatial displacements" (Sobin, *Voyaging*, p. 16). Natural elements, as Heraclitus likewise pointed out, transform into one another, with water becoming air during evaporation, and air turning to rain or fire. Sobin signals these metamorphoses in phrases of equivalence—earth *as* air, portrait of the self *as* instrument,—in "Of the Four-Winged Cherubim as Signature."

Such substitution and revelation occurs on a linguistic level, too. In a phrase like "(aloes, oleanders)," which occupies its own line, one word is composed entirely of letters enclosed in its counterpart (Sobin, *Voyaging*, p. 18). Sobin exploits other verbal similarities: "draft-star, our speculated drift," a line from "Transparent Itineraries: 1984," opens and closes with words only a vowel from identical, while farther down is "piled hearts, that heaped linen," where "hearts" and "heaped" each enclose "hea-" and both are framed by the palimpsest "-il-" / "-li-" (Sobin, *Voyaging*, p. 23). "Ode: For the Budding of Islands" is built on a sonorous conjugation, with "is / swiftness" morphing to "twist" and "hissed / syllables," then to "ciphers," "issues," "islands, / phosphors," and from there to "fixed," "flags of / our // forage," "be- / fore," "corals of metaphor" (Sobin, *Voyaging*, pp. 25–26). And

just as one part of speech can function as another in Sobin's work, here it is not flowers that bud, but islands.

As the book's title suggests, place and displacement have been integral to Sobin's notion of poetic work. In the early 1980s he translated *Ideograms in China* (1984) by the indomitable voyager Henri Michaux, while scouting locations throughout the Dordogne (a Michelin map and *The Cantos* in hand) for Laughlin, who was preparing to make a film about Pound. Sobin made three successive trips across the United States with his children, documented in "Along America's Edges." If "A Portrait of the Self …" is an account of his emergence as a poet, enabled by moving away from the States, then this ensuing section details how he "scattered" himself going back. Situated in Nantasket (Massachusetts), Rochester (New York), Albuquerque and Gallup (New Mexico), and even New York City's LaGuardia Airport, the poems trace—and erase—Sobin's "personal circuitry" across his native land. In his search for a "syntax equal to all that unhappening," recorded especially in "Road, Roadsides, and the Disparate Frames of a Sequence," the inability of language to "fix immensity" is posed against the forced disappearance of native Americans, with whose civilizations Sobin identifies (Sobin, *Voyaging*, pp. 86, 94, 89).

The volume's closing section is set—or unsettled—among the "living vestige" of Italy, a conceit that informs poems dedicated to Sobin's children and in memory of his parents (Sobin, *Voyaging*, p. 119). That country is likewise the site of *Sicilian Miniatures* (1986), a chapbook comprised of fifty-seven sensual, peripatetic quatrains. Trained on coins and vases, catacombs and *palazzo*, tin sheds and fortresses, the author remarks how "the ruins / gape, won't / close."

NON-BEING: POETRY IN THE NAME OF NOTHING

Eight poems or sequential sections in Sobin's fifth volume begin with the word "no" or its variants. A hymn to emptiness, absence, and the *unheimlich*, obfuscated or unrecoverable origin,

unnaming and the nameless, *Breaths' Burials* (1995) undertakes a "burgeoning," as one poem states, "about the // nihil, the / nullitas" (Sobin, *Breaths' Burials*, p. 51). According to Robert Baker in a review titled "The Muse of Aboutness," for Sobin "elision represents the metaphysical paradox at the center of a poetry that constantly moves towards the inexpressible" (*American Book Review*, p. 28). Sobin's fascination with "that apophatic night," "clamped lids of the naught, " and "dark daisy-chains of the *nicht*" places him in conversation with negative theologians, from Dionysius the Areopagite to Saint John of the Cross, who posit that humankind can know *that* God exists but never *what* He is, that God can be thought only in terms of what He is not, and that to communicate with the ineffable requires enduring a dark night of suffering (Sobin, *Breaths'*, pp. 55, 50, 57). Many of Sobin's poems conclude with an italicized passage, structured as a secular prayer or prose statement not unlike, say, the supplications perforating Saint Augustine's *Confessions* (397 AD) or the arguments that end Traherne's *Thanksgivings* (1699). "*the null : the null, at / last, ebullient*," reads the close of "Poesis : A Conceit," Sobin recoding mystical self-divestment as an artistic posture, whereby flesh is rendered word, "*and / you, little // more than this body you'd / tease— mass, / cajole—through the narrow stalk of / so // much / muttered syllable*" (Sobin, *Breaths'*, p. 61).

Sobin's increasing commitment to negativity, however, is far from any orthodox, systematic, or sustained theology. He works among an array of writers—Jacques Derrida, Paul Celan, Maurice Blanchot, Martin Heidegger, Wallace Stevens, Emily Dickinson—whose texts unfold what continental philosophy has begun elaborating as "religion without religion." Featuring structural parallels to spiritual transcendence, but missing the divine, dogmatic center, such writing retains a recognizably theological paradigm while supplanting its traditional content. Sobin's invocation to "*mother of no one*," like his "Psalmodic" and myriad lyrics to "no one's light," replace an omnipotent, godly presence with an anonymous impersonality, reinscribing the ascetic imperative

to "shed identity" as an aesthetic call to "recognize our own anonymity" (Sobin, *Breaths'*, pp. 20, 51, 76). What was "sacred, once," he claims in "Eckhart," invoking the German theologian, has since "dissolved ... down / through the / fresh definitions," which however diluted or "dull" are nonetheless the "vestige" remaining (Sobin, *Breaths'*, 65). "Transparent Itineraries: 1992" says it unequivocally: "the divine, you knew, was never more than the nominal substitute for those wordless expanses" (Sobin, *Breaths'*, p. 57).

Speaking in an interview with Leonard Schwartz about the necessity of this surrogate, Sobin notes, "Since at least the outset of the Neolithic, ten thousand years earlier, human societies have addressed—in supplication—invisible auditoria. Have basked in the radiance of some form of immanent response" (*Verse*, p. 110). Whether propitiatory, thaumaturgic, or redemptive, Sobin continues, such replies

have served humankind as the indispensable complement to an all-too-precarious existence on earth. They were, for millennia, one's omniscient mirror. That this mirror has undergone eclipse and, along with it, deprived us of our most privileged form of address, few would deny. What hasn't vanished, however, is the need—call it the psychic imperative—that such an address exist. Long after the addressee has vanished, after the omniscient mirror has dissolved and its transcendent dimension been dismantled, demystified, deconstructed, there remains—I insist—that psychic imperative deeply inscribed within the innermost regions of our being. We can't do, it would seem, without something that isn't. ... Only in the poem, I find, in so many stray bars of speculative music, can that trajectory still be traced.

Sobin's nihil is an invisible looking-glass in which people still recognize themselves. If that mirror seems distant from us, argues Philip Crick in *Evolving the Idol: The Poetry of Gustaf Sobin* (1984), this is so it might, in its separation, turn to face us (p. 12). And if trading scripture, psalm, and prayer for that other supreme fiction, poetry, while swapping abundance for nothingness, means our world is now merely "decor" and "empty / gesture," as the sequence "Lines from Pietro Longhi" worries, where the self seems less

alive than "some life-sized rendering" on a stage, we should recall, Sobin cautions, that this "nearly a / world" is also our only one (Sobin, *Breaths'*, pp. 55, 6).

Moreover, his allusion to a "*late country*," to "living / as you did, towards the very end, at the / earth's // virtual completion," certainly evokes Hegel's fulfillment of history (Sobin, *Breaths'*, pp. 90, 96). Sobin's later poetry might be considered in relation to the Hegelian reflexivity by which a concept, not least of all the self, becomes what it is only at the end of a dialectical movement, after having passed through successive alterities. Indeed, Sobin speaks in "Odes of Estrangement" about being "worked free" of one's "moorings," of having "followed yourself / through your own, displaced / worksites," where "alternately, you / are and / aren't," and of having finally, "in the name of / nothing, ... reached / this abundance" (Sobin, *Breaths'*, pp. 85, 90, 86, 97).

The poet, "charged / with emptiness," as Sobin says elsewhere in *Breaths' Burials*, assays to "pour / the sounds back" into the world, that objects might once again stand where linguistic representation had shadowed them. In finding for every object its "voided counterpart"—not ideation but a noise preceding speech, a "language-with- / out"—the breath will "absolve," Sobin declares, "its least / syllable" from the mimetic appropriation formerly leveled against things. He announces this restorative dynamic in the poem's title: "Absolution." As the philosopher Giorgio Agamben elucidates in "**Se*: Hegel's Absolute and Heidegger's *Ereignis*" (*Potentialities: Collected Essays in Philosophy*, 1999), the word "absolute" hails from the Latin verb *solvo*, or *se-luo*, which indicates a loosening that leads something back to its own proper, or absolves it. Plural and possessive in the title of Sobin's volume, the breaths undergo burials: not because, like some dead language, they too have gone to their rest, but rather in order to realize themselves, to come back from the night of their inner divisions, into their own: to "let, let / one // another out" (Sobin, *Breaths'*, p. 82).

Vigilant against "all-reductive, all-exclusive rationality," Sobin generally spoke of his poems

in terms of intuitive, organic development, of writing as obeying "an inherent tendency within language to unspell, unspeak, divest itself of its own nomenclature in an attempt to touch upon the untouchable, utter the unutterable" (Schwartz, p. 107–108, 112). He claimed not only that a poem "begins with the perception of a single palpable object or phenomenon," from which its lines "evolve," but also that "the more that initial image expresses a palpable reality, the more it permits—even provokes—an impalpable reflection." His annual "Transparent Itineraries," constructed as bricolage, for the most part proved the sole exception to his usual directive, "don't write a poem: grow it … the poem grows out of the poem, not out of one's own, particular intellect" (Sobin, *Talisman*, p. 41).

Marking a procedural departure for Sobin, however, *Towards the Blanched Alphabets* (1998) partakes of extended intellectual, if not academic, exploration. "Reading Sarcophagi: An Essay" poetically traces half a millennium of history to Constantine's conversion, spanning eleven pages and featuring endnotes, signaled by number within the text. Similarly, the even longer "Late Bronze, Early Iron: A Journey Book" examines the emergence, between 700 and 550 BC, of the "mercantile exchange system, undermining every form of autonomous economy," naming along the way specific sites: Lattara, St. Marcel-sur-Aude, Aigues-Vives, Cabezac. Reaching less for the ineffable than for an irretrievable history, many poems in the volume eschew a seminal object of meditative contemplation characteristic of Sobin's earlier, haiku-like lyrics, and instead pursue, with increasing abstraction and logic, the decline of entire societies.

That is not to say that the volume avoids singing of "that *isn't* that // *is*," which "run[s] inextricable / through the living mass," or that Sobin neglects the "word-wordless" silence and the "richly invested naught" that condition and lure the lyric (Sobin, *Towards*, pp. 3, 8, 20). For Sobin, "poetry not only bears the null within itself as silence," argues Baker in a 1999 review, "but must encounter nothingness as the very horizon of its own existence" ("The Open Vocable," *American Book Review*, p. 10). It is appropriate that Sobin frequently mentions "aura," including once with reference to Walter Benjamin and once evoking the goddess Aura, for his poems are obsessed by "lost adequation," "vacua," "self-generated ephemera," and "rippling / chimera" (Sobin, *Towards*, pp. 105, 103, 107, 120). Pitched from a vantage of "aftermath" and "afterworld," their desire to "precede vestige" recalls the constellation of "aura" with "aurora" and "aural," hinting that humanity's unsharded authenticity is to be found in the dawn of civilization, before the immediacy of voice was scuttled by the deferral, repeatability, and unverifiability of the written (Sobin, *Towards*, pp. 30, 32).

Yet even as he "pillage[s] history for its / lost dicta, abolished alphabets," lamenting that language, co-opted by the capitalist project, has since become utilitarian, Sobin sees the poem moving not backward but forward: "already, the poem, basking in / its idol of syllables, exists in a / future you'd never, otherwise, have / known" (12–13). Eirik Steinhoff astutely situates Sobin's late work between the romantic belief that archaic objects permit entry into an antediluvian moment of linguistic transparency and poststructuralist skepticism about language's ability to refer (*Chicago Review*, p. 118). Similarly, Sobin places himself between "sumptuous shelters of the exclusively / acoustic" and "broken // grammar," between "breath's // transparent coinage" and "misnomer," between "reciprocal signifiers" and "arbitrary imprint," between "people who'd existed, no doubt, in the very glow of their own voices" and "living in the resonance of an absentee's pronoun" (Sobin, *Towards*, pp. 75, 102, 6, 104, 81, 17, 41, 21). The notion of interval is regularly thematized by Sobin, who claims humanity is both lodged and dislocated between two languages. Roughly corresponding to the "saying" and the "said" theorized by Emmanuel Lévinas in his 1974 volume *Autrement qu'être; ou, Au-delà de l'essence* (*Otherwise Than Being; or, Beyond Essence*), Sobin posits an "uninterruptedly mute" *urspracht* that is present, but never exhausted, in "our own" speech (Sobin, *Towards*, pp. 63, 7). Words are only the ontological echo or "antiphon" to a primeval language that is beyond being. Sobin

believes that only poetry—in which the subject seeks not to give signs but to become one, expelled out of all dwelling toward the other—can attempt the restoration of "saying."

Reviewers have noted the lack of long sequences and relative brevity of each poem in *In the Name of the Neither* (2002), though as a whole it continues to privilege ideation and highly speculative rhetoric, opening with epigraphs from Plotinus and Benjamin about periphrasis. Nonetheless, the book has an air of erotic desperation, of couples conjoining in a disjointed world, that had been most overt in *Articles of Light & Elation* (1998). A cycle of forty-six highly alliterative and assonantal lyrics, addressed to an unnamed "you," that latter book glorifies "ankles / arched flat and fingers, in / that furious arabesque, forked," as two lovers "pummelled weightless" the "piled weight of / our lives," trying to "quit sequence" in favor of eternity and to "end, this / distance, this / 'self' as separate" (Sobin, *Articles*, pp. 6, 9, 28, 13). While *In the Name* mostly avoids *Articles*'s baroque diction, it still shares the project of "working our- / selves out- / ward" in pursuit of "that single, ir- / repressible instant; what knows, indeed, / neither // antecedent nor / sequel" (Sobin, *Name*, pp. 14, 24).

This notion of "neither" assumed tremendous importance in Sobin's latter work, catalyzing and coalescing his convictions that poetry generates energy in heading toward its reception, that a poem issues from no one and needs a destination, that things and language are inherently reciprocal, that the self is other even unto itself. "The 'neither'," he explained, "occurs any time one of those paired counterpoints … meet in such perfect equanimity that they tend to cancel one another out. The very tension that constitutes the energy field for these polaric opposites undergoes, at such moments, release" (Schwartz, p. 112). Inside this description resounds Martin Buber's pairing of I-and-Thou, as well as the ethical *autrui* of Lévinas. The grammatical form of the subject, Lévinas avers in *Otherwise Than Being*, is not merely reflexive—it is an "accusative that derives from no nominative." This "*se- accusative*," or the subject described "from the first in the accusative form," indicates that the self is constitutively "under accusation": standing before and living for the other, radically exposed to him and ever in his debt, not absolved but guilty (Lévinas, pp. 11, 53). Of the relation between self and other in his poetry, "the 'you,'" Sobin explained, "deliberately playing on its own ambivalence—invites the two, ever-estranged participants in any given text to a certain complicity" (cf. Mills). Sometimes using "neither" as a verb, he has likewise employed the Chinese cosmological terminology of yin and yang to characterize this mutually voiding, mutually affirmative rapport, this "vis-à-vis" by which we are "vouchsafed" (Sobin, *Name*, p. 53).

Trust in the efficacy of symbiotic models has been present in Sobin's poetry from the moment he calibrated breath as its measure. Just as humans exhale the carbon that plants need, while flora expels the oxygen fauna breathes, so does the poet "convert" the external world's "waves of non-vocal utterance" into "articulated speech-music," before throwing them "back, wave-like, toward their source" (Crick, p. 11). It is by this natural cycle that, as Sobin's "Article of Faith" professes, "nothing / ends" (Sobin, *Name*, p. 57).

LOCATION OR LOCUTION: ESSAYS

It is not surprising that Sobin's last pair of poetry books published before his death, containing poems like "Barroco: An Essay" and "On Imminence: An Essay," were written concurrently with a research project on Gallo-Roman antiquity. Asked how his poetry relates to his nonfiction prose, Sobin proffered that whereas poems "draw essentially from the present, attempting—in their speculative movement forth—to track intent, extrapolate meaning, speculate on what might be called the ontologically withheld," the essays "draw from the past in an attempt to elucidate the present" (Schwartz, p. 110).

Part anthropological treatise, part eco-poetic apologia, rigorously historical and reservedly hopeful, *Luminous Debris: Reflecting on Vestige in Provence and Languedoc* (1999) comprises twenty-six essays spanning nearly four hundred thousand years of civilization as attested by

vestige between Nice and Narbonne. "The artifacts 'speak' if we know how to 'listen,'" Sobin says in his introduction. "The artifacts themselves are like words. They only await translation" (Sobin, *Luminous Debris*, pp. 3–6). Seeking to unearth vestige, in the dual sense of digging up and revealing, before it vanishes forever, Sobin desires also to preserve the past respectfully, that it not become mere spectacle or commercial ware. Less an archaeologist than a self-proclaimed "*archiviste*" and "*flaneur*" among stacks of print material, Sobin nonetheless traces the objects and instances that, in generating "reflection, reference," might "serve as a kind of resuscitated mirror," whereby we can "situate our own existence today." Such an exercise in the existential has never been more urgent: "Adrift in a world of semiotic vacuity, lost to ourselves in the midst of so much electronic overload," Sobin diagnoses, "we've begun, as if intuitively, haunting museums, consulting archives," sifting and valorizing the past "as never before," that it might substantiate a present otherwise in "default."

Sobin commits to a "*vertical* reading" of southeastern France, delving down for the "underwritten," not so much the world before ours as the one beneath. Sigmund Freud hence occasionally supplies a useful nomenclature, and to contextualize his arguments Sobin also calls on Plutarch, Pliny the Elder, Vitruvius, Sir Thomas Browne, Friedrich Schiller, Jean-Jacques Rousseau, Rainer Maria Rilke, Emile Benveniste, and Mircea Eliade. Regretting his sometimes abstract rhetoric, Margaret Todd Maitland, in *Hungry Mind Review*, nevertheless sees Sobin as "working in an honorable French philosophical tradition" that includes Gaston Bachelard's *The Poetics of Space* (1958), investigating the archetypal power of quotidian things (58). She claims Sobin has reinvigorated a nineteenth-century, "lyrical" approach to archaeology, rather than practicing its lamentably "statistical," current variety.

In his examination of the receding world, Sobin scrutinizes windbreaks, pictographs and toponyms, stelae and tesserae, aqueducts, urns, earrings, votive mirrors. Pursuing our lost ontology across a now "gameless wasteland," Sobin rediscovers an Eden where, contra our current state of linguistic deconstruction, abuse, and decay, "every 'signifier' seems to have elicited its equivalent 'signified,' every point its perfectly matched counterpoint" (Sobin, *Luminous*, p. 24, 91). Nor was this "tightly woven system of reciprocities" limited to verbal coherence. Sobin sees symbiosis permeating the entire prehistoric milieu. "If I'd come to read the aboriginal arrowhead not as a word but as a kind of hyphen drawn between two discrete quantities" Sobin writes in "The First Hunters and the Last," questioning his own analogy of landscape and language, "between society and nature, the bestowed and the bestower—the connective itself implied agreement, reciprocity, trust. It implied a contract of sorts in which a lesser entity (ourselves) was granted permission to subsist upon the bounty of a greater entity (nature)" (Sobin, *Luminous*, p. 28).

As with all such ancient contracts, Sobin esteems, it has long since been revoked, leaving us to gather the scattered shards by which it might be coaxed to endure a little longer. That it has taken a few cursory centuries to deface what required hundreds of thousands of patient, meticulous years to construct is the most pressing, prescient observation leveled by Sobin. *Luminous Debris* constantly solemnizes the "immensely delicate balance," as "Terremare" states, "that must be met by any society in its relation to all the forces, natural or not, by which it is surrounded" (Sobin, *Luminous*, p. 107).

In the end, Sobin considers signifying and site as mutually enabling. His search for the world's "inherent discourse," like the concomitant quest for some "synthesizing grammar" by which to read its architectural and natural features, transcends metaphor (Sobin, *Luminous*, p. 203, 204). He cannot make up his mind whether his excavations are in pursuit of "a *location* or a *locution*," as he admits in "Aeria the Evanescent" (Sobin, *Luminous*, p. 170). The fact that those two words vary by only a vowel articulates important, if competing, points: that locus and lingua, place and patois, take their first and final

bearings from one another; and that the difference installed by a single letter is enormously significant.

VANISHING STARS: FICTION

"If poetry could be called the realm of the unexpected," Sobin posited to Edward Foster, then "prose, at least as I see it, is that of the plan, the foreseen" (Foster, p. 34). The author of four novels, Sobin claimed to "always know what I'm after in fiction," which he dubbed poetry's "total opposite." Indeed, Jane Solanus's brief, favorable review of his *Venus Blue* (1991) notes, "There is a *lot* of academic calculation about American poet Gustaf Sobin's first novel" (Jane Solanus, *Time Out*). The themes and methods of his fiction, however, are not always markedly distinct from his poetry's. His procedure of structuring lyrics vertically has been "influenced by film," he conceded, where "cadence is determined by an inexorable movement downward," one image replacing another (cf. Mills). How appropriate, then, that Douglas Messerli, in the *Los Angeles Times Book Review*, argues, "*Venus Blue* is less a novel about filmmaking than it is a film cloaked in the language of fiction."

Two of Sobin's novels are set in Hollywood, two in Provence—a perfect symmetry of his coasts. "Sobin writes like a man torn between two cultures," claims John Nicholson in the London *Times*. "His languorous prose owes little to his New World origins, though his fascination with the minutiae of studio life and his admiration for *film noir* belong to the universal tradition of the cineaste." *Venus Blue* is the story of a late 1930s starlet named Molly Lamanna, a living principle of disappearance and dissimulation, and the efforts of two others to comprehend if not capture her: the writer Millicent Rappaport, whose love for the B-movie actress borders on mania, and the memorabilia collector Stefan Hollander, who reads Millicent's journals fifty years later. A bush pilot addicted to night flying, Molly has an "elusive and apparently unqualifiable" essence, spurred by having twice experienced shocks resulting in amnesia (Sobin, *Venus Blue*, p. 3). Unable to look back, she hurtles forward.

Seeming to "slip, each time, through logic, language, through all the systems we've ever invented for the simple purpose of determining, with increasing rigour, our arbitrary realities" (Sobin, *Venus*, p. 190), Molly exemplifies Denis Diderot's paradox: that to perform a character, an actor must possess no personality of her own. More acutely, Molly stands in for a kind of deity—her name itself contains "manna"—presiding over a quasi-spiritual tale of stolen origin, desire, impossibility, and the allure of an "idol" that is *hors catégorie* (Sobin, *Venus*, pp. 157, 96). Her seductive vacuity, moreover, has the dual effect of reducing others and creating replicas. Molly has a doppelgänger, Vivien Voigt, to aid her subterfuge, while Millicent, feeling herself "slipping," discovers that, since Molly's given name was Mildred Pearl, she shares with her quarry the moniker "Milly."

The novel mobilizes other concerns dear to Sobin. "Paralleling the attempt to discover Molly Lamanna's history is an inquiry into language," Messerli argues, "the *means* of art to define and describe its subject." As Zoë English elaborates in "Essence, Absence, and Sobin's *Venus Blue*," that Milly's narrative arrives twice-removed, by way of a journal read by Hollander, enacts Sobin's "conviction that language can convey a genuine sense of 'presence' only through the writer's dislocation from the work" (*Talisman*, p. 60). Second, the novel hearkens toward an *age d'ôr*. While the edenic, earlier world is cinematic and fictional here, rather than an actual antiquity, it is nonetheless proposed as a soteriological ideal among an otherwise corrupt, capitalistic modernity "raised upon a vision of sheer mythlessness" and on the edge of world war (Sobin, *Venus*, p. 143). Concomitant with this nostalgia is the novel's indulgence in "the bone heap" of screen archives, "an underworld, a cryptic substratum composed of pure minutiae," where the curator plays Pluto to secular relic hunters (Sobin, *Venus*, pp. 8–9). "Here," Sobin states, in rhetoric evoking *Luminous Debris*,

resides everything one might possibly need to reconstitute—even a half-century later—the daily lives of particular actors or actresses. ... Once within (or, more exactly, once under, for one didn't enter

the archives: one delved, one plummeted), it wasn't so much an act of scholarship that was called for, as that, precisely, of an exhumation.

An epigraph, by Roland Barthes, to Sobin's other novel about an actress announces similar preoccupations: "Garbo's face constitutes a kind of summation of the flesh that one can neither attain nor abandon." The novel's epigraphs mark the only moment of *In Pursuit of a Vanishing Star* (2002) where Greta Garbo's name is mentioned, testifying no less to Sobin's belief in aesthetic indirection and apposite privacy than to the iconic inaccessibility—even to herself, the novel hazards—of the woman known as the "Divine One" (Sobin, *Pursuit*, p. 6). The narrator Philip Nilson, a modern-day filmmaker, in seeking to portray Garbo's 1924 stay in Constantinople with Maurice Stiller, resolves to reveal her face only at the end, and then merely in the reflection cast by the glass framing a photograph. Other items corroborating Garbo's deified status include the fantasy of a "last living witness" and the facts that "Episode in Constantinople," which so obsesses Nilson, was a silent film, that it went unfinished, and that no footage remains.

If Garbo's anonymity, abetted by the multiple pseudonyms she assumes in order to travel undetected, paradoxically renders her singular, the other characters double one another, in a Proustian relay of plurality and repetition. Nilson is paired with Phil Silverstein, who shares his first name and is married to his former wife, Laura. She, in turn, had been a "stand-in spouse for a lost beloved," reminding Nilson of an unrequited childhood love for his half-sister Leila (Sobin, *Pursuit*, p. 15). Leila died young of a blood disorder, thereby continuing "to serve," by Nilson's reckoning, "as a model for each and every woman I ever encountered" (Sobin, *Pursuit*, p. 31). In this, Leila is like the Annabel reprised by Humbert Humbert as Lolita in Vladimir Nabokov's *Lolita* (1955)—where both girls are already consciously figured as revisions of Edgar Allan Poe's nymphette, Annabel Lee. Nilson even mistakes a film negative of his mother for Leila. "Wasn't that, though, a game that each of us played," he asks: "a game of semblances in which one life gets piled—superimposed—upon the next? A game, that is, wherein each successive rapport grows more and more remote, vicarious, insubstantial: an endless series of pseudo-replications?" If Garbo is an "idol," archetypal and irreplaceable, she is so because moviegoers live in an era when collective spiritual adulation has long since vanished, leaving people, in "default of that single, singular presence," to "substitute" and fabricate "sublimated personifications" (Sobin, *Pursuit*, p. 129).

Alan Riding's article on Sobin in the *New York Times* in March 2000 notes that the novel was originally titled "For Her Lashes Alone." Not unlike Sobin's other writings, *Pursuit* is deeply engaged with "the fragility of human relationships," as he explores how passions "depend on something as slight as the arch of an eyebrow," how iconic "immensities" emerge out of "lashes and light" (Sobin, *Pursuit*, pp. 13, 64). In an unusual case of Hollywood finding its way into Sobin's poetry, "On *Imagerie*: Esther Williams, 1944," published in *The Faber Book of Movie Verse* (1993), likewise venerates a sex symbol's elbows, hair, and hands. Recollecting that Williams taught him to swim at the Beverly Hills Hotel when he was eight, Sobin discovers "ob- / fuscated worlds" in every sensual move, in "the / milkiest / emulsions," of the MGM aquatic star (pp. 203–204, 244).

The influences to which reviewers have alluded in situating Sobin's novels are myriad, themselves constituting the "bizarrerie" that the *Independent on Sunday* labeled his fictional debut. That paper viewed *Venus Blue* as an unlikely blend of F. Scott Fitzgerald and the director Billy Wilder, while Doris Lynch said in *Library Journal* that its "sensual focus" recalls Lawrence Durrell. More surprising are the literary antecedents and divergent linguistic values attributed to *The Fly-Truffler* (1999), which was an unexpected success, garnering attention in Hollywood as well as from the Académie d'Aix-en-Provence, which awarded the book its highest literary prize. Christopher Lehmann-Haupt of the *New York Times* saw Nabokov in its "detail," *Publishers Weekly* heard the "gothic strains" of Poe, the *New Yorker* detected "magic realism," and Catherine

GUSTAF SOBIN

Kasper tasted Proust's *madeleine* in the book's mushrooms and "lush imagery" (*Rain Taxi*, p. 27). On the level of language, all critics seemed to agree with Lehmann-Haupt that the novel is "mesmerizing" and "haunting," and nearly everyone concurred with William Corbett in the *Boston Phoenix* that the real protagonist is the very language itself. Whereas Corbett praised the book's "spare, lucid prose," however, as resembling the ancient Provençal language likewise characterized by "exquisite economy," the *New Yorker* pronounced the book worthwhile "despite a few spells of overblown prose." Similarly, while *Publishers Weekly* proffered that "Sobin's prose is dense and aromatic, his descriptions gorgeously verging on the purple," the *Los Angeles Times Book Review*, to the contrary, found it "wintry." Speaking most judiciously, Judith Bishop has remarked of Sobin's style, "Bordering on the excessive, the result is nonetheless entirely congruent with its end: to render palpable language's ineffectual reaching after states of being whose nature—emanating light and energy, producing effects the traces of which alone linger—is to dissipate" (*Verse*, p. 247).

Sobin's earlier novel of southern France, *Dark Mirrors* (1992), was received as "the perfect antidote to the ersatz Provence" depicted by Peter Mayle (Alannah Hopkin, *Financial Times*). It was inevitable that Sobin's book, because of its setting, would evoke the 1990 bestseller *A Year in Provence*, but contrast far outweighs any commonality, since Sobin's novel deploys psychologically complex amours, symbolic collapses, and an entire metafiction. Indeed, what Sobin said of *The Fly-Truffler* is true of *Dark Mirrors*, that it "isn't about a year in Provence" but "about an eternity" (Riding, *New York Times*).

Flush with conviction about the fragile, dissipating, authentic artistic temperament, the decency of life led in comportment with the land, and the gift that one person is to another, *Dark Mirrors* cannot but be elegiac. If the story "seems to come from an era of aesthetic concentration that has nothing in common with our own *fin de siècle*," though, it is only partly because the narrative is split among a distant mid-sixteenth century, the postwar twentieth, and the present

day (May, the *Times*). The mirror of the title reflects a bygone era "that existed before its least living particle had been appraised," when "the world was still rooted to something that resembled an earth. When whatever grew, grew through the toil and tending of human hands. When the work of those hands not only created but substantiated existence, and gave to the smallest thing its own, specific dignity" (Sobin, *Dark Mirrors*, p. 19). This vision recalls Traherne and John Clare, but it is qualified by the Pauline notion of seeing darkly. Each character, in an act of generosity, holds a looking-glass to the other, that the other may finally see herself, but the resulting portrait, if clear, is often ugly. Most of the personages—from the Nazi collaborator Emmanuel St. Chamas to the Catholic Church that protects him, from the lovers engaged in a parallel pair of illicit affairs to the spouses that drove them to it—are morally compromised in severe, if forgivable, ways. Hence they frequently devise alternative identities, evading who they are, through what *The Fly-Truffler* refers to as "a deep fictive complicity together" (58).

Philippe Cabassac, the troubled protagonist of that novel, lives on a steady diet of fantasy. Nearly fifty, a professor of Provençal linguistics in nearby Avignon, he harvests truffles between mid-November and early March, since eating them creates the condition for dreaming about his dead wife, Julieta. Initially his hallucinations are accidental and fragmentary, but over time the discrete, disconnected dreams grow more protracted and eventually sequential, until Cabassac is purposefully devoting his wakefulness in preparation for sleep, since it is only oneirically that he can conduct an entire life, or afterlife, with his lost beloved.

In Cabassac's association of the tuber and his late wife, "one buried thing for another," Sobin renders modern the myth of Demeter, as well as the tale of Orpheus and Eurydice, while evoking Dante's unrequited love for Beatrice. Additionally, Cabassac's "highly codified set of ceremonial gestures," beginning with cooking his truffle omelet lightly, indicates a "residual vestige ... of Christianity," if not an oblique *ars poetica* (Sobin, *Fly*, p. 134, 128). More broadly, though,

Sobin builds a bridge between past and present, living and dead, what is vanished and what returns, in order to illustrate the impulse of desire and the utter necessity of care (Sobin, *Fly*, p. 17). Under constant threat of extinction, the Gallo-Romanic language that Cabassac teaches, a "dying idiom" that Julieta too had studied and that had established the couple's "intimacy," is itself a remnant that endures, if barely, here and now: a "breath relic" (Sobin, *Fly*, p. 49, 63). The farmhouse that has been in Cabassac's family for eight generations is yet another instance of luminous debris, "a kind of living organism," and every year, pressured by debt in an increasingly commercial Provence, he is forced to sell bits of the estate, until by novel's end it is plowed under to become a golf course (Sobin, *Fly*, p. 20).

Shuttling between dereliction and delight, certain that the smallest object is often an "obscure cryptogram," *The Fly-Truffler* dramatizes many of Sobin's recurring concerns (14). The psychoanalytic tropes of interpersonal sublimation and displacement are played against ontotheological tropes of gathering, givenness, unconcealment. The presence of mirrors and the positing of idol and icon once again put a phenomenology into play. On a sociopolitical plane, the book critiques the personal derangement and societal deracination leveled by modernity, in which capital is king and history consigned to the crypt. And as ever in Sobin, always under the fascination of what withdraws, there is the belief, or at least the hope, that language, however ancient or evanescent, may resuscitate an "otherwise obliterated heritage" (Sobin, *Fly*, p. 53).

Selected Biliography

WORKS OF GUSTAV SOBIN

POETRY

Wind Chrysalid's Rattle. New York: Montemora, 1980.
Celebration of the Sound Through. New York: Montemora, 1982.

The Earth as Air. New York: New Directions, 1984.
Voyaging Portraits. New York: New Directions, 1988.
Breaths' Burials. New York: New Directions, 1995.
By the Bias of Sound: Selected Poems 1974–1994. New York: New Directions, 1995.
Towards the Blanched Alphabets. Jersey City, N.J.: Talisman, 1998.
In the Name of the Neither. Jersey City, N.J.: Talisman, 2002.
The Places as Preludes. Jersey City, N.J.: Talisman, 2005.

FICTION

Venus Blue. London: Bloomsbury, 1991; Boston: Little Brown, . (Citations taken from Bloomsbury edition, 1991.)
Dark Mirrors: A Novel of Provence. London: Bloomsbury, 1992.
The Fly-Truffler. London: Bloomsbury, 1999; New York: Norton, 2000. (Citations taken from Norton edition, 2000.)
In Pursuit of a Vanishing Star. New York: Norton, 2002.

NONFICTION

Luminous Debris: Reflecting on Vestige in Provence and Languedoc. Berkeley and Los Angeles: University of California Press, 1999.
Ambrogio Magnaghi. Milan: Skira, 2004. (Sobin selected the works and wrote the accompanying monograph, "The Miracle Depicted," pp. 9–23.)

POETRY CHAPBOOKS AND PAMPHLETS

Telegrams. London: Bond, 1963. (Edition of two hundred privately printed copies.)
Ascension. Ribaute-les-Tavernes, France: PAB, 1964. (Seventeen signed, numbered copies, with an original etching.)
Caesurae: Midsummer. Plymouth, U.K.: Shearsman/Blue Guitar, 1981. (Reprinted in *Celebration of the Sound Through.*)
Ten Sham Haikus. New York: Grenfell, 1983. (Letterpress edition of twenty-nine signed and numbered copies.)
Carnets 1979–1982. Plymouth, U.K.: Shearsman, 1984. (Sequence reprinted in *The Earth as Air.*)
Nile. London and Plymouth, U.K.: Oasis/Shearsman, 1984. (Poem reprinted in *Voyaging Portraits.*)
Sicilian Miniatures. San Francisco: Cadmus, 1986. (Signed edition of two hundred copies.)
Blown Letters, Driven Alphabets. Plymouth, U.K.: Shearsman, 1994. (Contains "Transparent Itineraries" 1991 and 1992, as well as "On the Nature of the Iconic," all reprinted in *Breaths' Burials.*)
A World of Letters. Sacramento: Arcturus, 1998. (Letterpress

edition. Contains four poems reprinted in *Towards the Blanched Alphabets* and one reprinted in *In the Name of the Neither*.)

Articles of Light & Elation. San Francisco: Cadmus, 1998. (Trade edition, as well as a signed edition limited to fifty numbered and twenty-six lettered copies.)

OTHER WORKS

The Tale of the Yellow Triangle. Illustrated by Jolaine Meyer. New York: Braziller, 1973. (Children's book.)

Ideograms in China, by Henri Michaux. New York: New Directions, 1984. (Translation from the French by Sobin.)

"A Few Stray Comments on the Cultivation of the Lyric (in Answer to a Young Poet Who Asked for Them)." *Talisman* 10 (spring 1993): 41–44. (Statement of poetics.)

"On *Imagerie*: Esther Williams, 1944." In *The Faber Book of Movie Verse*, edited by Philip French and Ken Wlaschin, 203–204. London: Faber and Faber, 1993. (Poem.)

INTERVIEWS

Foster, Edward. *Talisman* 10:26–39 (spring 1993).

Hilbert, Ernest. "To Destroy an Object of Desire: A Conversation with Gustaf Sobin on His Novel *The Fly-Truffler*." *NC1*:150–156 (summer 2002).

Mills, Tedi López. In *Matrices de Viento y de Sombra*. Mexico City: Hotel Ambos Mundos, 1999. (As this interview was translated into Spanish for the book, all citations within the above article refer to Gustaf Sobin's original; they are hence unpaginated.)

Schwartz, Leonard. *Verse* 20, no. 2-3:106–112 (2004).

CRITICAL AND BIOGRAPHICAL STUDIES

Andrews, Ruth. "*Towards the Blanchet Alphabets* and *Articles of Light & Elation*." *Rain Taxi* (www.raintaxi.com), summer 1999.

Baker, Robert. "The Open Vocable." *American Book Review* 20, no. 2:4,10 (January–February 1999). (Review of *Towards the Blanchet Alphabets*.)

———. "*Luminous Debris*." *Rain Taxi* (www.raintaxi.com), fall 2000.

———. "The Muse of Aboutness." *American Book Review* (2002): 26, 28. (Review of *In the Name of the Neither*.)

Beam, Jeffery. "*Luminous Debris*." *Oyster Boy Review* 13:56 (summer 2001).

Bishop, Judith. "*In Pursuit of a Vanishing Star*." *Verse* 20, no. 2–3:245–247 (2004).

Christensen, Paul. "A Noble Wave." *Temblor* 7 (1988).

——— "Restructuring Paradise." *Parnassus* 14, no. 2:131–149 (1988). (Review of *The Earth as Air* and *Voyaging Portraits*.)

Connolly, Cressida. "First Novels: From Schoolgirls to Sirens." *Marie Claire*, January 1991. (Review of *Venus Blue*.)

Cooke, Judy. "Thoroughly Mysterious Molly." *Guardian* (London), January 10, 1991. (Review of *Venus Blue* et al.)

Corbett, William. "Gustaf Sobin's Spirit World." *Boston Phoenix*, March 10, 2000. (Review of *The Fly-Truffler*.)

Crick, Philip. *Evolving the Idol: The Poetry of Gustaf Sobin*. London and Plymouth: Oasis/ Shearsman, 1984. (Fifteen-page essay with brief bibliography of Sobin's early work.)

English, Zoë. "Essence, Absence, and Sobin's *Venus Blue*." *Talisman* 10:60–62 (spring 1993).

Foley, Jack. *Alsop Review* (http://www.alsopreview.com/ columns/foley/jfsobin.html). (Review of *Luminous Debris*.)

Greilsamer, Laurent. *L'éclair au front: La Vie de René Char*. Paris: Fayard, 2004. (This biography of Char contains myriad references to Sobin.)

HB. "Novels in Brief." *Independent on Sunday*, January 13, 1991. (Review of *Venus Blue*.)

Hopkin, Alannah. "Doves and Doom." *Financial Times*, August 8, 1992. (Review of *Dark Mirrors*.)

"*Dark Mirrors*." *Hull Daily Mail*, August 15, 1992.

Januzzi, Marisa. "Luminous Cargo: Gustaf Sobin, 'A Portrait of the Self as Instrument of Its Syllables.'" *Talisman* 10:69–72 (spring 1993).

Joron, Andrew and Andrew Zawacki (eds.) "Miracle of Measure Ascendant: A Festschrift for Gustaf Sobin." Jersey City: Talisman House, 2005. (This small anthology contains tributes from two dozen writers. It was reprinted on pages 24–82 of *Talisman: A Journal of Contemporary Poetry and Poetics* 30&31 (fall 2005–winter 2006).

Kasper, Catherine. "*The Fly-Truffler*." *Rain Taxi Review of Books* 5, no. 1:27 (spring 2000).

Lehmann-Haupt, Christopher. "Going Beneath the Surface to Retrieve a Lost Love." *New York Times*, February 7, 2000, p. B6. (Review of *The Fly-Truffler*.)

"*The Fly-Truffler*." *Los Angeles Times Book Review*, January 23, 2000, p. 11.

Lutkus, Tony. "On Gustaf Sobin." *Talisman* 10:66–68 (spring 1993).

Lynch, Doris. "*Venus Blue*." *Library Journal*, January 1992, p. 178.

Ma, Ming-Qian. "The Dialectic of 'Saying So Little': Gustaf Sobin's Poetics of 'Toward.' " *Talisman* 10:54–59 (spring 1993).

Maitland, Margaret Todd. "Creatures of Innate Longing." *Hungry Mind Review*, winter 1999, pp. 57–58. (Review of *Luminous Debris*.)

Marcus, Ben. "A Truffling Affair." *Village Voice*, February 16–22, 2000, p. 62. (Review of *The Fly-Truffler*.)

May, Derwent. "Flying the Nest of Love." *Times* (London), September 10, 1992. (Review of *Dark Mirrors*.)

McCreary, Chris. "*In Pursuit of a Vanishing Star*." *Rain Taxi Review of Books* 7, no. 1:33 (spring 2002).

Messerli, Douglas. "Swinging on a Starlet." *Los Angeles Times Book Review*, April 19, 1992, p. 11. (Review of *Venus Blue*.)

Miller, Sandra. "*The Fly-Truffler*." *Verse* 19, no. 1–2:197–199 (2002).

Miller, Tyrus. "Gustaf Sobin." *Contemporary Poets*. 5th ed., edited by Tracy Chevalier, 934–935. Chicago and London: St. James Press, 1991.

Mobilio, Albert. "*Towards the Blanched Alphabets*." *Village Voice Literary Supplement* (December 1998).

Muratori, Fred. "The Cadence of Disclosure." *American Book Review* 17, no. 3:21 (February–March 1996). (Review of *By the Bias of Sound* et al.)

"*The Fly-Truffler*." *New Yorker*, March 20, 2000. p. 139.

Nicholson, John. "A la recherche de la bimbo perdue." *Times* (London), January 10, 1991. (Review of *Venus Blue*.)

Oderman, Kevin. "Gustaf Sobin: 'For Winnowing the Clotted Salt By.' " *North Dakota Quarterly* 55, no. 4:52–58 (1987).

"*The Fly-Truffler*." *Publishers Weekly*, December 13, 1999, p. 65.

Riding, Alan. "Where Dreams Are Induced by Light, Land, and Truffles." *New York Times*, March 28, 2000. (Human interest story on Sobin and *The Fly-Truffler*.)

Smith Nash, Susan. "Gustaf Sobin and a Consolation of Imagerie." *Talisman* 10:52–53 (spring 1993).

Solanas, Jane. " *Venus Blue*." *Time Out* (London), January 2–9, 1991.

Steinhoff, Eirik. "*Towards the Blanched Alphabets*." *Chicago Review* 46, no. 2:117–121 (2000).

Tritica, John. "At Each Instant's Extremity: The Tentative Edges of a Practice." *Talisman* 10:63–65 (spring 1993).

Wallace, Mark. "*Towards the Blanched Alphabets*." *Verse* 16, no 3–17, no. 1:189–193 (2000).

Zawacki, Andrew. "*Towards the Blanched Alphabets*." *Boston Review* 24, no. 6:56–58 (December 1999–January 2000).

Index

Arabic numbers printed in bold-face type refer to extended treatment of a subject.

"A" (Zukofsky), **Supp. III Part 2:** 611, 612, 614, 617, 619, 620, 621, 622, 623, 624, 626, 627, 628, 629, 630, 631; **Supp. IV Part 1:** 154; **Supp. XVI:**287

Aal, Katharyn, **Supp. IV Part 1:** 332

Aaron, Daniel, **IV:** 429; **Supp. I Part 2:** 647, 650

Aaron's Rod (Lawrence), **Supp. I Part 1:** 255

Abacus (Karr), **Supp. XI:** 240–242, 248, 254

Abádi-Nagy, Zoltán, **Supp. IV Part 1:** 280, 289, 291

"Abandoned House, The" (L. Michaels), **Supp. XVI:** 214

"Abandoned Newborn, The" (Olds), **Supp. X:** 207

Abbey, Edward, **Supp. VIII:** 42; **Supp. X:** 24, 29, 30, 31, 36; **Supp. XIII:** 1–18; **Supp. XIV:**179

Abbey's Road (Abbey), **Supp. XIII:** 12

Abbott, Edith, **Supp. I Part 1:** 5

Abbott, George, **Supp. IV Part 2:** 585

Abbott, Grace, **Supp. I Part 1:** 5

Abbott, Jack Henry, **Retro. Supp. II:** 210

Abbott, Jacob, **Supp. I Part 1:** 38, 39

Abbott, Lyman, **III:** 293

Abbott, Sean, **Retro. Supp. II:** 213

ABC of Color, An: Selections from Over a Half Century of Writings (Du Bois), **Supp. II Part 1:** 186

ABC of Reading (Pound), **III:** 468, 474–475

"Abdication, An" (Merrill), **Supp. III Part 1:** 326

Abel, Lionel, **Supp. XIII:** 98

Abel, Sam, **Supp. XIII:** 199

Abelard, Peter, **I:** 14, 22

Abeles, Sigmund, **Supp. VIII:** 272

Abercrombie, Lascelles, **III:** 471; **Retro. Supp. I:** 127, 128

Abernathy, Milton, **Supp. III Part 2:** 616

Abernon, Edgar Vincent, Viscount d',

Supp. XVI:191

Abhau, Anna. *See* Mencken, Mrs. August (Anna Abhau)

"Ability" (Emerson), **II:** 6

Abingdon, Alexander, **Supp. XVI:**99

Abish, Walter, **Supp. V:** 44

"Abishag" (Glück), **Supp. V:** 82

"Abortion, The" (Sexton), **Supp. II Part 2:** 682

"Abortions" (Dixon), **Supp. XII:** 153

"About C. D. Wright" (Colburn), **Supp. XV:** 341

"About Hospitality" (Jewett), **Retro. Supp. II:** 131

"About Kathryn" (Dubus), **Supp. VII:** 91

About the House (Auden), **Supp. II Part 1:** 24

About Town: "The New Yorker" and the World It Made (Yagoda), **Supp. VIII:** 151

"Above Pate Valley" (Snyder), **Supp. VIII:** 293

Above the River (Wright), **Supp. III Part 2:** 589, 606

"Abraham" (Schwartz), **Supp. II Part 2:** 663

Abraham, Nelson Algren. *See* Algren, Nelson

"Abraham Davenport" (Whittier), **Supp. I Part 2:** 699

"Abraham Lincoln" (Emerson), **II:** 13

Abraham Lincoln: The Prairie Years (Sandburg), **III:** 580, 587–589, 590

Abraham Lincoln: The Prairie Years and the War Years (Sandburg), **III:** 588, 590

Abraham Lincoln: The War Years (Sandburg), **III:** 588, 589–590

"Abraham Lincoln Walks at Midnight" (Lindsay), **Supp. I Part 2:** 390–391

"Abram Morrison" (Whittier), **Supp. I Part 2:** 699

Abramovich, Alex, **Supp. X:** 302, 309

Abrams, M. H., **Supp. XVI:**19

Abridgment of Universal Geography,

An: Together with Sketches of History (Rowson), **Supp. XV:** 243

"Absalom" (Rukeyser), **Supp. VI:** 278–279

Absalom, Absalom! (Faulkner), **II:** 64, 65–67, 72, 223; **IV:** 207; **Retro. Supp. I:** 75, 81, 82, 84, 85, 86, 87, 88, 89, 90, 92, 382; **Supp. V:** 261; **Supp. X:** 51; **Supp. XIV:**12–13

"Absence of Mercy" (Stone), **Supp. V:** 295

"Absentee, The" (Levertov), **Supp. III Part 1:** 284

Absentee Ownership (Veblen), **Supp. I Part 2:** 642

"Absent-Minded Bartender" (X. J. Kennedy), **Supp. XV:** 159

"Absent Thee from Felicity Awhile" (Wylie), **Supp. I Part 2:** 727, 729

"Absolution" (Fitzgerald), **Retro. Supp. I:** 108

"Absolution" (Sobin), **Supp. XVI:**289

"Abuelita's Ache" (Mora), **Supp. XIII:** 218

Abysmal Brute, The (London), **II:** 467

"Academic Story, An" (Simpson), **Supp. IX:** 279–280

"Academic Zoo, The: Theory—in Practice" (Epstein), **Supp. XIV:**107–108, 109

"Accident" (Minot), **Supp. VI:** 208–209

"Accident, The" (Southern), **Supp. XI:** 295

"Accident, The" (Strand), **Supp. IV Part 2:** 624

Accident/A Day's News (Wolf), **Supp. IV Part 1:** 310

Accidental Tourist, The (Tyler), **Supp. IV Part 2:** 657, 668–669; **Supp. V:** 227

Accordion Crimes (Proulx), **Supp. VII:** 259–261

"Accountability" (Dunbar), **Supp. II Part 1:** 197, 204

"Account of the Method of Drawing Birds" (Audubon), **Supp. XVI:**12

"Accusation, The" (Wright), **Supp. III Part 2:** 595

"Accusation of the Inward Man, The" (Taylor), **IV:** 156

"Accusing Message from Dead Father" (Karr), **Supp. XI:** 244

Ace, Goodman, **Supp. IV Part 2:** 574

Achievement in American Poetry (Bogan), **Supp. III Part 1:** 63–64

Acker, Kathy, **Supp. XII:** 1–20

Ackerman, Diane, **Supp. XIII:** 154

"Acknowledgment" (Lanier), **Supp. I Part 1:** 364

Ackroyd, Peter, **Supp. V:** 233

"Acquaintance in the Heavens, An" (Dillard), **Supp. VI:** 34

"Acquainted with the Night" (Frost), **II:** 155; **Retro. Supp. I:** 137

Across Spoon River (Masters), **Supp. I Part 2:** 455, 457, 459, 460, 466, 474–475, 476

Across the Layers: Poems Old and New (Goldbarth), **Supp. XII:** 181, 187–189

Across the River and into the Trees (Hemingway), **I:** 491; **II:** 255–256, 261; **Retro. Supp. I:** 172, 184–185

"Actfive" (MacLeish), **III:** 18–19, 22

Actfive and Other Poems (MacLeish), **III:** 3, 17–19, 21

Action (Shepard), **Supp. III Part 2:** 446

Active Anthology (Pound), **Supp. III Part 2:** 617

Active Service (Crane), **I:** 409

Acton, Patricia Nassif, **Supp. X:** 233

Actual, The (Bellow), **Retro. Supp. II:** 33

"Actual Experience, Preferred Narratives" (Julier), **Supp. IV Part 1:** 211

Acuff, Roy, **Supp. V:** 335

Ada (Nabokov), **Retro. Supp. I:** 265, 266, 270, 276–277, 278, 279

"Ada" (Stein), **IV:** 43

Ada; or Ardor (Nabokov), **III:** 247

"Adagia" (Stevens), **IV:** 78, 80, 88, 92

"Adam" (Hecht), **Supp. X:** 62

"Adam" (W. C. Williams), **Retro. Supp. I:** 422, 423

"Adam and Eve" (Eugene), **Supp. X:** 204

"Adam and Eve" (Shapiro), **Supp. II Part 2:** 708, 712

"Adamantine Practice of Poetry, The" (Wright), **Supp. XV:** 341–342, 343–344

Adam Bede (Eliot), **II:** 181

Adamé, Leonard, **Supp. XIII:** 316

Adam & Eve & the City (W. C. Williams), **Retro. Supp. I:** 423

"Adamic Purity as Double Agent" (Whalen-Bridge), **Retro. Supp. II:** 211–212

Adams, Althea. *See* Thurber, Mrs. James (Althea Adams)

Adams, Annie. *See* Fields, Annie Adams

Adams, Brooks, **Supp. I Part 2:** 484

Adams, Charles, **Supp. I Part 2:** 644

Adams, Charles Francis, **I:** 1, 4; **Supp. I Part 2:** 484

Adams, Franklin P., **Supp. I Part 2:** 653; **Supp. IX:** 190; **Supp. XV:** 294, 297

Adams, Henry, **I:** 1–24, 111, 243, 258; **II:** 278, 542; **III:** 396, 504; **IV:** 191, 349; **Retro. Supp. I:** 53, 59; **Retro. Supp. II:** 207; **Supp. I Part 1:** 299–300, 301, 314; **Supp. I Part 2:** 417, 492, 543, 644; **Supp. II Part 1:** 93–94, 105; **Supp. III Part 2:** 613; **Supp. IV Part 1:** 31, 208

Adams, Henry B., **Supp. I Part 1:** 369

Adams, J. Donald, **IV:** 438

Adams, James Truslow, **Supp. I Part 2:** 481, 484, 486

Adams, John, **I:** 1; **II:** 103, 301; **III:** 17, 473; **Supp. I Part 2:** 483, 506, 507, 509, 510, 511, 517, 518, 520, 524

Adams, John Luther, **Supp. XII:** 209

Adams, John Quincy, **I:** 1, 3, 16–17; **Supp. I Part 2:** 685, 686

Adams, Léonie, **Supp. I Part 2:** 707; **Supp. V:** 79; **Supp. IX:** 229

Adams, Luella, **Supp. I Part 2:** 652

Adams, Mrs. Henry (Marian Hooper), **I:** 1, 5, 10, 17–18

Adams, Phoebe, **Supp. IV Part 1:** 203; **Supp. VIII:** 124

Adams, Samuel, **Supp. I Part 2:** 516, 525

Adams, Timothy Dow, **Supp. XVI:** 67, 69

"Ad Castitatem" (Bogan), **Supp. III Part 1:** 50

Addams, Jane, **Supp. I Part 1:** 1–26; **Supp. XI:** 200, 202

Addams, John Huy, **Supp. I Part 1:** 2

"Addendum" (Wright), **Supp. V:** 339

Addiego, John, **Supp. XII:** 182

Adding Machine, The (Rice), **I:** 479

Adding Machine, The: Selected Essays (Burroughs), **Supp. III Part 1:** 93, 97

Addison, Joseph, **I:** 8, 105, 106–107, 108, 114, 131, 300, 304; **III:** 430

"Addressed to a Political Shrimp, or, Fly upon the Wheel" (Freneau),

Supp. II Part 1: 267

"Address to My Soul" (Wylie), **Supp. I Part 2:** 729

Address to the Government of the United States on the Cession of Louisiana to the French, An (Brown), **Supp. I Part 1:** 146

"Address to the Scholars of New England" (Ransom), **III:** 491

"Address with Exclamation Points, A" (Simic), **Supp. VIII:** 283

"Adjutant Bird, The" (Banks), **Supp. V:** 5

Adkins, Nelson F., **II:** 20

Adler, Alfred, **I:** 248

Adler, Betty, **III:** 103

Adler, George J., **III:** 81

Adler, Renata, **Supp. X:** 171

Admiral of the Ocean Sea: A Life of Christopher Columbus (Morison), **Supp. I Part 2:** 486–488

"Admirals" (Chabon), **Supp. XI:** 72

"Admonition, An" (Brodsky), **Supp. VIII:** 33

"Adolescence" (Bidart), **Supp. XV:** 32

"Adolescence" (Dove), **Supp. IV Part 1:** 245

"Adolescence" (Olds), **Supp. X:** 211

"Adolescence II" (Dove), **Supp. IV Part 1:** 242, 244–245

Adolescent's Christmas, An: 1944 (C. Bly), **Supp. XVI:** 31–32

"Adolf Eichmann" (Carruth), **Supp. XVI:** 47

"Adonais" (Shelley), **II:** 516, 540

Adorno, Theodor, **Supp. I Part 2:** 645, 650; **Supp. IV Part 1:** 301

"Adrienne Rich: The Poetics of Change" (Gelpi), **Supp. I Part 2:** 554

"Adultery" (Banks), **Supp. V:** 15

"Adultery" (Dubus), **Supp. VII:** 85

Adultery and Other Choices (Dubus), **Supp. VII:** 83–85

Adulthood Rites (O. Butler), **Supp. XIII:** 63, 64–65

Adult Life of Toulouse Lautrec by Henri Toulouse Lautrec, The (Acker), **Supp. XII:** 5, 6, 8–9

Adventure (London), **II:** 466

Adventures in Ancient Egypt (Goldbarth), **Supp. XII:** 191

Adventures in Value (Cummings), **I:** 430

"Adventures of a Book Reviewer" (Cowley), **Supp. II Part 1:** 137, 142

Adventures of Augie March, The (Bellow), **I:** 144, 147, 149, 150, 151, 152–153, 154, 155, 157, 158–159, 164; **Retro. Supp. II:** 19, 20, 22–

23, 24, 30; **Supp. VIII:** 234, 236–237

Adventures of a Young Man (Dos Passos), **I:** 488, 489, 492

Adventures of Captain Bonneville (Irving), **II:** 312

Adventures of Huckleberry Finn, The (Twain), **I:** 307, 506; **II:** 26, 72, 262, 266–268, 290, 418, 430; **III:** 101, 112–113, 357, 554, 558, 577; **IV:** 198, 201–204, 207; **Retro. Supp. I:** 188; **Retro. Supp. II:** 121; **Supp. I Part 1:** 247; **Supp. IV Part 1:** 247, 257; **Supp. IV Part 2:** 502; **Supp. V:** 131; **Supp. VIII:** 198; **Supp. X:** 230; **Supp. XII:** 16; **Supp. XVI:**222

Adventures of Jimmy (Broughton), **Supp. XV:** 146

Adventures of Roderick Random, The (Smollett), **I:** 134

Adventures of the Letter I (Simpson), **Supp. IX:** 266, 273–274

Adventures of Tom Sawyer, The (Twain), **II:** 26; **III:** 223, 572, 577; **IV:** 199–200, 203, 204; **Supp. I Part 2:** 456, 470; **Supp. XVI:**66

Adventures While Preaching the Gospel of Beauty (Lindsay), **Supp. I Part 2:** 374, 376, 381, 382–384, 389, 399

Adventures with Ed (Loeffler), **Supp. XIII:** 1

Advertisements for Myself (Mailer), **III:** 27, 35–38, 41–42, 45, 46; **Retro. Supp. II:** 196, 199, 200, 202, 203, 212; **Supp. IV Part 1:** 90, 284; **Supp. XIV:**157

"Advertisements for Myself on the Way Out" (Mailer), **III:** 37

"Advice to a Prophet" (Wilbur), **Supp. III Part 2:** 555–557

Advice to a Prophet and Other Poems (Wilbur), **Supp. III Part 2:** 554–558

"Advice to a Raven in Russia" (Barlow), **Supp. II Part 1:** 65, 74, 80, 83

"Advice to Players" (Bidart), **Supp. XV:** 35

Advice to the Lovelorn (film), **Retro. Supp. II:** 328

Advice to the Privileged Orders, Part I (Barlow), **Supp. II Part 1:** 80

"Aeneas and Dido" (Brodsky), **Supp. VIII:** 24–25

"Aeneas at Washington" (Tate), **IV:** 129

Aeneid (Virgil), **I:** 396; **II:** 542; **III:** 124; **Supp. XV:** 23

Aeneus Tacticus, **I:** 136

Aerial View (Barabtarlo), **Retro. Supp. I:** 278

"Aeria the Evanescent" (Sobin), **Supp. XVI:**292

Aeschylus, **I:** 274, 433; **III:** 398; **IV:** 358, 368, 370; **Retro. Supp. I:** 65; **Supp. I Part 2:** 458, 494

Aesop, **I:** 387; **II:** 154, 169, 302; **III:** 587

Aesthetic (Croce), **III:** 610

"Aesthetics" (Mumford), **Supp. II Part 2:** 476

"Aesthetics of Silence, The" (Sontag), **Supp. III Part 2:** 459

"Aesthetics of the Shah" (Olds), **Supp. X:** 205

"Affair at Coulter's Notch, The" (Bierce), **I:** 202

Affaire de viol, Une (C. Himes). See *Case of Rape, A* (C. Himes)

"Affair of Outposts, An" (Bierce), **I:** 202

Affliction (Banks), **Supp. V:** 15, 16

Affluent Society, The (Galbraith), **Supp. I Part 2:** 648

"Aficionados, The" (Carver), **Supp. III Part 1:** 137

"Afloat" (Beattie), **Supp. V:** 29

Afloat and Ashore (Cooper), **I:** 351, 355

Africa, Its Geography, People, and Products (Du Bois), **Supp. II Part 1:** 179

Africa, Its Place in Modern History (Du Bois), **Supp. II Part 1:** 179

"Africa, to My Mother" (D. Diop), **Supp. IV Part 1:** 16

African American Writers (Smith, ed.), **Supp. XIII:** 115, 127

"African Book" (Hemingway), **II:** 259

"African Chief, The" (Bryant), **Supp. I Part 1:** 168

"African Fragment" (Brooks), **Supp. III Part 1:** 85

African Queen, The (film), **Supp. XI:** 17

"African Roots of War, The" (Du Bois), **Supp. II Part 1:** 174

African Silences (Matthiessen), **Supp. V:** 203

African Treasury, An (Hughes, ed.), **Supp. I Part 1:** 344

"Afrika Revolution" (Baraka), **Supp. II Part 1:** 53

"AFRO-AMERICAN LYRIC" (Baraka), **Supp. II Part 1:** 59

After All: Last Poems (Matthews), **Supp. IX:** 155, 167–169

After and Before the Lightning (Ortiz),

Supp. IV Part 2: 513

"After a Party" (Salinas), **Supp. XIII:** 327

"After Apple-Picking" (Frost), **Retro. Supp. I:** 126, 128

"After Arguing against the Contention That Art Must Come from Discontent" (Stafford), **Supp. XI:** 327

After Confession: Poetry as Autobiography (Harris), **Supp. XIV:**269

After Confession: Poetry as Autobiography (K. Sontag and D. Graham), **Supp. XV:** 104

After Experience (Snodgrass), **Supp. VI:** 314–316, 317

"After great pain, a formal feeling comes" (Dickinson), **Retro. Supp. I:** 37

"After Hearing a Waltz by Bartók" (Lowell), **II:** 522

After Henry (Didion), **Supp. IV Part 1:** 195, 196, 199, 207, 208, 211

"After Henry" (Didion), **Supp. IV Part 1:** 211

"After Holbein" (Wharton), **IV:** 325; **Retro. Supp. I:** 382

After Ikkyu and Other Poems (Harrison), **Supp. VIII:** 42

"After-Image" (Caldwell), **I:** 309

After-Images: Autobiographical Sketches (Snodgrass), **Supp. VI:** 314, 319–323, 324, 326–327

After I's (Zukofsky), **Supp. III Part 2:** 628, 629

Afterlife (Monette), **Supp. X:** 153

Afterlife (Updike), **Retro. Supp. I:** 322

Afterlife, The (Levis), **Supp. XI:** 259, 260–264

"After Magritte" (McClatchy), **Supp. XII:** 264

"After Making Love" (Dunn), **Supp. XI:** 153

Aftermath (Longfellow), **II:** 490

"Aftermath" (Longfellow), **II:** 498

"Afternoon" (Ellison), **Supp. II Part 1:** 238

"Afternoon at MacDowell" (Kenyon), **Supp. VII:** 159

"Afternoon Miracle, An" (O. Henry), **Supp. II Part 1:** 390

Afternoon of a Faun (Hearon), **Supp. VIII:** 63–64

Afternoon of an Author: A Selection of Uncollected Stories and Essays (Fitzgerald), **II:** 94

"Afternoon of a Playwright" (Thurber), **Supp. I Part 2:** 620

Afternoon of the Unreal (Salinas), **Supp. XIII:** 311, 316–318

"Afternoon with the Old Man, An"

(Dubus), **Supp. VII:** 84

"After Punishment Was Done with Me" (Olds), **Supp. X:** 213

"After Reading *Barely and Widely*," (Zukofsky), **Supp. III Part 2:** 625, 631

"After Reading 'In the Clearing' for the Author, Robert Frost" (Corso), **Supp. XII:** 130

"After Reading *Mickey in the Night Kitchen* for the Third Time before Bed" (Dove), **Supp. IV Part 1:** 249

"After Reading Tu Fu, I Go Outside to the Dwarf Orchard" (Wright), **Supp. V:** 343

"After Reading Wang Wei, I Go Outside to the Full Moon" (Wright), **Supp. V:** 343

After Shocks, Near Escapes (Dobyns), **Supp. XIII:** 80–82

"After Song, An" (W. C. Williams), **Retro. Supp. I:** 413

After Strange Gods (Eliot), **I:** 588

After Such Knowledge: Memory, History, and the Legacy of the Holocaust (E. Hoffman), **Supp. XVI:**152–153, 158–161

"After the Alphabets" (Merwin), **Supp. III Part 1:** 356

"After the Argument" (Dunn), **Supp. XI:** 149

"After the Baptism" (C. Bly), **Supp. XVI:**40

"After the Burial" (Lowell), **Supp. I Part 2:** 409

"After the Curfew" (Holmes), **Supp. I Part 1:** 308

"After the Death of John Brown" (Thoreau), **IV:** 185

"After the Denim" (Carver), **Supp. III Part 1:** 144

"After the Dentist" (Swenson), **Supp. IV Part 2:** 645

After the Fall (A. Miller), **III:** 148, 149, 156, 161, 162, 163–165, 166

"After the Fire" (Merrill), **Supp. III Part 1:** 328

"After the Flood" (Sanders), **Supp. XVI:**274–275

After the Fox (film), **Supp. IV Part 2:** 575

After the Genteel Tradition (Cowley), **Supp. II Part 1:** 143

"After the Heart's Interrogation" (Komunyakaa), **Supp. XIII:** 120

After the Lost Generation: A Critical Study of the Writers of Two Wars (Aldridge), **Supp. IV Part 2:** 680

"After the Night Office—Gethsemani

Abbey" (Merton), **Supp. VIII:** 195–196

"After the Persian" (Bogan), **Supp. III Part 1:** 64

"After the Pleasure Party" (Melville), **III:** 93

"After the Resolution" (Dunn), **Supp. XI:** 151

After the Stroke (Sarton), **Supp. VIII:** 264

"After the Surprising Conversions" (Lowell), **I:** 544, 545; **II:** 550; **Retro. Supp. II:** 187

"After 37 Years My Mother Apologizes for My Childhood" (Olds), **Supp. X:** 208

Afterthoughts (L. P. Smith), **Supp. XIV:**339, 345

"Afterthoughts on the Rosenbergs" (Fiedler), **Supp. XIII:** 99

"After Twenty Years" (Rich), **Supp. I Part 2:** 559–560

"Afterwake, The" (Rich), **Supp. I Part 2:** 553

"Afterward" (Wharton), **Retro. Supp. I:** 372

"After Working Long" (Kenyon), **Supp. VII:** 170

"After Yitzl" (Goldbarth), **Supp. XII:** 186

"After You, My Dear Alphonse" (Jackson), **Supp. IX:** 119

"Again" (Dixon), **Supp. XII:** 157

"Again, Kapowsin" (Hugo), **Supp. VI:** 141

"Against" (Goldbarth), **Supp. XII:** 193

"Against Decoration" (Karr), **Supp. XI:** 248

Against Interpretation (Sontag), **Supp. III Part 2:** 451, 455; **Supp. XIV:**15

"Against Interpretation" (Sontag), **Supp. III Part 2:** 456–458, 463

"Against Modernity" (Ozick), **Supp. V:** 272

"Against Nature" (Karr), **Supp. XI:** 243

Against Nature (Updike), **Retro. Supp. I:** 323

Against the Cold (Bynner), **Supp. XV:** 51

"Against the Crusades" (Stern), **Supp. IX:** 300

Against the Current: As I Remember F. Scott Fitzgerald (Kroll Ring), **Supp. IX:** 63

Agamben, Giorgio, **Supp. XVI:**289

Agapida, Fray Antonio (pseudonym). *See* Irving, Washington

"Agassiz" (Lowell), **Supp. I Part 2:** 414, 416

Agassiz, Louis, **II:** 343; **Supp. I Part 1:** 312; **Supp. IX:** 180

Ăge cassant, L' (Char; Sobin, trans.), **Supp. XVI:**282

"Aged Wino's Counsel to a Young Man on the Brink of Marriage, The" (X. J. Kennedy), **Supp. XV:** 156

Agee, Emma, **I:** 26

Agee, James, **I:** 25–47, 293; **IV:** 215; **Supp. IX:** 109; **Supp. XIV:**92; **Supp. XV:** 143

"Agent, The" (Wilbur), **Supp. III Part 2:** 557–561

Age of Anxiety, The (Auden), **Supp. II Part 1:** 2, 19, 21

"Age of Conformity, The" (Howe), **Supp. VI:** 117

Age of Grief, The: A Novella and Stories (Smiley), **Supp. VI:** 292, 299–301

Age of Innocence, The (Wharton), **IV:** 320–322, 327–328; **Retro. Supp. I:** 372, 374, 380–381; **Supp. IV Part 1:** 23

Age of Longing, The (Koestler), **I:** 258

Age of Reason, The (Paine), **Supp. I Part 2:** 503, 515–517, 520

"Age of Strolling, The" (Stern), **Supp. IX:** 297

"Ages, The" (Bryant), **Supp. I Part 1:** 152, 155, 166, 167

"Aging" (Jarrell), **II:** 388

Aging and Gender in Literature (George), **Supp. IV Part 2:** 450

"Agio Neró" (Mora), **Supp. XIII:** 224

"Agitato ma non Troppo" (Ransom), **III:** 493

"Agnes of Iowa" (Moore), **Supp. X:** 165, 178

Agnes of Sorrento (Stowe), **Supp. I Part 2:** 592, 595–596

Agnon, S. Y., **Supp. V:** 266

"Agosta the Winged Man and Rasha the Black Dove" (Dove), **Supp. IV Part 1:** 246–247

Agrarian Justice (Paine), **Supp. I Part 2:** 517–518

"Agricultural Show, The" (McKay), **Supp. X:** 139

Agrippa: A Book of the Dead (W. Gibson), **Supp. XVI:**125

Agua Fresca: An Anthology of Raza Poetry (Rodríguez, ed.), **Supp. IV Part 2:** 540

Agua Santa/Holy Water (Mora), **Supp. XIII:** 222–225

Agüero Sisters, The (García), **Supp. XI:** 185–190

Aguiar, Sarah Appleton, **Supp. XIII:** 30

Ah, Wilderness! (O'Neill), **III:** 400–401; **Supp. IV Part 2:** 587

Ah, Wilderness!: The Frontier in American Literature (Humphrey), **Supp. IX:** 104

Ahearn, Barry, **Retro. Supp. I:** 415

Ahearn, Frederick L., Jr., **Supp. XI:** 184

Ahearn, Kerry, **Supp. IV Part 2:** 604

Ahmed Arabi Pasha, **I:** 453

Ahnebrink, Lars, **III:** 328

Ah Sin (Harte), **Supp. II Part 1:** 354–355

"Ah! Sun-flower" (Blake), **III:** 19

AIDS and Its Metaphors (Sontag), **Supp. III Part 2:** 452, 466–468

Aids to Reflection (Coleridge), **II:** 10

Aiieeeee! An Anthology of Asian-American Writers (The Combined Asian Resources Project), **Supp. X:** 292

Aiken, Conrad, **I:** 48–70, 190, 211, 243; **II:** 55, 530, 542; **III:** 458, 460; **Retro. Supp. I:** 55, 56, 57, 58, 60, 62; **Supp. X:** 50, 115; **Supp. XV:** 144, 297, 298, 302, 306, 309

"Aim Was Song, The" (Frost), **Retro. Supp. I:** 133

Ainsworth, Linda, **Supp. IV Part 1:** 274

Ainsworth, William, **III:** 423

Air-Conditioned Nightmare, The (H. Miller), **III:** 186

Airing Dirty Laundry (Reed), **Supp. X:** 241

"Air Plant, The" (Crane), **I:** 401

Air Raid: A Verse Play for Radio (MacLeish), **III:** 21

"Airs above the Ground" (Sarton), **Supp. VIII:** 261

Air Tight: A Novel of Red Russia. See We the Living (Rand)

"Airwaves" (Mason), **Supp. VIII:** 146

Airways, Inc. (Dos Passos), **I:** 482

Aitken, Robert, **Supp. I Part 2:** 504

Akhmadulina, Bella, **Supp. III Part 1:** 268

Akhmatova, Anna, **Supp. III Part 1:** 268, 269; **Supp. VIII:** 20, 21, 25, 27, 30

Akhmatova Translations, The (Kenyon), **Supp. VII:** 160

"Akhnilo" (Salter), **Supp. IX:** 260

Akins, Zoë, **Supp. XVI:**187

Aksenev, Vasily P., **Retro. Supp. I:** 278

"Al Aaraaf" (Poe), **III:** 426–427

Al Aaraaf, Tamerlane, and Minor Po-ems (Poe), **III:** 410

"Alain Locke: Bahá'í Philosopher" (Buck), **Supp. XIV:**199

Alain Locke: Faith and Philosophy (Buck), **Supp. XIV:**200

"Alain Locke and Cultural Pluralism" (Kallen), **Supp. XIV:**197

Alarcón, Justo, **Supp. IV Part 2:** 538, 539, 540

À la Recherche du Temps Perdu (Proust), **IV:** 428

"Alarm" (X. J. Kennedy), **Supp. XV:** 163

"Alastor" (Shelley), **Supp. I Part 2:** 728

"Alatus" (Wilbur), **Supp. III Part 2:** 563

"Alba" (Creeley), **Supp. IV Part 1:** 150

Albee, Edward, **I:** 71–96, 113; **II:** 558, 591; **III:** 281, 387; **IV:** 4, 230; **Retro. Supp. II:** 104; **Supp. VIII:** 331; **Supp. XIII:** 196, 197

Albers, Joseph, **Supp. IV Part 2:** 621

Alberti, Rafael, **Supp. XV:** 75

Albright, Margery, **Supp. I Part 2:** 613

"Album, The" (Morris), **III:** 220

Alcestiad, The (Wilder), **IV:** 357, 374

"Alchemist, The" (Bogan), **Supp. III Part 1:** 50

"Alchemist in the City, The" (Hopkins), **Supp. IV Part 2:** 639

Alchymist's Journal, The (Connell), **Supp. XIV:**80

"Alcmena" (Winters), **Supp. II Part 2:** 801

Alcott, Abba. *See* Alcott, Mrs. Amos Bronson (Abigail May)

Alcott, Amos Bronson, **II:** 7, 225; **IV:** 172, 173, 184; **Retro. Supp. I:** 217; **Supp. I Part 1:** 28, 29–32, 35, 39, 41, 45; **Supp. II Part 1:** 290; **Supp. XVI:**84, 89

Alcott, Anna. *See* Pratt, Anna

Alcott, Louisa May, **IV:** 172; **Supp. I Part 1:** 28–46; **Supp. IX:** 128; **Supp. XV:** 338; **Supp. XVI:**84

Alcott, May, **Supp. I Part 1:** 41

Alcott, Mrs. Amos Bronson (Abigail May), **IV:** 184; **Supp. I Part 1:** 29, 30, 31, 32, 35

Alcuin: A Dialogue (Brown), **Supp. I Part 1:** 126–127, 133

Alden, Hortense. *See* Farrell, Mrs. James T. (Hortense Alden)

Alden, John, **I:** 471; **II:** 502–503

"Alder Fork, The" (Leopold), **Supp. XIV:**186

Aldington, Mrs. Richard. *See* Doolittle, Hilda

Aldington, Perdita, **Supp. I Part 1:** 258

Aldington, Richard, **II:** 517; **III:** 458, 459, 465, 472; **Retro. Supp. I:** 63, 127; **Supp. I Part 1:** 257–262, 270

Aldo Leopold: His Life and Work (Meine), **Supp. XIV:**179

"Aldo Leopold's Intellectual Heritage" (Nash), **Supp. XIV:**191–192

Aldon, Raymond, **Supp. XV:** 297

Aldrich, Thomas Bailey, **II:** 400; **Supp. II Part 1:** 192; **Supp. XIV:**45

Aldrich, Tom, **Supp. I Part 2:** 415

Aldridge, John W., **Supp. I Part 1:** 196; **Supp. IV Part 1:** 286; **Supp. IV Part 2:** 680, 681; **Supp. VIII:** 189; **Supp. XI:** 228

Aleck Maury Sportsman (Gordon), **II:** 197, 200, 203–204

Alegría, Claribel, **Supp. IV Part 1:** 208

Aleichem, Sholom, **IV:** 3, 10; **Supp. IV Part 2:** 585

"Alert Lovers, Hidden Sides, and Ice Travelers: Notes on Poetic Form and Energy" (Dunn), **Supp. XI:** 153

"Aleš Debeljak" (Simic), **Supp. VIII:** 279

"Alex" (Oliver), **Supp. VII:** 232

Alexander, George, **II:** 331

Alexander, Michael, **Retro. Supp. I:** 293

"Alexander Crummell Dead" (Dunbar), **Supp. II Part 1:** 207, 208–209

Alexander's Bridge (Cather), **I:** 313, 314, 316–317, 326; **Retro. Supp. I:** 1, 6, 7, 8

Alexander the Great, **IV:** 322

"Alexandra" (Cather), **Retro. Supp. I:** 7, 9, 17

Alexandrov, V. E., **Retro. Supp. I:** 270

Algonquin Round Table, **Supp. IX:** 190, 191, 197

Algren, Nelson, **I:** 211; **Supp. V:** 4; **Supp. IX:** 1–18; **Supp. XII:** 126; **Supp. XIII:** 173; **Supp. XIV:**3

Alhambra, The (Irving), **II:** 310–311

Alias Grace (Atwood), **Supp. XIII:** 20, 31–32

Alice (film; Allen), **Supp. XV:** 2, 11

"Alice Doane's Appeal" (Hawthorne), **II:** 227

Alice in Wonderland (Carroll), **Supp. I Part 2:** 622

Alice's Adventures in Wonderland (Carroll), **Supp. XVI:**261

"Alicia and I Talking on Edna's Steps" (Cisneros), **Supp. VII:** 64

"Alicia Who Sees Mice" (Cisneros), **Supp. VII:** 60

Alien 3 (screenplay, W. Gibson), **Supp. XVI:**120, 124

Alison, Archibald, **Supp. I Part 1:** 151, 159

Alison's House (Glaspell), **Supp. III Part 1:** 182, 188, 189

Alive (screenplay, Shanley), **Supp. XIV:**316

Alive and Writing: Interviews with American Authors of the 1980s (McCaffery and Gregory), **Supp. X:** 260

"Alki Beach" (Hugo), **Supp. VI:** 135

ALL: The Collected Poems, 1956–1964 (Zukofsky), **Supp. III Part 2:** 630

ALL: The Collected Short Poems, 1923–1958 (Zukofsky), **Supp. III Part 2:** 629

Alla Breve Loving (Wright), **Supp. XV:** 339, 340

"Alla Breve Loving" (Wright), **Supp. XV:** 340

"All Around the Town" (Benét), **Supp. XI:** 48, 58

All at Sea (Lardner), **II:** 427

"All Boy" (Rawlings), **Supp. X:** 222

Allegiances (Stafford), **Supp. XI:** 322–323, 329

"Allegory of the Cave" (Dunn), **Supp. XI:** 150

"Allegro, L' " (Milton), **Supp. XIV:**8

Allen, Brooke, **Supp. VIII:** 153

Allen, Dick, **Supp. IX:** 279

Allen, Donald, **Supp. VIII:** 291; **Supp. XIII:** 112

Allen, Frank, **Supp. XI:** 126; **Supp. XII:** 186

Allen, Frederick Lewis, **Supp. I Part 2:** 655

Allen, Gay Wilson, **IV:** 352; **Supp. I Part 2:** 418

Allen, Paula Gunn. *See* Gunn Allen, Paula

Allen, Walter, **I:** 505; **III:** 352; **Supp. IV Part 2:** 685; **Supp. IX:** 231

Allen, Woody, **Supp. I Part 2:** 607, 623; **Supp. IV Part 1:** 205; **Supp. X:** 164; **Supp. XI:** 307; **Supp. XV:** 1–18

"Aller et Retour" (Barnes), **Supp. III Part 1:** 36

Aller Retour New York (H. Miller), **III:** 178, 182, 183

Alessandrini, Goffredo, **Supp. IV Part 2:** 520

Alleys of Eden, The (R. O. Butler), **Supp. XII:** 62, 62–64, 68

All God's Children Need Traveling Shoes (Angelou), **Supp. IV Part 1:** 2, 9–10, 12–13, 17

All God's Chillun Got Wings (O'Neill), **III:** 387, 391, 393–394

All Gone (Dixon), **Supp. XII:** 148, 149

"All Hallows" (Glück), **Supp. V:** 82

"All I Can Remember" (Jackson), **Supp. IX:** 115

"Alligators, The" (Updike), **IV:** 219

Allingham, John Till, **Supp. XV:** 243

"ALL IN THE STREET" (Baraka), **Supp. II Part 1:** 53

"All I Want" (Tapahonso), **Supp. IV Part 2:** 508

"All Little Colored Children Should Play the Harmonica" (Patchett), **Supp. XII:** 309

"All Mountains" (Doolittle), **Supp. I Part 1:** 271

All My Friends Are Going to Be Strangers (McMurtry), **Supp. V:** 224, 228, 229

All My Pretty Ones (Sexton), **Supp. II Part 2:** 678, 679–683

"All My Pretty Ones" (Sexton), **Supp. II Part 2:** 681–682

"All My Sad Captains" (Jewett), **Retro. Supp. II:** 134

All My Sons (A. Miller), **III:** 148, 149, 150, 151–153, 154, 155, 156, 158, 159, 160, 164, 166

"All Night, All Night" (Schwartz), **Supp. II Part 2:** 665

All Night Long (Caldwell), **I:** 297

"All Our Lost Children: Trauma and Testimony in the Performance of Childhood" (Pace), **Supp. XI:** 245

"All Out" (Hecht), **Supp. X:** 72

All Over (Albee), **I:** 91–94

"Allowance" (Minot), **Supp. VI:** 206, 207–208

"Alloy" (Rukeyser), **Supp. VI:** 279

"All Parrots Speak" (Bowles), **Supp. IV Part 1:** 89

Allport, Gordon, **II:** 363–364

All Quiet on the Western Front (Remarque), **Supp. IV Part 1:** 380, 381

"ALL REACTION IS DOOMED-!-!-!" (Baraka), **Supp. II Part 1:** 59

"All Revelation" (Frost), **II:** 160–162

All Shot Up (C. Himes), **Supp. XVI:**143, 144

"All Souls'" (Gioia), **Supp. XV:** 117

"All Souls" (Wharton), **IV:** 315–316; **Retro. Supp. I:** 382

"All Souls' Night" (Yeats), **Supp. X:** 69

All Souls' Rising (Bell), **Supp. X:** 12, 13–16, 17

"All-Star Literary Vaudeville" (Wilson), **IV:** 434–435

Allston, Washington, **II:** 298

All Stories Are True (Wideman), **Supp. X:** 320

"All That Is" (Wilbur), **Supp. III Part 2:** 563

"All the Bearded Irises of Life: Confessions of a Homospiritual" (Walker), **Supp. III Part 2:** 527

"All the Beautiful Are Blameless" (Wright), **Supp. III Part 2:** 597

All the Conspirators (Isherwood), **Supp. XIV:**156, 159, 160

All the Dark and Beautiful Warriors (Hansberry), **Supp. IV Part 1:** 360, 374

All the Days and Nights: The Collected Stories (Maxwell), **Supp. VIII:** 151, 158, 169

"All the Dead Dears" (Plath), **Retro. Supp. II:** 246; **Supp. I Part 2:** 537

All the Good People I've Left Behind (Oates), **Supp. II Part 2:** 510, 522, 523

"All the Hippos Were Boiled in Their Tanks" (Burroughs and Kerouac), **Supp. III Part 1:** 94

All the King's Men (Warren), **I:** 489; **IV:** 243, 248–249, 252; **Supp. V:** 261; **Supp. VIII:** 126; **Supp. X:** 1

All the Little Live Things (Stegner), **Supp. IV Part 2:** 599, 604, 605, 606, 609–610, 611, 613

All the Pretty Horses (film), **Supp. VIII:** 175

All the Pretty Horses (McCarthy), **Supp. VIII:** 175, 182–183, 188

All the Sad Young Men (Fitzgerald), **II:** 94; **Retro. Supp. I:** 108

"All the Time in the World" (Dubus), **Supp. VII:** 91

"All the Way to Flagstaff, Arizona" (Bausch), **Supp. VII:** 47, 49

"All This and More" (Karr), **Supp. XI:** 243

All Tomorrow's Parties (W. Gibson), **Supp. XVI:**119, 121, 123, 124, 130

"All Too Real" (Vendler), **Supp. V:** 189

All Trivia: Triva, More Trivia, Afterthoughts, Last Words (L. P. Smith), **Supp. XIV:**339

All-True Travels and Adventures of Lidie Newton (Smiley), **Supp. VI:** 292, 305–307

All We Need of Hell (Crews), **Supp. XI:** 114

Almack, Edward, **Supp. IV Part 2:** 435

al-Maghut, Muhammad, **Supp. XIII:** 278

"Almanac" (Swenson), **Supp. IV Part 2:** 641

Almanac of the Dead (Silko), **Supp. IV Part 2:** 558–559, 560, 561, 570–571

Almon, Bert, **Supp. IX:** 93

"Almost" (Untermeyer), **Supp. XV:** 304

Almost Revolution, The (Priaulx and Ungar), **Supp. XI:** 228

Alnilam (Dickey), **Supp. IV Part 1:** 176, 186, 188–189

"Alone" (Levine), **Supp. V:** 184, 185, 186

"Alone" (Poe), **Retro. Supp. II:** 266

"Alone" (Singer), **IV:** 15

"Alone" (Winters), **Supp. II Part 2:** 786, 811

Aloneness (Brooks), **Supp. III Part 1:** 85, 86

Alone with America (Corso), **Supp. XII:** 131

Alone with America (Howard), **Supp. IX:** 326

"Along America's Edges" (Sobin), **Supp. XVI:**288

"Along the Color Line" (Du Bois), **Supp. II Part 1:** 173

Along the Illinois (Masters), **Supp. I Part 2:** 472

"Alphabet" (Nye), **Supp. XIII:** 283

Alphabet, An (Doty), **Supp. XI:** 120

Alphabet of Grace, The (Buechner), **Supp. XII:** 52

"Alphabet of My Dead, An" (Pinsky), **Supp. VI:** 235, 250

"Alphabet of Subjects, An" (Zukofsky), **Supp. III Part 2:** 624

"Alpine Christ, The" (Jeffers), **Supp. II Part 2:** 415, 419

Alpine Christ and Other Poems, The (Jeffers), **Supp. II Part 2:** 419

"Alpine Idyll, An" (Hemingway), **II:** 249; **Retro. Supp. I:** 176

Al Que Quiere! (W. C. Williams), **Retro. Supp. I:** 414, 416, 417, 428

Alsop, Joseph, **II:** 579

"Altar, The" (Herbert), **Supp. IV Part 2:** 646

"Altar, The" (MacLeish), **III:** 4

"Altar Boy" (Fante), **Supp. XI:** 160, 164

"Altar of the Dead, The" (James), **Retro. Supp. I:** 229

"Altars in the Street, The" (Levertov), **Supp. III Part 1:** 280

Alter, Robert, **Supp. XII:** 167

Altgeld, John Peter, **Supp. I Part 2:** 382, 455

Althea (Masters), **Supp. I Part 2:** 455, 459

Altick, Richard, **Supp. I Part 2:** 423

Altieri, Charles, **Supp. VIII:** 297, 303

Altman, Robert, **Supp. IX:** 143

"Alto" (C. Frost), **Supp. XV:** 101

"Altra Ego" (Brodsky), **Supp. VIII:** 31–32

A Lume Spento (Pound), **Retro. Supp. I:** 283, 285

"Aluminum House" (F. Barthelme), **Supp. XI:** 26

Alvares, Mosseh, **Supp. V:** 11

Alvarez, A., **Supp. I Part 2:** 526, 527; **Supp. II Part 1:** 99; **Supp. IX:** 248

Alvarez, Julia, **Supp. VII:** 1–21; **Supp. XI:** 177

"Always a Rose" (L.-Y. Lee), **Supp. XV:** 215, 216

"Always in Good Humor" (Adams), **Supp. XV:** 294

Always Outnumbered, Always Outgunned (Mosley), **Supp. XIII:** 242

"Always the Stories" (Ortiz), **Supp. IV Part 2:** 499, 500, 502, 504, 512

Always the Young Strangers (Sandburg), **III:** 577–578, 579

Amadeus (Shaffer), **Supp. XIV:**330

"Amahl and the Night Visitors: A Guide to the Tenor of Love" (Moore), **Supp. X:** 167

"Am and Am Not" (Olds), **Supp. X:** 212

"Amanita, The" (Francis), **Supp. IX:** 81

Amaranth (Robinson), **III:** 509, 510, 512, 513, 522, 523

Amazing Adele, The (Barillet and Grédy; Loos, trans.), **Supp. XVI:**194

Amazing Adventures of Kavalier and Clay, The (Chabon), **Supp. XI:** 68, 76, 77–80

Amazing Science Fiction Stories, **Supp. XVI:**121

Amazons: An Intimate Memoir by the First Woman to Play in the National Hockey League (DeLillo), **Supp. VI:** 2

Ambassador of Peace, An (Abernon), **Supp. XVI:**191

Ambassadors, The (H. James), **II:** 320, 333–334, 600; **III:** 517; **IV:** 322; **Retro. Supp. I:** 215, 218, 219, 220, 221, 232–233

Ambelain, Robert, **Supp. I Part 1:** 260, 273, 274

Ambition: The Secret Passion (Epstein), **Supp. XIV:**113–114

"Ambition Bird, The" (Sexton), **Supp. II Part 2:** 693

Ambler, Eric, **III:** 57

Ambrose Holt and Family (Glaspell), **Supp. III Part 1:** 175, 181, 184, 187, 188

"Ambrose Seyffert" (Masters), **Supp. I Part 2:** 464

"Ambush" (Komunyakaa), **Supp. XIII:** 122

Amen Corner, The (Baldwin), **Retro. Supp. II:** 5, 7; **Supp. I Part 1:** 48, 51, 54, 55, 56

America (Benét), **Supp. XI:** 46, 47, 51

"America" (Ginsberg), **Supp. II Part 1:** 58–59, 317

"America" (song), **IV:** 410

"America, America!" (poem) (Schwartz), **Supp. II Part 2:** 665

"America, Commerce, and Freedom" (Rowson and Reinagle), **Supp. XV:** 240

"America, Seen Through Photographs, Darkly" (Sontag), **Supp. III Part 2:** 464

America: The Story of a Free People (Commager and Nevins), **I:** 253

"America! America!" (story) (Schwartz), **Supp. II Part 2:** 640, 658–659, 660

America and Americans (Steinbeck), **IV:** 52

"America and the Vidal Chronicles" (Pease), **Supp. IV Part 2:** 687

America as a Civilization (Lerner), **III:** 60

"America Independent" (Freneau), **Supp. II Part 1:** 261

America Is Worth Saving (Dreiser), **Retro. Supp. II:** 96

American, The (James), **I:** 226; **II:** 326–327, 328, 331, 334; **IV:** 318; **Retro. Supp. I:** 220, 221, 228, 376, 381

Americana (DeLillo), **Supp. VI:** 2, 3, 5, 6, 8, 13, 14

American Adam, The (R. W. B. Lewis), **II:** 457–458; **Supp. XIII:** 93

American Almanac (Leeds), **II:** 110

American Anthem (Doctorow and Suares), **Supp. IV Part 1:** 234

"American Apocalypse" (Gunn Allen), **Supp. IV Part 1:** 325

American Aristocracy (film), **Supp. XVI:**185–186

American Blood, (Nichols), **Supp. XIII:** 268

American Blues (T. Williams), **IV:** 381, 383

American Buffalo (Mamet), **Supp. XIV:**239, 241, 242, 244–245, 246, 254, 255

American Caravan: A Yearbook of American Literature (Mumford, ed.), **Supp. II Part 2:** 482

American Cause, The (MacLeish), **III:** 3

American Childhood, An (Dillard), **Supp. VI:** 19–21, 23, 24, 25, 26, 30, 31

"American Childhood in the Dominican Republic, An" (Alvarez), **Supp. VII:** 2, 5

American Child Supreme, An: The Education of a Liberation Ecologist (Nichols), **Supp. XIII:** 256, 257, 258, 264, 265, 266, 267, 268, 269

American Claimant, The (Twain), **IV:** 194, 198–199

American Crisis I (Paine), **Supp. I Part 2:** 508

American Crisis II (Paine), **Supp. I Part 2:** 508

American Crisis XIII (Paine), **Supp. I Part 2:** 509

"American Critic, The" (J. Spingarn), **I:** 266

American Culture, Canons, and the Case of Elizabeth Stoddard (Smith and Weinauer), **Supp. XV:** 270

American Daughter, An (Wasserstein), **Supp. XV:** 330–332, 333

American Democrat, The (Cooper), **I:** 343, 346, 347, 353

American Diary (Webb), **Supp. I Part 1:** 5

American Drama since World War II (Weales), **IV:** 385

American Dream, An (Mailer), **III:** 27, 33–34, 35, 39, 41, 43, 44; **Retro. Supp. II:** 203, 204–205

American Dream, The (Albee), **I:** 74–76, 77, 89, 94

"American Dreams" (Simpson), **Supp. IX:** 274

American Earth (Caldwell), **I:** 290, 308

"American Emperors" (Poirier), **Supp. IV Part 2:** 690

American Exodus, An (Lange and Taylor), **I:** 293

American Experience, The (Parkes), **Supp. I Part 2:** 617–618

American Express (Corso), **Supp. XII:** 129

"American Express" (Salter), **Supp. IX:** 260–261

"American Fear of Literature, The" (Lewis), **II:** 451

American Fictions (Hardwick), **Supp. X:** 171

American Fictions, 1940–1980 (Karl), **Supp. IV Part 1:** 384

"American Financier, The" (Dreiser), **II:** 428

American Folkways (book series), **I:** 290

American Heroine: The Life and Legend of Jane Addams (Davis), **Supp. I Part 1:** 1

American Historical Novel, The (Leisy), **Supp. II Part 1:** 125

"American Horse" (Erdrich), **Supp. IV Part 1:** 333

American Humor (Rourke), **IV:** 339, 352

American Hunger (Wright), **Supp. IV Part 1:** 11

American Indian Anthology, An (Tvedten, ed.), **Supp. IV Part 2:** 505

"American Indian Women: At the Center of Indigenous Resistance in Contemporary North America" (Jaimes and Halsey), **Supp. IV Part 1:** 331

"American in England, An" (Wylie), **Supp. I Part 2:** 707

American Jitters, The: A Year of the Slump (Wilson), **IV:** 427, 428

American Journal (Hayden), **Supp. II Part 1:** 367

American Journey: The Times of Robert F. Kennedy (Plimpton, ed.), **Supp. XVI:**245

"American Land Ethic, An" (Momaday), **Supp. IV Part 2:** 488

American Landscape, The, **Supp. I Part 1:** 157

American Language, The (Mencken), **II:** 289, 430; **III:** 100, 104, 105, 108, 111, 119–120

American Language, The: Supplement One (Mencken), **III:** 111

American Language, The: Supplement Two (Mencken), **III:** 111

"American Letter" (MacLeish), **III:** 13

"American Liberty" (Freneau), **Supp. II Part 1:** 257

American Literary History (Harrison), **Supp. VIII:** 37

American Mercury, **Supp. XI:** 163, 164

American Mind, The (Commager), **Supp. I Part 2:** 650

American Moderns: From Rebellion to Conformity (Geismar), **Supp. IX:** 15; **Supp. XI:** 223

"American Names" (Benét), **Supp. XI:** 47

American Nature Writers (Elder, ed.), **Supp. IX:** 25

American Nature Writers (Winter), **Supp. X:** 104

American Negro, The (W. H. Thomas), **Supp. II Part 1:** 168

American Notebooks, The (Hawthorne), **II:** 226

American Novel Since World War II, The (Klein, ed.), **Supp. XI:** 233

Americano, The (film), **Supp. XVI:**185

"American Original, An: Learning from a Literary Master" (Wilkinson), **Supp. VIII:** 164, 165, 168

American Ornithology (Wilson), **Supp. XVI:**4, 6

American Pastoral (P. Roth), **Retro. Supp. II:** 279, 289, 292–293; **Supp. XI:** 68

American Places (Porter, Stegner and Stegner), **Supp. IV Part 2:** 599

"American Poet" (Shapiro), **Supp. II Part 2:** 701

"American Poetry" (Simpson), **Supp. IX:** 272

American Poetry, 1922: A Miscellany (Untermeyer, ed.), **Supp. XV:** 306

"American Poetry and American Life" (Pinsky), **Supp. VI:** 239–240

American Poetry from the Beginning to Whitman (Untermeyer, ed.), **Supp. XV:** 310

American Poetry since 1900 (Untermeyer, ed.), **Supp. XV:** 306

American Poetry since 1945: A Critical Survey (Stepanchev), **Supp. XI:** 312

American Poetry since 1960 (Mesic), **Supp. IV Part 1:** 175

American Poets since World War II Dictionary of Literary Biography (Gwynn, ed.), **Supp. XV:** 343

American Primer, An (Boorstin), **I:** 253

American Primer, An (Whitman), **IV:** 348

"American Primitive" (W. J. Smith), **Supp. XIII:** 333

American Primitive: Poems (Oliver), **Supp. VII:** 234–237, 238

American Procession, An: The Major American Writers from 1830–1930—-the Crucial Century (Kazin), **Supp. VIII:** 105–106, 108

American Radio Company, The (radio show, Keillor), **Supp. XVI:**176–177

"American Realist Playwrights, The" (McCarthy), **II:** 562

American Register, or General Repository of History, Politics, and Science, The (Brown, ed.), **Supp. I**

Part 1: 146

American Renaissance (Matthiessen), **I:** 259–260; **III:** 310; **Supp. XIII:** 93

"American Rendezvous, An" (Beauvoir), **Supp. IX:** 4

American Scene, The (James), **II:** 336; **III:** 460; **Retro. Supp. I:** 232, 235

American Scenes (Kozlenko, ed.), **IV:** 378

"American Scholar, The" (Emerson), **I:** 239; **II:** 8, 12–13; **Retro. Supp. I:** 62, 74–75, 149, 298; **Retro. Supp. II:** 155; **Supp. I Part 2:** 420; **Supp. IX:** 227, 271; **Supp. XIV:**104

Americans in England; or, Lessons for Daughters (Rowson), **Supp. XV:** 240

"American Soldier, The" (Freneau), **Supp. II Part 1:** 269

American Songbag, The (Sandburg), **III:** 583

"American Student in Paris, An" (Farrell), **II:** 45

"American Sublime, The" (Stevens), **IV:** 74

"American Tar, The; or, The Press Gang Defeated" (Rowson and Taylor), **Supp. XV:** 238

"American Temperament, The" (Locke), **Supp. XIV:**211

American Tragedy, An (Dreiser), **I:** 497, 498, 499, 501, 502, 503, 511–515, 517, 518, 519; **III:** 251; **IV:** 35, 484; **Retro. Supp. II:** 93, 95, 104–108

"American Triptych" (Kenyon), **Supp. VII:** 165

"American Use for German Ideals" (Bourne), **I:** 228

American Village, The (Freneau), **Supp. II Part 1:** 256, 257

"American Village, The" (Freneau), **Supp. II Part 1:** 256

America's Coming-of-Age (Brooks), **I:** 228, 230, 240, 245, 258; **IV:** 427

America's Humor: From Poor Richard to Doonesbury (Blair and Hill), **Retro. Supp. II:** 286

"America's Part in World Peace" (Locke), **Supp. XIV:**208

America's Rome (Vance), **Supp. IV Part 2:** 684

America Was Promises (MacLeish), **III:** 16, 17

"Amerika" (Snyder), **Supp. VIII:** 301

Ames, Fisher, **Supp. I Part 2:** 486

Ames, Lois, **Supp. I Part 2:** 541, 547

Ames, William, **IV:** 158

Ames Stewart, Beatrice, **Supp. IX:** 200

Amichai, Yehuda, **Supp. XI:** 267

Amidon, Stephen, **Supp. XI:** 333

Amiel, Henri F., **I:** 241, 243, 250

Amis, Kingsley, **IV:** 430; **Supp. IV Part 2:** 688; **Supp. VIII:** 167; **Supp. XIII:** 93; **Supp. XV:** 117

Amis, Martin, **Retro. Supp. I:** 278

Ammons, A. R., **Supp. III Part 2:** 541; **Supp. VII:** 23–38; **Supp. IX:** 41, 42, 46; **Supp. XII:** 121; **Supp. XV:** 115

Ammons, Elizabeth, **Retro. Supp. I:** 364, 369; **Retro. Supp. II:** 140

"Among Children" (Levine), **Supp. V:** 192

Among My Books (Lowell), **Supp. I Part 2:** 407

"Among School Children" (Yeats), **III:** 249; **Supp. IX:** 52; **Supp. XIV:**8

"Among the Hills" (Whittier), **Supp. I Part 2:** 703

Among the Isles of Shoals (Thaxter), **Supp. XIII:** 152

"Among Those Present" (Benét), **Supp. XI:** 53

"Amoral Moralist" (White), **Supp. I Part 2:** 648

Amory, Cleveland, **Supp. I Part 1:** 316

Amory, Fred, **Supp. III Part 1:** 2

Amos (biblical book), **II:** 166

Amran, David, **Supp. XIV:**150

"Am Strand von Tanger" (Salter), **Supp. IX:** 257

"AMTRAK" (Baraka), **Supp. II Part 1:** 60

Amy and Isabelle (Strout), **Supp. X:** 86

Amy Lowell: Portrait of the Poet in Her Time (Gregory), **II:** 512

"Amy Lowell of Brookline, Mass." (Scott), **II:** 512

"Amy Wentworth" (Whittier), **Supp. I Part 2:** 694, 696

Anabase (Perse), **III:** 12

"Anabasis (I)" (Merwin), **Supp. III Part 1:** 342, 346

"Anabasis (II)" (Merwin), **Supp. III Part 1:** 342, 346

Anagrams: A Novel (Moore), **Supp. X:** 163, 164, 167, 169–171, 172

Analects (Confucius), **Supp. IV Part 1:** 14

Analects, The (Pound, trans.), **III:** 472

Analogy (J. Butler), **II:** 8

"Analysis of a Theme" (Stevens), **IV:** 81

Anarchiad, The, A Poem on the Restoration of Chaos and Substantial Night, in Twenty Four Books

(Barlow), **Supp. II Part 1:** 70

Anatomy Lesson, and Other Stories, The (Connell), **Supp. XIV:**84, 87, 89

"Anatomy Lesson, The" (Connell), **Supp. XIV:**84, 86, 87

Anatomy Lesson, The (P. Roth), **Retro. Supp. II:** 286, 290; **Supp. III Part 2:** 422–423, 425

Anatomy of Criticism (Frye), **Supp. XIII:** 19; **Supp. XIV:**15

Anatomy of Melancholy (Burton), **III:** 78

Anatomy of Nonsense, The (Winters), **Supp. II Part 2:** 811, 812

Anaya, Rudolfo A., **Supp. IV Part 2:** 502; **Supp. XIII:** 213, 220

Ancestors (Maxwell), **Supp. VIII:** 152, 168

"Ancestors, The" (Tate), **IV:** 128

Ancestral Voice: Conversations with N. Scott Momaday (Woodard), **Supp. IV Part 2:** 484, 485, 486, 489, 493

"Anchorage" (Harjo), **Supp. XII:** 220–221

Ancient Child, The: A Novel (Momaday), **Supp. IV Part 2:** 488, 489–491, 492, 493

"Ancient Egypt/Fannie Goldbarth" (Goldbarth), **Supp. XII:** 191–192

Ancient Evenings (Mailer), **Retro. Supp. II:** 206, 210, 213

Ancient Law, The (Glasgow), **II:** 179–180, 192

Ancient Musics (Goldbarth), **Supp. XII:** 191–192

"Ancient Semitic Rituals for the Dead" (Goldbarth), **Supp. XII:** 191–192

"Ancient World, The" (Doty), **Supp. XI:** 122

& (And) (Cummings), **I:** 429, 431, 432, 437, 445, 446, 448

Andersen, Hans Christian, **I:** 441; **Supp. I Part 2:** 622

Anderson, Charles R., **Supp. I Part 1:** 356, 360, 368, 371, 372

Anderson, Frances, **I:** 231

Anderson, Guy, **Supp. X:** 264, 265

Anderson, Henry J., **Supp. I Part 1:** 156

Anderson, Irwin M., **I:** 98–99

Anderson, Jon, **Supp. V:** 338

Anderson, Judith, **III:** 399

Anderson, Karl, **I:** 99, 103

Anderson, Margaret, **I:** 103; **III:** 471

Anderson, Margaret Bartlett, **III:** 171

Anderson, Mary Jane. *See* Lanier, Mrs. Robert Sampson (Mary Jane Anderson)

Anderson, Maxwell, **III:** 159

Anderson, Mrs. Irwin M., **I:** 98–99

Anderson, Mrs. Sherwood (Tennessee Mitchell), **I:** 100; **Supp. I Part 2:** 459, 460

Anderson, Quentin, **Retro. Supp. I:** 392

Anderson, Robert, **Supp. I Part 1:** 277; **Supp. V:** 108

Anderson, Sally, **Supp. XIII:** 95

Anderson, Sherwood, **I:** 97–120, 211, 374, 375, 384, 405, 423, 445, 480, 487, 495, 506, 518; **II:** 27, 38, 44, 55, 56, 68, 250–251, 263, 271, 289, 451, 456–457; **III:** 220, 224, 382–383, 453, 483, 545, 576, 579; **IV:** 27, 40, 46, 190, 207, 433, 451, 482; **Retro. Supp. I:** 79, 80, 177; **Supp. I Part 2:** 378, 430, 459, 472, 613; **Supp. IV Part 2:** 502; **Supp. V:** 12, 250; **Supp. VIII:** 39, 152; **Supp. IX:** 14, 309; **Supp. XI:** 159, 164; **Supp. XII:** 343; **Supp. XV:** 298; **Supp. XVI:** 17, 20

Anderson, T. J., **Supp. XIII:** 132

Anderssen, A., **III:** 252

"And Hickman Arrives" (Ellison), **Retro. Supp. II:** 118, 126; **Supp. II Part 1:** 248

And in the Hanging Gardens (Aiken), **I:** 63

"And It Came to Pass" (Wright), **Supp. XV:** 348

And I Worked at the Writer's Trade (Cowley), **Supp. II Part 1:** 137, 139, 141, 143, 147, 148

Andorra (Cameron), **Supp. XII:** 79, 81, 88–91

"—and Other Poets" (column; Untermeyer), **Supp. XV:** 294

"—and Other Poets" (Untermeyer), **Supp. XV:** 297

Andral, Gabriel, **Supp. I Part 1:** 302

Andre, Michael, **Supp. XII:** 117–118, 129, 132, 133–134

Andre's Mother (McNally), **Supp. XIII:** 206

Andress, Ursula, **Supp. XI:** 307

"Andrew Jackson" (Masters), **Supp. I Part 2:** 472

Andrews, Bruce, **Supp. IV Part 2:** 426

Andrews, Roy Chapman, **Supp. X:** 172

Andrews, Tom, **Supp. XI:** 317

Andrews, Wayne, **IV:** 310

Andrews, William L., **Supp. IV Part 1:** 13

Andreyev, Leonid Nikolaevich, **I:** 53; **II:** 425

Andria (Terence), **IV:** 363

"Andromache" (Dubus), **Supp. VII:** 84

"And Summer Will Not Come Again" (Plath), **Retro. Supp. II:** 242

"And That Night Clifford Died" (Levine), **Supp. V:** 195

And the Band Played On (Shilts), **Supp. X:** 145

"And the Moon Be Still as Bright" (Bradbury), **Supp. IV Part 1:** 106

"And the Sea Shall Give up Its Dead" (Wilder), **IV:** 358

And Things That Go Bump in the Night (McNally), **Supp. XIII:** 196–197, 205, 208

And to Think That I Saw It on Mulberry Street (Geisel), **Supp. XVI:** 100, 101, 104

"And *Ut Pictura Poesis* Is Her Name" (Ashbery), **Supp. III Part 1:** 19

"Anecdote and Storyteller" (Howe), **Supp. VI:** 127

"Anecdote of the Jar" (Stevens), **IV:** 83–84

"Anemone" (Rukeyser), **Supp. VI:** 281, 285

"Angel, The" (Buck), **Supp. II Part 1:** 127

"Angel and Unicorn and Butterfly" (Everwine), **Supp. XV:** 76

Angela's Ashes (McCourt), **Supp. XII:** 271–279, 283, 285

"Angel at the Grave, The" (Wharton), **IV:** 310; **Retro. Supp. I:** 365

"Angel Butcher" (Levine), **Supp. V:** 181

Angel City (Shepard), **Supp. III Part 2:** 432, 445

"Angel Is My Watermark!, The" (H. Miller), **III:** 180

Angell, Carol, **Supp. I Part 2:** 655

Angell, Katharine Sergeant. *See* White, Katharine

Angell, Roger, **Supp. I Part 2:** 655; **Supp. V:** 22; **Supp. VIII:** 139

Angel Landing (Hoffman), **Supp. X:** 82–83

"Angel Levine" (Malamud), **Supp. I Part 2:** 431, 432, 433–434, 437

Angel of Bethesda, The (Mather), **Supp. II Part 2:** 464

"Angel of the Bridge, The" (Cheever), **Supp. I Part 1:** 186–187

"Angel of the Odd, The" (Poe), **III:** 425

Angelo Herndon Jones (Hughes), **Retro. Supp. I:** 203

"Angel on the Porch, An" (Wolfe), **IV:** 451

Angelou, Maya, **Supp. IV Part 1:** 1–19; **Supp. XI:** 20, 245; **Supp. XIII:** 185; **Supp. XVI:** 259

"Angel Poem, The" (Stern), **Supp. IX:** 292

Angels and Earthly Creatures (Wylie), **Supp. I Part 2:** 709, 713, 724–730

Angels in America: A Gay Fantasia on National Themes (Kushner), **Supp. IX:** 131, 134, 141–146

"Angels of the Love Affair" (Sexton), **Supp. II Part 2:** 692

"Angel Surrounded by Paysans" (Stevens), **IV:** 93

Angel That Troubled the Waters, The (Wilder), **IV:** 356, 357–358

"Anger" (Creeley), **Supp. IV Part 1:** 150–152

Anger (Sarton), **Supp. VIII:** 256

"Anger against Children" (R. Bly), **Supp. IV Part 1:** 73

Angle of Ascent (Hayden), **Supp. II Part 1:** 363, 367, 370

"Angle of Geese" (Momaday), **Supp. IV Part 2:** 485

Angle of Geese and Other Poems (Momaday), **Supp. IV Part 2:** 487, 491

Angle of Repose (Stegner), **Supp. IV Part 2:** 599, 605, 606, 610–611

"*Angle of Repose* and the Writings of Mary Hallock Foote: A Source Study" (Williams-Walsh), **Supp. IV Part 2:** 611

Anglo-Saxon Century, The (Dos Passos), **I:** 474–475, 483

Angoff, Charles, **III:** 107

"Angola Question Mark" (Hughes), **Supp. I Part 1:** 344

Angry Wife, The (Sedges), **Supp. II Part 1:** 125

"Angry Women Are Building: Issues and Struggles Facing American Indian Women Today" (Gunn Allen), **Supp. IV Part 1:** 324

"Animal, Vegetable, and Mineral" (Bogan), **Supp. III Part 1:** 66

"Animal Acts" (Simic), **Supp. VIII:** 278

Animal and Vegetable Physiology Considered with Reference to Natural Theology (Roget), **Supp. I Part 1:** 312

Animal Dreams (Kingsolver), **Supp. VII:** 199, 204–207

Animal Magnetism (Prose), **Supp. XVI:** 251, 260

"Animals, The" (Merwin), **Supp. III Part 1:** 348

"Animals Are Passing from Our Lives" (Levine), **Supp. V:** 181, 182

Animals in That Country, The (Atwood), **Supp. XIII:** 20, 33

Animals of the Soul: Sacred Animals of the Oglala Sioux (Brown), **Supp. IV Part 2:** 487

"Animals You Eat, The" (X. J. Kennedy), **Supp. XV:** 169

"Animula" (Eliot), **Retro. Supp. I:** 64

Anita Loos Rediscovered (M. A. Loos), **Supp. XVI:**196

Ankor Wat (Ginsberg), **Supp. II Part 1:** 323

"Annabelle" (Komunyakaa), **Supp. XIII:** 117

"Annabel Lee" (Poe), **Retro. Supp. I:** 273; **Retro. Supp. II:** 266

Anna Christie (O'Neill), **III:** 386, 389, 390

Anna Karenina (Tolstoy), **I:** 10; **II:** 290; **Retro. Supp. I:** 225; **Supp. V:** 323

"Anna Karenina" (Trilling), **Supp. III Part 2:** 508

"Anna Who Was Mad" (Sexton), **Supp. II Part 2:** 692

"Ann Burlak" (Rukeyser), **Supp. VI:** 280

"Anne" (Davis), **Supp. XVI:**91, 92

"Anne" (Oliver), **Supp. VII:** 232

"Anne at the Symphony" (Shields), **Supp. VII:** 310

"Anne Bradstreet's Poetic Voices" (Requa), **Supp. I Part 1:** 107

Anne Sexton: The Artist and Her Critics (McClatchy), **Supp. XII:** 253

"Ann from the Street" (Dixon), **Supp. XII:** 146–147

"Ann Garner" (Agee), **I:** 27

"Anniad, The" (Brooks), **Supp. III Part 1:** 77, 78

Annie (musical), **Supp. IV Part 2:** 577

Annie Allen (Brooks), **Supp. III Part 1:** 76–79

Annie Dillard Reader, The (Dillard), **Supp. VI:** 23

Annie Hall (film; Allen), **Supp. IV Part 1:** 205; **Supp. XV:** 1, 2, 4, 5, 6–7, 14

Annie John (Kincaid), **Supp. VII:** 184–186, 193

Annie Kilburn, a Novel (Howells), **II:** 275, 286, 287

"Annihilation" (X. J. Kennedy), **Supp. XV:** 168

Anniversary (Shields), **Supp. VII:** 320, 322, 323, 324

"Annunciation, The" (Le Sueur), **Supp. V:** 130

Ann Vickers (Lewis), **II:** 453

"A No-Account Creole, A" (Chopin), **Retro. Supp. II:** 64

"Anodyne" (Komunyakaa), **Supp.**

XIII: 130

Another America/Otra America (Kingsolver), **Supp. VII:** 207–209

"Another Animal" (Swenson), **Supp. IV Part 2:** 639

Another Animal: Poems (Swenson), **Supp. IV Part 2:** 639–641, 649

Another Antigone (Gurney), **Supp. V:** 97, 98, 100, 101, 102, 105

"Another August" (Merrill), **Supp. III Part 1:** 326

"Another Beer" (Matthews), **Supp. IX:** 158

Another Country (Baldwin), **Retro. Supp. II:** 9–11, 14; **Supp. I Part 1:** 51, 52, 56–58, 63, 67, 337; **Supp. II Part 1:** 40; **Supp. VIII:** 349

"Another Language" (Jong), **Supp. V:** 131

Another Mother Tongue: Gay Words, Gay Worlds (Grahn), **Supp. IV Part 1:** 330

"Another Night in the Ruins" (Kinnell), **Supp. III Part 1:** 239, 251

"Another Old Woman" (W. C. Williams), **Retro. Supp. I:** 423

Another Part of the Forest (Hellman), **Supp. I Part 1:** 282–283, 297

Another Republic: 17 European and South American Writers (Strand, trans.), **Supp. IV Part 2:** 630

Another Roadside Attraction (Robbins), **Supp. X:** 259, 261, 262, 263, 264, 265–266, 267–269, 274, 275, 277, 284

"Another Spring Uncovered" (Swenson), **Supp. IV Part 2:** 644

Another Thin Man (film), **Supp. IV Part 1:** 355

Another Time (Auden), **Supp. II Part 1:** 15

Another Turn of the Crank (Berry), **Supp. X:** 25, 35

"Another upon the Same" (Taylor), **IV:** 161

"Another Voice" (Wilbur), **Supp. III Part 2:** 557

"Another Wife" (Anderson), **I:** 114

Another Woman (film; Allen), **Supp. XV:** 11

Another You (Beattie), **Supp. V:** 29, 31, 33–34

Anouilh, Jean, **Supp. I Part 1:** 286–288, 297

Ansky, S., **IV:** 6

Ansky, Shloime, **Supp. IX:** 131, 138

"Answer, The" (Jeffers), **Supp. III Part 2:** 423

Answered Prayers: The Unfinished Novel (Capote), **Supp. III Part 1:**

113, 125, 131–132; **Supp. XVI:**245

"Answering the Deer: Genocide and Continuance in the Poetry of American Indian Women" (Gunn Allen), **Supp. IV Part 1:** 322, 325

"Answer of Minerva, The: Pacifism and Resistance in Simone Weil" (Merton), **Supp. VIII:** 204

Antaeus (Wolfe), **IV:** 461

"Ante-Bellum Sermon, An" (Dunbar), **Supp. II Part 1:** 203–204

Antheil, George, **III:** 471, 472; **IV:** 404

Anthem (Rand), **Supp. IV Part 2:** 523

Anthology of Holocaust Literature (Glatstein, Knox, and Margoshes, eds.), **Supp. X:** 70

Anthology of Twentieth-Century Brazilian Poetry, An (Bishop and Brasil, eds.), **Retro. Supp. II:** 50; **Supp. I Part 1:** 94

Anthon, Kate, **I:** 452

Anthony, Andrew, **Supp. XVI:**235, 245, 246

Anthony, Saint, **III:** 395

Anthony, Susan B., **Supp. XI:** 200

"Anthropologist as Hero, The" (Sontag), **Supp. III Part 2:** 451

"Anthropology of Water, The" (Carson), **Supp. XII:** 102–103

Anthropos: The Future of Art (Cummings), **I:** 430

Antichrist (Nietzsche), **III:** 176

"Anti-Father" (Dove), **Supp. IV Part 1:** 246

"Anti-Feminist Woman, The" (Rich), **Supp. I Part 2:** 550

Antigone (Sophocles), **Supp. I Part 1:** 284; **Supp. X:** 249

Antin, David, **Supp. VIII:** 292; **Supp. XII:** 2, 8

Antin, Mary, **Supp. IX:** 227; **Supp. XVI:**148, 149

Anti-Oedipus: Capitalism and Schizophrenia (Deleuze and Guattari), **Supp. XII:** 4

Antiphon, The (Barnes), **Supp. III Part 1:** 43–44

"Antiquities" (Mather), **Supp. II Part 2:** 452

"Antiquity of Freedom, The" (Bryant), **Supp. I Part 1:** 168

"Antislavery Tocsin, An" (Douglass), **Supp. III Part 1:** 171

Antoine, Andre, **III:** 387

Antonioni, Michelangelo, **Supp. IV Part 1:** 46, 47, 48

Antony and Cleopatra (Shakespeare), **I:** 285

"Antony on Behalf of the Play" (Burke), **I:** 284

"An trentiesme de mon Eage, L" (MacLeish), **III:** 9

"Ants" (R. Bly), **Supp. IV Part 1:** 71

Anxiety of Influence, The (Bloom), **Supp. XIII:** 46

"Any City" (Untermeyer), **Supp. XV:** 296

"Any Object" (Swenson), **Supp. IV Part 2:** 640

"Any Porch" (Parker), **Supp. IX:** 194

Anything Else (film; Allen), **Supp. XV:** 2, 11

"Anywhere Out of This World" (Baudelaire), **II:** 552

Any Woman Can't (Wasserstein), **Supp. XV:** 322

Any Woman's Blues (Jong), **Supp. V:** 115, 123, 126

Anzaldúa, Gloria, **Supp. IV Part 1:** 330; **Supp. XIII:** 223

"Aphorisms on Society" (Stevens), **Retro. Supp. I:** 303

"Apiary IX" (C. Frost), **Supp. XV:** 106

Apollinaire, Guillaume, **I:** 432; **II:** 529; **III:** 196; **IV:** 80; **Retro. Supp. II:** 326; **Supp. XV:** 182

Apologies to the Iroquois (Wilson), **IV:** 429

"Apology" (C. Frost), **Supp. XV:** 103

"Apology, An" (Malamud), **Supp. I Part 2:** 435, 437

"Apology for Bad Dreams" (Jeffers), **Supp. II Part 2:** 427, 438

"Apology for Crudity, An" (Anderson), **I:** 109

Apology for Poetry (Sidney), **Supp. II Part 1:** 105

"Apostle of the Tules, An" (Harte), **Supp. II Part 1:** 356

"Apostrophe to a Dead Friend" (Kumin), **Supp. IV Part 2:** 442, 451, 452

"Apostrophe to a Pram Rider" (White), **Supp. I Part 2:** 678

"Apostrophe to Man (on reflecting that the world is ready to go to war again)" (Millay), **III:** 127

"Apostrophe to Vincentine, The" (Stevens), **IV:** 90

"Apotheosis" (Kingsolver), **Supp. VII:** 208

"Apotheosis of Martin Luther King, The" (Hardwick), **Supp. III Part 1:** 203–204

Appalachia (Wright), **Supp. V:** 333, 345

"Appalachian Book of the Dead III" (Wright), **Supp. V:** 345

"Appeal to Progressives, An" (Wilson), **IV:** 429

Appeal to Reason (Paine), **I:** 490

Appeal to the World, An (Du Bois), **Supp. II Part 1:** 184

Appearance and Reality (Bradley), **I:** 572

"Appendix to 'The Anniad'" (Brooks), **Supp. III Part 1:** 77

Apple, Max, **Supp. VIII:** 14

"Apple, The" (Kinnell), **Supp. III Part 1:** 250

Applebaum, Anne, **Supp. XVI:**153

Applegarth, Mabel, **II:** 465, 478

"Apple of Discord, The" (Humphrey), **Supp. IX:** 109

"Apple Peeler" (Francis), **Supp. IX:** 82

"Apple Rind" (C. Frost), **Supp. XV:** 102

Appleseed, Johnny (pseudonym). *See* Chapman, John (Johnny Appleseed)

Appleton, Nathan, **II:** 488

Appleton, Thomas Gold, **Supp. I Part 1:** 306; **Supp. I Part 2:** 415

"Apple Tree, The" (McCarriston), **Supp. XIV:**263, 268

"Applicant, The" (Plath), **Retro. Supp. II:** 252; **Supp. I Part 2:** 535, 544, 545

"Application, The" (Neugeboren), **Supp. XVI:**219, 220, 225

"Applications of the Doctrine" (Hass), **Supp. VI:** 100–101

Appointment, The (film), **Supp. IX:** 253

Appointment in Samarra (O'Hara), **III:** 361, 363–364, 365–367, 371, 374, 375, 383

Appreciation of Sarah Orne Jewett (Cary), **Retro. Supp. II:** 132

"Approaches, The" (Merwin), **Supp. III Part 1:** 350

"Approaching Artaud" (Sontag), **Supp. III Part 2:** 470–471

"Approaching Prayer" (Dickey), **Supp. IV Part 1:** 175

Approach to Literature, An: A Collection of Prose and Verse with Analyses and Discussions (Brooks, Warren, and Purser), **Supp. XIV:**4

"Approach to Thebes, The" (Kunitz), **Supp. III Part 1:** 265–267

Approach to Vedanta, An (Isherwood), **Supp. XIV:**157, 163, 164

"Après-midi d'un faune, L'" (Mallarmé), **III:** 8

"April" (Winters), **Supp. II Part 2:** 788

"April" (W. C. Williams), **Retro. Supp. I:** 422

April, Steve. See Lacy, Ed

April Galleons (Ashbery), **Supp. III Part 1:** 26

"April Galleons" (Ashbery), **Supp. III Part 1:** 26

April Hopes (Howells), **II:** 285, 289

"April Lovers" (Ransom), **III:** 489–490

"April Showers" (Wharton), **Retro. Supp. I:** 361

"April Today Main Street" (Olson), **Supp. II Part 2:** 581

April Twilights (Cather), **I:** 313; **Retro. Supp. I:** 5

"Apt Pupil" (King), **Supp. V:** 152

Arabian Nights, **I:** 204; **II:** 8; **Supp. I Part 2:** 584, 599; **Supp. IV Part 1:** 1

"Arabic Coffee" (Nye), **Supp. XIII:** 276

"Araby" (Joyce), **I:** 174; **Supp. VIII:** 15

Aragon, Louis, **I:** 429; **III:** 471; **Retro. Supp. II:** 85, 321

Arana-Ward, Marie, **Supp. VIII:** 84

Ararat (Glück), **Supp. V:** 79, 86–87

Arbre du voyageur, L' (W. J. Smith; Haussmann, trans.), **Supp. XIII:** 347

Arbus, Diane, **Supp. XII:** 188

Arbuthnott, John (pseudonym). *See* Henry, O.

"Arc, The" (Bidart), **Supp. XV:** 25–26, 27

Archaeologist of Morning (Olson), **Supp. II Part 2:** 557

"Archaic Maker, The" (Merwin), **Supp. III Part 1:** 357

"Archaic Torso of Apollo" (Rilke), **Supp. XV:** 148

"Archbishop, The" (Gioia), **Supp. XV:** 126, 127

Archer (television show), **Supp. IV Part 2:** 474

Archer, William, **IV:** 131; **Retro. Supp. I:** 228

Archer at Large (Macdonald), **Supp. IV Part 2:** 473

Archer in Hollywood (Macdonald), **Supp. IV Part 2:** 474

"Archetype and Signature: The Relationship of Poet and Poem" (Fiedler), **Supp. XIII:** 101

"Archibald Higbie" (Masters), **Supp. I Part 2:** 461

"Architect, The" (Bourne), **I:** 223

Arctic Dreams (Lopez), **Supp. V:** 211

Arctic Refuge: A Circle of Testimony (Haines), **Supp. XII:** 205

"Arcturus" (Connell), **Supp. XIV:**88

Arendt, Hannah, **II:** 544; **Retro. Supp. I:** 87; **Retro. Supp. II:** 28, 117; **Supp. I Part 2:** 570; **Supp. IV Part 1:** 386; **Supp. VIII:** 98, 99, 100, 243; **Supp. XII:** 166–167

Arensberg, Walter, **IV:** 408; **Retro. Supp. I:** 416

Aren't You Happy for Me? (Bausch), **Supp. VII:** 42, 51, 54

Areopagitica (Milton), **Supp. I Part 2:** 422

"Are You a Doctor?" (Carver), **Supp. III Part 1:** 139–141

"Are You Mr. William Stafford?" (Stafford), **Supp. XI:** 317

"Argonauts of 49, California's Golden Age" (Harte), **Supp. II Part 1:** 353, 355

"Arguments with the Gestapo Continued: II" (Wright), **Supp. XV:** 344

"Arguments with the Gestapo Continued: Literary Resistance" (Wright), **Supp. XV:** 344

Aria da Capo (Millay), **III:** 137–138

Ariadne's Thread: A Collection of Contemporary Women's Journals (Lifshin, ed.), **Supp. XVI:**37–38

Ariel (Plath), **Retro. Supp. II:** 250–255; **Supp. I Part 2:** 526, 539, 541; **Supp. V:** 79

"Ariel" (Plath), **Supp. I Part 2:** 542, 546

"Ariel Poems" (Eliot), **I:** 579

"Ariosto: Critical Notice of His Life and Genius" (Hunt), **Supp. XV:** 175

Ariosto, Ludovico, **Supp. XV:** 175

Arise, Arise (Zukofsky), **Supp. III Part 2:** 619, 629

Aristides. See Epstein, Joseph

"Aristocracy" (Emerson), **II:** 6

Aristocracy and Justice (More), **I:** 223

Aristophanes, **I:** 436; **II:** 577; **Supp. I Part 2:** 406

Aristotle, **I:** 58, 265, 280, 527; **II:** 9, 12, 198, 536; **III:** 20, 115, 145, 157, 362, 422, 423; **IV:** 10, 18, 74–75, 89; **Supp. I Part 1:** 104, 296; **Supp. I Part 2:** 423; **Supp. IV Part 1:** 391; **Supp. IV Part 2:** 526, 530; **Supp. X:** 78; **Supp. XI:** 249; **Supp. XII:** 106; **Supp. XIV:**242–243

Aristotle Contemplating the Bust of Homer (Rembrandt), **Supp. IV Part 1:** 390, 391

"Arkansas Traveller" (Wright), **Supp. V:** 334

"Arm, The" (X. J. Kennedy), **Supp. XV:** 169

"Armadillo, The" (Bishop), **Supp. I Part 1:** 93

Armadillo in the Grass (Hearon), **Supp. VIII:** 58–59

"Armageddon" (Ransom), **III:** 489, 492

Armah, Aiy Kwei, **Supp. IV Part 1:** 373

Armies of the Night, The (Mailer), **III:** 39–40, 41, 42, 44, 45, 46; **Retro. Supp. II:** 205, 206–207, 208; **Supp. IV Part 1:** 207; **Supp. XIV:**49, 162

"Arm in Arm" (Simpson), **Supp. IX:** 267–268

Arminius, Jacobus, **I:** 557

Armitage, Shelley, **Supp. IV Part 2:** 439

Arm of Flesh, The (Salter), **Supp. IX:** 251

"Armor" (Dickey), **Supp. IV Part 1:** 179

Armored Attack (film), **Supp. I Part 1:** 281

Arms, George W., **Supp. I Part 2:** 416–417

Armstrong, George, **Supp. I Part 2:** 386

Armstrong, Louis, **Retro. Supp. II:** 114

"'Arm the Paper Arm': Kenneth Koch's Postmodern Comedy" (Chinitz), **Supp. XV:** 180, 185

"Army" (Corso), **Supp. XII:** 117, 127

Army Brat (W. J. Smith), **Supp. XIII:** 331, 347

Arna Bontemps Langston Hughes: Letters 1925–1967 (Nichols), **Retro. Supp. I:** 194

Arner, Robert D., **Retro. Supp. II:** 62

Arnold, Edwin T., **Supp. VIII:** 189

Arnold, George W., **Supp. I Part 2:** 411

Arnold, Marilyn, **Supp. IV Part 1:** 220

Arnold, Matthew, **I:** 222, 228, 275; **II:** 20, 110, 338, 541; **III:** 604; **IV:** 349; **Retro. Supp. I:** 56, 325; **Supp. I Part 2:** 416, 417, 419, 529, 552, 602; **Supp. IX:** 298; **Supp. XIV:**11, 335

Arnold, Thurman, **Supp. I Part 2:** 645

Aronson, Steven M. L., **Supp. V:** 4

Around about America (Caldwell), **I:** 290

"Arrangement in Black and White" (Parker), **Supp. IX:** 198

"Arrival at Santos" (Bishop), **Retro. Supp. II:** 46; **Supp. IX:** 45–46

"Arrival of the Bee Box, The" (Plath), **Retro. Supp. II:** 255

Arrivistes, The: Poem 1940–1949 (Simpson), **Supp. IX:** 265, 267–268

"Arrow" (Dove), **Supp. IV Part 1:** 250

Arrowsmith (Lewis), **I:** 362; **II:** 445–446, 449

"Arsenal at Springfield, The" (Longfellow), **Retro. Supp. II:** 168

"Arson Plus" (Hammett), **Supp. IV Part 1:** 343

"Ars Poetica" (Dove), **Supp. IV Part 1:** 250

"Ars Poetica" (Dunn), **Supp. XI:** 154

"Ars Poetica" (MacLeish), **III:** 9–10

"Ars Poetica" (X. J. Kennedy), **Supp. XV:** 154

"*Ars Poetica:* A Found Poem" (Kumin), **Supp. IV Part 2:** 455

"Ars Poetica; or, Who Lives in the Ivory Tower" (McGrath), **Supp. X:** 117

"Ars Poetica: Some Recent Criticism" (Wright), **Supp. III Part 2:** 603

"Art" (Emerson), **II:** 13

"Art and Neurosis" (Trilling), **Supp. III Part 2:** 502

Art and Technics (Mumford), **Supp. II Part 2:** 483

Art & Ardor: Essays (Ozick), **Supp. V:** 258, 272

Art as Experience (Dewey), **I:** 266

Art by Subtraction (Reid), **IV:** 41

Art de toucher le clavecin, L' (Couperin), **III:** 464

Artemis to Actaeon and Other Verse (Wharton), **Retro. Supp. I:** 372

Arte of English Poesie (Puttenham), **Supp. I Part 1:** 113

Arthur, Anthony, **Supp. IV Part 2:** 606

Arthur Mervyn; or, Memoirs of the Year 1793 (Brown), **Supp. I Part 1:** 137–140, 144

"Article of Faith" (Sobin), **Supp. XVI:**291

Articles of Light & Elation (Sobin), **Supp. XVI:**291

Articulation of Sound Forms in Time (Howe), **Supp. IV Part 2:** 419, 431–433

"Artificer" (X. J. Kennedy), **Supp. XV:** 160

"Artificial Nigger, The" (O'Connor), **III:** 343, 351, 356, 358; **Retro. Supp. II:** 229, 232

Artist, The: A Drama without Words (Mencken), **III:** 104

"Artist of the Beautiful, The" (Hawthorne), **Retro. Supp. I:** 149

Artistry of Grief (Torsney), **Retro. Supp. I:** 224

"Artists' and Models' Ball, The" (Brooks), **Supp. III Part 1:** 72

"Art of Disappearing, The" (Nye), **Supp. XIII:** 287

Art of Fiction, The (Gardner), **Supp. VI:** 73

"Art of Fiction, The" (H. James), **Retro. Supp. I:** 226; **Retro. Supp. II:** 223

Art of Hunger, The (Auster), **Supp. XII:** 22

"Art of Keeping Your Mouth Shut, The" (Heller), **Supp. IV Part 1:** 383

"Art of Literature and Commonsense, The" (Nabokov), **Retro. Supp. I:** 271

Art of Living and Other Stories, The (Gardner), **Supp. VI:** 72

Art of Love, The (Koch), **Supp. XV:** 182

"Art of Love, The" (Koch), **Supp. XV:** 182

Art of Poetry, The (Koch), **Supp. XV:** 175–176, 178, 188

"Art of Poetry, The" (Koch), **Supp. XV:** 182

"Art of Poetry, The" (McClatchy), **Supp. XII:** 262

"Art of Romare Bearden, The" (Ellison), **Retro. Supp. II:** 123

"Art of Storytelling, The" (Simpson), **Supp. IX:** 277

Art of Sylvia Plath, The (Newman), **Supp. I Part 2:** 527

Art of the Moving Picture, The (Lindsay), **Supp. I Part 2:** 376, 391–392, 394; **Supp. XVI:**185

Art of the Novel (H. James), **Retro. Supp. I:** 227

"Art of Theodore Dreiser, The" (Bourne), **I:** 235

Art of the Personal Essay, The (Lopate, comp.), **Supp. XIII:** 280–281; **Supp. XVI:**266

Art of the Self, The: Essays a Propos "Steps" (Kosinski), **Supp. VII:** 222

Arts and Sciences (Goldbarth), **Supp. XII:** 184–186

"Art's Bread and Butter" (Benét), **Retro. Supp. I:** 108

Arvin, Newton, **I:** 259; **II:** 508; **Retro. Supp. I:** 19, 137

Asali, Muna, **Supp. XIII:** 121, 126

Asbury, Herbert, **Supp. IV Part 1:** 353

Ascent of F6, The (Auden), **Supp. II Part 1:** 11, 13

Ascent to Truth, The (Merton), **Supp. VIII:** 208

Asch, Nathan, **Supp. XV:** 133, 134

Asch, Sholem, **IV:** 1, 9, 11, 14; **Retro. Supp. II:** 299

Ascherson, Neal, **Supp. XII:** 167

As Does New Hampshire and Other Poems (Sarton), **Supp. VIII:** 259

"As Evening Lays Dying" (Salinas), **Supp. XIII:** 319

"As Flowers Are" (Kunitz), **Supp. III Part 1:** 265

"Ash" (Sobin), **Supp. XVI:**284–285

Ashbery, John, **Retro. Supp. I:** 313; **Supp. I Part 1:** 96; **Supp. III Part 1:** 1–29; **Supp. III Part 2:** 541; **Supp. IV Part 2:** 620; **Supp. VIII:** 272; **Supp. IX:** 52; **Supp. XI:** 139; **Supp. XIII:** 85; **Supp. XV:** 176, 177, 178, 188, 250

"Ashes" (Levine), **Supp. V:** 188

Ashes: Poems Old and New (Levine), **Supp. V:** 178, 188–189

"Ashes of the Beacon" (Bierce), **I:** 209

Ashford, Margaret Mary (Daisy), **II:** 426

Ash Wednesday (Eliot), **I:** 570, 574–575, 578–579, 580, 582, 584, 585; **Retro. Supp. I:** 64

"Ash Wednesday" (Eliot), **Supp. IV Part 2:** 436

"Ash Wednesday" (Garrett), **Supp. VII:** 109–110

"Ash Wednesday" (Merton), **Supp. VIII:** 199

Asian American Authors (Hsu and Palubinskas, eds.), **Supp. X:** 292

Asian American Heritage: An Anthology of Prose and Poetry (Wand), **Supp. X:** 292

Asian Figures (Mervin), **Supp. III Part 1:** 341

Asian Journal of Thomas Merton, The (Merton), **Supp. VIII:** 196, 206, 208

"Asian Peace Offers Rejected without Publication" (R. Bly), **Supp. IV Part 1:** 61

"Asides on the Oboe" (Stevens), **Retro. Supp. I:** 305

"As I Ebb'd with the Ocean of Life" (Whitman), **IV:** 342, 345–346; **Retro. Supp. I:** 404, 405

As I Lay Dying (Faulkner), **II:** 60–61, 69, 73, 74; **IV:** 100; **Retro. Supp. I:** 75, 82, 84, 85, 86, 88, 89, 91, 92; **Supp. IV Part 1:** 47; **Supp. VIII:** 37, 178; **Supp. IX:** 99, 103, 251; **Supp. XIV:**24

"As I Lay with My Head in Your Lap, Camerado" (Whitman), **IV:** 347

Asimov, Isaac, **Supp. IV Part 1:** 116; **Supp. XVI:**122

Asinof, Eliot, **II:** 424

Asirvatham, Sandy, **Supp. XVI:**249

"As Is the Daughter, So Is Her Mother" (Patchett), **Supp. XII:** 310

"As It Was in the Beginning" (Benét), **Supp. XI:** 56

"As I Walked Out One Evening" (Auden), **Supp. II Part 1:** 13; **Supp. XV:** 126

"As I Went Down by Havre de Grace" (Wylie), **Supp. I Part 2:** 723

"Ask Me" (Stafford), **Supp. XI:** 326–327

Ask Me Tomorrow (Cozzens), **I:** 365–367, 379

Ask the Dust (Fante), **Supp. XI:** 159, 160, 166, 167–169, 172, 173, 174

Ask Your Mama (Hughes), **Supp. I Part 1:** 339, 341–342

Ask Your Mama: 12 Moods for Jazz (Hughes), **Retro. Supp. I:** 210, 211

As Little Children (R. P. Smith), **Supp. XIV:**333

"As One Put Drunk into the Packet Boat" (Ashbery), **Supp. III Part 1:** 18

"Aspects of Robinson" (Kees), **Supp. XV:** 134

Aspects of the Novel (Forster), **Retro. Supp. I:** 232; **Supp. VIII:** 155

"Aspen and the Stream, The" (Wilbur), **Supp. III Part 2:** 555, 556

Aspern Papers, The (James), **Supp. V:** 101, 102

"Aspern Papers, The" (James), **Retro. Supp. I:** 219, 227, 228

Asphalt Georgics (Carruth), **Supp. XVI:**54

Asphalt Jungle (film, Huston), **Supp. XIII:** 174

"Asphodel" (Welty), **IV:** 265, 271

"Asphodel, That Greeny Flower" (W. C. Williams), **Retro. Supp. I:** 429

"Aspic and Buttermilk" (Olds), **Supp. X:** 213

Asquith, Herbert Henry, **Retro. Supp. I:** 59

"Ass" (Cisneros), **Supp. VII:** 67

Assante, Armand, **Supp. VIII:** 74

Assassins, The (Oates), **Supp. II Part 2:** 512, 517–519

"Assault" (Millay), **III:** 130–131

"Assemblage of Husbands and Wives, An" (Lewis), **II:** 455–456

Assembly (O'Hara), **III:** 361

Assignment, Wildlife (LaBastille), **Supp. X:** 99, 104

"Assimiliation in Recent American Jewish Autobiographies" (Krupnick), **Supp. XVI:**153

Assistant, The (Malamud), **Supp. I Part 2:** 427, 428, 429, 431, 435, 441–445, 451; **Supp. XVI:**220

Assommoir, L' (Zola), **II:** 291; **III:** 318

Assorted Prose (Updike), **IV:** 215–216, 218; **Retro. Supp. I:** 317, 319, 327

Astaire, Adele, **Supp. XVI:**187

Astor, Mary, **Supp. IV Part 1:** 356; **Supp. XII:** 173

Astoria, or, Anecdotes of an Enterprise beyond the Rocky Mountains (Irving), **II:** 312

"Astounding News by Electric Express via Norfolk! The Atlantic Crossed in Three Days Signal Triumph of Mr. Monck's Flying-Machine . . ." (Poe), **III:** 413, 420

Astraea (Holmes), **III:** 82

Astro, Richard, **Supp. I Part 2:** 429, 445

"Astrological Fricassee" (H. Miller), **III:** 187

Astrophil and Stella (Sidney), **Supp. XIV:**128

"As Weary Pilgrim" (Bradstreet), **Supp. I Part 1:** 103, 109, 122

As We Know (Ashbery), **Supp. III Part 1:** 9, 21–25

"As We Know" (Ashbery), **Supp. III Part 1:** 21–22

Aswell, Edward C., **IV:** 458, 459, 461

"Asylum, The" (Carruth), **Supp. XVI:**48–49

"As You Like It" (Chopin), **Supp. I Part 1:** 217

As You Like It (Shakespeare), **Supp. I Part 1:** 308

"At a Bar in Charlotte Amalie" (Updike), **IV:** 214

"At a Lecture" (Brodsky), **Supp. VIII:** 33

"At a March against the Vietnam War" (R. Bly), **Supp. IV Part 1:** 61

"At a Reading" (McClatchy), **Supp. XII:** 256–257

"Atavism of John Tom Little Bear, The" (O. Henry), **Supp. II Part 1:** 410

"At Chênière Caminada" (Chopin), **Supp. I Part 1:** 220

"At Chinese Checkers" (Berryman), **I:** 182

Atchity, Kenneth John, **Supp. XI:** 227

At Eighty-Two (Sarton), **Supp. VIII:** 264

"At Every Gas Station There Are Mechanics" (Dunn), **Supp. XI:** 144

At Fault (Chopin), **Retro. Supp. II:** 57, 60, 62–63; **Supp. I Part 1:** 207, 209–211, 220

At Heaven's Gate (Warren), **IV:** 243, 247–248, 251

Atheism Refuted: in a Discourse to Prove the Existence of God (Paine), **Supp. I Part 2:** 517

"Athénaïse" (Chopin), **Retro. Supp.**

II: 66, 67; **Supp. I Part 1:** 219–220

Atherton, Gertrude, **I:** 199, 207–208

Athey, Jean L., **Supp. XI:** 184

At Home: Essays, 1982–1988 (Vidal), **Supp. IV Part 2:** 682, 687, 688

"At Home With" (column; Leland), **Supp. XV:** 69

"At Kino Viejo, Mexico" (Ríos), **Supp. IV Part 2:** 541

Atkinson, Brooks, **IV:** 288; **Supp. IV Part 2:** 683

Atlantis (Doty), **Supp. XI:** 121, 126–129

"Atlantis" (Doty), **Supp. XI:** 127–128

Atlas, James, **Supp. V:** 233; **Supp. XV:** 25

Atlas Shrugged (Rand), **Supp. IV Part 2:** 517, 521, 523, 524–526, 528, 531

At Liberty (T. Williams), **IV:** 378

"At Melville's Tomb" (H. Crane), **I:** 393; **Retro. Supp. II:** 76, 78, 80, 82

"At Mother Teresa's" (Nye), **Supp. XIII:** 276

At Night the Salmon Move (Carver), **Supp. III Part 1:** 142

"At North Farm" (Ashbery), **Supp. III Part 1:** 1–2

At Paradise Gate (Smiley), **Supp. VI:** 292, 293–294

"At Paso Rojo" (Bowles), **Supp. IV Part 1:** 87

At Play in the Fields of the Lord (Matthiessen), **Supp. V:** 199, 202, 204–206, 212

"At Play in the Paradise of Bombs" (Sanders), **Supp. XVI:**272–273, 274, 277

"At Pleasure By" (Pinsky), **Supp. VI:** 245

At Risk (Hoffman), **Supp. X:** 87

"At Sea" (Hemingway), **II:** 258

"At Shaft 11" (Dunbar), **Supp. II Part 1:** 212

"At Slim's River" (Haines), **Supp. XII:** 208–209

"At St. Croix" (Dubus), **Supp. VII:** 83, 87

At Sundown (Whittier), **Supp. I Part 2:** 704

"At Sunset" (Simic), **Supp. VIII:** 282

Attebery, Brian, **Supp. IV Part 1:** 101

"At That Time, or The History of a Joke" (Paley), **Supp. VI:** 229–230

At the Back of the North Wind (Macdonald), **Supp. XIII:** 75

"At the Birth of an Age" (Jeffers), **Supp. II Part 2:** 432

"At the Bomb Testing Site" (Stafford), **Supp. XI:** 317–318, 321, 323

At the Bottom of the River (Kincaid),

Supp. VII: 182–184, 185

"At the 'Cadian Ball" (Chopin), **Retro. Supp. II:** 64, 65, 68

"At the Chelton-Pulver Game" (Auchincloss), **Supp. IV Part 1:** 27

"At the Drugstore" (Taylor), **Supp. V:** 323

At the Edge of the Body (Jong), **Supp. V:** 115, 130

At the End of the Open Road (Simpson), **Supp. IX:** 265, 269, 271–273, 277

At the End of This Summer: Poems 1948–1954, **Supp. XII:** 211

"At the End of War" (Eberhart), **I:** 522–523

"At the Executed Murderer's Grave" (Wright), **Supp. III Part 2:** 595, 597

"At the Fishhouses" (Bishop), **Retro. Supp. II:** 45; **Supp. I Part 1:** 90, 92

"At the Grave of My Guardian Angel: St. Louis Cemetery, New Orleans" (Levis), **Supp. XI:** 268–269

"At the Gym" (Doty), **Supp. XI:** 135

"At the Indian Store" (McCarriston), **Supp. XIV:**271

"At the Lake" (Oliver), **Supp. VII:** 244

"At the Landing" (Welty), **IV:** 265–266; **Retro. Supp. I:** 348

"At the Last" (Bynner), **Supp. XV:** 44

"At the Last Rites for Two Hot Rodders" (X. J. Kennedy), **Supp. XV:** 166

"At the Premiere" (Keillor), **Supp. XVI:**167

At the Root of Stars (Barnes), **Supp. III Part 1:** 34

"At the Slackening of the Tide" (Wright), **Supp. III Part 2:** 597

"At the Tomb of Walt Whitman" (Kunitz), **Supp. III Part 1:** 262

"At the Tourist Centre in Boston" (Atwood), **Supp. XIII:** 33

"At the Town Dump" (Kenyon), **Supp. VII:** 167

"At the Worcester Museum" (Pinsky), **Supp. VI:** 251

"Atticus Finch and the Mad Dog: Harper Lee's *To Kill a Mockingbird*" (Jones), **Supp. VIII:** 128

"Atticus Finch—Right and Wrong" (Freedman), **Supp. VIII:** 127–128

"Attic Which Is Desire, The" (W. C. Williams), **Retro. Supp. I:** 422

"At Times in Flight: A Parable" (H. Roth), **Supp. IX:** 234

Attitudes toward History (Burke), **I:** 274

Atwan, Robert, **Supp. XVI:**273, 277

"At White River" (Haines), **Supp. XII:** 208–209

Atwood, Margaret, **Supp. IV Part 1:** 252; **Supp. V:** 119; **Supp. XI:** 317; **Supp. XIII:** 19–39, 291, 306

"Atwood's Gorgon Touch" (Davey), **Supp. XIII:** 33

"Aubade" (McCarriston), **Supp. XIV:**271

"Aubade: November" (McCarriston), **Supp. XIV:**261–262

"Aubade: Opal and Silver" (Doty), **Supp. XI:** 129

"Aubade of an Early Homo Sapiens" (C. Frost), **Supp. XV:** 97–98

"Au Bal Musette" (Van Vechten), **Supp. II Part 2:** 735

Auchincloss, Hugh D., **Supp. IV Part 2:** 679

Auchincloss, Louis, **I:** 375; **III:** 66; **Retro. Supp. I:** 370, 373; **Supp. IV Part 1:** 21–38

"Auction" (Simic), **Supp. VIII:** 278

"Auction, The" (Crane), **I:** 411

"Auction Model 1934" (Z. Fitzgerald), **Supp. IX:** 61

Auden, W. H., **I:** 71, 381, 539; **II:** 367, 368, 371, 376, 586; **III:** 17, 134, 269, 271, 292, 476–477, 504, 527, 530, 542, 615; **IV:** 136, 138, 240, 430; **Retro. Supp. I:** 430; **Retro. Supp. II:** 183, 242, 244, 323; **Supp. I Part 1:** 270; **Supp. I Part 2:** 552, 610; **Supp. II Part 1:** 1–28; **Supp. III Part 1:** 2, 3, 14, 26, 60, 61, 64, 341; **Supp. III Part 2:** 591, 595; **Supp. IV Part 1:** 79, 84, 136, 225, 302, 313; **Supp. IV Part 2:** 440, 465; **Supp. V:** 337; **Supp. VIII:** 19, 21, 22, 23, 30, 32, 155, 190; **Supp. IX:** 94, 287, 288; **Supp. X:** 35, 57, 59, 115–116, 117, 118–119; **Supp. XI:** 243, 244; **Supp. XII:** 253, 264–265, 266, 269–270; **Supp. XIV:**156, 158, 160, 162, 163; **Supp. XV:** 74, 117–118, 139, 144, 186

"Auden's OED" (McClatchy), **Supp. XII:** 264–265

"Audition" (Alvarez), **Supp. VII:** 10

Audubon, John James, **III:** 210; **IV:** 265; **Supp. IX:** 171; **Supp. XVI:**1–14

Audubon, John Woodhouse, **Supp. XVI:**10

Audubon, Maria Rebecca, **Supp. XVI:**11

Audubon, Victor Gifford, **Supp. XVI:**10

Audubon and His Journals (M. Audu-bon, ed.), **Supp. XVI:**11, 12

Audubon Reader, The: The Best Writings of John James Audubon (Sanders, ed.), **Supp. XVI:**269

Auer, Jane. *See* Bowles, Jane

Auerbach, Eric, **III:** 453

Auerbach, Nina, **Supp. I Part 1:** 40

"August" (Oliver), **Supp. VII:** 235

"August" (Rich), **Supp. I Part 2:** 564

"August 1968" (Auden), **Supp. II Part 1:** 25

"August Darks, The" (Clampitt), **Supp. IX:** 43, 50–51, 52

Augustine, Saint, **I:** 279, 290; **II:** 537; **III:** 259, 270, 292, 300; **IV:** 69, 126; **Retro. Supp. I:** 247; **Supp. VIII:** 203; **Supp. XI:** 245; **Supp. XIII:** 89

August Snow (Price), **Supp. VI:** 264

"Au Jardin" (Pound), **III:** 465–466

Aunt Carmen's Book of Practical Saints (Mora), **Supp. XIII:** 227–229

"Aunt Cynthy Dallett" (Jewett), **II:** 393

"Aunt Gladys" (Karr), **Supp. XI:** 241

"Aunt Imogen" (Robinson), **III:** 521

"Aunt Jemima of the Ocean Waves" (Hayden), **Supp. II Part 1:** 368, 379

"Aunt Jennifer's Tigers" (Rich), **Supp. XV:** 252

Aunt Jo's Scrapbooks (Alcott), **Supp. I Part 1:** 43

"Aunt Mary" (Oliver), **Supp. VII:** 232

"Aunt Mary" (Stowe), **Supp. I Part 2:** 587

"Aunt Moon's Young Man" (Hogan), **Supp. IV Part 1:** 400

"Aunt Rectita's Good Friday" (X. J. Kennedy), **Supp. XV:** 166

"Aunt Sarah" (Lowell), **II:** 554

"Aunt Sue's Stories" (Hughes), **Retro. Supp. I:** 197, 199

"Aunt Violet's Canadian Honeymoon/ 1932" (Shields), **Supp. VII:** 311

"Aunt Violet's Things" (Shields), **Supp. VII:** 311–312

"Aurelia: Moon Jellies" (Mora), **Supp. XIII:** 224

Aurora Leigh (E. Browning), **Retro. Supp. I:** 33; **Supp. XI:** 197

Aurora Means Dawn (Sanders), **Supp. XVI:**268

Auroras of Autumn, The (Stevens), **Retro. Supp. I:** 297, 300, 309–312

"Auroras of Autumn, The" (Stevens), **Retro. Supp. I:** 311, 312; **Supp. III Part 1:** 12

Auslander, Joseph, **Supp. XIV:**120

"Auspex" (Frost), **Retro. Supp. I:** 122

"Auspex" (Lowell), **Supp. I Part 2:** 424

Austen, Jane, **I:** 130, 339, 375, 378; **II:** 272, 278, 287, 568–569, 577; **IV:** 8; **Retro. Supp. I:** 354; **Supp. I Part 1:** 267; **Supp. I Part 2:** 656, 715; **Supp. IV Part 1:** 300; **Supp. VIII:** 125, 167; **Supp. IX:** 128; **Supp. XII:** 310; **Supp. XV:** 338

Auster, Paul, **Supp. XII:** 21–39; **Supp. XIV:**292

Austerities (Simic), **Supp. VIII:** 276–278, 283

"Austerities" (Simic), **Supp. VIII:** 277

Austin, Mary Hunter, **Retro. Supp. I:** 7; **Supp. IV Part 2:** 503; **Supp. X:** 29; **Supp. XIII:** 154

"Authentic Unconscious, The" (Trilling), **Supp. III Part 2:** 512

Author and Agent: Eudora Welty and Diarmuid Russell (Kreyling), **Retro. Supp. I:** 342, 345, 347, 349–350

"Author at Sixty, The" (Wilson), **IV:** 426

"Author of 'Beltraffio,' The" (James), **Retro. Supp. I:** 227

"Author's House" (Fitzgerald), **Retro. Supp. I:** 98

"Author's Reflections, An: Willie Loman, Walter Younger, and He Who Must Live" (Hansberry), **Supp. IV Part 1:** 370

"Author to Her Book, The" (Bradstreet), **Supp. I Part 1:** 119; **Supp. V:** 117–118; **Supp. XV:** 125–126

"Autobiographical Note" (H. Miller), **III:** 174–175

"Autobiographical Notes" (Baldwin), **Supp. I Part 1:** 54

"Autobiographical Notes" (Holmes), **Supp. I Part 1:** 301

"Autobiographic Chapter, An" (Bourne), **I:** 236

Autobiography (Franklin), **II:** 102, 103, 108, 121–122, 302

Autobiography (James), **I:** 462

"Autobiography" (MacLeish), **III:** 20

Autobiography (Van Buren), **III:** 473

Autobiography (W. C. Williams), **Supp. I Part 1:** 254

Autobiography (Zukofsky), **Supp. III Part 2:** 627

"Autobiography in the Shape of a Book Review" (Bynner), **Supp. XV:** 40

"Autobiography of a Confluence, The" (Gunn Allen), **Supp. IV Part 1:** 321

Autobiography of Alice B. Toklas, The (Stein), **IV:** 26, 30, 35, 43; **Supp. IV Part 1:** 11, 81

Autobiography of an Ex-Colored Man,

The (Johnson), **Supp. II Part 1:** 33, 194

Autobiography of a Schizophrenic Girl (Renée), **Supp. XVI:**64, 66

Autobiography of Benjamin Franklin (Franklin), **Supp. IV Part 1:** 5

Autobiography of LeRoi Jones, The (Baraka), **Retro. Supp. I:** 411

Autobiography of Malcolm X (Little), **Supp. I Part 1:** 66; **Supp. X:** 27; **Supp. XIII:** 264

Autobiography of Mark Twain, The (Twain), **IV:** 209

Autobiography of My Mother, The (Kincaid), **Supp. VII:** 182, 188–190, 191, 192, 193

Autobiography of Red: A Novel in Verse (Carson), **Supp. XII:** 97, 106–110

Autobiography of Upton Sinclair, The (Sinclair), **Supp. V:** 276, 282

Autobiography of W. E. B. Du Bois, The (Du Bois), **Supp. II Part 1:** 159, 186

Autobiography of William Carlos Williams, The (W. C. Williams), **Retro. Supp. I:** 51, 428

Autocrat of the Breakfast-Table, The (Holmes), **Supp. I Part 1:** 306–307

"Automatic Gate, The" (Southern), **Supp. XI:** 294

"Automotive Passacaglia" (H. Miller), **III:** 186

"Autopsy Room, The" (Carver), **Supp. III Part 1:** 137

"Auto Wreck" (Shapiro), **Supp. II Part 2:** 706

"Autre Temps" (Wharton), **IV:** 320, 324

"Autumn Afternoon" (Farrell), **II:** 45

"Autumnal" (Eberhart), **I:** 540–541

"Autumn Begins in Martins Ferry, Ohio" (Wright), **Supp. III Part 2:** 599

"Autumn Courtship, An" (Caldwell), **I:** 309

Autumn Garden, The (Hellman), **Supp. I Part 1:** 285–286, 290

"Autumn Garden, The: Mechanics and Dialectics" (Felheim), **Supp. I Part 1:** 297

"Autumn Holiday, An" (Jewett), **II:** 391; **Retro. Supp. II:** 140–141

"Autumn Musings" (Harte), **Supp. II Part 1:** 336

"Autumn Within" (Longfellow), **II:** 499

"Autumn Woods" (Bryant), **Supp. I Part 1:** 164

"Au Vieux Jardin" (Aldington), **Supp.**

I Part 1: 257

"Aux Imagistes" (W. C. Williams), **Supp. I Part 1:** 266

Avakian, Aram, **Supp. XI:** 294, 295, 309

"Ave Atque Vale" (Bynner), **Supp. XV:** 49

Avedon, Richard, **Supp. I Part 1:** 58; **Supp. V:** 194; **Supp. X:** 15

Aveling, Edward, **Supp. XVI:**85

"Avenue" (Pinsky), **Supp. VI:** 248

Avenue Bearing the Initial of Christ into the New World: Poems 1946–1964 (Kinnell), **Supp. III Part 1:** 235, 239–241

"Avenue of the Americas" (Simic), **Supp. VIII:** 278

"Average Torture" (Karr), **Supp. XI:** 243

Avery, John, **Supp. I Part 1:** 153

"Avey" (Toomer), **Supp. IX:** 317

Avon's Harvest (Robinson), **III:** 510

Awake and Sing! (Odets), **Supp. II Part 2:** 530, 531, 536–538, 550; **Supp. IV Part 2:** 587

Awakening, The (Chopin), **Retro. Supp. I:** 10; **Retro. Supp. II:** 57, 59, 60, 67, 68–71, 73; **Supp. I Part 1:** 200, 201, 202, 211, 220–225; **Supp. V:** 304; **Supp. VIII:** 198; **Supp. XII:** 170

Awful Rowing Toward God, The (Sexton), **Supp. II Part 2:** 694–696

Awiakta, Marilou, **Supp. IV Part 1:** 319, 335

Awkward Age, The (James), **II:** 332; **Retro. Supp. I:** 229, 230–231

Axe Handles (Snyder), **Supp. VIII:** 303–305

Axel's Castle: A Study in the Imaginative Literature of 1870 to 1930 (Wilson), **I:** 185; **II:** 577; **IV:** 428, 431, 438, 439, 443; **Supp. VIII:** 101

"Ax-Helve, The" (Frost), **Retro. Supp. I:** 133

Azikewe, Nnamdi, **Supp. IV Part 1:** 361

"Aztec Angel" (Salinas), **Supp. XIII:** 314

Aztec Treasure House, The: New and Selected Essays (Connell), **Supp. XIV:**80, 97

B

B. F.'s Daughter (Marquand), **III:** 59, 65, 68, 69

Babbitt (Lewis), **II:** 442, 443–445, 446, 447, 449; **III:** 63–64, 394; **IV:** 326

Babbitt, Irving, **I:** 247; **II:** 456; **III:** 315, 461, 613; **IV:** 439; **Retro. Supp. I:** 55; **Supp. I Part 2:** 423

Babcock, Elisha, **Supp. II Part 1:** 69

Babel, Isaac, **IV:** 1; **Supp. IX:** 260; **Supp. XII:** 308–309

Babel, Isaak, **Supp. XIV:**83, 84

Babel to Byzantium (Dickey), **Supp. IV Part 1:** 177, 185

Babeuf, François, **Supp. I Part 2:** 518

"Babies, The" (Strand), **Supp. IV Part 2:** 625

Baby, Come on Inside (Wagoner), **Supp. IX:** 335

"Baby, The" (Barthelme), **Supp. IV Part 1:** 49

Baby Doll (T. Williams), **IV:** 383, 386, 387, 389, 395

"Baby Face" (Sandburg), **III:** 584

"Babylon Revisited" (Fitzgerald), **II:** 95; **Retro. Supp. I:** 109

"Baby or the Botticelli, The" (Gass), **Supp. VI:** 92

"Baby Pictures of Famous Dictators" (Simic), **Supp. VIII:** 276

"Baby's Breath" (Bambara), **Supp. XI:** 15, 16

"Babysitter, The" (Coover), **Supp. V:** 43–44

"Baby Villon" (Levine), **Supp. V:** 182

Bacall, Lauren, **Supp. IV Part 1:** 130

"Baccalaureate" (MacLeish), **III:** 4

Bacchae, The (Euripides), **Supp. VIII:** 182

Bach, Johann Sebastian, **Supp. I Part 1:** 363; **Supp. III Part 2:** 611, 612, 619

Bachardy, Don, **Supp. XIV:**166, 170, 172, 173

Bache, Richard, **Supp. I Part 2:** 504

Bachelard, Gaston, **Supp. XIII:** 225; **Supp. XVI:**292

Bachelor Girls (Wasserstein), **Supp. XV:** 327–328, 332

Bachman, John, **Supp. XVI:**10, 11

Bachmann, Ingeborg, **Supp. IV Part 1:** 310; **Supp. VIII:** 272

Bachofen, J. J., **Supp. I Part 2:** 560, 567

Back Bog Beast Bait (Shepard), **Supp. III Part 2:** 437, 438

Backbone (C. Bly), **Supp. XVI:**34–36, 37, 40, 41

Back Country, The (Snyder), **Supp. VIII:** 296–299

"Back fom the Argentine" (Leopold), **Supp. XIV:**186

"Background with Revolutionaries" (MacLeish), **III:** 14–15

Back in The World (Wolff), **Supp. VII:** 345

Back in the World (Wolff), **Supp. VII:** 344

"Backlash Blues, The" (Hughes), **Supp. I Part 1:** 343

"Backlash of Kindness, A" (Nye), **Supp. XIII:** 285, 286

Back to China (Fiedler), **Supp. XIII:** 102–103

Back to Methuselah (Shaw), **IV:** 64

"Backwacking: A Plea to the Senator" (Ellison), **Retro. Supp. II:** 126; **Supp. II Part 1:** 248

Backward Glance, A (Wharton), **Retro. Supp. I:** 360, 363, 366, 378, 380, 382

"Backward Glance o'er Travel'd Roads, A" (Whitman), **IV:** 348

Bacon, Francis, **II:** 1, 8, 11, 15–16, 111; **III:** 284; **Retro. Supp. I:** 247; **Supp. I Part 1:** 310; **Supp. I Part 2:** 388; **Supp. IX:** 104; **Supp. XIV:** 22, 210

Bacon, Helen, **Supp. X:** 57

Bacon, Leonard, **II:** 530

Bacon, Roger, **IV:** 69

"Bacterial War, The" (Nemerov), **III:** 272

Bad Boy Brawly Brown (Mosley), **Supp. XIII:** 237, 239, 240–241

Bad Boys (Cisneros), **Supp. VII:** 58

"Bad Dream" (Taylor), **Supp. V:** 320

Badè, William Frederic, **Supp. IX:** 178

"Bad Fisherman, The" (Wagoner), **Supp. IX:** 328

Bad for Each Other (film), **Supp. XIII:** 174

"Badger" (Clare), **II:** 387

Badger, A. G., **Supp. I Part 1:** 356

Bad Government and Silly Literature (C. Bly), **Supp. XVI:** 37, 38, 40

Badlands (film; Malick), **Supp. XV:** 351

"Bad Lay" (McCarriston), **Supp. XIV:** 267

Badley, Linda, **Supp. V:** 148

Bad Man, A (Elkin), **Supp. VI:** 47

Bad Man Ballad (Sanders), **Supp. XVI:** 268

Bad Man Blues: A Portable George Garrett (Garrett), **Supp. VII:** 111

"Bad Music, The" (Jarrell), **II:** 369

"Bad Woman, A" (Fante), **Supp. XI:** 165

Baeck, Leo, **Supp. V:** 260

Baecker, Diann L., **Supp. VIII:** 128

Baer, William, **Supp. XIII:** 112, 118, 129

Baez, Joan, **Supp. IV Part 1:** 200; **Supp. VIII:** 200, 202

Bag of Bones (King), **Supp. V:** 139, 148, 151

"Bagpipe Music" (MacNeice), **Supp. X:** 117

"Bahá'í Faith: Only Church in World That Does Not Discriminate" (Locke), **Supp. XIV:** 200

"Bahá'u'lláh in the Garden of Ridwan" (Hayden), **Supp. II Part 1:** 370, 378

Bahr, David, **Supp. XV:** 66

"Bailbondsman, The" (Elkin), **Supp. VI:** 49, 50, 58

Bailey, Gamaliel, **Supp. I Part 2:** 587, 590

Bailey, Peter, **Supp. XVI:** 69

Bailey, William, **Supp. IV Part 2:** 631, 634

Bailey's Café (Naylor), **Supp. VIII:** 226–228

Bailyn, Bernard, **Supp. I Part 2:** 484, 506

Bair, Deirdre, **Supp. X:** 181, 186, 187, 188, 192, 194, 195, 196, 197

Baird, Linnett, **Supp. XII:** 299

Baird, Peggy, **I:** 385, 401

Bakan, David, **I:** 59

Baker, Carlos, **II:** 259

Baker, David, **Supp. IX:** 298; **Supp. XI:** 121, 142, 153; **Supp. XII:** 175, 191–192

Baker, George Pierce, **III:** 387; **IV:** 453, 455

Baker, Gladys, **Supp. XIV:** 121

Baker, Houston A., Jr., **Retro. Supp. II:** 121; **Supp. IV Part 1:** 365; **Supp. X:** 324

Baker, Kevin, **Supp. XIV:** 96

Baker, Nicholson, **Supp. XIII:** 41–57

Baker, Robert, **Supp. XVI:** 288, 290

Bakerman, Jane S., **Supp. IV Part 2:** 468

Bakhtin, Mikhail, **Retro. Supp. II:** 273; **Supp. IV Part 1:** 301; **Supp. X:** 120, 239

Bakst, Léon, **Supp. IX:** 66

Bakunin, Mikhail Aleksandrovich, **IV:** 429

Balakian, Jan, **Supp. XV:** 327

Balbuena, Bernado de, **Supp. V:** 11

Balch, Emily Greene, **Supp. I Part 1:** 25

Balcony, The (Genet), **I:** 84

Bald Soprano, The (Ionesco), **I:** 74

Baldwin, David, **Supp. I Part 1:** 47, 48, 49, 50, 51, 54, 65, 66

Baldwin, James, **Retro. Supp. II:** 1–17; **Supp. I Part 1:** 47–71, 337, 341; **Supp. II Part 1:** 40; **Supp. III Part 1:** 125; **Supp. IV Part 1:** 1, 10, 11, 163, 369; **Supp. V:** 201; **Supp. VIII:** 88, 198, 235, 349; **Supp. X:** 136, 324; **Supp. XI:** 288, 294; **Supp. XIII:** 46, 111, 181, 186, 294; **Supp. XIV:** 54, 71, 73, 306; **Supp. XVI:** 135, 141, 143

Baldwin, Samuel, **Supp. I Part 1:** 48

Balitas, Vincent D., **Supp. XVI:** 222

Balkian, Nona, **Supp. XI:** 230

Ball, Gordon, **Supp. XIV:** 148

Ball, John, **Supp. XV:** 202

"Ballad: Between the Box Cars" (Warren), **IV:** 245

"Ballade" (MacLeish), **III:** 4

"Ballade at Thirty-Five" (Parker), **Supp. IX:** 192

"Ballade for the Duke of Orléans" (Wilbur), **Supp. III Part 2:** 556

"Ballade of Broken Flutes, The" (Robinson), **III:** 505

"Ballade of Meaty Inversions" (White), **Supp. I Part 2:** 676

"Ballad of Billie Potts, The" (Warren), **IV:** 241–242, 243, 253

"Ballad of Carmilhan, The" (Longfellow), **II:** 505

"ballad of chocolate Mabbie, the" (Brooks), **Supp. IV Part 1:** 15

"Ballad of Dead Ladies, The" (Villon), **Retro. Supp. I:** 286

"Ballad of East and West" (Kipling), **Supp. IX:** 246

"Ballad of Jesse Neighbours, The" (Humphrey), **Supp. IX:** 100

"Ballad of Jesus of Nazareth, A" (Masters), **Supp. I Part 2:** 459

"Ballad of John Cable and Three Gentlemen" (Merwin), **Supp. III Part 1:** 342

"Ballad of Nat Turner, The" (Hayden), **Supp. II Part 1:** 378

"Ballad of Pearl May Lee, The" (Brooks), **Supp. III Part 1:** 74, 75

Ballad of Remembrance, A (Hayden), **Supp. II Part 1:** 367

"Ballad of Remembrance, A" (Hayden), **Supp. II Part 1:** 368, 372, 373

"Ballad of Ruby, The" (Sarton), **Supp. VIII:** 259–260

"Ballad of Sue Ellen Westerfield, The" (Hayden), **Supp. II Part 1:** 364

Ballad of the Brown Girl, The (Cullen), **Supp. IV Part 1:** 167, 168, 169–170, 173

"Ballad of the Brown Girl, The" (Cullen), **Supp. IV Part 1:** 168

"Ballad of the Children of the Czar, The" (Schwartz), **Supp. II Part 2:** 649

"Ballad of the Girl Whose Name Is Mud" (Hughes), **Retro. Supp. I:** 205

"Ballad of the Goodly Fere," **III:** 458
"Ballad of the Harp-Weaver" (Millay), **III:** 135
"Ballad of the Sad Cafe, The" (McCullers), **II:** 586, 587, 588, 592, 595, 596–600, 604, 605, 606
"Ballad of the Sixties" (Sarton), **Supp. VIII:** 259
"Ballad of Trees and the Master, A" (Lanier), **Supp. I Part 1:** 370
"Ballad of William Sycamore, The" (Benét), **Supp. XI:** 44, 47
Ballads and Other Poems (Longfellow), **II:** 489; **III:** 412, 422; **Retro. Supp. II:** 157, 168
Ballads for Sale (Lowell), **II:** 527
"Ballads of Lenin" (Hughes), **Supp. I Part 1:** 331
Ballantyne, Sheila, **Supp. V:** 70
Ballard, J. G., **Supp. XVI:**123, 124
Ballard, Josephine. *See* McMurtry, Josephine
"Ballena" (Mora), **Supp. XIII:** 224
"Ballet in Numbers for Mary Ellen, A" (Karr), **Supp. XI:** 241
"Ballet of a Buffoon, The" (Sexton), **Supp. II Part 2:** 693
"Ballet of the Fifth Year, The" (Schwartz), **Supp. II Part 2:** 650
"Ball Game, The" (Creeley), **Supp. IV Part 1:** 140
"Balloon Hoax, The" (Poe), **III:** 413, 420
"Balm of Recognition, The: Rectifying Wrongs through Generations" (E. Hoffman, lecture), **Supp. XVI:**155
Balo (Toomer), **Supp. III Part 2:** 484
Balsan, Consuelo, **IV:** 313–314
Balthus, **Supp. IV Part 2:** 623
Balthus Poems, The (Dobyns), **Supp. XIII:** 87
Baltimore, Lord, **I:** 132
Balzac, Honoré de, **I:** 103, 123, 339, 376, 474, 485, 499, 509, 518; **II:** 307, 322, 324, 328, 336, 337; **III:** 61, 174, 184, 320, 382; **IV:** 192; **Retro. Supp. I:** 91, 217, 218, 235; **Retro. Supp. II:** 93; **Supp. I Part 2:** 647; **Supp. XVI:**72
Bambara, Toni Cade, **Supp. XI:** 1–23
Banana Bottom (McKay), **Supp. X:** 132, 139–140
Bananas (film; Allen), **Supp. XV:** 3, 4
Bancal, Jean, **Supp. I Part 2:** 514
Bancroft, George, **I:** 544; **Supp. I Part 2:** 479
Band of Angels (Warren), **IV:** 245, 254–255
Bang the Drum Slowly (Harris), **II:** 424–425

Banjo: A Story without a Plot (McKay), **Supp. X:** 132, 138–139
"Banjo Song, A" (Dunbar), **Supp. II Part 1:** 197
Bankhead, Tallulah, **IV:** 357; **Supp. IV Part 2:** 574
"Banking Potatoes" (Komunyakaa), **Supp. XIII:** 126
"Bank of England Restriction, The" (Adams), **I:** 4
Banks, Joanne Trautmann, **Supp. XIII:** 297
Banks, Russell, **Supp. V:** 1–19, 227; **Supp. IX:** 153; **Supp. X:** 85; **Supp. XI:** 178; **Supp. XII:** 295, 309, 343
"Banned Poem" (Nye), **Supp. XIII:** 282
Bannon, Barbara, **Supp. XI:** 228
"Banyan" (Swenson), **Supp. IV Part 2:** 651, 652
"Baptism" (Olsen). *See* "O Yes" (Olsen)
Baptism, The (Baraka), **Supp. II Part 1:** 40, 41–42, 43
Baptism of Desire (Erdrich), **Supp. IV Part 1:** 259
"B.A.R. Man, The" (Yates), **Supp. XI:** 341
Barabtarlo, Gennady, **Retro. Supp. I:** 278
Baraka, Imamu Amiri (LeRoi Jones), **Retro. Supp. I:** 411; **Retro. Supp. II:** 280; **Supp. I Part 1:** 63; **Supp. II Part 1:** 29–63, 247, 250; **Supp. III Part 1:** 83; **Supp. IV Part 1:** 169, 244, 369; **Supp. VIII:** 295, 329, 330, 332; **Supp. X:** 324, 328; **Supp. XIII:** 94; **Supp. XIV:**125, 144
"Bar at the Andover Inn, The" (Matthews), **Supp. IX:** 168
"Barbados" (Marshall), **Supp. XI:** 281
"Barbara Frietchie" (Whittier), **Supp. I Part 2:** 695–696
Barbarella (film), **Supp. XI:** 293, 307–308
"Barbarian Status of Women, The" (Veblen), **Supp. I Part 2:** 636–637
Barbarous Coast, The (Macdonald), **Supp. IV Part 2:** 472, 474
Barbary Shore (Mailer), **III:** 27, 28, 30–31, 33, 35, 36, 40, 44; **Retro. Supp. II:** 199–200, 207; **Supp. XIV:**162
Barber, David, **Supp. IV Part 2:** 550; **Supp. XII:** 188–189
Barber, Rowland, **Supp. IV Part 2:** 581
Barber, Samuel, **Supp. IV Part 1:** 84

"Barclay of Ury" (Whittier), **Supp. I Part 2:** 693
Bard of Savagery, The: Thorstein Veblen and Modern Social Theory (Diggins), **Supp. I Part 2:** 650
"Barefoot Boy, The" (Whittier), **Supp. I Part 2:** 691, 699–700
Barefoot in the Park (Simon), **Supp. IV Part 2:** 575, 578–579, 586, 590
Bare Hills, The (Winters), **Supp. II Part 2:** 786, 788
"Bare Hills, The" (Winters), **Supp. II Part 2:** 790
Barely and Widely (Zukofsky), **Supp. III Part 2:** 627, 628, 635
Barenblat, Rachel, **Supp. XIII:** 274
Barfield, Owen, **III:** 274, 279
"Bargain Lost, The" (Poe), **III:** 411
Barillas, William, **Supp. XIV:**177
Barillet, Pierre, **Supp. XVI:**194
Barker, Arthur, **Supp. XIII:** 167
Barker, Clive, **Supp. V:** 142
"Barking Man" (Bell), **Supp. X:** 9
Barking Man and Other Stories (Bell), **Supp. X:** 9
Barksdale, Richard, **Retro. Supp. I:** 202, 205; **Supp. I Part 1:** 341, 346
Barlow, Joel, **Supp. I Part 1:** 124; **Supp. I Part 2:** 511, 515, 521; **Supp. II Part 1:** 65–86, 268
Barlow, Ruth Baldwin (Mrs. Joel Barlow), **Supp. II Part 1:** 69
Barnaby Rudge (Dickens), **III:** 421
Barnard, Frederick, **Supp. I Part 2:** 684
Barnard, Rita, **Retro. Supp. II:** 324
Barn Blind (Smiley), **Supp. VI:** 292–293
"Barn Burning" (Faulkner), **II:** 72, 73; **Supp. IV Part 2:** 682
Barnes, Djuna, **Supp. III Part 1:** 31–46; **Supp. IV Part 1:** 79, 80; **Supp. XVI:**282
Barnett, Claudia, **Supp. XV:** 323, 330, 334
Barnett, Samuel, **Supp. I Part 1:** 2
Barnstone, Tony, **Supp. XIII:** 115, 126
Barnstone, Willis, **Supp. I Part 2:** 458
Barnum, P. T., **Supp. I Part 2:** 703
Baroja, Pío, **I:** 478
"Baroque Comment" (Bogan), **Supp. III Part 1:** 56, 58
"Baroque Sunburst, A" (Clampitt), **Supp. IX:** 49
"Baroque Wall-Fountain in the Villa Sciarra, A" (Wilbur), **Supp. III Part 2:** 553
Barr, Robert, **I:** 409, 424
Barracks Thief, The (Wolff), **Supp. VII:** 344–345

Barren Ground (Glasgow), **II:** 174, 175, 178, 179, 184–185, 186, 187, 188, 189, 191, 192, 193, 194; **Supp. X:** 228

Barrés, Auguste M., **I:** 228

Barresi, Dorothy, **Supp. XV:** 100, 102

Barrett, E. B., **Supp. XV:** 309

Barrett, Elizabeth, **Supp. IV Part 2:** 430

Barrett, George, **Supp. IX:** 250

Barrett, Ralph, **Supp. I Part 2:** 462

Barrier of a Common Language: An American Looks at Contemporary British Poetry (Gioia), **Supp. XV:** 112, 116–117

"Barroco: An Essay" (Sobin), **Supp. XVI:**291

Barron, Jonathan, **Supp. IX:** 299

Barrow, John, **II:** 18

Barrus, Clara, **I:** 220

Barry, Iris, **Supp. XIII:** 170

Barry, Philip, **Retro. Supp. I:** 104; **Supp. IV Part 1:** 83; **Supp. V:** 95

Barstow, Elizabeth Drew. See Stoddard, Elizabeth

Bartas, Seigneur du, **IV:** 157

Barth, John, **I:** 121–143; **Supp. I Part 1:** 100; **Supp. III Part 1:** 217; **Supp. IV Part 1:** 48, 379; **Supp. V:** 39, 40; **Supp. IX:** 208; **Supp. X:** 263, 301, 302, 307; **Supp. XI:** 309; **Supp. XII:** 29, 289, 316; **Supp. XIII:** 41, 101, 104

Barth, Karl, **III:** 40, 258, 291, 303, 309; **IV:** 225; **Retro. Supp. I:** 325, 326, 327

Barth, Robert C., **Supp. XV:** 169

Barthé, Richmond, **Retro. Supp. II:** 115

Barthelme, Donald, **Supp. IV Part 1:** 39–58, 227; **Supp. V:** 2, 39, 44; **Supp. VIII:** 75, 138; **Supp. X:** 263; **Supp. XI:** 25; **Supp. XII:** 29; **Supp. XIII:** 41, 46; **Supp. XVI:**206

Barthelme, Frederick, **Supp. XI:** 25–41

Barthelme, Peter, **Supp. XI:** 25

Barthelme, Steven, **Supp. XI:** 25, 27, 37

Barthes, Roland, **Supp. IV Part 1:** 39, 119, 126; **Supp. XIII:** 83; **Supp. XVI:**285, 294

Bartholomew and the Oobleck (Geisel), **Supp. XVI:**104

"Bartleby, the Scrivener; A Story of Wall-Street" (Melville), **III:** 88–89; **Retro. Supp. I:** 255

Bartleby in Manhattan and Other Essays (Hardwick), **Supp. III Part 1:** 204, 210

Bartlet, Phebe, **I:** 562

Bartlett, Lee, **Supp. VIII:** 291

Bartlett, Mary Dougherty, **Supp. IV Part 1:** 335

Barton, Bruce, **III:** 14; **Retro. Supp. I:** 179

Barton, Priscilla. *See* Morison, Mrs. Samuel Eliot (Priscilla Barton)

Barton, Ralph, **Supp. XVI:**195

Barton, Rev. William E., **Retro. Supp. I:** 179

Bartov, Omer, **Supp. XVI:**153–154

Bartram, John, **Supp. I Part 1:** 244

Bartram, William, **II:** 313; **Supp. IX:** 171; **Supp. X:** 223

Barzun, Jacques, **Supp. XIV:**54

"Basement" (Bambara), **Supp. XI:** 5

"Base of All Metaphysics, The" (Whitman), **IV:** 348

"Base Stealer, The" (Francis), **Supp. IX:** 82

Bashevis, Isaac. *See* Singer, Isaac Bashevis

Basil Stories, The (Fitzgerald), **Retro. Supp. I:** 109

Basin and Range (McPhee), **Supp. III Part 1:** 309

"Basin of Eggs, A" (Swenson), **Supp. IV Part 2:** 645

"Basket, The" (Lowell), **II:** 522

"Basketball and Beefeaters" (McPhee), **Supp. III Part 1:** 296

"Basketball and Poetry: The Two Richies" (Dunn), **Supp. XI:** 140

"Basketball Player" (L. Michaels), **Supp. XVI:**209

Baskin, Leonard, **Supp. X:** 58, 71; **Supp. XV:** 348

Bass, Rick, **Supp. XIV:**227; **Supp. XVI:**15–29

Basso, Hamilton, **Retro. Supp. I:** 80

Bastard, The (Caldwell), **I:** 291, 292, 308

"Bat, The" (Kenyon), **Supp. VII:** 168

Bataille, Georges, **Supp. VIII:** 4; **Supp. XII:** 1

"Batard" (London), **II:** 468–469

Bate, W. J., **II:** 531

Bates, Arlo, **Retro. Supp. I:** 35

Bates, Blanche, **Supp. XVI:**182

Bates, Kathy, **Supp. XIII:** 207

Bates, Lee, **Retro. Supp. II:** 46

Bates, Milton J., **Supp. XII:** 62

Bates, Sylvia Chatfield, **II:** 586

Bateson, Gregory, **Supp. XV:** 146

"Bath, The" (Carver), **Supp. III Part 1:** 144, 145

"Bath, The" (Snyder), **Supp. VIII:** 302

Bathwater Wine (Coleman), **Supp. XI:** 83, 90, 91

"Batter my heart, three person'd God"

(Donne), **Supp. I Part 2:** 726

"Battle, The" (Simpson), **Supp. IX:** 268–269

Battlefield Where the Moon Says I Love You, The (Stanford), **Supp. XV:** 345

Battle-Ground, The (Glasgow), **II:** 175, 176, 177, 178, 193

"Battle Hymn of the Republic" (Sandburg), **III:** 585

"Battle Hymn of the Republic, The" (Howe), **III:** 505

"Battle Hymn of the Republic, The" (Updike), **Retro. Supp. I:** 324

Battle of Angels (T. Williams), **IV:** 380, 381, 383, 385, 386, 387

"Battle of Lovell's Pond, The" (Longfellow), **II:** 493

Battle of the Atlantic, The (Morison), **Supp. I Part 2:** 490

"Battle of the Baltic, The" (Campbell), **Supp. I Part 1:** 309

"Battle of the Bunker, The" (Snodgrass), **Supp. VI:** 319–320

"***Battle of the Century!!!, The***" (Goldbarth), **Supp. XII:** 193

Battle-Pieces and Aspects of the War (Melville), **II:** 538–539; **III:** 92; **IV:** 350; **Retro. Supp. I:** 257

"Battler, The" (Hemingway), **II:** 248; **Retro. Supp. I:** 175

"Baudelaire" (Schwartz), **Supp. II Part 2:** 663

Baudelaire, Charles, **I:** 58, 63, 384, 389, 420, 569; **II:** 543, 544–545, 552; **III:** 137, 141–142, 143, 409, 417, 418, 421, 428, 448, 466, 474; **IV:** 74, 79, 80, 87, 211, 286; **Retro. Supp. I:** 56, 90; **Retro. Supp. II:** 261, 262, 322, 326; **Supp. I Part 1:** 271; **Supp. III Part 1:** 4, 6, 105; **Supp. XIII:** 77, 284

Baudelaire, Charles-Pierre, **Supp. XV:** 165

Baudrillard, Jean, **Supp. IV Part 1:** 45

Bauer, Dale, **Retro. Supp. I:** 381

Bauer, Douglas, **Supp. XII:** 290

Baum, L. Frank, **Supp. I Part 2:** 621; **Supp. IV Part 1:** 101, 113; **Supp. XII:** 42

Baumann, Walter, **III:** 478

Bausch, Richard, **Supp. VII:** 39–56

Bawer, Bruce, **Supp. VIII:** 153; **Supp. IX:** 135; **Supp. X:** 187

Baxter, Charles, **Supp. XII:** 22; **Supp. XIV:**89, 92

Baxter, John, **Supp. XI:** 302

Baxter, Richard, **III:** 199; **IV:** 151, 153; **Supp. I Part 2:** 683

"Baxter's Procrustes" (Chesnutt), **Supp. XIV:**76

"Bay City Blues" (Chandler), **Supp. IV Part 1:** 129

Baylies, William, **Supp. I Part 1:** 153

Baym, Nina, **Supp. IV Part 2:** 463; **Supp. X:** 229; **Supp. XVI:**92

Bayou Folk (Chopin), **Retro. Supp. II:** 64–65, 73; **Supp. I Part 1:** 200, 216, 218

Baziotes, William, **Supp. XV:** 144

Beach, Joseph Warren, **I:** 309, 500; **II:** 27; **III:** 319

Beach, Sylvia, **IV:** 404; **Retro. Supp. I:** 109, 422

"Beach Women, The" (Pinsky), **Supp. VI:** 241

"Beaded Pear, The" (Simpson), **Supp. IX:** 276

Beagle, Peter, **Supp. X:** 24

Beam, Jeffrey, **Supp. XII:** 98

Beaman, E. O., **Supp. IV Part 2:** 604

Bean, Michael, **Supp. V:** 203

Bean, Robert Bennett, **Supp. II Part 1:** 170

Bean Eaters, The (Brooks), **Supp. III Part 1:** 79–81

Be Angry at the Sun (Jeffers), **Supp. II Part 2:** 434

"Beanstalk Country, The" (T. Williams), **IV:** 383

Bean Trees, The (Kingsolver), **Supp. VII:** 197, 199–201, 202, 207, 209

"Bear" (Hogan), **Supp. IV Part 1:** 412

Bear, The (Faulkner), **Supp. VIII:** 184

"Bear, The" (Faulkner), **II:** 71–72, 73, 228; **IV:** 203; **Supp. IV Part 2:** 434; **Supp. IX:** 95; **Supp. X:** 30; **Supp. XIV:**32

"Bear, The" (Kinnell), **Supp. III Part 1:** 244

"Bear, The" (Momaday), **Supp. IV Part 2:** 480, 487

Bear and His Daughter: Stories (Stone), **Supp. V:** 295, 308

Beard, Charles, **I:** 214; **IV:** 429; **Supp. I Part 2:** 481, 490, 492, 632, 640, 643, 647

Beard, James, **I:** 341

Beard, Mary, **Supp. I Part 2:** 481

"Bearded Oaks" (Warren), **IV:** 240

Bearden, Romare, **Retro. Supp. I:** 209; **Supp. VIII:** 337, 342

"Beard of Bees, A" (X. J. Kennedy), **Supp. XV:** 171

Beardon, Romare, **Supp. XV:** 144

Beardsley, Aubrey, **II:** 56; **IV:** 77

Beaser, Robert, **Supp. XV:** 259

"Beast" (Swenson), **Supp. IV Part 2:** 639

"Beast & Burden, The: Seven Improvisations" (Komunyakaa), **Supp.**

XIII: 120, 121

Beast God Forgot to Invent, The (Harrison), **Supp. VIII:** 37, 46, 51–52

Beast in Me, The (Thurber), **Supp. I Part 2:** 615

"Beast in the Jungle, The" (James), **I:** 570; **II:** 335; **Retro. Supp. I:** 235; **Supp. V:** 103–104

Beast in View (Rukeyser), **Supp. VI:** 272, 273, 279, 280

Beasts of Bethlehem, The (X. J. Kennedy), **Supp. XV:** 163

"Beat! Beat! Drums!" (Whitman), **III:** 585

Beat Down to Your Soul: What Was the Beat Generation? (Charters, ed.), **Supp. XIV:**152

Beaton, Cecil, **Supp. XVI:**191

"Beatrice Palmato" (Wharton), **Retro. Supp. I:** 379

Beats, The (Krim, ed.), **Supp. XV:** 338

Beattie, Ann, **Supp. V:** 21–37; **Supp. XI:** 26; **Supp. XII:** 80, 139, 294

Beatty, General Sam, **I:** 193

Beaty, Jerome, **Supp. IV Part 1:** 331

"Beau Monde of Mrs. Bridge, The" (Connell), **Supp. XIV:**88, 89

Beaumont, Francis, **Supp. I Part 2:** 422

"Beauties of Santa Cruz, The" (Freneau), **Supp. II Part 1:** 260

Beautiful and Damned, The (Fitzgerald), **II:** 88, 89–91, 93, 263; **Retro. Supp. I:** 103–105, 105, 106, 110; **Supp. IX:** 56, 57

Beautiful Changes, The (Wilbur), **Supp. III Part 2:** 544–550

"Beautiful Changes, The" (Wilbur), **Supp. III Part 2:** 549, 550

"Beautiful Child, A" (Capote), **Supp. III Part 1:** 113, 125

"Beautiful & Cruel" (Cisneros), **Supp. VII:** 63, 67

"Beautiful Woman Who Sings, The" (Gunn Allen), **Supp. IV Part 1:** 326

"Beauty" (Emerson), **II:** 2, 5

"Beauty" (Sanders), **Supp. XVI:**277

"Beauty" (Wylie), **Supp. I Part 2:** 710

"Beauty and the Beast" (Dove), **Supp. IV Part 1:** 245

"Beauty and the Beast" (fairy tale), **IV:** 266; **Supp. X:** 88

"Beauty and the Shoe Sluts" (Karr), **Supp. XI:** 250

Beauty of the Husband, The: A Fictional Essay in Twenty-Nine Tangos (Carson), **Supp. XII:** 113–114

Beauty's Punishment (Rice), **Supp. VII:** 301

Beauty's Release: The Continued Erotic Adventures of Sleeping Beauty (Rice), **Supp. VII:** 301

Beauvoir, Simone de, **IV:** 477; **Supp. I Part 1:** 51; **Supp. III Part 1:** 200–201, 208; **Supp. IV Part 1:** 360; **Supp. IX:** 4

"Be Careful" (Zach; Everwine, trans.), **Supp. XV:** 86

Be Careful How You Live (Lacy), **Supp. XV:** 203–204

"Because I could not stop for Death—" (Dickinson), **Retro. Supp. I:** 38–40, 41, 43, 44

"Because It Happened" (Goldbarth), **Supp. XII:** 192

"Because of Libraries We Can Say These Things" (Nye), **Supp. XIII:** 283

"Because You Mentioned the Spiritual Life" (Dunn), **Supp. XI:** 154

Bech: A Book (Updike), **IV:** 214; **Retro. Supp. I:** 329, 335

Beck, Dave, **I:** 493

Beck, Jack, **Supp. IV Part 2:** 560

Becker, Carl, **Supp. I Part 2:** 492, 493

Becker, Paula. *See* Modersohn, Mrs. Otto (Paula Becker)

Beckett, Samuel, **I:** 71, 91, 142, 298, 461; **III:** 387; **IV:** 95; **Retro. Supp. I:** 206; **Supp. IV Part 1:** 297, 368–369; **Supp. IV Part 2:** 424; **Supp. V:** 23, 53; **Supp. XI:** 104; **Supp. XII:** 21, 150–151; **Supp. XIII:** 74; **Supp. XIV:**239

Beckett, Tom, **Supp. IV Part 2:** 419

Beckford, William, **I:** 204

Beckonings (Brooks), **Supp. III Part 1:** 85

"Becky" (Toomer), **Supp. III Part 2:** 481, 483; **Supp. IX:** 312

Becoming a Man: Half a Life Story (Monette), **Supp. X:** 146, 147, 149, 151, 152, 155–157

"Becoming a Meadow" (Doty), **Supp. XI:** 124–125

"Becoming and Breaking: Poet and Poem" (Ríos), **Supp. IV Part 2:** 539

Becoming Canonical in American Poetry (Morris), **Retro. Supp. I:** 40

Becoming Light: New and Selected Poems (Jong), **Supp. V:** 115

Bécquer, Gustavo Adolfo, **Supp. XIII:** 312

"Bed, The" (Dixon), **Supp. XII:** 154

Beddoes, Thomas Lovell, **III:** 469; **Retro. Supp. I:** 285

Bedichek, Roy, **Supp. V:** 225

Bedient, Calvin, **Supp. IX:** 298; **Supp. XII:** 98

"Bed in the Sky, The" (Snyder), **Supp. VIII:** 300

Bednarik, Joseph, **Supp. VIII:** 39

"Bedrock" (Proulx), **Supp. VII:** 253

"Bee, The" (Lanier), **Supp. I Part 1:** 364

Beecher, Catharine, **Supp. I Part 2:** 581, 582–583, 584, 586, 588, 589, 591, 599; **Supp. X:** 103; **Supp. XI:** 193

Beecher, Charles, **Supp. I Part 2:** 588, 589

Beecher, Edward, **Supp. I Part 2:** 581, 582, 583, 584, 588, 591

Beecher, Harriet. *See* Stowe, Harriet Beecher

Beecher, Henry Ward, **II:** 275; **Supp. I Part 2:** 581; **Supp. XI:** 193

Beecher, Lyman, **Supp. I Part 2:** 580–581, 582, 583, 587, 588, 599; **Supp. XI:** 193

Beecher, Mrs. Lyman (Roxanna Foote), **Supp. I Part 2:** 580–581, 582, 588, 599

Beeching, Jack, **Supp. X:** 114, 117, 118, 123, 125, 126

"Beehive" (Toomer), **Supp. IX:** 317

"Bee Hunt, The" (Irving), **II:** 313

"Beekeeper's Daughter, The" (Plath), **Retro. Supp. II:** 246–247

"Bee Meeting, The" (Plath), **Retro. Supp. II:** 254–255

Bee Poems (Plath), **Retro. Supp. II:** 254–255

Beer, Thomas, **I:** 405

Beerbohm, Max, **III:** 472; **IV:** 436; **Supp. I Part 2:** 714

"Beer in the Sergeant Major's Hat, or The Sun Also Sneezes" (Chandler), **Supp. IV Part 1:** 121

Beethoven, Ludwig van, **II:** 536; **III:** 118; **IV:** 274, 358; **Supp. I Part 1:** 363; **Supp. VIII:** 103

Beet Queen, The (Erdrich), **Supp. IV Part 1:** 259, 260, 264–265, 266, 273, 274, 275

Befo' de War: Echoes in Negro Dialect (Gordon), **Supp. II Part 1:** 201

"Before" (Goldbarth), **Supp. XII:** 175

"Before" (Snyder), **Supp. VIII:** 301

Before Adam (London), **II:** 466

Before Disaster (Winters), **Supp. II Part 2:** 786, 800

"Before Disaster" (Winters), **Supp. II Part 2:** 801, 815

"Before I Knocked" (D. Thomas), **III:** 534

"Before March" (MacLeish), **III:** 15

Before My Life Began (Neugeboren), **Supp. XVI:** 224–225

"Before the Altar" (Lowell), **II:** 516

"Before the Birth of one of her children" (Bradstreet), **Supp. I Part 1:** 118

"Before the Sky Darkens" (Dunn), **Supp. XI:** 155

"Begat" (Sexton), **Supp. II Part 2:** 693

Beggar on Horseback (Kaufman and Connelly), **III:** 394

"Beggar Said So, The" (Singer), **IV:** 12

Beggars in the House of Plenty (Shanley), **Supp. XIV:** 316, 327–328

Beggar's Opera, The (Gay), **Supp. I Part 2:** 523

Begiebing, Robert, **Retro. Supp. II:** 210

Begin Again (Paley), **Supp. VI:** 221

"Beginning and the End, The" (Jeffers), **Supp. II Part 2:** 420–421, 424

"Beginning of Decadence, The" (Jeffers), **Supp. II Part 2:** 420

"Beginning of Enthusiasm, The" (Salinas), **Supp. XIII:** 327–328

Beginning of Wisdom, The (Benét), **I:** 358; **Supp. XI:** 44

Be Glad You're Neurotic (Bisch), **Supp. I Part 2:** 608

"Begotten of the Spleen" (Simic), **Supp. VIII:** 277

"Behaving Like a Jew" (Stern), **Supp. IX:** 290–291, 294

"Behavior" (Emerson), **II:** 2, 4

Behavior of Titans, The (Merton), **Supp. VIII:** 201

Behind a Mask (Alcott), **Supp. I Part 1:** 36–37, 43–44

"Behind a Wall" (Lowell), **II:** 516

Behind the Movie Camera (radio show), **Supp. XV:** 147

"Behold the Key" (Malamud), **Supp. I Part 2:** 437

Behrendt, Stephen, **Supp. X:** 204

Behrman, S. N., **Supp. V:** 95

Beidler, Peter G., **Supp. IV Part 2:** 557

Beidler, Philip D., **Supp. XII:** 69

Beige Dolorosa (Harrison), **Supp. VIII:** 40, 51

Beiles, Sinclair, **Supp. XII:** 129

Beiliss, Mendel, **Supp. I Part 2:** 427, 446, 447, 448

"Being a Lutheran Boy-God in Minnesota" (R. Bly), **Supp. IV Part 1:** 59, 67

Being and Race (Johnson), **Supp. VI:** 193, 199

Being and Time (Heidegger), **Supp. VIII:** 9

Being Busted (Fiedler), **Supp. XIII:** 95, 102, 104

Being John Malkovich (Kaufman), **Supp. XV:** 16

Being There (Kosinski), **Supp. VII:** 215, 216, 222–223

Beiswanger, George, **Retro. Supp. II:** 220

Belasco, David, **Supp. XVI:** 182

Bel Canto (Patchett), **Supp. XII:** 307, 310, 320–322

"Beleaguered City, The" (Longfellow), **II:** 498

Belfry of Bruges, The, and Other Poems (Longfellow), **II:** 489; **Retro. Supp. II:** 157, 168

"Belief" (Levine), **Supp. V:** 186, 190

"Beliefs of Writers, The" (Doctorow), **Supp. IV Part 1:** 235–236

"Believers, The/Los Creyentes" (Kingsolver), **Supp. VII:** 208

Belinda (Rice), **Supp. VII:** 301–302

"Belinda's Petition" (Dove), **Supp. IV Part 1:** 245

"Belita" (Ríos), **Supp. IV Part 2:** 541

Belitt, Ben, **Supp. XII:** 260

Bell, Clive, **IV:** 87

Bell, Daniel, **Supp. I Part 2:** 648

Bell, George Kennedy Allen, **Retro. Supp. I:** 65

Bell, Madison Smartt, **Supp. X:** 1–20

Bell, Marvin, **Supp. V:** 337, 339; **Supp. IX:** 152; **Supp. XI:** 316

Bell, Michael, **Retro. Supp. II:** 139

Bell, Pearl, **Supp. XI:** 233

Bell, Quentin, **Supp. I Part 2:** 636

Bell, Whitfield J., Jr., **II:** 123

Bellafante, Gina, **Supp. VIII:** 85

Bellamy, Edward, **II:** 276; **Supp. I Part 2:** 641; **Supp. XI:** 200, 203

Bellarosa Connection, The (Bellow), **Retro. Supp. II:** 31, 32

"Belle Dollinger" (Masters), **Supp. I Part 2:** 463

Belleforest, François de, **IV:** 370

"Belle Zoraïde, La" (Chopin), **Supp. I Part 1:** 215–216

Bell Jar, The (Plath), **Retro. Supp. II:** 242, 249–250; **Supp. I Part 2:** 526, 527, 529, 531–536, 539, 540, 541, 542, 544

Belloc, Hilary, **III:** 176; **IV:** 432

Bellow, Saul, **I:** 113, 138–139, 144–166, 375, 517; **II:** 579; **III:** 40; **IV:** 3, 19, 217, 340; **Retro. Supp. II:** 19–36, 118, 279, 307, 324; **Supp. I Part 2:** 428, 451; **Supp. II Part 1:** 109; **Supp. IV Part 1:** 30; **Supp. V:**

258; **Supp. VIII:** 98, 176, 234, 236–
237, 245; **Supp. IX:** 212, 227;
Supp. XI: 64, 233; **Supp. XII:** 159,
165, 170, 310; **Supp. XIII:** 106;
Supp. XV: 143; **Supp. XVI:**208
Bellows, George, **Supp. XV:** 295
"Bells, The" (Poe), **III:** 593; **Retro.
Supp. II:** 266; **Supp. I Part 2:** 388
"Bells, The" (Sexton), **Supp. II Part
2:** 673
"Bells for John Whiteside's Daughter"
(Ransom), **III:** 490
"Bells of Lynn, The" (Longfellow), **II:**
498
"Bells of San Blas, The" (Longfellow),
II: 490–491, 493, 498
"Bell Tower, The" (Melville), **III:** 91
"Belly, The" (Dobyns), **Supp. XIII:** 87
"Belonging Kind, The" (W. Gibson and
J. Shirley), **Supp. XVI:**123
Beloved (Morrison), **Supp. III Part 1:**
364, 372–379; **Supp. IV Part 1:**
13–14; **Supp. V:** 259; **Supp. VIII:**
343; **Supp. XIII:** 60
*Beloved Lady: A History of Jane Add-
ams' Ideas on Reform and Peace*
(Farrell), **Supp. I Part 1:** 24
Beloved Stranger, The (Bynner), **Supp.
XV:** 44, 50
Benchley, Robert, **I:** 48, 482; **II:** 435;
III: 53; **Supp. IX:** 190, 195, 204
Benda, W. T., **Retro. Supp. I:** 13
Bend Sinister (Nabokov), **III:** 253–
254; **Retro. Supp. I:** 265, 266, 270
"Beneath the Sidewalk" (Dunn), **Supp.
XI:** 145
"Beneath the Smooth Skin of America"
(Sanders), **Supp. XVI:**275
Benedict, Ruth, **Supp. IX:** 229
Benefactor, The (Sontag), **Supp. III
Part 2:** 451, 455, 468, 469
"Benefit Performance" (Malamud),
Supp. I Part 2: 431
Benét, Laura, **Supp. XI:** 44
Benét, Rosemary, **Supp. XI:** 44, 51
Benét, Stephen Vincent, **I:** 358; **II:**
177; **III:** 22; **IV:** 129; **Supp. XI:**
43–61
Benét, William Rose, **II:** 530; **Retro.
Supp. I:** 108; **Supp. I Part 2:** 709;
Supp. XI: 43, 44; **Supp. XIV:**119,
122, 129
Ben Franklin's Wit and Wisdom
(Franklin), **II:** 111
Ben-Hur (film), **Supp. IV Part 2:** 683
Benigna Machiavelli (Gilman), **Supp.
XI:** 201, 208
Benitez, R. Michael, **Retro. Supp. II:**
264
Benito Cereno (Lowell), **II:** 546;

Retro. Supp. II: 181
"Benito Cereno" (Melville), **III:** 91;
Retro. Supp. I: 255; **Retro. Supp.
II:** 188
Benito's Dream Bottle (Nye), **Supp.
XIII:** 278
"Bênitou's Slave, The" (Chopin),
Retro. Supp. II: 64
Benjamin, Walter, **Supp. IX:** 133;
Supp. XVI:290, 291
Benjamin Franklin (Van Doren), **Supp.
I Part 2:** 486
"Benjamin Pantier" (Masters), **Supp. I
Part 2:** 461
Bennett, Anne Virginia, **II:** 184
Bennett, Arnold, **I:** 103; **II:** 337; **Supp.
XVI:**190
Bennett, Elizabeth, **Supp. VIII:** 58
Bennett, Patrick, **Supp. V:** 225
Bennett, Paula, **Retro. Supp. I:** 29, 33,
42
Bennett, William, **Supp. VIII:** 245
Benson, Jackson J., **Supp. IV Part 2:**
613
Benstock, Shari, **Retro. Supp. I:** 361,
368, 371, 382
Bentham, Jeremy, **I:** 279; **Supp. I Part
2:** 635
Bentley, Eric R., **IV:** 396
Bentley, Nelson, **Supp. IX:** 324
Bentley, Richard, **III:** 79, 86
Benton, Robert, **Supp. IV Part 1:** 236
"Bent Tones" (Wright), **Supp. XV:** 346
Benveniste, Emile, **Supp. XVI:**292
Benzel, Jan, **Supp. XVI:**112
Beowulf, **Supp. II Part 1:** 6
Beran, Carol, **Supp. XIII:** 25
"Berck-Plage" (Plath), **Retro. Supp.
II:** 253–254
Bercovitch, Sacvan, **Retro. Supp. I:**
408; **Retro. Supp. II:** 325, 330;
Supp. I Part 1: 99; **Supp. I Part 2:**
659
Berdyaev, Nikolai, **I:** 494; **III:** 292
"Bereaved Apartments" (Kingsolver),
Supp. VII: 203
"Bereavement in their death to feel"
(Dickinson), **Retro. Supp. I:** 43, 44
"Berenice" (Poe), **III:** 415, 416, 425;
Retro. Supp. II: 270
Bérénice (Racine), **II:** 573
Berenson, Bernard, **Retro. Supp. I:**
381; **Supp. IV Part 1:** 314; **Supp.
XIV:**335, 336, 337
Berg, James, **Supp. XIV:**157, 159
Berg, Stephen, **Supp. IV Part 1:** 60
Berger, Charles, **Retro. Supp. I:** 311
Berger, John, **Supp. XVI:**284
Berger, Roger, **Supp. XIII:** 237

Berger, Thomas, **III:** 258; **Supp. XII:**
171
Bergman, Ingmar, **I:** 291; **Supp. XV:**
7, 8, 12
Bergson, Henri, **I:** 224; **II:** 163, 165,
166, 359; **III:** 8, 9, 488, 619; **IV:**
86, 122, 466, 467; **Retro. Supp. I:**
55, 57, 80; **Supp. IV Part 1:** 42
Berkeley, Anthony, **Supp. IV Part 1:**
341
Berkeley, George, **II:** 10, 349, 357,
480, 554
Berkman, Leonard, **Supp. XV:** 321
Berkowitz, Gerald, **Supp. IV Part 2:**
590
Berlin Alexanderplatz (Döblin), **Supp.
XV:** 137
Berlin Stories (Isherwood), **Supp. IV
Part 1:** 82; **Supp. XIV:**155, 156,
161, 162, 164, 165
Berlioz, Hector, **Supp. XV:** 33
Berlyne, Daniel E., **Supp. I Part 2:**
672
Bernard Clare (Farrell), **II:** 38, 39
Bernard of Clairvaux, Saint, **I:** 22; **II:**
538
Bernays, Thekla, **Retro. Supp. II:** 65
Berne, Suzanne, **Supp. XII:** 320
Berneis, Peter, **IV:** 383
Bernhard, Brendan, **Supp. XIV:**163
Bernhardt, Sarah, **I:** 484; **Retro. Supp.
I:** 377
Bernice (Glaspell), **Supp. III Part 1:**
179
"Bernice Bobs Her Hair" (Fitzgerald),
II: 88; **Retro. Supp. I:** 103
Bernstein, Aline, **IV:** 455, 456
Bernstein, Andrea, **Supp. IX:** 146
Bernstein, Charles, **Supp. IV Part 2:**
421, 426
Bernstein, Elizabeth, **Supp. XII:** 318
Bernstein, Leonard, **I:** 28; **Supp. I
Part 1:** 288, 289; **Supp. IV Part 1:**
83, 84
Bernstein, Melvin, **Supp. XIV:**41, 46
Bernstein, Michael André, **Retro.
Supp. I:** 427
Bernstein, Richard, **Supp. IX:** 253,
262; **Supp. XII:** 113; **Supp. XIV:**33
Berrett, Jesse, **Supp. XIII:** 241, 242
Berrigan, Ted, **Supp. XIV:**150
"Berry" (Hughes), **Supp. I Part 1:**
329, 330
Berry, Faith, **Retro. Supp. I:** 194, 201
Berry, Walter, **IV:** 313–314, 326
Berry, Wendell, **Supp. VIII:** 304;
Supp. X: 21–39; **Supp. XII:** 202;
Supp. XIII: 1–2; **Supp. XIV:**179;
Supp. XVI:39, 56

"Berry Feast, A" (Snyder), **Supp. VIII:** 289, 297

Berryman, John, **I:** 167–189, 405, 441–442, 521; **II:** 554; **III:** 273; **IV:** 138, 430; **Retro. Supp. I:** 430; **Retro. Supp. II:** 175, 178; **Supp. I Part 2:** 546; **Supp. II Part 1:** 109; **Supp. III Part 2:** 541, 561, 595, 596, 603; **Supp. IV Part 2:** 620, 639; **Supp. V:** 179–180, 337; **Supp. IX:** 152; **Supp. XI:** 240; **Supp. XV:** 93

Berryman, Mrs. John, **I:** 168–169

Berryman's Sonnets (Berryman), **I:** 168, 175–178

"Berry Territory" (Snyder), **Supp. VIII:** 304

Berthoff, Warner, **Supp. I Part 1:** 133

Bertolucci, Bernardo, **Supp. IV Part 1:** 94

"Bertrand Hume" (Masters), **Supp. I Part 2:** 463–464

"Best, the Most, The" (Carruth), **Supp. XVI:**59

Best American Essays 1987, The (G. Talese and R. Atwan, eds.), **Supp. XVI:**273

Best American Essays 1988, The (Dillard, ed.), **Supp. VIII:** 272

Best American Essays 1993, The (J. Epstein, ed.), **Supp. XVI:**275

Best American Essays 1997, The (Frazier, ed.), **Supp. VIII:** 272

Best American Essays 1999, The (E. Hoagland and R. Atwan, eds.), **Supp. XVI:**277

Best American Essays for College Students, The (R. Atwan, ed.), **Supp. XVI:**273

Best American Poetry, The: 1988 (Ashbery, ed.), **Supp. III Part 1:** 26

Best American Short Stories, **I:**174; **II:** 587; **III:** 443; **Supp. IV Part 1:** 102, 315; **Supp. IX:** 114; **Supp. X:** 301

Best American Short Stories, 1915–1050, The, **Supp. IX:** 4

Best American Short Stories 1965, The (Foley, ed.), **Supp. XVI:**225

Best American Short Stories 1983, The (A. Tyler, ed.), **Supp. XVI:**37

Best American Short Stories 1988, The (Helprin, ed.), **Supp. XVI:**16

Best American Short Stories 1991, The (Adams and Kenison, eds.), **Supp. XVI:**256

Best American Short Stories 2001, The (Kenison and Kingsover, eds.), **Supp. XVI:**24

Best American Short Stories of 1942, The, **Supp. V:** 316

Best American Short Stories of 1944, The, **Supp. IX:** 119

Best American Short Stories of the Century (Updike, ed.), **Supp. X:** 163

Best American Short Stories of the Eighties, The (Ravenal, ed.), **Supp. IV Part 1:** 93

"Best China Saucer, The" (Jewett), **Retro. Supp. II:** 145–146

Bester, Alfred, **Supp. XVI:**123

Best Hour of the Night, The (Simpson), **Supp. IX:** 277–279

Bestiaire, Le (Apollinaire), **IV:** 80

Bestiary, A (Wilbur), **Supp. III Part 2:** 552

"Bestiary for the Fingers of My Right Hand" (Simic), **Supp. VIII:** 274, 275

Best Man, The: A Play About Politics (Vidal), **Supp. IV Part 2:** 683

"Best of Everything, The" (Yates), **Supp. XI:** 341

Best of Plimpton (Plimpton), **Supp. XVI:**238, 239, 240

Best Short Plays, The (Mayorga), **IV:** 381

Best Short Stories, The (O'Brien, ed.), **I:** 289

Best Short Stories by Negro Writers, The (Hughes, ed.), **Supp. I Part 1:** 345

Best That Ever Did It, The (Lacy), **Supp. XV:** 201–202

Best Times, The: An Informal Memoir (Dos Passos), **I:** 475, 482

Best Words, Best Order: Essays on Poetry (Dobyns), **Supp. XIII:** 74, 76–78, 87

Best Years of Our Lives, The (film; Wyler), **Supp. XV:** 195

"BETANCOURT" (Baraka), **Supp. II Part 1:** 33, 34

Bête humaine, La (Zola), **III:** 316, 318

"Bethe" (Hellman), **Supp. I Part 1:** 293

Bethea, David, **Supp. VIII:** 27

Bethel Merriday (Lewis), **II:** 455

Bethke, Bruce, **Supp. XVI:**121

Bethlehem in Broad Daylight (Doty), **Supp. XI:** 121, 122–123

Bethune, Mary McLeod, **Retro. Supp. I:** 197; **Supp. I Part 1:** 333

Bethurum, Dorothy, **IV:** 121

"Betrayal" (Lanier), **Supp. I Part 1:** 364

"Betrothed" (Bogan), **Supp. III Part 1:** 49–51

Bettelheim, Bruno, **Supp. I Part 2:** 622; **Supp. X:** 77, 84; **Supp. XIV:**126; **Supp. XVI:**33

Better Days (Price), **Supp. VI:** 264

Better Sort, The (James), **II:** 335

"Better Things in Life, The" (Loos), **Supp. XVI:**194

Betty Leicester (Jewett), **II:** 406

Betty Leicester's Christmas (Jewett), **II:** 406; **Retro. Supp. II:** 145

Between Angels (Dunn), **Supp. XI:** 149–159

"Between Angels" (Dunn), **Supp. XI:** 150

Between Fantoine and Agapa (Pinget), **Supp. V:** 39

"Between Memory and History: A Writer's Voice" (Kreisler), **Supp. XVI:**155

"Between the Porch and the Altar" (Lowell), **II:** 540–541

"Between the World and Me" (Wright), **Supp. II Part 1:** 228

Between Time and Timbuktu (Vonnegut), **Supp. II Part 2:** 753, 759

Bevis, Howard L., **Supp. I Part 2:** 611

Bevis, John, **Supp. I Part 2:** 503

"Bewitched" (Wharton), **IV:** 316

Bewley, Marius, **I:** 336

Beyle, Marie Henri. *See* Stendhal

Beyond (Goldbarth), **Supp. XII:** 192

Beyond Black Bear Lake (LaBastille), **Supp. X:** 95, 99–102, 108

"Beyond Charles River to the Acheron" (Lowell), **II:** 541

Beyond Criticism (Shapiro), **Supp. II Part 2:** 703, 711

Beyond Culture (Trilling), **Supp. III Part 2:** 508–512

Beyond Desire (Anderson), **I:** 111

Beyond Document: The Art of Nonfiction Film (Warren, ed.), **Supp. IV Part 2:** 434

Beyond Good and Evil (Nietzsche), **Supp. IV Part 2:** 519

"Beyond Harm" (Olds), **Supp. X:** 210

"Beyond the Alps" (Lowell), **II:** 547, 550

"Beyond the Bayou" (Chopin), **Supp. I Part 1:** 215

Beyond the Horizon (O'Neill), **III:** 389

Beyond the Hundredth Meridian: John Wesley Powell and the Second Opening of the West (Stegner), **Supp. IV Part 2:** 599, 603–604, 611

"Beyond the Kittery Bridge" (Hatlen), **Supp. V:** 138

Beyond the Law (film) (Mailer), **Retro. Supp. II:** 205

"Beyond the Sea (at the sanatorium)" (Salinas), **Supp. XIII:** 325

Beyond the Wall: Essays from the Out-

side (Abbey), **Supp. XIII:** 13

Beyond the Writers' Workshop: New Ways to Write Creative Nonfiction (C. Bly), **Supp. XVI:**41

Beyond Tragedy (Niebuhr), **III:** 300–303

Bezner, Kevin, **Supp. XII:** 202

Bhagavad Gita, **III:** 566; **IV:** 183

"Biafra: A People Betrayed" (Vonnegut), **Supp. II Part 2:** 760

Bianchi, Martha Dickinson, **I:** 470; **Retro. Supp. I:** 35, 37, 38

Bible, **I:** 191, 280, 414, 421, 490, 506; **II:** 6, 12, 15, 17, 108, 231, 237, 238, 252, 267, 302; **III:** 28, 199, 308–309, 341, 343, 350, 356, 402, 492, 519, 565, 577; **IV:** 11, 13, 42, 57, 60, 67, 152, 153, 154, 155, 164, 165, 296, 337, 341, 367, 369, 370, 371, 438; **Retro. Supp. I:** 91; **Supp. I Part 1:** 4, 6, 63, 101, 104, 105, 113, 193, 369; **Supp. I Part 2:** 388, 433, 494, 515, 516, 517, 583, 584, 587, 589, 653, 689, 690, 691; **Supp. IV Part 1:** 284; **Supp. VIII:** 20; **Supp. IX:** 246; **Supp. XIV:**225. *See also* names of biblical books; New Testament; Old Testament

Biblia Americana (Mather), **Supp. II Part 2:** 442

Biblical Dialogues between a Father and His Family (Rowson), **Supp. XV:** 245–246

Bibliography of the King's Book, A; or, Eikon Basilike (Almack), **Supp. IV Part 2:** 435

"Bibliography of the King's Book, A, or, Eikon Basilike" (Howe), **Supp. IV Part 2:** 435

Bickel, Freddy. *See* March, Fredric

Bidart, Frank, **Retro. Supp. II:** 48, 50, 52, 182, 183, 184; **Supp. XV:** 19–37

Bid Me to Live (Doolittle), **Supp. I Part 1:** 258, 260, 268, 269, 270

"*Bien* Pretty" (Cisneros), **Supp. VII:** 70

"Bienvenidos" (Mora), **Supp. XIII:** 220

Bierce, Albert, **I:** 191, 209

Bierce, Ambrose, **I:** 190–213, 419; **II:** 74, 264, 271; **IV:** 350; **Retro. Supp. II:** 72

Bierce, Day, **I:** 195, 199

Bierce, General Lucius Verus, **I:** 191

Bierce, Helen, **I:** 210

Bierce, Leigh, **I:** 195, 198, 208

Bierce, Marcus, **I:** 190, 191

Bierce, Mrs. Ambrose, **I:** 194–195, 199

Bierce, Mrs. Marcus, **I:** 190, 191

Biffle, Kent, **Supp. V:** 225

"Bi-Focal" (Stafford), **Supp. XI:** 318, 321

Big as Life (Doctorow), **Supp. IV Part 1:** 231, 234

"Big Bite" (Mailer), **Retro. Supp. II:** 204

"Big Blonde" (Parker), **Supp. IX:** 189, 192, 193, 195, 196, 203

Big Bozo, The (Glaspell), **Supp. III Part 1:** 182

Bigelow, Gordon, **Supp. X:** 222, 227, 229

Bigelow, Jacob, **Supp. I Part 1:** 302

Bigelow Papers, Second Series, The (Lowell), **Supp. I Part 2:** 406, 415–416

Bigelow Papers, The (Lowell), **Supp. I Part 2:** 406, 407, 408, 410, 411–412, 415, 417, 424

Big Fix, The (Lacy), **Supp. XV:** 204–205

Bigfoot Dreams (Prose), **Supp. XVI:**253–254

Big Funk, The: A Casual Play (Shanley), **Supp. XIV:**316, 327

Big Gold Dream, The (C. Himes), **Supp. XVI:**143, 144

"Bight, The" (Bishop), **Retro. Supp. II:** 38, 45

Big Hunger: Stories 1932–1959 (Fante), **Supp. XI:** 160

Big Knife, The (Odets), **Supp. II Part 2:** 546, 547, 548

Big Knockover, The (Hammett), **Supp. I Part 1:** 292; **Supp. IV Part 1:** 344, 345, 356

Big Laugh, The (O'Hara), **III:** 362, 373–375

Big Man (Neugeboren), **Supp. XVI:**219, 220, 221, 225

Big Money, The (Dos Passos), **I:** 482, 483, 486–487, 489; **Supp. I Part 2:** 646, 647

"Big Rock Candy Figgy Pudding Pitfall, The" (Didion), **Supp. IV Part 1:** 195

Big Rock Candy Mountain, The (Stegner), **Supp. IV Part 2:** 596, 597, 598, 599, 600, 603, 604, 605, 606–607, 608, 610–611

Bigsby, C. W. E. (Christopher), **Supp. IX:** 137, 140; **Supp. XV:** 332

Big Sea, The (Hughes), **Retro. Supp. I:** 195, 197, 199, 201, 204; **Supp. I Part 1:** 322, 332, 333; **Supp. II Part 1:** 233–234

Big Sky, The (Mora), **Supp. XIII:** 221

Big Sleep, The (Chandler), **Supp. IV Part 1:** 122–125, 127, 128, 134

Big Sleep, The (film), **Supp. IV Part 1:** 130

Big Sur (Kerouac), **Supp. III Part 1:** 230

Big Sur and the Oranges of Hieronymous Bosch (H. Miller), **III:** 189–190

Big Town, The (Lardner), **II:** 426, 429

"Big Two-Hearted River" (Hemingway), **II:** 249; **Retro. Supp. I:** 170–171; **Supp. IX:** 106; **Supp. XIV:**227, 235

"Big Wind" (Roethke), **III:** 531

"Big Winner Rises Late, The" (Dunn), **Supp. XI:** 146

"Bilingual Christmas" (Mora), **Supp. XIII:** 216–217

"Bilingual Sestina" (Alvarez), **Supp. VII:** 10

"Bill" (Winters), **Supp. II Part 2:** 792

"Bill, The" (Malamud), **Supp. I Part 2:** 427, 430, 434

"Billie Holiday" (Carruth), **Supp. XVI:**50

Billings, Gladys. *See* Brooks, Mrs. Van Wyck

Bill of Rites, a Bill of Wrongs, a Bill of Goods, A (Morris), **III:** 237

"Bill's Beans" (Nye), **Supp. XIII:** 283

"Billy" (Gordon), **Supp. IV Part 1:** 306

"Billy" (McCarriston), **Supp. XIV:**265

Billy Bathgate (Doctorow), **Supp. IV Part 1:** 217, 219, 222, 224, 227, 229–231, 231, 232, 233, 238

Billy Bathgate (film), **Supp. IV Part 1:** 236

Billy Budd, Sailor (Melville), **III:** 40, 93–95; **IV:** 105; **Retro. Supp. I:** 249, 258–260

Billy Phelan's Greatest Game (W. Kennedy), **Supp. VII:** 131, 132, 134, 135, 142–147, 149, 151, 153, 155

Billy the Kid, **Supp. IV Part 2:** 489, 490, 492

Biloxi Blues (Simon), **Supp. IV Part 2:** 576, 577, 584, 586–587, 590

"Bimini" (Hemingway), **II:** 258

Bingham, Anne, **Supp. XV:** 239

Bingham, Millicent Todd, **I:** 470; **Retro. Supp. I:** 36

Bingo Palace, The (Erdrich), **Supp. IV Part 1:** 259, 260, 261, 263–264, 265, 266–267, 268–269, 270, 271–273, 274, 275

"Binsey Poplars" (Hopkins), **Supp. I Part 1:** 94; **Supp. IV Part 2:** 639

Binswanger, Ludwig, **Supp. XV:** 26

Biographia Literaria (Coleridge), **II:**

10; **Retro. Supp. I:** 308

"Biography" (Francis), **Supp. IX:** 77

"Biography" (Pinsky), **Supp. VI:** 235, 236, 239, 241, 243, 249, 250

Biography and Poetical Remains of the Late Margaret Miller Davidson (Irving), **II:** 314

"Biography in the First Person" (Dunn), **Supp. XI:** 144

"Biography of an Armenian Schoolgirl" (Nye), **Supp. XIII:** 275, 280

"Biography of a Story" (Jackson), **Supp. IX:** 113

Biondi, Joann, **Supp. XI:** 103

"Biopoetics Sketch for *Greenfield Review*" (Harjo), **Supp. XII:** 216

"Birchbrook Mill" (Whittier), **Supp. I Part 2:** 699

"Birches" (Frost), **II:** 154; **Retro. Supp. I:** 132; **Supp. XIII:** 147

Bird, Alan, **Supp. I Part 1:** 260

Bird, Gloria, **Supp. XII:** 216

Bird, Isabella, **Supp. X:** 103

Bird, Robert M., **III:** 423

"Bird, The" (Simpson), **Supp. IX:** 269–270

"Bird, the Bird, the Bird, The" (Creeley), **Supp. IV Part 1:** 149

"Bird came down the Walk, A" (Dickinson), **Retro. Supp. I:** 37

"Bird Frau, The" (Dove), **Supp. IV Part 1:** 245

"Bird in Hand" (screen story) (West and Ingster), **Retro. Supp. II:** 330

Bird Kingdom of the Mayas (LaBastille), **Supp. X:** 96

Birds and Beasts (W. J. Smith), **Supp. XIII:** 346

Bird's Nest, The (Jackson), **Supp. IX:** 124–125

Birds of America (McCarthy), **II:** 579–583; **Supp. X:** 177

Birds of America (Moore), **Supp. X:** 163, 165, 167, 168, 171, 177–179

Birds of America, The (Audubon), **Supp. XVI:** 5–6, 7, 9, 10, 12, 13

"Birds of Killingsworth, The" (Longfellow), **Retro. Supp. II:** 164

Birds of North America (Audubon Society), **Supp. X:** 177

"Birds of Vietnam, The" (Carruth), **Supp. XVI:** 55

"Bird-Witted" (Moore), **III:** 214

Birkerts, Sven, **Supp. IV Part 2:** 650; **Supp. V:** 212; **Supp. VIII:** 85; **Supp. X:** 311

Birkhead, L. M., **III:** 116

"Birmingham Sunday" (Hughes), **Supp. I Part 1:** 343

Birnbaum, Henry, **Supp. XII:** 128

Birnbaum, Robert, **Supp. X:** 13; **Supp. XVI:** 75

Birney, James G., **Supp. I Part 2:** 587, 588

Birstein, Ann, **Supp. VIII:** 100

"Birthday, A" (Untermeyer), **Supp. XV:** 296

Birthday Basket for Tía, A (Mora), **Supp. XIII:** 221

"Birthday Cake" (Carruth), **Supp. XVI:** 59

"Birthday Cake for Lionel, A" (Wylie), **Supp. I Part 2:** 721

"Birthday Girl: 1950" (McCarriston), **Supp. XIV:** 261

"Birthday of Mrs. Pineda, The" (Ríos), **Supp. IV Part 2:** 542, 546

"Birthday Poem, A" (Hecht), **Supp. X:** 64

"Birthday Present, A" (Plath), **Supp. I Part 2:** 531

"Birthmark, The" (Ellison), **Retro. Supp. II:** 116; **Supp. II Part 1:** 237–238

"Birth-mark, The" (Hawthorne), **Retro. Supp. I:** 152

Birth-mark, The: Unsettling the Wilderness in American Literary History (Howe), **Supp. IV Part 2:** 422, 431, 434

Birth of a Nation, The (film), **Supp. I Part 1:** 66

Birth of the Poet, The (Gordon), **Supp. XII:** 7

Birth of Tragedy, The (Nietzsche), **Supp. IV Part 1:** 105, 110; **Supp. IV Part 2:** 519; **Supp. VIII:** 182

"Birth of Venus, The" (Botticelli), **IV:** 410

"Birth of Venus, The" (Rukeyser), **Supp. VI:** 281

"Birthplace Revisited" (Corso), **Supp. XII:** 123

"Birthright" (McKay), **Supp. X:** 136

Bisch, Louis E., **Supp. I Part 2:** 608

Bishop, Elizabeth, **Retro. Supp. I:** 140, 296, 303; **Retro. Supp. II:** 37–56, 175, 178, 189, 233, 234, 235; **Supp. I Part 1:** 72–97, 239, 320, 326; **Supp. III Part 1:** 6, 7, 10, 18, 64, 239, 320, 326; **Supp. III Part 2:** 541, 561; **Supp. IV Part 1:** 249, 257; **Supp. IV Part 2:** 439, 626, 639, 641, 644, 647, 651, 653; **Supp. V:** 337; **Supp. IX:** 40, 41, 45, 47, 48; **Supp. X:** 58; **Supp. XI:** 123, 136; **Supp. XIII:** 115, 348; **Supp. XV:** 20–21, 100, 101, 112, 119, 249, 251

Bishop, James, Jr., **Supp. XIII:** 1, 5, 6, 7, 9, 11, 15

Bishop, John Peale, **I:** 432, 440; **II:** 81, 85, 86–87, 91, 209; **IV:** 35, 140, 427; **Retro. Supp. I:** 109; **Supp. I Part 2:** 709

Bishop, John W., **Supp. I Part 1:** 83

Bishop, Judith, **Supp. XVI:** 295

Bishop, Morris, **Supp. I Part 2:** 676

Bishop, William Thomas, **Supp. I Part 1:** 83

"Bishop Orders His Tomb at St. Praxed's Church, The" (R. Browning), **Supp. XV:** 127

"Bishop's Beggar, The" (Benét), **Supp. XI:** 56

"Bismarck" (Chapman), **Supp. XIV:** 52, 53

Bismark, Otto von, **Supp. I Part 2:** 643

"Bistro Styx, The" (Dove), **Supp. IV Part 1:** 250–251

Bitov, Andrei, **Retro. Supp. I:** 278

Bits of Gossip (Davis), **Supp. XVI:** 82–83, 84, 85, 89

"Bitter Drink, The" (Dos Passos), **Supp. I Part 2:** 647

"Bitter Farce, A" (Schwartz), **Supp. II Part 2:** 640, 657–658

"Bitter Pills for the Dark Ladies" (Jong), **Supp. V:** 118

Bitterroot (Burke), **Supp. XIV:** 34, 35

Bitter Victory (Hardy; Kinnell, trans.), **Supp. III Part 1:** 235

Bitzer, G. W. "Billy," **Supp. XVI:** 183

Bixby, Horace, **IV:** 194

Bjorkman, Frances Maule, **Supp. V:** 285

Bjorkman, Stig, **Supp. XV:** 6

Björnson, Björnstjerne, **II:** 275

Black 100, The (Salley), **Supp. XIV:** 195

Blackamerican Literature, 1760-Present (R. Miller), **Supp. X:** 324

Black American Literature Forum, **Supp. XI:** 86, 92, 93

"Black and Tan" (Bell), **Supp. X:** 9

Black Armour (Wylie), **Supp. I Part 2:** 708, 709, 712–714, 729

"Black Art" (Baraka), **Supp. II Part 1:** 49, 50–51, 59, 60

"Black Art, The" (Sexton), **Supp. II Part 2:** 682

"Black Ball, The" (Ellison), **Retro. Supp. II:** 124

Black Bart and the Sacred Hills (Wilson), **Supp. VIII:** 330, 331

Black Beetles in Amber (Bierce), **I:** 204, 209

"Blackberries" (Komunyakaa), **Supp. XIII:** 126

"Blackberry Eating" (Kinnell), **Supp. III Part 1:** 250

Blackberry Winter (Warren), **IV:** 243, 251, 252

Black Betty (Mosley), **Supp. XIII:** 237, **Supp. XIII:** 240, 243

"Black Birch in Winter, A" (Wilbur), **Supp. III Part 2:** 561

Black Boy (Wright), **IV:** 477, 478, 479, 480–482, 488, 489, 494; **Retro. Supp. II:** 117; **Supp. II Part 1:** 235–236; **Supp. IV Part 1:** 11

"Black Boys and Native Sons" (Howe), **Retro. Supp. II:** 112

Blackburn, Alex, **Supp. XIII:** 112

Blackburn, William, **IV:** 100

"Black Buttercups" (Clampitt), **Supp. IX:** 42

Black Cargo, The (Marquand), **III:** 55, 60

Black Cargoes: A History of the Atlantic Slave Trade (Cowley), **Supp. II Part 1:** 140

"Black Cat, The" (Poe), **III:** 413, 414, 415; **Retro. Supp. II:** 264, 267, 269, 270

Black Cherry Blues (Burke), **Supp. XIV:** 30

"Black Christ, The" (Cullen), **Supp. IV Part 1:** 170, 171–172

Black Christ and Other Poems, The (Cullen), **Supp. IV Part 1:** 166, 170

"Black Cottage, The" (Frost), **Retro. Supp. I:** 128

"BLACK DADA NIHILISMUS" (Baraka), **Supp. II Part 1:** 39, 41

"Black Death" (Hurston), **Supp. VI:** 153

Black Dog, Red Dog (Dobyns), **Supp. XIII:** 87, 88–89

"Black Dog, Red Dog" (Dobyns), **Supp. XIII:** 89

"Black Earth" (Moore), **III:** 197, 212

Black Fire (Jones and Neal, eds.), **Supp. X:** 324, 328

Black Fire: An Anthology of Afro American Writing (Baraka, ed.), **Supp. II Part 1:** 53

Black Flame, The (Du Bois), **Supp. II Part 1:** 159, 185–186

Black Folk, Then and Now: An Essay in the History and Sociology of the Negro Race (Du Bois), **Supp. II Part 1:** 159, 178, 183, 185

"Black Fox, The" (Whittier), **Supp. I Part 2:** 692

Black Freckles (Levis), **Supp. XI:** 257, 271

"Black Gang," **IV:** 406, 407

Black Genius (Mosley, ed.), **Supp.**

XIII: 246

"Black Hood, The" (Francis), **Supp. IX:** 83, 91

Black House, The (Theroux), **Supp. VIII:** 319

Black Humor (Johnson), **Supp. VI:** 187, 199

Black Image in the White Mind, The (Fredrickson), **Supp. I Part 2:** 589

"Black Is My Favorite Color" (Malamud), **Supp. I Part 2:** 437

"Black Jewel, The" (Merwin), **Supp. III Part 1:** 355

Black Lamb and Grey Falcon (R. West), **Supp. XVI:** 152

Black Light (Kinnell), **Supp. III Part 1:** 235, 243

"Blacklist and the Cold War, The" (Kramer), **Supp. I Part 1:** 295

Black Literature in America (Baker), **Supp. X:** 324

Black Magic, A Pictorial History of the Negro in American Entertainment (Hughes), **Supp. I Part 1:** 345

Black Magic: Collected Poetry 1961–1967 (Baraka), **Supp. II Part 1:** 45, 49–50

"Blackmailers Don't Shoot" (Chandler), **Supp. IV Part 1:** 121–122

Black Manhattan (Johnson), **Supp. IV Part 1:** 169

Black Mass, A (Baraka), **Supp. II Part 1:** 46, 48–49, 56, 57

"Black Mesa, The" (Merrill), **Supp. III Part 1:** 328

Black Metropolis (Cayton and Drake), **IV:** 475, 486, 488

Black Misery (Hughes), **Supp. I Part 1:** 336

Blackmur, Helen Dickson (Mrs. R. P. Blackmur), **Supp. II Part 1:** 90

Blackmur, Richard P., **I:** 50, 63, 67, 280, 282, 386, 455, 472; **II:** 320, 537; **III:** 194, 208, 462, 478, 497; **Supp. II Part 1:** 87–112, 136; **Supp. II Part 2:** 543, 643; **Supp. XII:** 45

Black Music (Baraka), **Supp. II Part 1:** 47, 51

Black Nativity (Hughes), **Retro. Supp. I:** 196

Black No More (Schuyler), **Supp. XVI:** 142

Black on Black: "Baby Sister" and Selected Writings (C. Himes), **Supp. XVI:** 145

"Blackout" (Hay), **Supp. XIV:** 121

"Black Panther" (Hughes), **Retro. Supp. I:** 211

"Black Petal" (L.-Y. Lee), **Supp. XV:** 224–225

Black Power (Wright), **IV:** 478, 488, 494

"Black Rainbow, A: Modern Afro-American Poetry" (Dove and Waniek), **Supp. IV Part 1:** 244

Black Reconstruction (Du Bois), **Supp. II Part 1:** 159, 162, 171, 182

Black Riders and Other Lines, The (Crane), **I:** 406, 419

"Black Rook in Rainy Weather" (Plath), **Supp. I Part 2:** 543, 544

Blacks (Brooks), **Supp. III Part 1:** 69, 72, 86, 87

Blacks, The (Genet), **Supp. IV Part 1:** 8

Black Skin, White Masks (Fanon), **Retro. Supp. II:** 118

Black Sleuth, The (J. Bruce), **Supp. XVI:** 143

Black Spear, The (Hayden), **Supp. II Part 1:** 375

Black Spring (H. Miller), **III:** 170, 175, 178, 180–182, 183, 184; **Supp. X:** 187

"Black Stone Lying on a White Stone" (Vallejo), **Supp. XIII:** 324

Black Sun (Abbey), **Supp. XIII:** 4, 8–9, 17

"Black Swan, The" (Jarrell), **II:** 382

Black Swan, The (Merrill), **Supp. III Part 1:** 319, 320

"Black Tambourine" (Crane), **I:** 387–388; **II:** 371

"Black Tuesday" (Swenson), **Supp. IV Part 2:** 646

Black Voices (Chapman), **IV:** 485

"Blackwater Mountain" (Wright), **Supp. V:** 335, 340

"Black Wedding, The" (Singer), **IV:** 12–13

Blackwell, Alice Stone, **Supp. XI:** 195, 197

Blackwell, Elizabeth, **Retro. Supp. II:** 146

Black Woman, The (Bambara, ed.), **Supp. XI:** 1

"Black Workers" (Hughes), **Retro. Supp. I:** 202

"Black Writer and the Southern Experience, The" (Walker), **Supp. III Part 2:** 521

Black Zodiac (Wright), **Supp. V:** 333, 344, 345

Blade Runner (film), **Supp. XI:** 84

Blaine, Anita McCormick, **Supp. I Part 1:** 5

Blaine, Nell, **Supp. XV:** 179

Blair, Hugh, **II:** 8, 17; **Supp. I Part 2:** 422

Blair, Robert, **Supp. I Part 1:** 150

Blair, Walter, **II:** 20; **Retro. Supp. II:** 286

Blaisdell, Gus, **Supp. XIV:**87

Blake, **Supp. XVI:**282

Blake, William, **I:** 381, 383, 389, 390, 398, 447, 476, 525, 526, 533; **II:** 321; **III:** 5, 19, 22, 195, 196, 197, 205, 485, 528, 540, 544–545, 567, 572; **IV:** 129; **Retro. Supp. II:** 76, 300; **Supp. I Part 1:** 80; **Supp. I Part 2:** 385, 514, 517, 539, 552, 708; **Supp. V:** 208, 257, 258; **Supp. VIII:** 26, 99, 103; **Supp. X:** 120; **Supp. XII:** 45; **Supp. XIV:**344

Blakely, Barbara, **Supp. XIII:** 32

Blanc, Marie Thérèse, **Retro. Supp. II:** 135

Blanc-Bentzon, Mme. Thérèse, **II:** 405

Blanchard, Paula, **Retro. Supp. II:** 131, 133–134, 135

Blanchot, Maurice, **Supp. XVI:**288

Blancs, Les (Hansberry), **Supp. IV Part 1:** 359, 364, 365, 369, 372–374

Blancs, Les: The Collected Last Plays of Lorraine Hansberry (Nemiroff, ed.), **Supp. IV Part 1:** 365, 368, 374

"'Blandula, Tenulla, Vagula'" (Pound), **III:** 463; **Supp. V:** 336, 337, 345

Blankenship, Tom, **IV:** 193

Blanshard, Rufus A., **I:** 67

Blauvelt, William Satake, **Supp. V:** 171, 173

Blavatsky, Elena Petrovna, **III:** 176

"Blazing in Gold and Quenching in Purple" (Dickinson), **Retro. Supp. I:** 30

Bleak House (Dickens), **II:** 291; **Supp. IV Part 1:** 293

Blechman, Burt, **Supp. I Part 1:** 290

"Bleeder" (Dobyns), **Supp. XIII:** 88

"Bleeding" (Swenson), **Supp. IV Part 2:** 646–647

"Blessed Is the Man" (Moore), **III:** 215

"Blessed Man of Boston, My Grandmother's Thimble, and Fanning Island, The" (Updike), **IV:** 219

"Blessing, A" (Wright), **Supp. III Part 2:** 600, 606

"Blessing the Animals" (Komunyakaa), **Supp. XIII:** 129–130

"Blessing the Children" (Hogan), **Supp. IV Part 1:** 401

Bless Me, Ultima (Anya), **Supp. XIII:** 220

Blew, Mary Clearman, **Supp. XIV:**227

Bligh, S. M., **I:** 226

Blind Assassin, The (Atwood), **Supp. XIII:** 20, 32

Blind Bow-Boy, The (Van Vechten), **Supp. II Part 2:** 737, 740–742

Blind Date (Kosinski), **Supp. VII:** 215, 224–225

Blind Lion, The (Gunn Allen), **Supp. IV Part 1:** 324

"Blind Man's Holiday" (O. Henry), **Supp. II Part 1:** 401

Blind Man with a Pistol (C. Himes), **Supp. XVI:**143, 144

Blindness and Insight (de Man), **Retro. Supp. I:** 67

"Blind Poet, The: Sidney Lanier" (Warren), **Supp. I Part 1:** 371, 373

"Blind Tom" (Davis), **Supp. XVI:**89, 90

Blithedale Romance, The (Hawthorne), **II:** 225, 231, 239, 241–242, 271, 282, 290; **IV:** 194; **Retro. Supp. I:** 63, 149, 152, 156–157, 162–163; **Supp. I Part 2:** 579; **Supp. II Part 1:** 280; **Supp. VIII:** 153, 201

Blitzstein, Marc, **Supp. I Part 1:** 277

Blix (Norris), **III:** 314, 322, 327, 328, 333

Blixen, Karen Denisen Baroness. *See* Dinesen, Isak

"Blizzard in Cambridge" (Lowell), **II:** 554

Blok, Aleksandr Aleksandrovich, **IV:** 443

Blonde Bait (Lacy), **Supp. XV:** 204

Blondin, Antoine, **Supp. XVI:**230

"Blood" (Singer), **IV:** 15, 19

Blood, Tin, Straw (Olds), **Supp. X:** 212–215

Blood and Guts in High School (Acker), **Supp. XII:** 5, 6, 11–12

"Blood Bay, The" (Proulx), **Supp. VII:** 262–263

"Blood-Burning Moon" (Toomer), **Supp. III Part 2:** 483; **Supp. IX:** 314–315

"Bloodchild" (O. Butler), **Supp. XIII:** 61, 69–70

Bloodchild and Other Stories (O. Butler), **Supp. XIII:** 69

"Blood Donor" (Hay), **Supp. XIV:**121

Blood for a Stranger (Jarrell), **II:** 367, 368–369, 370–371, 375, 377

Blood Issue (Crews), **Supp. XI:** 103

Bloodlines (Wright), **Supp. V:** 332, 335, 340

Blood Meridian; or, The Evening Redness in the West (McCarthy), **Supp. VIII:** 175, 177, 180–182, 188, 190

"Blood of the Conquistadores, The"

(Alvarez), **Supp. VII:** 7

"Blood of the Lamb, The" (hymn), **Supp. I Part 2:** 385

Blood of the Martyr (Crane), **I:** 422

"Blood of the Martyrs, The" (Benét), **Supp. XI:** 56, 58

Blood of the Prophets, The (Masters), **Supp. I Part 2:** 458, 459, 461

Blood on the Forge (Attaway), **Supp. II Part 1:** 234–235

"Blood Returns, The" (Kingsolver), **Supp. VII:** 209

Bloodshed and Three Novellas (Ozick), **Supp. V:** 259–260, 261, 266–268

"Blood Stains" (Francis), **Supp. IX:** 86

Bloody Crossroads, The: Where Literature and Politics Meet (Podhoretz), **Supp. VIII:** 241–242

Bloom, Alice, **Supp. IV Part 1:** 308

Bloom, Allan, **Retro. Supp. II:** 19, 30, 31, 33–34

Bloom, Claire, **Retro. Supp. II:** 281; **Supp. IX:** 125

Bloom, Harold, **Retro. Supp. I:** 67, 193, 299; **Retro. Supp. II:** 81, 210, 262; **Supp. IV Part 2:** 620, 689; **Supp. V:** 178, 272; **Supp. VIII:** 180; **Supp. IX:** 146, 259; **Supp. XII:** 261; **Supp. XIII:** 46, 47; **Supp. XIV:**14; **Supp. XV:** 134

Bloom, Larry, **Supp. XIII:** 133

Bloom, Leopold, **I:** 27, 150; **III:** 10

Bloom, Lynn Z., **Supp. IV Part 1:** 6

Bloomfield, Leonard, **I:** 64

Bloomingdale Papers, The (Carruth), **Supp. XVI:**48–50

"Blossom and Fruit" (Benét), **Supp. XI:** 52–53

Blotner, Joseph, **Retro. Supp. I:** 88

Blouin, Lenora, **Supp. VIII:** 266

Blue Angel (Prose), **Supp. XVI:**249, 259–260

"Blue Battalions, The" (Crane), **I:** 419–420

"Bluebeard" (Barthelme), **Supp. IV Part 1:** 47

"Bluebeard" (Millay), **III:** 130

"Blueberries" (Frost), **Retro. Supp. I:** 121, 128

Blue Calhoun (Price), **Supp. VI:** 265–266

Blue City (Macdonald, under Millar), **Supp. IV Part 2:** 466–467

Blue Dahlia, The (Chandler), **Supp. IV Part 1:** 130

Blue Estuaries, The: Poems, 1923–1968 (Bogan), **Supp. III Part 1:** 48, 57, 66

Blue Hammer, The (Macdonald), **Supp.**

IV Part 2: 462

"Blue Hotel, The" (Crane), **I:** 34, 415–416, 423

"Blue Hour, The" (Komunyakaa), **Supp. XIII:** 130

Blue in the Face (Auster), **Supp. XII:** 21

Blue Jay's Dance, The: A Birth Year (Erdrich), **Supp. IV Part 1:** 259–260, 265, 270, 272

"Blue Juniata" (Cowley), **Supp. II Part 1:** 144

Blue Juniata: Collected Poems (Cowley), **Supp. II Part 1:** 140

Blue Light (Mosley), **Supp. XIII:** 245–247, 248, 249

"Blue Light Lounge Sutra for the Performance Poets at Harold Park Hotel" (Komunyakaa), **Supp. XIII:** 125

"Blue Meridian" (Toomer), **Supp. III Part 2:** 476, 487; **Supp. IX:** 320

"Blue Moles" (Plath), **Supp. I Part 2:** 539

Blue Mountain Ballads (music) (Bowles), **Supp. IV Part 1:** 84

Blue Movie (Southern), **Supp. XI:** 309

"Blue Notes" (Matthews), **Supp. IX:** 169

Blue Pastures (Oliver), **Supp. VII:** 229–230, 245

"Blueprints" (Kingsolver), **Supp. VII:** 203

Blue Rhine, Black Forest (Untermeyer), **Supp. XV:** 310

"Blue Ribbon at Amesbury, A" (Frost), **Retro. Supp. I:** 138

"Blues Ain't No Mockin Bird" (Bambara), **Supp. XI:** 3

"Blues Chant Hoodoo Rival" (Komunyakaa), **Supp. XIII:** 117, 118

"Blues for Another Time" (Dunn), **Supp. XI:** 148

"Blues for Jimmy" (McGrath), **Supp. X:** 116

"Blues for John Coltraine, Dead at 41" (Matthews), **Supp. IX:** 157

Blues for Mister Charlie (Baldwin), **Retro. Supp. II:** 8; **Supp. I Part 1:** 48, 61–62, 63

"Blues for Warren" (McGrath), **Supp. X:** 116

Blues If You Want (Matthews), **Supp. IX:** 155, 163–165

"Blues I'm Playing, The" (Hughes), **Retro. Supp. I:** 204

"Blue Sky, The" (Snyder), **Supp. VIII:** 306

"Blues on a Box" (Hughes), **Retro.**

Supp. I: 208

"Blues People" (Ellison), **Retro. Supp. II:** 124

Blues People: Negro Music in White America (Baraka), **Retro. Supp. II:** 124; **Supp. II Part 1:** 30, 31, 33–35, 37, 41, 42, 53

Bluest Eye, The (Morrison), **Supp. III Part 1:** 362, 363–367, 379; **Supp. IV Part 1:** 2, 253; **Supp. VIII:** 213, 214, 227; **Supp. XI:** 4, 91

Bluestone, George, **Supp. IX:** 7, 15

Blue Swallows, The (Nemerov), **III:** 269, 270, 271, 274–275, 278, 284, 286–288

Blue Voyage (Aiken), **I:** 53, 56

Blum, Gustav, **Supp. XV:** 194

Blum, Morgan, **I:** 169

Blum, W. C (pseudonym). *See* Watson, James Sibley, Jr.

Blumenthal, Nathaniel. *See* Branden, Nathaniel

Blumenthal, Sidney, **Supp. VIII:** 241

Blunt, Wilfrid Scawen, **III:** 459

Bly, Carol, **Supp. XVI:**31–43

Bly, Robert, **I:** 291; **Supp. III Part 2:** 599; **Supp. IV Part 1:** 59–77, 177; **Supp. IV Part 2:** 623; **Supp. V:** 332; **Supp. VIII:** 279; **Supp. IX:** 152, 155, 265, 271, 290; **Supp. X:** 127; **Supp. XI:** 142; **Supp. XIII:** 284; **Supp. XV:** 74, 176; **Supp. XVI:**32, 36, 39, 177, 212, 230

"B Negative" (X. J. Kennedy), **Supp. XV:** 156–157

"Boarder, The" (Simpson), **Supp. IX:** 269

Boarding House Blues (Farrell), **II:** 30, 43, 45

Boas, Franz, **I:** 214; **Supp. I Part 2:** 641; **Supp. VIII:** 295; **Supp. IX:** 329; **Supp. XIV:**199, 209, 210

"Boat, The" (Oliver), **Supp. VII:** 247

"Boat, The" (Sexton), **Supp. II Part 2:** 692

Boating Party, The (Renoir), **Supp. XII:** 188

Boat of Quiet Hours, The (Kenyon), **Supp. VII:** 167–169, 171

"Boat of Quiet Hours, The" (Kenyon), **Supp. VII:** 168

"Bob and Spike" (Wolfe), **Supp. III Part 2:** 580

Bobrowski, Johannes, **Supp. XV:** 78

Bob the Gambler (F. Barthelme), **Supp. XI:** 30, 31, 32, 34–35, 36–37

Boccaccio, Giovanni, **III:** 283, 411; **IV:** 230

Bocock, Maclin, **Supp. X:** 79

Bodelson, Anders, **Supp. XVI:**33

Bodenheim, Maxwell, **II:** 42, 530; **Retro. Supp. I:** 417; **Supp. I Part 1:** 257

"Bodies" (Oates), **Supp. II Part 2:** 520

"Bodies and Souls: The Haitian Revolution and Madison Smartt Bell's *All Souls' Rising*" (Trouillot), **Supp. X:** 14

Bodies of Work: Essays (Acker), **Supp. XII:** 7

Bodily Harm (Atwood), **Supp. XIII:** 25–27

Bodley Head Jack London (London), **II:** 483

Body (Crews), **Supp. XI:** 108–109

"Body, The" (Heldreth), **Supp. V:** 151

Body and Soul (Conroy), **Supp. XVI:**63, 72–74, 77

"Body and Soul: A Meditation" (Kumin), **Supp. IV Part 2:** 442, 452

Body and the Song, The (Bishop), **Retro. Supp. II:** 40

"Body Bright" (Sanders), **Supp. XVI:**276

Body of This Death: Poems (Bogan), **Supp. III Part 1:** 47, 49–52, 58

Body of Waking (Rukeyser), **Supp. VI:** 274, 281

"Body of Waking" (Rukeyser), **Supp. VI:** 279

Body Rags (Kinnell), **Supp. III Part 1:** 235, 236, 243–245, 250, 253, 254

"Body's Curse, The" (Dobyns), **Supp. XIII:** 87

"Body's Weight, The" (Dobyns), **Supp. XIII:** 89

Body Traffic (Dobyns), **Supp. XIII:** 87, 89

"'Body with the Lamp Lit Inside, The'" (Mills), **Supp. IV Part 1:** 64

Boehme, Jakob, **I:** 10

Bogan, Louise, **I:** 169, 185; **Retro. Supp. I:** 36; **Supp. I Part 2:** 707, 726; **Supp. III Part 1:** 47–68; **Supp. VIII:** 171, 265; **Supp. IX:** 229; **Supp. X:** 58, 102; **Supp. XIII:** 347; **Supp. XIV:**129

Bogan, Major Benjamin Lewis, **IV:** 120

Bogart, Humphrey, **Supp. I Part 2:** 623; **Supp. IV Part 1:** 130, 356

Bogdanovich, Peter, **Supp. V:** 226

Bogey Man, The (Plimpton), **Supp. XVI:**241

Boggs, Francis W., **Supp. XVI:**182

"Bohemian, The" (Harte), **Supp. II Part 1:** 339

"Bohemian Girl, The" (Cather), **Retro. Supp. I:** 7

"Bohemian Hymn, The" (Emerson), **II:** 19

"Boids and Beasties" (Geisel), **Supp. XVI:**100

Boissevain, Eugen, **III:** 124

Boit, Edward, **Retro. Supp. I:** 366

Bojorquez, Jennifer, **Supp. XII:** 318

Boker, George, **Supp. XV:** 269

"Bold Words at the Bridge" (Jewett), **II:** 394

Boleslavsky, Richard, **Supp. XIV:**240, 243

Boleyn, Anne, **Supp. I Part 2:** 461

Bolick, Katie, **Supp. XVI:**167

Bolivar, Simon, **Supp. I Part 1:** 283, 284, 285

Bolton, Guy, **Supp. I Part 1:** 281

Bolts of Melody: New Poems of Emily Dickinson (Todd and Bingham, eds.), **I:** 470; **Retro. Supp. I:** 36

"Bomb" (Corso), **Supp. XII:** 117, 124, 125–126, 127

Bombs Away (Steinbeck), **IV:** 51–52

"Bona and Paul" (Toomer), **Supp. IX:** 307, 318–319

Bonaparte, Marie, **III:** 418; **Retro. Supp. II:** 264, 266

"Bon-Bon" (Poe), **III:** 425

Bondsman, The (Massinger), **Supp. XV:** 238

Bone, Robert, **Supp. IX:** 318–319; **Supp. XI:** 283

Bone by Bone (Matthiessen), **Supp. V:** 199, 212, 213, 214

Boners (Abingdon). See *Schoolboy Howlers* (Abingdon)

"Bones" (Goldbarth), **Supp. XII:** 173–174

"Bones and Jewels" (Monette), **Supp. X:** 159

"Bones and Shells" (Sanders), **Supp. XVI:**271–272

"Bones of a House" (Cowley). See "Blue Juniata"

Bonetti, Kay, **Supp. VIII:** 47, 152, 159, 160, 165, 168, 170, 223; **Supp. XII:** 61; **Supp. XIV:**232, 234

Bonfire of the Vanities, The (Wolfe), **Supp. III Part 2:** 584–586

Bonheur, Rosa, **Supp. XV:** 276

Bonhoeffer, Dietrich, **Supp. VIII:** 198

Boni, Charles, **Supp. XIV:**288

Boni and Liveright, **Retro. Supp. I:** 59, 80, 178

Bonicelli, Vittorio, **Supp. XI:** 307

Bonifacius (Mather), **Supp. II Part 2:** 461, 464

Bonnefoy, Yves, **Supp. III Part 1:** 235, 243

Bonner, Robert, **Retro. Supp. I:** 246

Bonneville, Mme. Marguerite, **Supp. I Part 2:** 520, 521

Bonneville, Nicolas de, **Supp. I Part 2:** 511, 518, 519

Bonney, William. See Billy the Kid

Bontemps, Arna, **Retro. Supp. I:** 194, 196, 203; **Supp. I Part 1:** 325; **Supp. IV Part 1:** 170; **Supp. IX:** 306, 309

Book, A (Barnes), **Supp. III Part 1:** 36, 39, 44

Book about Myself, A (Dreiser), **I:** 515; **Retro. Supp. II:** 104

"Book as a Container of Consciousness, The" (Gass), **Supp. VI:** 92

Booker, Keith, **Supp. XV:** 197

"Bookies, Beware!" (Heller), **Supp. IV Part 1:** 383

Book of American Negro Poetry, The (Johnson), **Supp. IV Part 1:** 165, 166

Book of Americans, A (Benét), **Supp. XI:** 46, 47, 51

Book of Beb, The (Buechner), **Supp. XII:** 53

Book of Breeething, The (Burroughs), **Supp. III Part 1:** 97, 103

Book of Burlesques, A (Mencken), **III:** 104

Book of Common Prayer, A (Didion), **Supp. IV Part 1:** 196, 198, 203–205, 207, 208

Book of Daniel, The (Doctorow), **Supp. IV Part 1:** 218, 219, 220–222, 227, 231, 237–238, 238; **Supp. V:** 45

Book of Dreams (Kerouac), **Supp. III Part 1:** 225

"Book of Ephraim, The" (Merrill), **Supp. III Part 1:** 330–334

Book of Folly, The (Sexton), **Supp. II Part 2:** 691, 692–694

Book of Gods and Devils, The (Simic), **Supp. VIII:** 281

Book of Guys, The (Keillor), **Supp. XVI:**177

"Book of Hours of Sister Clotilde, The" (Lowell), **II:** 522

Book of Jamaica, The (Banks), **Supp. V:** 11, 12, 16

"Book of Life" (Bidart), **Supp. XV:** 23

Book of Living Verse, The; English and American Poetry from the Thirteenth Century to the Present Day (Untermeyer, ed.), **Supp. XV:** 310

Book of Love, A (Vildrac; Bynner, trans.), **Supp. XV:** 50

Book of Lyrics (Bynner), **Supp. XV:** 51

Book of Medicines, The (Hogan), **Supp.**

IV Part 1: 397, 410, 411–414

"Book of Medicines, The" (Hogan), **Supp. IV Part 1:** 412, 413

"Book of Memory, The" (Auster), **Supp. XII:** 21–22

Book of My Nights (L.-Y. Lee), **Supp. XV:** 215, 223–226

Book of Negro Folklore, The (Hughes, ed.), **Supp. I Part 1:** 345

Book of Nightmares, The (Kinnell), **Supp. III Part 1:** 235, 236, 243, 244, 246–254

Book of Prefaces, A (Mencken), **III:** 99–100, 105

Book of Repulsive Women, The (Barnes), **Supp. III Part 1:** 33

Book of Roses, The (Parkman), **Supp. II Part 2:** 597, 598

Book of the Body, The (Bidart), **Supp. XV:** 21, 25–27

"Book of the Dead, The" (Rukeyser), **Supp. VI:** 272, 278, 279; **Supp. XV:** 349

"Book of the Grotesque, The" (Anderson), **I:** 106

Book of the Homeless, The (Wharton), **Retro. Supp. I:** 377

Book of the Hopi (Waters), **Supp. X:** 124

Book of Tobit (Bible), **Supp. XII:** 54

Book of Verses, A (Masters), **Supp. I Part 2:** 458

Book of Yaak, The (Bass), **Supp. XVI:**18–19

"Book of Yolek, The" (Hecht), **Supp. X:** 69, 70–71

"Books Considered" (Bloom), **Supp. I Part 1:** 96

Books in My Life, The (H. Miller), **II:** 176, 189

"Books/P,L,E, The" (Goldbarth), **Supp. XII:** 190

Bookviews, **Supp. XI:** 216

"Boom" (Nemerov), **III:** 278

Boom! (T. Williams), **IV:** 383

Boom Town (Wolfe), **IV:** 456

"Boom Town" (Wolfe), **IV:** 469

Boone, Daniel, **II:** 207; **III:** 444; **IV:** 192, 193

Boorstin, Daniel, **I:** 253

Booth, Charles, **Supp. I Part 1:** 13

Booth, General William, **Supp. I Part 2:** 384, 386

Booth, John Wilkes, **III:** 588

Booth, Philip, **I:** 522; **Supp. IX:** 269; **Supp. XI:** 141; **Supp. XIII:** 277; **Supp. XV:** 92

Borah, William, **III:** 475

Borden, Lizzie, **II:** 5

Borderlands/La Frontera: The New

Mestiza (Anzaldúa), **Supp. XIII:** 223

Borders (Mora), **Supp. XIII:** 213, 215–217

Border Trilogy (McCarthy), **Supp. VIII:** 175, 182

Borel, Pétrus, **III:** 320

Borges, Jorge Luis, **I:** 123, 135, 138, 140, 142; **Supp. III Part 2:** 560; **Supp. IV Part 2:** 623, 626, 630; **Supp. V:** 238; **Supp. VIII:** 15, 348, 349; **Supp. XII:** 21, 147; **Supp. XV:** 34; **Supp. XVI:**201, 206

"Borges and I" (Bidart), **Supp. XV:** 34, 35

"Borinken Blues" (Komunyakaa), **Supp. XIII:** 117

"Born a Square: The Westerner's Dilemma" (Stegner), **Supp. IV Part 2:** 595; **Supp. V:** 224

"Born Bad" (Cisneros), **Supp. VII:** 62

Borrowed Time: An AIDS Memoir (Monette), **Supp. X:** 145, 146, 147, 152, 154, 155

"Bosque del Apache Wildlife Refuge" (Mora), **Supp. XIII:** 218

"Boston" (Hardwick), **Supp. III Part 1:** 201

Boston (Sinclair), **Supp. V:** 282, 288–289

Boston, B. H., **Supp. XIII:** 312

Boston Adventure (Stafford), **Retro. Supp. II:** 177, 178

"Boston Common" (Berryman), **I:** 172

"Boston Hymn" (Emerson), **II:** 13, 19

Bostonians, The (James), **I:** 9; **II:** 282; **IV:** 202; **Retro. Supp. I:** 216, 225

Boston Marriage (Mamet), **Supp. XIV:**247

"Boston Nativity, The" (Lowell), **II:** 538

Boswell: A Modern Comedy (Elkin), **Supp. VI:** 42, 44–45, 57

Boswell, James, **IV:** 431; **Supp. I Part 2:** 656

Bosworth, Patricia, **Supp. IV Part 2:** 573, 591

Botticelli (McNally), **Supp. XIII:** 197

Botticelli, Sandro, **IV:** 410; **Retro. Supp. I:** 422

"Botticellian Trees, The" (W. C. Williams), **Retro. Supp. I:** 422

"Bottle of Milk for Mother, A" (Algren), **Supp. IX:** 3

"Bottle of Perrier, A" (Wharton), **IV:** 316

"Bottles" (Kenyon), **Supp. VII:** 171

Bottom: On Shakespeare (Zukofsky), **Supp. III Part 2:** 622, 624, 625, 626, 627, 629

"Bottom Line, The" (Elkin), **Supp. VI:** 52, 53

Boucher, Anthony, **Supp. IV Part 2:** 473; **Supp. XV:** 203, 205

Boulanger, Nadia, **Supp. IV Part 1:** 81

"Boulot and Boulette" (Chopin), **Supp. I Part 1:** 211

Boulton, Agnes, **III:** 403

Bound East for Cardiff (O'Neill), **III:** 388

"Bouquet, The" (Stevens), **IV:** 90

"Bouquet of Roses in Sunlight" (Stevens), **IV:** 93

Bourdin, Henri L., **Supp. I Part 1:** 251

Bourgeois Poet, The (Shapiro), **Supp. II Part 2:** 701, 703, 704, 713, 714–716

Bourget, James, **IV:** 319

Bourget, Paul, **II:** 325, 338; **IV:** 311, 315; **Retro. Supp. I:** 224, 359, 373

Bourjaily, Vance, **III:** 43; **Supp. IX:** 260

Bourke-White, Margaret, **I:** 290, 293, 295, 297

Bourne, Charles Rogers, **I:** 215

Bourne, Mrs. Charles Rogers, **I:** 215

Bourne, Randolph, **I:** 214–238, 243, 245, 246–247, 251, 259; **Supp. I Part 2:** 524; **Supp. XV:** 141, 298, 301

Bowden, Charles, **Supp. XIII:** 17

Bowditch, Nathaniel, **Supp. I Part 2:** 482

Bowen, Barbara, **Supp. IX:** 311

Bowen, Elizabeth, **Retro. Supp. I:** 351; **Supp. IV Part 1:** 299; **Supp. VIII:** 65, 165, 251, 265; **Supp. IX:** 128

Bowen, Francis, **Supp. I Part 2:** 413

Bowen, Louise de Koven, **Supp. I Part 1:** 5

Bowen, Michael, **Supp. VIII:** 73

Bowers, John, **Supp. XI:** 217–218

"Bowlers Anonymous" (Dobyns), **Supp. XIII:** 86

Bowles, Jane (Jane Auer), **II:** 586; **Supp. IV Part 1:** 89, 92

Bowles, Paul, **I:** 211; **II:** 586; **Supp. II Part 1:** 17; **Supp. IV Part 1:** 79–99

Bowles, Samuel, **I:** 454, 457; **Retro. Supp. I:** 30, 32, 33

"Bowl of Blood, The" (Jeffers), **Supp. II Part 2:** 434

"Bowls" (Moore), **III:** 196

Bowman, James, **I:** 193

"Bows to Drouth" (Snyder), **Supp. VIII:** 303

Box, Edgar (pseudonym). *See* Vidal, Gore

Box and Quotations from Chairman Mao Tse-tung (Albee), **I:** 89–91, 94

Box Garden, The (Shields), **Supp. VII:** 314–315, 320

"Box Seat" (Toomer), **Supp. III Part 2:** 484; **Supp. IX:** 316, 318

Boy, A (Ashbery), **Supp. III Part 1:** 5

Boyce, Horace, **II:** 136

Boyd, Brian, **Retro. Supp. I:** 270, 275

Boyd, Janet L., **Supp. X:** 229

Boyd, Nancy (pseudonym). *See* Millay, Edna St. Vincent

Boyd, Thomas, **I:** 99; **IV:** 427

Boyesen, H. H., **II:** 289

"Boyhood" (Farrell), **II:** 28

"Boy in France, A" (Salinger), **III:** 552–553

Boy in the Water (Dobyns), **Supp. XIII:** 75, 84

Boyle, Kay, **IV:** 404

Boyle, T. C. (Thomas Coraghessan), **Supp. VIII:** 1–17

Boyle, Thomas John. *See* Boyle, T. C.

Boynton, H. W., **Supp. IX:** 7

Boynton, Percy Holmes, **Supp. I Part 2:** 415

"Boy on a Train" (Ellison), **Retro. Supp. II:** 124

"Boy Riding Forward Backward" (Francis), **Supp. IX:** 82

"Boys and Girls" (Cisneros), **Supp. VII:** 59–60

Boy's Froissart, The (Lanier), **Supp. I Part 1:** 361

Boy's King Arthur, The (Lanier), **Supp. I Part 1:** 361

Boy's Mabinogion, The (Lanier), **Supp. I Part 1:** 361

"Boys of '29, The" (Holmes), **Supp. I Part 1:** 308

Boys of '76, The (Coffin), **III:** 577

Boy's Percy, The (Lanier), **Supp. I Part 1:** 361

Boy's Town (Howells), **I:** 418

Boy's Will, A (Frost), **II:** 152, 153, 155–156, 159, 164, 166; **Retro. Supp. I:** 124, 127, 128, 131; **Retro. Supp. II:** 168

"Boy Who Wrestled with Angels, The" (Hoffman), **Supp. X:** 90

"Boy with One Shoe, The" (Jewett), **Retro. Supp. II:** 132

"Brace, The" (Bausch), **Supp. VII:** 48

Bracebridge Hall, or, The Humorists (Irving), **I:** 339, 341; **II:** 308–309, 313

Bracher, Frederick, **I:** 378, 380; **Supp. I Part 1:** 185

Brackenridge, Hugh Henry, **Supp. I Part 1:** 124, 127, 145; **Supp. II**

Part 1: 65

Brackett, Leigh, **Supp. IV Part 1:** 130

Bradbury, John M., **I:** 288–289; **IV:** 130, 135

Bradbury, Malcolm, **Supp. VIII:** 124

Bradbury, Ray, **Supp. I Part 2:** 621–622; **Supp. IV Part 1:** 101–118; **Supp. XVI:** 122

Braddon, Mary E., **Supp. I Part 1:** 35, 36

Bradfield, Scott, **Supp. VIII:** 88

Bradford, Gamaliel, **I:** 248, 250

Bradford, Roark, **Retro. Supp. I:** 80

Bradford, William, **Retro. Supp. II:** 161, 162; **Supp. I Part 1:** 110, 112; **Supp. I Part 2:** 486, 494

Bradlee, Ben, **Supp. V:** 201

Bradley, Bill, **Supp. VIII:** 47

Bradley, F. H., **Retro. Supp. I:** 57, 58

Bradley, Francis Herbert, **I:** 59, 567–568, 572, 573

Bradshaw, Barbara, **Supp. XIII:** 313

Bradstreet, Anne, **I:** 178–179, 180, 181, 182, 184; **III:** 505; **Retro. Supp. I:** 40; **Supp. I Part 1:** 98–123, 300; **Supp. I Part 2:** 484, 485, 496, 546, 705; **Supp. V:** 113, 117–118; **Supp. XIII:** 152; **Supp. XIV:** 128

Bradstreet, Elizabeth, **Supp. I Part 1:** 108, 122

Bradstreet, Mrs. Simon. *See* Bradstreet, Anne

Bradstreet, Simon, **I:** 178; **Supp. I Part 1:** 103, 110, 116

Brady, Alice, **III:** 399

"Bragdowdy and the Busybody, The" (Thurber), **Supp. I Part 2:** 617

"Brahma" (Emerson), **II:** 19, 20

Brahms, Johannes, **III:** 118, 448

"Braiding" (L.-Y. Lee), **Supp. XV:** 214

"Brain and the Mind, The" (James), **II:** 346

Brainard, Joe, **Supp. XV:** 33

"Brain Damage" (Barthelme), **Supp. IV Part 1:** 44

"Brain to the Heart, The" (Komunyakaa), **Supp. XIII:** 120

Braithewaite, W. S., **Retro. Supp. I:** 131

Braithwaite, William Stanley, **Supp. IX:** 309; **Supp. XV:** 296–297, 301–302, 305, 306

Brakhage, Stan, **Supp. XII:** 2

Brame, Gloria, **Supp. XV:** 113

Bramer, Monte, **Supp. X:** 152

Branch Will Not Break, The (Wright), **Supp. III Part 2:** 596, 598–601; **Supp. IV Part 1:** 60; **Supp. IX:** 159

Brancusi, Constantin, **III:** 201; **Retro.**

Supp. I: 292

Brande, Dorothea, **Supp. I Part 2:** 608

Branden, Nathaniel, **Supp. IV Part 2:** 526, 528

"Brand-Name Blues" (Kaufmann), **Supp. XI:** 39

Brand New Life, A (Farrell), **II:** 46, 48

Brando, Marlon, **II:** 588; **Supp. IV Part 2:** 560

Brandon, Henry, **Supp. I Part 2:** 604, 612, 618

Brandt, Alice, **Supp. I Part 1:** 92

Brandt, Carl, **Supp. XI:** 45

Brant, Sebastian, **III:** 447, 448

Braque, Georges, **III:** 197; **Supp. IX:** 66

Brashford, Jake, **Supp. X:** 252

Brasil, Emanuel, **Supp. I Part 1:** 94

"Brasília" (Plath), **Supp. I Part 2:** 544, 545

"Brass Buttons" (McCoy), **Supp. XIII:** 161

"Brass Candlestick, The" (Francis), **Supp. IX:** 89

Brass Check, The (Sinclair), **Supp. V:** 276, 281, 282, 284–285

"Brass Ring, The" (Carver), **Supp. III Part 1:** 137

"Brass Spittoons" (Hughes), **Supp. I Part 1:** 326–327

Brats (X. J. Kennedy), **Supp. XV:** 163

Brautigan, Richard, **III:** 174; **Supp. VIII:** 42, 43; **Supp. XII:** 139; **Supp. XVI:** 172

Brave Cowboy, The (Abbey), **Supp. XIII:** 4–5

Brave New World (Huxley), **II:** 454; **Supp. XIII:** 29

"Brave New World" (MacLeish), **III:** 18

Bravery of Earth, A (Eberhart), **I:** 522, 524, 525, 526, 530

"Brave Words for a Startling Occasion" (Ellison), **Retro. Supp. II:** 118

Braving the Elements (Merrill), **Supp. III Part 1:** 320, 323, 325–327, 329

Bravo, The (Cooper), **I:** 345–346, 348

"Bravura" (Francis), **Supp. IX:** 90

Brawley, Benjamin, **Supp. I Part 1:** 327, 332

Brawne, Fanny, **I:** 284; **II:** 531

Braxton, Joanne, **Supp. IV Part 1:** 12, 15

Brazil (Bishop), **Retro. Supp. II:** 45; **Supp. I Part 1:** 92

"Brazil" (Marshall), **Supp. XI:** 281

Brazil (Updike), **Retro. Supp. I:** 329, 330, 334

"Brazil, January 1, 1502" (Bishop), **Retro. Supp. II:** 47

Braziller, George, **Supp. X:** 24

Brazzi, Rossano, **Supp. IV Part 2:** 520

"Bread" (Dickey), **Supp. IV Part 1:** 182

"Bread" (Olds), **Supp. X:** 206

"Bread Alone" (Wylie), **Supp. I Part 2:** 727

Bread in the Wilderness (Merton), **Supp. VIII:** 197, 208

Bread of Idleness, The (Masters), **Supp. I Part 2:** 460

"Bread of This World, The" (McGrath), **Supp. X:** 119, 127

Bread of Time, The (Levine), **Supp. V:** 180

Bread without Sugar (Stern), **Supp. IX:** 297–298

"Break, The" (Sexton), **Supp. II Part 2:** 689

Breakfast at Tiffany's (Capote), **Supp. III Part 1:** 113, 117, 119–121, 124, 126

Breakfast of Champions (Vonnegut), **Supp. II Part 2:** 755, 759, 769, 770, 777–778

Breaking and a Death, A (Kees), **Supp. XV:** 145

Breaking and Entering (X. J. Kennedy), **Supp. XV:** 153, 160–162

Breaking Hard Ground (D. Hunter), **Supp. XVI:** 38

Breaking Ice (McMillan, ed.), **Supp. XIII:** 182–183

Breaking Open (Rukeyser), **Supp. VI:** 274, 281

"Breaking Open" (Rukeyser), **Supp. VI:** 286

Breaking Ranks: A Political Memoir (Podhoretz), **Supp. VIII:** 239–241, 245

"Breaking the Code of Silence: Ideology and Women's Confessional Poetry" (Harris), **Supp. XIV:** 269

"Breaking Up of the Winships, The" (Thurber), **Supp. I Part 2:** 616

Breast, The (Roth), **Retro. Supp. II:** 287–288; **Supp. III Part 2:** 416, 418

"Breast, The" (Sexton), **Supp. II Part 2:** 687

"Breasts" (Simic), **Supp. VIII:** 275

"Breath" (Levine), **Supp. V:** 185

Breathe No More, My Lady (Lacy), **Supp. XV:** 203

Breathing Lessons (Tyler), **Supp. IV Part 2:** 669–670

Breathing the Water (Levertov), **Supp. III Part 1:** 274, 283, 284

Breath's Burials (Sobin), **Supp. XVI:** 288–289

Breaux, Zelia, **Retro. Supp. II:** 114
Brecht, Bertolt, **I:** 60, 301; **III:** 161, 162; **IV:** 394; **Supp. I Part 1:** 292; **Supp. II Part 1:** 10, 26, 56; **Supp. IV Part 1:** 359; **Supp. IX:** 131, 133, 140; **Supp. X:** 112; **Supp. XIII:** 206, 286; **Supp. XIV:**162
Breen, Joseph I., **IV:** 390
Breit, Harvey, **I:** 433; **III:** 575; **Retro. Supp. II:** 230
Bremer, Fredrika, **Supp. I Part 1:** 407
Brendan: A Novel (Buechner), **Supp. XII:** 53
Brennan, Matthew, **Supp. XV:** 113, 125
Brent, Linda, **Supp. IV Part 1:** 12, 13
Brentano, Franz, **II:** 350; **Supp. XIV:**198, 199
Brer Rabbit (tales), **Supp. IV Part 1:** 11, 13; **Supp. XIV:**88
Breslin, James E. B., **Retro. Supp. I:** 430
Breslin, John B., **Supp. IV Part 1:** 308
Breslin, Paul, **Supp. VIII:** 283
Bresson, Robert, **Supp. IV Part 1:** 156
"Bresson's Movies" (Creeley), **Supp. IV Part 1:** 156–157
Breton, André, **III:** 425; **Supp. XIII:** 114
Brett, George, **II:** 466; **Supp. V:** 286
Brevoort, Henry, **II:** 298
Brew, Kwesi, **Supp. IV Part 1:** 10, 16
Brewer, Gaylord, **Supp. XV:** 330
"Brewing of Soma, The" (Whittier), **Supp. I Part 2:** 704
Brewsie and Willie (Stein), **IV:** 27
Brewster, Martha, **Supp. I Part 1:** 114
"Brian Age 7" (Doty), **Supp. XI:** 136
"Briar Patch, The" (Warren), **IV:** 237
Briar Rose (Coover), **Supp. V:** 52
"Briar Rose (Sleeping Beauty)" (Sexton), **Supp. II Part 2:** 690
Brice, Fanny, **II:** 427
"Brick, The" (Nye), **Supp. XIII:** 276
"Bricklayer in the Snow" (Fante), **Supp. XI:** 164–165
"Brick Layer's Lunch Hour, The" (Ginsberg), **Supp. II Part 1:** 318
Brickman, Marshall, **Supp. XV:** 5
"Bricks, The" (Hogan), **Supp. IV Part 1:** 413
"Bridal Ballad, The" (Poe), **III:** 428
Bridal Dinner, The (Gurney), **Supp. V:** 109, 110
"Bride Comes to Yellow Sky, The" (Crane), **I:** 34, 415, 416, 423
"Bride in the 30's, A" (Auden), **Supp. II Part 1:** 9
Bride of Lammermoor (Scott), **II:** 291

Bride of Samoa (film), **Supp. IV Part 1:** 82
Bride of the Innisfallen, The (Welty), **IV:** 261, 275–279
"Bride of the Innisfallen, The" (Welty), **IV:** 278–279; **Retro. Supp. I:** 353
Bride of the Innisfallen, The, and Other Stories (Welty), **Retro. Supp. I:** 352–353, 355
Brides of the South Wind: Poems 1917–1922 (Jeffers), **Supp. II Part 2:** 419
Bridge, Horatio, **II:** 226
"BRIDGE, THE" (Baraka), **Supp. II Part 1:** 32, 36
Bridge, The (H. Crane), **I:** 62, 109, 266, 385, 386, 387, 395–399, 400, 402; **IV:** 123, 341, 418, 419, 420; **Retro. Supp. I:** 427; **Retro. Supp. II:** 76, 77, 81, 83, 84–87; **Supp. V:** 342; **Supp. IX:** 306
Bridge at Remagen, The (film), **Supp. XI:** 343
"Bridge Burners, The" (Van Vechten), **Supp. II Part 2:** 733
Bridge of San Luis Rey, The (Wilder), **I:** 360; **IV:** 356, 357, 360–363, 365, 366
Bridge of Years, The (Sarton), **Supp. VIII:** 253
"Bridges" (Kingsolver), **Supp. VII:** 208
Bridges, Harry, **I:** 493
Bridges, Lloyd, **Supp. XV:** 202
Bridges, Robert, **II:** 537; **III:** 527; **Supp. I Part 2:** 721; **Supp. II Part 1:** 21; **Supp. XIV:**336, 341, 342, 343
Bridgman, P. W., **I:** 278
"Bridle, The" (Carver), **Supp. III Part 1:** 138
"Brief and Blameless Outline of the Ontogeny of Crow, A" (Wright), **Supp. XV:** 347
"Brief Début of Tildy, The" (O. Henry), **Supp. II Part 1:** 408
"Brief Encounters on the Inland Waterway" (Vonnegut), **Supp. II Part 2:** 760
Briefings (Ammons), **Supp. VII:** 29
Brief Interviews with Hideous Men (Wallace), **Supp. X:** 308–310
"Brief Interviews with Hideous Men" (Wallace), **Supp. X:** 309
"Briefly It Enters, and Briefly Speaks" (Kenyon), **Supp. VII:** 174
Briffault, Robert, **Supp. I Part 2:** 560, 567
"Brigade de Cuisine" (McPhee), **Supp. III Part 1:** 307–308
Brigadier and the Golf Widow, The

(Cheever), **Supp. I Part 1:** 184–185, 192
Briggs, Charles F., **Supp. I Part 2:** 411
brigham, besmilr, **Supp. XV:** 349
"Bright and Morning Star" (Wright), **IV:** 488
Bright Book of Life: American Novelists and Storytellers from Hemingway to Mailer (Kazin), **Supp. VIII:** 102, 104
Bright Center of Heaven (Maxwell), **Supp. VIII:** 153–155, 164
Brighton Beach Memoirs (Simon), **Supp. IV Part 2:** 576, 577, 584, 586–587, 590
Bright Procession (Sedges), **Supp. II Part 1:** 125
Bright Room Called Day, A (Kushner), **Supp. IX:** 133, 138–141, 142
"Brilliance" (Doty), **Supp. XI:** 124, 128
"Brilliant Leaves" (Gordon), **II:** 199
"Brilliant Sad Sun" (W. C. Williams), **Retro. Supp. I:** 422
"Bringing Back the Trumpeter Swan" (Kumin), **Supp. IV Part 2:** 454
Bringing It All Back Home (McNally), **Supp. XIII:** 197–198
"Bringing the Strange Home" (Dunn), **Supp. XI:** 141
"Bring the Day!" (Roethke), **III:** 536
Brinkley, Douglas, **Supp. XIII:** 9
Brinkmeyer, Robert H., Jr., **Supp. XI:** 38
Brinnin, John Malcolm, **IV:** 26, 27, 28, 42, 46; **Supp. XV:** 139
Brissot, Jacques Pierre, **Supp. I Part 2:** 511
"Britain's Negro Problem in Sierra Leone" (Du Bois), **Supp. I Part 1:** 176
"British Guiana" (Marshall), **Supp. XI:** 281–282
"British Poets, The" (Holmes), **Supp. I Part 1:** 306
"British Prison Ship, The" (Freneau), **Supp. II Part 1:** 261
Brittan, Gordon G., Jr., **Supp. XIV:**234
Britten, Benjamin, **II:** 586; **Supp. II Part 1:** 17; **Supp. IV Part 1:** 84
Broadwater, Bowden, **II:** 562
Broadway, Broadway (McNally). *See It's Only a Play* (McNally)
Broadway, J. William, **Supp. V:** 316
Broadway Bound (Simon), **Supp. IV Part 2:** 576, 577, 584, 586–587, 590
Broadway Danny Rose (film; Allen), **Supp. XV:** 9

"Broadway Sights" (Whitman), **IV:** 350

Broccoli, Albert R. "Cubby," **Supp. XI:** 307

Bröck, Sabine, **Supp. XI:** 275, 277, 278

Brodhead, Richard, **Retro. Supp. II:** 139; **Supp. XIV:**61

Brodkey, Harold, **Supp. VIII:** 151; **Supp. X:** 160

Brodskii, Iosif Alexsandrovich. *See* Brodsky, Joseph

Brodsky, Joseph, **Supp. VIII:** 19–35; **Supp. X:** 65, 73; **Supp. XV:** 134, 135, 256

Brody, Alter, **Supp. XV:** 302, 307

Brodyar, Anatole, **Supp. XIV:**106

"Brokeback Mountain" (Proulx), **Supp. VII:** 264–265

"Broken Balance, The" (Jeffers), **Supp. II Part 2:** 426

"Broken Field Running" (Bambara), **Supp. XI:** 10, 11

Broken Frieze, The (Everwine), **Supp. XV:** 74, 75, 89

Broken Ground, The (Berry), **Supp. X:** 30

"Broken Home, The" (Merrill), **Supp. III Part 1:** 319, 325

"Broken Oar, The" (Longfellow), **Retro. Supp. II:** 169

"Broken Promise" (MacLeish), **III:** 15

Broken Span, The (W. C. Williams), **IV:** 419; **Retro. Supp. I:** 424

"Broken Tower, The" (H. Crane), **I:** 385, 386, 400, 401–402; **Retro. Supp. II:** 89, 90

Broken Vessels (Dubus), **Supp. VII:** 90–91; **Supp. XI:** 347

"Broken Vessels" (Dubus), **Supp. VII:** 90

"Broker" (H. Roth), **Supp. IX:** 234

Bromfield, Louis, **IV:** 380

"Brompton Cocktail" (Mamet), **Supp. XIV:**252

Bromwich, David, **Retro. Supp. I:** 305; **Supp. XII:** 162

"Broncho That Would Not Be Broken, The" (Lindsay), **Supp. I Part 2:** 383

Bronk, William, **Supp. XV:** 115

Brontë, Anne, **Supp. IV Part 2:** 430

Brontë, Branwell, **I:** 462

Brontë, Charlotte, **I:** 458; **II:** 175; **Supp. IV Part 2:** 430; **Supp. IX:** 128; **Supp. XII:** 104, 303; **Supp. XV:** 338; **Supp. XVI:**158

Brontë, Emily, **I:** 458; **Retro. Supp. I:** 43; **Supp. IV Part 2:** 430; **Supp. IX:** 128; **Supp. X:** 78, 89; **Supp. XV:** 338

"Bronze" (Francis), **Supp. IX:** 76

"Bronze" (Merrill), **Supp. III Part 1:** 336

Bronze Booklets on the History, Problems, and Cultural Contributions of the Negro series, **Supp. XIV:**202

"Bronze Buckaroo, The" (Baraka), **Supp. II Part 1:** 49

"Bronze Horses, The" (Lowell), **II:** 524

"Bronze Tablets" (Lowell), **II:** 523

Bronzeville Boys and Girls (Brooks), **Supp. III Part 1:** 79

"Bronzeville Mother Loiters in Mississippi, A. Meanwhile, a Mississippi Mother Burns Bacon" (Brooks), **Supp. III Part 1:** 80

"Brooch, The" (Singer), **IV:** 20

Brook, Peter, **Retro. Supp. II:** 182

Brooke, Rupert, **II:** 82; **III:** 3

Brook Evans (Glaspell), **Supp. III Part 1:** 182–185

"Brooking Likeness" (Glück), **Supp. V:** 85

"Brooklyn" (Marshall), **Supp. XI:** 281, 282

Brooks, Cleanth, **I:** 280, 282; **III:** 517; **IV:** 236, 279; **Retro. Supp. I:** 40, 41, 90; **Retro. Supp. II:** 235; **Supp. I Part 2:** 423; **Supp. III Part 2:** 542; **Supp. V:** 316; **Supp. IX:** 153, 155; **Supp. X:** 115, 123; **Supp. XIV:**1–20

Brooks, David, **Supp. IV Part 2:** 623, 626, 630; **Supp. VIII:** 232

Brooks, Gwendolyn, **Retro. Supp. I:** 208; **Supp. III Part 1:** 69–90; **Supp. IV Part 1:** 2, 15, 244, 251, 257; **Supp. XI:** 1, 278; **Supp. XIII:** 111, 112, 296; **Supp. XIV:**73

Brooks, Mel, **Supp. IV Part 1:** 390; **Supp. IV Part 2:** 591

Brooks, Mrs. Van Wyck (Eleanor Kenyon Stimson), **I:** 240, 245, 250, 252

Brooks, Mrs. Van Wyck (Gladys Billings), **I:** 258

Brooks, Paul, **Supp. IX:** 26, 31, 32

Brooks, Phillips, **II:** 542; **Retro. Supp. II:** 134; **Supp. XIII:** 142

Brooks, Van Wyck, **I:** 106, 117, 215, 222, 228, 230, 231, 233, 236, 239–263, 266, 480; **II:** 30, 271, 285, 309, 337, 482; **III:** 394, 606; **IV:** 171, 312, 427, 433; **Retro. Supp. II:** 46, 137; **Supp. I Part 2:** 423, 424, 650; **Supp. II Part 1:** 137; **Supp. VIII:** 98, 101; **Supp. XIV:**11; **Supp. XV:** 298, 301

Broom of the System, The (Wallace),

Supp. X: 301, 302–305, 310

"Brooms" (Simic), **Supp. VIII:** 275

Brosnan, Jim, **II:** 424–425

Brother Carl (Sontag), **Supp. III Part 2:** 452

"Brother Death" (Anderson), **I:** 114

Brotherhood of the Grape, The (Fante), **Supp. XI:** 160, 171–172

"Brothers" (Anderson), **I:** 114

Brothers, The (F. Barthelme), **Supp. XI:** 25, 28, 29, 30, 32–33

Brothers and Keepers (Wideman), **Supp. X:** 320, 321–322, 323, 325–327, 328, 329–330, 331, 332

Brothers Ashkenazi, The (Singer), **IV:** 2

Brothers Karamazov, The (Dostoyevsky), **II:** 60; **III:** 146, 150, 283; **Supp. IX:** 102, 106; **Supp. XI:** 172; **Supp. XII:** 322

Brother to Dragons: A Tale in Verse and Voices (Warren), **IV:** 243–244, 245, 246, 251, 252, 254, 257

Broughton, James, **Supp. XV:** 146

Broughton, Rhoda, **II:** 174; **IV:** 309, 310

Broun, Heywood, **I:** 478; **II:** 417; **IV:** 432; **Supp. IX:** 190

Broussais, François, **Supp. I Part 1:** 302

Browder, Earl, **I:** 515

Brower, David, **Supp. X:** 29

Brower, Reuben, **Supp. XV:** 20

Brown, Alice, **II:** 523; **Retro. Supp. II:** 136

Brown, Andrew, **Supp. XVI:**150

Brown, Ashley, **Retro. Supp. II:** 48; **Supp. I Part 1:** 79, 80, 82, 84, 92

Brown, Charles Brockden, **I:** 54, 211, 335; **II:** 74, 267, 298; **III:** 415; **Supp. I Part 1:** 124–149; **Supp. II Part 1:** 65, 292

Brown, Clifford, **Supp. V:** 195

Brown, Dee, **Supp. IV Part 2:** 504

Brown, Elijah, **Supp. I Part 1:** 125

Brown, George Douglas, **III:** 473

Brown, Harry, **Supp. IV Part 2:** 560

Brown, Harvey, **Supp. XIV:**148

Brown, John, **II:** 13; **IV:** 125, 126, 172, 237, 249, 254; **Supp. I Part 1:** 345; **Supp. VIII:** 204

Brown, Joseph Epes, **Supp. IV Part 2:** 487

Brown, Leonard, **Supp. IX:** 117

Brown, Mary Armitt, **Supp. I Part 1:** 125

Brown, Mrs. Charles Brockden (Elizabeth Linn), **Supp. I Part 1:** 145, 146

Brown, Percy, **II:** 20

Brown, Robert E., **Supp. X:** 12

Brown, Scott, **Supp. XI:** 178

Brown, Slater, **IV:** 123; **Retro. Supp. II:** 79

Brown, Solyman, **Supp. I Part 1:** 156

Brown, Sterling, **Retro. Supp. I:** 198; **Supp. IV Part 1:** 169; **Supp. XIV:**202

Brown: The Last Discovery of America (Rodriguez), **Supp. XIV:**297, 298, 300, 305–309, 310, 311–312

Brown, Tina, **Supp. XVI:**176–177

Brown, Wesley, **Supp. V:** 6

Brown Decades, The (Mumford), **Supp. II Part 2:** 475, 478, 491–492

Brown Dog (Harrison), **Supp. VIII:** 51

Brown Dog of the Yaak: Essays on Art and Activism (Bass), **Supp. XVI:**22

"Brown Dwarf of Rügen, The" (Whittier), **Supp. I Part 2:** 696

Browne, Charles Farrar, **II:** 289; **IV:** 193, 196

Browne, Roscoe Lee, **Supp. VIII:** 345

Browne, Thomas, **II:** 15–16, 304; **III:** 77, 78, 198, 487; **IV:** 147; **Supp. IX:** 136; **Supp. XII:** 45; **Supp. XVI:**292

Browne, William, **Supp. I Part 1:** 98

Brownell, W. C., **II:** 14

Brownell, William Crary, **Retro. Supp. I:** 365, 366

Brown Girl, Brownstones (Marshall), **Supp. XI:** 275, 276, 278–280, 282

Brownies' Book, The (Hughes), **Supp. I Part 1:** 321

Browning, Elizabeth Barrett, **I:** 458, 459; **Retro. Supp. I:** 33, 43

Browning, Robert, **I:** 50, 66, 103, 458, 460, 468; **II:** 338, 478, 522; **III:** 5, 8, 467, 469, 484, 511, 521, 524, 606, 609; **IV:** 135, 245, 366, 416; **Retro. Supp. I:** 43, 55, 217; **Retro. Supp. II:** 188, 190; **Supp. I Part 1:** 2, 6, 79, 311; **Supp. I Part 2:** 416, 468, 622; **Supp. III Part 1:** 5, 6; **Supp. IV Part 2:** 430; **Supp. X:** 65; **Supp. XV:** 92, 250, 275

Brownmiller, Susan, **Supp. X:** 252

"Brown River, Smile" (Toomer), **Supp. IV Part 1:** 16

Brownstone Eclogues and Other Poems (Aiken), **I:** 65, 67

Broyard, Anatole, **Supp. IV Part 1:** 39; **Supp. VIII:** 140; **Supp. X:** 186; **Supp. XI:** 348; **Supp. XVI:**213

Bruccoli, Matthew, **Retro. Supp. I:** 98, 102, 105, 114, 115, 359; **Supp. IV Part 2:** 468, 470

Bruce, John Edward, **Supp. XVI:**143

Bruce, Lenny, **Supp. VIII:** 198

Bruce, Virginia, **Supp. XII:** 173

Bruce-Novoa, Juan, **Supp. VIII:** 73, 74

Bruchac, Joseph, **Supp. IV Part 1:** 261, 319, 320, 321, 322, 323, 325, 328, 398, 399, 403, 408, 414; **Supp. IV Part 2:** 502, 506

Brueghel, Pieter, **I:** 174; **Supp. I Part 2:** 475

Brueghel, Pieter, the Elder, **Retro. Supp. I:** 430

Bruell, Edwin, **Supp. VIII:** 126

Brugh, Spangler Arlington. See Taylor, Robert

"Bruja: Witch" (Mora), **Supp. XIII:** 214, 220, 221, **Supp. XIII:** 222

Brulé, Claude, **Supp. XI:** 307

Brumer, Andy, **Supp. XIII:** 88

Brunner, Emil, **III:** 291, 303

Brustein, Robert, **Supp. VIII:** 331

Brutus, **IV:** 373, 374; **Supp. I Part 2:** 471

"Brutus and Antony" (Masters), **Supp. I Part 2:** 472

"Bryan, Bryan, Bryan, Bryan" (Lindsay), **Supp. I Part 2:** 394, 395, 398

Bryan, George, **Retro. Supp. II:** 76

Bryan, Sharon, **Supp. IX:** 154

Bryan, William Jennings, **I:** 483; **IV:** 124; **Supp. I Part 2:** 385, 395–396, 455, 456

Bryant, Austin, **Supp. I Part 1:** 152, 153

Bryant, Frances, **Supp. I Part 1:** 153

Bryant, Louise, **Supp. X:** 136

Bryant, Mrs. William Cullen (Frances Fairchild), **Supp. I Part 1:** 153, 169

Bryant, Peter, **Supp. I Part 1:** 150, 151, 152, 153. *See also* George, Peter

Bryant, William Cullen, **I:** 335, 458; **II:** 311; **III:** 81; **IV:** 309; **Retro. Supp. I:** 217; **Retro. Supp. II:** 155; **Supp. I Part 1:** 150–173, 312, 362; **Supp. I Part 2:** 413, 416, 420; **Supp. IV Part 1:** 165; **Supp. XIII:** 145

Bryer, Jackson R., **Supp. IV Part 2:** 575, 583, 585, 586, 589, 591; **Supp. XIII:** 200, **Supp. XIII:** 205

Bryher, Jackson R. (pseudonym). *See* Ellerman, Winifred

"Bubbs Creek Haircut" (Snyder), **Supp. VIII:** 306

Buber, Martin, **II:** 228; **III:** 45, 308, 528; **IV:** 11; **Supp. I Part 1:** 83, 88; **Supp. XVI:**291

Buccaneers, The (Wharton), **IV:** 327; **Retro. Supp. I:** 382

Buchanan Dying (Updike), **Retro. Supp. I:** 331, 335

Buchbinder, David, **Supp. XIII:** 32

Buchwald, Art, **Supp. XII:** 124–125; **Supp. XVI:**110–111

Buchwald, Emilie, **Supp. XVI:**35, 36

Buck, Dudley, **Supp. I Part 1:** 362

Buck, Gene, **II:** 427

Buck, Pearl S., **Supp. II Part 1:** 113–134; **Supp. XIV:**274

"Buckdancer's Choice" (Dickey), **Supp. IV Part 1:** 191

Buckdancer's Choice (Dickey), **Supp. IV Part 1:** 176, 177, 178, 180

Bucke, Richard Maurice, **Retro. Supp. I:** 407

"Buck Fever" (Humphrey), **Supp. IX:** 109

"Buck in the Snow, The" (Millay), **III:** 135

Buckley, Christopher, **Supp. IX:** 169; **Supp. XI:** 257, 329; **Supp. XV:** 76–77, 86

Buckminster, Joseph, **Supp. II Part 1:** 66–67, 69

Bucknell, Katherine, **Supp. XIV:**170

Bucolics (Auden), **Supp. II Part 1:** 21, 24

Budd, Louis J., **IV:** 210

Buddha, **I:** 136; **II:** 1; **III:** 173, 179, 239, 567; **Supp. I Part 1:** 363; **Supp. I Part 2:** 397

"Buddha's Last Instruction, The" (Oliver), **Supp. VII:** 239

Budding Prospects: A Pastoral (Boyle), **Supp. VIII:** 8–9

Buechner, Frederick, **III:** 310; **Supp. XII:** 41–59

Buell, Lawrence, **Supp. V:** 209; **Supp. IX:** 29; **Supp. XV:** 269, 282

"Buffalo, The" (Moore), **III:** 215

"Buffalo Bill." *See* Cody, William

Buffalo Girls (McMurtry), **Supp. V:** 229

Buffalo Girls (screenplay) (McMurtry), **Supp. V:** 232

Buffett, Jimmy, **Supp. VIII:** 42

Buffon, Comte de, **II:** 101

Buford, Fanny McConnell, **Retro. Supp. II:** 117

Bugeja, Michael, **Supp. X:** 201

Bugged for Murder (Lacy), **Supp. XV:** 205

"Buglesong" (Stegner), **Supp. IV Part 2:** 606

"Buick" (Shapiro), **Supp. II Part 2:** 705

"Builders" (Yates), **Supp. XI:** 342–343

Builders, The (Glasgow), **II:** 183–184, 193

"Builders, The" (Hay), **Supp. XIV:**125

Builders of the Bay Colony (Morison), **Supp. I Part 2:** 484–485

"Builders of the Bridge, The" (Mumford), **Supp. II Part 2:** 475

"Building" (Snyder), **Supp. VIII:** 305

"Building, Dwelling, Thinking" (Heidegger), **Retro. Supp. II:** 87

Building a Character (Stanislavsky), **Supp. XIV:**243

"Building of the Ship, The" (Longfellow), **II:** 498; **Retro. Supp. II:** 159, 167, 168

"Build Soil" (Frost), **Retro. Supp. I:** 138, 139

"Build Soil" (Snyder), **Supp. VIII:** 304

Build-Up, The (W. C. Williams), **Retro. Supp. I:** 423

Bukowski, Charles, **Supp. III Part 1:** 147; **Supp. XI:** 159, 161, 172, 173

Bulgakov, Mikhail, **Supp. XIV:**97

"Bulgarian Poetess, The" (Updike), **IV:** 215, 227; **Retro. Supp. I:** 329

Bull, Ole, **II:** 504

"Bulldozer, The" (Francis), **Supp. IX:** 87

"Bullet in the Brain" (Wolff), **Supp. VII:** 342–343

Bullet Park (Cheever), **Supp. I Part 1:** 185, 187–193, 194, 195

Bullets over Broadway (film; Allen), **Supp. XV:** 12, 12–13

Bullfight, The (Mailer), **Retro. Supp. II:** 205

Bullins, Ed, **Supp. II Part 1:** 34, 42

Bullock, Sandra, **Supp. X:** 80

"Bull-Roarer, The" (Stern), **Supp. IX:** 297

"Bully, The" (Dubus), **Supp. VII:** 84

"Bulsh" (X. J. Kennedy), **Supp. XV:** 161

Bultmann, Rudolf, **III:** 309

Bulwark, The (Dreiser), **I:** 497, 506, 516–517; **Retro. Supp. II:** 95, 96, 105, 108

Bulwer-Lytton, Edward George, **IV:** 350

"Bums in the Attic" (Cisneros), **Supp. VII:** 62

Bunche, Ralph, **Supp. I Part 1:** 343; **Supp. XIV:**202

"Bunchgrass Edge of the World, The" (Proulx), **Supp. VII:** 263

"Bunner Sisters, The" (Wharton), **IV:** 317

Bunting, Basil, **Retro. Supp. I:** 422; **Supp. III Part 2:** 616, 620, 624; **Supp. XIV:**286

Buñuel, Luis, **III:** 184; **Retro. Supp. II:** 337

Bunyan, John, **I:** 445; **II:** 15, 104, 228; **IV:** 80, 84, 156, 437; **Supp. I Part 1:** 32

Burana, Lily, **Supp. XI:** 253

Burbank, Luther, **I:** 483

Burbank, Rex, **IV:** 363

Burchfield, Alice, **Supp. I Part 2:** 652, 660

Burden of Southern History, The (Woodward), **Retro. Supp. I:** 75

Burdens of Formality, The (Lea, ed.), **Supp. X:** 58

Burger, Gottfried August, **II:** 306

Burgess, Anthony, **Supp. IV Part 1:** 227; **Supp. IV Part 2:** 685; **Supp. V:** 128

Burgh, James, **Supp. I Part 2:** 522

"Burglar of Babylon, The" (Bishop), **Retro. Supp. II:** 47; **Supp. I Part 1:** 93

Burgum, E. B., **IV:** 469, 470

Buried Child (Shepard), **Supp. III Part 2:** 433, 447, 448; **Supp. XIV:**327

"Buried Lake, The" (Tate), **IV:** 136

Burke, Edmund, **I:** 9; **III:** 310; **Supp. I Part 2:** 496, 511, 512, 513, 523; **Supp. II Part 1:** 80

Burke, James Lee, **Supp. XIV:**21–38

Burke, Kenneth, **I:** 264–287, 291; **III:** 497, 499, 546; **IV:** 123, 408; **Retro. Supp. I:** 297; **Retro. Supp. II:** 117, 120; **Supp. I Part 2:** 630; **Supp. II Part 1:** 136; **Supp. VIII:** 105; **Supp. IX:** 229; **Supp. XIV:**3

Burley, Justin, **Supp. XVI:**158

"Burly Fading One, The" (Hayden), **Supp. II Part 1:** 366

"Burned" (Levine), **Supp. V:** 186, 192

"Burned Diary, The" (Olds), **Supp. X:** 215

Burnett, David, **Supp. XI:** 299

Burnett, Frances Hodgson, **Supp. I Part 1:** 44

Burnett, Whit, **III:** 551; **Supp. XI:** 294

Burney, Fanny, **Supp. XV:** 232

Burnham, James, **Supp. I Part 2:** 648

Burnham, John Chynoweth, **I:** 59

"Burning, The" (Welty), **IV:** 277–278; **Retro. Supp. I:** 353

Burning Angel (Burke), **Supp. XIV:**30, 32

Burning Bright (Steinbeck), **IV:** 51, 61–62

Burning Bush (Untermeyer), **Supp. XV:** 309

"Burning Bush" (Untermeyer), **Supp. XV:** 309

Burning Chrome (W. Gibson), **Supp. XVI:**118, 122, 128

"Burning Chrome" (W. Gibson), **Supp. XVI:**117, 120, 123, 124, 128

Burning City (Benét), **Supp. XI:** 46, 58

Burning Daylight (London), **II:** 474, 481

Burning House, The (Beattie), **Supp. V:** 29

"Burning Ladder, The" (Gioia), **Supp. XV:** 118

Burning Mystery of Anna in 1951, The (Koch), **Supp. XV:** 182–183

"Burning of Paper Instead of Children, The" (Rich), **Supp. I Part 2:** 558

Burning the Days: Recollections (Salter), **Supp. IX:** 245, 246, 248, 260, 261–262

"Burning the Small Dead" (Snyder), **Supp. VIII:** 298

Burns, David, **III:** 165–166

Burns, Ken, **Supp. XIV:**14

Burns, Michael, **Supp. XV:** 339

Burns, Robert, **II:** 150, 306; **III:** 592; **IV:** 453; **Supp. I Part 1:** 158; **Supp. I Part 2:** 410, 455, 683, 685, 691, 692; **Supp. IX:** 173; **Supp. XII:** 171; **Supp. XIII:** 3

Burnshaw, Stanley, **Retro. Supp. I:** 298, 303; **Supp. III Part 2:** 615

"Burn the Cities" (West), **Retro. Supp. II:** 338

Burnt Norton (Eliot), **I:** 575, 580–581, 582, 584, 585; **III:** 10

"Burnt Norton" (Eliot), **Retro. Supp. I:** 66; **Supp. XV:** 216

Burnt-Out Case, A (Greene), **Supp. VIII:** 4

"Burnt-out Spa, The" (Plath), **Retro. Supp. II:** 246

Burr, Aaron, **I:** 7, 549, 550; **II:** 300; **IV:** 264; **Supp. I Part 2:** 461, 483

Burr: A Novel (Vidal), **Supp. IV Part 2:** 677, 682, 684, 685, 687, 688, 689, 691

Burr Oaks (Eberhart), **I:** 533, 535

Burroughs, Edgar Rice, **Supp. IV Part 1:** 101

Burroughs, John, **I:** 220, 236, 506; **IV:** 346; **Supp. IX:** 171

Burroughs, William S., **III:** 45, 174, 258; **Supp. II Part 1:** 320, 328; **Supp. III Part 1:** 91–110, 217, 226; **Supp. IV Part 1:** 79, 87, 90; **Supp. XI:** 297, 308; **Supp. XII:** 1, 3, 118, 121, 124, 129, 131, 136; **Supp. XIV:**137, 140–141, 143–144, 150; **Supp. XVI:**123, 135

Burrow, Trigant, **Supp. II Part 1:** 6

Burrows, Ken, **Supp. V:** 115

Burson, Claudia, **Supp. XV:** 343

Burt, Stephen, **Supp. XV:** 341, 342, 345, 347, 351

Burt, Steve, **Supp. V:** 83

Burtis, Thomson, **Supp. XIII:** 163

Burton, Robert, **II:** 535; **III:** 77, 78; **Supp. I Part 1:** 349

Burton, William Evans, **III:** 412

"Burying Ground by the Ties" (MacLeish), **III:** 14

Bury My Heart at Wounded Knee (Brown), **Supp. IV Part 2:** 504

Bury the Dead (Shaw), **IV:** 381

"Bus Along St. Clair: December, A" (Atwood), **Supp. XIII:** 33

Busch, Frederick, **Supp. X:** 78; **Supp. XII:** 343

Bush, Barney, **Supp. XII:** 218, 222

Bush, Douglas, **Supp. I Part 1:** 268; **Supp. XIV:**10

"Busher Comes Back, The" (Lardner), **II:** 422

"Busher's Letters Home, A" (Lardner), **II:** 418–419, 421

"Business and Poetry" (Gioia), **Supp. XV:** 113, 115

"Business Deal" (West), **IV:** 287

"Business Man, A" (Jewett), **Retro. Supp. II:** 132

Buss, Helen M., **Supp. IV Part 1:** 12

Butcher, Margaret Just, **Supp. XIV:**203

"Butcher, The" (Southern), **Supp. XI:** 294

"Butcher Shop" (Simic), **Supp. VIII:** 273

But Gentlemen Marry Brunettes (Loos), **Supp. XVI:**190–191

Butler, Benjamin, **I:** 457

Butler, Dorothy. *See* Farrell, Mrs. James T. (Dorothy Butler)

Butler, Elizabeth, **Supp. I Part 1:** 260

Butler, Ethel, **Supp. XIV:**125

Butler, James D., **Supp. IX:** 175

Butler, Joseph, **II:** 8, 9

Butler, Judith, **Supp. XII:** 6

Butler, Maud. *See* Falkner, Mrs. Murray C. (Maud Butler)

Butler, Nicholas Murray, **I:** 223; **Supp. I Part 1:** 23; **Supp. III Part 2:** 499

Butler, Octavia, **Supp. XIII:** 59–72

Butler, Robert Olen, **Supp. XII:** 61–78, 319

Butler, Samuel, **II:** 82, 86; **IV:** 121, 440; **Supp. VIII:** 171

Butler-Evans, Elliot, **Retro. Supp. II:** 121

"But Only Mine" (Wright), **Supp. III Part 2:** 595

Butscher, Edward, **Supp. I Part 2:** 526

Butter Battle Book, The (Geisel), **Supp. XVI:**110

"Buttercups" (Lowell), **Retro. Supp. II:** 187

Butterfield 8 (O'Hara), **III:** 361

Butterfield, R. W., **I:** 386

Butterfield, Stephen, **Supp. IV Part 1:** 3, 11

Butterfly (Harvey), **Supp. XIII:** 184

"Butterfly, The" (Brodksy), **Supp. VIII:** 26

"Butterfly and the Traffic Light, The" (Ozick), **Supp. V:** 263, 265

"Butterfly-toed Shoes" (Komunyakaa), **Supp. XIII:** 126

Butter Hill and Other Poems (Francis), **Supp. IX:** 88, 89

Buttons, Red, **Supp. IV Part 2:** 574

Buttrick, George, **III:** 301; **Supp. XII:** 47–48

"But What Is the Reader to Make of This?" (Ashbery), **Supp. III Part 1:** 25

Butz, Earl, **Supp. X:** 35

"Buz" (Alcott), **Supp. I Part 1:** 43

By Avon River (Doolittle), **Supp. I Part 1:** 272

"By Blue Ontario's Shore" (Whitman), **Retro. Supp. I:** 399, 400

"By Disposition of Angels" (Moore), **III:** 214

"By Earth" (Olds), **Supp. X:** 214

"By Fire" (Olds), **Supp. X:** 214

Bygones (Untermeyer), **Supp. XV:** 304, 308–309, 312, 313

By Land and by Sea (Morison), **Supp. I Part 2:** 492

By-Line: Ernest Hemingway (Hemingway), **II:** 257–258

By Love Possessed (Cozens), **I:** 358, 365, 372–374, 375, 376, 377, 378, 379

"By Morning" (Swenson), **Supp. IV Part 2:** 642

"By Night" (Francis), **Supp. IX:** 76

Bynner, Witter, **II:** 513, 527; **Supp. XIII:** 347; **Supp. XV:** 39–54

Byrd, William, **Supp. IV Part 2:** 425

Byrne, Donn, **IV:** 67

Byron, George Gordon, Lord, **I:** 343, 568, 577; **II:** 135, 193, 296, 301, 303, 310, 315, 331, 566; **III:** 82, 137, 170, 409, 410, 412, 469; **IV:** 245, 435; **Supp. I Part 1:** 150, 312, 349; **Supp. I Part 2:** 580, 591, 683, 685, 719; **Supp. XIII:** 139; **Supp. XVI:**188, 203, 206, 210

"Byron's Cain" (L. Michaels), **Supp. XVI:**203

"Bystanders" (Matthews), **Supp. IX:** 160

By the Bias of Sound (Sobin), **Supp. XVI:**281

By the North Gate (Oates), **Supp. II Part 2:** 504

"By the Waters of Babylon" (Benét), **Supp. XI:** 56, 58

By the Waters of Manhattan (Reznikoff), **Supp. XIV:**288, 293, 294

By the Waters of Manhattan: An Annual (Reznikoff), **Supp. XIV:**277, 280, 289

By the Waters of Manhattan: Selected Verse (Reznikoff), **Supp. XIV:**281, 291

By the Well of Living and Seeing: New and Selected Poems 1918–1973 (Reznikoff), **Supp. XIV:**281, 287–288, 295

By the Well of Living and Seeing and the Fifth Book of the Maccabees (Reznikoff), **Supp. XIV:**281

By Way of Orbit (O'Neill), **III:** 405

C

"C 33" (H. Crane), **I:** 384; **Retro. Supp. II:** 76

Cabala, The (Wilder), **IV:** 356, 358–360, 369, 374

Cabaret (film), **Supp. XIV:**155, 162

Cabaret (play), **Supp. XIV:**162

Cabbages and Kings (O. Henry), **Supp. II Part 1:** 394, 409

Cabell, James Branch, **II:** 42; **III:** 394; **IV:** 67, 359, 360; **Retro. Supp. I:** 80; **Supp. I Part 2:** 613, 714, 718, 721; **Supp. X:** 223

"Cabin, The" (Carver), **Supp. III Part 1:** 137, 146

Cabin, The: Reminiscence and Diversions (Mamet), **Supp. XIV:**240

Cabinet of Dr. Caligari, The (film), **Retro. Supp. I:** 268

Cable, George Washington, **II:** 289; **Retro. Supp. II:** 65; **Supp. I Part 1:** 200; **Supp. II Part 1:** 198; **Supp. XIV:**63

Cables to the Ace; or, Familiar Liturgies of Misunderstanding (Merton), **Supp. VIII:** 208

Cabot, James, **II:** 14; **IV:** 173

Cabot, John, **Supp. I Part 2:** 496, 497

Cactus Flower (Barillet and Grédy), **Supp. XVI:**194

"Caddy's Diary, A" (Lardner), **II:** 421–422

Cadieux, Isabelle, **Supp. XIII:** 127

"Cadence" (Dubus), **Supp. VII:** 84–85

"Cadillac Flambé" (Ellison), **Retro.**

Supp. II: 119, 126; **Supp. II Part 1:** 248

Cadillac Jack (McMurtry), **Supp. V:** 225

Cadillac Jukebox (Burke), **Supp. XIV:**32

Cadle, Dean, **Supp. I Part 2:** 429

Cady, Edwin H., **II:** 272

"Caedmon" (Garrett), **Supp. VII:** 96–97

Caesar, Julius, **II:** 12, 502, 561–562; **IV:** 372, 373

Caesar, Sid, **Supp. IV Part 2:** 574, 591

"Cafeteria, The" (Singer), **Retro. Supp. II:** 316

Cage, John, **Supp. IV Part 1:** 84; **Supp. V:** 337, 341

"Cage and the Prairie: Two Notes on Symbolism, The" (Bewley), **Supp. I Part 1:** 251

Cage of Spines, A (Swenson), **Supp. IV Part 2:** 641–642, 647

Cagney, James, **Supp. IV Part 1:** 236; **Supp. XIII:** 174

Cagney, William, **Supp. XIII:** 174

Cahalan, James, **Supp. XIII:** 1, 2, 3, 4, 12

Cahan, Abraham, **Supp. IX:** 227; **Supp. XIII:** 106

Cahill, Tim, **Supp. XIII:** 13

Cain, James M., **III:** 99; **Supp. IV Part 1:** 130; **Supp. XI:** 160; **Supp. XIII:** 159, 165

Cairns, Huntington, **III:** 103, 108, 114, 119

Cairo! Shanghai! Bombay! (Williams and Shapiro), **IV:** 380

Cake (Bynner), **Supp. XV:** 50

Cakes and Ale (Maugham), **III:** 64

Calabria, Frank, **Supp. XIII:** 164

Calamity Jane (Martha Jane Canary), **Supp. V:** 229–230; **Supp. X:** 103

"Calamus" (Whitman), **IV:** 342–343; **Retro. Supp. I:** 52, 403, 404, 407

Calasso, Roberto, **Supp. IV Part 1:** 301

Calderón, Hector, **Supp. IV Part 2:** 544

Caldwell, Christopher, **Supp. IV Part 1:** 211

Caldwell, Erskine, **I:** 97, 211, 288–311; **IV:** 286; **Supp. IV Part 2:** 601

Caldwell, Mrs. Erskine (Helen Lannegan), **I:** 289

Caldwell, Mrs. Erskine (Margaret Bourke-White), **I:** 290, 293–295, 297

Caldwell, Mrs. Erskine (Virginia Fletcher), **I:** 290

Caldwell, Reverend Ira Sylvester, **I:** 289, 305

Caldwell, Zoe, **Supp. XIII:** 207

Caleb Williams (Godwin), **III:** 415

"Calendar" (Creeley), **Supp. IV Part 1:** 158

Calendar of Saints for Unbelievers, A (Wescott), **Supp. XIV:**342

Calhoun, John C., **I:** 8; **III:** 309

"Caliban in the Coal Mines" (Untermeyer), **Supp. XV:** 296

"California" (Carruth), **Supp. XVI:**56

"California" (Didion), **Supp. IV Part 1:** 195

"California, This Is Minnesota Speaking" (Dunn), **Supp. XI:** 146

California and Oregon Trail, The (Parkman), **Supp. I Part 2:** 486

"California Hills in August" (Gioia), **Supp. XV:** 118–119

Californians (Jeffers), **Supp. II Part 2:** 415, 418, 420

"California Oaks, The" (Winters), **Supp. II Part 2:** 798

"California Plush" (Bidart), **Supp. XV:** 23

"California Republic" (Didion), **Supp. IV Part 1:** 205

"California Requiem, A" (Gioia), **Supp. XV:** 126

California Suite (film), **Supp. IV Part 2:** 589

California Suite (Simon), **Supp. IV Part 2:** 581, 582

"Caligula" (Lowell), **II:** 554

Callahan, John F., **Retro. Supp. II:** 119, 126, 127

"Call at Corazón" (Bowles), **Supp. IV Part 1:** 82, 87

Calle, Sophia, **Supp. XII:** 22

"Called Back" (Kazin), **Supp. VIII:** 104

Calley, Captain William, **II:** 579

Calley, John, **Supp. XI:** 305

Callicott, J. Baird, **Supp. XIV:**184

Calligrammes (Apollinaire), **I:** 432

"Calling Jesus" (Toomer), **Supp. III Part 2:** 484

Calling Myself Home (Hogan), **Supp. IV Part 1:** 397, 399, 400, 401, 413

Call It Experience (Caldwell), **I:** 290–291, 297

"Call It Fear" (Harjo), **Supp. XII:** 220

Call It Sleep (H. Roth), **Supp. VIII:** 233; **Supp. IX:** 227, 228, 229–231; **Supp. XIII:** 106

"Call Letters: Mrs. V. B." (Angelou), **Supp. IV Part 1:** 15

Call Me Ishmael (Olson), **Supp. II Part 2:** 556

Call of the Gospel, The (Mather), **Supp. II Part 2:** 448

Call of the Wild, The (London), **II:** 466, 470–471, 472, 481

"Call of the Wild, The" (Snyder), **Supp. VIII:** 301

"Calloway's Code" (O. Henry), **Supp. II Part 1:** 404

"Call to Arms" (Mumford), **Supp. II Part 2:** 479

Call to Arms, The (film), **Retro. Supp. I:** 325

Calmer, Ned, **Supp. XI:** 219

Calvert, George H., **Supp. I Part 1:** 361

Calverton, V. F., **Supp. VIII:** 96

Calvin, John, **II:** 342; **IV:** 160, 490

Calvino, Italo, **Supp. IV Part 2:** 623, 678

Cambridge Edition of the Works of F. Scott Fitzgerald, The (Bruccoli, ed.), **Retro. Supp. I:** 115

"Cambridge Thirty Years Ago" (Lowell), **Supp. I Part 2:** 419

Cambridge University Press, **Retro. Supp. I:** 115

"Camellia Sabina" (Moore), **III:** 208, 215

"Cameo Appearance" (Simic), **Supp. VIII:** 283

Camera Obscura (Nabokov), **III:** 255

Cameron, Elizabeth, **I:** 10, 17

Cameron, Kenneth W., **II:** 16

Cameron, Peter, **Supp. XII:** 79–95

Cameron, Sharon, **Retro. Supp. I:** 43; **Retro. Supp. II:** 40

Camerson, Don, **I:** 10, 17

Camino, Léon Felipe, **Retro. Supp. II:** 89

Camino Real (T. Williams), **IV:** 382, 385, 386, 387, 388, 391, 392, 395, 398

Camões, Luiz Vaz de, **II:** 133; **Supp. I Part 1:** 94

"Camouflaging the Chimera" (Komunyakaa), **Supp. XIII:** 122–123

Camp, James, **Supp. XV:** 165

Camp, Walter, **II:** 423

Campana, Dino, **Supp. V:** 337

Campbell, Alan, **Supp. IV Part 1:** 353; **Supp. IX:** 196, 198, 201

Campbell, Alexander, **Supp. I Part 2:** 381, 395

Campbell, Donna, **Retro. Supp. II:** 139

Campbell, Helen, **Supp. XI:** 200, 206

Campbell, James, **Supp. XII:** 127

Campbell, James Edwin, **Supp. II Part 1:** 202

Campbell, Joanna (pseudo.). See Bly, Carol

Campbell, Joseph, **I:** 135; **IV:** 369, 370; **Supp. IX:** 245

Campbell, Lewis, **III:** 476

Campbell, Thomas, **II:** 8, 303, 314; **III:** 410; **Supp. I Part 1:** 309, 310

Campbell, Virginia, **Supp. XIII:** 114

Campbell (Hale), Janet, **Supp. IV Part 2:** 503

"Campers Leaving: Summer 1981" (Kenyon), **Supp. VII:** 169

"Camp Evergreen" (Kenyon), **Supp. VII:** 168

"Camping in Madera Canyon" (Swenson), **Supp. IV Part 2:** 649

Campion, Thomas, **I:** 439; **Supp. VIII:** 272

Camus, Albert, **I:** 53, 61, 292, 294, 494; **II:** 57, 244; **III:** 292, 306, 453; **IV:** 6, 211, 236, 442, 487; **Retro. Supp. I:** 73; **Retro. Supp. II:** 20; **Supp. I Part 2:** 621; **Supp. VIII:** 11, 195, 241; **Supp. XI:** 96; **Supp. XIII:** 74, 165, 233, 247

Camuto, Christopher, **Supp. V:** 212–213

Canada Fragrant with Resin, **Supp. XVI:**149

"Canadian Mosaic, The" (Beran), **Supp. XIII:** 25

"Canadians and Pottawatomies" (Sandburg), **III:** 592–593

"Can a Good Wife Be a Good Sport?" (T. Williams), **IV:** 380

"Canal, The: A Poem on the Application of Physical Science to Political Economy" (Barlow), **Supp. II Part 1:** 73

Canary, Martha Jane. See Calamity Jane (Martha Jane Canary)

"Canary for One, A" (Hemingway), **Retro. Supp. I:** 170, 189

Canary in a Cat House (Vonnegut), **Supp. II Part 2:** 758

"Canary in Bloom" (Dove), **Supp. IV Part 1:** 248

Canby, Henry Seidel, **IV:** 65, 363

"Cancer" (McClatchy), **Supp. XII:** 266

"Cancer Match, The" (Dickey), **Supp. IV Part 1:** 182

"Canción y Glosa" (Merwin), **Supp. III Part 1:** 342

Candide (Hellman), **I:** 28; **Supp. I Part 1:** 288–289, 292

Candide (Voltaire), **Supp. I Part 1:** 288–289; **Supp. XI:** 297; **Supp. XVI:**189

Candide (Voltaire; Wilbur, trans.),

Supp. III Part 2: 560

Candle in the Cabin, The (Lindsay), **Supp. I Part 2:** 398, 400

"Candles" (Plath), **Retro. Supp. II:** 248, 257

Candles in Babylon (Levertov), **Supp. III Part 1:** 283

Candles in the Sun (T. Williams), **IV:** 381

Candles of Your Eyes, The (Purdy), **Supp. VII:** 278

Candy (Southern), **Supp. XI:** 297, 298–299, 305

"Candy-Man Beechum" (Caldwell), **I:** 309

Cane (Toomer), **Supp. III Part 2:** 475, 481–486, 488; **Supp. IV Part 1:** 164, 168; **Supp. IX:** 305, 306, 307, 308–320

"Cane in the Corridor, The" (Thurber), **Supp. I Part 2:** 616

Canfield, Cass, **Supp. I Part 2:** 668

Canfield, Dorothy, **Retro. Supp. I:** 4, 11, 14, 18. *See also* Fisher, Dorothy Canfield

Can Grande's Castle (Lowell), **II:** 518, 524

"Canicula di Anna" (Carson), **Supp. XII:** 101–102

"Canis Major" (Frost), **Retro. Supp. I:** 137

Cannery Row (Steinbeck), **IV:** 50, 51, 64–65, 66, 68

Cannibal Galaxy, The (Ozick), **Supp. V:** 270

Cannibals and Christians (Mailer), **III:** 38–39, 40, 42; **Retro. Supp. II:** 203, 204, 205

Canning, George, **I:** 7, 8

Canning, Richard, **Supp. X:** 147

Cannon, Jimmy, **II:** 424

Cannon, Steve, **Retro. Supp. II:** 111

Cannon between My Knees, A (Gunn Allen), **Supp. IV Part 1:** 324

Canolle, Jean, **Supp. XVI:**194

"Canonization, The" (Donne), **Supp. XIV:**8

"Can Poetry Matter?" (Gioia), **Supp. XV:** 113, 114

Can Poetry Matter?: Essays on Poetry and American Culture (Gioia), **Supp. XV:** 112, 113–115

"Canso" (Merwin), **Supp. III Part 1:** 344

Can Such Things Be? (Bierce), **I:** 203, 204, 205, 209

Canterbury Tales (Chaucer), **II:** 504; **III:** 411; **IV:** 65

"Canto Amor" (Berryman), **I:** 173

Canto I (Pound), **III:** 469, 470; **Retro.**

Supp. I: 286

Canto II (Pound), **III:** 470

Canto III (Pound), **III:** 470

Canto IV (Pound), **III:** 470

Canto VIII (Pound), **III:** 472

Canto IX (Pound), **III:** 472

Canto X (Pound), **III:** 472

Canto XIII (Pound), **III:** 472

Canto XXXIX (Pound), **III:** 468

Canto LXV (Pound), **Retro. Supp. I:** 292

Canto LXXXI (Pound), **III:** 459; **Retro. Supp. I:** 293

Cantor, Lois, **Supp. IV Part 1:** 285

Cantos (Pound), **I:** 482; **III:** 13–14, 17, 457, 462, 463, 466, 467, 469–470, 472–473, 474, 475, 476, 492; **Retro. Supp. I:** 284, 292, 292–293, 293, 427; **Supp. I Part 1:** 272; **Supp. II Part 1:** 5; **Supp. II Part 2:** 420, 557, 564, 644; **Supp. IV Part 1:** 153; **Supp. V:** 343, 345; **Supp. VIII:** 305; **Supp. XIV:**55, 96; **Supp. XV:** 349

"Cantus Planis" (Pound), **III:** 466

Cantwell, Robert, **Retro. Supp. I:** 85; **Supp. VIII:** 96; **Supp. XIII:** 292

"Can You Carry Me" (O'Hara), **III:** 369

Canzoneri, Robert, **IV:** 114, 116

Canzoni (Pound), **Retro. Supp. I:** 286, 288, 413

"Cap" (Shaw), **Supp. IV Part 1:** 345

"Cape Breton" (Bishop), **Supp. I Part 1:** 92; **Supp. IX:** 45

Cape Cod (Thoreau), **II:** 540

"Cape Cod, Rome, and Jerusalem" (Chapman), **Supp. XIV:**55

Capitalism: The Unknown Ideal (Rand), **Supp. IV Part 2:** 518, 527, 531, 532

Caponi, Gena Dagel, **Supp. IV Part 1:** 95

Capote, Truman, **Supp. I Part 1:** 291, 292; **Supp. III Part 1:** 111–133; **Supp. III Part 2:** 574; **Supp. IV Part 1:** 198, 220; **Supp. VIII:** 105; **Supp. XII:** 43, 249; **Supp. XV:** 146; **Supp. XVI:**245–246

Capouya, Emile, **Supp. I Part 1:** 50

Cappetti, Carla, **Supp. IX:** 4, 8

Capra, Frank, **Supp. XVI:**102

Capra, Fritjof, **Supp. X:** 261

Capron, Marion, **Supp. IX:** 193

"Capsule History of Conservation, A" (Stegner), **Supp. IV Part 2:** 600

"Captain Carpenter" (Ransom), **III:** 491

Captain Craig (Robinson), **III:** 508, 523; **Supp. II Part 1:** 192

"Captain Jim's Friend" (Harte), **Supp. II Part 1:** 337

"Captain Jones's Invitation" (Freneau), **Supp. II Part 1:** 261

"Captain's Son, The" (Taylor), **Supp. V:** 314, 325, 327

"Captain's Wife, The" (Salter), **Supp. IX:** 261

"Capt Christopher Levett (of York)" (Olson), **Supp. II Part 2:** 576, 577

Captive Israel (Reznikoff), **Supp. XIV:**283

"Captivity and Restoration of Mrs. Mary Rowlandson, The" (Howe), **Supp. IV Part 2:** 419, 431, 434

"Captivity of the Fly" (MacLeish), **III:** 19

"Captured Goddess, The" (Lowell), **II:** 520

Caputi, Jane, **Supp. IV Part 1:** 334, 335

Caputo, Philip, **Supp. XI:** 234

Capuzzo, Michael, **Supp. XIII:** 254

Car (Crews), **Supp. XI:** 110–111

Carabi, Angels, **Supp. VIII:** 223; **Supp. XII:** 215

"Caramels" (Zinberg), **Supp. XV:** 195

"Caravaggio: Swirl & Vortex" (Levis), **Supp. XI:** 258, 269

Caravan (Bynner), **Supp. XV:** 50

Carby, Hazel B., **Supp. IV Part 1:** 13

"Carcassonne" (Faulkner), **Retro. Supp. I:** 81

Card, Antha E., **Supp. I Part 2:** 496

Cárdenas, Lupe, **Supp. IV Part 2:** 538, 539, 540

Cardinale, Ernesto, **Supp. XII:** 225

"Cardinal Ideograms" (Swenson), **Supp. IV Part 2:** 645

"Cards" (Beattie), **Supp. V:** 31

"Career Woman" (Hay), **Supp. XIV:**131

"Careful" (Carver), **Supp. III Part 1:** 138

Careful and Strict Enquiry into the Modern Prevailing Notions of That Freedom of Will, Which Is Supposed to be Essential to Moral Agency, Vertue and Vice, Reward and Punishment, Praise and Blame, A (Edwards), **I:** 549, 557, 558, 562

Carel: A Poem and Pilgrimage in the Holy Land (Melville), **III:** 92–93

"Carentan O Carentan" (Simpson), **Supp. IX:** 267

Carew, Thomas, **IV:** 453

Carey, Gary, **Supp. XVI:**186

Carey, Mathew, **Supp. XV:** 238

"Car Games" (Conroy), **Supp. XVI:**72

Cargill, Oscar, **Supp. II Part 1:** 117

Caribbean as Columbus Saw It (Morison and Obregon), **Supp. I Part 2:** 488

Caribou Rising: Defending the Porcupine Herd, Gwich-'in Culture, and the Arctic National Wildlife Refuge (Bass), **Supp. XVI:**27–28, 28

Carl, K. A., **III:** 475

"Carlos Who Died, and Left Only This, The" (Ríos), **Supp. IV Part 2:** 547

Carlotta (empress of Mexico), **Supp. I Part 2:** 457

Carl Sandburg (Golden), **III:** 579

Carlson, Susan L., **Supp. XV:** 323

Carlyle, Thomas, **I:** 103, 279; **II:** 5, 7, 11, 15–16, 17, 20, 145, 315; **III:** 82, 84, 85, 87; **IV:** 169, 182, 338, 350; **Retro. Supp. I:** 360, 408; **Supp. I Part 1:** 2, 349; **Supp. I Part 2:** 410, 422, 482, 485, 552

"Carma" (Toomer), **Supp. III Part 2:** 481–483; **Supp. IX:** 312–313

"Carmen de Boheme" (Crane), **I:** 384

Carmen Jones (film), **Supp. I Part 1:** 66

Carmina Burana, **Supp. X:** 63

Carnegie, Andrew, **I:** 483; **IV:** 192; **Supp. I Part 2:** 639, 644; **Supp. V:** 285

Carnegie, Dale, **Supp. I Part 2:** 608

"Carnegie Hall: Rescued" (Moore), **III:** 215

Carne-Ross, D. S., **Supp. I Part 1:** 268, 269

Carnes, Mark C., **Supp. X:** 14

"Carnets" poems (Sobin), **Supp. XVI:**286–287

Carnovsky, Morris, **III:** 154

Caroling Dusk: An Anthology of Verse by Negro Poets (Cullen), **Supp. IV Part 1:** 166, 169

"Carol of Occupations" (Whitman), **I:** 486

"Carpe Diem" (Frost), **Supp. XII:** 303

"Carpe Noctem, if You Can" (Thurber), **Supp. I Part 2:** 620

Carpenter, Dan, **Supp. V:** 250

Carpenter, David, **Supp. VIII:** 297

Carpenter, Frederic I., **II:** 20

Carpentered Hen and Other Tame Creatures, The (Updike), **IV:** 214; **Retro. Supp. I:** 320

Carpenter's Gothic (Gaddis), **Supp. IV Part 1:** 288, 289–291, 293, 294

Carr, Dennis W., **Supp. IV Part 2:** 560

Carr, Elias, **Supp. XIV:**57

Carr, Rosemary. *See* Benét, Rosemary

Carrall, Aaron, **Supp. IV Part 2:** 499

Carrel, Alexis, **IV:** 240

"Carrell/Klee/and Cosmos's Groom" (Goldbarth), **Supp. XII:** 183

"Carriage from Sweden, A" (Moore), **III:** 212

Carrie (King), **Supp. V:** 137

Carried Away (Harrison), **Supp. VIII:** 39

Carrier of Ladders (Merwin), **Supp. III Part 1:** 339, 346, 350–352, 356, 357

"Carriers of the Dream Wheel" (Momaday), **Supp. IV Part 2:** 481

Carriers of the Dream Wheel: Contemporary Native American Poetry (Niatum, ed.), **Supp. IV Part 2:** 484, 505

Carrington, Carroll, **I:** 199

"Carrion Spring" (Stegner), **Supp. IV Part 2:** 604

Carroll, Charles, **Supp. I Part 2:** 525

Carroll, Lewis, **I:** 432; **II:** 431; **III:** 181; **Supp. I Part 1:** 44; **Supp. I Part 2:** 622, 656; **Supp. XVI:**103

"Carrots, Noses, Snow, Rose, Roses" (Gass), **Supp. VI:** 87

Carrouges, Michel, **Supp. IV Part 1:** 104

"Carrousel, The" (Rilke), **III:** 558

Carruth, Hayden, **Supp. IV Part 1:** 66; **Supp. VIII:** 39; **Supp. IX:** 291; **Supp. XIII:** 112; **Supp. XIV:**273–274; **Supp. XVI:**45–61

Carruth, Joe-Anne McLaughlin, **Supp. XVI:**47

"Carry" (Hogan), **Supp. IV Part 1:** 412

"Carrying On" (Dunn), **Supp. XI:** 145

Cars of Cuba (García), **Supp. XI:** 190

Carson, Anne, **Supp. XII:** 97–116; **Supp. XV:** 252

Carson, Johnny, **Supp. IV Part 2:** 526

Carson, Rachel, **Supp. V:** 202; **Supp. IX:** 19–36; **Supp. X:** 99; **Supp. XVI:**36

Carson, Tom, **Supp. XI:** 227

Cart, Michael, **Supp. X:** 12

Carter, Elliott, **Supp. III Part 1:** 21

Carter, Hodding, **Supp. XIV:**2

Carter, Jimmy, **Supp. I Part 2:** 638; **Supp. XIV:**107

Carter, Marcia, **Supp. V:** 223

Carter, Mary, **Supp. IV Part 2:** 444

Carter, Stephen, **Supp. XI:** 220

Cartesian Sonata and Other Novellas (Gass), **Supp. VI:** 92–93

Cartier, Jacques, **Supp. I Part 2:** 496, 497

Cartier-Bresson, Henri, **Supp. VIII:** 98

"Cartographies of Silence" (Rich), **Supp. I Part 2:** 571–572

Cartwright, Louis, **Supp. XIV:**147, 149, 151

Carver, Raymond, **Supp. III Part 1:** 135–151; **Supp. IV Part 1:** 342; **Supp. V:** 22, 23, 220, 326; **Supp. VIII:** 15; **Supp. X:** 85, 167; **Supp. XI:** 26, 65, 116, 153; **Supp. XII:** 79, 139, 289, 294

Cary, Alice, **Retro. Supp. II:** 145; **Supp. XV:** 273

Cary, Phoebe, **Supp. XV:** 273

Cary, Richard, **Retro. Supp. II:** 132, 137

"Casabianca" (Bishop), **Retro. Supp. II:** 42; **Supp. I Part 1:** 86

Casablanca (film), **Supp. VIII:** 61; **Supp. XV:** 14

Case of Rape, A (C. Himes), **Supp. XVI:**143

Case of the Crushed Petunias, The (T. Williams), **IV:** 381

Case of the Officers of Excise (Paine), **Supp. I Part 2:** 503–504

Casey, John, **Supp. X:** 164

Cash, Arthur, **Supp. IV Part 1:** 299

Cashman, Nellie, **Supp. X:** 103

Casiero, Robert, **Supp. XIV:**167

Casino Royale (film), **Supp. XI:** 306–307

Caskey, William, **Supp. XIV:**166

"Cask of Amontillado, The" (Poe), **II:** 475; **III:** 413; **Retro. Supp. II:** 268, 269, 270, 273

Casper, Robert N., **Supp. XV:** 339, 347

Cassada (Salter), **Supp. IX:** 251–252

Cassady, Carolyn, **Supp. XIV:**150

Cassady, Neal, **Supp. II Part 1:** 309, 311; **Supp. XIV:**137, 144

"Cassandra Southwick" (Whittier), **Supp. I Part 2:** 693

Cassell, Verlin, **Supp. XI:** 315

Cassill, R. V., **Supp. V:** 323

Cassirer, Ernst, **I:** 265; **IV:** 87, 89

Cass Timberlane (Lewis), **II:** 455–456

Cast a Cold Eye (McCarthy), **II:** 566

Castaway (Cozzens), **I:** 363, 370, 374, 375, 379

"Caste in America" (Du Bois), **Supp. II Part 1:** 169

Castiglione, Baldassare, **I:** 279; **III:** 282

"Castilian" (Wylie), **Supp. I Part 2:** 714

Castillo, Ana, **Supp. XI:** 177

"Castle in Lynn, A" (McCarriston), **Supp. XIV:**265, 268

"Castles and Distances" (Wilbur), **Supp. III Part 2:** 550

Castle Sinister (Marquand), **III:** 58

Cast of Thousands (Loos), **Supp.**

XVI:192, 193, 195

Castro, Fidel, **II:** 261, 434

Cast the First Stone (C. Himes), **Supp. XVI:**135, 137–138

"Casual Incident, A" (Hemingway), **II:** 44

"Cat, The" (Matthews), **Supp. IX:** 157–158

Cat, You Better Come Home (Keillor), **Supp. XVI:**177

"Catbird Seat, The" (Thurber), **Supp. I Part 2:** 623

"Catch" (Francis), **Supp. IX:** 82

Catch-22 (Heller), **III:** 558; **Supp. IV Part 1:** 379, 380, 381–382, 383, 384–386, 387, 390, 391, 392, 393, 394; **Supp. V:** 244, 248; **Supp. XII:** 167–168

Catcher in the Rye, The (Salinger), **I:** 493; **III:** 551, 552, 553–558, 567, 571; **Retro. Supp. I:** 102; **Retro. Supp. II:** 222, 249; **Supp. I Part 2:** 535; **Supp. V:** 119; **Supp. VIII:** 242; **Supp. XI:** 65

"Catching Frogs" (Kenyon), **Supp. VII:** 170

catechism of d neoamerican hoodoo church (Reed), **Supp. X:** 240, 241

Catered Affair, The (film), **Supp. IV Part 2:** 683

"Cathay" (Goldbarth), **Supp. XII:** 185, 186

Cathay (Pound), **II:** 527; **Retro. Supp. I:** 289

Cathedral (Carver), **Supp. III Part 1:** 144–146; **Supp. XII:** 139

"Cathedral" (Carver), **Supp. III Part 1:** 144–145

Cathedral, The (Lowell), **Supp. I Part 2:** 407, 416–417

Cather, Willa, **I:** 312–334, 405; **II:** 96, 177, 404, 412; **III:** 453; **IV:** 190; **Retro. Supp. I:** 1–23, 355, 382; **Retro. Supp. II:** 71, 136; **Supp. I Part 2:** 609, 719; **Supp. IV Part 1:** 31; **Supp. VIII:** 101, 102, 263; **Supp. X:** 103; **Supp. XIII:** 253; **Supp. XIV:**112; **Supp. XV:** 40, 51; **Supp. XVI:**226

Catherine, Saint, **II:** 211

Catherine II, **Supp. I Part 2:** 433

Catholic Art and Culture (Watkin), **Retro. Supp. II:** 187

"Catholic Novelist in the Protestant South, The" (O'Connor), **Retro. Supp. II:** 223, 224

"Cathy Queen of Cats" (Cisneros), **Supp. VII:** 59

Cat Inside, The (Burroughs), **Supp. III Part 1:** 105

Cat in the Hat, The (Geisel), **Supp. XVI:**106–107, 112

Cat in the Hat Come Back, The (Geisel), **Supp. XVI:**107

"Cat in the Hat for President, The" (Coover), **Supp. V:** 44, 46–47

Cat in The Hat Songbook, The (Geisel), **Supp. XVI:**104

Cato, **II:** 114, 117

Cat on a Hot Tin Roof (T. Williams), **II:** 190; **IV:** 380, 382, 383, 386, 387, 389, 390, 391, 394, 395, 397–398

"Cat People: What Dr. Seuss Really Taught Us" (Menand), **Supp. XVI:**106

Cat's Cradle (Vonnegut), **Supp. II Part 2:** 758, 759, 767–768, 770, 771, 772; **Supp. V:** 1

Cat's Eye (Atwood), **Supp. XIII:** 29–30

"Cat's Meow, A" (Brodsky), **Supp. VIII:** 31

Cat's Quizzer, The (Geisel), **Supp. XVI:**111

"Catterskill Falls" (Bryant), **Supp. I Part 1:** 160

Catullus, **Supp. XII:** 2, 13, 112; **Supp. XV:** 23, 27, 35, 36

Catullus (Gai Catulli Veronensis Liber) (Zukofsky), **Supp. III Part 2:** 625, 627, 628, 629

"Catullus: *Carmina*" (Carson), **Supp. XII:** 112

"*Catullus: Excrucior*" (Bidart), **Supp. XV:** 32, 35

Catullus, Gaius Valerius, **I:** 381; **Supp. I Part 1:** 261; **Supp. I Part 2:** 728

"Cat Who Aspired to Higher Things, The" (X. J. Kennedy), **Supp. XV:** 163

Caudwell, Christopher, **Supp. X:** 112

"Caul, The" (Banks), **Supp. V:** 10–11

Cause for Wonder (Morris), **III:** 232–233

"Causerie" (Tate), **IV:** 129

Causes and Consequences (Chapman), **Supp. XIV:**41, 49, 51

"Causes of American Discontents before 1768, The" (Franklin), **II:** 120

Causley, Charles, **Supp. XV:** 117

Cavafy, Constantine P., **Supp. IX:** 275; **Supp. XI:** 119, 123

Cavalcade of America, The (radio program), **III:** 146

Cavalcanti (Pound, opera), **Retro. Supp. I:** 287

Cavalcanti, Guido, **I:** 579; **III:** 467; **Supp. III Part 2:** 620, 621, 622, 623

Cavalieri, Grace, **Supp. IV Part 2:** 630, 631

"Cavalry Crossing the Ford" (Whitman), **IV:** 347

"Cave, The" (Bass), **Supp. XVI:**23

Cave, The (Warren), **IV:** 255–256

Cavell, Stanley, **Retro. Supp. I:** 306–307, 309

Cavender's House (Robinson), **III:** 510

Caviare at the Funeral (Simpson), **Supp. IX:** 266, 276–277

"Cawdor" (Jeffers), **Supp. II Part 2:** 431

Caxton, William, **III:** 486

Cayton, Horace, **IV:** 475, 488

Cazamian, Louis, **II:** 529

Celan, Paul, **Supp. X:** 149; **Supp. XII:** 21, 110–111; **Supp. XVI:**284–285, 288

"Celebrated Jumping Frog of Calaveras County, The" (Twain), **IV:** 196

Celebrated Jumping Frog of Calaveras County, The, and Other Sketches (Twain), **IV:** 197

Celebration (Crews), **Supp. XI:** 103, 108

Celebration at Dark (W. J. Smith), **Supp. XIII:** 332

"Celebration for June 24th" (McGrath), **Supp. X:** 116

Celebration of the Sound Through (Sobin), **Supp. XVI:**284–285

Celebrations after the Death of John Brennan (X. J. Kennedy), **Supp. XV:** 165

Celebrity (film; Allen), **Supp. XV:** 11

"Celery" (Stein), **IV:** 43

"Celestial Games" (Conroy), **Supp. XVI:**72

"Celestial Globe" (Nemerov), **III:** 288

Celestial Navigation (Tyler), **Supp. IV Part 2:** 662–663, 671

"Celestial Railroad, The" (Hawthorne), **Retro. Supp. I:** 152; **Supp. I Part 1:** 188

Celibate Season, A (Shields), **Supp. VII:** 323, 324

Cellini (Shanley), **Supp. XIV:**316, 329–330

"Cemetery at Academy, California" (Levine), **Supp. V:** 182

Cemetery Nights (Dobyns), **Supp. XIII:** 85, 87, 89

"Censors As Critics: *To Kill a Mockingbird* As a Case Study" (May), **Supp. VIII:** 126

"Census-Taker, The" (Frost), **Retro. Supp. I:** 129

"Centaur, The" (Swenson), **Supp. IV Part 2:** 641

Centaur, The (Updike), **IV:** 214, 216, 217, 218, 219–221, 222; **Retro. Supp. I:** 318, 322, 324, 331, 336

"Centennial Meditation of Columbia, The" (Lanier), **Supp. I Part 1:** 362

Centeno, Agusto, **IV:** 375

"Centipede" (Dove), **Supp. IV Part 1:** 246

"Central Man, The" (Bloom), **Supp. IV Part 2:** 689

"Central Park" (Lowell), **II:** 552

Central Park (Wasserstein and Drattel), **Supp. XV:** 333

Central Park West (Allen), **Supp. XV:** 13

Century of Dishonor, A (Jackson), **Retro. Supp. I:** 31

"Cerebral Snapshot, The" (Theroux), **Supp. VIII:** 313

"Ceremonies" (Rukeyser), **Supp. VI:** 279

Ceremony (Silko), **Supp. IV Part 1:** 274, 333; **Supp. IV Part 2:** 557–558, 558–559, 559, 561–566, 570

Ceremony (Wilbur), **Supp. III Part 2:** 550–551

"Ceremony, The" (Harjo), **Supp. XII:** 230

"Ceremony, The—Anatomy of a Massacre" (E. Hoffman, play), **Supp. XVI:**160

Ceremony in Lone Tree (Morris), **III:** 229–230, 232, 238, 558

Ceremony of Brotherhood, A (Anaya and Ortiz, eds.), **Supp. IV Part 2:** 502

Cerf, Bennett, **III:** 405; **IV:** 288; **Retro. Supp. II:** 330; **Supp. XIII:** 172

"Certain Attention to the World, A" (Haines), **Supp. XII:** 201

Certain Distance, A (Francis), **Supp. IX:** 85

"Certain Music, A" (Rukeyser), **Supp. VI:** 273

Certain Noble Plays of Japan (Pound), **III:** 458

Certain People (Wharton), **Retro. Supp. I:** 382

"Certain Poets" (MacLeish), **III:** 4

"Certain Testimony" (Bausch), **Supp. VII:** 48

Certificate, The (Singer), **IV:** 1; **Retro. Supp. II:** 314–315

Cervantes, Lorna Dee, **Supp. IV Part 2:** 545

Cervantes, Miguel de, **I:** 130, 134; **II:** 8, 272, 273, 276, 289, 302, 310, 315; **III:** 113, 614; **IV:** 367; **Retro. Supp. I:** 91; **Supp. I Part 2:** 406; **Supp. V:** 277; **Supp. XIII:** 17

Césaire, Aimé, **Supp. X:** 132, 139; **Supp. XIII:** 114

"Cesarean" (Kenyon), **Supp. VII:** 173

Cézanne, Paul, **II:** 576; **III:** 210; **IV:** 26, 31, 407; **Supp. V:** 333, 341–342

Chabon, Michael, **Supp. XI:** 63–81; **Supp. XVI:**259

Chaboseau, Jean, **Supp. I Part 1:** 260

Chaikin, Joseph, **Supp. III Part 2:** 433, 436–437

"Chain, The" (Kumin), **Supp. IV Part 2:** 452

Chainbearer, The (Cooper), **I:** 351, 352–353

"Chain of Love, A" (Price), **Supp. VI:** 258–259, 260

Chains of Dew (Glaspell), **Supp. III Part 1:** 181

Challacombe, Robert Hamilton, **III:** 176

Challenge (Untermeyer), **Supp. XV:** 296, 303

"Challenge" (Untermeyer), **Supp. XV:** 296

Chalmers, George, **Supp. I Part 2:** 514, 521

"Chambered Nautilus, The" (Holmes), **Supp. I Part 1:** 254, 307, 312–313, 314

Chamberlain, John, **Supp. I Part 2:** 647; **Supp. IV Part 2:** 525

Chamberlain, Neville, **II:** 589; **Supp. I Part 2:** 664

Chamber Music (Joyce), **III:** 16

Chambers, Richard, **Supp. III Part 2:** 610, 611, 612

Chambers, Whittaker, **Supp. III Part 2:** 610; **Supp. IV Part 2:** 526; **Supp. XV:** 143

"Champ, The" (Zinberg), **Supp. XV:** 193

"Champagne Regions" (Ríos), **Supp. IV Part 2:** 553

"Champion" (Lardner), **II:** 420–421, 428, 430

Champion, Laurie, **Supp. VIII:** 128

Champollion-Figeac, Jean Jacques, **IV:** 426

"Chance" (Doolittle), **Supp. I Part 1:** 271

Chance, Frank, **II:** 418

Chance Acquaintance, A (Howells), **II:** 278

"Chanclas" (Cisneros), **Supp. VII:** 61

Chandler, Raymond, **Supp. III Part 1:** 91; **Supp. IV Part 1:** 119–138, 341, 344, 345; **Supp. IV Part 2:** 461, 464, 469, 470, 471, 472, 473; **Supp. XI:** 160, 228; **Supp. XII:** 307; **Supp. XIII:** 159, 233; **Supp.**

XIV:21; **Supp. XV:** 119; **Supp. XVI:**122

Chaney, "Professor" W. H., **II:** 463–464

Chang, Leslie C., **Supp. IV Part 1:** 72

"Change, The: Kyoto-Tokyo Express" (Ginsberg), **Supp. II Part 1:** 313, 329

Changed Man, A (Prose), **Supp. XVI:**261–262

Changeling (Middleton), **Retro. Supp. I:** 62

"Changeling, The" (Lowell), **Supp. I Part 2:** 409

"Changeling, The" (Whittier), **Supp. I Part 2:** 697

Change of World, A (Rich), **Supp. I Part 2:** 551, 552

"Changes of Mind" (Baker), **Supp. XIII:** 52

"Change the Joke and Slip the Yoke" (Ellison), **Retro. Supp. II:** 118

Changing Light at Sandover, The (Merrill), **Supp. III Part 1:** 318, 319, 323, 327, 332, 335–336; **Supp. XII:** 269–270; **Supp. XV:** 264

"Changing Same, The" (Baraka), **Supp. II Part 1:** 47, 51, 53

Changing the Bully Who Rules the World: Reading and Thinking about Ethics (C. Bly), **Supp. XVI:**32, 39–40, 41

Chanler, Mrs. Winthrop, **I:** 22; **IV:** 325

Channing, Carol, **IV:** 357

Channing, Edward, **Supp. I Part 2:** 479–480

Channing, Edward Tyrrel, **Supp. I Part 1:** 155; **Supp. I Part 2:** 422

Channing, William Ellery, **I:** 336; **II:** 224, 495; **IV:** 172, 173, 176, 177; **Retro. Supp. I:** 54; **Supp. I Part 1:** 103; **Supp. I Part 2:** 589

Channing, William Henry, **IV:** 178; **Supp. II Part 1:** 280, 285

Chanson de Roland, La, **I:** 13

"Chanson un Peu Naïve" (Bogan), **Supp. III Part 1:** 50–51

"Chanteuse" (Doty), **Supp. XI:** 119

"Chant for May Day" (Hughes), **Supp. I Part 1:** 331

Chants (Mora), **Supp. XIII:** 214–215

Chaos (Dove), **Supp. IV Part 1:** 243

"Chaperone, The" (Van Vechten), **Supp. II Part 2:** 728

Chaplin, Charles Spencer, **I:** 27, 32, 43, 386, 447; **III:** 403; **Supp. I Part 2:** 607; **Supp. IV Part 1:** 146; **Supp. IV Part 2:** 574

"Chaplinesque" (H. Crane), **Retro. Supp. II:** 79

"Chapman" (Rukeyser), **Supp. VI:** 273

Chapman, Abraham, **IV:** 485

Chapman, George, **Supp. I Part 2:** 422

Chapman, John (Johnny Appleseed), **Supp. I Part 2:** 397

Chapman, John Jay, **IV:** 436; **Supp. XIV:**39–56

Chapman, Stephen, **Supp. XIII:** 12

Chappell, Fred, **Supp. IV Part 1:** 69; **Supp. XI:** 317

Chapters in a Mythology: The Poetry of Sylvia Plath (Kroll), **Supp. I Part 2:** 541–543

Chapters on Erie (Adams and Adams), **Supp. I Part 2:** 644

Chapter Two (Simon), **Supp. IV Part 2:** 575, 586

"Chapter VI" (Hemingway), **II:** 252

Char, René, **Supp. XVI:**282

"Character" (Emerson), **II:** 6

"Character of Presidents, The" (Doctorow), **Supp. IV Part 1:** 224

"Character of Socrates, The" (Emerson), **II:** 8–9

Character of the Poet, The (Simpson), **Supp. IX:** 273, 275, 278

"Characters in Fiction" (McCarthy), **II:** 562

"Charades" (Moore), **Supp. X:** 178

"Charge It" (Fante), **Supp. XI:** 164–165

Charlatan, The (Singer), **IV:** 1

"Charles" (Jackson), **Supp. IX:** 125

Charles Goodnight: Cowman and Plainsman (Haley), **Supp. V:** 226

Charles Simic: Essays on the Poetry (Weigl), **Supp. VIII:** 269

Charles the Bold, Duke of Burgundy, **III:** 487

Charleville, Victoria Verdon, **Supp. I Part 1:** 200–201, 205, 206, 210

Charley's Aunt (B. Thomas), **II:** 138

Charlie Chan Is Dead: An Anthology of Contemporary Asian American Fiction (Hagedorn), **Supp. X:** 292

"Charlie Christian Story, The" (Ellison), **Retro. Supp. II:** 121

"Charlie Howard's Descent" (Doty), **Supp. XI:** 122

Charlotte: A Tale of Truth (Rowson), **Supp. I Part 1:** 128; **Supp. XV:** 234–235, 238. See also *Charlotte Temple* (Rowson)

Charlotte's Daughter; or, The Three Orphans (Rowson), **Supp. XV:** 246

Charlotte's Web (White), **Supp. I Part 2:** 655, 656, 658, 667, 670

Charlotte Temple (Rowson), **Supp.**

XV: 229, 238–239. See also *Charlotte: A Tale of Truth* (Rowson)

Charm, The (Creeley), **Supp. IV Part 1:** 139, 141, 144, 149–150

Charmed Life, A (McCarthy), **II:** 571–574

Charms for the Easy Life (Gibbons), **Supp. X:** 45, 47–48

Charnel Rose, The (Aiken), **I:** 50, 57, 62

Charon's Cosmology (Simic), **Supp. VIII:** 276–278

Charterhouse, The (Percy), **Supp. III Part 1:** 388

Charvat, William, **II:** 244

Chase, Mary Ellen, **Retro. Supp. II:** 243, 245

Chase, Richard, **IV:** 202, 443; **Retro. Supp. I:** 40, 395

Chase, Salmon P., **Supp. I Part 2:** 584

Chase, Stuart, **Supp. I Part 2:** 609

Chase, The (Foote), **Supp. I Part 1:** 281

"Chaste Land, The" (Tate), **IV:** 122

Château, The (Maxwell), **Supp. VIII:** 152, 160, 165–167, 168, 169

Chatham, Russell, **Supp. VIII:** 40

Chatterdon, The Black Death, and Meriwether Lewis (Reznikoff), **Supp. XIV:**288

Chatterton, Thomas, **Supp. I Part 1:** 349; **Supp. I Part 2:** 410, 716

Chatterton, Wayne, **Supp. IX:** 2, 4, 11–12

Chatwin, Bruce, **Supp. VIII:** 322

Chaucer, Geoffrey, **I:** 131; **II:** 11, 504, 516, 542, 543; **III:** 283, 411, 473, 492, 521; **Retro. Supp. I:** 135, 426; **Supp. I Part 1:** 356, 363; **Supp. I Part 2:** 422, 617; **Supp. V:** 259; **Supp. XII:** 197

Chauncy, Charles, **I:** 546–547; **IV:** 147

Chavez, César, **Supp. V:** 199

Chávez, Denise, **Supp. IV Part 2:** 544; **Supp. XI:** 316

Chavez, Lydia, **Supp. VIII:** 75

Chavkin, Allan, **Supp. IV Part 1:** 259

Chavkin, Nancy Feyl, **Supp. IV Part 1:** 259

Chayefsky, Paddy, **Supp. XI:** 306

Cheang, Shu Lea, **Supp. XI:** 20

"Cheat Takes Over" (Leopold), **Supp. XIV:**189

"Cheers" (Carver), **Supp. III Part 1:** 138

Cheetham, James, **Supp. I Part 2:** 521

Cheever, Benjamin Hale, **Supp. I Part 1:** 175

Cheever, David W., **Supp. I Part 1:** 304

Cheever, Ezekiel, **Supp. I Part 1:** 174, 193

Cheever, Federico, **Supp. I Part 1:** 175

Cheever, Fred, **Supp. I Part 1:** 174

Cheever, Frederick L., **Supp. I Part 1:** 174

Cheever, John, **Retro. Supp. I:** 116, 333, 335; **Supp. I Part 1:** 174–199; **Supp. V:** 23, 95; **Supp. VIII:** 151; **Supp. IX:** 114, 208; **Supp. XI:** 65, 66, 99; **Supp. XII:** 140; **Supp. XIV:**93; **Supp. XV:** 119, 142

Cheever, Mary Liley, **Supp. I Part 1:** 174

Cheever, Mrs. John (Mary Winternitz), **Supp. I Part 1:** 175

Cheever, Susan. *See* Cowley, Susan Cheever (Susan Cheever)

Cheever Evening, A (Gurney), **Supp. V:** 95

Chekhov, Anton, **I:** 52, 90; **II:** 27, 38, 44, 49, 198, 542; **III:** 362, 467; **IV:** 17, 53, 359, 446; **Retro. Supp. I:** 5, 355; **Retro. Supp. II:** 299; **Supp. I Part 1:** 196; **Supp. II Part 1:** 6; **Supp. IV Part 2:** 585; **Supp. V:** 265; **Supp. VIII:** 153, 332; **Supp. IX:** 260, 265, 274; **Supp. XI:** 66; **Supp. XII:** 94, 307; **Supp. XIII:** 79; **Supp. XIV:**87, 242; **Supp. XV:** 320, 329

"Chekhov's Sense of Writing as Seen Through His Letters" (Dobyns), **Supp. XIII:** 77–78

"Chemin de Fer" (Bishop), **Retro. Supp. II:** 41; **Supp. I Part 1:** 80, 85, 86

Cheney, Brainard, **Retro. Supp. II:** 229

Chenzira, Ayoka, **Supp. XI:** 19

Chéri (Colette; stage adaptation, Loos), **Supp. XVI:**194

Cherkovski, Neeli, **Supp. XII:** 118, 132, 134

Chernyshevski, Nikolai, **III:** 261, 262, 263; **Retro. Supp. I:** 269

Cherokee Lottery, The: A Sequence of Poems (W. J. Smith), **Supp. XIII:** 340–344

Cherry (Karr), **Supp. XI:** 239, 251–254

Cherry Orchard, The (Chekhov), **IV:** 359, 426; **Supp. VIII:** 153

Cheslock, Louis, **III:** 99, 118, 119

Chesnutt, Charles Waddell, **Supp. II Part 1:** 174, 193, 211; **Supp. IV Part 1:** 257; **Supp. XIV:**57–78

"Chess House, The" (Dixon), **Supp. XII:** 139

Chessman, Caryl, **Supp. I Part 2:** 446

Chester, Alfred, **Retro. Supp. II:** 111, 112; **Supp. X:** 192

Chesterfield, Lord, **II:** 36

Chesterton, Gilbert Keith, **I:** 226; **IV:** 432

Cheuse, Alan, **Supp. IV Part 2:** 570

Chevigny, Bell Gale, **Supp. XI:** 283

"Chicago" (Sandburg), **III:** 581, 592, 596; **Supp. III Part 1:** 71

Chicago (Shepard), **Supp. III Part 2:** 439

Chicago: City on the Make (Algren), **Supp. IX:** 1, 3

"*Chicago Defender* Sends a Man to Little Rock, The" (Brooks), **Supp. III Part 1:** 80–81

"Chicago Hamlet, A" (Anderson), **I:** 112

Chicago Loop (Theroux), **Supp. VIII:** 324

"Chicago Picasso, The" (Brooks), **Supp. III Part 1:** 70–71, 84

Chicago Poems (Sandburg), **III:** 579, 581–583, 586

"Chicano/Borderlands Literature and Poetry" (Ríos), **Supp. IV Part 2:** 537, 538, 542, 545

Chick, Nancy, **Supp. IV Part 1:** 1

"Chickamauga" (Bierce), **I:** 201

"Chickamauga" (Wolfe), **IV:** 460

Chickamauga (Wright), **Supp. V:** 333, 343–344

"Chickamauga" (Wright), **Supp. V:** 334

"Chiefly about War Matters" (Hawthorne), **II:** 227; **Retro. Supp. I:** 165

"Child" (Plath), **Supp. I Part 2:** 544

Child, Lydia Maria, **Supp. XIII:** 141

"Child, The" (Ríos), **Supp. IV Part 2:** 543

"Child by Tiger, The" (Wolfe), **IV:** 451

"Childhood" (Wright), **Supp. V:** 341

Childhood, A: The Biography of a Place (Crews), **Supp. XI:** 102–103, 245

"Childhood, When You Are in It . . ." (Kenyon), **Supp. VII:** 160, 170

"Childhood Sketch" (Wright), **Supp. III Part 2:** 589

"Child Is Born, A" (Benét), **Supp. XI:** 46

"Child Is the Meaning of This Life, The" (Schwartz), **Supp. II Part 2:** 659–660

"Childlessness" (Merrill), **Supp. III Part 1:** 323

"Childless Woman" (Plath), **Supp. I Part 2:** 544

Child-Life (Whittier and Larcom, eds.), **Supp. XIII:** 142

Child-Life in Prose (Whittier and Larcom, eds.), **Supp. XIII:** 142

Childlike Life of the Black Tarantula, The (Acker), **Supp. XII:** 4, 6, 7–8

"Child Margaret" (Sandburg), **III:** 584

"Child of Courts, The" (Jarrell), **II:** 378, 379, 381

Child of God (McCarthy), **Supp. VIII:** 177–178

"CHILD OF THE THIRTIES" (Baraka), **Supp. II Part 1:** 60

"Child on Top of a Greenhouse" (Roethke), **III:** 531

Children (Gurney), **Supp. V:** 95, 96

"Children" (Stowe), **Supp. I Part 2:** 587

Children, The (Wharton), **IV:** 321, 326; **Retro. Supp. I:** 381

"Children, the Sandbar, That Summer" (Rukeyser), **Supp. VI:** 274

Children and Others (Cozzens), **I:** 374

Children Is All (Purdy), **Supp. VII:** 277, 278, 282

"Children of Adam" (Whitman), **IV:** 342; **Retro. Supp. I:** 403, 405

Children of Light (Stone), **Supp. V:** 304–306

Children of Light and the Children of Darkness, The (Niebuhr), **III:** 292, 306, 310

Children of the Frost (London), **II:** 469, 483

"Children of the Lord's Supper, The" (Tegnér), **Retro. Supp. II:** 155, 157

Children of the Market Place (Masters), **Supp. I Part 2:** 471

"Children on Their Birthdays" (Capote), **Supp. III Part 1:** 114, 115

"Children Selecting Books in a Library" (Jarrell), **II:** 371

Children's Hour, The (Hellman), **Supp. I Part 1:** 276–277, 281, 286, 297

"Children's Rhymes" (Hughes), **Supp. I Part 1:** 340

Childress, Mark, **Supp. X:** 89

Child's Garden of Verses, A (Stevenson), **Supp. IV Part 1:** 298, 314; **Supp. XIII:** 75

"Child's Reminiscence, A" (Whitman), **IV:** 344

Childwold (Oates), **Supp. II Part 2:** 519–520

Chill, The (Macdonald), **Supp. IV Part 2:** 473

Chills and Fever (Ransom), **III:** 490, 491–492, 493

Chilly Scenes of Winter (Beattie), **Supp. V:** 21, 22, 23, 24, 26, 27

Chime of Words, A: The Letters of Logan Pearsall Smith (Tribble, ed.), **Supp. XIV:**348–349

Chimera (C. Frost), **Supp. XV:** 94, 95, 100

"Chimes for Yahya" (Merrill), **Supp. III Part 1:** 329

Chin, Frank, **Supp. V:** 164, 172

"China" (Johnson), **Supp. VI:** 193–194

"Chinaman's Hat" (Kingston), **Supp. V:** 169

China Men (Kingston), **Supp. V:** 157, 158, 159, 160, 161, 164–169; **Supp. X:** 292; **Supp. XV:** 220

China Trace (Wright), **Supp. V:** 332, 340, 341, 342

Chinese Classics (Legge), **III:** 472

Chinese Materia Medica (P. Smith), **III:** 572

"Chinese Nightingale, The" (Lindsay), **Supp. I Part 2:** 392–393, 394

Chinese Nightingale and Other Poems, The (Lindsay), **Supp. I Part 2:** 392

Chinese Siamese Cat, The (Tan), **Supp. X:** 289

Chinese Translations, The (Bynner), **Supp. XV:** 47, 52

Chinitz, David, **Supp. XV:** 180, 185

"Chinoiseries" (Lowell), **II:** 524–525

Chip (Untermeyer), **Supp. XV:** 310

Chirico, Giorgio de, **Supp. III Part 1:** 14

Chirico, Miriam M., **Supp. XV:** 323

"Chiron" (Winters), **Supp. II Part 2:** 801

Chodorov, Jerome, **IV:** 274

"Choice, The" (Karr), **Supp. XI:** 251

"Choice of Profession, A" (Malamud), **Supp. I Part 2:** 437

Chomei, Kamo No, **IV:** 170, 171, 184

Chomsky, Noam, **Supp. IV Part 2:** 679

Choosing not Choosing (Cameron), **Retro. Supp. I:** 43

Chopin, Felix, **Supp. I Part 1:** 202

Chopin, Frédéric, **Supp. I Part 1:** 363

Chopin, Jean, **Supp. I Part 1:** 206

Chopin, Kate, **II:** 276; **Retro. Supp. I:** 10, 215; **Retro. Supp. II:** 57–74; **Supp. I Part 1:** 200–226; **Supp. V:** 304; **Supp. X:** 227

"Choral: The Pink Church" (W. C. Williams), **Retro. Supp. I:** 428

"Chord" (Merwin), **Supp. III Part 1:** 356

"Chords and Dischords" (column; Untermeyer), **Supp. XV:** 294

Choruses from Iphigenia in Aulis (Doolittle, trans.), **Supp. I Part 1:** 257, 268, 269

"Chosen Blindness" (Karr), **Supp. XI:** 251

Chosen Country (Dos Passos), **I:** 475, 490–491

Chosen Place, The Timeless People, The (Marshall), **Supp. XI:** 275, 276, 282–284

Choson (Lowell), **II:** 513

Choukri, Mohamed, **Supp. IV Part 1:** 92

Chovteau, Mane Thérèse, **Supp. I Part 1:** 205

Chrisman, Robert, **Supp. IV Part 1:** 1

Christabel (Coleridge), **Supp. IV Part 2:** 465

"Christ for Sale" (Lowell), **II:** 538

Christian, Graham, **Supp. XII:** 193

Christian Dictionary, A (Wilson), **IV:** 153

"Christian in World Crisis, The" (Merton), **Supp. VIII:** 203

Christianity and Power Politics (Niebuhr), **III:** 292, 303

"Christianity and the Survival of Creation" (Berry), **Supp. X:** 30

"Christian Minister, The" (Emerson), **II:** 10

Christian Philosopher, The (Mather), **Supp. II Part 2:** 463–464

Christian Realism and Practical Problems (Niebuhr), **III:** 292, 308

"Christian Roommates, The" (Updike), **IV:** 226–227; **Retro. Supp. I:** 319, 323

Christiansen, Carrie, **I:** 210

Christian's Secret of a Happy Life, The (H. W. Smith), **Supp. XIV:**333–334

Christie, Agatha, **Supp. IV Part 1:** 341; **Supp. IV Part 2:** 469

Christine (King), **Supp. V:** 139, 148

"Christ Light, The" (Chopin), **Retro. Supp. II:** 61

"Christmas 1944" (Levertov), **Supp. III Part 1:** 274

"Christmas, or the Good Fairy" (Stowe), **Supp. I Part 2:** 586

"Christmas Banquet, The" (Hawthorne), **II:** 227

Christmas Card, A (Theroux), **Supp. VIII:** 322

Christmas Carol, A (Dickens), **Retro. Supp. I:** 196; **Supp. I Part 2:** 409–410; **Supp. X:** 252, 253

"Christmas Eve at Johnson's Drugs N Goods" (Bambara), **Supp. XI:** 11–12

"Christmas Eve in the Time of War: A Capitalist Meditates by a Civil War Monument" (Lowell), **II:** 538

"Christmas Eve under Hooker's Statue" (Lowell), **II:** 539–540

"Christmas Gift" (Warren), **IV:** 252–253

"Christmas Greeting, A" (Wright), **Supp. III Part 2:** 601

"Christmas Hymn, A" (Wilbur), **Supp. III Part 2:** 557

Christmas Memory, A (Capote), **Supp. III Part 1:** 118, 119, 129

"Christmass Poem" (West), **Retro. Supp. II:** 338

Christmas Story (Mencken), **III:** 111

"Christmas to Me" (Lee), **Supp. VIII:** 113

Christographia (Taylor), **IV:** 164–165

"*Christ on the Cross*/Nuestro Señor Crucificado" (Mora), **Supp. XIII:** 229

Christopher and His Kind: 1929–1939 (Isherwood), **Supp. XIV:**157, 163, 164, 171

"Christopher Cat" (Cullen), **Supp. IV Part 1:** 173

Christopher Columbus, Mariner (Morison), **Supp. I Part 2:** 488

Christopher Isherwood: A Critical Biography (Finney), **Supp. XIV:**158

Christophersen, Bill, **Supp. IX:** 159, 167; **Supp. XI:** 155; **Supp. XIII:** 87

"Christ's Passion" (Karr), **Supp. XI:** 251

Christus: A Mystery (Longfellow), **II:** 490, 493, 495, 505–507; **Retro. Supp. II:** 161, 165, 166

Chroma (F. Barthelme), **Supp. XI:** 30, 33, 34

"Chroma" (F. Barthelme), **Supp. XI:** 31

"Chronicle of Race Relations, A" (Du Bois), **Supp. II Part 1:** 182

Chronicle of the Conquest of Granada (Irving), **II:** 310

"Chronologues" (Goldbarth), **Supp. XII:** 183, 184

"Chrysanthemums, The" (Steinbeck), **IV:** 53

"Chrysaor" (Longfellow), **II:** 498

Chu, Louis, **Supp. X:** 291

Chuang, Hua, **Supp. X:** 291

Chuang-Tzu, **Supp. VIII:** 206

"Chunk of Amethyst, A" (R. Bly), **Supp. IV Part 1:** 72

Church, Margaret, **IV:** 466

"Church and the Fiction Writer, The" (O'Connor), **Retro. Supp. II:** 223, 233

Churchill, Charles, **Supp. XV:** 232

Churchill, Winston, **I:** 9, 490; **Supp. I Part 2:** 491

Church of Dead Girls, The (Dobyns), **Supp. XIII:** 75, 83–84

"Church Porch, The" (Herbert), **IV:** 153

Church Psalmody, Selected from Dr. Watts and Other Authors (Mason and Greene, ed.), **I:** 458

Ciannic, Saint, **II:** 215

Ciano, Edda, **IV:** 249

Ciardi, John, **I:** 169, 179, 535; **III:** 268; **Supp. IV Part 1:** 243; **Supp. IV Part 2:** 639; **Supp. IX:** 269, 324; **Supp. XII:** 119

Cicada (Haines), **Supp. XII:** 206–207

"Cicadas" (Wilbur), **Supp. III Part 2:** 549

Cicero, **I:** 279; **II:** 8, 14–15; **III:** 23; **Supp. I Part 2:** 405

Cider House Rules, The (Irving), **Supp. VI:** 164, 173–175

"Cigales" (Wilbur), **Supp. III Part 2:** 549

"Cigarette" (L. Michaels), **Supp. XVI:**214

Cimarron, Rose (Burke), **Supp. XIV:**22, 35

"Cimetière Marin, Le" (Valéry), **IV:** 91–92

Cimino, Michael, **Supp. X:** 126

Cincinnati Kid, The (film), **Supp. XI:** 306

"Cinderella" (Jarrell), **II:** 386

"Cinderella" (Perrault), **IV:** 266, 267

"Cinderella" (Sexton), **Supp. II Part 2:** 691

"Cinema, The" (Salter), **Supp. IX:** 257

Cinema of Tony Richardson, The: Essays and Interviews (Phillips), **Supp. XI:** 306

Cinthio, **IV:** 370

Ciolkowski, Laura, **Supp. XVI:**24

CIOPW (Cummings), **I:** 429

"Circe" (Welty), **Retro. Supp. I:** 353

Circle Game, The (Atwood), **Supp. XIII:** 20, 33

"Circle in the Fire, A" (O'Connor), **III:** 344–345, 349–350, 351, 353, 354; **Retro. Supp. II:** 229, 232

"Circle of Breath" (Stafford), **Supp. XI:** 318, 322

"Circles" (Emerson), **I:** 455, 460

"Circles" (Lowell), **II:** 554

"Circus, The" (Porter), **III:** 443, 445

"Circus Animals' Desertion" (Yeats), **I:** 389

"Circus in the Attic" (Warren), **IV:** 253

Circus in the Attic, The (Warren), **IV:** 243, 251–253

"Circus in Three Rings" (Plath), **Retro. Supp. II:** 243; **Supp. I Part 2:** 536

Circus of Needs, A (Dunn), **Supp. XI:** 147–148

"Cirque d'Hiver" (Bishop), **Supp. I Part 1:** 85

Cisneros, Sandra, **Supp. IV Part 2:** 544; **Supp. VII:** 57–73; **Supp. XI:** 177

Cities of the Interior (Nin), **Supp. X:** 182

Cities of the Plain (McCarthy), **Supp. VIII:** 175, 186–187

Cities of the Red Night (Burroughs), **Supp. III Part 1:** 106

"Citizen Cain" (Baraka), **Supp. II Part 1:** 49

Citizen Kane (film), **Retro. Supp. I:** 115; **Supp. V:** 251; **Supp. XI:** 169

"Citizen of the World" (Goldsmith), **II:** 299

"City" (Francis), **Supp. IX:** 87

City and the Pillar, The (Vidal), **Supp. IV Part 2:** 677, 680–681; **Supp. XIV:**170

"*City and the Pillar, The,* as Gay Fiction" (Summers), **Supp. IV Part 2:** 680–681

City Boy (L. Michaels), **Supp. XVI:**212

"City Boy" (L. Michaels), **Supp. XVI:**203–204

City in History, The (Mumford), **Supp. II Part 2:** 495

"City in the Sea, The" (Poe), **III:** 411; **Retro. Supp. II:** 274

City in Which I Love You, The (L.-Y. Lee), **Supp. XV:** 212, 215–220

"City in Which I Love You, The" (L.-Y. Lee), **Supp. XV:** 215, 217–218

City Life (Barthelme), **Supp. IV Part 1:** 44, 47

"City of Change, A" (Bynner), **Supp. XV:** 45

City of Glass (Auster), **Supp. XII:** 22, 24–26

City of God, The (St. Augustine), **IV:** 126

City of the Living and Other Stories, The (Stegner), **Supp. IV Part 2:** 599, 609, 613

City of Words: American Fiction 1950-1970 (T. Tanner), **Supp. XVI:**69

City of Your Final Destination, The (Cameron), **Supp. XII:** 79, 82, 91–94

"City on a Hill" (Lowell), **II:** 552

"City Person Encountering Nature, A" (Kingston), **Supp. V:** 170

"City Planners, The" (Atwood), **Supp. XIII:** 33

City Without Walls (Auden), **Supp. II Part 1:** 24

Civil Disobedience (Thoreau), **IV:** 185; **Supp. I Part 2:** 507

Civilization in the United States (Stearns), **I:** 245

"Civil Rights" (Lanier), **Supp. I Part 1:** 357

Cixous, Hélène, **Supp. X:** 102; **Supp. XIII:** 297; **Supp. XV:** 347

Claiborne, William, **I:** 132

Claiming of Sleeping Beauty, The (Rice), **Supp. VII:** 301

Clampitt, Amy, **Supp. IX:** 37–54; **Supp. X:** 120; **Supp. XI:** 249; **Supp. XV:** 251, 256

Clancy's Wake, At (Crane), **I:** 422

"Clandeboye" (Leopold), **Supp. XIV:**189

Clara Howard; or, The Enthusiasm of Love (Brown), **Supp. I Part 1:** 145

Clara's Ole Man (Bullins), **Supp. II Part 1:** 42

Clare, John, **II:** 387; **III:** 528; **Supp. XVI:**295

Clarel: A Poem and Pilgrimage in the Holy Land (Melville), **Retro. Supp. I:** 257

Clarissa (Richardson), **II:** 111; **Supp. I Part 2:** 714; **Supp. V:** 127; **Supp. XV:** 231

Clark, Alex, **Supp. XII:** 307

Clark, Charles, **I:** 470

Clark, Eleanor. *See* Warren, Mrs. Robert Penn (Eleanor Clark)

Clark, Francis Edward, **II:** 9

Clark, Geoffrey, **Supp. XI:** 342

Clark, Harry Hayden, **Supp. I Part 2:** 423

Clark, John Bates, **Supp. I Part 2:** 633

Clark, Kenneth, **Supp. XIV:**342, 348

Clark, Thomas, **Supp. III Part 2:** 629; **Supp. IV Part 1:** 140, 145, 147

Clark, Walter, **Supp. XI:** 315

Clark, William, **III:** 14; **IV:** 179, 283

Clark, Willis Gaylord, **Supp. I Part 2:** 684

Clarke, James Freeman, **Supp. II Part 1:** 280

Clarke, John, **Supp. IV Part 1:** 8

Clarke, John J., **III:** 356

Clarke, Samuel, **II:** 108

Clark Lectures, **Retro. Supp. I:** 65

Clash by Night (Odets), **Supp. II Part 2:** 531, 538, 544–546, 550, 551

Classical Tradition, The (Highet), **Supp. I Part 1:** 268

Classic Ballroom Dances (Simic),

Supp. VIII: 271, 276–278, 283
Classics and Commercials: A Literary Chronicle of the Forties (Wilson), **IV:** 433
"CLASS STRUGGLE" (Baraka), **Supp. III Part 1:** 55
Claudel, Paul, **I:** 60
Claudelle Inglish (Caldwell), **I:** 304
Clavel, Marcel, **I:** 343
"CLAY" (Baraka), **Supp. II Part 1:** 54
Clay, Henry, **I:** 8; **Supp. I Part 2:** 684, 686
Clay's Ark (O. Butler), **Supp. XIII:** 63
Clayton, John J., **Supp. IV Part 1:** 238
"Clean, Well Lighted Place, A" (Hemingway), **Retro. Supp. I:** 181
"Clear, with Light Variable Winds" (Lowell), **II:** 522
"Clear Days" (White), **Supp. I Part 2:** 664, 665
Clearing (Berry), **Supp. X:** 22
"Clearing, A" (Simpson), **Supp. IX:** 280
"Clearing, The" (Kenyon), **Supp. VII:** 174
"Clearing the Title" (Merrill), **Supp. III Part 1:** 336
"Clearing Up the Question of Stesichoros' Blinding by Helen" (Carson), **Supp. XII:** 107–108
"Clear Morning" (Glück), **Supp. V:** 88
"Clearness" (Wilbur), **Supp. III Part 2:** 544, 550
"Clear Night" (Wright), **Supp. V:** 341
Clear Pictures: First Loves, First Guides (Price), **Supp. VI:** 253, 254, 255, 256, 265
Clear Springs (Mason), **Supp. VIII:** 134–136, 137–138, 139, 147
Cleaver, Eldridge, **Retro. Supp. II:** 12; **Supp. IV Part 1:** 206; **Supp. X:** 249
"Cleaving, The" (L.-Y. Lee), **Supp. XV:** 215, 218–220
Cleland, John, **Supp. V:** 48, 127
Clemenceau, Georges, **I:** 490
Clemens, Jane, **I:** 247
Clemens, Mrs. Samuel Langhorne (Olivia Langdon), **I:** 197, 208, 247; **Supp. I Part 2:** 457
Clemens, Orion, **IV:** 193, 195
Clemens, Samuel Langhorne. *See* Twain, Mark
Clemens, Susie, **IV:** 208
Clementine Recognitions (novel), **Supp. IV Part 1:** 280
Clements, Colin Campbell, **Supp. XVI:**190

Clemons, Walter, **Supp. IV Part 1:** 305, 307
Cleopatra, **III:** 44; **IV:** 373; **Supp. I Part 1:** 114
"Clepsydra" (Ashbery), **Supp. III Part 1:** 10–15
"Clerks, The" (Robinson), **III:** 517–518
Cleveland, Carol, **Supp. IX:** 120, 125
Cleveland, Ceil, **Supp. V:** 222
Cleveland, Grover, **II:** 126, 128, 129, 130, 137, 138; **Supp. I Part 2:** 486
"Clever Magician Carrying My Heart, A" (Salinas), **Supp. XIII:** 323
Clifford, Craig, **Supp. IX:** 99
Clift, Montgomery, **III:** 161
Climate of Monastic Prayer, The (Merton), **Supp. VIII:** 205, 207
"Climber, The" (Mason), **Supp. VIII:** 140–141
"Climbing the Tower" (Crews), **Supp. XI:** 102
Clinton, De Witt, **I:** 338
"Clipped Wings" (H. Miller), **III:** 176–177
Clive, Robert, **Supp. I Part 2:** 505
Clock Winder, The (Tyler), **Supp. IV Part 2:** 661–662, 670
Clock Without Hands (McCullers), **II:** 587–588, 604–606
Clockwork Orange, A (Burgess), **Supp. XIII:** 29
Clorindy (Cook), **Supp. II Part 1:** 199
"Close Calls" (Wolff), **Supp. VII:** 332–333
"Closed Book, A" (Mosley), **Supp. XIII:** 237
Close Range: Wyoming Stories (Proulx), **Supp. VII:** 261–265
Close the Book (Glaspell), **Supp. III Part 1:** 179
"Close the Book" (Lowell), **II:** 554
Close to Shore: A True Story of Terror in an Age of Innocence (Capuzzo), **Supp. XIII:** 254
Closet Writing & Gay Reading: The Case of Melville's Pierre (Creech), **Retro. Supp. I:** 254
Closing Circle, The (Commoner), **Supp. XIII:** 264
Closing of the American Mind, The (Bloom), **Retro. Supp. II:** 19, 30, 31
"Closing of the Rodeo, The" (W. J. Smith), **Supp. XIII:** 332
Closing Time (Heller), **Supp. IV Part 1:** 382, 386, 391–394
Closset, Marie, **Supp. VIII:** 251, 265
"Cloud, The" (Shelley), **Supp. I Part 2:** 720

"Cloud and Fame" (Berryman), **I:** 173
Cloud Forest, The: A Chronicle of the South American Wilderness (Matthiessen), **Supp. V:** 202, 204
"Cloud on the Way, The" (Bryant), **Supp. I Part 1:** 171
"Cloud River" (Wright), **Supp. V:** 341
"Clouds" (Levine), **Supp. V:** 184
Cloudsplitter (Banks), **Supp. V:** 16
"Clover" (Lanier), **Supp. I Part 1:** 362–364
Clover and Other Poems (Lanier), **Supp. I Part 1:** 362
"Clown" (Corso), **Supp. XII:** 127
Clown in the Belfry, The: Writings on Faith and Fiction (Buechner), **Supp. XII:** 53
Cluck, Julia, **Supp. I Part 2:** 728
Clum, John M., **Supp. XIII:** 200, 201, 209
Cluny, Hugo, **IV:** 290
Clurman, Harold, **I:** 93; **IV:** 381, 385
Clytus, Radiclani, **Supp. XIII:** 128, **Supp. XIII:** 129, 132
"Coal: Beginning and End" (Winters), **Supp. II Part 2:** 791
Coale, Howard, **Supp. XIII:** 15
"Coast, The" (column), **Supp. IV Part 1:** 198
"Coast Guard's Cottage, The" (Wylie), **Supp. I Part 2:** 723
Coast of Trees, A (Ammons), **Supp. VII:** 24, 34
"Coast-Range Christ, The" (Jeffers), **Supp. II Part 2:** 414, 419
"Coast-Road, The" (Jeffers), **Supp. II Part 2:** 425
"Coat, The" (Everwine), **Supp. XV:** 80
Coates, Joseph, **Supp. VIII:** 80
Coates, Robert, **I:** 54; **IV:** 298
"Coatlicue's Rules: Advice from an Aztec Goddess" (Mora), **Supp. XIII:** 223
"Coats" (Kenyon), **Supp. VII:** 172
Cobb, Lee J., **III:** 153
Cobb, Ty, **III:** 227, 229
Cobbett, William, **Supp. I Part 2:** 517; **Supp. XV:** 237
"Cobbler Keezar's Vision" (Whittier), **Supp. I Part 2:** 699
"Cobweb, The" (Carver), **Supp. III Part 1:** 148
Cobwebs From an Empty Skull (Bierce), **I:** 195
Coccimiglio, Vic, **Supp. XIII:** 114
"Cock-a-Doodle-Doo!" (Melville), **III:** 89
"Cockayne" (Emerson), **II:** 6
"Cock-Crow" (Gordon), **II:** 219
Cock Pit (Cozzens), **I:** 359, 378, 379

Cockpit (Kosinski), **Supp. XII:** 21

Cockpit: A Novel (Kosinski), **Supp. VII:** 215, 223–224, 225

"Cock Robin Takes Refuge in the Storm House" (Snodgrass), **Supp. VI:** 319

Cocktail Hour, The (Gurney), **Supp. V:** 95, 96, 100, 101, 103, 105, 108

Cocktail Hour and Two Other Plays: Another Antigone and *The Perfect Party* (Gurney), **Supp. V:** 100

Cocktail Party, The (Eliot), **I:** 571, 582–583; **III:** 21; **Retro. Supp. I:** 65; **Supp. V:** 101, 103

Cocteau, Jean, **III:** 471; **Retro. Supp. I:** 82, 378; **Supp. IV Part 1:** 82; **Supp. XVI:**135

"Coda: Wilderness Letter" (Stegner), **Supp. IV Part 2:** 595

"Code, The" (Frost), **Retro. Supp. I:** 121, 128

Codman, Florence, **Supp. II Part 1:** 92, 93

Codman, Ogden, Jr., **Retro. Supp. I:** 362, 363

Cody, William ("Buffalo Bill"), **I:** 440; **III:** 584; **Supp. V:** 230

Coffey, Michael, **Supp. V:** 243; **Supp. XV:** 65

Coffey, Warren, **III:** 358

Coffin, Charles, **III:** 577

Cogan, David J., **Supp. IV Part 1:** 362

Coghill, Nevill, **Supp. II Part 1:** 4; **Supp. XIV:**13

Cohan, George M., **II:** 427; **III:** 401

Cohen, Edward M., **Supp. XVI:**212

Cohen, Esther, **Supp. XV:** 323

Cohen, Hettie, **Supp. II Part 1:** 30

Cohen, Marty, **Supp. X:** 112

Cohen, Norman J., **Supp. IX:** 132, 143

Cohen, Rosetta, **Supp. XV:** 257

Cohen, Sarah Blacher, **Supp. V:** 273

"Coin" (Goldbarth), **Supp. XII:** 187

Coindreau, Maurice, **III:** 339

Coiner, Constance, **Supp. XIII:** 297, 302

Coit, Lille Hitchcock, **Supp. X:** 103

"Coitus" (Pound), **III:** 466

Colburn, Nadia Herman, **Supp. XV:** 339, 341, 347

"Cold, The" (Kenyon), **Supp. VII:** 164

"Cold, The" (Winters), **Supp. II Part 2:** 790–791, 809, 811

"Cold-blooded Creatures" (Wylie), **Supp. I Part 2:** 729

Colden, Cadwallader, **Supp. I Part 1:** 250

"Colder the Air, The" (Bishop), **Supp. I Part 1:** 86

Cold Feet (Harrison), **Supp. VIII:** 39

Cold Frame (C. Frost), **Supp. XV:** 93, 96

Cold Ground Was My Bed Last Night (Garrett), **Supp. VII:** 98

"Cold Ground Was My Bed Last Night" (Garrett), **Supp. VII:** 100

"Cold Night, The" (W. C. Williams), **Retro. Supp. I:** 418

"Cold Plunge into Skin Diving, A" (Knowles), **Supp. XII:** 241

Cold Spring, A (Bishop), **Retro. Supp. II:** 45

Cold Springs Harbor (Yates), **Supp. XI:** 348

Cold War American Poetry, **Supp. V:** 182

Cold War and the Income Tax, The (Wilson), **IV:** 430

Cole, Goody, **Supp. I Part 2:** 696–697

Cole, Lester, **Retro. Supp. II:** 329

Cole, Nat King, **Retro. Supp. I:** 334; **Supp. X:** 255

Cole, Thomas, **Supp. I Part 1:** 156, 158, 171

"Coleman" (Karr), **Supp. XI:** 244

Coleman, Wanda, **Supp. XI:** 83–98

Coleridge, Samuel Taylor, **I:** 283, 284, 447, 522; **II:** 7, 10, 11, 19, 71, 169, 273, 301, 502, 516, 549; **III:** 77, 83–84, 424, 461, 488, 523; **IV:** 74, 173, 250, 349, 453; **Retro. Supp. I:** 65, 308; **Supp. I Part 1:** 31, 311, 349; **Supp. I Part 2:** 376, 393, 422; **Supp. IV Part 2:** 422, 465; **Supp. V:** 258; **Supp. IX:** 38, 50; **Supp. XIII:** 139; **Supp. XIV:**21–22; **Supp. XV:** 250

Coles, Katharine, **Supp. IV Part 2:** 630

Colette, **Supp. VIII:** 40, 171

Colette, Sidonie-Gabrielle, **Supp. XVI:**193–194

"Coliseum, The" (Poe), **III:** 411

Collage of Dreams (Spencer), **Supp. X:** 196

"Collapse of Tomorrow, The" (Mumford), **Supp. II Part 2:** 482

"Collected by a Valetudinarian" (E. Stoddard), **Supp. XV:** 286–287

Collected Earlier Poems (Hecht), **Supp. X:** 58, 59

Collected Earlier Poems (W. C. Williams), **Retro. Supp. I:** 414, 428

Collected Earlier Poems 1940–1960 (Levertov), **Supp. III Part 1:** 273, 275

Collected Essays (Tate), **IV:** 133–134

Collected Essays of Ralph Ellison, The (Ellison), **Retro. Supp. II:** 119

Collected Essays of Robert Creeley,

The (Creeley), **Supp. IV Part 1:** 153, 154

Collected Later Poems (W. C. Williams), **Retro. Supp. I:** 428

Collected Plays (A. Miller), **III:** 158

Collected Plays, 1974–1983 (Gurney), **Supp. V:** 99

Collected Poems (Aiken), **I:** 50

Collected Poems (Burke), **I:** 269

Collected Poems (Cummings), **I:** 430, 439, 441

Collected Poems (Doolittle), **Supp. I Part 1:** 264–267, 269

Collected Poems (Frost), **Retro. Supp. I:** 136

Collected Poems (Kees; Justice, ed.), **Supp. XV:** 134

Collected Poems (Lindsay), **Supp. I Part 2:** 380, 387, 392, 396–397, 400

Collected Poems (Lowell), **Supp. XV:** 20

Collected Poems (Moore), **III:** 194, 215

Collected Poems (Price), **Supp. VI:** 267

Collected Poems (Simpson), **Supp. IX:** 279

Collected Poems (Winters), **Supp. II Part 2:** 791, 810

Collected Poems (Wright), **Supp. III Part 2:** 602

Collected Poems (W. C. Williams), **IV:** 415; **Retro. Supp. I:** 430

Collected Poems (Yeats), **Supp. XV:** 152

Collected Poems 1909–1935 (Eliot), **I:** 580; **Retro. Supp. I:** 66

Collected Poems 1909–1962 (Eliot), **I:** 583

Collected Poems 1917–1952 (MacLeish), **III:** 3, 4, 19

Collected Poems 1921–1931 (W. C. Williams), **Retro. Supp. I:** 422; **Supp. XIV:**285

Collected Poems 1930–1960 (Eberhart), **I:** 522, 525–526, 540, 541

Collected Poems, 1923–1953 (Bogan), **Supp. III Part 1:** 64

Collected Poems, 1936–1976 (Francis), **Supp. IX:** 77, 80, 87

Collected Poems: 1939–1989 (W. J. Smith), **Supp. XIII:** 332, 340, 343, 345

Collected Poems: 1940–1978 (Shapiro), **Supp. II Part 2:** 703, 717

Collected Poems: 1951–1971 (Ammons), **Supp. VII:** 24, 26–29, 32, 33

Collected Poems: 1956–1976

(Wagoner), **Supp. IX:** 323, 328–329

Collected Poems, The (Stevens), **III:** 273; **IV:** 75, 76, 87, 93; **Retro. Supp. I:** 296, 309

Collected Poems of Amy Clampitt, The (Clampitt), **Supp. IX:** 37, 44, 53

Collected Poems of George Garrett (Garrett), **Supp. VII:** 109

Collected Poems of Hart Crane, The (Crane), **I:** 399–402

Collected Poems of James Agee, The (Fitzgerald, ed.), **I:** 27–28

Collected Poems of James T. Farrell, The (Farrell), **II:** 45

Collected Poems of Langston Hughes, The (Rampersad and Roessel, ed.), **Retro. Supp. I:** 194, 196, 212

Collected Poems of Muriel Rukeyser, The (Rukeyser), **Supp. VI:** 274

Collected Poems of Thomas Merton, The, **Supp. VIII:** 207, 208

Collected Poetry (Auden), **Supp. II Part 1:** 18

Collected Prose (Wright), **Supp. III Part 2:** 596

Collected Prose, The (Bishop), **Retro. Supp. II:** 51

Collected Recordings (W. C. Williams), **Retro. Supp. I:** 431

Collected Shorter Poems, 1946-1991 (Carruth), **Supp. XVI:**47

Collected Short Stories, The (Wharton), **Retro. Supp. I:** 362, 363, 366

Collected Sonnets (Millay), **III:** 136–137

Collected Stories, 1939–1976 (Bowles), **Supp. IV Part 1:** 92

Collected Stories, The (Paley), **Supp. VI:** 218

Collected Stories, The (Price), **Supp. VI:** 266

Collected Stories, The (Theroux), **Supp. VIII:** 318

Collected Stories, The (Wharton), **Retro. Supp. I:** 361

Collected Stories of Eudora Welty, The (Welty), **Retro. Supp. I:** 355

Collected Stories of Isaac Bashevis Singer (Singer), **Retro. Supp. II:** 307–308

Collected Stories of Katherine Anne Porter (Porter), **III:** 454

Collected Stories of Peter Taylor (Taylor), **Supp. V:** 314, 320, 323–324, 325, 326

Collected Stories of Richard Yates, The, **Supp. XI:** 349

Collected Stories of Wallace Stegner (Stegner), **Supp. IV Part 2:** 599, 605

Collected Stories of William Faulkner (Faulkner), **II:** 72; **Retro. Supp. I:** 75

Collected Stories of William Humphrey, The (Humphrey), **Supp. IX:** 106

Collected Works (Bierce), **I:** 204, 208–210

Collected Works of Buck Rogers in the 25th Century, The (Bradbury), **Supp. IV Part 1:** 101

Collected Writings, The (Z. Fitzgerald; Bruccoli, ed.), **Supp. IX:** 65, 68

Collecting the Animals (Everwine), **Supp. XV:** 73, 75, 78–81, 85, 88

Collection of Epigrams, **II:** 111

Collection of Poems, on American Affairs, and a Variety of Other Subjects . . . (Freneau), **Supp. II Part 1:** 274

Collection of Select Aphorisms and Maxims (Palmer), **II:** 111

"Collectors" (Carver), **Supp. III Part 1:** 141–142

Collingwood, R. G., **I:** 278

Collins, Billy, **Supp. XI:** 143; **Supp. XIV:**123

Collins, Doug, **Supp. V:** 5

Collins, Eddie, **II:** 416

Collins, Richard, **Supp. XI:** 171

Collins, Wilkie, **Supp. I Part 1:** 35, 36; **Supp. IV Part 1:** 341

Collins, William, **Supp. I Part 2:** 714

Collinson, Peter, **II:** 114

Collinson, Peter (pseudonym). *See* Hammett, Dashiell

Colloff, Pamela, **Supp. XIII:** 281

Colloque Sentimental (ballet), **Supp. IV Part 1:** 83

"Colloquy" (Kees), **Supp. XV:** 133

"Colloquy in Black Rock" (Lowell), **II:** 535; **Retro. Supp. II:** 178

"Colloquy of Monos and Una, The" (Poe), **III:** 412

Colonel's Dream, The (Chesnutt), **Supp. XIV:**63, 75–76

Colônia, Regina, **Retro. Supp. II:** 53

Color (Cullen), **Supp. IV Part 1:** 164, 166, 167, 168

"Color: The Unfinished Business of Democracy" (Locke), **Supp. XIV:**202, 207

"Colorado" (Beattie), **Supp. V:** 27

Color and Democracy: Colonies and Peace (Du Bois), **Supp. II Part 1:** 184, 185

Color Curtain, The (Wright), **IV:** 478, 488

"Colored Americans" (Dunbar), **Supp. II Part 1:** 197

"Color Line, The" (Douglass), **Supp. III Part 1:** 163–165

Color Line, The (W. B. Smith), **Supp. II Part 1:** 168

Color of a Great City, The (Dreiser), **Retro. Supp. II:** 104

Color of Darkness (Purdy), **Supp. VII:** 271

Color Purple, The (Walker), **Supp. III Part 2:** 517, 518, 520, 525–529, 532–537; **Supp. VIII:** 141; **Supp. X:** 252, 330

Color Schemes (Cheang; film), **Supp. XI:** 20

"Colors of Night, The" (Momaday), **Supp. IV Part 2:** 490

"Colors without Objects" (Swenson), **Supp. IV Part 2:** 645

Colossus, The (Plath), **Retro. Supp. II:** 245–247; **Supp. I Part 2:** 529, 531, 536, 538, 540; **Supp. V:** 79; **Supp. XI:** 317

"Colossus, The" (Plath), **Retro. Supp. II:** 250

Colossus of Maroussi, The (H. Miller), **III:** 178, 185–186

"Colt, The" (Stegner), **Supp. IV Part 2:** 600

Coltelli, Laura, **Supp. IV Part 1:** 323, 330, 335, 409; **Supp. IV Part 2:** 493, 497, 559

Colter: The True Story of the Best Dog I Ever Had (Bass), **Supp. XVI:**23

Coltrane, John, **Supp. VIII:** 197

Colum, Mary, **I:** 246, 252, 256; **Supp. I Part 2:** 708, 709

Columbiad, The (Barlow), **Supp. II Part 1:** 67, 72, 73, 74, 75–77, 79

Columbia History of the American Novel, **Supp. XV:** 270

Columbia Literary History of the United States, **Supp. XV:** 270

"Columbian Ode" (Dunbar), **Supp. II Part 1:** 199

"Columbia U Poesy Reading—1975" (Corso), **Supp. XII:** 134

Columbus, Christopher, **I:** 253; **II:** 6, 310; **III:** 8; **Supp. I Part 2:** 397, 479, 480, 483, 486–488, 491, 495, 497, 498

"Columbus to Ferdinand" (Freneau), **Supp. II Part 1:** 255

Comanche Moon (McMurtry), **Supp. V:** 232

"Come, Break With Time" (Bogan), **Supp. III Part 1:** 52

Come Along with Me (Jackson), **Supp. IX:** 117, 118, 122

Come Back, Charleston Blue (film), **Supp. XVI:**144

Comeback, The (Gurney), **Supp. V:** 97

"Come Back to the Raft Ag'in, Huck

Honey!" (Fiedler), **Supp. XIII:** 93, 96–97, 101

Come Blow Your Horn (Simon), **Supp. IV Part 2:** 574, 575, 577, 578, 586, 587, 591

"Come Dance with Me in Ireland" (Jackson), **Supp. IX:** 119

"Comedian as the Letter C, The" (Stevens), **IV:** 84–85, 88; **Retro. Supp. I:** 297, 301, 302

"Comedy Cop" (Farrell), **II:** 45

"Comedy's Greatest Era" (Agee), **I:** 31

"Come In" (Frost), **Retro. Supp. I:** 139

"Come On, Baby" (Zinberg), **Supp. XV:** 195

"Come on Back" (Gardner), **Supp. VI:** 73

"Come Out into the Sun" (Francis), **Supp. IX:** 82

Come Out into the Sun: Poems New and Selected (Francis), **Supp. IX:** 82–83

"Come out the Wilderness" (Baldwin), **Supp. I Part 1:** 63

Comer, Anjanette, **Supp. XI:** 305

Comer, Cornelia, **I:** 214

"Come Shining: The Spiritual South" (exhibition; Luster), **Supp. XV:** 350

Come with Me: Poems for a Journey (Nye), **Supp. XIII:** 279

"Comforts of Home, The" (O'Connor), **III:** 349, 351, 355; **Retro. Supp. II:** 237

Comic Artist, The (Glaspell and Matson), **Supp. III Part 1:** 182

"Comic Imagination of the Young Dickens, The" (Wright), **Supp. III Part 2:** 591

"Comic Textures and Female Communities 1937 and 1977: Clare Boothe and Wendy Wasserstein" (Carlson), **Supp. XV:** 323

Comic Tragedies (Alcott), **Supp. I Part 1:** 33

"Coming Close" (Levine), **Supp. V:** 192

Coming Forth by Day of Osiris Jones, The (Aiken), **I:** 59

"Coming Home" (Gordon), **Supp. IV Part 1:** 309

"Coming Home to Vermont" (McCarriston), **Supp. XIV:** 269

"Coming in From the Cold" (Walker), **Supp. III Part 2:** 526

Coming into Eighty (Sarton), **Supp. VIII:** 262

"Coming into Eighty" (Sarton), **Supp. VIII:** 262

Coming into the Country (McPhee),

Supp. III Part 1: 298, 301–306, 309, 310

Coming Into Writing (Cixous), **Supp. X:** 102

Coming of Age in Mississippi (Moody), **Supp. IV Part 1:** 11

Comings Back (Goldbarth), **Supp. XII:** 180

Coming to Canada: Poems (Shields), **Supp. VII:** 311–312

"Coming to Canada—Age Twenty Two" (Shields), **Supp. VII:** 311

"Coming to the Morning" (Merwin), **Supp. III Part 1:** 356

"Coming to This" (Strand), **Supp. IV Part 2:** 627

Comiskey, Charles, **II:** 422

Commager, Henry Steele, **I:** 253; **Supp. I Part 1:** 372; **Supp. I Part 2:** 484, 647, 650

Command the Morning (Buck), **Supp. II Part 1:** 125

"Commencement Address, A" (Brodsky), **Supp. VIII:** 31

"Commencement Day Address, The" (Schwartz), **Supp. II Part 2:** 660

Commentaries (Caesar), **II:** 502, 561

"Commentary" (Auden), **Supp. II Part 1:** 13

"Comment on Curb" (Hughes), **Supp. I Part 1:** 340

"Commerce" (Nye), **Supp. XIII:** 281

Commins, Saxe, **Retro. Supp. I:** 73; **Retro. Supp. II:** 337

Commodity of Dreams & Other Stories, A (Nemerov), **III:** 268–269, 285

Common Carnage (Dobyns), **Supp. XIII:** 87

"Common Ground, A" (Levertov), **Supp. III Part 1:** 277

"Common Life, The" (Auden), **Supp. IV Part 1:** 302, 313

Common Room, A: Essays 1954–1987 (Price), **Supp. VI:** 264–265, 267

Commons, John, **Supp. I Part 2:** 645

Common Sense (Paine), **II:** 117; **Supp. I Part 1:** 231; **Supp. I Part 2:** 505, 506–508, 509, 513, 516, 517, 521

"Communication" (Dobyns), **Supp. XIII:** 91

"Communion" (Dubus), **Supp. VII:** 91

Communion (Mora), **Supp. XIII:** 217–219

Communist Manifesto, The (Marx), **II:** 463

"Community Life" (Moore), **Supp. X:** 178

"Community of Glaciers, The" (Bass), **Supp. XVI:** 23

Comnes, Gregory, **Supp. IV Part 1:**

283, 284, 291

"Companions, The" (Nemerov), **III:** 269, 278, 287

Company of Poets, A (Simpson), **Supp. IX:** 265, 275

Company of Women, The (Gordon), **Supp. IV Part 1:** 302–304, 304, 306, 313

Company She Keeps, The (McCarthy), **II:** 562, 563–566

Compass Flower, The (Merwin), **Supp. III Part 1:** 353, 357

"Compassionate Friendship" (Doolittle), **Supp. I Part 1:** 257, 258, 259, 260, 271

"Compatibility" (C. Frost), **Supp. XV:** 103

"Compendium" (Dove), **Supp. IV Part 1:** 248

"Complaint" (W. C. Williams), **Retro. Supp. I:** 418

"Complete Birth of the Cool, The" (Wright), **Supp. XV:** 343, 344

Complete Collected Poems of William Carlos Williams, 1906–1938, The (W. C. Williams), **Retro. Supp. I:** 424

"Complete Destruction" (W. C. Williams), **IV:** 413

"Complete Life of John Hopkins, The" (O. Henry), **Supp. II Part 1:** 405

Complete Poems (Frost), **II:** 155, 164

Complete Poems (Reznikoff), **Supp. XIV:** 281

Complete Poems (Sandburg), **III:** 590–592, 594, 596

Complete Poems, The (Bishop), **Retro. Supp. II:** 49; **Supp. I Part 1:** 72, 82, 94

Complete Poems, The (Bradbury), **Supp. IV Part 1:** 105

Complete Poems, The: 1927–1979 (Bishop), **Retro. Supp. II:** 51

Complete Poems of Emily Dickinson, The (Bianchi and Hampson, eds.), **Retro. Supp. I:** 35

Complete Poems of Emily Dickinson, The (Johnson, ed.), **I:** 470

Complete Poems of Frederick Goddard Tuckerman, The (Momaday), **Supp. IV Part 2:** 480

Complete Poems of Hart Crane, **Retro. Supp. II:** 81

Complete Poems to Solve, The (Swenson), **Supp. IV Part 2:** 652

Complete Poetical Works (Hulme), **III:** 464

Complete Poetical Works (Longfellow), **Retro. Supp. II:** 154

Complete Poetical Works (Lowell), **II:**

512, 516–517

Complete Poetical Works of Amy Lowell, The, **Supp. XV:** 295–296

Complete Stories (O'Connor), **Supp. X:** 1

Complete Tragedies, The: Euripedes II, **Supp. XV:** 50

"Complete with Starry Night and Bourbon Shots" (Goldbarth), **Supp. XII:** 192–193

Complete Works of Kate Chopin, The (Seyersted, ed.), **Supp. I Part 1:** 212, 225

Complete Works of the Gawain-Poet (Gardner), **Supp. VI:** 64, 65

"Complex Histories, Contested Memories: Some Reflections on Remembering Difficult Pasts" (E. Hoffman, lecture), **Supp. XVI:**155

"Complicated Thoughts About a Small Son" (White), **Supp. I Part 2:** 678

"Compliments of the Season" (O. Henry), **Supp. II Part 1:** 392, 399

"Compline" (Auden), **Supp. II Part 1:** 23

Composition as Explanation (Stein), **IV:** 32, 33, 38

"Composition as Explanation" (Stein), **IV:** 27, 28

"Compounding *of* Consciousness" (James), **II:** 358–359

Comprehensive Bibliography (Hanneman), **II:** 259

Compton-Burnett, Ivy, **I:** 93; **II:** 580

"Comrade Laski, C.P.U.S.A. [M.L.]" (Didion), **Supp. IV Part 1:** 200

Comstock, Anthony, **Retro. Supp. II:** 95

Comus (Milton), **II:** 12; **Supp. I Part 2:** 622

Conan Doyle, Arthur. *See* Doyle, Arthur Conan

Conceptions of Reality in Modern American Poetry (Dembo), **Supp. I Part 1:** 272

"Concept of Character in Fiction, The" (Gass), **Supp. VI:** 85, 86

Concept of Dread, The (Kierkegaard), **III:** 305

Concerning Children (Gilman), **Supp. XI:** 206

"Concerning Necessity" (Carruth), **Supp. XVI:**57

"Concerning Some Recent Criticism of His Work" (Doty), **Supp. XI:** 131

Concerning the End for Which God Created the World (Edwards), **I:** 549, 557, 559

Concerto for Two Pianos, Winds, and

Percussion (Bowles), **Supp. IV Part 1:** 83

Conchologist's First Book, The (Poe), **III:** 412

Conclusive Evidence (Nabokov), **III:** 247–250, 252

"Concord Hymn" (Emerson), **II:** 19

"Concrete Universal, The: Observations on the Understanding of Poetry" (Ransom), **III:** 480

Concurring Beasts (Dobyns), **Supp. XIII:** 76

Condensed Novels and Other Papers (Harte), **Supp. II Part 1:** 342

"Condition, The" (Karmi; Everwine, trans.), **Supp. XV:** 78

Condition of Man, The (Mumford), **Supp. II Part 2:** 483, 484, 486, 495–496, 498

"Condolence" (Parker), **Supp. IX:** 191

"Condominium, The" (Elkin), **Supp. VI:** 49, 50–51, 55, 56

Condon, Charles R., **Supp. XIII:** 163

Condor and the Cows, The: A South American Travel Diary (Isherwood and Caskey), **Supp. XIV:**166

"Condor and the Guests, The" (Connell), **Supp. XIV:**86

Condorcet, Marquis de, **Supp. I Part 2:** 511

Conduct of Life, The (Emerson), **II:** 1–5, 8

Conduct of Life, The (Mumford), **Supp. II Part 2:** 485, 496–497

"Conductor of Nothing, The" (Levine), **Supp. V:** 189

"Conference Male, The" (Mora), **Supp. XIII:** 218

"Confessional" (Bidart), **Supp. XV:** 29–30, 31

Confession de Claude, La (Zola), **I:** 411

"Confession of a House-Breaker, The" (Jewett), **Retro. Supp. II:** 146–147

Confession of Jereboam O. Beauchamp, The (pamphlet), **IV:** 253

Confessions (Augustine), **I:** 279; **Supp. XVI:**288

Confessions (Rousseau), **I:** 226

Confessions of a Barbarian: Selections from the Journals of Edward Abbey, 1951–1989 (Abbey; Petersen, ed.), **Supp. XIII:** 2, 4

"Confessions of a Latina Author" (Mora), **Supp. XIII:** 221

Confessions of Nat Turner, The (Styron), **IV:** 98, 99, 105, 113–117; **Supp. X:** 16, 250

Confetti (Mora), **Supp. XIII:** 221

Confidence (James), **II:** 327, 328

Confidence-Man, The (Melville), **III:** 91; **Retro. Supp. I:** 255–256, 257; **Retro. Supp. II:** 121; **Supp. XIV:**49

Confidence Man, The (Van Vechten), **Supp. II Part 2:** 737

Confidential Clerk, The (Eliot), **I:** 570, 571–572, 583, 584; **Retro. Supp. I:** 65

Confident Years, 1885–1915, The (Brooks), **I:** 257, 259; **Supp. I Part 2:** 650

"Configurations" (Ammons), **Supp. VII:** 28

Confronting the Horror: The Novels of Nelson Algren (Giles), **Supp. IX:** 11, 15

Confucius, **II:** 1; **III:** 456, 475; **Supp. IV Part 1:** 14

Confusion (Cozzens), **I:** 358, 359, 377, 378

Congo (film), **Supp. IV Part 1:** 83

Congo (screenplay, Shanley), **Supp. XIV:**316

"Congo, The" (Lindsay), **Supp. I Part 2:** 388–389, 392, 395

Congo and Other Poems, The (Lindsay), **Supp. I Part 2:** 379, 382, 389, 390, 391

"Congress of the Insomniacs, The" (Simic), **Supp. VIII:** 281–282

Congreve, William, **III:** 195; **Supp. V:** 101

Coningsby (Disraeli), **II:** 127

Conjectures of a Guilty Bystander (Merton), **Supp. VIII:** 197, 206, 207

Conjugal Bliss: A Comedy of Marital Arts (Nichols), **Supp. XIII:** 269

"Conjugation of the Paramecium, The" (Rukeyser), **Supp. VI:** 271

"Conjuration" (Wilbur), **Supp. III Part 2:** 551

Conjure (Reed), **Supp. X:** 240, 242

Conjure (recording), **Supp. X:** 241

Conjure-Man Dies, The (R. Fisher), **Supp. XVI:**143

Conjure Woman, The (Chesnutt), **Supp. II Part 1:** 193; **Supp. XIV:**57, 58–61, 62, 63

Conklin, Grof, **Supp. I Part 2:** 672

Conkling, Hilda, **II:** 530

Conkling, Roscoe, **III:** 506

Conley, Robert J., **Supp. V:** 232

Conley, Susan, **Supp. XIII:** 111, 112

Connaroe, Joel, **Supp. IV Part 2:** 690

"Connecticut Lad, A" (White), **Supp. I Part 2:** 677

"Connecticut Valley" (Cowley), **Supp. II Part 1:** 141–142

Connecticut Yankee in King Arthur's

Court, A (Twain), **I:** 209; **II:** 276; **IV:** 205

Connell, Evan S., **Supp. XIV:**79–100

Connell, Norreys (pseudonym). *See* O'Riordan, Conal Holmes O'Connell

Connelly, Marc, **III:** 394; **Supp. I Part 2:** 679; **Supp. IX:** 190

Connoisseur, The (Connell), **Supp. XIV:**87

"Connoisseur of Chaos" (Stevens), **IV:** 89; **Retro. Supp. I:** 306

Connolly, Cyril, **Supp. XIV:**158, 343, 348

Connors, Elizabeth. *See* Lindsay, Mrs. Vachel (Elizabeth Connors)

Conover, Roger, **Supp. I Part 1:** 95

Conquering Horse (Manfred), **Supp. X:** 126

"Conqueror Worm, The" (Poe), **Retro. Supp. II:** 261

Conquest of Canaan (Dwight), **Supp. I Part 1:** 124

Conquistador (MacLeish), **III:** 2, 3, 13–14, 15

Conrad, Alfred, **Retro. Supp. II:** 245

Conrad, Alfred H., **Supp. I Part 2:** 552

Conrad, David, **Supp. I Part 2:** 552

Conrad, Jacob, **Supp. I Part 2:** 552

Conrad, Joseph, **I:** 123, 343, 394, 405, 409, 415, 421, 485, 506, 575–576, 578; **II:** 58, 73, 74, 91, 92, 144, 263, 320, 338, 595; **III:** 28, 102, 106, 328, 464, 467, 491, 512; **IV:** 476; **Retro. Supp. I:** 80, 91, 106, 108, 231, 274, 377; **Retro. Supp. II:** 222; **Supp. I Part 1:** 292; **Supp. I Part 2:** 621, 622; **Supp. IV Part 1:** 197, 341; **Supp. IV Part 2:** 680; **Supp. V:** 249, 251, 262, 298, 307, 311; **Supp. VIII:** 4, 310; **Supp. XIV:**112; **Supp. XVI:**158, 212

Conrad, Paul, **Supp. I Part 2:** 552

Conrad, Peter, **Supp. IV Part 2:** 688

"Conrad Aiken: From Savannah to Emerson" (Cowley), **Supp. II Part 1:** 43

Conroy, Frank, **Supp. VIII:** 145; **Supp. XI:** 245; **Supp. XVI:**63–78

Conscience with the Power and Cases thereof (Ames), **IV:** 158

"Conscientious Objector, The" (Shapiro), **Supp. II Part 2:** 710

"Consciousness and Dining" (Harrison), **Supp. VIII:** 46

"Conscription Camp" (Shapiro), **Supp. II Part 2:** 705

"Consejos de Nuestra Señora de Guadalupe: Counsel from the Brown Virgin" (Mora), **Supp. XIII:** 224

"Conservation Esthetic" (Leopold), **Supp. XIV:**179, 181, 186, 189–190

"Conserving Natural and Cultural Diversity: The Prose and Poetry of Pat Mora" (Murphy), **Supp. XIII:** 214

"Considerations by the Way" (Emerson), **II:** 2, 5

Considine, Bob, **II:** 424

"Consolation" (Bausch), **Supp. VII:** 48

"Consolations" (Stafford), **Supp. XI:** 329

"Conspiracy of History, The: E. L. Doctorow's *The Book of Daniel*" (Levine), **Supp. IV Part 1:** 221

Conspiracy of Kings, The (Barlow), **Supp. II Part 1:** 80

Conspiracy of Pontiac, The (Parkman), **Supp. II Part 2:** 590, 595, 596, 599–600

Constab Ballads (McKay), **Supp. X:** 131, 133

Constance (Kenyon), **Supp. VII:** 170–172

Construction of Boston, The (Koch), **Supp. XV:** 187

"Constructive Work" (Du Bois), **Supp. II Part 1:** 172

"Consumer's Report" (X. J. Kennedy), **Supp. XV:** 161–162

"Consumption" (Bryant), **Supp. I Part 1:** 169–170

"Contagiousness of Puerperal Fever, The" (Holmes), **Supp. I Part 1:** 303–304

"Contemplation in a World of Action" (Merton), **Supp. VIII:** 204

"Contemplation of Poussin" (Sarton), **Supp. VIII:** 261

"Contemplations" (Bradstreet), **Supp. I Part 1:** 112, 113, 119–122

Contemporaries (Kazin), **Supp. VIII:** 102, 103–104

Contemporary American Playwrights (Bigsby), **Supp. XV:** 332

Contemporary American Poetry (Poulin, ed.), **Supp. IX:** 272; **Supp. XI:** 259

"Contentment" (Holmes), **Supp. I Part 1:** 307

"Contest, The" (Paley), **Supp. VI:** 223, 230, 231

"Contest for Aaron Gold, The" (Roth), **Supp. III Part 2:** 403

Continental Drift (Banks), **Supp. V:** 13–14, 16, 227

Continental Op, The (Hammett), **Supp. IV Part 1:** 344

Continuity of American Poetry, The (Pearce), **Supp. I Part 1:** 111; **Supp. I Part 2:** 475

Continuous Harmony, A: Essays Cultural and Agricultural (Berry), **Supp. X:** 33

Continuous Life, The (Strand), **Supp. IV Part 2:** 630, 631–633

Contoski, Victor, **Supp. XII:** 181

"Contract" (Lardner), **II:** 432

"Contraption, The" (Swenson), **Supp. IV Part 2:** 643

"Contrariness of the Mad Farmer, The" (Berry), **Supp. X:** 35

"Contrition" (Dubus), **Supp. VII:** 84

"Control Burn" (Snyder), **Supp. VIII:** 301

"Control Is the Mainspring" (Komunyakaa), **Supp. XIII:** 122, 124

"Controlling the 'Sloppiness of Things' in Frank Conroy's *Stop-Time*" (Strychacz), **Supp. XVI:**69–70

Control of Nature, The (McPhee), **Supp. III Part 1:** 310–313

"Conventional Wisdom, The" (Elkin), **Supp. VI:** 52–53

"Convergence" (Ammons), **Supp. VII:** 28

"Convergence of the Twain, The" (Hardy), **Supp. VIII:** 31, 32

Conversation (Aiken), **I:** 54

Conversation at Midnight (Millay), **III:** 138

"Conversation of Eiros and Charmion, The" (Poe), **III:** 412

"Conversation on Conversation" (Stowe), **Supp. I Part 2:** 587

"Conversations in Moscow" (Levertov), **Supp. III Part 1:** 282

Conversations on Some of the Old Poets (Lowell), **Supp. I Part 2:** 405

Conversations with Byron (Blessington), **Retro. Supp. II:** 58

Conversations with Eudora Welty (Prenshaw, ed.), **Retro. Supp. I:** 339, 340, 341, 342, 343, 352, 354

"Conversations with Helmholtz" (Allen), **Supp. XV:** 15

Conversations with Ishmael Reed (Dick and Singh, eds.), **Supp. X:** 244

Conversations with James Baldwin (Standley and Pratt, eds.), **Retro. Supp. II:** 6

Conversations with Richard Wilbur (Wilbur), **Supp. III Part 2:** 542–543

"Conversation with My Father, A" (Paley), **Supp. VI:** 220

"Conversion of the Jews, The" (Roth), **Retro. Supp. II:** 281; **Supp. III Part 2:** 404, 406

Convict, The: Stories (Burke), **Supp. XIV:**25

Conway, Jill, **Supp. I Part 1:** 19

Coode, John, **I:** 132

Cook, Bruce, **Supp. XII:** 130, 131, 133–134

Cook, Captain James, **I:** 2

Cook, Eleanor, **Retro. Supp. I:** 311

Cook, Elisha, **Supp. IV Part 1:** 356

Cook, Elizabeth Christine, **II:** 106

Cook, Mercer, **Supp. IV Part 1:** 368

Cooke, Alistair, **III:** 113, 119, 120

Cooke, Delmar G., **II:** 271

Cooke, Grace MacGowan, **Supp. V:** 285

Cooke, Philip Pendleton, **III:** 420

Cooke, Rose Terry, **II:** 401; **Retro. Supp. II:** 51, 136, 138; **Supp. XIII:** 152

"Cookie" (Taylor), **Supp. V:** 320

"Cookies, The" (Nye), **Supp. XIII:** 281

Cook-Lynn, Elizabeth, **Supp. IV Part 1:** 325

Coolbrith, Ina, **I:** 193, 196

"Coole Park" (Yeats), **Supp. VIII:** 155, 159

"Coole Park and Ballylee" (Yeats), **Supp. VIII:** 156

Cooley, John, **Supp. V:** 214

Cooley, Peter, **Supp. XIII:** 76

Coolidge, Calvin, **I:** 498; **II:** 95; **Supp. I Part 2:** 647

Cooling Time: An American Poetry Vigil (Wright), **Supp. XV:** 353

"Cool Million, A" (screen story) (West and Ingster), **Retro. Supp. II:** 330

Cool Million, A (West), **III:** 425; **IV:** 287, 288, 297–299, 300; **Retro. Supp. II:** 321, 322–323, 328, 335–337

"Cool Tombs" (Sandburg), **III:** 554

Coon, Ross, **IV:** 196

Cooney, Seamus, **Supp. XIV:**289

"Coon Hunt" (White), **Supp. I Part 2:** 669

Co-op (Sinclair), **Supp. V:** 290

Cooper, Bernard, **Supp. XI:** 129

Cooper, Gary, **Supp. IV Part 2:** 524

Cooper, James Fenimore, **I:** 211, 257, 335–357; **II:** 74, 277, 295–296, 302, 306, 309, 313, 314; **III:** 51; **IV:** 205, 333; **Retro. Supp. I:** 246; **Retro. Supp. II:** 160; **Supp. I Part 1:** 141, 155, 156, 158, 171, 372; **Supp. I Part 2:** 413, 495, 579, 585, 652, 660; **Supp. IV Part 1:** 80; **Supp.**

IV Part 2: 463, 469; **Supp. V:** 209–210; **Supp. VIII:** 189; **Supp. XIV:**227

Cooper, Jane, **Supp. XV:** 259

Cooper, Mrs. James Fenimore (Susan A. De Lancey), **I:** 338, 351, 354

Cooper, Mrs. William, **I:** 337

Cooper, Rand Richards, **Supp. XVI:**74

Cooper, Susan Fenimore, **I:** 337, 354

Cooper, William, **I:** 337–338, 351

Coover, Robert, **Supp. IV Part 1:** 388; **Supp. V:** 39–55; **Supp. XII:** 152; **Supp. XIV:**96

Copacetic (Komunyakaa), **Supp. XIII:** 116–118, 126

Cope, Wendy, **Supp. XV:** 117

Copland, Aaron, **II:** 586; **Supp. I Part 1:** 281; **Supp. III Part 2:** 619; **Supp. IV Part 1:** 79, 80–81, 84

Coplas de Don Jorge Manrique (Longfellow, trans.), **II:** 488, 492

Coppée, François Edouard Joachim, **II:** 325

Copperhead, The (Frederic), **II:** 134–135

Copper Sun (Cullen), **Supp. IV Part 1:** 167, 168

Coppola, Francis Ford, **Supp. XI:** 171, 172; **Supp. XII:** 75

Coprolites (Goldbarth), **Supp. XII:** 177–178, 180, 183

Coral and Captive Israel (Reznikoff), **Supp. XIV:**288

"Coral Ring, The" (Stowe), **Supp. I Part 2:** 586

"Cora Unashamed" (Hughes), **Supp. I Part 1:** 329, 330

"Corazón del Corrido" (Mora), **Supp. XIII:** 225

Corban Ephphata (Li Lin Lee), **Supp. XV:** 225

Corbett, Gentlemen Jim, **II:** 416

Corbett, William, **Supp. XI:** 248; **Supp. XVI:**286, 295

Corbière, Jean Antoine, **II:** 354–355, 528

Cording, Robert, **Supp. IX:** 328; **Supp. XII:** 184

Corelli, Marie, **III:** 579

Corey, Lewis, **Supp. I Part 2:** 645

"Corinna's Going a-Maying" (Herrick), **Supp. XIV:**8, 9

"Coriolan" (Eliot), **I:** 580

"Coriolanus and His Mother" (Schwartz), **Supp. II Part 2:** 643, 644–645

"Corkscrew" (Hammett), **Supp. IV Part 1:** 345, 347

Corkum, Gerald, **I:** 37

"Corky's Brother" (Neugeboren),

Supp. XVI:225

Corky's Brother (Neugeboren), **Supp. XVI:**225

Corliss, Richard, **Supp. VIII:** 73

Corman, Cid, **Supp. III Part 2:** 624, 625, 626, 627, 628; **Supp. IV Part 1:** 144; **Supp. VIII:** 292; **Supp. XV:** 74, 153

"Corn" (Lanier), **Supp. I Part 1:** 352, 353, 354, 356–361, 364, 366

Corn, Alfred, **Supp. IX:** 156; **Supp. XV:** 250

Corneille, Pierre, **Supp. I Part 2:** 716; **Supp. IX:** 131

Cornell, Esther, **I:** 231

Cornell, Katherine, **IV:** 356

"Corners" (Dunn), **Supp. XI:** 148

Cornhuskers (Sandburg), **III:** 583–585

"Corn-Planting, The" (Anderson), **I:** 114

"Corporal of Artillery" (Dubus), **Supp. VII:** 84, 85

"Corpse Plant, The" (Rich), **Supp. I Part 2:** 555

Corpus Christi (McNally), **Supp. XIII:** 205–206, 209

Corradi, Juan, **Supp. IV Part 1:** 208

"Correspondences" (Baudelaire), **I:** 63

"Corrido de Gregorio Cortez" (Mora), **Supp. XIII:** 225

"Corrigenda" (Komunyakaa), **Supp. XIII:** 115, 116

Corruption City (McCoy), **Supp. XIII:** 175

Corso, Gregory, **Supp. II Part 1:** 30; **Supp. IV Part 1:** 90; **Supp. XII:** 117–138; **Supp. XIV:**150; **Supp. XVI:**135

Corsons Inlet (Ammons), **Supp. VII:** 25–26, 28–29, 36

"Corsons Inlet" (Ammons), **Supp. VII:** 25–26

Cortázar, Julio, **Retro. Supp. I:** 278

"Cortège for Rosenbloom" (Stevens), **IV:** 81

Cortez, Hernando, **III:** 2

Coser, Lewis, **Supp. I Part 2:** 650

Cosgrave, Patrick, **Retro. Supp. II:** 185

Cosmic Optimism: A Study of the Interpretation of Evolution by American Poets from Emerson to Robinson (Conner), **Supp. I Part 1:** 73

Cosmological Eye, The (H. Miller), **III:** 174, 184

"Cosmological Eye, The" (H. Miller), **III:** 183

"Cosmos" (Beattie), **Supp. V:** 35

"Cost, The" (Hecht), **Supp. X:** 62–63

Costello, Bonnie, **Retro. Supp. II:** 40

Costner, Kevin, **Supp. VIII:** 45

"Cost of Living, The" (Malamud), **Supp. I Part 2:** 429, 437

Cott, Jonathan, **Supp. XVI:**104, 106

"Cottage Street, 1953" (Wilbur), **Supp. III Part 2:** 543, 561

"Cottagette, The" (Gilman), **Supp. XI:** 207

Cotten, Joseph, **Supp. IV Part 2:** 524

Cotter, James Finn, **Supp. X:** 202

Cotton, John, **Supp. I Part 1:** 98, 101, 110, 111, 116

Cotton, Joseph, **Supp. XII:** 160

Cotton, Seaborn, **Supp. I Part 1:** 101

Cotton Comes to Harlem (C. Himes), **Supp. XVI:**143, 144

Cotton Comes to Harlem (film, O. Davis), **Supp. XVI:**144

"Cotton Song" (Toomer), **Supp. IX:** 312

Couch, W. T., **Supp. X:** 46

Coughlin, Ruth Pollack, **Supp. VIII:** 45

Coulette, Henri, **Supp. V:** 180; **Supp. XIII:** 312; **Supp. XV:** 74, 75

Coultrap-McQuin, Susan, **Supp. XVI:**85, 92

"Council of State, A" (Dunbar), **Supp. II Part 1:** 211, 213

"Count Dracula" (Allen), **Supp. XV:** 15

"Countee Cullen at 'The Heights'" (Tuttleton), **Supp. IV Part 1:** 166

Counterfeiters, The (Gide), **Supp. IV Part 1:** 80; **Supp. IV Part 2:** 681

"Countering" (Ammons), **Supp. VII:** 28

Counterlife, The (Roth), **Retro. Supp. II:** 279, 280, 291; **Supp. III Part 2:** 424–426

Counter-Statement (Burke), **I:** 270–272; **IV:** 431

"Countess, The" (Whittier), **Supp. I Part 2:** 691, 694

Count Frontenac and New France Under Louis XIV (Parkman), **Supp. II Part 2:** 607, 609–610

"Counting Small-Boned Bodies" (R. Bly), **Supp. IV Part 1:** 62

"Counting the Children" (Gioia), **Supp. XV:** 122–123

"Counting the Mad" (Justice), **Supp. VII:** 117

Count of Monte Cristo, The (Dumas), **III:** 386, 396

"Countries We Live In, The" (Zach; Everwine, trans.), **Supp. XV:** 87

"Country Boy in Boston, The" (Howells), **II:** 255

Country By-Ways (Jewett), **II:** 402

Country Doctor, A (Jewett), **II:** 391, 392, 396, 404–405; **Retro. Supp. II:** 131, 141, 146

"Country Full of Swedes" (Caldwell), **I:** 297, 309

Country Girl, The (Odets), **Supp. II Part 2:** 546, 547, 548–549

"Country House" (Kumin), **Supp. IV Part 2:** 446

"Country Husband, The" (Cheever), **Supp. I Part 1:** 184, 189

"Country Marriage" (C. Frost), **Supp. XV:** 99

Countrymen of Bones (R. O. Butler), **Supp. XII:** 62, 65–66

"Country Mouse, The" (Bishop), **Retro. Supp. II:** 37, 38, 51

Country Music: Selected Early Poems (Wright), **Supp. V:** 332, 335, 338, 342

Country of a Thousand Years of Peace, The (Merrill), **Supp. III Part 1:** 321, 322, 331

"Country of Elusion, The" (O. Henry), **Supp. II Part 1:** 407

Country Of Language, The (Sanders), **Supp. XVI:**277

Country of Marriage, The (Berry), **Supp. X:** 33

Country of the Pointed Firs, The (Jewett), **II:** 392, 399, 405, 409–411; **Retro. Supp. I:** 6; **Retro. Supp. II:** 134, 136, 139, 140, 141, 145, 146, 147; **Supp. VIII:** 126; **Supp. XIII:** 152

"Country Printer, The" (Freneau), **Supp. II Part 1:** 269

"Country Wife, The" (Gioia), **Supp. XV:** 120

Count Zero (W. Gibson), **Supp. XVI:**119, 126–127, 129

Coup, The (Updike), **Retro. Supp. I:** 331, 334, 335

"Coup de Grâce, The" (Bierce), **I:** 202

Couperin, François, **III:** 464

"Couple, The" (Olds), **Supp. X:** 206

"Couple of Hamburgers, A" (Thurber), **Supp. I Part 2:** 616

"Couple of Nuts, A" (Z. Fitzgerald), **Supp. IX:** 58, 71, 72

Couples (Updike), **IV:** 214, 215, 216, 217, 227, 229–230; **Retro. Supp. I:** 320, 327, 330; **Supp. XII:** 296

Cournos, John, **III:** 465; **Supp. I Part 1:** 258

"Course in Creative Writing, A" (Stafford), **Supp. XI:** 327

"Course of a Particular, The" (Stevens), **Retro. Supp. I:** 312

"Coursier de Jeanne d'Arc, Le" (McCarriston), **Supp. XIV:**267–268

Courtier, The (Castiglione), **III:** 282

"'Courtin,' The" (Lowell), **Supp. I Part 2:** 415

"Courting of Sister Wisby, The" (Jewett), **Retro. Supp. II:** 134, 135, 146

"Courtship" (Dove), **Supp. IV Part 1:** 248

"Courtship, Diligence" (Dove), **Supp. IV Part 1:** 248

Courtship of Miles Standish, The (Longfellow), **II:** 489, 502–503; **Retro. Supp. II:** 155, 161–162, 163, 166, 168

"Cousin Aubrey" (Taylor), **Supp. V:** 328

Cousine Bette (Balzac), **Retro. Supp. II:** 98

Couturier, Maurice, **Supp. IV Part 1:** 44

Covarrubias, Miguel, **Supp. XVI:**187

"Covered Bridges" (Kingsolver), **Supp. VII:** 203

Cowan, Lester, **III:** 148

Cowan, Louise, **IV:** 120, 125

Coward, Noel, **Retro. Supp. I:** 65; **Supp. I Part 1:** 332; **Supp. V:** 101; **Supp. XV:** 329

"Cowardice" (Theroux), **Supp. VIII:** 313

Cowboy Mouth (Shepard), **Supp. III Part 2:** 441–442

"Cowboys" (Salter). *See* "Dirt" (Salter)

Cowboys (Shepard), **Supp. III Part 2:** 432

Cowboys #2 (Shepard), **Supp. III Part 2:** 437, 438

Cowell, Henry, **Supp. IV Part 1:** 80, 82

Cowen, Wilson Walker, **Supp. IV Part 2:** 435

Cowie, Alexander, **IV:** 70

"Cow in Apple Time, The" (Frost), **II:** 154; **Retro. Supp. I:** 131

Cowl, Jane, **IV:** 357

Cowley, Abraham, **III:** 508; **IV:** 158; **Supp. I Part 1:** 357

Cowley, Malcolm, **I:** 246, 253, 254, 255, 256, 257, 283, 385; **II:** 26, 57, 94, 456; **III:** 606; **IV:** 123; **Retro. Supp. I:** 73, 91, 97; **Retro. Supp. II:** 77, 83, 89, 221, 330; **Supp. I Part 1:** 174; **Supp. I Part 2:** 609, 610, 620, 647, 654, 678; **Supp. II Part 1:** 103, 135–156; **Supp. VIII:** 96; **Supp. XV:** 142

Cowley, Marguerite Frances Baird

(Mrs. Malcolm Cowley), **Supp. I Part 2:** 615; **Supp. II Part 1:** 138, 139

Cowley, Muriel Maurer (Mrs. Malcolm Cowley), **Supp. II Part 1:** 139

Cowley, Susan Cheever (Susan Cheever), **Supp. I Part 1:** 175; **Supp. IX:** 133

Cowper, William, **II:** 17, 304; **III:** 508, 511; **Supp. I Part 1:** 150, 151, 152; **Supp. I Part 2:** 539

"Cow Wandering in the Bare Field, The" (Jarrell), **II:** 371, 388

Cox, Martha Heasley, **Supp. IX:** 2, 4, 11–12

Cox, Sidney, **Retro. Supp. I:** 131

Cox, Stephen, **Supp. IV Part 2:** 523, 524

Coxey, Jacob, **II:** 464

"Coxon Fund, The" (James), **Retro. Supp. I:** 228

Coyne, Patricia, **Supp. V:** 123

"Coyote Ortiz: *Canis latrans latrans* in the Poetry of Simon Ortiz" (P. C. Smith), **Supp. IV Part 2:** 509

Coyote's Daylight Trip (Gunn Allen), **Supp. IV Part 1:** 320, 324

Coyote Was Here (Ortiz), **Supp. IV Part 2:** 499

Cozzens, James Gould, **I:** 358–380; **II:** 459

Crabbe, George, **II:** 304; **III:** 469, 508, 511, 521

"Crab-Boil" (Dove), **Supp. IV Part 1:** 249

"Cracked Looking-Glass, The" (Porter), **III:** 434, 435, 446

"Cracker Chidlings" (Rawlings), **Supp. X:** 224, 228

Cracks (Purdy), **Supp. VII:** 277–278

"Crack-Up, The" (Fitzgerald), **I:** 509; **Retro. Supp. I:** 113, 114

Crack-Up, The (Fitzgerald), **II:** 80; **III:** 35, 45; **Retro. Supp. I:** 113, 115; **Supp. V:** 276; **Supp. IX:** 61

"Crack-up of American Optimism, The: Vachel Lindsay, the Dante of the Fundamentalists" (Viereck), **Supp. I Part 2:** 403

Cradle Will Rock, The (Blitzstein), **Supp. I Part 1:** 277, 278

Craft of Fiction, The (Lubbock), **I:** 504; **Supp. VIII:** 165

Craft of Peter Taylor, The (McAlexander, ed.), **Supp. V:** 314

Craig, Gordon, **III:** 394

Crain, Jane Larkin, **Supp. V:** 123; **Supp. XII:** 167, 168

Cram, Ralph Adams, **I:** 19

Cramer, Stephen, **Supp. XI:** 139

Cramer, Steven, **Supp. XV:** 26

Crandall, Reuben, **Supp. I Part 2:** 686

Crane, Agnes, **I:** 406

Crane, Edmund, **I:** 407

Crane, Hart, **I:** 61, 62, 97, 109, 116, 266, 381–404; **II:** 133, 215, 306, 368, 371, 536, 542; **III:** 260, 276, 453, 485, 521; **IV:** 122, 123–124, 127, 128, 129, 135, 139, 140, 141, 341, 380, 418, 419; **Retro. Supp. I:** 427; **Retro. Supp. II:** 75–91; **Supp. I Part 1:** 86; **Supp. II Part 1:** 89, 152; **Supp. III Part 1:** 20, 63, 350; **Supp. V:** 342; **Supp. VIII:** 39; **Supp. IX:** 38, 229, 320; **Supp. X:** 115, 116, 120; **Supp. XI:** 123, 131; **Supp. XII:** 198; **Supp. XV:** 138

Crane, Jonathan, Jr., **I:** 407

Crane, Jonathan Townley, **I:** 406

Crane, Luther, **I:** 406

Crane, Milton, **Supp. XV:** 144

Crane, Mrs. Jonathan Townley, **I:** 406

Crane, Nellie, **I:** 407

Crane, R. S., **Supp. I Part 2:** 423

Crane, Stephen, **I:** 34, 169–170, 201, 207, 211, 405–427, 477, 506, 519; **II:** 58, 144, 198, 262, 263, 264, 276, 289, 290, 291; **III:** 314, 317, 334, 335, 454, 505, 585; **IV:** 207, 208, 256, 350, 475; **Retro. Supp. I:** 231, 325; **Retro. Supp. II:** 97, 123; **Supp. I Part 1:** 314; **Supp. III Part 2:** 412; **Supp. IV Part 1:** 350, 380; **Supp. IV Part 2:** 680, 689, 692; **Supp. VIII:** 98, 105; **Supp. IX:** 1, 14; **Supp. X:** 223; **Supp. XI:** 95; **Supp. XII:** 50; **Supp. XIV:** 21, 50, 51, 227

Crane, William, **I:** 407

Cranford (Gaskell), **Supp. IX:** 79

Crashaw, William, **IV:** 145, 150, 151, 165

"Crash Report" (McGrath), **Supp. X:** 116

Crater, The (Cooper), **I:** 354, 355

Cratylus (Plato), **II:** 10

"Craven Street Gazette" (Franklin), **II:** 119

Crawdad Creek (Sanders), **Supp. XVI:** 269

Crawford, Brad, **Supp. XI:** 133

Crawford, Eva, **I:** 199

Crawford, F. Marion, **III:** 320

Crawford, Joan, **Supp. I Part 1:** 67

Crawford, Kathleen, **I:** 289

"Crayon House" (Rukeyser), **Supp. VI:** 273

Crayon Miscellany, The (Irving), **II:** 312–313

"Crazy about her Shrimp" (Simic), **Supp. VIII:** 282

"Crazy Cock" (H. Miller), **III:** 177

Crazy Gypsy (Salinas), **Supp. XIII:** 311, 313–315, 316

"Crazy Gypsy" (Salinas), **Supp. XIII:** 313–314

Crazy Horse, **Supp. IV Part 2:** 488, 489

Crazy Horse (McMurtry), **Supp. V:** 233

Crazy Horse in Stillness (Heyen), **Supp. XIII:** 344

"Crazy in the Stir" (C. Himes), **Supp. XVI:** 137

Crazy Kill, The (C. Himes), **Supp. XVI:** 143

Creating a Role (Stanislavsky), **Supp. XIV:** 243

"Creation, According to Coyote, The" (Ortiz), **Supp. IV Part 2:** 505

Creation: A Novel (Vidal), **Supp. IV Part 2:** 677, 685, 688

"Creation of Anguish" (Nemerov), **III:** 269

"Creation Story" (Gunn Allen), **Supp. IV Part 1:** 325

"Creative and Cultural Lag" (Ellison), **Retro. Supp. II:** 116; **Supp. II Part 1:** 229

Creative Criticism (Spingarn), **I:** 266

"Creative Democracy" (Locke), **Supp. XIV:** 208

Creative Present, The (Balkian and Simmons, eds.), **Supp. XI:** 230

Creatures in an Alphabet (illus. Barnes), **Supp. III Part 1:** 43

"Credences of Summer" (Stevens), **IV:** 93–94

"Credo" (Bynner), **Supp. XV:** 50

"Credo" (Du Bois), **Supp. II Part 1:** 169

"Credo" (Jeffers), **Supp. II Part 2:** 424

"Credos and Curios" (Thurber), **Supp. I Part 2:** 606, 613

Creech, James, **Retro. Supp. I:** 254

"Creed for Americans, A" (Benét), **Supp. XI:** 52

"Creed of a Beggar, The" (Lindsay), **Supp. I Part 2:** 379

Creekmore, Hubert, **II:** 586

Creeley, Robert, **Retro. Supp. I:** 411; **Supp. II Part 1:** 30; **Supp. III Part 1:** 2; **Supp. III Part 2:** 622, 626, 629; **Supp. IV Part 1:** 139–161, 322, 325; **Supp. XI:** 317; **Supp. XIII:** 104, 112; **Supp. XIV:** 150; **Supp. XVI:** 283

Creelman, James Ashmore, **Supp. XVI:** 186–187

"Cremona Violin, The" (Lowell), **II**: 523

"Crêpe de Chine" (Doty), **Supp. XI**: 128

"Cressy" (Harte), **Supp. II Part 1**: 354, 356

"Cretan Woman, The" (Jeffers), **Supp. II Part 2**: 435

Crèvecoeur, Michel-Guillaume Jean de, **I**: 229; **Supp. I Part 1**: 227–252

Crèvecoeur's Eighteenth-Century Travels in Pennsylvania and New York (Adams), **Supp. I Part 1**: 251

Crevel, René, **Supp. XIV**:343

Crewe Train (Macaulay), **Supp. XII**: 88

Crews, Harry, **Supp. X**: 11, 12; **Supp. XI**: 99–117, 245

Crichton, Michael, **Supp. XIV**:316

Crick, Philip, **Supp. XVI**:289

"Crickets" (R. O. Butler), **Supp. XII**: 71

Criers and Kibitzers, Kibitzers and Criers (Elkin), **Supp. VI**: 45–46, 57

Crime and Punishment (Dostoyevsky), **II**: 60, 130; **IV**: 484; **Supp. IV Part 2**: 525; **Supp. VIII**: 282; **Supp. XII**: 281

Crimes and Misdemeanors (film; Allen), **Supp. XV**: 1, 2, 11, 12

Crisis papers (Paine), **Supp. I Part 2**: 508–509, 510

"Criteria of Negro Arts" (Du Bois), **Supp. II Part 1**: 181

"Critiad, The" (Winters), **Supp. II Part 2**: 794, 799

Critical Anthology A (Untermeyer), **Supp. XV**: 310

Critical Essays on Charlotte Perkins Gilman (Karpinski, ed.), **Supp. XI**: 201

Critical Essays on Peter Taylor (McAlexander), **Supp. V**: 319, 320, 323–324

Critical Essays on Robert Bly (Davis), **Supp. IV Part 1**: 64, 69

Critical Essays on Wallace Stegner (Arthur), **Supp. IV Part 2**: 606

Critical Fable, A (Lowell), **II**: 511–512, 527, 529–530

Critical Guide to Leaves of Grass, A (J. Miller), **IV**: 352

Critical Response to Joan Didion, The (Felton), **Supp. IV Part 1**: 210

Critical Temper of Alain Locke, The: A Selection of His Essays on Art and Culture (Stewart, ed.), **Supp. XIV**:196, 210–211, 213

"Critic as Artist, The" (Wilde), **Supp. X**: 189

Criticism and Fiction (Howells), **II**: 288

Criticism and Ideology (Eagleton), **Retro. Supp. I**: 67

Criticism in the Borderlands (Calderón and Saldívar, eds.), **Supp. IV Part 2**: 544

"Critics, The" (Jong), **Supp. V**: 119

"Critics and Connoisseurs" (Moore), **III**: 209

Critic's Notebook, A (Howe), **Supp. VI**: 126–128

"Critic's Task, The" (Kazin), **Supp. VIII**: 103

"Critic Who Does Not Exist, The" (Wilson), **IV**: 431

"Critique de la Vie Quotidienne" (Barthelme), **Supp. IV Part 1**: 50

Critique of Pure Reason (Kant), **Supp. XVI**:184

Croce, Benedetto, **I**: 58, 255, 265, 273, 281; **III**: 610

Crockett, Davy, **II**: 307; **III**: 227; **IV**: 266; **Supp. I Part 2**: 411

Crofter and the Laird, The (McPhee), **Supp. III Part 1**: 301–302, 307

Croly, Herbert, **I**: 229, 231, 235; **IV**: 436

Cromwell, Oliver, **IV**: 145, 146, 156; **Supp. I Part 1**: 111

Cronin, Dr. Archibald, **III**: 578

Cronin, Justin, **Supp. X**: 10

Crooke, Dr. Helkiah, **Supp. I Part 1**: 98, 104

Crooks, Alan, **Supp. V**: 226

Crooks, Robert, **Supp. XIII**: 237

"Crop, The" (O'Connor), **Retro. Supp. II**: 223–225

Crosby, Caresse, **I**: 385; **III**: 473; **Retro. Supp. II**: 85; **Supp. XII**: 198

Crosby, Harry, **I**: 385; **Retro. Supp. II**: 85

"Cross" (Hughes), **Supp. I Part 1**: 325

Crossan, John Dominic, **Supp. V**: 251

"Cross Country Snow" (Hemingway), **II**: 249

Cross Creek (Rawlings), **Supp. X**: 223, 226, 228, 231–232, 233, 234, 235

Cross Creek Cookery (Rawlings), **Supp. X**: 233

Crossing, The (McCarthy), **Supp. VIII**: 175, 184–186

"Crossing, The" (Swenson), **Supp. IV Part 2**: 644

"Crossing Brooklyn Ferry" (Whitman), **IV**: 333, 340, 341; **Retro. Supp. I**: 389, 396, 397, 400–401

"Crossing into Poland" (Babel), **Supp. XIV**:84

Crossings (Chuang), **Supp. X**: 291

"Crossings" (Hogan), **Supp. IV Part 1**: 412

Crossing the Water (Plath), **Retro. Supp. II**: 248; **Supp. I Part 2**: 526, 538

Crossing to Safety (Stegner), **Supp. IV Part 2**: 599, 606, 612, 613–614

"Cross of Snow, The" (Longfellow), **II**: 490; **Retro. Supp. II**: 169–170

"Crossover" (O. Butler), **Supp. XIII**: 61

"Cross-Roads, The" (Lowell), **II**: 523

"Crossroads of the World Etc." (Merwin), **Supp. III Part 1**: 347, 348

Cross-Section (Seaver), **IV**: 485

Cross the Border, Close the Gap (Fiedler), **Supp. XIII**: 104

Cross Ties (X. J. Kennedy), **Supp. XV**: 165, 166–167

"Cross Ties" (X. J. Kennedy), **Supp. XV**: 158

"Croup" (Karr), **Supp. XI**: 243

Crouse, Russel, **III**: 284

"Crow" (Hogan), **Supp. IV Part 1**: 405

Crow (Hughes), **Supp. XV**: 347, 348

"Crow, The" (Creeley), **Supp. IV Part 1**: 148–149

Crow and the Heart, The (Carruth), **Supp. XVI**:47–48

"Crowded Street, The" (Bryant), **Supp. I Part 1**: 168

Crowder, A. B., **Supp. XI**: 107

"Crow Jane" (Baraka), **Supp. II Part 1**: 38

Crowninshield, Frank, **III**: 123; **Supp. IX**: 201

Crown of Columbus (Erdrich and Dorris), **Supp. IV Part 1**: 260

"Crows, The" (Bogan), **Supp. III Part 1**: 50, 51

Crucial Instances (Wharton), **Retro. Supp. I**: 365, 367

Crucible, The (A. Miller), **III**: 147, 148, 155, 156–158, 159, 166; **Supp. XIII**: 206

"Crucifix in the Filing Cabinet" (Shapiro), **Supp. II Part 2**: 712

"Crude Foyer" (Stevens), **Retro. Supp. I**: 310

"Cruel and Barbarous Treatment" (McCarthy), **II**: 562, 563

Cruise of the Dazzler, The (London), **II**: 465

Cruise of the Snark, The (London), **II**: 476–477

"Cruising with the Beach Boys" (Gioia), **Supp. XV**: 118

"'Crumbling Idols' by Hamlin Garland" (Chopin), **Supp. I Part 1:** 217

"Crusade of the Excelsior, The" (Harte), **Supp. II Part 1:** 336, 354

"Crusoe in England" (Bishop), **Retro. Supp. II:** 50; **Supp. I Part 1:** 93, 95, 96; **Supp. III Part 1:** 10, 18

Cry, the Beloved Country (Paton), **Supp. VIII:** 126

Cryer, Dan, **Supp. VIII:** 86, 88; **Supp. XII:** 164

Crying of Lot 49, The (Pynchon), **Supp. II Part 2:** 618, 619, 621, 630–633

"Crying Sisters, The" (Rand), **Supp. IV Part 2:** 524

"Crying Wolf" (C. Frost), **Supp. XV:** 101

Cryptogram, The (Mamet), **Supp. XIV:** 240, 247, 255

"Crystal, The" (Aiken), **I:** 60

"Crystal, The" (Lanier), **Supp. I Part 1:** 364, 370

"Crystal Cage, The" (Kunitz), **Supp. III Part 1:** 258

"Crytal" (Sobin), **Supp. XVI:** 283

Cry to Heaven (Rice), **Supp. VII:** 300–301

"Cuba" (Hemingway), **II:** 258

"Cuba Libre" (Baraka), **Supp. II Part 1:** 33

Cudjoe, Selwyn, **Supp. IV Part 1:** 6

"Cudjo's Own Story of the Last American Slaver" (Hurston), **Supp. VI:** 153

Cudlipp, Thelma, **I:** 501

Cudworth, Ralph, **II:** 9, 10

"Cuentista" (Mora), **Supp. XIII:** 224

"Cuento de agua santa, Un" (Mora), **Supp. XIII:** 224

Cujo (King), **Supp. V:** 138–139, 143, 149, 152

Cukor, George, **Supp. XVI:** 192

Cullen, Countee, **Retro. Supp. I:** 207; **Retro. Supp. II:** 114; **Supp. I Part 1:** 49, 325; **Supp. III Part 1:** 73, 75, 76; **Supp. IV Part 1:** 163–174; **Supp. IX:** 306, 309; **Supp. X:** 136, 140; **Supp. XIII:** 186

"Cultivation of Christmas Trees, The" (Eliot), **I:** 579

"Cult of the Best, The" (Arnold), **I:** 223

"Cultural Exchange" (Hughes), **Supp. I Part 1:** 341

"Cultural Pluralism: A New Americanism" (Locke), **Supp. XIV:** 195

"Cultural Relativism and Ideological Peace" (Locke), **Supp. XIV:** 202, 212

"Culture" (Emerson), **III:** 2, 4

"Culture, Self, and Style" (Gass), **Supp. VI:** 88

"Culture and Religion" (Olds), **Supp. X:** 214

Culture of Cities, The (Mumford), **Supp. II Part 2:** 492, 494–495

Cummings, E. E., **I:** 44, 48, 64, 105, 176, 428–450, 475, 477, 482, 526; **III:** 20, 196, 476; **IV:** 384, 402, 415, 427, 433; **Retro. Supp. II:** 178, 328; **Supp. I Part 2:** 622, 678; **Supp. III Part 1:** 73; **Supp. IV Part 2:** 637, 641; **Supp. IX:** 20; **Supp. XV:** 312, 338

Cummings, Robert, **Supp. IV Part 2:** 524

Cunard, Lady, **III:** 459

Cunningham, J. V., **Supp. XV:** 169

Cunningham, Merce, **Supp. IV Part 1:** 83; **Supp. XV:** 187

Cunningham, Michael, **Supp. XII:** 80; **Supp. XV:** 55–71

Cup of Gold (Steinbeck), **IV:** 51, 53, 61–64, 67

"Cupola, The" (Bogan), **Supp. III Part 1:** 53

"Curandera" (Mora), **Supp. XIII:** 214, 222

Curé de Tours, Le (Balzac), **I:** 509

Cure for Dreams, A: A Novel (Gibbons), **Supp. X:** 45–47, 48, 50

Curie, Marie, **IV:** 420, 421; **Supp. I Part 2:** 569

Curie, Pierre, **IV:** 420

Curiosa Americana (Mather), **Supp. II Part 2:** 463

Curiosities (Matthews), **Supp. IX:** 151, 152

"Curious Case of Sidd Finch, The" (Plimpton), **Supp. XVI:** 244

"Curious Shifts of the Poor" (Dreiser), **Retro. Supp. II:** 97

"Currents and Counter-Currents in Medical Science" (Holmes), **Supp. I Part 1:** 305

"Curried Cow" (Bierce), **I:** 200

Curry, Professor W. C., **IV:** 122

Curse of the Jade Scorpion, The (film; Allen), **Supp. XV:** 11

Curse of the Starving Class (Shepard), **Supp. III Part 2:** 433, 447–448

"Curse on a Thief, A" (X. J. Kennedy), **Supp. XV:** 171

"Curtain, The" (Chandler), **Supp. IV Part 1:** 122

Curtain Calls: British and American Women and the Theater, 1660–1820 (Saar), **Supp. XV:** 237

Curtain of Green, A (Welty), **IV:** 261–

264, 268, 283

"Curtain of Green, A" (Welty), **IV:** 263–264

Curtain of Green and Other Stories, A (Welty), **Retro. Supp. I:** 343, 344, 345, 346, 347, 355

Curtain of Trees (opera), **Supp. IV Part 2:** 552

"Curtain Raiser, A" (Stein), **IV:** 43, 44

"Curtains" (Cisneros), **Supp. VII:** 66

Curtin, John, **Supp. IX:** 184

Curtis, George William, **Supp. I Part 1:** 307

Curve (Goldbarth), **Supp. XII:** 181

Curve of Binding Energy, The (McPhee), **Supp. III Part 1:** 301

Curzon, Mary, **III:** 52

Cushing, Caleb, **Supp. I Part 2:** 684, 686

Cushman, Howard, **Supp. I Part 2:** 652

Cushman, Stephen, **Retro. Supp. I:** 430

"Custard Heart, The" (Parker), **Supp. IX:** 201

Custer, General George, **I:** 489, 491

Custer Died for Your Sins (Deloria), **Supp. IV Part 1:** 323; **Supp. IV Part 2:** 504

"Custom House, The" (Hawthorne), **II:** 223; **Retro. Supp. I:** 147–148, 157

Custom of the Country, The (Wharton), **IV:** 318; **Retro. Supp. I:** 374, 375–376

"Cut" (Plath), **Retro. Supp. II:** 253

"Cut-Glass Bowl, The" (Fitzgerald), **II:** 88

Cutting, Bronson, **III:** 600

"Cuttings, *later*" (Roethke), **III:** 532

"Cyberpunk" (Bethke), **Supp. XVI:** 121

Cyberspace trilogy (W. Gibson). See Sprawl trilogy (W. Gibson)

"Cycles, The" (Pinsky), **Supp. VI:** 250–252

Cynic's Word Book, The (Bierce), **I:** 197, 205, 208, 209, 210

Cynthia Ozick (Lowin), **Supp. V:** 273

Cynthia Ozick's Comic Art (Cohen), **Supp. V:** 273

Cynthia Ozick's Fiction (Kauvar), **Supp. V:** 273

D

"D. H. Lawrence" (Bynner), **Supp. XV:** 46

D. H. Lawrence: An Unprofessional Study (Nin), **Supp. X:** 182–183

D. H. Lawrence: The World of the Major Novels (Sanders), **Supp. XVI:** 267

Dacey, Philip, **Supp. IV Part 1:** 70
Dacier, André, **II:** 10
"Dad" (Cullen), **Supp. IV Part 1:** 167
"Daddy" (Plath), **Retro. Supp. II:** 250–251; **Supp. I Part 2:** 529, 542, 545, 546; **Supp. II Part 2:** 688
"Daemon, The" (Bogan), **Supp. III Part 1:** 58, 61
"Daemon Lover, The" (Jackson), **Supp. IX:** 116–117
"Daffodils" (Wordsworth), **Supp. XIII:** 284
"Daffy Duck in Hollywood" (Ashbery), **Supp. III Part 1:** 18
D'Agata, John, **Supp. XII:** 97, 98
Dago Red (Fante), **Supp. XI:** 160, 169
Dahl, Roald, **Supp. IX:** 114
Dahlberg, Edward, **I:** 231; **Retro. Supp. I:** 426; **Supp. III Part 2:** 624; **Supp. XIV:**148
Dahlberg, R'lene, **Supp. XIV:**148
Daiches, David, **Retro. Supp. II:** 243; **Supp. I Part 2:** 536
Daily Horoscope (Gioia), **Supp. XV:** 112, 118–121, 126
"Daily Horoscope" (Gioia), **Supp. XV:** 119
Daily Modernism (Podnieks), **Supp. X:** 189
Dain Curse, The (Hammett), **Supp. IV Part 1:** 348
"Daisies" (Glück), **Supp. V:** 88
"Daisy" (Oates), **Supp. II Part 2:** 523
Daisy-Head Mayzie (Geisel), **Supp. XVI:**112
Daisy Miller (James), **Retro. Supp. I:** 216, 220, 222, 223, 228, 231
"Daisy Miller" (James), **II:** 325, 326, 327, 329; **IV:** 316
Dale, Charlie, **Supp. IV Part 2:** 584
Dali, Salvador, **II:** 586; **Supp. IV Part 1:** 83; **Supp. XIII:** 317
Dalibard, Thomas-François, **II:** 117
"Dallas-Fort Worth: Redband and Mistletoe" (Clampitt), **Supp. IX:** 45
"Dalliance of Eagles, The" (Whitman), **IV:** 348
Dalva (Harrison), **Supp. VIII:** 37, 45, 46, 48–49
Daly, Carroll John, **Supp. IV Part 1:** 343, 345
Daly, John, **II:** 25, 26
Daly, Julia Brown, **II:** 25, 26
"Dalyrimple Goes Wrong" (Fitzgerald), **II:** 88
"Dam, The" (Rukeyser), **Supp. VI:** 283
Damas, Leon, **Supp. X:** 139
Damascus Gate (Stone), **Supp. V:** 308–311

Damballah (Wideman), **Supp. X:** 319, 320, 321, 322, 323, 326, 327, 331, 333–334
Damnation of Theron Ware, The (Frederic), **II:** 140–143, 144, 146, 147; **Retro. Supp. I:** 325
"Damned Thing, The" (Bierce), **I:** 206
Damon, Matt, **Supp. VIII:** 175
Damon, S. Foster, **I:** 26; **II:** 512, 514, 515
"Damon and Vandalia" (Dove), **Supp. IV Part 1:** 252
Dana, H. W. L., **I:** 225
Dana, Richard Henry, **I:** 339, 351; **Supp. I Part 1:** 103, 154, 155; **Supp. I Part 2:** 414, 420
Dana, Richard Henry, Jr., **III:** 81
Dana, Robert, **Supp. V:** 178, 180
"Dana Gioia and Fine Press Printing" (Peich), **Supp. XV:** 117
"Dance, The" (Crane), **I:** 109
"Dance, The" (Roethke), **III:** 541
Dance of Death, The (Auden), **Supp. II Part 1:** 10
Dance of Death, The (Bierce and Harcourt), **I:** 196
Dance of the Sleepwalkers (Calabria), **Supp. XIII:** 164
"Dance of the Solids, The" (Updike), **Retro. Supp. I:** 323
Dances with Wolves (film), **Supp. X:** 124
Dancing After Hours (Dubus), **Supp. VII:** 91
Dancing Bears, The (Merwin), **Supp. III Part 1:** 343–344
Dancing on the Stones (Nichols), **Supp. XIII:** 256, 257, 259, 267, 269
"Dancing the Jig" (Sexton), **Supp. II Part 2:** 692
Dandelion Wine (Bradbury), **Supp. IV Part 1:** 101, 109–110
Dandurand, Karen, **Retro. Supp. I:** 30
"Dandy Frightening the Squatters, The" (Twain), **IV:** 193–194
Dangerous Crossroads (film), **Supp. XIII:** 163
Dangerous Moonlight (Purdy), **Supp. VII:** 278
"Dangerous Road Before Martin Luther King" (Baldwin), **Supp. I Part 1:** 52
"Dangerous Summer, The" (Hemingway), **II:** 261
"Dangers of Authorship, The" (Blackmur), **Supp. II Part 1:** 147
Dangling Man (Bellow), **I:** 144, 145, 147, 148, 150–151, 153–154, 158, 160, 161, 162, 163; **Retro. Supp.**

II: 19, 20–21, 22, 23; **Supp. VIII:** 234
Daniel (biblical book), **Supp. I Part 1:** 105
Daniel (film), **Supp. IV Part 1:** 236
Daniel, Arnaut, **III:** 467
Daniel, Robert W., **III:** 76
Daniel, Samuel, **Supp. I Part 1:** 369
Daniel Deronda (Eliot), **I:** 458
Danielson, Linda, **Supp. IV Part 2:** 569
D'Annunzio, Gabriele, **II:** 515
Danny and the Deep Blue Sea: An Apache Dance (Shanley), **Supp. XIV:**315, 318–319, 320, 321, 323, 324
Danny O'Neill pentalogy (Farrell), **II:** 35–41
Danse Macabre (King), **Supp. IV Part 1:** 102; **Supp. V:** 144
"Danse Russe" (W. C. Williams), **IV:** 412–413
"Dans le Restaurant" (Eliot), **I:** 554, 578
Dans l'ombre des cathédrales (Ambelain), **Supp. I Part 1:** 273
Dante Alighieri, **I:** 103, 136, 138, 250, 384, 433, 445; **II:** 8, 274, 278, 289, 490, 492, 493, 494, 495, 504, 508, 524, 552; **III:** 13, 77, 124, 182, 259, 278, 448, 453, 467, 533, 607, 609, 610–612, 613; **IV:** 50, 134, 137, 138, 139, 247, 437, 438; **Retro. Supp. I:** 62, 63, 64, 66, 360; **Retro. Supp. II:** 330; **Supp. I Part 1:** 256, 363; **Supp. I Part 2:** 422, 454; **Supp. III Part 2:** 611, 618, 621; **Supp. IV Part 2:** 634; **Supp. V:** 277, 283, 331, 338, 345; **Supp. VIII:** 27, 219–221; **Supp. X:** 120, 121, 125; **Supp. XII:** 98; **Supp. XV:** 254
Danziger, Adolphe, **I:** 199–200
Dar (Nabokov), **III:** 246, 255
"Dare's Gift" (Glasgow), **II:** 190
Dark Angel, The (Bolton), **Supp. I Part 1:** 281
"Dark Angel Travels With Us to Canada and Blesses Our Vacation, The" (Dunn), **Supp. XI:** 146
Dark Carnival (Bradbury), **Supp. IV Part 1:** 102
Darker (Strand), **Supp. IV Part 2:** 619, 626–628
Darker Face of the Earth, The (Dove), **Supp. IV Part 1:** 255–257
Dark Green, Bright Red (Vidal), **Supp. IV Part 2:** 677
Dark Half, The (King), **Supp. V:** 141
Dark Harbor: A Poem (Strand), **Supp.**

IV Part 2: 633–634

"Dark Hills, The" (Robinson), **III:** 523

Dark Horses (X. J. Kennedy), **Supp. XV:** 167–170

Dark Laughter (Anderson), **I:** 111, 116; **II:** 250–251

"Darkling Alphabet, A" (Snodgrass), **Supp. VI:** 323

Darkling Child (Merwin and Milroy), **Supp. III Part 1:** 346

"Darkling Summer, Ominous Dusk, Rumorous Rain" (Schwartz), **Supp. II Part 2:** 661

"Darkling Thrush" (Hardy), **Supp. IX:** 40

"Dark Men, The" (Dubus), **Supp. VII:** 86

Dark Mirrors (Sobin), **Supp. XVI:**295

Darkness and the Light, The (Hecht), **Supp. X:** 58

"Darkness on the Edge of Town" (O'Brien), **Supp. V:** 246

Darkness under the Trees/Walking behind the Spanish (Salinas), **Supp. XIII:** 311, 319–324

"Dark Night" (St. John of the Cross), **Supp. XV:** 30

Dark Night of the Soul, The (St. John of the Cross), **I:** 1, 585

"Dark Ones" (Dickey), **Supp. IV Part 1:** 182

Dark Princess: A Romance (Du Bois), **Supp. II Part 1:** 179, 181–182

Dark Room, The (T. Williams), **IV:** 381

"Dark Summer" (Bogan), **Supp. III Part 1:** 51, 53

Dark Summer: Poems (Bogan), **Supp. III Part 1:** 52–53, 57

"Dark Tower, The" (column), **Supp. IV Part 1:** 168, 170

Dark Tower, The: The Gunslinger (King), **Supp. V:** 152

Dark Tower IV, The: Wizard and Glass (King), **Supp. V:** 139

Dark Tunnel, The (Macdonald, under Millar), **Supp. IV Part 2:** 465, 466

"Dark TV Screen" (Simic), **Supp. VIII:** 282

"Dark Voyage, The" (McLay), **Supp. XIII:** 21

"Dark Walk, The" (Taylor), **Supp. V:** 320–321, 322, 326

Darkwater: Voices from Within the Veil (Du Bois), **Supp. II Part 1:** 178, 180, 183

Dark Waves and Light Matter (Goldbarth), **Supp. XII:** 176, 193

Dark World (Carruth), **Supp. XVI:**55

"Darling" (Nye), **Supp. XIII:** 283–284

"Darling, The" (Chekhov), **Supp. IX:** 202

Darling-Darling (Barillet and Grédy; Loos, trans.), **Supp. XVI:**194

Darnell, Linda, **Supp. XII:** 173

Darragh, Tina, **Supp. IV Part 2:** 427

Darreu, Robert Donaldson, **Supp. II Part 1:** 89, 98, 102

Darrow, Clarence, **Supp. I Part 1:** 5; **Supp. I Part 2:** 455

Darwin, Charles, **I:** 457; **II:** 323, 462, 481; **III:** 226, 231; **IV:** 69, 304; **Retro. Supp. I:** 254; **Retro. Supp. II:** 60, 65; **Supp. I Part 1:** 368; **Supp. IX:** 180; **Supp. XI:** 203; **Supp. XVI:**13

"Darwin in 1881" (Schnackenberg), **Supp. XV:** 253, 254, 258

Daryush, Elizabeth, **Supp. V:** 180

Dash, Julie, **Supp. XI:** 17, 18, 20

Dashell, Alfred, **Supp. X:** 224

"DAS KAPITAL" (Baraka), **Supp. II Part 1:** 55

Datlow, Ellen, **Supp. XVI:**123

"Datum Centurio" (Wallace), **Supp. X:** 309

Daudet, Alphonse, **II:** 325, 338

"Daughter" (Caldwell), **I:** 309

"Daughter in the House" (X. J. Kennedy), **Supp. XV:** 160

Daughter of Earth (Smedly), **Supp. XIII:** 295

Daughter of the Snows, A (London), **II:** 465, 469–470

"Daughters" (Anderson), **I:** 114

Daughters (Marshall), **Supp. XI:** 275, 276, 277, 286–288, 289, 290

Daughters, I Love You (Hogan), **Supp. IV Part 1:** 397, 399, 401

"Daughters of Invention" (Alvarez), **Supp. VII:** 9

Daughters of the Dust (Dash; film), **Supp. XI:** 17, 18

Daumier, Honoré, **IV:** 412

Dave, R. A., **Supp. VIII:** 126

Davenport, Abraham, **Supp. I Part 2:** 699

Davenport, Gary, **Supp. IX:** 98

Davenport, Guy, **Supp. XIV:**96

Davenport, Herbert J., **Supp. I Part 2:** 642

Davenport, James, **I:** 546

Daves, E. G., **Supp. I Part 1:** 369

Davey, Frank, **Supp. XIII:** 33

"David" (Garrett), **Supp. VII:** 109–110

"David" (Gordon), **Supp. IV Part 1:** 298–299

"David and Agnes, a Romance" (Keillor), **Supp. XVI:**175

David Copperfield (Dickens), **I:** 458;

II: 290; **Retro. Supp. I:** 33; **Supp. XVI:**65, 72

"David Crockett's Other Life" (Nye), **Supp. XIII:** 282

Davideis (Cowley), **IV:** 158

David Harum (Westcott), **I:** 216

"David Lynch Keeps His Head" (Wallace), **Supp. X:** 314

David Show, The (Gurney), **Supp. V:** 97

Davidson, Cathy, **Supp. XV:** 238

Davidson, Donald, **I:** 294; **III:** 495, 496; **IV:** 121, 122, 124, 125, 236; **Supp. II Part 1:** 139; **Supp. XIV:**2

Davidson, John, **Retro. Supp. I:** 55

Davidson, Michael, **Supp. VIII:** 290, 293, 294, 302–303

Davidson, Sara, **Supp. IV Part 1:** 196, 198, 203

Davidsz de Heem, Jan, **Supp. XI:** 133

Davie, Donald, **III:** 478; **Supp. IV Part 2:** 474; **Supp. V:** 331; **Supp. X:** 55, 59

Davies, Arthur, **III:** 273

Davies, Marion, **Supp. XVI:**186

Davies, Sir John, **III:** 541

Da Vinci, Leonardo, **I:** 274; **II:** 536; **III:** 210

Davis, Allen F., **Supp. I Part 1:** 1, 7

Davis, Allison, **Supp. I Part 1:** 327

Davis, Angela, **Supp. I Part 1:** 66; **Supp. X:** 249

Davis, Bette, **I:** 78; **Supp. I Part 1:** 67

Davis, Bill, **Supp. XIII:** 267

Davis, Christina, **Supp. XV:** 264

Davis, Donald, **Supp. XIII:** 93

Davis, Elizabeth Gould, **Supp. I Part 2:** 567

Davis, George, **II:** 586

Davis, Glover, **Supp. V:** 180, 182, 186

Davis, Jefferson, **II:** 206; **IV:** 122, 125, 126

Davis, Jordan, **Supp. XV:** 178, 181, 186, 188

Davis, Katie, **Supp. VIII:** 83

Davis, L. J., **Supp. XI:** 234

Davis, Lydia, **Supp. XII:** 24

Davis, Miles, **Supp. XV:** 346

Davis, Ossie, Jr., **Supp. IV Part 1:** 362; **Supp. XVI:**144

Davis, Rebecca Harding, **Supp. I Part 1:** 45; **Supp. XIII:** 292, 295, 305; **Supp. XVI:**79–96

Davis, Richard Harding, **III:** 328; **Supp. II Part 1:** 393; **Supp. XVI:**85

Davis, Robert Gorham, **II:** 51; **IV:** 108

Davis, Stuart, **IV:** 409; **Supp. XV:** 295

Davis, Thulani, **Supp. XI:** 179; **Supp. XIII:** 233, 234, 239

Davis, William V., **Supp. IV Part 1:**

63, 64, 68, 69, 70

Dawn (Dreiser), **I:** 498, 499, 503, 509, 515, 519

Dawn (O. Butler), **Supp. XIII:** 63, 64

"Dawnbreaker" (Hayden), **Supp. II Part 1:** 370

"Dawn Patrol: A Review of the Literature of the Negro for 1948" (Locke), **Supp. XIV:**211

Dawn Patrol, The (film), **Supp. XIV:**81

Dawson, Edward, **IV:** 151

Dawson, Emma, **I:** 199

Dawson, Ruth, **Supp. XI:** 120

Day, Dorothy, **II:** 215; **Supp. I Part 2:** 524; **Supp. X:** 142

Day, Georgiana, **Supp. I Part 2:** 585

Dayan, Joan, **Retro. Supp. II:** 270

Day Book, A (Creeley), **Supp. IV Part 1:** 155

"Daybreak" (Kinnell), **Supp. III Part 1:** 250

"Daybreak Blues" (Kees), **Supp. XV:** 133

"Daybreak in Alabama" (Hughes), **Retro. Supp. I:** 211; **Supp. I Part 1:** 344

Day by Day (Lowell), **Retro. Supp. II:** 184, 186, 191

"Day-Care Field Trip: Aquarium" (Karr), **Supp. XI:** 243

"Day-Dream, A" (Bryant), **Supp. I Part 1:** 160

"Day for Poetry and Song, A" (Douglass), **Supp. III Part 1:** 172

Day Late and a Dollar Short, A (McMillan), **Supp. XIII:** 184, **Supp. XIII:** 185, 191–192

"Day longs for the evening, The" (Levertov), **Supp. III Part 1:** 274

Day of a Stranger (Merton), **Supp. VIII:** 203

"Day of Days, A" (James), **II:** 322

Day of Doom (Wigglesworth), **IV:** 147, 155, 156

Day of the Body (C. Frost), **Supp. XV:** 93, 98–100, 106

Day of the Locust, The (West), **I:** 298; **IV:** 288, 299–306; **Retro. Supp. II:** 321, 323, 324, 329, 337–338; **Supp. II Part 2:** 626; **Supp. XI:** 296; **Supp. XII:** 173; **Supp. XIII:** 170; **Supp. XIV:**328

"Day on the Big Branch, A" (Nemerov), **III:** 275–276

"Day on the Connecticut River, A" (Merrill), **Supp. III Part 1:** 336

Day Room, The (DeLillo), **Supp. VI:** 4

"Days" (Emerson), **II:** 19, 20

Days: Tangier Journal, 1987–1989 (Bowles), **Supp. IV Part 1:** 94

"Days and Nights" (Koch), **Supp. XV:** 179, 180

"Days and Nights: A Journal" (Price), **Supp. VI:** 265

Days Before, The (Porter), **III:** 433, 453

"Days of 1935" (Merrill), **Supp. III Part 1:** 325, 328

"Days of 1964" (Merrill), **Supp. III Part 1:** 328, 352

"Days of 1971" (Merrill), **Supp. III Part 1:** 328

"Days of 1981" (Doty), **Supp. XI:** 123

"Days of 1941 and '44" (Merrill), **Supp. III Part 1:** 336

"Days of Awe: The Birth of Lucy Jane" (Wasserstein), **Supp. XV:** 332

"Days of Edward Hopper" (Haines), **Supp. XII:** 210

"Days of Heaven" (Bass), **Supp. XVI:**20

Days of Obligation: An Argument with My Mexican Father (Rodriguez), **Supp. XIV:**298, 300, 302–305, 307, 310

Days of Our Lives (soap opera), **Supp. XI:** 83

Days of Our Lives Lie in Fragments: New and Old Poems (Garrett), **Supp. VII:** 109–110, 111

Days of the Phoenix (Brooks), **I:** 266

Days of Wine and Roses (J. P. Miller), **Supp. XIII:** 262

Days to Come (Hellman), **Supp. I Part 1:** 276, 277–278

Days without End (O'Neill), **III:** 385, 391, 397

"Day's Work, A" (Capote), **Supp. III Part 1:** 120

"Day's Work, A" (Porter), **III:** 443, 446

"Day the Presidential Candidate Came to Ciudad Tamaulipas, The" (Caldwell), **I:** 309

Day the World ended, The (Coover), **Supp. V:** 1

"Day with Conrad Green, A" (Lardner), **II:** 428–429, 430

"Deacon's Masterpiece, The" (Holmes), **Supp. I Part 1:** 302, 307

"Dead, The" (Joyce), **I:** 285; **III:** 343

Dead and the Living, The (Olds), **Supp. X:** 201, 204–206, 207

"Dead Body, The" (Olds), **Supp. X:** 210

"Dead by the Side of the Road, The" (Snyder), **Supp. VIII:** 301

Dead End (Kingsley), **Supp. I Part 1:** 277, 281

Dead Father, The (Barthelme), **Supp.**

IV Part 1: 43, 47, 50–51

"Dead Fiddler, The" (Singer), **IV:** 20

Dead Fingers Talk (Burroughs), **Supp. III Part 1:** 103

"Dead Hand" series (Sinclair), **Supp. V:** 276, 277, 281

"Dead Languages, The" (Humphrey), **Supp. IX:** 109

Dead Lecturer, The (Baraka), **Supp. II Part 1:** 31, 33, 35–37, 49

Deadline at Dawn (Odets), **Supp. II Part 2:** 546

"Dead-Lock and Its Key, A" (E. Stoddard), **Supp. XV:** 286

"Dead Loon, The" (Bynner), **Supp. XV:** 44–45

Deadly Affair, A (Lacy), **Supp. XV:** 205–206

Dead Man's Walk (McMurtry), **Supp. V:** 231, 232

Dead Man's Walk (screenplay; McMurtry and Ossana), **Supp. V:** 231

Dead Man Walking (opera libretto, McNally), **Supp. XIII:** 207

Dead Souls (Gogol), **I:** 296

"Dead Souls on Campus" (Kosinski), **Supp. VII:** 222

"Dead Wingman, The" (Jarrell), **II:** 374

"Dead Yellow Women" (Hammett), **Supp. IV Part 1:** 345

Dead Zone, The (King), **Supp. V:** 139, 143, 144, 148, 152

Dean, James, **I:** 493

Dean, Man Mountain, **II:** 589

Deane, Silas, **Supp. I Part 2:** 509, 524

"Dean of Men" (Taylor), **Supp. V:** 314, 323

Dean's December, The (Bellow), **Retro. Supp. II:** 30–31

"Dear Adolph" (Benét), **Supp. XI:** 46

"Dear America" (Ortiz), **Supp. IV Part 2:** 503

"Dearest M—" (Carruth), **Supp. XVI:**59

"Dear Judas" (Jeffers), **Supp. II Part 2:** 431–432, 433

Dear Juliette (Sarton), **Supp. VIII:** 265

Dear Lovely Death (Hughes), **Retro. Supp. I:** 203; **Supp. I Part 1:** 328

"Dear Villon" (Corso), **Supp. XII:** 135

"Dear World" (Gunn Allen), **Supp. IV Part 1:** 321

Death (Allen), **Supp. XV:** 3

"Death" (Corso), **Supp. XII:** 127

"Death" (Lowell), **II:** 536

"Death" (Mailer), **III:** 38

"Death" (West), **IV:** 286

"Death" (W. C. Williams), **Retro.**

Supp. I: 422

"Death and Absence" (Glück), **Supp. V:** 82

Death and Taxes (Parker), **Supp. IX:** 192

"Death and the Child" (Crane), **I:** 414

"Death as a Society Lady" (Hecht), **Supp. X:** 71–72

Death before Bedtime (Vidal, under pseudonym Box), **Supp. IV Part 2:** 682

"Death Be Not Proud" (Donne), **Supp. XVI:**158

"Death by Water" (Eliot), **I:** 395, 578

Death Comes for the Archbishop (Cather), **I:** 314, 327, 328–330; **Retro. Supp. I:** 16–18, 21; **Supp. XIII:** 253

Death in the Afternoon (Hemingway), **II:** 253; **IV:** 35; **Retro. Supp. I:** 182; **Supp. VIII:** 182; **Supp. XVI:**205

"Death in the Country, A" (Benét), **Supp. XI:** 53–54

Death in the Family, A (Agee), **I:** 25, 29, 42, 45

Death in the Fifth Position (Vidal, under pseudonym Box), **Supp. IV Part 2:** 682

"Death in the Woods" (Anderson), **I:** 114, 115

Death in the Woods and Other Stories (Anderson), **I:** 112, 114, 115

Death in Venice (Mann), **III:** 231; **Supp. IV Part 1:** 392; **Supp. V:** 51

"Death in Viet Nam" (Salinas), **Supp. XIII:** 315

"Death in Winter" (C. Frost), **Supp. XV:** 98

Death Is a Lonely Business (Bradbury), **Supp. IV Part 1:** 102, 103, 111–112, 115

"Death Is Not the End" (Wallace), **Supp. X:** 309

Death Kit (Sontag), **Supp. III Part 2:** 451, 468–469

Death Likes It Hot (Vidal, under pseudonym Box), **Supp. IV Part 2:** 682

"*Death*/Muerta" (Mora), **Supp. XIII:** 228

Death Notebooks, The (Sexton), **Supp. II Part 2:** 691, 694, 695

"Death of a Jazz Musician" (W. J. Smith), **Supp. XIII:** 334

Death of a Kinsman, The (Taylor), **Supp. V:** 324, 326

"Death of an Old Seaman" (Hughes), **Retro. Supp. I:** 199

"Death of a Pig" (White), **Supp. I Part 2:** 665–668

Death of a Salesman (A. Miller), **I:** 81; **III:** 148, 149, 150, 153–154, 156, 157, 158, 159, 160, 163, 164, 166; **IV:** 389; **Supp. IV Part 1:** 359; **Supp. XIV:**102, 239, 254, 255; **Supp. XV:** 205

"Death of a Soldier, The" (Stevens), **Retro. Supp. I:** 299, 312. *see also* "Lettres d'un Soldat" (Stevens)

"Death of a Soldier, The" (Wilson), **IV:** 427, 445

"Death of a Toad" (Wilbur), **Supp. III Part 2:** 550

"Death of a Traveling Salesman" (Welty), **IV:** 261; **Retro. Supp. I:** 344

"Death of a Young Son by Drowning" (Atwood), **Supp. XIII:** 33

Death of Bessie Smith, The (Albee), **I:** 76–77, 92

Death of Billy the Kid, The (Vidal), **Supp. IV Part 2:** 683

Death of Cock Robin, The (Snodgrass), **Supp. VI:** 315, 317–319, 324

"Death of General Wolfe, The" (Paine), **Supp. I Part 2:** 504

"Death of Halpin Frayser, The" (Bierce), **I:** 205

"Death of Justina, The" (Cheever), **Supp. I Part 1:** 184–185

Death of Life, The (Barnes), **Supp. III Part 1:** 34

Death of Malcolm X, The (Baraka), **Supp. II Part 1:** 47

"Death of Marilyn Monroe, The" (Olds), **Supp. X:** 205

"Death of Me, The" (Malamud), **Supp. I Part 2:** 437

"Death of Slavery, The" (Bryant), **Supp. I Part 2:** 168–169

"Death of St. Narcissus, The" (Eliot), **Retro. Supp. I:** 291

"Death of the Ball Turret Gunner, The" (Jarrell), **II:** 369–370, 372, 374, 375, 376, 378

"Death of the Fathers, The" (Sexton), **Supp. II Part 2:** 692

"Death of the Flowers, The" (Bryant), **Supp. I Part 1:** 170

Death of the Fox (Garrett), **Supp. VII:** 99, 101–104, 108

"Death of the Hired Man, The" (Frost), **III:** 523; **Retro. Supp. I:** 121, 128; **Supp. IX:** 261

Death of the Kapowsin Tavern (Hugo), **Supp. VI:** 133–135

"Death of the Kapowsin Tavern" (Hugo), **Supp. VI:** 137, 141

"Death of the Lyric, The: The Achieve-ment of Louis Simpson" (Jarman and McDowell), **Supp. IX:** 266, 270, 276

"Death of Venus, The" (Creeley), **Supp. IV Part 1:** 143, 144–145

"Death on All Fronts" (Ginsberg), **Supp. II Part 1:** 326

"Deaths" (Dunn), **Supp. XI:** 147

"Death Sauntering About" (Hecht), **Supp. X:** 72

Deaths for the Ladies (and Other Disasters) (Mailer), **Retro. Supp. II:** 203

Death's Jest-Book (Beddoes), **Retro. Supp. I:** 285

Death Song (McGrath), **Supp. X:** 127

"Death the Carnival Barker" (Hecht), **Supp. X:** 72

"Death the Film Director" (Hecht), **Supp. X:** 72

"Death the Judge" (Hecht), **Supp. X:** 72

"Death the Mexican Revolutionary" (Hecht), **Supp. X:** 72

"Death the Oxford Don" (Hecht), **Supp. X:** 72

"Death the Painter" (Hecht), **Supp. X:** 72

Death the Proud Brother (Wolfe), **IV:** 456

"Death to Van Gogh's Ear!" (Ginsberg), **Supp. II Part 1:** 320, 322, 323

"Death Warmed Over!" (Bradbury), **Supp. IV Part 1:** 104–105, 112

Débâcle, La (Zola), **III:** 316

"Debate with the Rabbi" (Nemerov), **III:** 272

Debeljak, Aleš, **Supp. VIII:** 272

De Bellis, Jack, **Supp. I Part 1:** 366, 368, 372

De Bosis, Lauro, **IV:** 372

"Debriefing" (Sontag), **Supp. III Part 2:** 468–470

Debs, Eugene, **I:** 483, 493; **III:** 580, 581; **Supp. I Part 2:** 524; **Supp. IX:** 1, 15

Debt to Pleasure, The (Lanchester), **Retro. Supp. I:** 278

Debussy, Claude, **Retro. Supp. II:** 266; **Supp. XIII:** 44

Decameron (Boccaccio), **III:** 283, 411; **Supp. IX:** 215

"Deceased" (Hughes), **Retro. Supp. I:** 208

"December" (Oliver), **Supp. VII:** 245

"December 1, 1994" (Stern), **Supp. IX:** 299

"December Eclogue" (Winters), **Supp. II Part 2:** 794

Deception (Roth), **Retro. Supp. II:** 291; **Supp. III Part 2:** 426–427

"Deceptions" (Dobyns), **Supp. XIII:** 77

De Chiara, Ann. *See* Malamud, Mrs. Bernard (Ann de Chiara)

De Chirico, Giorgio, **Supp. XIII:** 317

"Decided Loss, A" (Poe), **II:** 411

"Decisions to Disappear" (Dunn), **Supp. XI:** 144

"Decisive Moment, The" (Auster), **Supp. XIV:**292

Decker, James A., **Supp. III Part 2:** 621

Declaration of Gentlemen and Merchants and Inhabitants of Boston, and the Country Adjacent, A (Mather), **Supp. II Part 2:** 450

"Declaration of Paris, The" (Adams), **I:** 4

Declaration of the Rights of Man and the Citizen, **Supp. I Part 2:** 513, 519

Declaration of Universal Peace and Liberty (Paine), **Supp. I Part 2:** 512

Decline and Fall (Waugh), **Supp. I Part 2:** 607; **Supp. XV:** 142

Decline and Fall of the English System of Finance, The (Paine), **Supp. I Part 2:** 518

Decline and Fall of the Roman Empire, The (Gibbons), **Supp. III Part 2:** 629

"Decline of Book Reviewing, The" (Hardwick), **Supp. III Part 1:** 201–202

Decline of the West, The (Spengler), **I:** 270; **IV:** 125

Deconstructing Harry (film; Allen), **Supp. XV:** 12, 13

"Décor" (X. J. Kennedy), **Supp. XV:** 171

"Decoration Day" (Jewett), **II:** 412; **Retro. Supp. II:** 138

Decoration of Houses, The (Wharton and Codman), **IV:** 308; **Retro. Supp. I:** 362, 363–364, 366

"Decoy" (Ashbery), **Supp. III Part 1:** 13–14

"De Daumier-Smith's Blue Period" (Salinger), **III:** 560–561

"Dedication and Household Map" (Erdrich), **Supp. IV Part 1:** 272

"Dedication Day" (Agee), **I:** 34

"Dedication for a Book" (Hay), **Supp. XIV:**125

"Dedication for a Book of Criticism" (Winters), **Supp. II Part 2:** 801

"Dedication in Postscript, A" (Winters), **Supp. II Part 2:** 801

Dedications and Other Darkhorses (Komunyakaa), **Supp. XIII:** 112, 113–114

"Dedication to Hunger" (Glück), **Supp. V:** 83

"Dedication to My Wife, A" (Eliot), **I:** 583

Dee, Ruby, **Supp. IV Part 1:** 362

Deeds of Utmost Kindness (Gander), **Supp. XV:** 340

"Deep Breath at Dawn, A" (Hecht), **Supp. X:** 58

Deeper into Movies: The Essential Kael Collection from '69 to '72 (Kael), **Supp. IX:** 253

"Deeper Wisdom, The" (Hay), **Supp. XIV:**129

Deep Green Sea (R. O. Butler), **Supp. XII:** 62, 74

Deephaven (Jewett), **II:** 398–399, 400, 401, 410, 411; **Retro. Supp. II:** 133, 134, 135, 136, 137, 138, 140, 141, 143, 144

"Deep Sight and Rescue Missions" (Bambara), **Supp. XI:** 18–19

Deep Sightings and Rescue Missions: Fiction, Essays, and Conversations (Bambara), **Supp. XI:** 1, 3, 14–20

Deep Sleep, The (Morris), **III:** 224–225

Deep South (Caldwell), **I:** 305, 309, 310

Deepstep Come Shining (Wright), **Supp. XV:** 337, 341, 344, 349–350, 351, 353

"Deep Water" (Marquand), **III:** 56

"Deep Woods" (Nemerov), **III:** 272–273, 275

"Deer at Providencia, The" (Dillard), **Supp. VI:** 28, 32

"Deer Dancer" (Harjo), **Supp. XII:** 224–225

"Deer Ghost" (Harjo), **Supp. XII:** 225

Deer Park, The (Mailer), **I:** 292; **III:** 27, 31–33, 35–36, 37, 39, 40, 42, 43, 44; **Retro. Supp. II:** 200–202, 205, 207, 211

Deer Park, The: A Play (Mailer), **Retro. Supp. II:** 205

Deer Pasture, The (Bass), **Supp. XVI:**15, 16, 23

Deerslayer, The (Cooper), **I:** 341, 349, 350, 355; **Supp. I Part 1:** 251

"Defence of Poesy, The" (Sidney), **Supp. V:** 250

"Defence of Poetry" (Longfellow), **II:** 493–494

"Defender of the Faith" (Roth), **Retro. Supp. II:** 281; **Supp. III Part 2:** 404, 407, 420

"Defenestration in Prague" (Matthews), **Supp. IX:** 168

Defenestration of Prague (Howe), **Supp. IV Part 2:** 419, 426, 429–430

Defense, The (Nabokov), **III:** 251–252; **Retro. Supp. I:** 266, 268, 270–272

"Defense of Poetry" (Francis), **Supp. IX:** 83–84

Defiant Ones, The (film), **Supp. I Part 1:** 67

"Defining the Age" (Davis), **Supp. IV Part 1:** 64

"Definition" (Ammons), **Supp. VII:** 28

Defoe, Daniel, **I:** 204; **II:** 104, 105, 159, 304–305; **III:** 113, 423; **IV:** 180; **Supp. I Part 2:** 523; **Supp. V:** 127

De Forest, John William, **II:** 275, 280, 288, 289; **IV:** 350

Degas, Brian, **Supp. XI:** 307

Degler, Carl, **Supp. I Part 2:** 496

"Degrees of Fidelity" (Dunn), **Supp. XI:** 148, 156

Deguy, Michel, **Supp. XV:** 178

De Haven, Tom, **Supp. XI:** 39; **Supp. XII:** 338–339

Deitch, Joseph, **Supp. VIII:** 125

"Dejection" (Coleridge), **II:** 97

DeJong, Constance, **Supp. XII:** 4

DeJong, David Cornel, **I:** 35

de Kooning, Willem, **Supp. XII:** 198; **Supp. XV:** 177, 178

Delacroix, Henri, **I:** 227

De La Mare, Walter, **III:** 429; **Supp. II Part 1:** 4

Delamotte, Eugenia C., **Supp. XI:** 279

De Lancey, James, **I:** 338

De Lancey, Mrs. James (Anne Heathcote), **I:** 338

De Lancey, Susan A. *See* Cooper, Mrs. James Fenimore

De Lancey, William Heathcote, **I:** 338, 353

Delano, Amasa, **III:** 90

Delattre, Roland A., **I:** 558

De Laurentiis, Dino, **Supp. XI:** 170, 307

De la Valdéne, Guy, **Supp. VIII:** 40, 42

De l'éducation d'un homme sauvage (Itard), **Supp. I Part 2:** 564

"Delft" (Goldbarth), **Supp. XII:** 189

Delft: An Essay-Poem (Goldbarth), **Supp. XII:** 187

Delicate Balance, A (Albee), **I:** 86–89, 91, 93, 94

Delicate Balance, The (Hay), **Supp.**

XIV:121, 122, 124, 129, 133–134
"Delicate Balance, The" (Hay), **Supp. XIV:**122
"Delicate Prey, The" (Bowles), **Supp. IV Part 1:** 86
Delicate Prey and Other Stories, The (Bowles), **Supp. IV Part 1:** 86–87
Délie (Scève), **Supp. III Part 1:** 11
DeLillo, Don, **Retro. Supp. I:** 278; **Retro. Supp. II:** 279; **Supp. VI:** 1–18; **Supp. IX:** 212; **Supp. XI:** 68; **Supp. XII:** 21, 152
DeLisle, Anne, **Supp. VIII:** 175
Deliverance (Dickey), **Supp. IV Part 1:** 176, 186–188, 190; **Supp. X:** 30
Deliverance, The (Glasgow), **II:** 175, 176, 177–178, 181
"Delivering" (Dubus), **Supp. VII:** 87
Dell, Floyd, **I:** 103, 105; **Supp. I Part 2:** 379; **Supp. XV:** 295
Della Francesca, Piero, **Supp. XV:** 262
"Della Primavera Trasportata al Morale" (W. C. Williams), **Retro. Supp. I:** 419, 422
DeLoria, Philip J., **Supp. XIV:**306
Deloria, Vine, Jr., **Supp. IV Part 1:** 323; **Supp. IV Part 2:** 504
"Delta Autumn" (Faulkner), **II:** 71
"Delta Factor, The" (Percy), **Supp. III Part 1:** 386
Delta of Venus: Erotica (Nin), **Supp. X:** 192, 195
Delta Wedding (Welty), **IV:** 261, 268–271, 273, 281; **Retro. Supp. I:** 349–350, 351
Delusions (Berryman), **I:** 170
de Man, Paul, **Retro. Supp. I:** 67
DeMarinis, Rick, **Supp. XIV:**22
DeMars, James, **Supp. IV Part 2:** 552
Dembo, L. S., **I:** 386, 391, 396, 397, 398, 402; **III:** 478; **Supp. I Part 1:** 272; **Supp. XIV:**277, 282, 288, 290
Demetrakopoulous, Stephanie A., **Supp. IV Part 1:** 12
DeMille, Cecil B., **Supp. IV Part 2:** 520; **Supp. XV:** 42
Demme, Jonathan, **Supp. V:** 14
Democracy (Adams), **I:** 9–10, 20; **Supp. IV Part 1:** 208
Democracy (Didion), **Supp. IV Part 1:** 198, 208–210
"Democracy" (Lowell), **Supp. I Part 2:** 419
Democracy and Education (Dewey), **I:** 232
Democracy and Other Addresses (Lowell), **Supp. I Part 2:** 407
Democracy and Social Ethics (Addams), **Supp. I Part 1:** 8–11
Democracy in America (Tocqueville),

Retro. Supp. I: 235; **Supp. XIV:**306
Democratic Vistas (Whitman), **IV:** 333, 336, 348–349, 351, 469; **Retro. Supp. I:** 408; **Supp. I Part 2:** 456
Democritus, **I:** 480–481; **II:** 157; **III:** 606; **Retro. Supp. I:** 247
"Demon Lover, The" (Rich), **Supp. I Part 2:** 556
"Demonstrators, The" (Welty), **IV:** 280; **Retro. Supp. I:** 355
DeMott, Benjamin, **Supp. IV Part 1:** 35; **Supp. V:** 123; **Supp. XIII:** 95; **Supp. XIV:**106
DeMott, Robert, **Supp. VIII:** 40, 41
Demuth, Charles, **IV:** 404; **Retro. Supp. I:** 412, 430
"Demystified Zone" (Paley), **Supp. VI:** 227
Denmark Vesey (opera) (Bowles), **Supp. IV Part 1:** 83
Denney, Joseph Villiers, **Supp. I Part 2:** 605
Denney, Reuel, **Supp. XII:** 121
Dennie, Joseph, **II:** 298; **Supp. I Part 1:** 125
Denniston, Dorothy Hamer, **Supp. XI:** 276, 277
"Den of Lions" (Plath), **Retro. Supp. II:** 242
"Dental Assistant, The" (Simpson), **Supp. IX:** 280
Den Uyl, Douglas, **Supp. IV Part 2:** 528, 530
"Deodand, The" (Hecht), **Supp. X:** 65
"Departing" (Cameron), **Supp. XII:** 81
"Departure" (Glück), **Supp. V:** 89
"Departure" (Plath), **Supp. I Part 2:** 537
"Departure, The" (Freneau), **Supp. II Part 1:** 264
"Departure from Hydra, The" (Koch), **Supp. XV:** 180–181
Departures (Justice), **Supp. VII:** 124–127
Departures and Arrivals (Shields), **Supp. VII:** 320, 322
"Depressed by a Book of Bad Poetry, I Walk Toward an Unused Pasture and Invite the Insects to Join Me" (Wright), **Supp. III Part 2:** 600
"Depressed Person, The" (Wallace), **Supp. X:** 309
"Depression Days" (Mora), **Supp. XIII:** 224–225
De Puy, John, **Supp. XIII:** 12
D'Erasmo, Stacey, **Supp. IX:** 121
De Reilhe, Catherine, **Supp. I Part 1:** 202
De Rerum Natura (Lucretius), **II:** 162

"De Rerum Virtute" (Jeffers), **Supp. II Part 2:** 424
De Rioja, Francisco, **Supp. I Part 1:** 166
"Derivative Sport in Tornado Alley" (Wallace), **Supp. X:** 314
Derleth, August, **Supp. I Part 2:** 465, 472
Deronda, Daniel, **II:** 179
Derrida, Jacques, **Supp. IV Part 1:** 45; **Supp. XV:** 215, 224; **Supp. XVI:**285, 288
Deruddere, Dominique, **Supp. XI:** 173
Der Wilde Jäger (Bürger), **II:** 306
Derzhavin, Gavrila Romanovich, **Supp. VIII:** 27
Desai, Anita, **Supp. XVI:**156, 157, 158
De Santis, Christopher, **Retro. Supp. I:** 194
Descartes, René, **I:** 255; **III:** 618–619; **IV:** 133
Descendents, The (Glasgow), **II:** 173, 174–175, 176
Descending Figure (Glück), **Supp. V:** 83–84
"Descending Theology: Christ Human" (Karr), **Supp. XI:** 251
"Descending Theology: The Garden" (Karr), **Supp. XI:** 251
"Descent, The" (W. C. Williams), **Retro. Supp. I:** 428, 429
"Descent from the Cross" (Eliot), **Retro. Supp. I:** 57, 58
"Descent in the Maelström, A" (Poe), **Retro. Supp. II:** 274
"Descent into Proselito" (Knowles), **Supp. XII:** 237
"Descent into the Maelström, A" (Poe), **III:** 411, 414, 416, 424
Descent of Man (Boyle), **Supp. VIII:** 1, 12–13
"Descent of Man" (Boyle), **Supp. VIII:** 14
Descent of Man, The (Darwin), **Supp. XIV:**192
Descent of Man, The (Wharton), **IV:** 311; **Retro. Supp. I:** 367
Descent of Man and Other Stories, The (Wharton), **Retro. Supp. I:** 367
Descent of Winter, The (W. C. Williams), **Retro. Supp. I:** 419, 428
De Schloezer, Doris, **III:** 474
"Description" (Doty), **Supp. XI:** 126
"Description of the great Bones dug up at Clavarack on the Banks of Hudsons River A.D. 1705, The" (Taylor), **IV:** 163, 164
"Description without Place" (Stevens), **Retro. Supp. I:** 422

"Desert" (Hughes), **Retro. Supp. I:** 207

"Deserted Cabin" (Haines), **Supp. XII:** 203

Deserted Village, The (Goldsmith), **II:** 304

Desert Is My Mother, The/El desierto es mi madre (Mora), **Supp. XIII:** 214, 221

Desert Music, The (W. C. Williams), **IV:** 422; **Retro. Supp. I:** 428, 429

"Desert Music, The" (W. C. Williams), **Retro. Supp. I:** 428, 429

"Desert Places" (Frost), **II:** 159; **Retro. Supp. I:** 121, 123, 129, 138, 299; **Supp. XIV:**229

Desert Rose, The (McMurtry), **Supp. V:** 225, 231

Desert Solitaire (Abbey), **Supp. X:** 30; **Supp. XIII:** 7–8, 12; **Supp. XIV:**177, 179

"Design" (Frost), **II:** 158, 163; **Retro. Supp. I:** 121, 126, 138, 139; **Supp. IX:** 81

"Designated National Park, A" (Ortiz), **Supp. IV Part 2:** 509

"Designs on a Point of View" (Everwine), **Supp. XV:** 76

Des Imagistes (Pound), **II:** 513; **Supp. I Part 1:** 257, 261, 262

"Desire" (Beattie), **Supp. V:** 29

Desire (Bidart), **Supp. XV:** 32–34, 35

"Desire" (Everwine), **Supp. XV:** 85

"Désirée's Baby" (Chopin), **Retro. Supp. II:** 64, 65; **Supp. I Part 1:** 213–215

Desire under the Elms (O'Neill), **III:** 387, 390

"Desolate Field, The" (W. C. Williams), **Retro. Supp. I:** 418

"Desolation, A" (Ginsberg), **Supp. II Part 1:** 313

Desolation Angels (Kerouac), **Supp. III Part 1:** 218, 225, 230

"Desolation Is a Delicate Thing" (Wylie), **Supp. I Part 2:** 729

Despair (Nabokov), **Retro. Supp. I:** 270, 274

"Despisals" (Rukeyser), **Supp. VI:** 282

Des Pres, Terrence, **Supp. X:** 113, 120, 124

"Destiny and the Lieutenant" (McCoy), **Supp. XIII:** 171

"Destruction of Kreshev, The" (Singer), **IV:** 13; **Retro. Supp. II:** 307

Destruction of the European Jews, The (Hilberg), **Supp. V:** 267

"Destruction of the Goetheanum, The" (Salter), **Supp. IX:** 257

"Destruction of the Long Branch, The"

(Pinsky), **Supp. VI:** 239, 240, 243–244, 245, 247, 250

Destructive Element, The (Spender), **Retro. Supp. I:** 216

"Detail & Parody for the poem 'Paterson'" (W. C. Williams), **Retro. Supp. I:** 424

Detmold, John, **Supp. I Part 2:** 670

Deuce, The (R. O. Butler), **Supp. XII:** 62, 69–70, 72

Deus Lo Volt! (Connell), **Supp. XIV:**80, 81, 95

Deuteronomy (biblical book), **II:** 166

Deutsch, Andre, **Supp. XI:** 297, 301

Deutsch, Babette, **Supp. I Part 1:** 328, 341

Deutsch, Michel, **Supp. IV Part 1:** 104

Deutsche, Babette, **Supp. XV:** 305

"Devaluation Blues: Ruminations on Black Families in Crisis" (Coleman), **Supp. XI:** 87

Devane, William, **Supp. XI:** 234

"Development of the Literary West" (Chopin), **Retro. Supp. II:** 72

"Development of the Modern English Novel, The" (Lanier), **Supp. I Part 1:** 370–371

DeVeriante (Herbert of Cherbury), **II:** 108

"Devil and Daniel Webster, The" (Benét), **III:** 22; **Supp. XI:** 45–46, 47, 50–51, 52

Devil and Daniel Webster and Other Writings, The (Benét), **Supp. XI:** 48

"Devil and Tom Walker, The" (Irving), **II:** 309–310

Devil At Large, The: Erica Jong on Henry Miller (Jong), **Supp. V:** 115, 131

Devil Finds Work, The (Baldwin), **Retro. Supp. II:** 14; **Supp. I Part 1:** 48, 52, 66–67

Devil in a Blue Dress (Mosley), **Supp. XIII:** 237, 239

"Devil in Manuscript, The" (Hawthorne), **II:** 226; **Retro. Supp. I:** 150–151

Devil in Paradise, A (H. Miller), **III:** 190

"Devil in the Belfry, The" (Poe), **III:** 425; **Retro. Supp. II:** 273

"Devil Is a Busy Man, The" (Wallace), **Supp. X:** 309

Devil's Dictionary, The (Bierce), **I:** 196, 197, 205, 208, 209, 210

Devil's Stocking, The (Algren), **Supp. IX:** 5, 16

Devil's Tour, The (Karr), **Supp. XI:** 240, 242–244

Devil Tree, The (Kosinski), **Supp. VII:**

215, 222, 223

"Devising" (Ammons), **Supp. VII:** 28

De Voto, Bernard, **I:** 247, 248; **II:** 446; **Supp. IV Part 2:** 599, 601

"Devout Meditation in Memory of Adolph Eichmann, A" (Merton), **Supp. VIII:** 198, 203

De Vries, Peter, **Supp. I Part 2:** 604

Dewberry, Elizabeth, **Supp. XII:** 62, 72

Dewey, John, **I:** 214, 224, 228, 232, 233, 266, 267; **II:** 20, 27, 34, 229, 361; **III:** 112, 294–295, 296, 303, 309–310, 599, 605; **IV:** 27, 429; **Supp. I Part 1:** 3, 5, 7, 10, 11, 12, 24; **Supp. I Part 2:** 493, 641, 647, 677; **Supp. V:** 290; **Supp. IX:** 179; **Supp. XIV:**3; **Supp. XV:** 41

Dewey, Joseph, **Supp. IX:** 210

Dewey, Thomas, **IV:** 161

Dexter, Peter, **Supp. XIV:**221

De Young, Charles, **I:** 194

Dhairyam, Sagari, **Supp. IV Part 1:** 329, 330

Dharma Bums, The (Kerouac), **Supp. III Part 1:** 230, 231; **Supp. VIII:** 289, 305

D'Houdetot, Madame, **Supp. I Part 1:** 250

"Diabetes" (Dickey), **Supp. IV Part 1:** 182

Diaghilev, Sergei, **Supp. I Part 1:** 257

Dial (publication), **I:** 58, 109, 115, 116, 215, 231, 233, 245, 261, 384, 429; **II:** 8, 430; **III:** 194, 470, 471, 485; **IV:** 122, 171, 427; **Retro. Supp. I:** 58; **Retro. Supp. II:** 78; **Supp. I Part 2:** 642, 643, 647; **Supp. II Part 1:** 168, 279, 291; **Supp. II Part 2:** 474; **Supp. III Part 2:** 611

"Dialectics of Love, The" (McGrath), **Supp. X:** 116

"Dialogue" (Rich), **Supp. I Part 2:** 560

Dialogue, A (Baldwin and Giovanni), **Supp. I Part 1:** 66

"Dialogue: William Harvey; Joan of Arc" (Goldbarth), **Supp. XII:** 178

"Dialogue Between Franklin and the Gout" (Franklin), **II:** 121

"Dialogue Between General Wolfe and General Gage in a Wood near Boston, A" (Paine), **Supp. I Part 2:** 504

"Dialogue between Old England and New" (Bradstreet), **Supp. I Part 1:** 105–106, 110–111, 116

"Dialogue between the Writer and a Maypole Dresser, A" (Taylor), **IV:** 155

Dialogues (Bush, ed.), **III:** 4

Dialogues in Limbo (Santayana), **III:** 606

"Diamond as Big as the Ritz, The" (Fitzgerald), **II:** 88–89

Diamond Cutters and Other Poems, The (Rich), **Supp. I Part 2:** 551, 552, 553

"Diamond Guitar, A" (Capote), **Supp. III Part 1:** 124

"Diana and Persis" (Alcott), **Supp. I Part 1:** 32, 41

Diaries of Charlotte Perkins Gilman (Knight, ed.), **Supp. XI:** 201

Diary of a Chambermaid, The (film; Renoir), **Supp. XVI:**193

Diary of Anaïs Nin, The (1931–1974), **Supp. X:** 181, 185–189, 191, 192, 193, 195

Diary of a Rapist, The: A Novel (Connell), **Supp. XIV:**80, 82, 94

Diary of a Yuppie (Auchincloss), **Supp. IV Part 1:** 31, 32–33

Diary of "Helena Morley," The (Bishop, trans.), **Retro. Supp. II:** 45, 51; **Supp. I Part 1:** 92

Díaz del Castillo, Bernál, **III:** 13, 14

Dick, Philip K., **Supp. XVI:**123

Dickens, Charles, **I:** 152, 198, 505; **II:** 98, 179, 186, 192, 271, 273–274, 288, 290, 297, 301, 307, 316, 322, 559, 561, 563, 577, 582; **III:** 146, 247, 325, 368, 411, 421, 426, 572, 577, 613–614, 616; **IV:** 21, 192, 194, 211, 429; **Retro. Supp. I:** 33, 91, 218; **Retro. Supp. II:** 204; **Supp. I Part 1:** 13, 34, 35, 36, 41, 49; **Supp. I Part 2:** 409, 523, 579, 590, 622, 675; **Supp. IV Part 1:** 293, 300, 341; **Supp. IV Part 2:** 464; **Supp. VIII:** 180; **Supp. IX:** 246; **Supp. XI:** 277; **Supp. XII:** 335, 337; **Supp. XIII:** 233; **Supp. XV:** 62; **Supp. XVI:**63, 65–66, 72–73, 202

Dickey, James, **I:** 29, 535; **III:** 268; **Retro. Supp. II:** 233; **Supp. III Part 1:** 354; **Supp. III Part 2:** 541, 597; **Supp. IV Part 1:** 175–194; **Supp. V:** 333; **Supp. X:** 30; **Supp. XI:** 312, 317; **Supp. XV:** 115, 348

Dick Gibson Show, The (Elkin), **Supp. VI:** 42, 48–49

Dickie, Margaret, **Retro. Supp. II:** 53, 84

Dickinson, Donald, **Retro. Supp. I:** 206, 212

Dickinson, Edward, **I:** 451–452, 453

Dickinson, Emily, **I:** 384, 419, 433, 451–473; **II:** 272, 276, 277, 530; **III:** 19, 194, 196, 214, 493, 505, 508, 556, 572, 576; **IV:** 134, 135, 331, 444; **Retro. Supp. I:** 25–50; **Retro. Supp. II:** 39, 40, 43, 45, 50, 76, 134, 155, 170; **Supp. I Part 1:** 29, 79, 188, 372; **Supp. I Part 2:** 375, 546, 609, 682, 691; **Supp. II Part 1:** 4; **Supp. III Part 1:** 63; **Supp. III Part 2:** 600, 622; **Supp. IV Part 1:** 31, 257; **Supp. IV Part 2:** 434, 637, 641, 643; **Supp. V:** 79, 140, 332, 335; **Supp. VIII:** 95, 104, 106, 108, 198, 205, 272; **Supp. IX:** 37, 38, 53, 87, 90; **Supp. XII:** 226; **Supp. XIII:** 153, 339; **Supp. XIV:**45, 127–128, 133, 261, 284; **Supp. XV:** 287, 303, 309; **Supp. XVI:**288

Dickinson, Gilbert, **I:** 469

Dickinson, Goldsworthy Lowes, **Supp. XIV:**336

Dickinson, Lavinia Norcross, **I:** 451, 453, 462, 470

Dickinson, Mrs. Edward, **I:** 451, 453

Dickinson, Mrs. William A. (Susan Gilbert), **I:** 452, 453, 456, 469, 470

Dickinson, William Austin, **I:** 451, 453, 469

Dickinson and the Strategies of Reticence (Dobson), **Retro. Supp. I:** 29, 42

Dickson, Helen. *See* Blackmur, Helen Dickson

Dickstein, Morris, **Supp. XIII:** 106

"Dick Whittington and His Cat," **Supp. I Part 2:** 656

"DICTATORSHIP OF THE PROLETARIAT, THE" (Baraka), **Supp. II Part 1:** 54

Dictionary of Literary Biography (Kibler, ed.), **Supp. IX:** 94, 109; **Supp. XI:** 297

Dictionary of Literary Biography (Knight), **Supp. XIV:**144

Dictionary of Modern English Usage, A (Fowler), **Supp. I Part 2:** 660

"Dictum: For a Masque of Deluge" (Merwin), **Supp. III Part 1:** 342–343

"Didactic Poem" (Levertov), **Supp. III Part 1:** 280

Diderot, Denis, **II:** 535; **IV:** 440; **Supp. XVI:**293

Did I Ever Tell You How Lucky You Are? (Geisel), **Supp. XVI:**109

Didion, Joan, **Retro. Supp. I:** 116; **Retro. Supp. II:** 209; **Supp. I Part 1:** 196, 197; **Supp. III Part 1:** 302; **Supp. IV Part 1:** 195–216; **Supp. XI:** 221; **Supp. XII:** 307

Dido, **I:** 81

"Did You Ever Dream Lucky?" (Ellison), **Supp. II Part 1:** 246

"Die-Hard, The" (Benét), **Supp. XI:** 54–55, 56

Diehl, Digby, **Supp. IV Part 1:** 204

Dien Cai Dau (Komunyakaa), **Supp. XIII:** 121, 122–124, 125, 131, 132

"Dies Irae" (Lowell), **II:** 553

Die Zeit Ohne Beispiel, (Goebbels), **III:** 560

Difference Engine, The (W. Gibson and B. Sterling), **Supp. XVI:**121, 124, 128–129

Different Drummer, A (Larkin; film), **Supp. XI:** 20

Different Fleshes (Goldbarth), **Supp. XII:** 181–182, 188

Different Hours (Dunn), **Supp. XI:** 139, 142, 143, 155

Different Seasons (King), **Supp. V:** 148, 152

Different Ways to Pray (Nye), **Supp. XIII:** 274, 275, 277, 285, 287

"Different Ways to Pray" (Nye), **Supp. XIII:** 275

"Difficulties of a Statesman" (Eliot), **I:** 580

"Difficulties of Modernism and the Modernism of Difficulty" (Poirier), **Supp. II Part 1:** 136

Diff'rent (O'Neill), **III:** 389

DiGaetani, John L., **Supp. XIII:** 200

"Digging" (Sanders), **Supp. XVI:**272

"Digging in the Garden of Age I Uncover a Live Root" (Swenson), **Supp. IV Part 2:** 649

Diggins, John P., **Supp. I Part 2:** 650

"Dignity of Life, The" (C. Bly), **Supp. XVI:**34, 36–37

Digregorio, Charles, **Supp. XI:** 326

"Dilemma of Determinism, The" (James), **II:** 347–348, 352

"Dilemma of the Negro Writer, The" (speech, C. Himes), **Supp. XVI:**140

"Dilettante, The" (Wharton), **IV:** 311, 313

"Dilettante, The: A Modern Type" (Dunbar), **Supp. II Part 1:** 199

Dillard, Annie, **Supp. VI:** 19–39; **Supp. VIII:** 272; **Supp. X:** 31; **Supp. XIII:** 154

Dillard, R. H. W., **Supp. XII:** 16

Dillman, Bradford, **III:** 403; **Supp. XII:** 241

Dillon, Brian, **Supp. X:** 209

Dillon, George, **III:** 141; **Supp. III Part 2:** 621

Dillon, Millicent, **Supp. IV Part 1:** 95

Dilsaver, Paul, **Supp. XIII:** 112

Dilthey, Wilhelm, **I:** 58

Dime-Store Alchemy: The Art of Joseph Cornell, **Supp. VIII:** 272

"Diminuendo" (Dunn), **Supp. XI:** 152–153

"Dimout in Harlem" (Hughes), **Supp. I Part 1:** 333

Dinesen, Isak, **IV:** 279; **Supp. VIII:** 171; **Supp. XVI:**250

Dining Room, The (Gurney), **Supp. V:** 105–106

"Dinner at ———, A" (O. Henry), **Supp. II Part 1:** 402

"Dinner at Sir Nigel's" (Bowles), **Supp. IV Part 1:** 94

Dinner at the Homesick Restaurant (Tyler), **Supp. IV Part 2:** 657, 667–668

"Dinner at Uncle Borris's" (Simic), **Supp. VIII:** 272

Dinner Bridge (Lardner), **II:** 435

Dinosaur Tales (Bradbury), **Supp. IV Part 1:** 103

"Diogenes Invents a Game" (Karr), **Supp. XI:** 240–241

"Diogenes Tries to Forget" (Karr), **Supp. XI:** 241

Dionysis in Doubt (Robinson), **III:** 510

Diop, Birago, **Supp. IV Part 1:** 16

Diop, David, **Supp. IV Part 1:** 16

Di Prima, Diane, **Supp. III Part 1:** 30; **Supp. XIV:**125, 144, 148, 150

Direction of Poetry, The: An Anthology of Rhymed and Metered Verse Written in the English Language since 1975 (Richman, ed.), **Supp. XV:** 250, 251

Direction of Poetry, The: Rhymed and Metered Verse Written in the English Language since 1975 (Richman), **Supp. XI:** 249

"Directive" (Bishop), **Retro. Supp. II:** 42

"Directive" (Frost), **III:** 287; **Retro. Supp. I:** 140; **Supp. VIII:** 32, 33

"Dire Cure" (Matthews), **Supp. IX:** 168

"Dirge" (Dunbar), **Supp. II Part 1:** 199

"Dirge without Music" (Millay), **III:** 126

"Dirt" (Salter), **Supp. IX:** 257, 260, 261

"Dirt and Desire: Essay on the Phenomenology of Female Pollution in Antiquity" (Carson), **Supp. XII:** 111

"Dirty English Potatoes" (X. J. Kennedy), **Supp. XV:** 165

"Dirty Memories" (Olds), **Supp. X:** 211

Dirty Story (Shanley), **Supp. XIV:**316, 331

"Dirty Word, The" (Shapiro), **Supp. II Part 2:** 710

Disappearance of the Jews, The (Mamet), **Supp. XIV:**249–250, 250–251, 252, 254

Disappearances (Auster), **Supp. XII:** 23

"Disappearances" (Hogan), **Supp. IV Part 1:** 401

Disappearing Acts (McMillan), **Supp. XIII:** 182, 183, 188–189, 192

Disappearing Ink: Poetry at the End of Print Culture (Gioia), **Supp. XV:** 112

"Disappointment, The" (Creeley), **Supp. IV Part 1:** 143

"Disappointment and Desire" (R. Bly), **Supp. IV Part 1:** 71

"Discards" (Baker), **Supp. XIII:** 53, 55–56

Discerning the Signs of the Times (Niebuhr), **III:** 300–301, 307–308

"Disciple of Bacon, The" (Epstein), **Supp. XII:** 163–164

"Discordants" (Aiken), **I:** 65

Discourse on Method (Descartes), **I:** 255

"Discourtesies" (Kirsch), **Supp. XV:** 341

"Discovering Theme and Structure in the Novel" (Schuster), **Supp. VIII:** 126

"Discovery" (Freneau), **Supp. II Part 1:** 258

"Discovery of the Madeiras, The" (Frost), **Retro. Supp. I:** 139

"Discovery of What It Means to Be an American, The" (Baldwin), **Supp. I Part 1:** 54–55

Discovery! The Search for Arabian Oil (Stegner), **Supp. IV Part 2:** 599

"Discrete Series" (Zukofsky), **Supp. III Part 2:** 616

"Discretions of Alcibiades" (Pinsky), **Supp. VI:** 241

"Disease, The" (Rukeyser), **Supp. VI:** 279

Disenchanted, The (Schulberg), **II:** 98; **Retro. Supp. I:** 113

Disenchantments: An Anthology of Modern Fairy Tale Poetry (Mieder), **Supp. XIV:**126

"Dish of Green Pears, A" (Ríos), **Supp. IV Part 2:** 552

"Disillusion and Dogma" (Untermeyer), **Supp. XV:** 306

Dismantling the Silence (Simic), **Supp. VIII:** 273–274, 275, 276

Disney, Walt, **III:** 275, 426

"Disney of My Mind" (Chabon), **Supp. XI:** 63

Dispatches (Herr), **Supp. XI:** 245

"Displaced Person, The" (O'Connor), **III:** 343–344, 350, 352, 356; **Retro. Supp. II:** 229, 232, 236

"Disposal" (Snodgrass), **Supp. VI:** 314

Dispossessed, The (Berryman), **I:** 170, 172, 173, 174, 175, 176, 178

"Disquieting Muses, The" (Plath), **Supp. I Part 2:** 538

Disraeli, Benjamin, **II:** 127

Dissent (Didion), **Supp. IV Part 1:** 208

"Dissenting Opinion on Kafka, A" (Wilson), **IV:** 437–438

Dissent in Three American Wars (Morison, Merk, and Freidel), **Supp. I Part 2:** 495

Dissertation on Liberty and Necessity, Pleasure and Pain, A (Franklin), **II:** 108

Dissertations on Government; the Affairs of the Bank: and Paper Money (Paine), **Supp. I Part 2:** 510

"Distance" (Carver), **Supp. III Part 1:** 146

"Distance" (Everwine), **Supp. XV:** 85

"Distance" (Paley), **Supp. VI:** 222

"Distance, The" (Karr), **Supp. XI:** 241

"Distance from the Sea, A" (Kees), **Supp. XV:** 147

"Distance Nowhere" (Hughes), **Retro. Supp. I:** 207

"Distant Episode, A" (Bowles), **Supp. IV Part 1:** 84–85, 86, 90

Distant Episode, A: The Selected Stories (Bowles), **Supp. IV Part 1:** 79

Distinguished Guest, The (Miller), **Supp. XII:** 299–301

Distortions (Beattie), **Supp. V:** 21, 23, 24, 25, 27

"Distrest Shepherdess, The" (Freneau), **Supp. II Part 1:** 258

District of Columbia (Dos Passos), **I:** 478, 489–490, 492

Disturber of the Peace (Manchester), **III:** 103

Disturbing the Peace (Yates), **Supp. XI:** 345, 346

"Diver, The" (Hayden), **Supp. II Part 1:** 368, 372, 373

"Divided Life of Jean Toomer, The" (Toomer), **Supp. III Part 2:** 488

Divina Commedia (Longfellow, trans.), **II:** 490, 492, 493

"Divine Collaborator" (Simic), **Supp. VIII:** 282

Divine Comedies (Merrill), **Supp. III**

Part 1: 324, 329–332

Divine Comedy (Dante), **I:** 137, 265, 400, 446; **II:** 215, 335, 490, 492, 493; **III:** 13, 448, 453; **Supp. V:** 283, 331, 338, 345; **Supp. X:** 253; **Supp. XIV:**6

"Divine Image, The" (Blake), **Supp. V:** 257

Divine Pilgrim, The (Aiken), **I:** 50, 55

Divine Tragedy, The (Longfellow), **II:** 490, 500, 505, 506, 507; **Retro. Supp. II:** 165, 166

Divine Weekes and Workes (Sylvester, trans.), **Supp. I Part 1:** 104

Divine Weeks (Du Bartas), **IV:** 157–158

Diving into the Wreck: Poems 1971–1972 (Rich), **Supp. I Part 2:** 550, 559–565, 569; **Supp. XV:** 252

Diving Rock on the Hudson, A (H. Roth), **Supp. IX:** 236, 237–238

"Divinity in Its Fraying Fact, A" (Levis), **Supp. XI:** 271

"Divinity School Address" (Emerson), **II:** 12–13

"Divisions upon a Ground" (Hecht), **Supp. X:** 58

"Divorce" (Karr), **Supp. XI:** 244

Divorced in America: Marriage in an Age of Possibility (Epstein), **Supp. XIV:**113

Dix, Douglas Shields, **Supp. XII:** 14

Dixie City Jam (Burke), **Supp. XIV:**32

Dixon, Ivan, **Supp. IV Part 1:** 362

Dixon, Stephen, **Supp. XII:** 139–158

Dixon, Terrell F., **Supp. XVI:**21

Dixon, Thomas, Jr., **Supp. II Part 1:** 169, 171, 177

Djinn (Robbe-Grillet), **Supp. V:** 48

D'Lugoff, Burt, **Supp. IV Part 1:** 362, 370

Do, Lord, Remember Me (Garrett), **Supp. VII:** 98–100, 110

"Doaksology, The" (Wolfe), **IV:** 459

Dobie, J. Frank, **Supp. V:** 225; **Supp. XIII:** 227

Döblin, Alfred, **Supp. XV:** 137

Dobriansky, Lev, **Supp. I Part 2:** 648, 650

Dobson, Joanne, **Retro. Supp. I:** 29, 31, 42

Dobyns, Stephen, **Supp. XIII:** 73–92

"Docking at Palermo" (Hugo), **Supp. VI:** 137–138

"Dock Rats" (Moore), **III:** 213

"Dock-Witch, The" (Ozick), **Supp. V:** 262, 264

"Doc Mellhorn and the Pearly Gates" (Benét), **Supp. XI:** 55

"Doctor, The" (Dubus), **Supp. VII:** 80–81

"Doctor and the Doctor's Wife, The" (Hemingway), **II:** 248; **Retro. Supp. I:** 174, 175

Doctor Breen's Practice, a Novel (Howells), **I:** 282

Doctor Faustus (Mann), **III:** 283

Doctor Jazz (Carruth), **Supp. XVI:**47, 59

"Doctor Jekyll" (Sontag), **Supp. III Part 2:** 469

"Doctor Leavis and the Moral Tradition" (Trilling), **Supp. III Part 2:** 512–513

Doctor Martino and Other Stories (Faulkner), **II:** 72; **Retro. Supp. I:** 84

"Doctor of the Heart, The" (Sexton), **Supp. II Part 2:** 692

Doctorow, E. L., **Retro. Supp. I:** 97; **Supp. III Part 2:** 590, 591; **Supp. IV Part 1:** 217–240; **Supp. V:** 45; **Supp. XVI:**73

Doctor Sax (Kerouac), **Supp. III Part 1:** 220–222, 224–227

Doctor Sleep (Bell), **Supp. X:** 9–11

"Doctors' Row" (Aiken), **I:** 67

Doctor's Son and Other Stories, The (O'Hara), **III:** 361

Doctor Stories, The (W. C. Williams), **Retro. Supp. I:** 424

"Doctor's Wife, The" (Ozick), **Supp. V:** 262, 265

Doctor Zhivago (Pasternak), **IV:** 434, 438, 443

"Documentary" (Simic), **Supp. VIII:** 282

Dodd, Elizabeth, **Supp. V:** 77

Dodd, Wayne, **Supp. IV Part 2:** 625

Dodson, Owen, **Supp. I Part 1:** 54

Dodsworth (Lewis), **II:** 442, 449–450, 453, 456

Doenitz, Karl, **Supp. I Part 2:** 491

Does Civilization Need Religion? (Niebuhr), **III:** 293–294

"Does 'Consciousness' Exist?" (James), **II:** 356

"Does Education Pay?" (Du Bois), **Supp. II Part 1:** 159

Dog (Shepard), **Supp. III Part 2:** 434

"Dog Act, The" (Komunyakaa), **Supp. XIII:** 114–115

"Dog and the Playlet, The" (O. Henry), **Supp. II Part 1:** 399

Dog Beneath the Skin, The (Auden), **Supp. II Part 1:** 10

"Dog Creek Mainline" (Wright), **Supp. V:** 340

"Dogfight" (W. Gibson and Swanwick),

Supp. XVI:128

Dog in the Manger, The (Vega; Merwin, trans.), **Supp. III Part 1:** 341, 347

Dogs Bark, but the Caravan Rolls On (Conroy), **Supp. XVI:**63, 70, 74, 75–76

Dogs Bark, The: Public People and Private Places (Capote), **Supp. III Part 1:** 120, 132

Dog Soldiers (Stone), **Supp. V:** 298, 299–301

"Dog Stories" (Prose), **Supp. XVI:**256

Dog & the Fever, The (Quevedo), **Retro. Supp. I:** 423

"Dogwood, The" (Levertov), **Supp. III Part 1:** 276

"Dogwood Tree, The: A Boyhood" (Updike), **IV:** 218; **Retro. Supp. I:** 318, 319

Doig, Ivan, **Supp. XIV:**227

"Doing Battle with the Wolf" (Coleman), **Supp. XI:** 87–88

Doing Literary Business: American Women Writers in the Nineteenth Century (Coultrap-McQuin), **Supp. XVI:**85

Doings and Undoings (Podhoretz), **Supp. VIII:** 236–237

Dolan, Jill, **Supp. XV:** 327

"Dolce Far' Niente" (Humphrey), **Supp. IX:** 106

Dolci, Carlo, **III:** 474–475

"Dollhouse, The" (Haines), **Supp. XII:** 204

Dollmaker's Ghost, The (Levis), **Supp. XI:** 259, 260, 264–268

Doll's House, A (Ibsen), **III:** 523; **IV:** 357; **Supp. XVI:**182

Dolmetsch, Arnold, **III:** 464

Dolores Claiborne (King), **Supp. V:** 138, 141, 147, 148, 149–150, 152

"Dolph Heyliger" (Irving), **II:** 309

Dolphin, The (Lowell), **Retro. Supp. II:** 183, 186, 188, 190–191; **Supp. XII:** 253–254

"Dolphins" (Francis), **Supp. IX:** 83

Dome of Many-Coloured Class, A (Lowell), **II:** 515, 516–517

Domesday Book (Masters), **Supp. I Part 2:** 465, 466–469, 471, 473, 476

"Domestic Economy" (Gilman), **Supp. XI:** 206

"Domestic Manners" (Hardwick), **Supp. III Part 1:** 211

"Dominant White, The" (McKay), **Supp. X:** 134

Dominguez, Robert, **Supp. VIII:** 83

Dominique, Jean. *See* Closset, Marie

Donahue, Phil, **Supp. IV Part 2:** 526;

Supp. X: 311

Doña Perfecta (Galdós), **II:** 290

Dong, Stella, **Supp. XVI:**222

Don Juan (Byron), **Supp. XV:** 259

"DON JUAN IN HELL" (Baraka), **Supp. II Part 1:** 33

Donkey of God, The (Untermeyer), **Supp. XV:** 310

"Donna mi Prega" (Cavalcanti), **Supp. III Part 2:** 620, 621, 622

Donn-Byrne, Brian Oswald. *See* Byrne, Donn

Donne, John, **I:** 358–359, 384, 389, 522, 586; **II:** 254; **III:** 493; **IV:** 83, 88, 135, 141, 144, 145, 151, 156, 165, 331, 333; **Retro. Supp. II:** 76; **Supp. I Part 1:** 80, 364, 367; **Supp. I Part 2:** 421, 424, 467, 725, 726; **Supp. III Part 2:** 614, 619; **Supp. VIII:** 26, 33, 164; **Supp. IX:** 44; **Supp. XII:** 45, 159; **Supp. XIII:** 94, 130; **Supp. XIV:**122; **Supp. XV:** 92, 251; **Supp. XVI:**158, 204

Donne's Sermons: Selected Passages (L. P. Smith, ed.), **Supp. XIV:**342

Donoghue, Denis, **I:** 537; **Supp. IV Part 1:** 39; **Supp. VIII:** 105, 189

Donohue, H. E. F., **Supp. IX:** 2, 3, 15, 16

Donovan, Josephine, **Retro. Supp. II:** 138, 139, 147

Don Quixote (Cervantes), **I:** 134; **II:** 291, 434; **III:** 113, 614; **Supp. I Part 2:** 422; **Supp. IX:** 94

Don Quixote: Which Was a Dream (Acker), **Supp. XII:** 5, 12–14

Don't Ask (Levine), **Supp. V:** 178

Don't Ask Questions (Marquand), **III:** 58

Don't Bet on the Prince: Contemporary Feminist Fairy Tales in North America and England (Zipes), **Supp. XIV:**126

Don't Drink the Water (Allen), **Supp. XV:** 3, 14

"Don't Shoot the Warthog" (Corso), **Supp. XII:** 123

"Don't Tell Mother" (Wasserstein), **Supp. XV:** 319

"Don't Worry About the Kids" (Neugeboren), **Supp. XVI:**226

Don't Worry About the Kids (Neugeboren), **Supp. XVI:**226

Don't You Want to Be Free? (Hughes), **Retro. Supp. I:** 203; **Supp. I Part 1:** 339

"Doodler, The" (Merrill), **Supp. III Part 1:** 321

Doolan, Moira, **Retro. Supp. II:** 247

Doolittle, Hilda (H. D.), **II:** 517, 520–521; **III:** 194, 195–196, 457, 465; **IV:** 404, 406; **Retro. Supp. I:** 288, 412, 413, 414, 415, 417; **Supp. I Part 1:** 253–275; **Supp. I Part 2:** 707; **Supp. III Part 1:** 48; **Supp. III Part 2:** 610; **Supp. IV Part 1:** 257; **Supp. V:** 79; **Supp. XV:** 43, 249, 301, 302

Doolittle, Thomas, **IV:** 150

"Doomed by Our Blood to Care" (Orfalea), **Supp. XIII:** 278

"Doomsday" (Plath), **Retro. Supp. II:** 242

Doomsters, The (Macdonald), **Supp. IV Part 2:** 462, 463, 472, 473

"Door, The" (Creeley), **Supp. IV Part 1:** 145, 146, 156–157

"Door, The" (White), **Supp. I Part 2:** 651, 675–676

"Door in the Dark, The" (Frost), **II:** 156

Door in the Hive, A (Levertov), **Supp. III Part 1:** 283, 284

"Door of the Trap, The" (Anderson), **I:** 112

"Doors, Doors, Doors" (Sexton), **Supp. II Part 2:** 681

Doors, The, **Supp. X:** 186

"Doorways into the Depths" (Sanders), **Supp. XVI:**272

Doreski, William, **Retro. Supp. II:** 185

Dorfman, Ariel, **Supp. IX:** 131, 138

Dorfman, Joseph, **Supp. I Part 2:** 631, 647, 650

Dorman, Jen, **Supp. XI:** 240

Dorn, Edward, **Supp. IV Part 1:** 154

Dorr, Julia, **Supp. XV:** 286

Dorris, Michael, **Supp. IV Part 1:** 260, 272

Dos Passos, John, **I:** 99, 288, 374, 379, 474–496, 517, 519; **II:** 74, 77, 89, 98; **III:** 2, 28, 29, 70, 172, 382–383; **IV:** 340, 427, 433; **Retro. Supp. I:** 105, 113, 187; **Retro. Supp. II:** 95, 196; **Supp. I Part 2:** 646; **Supp. III Part 1:** 104, 105; **Supp. V:** 277; **Supp. VIII:** 101, 105; **Supp. XIV:**24; **Supp. XV:** 135, 137, 182

"Dos Passos: Poet Against the World" (Cowley), **Supp. II Part 1:** 143, 145

Dostoyevsky, Fyodor, **I:** 53, 103, 211, 468; **II:** 60, 130, 275, 320, 587; **III:** 37, 61, 155, 174, 176, 188, 189, 267, 272, 283, 286, 354, 357, 358, 359, 467, 571, 572; **IV:** 1, 7, 8, 17, 21, 50, 59, 106, 110, 128, 134, 285, 289, 476, 485, 491; **Retro. Supp. II:** 20, 204, 299; **Supp. I Part 1:** 49; **Supp. I Part 2:** 445, 466; **Supp. IV Part 2:** 519, 525; **Supp. VIII:** 175; **Supp.** X: 4–5; **Supp. XI:** 161; **Supp. XII:** 322; **Supp. XVI:**63

Doty, M. R. *See* Dawson, Ruth; Doty, Mark

Doty, Mark, **Supp. IX:** 42, 300; **Supp. XI:** 119–138

Double, The (Dostoyevsky), **Supp. IX:** 105

"Double, The" (Levis), **Supp. XI:** 260, 261–263

Double, The (Rank), **Supp. IX:** 105

Double Agent, The (Blackmur), **Supp. II Part 1:** 90, 108, 146

Double Axe, The (Jeffers), **Supp. II Part 2:** 416, 434

Doubleday, Frank, **I:** 500, 502, 515, 517; **III:** 327

Doubleday, Mrs. Frank, **I:** 500

Double Down (F. and S. Barthelme), **Supp. XI:** 27, 34, 35, 36–38

Double Dream of Spring, The (Ashbery), **Supp. III Part 1:** 11–13

Double Fold: Libraries and the Assault on Paper (Baker), **Supp. XIII:** 52, 56

Double Game (Calle), **Supp. XII:** 22

"Double Gap, The" (Auchincloss), **Supp. IV Part 1:** 33

"Double-Headed Snake of Newbury, The" (Whittier), **Supp. I Part 2:** 698

Double Honeymoon (Connell), **Supp. XIV:**80, 87

Double Image, The (Levertov), **Supp. III Part 1:** 274, 276

"Double Image, The" (Sexton), **Supp. II Part 2:** 671, 677–678

Double Indemnity (film), **Supp. IV Part 1:** 130

"Double Limbo" (Komunyakaa), **Supp. XIII:** 132

Double Man, The (Auden), **Supp. III Part 1:** 16; **Supp. X:** 118

"Double Ode" (Rukeyser), **Supp. VI:** 282–283, 286

Double Persephone (Atwood), **Supp. XIII:** 19

Doubles in Literary Psychology (Tymms), **Supp. IX:** 105

Double Vision: American Thoughts Abroad (Knowles), **Supp. XII:** 249

"Doubt on the Great Divide" (Stafford), **Supp. XI:** 322

Dougherty, Steve, **Supp. X:** 262

Douglas, Aaron, **Supp. I Part 1:** 326

Douglas, Alfred, **Supp. X:** 151

Douglas, Ann, **Supp. XII:** 136

Douglas, Claire, **III:** 552

Douglas, George (pseudonym). *See* Brown, George Douglas

Douglas, Kirk, **Supp. XIII:** 5–6

Douglas, Lloyd, **IV:** 434

Douglas, Melvyn, **Supp. V:** 223

Douglas, Michael, **Supp. XI:** 67

Douglas, Paul, **III:** 294

Douglas, Stephen A., **III:** 577, 588–589; **Supp. I Part 2:** 456, 471

Douglas, William O., **III:** 581

Douglass, Frederick, **Supp. I Part 1:** 51, 345; **Supp. I Part 2:** 591; **Supp. II Part 1:** 157, 195, 196, 292, 378; **Supp. III Part 1:** 153–174; **Supp. IV Part 1:** 1, 2, 13, 15, 256; **Supp. VIII:** 202

Douglass Pilot, The (Baldwin, ed.), **Supp. I Part 1:** 49

Dove, Belle, **I:** 451

Dove, Rita, **Supp. IV Part 1:** 241–258

"Dover Beach" (Arnold), **Retro. Supp. I:** 325

Dow, Lorenzo, **IV:** 265

Dowd, Douglas, **Supp. I Part 2:** 645, 650

"Do We Understand Each Other?" (Ginsberg), **Supp. II Part 1:** 311

Dowie, William, **Supp. V:** 199

Do with Me What You Will (Oates), **Supp. II Part 2:** 506, 515–517

Dowling, Eddie, **IV:** 394

Down and Out (Shanley), **Supp. XIV:**317

"Down at City Hall" (Didion), **Supp. IV Part 1:** 211

"Down at the Cross" (Baldwin), **Retro. Supp. II:** 1, 2, 7, 12, 13, 15; **Supp. I Part 1:** 60, 61

"Down at the Dinghy" (Salinger), **III:** 559, 563

"Down by the Station, Early in the Morning" (Ashbery), **Supp. III Part 1:** 25

Downhill Racer (film), **Supp. IX:** 253

"Down in Alabam" (Bierce), **I:** 193

Downing, Ben, **Supp. XII:** 175, 189, 190–191

Downing, Major Jack (pseudonym). *See* Smith, Seba

Down in My Heart (Stafford), **Supp. XI:** 313, 315

Down Mailer's Way (Solotaroff), **Retro. Supp. II:** 203

Down the Rabbit Hole: Adventures and Misadventures in the Realm of Children's Literature (Lanes), **Supp. XVI:**104

Down There on a Visit (Isherwood), **Supp. XIV:**159, 161, 164, 168–169, 170, 171

Down the River (Abbey), **Supp. XIII:** 12–13

"Down the River with Henry Thoreau" (Abbey), **Supp. XIII:** 12–13

Down These Mean Streets (P. Thomas), **Supp. XIII:** 264

Down the Starry River (Purdy), **Supp. VII:** 278

"Downward Path to Wisdom, The" (Porter), **III:** 442, 443, 446

"Down Where I Am" (Hughes), **Supp. I Part 1:** 344

Dowson, Ernest C., **I:** 384

Doyle, Arthur Conan, **Retro. Supp. I:** 270; **Supp. IV Part 1:** 128, 341; **Supp. IV Part 2:** 464, 469; **Supp. XI:** 63

Doyle, C. W., **I:** 199

"Dr. Bergen's Belief" (Schwartz), **Supp. II Part 2:** 650

"Dr. Jack-o'-Lantern" (Yates), **Supp. XI:** 340–341

Dr. Seuss. See Geisel, Theodor Seuss (Dr. Seuss)

Dr. Seuss and Mr. Geisel (J. and N. Morgan), **Supp. XVI:**103

Dr. Seuss Goes to War: The World War II Editorial Cartoons of Theodor Seuss Geisel (Minear), **Supp. XVI:**101

Dr. Seuss's ABC (Geisel), **Supp. XVI:**99

Dr. Strangelove; or, How I Learned to Stop Worrying and Love the Bomb (film), **Supp. XI:** 293, 301–305

"Draba" (Leopold), **Supp. XIV:**186

Drabble, Margaret, **Supp. IV Part 1:** 297, 299, 305

Drabelle, Dennis, **Supp. XIII:** 13

Drach, Ivan, **Supp. III Part 1:** 268

Dracula (film), **Supp. IV Part 1:** 104

"Draft Horse, The" (Frost), **Retro. Supp. I:** 141

"Draft Lyrics for *Candide*" (Agee), **I:** 28

Draft of XVI Cantos, A (Pound), **III:** 472; **Retro. Supp. I:** 292

Draft of XXX Cantos, A (Pound), **III:** 196; **Retro. Supp. I:** 292

Drafts &Fragments (Pound), **Retro. Supp. I:** 293

Dragon Country (T. Williams), **IV:** 383

Dragon Seed (Buck), **Supp. II Part 1:** 124

Dragon's Teeth (Sinclair), **Supp. V:** 290

Drake, Benjamin, **Supp. I Part 2:** 584

Drake, Daniel, **Supp. I Part 2:** 584

Drake, Sir Francis, **Supp. I Part 2:** 497

Drake, St. Clair, **IV:** 475

Drake, William, **Supp. XV:** 295

Dramatic Duologues (Masters), **Supp. I Part 2:** 461

Drattel, Deborah, **Supp. XV:** 333

Drat These Brats (X. J. Kennedy), **Supp. XV:** 163

"Draught" (Cowley), **Supp. II Part 1:** 141, 142

Drayton, Michael, **IV:** 135; **Retro. Supp. II:** 76

"Dreadful Has Already Happened, The" (Strand), **Supp. IV Part 2:** 627

"Dream, A" (Ginsberg), **Supp. II Part 1:** 312

"Dream, A" (Tate), **IV:** 129

"Dream, The" (Hayden), **Supp. II Part 1:** 368, 377

Dream at the End of the World, The: Paul Bowles and the Literary Renegades in Tangier (Green), **Supp. IV Part 1:** 95

"Dream Avenue" (Simic), **Supp. VIII:** 282

"Dream Boogie" (Hughes), **Retro. Supp. I:** 208; **Supp. I Part 1:** 339–340

"Dreambook Bestiary" (Komunyakaa), **Supp. XIII:** 120

Dreamer (Johnson), **Supp. VI:** 186, 196–199

dreamer examines his pillow, the (Shanley), **Supp. XIV:**315, 327

"Dreamer in a Dead Language" (Paley), **Supp. VI:** 217

Dreaming in Cuban (García), **Supp. XI:** 178, 179–185, 190

"Dreaming of Hair" (L.-Y. Lee), **Supp. XV:** 214

"Dreaming the Breasts" (Sexton), **Supp. II Part 2:** 692

"Dream Interpreted, The" (Paine), **Supp. I Part 2:** 505

Dream Jumbo (Longo), **Supp. XVI:**124

Dream Keeper, The (Hughes), **Supp. I Part 1:** 328, 332, 333, 334

Dream Keeper and Other Poems, The (Hughes), **Retro. Supp. I:** 201, 202

Dreamland (Baker), **Supp. XIV:**96

"Dream-Land" (Poe), **Retro. Supp. II:** 274

Dream Life of Balso Snell, The (West), **IV:** 286, 287, 288–290, 291, 297; **Retro. Supp. II:** 321, 322, 327, 328, 330–332

Dream of a Common Language, The: Poems, 1974–1977 (Rich), **Supp. I Part 2:** 551, 554, 569–576

Dream of Arcadia: American Writers and Artists in Italy (Brooks), **I:** 254

Dream of Governors, A (Simpson), **Supp. IX:** 265, 269–270

"Dream of Italy, A" (Masters), **Supp. I Part 2:** 458

"Dream of Mourning, The" (Glück), **Supp. V:** 84

"Dream of the Blacksmith's Room, A" (R. Bly), **Supp. IV Part 1:** 73

"Dream of the Cardboard Lover" (Haines), **Supp. XII:** 204

Dream of the Golden Mountains, The (Cowley), **Supp. II Part 1:** 139, 141, 142, 144

"Dream Pang, A" (Frost), **II:** 153

"Dreams About Clothes" (Merrill), **Supp. III Part 1:** 328–329

Dreams from Bunker Hill (Fante), **Supp. XI:** 160, 166, 172–173

"Dreams of Adulthood" (Ashbery), **Supp. III Part 1:** 26

"Dreams of Glory on the Mound" (Plimpton), **Supp. XVI:**238–239

"Dreams of Math" (Kenyon), **Supp. VII:** 160–161

"Dreams of the Animals" (Atwood), **Supp. XIII:** 33

"Dream Variations" (Hughes), **Retro. Supp. I:** 198; **Supp. I Part 1:** 323

"Dream Vision" (Olsen), **Supp. XIII:** 295–296

Dream Work (Oliver), **Supp. VII:** 234–235, 236–238, 240

Dred: A Tale of the Great Dismal Swamp (Stowe), **Supp. I Part 2:** 592

Dreiser, Theodore, **I:** 59, 97, 109, 116, 355, 374, 375, 475, 482, 497–520; **II:** 26, 27, 29, 34, 38, 44, 74, 89, 93, 180, 276, 283, 428, 444, 451, 456–457, 467–468; **III:** 40, 103, 106, 251, 314, 319, 327, 335, 453, 576, 582; **IV:** 29, 35, 40, 135, 208, 237, 475, 482, 484; **Retro. Supp. I:** 325, 376; **Retro. Supp. II:** 93–110, 114, 322; **Supp. I Part 1:** 320; **Supp. I Part 2:** 461, 468; **Supp. III Part 2:** 412; **Supp. IV Part 1:** 31, 236, 350; **Supp. IV Part 2:** 689; **Supp. V:** 113, 120; **Supp. VIII:** 98, 101, 102; **Supp. IX:** 1, 14, 15, 308; **Supp. XI:** 207; **Supp. XIV:**111

"Drenched in Light" (Hurston), **Supp. VI:** 150–151

Dresser, Paul, **Retro. Supp. II:** 94, 103

Dress Gray (Truscott), **Supp. IV Part 2:** 683

Dress Gray (teleplay), **Supp. IV Part 2:** 683

"Dressing for Dinner" (Ríos), **Supp. IV Part 2:** 548

Dressing Up for the Carnival (Shields), **Supp. VII:** 328

Drew, Bettina, **Supp. IX:** 2, 4

Drew, Elizabeth, **Retro. Supp. II:** 242, 243

Drexler, Eric, **Supp. XVI:**121

Dreyfus, Alfred, **Supp. I Part 2:** 446

Drift and Mastery (Lippmann), **I:** 222–223

"Driftwood" (C. Frost), **Supp. XV:** 106–107

"Drinker, The" (Lowell), **II:** 535, 550

"Drinking Cold Water" (Everwine), **Supp. XV:** 80–81

"Drinking from a Helmet" (Dickey), **Supp. IV Part 1:** 180

Drinking Gourd, The (Hansberry), **Supp. IV Part 1:** 359, 365–367, 374

Drinks before Dinner (Doctorow), **Supp. IV Part 1:** 231, 234–235

Drive, He Said (Larner), **Supp. XVI:**220

"Drive Home, The" (Banks), **Supp. V:** 7

"Driver" (Merrill), **Supp. III Part 1:** 331

"Driving through Minnesota during the Hanoi Bombings" (R. Bly), **Supp. IV Part 1:** 61

"Driving through Oregon" (Haines), **Supp. XII:** 207

"Driving toward the Lac Qui Parle River" (R. Bly), **Supp. IV Part 1:** 61

"Drone" (Coleman), **Supp. XI:** 85–86

"Drowned Man, The: Death between Two Rivers" (McGrath), **Supp. X:** 116

"Drowning 1954" (Keillor), **Supp. XVI:**172

Drowning Pool, The (film), **Supp. IV Part 2:** 474

Drowning Pool, The (Macdonald), **Supp. IV Part 2:** 470, 471

Drowning Season, The (Hoffman), **Supp. X:** 82

Drowning with Others (Dickey), **Supp. IV Part 1:** 176, 178, 179

"Drowsy Day, A" (Dunbar), **Supp. II Part 1:** 198

Drugiye Berega (Nabokov), **III:** 247–250, 252

"Drug Shop, The, or Endymion in Edmonstoun" (Benét), **Supp. XI:** 43

"Drug Store" (Shapiro), **Supp. II Part 2:** 705

"Drugstore in Winter, A" (Ozick), **Supp. V:** 272

Drukman, Steven, **Supp. XIII:** 195, 197, 202

"Drum" (Hogan), **Supp. IV Part 1:** 413

"Drum, The" (Alvarez), **Supp. VII:** 7

"Drumlin Woodchuck, A" (Frost), **II:** 159–160; **Retro. Supp. I:** 138

Drummond, William, **Supp. I Part 1:** 369

Drummond de Andrade, Carlos, **Supp. IV Part 2:** 626, 629, 630

Drum-Taps (Whitman), **IV:** 346, 347, 444; **Retro. Supp. I:** 406

"Drunken Fisherman, The" (Lowell), **II:** 534, 550

"Drunken Sisters, The" (Wilder), **IV:** 374

Drunk in the Furnace, The (Merwin), **Supp. III Part 1:** 345–346

"Drunk in the Furnace, The" (Merwin), **Supp. III Part 1:** 346

Druten, John van, **Supp. XIV:**162

Dryden, John, **II:** 111, 542, 556; **III:** 15; **IV:** 145; **Retro. Supp. I:** 56; **Supp. I Part 1:** 150; **Supp. I Part 2:** 422; **Supp. IX:** 68; **Supp. XIV:**5; **Supp. XV:** 258

Drye, Captain Frank, **Retro. Supp. II:** 115

Dry Salvages, The (Eliot), **I:** 581

"Dry Salvages, The" (Eliot), **Retro. Supp. I:** 66

"Dry September" (Faulkner), **II:** 72, 73

Dry Sun, Dry Wind (Wagoner), **Supp. IX:** 323, 324

D'Souza, Dinesh, **Supp. X:** 255

"Dual" (Goldbarth), **Supp. XII:** 188

"Dual Curriculum" (Ozick), **Supp. V:** 270

"Dualism" (Reed), **Supp. X:** 242

Duane's Depressed (McMurtry), **Supp. V:** 233

Du Bartas, Guillaume, **Supp. I Part 1:** 98, 104, 111, 118, 119

Duberman, Martin, **Supp. I Part 2:** 408, 409

"Dubin's Lives" (Malamud), **Supp. I Part 2:** 451

Dubliners (Joyce), **I:** 130, 480; **III:** 471; **Supp. VIII:** 146

"Dubliners" (J. Joyce), **Supp. XVI:**41

Du Bois, Nina Gomer (Mrs. W. E. B. Du Bois), **Supp. II Part 1:** 158; **Supp. XIV:** 200

Du Bois, Shirley Graham (Mrs. W. E. B. Du Bois), **Supp. II Part 1:** 186

Du Bois, W. E. B., **I:** 260; **Supp. I Part 1:** 5, 345; **Supp. II Part 1:** 33, 56, 61, 157–189, 195; **Supp. IV Part 1:** 9, 164, 170, 362; **Supp. X:** 133, 134, 137, 139, 242; **Supp.**

XIII: 185, **Supp. XIII:** 186, 233, 238, 243, 244, 247; **Supp. XIV:**54, 69, 72, 201, 202; **Supp. XVI:**135

Dubreuil, Jean, **Supp. IV Part 2:** 425

Dubus, Andre, **Supp. VII:** 75–93; **Supp. XI:** 347,**Supp. XI:** 349; **Supp. XIV:**21

Duchamp, Marcel, **IV:** 408; **Retro. Supp. I:** 416, 417, 418, 430; **Supp. IV Part 2:** 423, 424; **Supp. XII:** 124; **Supp. XV:** 157

"Duchess at Prayer, The" (Wharton), **Retro. Supp. I:** 365

Duchess of Malfi, The (Webster), **IV:** 131

Duck Soup (film), **Supp. IV Part 1:** 384

Duck Variations, The (Mamet), **Supp. XIV:**239, 240, 249

Dudley, Anne. *See* Bradstreet, Anne

Dudley, Joseph, **III:** 52

Dudley, Thomas, **III:** 52; **Supp. I Part 1:** 98, 99, 110, 116

"Duet, With Muffled Brake Drums" (Updike), **Retro. Supp. I:** 319

Duet for Cannibals (Sontag), **Supp. III Part 2:** 452, 456

Duffey, Bernard, **Supp. I Part 2:** 458, 471

Duffus, R. L., **Supp. I Part 2:** 650

Duffy, Martha, **Supp. IV Part 1:** 207

Duffy, William, **Supp. XVI:**32

Du Fu (Tu Fu), **Supp. XV:** 217

Dufy, Raoul, **I:** 115; **IV:** 80

Dugan, Alan, **Supp. XIII:** 76

Dugan, James, **Supp. XV:** 197

Duhamel, Marcel, **Supp. XVI:**135, 143

Dujardin, Edouard, **I:** 53

"Duke de l'Omelette, The" (Poe), **III:** 411, 425

"Duke in His Domain, The" (Capote), **Supp. III Part 1:** 113, 126

Duke of Deception, The (G. Wolff), **Supp. II Part 1:** 97; **Supp. XI:** 246

"Duke's Child, The" (Maxwell), **Supp. VIII:** 172

Duluth (Vidal), **Supp. IV Part 2:** 677, 685, 689, 691–692

Dumas, Alexandre, **III:** 386

"Dumb Oax, The" (Lewis), **Retro. Supp. I:** 170

"Dummy, The" (Sontag), **Supp. III Part 2:** 469

"Dump Ground, The" (Stegner), **Supp. IV Part 2:** 601

Dunbar, Alice Moore (Mrs. Paul Laurence Dunbar), **Supp. II Part 1:** 195, 200, 217

Dunbar, Paul Laurence, **Supp. I Part 1:** 320; **Supp. II Part 1:** 174, 191–219; **Supp. III Part 1:** 73; **Supp. IV Part 1:** 15, 165, 170; **Supp. X:** 136; **Supp. XI:** 277; **Supp. XIII:** 111

Duncan, Harry, **Supp. XV:** 75

Duncan, Isadora, **I:** 483; **Supp. XV:** 42, 50

Duncan, Robert, **Retro. Supp. II:** 49; **Supp. III Part 2:** 625, 626, 630, 631; **Supp. VIII:** 304; **Supp. XVI:**282–283

Dunciad, The (Pope), **I:** 204

Dunford, Judith, **Supp. VIII:** 107

Dunlap, William, **Supp. I Part 1:** 126, 130, 137, 141, 145

Dunn, Stephen, **Supp. XI:** 139–158

Dunne, Finley Peter, **II:** 432

Dunne, John Gregory, **Supp. IV Part 1:** 197, 198, 201, 203, 207

"Dunnet Shepherdess, A" (Jewett), **II:** 392–393; **Retro. Supp. II:** 139

Dunning, Stephen, **Supp. XIV:**126

Dunning, William Archibald, **Supp. II Part 1:** 170; **Supp. XIV:**48

Dunnock, Mildred, **III:** 153

Dunster, Henry, **Supp. I Part 2:** 485

"Duo Tried Killing Man with Bacon" (Goldbarth), **Supp. XII:** 176

Dupee, F. W., **I:** 254; **II:** 548; **Supp. VIII:** 231; **Supp. IX:** 93, 96

DuPlessis, Rachel Blau, **Supp. IV Part 2:** 421, 426, 432; **Supp. XVI:**284

Duplicate Keys (Smiley), **Supp. VI:** 292, 294–296

Duplications, The (Koch), **Supp. XV:** 181, 183, 186

Durable Fire, A (Sarton), **Supp. VIII:** 260

Durand, Asher, B., **Supp. I Part 1:** 156, 157

Durand, Régis, **Supp. IV Part 1:** 44

"Durango Suite" (Gunn Allen), **Supp. IV Part 1:** 326

"Durations" (Matthews), **Supp. IX:** 152–153, 154

Dürer, Albrecht, **III:** 212; **Supp. XII:** 44

"During Fever" (Lowell), **II:** 547

Durkheim, Émile, **I:** 227; **Retro. Supp. I:** 55, 57; **Supp. I Part 2:** 637, 638

Durrell, Lawrence, **III:** 184, 190; **IV:** 430; **Supp. X:** 108, 187; **Supp. XVI:**294

Dürrenmatt, Friedrich, **Supp. IV Part 2:** 683

Duse, Eleonora, **II:** 515, 528

Dusk and Other Stories (Salter), **Supp. IX:** 260–261

Dusk of Dawn: An Essay Toward an Autobiography of a Race Concept (Du Bois), **Supp. II Part 1:** 159, 183, 186

"Dusting" (Alvarez), **Supp. VII:** 4

"Dusting" (Dove), **Supp. IV Part 1:** 247, 248

"Dusting" (Schnackenberg), **Supp. XV:** 256

"Dust of Snow" (Frost), **II:** 154

Dust Tracks on a Road (Hurston), **Supp. IV Part 1:** 5, 11; **Supp. VI:** 149, 151, 158–159

"Dusty Braces" (Snyder), **Supp. VIII:** 302

Dutchman (Baraka), **Supp. II Part 1:** 38, 40, 42–44, 54, 55

"Dutch Nick Massacre, The" (Twain), **IV:** 195

"Dutch Picture, A" (Longfellow), **Retro. Supp. II:** 171

Dutton, Charles S., **Supp. VIII:** 332, 342

Dutton, Clarence Earl, **Supp. IV Part 2:** 598

Duvall, Robert, **Supp. V:** 227

"Duwamish" (Hugo), **Supp. VI:** 136

"Duwamish, Skagit, Hoh" (Hugo), **Supp. VI:** 136–137

"Duwamish No. 2" (Hugo), **Supp. VI:** 137

Duyckinck, Evert, **III:** 77, 81, 83, 85; **Retro. Supp. I:** 155, 247, 248; **Supp. I Part 1:** 122, 317

Duyckinck, George, **Supp. I Part 1:** 122

"Dvonya" (Simpson), **Supp. IX:** 274

Dwellings: A Spiritual History of the Living World (Hogan), **Supp. IV Part 1:** 397, 410, 415–416, 417

Dwight, Sereno E., **I:** 547

Dwight, Timothy, **Supp. I Part 1:** 124; **Supp. I Part 2:** 516, 580; **Supp. II Part 1:** 65, 69

Dworkin, Andrea, **Supp. XII:** 6

Dwyer, Jim, **Supp. XVI:**16, 19

Dybbuk, A, or Between Two Worlds: Dramatic Legend in Four Acts (Kushner), **Supp. IX:** 138

Dybbuk, The (Ansky), **IV:** 6

Dyer, Geoff, **Supp. X:** 169

Dyer, R. C., **Supp. XIII:** 162

Dying Animal, The (Roth), **Retro. Supp. II:** 288

"Dying Elm, The" (Freneau), **Supp. II Part 1:** 258

"Dying Indian, The" (Freneau), **Supp. II Part 1:** 262

"Dying Man, The" (Roethke), **III:** 540, 542, 543–545

Dylan, Bob, **Supp. VIII:** 202; **Supp. XIII:** 114, 119; **Supp. XV:** 349, 350
Dynamo (O'Neill), **III:** 396
"Dysfunctional Nation" (Karr), **Supp. XI:** 245
Dyson, A. E., **Retro. Supp. II:** 247
E
E. E. Cummings (Marks), **I:** 438
E. E. Cummings: A Miscellany (Cummings), **I:** 429, 441
E. E. Cummings: A Miscellany, Revised (Cummings), **I:** 429
E. L. Doctorow (Harter and Thompson), **Supp. IV Part 1:** 217
E. M. Forster (Trilling), **Supp. III Part 2:** 496, 501, 504
"Each and All" (Emerson), **II:** 19
Each in His Season (Snodgrass), **Supp. VI:** 324, 327
"Each Like a Leaf" (Swenson), **Supp. IV Part 2:** 644
Eager, Allen, **Supp. XI:** 294
"Eagle, The" (Tate), **IV:** 128
"Eagle and the Mole, The" (Wylie), **Supp. I Part 2:** 710, 711, 713, 714, 729
Eagle as Wide as the World, The (X. J. Kennedy), **Supp. XV:** 162, 164
"Eagle Poem" (Harjo), **Supp. XII:** 224, 226
"Eagles" (Dickey), **Supp. IV Part 1:** 186
Eagle's Mile, The (Dickey), **Supp. IV Part 1:** 178, 185–186
"Eagle That Is Forgotten, The" (Lindsay), **Supp. I Part 2:** 382, 387
Eagleton, Terry, **Retro. Supp. I:** 67
Eakin, Paul John, **Supp. VIII:** 167, 168; **Supp. XIII:** 225; **Supp. XVI:**70
Eakins, Thomas, **Supp. XIV:**338
Eames, Roscoe, **II:** 476
"Earl: My Life with a Louse" (Keillor), **Supp. XVI:**176
"Earl Painter" (Banks), **Supp. V:** 14–15
"Early Adventures of Ralph Ringwood, The" (Irving), **II:** 314
Early Ayn Rand, The: A Selection of Her Unpublished Fiction (Rand), **Supp. IV Part 2:** 520
Early Dark (Price), **Supp. VI:** 262
Early Diary of Anaïs Nin, The, **Supp. X:** 184, 192
Early Elkin (Elkin), **Supp. VI:** 42–43, 45
"Early Evenin' Blues" (Hughes), **Retro. Supp. I:** 205
"Early History of a Seamstress" (Reznikoff), **Supp. XIV:**277, 289
"Early History of a Sewing-Machine

Operator" (Reznikoff), **Supp. XIV:**277
Early History of a Sewing-Machine Operator (Reznikoff), **Supp. XIV:**289
"Early History of a Writer" (Reznikoff), **Supp. XIV:**278, 290
"Early in the Morning" (L.-Y. Lee), **Supp. XV:** 214
Early Lectures of Ralph Waldo Emerson, The (Emerson), **II:** 11
Early Lives of Melville, The (Sealts), **Retro. Supp. I:** 257
Early Martyr and Other Poems, An (W. C. Williams), **Retro. Supp. I:** 423
"Early Morning: Cape Cod" (Swenson), **Supp. IV Part 2:** 641
"Early Spring between Madison and Bellingham" (R. Bly), **Supp. IV Part 1:** 71
Earnhardt, Dale, **Supp. XII:** 310
Earnshaw, Doris, **Supp. IV Part 1:** 310
"Earth" (Bryant), **Supp. I Part 1:** 157, 164, 167
"Earth, The" (Sexton), **Supp. II Part 2:** 696
"Earth and Fire" (Berry), **Supp. X:** 27
Earth as Air, The: An Ars Poetica (Sobin), **Supp. XVI:**285–286
"Earth Being" (Toomer), **Supp. IX:** 320
"Earthly Care a Heavenly Discipline" (Stowe), **Supp. I Part 2:** 586
"Earthly City of the Jews, The" (Kazin), **Retro. Supp. II:** 286
Earthly Possessions (Tyler), **Supp. IV Part 2:** 665–666, 671
Earth Power Coming (Ortiz, ed.), **Supp. IV Part 2:** 502
"Earth's Holocaust" (Hawthorne), **II:** 226, 231, 232, 242; **III:** 82; **Retro. Supp. I:** 152
East Coker (Eliot), **I:** 580, 581, 582, 585, 587
"East Coker" (Eliot), **Retro. Supp. I:** 66; **Supp. VIII:** 195, 196
"Easter" (Toomer), **Supp. III Part 2:** 486
"Easter, an Ode" (Lowell), **II:** 536
"Easter Morning" (Ammons), **Supp. VII:** 34
"Easter Morning" (Clampitt), **Supp. IX:** 45
"Easter Ode, An" (Dunbar), **Supp. II Part 1:** 196
Easter Parade, The (Yates), **Supp. XI:** 346, 349
"Easter Sunday: Recollection" (Gunn Allen), **Supp. IV Part 1:** 322
"Easter Wings" (Herbert), **Supp. IV**

Part 2: 646
"East European Cooking" (Simic), **Supp. VIII:** 277
East Is East (Boyle), **Supp. VIII:** 1–3
Eastlake, William, **Supp. XIII:** 12
East Lynne (Wood), **Supp. I Part 1:** 35, 36; **Supp. I Part 2:** 459, 462; **Supp. XVI:**182
Eastman, Elaine Goodale, **Supp. X:** 103
Eastman, Max, **Supp. III Part 2:** 620; **Supp. X:** 131, 134, 135, 137; **Supp. XV:** 295; **Supp. XVI:**185
East of Eden (Steinbeck), **IV:** 51, 56–57, 59
"East of the Sun and West of the Moon" (Merwin), **Supp. III Part 1:** 344
Easton, Alison, **Retro. Supp. II:** 143, 144, 145
Easton, Bret Ellis, **Supp. XI:** 65
Easton, Robert, **Supp. IV Part 2:** 461, 474
East Wind (Lowell), **II:** 527
East Wind: West Wind (Buck), **Supp. II Part 1:** 114–115
Easy Rawlins mysteries, **Supp. XIII:** 236, 237–241, 242
Easy Rider (film), **Supp. XI:** 293, 308, 309
Eat a Bowl of Tea (Chu), **Supp. X:** 291
"Eating " (Bass), **Supp. XVI:**23–24
"Eating Alone" (L.-Y. Lee), **Supp. XV:** 214
Eating Naked (Dobyns), **Supp. XIII:** 78–79
"Eating Out" (L. Michaels), **Supp. XVI:**209
"Eating Poetry" (Strand), **Supp. IV Part 2:** 626
"Eating the Whole" (C. Frost), **Supp. XV:** 101
"Eating Together" (L.-Y. Lee), **Supp. XV:** 214
"Eating with My Fingers" (C. Frost), **Supp. XV:** 97
Eaton, Edith, **Supp. X:** 291
Eaton, Peggy, **Supp. I Part 2:** 461
Eaton, Winnifred, **Supp. X:** 291
"Eatonville Anthology, The" (Hurston), **Supp. VI:** 152
"Ebb and Flow, The" (Taylor), **IV:** 161
"Ebenezer Marsh, 1725" (Schnackenberg), **Supp. XV:** 256
Eben Holden (Bacheller), **I:** 216
Eberhardt, Isabelle, **Supp. IV Part 1:** 92
Eberhart, Mrs., **I:** 521–522, 530
Eberhart, Richard, **I:** 521–543; **II:** 535–536; **III:** 527; **IV:** 416; **Retro.**

Supp. II: 176, 178; **Supp. I Part 1:** 83; **Supp. XII:** 119

Eble, Kenneth E., **Supp. I Part 1:** 201

Eccentricities of a Nightingale (T. Williams), **IV:** 382, 385, 397, 398

Ecclesiastica Historia Integram Ecclesiae (Taylor), **IV:** 163

"Echart" (Sobin), **Supp. XVI:**289

"Echo, The" (Bowles), **Supp. IV Part 1:** 84, 86, 87

Echoes inside the Labyrinth (McGrath), **Supp. X:** 127

Eckehart, Meister, **Supp. XV:** 225

Eckhart, Maria, **Supp. V:** 212

Eclipse (Hogan), **Supp. IV Part 1:** 397, 400, 402

Eclipse, a Nightmare (Montalembert), **Supp. XV:** 349

Eclogues (Virgil), **Supp. VIII:** 31

"Ecologue" (Ginsberg), **Supp. II Part 1:** 326

"Ecologues of These States 1969–1971" (Ginsberg), **Supp. II Part 1:** 325

"Economics of Negro Emancipation in the United States, The" (Du Bois), **Supp. II Part 1:** 174

"Economic Theory of Women's Dress, The" (Veblen), **Supp. I Part 2:** 636

Economy of the Unlost: Reading Simonides of Keos with Paul Celan (Carson), **Supp. XII:** 110–111

Ecotactics: The Sierra Club Handbook for Environmental Activists (Mitchell and Stallings, eds.), **Supp. IV Part 2:** 488

"Ecstasy" (Olds), **Supp. X:** 206

"Ecstatic" (Komunyakaa), **Supp. XIII:** 131

Edda, **Supp. X:** 114

Eddy, Mary Baker, **I:** 583; **III:** 506

Edel, Leon, **I:** 20; **II:** 338–339; **Retro. Supp. I:** 218, 224, 231

Edelberg, Cynthia, **Supp. IV Part 1:** 155

"Eden and My Generation" (Levis), **Supp. XI:** 270

Edenbaum, Robert, **Supp. IV Part 1:** 352

Eden Tree (Bynner), **Supp. XV:** 42, 51

Eder, Richard, **Supp. XII:** 189; **Supp. XV:** 62, 187, 259, 261

Edgar Huntly; or, Memoirs of a Sleep-Walker (Brown), **Supp. I Part 1:** 140–144, 145

"Edge" (Plath), **Retro. Supp. II:** 256; **Supp. I Part 2:** 527, 547

Edge, Mary E., **II:** 316

"Edge of the Great Rift, The" (Theroux), **Supp. VIII:** 325

Edge of the Sea, The (Carson), **Supp. IX:** 19, 25–31, 32

Edgers, Geoff, **Supp. XV:** 113

Edgeworth, Maria, **II:** 8; **Supp. XV:** 231

Edible Woman, The (Atwood), **Supp. XIII:** 19, 20, 20–21

"Edict by the King of Prussia, An" (Franklin), **II:** 120

Edie: An American Biography (Stein), **Supp. XVI:**245

Edison, Thomas A., **I:** 483; **Supp. I Part 2:** 392

Edith Wharton (Joslin), **Retro. Supp. I:** 376

Edith Wharton: A Biography (Lewis), **Retro. Supp. I:** 362

Edith Wharton: A Woman in Her Time (Auchincloss), **Retro. Supp. I:** 370

Edith Wharton: Matters of Mind and Spirit (Singley), **Retro. Supp. I:** 373

Edith Wharton: Traveller in the Land of Letters (Goodwyn), **Retro. Supp. I:** 370

Edith Wharton's Argument with America (Ammons), **Retro. Supp. I:** 364

Edith Wharton's Brave New Politics (Bauer), **Retro. Supp. I:** 381

Edith Wharton's Letters from the Underworld (Waid), **Retro. Supp. I:** 360

"Editing and Glosses" (Reznikoff), **Supp. XIV:**283

Editing of Emily Dickinson, The (Franklin), **Retro. Supp. I:** 41

"Editor and the Schoolma'am, The" (Frederic), **II:** 130

"Editor's Easy Chair" (Howells), **II:** 276

"Editor's Study, The" (Howells), **II:** 275, 276, 285

"Editor Whedon" (Masters), **Supp. I Part 2:** 463

Edlin, Mari, **Supp. X:** 266

Edman, Irwin, **III:** 605

Edmond (Mamet), **Supp. XIV:**241, 248, 249, 250

Edmundson, Mark, **Retro. Supp. II:** 262

Edsel (Shapiro), **Supp. II Part 2:** 703, 704, 717–719

Edson, Russell, **Supp. VIII:** 279

"Educated American Woman, An" (Cheever), **Supp. I Part 1:** 194

Education and Living (Bourne), **I:** 252

"Education by Poetry" (Frost), **Supp. XV:** 215

"Education of a Storyteller, The" (Bambara), **Supp. XI:** 20

Education of Black People, The (Du Bois), **Supp. II Part 1:** 186

Education of Harriet Hatfield, The (Sarton), **Supp. VIII:** 257–258

Education of Henry Adams, The (Adams), **I:** 1, 5, 6, 11, 14, 15–18, 19, 20–21, 111; **II:** 276; **III:** 504; **Retro. Supp. I:** 53, 59; **Supp. IX:** 19; **Supp. XIV:**299

"Education of Mingo, The" (Johnson), **Supp. VI:** 193, 194

"Education of Norman Podhoretz, The" (Goldberg), **Supp. VIII:** 238

Education of Oscar Fairfax, The (Auchincloss), **Supp. IV Part 1:** 25, 36

"Education of the Poet" (Glück), **Supp. V:** 78, 80

Education sentimentale (Flaubert), **III:** 315

"Education the Imagination" (Koch), **Supp. XV:** 175–176, 177

Edwards, Eli. *See* McKay, Claude

Edwards, Esther, **I:** 545

Edwards, John, **I:** 478

Edwards, Jonathan, **I:** 544–566; **II:** 432; **Retro. Supp. II:** 187; **Supp. I Part 1:** 301, 302; **Supp. I Part 2:** 552, 594, 700; **Supp. IV Part 2:** 430; **Supp. VIII:** 205

Edwards, Sarah, **I:** 545

Edwards, Thomas, **Supp. XV:** 20

Edwards, Thomas R., **Supp. XVI:**207

Edwards, Timothy, **I:** 545

Edwards-Yearwood, Grace, **Supp. VIII:** 81

"Edwin Arlington Robinson" (Cowley), **Supp. II Part 1:** 144

Edwin Arlington Robinson (Winters), **Supp. II Part 2:** 812

Edwin Booth (play), **Supp. IV Part 1:** 89

"Effects of Analogy" (Stevens), **Retro. Supp. I:** 297

Effluences from the Sacred Caves; More Selected Essays and Reviews (Carruth), **Supp. XVI:**46

"Effort at Speech between Two People" (Rukeyser), **Supp. VI:** 276, 284

"Efforts of Affection" (Moore), **III:** 214

"Efforts of Affection: A Memoir of Marianne Moore" (Bishop), **Retro. Supp. II:** 52

"Egg, The" (Anderson), **I:** 113, 114

"Egg, The" (Snyder), **Supp. VIII:** 302

"Eggplant Epithalamion, The" (Jong), **Supp. V:** 119

"Eggs" (Olds), **Supp. X:** 206

"Eggshell" (Stern), **Supp. IX:** 299

Egoist, The (Meredith), **II:** 186

Egorova, Lubov, **Supp. IX:** 58

"Egotism, or the Bosom Sergent" (Hawthorne), **II:** 227, 239

"Egyptian Pulled Glass Bottle in the Shape of a Fish, An" (Moore), **III:** 195, 213

Ehrenfels, Christian von, **Supp. XIV:**198

Ehrenpreis, Irvin, **Supp. XII:** 128

Ehrlich, Gretel, **Supp. XIV:**227

Eichmann, Adolf, **Supp. XII:** 166

Eichmann in Jerusalem (Arendt), **Retro. Supp. II:** 28; **Supp. VIII:** 243; **Supp. XII:** 166

"Eichmann in New York: The New York Intellectuals and the Hannah Arendt Controversy" (Rabinbach), **Supp. XII:** 166

"Eidolon" (Warren), **IV:** 239

Eight Cousins (Alcott), **Supp. I Part 1:** 29, 38, 42, 43

18 Poems from the Quechua (Strand, trans.), **Supp. IV Part 2:** 630

1876: A Novel (Vidal), **Supp. IV Part 2:** 677, 684, 688, 689, 691, 692

"18 West 11th Street" (Merrill), **Supp. III Part 1:** 323, 328

"Eighth Air Force" (Jarrell), **II:** 373–374, 377

Eight Harvard Poets, **I:** 429, 475

"Eighth Ditch, The" (Baraka), **Supp. II Part 1:** 40

"'80s Pastoral: Frederick Barthelme's *Moon Deluxe* Ten Years On" (Peters), **Supp. XI:** 39

Eight Men (Wright), **IV:** 478, 488, 494

80 Flowers (Zukofsky), **Supp. III Part 2:** 631

Eikon Basilike, The, **Supp. IV Part 2:** 435

Eileen (Masters), **Supp. I Part 2:** 460

Eimi (Cummings), **I:** 429, 433, 434, 439–440

"Einstein" (MacLeish), **III:** 5, 8, 10–11, 18–19

Einstein, Albert, **I:** 493; **III:** 8, 10, 21, 161; **IV:** 69, 375, 410, 411, 421; **Retro. Supp. I:** 63; **Supp. I Part 2:** 609, 643; **Supp. III Part 2:** 621; **Supp. V:** 290; **Supp. XII:** 45

Eiseley, Loren, **III:** 227–228

Eisenhower, Dwight D., **I:** 136, 376; **II:** 548; **III:** 215; **IV:** 75; **Supp. I Part 1:** 291; **Supp. III Part 2:** 624; **Supp. V:** 45

Eisenstein, Sergei, **I:** 481

Eisinger, Chester E., **I:** 302; **II:** 604;

Supp. IX: 15

Eisner, Douglas, **Supp. X:** 155

Elam, Angela, **Supp. XI:** 290

El Bernardo (Balbuena), **Supp. V:** 11

Elbert, Sarah, **Supp. I Part 1:** 34, 41

Elder, Donald, **II:** 417, 426, 435, 437; **Supp. XV:** 137

Elder, John, **Supp. IX:** 25

Elder, Lonne, III, **Supp. IV Part 1:** 362

Elder, Richard, **Supp. XII:** 172

"Elder Sister, The" (Olds), **Supp. X:** 205–206

Elder Statesman, The (Eliot), **I:** 572, 573, 583; **Retro. Supp. I:** 53, 65

Eldredge, Kay, **Supp. IX:** 254, 259

Eldridge, Florence, **III:** 154, 403; **IV:** 357

Eleanor of Aquitaine, **III:** 470

Eleanor of Guienne, **I:** 14

"Elect, The" (Taylor), **Supp. V:** 323

"Elections, Nicaragua, 1984" (Kingsolver), **Supp. VII:** 208

Elective Affinities (Goethe; Bogan and Mayer, trans.), **Supp. III Part 1:** 63

Electra (Euripides), **III:** 398

Electra (Sophocles), **III:** 398; **IV:** 370; **Supp. IX:** 102

"Electra on Azalea Path" (Plath), **Supp. I Part 2:** 538

"Electrical Storm" (Bishop), **Supp. I Part 1:** 93

"Electrical Storm" (Hayden), **Supp. II Part 1:** 370

"Electric Arrows" (Proulx), **Supp. VII:** 256

"Electricity Saviour" (Olds), **Supp. X:** 215

Electric Kool-Aid Acid Test, The (Wolfe), **Supp. III Part 2:** 575–577, 582–584; **Supp. XI:** 239

Electric Lady, The (film), **Supp. XI:** 309

Elegant Extracts (Knox), **II:** 8

Elegiac Feelings American (Corso), **Supp. XII:** 131–134

"Elegiac Fragments" (Everwine), **Supp. XV:** 89

Elegies (Rukeyser), **Supp. VI:** 273

"Elegies" (Rukeyser), **Supp. VI:** 272

"Elegies for Paradise Valley" (Hayden), **Supp. II Part 1:** 363

"Elegy" (Bidart), **Supp. XV:** 25, 29

Elegy (Levis), **Supp. XI:** 257, 259, 261, 271–272

"Elegy" (Merwin), **Supp. III Part 1:** 351

"Elegy" (Stafford), **Supp. XI:** 322

"Elegy" (Tate), **IV:** 128

"Elegy, for the U.S.N. Dirigible, Ma-

con, An" (Winters), **Supp. II Part 2:** 810

"Elegy Ending in the Sound of a Skipping Rope" (Levis), **Supp. XI:** 271–272

"Elegy for D. H. Lawrence, An" (W. C. Williams), **Retro. Supp. I:** 421

"Elegy for My Father" (Strand), **Supp. IV Part 2:** 628

"Elegy for My Mother" (Wagoner), **Supp. IX:** 330

Elegy for September, An (Nichols), **Supp. XIII:** 268

"Elegy for Thelonious" (Komunyakaa), **Supp. XIII:** 118

"Elegy for the U.S.N. Dirigible, Macon, A" (Winters), **Supp. II Part 2:** 810

"Elegy of Last Resort" (Nemerov), **III:** 271

"Elegy with a Thimbleful of Water in the Cage" (Levis), **Supp. XI:** 272

Elegy Written in a Country Churchyard (Gray), **I:** 68

"Elegy Written in a Country Churchyard" (Gray), **Supp. XIV:**8

"Elementary Scene, The" (Jarrell), **II:** 387, 388, 389

"Elements" (Frank), **Supp. X:** 213

Elements of Style, The (Strunk), **Supp. I Part 2:** 670

"Elenita, Cards, Palm, Water" (Cisneros), **Supp. VII:** 64

"Eleonora" (Poe), **III:** 412

Eleothriambos (Lee), **IV:** 158

"Elephants" (Moore), **III:** 203

"Elevator, The" (Dixon), **Supp. XII:** 154

"Elevator Boy" (Hughes), **Retro. Supp. I:** 200; **Supp. I Part 1:** 326

"Eleven" (Cisneros), **Supp. VII:** 69

Eleven Essays in the European Novel (Blackmur), **Supp. II Part 1:** 91, 111

Eleven Kinds of Loneliness (Yates), **Supp. XI:** 340–343, 349

Eleven Poems on the Same Theme (Warren), **IV:** 239–241

"Eleven Times a Poem" (Corso), **Supp. XII:** 132, 133

El Greco (Doménikos Theotokópoulos), **I:** 387; **III:** 212

"El-Hajj Malik El-Shabazz" (Hayden), **Supp. II Part 1:** 379

"Eli, the Fanatic" (Roth), **Supp. III Part 2:** 407–408

Eliade, Mircea, **Supp. XVI:**292

Eliot, Charles W., **I:** 5; **II:** 345; **Supp. I Part 2:** 479; **Supp. IX:** 94

Eliot, Charles William, **Retro. Supp. I:** 55

Eliot, George, **I:** 375, 458, 459, 461, 467; **II:** 179, 181, 191–192, 275, 319, 324, 338, 577; **IV:** 311, 322; **Retro. Supp. I:** 218, 220, 225; **Supp. I Part 1:** 370; **Supp. I Part 2:** 559, 579; **Supp. IV Part 1:** 31, 297; **Supp. IV Part 2:** 677; **Supp. V:** 258; **Supp. IX:** 38, 43, 51; **Supp. XI:** 68; **Supp. XII:** 335; **Supp. XIV:**344

Eliot, T. S., **I:** 48, 49, 52, 59, 60, 64, 66, 68, 105, 107, 215–216, 236, 243, 256, 259, 261, 266, 384, 386, 395, 396, 399, 403, 430, 433, 441, 446, 475, 478, 479, 482, 521, 522, 527, 567–591; **II:** 65, 96, 158, 168, 316, 371, 376, 386, 529, 530, 532, 537, 542, 545; **III:** 1, 4, 5, 6, 7–8, 9, 10, 11, 14, 17, 20, 21, 23, 26, 34, 174, 194, 195–196, 205–206, 220, 236, 239, 269, 270–271, 277–278, 301, 409, 428, 435, 436, 453, 456–457, 459–460, 461–462, 464, 466, 471, 476, 478, 485, 488, 492, 493, 498, 504, 509, 511, 517, 524, 527, 539, 572, 575, 586, 591, 594, 600, 613; **IV:** 27, 74, 82, 83, 95, 122, 123, 127, 129, 134, 138, 140, 141, 191, 201, 237, 331, 379, 402, 403, 418, 419, 420, 430, 431, 439, 442, 491; **Retro. Supp. I:** 51–71, 74, 80, 89, 91, 171, 198, 210, 283, 289, 290, 292, 296, 298, 299, 311, 324, 359, 411, 413, 414, 416, 417, 420, 428; **Retro. Supp. II:** 79, 178, 189, 262, 326; **Supp. I Part 1:** 257, 264, 268, 270, 274, 299; **Supp. I Part 2:** 423, 455, 536, 554, 624, 659, 721; **Supp. II Part 1:** 1, 4, 8, 20, 30, 91, 98, 103, 136, 314; **Supp. III Part 1:** 9, 10, 26, 31, 37, 41, 43, 44, 48, 62–64, 73, 91, 99–100, 105–106, 273; **Supp. III Part 2:** 541, 611, 612, 617, 624; **Supp. IV Part 1:** 40, 47, 284, 380, 404; **Supp. IV Part 2:** 436; **Supp. V:** 79, 97, 101, 338, 343, 344; **Supp. VIII:** 19, 21, 93, 102, 105, 182, 195, 205, 290, 292; **Supp. IX:** 158–159, 229; **Supp. X:** 59, 115, 119, 124, 187, 324; **Supp. XI:** 242; **Supp. XII:** 45, 159, 198, 308; **Supp. XIII:** 77, 104, 115, 332, 341–342, 344, 346; **Supp. XIV:**5, 13, 107, 287, 290, 306, 347; **Supp. XV:** 20,**Supp. XV:** 251, 51, 139, 177, 181, 186, 216, 218, 250, 258, 298, 302, 303, 306, 307; **Supp. XVI:**158–159, 204, 207, 282

Eliot's Early Years (Gordon), **Retro. Supp. I:** 55

"Elizabeth" (Longfellow), **I:** 502

"Elizabeth, 1905" (Schnackenberg), **Supp. XV:** 253, 256

Elizabeth Appleton (O'Hara), **III:** 362, 364, 375–377

"Elizabeth Bishop (1911–1979)" (Merrill), **Retro. Supp. II:** 53

"Elizabeth Bishop in Brazil" (Brown), **Supp. I Part 1:** 96

"Elizabeth Bishop's *North & South*" (Lowell), **Retro. Supp. II:** 40–41

"Elizabeth Gone" (Sexton), **Supp. II Part 2:** 674, 681

Elizabeth Stoddard and the Boundaries of Bourgeois Culture (Mahoney), **Supp. XV:** 270

Elk Heads on the Wall (Ríos), **Supp. IV Part 2:** 540

Elkin, Stanley, **Supp. VI:** 41–59

"Elk Song" (Hogan), **Supp. IV Part 1:** 406

Ella in Bloom (Hearon), **Supp. VIII:** 70–71

Elledge, Jim, **Supp. XIII:** 88

Ellen Foster: A Novel (Gibbons), **Supp. X:** 41, 42–44, 46, 47, 49, 50

Ellen Rogers (Farrell), **II:** 42–43

"Ellen's Dream" (Gioia), **Supp. XV:** 128

"Ellen West" (Bidart), **Supp. XV:** 26–27

Eller, Ernest, **Supp. I Part 2:** 497

Ellerman, Winifred, **Supp. I Part 1:** 258–259. *See also* McAlmon, Mrs. Robert (Winifred Ellerman)

"*El libro de la sexualidad*" (Simic), **Supp. VIII:** 283

Ellington, Duke, **Retro. Supp. II:** 115; **Supp. IV Part 1:** 360; **Supp. IX:** 164

Elliot, Charles, **Supp. V:** 161

Elliot, George P., **Supp. XV:** 92

Elliott, George B., **III:** 478

"Ellipsis" (C. Frost), **Supp. XV:** 107

Ellis, Albert, **Supp. IV Part 2:** 527

Ellis, Anne, **Supp. XVI:**38

Ellis, Bret Easton, **Supp. XII:** 81

Ellis, Brett Easton, **Supp. X:** 7

Ellis, Charles, **Supp. I Part 1:** 99

Ellis, Havelock, **II:** 276

Ellis, John Harvard, **Supp. I Part 1:** 103

Ellis, Katherine, **IV:** 114

Ellison, Harlan, **Supp. XIII:** 61

Ellison, Ralph, **IV:** 250, 493; **Retro. Supp. II:** 3, 111–130; **Supp. II Part 1:** 33, 221–252; **Supp. IV, Part 1:** 374; **Supp. VIII:** 105, 245; **Supp. IX:** 114, 316; **Supp. X:** 324; **Supp. XI:** 18, 92, 275; **Supp. XIII:** 186, 233, 305; **Supp. XIV:**306; **Supp. XV:** 194; **Supp. XVI:**135, 139

Ellmann, Maud, **Supp. IV Part 1:** 302

Ellmann, Richard, **Supp. VIII:** 105; **Supp. XV:** 74

Ellroy, James, **Supp. XIV:**26

Elman, Richard, **Supp. V:** 40

"Elmer" (Faulkner), **Retro. Supp. I:** 79, 80

Elmer Gantry (Lewis), **I:** 26, 364; **II:** 447–449, 450, 455

Elmer the Great (Lardner), **II:** 427

"Elms" (Glück), **Supp. V:** 85

Eloges (Perse), **Supp. XIII:** 344

"Eloquence of Grief, An" (Crane), **I:** 411

"El Río Grande" (Mora), **Supp. XIII:** 224

"*El* Round up" (Alvarez), **Supp. VII:** 11

"El Salvador: Requiem and Invocation" (Levertov), **Supp. III Part 1:** 284

Elsasser, Henry, **I:** 226

"Elsa Wertman" (Masters), **Supp. I Part 2:** 462–463

Elsie John and Joey Martinez: Two Stories (Huncke), **Supp. XIV:**148

Elsie Venner (Holmes), **Supp. I Part 1:** 243, 315–316

Elton, Charles, **Supp. XIV:**192

Éluard, Paul, **III:** 528; **Supp. IV Part 1:** 80

Elvins, Kells, **Supp. III Part 1:** 93, 101

Ely, Richard T., **Supp. I Part 1:** 5; **Supp. I Part 2:** 640, 645

"Emancipation. A Life Fable" (Chopin), **Retro. Supp. II:** 59; **Supp. I Part 1:** 207–208

"Emancipation in the British West Indies" (Emerson), **II:** 13

"Emancipation Proclamation, The" (Emerson), **II:** 13

Emanuel, James, **Supp. I Part 1:** 346

Embargo, The (Bryant), **Supp. I Part 1:** 152–153

Embarrassments (James), **Retro. Supp. I:** 229

Embezzler, The (Auchincloss), **Supp. IV Part 1:** 24, 30–31

"Embroidery, The" (C. Frost), **Supp. XV:** 97

"Emerald" (Doty), **Supp. XI:** 131

"Emerald, The" (Merrill), **Supp. III Part 1:** 328

"Emergence of Flight from Aristotle's

Mud, The" (Goldbarth), **Supp. XII:** 190

"Emergency Haying" (Carruth), **Supp. XVI:**55

"Emergency Room" (Mora), **Supp. XIII:** 218

"Emerging Voices: The Teaching of Writing" (Mora), **Supp. XIII:** 220

Emerson, and Other Essays (Chapman), **Supp. XIV:**41–44

Emerson, Ellen, **Supp. I Part 1:** 33

Emerson, John, **Supp. XVI:**185, 186, 190, 192

Emerson, Ralph Waldo, **I:** 98, 217, 220, 222, 224, 228, 239, 246, 251, 252, 253, 257, 260, 261, 283, 386, 397, 402, 424, 433, 444, 447, 455, 458, 460–461, 463, 464, 485, 561; **II:** 1–24, 49, 92, 127–128, 169, 170, 226, 233, 237, 273–274, 275, 278, 289, 295, 301, 313, 315, 336, 338, 344, 402, 491, 503; **III:** 53, 82, 171, 174, 260, 277, 409, 424, 428, 453, 454, 507, 576–577, 606, 614; **IV:** 60, 167, 169, 170, 171, 172, 173– 174, 176, 178, 183, 186, 187, 192, 201, 202, 211, 335, 338, 340, 342, 350; **Retro. Supp. I:** 34, 53, 54, 57, 62, 74–75, 76, 125, 148–149, 152– 153, 159, 217, 250, 298, 392, 400, 403; **Retro. Supp. II:** 96, 113, 135, 142, 155, 207, 262; **Supp. I Part 1:** 2, 28–29, 31, 33, 188, 299, 308–309, 317, 358, 365, 366, 368; **Supp. I Part 2:** 374, 383, 393, 407, 413, 416, 420, 422, 474, 482, 580, 582, 602, 659, 679; **Supp. II Part 1:** 280, 288; **Supp. III Part 1:** 387; **Supp. IV Part 2:** 439, 597, 619; **Supp. V:** 118; **Supp. VIII:** 42, 105, 106, 108, 198, 201, 204, 205, 292; **Supp. IX:** 38, 90, 175, 176, 181; **Supp. X:** 42, 45, 121, 223; **Supp. XI:** 203; **Supp. XIII:** 141, 145, 233, 246, **Supp. XIII:** 247; **Supp. XIV:**41–44, 46, 54, 104, 177; **Supp. XV:** 219, 224; **Supp. XVI:**84

"Emerson and the Essay" (Gass), **Supp. VI:** 88

"Emerson the Lecturer" (Lowell), **Supp. I Part 2:** 420, 422

Emerson-Thoreau Award, **Retro. Supp. I:** 67

Emery, Clark, **III:** 478

"Emigre in Autumn, An" (Gioia), **Supp. XV:** 120

Emily Dickinson: Woman Poet (Bennett), **Retro. Supp. I:** 42

"Emily Dickinson and Class" (Erkkila), **Retro. Supp. I:** 42–43

Emily Dickinson Editorial Collective, **Retro. Supp. I:** 47

Emily Dickinson in Southern California (X. J. Kennedy), **Supp. XV:** 164– 165

Eminent Victorians (Strachey), **Supp. I Part 2:** 485

"Emma and Eginhard" (Longfellow), **III:** 505

"Emma Enters a Sentence of Elizabeth Bishop's" (Gass), **Supp. VI:** 93

Emperor Jones, The (O'Neill), **II:** 278; **III:** 391, 392

Emperor of Haiti (Hughes), **Supp. I Part 1:** 339

"Emperor of Ice Cream, The" (Stevens), **IV:** 76, 80–81

"Emperors" (Dunn), **Supp. XI:** 155

"Emperor's New Clothes, The" (Anderson), **I:** 441

"Empire" (Ford), **Supp. V:** 69

Empire: A Novel (Vidal), **Supp. IV Part 2:** 677, 684, 686, 690

"Empire Builders" (MacLeish), **III:** 14

Empire Falls (Russo), **Supp. XII:** 339– 343

Empire of Summer, The (Doty), **Supp. XI:** 120

Empire of the Senseless (Acker), **Supp. XII:** 5, 6, 14–16

"Empires" (Simic), **Supp. VIII:** 282

"Emporium" (Shapiro), **Supp. II Part 2:** 705

Empress of the Splendid Season (Hijuelos), **Supp. VIII:** 86–89

Empson, William, **I:** 522, 533; **II:** 536; **III:** 286, 497, 498, 499; **IV:** 136, 431; **Retro. Supp. I:** 263; **Retro. Supp. II:** 253; **Supp. XVI:**190

"Empty Hills, The" (Winters), **Supp. II Part 2:** 792, 793, 796

Empty Mirror, Early Poems (Ginsberg), **Supp. II Part 1:** 308, 311, 313–314, 319, 329

"Empty Room" (Hughes), **Supp. I Part 1:** 337

"Empty Threat, An" (Frost), **II:** 159

"Encantadas, The" (Melville), **III:** 89

Enchanter, The (Nabokov), **Retro. Supp. I:** 266

"Encomium Twenty Years Later" (Tate), **I:** 381

"Encounter, The" (Pound), **III:** 466

Encounter in April (Sarton), **Supp. VIII:** 259

"Encounter in April" (Sarton), **Supp. VIII:** 259

"Encountering the Sublime" (McClatchy), **Supp. XII:** 261

"Encounter on the Seine: Black Meets Brown" (Baldwin), **Retro. Supp. II:** 2

Encounters with Chinese Writers (Dillard), **Supp. VI:** 19, 23, 31

Encounters with the Archdruid (McPhee), **Supp. III Part 1:** 292– 294, 301; **Supp. X:** 30

"End, The" (Olds), **Supp. X:** 205

"Endangered Species" (Mora), **Supp. XIII:** 219–220

Endecott and the Red Cross (Lowell), **II:** 545

Endgame (Beckett), **Supp. XIII:** 196

"Endgame" (Tan), **Supp. X:** 290

"Endicott and the Red Cross" (Hawthorne), **Retro. Supp. II:** 181, 187–188

"End of Books, The" (Coover), **Supp. V:** 53

End of Education, The (Postman), **Supp. XI:** 275

"End of Season" (Warren), **IV:** 239– 240

"End of Something, The" (Hemingway), **II:** 248

End of the Affair, The (Greene), **Supp. XI:** 99

End of the Age of Innocence, The (Price), **Retro. Supp. I:** 377

"End of the Line, The" (Jarrell), **III:** 527

"End of the Rainbow, The" (Jarrell), **II:** 386

End of the Road (film), **Supp. XI:** 309

End of the Road, The (Barth), **I:** 121, 122, 126–131; **Supp. XI:** 309

"End of the World, The" (Gioia), **Supp. XV:** 126

"End of the World, The" (MacLeish), **III:** 8

Endor (Nemerov), **III:** 269, 270, 279

"Ends" (Dixon), **Supp. XII:** 153

End to Innocence, An: Essays on Culture and Politics (Fiedler), **Supp. XIII:** 98–99

Endure: The Diaries of Charles Walter Stetson (Stetson), **Supp. XI:** 196

"Enduring Chill, The" (O'Connor), **III:** 349, 351, 357; **Retro. Supp. II:** 236

Enduring Vision of Norman Mailer, The (Leeds), **Retro. Supp. II:** 204

Endymion (Keats), **IV:** 405; **Retro. Supp. I:** 412

End Zone (DeLillo), **Supp. VI:** 2, 3, 4, 10, 11, 12

Enemies: A Love Story (Singer), **IV:** 1; **Retro. Supp. II:** 310–311

Enemy, The: Time (T. Williams), **IV:** 391

Enemy of the People, An (adapt.

Miller), **III:** 154–156

"Energy Vampire" (Ginsberg), **Supp. II Part 1:** 326

"Enforcement of the Slave Trade Laws, The" (Du Bois), **Supp. II Part 1:** 161

"Engaging the Past" (Bell), **Supp. X:** 17

Engel, Bernard F., **I:** 532

Engels, Friedrich, **IV:** 429, 443–444; **Supp. I Part 1:** 13

Engineer of Beasts, The (Sanders), **Supp. XVI:**270

Engineer of Moonlight (DeLillo), **Supp. VI:** 4

Engineers and the Price System, The (Veblen), **I:** 475–476; **Supp. I Part 2:** 638, 642, 648

Engines of Creation: the Coming Era of Nanotechnology (Drexler), **Supp. XVI:**121

"England" (Moore), **III:** 203, 207, 214

Engle, Paul, **III:** 542; **Retro. Supp. II:** 220, 221; **Supp. V:** 337; **Supp. XI:** 315; **Supp. XIII:** 76

English, Zoë, **Supp. XVI:**293

English Elegy, The: Studies in the Genre from Spenser to Yeats (Sacks), **Supp. IV Part 2:** 450

English Hours (James), **II:** 337; **Retro. Supp. I:** 235

English Language, The (L. P. Smith), **Supp. XIV:**341

Englishmen of Letters (James), **II:** 327

English Notebooks, The (Hawthorne), **II:** 226, 227–228

English Novel, The (Lanier), **Supp. I Part 1:** 371

English Poets, The: Lessing, Rousseau (Lowell), **Supp. I Part 2:** 407

English Prosody and Modern Poetry (Shapiro), **Supp. II Part 2:** 710

English Traits (Emerson), **II:** 1, 5, 6–7, 8

"English Writers on America" (Irving), **II:** 308

Engstrand, Stuart, **Supp. I Part 1:** 51

"Enoch and the Gorilla" (O'Connor), **Retro. Supp. II:** 225

Enormous Changes at the Last Minute (Paley), **Supp. VI:** 218

"Enormous Changes at the Last Minute" (Paley), **Supp. VI:** 226, 232

"Enormous Radio, The" (Cheever), **Supp. I Part 1:** 175–177, 195

Enormous Radio and Other Stories, The (Cheever), **Supp. I Part 1:** 175–177

Enormous Room, The (Cummings), **I:** 429, 434, 440, 445, 477

"Enough for a Lifetime" (Buck), **Supp. II Part 1:** 127

Enough Rope (Parker), **Supp. IX:** 189, 192

Enquiry Concerning Political Justice (Godwin), **Supp. I Part 1:** 126, 146

Entered From the Sun (Garrett), **Supp. VII:** 105–106, 107–109

"Entering the Kingdom" (Oliver), **Supp. VII:** 234

Entertaining Strangers (Gurney), **Supp. V:** 98, 99

Enter without Desire (Lacy), **Supp. XV:** 201

Entrance: Four Chicano Poets, **Supp. XIII:** 316

Entrance to Porlock, The (Buechner), **Supp. XII:** 52

Entries (Berry), **Supp. X:** 23

"Entropy" (Pynchon), **Supp. II Part 2:** 619, 621

Environmental Imagination, The (Buell), **Supp. V:** 209; **Supp. IX:** 29

"Envoys, The" (Merrill), **Supp. III Part 1:** 326

"Envy; or, Yiddish in America" (Ozick), **Supp. V:** 263, 265–266

"Eolian Harp, The" (Coleridge), **I:** 284

"Eototo" (Sobin), **Supp. XVI:**283–284

"Ephemera, The" (Franklin), **II:** 121

Ephesians (biblical book), **Supp. I Part 1:** 117

Epictetus, **III:** 566

"Epicurean, The" (Auchincloss), **Supp. IV Part 1:** 25

Epicurus, **I:** 59

"Epigram" (Lowell), **II:** 550

"Epilogue" (Lowell), **Retro. Supp. II:** 191

"Epimanes" (Poe), **III:** 411

"Epimetheus" (Longfellow), **II:** 494

"Epiphany" (X. J. Kennedy), **Supp. XV:** 166, 167

"Epipsychidion" (Shelley), **Supp. I Part 2:** 718

Episode in Palmetto (Caldwell), **I:** 297, 307

"Epistle" (L.-Y. Lee), **Supp. XV:** 212

Epistle to a Godson (Auden), **Supp. II Part 1:** 24

"Epistle to Be Left in the Earth" (MacLeish), **III:** 13

"Epistle to George William Curtis" (Lowell), **Supp. I Part 2:** 416

"Epistle to Léon-Paul Fargue" (MacLeish), **III:** 15

"Epitaph Ending in And, The" (Stafford), **Supp. XI:** 321–322

Epitaph for a Desert Anarchist (Bishop), **Supp. XIII:** 1

"Epitaph for Fire and Flower" (Plath), **Supp. I Part 2:** 537

"Epitaph for the Race of Man" (Millay), **III:** 127–128

"Epithalamium" (Auden), **Supp. II Part 1:** 15

"Epstein" (Roth), **Retro. Supp. II:** 281; **Supp. III Part 2:** 404, 406–407, 412, 422

Epstein, Jason, **Supp. VIII:** 233

Epstein, Joseph, **Supp. IV Part 2:** 692; **Supp. VIII:** 236, 238; **Supp. XIV:**101–117; **Supp. XVI:**230, 275

Epstein, Leslie, **Supp. XII:** 159–174

Epstein, Philip, **Supp. XII:** 159

"Equal in Paris" (Baldwin), **Retro. Supp. II:** 3; **Supp. I Part 1:** 52

"Equals" (Untermeyer), **Supp. XV:** 304

"Equations of the Light" (Gioia), **Supp. XV:** 125

"Equilibrists, The" (Ransom), **III:** 490, 494

"Equipment for Pennies" (H. Roth), **Supp. IX:** 233

Erasmus, Desiderius, **Supp. XV:** 258

"Erat Hora" (Pound), **III:** 463; **Retro. Supp. I:** 413

Erdrich, Louise, **Supp. IV Part 1:** 259–278, 333, 404; **Supp. X:** 290

"Erectus" (Karr), **Supp. XI:** 243

"Ere Sleep Comes Down to Soothe the Weary Eyes" (Dunbar), **Supp. II Part 1:** 199, 207–208

Erikson, Erik, **I:** 58, 214, 218

Erisman, Fred, **Supp. VIII:** 126

Erkkila, Betsy, **Retro. Supp. I:** 42

"Ernest: or Parent for a Day" (Bourne), **I:** 232

Ernst, Max, **Retro. Supp. II:** 321

"Eros" (Komunyakaa), **Supp. XIII:** 130

"Eros and Anteros" (E. Stoddard), **Supp. XV:** 283

Eros and Civilization (Marcuse), **Supp. XII:** 2

"Eros at Temple Stream" (Levertov), **Supp. III Part 1:** 278–279

Eros the Bittersweet (Carson), **Supp. XII:** 97, 98–99

"Eros Turannos" (Robinson), **III:** 510, 512, 513–516, 517, 518

"Eroticism in Women" (Nin), **Supp. X:** 195

"Errand" (Carver), **Supp. III Part 1:** 149

Erskine, Albert, **IV:** 261; **Retro. Supp. II:** 117

Erskine, John, **I:** 223; **Supp. X:** 183; **Supp. XIV:**120

Erstein, Hap, **Supp. IV Part 2:** 589, 590

"Escape" (MacLeish), **III:** 4

Escape Artist, The (Wagoner), **Supp. IX:** 324, 334–335

Escher, M. C., **Supp. XII:** 26; **Supp. XVI:**102

"Escudilla" (Leopold), **Supp. XIV:**188

Eshleman, Clayton, **Supp. XVI:**284

Espen, Hal, **Supp. X:** 15

Espey, John, **III:** 463, 468, 478

Essais (Renouvier), **II:** 344–345

"Essay: The Love of Old Houses" (Doty), **Supp. XI:** 136

Essay Concerning Human Understanding, An (Locke), **I:** 554; **II:** 8, 348–349

Essay on American Poetry (Brown), **Supp. I Part 1:** 156

"Essay on Aristocracy" (Paine), **Supp. I Part 2:** 515

"Essay on Friendship, An" (McClatchy), **Supp. XII:** 258–259

"Essay on Love" (Carruth), **Supp. XVI:**56

Essay on Man (Pope), **II:** 111; **Supp. I Part 2:** 516

"Essay on Marriage" (Carruth), **Supp. XVI:**48

Essay on Our Changing Order (Veblen), **Supp. I Part 2:** 629, 642

"Essay on Poetics" (Ammons), **Supp. VII:** 29–31

Essay on Projects (Defoe), **II:** 104

"Essay on Psychiatrists" (Pinsky), **Supp. VI:** 237, 238, 241, 242, 249, 250

Essay on Rime (Shapiro), **I:** 430; **Supp. II Part 2:** 702, 703, 708–711

"Essay on Sanity" (Dunn), **Supp. XI:** 147

"Essay on the Character of Robespierre" (Paine), **Supp. I Part 2:** 515

Essay on the Chinese Written Character (Fenollosa), **III:** 474

"Essay on What I Think About Most" (Carson), **Supp. XII:** 111–112

Essays (Emerson), **II:** 1, 7, 8, 12–13, 15, 21

Essays, Speeches, and Public Letters by William Faulkner (Meriweather, ed.), **Retro. Supp. I:** 77

Essays in Anglo-Saxon Law (Adams), **I:** 5

Essays in London (James), **II:** 336

Essays in Radical Empiricism (James), **II:** 355, 356–357

Essays on Norman Mailer (Lucid),

Retro. Supp. II: 195

Essays on the Nature and Principles of Taste (Alison), **Supp. I Part 1:** 151

Essays to Do Good (Mather), **II:** 104; **Supp. II Part 2:** 461, 467

"Essay Toward a Point of View, An" (Brooks), **I:** 244

"Essence, Absence, and Sobin's *Venus Blue*" (English), **Supp. XVI:**293

Essential Haiku, The (Hass), **Supp. VI:** 102

Essential Keats (Levine, ed.), **Supp. V:** 179

"Essential Oils—are wrung" (Dickinson), **I:** 471; **Retro. Supp. I:** 43, 46

"Essentials" (Toomer), **Supp. III Part 2:** 486

Essentials: A Philosophy of Life in Three Hundred Definitions and Aphorisms (Toomer), **Supp. III Part 2:** 486

Essentials: Definitions and Aphorisms (Toomer), **Supp. IX:** 320

"Essentials of Spontaneous Prose" (Kerouac), **Supp. III Part 1:** 227–228

"Estate Sale" (Nye), **Supp. XIII:** 283

Estess, Sybil, **Supp. IV Part 2:** 449, 452

Esther (Adams), **I:** 9–10, 20

"Esther" (Toomer), **Supp. IX:** 313–314

"Esthétique du Mal" (Stevens), **IV:** 79; **Retro. Supp. I:** 300, 311, 312

"Estoy-eh-muut and the Kunideeyahs (Arrowboy and the Destroyers)" (film), **Supp. IV Part 2:** 560

Estrada, Genaro, **Retro. Supp. II:** 89

Estray, The (Longfellow, ed.), **Retro. Supp. II:** 155

Esty, William, **III:** 358

"Etching, An" (Masters), **Supp. I Part 2:** 458

"Eternal Goodness, The" (Whittier), **Supp. I Part 2:** 704

"Eternity, An" (W. C. Williams), **Retro. Supp. I:** 423

"Eternity Is Now" (Roethke), **III:** 544–545

"Ethan Brand" (Hawthorne), **II:** 227

Ethan Frome (Wharton), **IV:** 316–317, 327; **Retro. Supp. I:** 372–373; **Supp. IX:** 108

Ethics (Spinoza), **IV:** 12; **Retro. Supp. II:** 300

"Ethics of Culture, The" (Locke), **Supp. XIV:**211

Etulain, Richard, **Supp. IV Part 2:** 597, 601, 604, 606, 607, 608, 610, 611

Euclid, **III:** 6, 620

"Euclid Alone Has Looked on Beauty Bare" (Millay), **III:** 133

Eugene, Frank, **Supp. X:** 204

Eugene Onegin (Pushkin), **III:** 246, 263

Eugene Onegin (Pushkin; Nabokov, trans.), **Retro. Supp. I:** 266, 267, 272

Eugénie, Empress, **IV:** 309

Eugénie Grandet (Balzac), **II:** 328

"Eugénie Grandet" (Barthelme), **Supp. IV Part 1:** 47

"Eulogy for Richard Hugo (1923–1982)" (Wagoner), **Supp. IX:** 330–331

"Eulogy on the Flapper" (Z. Fitzgerald), **Supp. IX:** 71

Eumenides (Aeschylus), **Retro. Supp. I:** 65

"E Unibus Pluram: Television and U.S. Fiction" (Wallace), **Supp. X:** 315–316

"Euphemisms" (Matthews), **Supp. IX:** 167–168

Eureka (Poe), **III:** 409, 424, 428–429

Eurekas (Goldbarth), **Supp. XII:** 181

Euripides, **I:** 325; **II:** 8, 282, 543; **III:** 22, 145, 398; **IV:** 370; **Supp. I Part 1:** 268, 269, 270; **Supp. I Part 2:** 482; **Supp. V:** 277

"Euripides and Professor Murray" (Eliot), **Supp. I Part 1:** 268

"Euripides—A Playwright" (West), **IV:** 286; **Retro. Supp. II:** 326

"Europe" (Ashbery), **Supp. III Part 1:** 7–10, 13, 18

European Discovery of America, The: The Northern Voyages (Morison), **Supp. I Part 2:** 496–497

European Discovery of America, The: The Southern Voyages (Morison), **Supp. I Part 2:** 497

Europeans, The (James), **I:** 452; **II:** 327, 328; **Retro. Supp. I:** 216, 220

"Europe! Europe!" (Ginsberg), **Supp. II Part 1:** 320, 322

Europe of Trusts, The: Selected Poems (Howe), **Supp. IV Part 2:** 420, 422, 426

Europe without Baedeker (Wilson), **IV:** 429

Eurydice in the Underworld (Acker), **Supp. XII:** 7

Eustace, Saint, **II:** 215

Eustace Chisholm and the Works (Purdy), **Supp. VII:** 273–274, 279–280

"Euthanasia" (Tate), **IV:** 122

Eva-Mary (McCarriston), **Supp.**

XIV:259, 260, 263–268

"Evangeline" (Dixon), **Supp. XII:** 153

Evangeline (Longfellow), **II:** 489, 501–502; **Retro. Supp. II:** 155, 156–159, 162, 164; **Supp. I Part 2:** 586

Evanier, David, **Supp. XVI:**212

Evans, Mary Ann. *See* Eliot, George

Evans, Oliver, **Supp. IV Part 1:** 85, 91

Evans, Sandy, **Supp. XIII:** 129

Evans, Walker, **I:** 36, 38, 293; **Retro. Supp. II:** 85

"Eve" (W. C. Williams), **Retro. Supp. I:** 423

Even Cowgirls Get the Blues (Robbins), **Supp. X:** 259, 260, 261, 262–263, 264, 266, 269–271, 272, 274, 277, 284; **Supp. XIII:** 11

"Evening" (Carver), **Supp. III Part 1:** 148

Evening (Minot), **Supp. VI:** 204–205, 208, 213–215

"Evening at a Country Inn" (Kenyon), **Supp. VII:** 167

"Evening in a Sugar Orchard" (Frost), **Retro. Supp. I:** 133

"Evening in Nuevo Leon, An" (Caldwell), **I:** 309

"Evening in the Sanitarium" (Bogan), **Supp. III Part 1:** 61

"Evening of the 4th of July, The" (Kees), **Supp. XV:** 140, 142

"Evening on the Cote d'Azur" (Yates), **Supp. XI:** 349

Evening Performance, An: New and Selected Short Stories (Garrett), **Supp. VII:** 109

"Evenings at Home" (Hardwick), **Supp. III Part 1:** 195–196

"Evening's at Seven, The" (Thurber), **Supp. I Part 2:** 616

"Evening Star" (Bogan), **Supp. III Part 1:** 56

Evening Star, The (McMurtry), **Supp. V:** 230

Evening Star, The (screenplay) (McMurtry), **Supp. V:** 232

"Evening Sun" (Kenyon), **Supp. VII:** 168

Evening Sun Turned Crimson, The (Huncke), **Supp. XIV:**140, 149–150

"Evening Sun Turned Crimson, The" (Huncke), **Supp. XIV:**137–138, 139

"Evening Wind, The" (Bryant), **Supp. I Part 1:** 164

"Evening without Angels" (Stevens), **Retro. Supp. I:** 302

Evening with Richard Nixon, An (Vidal), **Supp. IV Part 2:** 683

"Even Sea, The" (Swenson), **Supp. IV Part 2:** 641

Even Stephen (Perelman and West), **Retro. Supp. II:** 328

"Event, An" (Wilbur), **Supp. III Part 2:** 547, 554

"Event, The" (Dove), **Supp. IV Part 1:** 242, 247–248

"Eventide" (Brooks), **Supp. III Part 1:** 73

"Eventide" (Purdy), **Supp. VII:** 270

"Event Itself, The" (Carruth), **Supp. XVI:**47

Eve of Saint Agnes, The (Keats), **II:** 82, 531

"Eve of St. Agnes, The" (Clampitt), **Supp. IX:** 40

"Ever a Bridegroom: Reflections on the Failure of Texas Literature" (McMurtry), **Supp. V:** 225

Everett, Alexander Hill, **Supp. I Part 1:** 152

Everlasting Story of Nory, The (Baker), **Supp. XIII:** 52, **Supp. XIII:** 53–55

Ever-Present Past, The (Hamilton), **Supp. XVI:**196

Evers, Medgar, **IV:** 280; **Retro. Supp. II:** 13; **Supp. I Part 1:** 52, 65

Everwine, Peter, **Supp. V:** 180; **Supp. XIII:** 312; **Supp. XV:** 73–90

"Everybody's Protest Novel" (Baldwin), **Retro. Supp. II:** 4; **Supp. I Part 1:** 50, 51

"Everybody's Reading Li Po' Silkscreened on a Purple T-Shirt" (Komunyakaa), **Supp. XIII:** 120

Everybody's Story: Writing by Older Minnesotans (C. Bly, ed.), **Supp. XVI:**38

"Everybody Was Very Nice" (Benét), **Supp. XI:** 53

"Every-Day Girl, A" (Jewett), **Retro. Supp. II:** 132

"Everyday Use" (Walker), **Supp. III Part 2:** 534

"Every-Day Work" (Jewett), **Retro. Supp. II:** 132

Everyone Says I Love You (film; Allen), **Supp. XV:** 11

Every Pleasure (Goldbarth), **Supp. XII:** 181

Every Soul Is a Circus (Lindsay), **Supp. I Part 2:** 384, 394, 399

"Everything Is a Human Being" (Walker), **Supp. III Part 2:** 527

Everything Is Illuminated (Foer), **Supp. XII:** 169

"Everything Stuck to Him" (Carver), **Supp. III Part 1:** 143

Everything That Rises Must Converge (O'Connor), **III:** 339, 348–349, 350–351; **Retro. Supp. II:** 235, 236–237

"Everything That Rises Must Converge" (O'Connor), **III:** 349, 352, 357; **Retro. Supp. II:** 236

Everything You Always Wanted to Know about Sex (film; Allen), **Supp. XV:** 4–5, 13

Eve's Diary (Twain), **IV:** 208–209

"Eve Speaks" (Untermeyer), **Supp. XV:** 300

"Eve the Fox" (Gunn Allen), **Supp. IV Part 1:** 331

"Evidence" (Harjo), **Supp. XII:** 219

Evidence of the Senses, The (Kelley), **Supp. IV Part 2:** 529

Evidence of Things Not Seen, The (Baldwin), **Retro. Supp. II:** 15

"Evil Seekers, The" (Sexton), **Supp. II Part 2:** 696

"Evolution" (Swenson), **Supp. IV Part 2:** 639

Evolving the Idol: The Poetry of Gustaf Sobin (Crick), **Supp. XVI:**289

Ewing, Jon, **Supp. X:** 253

Ewings, The (O'Hara), **III:** 383

"Examination at the Womb Door" (Hughes), **Supp. XV:** 347

"Examination of the Hero in a Time of War" (Stevens), **Retro. Supp. I:** 305–306, 308

"Excavation of Troy" (MacLeish), **III:** 18

Excellent Becomes the Permanent, The (Addams), **Supp. I Part 1:** 25

"Excelsior" (Longfellow), **Retro. Supp. II:** 169

"Excerpts from Swan Lake" (Cameron), **Supp. XII:** 80, 84

"Excerpts from the Epistemology Workshops" (Rand), **Supp. IV Part 2:** 529

"Excess of Charity" (Wylie), **Supp. I Part 2:** 720

"Exchange, The" (Swenson), **Supp. IV Part 2:** 644

"Exclusive" (Olds), **Supp. X:** 206

"Excrement Poem, The" (Kumin), **Supp. IV Part 2:** 448

"Excursion" (Garrett), **Supp. VII:** 100

Excursions (Thoreau), **IV:** 188

"Excursus of Reassurance in Begonia Time, An" (Carruth), **Supp. XVI:**58

Executioner's Song, The (Mailer), **Retro. Supp. II:** 108, 209

Exercises in History, Chronology, and Biography, in Question and Answer (Rowson), **Supp. XV:** 245

Ex-Friends: Falling Out with Allen

Ginsberg, Lionel and Diana Trilling, Lillian Hellman, Hannah Arendt, and Norman Mailer (Podhoretz), **Supp. VIII:** 239, 242–244

"Exhausted Bug, The" (R. Bly), **Supp. IV Part 1:** 73

"Exhortation" (Bogan), **Supp. III Part 1:** 58

"Exhortation" (McKay), **Supp. X:** 135

"Exile" (Gass), **Supp. VI:** 92

"Exile" (Oates), **Supp. II Part 2:** 523

Exile, The (Buck), **Supp. II Part 1:** 119, 131

"Exiles, The" (Bradbury), **Supp. IV Part 1:** 113

"Exiles, The" (Whittier), **Supp. I Part 2:** 692–693

Exiles and Fabrications (Scott), **II:** 512

Exile's Daughter, The (Spencer), **Supp. II Part 1:** 121

"Exile's Departure, The" (Whittier), **Supp. I Part 2:** 683

Exiles from Paradise: Zelda and Scott Fitzgerald (Mayfield), **Supp. IX:** 65

"Exile's Letter" (Karr), **Supp. XI:** 241

Exile's Return (Cowley), **Supp. III Part 1:** 136, 138, 140, 141, 144, 147, 148

"Exile's Return, The" (Lowell), **II:** 539; **Retro. Supp. II:** 187

"Existences" (Stafford), **Supp. XI:** 324

Exit into History (Hoffman), **Supp. XVI:** 148, 150, 151–153

Exit to Eden (Rampling), **Supp. VII:** 301–302

Exley, Frederick, **Supp. XVI:** 69

Exodus (biblical book), **IV:** 300

Exodus (Uris), **Supp. IV Part 1:** 379

"Exorcism" (Snodgrass), **Supp. VI:** 314

"Exorcism, An" (Malamud), **Supp. I Part 2:** 435

Exorcist, The (film), **Supp. I Part 1:** 66

"Expanses" (Dickey), **Supp. IV Part 1:** 186

"Ex Parte" (Lardner), **II:** 432

"Expatiation on the Combining of Weathers at Thirty-seventh and Indiana Where the Southern More or Less Crosses the Dog, The" (Carruth), **Supp. XVI:** 51–52

"Expectant Father Compares His Wife to a Rabbit, An" (White), **Supp. I Part 2:** 678

"Expedition to the Pole, An" (Dillard), **Supp. VI:** 32, 34

"Expelled" (Cheever), **Supp. I Part 1:** 174, 186

Expense of Greatness, The (Blackmur), **Supp. II Part 1:** 90, 107

Expense of Vision, The (Holland), **Retro. Supp. I:** 216

"Expensive Gifts" (Miller), **Supp. XII:** 294

"Expensive Moment, The" (Paley), **Supp. VI:** 222, 227–228, 230

Expensive People (Oates), **Supp. II Part 2:** 509, 510–511

"Experience" (Emerson), **Supp. XIV:** 42

"Experience and Fiction" (Jackson), **Supp. IX:** 121

"Experience and the Objects of Knowledge in the Philosophy of F. H. Bradley" (Eliot), **I:** 572; **Retro. Supp. I:** 59

Experience of Literature, The (Trilling), **Supp. III Part 2:** 493

"Experiences and Principles of an Historian" (Morison), **Supp. I Part 2:** 492

Experimental Death Unit # 1 (Baraka), **Supp. II Part 1:** 46

"Experimental Life, The" (Bourne), **I:** 217, 220

"Experiment in Misery, An" (S. Crane), **I:** 411; **Retro. Supp. II:** 97

Experiments and Observations on Electricity (Franklin), **II:** 102, 114–115

"Expiation" (Wharton), **Retro. Supp. I:** 367

"Explaining Evil" (Gordon), **Supp. IV Part 1:** 310

"Explanation" (Stevens), **IV:** 79

Explanation of America, An (Pinsky), **Supp. VI:** 237, 241–243

Exploding Gravy (X. J. Kennedy), **Supp. XV:** 163

"Exploit" (Wharton), **IV:** 324

"Exploration in the Great Tuolumne Cañon" (Muir), **Supp. IX:** 181

"Explorer, The" (Brooks), **Supp. III Part 1:** 79–80

"Exploring the Magalloway" (Parkman), **Supp. II Part 2:** 591

Expositor's Bible, The (G. A. Smith), **III:** 199

Expressions of Sea Level (Ammons), **Supp. VII:** 24, 28, 36

Extract from Captain Stormfield's Visit to Heaven (Twain), **IV:** 209–210

Extracts from Adam's Diary (Twain), **IV:** 208–209

"Exulting, The" (Roethke), **III:** 544

"Eye, The" (Bowles), **Supp. IV Part 1:** 93

Eye, The (Nabokov), **III:** 251

Eye-Beaters, Blood, Victory, Madness, Buckhead and Mercy, The (Dickey), **Supp. IV Part 1:** 178, 182–183

"Eye for an Eye, An" (Humphrey), **Supp. IX:** 108

"Eye in the Rock, The" (Haines), **Supp. XII:** 208, 209

"Eye-Mote, The" (Plath), **Retro. Supp. II:** 246, 247

"Eye of Paris, The" (H. Miller), **III:** 183–184

Eye of the Poet, The: Six Views of the Art and Craft of Poetry (Citino, ed.), **Supp. XIII:** 115

"Eye of the Rock, The" (Haines), **Supp. XII:** 208

"Eye of the Story, The" (Porter), **IV:** 279

Eye of the Story, The: Selected Essays and Reviews (Welty), **Retro. Supp. I:** 339, 342, 344, 345, 346, 351, 354, 355, 356

"Eyes, The" (Wharton), **IV:** 315

"Eyes like They Say the Devil Has" (Ríos), **Supp. IV Part 2:** 543, 544

Eyes of the Dragon, The (King), **Supp. V:** 139, 152

Eyes of the Heart: A Memoir of the Lost and Found (Buechner), **Supp. XII:** 53

"Eyes of Zapata" (Cisneros), **Supp. VII:** 70

"Eyes to See" (Cozzens), **I:** 374

Eye-to-Eye (Nye), **Supp. XIII:** 274

Eysturoy, Annie O., **Supp. IV Part 1:** 321, 322, 323, 328

Ezekiel (biblical book), **II:** 541

Ezekiel, Mordecai, **Supp. I Part 2:** 645

"Ezra Pound" (Bynner), **Supp. XV:** 49

"Ezra Pound: His Cantos" (Zukofsky), **Supp. III Part 2:** 612, 619, 622

Ezra Pound's Mauberley (Espey), **III:** 463

"Ezra Pound's Very Useful Labors" (Schwartz), **Supp. II Part 2:** 644

F

"F. S. F., 1896–1996, R.I.P." (Doctorow), **Retro. Supp. I:** 97

F. Scott Fitzgerald: A Critical Portrait (Piper), **Supp. IX:** 65

Faas, Ekbert, **Supp. VIII:** 292

"Fabbri Tape, The" (Auchincloss), **Supp. IV Part 1:** 21–22

Faber, Geoffrey, **Retro. Supp. I:** 63

Faber Book of Movie Verse, The (French and Wlaschin, eds.), **Supp. XVI:** 294

"Fable" (Merwin), **Supp. III Part 1:** 343

"Fable" (Wylie), **Supp. I Part 2:** 714

Fable, A (Faulkner), **II:** 55, 73; **Retro. Supp. I:** 74

"Fable, A" (Glück), **Supp. V:** 86

"Fable, The" (Winters), **Supp. II Part 2:** 792, 793, 796

Fable for Critics, A (Lowell), **Supp. I Part 2:** 406, 407–408, 409, 412–413, 416, 420, 422

"Fable of the War, A" (Nemerov), **III:** 272

Fables (Gay), **II:** 111

Fables and Distances: New and Selected Essays (Haines), **Supp. XII:** 197, 199, 207–208, 211

Fables for Our Time (Thurber), **Supp. I Part 2:** 610

Fables of Identity: Studies in Poetic Mythology (Frye), **Supp. X:** 80

Fables of La Fontaine, The (Moore), **III:** 194, 215

"Fables of Representation: Poetry of the New York School" (Hoover), **Supp. XV:** 179

"Fables of the Fallen Guy" (Rosaldo), **Supp. IV Part 2:** 544

"Fables of the Moscow Subway" (Nemerov), **III:** 271

Fabulators, The (Scholes), **Supp. V:** 40

Fabulous Small Jews (Epstein), **Supp. XIV:**112

Face against the Glass, The (Francis), **Supp. IX:** 80–81

Face of Time, The (Farrell), **II:** 28, 34, 35, 39

Faces of Jesus, The (Buechner), **Supp. XII:** 53

Fachinger, Petra, **Supp. XVI:**153

"Facing It" (Komunyakaa), **Supp. XIII:** 117, 124, 125

"Facing West from California's Shores" (Jeffers), **Supp. II Part 2:** 437–438

"Fact in Fiction, The" (McCarthy), **II:** 562

"Facts" (Levine), **Supp. V:** 193

"Facts" (Oliver), **Supp. VII:** 231–232

"Facts" (Snyder), **Supp. VIII:** 301

"Facts, The" (Lardner), **II:** 431

Facts, The: A Novelist's Autobiography (Roth), **Retro. Supp. II:** 280, 291; **Supp. III Part 2:** 401, 405, 417, 426

"Facts and Traditions Respecting the Existence of Indigenous Intermittent Fever in New England" (Holmes), **Supp. I Part 1:** 303

"Facts in the Case of M. Valdemar, The" (Poe), **III:** 416

Faderman, Lillian, **Retro. Supp. II:** 135; **Supp. XIII:** 313

Fadiman, Clifton, **II:** 430, 431, 443, 591–592; **Supp. IX:** 8; **Supp. XVI:**100, 106

"Fado" (McClatchy), **Supp. XII:** 265–266

Faerie Queene, The (Spenser), **III:** 487; **IV:** 253; **Supp. XIV:**6; **Supp. XV:** 181

Faery, Rebecca Blevins, **Retro. Supp. I:** 374

Fagan, Kathy, **Supp. V:** 180; **Supp. XV:** 73

Fahrenheit 451 (Bradbury), **Supp. IV Part 1:** 101, 102, 104, 107–109, 110, 113; **Supp. XIII:** 29

"Failure" (Gioia), **Supp. XV:** 125

"Failure" (Zach; Everwine, trans.), **Supp. XV:** 86

"Failure of David Barry, The" (Jewett), **Retro. Supp. II:** 132

Fainlight, Ruth, **Supp. XV:** 261, 264

Faint Perfume (Gale), **Supp. I Part 2:** 613

Fair, Bryan K., **Supp. VIII:** 128

Fairbanks, Douglas, **Supp. XVI:**185, 186

Fairchild, Frances. *See* Bryant, Mrs. William Cullen (Frances Fairchild)

Fairchild, Hoxie, **Supp. XIV:**120

Fairfield, Flora (pseudonym). *See* Alcott, Louisa May

Fairly Conventional Woman, A (Shields), **Supp. VII:** 312, 316, 318

"Fairly Sad Tale, A" (Parker), **Supp. IX:** 192

Fair Warning (R. O. Butler), **Supp. XII:** 62, 75–76

Faith (Goldbarth), **Supp. XII:** 181, 182–183

Faith and History (Niebuhr), **III:** 308

Faith and the Good Thing (Johnson), **Supp. VI:** 187, 188–190, 191, 193, 194, 196

Faith for Living (Mumford), **Supp. II Part 2:** 479–480

Faithful Narrative of the Surprising Works of God in the Conversion of Many Hundred Souls in Northampton, and the Neighboring Towns and Villages of New-Hampshire in New-England, A (Edwards), **I:** 545, 562

"Faith Healer" (Komunyakaa), **Supp. XIII:** 117

"Faith in a Tree" (Paley), **Supp. VI:** 217–218, 224, 230

"Faith in Search of Understanding"

(Updike), **Retro. Supp. I:** 327

"Faith of an Historian" (Morison), **Supp. I Part 2:** 492

Falcoff, Mark, **Supp. VIII:** 88

Falcon (Hammett), **Supp. IV Part 1:** 351

Falconer (Cheever), **Supp. I Part 1:** 176, 193–195, 196

Falconer, A. F., **Supp. XIV:**2

"Falcon of Ser Federigo, The" (Longfellow), **II:** 505

Falk, Peter, **Supp. XI:** 174

Falkner, Dean, **II:** 55

Falkner, John, **II:** 55

Falkner, Mrs. Murray C. (Maud Butler), **II:** 55

Falkner, Murray, **II:** 55

Falkner, Murray C., **II:** 55

Falkner, William C., **II:** 55

"Fall" (Francis), **Supp. IX:** 76

"Fall 1961" (Lowell), **II:** 550

"Fall, The" (Bass), **Supp. XVI:**25

"Fallen Western Star: The Decline of San Francisco as a Literary Region" (Gioia), **Supp. XV:** 112, 115–116

"Fallen Western Star" Wars, The: A Debate about Literary California (Foley, ed.), **Supp. XV:** 112, 116

"Fall in Corrales" (Wilbur), **Supp. III Part 2:** 556

Falling (Dickey), **Supp. IV Part 1:** 178, 181–182

"Falling" (Dickey), **Supp. IV Part 1:** 182

"Falling Asleep over the Aeneid" (Lowell), **II:** 542; **Retro. Supp. II:** 188

Falling in Place (Beattie), **Supp. V:** 28–29

"Falling into Holes in Our Sentences" (R. Bly), **Supp. IV Part 1:** 71

"Fall Journey" (Stafford), **Supp. XI:** 322

Fall of America, The: 1965–1971 (Ginsberg), **Supp. II Part 1:** 323, 325, 327; **Supp. XV:** 264

Fall of Eve, The (Loos), **Supp. XVI:**187

Fall of the City, The: A Verse Play for Radio (MacLeish), **III:** 20

"Fall of the House of Usher, The" (Poe), **III:** 412, 414, 415, 419; **Retro. Supp. II:** 270

Fall of the Magicians, The (Kees), **Supp. XV:** 144

Fallows, James, **Supp. VIII:** 241

Fall Quarter (Kees), **Supp. XV:** 141

Fall & Rise (Dixon), **Supp. XII:** 147–148, 148, 153, 157

"Falls, The" (Olds), **Supp. X:** 215

"Falls Fight, The" (Howe), **Supp. IV Part 2:** 431–432

Falon, Janet Ruth, **Supp. IV Part 2:** 422

"False Dawn" (Wharton), **Retro. Supp. I:** 381

"False Documents" (Doctorow), **Supp. IV Part 1:** 220, 236

"False Leads" (Komunyakaa), **Supp. XIII:** 116

Fame & Folly: Essays (Ozick), **Supp. V:** 272

"Familiar Epistle to a Friend, A" (Lowell), **Supp. I Part 2:** 416

Familiar Territory: Observations on American Life (Epstein), **Supp. XIV:**106

"Family" (Sanders), **Supp. XVI:**276

"Family" (Wilson), **IV:** 426

"Family Affair, A" (Chopin), **Retro. Supp. II:** 71

Family Arsenal, The (Theroux), **Supp. VIII:** 322

Family Chronicle: An Odyssey from Russia to America (Reznikoff), **Supp. XIV:**277, 288, 289

"Family History" (Mora), **Supp. XIII:** 217

"Family History, A" (Davis), **Supp. XVI:**82

Family Life (Banks), **Supp. V:** 7

"Family Matters" (Alvarez), **Supp. VII:** 10

Family Moskat, The (Singer), **IV:** 1, 17, 20, 46; **Retro. Supp. II:** 304

"Family of Little Feet, The" (Cisneros), **Supp. VII:** 61

Family Party, A (O'Hara), **III:** 362

Family Pictures (Brooks), **Supp. III Part 1:** 69, 85, 86

Family Pictures (Miller), **Supp. XII:** 291, 295–297, 299

"Family Reunion" (X. J. Kennedy), **Supp. XV:** 169

Family Reunion, The (Eliot), **I:** 570–571, 572, 581, 584, 588; **Retro. Supp. I:** 62, 65

"Family Secrets" (Kingsolver), **Supp. VII:** 208

"Family Sideshow, The" (Karr), **Supp. XI:** 245

"Family Ties" (Mora), **Supp. XIII:** 215

"Family Tree" (Komunyakaa), **Supp. XIII:** 117–118, 126

"Family Wasserstein, The" (Hoban), **Supp. XV:** 319, 325

Famous American Negroes (Hughes), **Supp. I Part 1:** 345

"Famous Gilson Bequest, The" (Bierce), **I:** 204

Famous Negro Music Makers (Hughes), **Supp. I Part 1:** 345

"Famous New York Trials" (Ellison), **Supp. II Part 1:** 230

Fanatics, The (Dunbar), **Supp. II Part 1:** 213–214

Fancher, Edwin, **Retro. Supp. II:** 202

Fancher, Lou, **Supp. XVI:**177

"Fancy and Imagination" (Poe), **III:** 421

"Fancy Flights" (Beattie), **Supp. V:** 25

"Fancy's Show Box" (Hawthorne), **II:** 238

"Fancy Woman, The" (Taylor), **Supp. V:** 316–317, 319, 323

"Fang" (Goldbarth), **Supp. XII:** 190

Fanny: Being the True History of the Adventures of Fanny Hackabout-Jones (Jong), **Supp. V:** 115, 127

Fanny Hill (Cleland), **Supp. V:** 48, 127

Fan of Swords, The (al-Maghut), **Supp. XIII:** 278

Fanon, Frantz, **Retro. Supp. II:** 118; **Supp. X:** 131, 141

Fanshawe (Hawthorne), **II:** 223–224; **Retro. Supp. I:** 149, 151

Fan's Notes, A (Exley), **Supp. XVI:**69

"Fantasia on 'The Nut-Brown Maid'" (Ashbery), **Supp. III Part 1:** 19

"Fantasia on the Relations between Poetry and Photography" (Strand), **Supp. IV Part 2:** 631

"Fantastic Fables" (Bierce), **I:** 209

Fante, John, **Supp. XI:** 159–176

Faraday, Michael, **I:** 480–481

"Farewell" (Emerson), **II:** 13

Farewell, My Lovely (Chandler), **Supp. IV Part 1:** 122, 125–126, 127, 128, 130

"Farewell, My Lovely!" (White), **Supp. I Part 2:** 661–663, 665

"Farewell Performance" (Merrill), **Supp. III Part 1:** 336–337

Farewell-Sermon Preached at the First Precinct in Northampton, after the People's Publick Rejection of their Minister, A (Edwards), **I:** 548, 562

"Farewell Sweet Dust" (Wylie), **Supp. I Part 2:** 727–728

Farewell to Arms, A (Hemingway), **I:** 212, 421, 476, 477; **II:** 68–69, 248–249, 252–253, 254, 255, 262, 265; **Retro. Supp. I:** 171, 178, 180–182, 187, 189; **Retro. Supp. II:** 108; **Supp. IV Part 1:** 380–381, 381; **Supp. VIII:** 179; **Supp. XII:** 241–242

"Farewell to Miles" (Berryman), **I:** 173

Farewell to Reform (Chamberlain), **Supp. I Part 2:** 647

Farewell to Sport (Gallico), **Supp. XVI:**238

"Farewell to the Middle Class" (Updike), **Retro. Supp. I:** 321

Far Field, The (Roethke), **III:** 528, 529, 539, 545, 547–548

"Far Field, The" (Roethke), **III:** 537, 540

Far-Flung (Cameron), **Supp. XII:** 81

Far from the Madding Crowd (Hardy), **II:** 291

Faris, Athénaíse Charleville, **Supp. I Part 1:** 204

Farley, Abbie, **I:** 458

Farley, Harriet, **Supp. XIII:** 140

"Farm, The" (Creeley), **Supp. IV Part 1:** 155

Farmer (Harrison), **Supp. VIII:** 39, 44–45

Farmer, Frances, **Supp. XV:** 196–197

Farmer, Richard, **Supp. XIV:**2

"Farmer and the Fox, The" (Leopold), **Supp. XIV:**188

"Farmers' Daughters, The" (W. C. Williams), **Retro. Supp. I:** 423

Farmers Hotel, The (O'Hara), **III:** 361

"Farmer's Sorrow, A" (Jewett), **Retro. Supp. II:** 132

"Farmer's Wife, The" (Sexton), **Supp. II Part 2:** 676

"Farm Implements and Rutabagas in a Landscape" (Ashbery), **Supp. III Part 1:** 13

Farming: A Hand Book (Berry), **Supp. X:** 31, 35

"Farm on the Great Plains, The" (Stafford), **Supp. XI:** 322

Farnol, Jeffrey, **Supp. I Part 2:** 653

Far North (Shepard), **Supp. III Part 2:** 433, 435

"Far Northern Birch, The" (Francis), **Supp. IX:** 90

Farnsworth, Elizabeth, **Supp. XI:** 139

"Farrago" (Kees), **Supp. XV:** 145

Farrand, Max, **II:** 122

Farrar, Geraldine, **Retro. Supp. I:** 10

Farrar, John, **II:** 191; **Supp. XI:** 47

Farrell, Barry, **Supp. XIV:**142

Farrell, James Francis, **II:** 25, 26

Farrell, James T., **I:** 97, 288, 475, 508, 517, 519; **II:** 25–53, 416, 424; **III:** 28, 114, 116, 118, 119, 317, 382; **IV:** 211, 286; **Retro. Supp. II:** 196, 327; **Supp. I Part 2:** 679; **Supp. VIII:** 96, 97; **Supp. XIV:**3; **Supp. XV:** 141

Farrell, John, **II:** 26

Farrell, John C., **Supp. I Part 1:** 24

Farrell, Kate, **Supp. XV:** 187–188,**Supp. XV:** 190

Farrell, Kevin, **II:** 26

Farrell, Mary, **II:** 25

Farrell, Mrs. James T. (Dorothy Butler), **II:** 26

Farrell, Mrs. James T. (Hortense Alden), **II:** 26, 27, 45, 48

"Far Rockaway" (Schwartz), **Supp. II Part 2:** 649

Farrow, Mia, **Supp. XV:** 8, 10

Far Side of the Dollar, The (Macdonald), **Supp. IV Part 2:** 473

Farther Off from Heaven (Humphrey), **Supp. IX:** 93, 96, 101, 103–104, 105, 109

Far Tortuga (Matthiessen), **Supp. V:** 201, 206–207

"Fascinating Fascism" (Sontag), **Supp. III Part 2:** 465

"Fascination of Cities, The" (Hughes), **Supp. I Part 1:** 325

Fashion, Power, Guilt and the Charity of Families (Shields), **Supp. VII:** 323

Fasman, Jonathan, **Supp. V:** 253

Fast, Howard, **Supp. I Part 1:** 295

Fast, Jonathan, **Supp. V:** 115

Fast and Loose (Wharton), **Retro. Supp. I:** 361

"Fastest Runner on Sixty-first Street, The" (Farrell), **II:** 45

"Fat" (Carver), **Supp. III Part 1:** 141

Fatal Interview (Millay), **III:** 128–129, 130

"Fatality" (Bausch), **Supp. VII:** 54

Fatal Lady (film), **Supp. XIII:** 166

"Fate" (Emerson), **II:** 2–3, 4, 16; **Supp. XIV:**42

"Fate" (Koch), **Supp. XV:** 183

"Fate" (Mailer), **Retro. Supp. II:** 207

"Fate of Pleasure, The" (Trilling), **Supp. III Part 2:** 510

Fate of the Jury, The (Masters), **Supp. I Part 2:** 466, 468, 469

"Fat Girl, The" (Dubus), **Supp. VII:** 84, 85

"Father" (Levine), **Supp. V:** 188

"Father" (Sanders), **Supp. XVI:**277

"Father" (Walker), **Supp. III Part 2:** 522

"Father, The" (Carver), **Supp. III Part 1:** 137, 140

Father, The (Olds), **Supp. X:** 209–211

"Father Abraham" (Faulkner), **Retro. Supp. I:** 81, 82

Fatheralong: A Meditation on Fathers and Sons, Race and Society (Wideman), **Supp. X:** 320, 332–333, 334, 335

"Father and Daughter" (Eberhart), **I:** 539

Father and Glorious Descendant (Lowe), **Supp. X:** 291

"Father and Son" (Eberhart), **I:** 539

Father and Son (Farrell), **II:** 34, 35, 290, 291

Father and Son (Gosse), **Supp. VIII:** 157

"Father and Son" (Hughes), **Retro. Supp. I:** 204; **Supp. I Part 1:** 329, 339

"Father and Son" (Kunitz), **Supp. III Part 1:** 262

"Father and Son" (Schwartz), **Supp. II Part 2:** 650

Father Bombo's Pilgrimage to Mecca (Freneau), **Supp. II Part 1:** 254

"Father Guzman" (Stern), **Supp. IX:** 293, 296

"Father out Walking on the Lawn, A" (Dove), **Supp. IV Part 1:** 246

"Fathers" (Creeley), **Supp. IV Part 1:** 157–158

Fathers, The (Tate), **IV:** 120, 127, 130, 131–133, 134, 141; **Supp. X:** 52

"Fathers and Sons" (Hemingway), **II:** 249, 265–266; **Retro. Supp. I:** 175

"Father's Body, The" (Dickey), **Supp. IV Part 1:** 176

"Father's Story, A" (Dubus), **Supp. VII:** 88

"Father's Voice" (Stafford), **Supp. XI:** 322

"Fat Lady, The" (Carruth), **Supp. XVI:**48

"Fat Man, Floating" (Dunn), **Supp. XI:** 144

Faulkner: A Collection of Critical Essays (Warren), **Retro. Supp. I:** 73

Faulkner, Barry, **Supp. XV:** 41

Faulkner, William, **I:** 54, 97, 99, 105, 106, 115, 117, 118, 123, 190, 204–205, 211, 288, 289, 291, 292, 297, 305, 324, 374, 378, 423, 480, 517; **II:** 28, 51, 54–76, 131, 174, 194, 217, 223, 228, 230, 259, 301, 306, 431, 458–459, 542, 594, 606; **III:** 45, 70, 108, 164, 218, 220, 222, 236–237, 244, 292, 334, 350, 382, 418, 453, 454, 482, 483; **IV:** 2, 4, 33, 49, 97, 98, 100, 101, 120, 131, 203, 207, 211, 217, 237, 257, 260, 261, 279, 280, 352, 461, 463; **Retro. Supp. I:** 73–95, 215, 339, 347, 356, 379, 382; **Retro. Supp. II:** 19, 221, 326; **Supp. I Part 1:** 196, 197, 242, 372; **Supp. I Part 2:** 450, 621; **Supp. III Part 1:** 384–385, 396; **Supp. IV Part 1:** 47, 130, 257, 342; **Supp. IV Part 2:** 434, 463, 468, 502, 677, 682; **Supp. V:** 58, 59, 138, 210, 226, 237, 261, 262, 334–336; **Supp. VIII:** 37, 39, 40, 104, 105, 108, 175, 176, 180, 181, 183, 184, 188, 189, 215; **Supp. IX:** 20, 95; **Supp. X:** 44, 228; **Supp. XI:** 92, 247; **Supp. XII:** 16, 289, 310, 313; **Supp. XIII:** 100, 169; **Supp. XIV:**1, 12–13, 21, 24, 93, 306; **Supp. XV:** 92, 135, 338; **Supp. XVI:**148, 189

Faulkner at Nagano (Jelliffe, ed.), **I:** 289; **II:** 63, 65

Faulkner-Cowley File, The: Letters and Memories 1944–1962 (Cowley, ed.), **Retro. Supp. I:** 73, 92; **Supp. II Part 1:** 140, 141

"Faun" (Plath), **Supp. I Part 2:** 537

"Fauna" (Jeffers), **Supp. II Part 2:** 415

Fauset, Jessie, **Supp. I Part 1:** 321, 325; **Supp. IV Part 1:** 164

Faust (Goethe), **I:** 396; **II:** 489; **III:** 395; **Supp. II Part 1:** 16; **Supp. IX:** 141

Faust, Clarence H., **II:** 20

Faute de l'Abbé Mouret, La (Zola), **III:** 322

Favor Island (Merwin), **Supp. III Part 1:** 346, 347

"Favrile" (Doty), **Supp. XI:** 131

Fay, Bernard, **IV:** 41

"Fear, The" (Frost), **Retro. Supp. I:** 128

"Fear & Fame" (Levine), **Supp. V:** 192

Fearful Child, The (C. Frost), **Supp. XV:** 96, 97, 106

"Fearful Child, The" (C. Frost), **Supp. XV:** 96

Fearing, Kenneth, **Supp. XV:** 138

"Fearless" (Mosley), **Supp. XIII:** 241

Fearless Jones (Mosley), **Supp. XIII:** 241–242

Fear of Fifty: A Midlife Memoir (Jong), **Supp. V:** 114, 115, 116, 131

Fear of Flying (Jong), **Supp. V:** 113, 115, 116, 119–123, 124, 129

"Feast, The" (Kinnell), **Supp. III Part 1:** 239, 250

Feast of All Saints, The (Rice), **Supp. VII:** 299–301

Feast of Snakes, A (Crews), **Supp. XI:** 102, 107–108

"Feast of Stephen, The" (Hecht), **Supp. X:** 63–64

"Featherbed for Critics, A" (Blackmur), **Supp. II Part 1:** 93, 151

Feather Crowns (Mason), **Supp. VIII:** 146–147

"Feathers" (Carver), **Supp. III Part 1:** 145

Feathers (Van Vechten), **Supp. II Part 2:** 736, 749

"Feathers, The" (Hogan), **Supp. IV Part 1:** 416

"February" (Ellison), **Supp. II Part 1:** 229

"February: Thinking of Flowers" (Kenyon), **Supp. VII:** 171

February in Sydney (Komunyakaa), **Supp. XIII:** 124–125, 129

"February in Sydney" (Komunyakaa), **Supp. XIII:** 125

"February 14th" (Levine), **Supp. V:** 194

"Feces" (McClatchy), **Supp. XII:** 266, 267–268

Fechner, Gustav, **II:** 344, 355, 358, 359, 363

Feder, Lillian, **IV:** 136; **Supp. XVI:**49, 50

Federal Arts Project, **Supp. III Part 2:** 618

Federigo, or, The Power of Love (Nemerov), **III:** 268, 276, 282, 283–284, 285

"Fedora" (Chopin), **Supp. I Part 1:** 220

Fedorko, Kathy A., **Retro. Supp. I:** 361, 374

"Feeling and Precision" (Moore), **III:** 206

"Feeling of Effort, The" (James), **II:** 349

"Feel Like a Bird" (Swenson), **Supp. IV Part 2:** 639

"Feel Me" (Swenson), **Supp. IV Part 2:** 647

Feeney, Mary, **Supp. IX:** 152, 154

Feinstein, Sascha, **Supp. XIII:** 125

Feldman, Charles K., **Supp. XI:** 307

Fellini, Federico, **Supp. XII:** 172; **Supp. XV:** 8

"Fellow Citizens" (Sandburg), **III:** 553

Fellows, John, **Supp. I Part 2:** 520

"Felo de Se" (Wylie), **Supp. I Part 2:** 727, 729

Felton, Sharon, **Supp. IV Part 1:** 210

"Female Author" (Plath), **Retro. Supp. II:** 243

"Female Frailty" (Freneau), **Supp. II Part 1:** 258

"Female Laughter and Comic Possibilities: *Uncommon Women and Others*" (Chirico), **Supp. XV:** 323

Female Patriot, The; or, Nature's Rights (Rowson), **Supp. XV:** 237–238

"Female Voice in *To Kill a Mockingbird*, The: Narrative Strategies in Film and Novel" (Shakelford), **Supp. VIII:** 129

"Feminine Landscape of Leslie Marmon Silko's *Ceremony*, The" (Gunn Allen), **Supp. IV Part 1:** 324

Feminism and the Politics of Literary Reputation: The Example of Erica Jong (Templin), **Supp. V:** 116

"Feminismo" (Robbins), **Supp. X:** 272

"Feminist Criticism in the Wilderness" (Showalter), **Supp. X:** 97

"Fence, The" (Oliver), **Supp. VII:** 232

"Fence Posts" (Snyder), **Supp. VIII:** 304

Fences (Wilson), **Supp. VIII:** 329, 330, 331, 334–337, 350

Fenick, Elizabeth, **Retro. Supp. II:** 221

"Fenimore Cooper's Literary Offenses" (Twain), **IV:** 204–205

Fenollosa, Ernest, **III:** 458, 465, 466, 474, 475, 477; **Retro. Supp. I:** 289; **Supp. IV Part 1:** 154

Fenollosa, Mrs. Ernest, **III:** 458

Fenton, Charles, **Supp. XI:** 43

Fenton, James, **Supp. XV:** 117

Ferdinand: Including "It Was" (Zukofsky), **Supp. III Part 2:** 630

"Fergus" (Bourne), **I:** 229

Ferguson, James, **Supp. I Part 2:** 503

Ferguson, Otis, **Supp. IX:** 7

Ferguson, William, **Supp. XII:** 189

Ferguson Affair, The (Macdonald), **Supp. IV Part 2:** 473

Fergusson, Francis, **I:** 265, 440; **Supp. XV:** 20

Ferlinghetti, Lawrence, **Supp. IV Part 1:** 90; **Supp. VIII:** 290, 292; **Supp. XII:** 121, 125; **Supp. XIII:** 275

Fermata, The (Baker), **Supp. XIII:** 49–52, 54

"Fern" (Toomer), **Supp. III Part 2:** 481; **Supp. IX:** 313

Fern, Fanny, **Retro. Supp. I:** 246; **Supp. V:** 122

Fernández, Enrique, **Supp. VIII:** 73

Fernandez, Ramon, **Retro. Supp. I:** 302, 303; **Supp. XVI:**214

"Fern-Beds in Hampshire Country" (Wilbur), **Supp. III Part 2:** 558

"Fern Hill" (D. Thomas), **IV:** 93

"Fern-Life" (Larcom), **Supp. XIII:** 143

Ferragammo, Salvatore, **Supp. XVI:**192

Ferreo, Guglielmo, **Supp. I Part 2:** 481

Fessenden, Thomas Green, **II:** 300

Fessier, Michael, **Supp. XIII:** 164

"Festival Aspect, The" (Olson), **Supp. II Part 2:** 585

"Festival of Regrets, The" (Wasserstein), **Supp. XV:** 333

Fetching the Dead (Sanders), **Supp. XVI:**269

Fêtes galantes (Verlaine), **IV:** 79

"Fetish" (McClatchy), **Supp. XII:** 256

Fetterley, Judith, **Retro. Supp. II:** 139

"Feud" (Zinberg), **Supp. XV:** 195

"Fever" (Carver), **Supp. III Part 1:** 145

"Fever 103°" (Plath), **Supp. I Part 2:** 541

Fever: Twelve Stories (Wideman), **Supp. X:** 320

Fever Pitch (Hornby), **Supp. XII:** 286

"Few Don'ts by an Imagiste, A" (Pound), **III:** 465; **Retro. Supp. I:** 288; **Supp. I Part 1:** 261–262

"Few Stray Comments on the Cultivation of the Lyric, A" (Sobin), **Supp. XVI:**285

"Few Words of Introduction, A" (McNally), **Supp. XIII:** 198–199

Fiamengo, Janice, **Supp. XIII:** 35

Fiber (Bass), **Supp. XVI:**22

"Fiber: A Post-Pastoral Georgic" (Gifford), **Supp. XVI:**22

Ficke, Arthur Davison, **Supp. XIII:** 347; **Supp. XV:** 40, 42, 43, 46, 48, 49

"Fiction" (Stafford), **Supp. XI:** 327

"Fiction: A Lens on Life" (Stegner), **Supp. IV Part 2:** 595, 596, 600

Fiction and the Figures of Life (Gass), **Supp. VI:** 85

Fiction of Joseph Heller, The (Seed), **Supp. IV Part 1:** 391

Fiction of Paule Marshall, The (Denniston), **Supp. XI:** 276

Fiction of the Forties (Eisinger), **I:** 302; **II:** 604

Fictions in Autobiography: Studies in the Art of Self-Invention (Eakin), **Supp. XVI:**70

"Fiction Writer and His Country, The" (O'Connor), **III:** 342; **Retro. Supp. II:** 223, 225; **Supp. II Part 1:** 148

Fidelity (Glaspell), **Supp. III Part 1:** 177

Fiedler, Leslie A., **II:** 27; **III:** 218; **Retro. Supp. II:** 280, 324; **Supp. II Part 1:** 87; **Supp. IV Part 1:** 42, 86; **Supp. IX:** 3, 227; **Supp. X:** 80; **Supp. XIII:** 93–110; **Supp. XIV:**11

Fiedler on the Roof: Essays on Literature and Jewish Identity (Fiedler), **Supp. XIII:** 106–107

"Fie! Fie! Fi-Fi!" (Fitzgerald), **Retro. Supp. I:** 100

Field, Eugene, **Supp. II Part 1:** 197

Field, John, **IV:** 179

"Field Events" (Bass), **Supp. XVI:**19

"Field Full of Black Cats, A" (C. Frost), **Supp. XV:** 101

Field Guide, (Hass), **Supp. VI:** 97–98, 99–101, 102, 103, 106

Field Guide to Contemporary Poetry and Poetics (Friebert and Young, eds.), **Supp. XI:** 270

"Field Guide to the Western Birds" (Stegner), **Supp. IV Part 2:** 609

Fielding, Henry, **I:** 134; **II:** 302, 304–305; **III:** 61; **Supp. I Part 2:** 421, 422, 656; **Supp. IV Part 2:** 688; **Supp. V:** 127; **Supp. IX:** 128; **Supp. XI:** 277

Fielding, Richard, **Supp. XV:** 232

"Field-larks and Blackbirds" (Lanier), **Supp. I Part 1:** 355

Field of Honor (Hay), **Supp. XIV:**120–121, 125, 130

"Field of Honor" (Hay), **Supp. XIV:**120–121, 129–130

Field of Vision, The (Morris), **III:** 226–228, 229, 232, 233, 238

"Field Report" (Corso), **Supp. XII:** 124, 136

"Fields" (Wright), **Supp. XV:** 342

Fields, Annie Adams, **II:** 401, 402, 403–404, 406, 412; **IV:** 177; **Retro. Supp. II:** 134, 135, 142; **Supp. I Part 1:** 317; **Supp. XVI:**84, 88

Fields, James T., **II:** 274, 279, 402–403; **Retro. Supp. II:** 135; **Supp. I Part 1:** 317; **Supp. XIII:** 150; **Supp. XVI:**84, 88

Fields, Joseph, **IV:** 274

Fields, Mrs. James T., **Supp. XIV:**44, 46. *See* Fields, Annie Adams

Fields, W. C., **II:** 427; **IV:** 335

"Fields at Dusk, The" (Salter), **Supp. IX:** 260

Fields of Wonder (Hughes), **Retro. Supp. I:** 206, 207; **Supp. I Part 1:** 333–334

Fierce Invalids Home from Hot Climates (Robbins), **Supp. X:** 267, 276–277, 282–285

Fiery Chariot, The (Hurston), **Supp. VI:** 155–156

15 Poems (Banks), **Supp. V:** 5

"Fifteenth Farewell" (Bogan), **Supp. III Part 1:** 51, 58

"Fifth Avenue, Uptown" (Baldwin), **Supp. I Part 1:** 52

"Fifth Avenue—Spring Afternoon" (Untermeyer), **Supp. XV:** 296

Fifth Book of Peace, The (Kingston), **Supp. V:** 173

Fifth Chinese Daughter (Wong), **Supp. X:** 291

Fifth Column, The (Hemingway), **II:**

254, 258; **Retro. Supp. I:** 184

"Fifth Column of the Fencerow" (Leopold), **Supp. XIV:**185

Fifth Decad of Cantos, The (Pound), **Retro. Supp. I:** 292

"Fifth Movement: *Autobiography*" (Zukofsky), **Supp. III Part 2:** 611

Fifth Sunday (Dove), **Supp. IV Part 1:** 251, 252–253

"Fifth Sunday" (Dove), **Supp. IV Part 1:** 252

Fifty Best American Short Stories (O'Brien), **III:** 56

"Fifty Dollars" (Elkin), **Supp. VI:** 43–44

"55 Miles to the Gas Pump" (Proulx), **Supp. VII:** 264

55 Poems (Zukofsky), **Supp. III Part 2:** 611, 621

"Fifty Grand" (Hemingway), **II:** 250, 424; **Retro. Supp. I:** 177

50 Poems (Cummings), **I:** 430, 440, 442–443, 444–445, 446

"Fifty Suggestions" (Poe), **Retro. Supp. II:** 266

"52 Oswald Street" (Kinnell), **Supp. III Part 1:** 251

"Fifty Years Among the Black Folk" (Du Bois), **Supp. II Part 1:** 169

"Fifty Years of American Poetry" (Jarrell), **Retro. Supp. I:** 52

Fight, The (Mailer), **Retro. Supp. II:** 207, 208

Fight Back: For the Sake of the People, For the Sake of the Land (Ortiz), **Supp. IV Part 2:** 497, 498, 499, 503, 510–512, 514

"Fighters, The" (Zinberg), **Supp. XV:** 193

Fight for Freedom (Hughes), **Supp. I Part 1:** 345

Fightin': New and Collected Stories (Ortiz), **Supp. IV Part 2:** 513

Fighting Angel (Buck), **Supp. II Part 1:** 119, 131

Fighting France; From Dunkerque to Belfort (Wharton), **Retro. Supp. I:** 377, 378

"Figlia che Piange, La" (Eliot), **I:** 570, 584; **III:** 9

Figliola, Samantha, **Supp. V:** 143

"Figure a Poem Makes, The" (Frost), **Retro. Supp. I:** 139

"Figured Wheel, The" (Pinsky), **Supp. VI:** 243, 244, 245, 246

Figured Wheel, The: New and Collected Poems (Pinsky), **Supp. VI:** 247–248

"Figure in the Carpet, The" (James), **Retro. Supp. I:** 228, 229

"Figure in the Doorway, The" (Frost), **Retro. Supp. I:** 138

Figures from the Double World (McGrath), **Supp. X:** 118–119

"Figures in the Clock, The" (McCarthy), **II:** 561–562

Figures Made Visible in the Sadness of Time (Everwine), **Supp. XV:** 75, 88

Figures of Time (Hayden), **Supp. II Part 1:** 367

"Filling Out a Blank" (Wagoner), **Supp. IX:** 324

Fillmore, Millard, **III:** 101

Film Flam: Essays on Hollywood (McMurtry), **Supp. V:** 228

Films of Ayn Rand, The (Cox), **Supp. IV Part 2:** 524

Filo, John, **Supp. XII:** 211

Filson, John, **Retro. Supp. I:** 421

Final Beast, The (Buechner), **Supp. XII:** 49–51

"Finale" (Longfellow), **II:** 505, 506–507

"Final Fear" (Hughes), **Supp. I Part 1:** 338

Final Harvest: Emily Dickinson's Poems (Johnson, ed.), **I:** 470, 471

Final Payments (Gordon), **Supp. IV Part 1:** 297, 299, 300–302, 304, 306, 314

"Final Report, A" (Maxwell), **Supp. VIII:** 169

"Final Soliloquy of the Interior Paramour" (Stevens), **Retro. Supp. I:** 312

Final Solution, The (Reitlinger), **Supp. XII:** 161

Financier, The (Dreiser), **I:** 497, 501, 507, 509; **Retro. Supp. II:** 94, 101–102, 105

Finch, Robert, **Supp. XIV:**186–187

Find a Victim (Macdonald), **Supp. IV Part 2:** 467, 472, 473

Fin de Chéri, La (Colette; stage adaptation, Loos), **Supp. XVI:**194

"Fin de Saison Palm Beach" (White), **Supp. I Part 2:** 673

Finding a Form (Gass), **Supp. VI:** 91–92, 93

Finding a Girl in America (Dubus), **Supp. VII:** 85–88

"Finding a Girl in America" (Dubus), **Supp. VII:** 87

"Finding Beads" (Hogan), **Supp. IV Part 1:** 400

"Finding of Zach, The" (Dunbar), **Supp. II Part 1:** 212

Findings and Keepings: Analects for an Autobiography (Mumford), **Supp. II Part 2:** 483

Finding the Center: Narrative Poetry of the Zuni Indians (Tedlock), **Supp. IV Part 2:** 509

Finding the Islands (Merwin), **Supp. III Part 1:** 353, 357

"Finding the Place: A Migrant Childhood" (Stegner), **Supp. IV Part 2:** 597

"Find the Woman" (Macdonald, under Millar), **Supp. IV Part 2:** 466

Fine, David, **Supp. XI:** 160

Fine Clothes to the Jew (Hughes), **Retro. Supp. I:** 200, 201, 203, 205; **Supp. I Part 1:** 326–328

"Fine Old Firm, A" (Jackson), **Supp. IX:** 120

Finer Grain, The (James), **II:** 335

Fine Writing (L. P. Smith), **Supp. XIV:**347

"Finis" (X. J. Kennedy), **Supp. XV:** 169

Finished Man, The (Garrett), **Supp. VII:** 96, 97–98

Fink, Mike, **IV:** 266

Finley, John H., **II:** 418

Finn, David, **Supp. VIII:** 106–107

Finnegans Wake (Joyce), **III:** 7, 12, 14, 261; **IV:** 182, 369–370, 418, 421; **Supp. I Part 2:** 620; **Supp. II Part 1:** 2; **Supp. XIII:** 191

Finney, Brian, **Supp. XIV:**158, 160, 161, 165, 166, 167, 169

"Finnish Rhapsody" (Ashbery), **Supp. III Part 1:** 26

Finster, Howard, **Supp. XV:** 349

Firbank, Ronald, **IV:** 77, 436

"Fire" (Hughes), **Supp. I Part 1:** 327

Fire: From "A Journal of Love," the Unexpurgated Diary of Anaïs Nin, 1934–1937, **Supp. X:** 184, 185, 189, 194, 195

"Fire and Cloud" (Wright), **IV:** 488

"Fire and Ice" (Frost), **II:** 154; **Retro. Supp. I:** 133

Fire and Ice (Stegner), **Supp. IV Part 2:** 598, 607–608

"Fire and the Cloud, The" (Hurston), **Supp. VI:** 158

"Fire and the Hearth, The" (Faulkner), **II:** 71

Firebird (Doty), **Supp. XI:** 119–120, 121, 132–133, 134

"Firebombing, The" (Dickey), **Supp. IV Part 1:** 180–181, 187, 189–190

"Fireborn Are at Home in Fire, The" (Sandburg), **III:** 591

"Fire Chaconne" (Francis), **Supp. IX:** 87

Firecrackers (Van Vechten), **Supp. II Part 2:** 740, 742–744, 749

"Fireman, The " (Bass), **Supp. XVI:**24

Fireman's Wife and Other Stories, The (Bausch), **Supp. VII:** 48, 54

Fire Next Time, The (Baldwin), **Retro. Supp. II:** 5, 8, 9; **Supp. I Part 1:** 48, 49, 52, 60–61

"Fire Next Time, The" (Baldwin). *See* "Down at the Cross" (Baldwin)

"Fire of Driftwood, The" (Longfellow), **II:** 499; **Retro. Supp. II:** 159, 168

"Fire of Life" (McCullers), **II:** 585

Fire on the Mountain (Abbey), **Supp. XIII:** 6

"Fire Poem" (Merrill), **Supp. III Part 1:** 321

"Fires" (Bass), **Supp. XVI:**20

"Fires" (Carver), **Supp. III Part 1:** 136–139, 147

Fires: Essays, Poems, Stories (Carver), **Supp. III Part 1:** 136, 140, 142, 146–147

Fire Screen, The (Merrill), **Supp. III Part 1:** 319, 325–329

"Fire Season" (Didion), **Supp. IV Part 1:** 199

"Fire Sequence" (Winters), **Supp. II Part 2:** 791, 796, 800

Fire Sermon (Morris), **III:** 238–239

"Fire Sermon, The" (Eliot), **Retro. Supp. I:** 60–61

Fireside Travels (Lowell), **Supp. I Part 2:** 407, 419–420

Firestarter (King), **Supp. V:** 140, 141, 144; **Supp. IX:** 114

"fire the bastards" (Green), **Supp. IV Part 1:** 285

"Fire-Truck, A" (Wilbur), **Supp. III Part 2:** 556

"Fireweed" (Clampitt), **Supp. IX:** 44–45

"Firewood" (Banks), **Supp. V:** 15

"Fireworks" (Ford), **Supp. V:** 69

"Fireworks" (Shapiro), **Supp. II Part 2:** 707

Fireworks: A History and Celebration (Plimpton), **Supp. XVI:**245

Fir-Flower Tablets (Lowell), **II:** 512, 526–527

Firkins, Oscar W., **II:** 271; **Supp. XV:** 297, 309

"Firmament, The" (Bryant), **Supp. I Part 1:** 162

Firmat, Gustavo Pérez, **Supp. VIII:** 76, 77, 79; **Supp. XI:** 184

"First American, The" (Toomer), **Supp. III Part 2:** 480, 487

"First Birth" (Olds), **Supp. X:** 212

First Book of Africa, The (Hughes), **Supp. I Part 1:** 344–345

First Book of Jazz, The (Hughes), **Supp. I Part 1:** 345

First Book of Negroes, The (Hughes), **Supp. I Part 1:** 345

First Book of Rhythms, The (Hughes), **Supp. I Part 1:** 345

First Book of the West Indies, The (Hughes), **Supp. I Part 1:** 345

Firstborn (Glück), **Supp. V:** 80, 81, 82, 84

"Firstborn" (Wright), **Supp. V:** 340

"First Chaldaic Oracle" (Carson), **Supp. XII:** 111

"First Communion" (Fante), **Supp. XI:** 160

"First Confession" (X. J. Kennedy), **Supp. XV:** 154–155

"First Day of School, The" (Gibbons), **Supp. X:** 41, 42

"First Death in Nova Scotia" (Bishop), **Supp. I Part 1:** 73

"First Formal" (Olds), **Supp. X:** 212

First Four Books of Poems, The (Glück), **Supp. V:** 81, 83

"First Grade" (Stafford), **Supp. XI:** 328

"First Hawaiian Bank" (Nye), **Supp. XIII:** 278

"First Heat" (Taylor), **Supp. V:** 323

"First Hour of the Night, The" (Bidart), **Supp. XV:** 30–32

"First Hunters and the Last, The" (Sobin), **Supp. XVI:**292

"First Job, The" (Cisneros), **Supp. VII:** 62

"1st Letter on Georges" (Olson), **Supp. II Part 2:** 578

First Light (Wagoner), **Supp. IX:** 330

"First Love" (Welty), **IV:** 264; **Retro. Supp. I:** 347

First Love: A Lyric Sequence (Untermeyer), **Supp. XV:** 295

First Man, The (O'Neill), **III:** 390

First Manifesto (McGrath), **Supp. X:** 115

"First Meditation" (Roethke), **III:** 545–546

"First Noni Daylight, The" (Harjo), **Supp. XII:** 219

"First Passover" (Longfellow), **II:** 500–501

"First Person Female" (Harrison), **Supp. VIII:** 40, 41, 48

"First Place, The" (Wagoner), **Supp. IX:** 328

First Poems (Buechner), **Supp. XII:** 45

First Poems (Merrill), **Supp. III Part 1:** 318–321, 323

First Poems 1946–1954 (Kinnell), **Supp. III Part 1:** 235, 238–239

"First Praise" (W. C. Williams), **Retro. Supp. I:** 413

First Principles (Spencer), **Supp. I Part 1:** 368

"First Ride and First Walk" (Goldbarth), **Supp. XII:** 182–183

"First Seven Years, The" (Malamud), **Supp. I Part 2:** 431

"First Sex" (Olds), **Supp. X:** 208

"First Snow in Alsace" (Wilbur), **Supp. III Part 2:** 545, 546, 559

"First Song" (Kinnell), **Supp. III Part 1:** 239

"First Spade in the West, The" (Fiedler), **Supp. XIII:** 103

"First Steps" (McClatchy), **Supp. XII:** 256

First There Is the Need (Reznikoff), **Supp. XIV:**291

"First Things First" (Auden), **Supp. II Part 1:** 13

"First Thought, Best Thought" (Ginsberg), **Supp. II Part 1:** 327

"First Time I Saw Paris, The" (Fante), **Supp. XI:** 174

"First Travels of Max" (Ransom), **III:** 490–491

"First Tycoon of Teen, The" (Wolfe), **Supp. III Part 2:** 572

"First Views of the Enemy" (Oates), **Supp. II Part 2:** 508

"First Wife, The" (Buck), **Supp. II Part 1:** 127

First Words before Spring (Untermeyer), **Supp. XV:** 310

"First World War" (White), **Supp. I Part 2:** 665

"Fish" (F. Barthelme), **Supp. XI:** 26

"Fish" (Levis), **Supp. XI:** 259–260

Fish, Stanley, **Supp. IV Part 1:** 48; **Supp. XIV:**14, 15

"Fish, The" (Bishop), **Supp. XV:** 100, 102

"Fish, The" (Moore), **III:** 195, 197, 209, 211, 213–214

"Fish, The" (Oliver), **Supp. VII:** 236

"Fish, The/Lago Chapala" (Everwine), **Supp. XV:** 82–83

"Fish and Shadow" (Pound), **III:** 466

Fishburne, Laurence, **Supp. VIII:** 345

"Fish Cannery" (Fante), **Supp. XI:** 167

Fisher, Alexander Metcalf, **Supp. I Part 2:** 582

Fisher, Alfred, **Retro. Supp. II:** 243

Fisher, Craig, **Supp. V:** 125

Fisher, Dorothy Canfield, **Retro. Supp. I:** 21, 133; **Supp. II Part 1:** 117. *See also* Canfield, Dorothy

Fisher, Mary, **Supp. I Part 2:** 455

Fisher, Phillip, **Retro. Supp. I:** 39

Fisher, Rudolph, **Retro. Supp. I:** 200; **Supp. I Part 1:** 325; **Supp. X:** 139; **Supp. XVI:**143

Fisher, Vardis, **Supp. IV Part 2:** 598

Fisher King, The (Marshall), **Supp. XI:** 275–276, 288–290

"Fisherman, The" (Merwin), **Supp. II Part 1:** 346

"Fisherman and His Wife, The" (Welty), **IV:** 266

"Fisherman from Chihuahua, The" (Connell), **Supp. XIV:**86

"Fishing" (Harjo), **Supp. XII:** 227–228

"Fish in the Stone, The" (Dove), **Supp. IV Part 1:** 245, 257

"Fish in the unruffled lakes" (Auden), **Supp. II Part 1:** 8–9

"Fish R Us" (Doty), **Supp. XI:** 135

Fisk, James, **I:** 4, 474

Fiske, John, **Supp. I Part 1:** 314; **Supp. I Part 2:** 493

"Fit Against the Country, A" (Wright), **Supp. III Part 2:** 591–592, 601

Fitch, Clyde, **Supp. IV Part 2:** 573

Fitch, Elizabeth. *See* Taylor, Mrs. Edward (Elizabeth Fitch)

Fitch, James, **IV:** 147

Fitch, Noël Riley, **Supp. X:** 186, 187

Fitts, Dudley, **I:** 169, 173; **Supp. I Part 1:** 342, 345; **Supp. XIII:** 346

FitzGerald, Edward, **Supp. I Part 2:** 416; **Supp. III Part 2:** 610

Fitzgerald, Ella, **Supp. XIII:** 132

Fitzgerald, F. Scott, **I:** 107, 117, 118, 123, 188, 221, 288, 289, 358, 367, 374–375, 382, 423, 476, 482, 487, 495, 509, 511; **II:** 77–100, 257, 263, 272, 283, 415, 416, 417–418, 420, 425, 427, 430, 431, 432, 433, 434, 436, 437, 450, 458–459, 482, 560; **III:** 2, 26, 35, 36, 37, 40, 44, 45, 69, 106, 244, 284, 334, 350–351, 453, 454, 471, 551, 552, 572; **IV:** 27, 49, 97, 101, 126, 140, 191, 222, 223, 287, 297, 427, 471; **Retro. Supp. I:** 1, 74, 97–120, 178, 180, 186, 215, 359, 381; **Retro. Supp. II:** 257, 321, 326, 328; **Supp. I Part 1:** 196, 197; **Supp. I Part 2:** 622; **Supp. III Part 2:** 409, 411, 585; **Supp. IV Part 1:** 123, 197, 200, 203, 341; **Supp. IV Part 2:** 463, 468, 607, 689; **Supp. V:** 23, 95, 226, 251, 262, 276, 313; **Supp. VIII:** 101, 103, 106, 137; **Supp. IX:** 15, 20, 55, 57–63, 199; **Supp. X:** 225; **Supp. XI:** 65, 221, 334; **Supp. XII:** 42, 173, 295; **Supp. XIII:** 170, 263;

Supp. XV: 135; **Supp. XVI:**64, 75, 191, 192, 294

Fitzgerald, Robert, **I:** 27–28; **III:** 338, 348; **Retro. Supp. II:** 179, 221, 222, 223, 228, 229; **Supp. IV Part 2:** 631; **Supp. XV:** 112, 249

"Fitzgerald: The Romance of Money" (Cowley), **Supp. II Part 1:** 143

Fitzgerald, Zelda (Zelda Sayre), **I:** 482; **II:** 77, 79, 82–85, 88, 90–91, 93, 95; **Supp. IV Part 1:** 310; **Supp. IX:** 55–73; **Supp. X:** 172. *See also* Sayre, Zelda

"Fitzgerald's Tragic Sense" (Schorer), **Retro. Supp. I:** 115

Five Came Back (West), **IV:** 287

Five Corners (screenplay, Shanley), **Supp. XIV:**316

5 Detroits (Levine), **Supp. V:** 178

"Five Dollar Guy, The" (W. C. Williams), **Retro. Supp. I:** 423

Five Easy Pieces (film), **Supp. V:** 26

"Five Elephants" (Dove), **Supp. IV Part 1:** 244–245

Five Groups of Verse (Reznikoff), **Supp. XIV:**279, 282

500 Hundred Hats of Bartholomew Cubbins, The (Geisel), **Supp. XVI:**100

Five Hundred Scorpions (Hearon), **Supp. VIII:** 57, 65, 66

Five Indiscretions (Ríos), **Supp. IV Part 2:** 545–547

Five Men and Pompey (Benét), **Supp. XI:** 43, 44

Five Plays (Hughes), **Retro. Supp. I:** 197, 209

Five Temperaments (Kalstone), **Retro. Supp. II:** 40

5,000 Fingers of Dr. T, The (film), **Supp. XVI:**103

Five Young American Poets, **I:** 170; **II:** 367

Fixer, The (Malamud), **Supp. I Part 2:** 428, 435, 445, 446–448, 450, 451

Fjellestad, Danuta Zadworna, **Supp. XVI:**150

Flaccus, Kimball, **Retro. Supp. I:** 136

Flacius, Matthias, **IV:** 163

"Flagellant's Song" (X. J. Kennedy), **Supp. XV:** 165

Flag for Sunrise, A (Stone), **Supp. V:** 301–304

Flag of Childhood, The: Poems from the Middle East (Nye, ed.), **Supp. XIII:** 280

"Flag of Summer" (Swenson), **Supp. IV Part 2:** 645

Flagons and Apples (Jeffers), **Supp. II Part 2:** 413, 414, 417–418

Flags in the Dust (Faulkner), **Retro. Supp. I:** 81, 82, 83, 86, 88
Flamel, Nicolas, **Supp. XII:** 178
Flaming Corsage, The (W. Kennedy), **Supp. VII:** 133, 153–156
Flammarion, Camille, **Supp. I Part 1:** 260
Flanagan, John T., **Supp. I Part 2:** 464, 465, 468
Flanner, Janet, **Supp. XVI:**195
"Flannery O'Connor: Poet to the Outcast" (Sister Rose Alice), **III:** 348
Flappers and Philosophers (Fitzgerald), **II:** 88; **Retro. Supp. I:** 103; **Supp. IX:** 56
Flash and Filigree (Southern), **Supp. XI:** 295, 296–297
"Flashcards" (Dove), **Supp. IV Part 1:** 250
Flash Fiction: Seventy-two Very Short Stories (J. Thomas, ed.), **Supp. XVI:**268
Flatt, Lester, **Supp. V:** 335
Flaubert, Gustave, **I:** 66, 123, 130, 272, 312, 314, 315, 477, 504, 506, 513, 514; **II:** 182, 185, 194, 198–199, 205, 209, 230, 289, 311, 316, 319, 325, 337, 392, 401, 577, 594; **III:** 196, 207, 251, 315, 461, 467, 511, 564; **IV:** 4, 29, 31, 37, 40, 134, 285, 428; **Retro. Supp. I:** 5, 215, 218, 222, 225, 235, 287; **Supp. III Part 2:** 411, 412; **Supp. XI:** 334; **Supp. XIV:**87, 336
"Flavia and Her Artists" (Cather), **Retro. Supp. I:** 5
Flavoring of New England, The (Brooks), **I:** 253, 256
Flavor of Man, The (Toomer), **Supp. III Part 2:** 487
Flaxman, Josiah, **Supp. I Part 2:** 716
"Flèche d'Or" (Merrill), **Supp. III Part 1:** 328
Flecker, James Elroy, **Supp. I Part 1:** 257
"Flee on Your Donkey" (Sexton), **Supp. II Part 2:** 683, 685
Fleming, Ian, **Supp. XI:** 307
Fleming, Rene, **Supp. XII:** 321
Flesch, Rudolf, **Supp. XVI:**105, 106
Flesh and Blood (Cunningham), **Supp. XV:** 63–65
Flesh and Blood (play; Cunnigham and Gaitens), **Supp. XV:** 65
"Fleshbody" (Ammons), **Supp. VII:** 27
Fletcher, H. D., **II:** 517, 529
Fletcher, John, **Supp. IV Part 2:** 621
Fletcher, John Gould, **I:** 243; **II:** 517, 529; **III:** 458; **Supp. I Part 1:** 263;

Supp. I Part 2: 422; **Supp. XV:** 298, 302, 306, 307, 308
Fletcher, Phineas, **Supp. I Part 1:** 369
Fletcher, Virginia. *See* Caldwell, Mrs. Erskine (Virginia Fletcher)
Fleurs du mal, Les (Beaudelaire; Millay and Dillon, trans.), **III:** 141–142
"Flight" (Updike), **IV:** 218, 222, 224; **Retro. Supp. I:** 318
"Flight, The" (Haines), **Supp. XII:** 204–205
"Flight, The" (Roethke), **III:** 537–538
Flight among the Tombs (Hecht), **Supp. X:** 58, 71–74
"Flight for Freedom" (McCoy), **Supp. XIII:** 170
"Flight from Byzantium" (Brodsky), **Supp. VIII:** 30–31
"Flight of Besey Lane, The" (Jewett), **Retro. Supp. II:** 139
Flight of the Rocket, The (Fitzgerald), **II:** 89
Flight to Canada (Reed), **Supp. X:** 240, 249–252
Flint, F. S., **II:** 517; **III:** 459, 464, 465; **Retro. Supp. I:** 127; **Supp. I Part 1:** 261, 262
Flint, R. W., **Supp. XVI:**47, 49, 57
"Flitting Flies" (X. J. Kennedy), **Supp. XV:** 166, 167
Flivver King, The (Sinclair), **Supp. V:** 290
Floating House, The (Sanders), **Supp. XVI:**269
Floating Light Bulb, The (Allen), **Supp. XV:** 2, 3, 13
Floating Opera, The (Barth), **I:** 121, 122–126, 127, 129, 130, 131
"Floating Poem, Unnumbered, The" (Rich), **Supp. I Part 2:** 572–573
"Floating Trees" (Wright), **Supp. XV:** 348
Flood (Matthews), **Supp. IX:** 154, 160–161
Flood (Warren), **IV:** 252, 256–257
"Flood of Years, The" (Bryant), **Supp. I Part 1:** 159, 170, 171; **Supp. I Part 2:** 416
"Floor and the Ceiling, The" (W. J. Smith), **Supp. XIII:** 345, 346
"Floor Plans" (Komunyakaa), **Supp. XIII:** 114
"Floral Decorations for Bananas" (Stevens), **IV:** 8
Florida (Acker), **Supp. XII:** 5
"Florida" (Bishop), **Retro. Supp. II:** 43
"Florida Road Workers" (Hughes),

Retro. Supp. I: 203
"Florida Sunday, A" (Lanier), **Supp. I Part 1:** 364, 366
"Flossie Cabanis" (Masters), **Supp. I Part 2:** 461–462
Flow Chart (Ashbery), **Supp. VIII:** 275
"Flowchart" (Ashbery), **Supp. III Part 1:** 26
Flower, Fruit, and Thorn Pieces (Richter), **Supp. XVI:**182
Flower-de-Luce (Longfellow), **II:** 490
Flower Fables (Alcott), **Supp. I Part 1:** 33
"Flower-Fed Buffaloes, The" (Lindsay), **Supp. I Part 2:** 398
"Flower Garden" (Jackson), **Supp. IX:** 119
"Flower-gathering" (Frost), **II:** 153
Flower Herding on Mount Monadnock (Kinnell), **Supp. III Part 1:** 235, 239, 241–244
"Flower Herding on Mount Monadnock" (Kinnell), **Supp. III Part 1:** 242
"Flowering Death" (Ashbery), **Supp. III Part 1:** 22
"Flowering Dream, The" (McCullers), **II:** 591
"Flowering Judas" (Porter), **III:** 434, 435–436, 438, 441, 445, 446, 450–451
Flowering Judas and Other Stories (Porter), **III:** 433, 434
Flowering of New England, The (Brooks), **IV:** 171–172; **Supp. VIII:** 101
Flowering of the Rod (Doolittle), **Supp. I Part 1:** 272
Flowering Peach, The (Odets), **Supp. II Part 2:** 533, 547, 549–550
"Flowering Plum" (Glück), **Supp. V:** 82
"Flowers for Marjorie" (Welty), **IV:** 262
"Flowers of the Fallow" (Larcom), **Supp. XIII:** 143, 145–146
"Flowers Well if anybody" (Dickinson), **Retro. Supp. I:** 30
"Fly, The" (Kinnell), **Supp. III Part 1:** 249
"Fly, The" (Shapiro), **Supp. II Part 2:** 705
"Fly, The" (Simic), **Supp. VIII:** 278
Flye, Father James Harold, **I:** 25, 26, 35–36, 37, 42, 46; **IV:** 215
"Fly in Buttermilk, A" (Baldwin), **Retro. Supp. II:** 8
"Flying High" (Levertov), **Supp. III Part 1:** 284

"Flying Home" (Ellison), **Retro. Supp. II:** 117, 125–126; **Supp. II Part 1:** 235, 238–239

"Flying Home" (Kinnell), **Supp. III Part 1:** 250

"Flying Home" and Other Stories (Ellison), **Retro. Supp. II:** 119, 124

"Flying Home from Utah" (Swenson), **Supp. IV Part 2:** 645

"Flying over Clouds" (Gioia), **Supp. XV:** 118

"Flying to Hanoi" (Rukeyser), **Supp. VI:** 279

Fly-Truffler, The (Sobin), **Supp. XVI:**294–295, 296

Foata, Anne, **Supp. XI:** 104

Focillon, Henri, **IV:** 90

Focus (A. Miller), **III:** 150–151, 156

Foer, Jonathan Safran, **Supp. XII:** 169

Foerster, Norman, **I:** 222; **Supp. I Part 2:** 423, 424; **Supp. IV Part 2:** 598

"Fog" (Sandburg), **III:** 586

"Fog Galleon" (Komunyakaa), **Supp. XIII:** 127

"Foggy Lane, The" (Simpson), **Supp. IX:** 274

Folded Leaf, The (Maxwell), **Supp. III Part 1:** 62; **Supp. VIII:** 159–162

Folding Star, The (Hollinghurst), **Supp. XIII:** 52

Foley, Jack, **Supp. X:** 125; **Supp. XV:** 112, 116

Foley, Martha, **II:** 587; **Supp. XVI:**225

Folks from Dixie (Dunbar), **Supp. II Part 1:** 211–212

Folkways (Sumner), **III:** 102

Follain, Jean, **Supp. IX:** 152, 154

Follett, Wilson, **I:** 405; **Supp. XIII:** 173

Follower of Dusk (Salinas), **Supp. XIII:** 326

Following the Equator (Twain), **II:** 434; **IV:** 208

Folly (Minot), **Supp. VI:** 205, 208, 210–213

Folsom, Charles, **Supp. I Part 1:** 156

Folsom, Ed, **Retro. Supp. I:** 392

Folson, Marcia McClintock, **Retro. Supp. II:** 139

Fonda, Henry, **Supp. I Part 1:** 67; **Supp. IV Part 1:** 236

Fonda, Jane, **III:** 284; **Supp. XI:** 307

Fonda, Peter, **Supp. VIII:** 42; **Supp. XI:** 293, 308

Foner, Eric, **Supp. I Part 2:** 523

Fong and the Indians (Theroux), **Supp. VIII:** 314, 315, 316–317

Fontanne, Lynn, **III:** 397

Food and Drink (Untermeyer), **Supp. XV:** 310

Fool for Love (Shepard), **Supp. III Part 2:** 433, 447, 448

Fools (Simon), **Supp. IV Part 2:** 584–585

Fool's Progress, The: An Honest Novel (Abbey), **Supp. XIII:** 4, 13–15

Foot Book, The (Geisel), **Supp. XVI:**108

Foote, Horton, **Supp. I Part 1:** 281; **Supp. VIII:** 128, 129

Foote, Mary Hallock, **Retro. Supp. II:** 72; **Supp. IV Part 2:** 611

Foote, Roxanna. *See* Beecher, Mrs. Lyman (Roxanna Foote)

Foote, Samuel, **Supp. I Part 2:** 584

Foote, Stephanie, **Retro. Supp. II:** 139

"Foot Fault" (pseudonym). *See* Thurber, James

Footing on This Earth, A (Hay), **Supp. XIV:**125, 126, 130

"Footing up a Total" (Lowell), **II:** 528

"Footnote to Howl" (Ginsberg), **Supp. II Part 1:** 316–317

"Footnote to Weather Forecasts, A" (Brodsky), **Supp. VIII:** 32

Footprints (Hearon), **Supp. VIII:** 69–70

Footprints (Levertov), **Supp. III Part 1:** 272, 281

"Footsteps of Angels" (Longfellow), **II:** 496

For a Bitter Season: New and Selected Poems (Garrett), **Supp. VII:** 99–100

"For a Dead Kitten" (Hay), **Supp. XIV:**119–120

"For a Dead Lady" (Robinson), **III:** 508, 513, 517

"For a Ghost Who Once Placed Bets in the Park" (Levis), **Supp. XI:** 265

"For a Lamb" (Eberhart), **I:** 523, 530, 531

"For All" (Snyder), **Supp. VIII:** 304

"For All Tuesday Travelers" (Cisneros), **Supp. VII:** 67–68

"For a Lost Child" (Stafford), **Supp. XI:** 329

"For a Marriage" (Bogan), **Supp. III Part 1:** 52

"For an Emigrant" (Jarrell), **II:** 371

"For Anna Akmatova" (Lowell), **II:** 544

"For Anna Mae Pictou Aquash, Whose Spirit Is Present Here and in the Dappled Stars" (Harjo), **Supp. XII:** 225

"For Anne, at a Little Distance" (Haines), **Supp. XII:** 207

"For Annie" (Poe), **III:** 427; **Retro.**

Supp. II: 263

"For a Southern Man" (Cisneros), **Supp. VII:** 67

"For Bailey" (Angelou), **Supp. IV Part 1:** 15

Forbes, Malcolm, **Supp. IV Part 1:** 94

"Forbidden, The" (Glück), **Supp. XIV:**269

"For Bill Nestrick (1940–96)" (Bidart), **Supp. XV:** 35

For Bread Alone (Choukri), **Supp. IV Part 1:** 92

Force of Spirit, The (Sanders), **Supp. XVI:**277–278

Forché, Carolyn, **Supp. IV Part 1:** 208

Ford, Arthur, **Supp. IV Part 1:** 140

Ford, Ford Madox, **I:** 288, 405, 409, 417, 421, 423; **II:** 58, 144, 198, 257, 263, 265, 517, 536; **III:** 458, 464–465, 470–471, 472, 476; **IV:** 27, 126, 261; **Retro. Supp. I:** 127, 177, 178, 186, 231, 286–287, 418; **Supp. II Part 1:** 107; **Supp. III Part 2:** 617; **Supp. VIII:** 107; **Supp. XIV:**3

Ford, Harrison, **Supp. VIII:** 323

Ford, Harry, **Supp. V:** 179; **Supp. XIII:** 76

Ford, Henry, **I:** 295, 480–481; **III:** 292, 293; **Supp. I Part 1:** 21; **Supp. I Part 2:** 644; **Supp. III Part 2:** 612, 613; **Supp. IV Part 1:** 223; **Supp. V:** 290

Ford, John, **Supp. I Part 2:** 422; **Supp. III Part 2:** 619

Ford, Richard, **Supp. IV Part 1:** 342; **Supp. V:** 22, 57–75

Ford, Webster (pseudonym). *See* Masters, Edgar Lee

"Fording and Dread" (Harrison), **Supp. VIII:** 41

"Ford Madox Ford" (Lowell), **II:** 547; **Retro. Supp. II:** 188

"For Dudley" (Wilbur), **Supp. III Part 2:** 558

Fordyce, David, **II:** 113

Foregone Conclusion, A (Howells), **II:** 278–279, 282

"Foreign Affairs" (Kunitz), **Supp. III Part 1:** 265

"Foreigner, A" (Bynner), **Supp. XV:** 46

"Foreigner, The" (Jewett), **II:** 409–410; **Retro. Supp. II:** 133, 142

"Foreign Shores" (Salter), **Supp. IX:** 260

Forensic and the Navigators (Shepard), **Supp. III Part 2:** 439

Foreseeable Future, The (Price), **Supp. VI:** 265

Foreseeable Futures (Matthews),

Supp. IX: 155, 163, 169
"For Esmé with Love and Squalor"
(Salinger), **III:** 560
"Forest" (Simic), **Supp. VIII:** 273
Forest, Jean-Claude, **Supp. XI:** 307
Forester's Letters (Paine), **Supp. I
Part 2:** 508
"Forest Hymn, A" (Bryant), **Supp. I
Part 1:** 156, 162, 163, 164, 165, 170
"Forest in the Seeds, The"
(Kingsolver), **Supp. VII:** 203
Forest of the South, The (Gordon), **II:**
197
"Forest of the South, The" (Gordon),
II: 199, 201
Forest without Leaves (Adams and
Haines), **Supp. XII:** 209
"Forever and the Earth" (Bradbury),
Supp. IV Part 1: 102
"Forever in That Year" (Carruth),
Supp. XVI:51
"For Fathers of Girls" (Dunn), **Supp.
XI:** 146
"For/From Lew" (Snyder), **Supp. VIII:**
303
"For Garrison Keillor, Fantasy Is a Lot
More Fun then Reality" (Letofsky),
Supp. XVI:167
"For George Santayana" (Lowell), **II:**
547
*Forgotten Helper, The: A Story for
Children* (Moore), **Supp. X:** 175
Forgotten Village, The (Steinbeck), **IV:**
51
Forgue, Guy J., **III:** 118, 119
"FOR HETTIE" (Baraka), **Supp. II
Part 1:** 32
"FOR HETTIE IN HER FIFTH
MONTH" (Baraka), **Supp. II Part
1:** 32, 38
"For Homer" (Corso), **Supp. XII:** 135
"For I'm the Boy" (Barthelme), **Supp.
IV Part 1:** 47
"For Jessica, My Daughter" (Strand),
Supp. IV Part 2: 629
"For John, Who Begs Me not to En-
quire Further" (Sexton), **Supp. II
Part 2:** 676
"For Johnny Pole on the Forgotten
Beach" (Sexton), **Supp. II Part 2:**
675
"For Joy to Leave Upon" (Ortiz),
Supp. IV Part 2: 508
"Fork" (Simic), **Supp. VIII:** 275
For Lancelot Andrewes (Eliot), **Retro.
Supp. I:** 64
For Lizzie and Harriet (Lowell),
Retro. Supp. II: 183, 186, 190
"Forlorn Hope of Sidney Lanier, The"
(Leary), **Supp. I Part 1:** 373

For Love (Creeley), **Supp. IV Part 1:**
139, 140, 142–145, 147–149, 150,
154
"For Love" (Creeley), **Supp. IV Part
1:** 145
For Love (Miller), **Supp. XII:** 297–
299, 299
For Love of Imabelle (C. Himes),
Supp. XVI:135, 143, 144
"Formal Elegy" (Berryman), **I:** 170
"Formalist Criticism: Its Principles and
Limits" (Burke), **I:** 282
Forman, Milos, **Supp. IV Part 1:** 236
"Form and Function of the Novel, The"
(Goldbarth), **Supp. XII:** 183
"For Marse Chouchoute" (Chopin),
Retro. Supp. II: 60
"For Mary Ann Youngren" (Bidart),
Supp. XV: 29
"Formation of a Separatist, I" (Howe),
Supp. IV Part 2: 427
"Form Is Emptiness" (Baraka), **Supp.
II Part 1:** 51
"For Mr. Death Who Stands with His
Door Open" (Sexton), **Supp. II Part
2:** 695
Forms of Discovery (Winters), **Supp.
II Part 2:** 812, 813
Forms of Fiction, The (Gardner and
Dunlap), **Supp. VI:** 64
"For My Children" (Karr), **Supp. XI:**
254
"For My Daughter" (Kees), **Supp. XV:**
141, 147
"For My Daughter" (Olds), **Supp. X:**
206
"For My Lover, Returning to His Wife"
(Sexton), **Supp. II Part 2:** 688
"For Night to Come" (Stern), **Supp.
IX:** 292
"For Once, Then, Something" (Frost),
II: 156–157; **Retro. Supp. I:** 126,
133, 134
"For Peg: A Remnant of Song Still
Distantly Sounding" (Carruth),
Supp. XVI:54
"For Pot-Boiling" (Hay), **Supp.
XIV:**128
"For Radicals" (Bourne), **I:** 221
"For Rainer Gerhardt" (Creeley), **Supp.
IV Part 1:** 142–143, 147
Forrestal, James, **I:** 491; **Supp. I Part
2:** 489
"For Richard After All" (Kingsolver),
Supp. VII: 208
"For Sacco and Vanzetti" (Kingsolver),
Supp. VII: 208
"Forsaken Merman" (Arnold), **Supp. I
Part 2:** 529
For Spacious Skies (Buck), **Supp. II**

Part 1: 131
Forster, E. M., **I:** 292; **IV:** 201; **Retro.
Supp. I:** 59, 232; **Supp. III Part 2:**
503; **Supp. V:** 258; **Supp. VIII:**
155, 171; **Supp. IX:** 128; **Supp.
XII:** 79, 81; **Supp. XIV:**159, 160,
163; **Supp. XV:** 62; **Supp. XVI:**236
Forster, John, **II:** 315
Fort, Paul, **II:** 518, 528, 529; **Retro.
Supp. I:** 55
"For the Ahkoond" (Bierce), **I:** 209
*For the Century's End: Poems 1990–
1999* (Haines), **Supp. XII:** 211–213
"For the Dedication of the New City
Library, Boston" (Holmes), **Supp. I
Part 1:** 308
"For the Fallen" (Levine), **Supp. V:**
188
*For the Health of the Land: Previously
Unpublished Essays and Other Writ-
ings* (Leopold), **Supp. XIV:**183
"For the Last Wolverine" (Dickey),
Supp. IV Part 1: 182
"For the Lovers of the Absolute"
(Simic), **Supp. VIII:** 278–279
"For the Man Cutting the Grass"
(Oliver), **Supp. VII:** 235
"For the Marriage of Faustus and
Helen" (H. Crane), **I:** 395–396, 399,
402; **Retro. Supp. II:** 78–79, 82
"For the Meeting of the National
Sanitary Association, 1860"
(Holmes), **Supp. I Part 1:** 307
For the New Intellectual (Rand), **Supp.
IV Part 2:** 521, 526–527, 527, 532
"For the New Railway Station in
Rome" (Wilbur), **Supp. III Part 2:**
554
"For the Night" (Kenyon), **Supp. VII:**
163
"For Theodore Roethke: 1908–1963"
(Lowell), **II:** 554
"For the Poem *Patterson*" (W. C.
Williams), **Retro. Supp. I:** 424
"For the Poets of Chile" (Levine),
Supp. V: 188
"FOR THE REVOLUTIONARY OUT-
BURST BY BLACK PEOPLE"
(Baraka), **Supp. II Part 1:** 55
"For the Sleepless" (Dunn), **Supp. XI:**
145
For the Time Being (Auden), **Supp. II
Part 1:** 2, 17, 18
For the Time Being (Dillard), **Supp.
VI:** 23, 27, 29, 32, 34–35
"For the Twentieth Century" (Bidart),
Supp. XV: 35
For the Union Dead (Lowell), **II:** 543,
550–551, 554, 555; **Retro. Supp.
II:** 181, 182, 186, 189; **Supp. X:** 53

"For the Union Dead" (Lowell), **II:** 551; **Retro. Supp. II:** 189

"For the Walking Dead" (Komunyakaa), **Supp. XIII:** 121

"For the West" (Snyder), **Supp. VIII:** 299

"For the Word Is Flesh" (Kunitz), **Supp. III Part 1:** 262–264

"Fortress, The" (Glück), **Supp. V:** 82

"Fortress, The" (Sexton), **Supp. II Part 2:** 682

Fortune, T. Thomas, **Supp. II Part 1:** 159

Fortune's Daughter (Hoffman), **Supp. X:** 77, 85

45 Mercy Street (Sexton), **Supp. II Part 2:** 694, 695, 697

Forty Poems Touching on Recent American History (Bly, ed.), **Supp. IV Part 1:** 61

42nd Parallel, The (Dos Passos), **I:** 482, 484–485

Forty Stories (Barthelme), **Supp. IV Part 1:** 47, 49, 53, 54

For Whom the Bell Tolls (Hemingway), **II:** 249, 254–255, 261; **III:** 18, 363; **Retro. Supp. I:** 115, 176–177, 178, 184, 187

Foscolo, Ugo, **II:** 543

Foss, Sam Walter, **Supp. II Part 1:** 197

"Fossils, The" (Kinnell), **Supp. III Part 1:** 244

Foster, Edward, **Supp. IV Part 2:** 431, 434; **Supp. XVI:**281, 293

Foster, Edward Halsey, **Supp. XII:** 120, 129, 130, 135

Foster, Emily, **II:** 309

Foster, Hannah, **Supp. XV:** 234

Foster, John Wilson, **Supp. XIII:** 32–33

Foster, Phil, **Supp. IV Part 2:** 574

Foster, Richard, **Supp. XV:** 269

Foster, Stephen, **Supp. I Part 1:** 100–101; **Supp. I Part 2:** 699

Foucault, Michel, **Supp. VIII:** 5; **Supp. XII:** 98; **Supp. XV:** 344; **Supp. XVI:**285

"Founder, The" (Stern), **Supp. IX:** 297

Founding of Harvard College, The (Morison), **Supp. I Part 2:** 485

"Fountain, The" (Bryant), **Supp. I Part 1:** 157, 165, 166, 168

Fountain, The (O'Neill), **III:** 391

Fountain and Other Poems, The (Bryant), **Supp. I Part 1:** 157

Fountainhead, The (film), **Supp. IV Part 2:** 524

Fountainhead, The (Rand), **Supp. IV Part 2:** 517, 521–523, 525, 531

Fountainhead, The: A Fiftieth Anniversary Celebration (Cox), **Supp. IV Part 2:** 523

"Fountain Piece" (Swenson), **Supp. IV Part 2:** 641

"Four Ages of Man, The" (Bradstreet), **Supp. I Part 1:** 111, 115

Four American Indian Literary Masters (Velie), **Supp. IV Part 2:** 486

"Four Beasts in One; the Homo Cameleopard" (Poe), **III:** 425

Four Black Revolutionary Plays (Baraka), **Supp. II Part 1:** 45; **Supp. VIII:** 330

"Four Brothers, The" (Sandburg), **III:** 585

Four Dogs and a Bone and the Wild Goose (Shanley), **Supp. XIV:**316, 328–329

"Four Evangelists, The" (Komunyakaa), **Supp. XIII:** 131

"Four for Sir John Davies" (Roethke), **III:** 540, 541

"Four Girls, The" (Alvarez), **Supp. VII:** 7

4-H Club (Shepard), **Supp. III Part 2:** 439

"Four Horse Songs" (Harjo), **Supp. XII:** 220

"400-Meter Free Style" (Kumin), **Supp. IV Part 2:** 442

Fourier, Charles, **II:** 342

"Four in a Family" (Rukeyser), **Supp. VI:** 272

Four in Hand: A Quartet of Novels (Warner), **Supp. VIII:** 164

"Four Lakes' Days" (Eberhart), **I:** 525

"Four Meetings" (James), **II:** 327

Four Million, The (O. Henry), **Supp. II Part 1:** 394, 408

"Four Monarchyes" (Bradstreet), **Supp. I Part 1:** 105, 106, 116

"Four Mountain Wolves" (Silko), **Supp. IV Part 2:** 561

Four of a Kind (Marquand), **III:** 54, 55

"Four of the Horsemen (Hypertense and Stroke, Coronary Occlusion and Cerebral Insult)" (Karr), **Supp. XI:** 250

"Four Poems" (Bishop), **Supp. I Part 1:** 92

"Four Preludes on Playthings of the Wind" (Sandburg), **III:** 586

Four Quartets (Eliot), **I:** 570, 576, 580–582, 585, 587; **II:** 537; **III:** 539; **Retro. Supp. I:** 66, 67; **Supp. II Part 1:** 1; **Supp. IV Part 1:** 284; **Supp. V:** 343, 344; **Supp. VIII:** 182, 195; **Supp. XIII:** 344; **Supp.**

XIV:167; **Supp. XV:** 216, 260, 266

Four Saints in Three Acts (Stein), **IV:** 30, 31, 33, 43, 44–45

"Four Seasons" (Bradstreet), **Supp. I Part 1:** 112–113

"Four Sides of One Story" (Updike), **Retro. Supp. I:** 328

"Four Skinny Trees" (Cisneros), **Supp. VII:** 64

"14: In A Dark Wood: Wood Thrushes" (Oliver), **Supp. VII:** 244

Fourteen Hundred Thousand (Shepard), **Supp. III Part 2:** 439

"14 Men Stage Head Winter 1624/ 25" (Olson), **Supp. II Part 2:** 574

Fourteen Sisters of Emilio Montez O'Brien, The (Hijuelos), **Supp. VIII:** 82–85

Fourteen Stories (Buck), **Supp. II Part 1:** 126

14 Stories (Dixon), **Supp. XII:** 141, 145–147

"Fourteenth Ward, The" (H. Miller), **III:** 175

Fourth Book of Peace, The (Kingston), **Supp. V:** 173

"Fourth Down" (Marquand), **III:** 56

Fourth Group of Verse, A (Reznikoff), **Supp. XIV:**282, 284

"Fourth of July in Maine" (Lowell), **II:** 535, 552–553

Fourth Wall, The (Gurney), **Supp. V:** 109–110

Fowler, Douglas, **Supp. IV Part 1:** 226, 227

Fowler, Gene, **Supp. VIII:** 290

Fowler, Henry Watson, **Supp. I Part 2:** 660

Fowler, Singrid, **Supp. VIII:** 249, 258

Fowler, Virginia C., **Supp. VIII:** 224

Fox, Alan, **Supp. XIII:** 120

Fox, Dixon Ryan, **I:** 337

Fox, Joe, **Supp. IX:** 259, 261

Fox, John, **Supp. XIII:** 166

Fox, Linda C., **Supp. XIII:** 217–218

Fox, Ruth, **Supp. I Part 2:** 619

"Fox, The" (Levine), **Supp. V:** 181, 189

Fox-Genovese, Elizabeth, **Supp. IV Part 1:** 286

Fox in Socks (Geisel), **Supp. XVI:**108, 112

Fox of Peapack, The (White), **Supp. I Part 2:** 676, 677–678

"Fox of Peapack, The" (White), **Supp. I Part 2:** 677

Foye, Raymond, **Supp. XIV:**150

Fraenkel, Michael, **III:** 178, 183

"Fragging" (Komunyakaa), **Supp. XIII:** 123

Fragile Beauty, A: John Nichols' Milagro Country: Text and Photographs from His Life and Work (Nichols), **Supp. XIII:** 268

"Fragility" (Shields), **Supp. VII:** 318

"Fragment" (Ashbery), **Supp. III Part 1:** 11, 13, 14, 19, 20

"Fragment" (Lowell), **II:** 516

"Fragment" (Ortiz), **Supp. IV Part 2:** 507

"Fragment of a Meditation" (Tate), **IV:** 129

"Fragment of an Agon" (Eliot), **I:** 579–580

"Fragment of a Prologue" (Eliot), **I:** 579–580

"Fragment of New York, 1929" (Eberhart), **I:** 536–537

"Fragments" (Emerson), **II:** 19

"Fragments for Fall" (Salinas), **Supp. XIII:** 320–321

"Fragments of a Hologram Rose" (W. Gibson), **Supp. XVI:**122, 123, 128

"Fragments of a Liquidation" (Howe), **Supp. IV Part 2:** 426

Fragonard, Jean Honoré, **III:** 275; **IV:** 79

Fraiman, Susan, **Supp. IV Part 1:** 324

"Frame for Poetry, A" (W. J. Smith), **Supp. XIII:** 333

France, Anatole, **IV:** 444; **Supp. I Part 2:** 631; **Supp. XIV:**79

France and England in North America (Parkman), **Supp. II Part 2:** 596, 600–605, 607, 613–614

Franchere, Hoyt C., **II:** 131

Franchiser, The (Elkin), **Supp. VI:** 51–52, 58

Franciosi, Robert, **Supp. XIV:**283

Francis, Lee, **Supp. IV Part 2:** 499

Francis, Richard, **Supp. XV:** 121

Francis, Robert, **Supp. IX:** 75–92

Francis of Assisi, Saint, **III:** 543; **IV:** 69, 375, 410; **Supp. I Part 2:** 394, 397, 441, 442, 443

Franco, Francisco, **II:** 261

Franconia (Fraser), **Retro. Supp. I:** 136

"Franconia" tales (Abbott), **Supp. I Part 1:** 38

Frank, Anne, **Supp. X:** 149

Frank, Frederick S., **Retro. Supp. II:** 273

Frank, James M., **Supp. XIV:**1

Frank, Jerome, **Supp. I Part 2:** 645

Frank, Joseph, **II:** 587

Frank, Mary, **Supp. X:** 213

Frank, Robert, **Supp. XI:** 295; **Supp. XII:** 127; **Supp. XIV:**150

Frank, Waldo, **I:** 106, 109, 117, 229, 236, 245, 259, 400; **Retro. Supp. II:** 77, 79, 83; **Supp. IX:** 308, 309, 311, 320; **Supp. XV:** 298

Frankel, Charles, **III:** 291

Frankel, Haskel, **Supp. I Part 2:** 448

Frankenberg, Lloyd, **I:** 436, 437, 445, 446; **III:** 194

Frankenheimer, John, **Supp. XI:** 343

Frankenstein (film), **Supp. IV Part 1:** 104

Frankenstein (Gardner), **Supp. VI:** 72

Frankenstein (Shelley), **Supp. XII:** 79

Frankfurter, Felix, **I:** 489

"Frankie" (Keillor), **Supp. XVI:**167

Frankie and Johnny (film), **Supp. XIII:** 206

Frankie and Johnny in the Clair de Lune (McNally), **Supp. XIII:** 200, 201

Franklin, Benjamin, **II:** 6, 8, 92, 101–125, 127, 295, 296, 302, 306; **III:** 74, 90; **IV:** 73, 193; **Supp. I Part 1:** 306; **Supp. I Part 2:** 411, 503, 504, 506, 507, 510, 516, 518, 522, 524, 579, 639; **Supp. VIII:** 202, 205; **Supp. XIII:** 150; **Supp. XIV:**306

Franklin, Cynthia, **Supp. IV Part 1:** 332

Franklin, R. W., **Retro. Supp. I:** 29, 41, 43, 47

Franklin, Ruth, **Supp. XVI:**160

Franklin, Sarah, **II:** 122

Franklin, Temple, **II:** 122

Franklin, William, **II:** 122; **Supp. I Part 2:** 504

Franklin Evans (Whitman), **Retro. Supp. I:** 393

"Frank O'Connor and *The New Yorker*" (Maxwell), **Supp. VIII:** 172

Franks, Lucinda, **Supp. XIII:** 12

"Frank Stanford of the Mulberry Family: An Arkansas Epilogue" (Wright), **Supp. XV:** 339–340

"Franny" (Salinger), **III:** 564, 565–566

Franny and Zooey (Salinger), **III:** 552, 564–567; **IV:** 216; **Supp. XIII:** 263

Franzen, Jonathan, **Retro. Supp. II:** 279

Fraser, G. S., **Supp. XII:** 128; **Supp. XIV:**162

Fraser, Joe, **III:** 46

Fraser, Marjorie Frost, **Retro. Supp. I:** 136

Frayn, Michael, **Supp. IV Part 2:** 582

Frazee, E. S., **Supp. I Part 2:** 381

Frazee, Esther Catherine. *See* Lindsay, Mrs. Vachel Thomas (Esther Catherine Frazee)

Frazer, Sir James G., **I:** 135; **II:** 204; **III:** 6–7; **IV:** 70; **Retro.**

Supp. I: 80; **Supp. I Part 1:** 18; **Supp. I Part 2:** 541

Frazier, Ian, **Supp. VIII:** 272

Freaks: Myths and Images of the Secret Self (Fiedler), **Supp. XIII:** 106, 107

"Freak Show, The" (Sexton), **Supp. II Part 2:** 695

Freddy's Book (Gardner), **Supp. VI:** 72

Frederic, Harold, **I:** 409; **II:** 126–149, 175, 276, 289; **Retro. Supp. I:** 325

"Frederick Douglass" (Dunbar), **Supp. II Part 1:** 197, 199

"Frederick Douglass" (Hayden), **Supp. II Part 1:** 363

Frederick the Great, **II:** 103; **Supp. I Part 2:** 433

Fredrickson, George M., **Supp. I Part 2:** 589

"Free" (O'Hara), **III:** 369

Free, and Other Stories (Dreiser), **Retro. Supp. II:** 104

Free Air (Lewis), **II:** 441

Freedman, Monroe H., **Supp. VIII:** 127

Freedman, Richard, **Supp. V:** 244

"Freedom" (White), **Supp. I Part 2:** 659

"Freedom, New Hampshire" (Kinnell), **Supp. III Part 1:** 238, 239, 251

"Freedom and Discipline" (Carruth), **Supp. XVI:**50

Freedom Is the Right to Choose: An Inquiry into the Battle for the American Future (MacLeish), **III:** 3

"Freedom's a Hard-Bought Thing" (Benét), **Supp. XI:** 47, 48

"Freedom's Plow" (Hughes), **Supp. I Part 1:** 346

"Free Fantasia: Tiger Flowers" (Hayden), **Supp. II Part 1:** 363, 366

Freeing of the Dust, The (Levertov), **Supp. III Part 1:** 281–282

"Free Lance, The" (Mencken), **III:** 104, 105

Free-Lance Pallbearers, The (Reed), **Supp. X:** 240, 242–243, 244

Freeloaders, The (Lacy), **Supp. XV:** 204

"Free Man" (Hughes), **Supp. I Part 1:** 333

Freeman, Chris, **Supp. XIV:**157, 159

Freeman, Douglas Southall, **Supp. I Part 2:** 486, 493

Freeman, Joseph, **II:** 26; **Supp. I Part 2:** 610

Freeman, Mary E. Wilkins, **II:** 401; **Supp. IX:** 79

Freeman, Mary Wilkins, **Retro. Supp. II:** 51, 136, 138

Freeman, Morgan, **Supp. XII:** 317

Freeman, Suzanne, **Supp. X:** 83

"Free Man's Worship, A" (Russell), **Supp. I Part 2:** 522

Freilicher, Jane, **Supp. XV:** 178

Freinman, Dorothy, **Supp. IX:** 94

Frémont, John Charles, **Supp. I Part 2:** 486

Fremont-Smith, Eliot, **Supp. XIII:** 263

Fremstad, Olive, **I:** 319; **Retro. Supp. I:** 10

French, Warren, **Supp. XII:** 118–119

French Connection, The (film), **Supp. V:** 226

French Leave (X. J. Kennedy), **Supp. XV:** 165

French Poets and Novelists (James), **II:** 336; **Retro. Supp. I:** 220

"French Scarecrow, The" (Maxwell), **Supp. VIII:** 169, 170

French Ways and Their Meaning (Wharton), **IV:** 319; **Retro. Supp. I:** 378

Freneau, Eleanor Forman (Mrs. Philip Freneau), **Supp. II Part 1:** 266

Freneau, Philip M., **I:** 335; **II:** 295; **Supp. I Part 1:** 124, 125, 127, 145; **Supp. II Part 1:** 65, 253–277

Frescoes for Mr. Rockefeller's City (MacLeish), **III:** 14–15

"Fresh Air" (Koch), **Supp. XV:** 181, 185

Fresh Air Fiend: Travel Writings, 1985–2000 (Theroux), **Supp. VIII:** 325

Fresh Brats (X. J. Kennedy), **Supp. XV:** 163

"Freshman" (Sanders), **Supp. XVI:** 277

Freud, Sigmund, **I:** 55, 58, 59, 66, 67, 135, 241, 242, 244, 247, 248, 283; **II:** 27, 370, 546–547; **III:** 134, 390, 400, 418, 488; **IV:** 7, 70, 138, 295; **Retro. Supp. I:** 80, 176, 253; **Retro. Supp. II:** 104; **Supp. I Part 1:** 13, 43, 253, 254, 259, 260, 265, 270, 315; **Supp. I Part 2:** 493, 527, 616, 643, 647, 649; **Supp. IV Part 2:** 450; **Supp. VIII:** 103, 196; **Supp. IX:** 102, 155, 161, 308; **Supp. X:** 193, 194; **Supp. XII:** 14–15; **Supp. XIII:** 75; **Supp. XIV:** 83; **Supp. XV:** 219; **Supp. XVI:** 157–158, 161, 292

Freud: The Mind of the Moralist (Sontag and Rieff), **Supp. III Part 2:** 455

"Freud: Within and Beyond Culture" (Trilling), **Supp. III Part 2:** 508

"Freud and Literature" (Trilling), **Supp. III Part 2:** 502–503

Freudian Psychology and Veblen's Social Theory, The (Schneider), **Supp. I Part 2:** 650

Freudian Wish and Its Place in Ethics, The (Holt), **I:** 59

"Freud's Room" (Ozick), **Supp. V:** 268

"Friday Morning Trial of Mrs. Solano, The" (Ríos), **Supp. IV Part 2:** 538, 548

Frieburger, William, **Supp. XIII:** 239

Friedenberg, Edgar Z., **Supp. VIII:** 240

Friedman, Bruce Jay, **I:** 161; **Supp. IV Part 1:** 379

Friedman, Lawrence S., **Supp. V:** 273

Friedman, Milton, **Supp. I Part 2:** 648

Friedman, Norman, **I:** 431–432, 435, 439

Friedman, Stan, **Supp. XII:** 186

Friedmann, Georges, **Supp. I Part 2:** 645

"Fried Sausage" (Simic), **Supp. VIII:** 270

Friend, Julius, **Retro. Supp. I:** 80

Friend, The (Coleridge), **II:** 10

"Friend Husband's Latest" (Sayre), **Retro. Supp. I:** 104

"Friendly Debate between a Conformist and a Non-Conformist, A" (Wild), **IV:** 155

"Friendly Neighbor" (Keillor), **Supp. XVI:** 172

Friend of the Earth (Boyle), **Supp. VIII:** 12, 16

"Friend of the Fourth Decade, The" (Merrill), **Supp. III Part 1:** 327

"Friends" (Beattie), **Supp. V:** 23, 27

"Friends" (Paley), **Supp. VI:** 219, 226

"Friends" (Sexton), **Supp. II Part 2:** 693

Friends: More Will and Magna Stories (Dixon), **Supp. XII:** 148, 149

Friend's Delight, The (Bierce), **I:** 195

"Friends from Philadelphia" (Updike), **Retro. Supp. I:** 319

"Friendship" (Emerson), **Supp. II Part 1:** 290

"Friends of Heraclitus, The" (Simic), **Supp. VIII:** 284

"Friends of Kafka, The" (Singer), **Retro. Supp. II:** 308

"Friends of the Family, The" (McCarthy), **II:** 566

"Friend to Alexander, A" (Thurber), **Supp. I Part 2:** 616

"Frigate Pelican, The" (Moore), **III:** 208, 210–211, 215

"Frill, The" (Buck), **Supp. XIV:** 274

"Fringe, The" (Bass), **Supp. XVI:** 19

Frobenius, Leo, **III:** 475; **Supp. III Part 2:** 620

Froebel, Friedrich, **Supp. XIV:** 52–53

Frog (Dixon), **Supp. XII:** 151

"Frog Dances" (Dixon), **Supp. XII:** 151

"Frog Pond, The" (Kinnell), **Supp. III Part 1:** 254

"Frog Takes a Swim" (Dixon), **Supp. XII:** 152

Frohock, W. M., **I:** 34, 42

Frolic of His Own, A (Gaddis), **Supp. IV Part 1:** 279, 291, 292–294

"From a Mournful Village" (Jewett), **Retro. Supp. II:** 146

"From an Old House in America" (Rich), **Supp. I Part 2:** 551, 565–567

From Another World (Untermeyer), **Supp. XV:** 293, 303, 310–311, 313

"From a Survivor" (Rich), **Supp. I Part 2:** 563

From A to Z (musical review; Allen), **Supp. XV:** 3, 13

From a Writer's Notebook (Brooks), **I:** 254

From Bauhaus to Our House (Wolfe), **Supp. III Part 2:** 580, 581, 584

From Bondage (H. Roth), **Supp. IX:** 236, 238–240

"From *Chants* to *Borders* to *Communion*" (Fox), **Supp. XIII:** 217–218

"From Chicago" (Anderson), **I:** 108–109

From Death to Morning (Wolfe), **IV:** 450, 456, 458

"From Feathers to Iron" (Kunitz), **Supp. III Part 1:** 261

"From Fifth Avenue Up" (Barnes), **Supp. III Part 1:** 33, 44

"From Gorbunov and Gorchakov" (Brodsky), **Supp. VIII:** 26

"From Grand Canyon to Burbank" (H. Miller), **III:** 186

"From Hell to Breakfast," **Supp. IX:** 326–327

From Here to Eternity (film), **Supp. XI:** 221

From Here to Eternity (Jones), **I:** 477; **Supp. XI:** 215, 216, 217, 218, 219–221, 223, 224, 226, 229, 230, 231, 232, 234

From Here to Eternity (miniseries), **Supp. XI:** 234

From Jordan's Delight (Blackmur), **Supp. II Part 1:** 91

Fromm, Erich, **I:** 58; **Supp. VIII:** 196

From Morn to Midnight (Kaiser), **I:** 479

"From Native Son to Invisible Man" (Locke), **Supp. IX:** 306

"From Pico, the Women: A Life" (Creeley), **Supp. IV Part 1:** 149

From Ritual to Romance (Weston), **II:** 540; **III:** 12; **Supp. I Part 2:** 439

From Room to Room (Kenyon), **Supp. VII:** 163–165, 166, 167

"From Room to Room" (Kenyon), **Supp. VII:** 159, 163–165

From Sand Creek: Rising in this Heart Which Is Our America (Ortiz), **Supp. IV Part 2:** 512–513

"From Sea Cliff, March" (Swenson), **Supp. IV Part 2:** 649

"From the Antigone" (Yeats), **III:** 459

From the Barrio: A Chicano Anthology (Salinas and Faderman, eds.), **Supp. XIII:** 313

"From the Childhood of Jesus" (Pinsky), **Supp. VI:** 244–245, 247

"From the Corpse Woodpiles, From the Ashes" (Hayden), **Supp. II Part 1:** 370

"From the Country to the City" (Bishop), **Supp. I Part 1:** 85, 86

"From the Cupola" (Merrill), **Supp. III Part 1:** 324–325, 331

"From the Dark Side of the Earth" (Oates), **Supp. II Part 2:** 510

"From the Diary of a New York Lady" (Parker), **Supp. IX:** 201

"From the Diary of One Not Born" (Singer), **IV:** 9

"From the East, Light" (Carver), **Supp. III Part 1:** 138

From the First Nine: Poems 1946–1976 (Merrill), **Supp. III Part 1:** 336

"From the Flats" (Lanier), **Supp. I Part 1:** 364

From the Flower Courtyard (Everwine), **Supp. XV:** 75

From the Heart of Europe (Matthiessen), **III:** 310

From the Meadow: Selected and New Poems (Everwine), **Supp. XV:** 75, 88–89

"From the Memoirs of a Private Detective" (Hammett), **Supp. IV Part 1:** 343

"From the Nursery" (Kenyon), **Supp. VII:** 171

"From the Poets in the Kitchen" (Marshall), **Supp. XI:** 277

From the Terrace (O'Hara), **III:** 362

"From the Thirties: Tillie Olsen and the Radical Tradition" (Rosenfelt), **Supp. XIII:** 296, 304

"From Trollope's Journal" (Bishop), **Retro. Supp. II:** 47

"Front, A" (Jarrell), **II:** 374

Front, The (film), **Supp. I Part 1:** 295

"Front and the Back Parts of the House, The" (Maxwell), **Supp. VIII:** 169

Frontier Eden (Bigelow), **Supp. X:** 227

"Frontiers of Culture" (Locke), **Supp. XIV:** 213

"Front Lines" (Snyder), **Supp. VIII:** 301

Frost, A. B., **Retro. Supp. II:** 72

"Frost: A Dissenting Opinion" (Cowley), **Supp. II Part 1:** 143

Frost: A Time to Talk (Francis), **Supp. IX:** 76, 85–86

Frost, Carol, **Supp. XV:** 91–109

"Frost: He Is Sometimes a Poet and Sometimes a Stump-Speaker" (News-Week), **Retro. Supp. I:** 137

Frost, Isabelle Moodie, **II:** 150, 151

Frost, Jeanie, **II:** 151

Frost, Richard, **Supp. XV:** 92

Frost, Robert, **I:** 26, 27, 60, 63, 64, 171, 229, 303, 326, 418; **II:** 55, 58, 150–172, 276, 289, 388, 391, 471, 523, 527, 529, 535; **III:** 5, 23, 67, 269, 271, 272, 275, 287, 453, 510, 523, 536, 575, 581, 591; **IV:** 140, 190, 415; **Retro. Supp. I:** 67, 121–144, 276, 287, 292, 298, 299, 311, 413; **Retro. Supp. II:** 40, 47, 50, 146, 178, 181; **Supp. I Part 1:** 80, 242, 263, 264; **Supp. I Part 2:** 387, 461, 699; **Supp. II Part 1:** 4, 19, 26, 103; **Supp. III Part 1:** 63, 74–75, 239, 253; **Supp. III Part 2:** 546, 592, 593; **Supp. IV Part 1:** 15; **Supp. IV Part 2:** 439, 445, 447, 448, 599, 601; **Supp. VIII:** 20, 30, 32, 98, 100, 104, 259, 292; **Supp. IX:** 41, 42, 75, 76, 80, 87, 90, 266, 308; **Supp. X:** 64, 65, 66, 74, 120, 172; **Supp. XI:** 43, 123, 150, 153, 312; **Supp. XII:** 130, 241, 303, 307; **Supp. XIII:** 143, 147, 334–335; **Supp. XIV:** 42, 122, 222, 229; **Supp. XV:** 21, 51, 65, 96, 212, 215, 250, 256, 293, 296, 299, 301, 302, 306, 348

Frost, William Prescott, **II:** 150–151

"Frost at Midnight" (Coleridge), **Supp. X:** 71

"Frost Flowers" (Kenyon), **Supp. VII:** 168

Frothingham, Nathaniel, **I:** 3

Frothingham, Octavius B., **IV:** 173

"Frozen City, The" (Nemerov), **III:** 270

"Frozen Fields, The" (Bowles), **Supp. IV Part 1:** 80

"Fruit Garden Path, The" (Lowell), **II:** 516

"Fruit of the Flower" (Cullen), **Supp. IV Part 1:** 167

Fruit of the Tree, The (Wharton), **IV:** 314–315; **Retro. Supp. I:** 367, 370–371, 373

"Fruit of Travel Long Ago" (Melville), **III:** 93

Fruits and Vegetables (Jong), **Supp. V:** 113, 115, 117, 118, 119

Frumkes, Lewis Burke, **Supp. XII:** 335–336

Fry, Christopher, **Supp. I Part 1:** 270

Fry, Roger, **Supp. XIV:** 336

Frye, Joanne, **Supp. XIII:** 292, 296, 298, 302

Frye, Northrop, **Supp. I Part 2:** 530; **Supp. II Part 1:** 101; **Supp. X:** 80; **Supp. XIII:** 19; **Supp. XIV:** 11, 15; **Supp. XVI:** 149, 156

Fryer, Judith, **Retro. Supp. I:** 379

Fuchs, Daniel, **Supp. XIII:** 106

Fuchs, Miriam, **Supp. IV Part 1:** 284

Fuehrer Bunker, The (Snodgrass), **Supp. VI:** 314, 315–317, 319–321

Fuel (Nye), **Supp. XIII:** 277, 282–284

"Fuel" (Nye), **Supp. XIII:** 283

Fuertes, Gloria, **Supp. V:** 178

Fugard, Athol, **Supp. VIII:** 330; **Supp. XIII:** 205

Fugitive Group, The (Cowan), **IV:** 120

Fugitive Kind, The (T. Williams), **IV:** 381, 383

Fugitives, The (group), **IV:** 122, 124, 125, 131, 237, 238

Fugitives, The: A Critical Account (Bradbury), **IV:** 130

"Fugitive Slave Law, The" (Emerson), **II:** 13

Fugitive's Return (Glaspell), **Supp. III Part 1:** 182–184

Fuller, B. A. G., **III:** 605

Fuller, Jesse "Lonecat," **Supp. XV:** 147

Fuller, Margaret, **I:** 261; **II:** 7, 276; **IV:** 172; **Retro. Supp. I:** 155–156, 163; **Retro. Supp. II:** 46; **Supp. I Part 2:** 524; **Supp. II Part 1:** 279–306; **Supp. IX:** 37

Fuller, Thomas, **II:** 111, 112

Fullerton Street (Wilson), **Supp. VIII:** 331

"Full Fathom Five" (Plath), **Supp. I Part 2:** 538

Full Measure: Modern Short Stories on Aging (D. Sennett, ed.), **Supp. XVI:** 37

Full Monty, The (musical, McNally), **Supp. XIII:** 207

"Full Moon" (Hayden), **Supp. II Part 1:** 370

"Full Moon: New Guinea" (Shapiro), **Supp. II Part 2:** 707

Full Moon and Other Plays (Price), **Supp. VI:** 266

"Full Moon and You're Not Here" (Cisneros), **Supp. VII:** 71–72

"Fullness of Life, The" (Wharton), **Retro. Supp. I:** 363

Full of Life (Fante), **Supp. XI:** 160

Full of Life (film), **Supp. XI:** 170

Full of Lust and Good Usage (Dunn), **Supp. XI:** 145–147

"Full Summer" (Olds), **Supp. X:** 212

Fulton, Robert, **Supp. I Part 2:** 519; **Supp. II Part 1:** 73

Function of Criticism, The (Winters), **Supp. II Part 2:** 812, 813

"Fundamentalism" (Tate), **IV:** 125

"Fundamental Project of Technology, The" (Kinnell), **Supp. III Part 1:** 253

"Funeral of Bobò, The" (Brodsky), **Supp. VIII:** 27, 28

"Funnel" (Sexton), **Supp. II Part 2:** 675

"Furious Seasons, The" (Carver), **Supp. III Part 1:** 137

Furious Seasons and Other Stories (Carver), **Supp. III Part 1:** 142, 143, 146

"Furious Versions" (L.-Y. Lee), **Supp. XV:** 215–217, 218, 220

"Furnished Room, The" (Hayden), **Supp. II Part 1:** 386–387, 394, 397, 399, 406, 408

"Furor Scribendi" (O. Butler), **Supp. XIII:** 70

Fur Person, The (Sarton), **Supp. VIII:** 264–265

Further Adventures with You (Wright), **Supp. XV:** 339, 342, 343–345

Further Fables for Our Time (Thurber), **Supp. I Part 2:** 612

"Further in Summer than the Birds" (Dickinson), **I:** 471

Further Poems of Emily Dickinson (Bianchi and Hampson, ed.), **Retro. Supp. I:** 35

Further Range, A (Frost), **II:** 155; **Retro. Supp. I:** 132, 136, 137, 138, 139

"Fury of Aerial Bombardment, The" (Eberhart), **I:** 535–536

"Fury of Flowers and Worms, The" (Sexton), **Supp. II Part 2:** 694

"Fury of Rain Storms, The" (Sexton), **Supp. II Part 2:** 695

Fury of the Jungle (film), **Supp. XIII:** 163

Fussell, Paul, **Supp. V:** 241

"Future, if Any, of Comedy, The" (Thurber), **Supp. I Part 2:** 620

Future is Ours, Comrade, The: Conversations with the Russians (Kosinski), **Supp. VII:** 215

Futureland: Nine Stories of an Imminent World (Mosley), **Supp. XIII:** 247–249

"Future Life, The" (Bryant), **Supp. I Part 1:** 170

Future Punishment of the Wicked, The (Edwards), **I:** 546

G

G. K. the DJ (Keillor), **Supp. XVI:**171

"Gabriel" (Rich), **Supp. I Part 2:** 557

Gabriel, Ralph H., **Supp. I Part 1:** 251

Gabriel, Trip, **Supp. V:** 212

Gabriel Conroy (Harte), **Supp. II Part 1:** 354

"Gabriel's Truth" (Kenyon), **Supp. VII:** 166

Gaddis, William, **Supp. IV Part 1:** 279–296; **Supp. IV Part 2:** 484; **Supp. V:** 52; **Supp. IX:** 208; **Supp. X:** 301, 302

Gadiot, Pud, **Supp. XI:** 295

Gain (Powers), **Supp. IX:** 212, 220–221

Gaines, Ernest, **Supp. X:** 250

Gaines, Ernest J., **Supp. X:** 24

Gaines, James R., **Supp. IX:** 190

Gaitens, Peter, **Supp. XV:** 65

Galamain, Ivan, **Supp. III Part 2:** 624

Galatea 2.2 (Powers), **Supp. IX:** 212, 219–220

"Galatea Encore" (Brodsky), **Supp. VIII:** 31

Galbraith, John Kenneth, **Supp. I Part 2:** 645, 650

Galdós, Benito Pérez. *See* Pérez Galdós, Benito

Gale, Zona, **Supp. I Part 2:** 613; **Supp. VIII:** 155

"Gale in April" (Jeffers), **Supp. II Part 2:** 423

Galignani, Giovanni Antonio, **II:** 315

Galileo Galilei, **I:** 480–481; **Supp. XII:** 180; **Supp. XIII:** 75

Gallagher, Tess, **Supp. XVI:**36

Gallant, Mavis, **Supp. VIII:** 151

Gallatin, Albert, **I:** 5

"Gallery" (Goldbarth), **Supp. XII:** 188

"Gallery of Real Creatures, A" (Thurber), **Supp. I Part 2:** 619

Gallico, Paul, **Supp. XVI:**238

Gallows Songs (Snodgrass), **Supp. VI:** 317

Gallup, Donald, **III:** 404, 478

Galsworthy, John, **III:** 70, 153, 382

Galton Case, The (Macdonald), **Supp. IV Part 2:** 463, 473, 474

"Gal Young 'Un" (Rawlings), **Supp. X:** 228

"Gambler, the Nun, and the Radio, The" (Hemingway), **II:** 250

"Gambler's Wife, The" (Dunbar), **Supp. II Part 1:** 196

Gambone, Philip, **Supp. XII:** 81

"Gambrel Roof, A" (Larcom), **Supp. XIII:** 144

"Game at Salzburg, A" (Jarrell), **II:** 384, 389

Game Management (Leopold), **Supp. XIV:**182

"Game of Catch, A" (Wilbur), **Supp. III Part 2:** 552

"Games in Frank Conroy's *Stop-Time*" (T. Adams), **Supp. XVI:**67

"Games Two" (Wilbur), **Supp. III Part 2:** 550

"Gamut, The" (Angelou), **Supp. IV Part 1:** 15

Gander, Forrest, **Supp. XV:** 339, 340, 342

Gandhi, Indira, **Supp. X:** 108

Gandhi, Mahatma, **III:** 179, 296–297; **IV:** 170, 185, 367; **Supp. VIII:** 203, 204; **Supp. X:** 27

Gandhi on Non-Violence (Merton, ed.), **Supp. VIII:** 204–205

"Gang of Mirrors, The" (Simic), **Supp. VIII:** 283

Gansevoort, Guert, **III:** 94

Gansevoort, Peter, **III:** 92

Garabedian, Michael, **Supp. XIII:** 115

Garbage (Ammons), **Supp. VII:** 24, 35–36

Garbage (Dixon), **Supp. XII:** 147, 148

Garbage Man, The (Dos Passos), **I:** 478, 479, 481, 493

Garber, Frederick, **Supp. IX:** 294–295

Garbo, Greta, **Supp. I Part 2:** 616

García, Cristina, **Supp. VIII:** 74; **Supp. XI:** 177–192

"García Lorca: A Photograph of the Granada Cemetery, 1966" (Levis), **Supp. XI:** 264

García Lorca, Federico. *See* Lorca, Federico García

García Márquez, Gabriel, **Supp. V:** 244; **Supp. VIII:** 81, 82, 84, 85; **Supp. XII:** 147, 310, 316, 322; **Supp. XIII:** 226

"Garden" (Marvell), **IV:** 161; **Supp. XVI:**204

"Garden, The" (Glück), **Supp. V:** 83

"Garden, The" (Strand), **Supp. IV Part 2:** 629

"Garden by Moonlight, The" (Lowell), **II:** 524

"Gardener Delivers a Fawn, The" (C. Frost), **Supp. XV:** 99

Gardener's Son, The (McCarthy), **Supp. VIII:** 187

"Gardenias" (Doty), **Supp. XI:** 122

"Gardenias" (Monette), **Supp. X:** 159

"Garden Lodge, The" (Cather), **I:** 316, 317

Garden of Adonis, The (Gordon), **II:** 196, 204–205, 209

Garden of Earthly Delights, A (Oates), **Supp. II Part 2:** 504, 507–509

"Garden of Eden" (Hemingway), **II:** 259

Garden of Eden, The (Hemingway), **Retro. Supp. I:** 186, 187–188

"Garden of the Moon, The" (Doty), **Supp. XI:** 122

"Gardens, The" (Oliver), **Supp. VII:** 236

"Gardens of Mont-Saint-Michel, The" (Maxwell), **Supp. VIII:** 169

"Gardens of the Villa D'Este, The" (Hecht), **Supp. X:** 59

"Gardens of Zuñi, The" (Merwin), **Supp. III Part 1:** 351

Gardiner, Judith Kegan, **Supp. IV Part 1:** 205

Gardner, Erle Stanley, **Supp. IV Part 1:** 121, 345

Gardner, Isabella, **IV:** 127

Gardner, John, **Supp. I Part 1:** 193, 195, 196; **Supp. III Part 1:** 136, 142, 146; **Supp. VI:** 61–76

Gardons, S. S. *See* Snodgrass, W. D.

Garfield, John, **Supp. XII:** 160

Garibaldi, Giuseppe, **I:** 4; **II:** 284

Garibay, Angel M., **Supp. XV:** 77

Garland, Hamlin, **I:** 407; **II:** 276, 289; **III:** 576; **Retro. Supp. I:** 133; **Retro. Supp. II:** 72; **Supp. I Part 1:** 217; **Supp. IV Part 2:** 502

Garland Companion, The (Zverev), **Retro. Supp. I:** 278

Garments the Living Wear (Purdy), **Supp. VII:** 278–279, 280–281

Garner, Dwight, **Supp. X:** 202

Garnett, Edward, **I:** 405, 409, 417; **III:** 27

Garrett, George P., **Supp. I Part 1:** 196; **Supp. VII:** 95–113; **Supp. X:** 3, 7; **Supp. XI:** 218

Garrigue, Jean, **Supp. XII:** 260

Garrison, Deborah, **Supp. IX:** 299

Garrison, Fielding, **III:** 105

Garrison, William Lloyd, **Supp. I Part

2:** 524, 588, 683, 685, 686, 687; **Supp. XIV:** 54

"Garrison of Cape Ann, The" (Whittier), **Supp. I Part 2:** 691, 694

Garry Moore Show (television show), **Supp. IV Part 2:** 575

"Garter Motif" (White), **Supp. I Part 2:** 673

Gartner, Zsuzsi, **Supp. X:** 276

Garvey, Marcus, **Supp. III Part 1:** 175, 180; **Supp. IV Part 1:** 168; **Supp. X:** 135, 136

Gas (Kaiser), **I:** 479

Gas-House McGinty (Farrell), **II:** 41–42

Gaskell, Elizabeth, A., **Supp. I Part 2:** 580

Gasoline (Corso), **Supp. XII:** 118, 121–123, 134

Gass, William H., **Supp. V:** 44, 52, 238; **Supp. VI:** 77–96; **Supp. IX:** 208; **Supp. XII:** 152; **Supp. XIV:** 305

Gassner, John, **IV:** 381; **Supp. I Part 1:** 284, 292

Gates, David, **Supp. V:** 24; **Supp. XIII:** 93; **Supp. XVI:** 73, 74

Gates, Elmer, **I:** 515–516

Gates, Henry Louis, **Retro. Supp. I:** 194, 195, 203; **Supp. X:** 242, 243, 245, 247

Gates, Lewis E., **III:** 315, 330

Gates, The (Rukeyser), **Supp. VI:** 271, 274, 281

"Gates, The" (Rukeyser), **Supp. VI:** 286

Gates, Tudor, **Supp. XI:** 307

Gates of Ivory, the Gates of Horn, The (McGrath), **Supp. X:** 118

Gates of Wrath, The; Rhymed Poems (Ginsberg), **Supp. II Part 1:** 311, 319

"Gathering of Dissidents, A" (Applebaum), **Supp. XVI:** 153

Gathering of Fugitives, A (Trilling), **Supp. III Part 2:** 506, 512

Gathering of Zion, The: The Story of the Mormon Trail (Stegner), **Supp. IV Part 2:** 599, 602–603

Gather Together in My Name (Angelou), **Supp. IV Part 1:** 2, 3, 4–6, 11

Gathorne-Hardy, Robert, **Supp. XIV:** 344, 347, 348, 349

Gaudier-Brzeska, Henri, **III:** 459, 464, 465, 477

Gauguin, Paul, **I:** 34; **IV:** 290; **Supp. IV Part 1:** 81; **Supp. XII:** 128

"Gauley Bridge" (Rukeyser), **Supp. VI:** 278

Gauss, Christian, **II:** 82; **IV:** 427, 439–440, 444

Gautier, Théophile, **II:** 543; **III:** 466, 467; **Supp. I Part 1:** 277

Gay, John, **II:** 111; **Supp. I Part 2:** 523; **Supp. XIV:** 337

Gay, Peter, **I:** 560

Gay, Sydney Howard, **Supp. I Part 1:** 158

Gay, Walter, **IV:** 317

Gayatri Prayer, The, **III:** 572

"Gay Chaps at the Bar" (Brooks), **Supp. III Part 1:** 74, 75

Gaylord, Winfield R., **III:** 579–580

"Gazebo" (Carver), **Supp. III Part 1:** 138, 144, 145

Gazer Within, The, and Other Essays by Larry Levis, **Supp. XI:** 270

Gazzara, Ben, **Supp. VIII:** 319

Gazzo, Michael V., **III:** 155

"Geese Gone Beyond" (Snyder), **Supp. VIII:** 304

"Gegenwart" (Goethe), **Supp. II Part 1:** 26

Geisel, Theodor Seuss (Dr. Seuss), **Supp. X:** 56; **Supp. XVI:** 97–115

Geismar, Maxwell, **II:** 178, 431; **III:** 71; **Supp. IX:** 15; **Supp. XI:** 223

Gelb, Arthur, **IV:** 380

Gelbart, Larry, **Supp. IV Part 2:** 591

Gelder, Robert Van, **Supp. XIII:** 166

Gelfant, Blanche H., **II:** 27, 41

Gelfman, Jean, **Supp. X:** 3

Gellhorn, Martha. *See* Hemingway, Mrs. Ernest (Martha Gellhorn)

Gelpi, Albert, **Supp. I Part 2:** 552, 554, 560

Gelpi, Barbara, **Supp. I Part 2:** 560

Gemini: an extended autobiographical statement on my first twenty-five years of being a black poet (Giovanni), **Supp. IV Part 1:** 11

"Gen" (Snyder), **Supp. VIII:** 302

"Gender Norms" (Radinovsky), **Supp. XV:** 285

"Gender of Sound, The" (Carson), **Supp. XII:** 106

"Genealogy" (Komunyakaa), **Supp. XIII:** 129

"General Aims and Theories" (Crane), **I:** 389

General Died at Dawn, The (Odets), **Supp. II Part 2:** 546

"General Gage's Confession" (Freneau), **Supp. II Part 1:** 257

"General Gage's Soliloquy" (Freneau), **Supp. II Part 1:** 257

General History of the Robberies and Murders of the Most Notorious

Pyrates from Their First Rise and Settlement in the Island of New Providence to the Present Year, A (Johnson), **Supp. V:** 128

"General William Booth Enters into Heaven" (Lindsay), **Supp. I Part 2:** 374, 382, 384, 385–388, 389, 392, 399

General William Booth Enters into Heaven and Other Poems (Lindsay), **Supp. I Part 2:** 379, 381, 382, 387–388, 391

"Generations of Men, The" (Frost), **Retro. Supp. I:** 128; **Supp. XIII:** 147

Generous Man, A (Price), **Supp. VI:** 259, 260, 261

Genesis (biblical book), **I:** 279; **II:** 540; **Retro. Supp. I:** 250, 256; **Supp. XII:** 54

"Genesis" (Stegner), **Supp. IV Part 2:** 604

Genesis: Book One (Schwartz), **Supp. II Part 2:** 640, 651–655

Genet, Jean, **I:** 71, 82, 83, 84; **Supp. IV Part 1:** 8; **Supp. XI:** 308; **Supp. XII:** 1; **Supp. XIII:** 74

"Genetic Expedition" (Dove), **Supp. IV Part 1:** 249, 257

"Genetics of Justice" (Alvarez), **Supp. VII:** 19

"Genial Host, The" (McCarthy), **II:** 564

"Genie in the Bottle, The" (Wilbur), **Supp. III Part 2:** 542

"Genius, The" (MacLeish), **III:** 19

Genius and Lust: A Journey through the Major Writings of Henry Miller (Mailer), **Retro. Supp. II:** 208

"Genius Child" (Hughes), **Retro. Supp. I:** 203

"Genius," The (Dreiser), **I:** 497, 501, 509–511, 519; **Retro. Supp. II:** 94–95, 102–103, 104, 105

"Genteel Tradition in American Philosophy, The" (Santayana), **I:** 222

"Gentle Communion" (Mora), **Supp. XIII:** 218–219

Gentle Crafter, The (O. Henry), **Supp. II Part 1:** 410

"Gentle Lena, The" (Stein), **IV:** 37, 40

Gentleman Caller, The (T. Williams), **IV:** 383

"Gentleman from Cracow, The" (Singer), **IV:** 9

"Gentleman of Bayou Têche, A" (Chopin), **Supp. I Part 1:** 211–212

"Gentleman of Shalott, The" (Bishop), **Supp. I Part 1:** 85, 86

Gentleman's Agreement (Hobson), **III:** 151

Gentlemen Prefer Blondes (Loos; musical adaptation), **Supp. XVI:**193

Gentlemen Prefer Blondes: The Illuminating Diary of a Professional Lady (Loos), **Supp. XVI:**181, 183, 186, 188–189

Gentlemen Prefer "Books" (J. Yeats), **Supp. XVI:**190

Gentry, Marshall Bruce, **Supp. IV Part 1:** 236

"Genuine Man, The" (Emerson), **II:** 10

Geo-Bestiary (Harrison), **Supp. VIII:** 53

"Geode" (Frost), **II:** 161

Geographical History of America, The (Stein), **IV:** 31, 45

Geography and Plays (Stein), **IV:** 29–30, 32, 43, 44

Geography III (Bishop), **Retro. Supp. II:** 50; **Supp. I Part 1:** 72, 73, 76, 82, 93, 94, 95

Geography of a Horse Dreamer (Shepard), **Supp. III Part 2:** 432

Geography of Home, The: California's Poetry of Place (Bluckey and Young, eds.), **Supp. XIII:** 313

Geography of Lograire, The (Merton), **Supp. VIII:** 208

Geography of the Heart (Johnson), **Supp. XI:** 129

"Geometric Poem, The" (Corso), **Supp. XII:** 132, 133–134

George, Diana Hume, **Supp. IV Part 2:** 447, 449, 450

George, Henry, **II:** 276; **Supp. I Part 2:** 518

George, Jan, **Supp. IV Part 1:** 268

George, Lynell, **Supp. XIII:** 234–235, 237, 249

George, Peter, **Supp. XI:** 302, 303, 304

George and the Dragon (Shanley), **Supp. XIV:**315

George Bernard Shaw: His Plays (Mencken), **III:** 102

George Mills (Elkin), **Supp. VI:** 53–54

"George Robinson: Blues" (Rukeyser), **Supp. VI:** 279

George's Mother (Crane), **I:** 408

"George Thurston" (Bierce), **I:** 202

George Washington Crossing the Delaware (Koch), **Supp. XV:** 186

"Georgia: Invisible Empire State" (Du Bois), **Supp. II Part 1:** 179

Georgia Boy (Caldwell), **I:** 288, 305–306, 308, 309, 310

"Georgia Dusk" (Toomer), **Supp. IX:** 309

"Georgia Night" (Toomer), **Supp. III** Part 2: 481

Georgia Scenes (Longstreet), **II:** 70, 313; **Supp. I Part 1:** 352

Georgics (Virgil), **Retro. Supp. I:** 135; **Supp. XVI:**22

Georgoudaki, Ekaterini, **Supp. IV Part 1:** 12

Gerald McBoing-Boing (film), **Supp. XVI:**102

"Geraldo No Last Name" (Cisneros), **Supp. VII:** 60–61

Gerald's Game (King), **Supp. V:** 141, 148–150, 151, 152

Gerald's Party (Coover), **Supp. V:** 49–50, 51, 52

Gérando, Joseph Marie de, **II:** 10

"Geranium" (O'Connor), **Retro. Supp. II:** 221, 236

Gerber, Dan, **Supp. VIII:** 39

Gerhardt, Rainer, **Supp. IV Part 1:** 142

"German Girls! The German Girls!, The" (MacLeish), **III:** 16

"German Refugee, The" (Malamud), **Supp. I Part 2:** 436, 437

"Germany's Reichswehr" (Agee), **I:** 35

Germinal (Zola), **III:** 318, 322

Gernsback, Hugo, **Supp. IV Part 1:** 101

"Gernsback Continuum, The" (W. Gibson), **Supp. XVI:**123, 128

"Gerontion" (Eliot), **I:** 569, 574, 577, 578, 585, 588; **III:** 9, 435, 436; **Retro. Supp. I:** 290; **Supp. XV:** 341; **Supp. XVI:**158–159

Gerry, Elbridge, **Supp. I Part 2:** 486

"Gerry's Jazz" (Komunyakaa), **Supp. XIII:** 125

Gershwin, Ira, **Supp. I Part 1:** 281

"Gert" (Monette), **Supp. X:** 158

Gertrude of Stony Island Avenue (Purdy), **Supp. VII:** 281–282

Gertrude Stein (Sprigge), **IV:** 31

Gertrude Stein: A Biography of Her Work (Sutherland), **IV:** 38

"Gertrude Stein and the Geography of the Sentence" (Gass), **Supp. VI:** 87

Gesell, Silvio, **III:** 473

"Gestalt at Sixty" (Sarton), **Supp. VIII:** 260

"Gesture toward an Unfound Renaissance, A" (Stafford), **Supp. XI:** 323

Getlin, Josh, **Supp. V:** 22; **Supp. VIII:** 75, 76, 78, 79

"Getting Along" (Larcom), **Supp. XIII:** 144

"Getting Along with Nature" (Berry), **Supp. X:** 31–32

"Getting Away from Already Pretty Much Being Away from It All"

(Wallace), **Supp. X:** 314–315

"Getting Born" (Shields), **Supp. VII:** 311

Getting Even (Allen), **Supp. XV:** 3, 14, 15

"Getting Lucky" (L. Michaels), **Supp. XVI:** 205, 209

"Getting Out of Jail on Monday" (Wagoner), **Supp. IX:** 327

"Getting There" (Plath), **Supp. I Part 2:** 539, 542

"Getting to the Poem" (Corso), **Supp. XII:** 135

Getty, J. Paul, **Supp. X:** 108

Getty, Norris, **Supp. XV:** 136–137, 138, 139, 142, 143, 145, 146

"Gettysburg: July 1, 1863" (Kenyon), **Supp. VII:** 172

Gettysburg, Manila, Acoma (Masters), **Supp. I Part 2:** 471

Ghachem, Malick, **Supp. X:** 17

"Ghazals: Homage to Ghalib" (Rich), **Supp. I Part 2:** 557

Ghost, The (Crane), **I:** 409, 421

"Ghost Chant, et alii" (Komunyakaa), **Supp. XIII:** 114

Ghost in the Music, A (Nichols), **Supp. XIII:** 267

"Ghostlier Demarcations, Keener Sounds" (Vendler), **Supp. I Part 2:** 565

"Ghostly Father, I Confess" (McCarthy), **II:** 565–566

Ghostly Lover, The (Hardwick), **Supp. III Part 1:** 194–196, 208, 209

"Ghost of the Buffaloes, The" (Lindsay), **Supp. I Part 2:** 393

Ghosts (Auster), **Supp. XII:** 22, 24, 26–27

Ghosts (Ibsen), **III:** 152

Ghosts (Wharton), **IV:** 316, 327

Ghost Town (Coover), **Supp. V:** 52–53

Ghost Writer, The (Roth), **Retro. Supp. II:** 22, 290, 291; **Supp. III Part 2:** 420–421

"G.I. Graves in Tuscany" (Hugo), **Supp. VI:** 138

Giachetti, Fosco, **Supp. IV Part 2:** 520

"Giacometti" (Wilbur), **Supp. III Part 2:** 551

Giacometti, Alberto, **Supp. VIII:** 168, 169

Giacomo, Padre, **II:** 278–279

Giant's House, The: A Romance (McCracken), **Supp. X:** 86

"Giant Snail" (Bishop), **Retro. Supp. II:** 49

Giant Weapon, The (Winters), **Supp. II Part 2:** 810

"Giant Woman, The" (Oates), **Supp. II Part 2:** 523

Gibbon, Edward, **I:** 4, 378; **IV:** 126; **Supp. I Part 2:** 503; **Supp. III Part 2:** 629; **Supp. XIII:** 75; **Supp. XIV:** 97

Gibbons, Kaye, **Supp. X:** 41–54; **Supp. XII:** 311

Gibbons, Reginald, **Supp. X:** 113, 124, 127; **Supp. XV:** 105

Gibbons, Richard, **Supp. I Part 1:** 107

"Gibbs" (Rukeyser), **Supp. VI:** 273

Gibbs, Barbara, **Supp. IV Part 2:** 644

Gibbs, Wolcott, **Supp. I Part 2:** 604, 618; **Supp. VIII:** 151

"GIBSON" (Baraka), **Supp. II Part 1:** 54

Gibson, Charles Dana, **Supp. X:** 184

Gibson, Graeme, **Supp. XIII:** 20

Gibson, Wilfrid W., **Retro. Supp. I:** 128

Gibson, William, **Supp. XVI:** 117–133

Giddins, Gary, **Supp. XIII:** 245

Gide, André, **I:** 271, 290; **II:** 581; **III:** 210; **IV:** 53, 289; **Supp. I Part 1:** 51; **Supp. IV Part 1:** 80, 284, 347; **Supp. IV Part 2:** 681, 682; **Supp. VIII:** 40; **Supp. X:** 187; **Supp. XIV:** 24, 348

Gideon Planish (Lewis), **II:** 455

Gielgud, John, **I:** 82; **Supp. XI:** 305

Gierow, Dr. Karl Ragnar, **III:** 404

Gifford, Bill, **Supp. XI:** 38

Gifford, Terry, **Supp. XVI:** 22

"Gift, The" (Creeley), **Supp. IV Part 1:** 153

"Gift, The" (Doolittle), **Supp. I Part 1:** 267

"Gift, The" (L.-Y. Lee), **Supp. XV:** 213, 214

Gift, The (Nabokov), **III:** 246, 255, 261–263; **Retro. Supp. I:** 264, 266, 268–270, 273, 274–275, 278

"Gift from the City, A" (Updike), **Retro. Supp. I:** 320

"Gift of God, The" (Robinson), **III:** 512, 517, 518–521, 524

Gift of the Black Folk, The: The Negroes in the Making of America (Du Bois), **Supp. II Part 1:** 179

"Gift of the Magi, The" (O. Henry), **Supp. II Part 1:** 394, 406, 408

"Gift of the *Osuo,* The" (Johnson), **Supp. VI:** 194

"Gift of the Prodigal, The" (Taylor), **Supp. V:** 314, 326

"Gift Outright, The" (Frost), **II:** 152; **Supp. IV Part 1:** 15

Gigi (Colette; stage adaptation, Loos), **Supp. XVI:** 193

"Gigolo" (Plath), **Retro. Supp. II:** 257

"Gila Bend" (Dickey), **Supp. IV Part 1:** 185–186

Gilbert, Jack, **Supp. IX:** 287

Gilbert, Peter, **Supp. IX:** 291, 300

Gilbert, Roger, **Supp. XI:** 124

Gilbert, Sandra M., **Retro. Supp. I:** 42; **Retro. Supp. II:** 324; **Supp. IX:** 66; **Supp. XV:** 270

Gilbert, Susan. *See* Dickinson, Mrs. William A.

Gilbert and Sullivan, **Supp. IV Part 1:** 389

Gil Blas (Le Sage), **II:** 290

Gilded Age, The (Twain), **III:** 504; **IV:** 198

Gilded Lapse of Time, A (Schnackenberg), **Supp. XV:** 258, 260–263

"Gilded Lapse of Time, A" (Schnackenberg), **Supp. XV:** 257

"Gilded Six-Bits, The" (Hurston), **Supp. VI:** 154–155

Gilder, R. W., **Retro. Supp. II:** 66; **Supp. I Part 2:** 418

Gildersleeve, Basil, **Supp. I Part 1:** 369

Giles, H. A., **Retro. Supp. I:** 289

Giles, James R., **Supp. IX:** 11, 15; **Supp. XI:** 219, 223–224, 228, 234

"Giles Corey of the Salem Farms" (Longfellow), **II:** 505, 506; **Retro. Supp. II:** 166, 167

Giles Goat-Boy (Barth), **I:** 121, 122–123, 129, 130, 134, 135–138; **Supp. V:** 39

Gill, Brendan, **Supp. I Part 2:** 659, 660

Gillespie, Nick, **Supp. XIV:** 298, 311

Gillette, Chester, **I:** 512

Gilligan, Carol, **Supp. XIII:** 216

Gillis, Jim, **IV:** 196

Gillis, Steve, **IV:** 195

Gilman, Charlotte Perkins, **Supp. I Part 2:** 637; **Supp. V:** 121, 284, 285; **Supp. XI:** 193–211; **Supp. XIII:** 295, 306; **Supp. XVI:** 84

Gilman, Daniel Coit, **Supp. I Part 1:** 361, 368, 370

Gilman, Richard, **IV:** 115; **Supp. IV Part 2:** 577; **Supp. XIII:** 100

Gilmore, Eddy, **Supp. I Part 2:** 618

Gilmore, Mikal, **Supp. XVI:** 123, 124

Gilpin, Charles, **III:** 392

Gilpin, Dewitt, **Supp. XV:** 197

Gilpin, Laura, **Retro. Supp. I:** 7

Gilpin, Sam, **Supp. V:** 213

Gilpin, William, **Supp. IV Part 2:** 603

"Gil's Furniture Bought & Sold" (Cisneros), **Supp. VII:** 61–62, 64

"Gimpel the Fool" (Singer), **IV:** 14; **Retro. Supp. II:** 22, 307

Gimpel the Fool and Other Stories (Singer), **IV:** 1, 7–9, 10, 12

"Gin" (Levine), **Supp. V:** 193

"Gingerbread House, The" (Coover), **Supp. V:** 42–43

Gingerbread Lady, The (Simon), **Supp. IV Part 2:** 580, 583–584, 588

Gingerich, Willard, **Supp. IV Part 2:** 510

Gingertown (McKay), **Supp. X:** 132, 139

Gingold, Hermione, **Supp. XV:** 13

Gingrich, Arnold, **Retro. Supp. I:** 113

Ginna, Robert, **Supp. IX:** 259

Ginsberg, Allen, **I:** 183; **Retro. Supp. I:** 411, 426, 427; **Retro. Supp. II:** 280; **Supp. II Part 1:** 30, 32, 58, 307–333; **Supp. III Part 1:** 2, 91, 96, 98, 100, 222, 226; **Supp. III Part 2:** 541, 627; **Supp. IV Part 1:** 79, 90, 322; **Supp. IV Part 2:** 502; **Supp. V:** 168, 336; **Supp. VIII:** 239, 242–243, 289; **Supp. IX:** 299; **Supp. X:** 120, 204; **Supp. XI:** 135, 297; **Supp. XII:** 118–119, 121–122, 124, 126, 130–131, 136, 182; **Supp. XIV:** 15, 53, 54, 125, 137, 141, 142, 143–144, 148, 150, 269, 280, 283; **Supp. XV:** 134, 177, 263; **Supp. XVI:** 123, 135

Gioia, Dana, **Supp. IX:** 279; **Supp. XII:** 209; **Supp. XIII:** 337; **Supp. XV:** 111–131, 251

Giono, Jean, **Supp. XVI:** 135

Giotto di Bondone, **Supp. I Part 2:** 438; **Supp. XI:** 126

Giovani, Regula, **Supp. XV:** 270

Giovanni, Nikki, **Supp. I Part 1:** 66; **Supp. II Part 1:** 54; **Supp. IV Part 1:** 11; **Supp. VIII:** 214

Giovanni's Room (Baldwin), **Retro. Supp. II:** 5, 6, 6–7, 8, 10; **Supp. I Part 1:** 51, 52, 55–56, 57, 60, 63, 67; **Supp. III Part 1:** 125

Giovannitti, Arturo, **I:** 476; **Supp. XV:** 299, 301, 302, 307

"Giraffe" (Swenson), **Supp. IV Part 2:** 651

Giraldi, Giovanni Battista. *See* Cinthio

"Girl" (Kincaid), **Supp. VII:** 182–183

"Girl, The" (Olds), **Supp. X:** 207

"Girl Friend Poems" (Wright), **Supp. XV:** 349

"Girl from Lynn Bathes Horse!!" (McCarriston), **Supp. XIV:** 266

"Girl from Red Lion, P.A., A" (Mencken), **III:** 111

Girl in Glass, The: Love Poems (W. J. Smith), **Supp. XIII:** 335

"Girl in the Grave, The" (McCoy), **Supp. XIII:** 170

Girl Like I, A (Loos), **Supp. XVI:** 181, 183, 184, 187, 194, 196

"Girl of the Golden West" (Didion), **Supp. IV Part 1:** 195, 208, 211

Girl of the Golden West, The (Puccini), **III:** 139

"Girl on a Scaffold" (C. Frost), **Supp. XV:** 98

"Girl on the Baggage Truck, The" (O'Hara), **III:** 371–372

Girls at Play (Theroux), **Supp. VIII:** 314, 315, 316, 317

"Girls at the Sphinx, The" (Farrell), **II:** 45

Girl Sleuth, The: A Feminist Guide (Mason), **Supp. VIII:** 133, 135, 139, 142

"Girl's Story, A" (Bambara), **Supp. XI:** 10–11

"Girl the Prince Liked, The" (Z. Fitzgerald), **Supp. IX:** 71

Girl Who Loved Tom Gordon, The (King), **Supp. V:** 138, 152

Girl with Curious Hair (Wallace), **Supp. X:** 301, 305–308

"Girl with Curious Hair" (Wallace), **Supp. X:** 306

"Girl with Silver Eyes, The" (Hammett), **Supp. IV Part 1:** 344, 345

"Girl with Talent, The" (Z. Fitzgerald), **Supp. IX:** 71

Girodias, Maurice, **III:** 171; **Supp. XI:** 297

Giroux, Robert, **Retro. Supp. II:** 177, 229, 235; **Supp. IV Part 1:** 280; **Supp. VIII:** 195; **Supp. XV:** 146

Gish, Dorothy, **Retro. Supp. I:** 103

Gish, Lillian, **Supp. XVI:** 184

Gissing, George, **II:** 138, 144

Gittings, Robert, **II:** 531

"Given" (C. Frost), **Supp. XV:** 96

"Give Us Back Our Country" (Masters), **Supp. I Part 2:** 472

"Give Way, Ye Gates" (Roethke), **III:** 536

"Give Your Heart to the Hawks" (Jeffers), **Supp. II Part 2:** 433

"Giving Blood" (Updike), **IV:** 226; **Retro. Supp. I:** 332

Giving Good Weight (McPhee), **Supp. III Part 1:** 307

"Giving in to You" (X. J. Kennedy), **Supp. XV:** 160

"Giving Myself Up" (Strand), **Supp. IV Part 2:** 627

Glackens, William, **Retro. Supp. II:** 103

Gladden, Washington, **III:** 293; **Supp. I Part 1:** 5

Gladstone, William Ewart, **Supp. I Part 2:** 419

"Gladys Poem, The" (Alvarez), **Supp. VII:** 10

"Glance at German 'Kultur,' A" (Bourne), **I:** 228

Glance Away, A (Wideman), **Supp. X:** 320

"Glance from the Bridge, A" (Wilbur), **Supp. III Part 2:** 551

Glance toward Shakespeare, A (Chapman), **Supp. XIV:** 44

Glanville-Hicks, Peggy, **Supp. IV Part 1:** 84

Glare (Ammons), **Supp. VII:** 35–36

Glasgow, Cary, **II:** 173, 182

Glasgow, Ellen, **II:** 173–195; **IV:** 328; **Supp. X:** 228, 234

Glasmon, Kubec, **Supp. XIII:** 166

Glaspell, Susan, **Supp. III Part 1:** 175–191; **Supp. X:** 46

"Glass" (Francis), **Supp. IX:** 80

Glass, Irony, and God (Carson), **Supp. XII:** 97, 104–106

"Glass Ark, The" (Komunyakaa), **Supp. XIII:** 129

Glass Bees, The (Jünger; Bogan and Mayer, trans.), **Supp. III Part 1:** 63

"Glass Blower of Venice" (Malamud), **Supp. I Part 2:** 450

"Glass Essay, The" (Carson), **Supp. XII:** 104–105

"Glass Face in the Rain, A: New Poems" (Stafford), **Supp. XI:** 327–328

Glass Key, The (Hammett), **Supp. IV Part 1:** 351–353

"Glass Meadows" (Bausch), **Supp. VII:** 53–54

Glass Menagerie, The (T. Williams), **I:** 81; **IV:** 378, 379, 380, 382, 383, 385, 386, 387, 388, 389, 390, 391, 392, 393–394, 395, 398; **Supp. IV Part 1:** 84

"Glass Mountain, The" (Barthelme), **Supp. IV Part 1:** 47

"Glass Tent, The" (Everwine), **Supp. XV:** 76

Glatstein, Jacob, **Supp. X:** 70

Glazer, Nathan, **Supp. VIII:** 93, 243

"Gleaners, The" (Merwin), **Supp. III Part 1:** 346

Gleanings in Europe (Cooper), **I:** 346

Gleason, Ralph J., **Supp. IX:** 16

Glenday, Michael, **Retro. Supp. II:** 210

Glengarry Glen Ross (film), **Supp. XIV:**242

Glengarry Glen Ross (Mamet), **Supp. XIV:**239, 240, 242, 245, 246, 250, 254, 255

Glimcher, Arne, **Supp. VIII:** 73

"Glimpses" (Jones), **Supp. XI:** 218

Glimpses of the Moon, The (Wharton), **II:** 189–190; **IV:** 322–323; **Retro. Supp. I:** 381

"Glimpses of Vietnamese Life" (Levertov), **Supp. III Part 1:** 282

Glisson, J. T., **Supp. X:** 234

Gloria Mundi (Frederic), **II:** 144–145

Gloria Naylor (Fowler), **Supp. VIII:** 224

Glorious Ones, The (Prose), **Supp. XVI:**251

Glory of Hera, The (Gordon), **II:** 196–197, 198, 199, 217–220

Glory of the Conquered, The (Glaspell), **Supp. III Part 1:** 176

Glossary of Literary Terms (Abrams), **Supp. XVI:**19

Glotfelty, Cheryll, **Supp. IX:** 25

Gluck, Christoph Willibald, **II:** 210, 211

Glück, Louise, **Supp. V:** 77–94; **Supp. VIII:** 272; **Supp. X:** 209; **Supp. XIV:**269; **Supp. XV:** 19, 252

"Glutton, The" (Shapiro), **Supp. II Part 2:** 705

"Glutton for Punishment, A" (Yates), **Supp. XI:** 341

Gnädiges Fräulein, The (T. Williams), **IV:** 382, 395, 398

Gnomes and Occasions (Nemerov), **III:** 269

Gnomologia (Fuller), **II:** 111

"Gnothis Seauton" (Emerson), **II:** 11, 18–19

Go (Holmes), **Supp. XIV:**144

"Goal of Intellectual Men, The" (Eberhart), **I:** 529–530

Go-Between, The (Hartley), **Supp. I Part 1:** 293

Gobineau, Joseph Arthur de, **Supp. XIV:**209

God (Allen), **Supp. XV:** 3

God and the American Writer (Kazin), **Supp. VIII:** 108–109

Godard, Jean-Luc, **Supp. I Part 2:** 558

Godbey (Masters), **Supp. I Part 2:** 472

God Bless You, Mr. Rosewater (Vonnegut), **Supp. II Part 2:** 758, 767, 768–769, 771, 772

Goddess Abides, The (Buck), **Supp. II Part 1:** 129, 131–132

Gödel, Kurt, **Supp. IV Part 1:** 43

Godfather (Puzo), **Supp. IV Part 1:** 390

"God in the Doorway" (Dillard), **Supp. VI:** 28

"God is a distant-stately Lover" (Dickinson), **I:** 471

Godkin, E. L., **II:** 274

God Knows (Heller), **Supp. IV Part 1:** 386, 388–389

God Made Alaska for the Indians (Reed), **Supp. X:** 241

God of His Fathers, The (London), **II:** 469

God of Vengeance (Asch), **IV:** 11

Go Down, Moses (Faulkner), **Retro. Supp. I:** 75, 82, 85, 86, 88, 89, 90, 92

"Go Down, Moses" (Faulkner), **II:** 71–72

Go Down, Moses (Hayden), **Supp. II Part 1:** 365

Go Down, Moses and Other Stories (Faulkner), **II:** 71; **Supp. X:** 52

"Go Down Death A Funeral Sermon" (Johnson), **Supp. IV Part 1:** 7

"God Rest Ye Merry, Gentlemen" (Hemingway), **IV:** 122

Godric (Buechner), **Supp. XII:** 53

Gods, The (Goldbarth), **Supp. XII:** 189, 190

Gods Arrive, The (Wharton), **IV:** 326–327; **Retro. Supp. I:** 382

"God Save the Rights of Man" (Freneau), **Supp. II Part 1:** 268

"Gods|Children" (Swenson), **Supp. IV Part 2:** 645

"God's Christ Theory" (Carson), **Supp. XII:** 106

God's Country and My People (Morris), **III:** 238

Gods Determinations touching his Elect: and the Elects Combat in their Conversion, and Coming up to God in Christ together with the Comfortable Effects thereof (Taylor), **IV:** 155–160, 165

God-Seeker, The (Lewis), **II:** 456

God's Favorite (Simon), **Supp. IV Part 2:** 575, 586, 588, 590

God's Little Acre (Caldwell), **I:** 288, 289, 290, 297, 298–302, 305–306, 309, 310

God's Man: A Novel in Wood Cuts (Ward), **I:** 31

Gods of Winter, The (Gioia), **Supp. XV:** 112, 121–125

"Gods of Winter, The" (Gioia), **Supp. XV:** 117

"God's Peace in November" (Jeffers), **Supp. II Part 2:** 420

"God Stiff" (Carson), **Supp. XII:** 106

God's Trombones (Johnson), **Supp. II Part 1:** 201

"God's Youth" (Untermeyer), **Supp. XV:** 296

"God the Father and the Empty House" (McCarriston), **Supp. XIV:**273

Godwin, William, **II:** 304; **III:** 415; **Supp. I Part 1:** 126, 146; **Supp. I Part 2:** 512, 513–514, 522, 709, 719

God without Thunder (Ransom), **III:** 495–496, 499

Goebbels, Josef, **III:** 560

Goebel, Irma, **Supp. X:** 95

Goen, C. C., **I:** 560

Goethe, Johann Wolfgang von, **I:** 181, 396, 587–588; **II:** 5, 6, 320, 344, 488, 489, 492, 502, 556; **III:** 395, 453, 607, 612, 616; **IV:** 50, 64, 173, 326; **Retro. Supp. I:** 360; **Retro. Supp. II:** 94; **Supp. I Part 2:** 423, 457; **Supp. II Part 1:** 26; **Supp. III Part 1:** 63; **Supp. IX:** 131, 308; **Supp. X:** 60; **Supp. XI:** 169

Go for the Body (Lacy), **Supp. XV:** 201, 204

Gogol, Nikolai, **I:** 296; **IV:** 1, 4; **Retro. Supp. I:** 266, 269; **Supp. VIII:** 14

Going, William T., **Supp. VIII:** 126

Going After Cacciato (O'Brien), **Supp. V:** 237, 238, 239, 244–246, 248, 249

Going All the Way (Wakefield), **Supp. VIII:** 43

"Going Critical" (Bambara), **Supp. XI:** 14

Going for the Rain (Ortiz), **Supp. IV Part 2:** 499, 505–508, 509, 514

"Going Home by Last Night" (Kinnell), **Supp. III Part 1:** 244

"Going Home in America" (Hardwick), **Supp. III Part 1:** 205

"Going North" (Salinas), **Supp. XIII:** 316

Going Places (L. Michaels), **Supp. XVI:**201, 203–206

"Going Places" (L. Michaels), **Supp. XVI:**203

Going South (Lardner and Buck), **II:** 427

Going To and Fro and Walking Up and Down (Reznikoff), **Supp. XIV:**280, 282, 284, 285

Going to Meet the Man (Baldwin), **Supp. I Part 1:** 60, 62–63

"Going to Meet the Man" (Baldwin), **Retro. Supp. II:** 8, 9; **Supp. I Part 1:** 62–63

"Going to Naples" (Welty), **IV:** 278; **Retro. Supp. I:** 352, 353

"Going to Shrewsbury" (Jewett), **II:** 393

"Going to the Bakery" (Bishop), **Supp. I Part 1:** 93

Going-to-the-Stars (Lindsay), **Supp. I Part 2:** 398

Going-to-the-Sun (Lindsay), **Supp. I Part 2:** 397–398

Going to the Territory (Ellison), **Retro. Supp. II:** 119, 123–124

"Going towards Pojoaque, A December Full Moon/72" (Harjo), **Supp. XII:** 218

"Going Under" (Dubus), **Supp. VII:** 83

"Gold" (Francis), **Supp. IX:** 82

Gold (O'Neill), **III:** 391

Gold, Michael, **II:** 26; **IV:** 363, 364, 365; **Retro. Supp. II:** 323; **Supp. I Part 1:** 331; **Supp. I Part 2:** 609; **Supp. XIV:**288

Goldbarth, Albert, **Supp. XII:** 175–195

Goldbarth's Book of Occult Phenomena (Goldbarth), **Supp. XII:** 181

Goldberg, S. L., **Supp. VIII:** 238

"Gold Bug, The" (Poe), **III:** 410, 413, 419, 420

Gold Bug Variations, The (Powers), **Supp. IX:** 210, 212, 216–217, 219

Gold Cell, The (Olds), **Supp. X:** 206–209

Gold Diggers, The (Monette), **Supp. X:** 153

Golde, Miss (Mencken's Secretary), **III:** 104, 107

Golden, Harry, **III:** 579, 581; **Supp. VIII:** 244

Golden, Mike, **Supp. XI:** 294, 295, 297, 299, 303

Golden Age, The (Gurney), **Supp. V:** 101–103

Golden Apples (Rawlings), **Supp. X:** 228–229, 230, 234

Golden Apples, The (Welty), **IV:** 261, 271–274, 281, 293; **Retro. Supp. I:** 341, 342, 343, 350–351, 352, 355

Golden Apples of the Sun, The (Bradbury), **Supp. IV Part 1:** 102, 103

Golden Book of Springfield, The (Lindsay), **Supp. I Part 2:** 376, 379, 395, 396

Golden Bough, The (Frazer), **II:** 204, 549; **III:** 6–7; **Supp. I Part 1:** 18; **Supp. IX:** 123; **Supp. X:** 124

Golden Bowl, The (James), **II:** 320, 333, 335; **Retro. Supp. I:** 215, 216, 218–219, 232, 234–235, 374

Golden Boy (Odets), **Supp. II Part 2:** 538, 539, 540–541, 546, 551

Golden Calves, The (Auchincloss), **Supp. IV Part 1:** 35

Golden Day, The (Mumford), **Supp. II Part 2:** 471, 475, 477, 483, 484, 488–489, 493

Golden Fleece, The (Gurney), **Supp. V:** 97

Golden Grove, The: Selected Passages from the Sermons and Writings of Jeremy Taylor (L. P. Smith), **Supp. XIV:**345

"Golden Heifer, The" (Wylie), **Supp. I Part 2:** 707

"Golden Honeymoon, The" (Lardner), **II:** 429–430, 431

Golden Journey, The (W. J. Smith and Bogan, comps.), **Supp. XIII:** 347

"Golden Lads" (Marquand), **III:** 56

Golden Legend, The (Longfellow), **II:** 489, 490, 495, 505, 506, 507; **Retro. Supp. II:** 159, 165, 166

Golden Mean and Other Poems, The (Tate and Wills), **IV:** 122

"Golden Retrievals" (Doty), **Supp. XI:** 132

Golden Shakespeare, The: An Anthology (L. P. Smith), **Supp. XIV:**349

Goldensohn, Lorrie, **Retro. Supp. II:** 51

Golden State (Bidart), **Supp. XV:** 21, 23–25

"Golden State" (Bidart), **Supp. XV:** 23, 24, 25

Golden States (Cunningham), **Supp. XV:** 55, 56–59, 63

Golden Treasury of Best Songs and Lyrical Poems in the English Language (Palgrave), **Retro. Supp. I:** 124

Golden Treasury of the Best Songs and Lyrical Poems in the English Language (Palgrave), **Supp. XIV:**340

Golden Whales of California and Other Rhymes in the American Language, The (Lindsay), **Supp. I Part 2:** 394–395, 396

"Goldfish Bowl, The" (Francis), **Supp. IX:** 78

Goldin Boys, The (Epstein), **Supp. XIV:**112

Golding, Arthur, **III:** 467, 468

Golding, William, **Supp. IV Part 1:** 297

Goldini, Carlo, **II:** 274

Goldkorn Tales (Epstein), **Supp. XII:** 163–164

Goldman, Albert, **Supp. XI:** 299

Goldman, Emma, **III:** 176, 177; **Supp. I Part 2:** 524

Goldman, William, **Supp. IV Part 2:** 474

"Gold Mountain Stories" project (Kingston), **Supp. V:** 164

Goldring, Douglas, **III:** 458

Goldsmith, Oliver, **II:** 273, 282, 299, 304, 308, 314, 315, 514; **Retro. Supp. I:** 335; **Supp. I Part 1:** 310; **Supp. I Part 2:** 503, 714, 716

Gold Standard and the Logic of Naturalism, The (Michaels), **Retro. Supp. I:** 369

Goldwater, Barry, **I:** 376; **III:** 38

Goldwyn, Samuel, **Retro. Supp. II:** 199; **Supp. I Part 1:** 281

Golem, The (Leivick), **IV:** 6

"Goliardic Song" (Hecht), **Supp. X:** 63

"Go Like This" (Moore), **Supp. X:** 165

Goll, Ivan, **Supp. III Part 1:** 235, 243–244; **Supp. III Part 2:** 621

Goncharova, Natalya, **Supp. IX:** 66

Goncourt, Edmond de, **II:** 325, 328; **III:** 315, 317–318, 321; **Retro. Supp. I:** 226

Goncourt, Jules de, **II:** 328; **III:** 315, 317–318, 321

Gone Fishin' (Mosley), **Supp. XIII:** 235–236, 240

"Gone to War" (E. Stoddard), **Supp. XV:** 282

"Gone West" (Rodriguez), **Supp. XIV:**308

Gone with the Wind (film), **Retro. Supp. I:** 113

Gone with the Wind (Mitchell), **II:** 177; **Retro. Supp. I:** 340

Gongora y Argote, Luis de, **II:** 552

Gonzalez, David, **Supp. VIII:** 85

Gooch, Brad, **Supp. XII:** 121

Good, George, **Supp. XI:** 306

"Good, the Plaid, and the Ugly, The" (Wasserstein), **Supp. XV:** 327

"Good and Not So Good, The" (Dunn), **Supp. XI:** 141

"Good Anna, The" (Stein), **IV:** 37, 40, 43

Good As Gold (Heller), **Supp. IV Part 1:** 386, 388, 394

Good Boys and Dead Girls and Other Essays (Gordon), **Supp. IV Part 1:** 309–310

"Good-by and Keep Cold" (Frost), **Retro. Supp. I:** 135

"Good-bye" (Emerson), **II:** 19

"Goodbye, Christ" (Hughes), **Retro. Supp. I:** 202, 203

Goodbye, Columbus (Roth), **Retro. Supp. II:** 280, 281, 290; **Supp. III Part 2:** 403–406; **Supp. XIV:**112

"Goodbye, Columbus" (Roth), **Supp. III Part 2:** 401, 404, 408–409, 411
Goodbye, Columbus and Five Short Stories (Roth), **Retro. Supp. II:** 279
"Goodbye, Goldeneye" (Swenson), **Supp. IV Part 2:** 651
"Goodbye, Mr. Chipstein" (Epstein), **Supp. XIV:**103, 108
"Goodbye, My Brother" (Cheever), **Supp. I Part 1:** 175, 177, 193
"Goodbye and Good Luck" (Paley), **Supp. VI:** 219, 223
Goodbye Girl, The (film), **Supp. IV Part 2:** 589
Goodbye Girl, The (musical), **Supp. IV Part 2:** 576, 588
Goodbye Girl, The (Simon), **Supp. IV Part 2:** 575
Goodbye Look, The (Macdonald), **Supp. IV Part 2:** 473, 474
"Good-Bye My Fancy" (Whitman), **IV:** 348
"Goodbye to All That" (Didion), **Supp. IV Part 1:** 197
Goodbye to All That (Graves), **I:** 477
Goodbye to Berlin (Isherwood), **Supp. XIV:**159, 161, 162, 169
"Good-Bye to the Mezzogiorno" (Auden), **Supp. II Part 1:** 19
"Goodbye to the Poetry of Calcium" (Wright), **Supp. III Part 2:** 599
"Good Company" (Matthews), **Supp. IX:** 160
"Good Country People" (O'Connor), **III:** 343, 350, 351, 352, 358; **Retro. Supp. II:** 229, 232
Good Day to Die, A (Harrison), **Supp. VIII:** 42–44, 45, 47
Good Doctor, The (Simon), **Supp. IV Part 2:** 575, 585
Good Earth, The (Buck), **Supp. I Part 1:** 49; **Supp. II Part 1:** 115–175, 118, 125, 132
Good European, The (Blackmur), **Supp. II Part 1:** 91
Good Evening Mr. & Mrs. America, and All the Ships at Sea (Bausch), **Supp. VII:** 41, 47, 52
Good Gray Poet, The (O'Connor), **Retro. Supp. I:** 407
Good Health and How We Won It (Sinclair), **Supp. V:** 285–286
Good Hearts (Price), **Supp. VI:** 259, 265
"Good Job Gone, A" (Hughes), **Retro. Supp. I:** 204
Good Journey, A (Ortiz), **Supp. IV Part 2:** 497, 499, 503, 505, 509–510, 514
Good Luck in Cracked Italian (Hugo),

Supp. VI: 133, 137–138
Goodman, Allegra, **Supp. XII:** 159; **Supp. XVI:**205
Goodman, Ellen, **Supp. XVI:**103
Goodman, Jenny, **Supp. XV:** 343, 344
Goodman, Paul, **I:** 218, 261; **III:** 39; **Supp. I Part 2:** 524; **Supp. VIII:** 239–240
Goodman, Philip, **III:** 105, 108
Goodman, Walter, **Supp. IV Part 2:** 532
Good Man Is Hard to Find, A (O'Connor), **III:** 339, 343–345
"Good Man Is Hard to Find, A" (O'Connor), **III:** 339, 344, 353; **Retro. Supp. II:** 230–231
Good Man Is Hard to Find and Other Stories, A (O'Connor), **Retro. Supp. II:** 229, 230–232
Good Morning, America (Sandburg), **III:** 592–593
"Good Morning, Major" (Marquand), **III:** 56
Good Morning, Midnight (Rhys), **Supp. III Part 1:** 43
"Good Morning, Revolution" (Hughes), **Retro. Supp. I:** 201, 203
Good Morning Revolution: Uncollected Writings of Social Protest (Hughes), **Retro. Supp. I:** 194, 201, 202, 209
Good Mother, The (Miller), **Supp. XII:** 289, 290–294, 299, 301
Good News (Abbey), **Supp. XIII:** 11–12
"Good News from New-England" (Johnson), **Supp. I Part 1:** 115
Good News of Death and Other Poems (Simpson), **Supp. IX:** 265, 268–269
Good Night, Willie Lee, I'll See You in the Morning (Walker), **Supp. III Part 2:** 520, 531
"Good Oak" (Leopold), **Supp. XIV:**185, 187, 191
Goodrich, Samuel G., **Supp. I Part 1:** 38
Good Scent from a Strange Mountain, A (R. O. Butler), **Supp. XII:** 62, 70–72
Good School, A (Yates), **Supp. XI:** 334, 346–347, 348, 349
"*Good Shepherdess, The*/La Buena Pastora" (Mora), **Supp. XIII:** 228–229
Good Will (Smiley), **Supp. VI:** 292, 299–300
Goodwin, K. L., **III:** 478
Goodwin, Stephen, **Supp. V:** 314, 316, 322, 323, 325
"Good Word for Winter, A" (Lowell),

Supp. I Part 2: 420
Goodwyn, Janet, **Retro. Supp. I:** 370
"Goophered Grapevine, The" (Chesnutt), **Supp. XIV:**57, 58–61
"Goose Fish, The" (Nemerov), **III:** 272, 284
"Goose Pond" (Kunitz), **Supp. III Part 1:** 262
Goose-Step, The (Sinclair), **Supp. V:** 276
Gordimer, Nadine, **Supp. XV:** 251
Gordon, A. R., **III:** 199
Gordon, Ambrose, **Supp. XV:** 144
Gordon, Caroline, **II:** 196–222, 536, 537; **III:** 454, 482; **IV:** 123, 126–127, 139, 282; **Retro. Supp. II:** 177, 222, 229, 233, 235; **Supp. II Part 1:** 139
Gordon, Charles G., **I:** 454
Gordon, Don, **Supp. X:** 119
Gordon, Eugene, **Supp. II Part 1:** 170
Gordon, Fran, **Supp. XIII:** 111
Gordon, James Morris, **II:** 197
Gordon, Lois, **Supp. IV Part 1:** 48; **Supp. V:** 46
Gordon, Lyndall, **Retro. Supp. I:** 55
Gordon, Mary, **Supp. IV Part 1:** 297–317
Gordon, Neil, **Supp. XVI:**156
Gordon, Peter, **Supp. XII:** 3–4, 4–5, 8
Gordon, Ruth, **IV:** 357
Gore, Thomas Pryor, **Supp. IV Part 2:** 679
Gorey, Edward, **IV:** 430, 436
Gorilla, My Love (Bambara), **Supp. XI:** 1, 2–7
"Gorilla, My Love" (Bambara), **Supp. XI:** 2, 3–4
Gorki, Maxim, **I:** 478; **II:** 49; **III:** 402; **IV:** 299; **Supp. I Part 1:** 5, 51
Gorney, Cynthia, **Supp. XVI:**112
Gorra, Michael, **Supp. V:** 71
Goslings, The (Sinclair), **Supp. V:** 276, 281
Go South to Sorrow (Rowan), **Supp. XIV:**306
Gospel According to Joe, The (Gurney), **Supp. V:** 99
"Gospel According to Saint Mark, The" (Gordon), **Supp. IV Part 1:** 310
Gospel according to the Son (Mailer), **Retro. Supp. II:** 213
"Gospel for the Twentieth Century, The" (Locke), **Supp. XIV:**206
"Gospel of Beauty, The" (Lindsay), **Supp. I Part 2:** 380, 382, 384, 385, 391, 396
Gospel Singer, The (Crews), **Supp. XI:** 102, 109

Gosse, Edmund, **II:** 538; **IV:** 350; **Supp. VIII:** 157

"Gossip" (Conroy), **Supp. XVI:**71–72

Gossips, Gorgons, and Crones: The Fates of the Earth (Caputi), **Supp. IV Part 1:** 335

Go Tell It on the Mountain (Baldwin), **Retro. Supp. II:** 1, 2, 3, 4–5, 7, 14; **Supp. I Part 1:** 48, 49, 50, 51, 52, 53–54, 55, 56, 57, 59, 61, 63, 64, 67; **Supp. II Part 1:** 170

Gotera, Vince, **Supp. XIII:** 115, 116, 119, 121, 127

Gothic Revival, The: An Essay on the History of Taste (Clark), **Supp. XIV:**348

Gothic Writers (Thomson, Voller, and Frank, eds.), **Retro. Supp. II:** 273

"Go to the Devil and Shake Yourself" (song), **Supp. I Part 2:** 580

"Go to the Shine That's on a Tree" (Eberhart), **I:** 523

Go to the Widow-Maker (Jones), **Supp. XI:** 214, 225–226, 227, 229, 233

Gottfried, Martin, **Supp. IV Part 2:** 584

Gotthelf, Allan, **Supp. IV Part 2:** 528

Gottlieb, Adolph, **Supp. XV:** 144

Gottlieb, Morton, **Supp. XVI:**196

Gottlieb, Robert, **Supp. IV Part 2:** 474

Gottschalk and the Grande Tarantelle (Brooks), **Supp. III Part 1:** 86

"Gottschalk and the Grande Tarantelle" (Brooks), **Supp. III Part 1:** 86–87

Gould (Dixon), **Supp. XII:** 152, 153

Gould, Edward Sherman, **I:** 346

Gould, Janice, **Supp. IV Part 1:** 322, 327; **Supp. XII:** 229

Gould, Jay, **I:** 4

Gould, Joe, **Supp. XV:** 143

Gourd Dancer, The (Momaday), **Supp. IV Part 2:** 481, 487, 491, 493

Gourmont, Remy de, **I:** 270, 272; **II:** 528, 529; **III:** 457, 467–468, 477; **Retro. Supp. I:** 55

Gouverneurs de la Rosée (Roumain), **Supp. IV Part 1:** 360, 367

"Governors of Wyoming, The" (Proulx), **Supp. VII:** 264

Goyen, William, **Supp. V:** 220

Grabhorn, Janet, **Supp. XV:** 142

"Grace" (Dubus), **Supp. VII:** 91

"Grace" (Harjo), **Supp. XII:** 224

Grace Notes (Dove), **Supp. IV Part 1:** 248–250, 252

"Graduation" (Dubus), **Supp. VII:** 84

Grady, Henry W., **Supp. I Part 1:** 370

Graeber, Laurel, **Supp. V:** 15

Graham, Billy, **I:** 308

Graham, David, **Supp. XV:** 104

Graham, Don, **Supp. XI:** 252, 254

Graham, Jorie, **Supp. IX:** 38, 52; **Supp. X:** 73; **Supp. XII:** 209; **Supp. XIII:** 85

Graham, Martha, **Supp. XI:** 152

Graham, Maryemma, **Retro. Supp. I:** 201, 204

Graham, Nan, **Supp. XII:** 272

Graham, Sheilah, **II:** 94; **Retro. Supp. I:** 97, 113–114, 115; **Supp. IX:** 63

Graham, Shirley, **Supp. I Part 1:** 51

Graham, Stephen, **Supp. I Part 2:** 397

Graham, Tom (pseudonym). *See* Lewis, Sinclair

Grahn, Judy, **Supp. IV Part 1:** 325, 330

Grainger, Percy, **Supp. I Part 2:** 386

Grain of Mustard Seed, A (Sarton), **Supp. VIII:** 259–260, 263

Gramar (Lowth), **II:** 8

Grammar of Motives, A (Burke), **I:** 272, 275, 276–278, 283, 284

Granados, Gabriel Bernal, **Supp. XV:** 350

Granberry, Edwin, **I:** 288

Grand Design, The (Dos Passos), **I:** 489–490

"Grande Malade, The" (Barnes), **Supp. III Part 1:** 36

"Grandfather" (Dunn), **Supp. XI:** 147

"Grandfather and Grandson" (Singer), **Retro. Supp. II:** 307

"Grandfather's Blessing" (Alvarez), **Supp. VII:** 2

"Grand Forks" (Simpson), **Supp. IX:** 280–281

"Grand Inquisitor" (Dostoyevsky), **IV:** 106

Grandissimes (Cable), **II:** 291

"Grand-Master Nabokov" (Updike), **Retro. Supp. I:** 317

"Grand Miracle, The" (Karr), **Supp. XI:** 251

"Grandmother" (Gunn Allen), **Supp. IV Part 1:** 320, 325

"Grandmother in Heaven" (Levine), **Supp. V:** 186

"Grandmother of the Sun: Ritual Gynocracy in Native America" (Gunn Allen), **Supp. IV Part 1:** 328

Grandmothers of the Light: A Medicine Woman's Sourcebook (Gunn Allen, ed.), **Supp. IV Part 1:** 332, 333–334

"Grandmother Songs, The" (Hogan), **Supp. IV Part 1:** 413

"Grandpa and the Statue" (A. Miller), **III:** 147

"Grandparents" (Lowell), **II:** 550

"Grandstand Complex, The" (McCoy),

Supp. XIII: 166

Grange, Red, **II:** 416

Granger's Index to Poetry (anthology), **Retro. Supp. I:** 37, 39

Grant, Lee, **Supp. XIII:** 295

Grant, Madison, **Supp. II Part 1:** 170

Grant, Richard, **Supp. X:** 282

Grant, Ulysses S., **I:** 4, 15; **II:** 542; **III:** 506, 584; **IV:** 348, 446; **Supp. I Part 2:** 418

Grantwood, **Retro. Supp. I:** 416, 417

"Grapes, The" (Hecht), **Supp. X:** 65–66

"Grape Sherbet" (Dove), **Supp. IV Part 1:** 246

Grapes of Wrath, The (Steinbeck), **I:** 301; **III:** 589; **IV:** 51, 53–55, 59, 63, 65, 67, 68, 69; **Supp. V:** 290; **Supp. XI:** 169; **Supp. XIV:**181; **Supp. XV:** 351

"Grapevine, The" (Ashbery), **Supp. III Part 1:** 4

"Grass" (Sandburg), **III:** 584

Grass, Günter, **Supp. VIII:** 40

"Grasse: The Olive Trees" (Wilbur), **Supp. III Part 2:** 550

Grass Harp, The (Capote), **Supp. III Part 1:** 114–117, 123

Grass Still Grows, The (A. Miller), **III:** 146

Gratitude to Old Teachers (R. Bly), **Supp. IV Part 1:** 73

Graupner, Gottlieb, **Supp. XV:** 240, 244

"Grave, A" (Moore), **III:** 195, 202, 208, 213

Grave, The (Blair), **Supp. I Part 1:** 150

"Grave, The" (Porter), **III:** 433, 443, 445–446

"Grave, The" (Winters), **Supp. II Part 2:** 795, 796

"Graven Image" (O'Hara), **III:** 320

Grave of the Right Hand, The (Wright), **Supp. V:** 332, 338, 339

"Grave Piece" (Eberhart), **I:** 533

Graves, Billy, **Supp. I Part 2:** 607

Graves, John, **Supp. V:** 220

Graves, Morris, **Supp. X:** 264

Graves, Peter, **Supp. IV Part 2:** 474

Graves, Rean, **Supp. I Part 1:** 326

Graves, Robert, **I:** 437, 477, 523; **Supp. I Part 2:** 541; **Supp. IV Part 1:** 280, 348; **Supp. IV Part 2:** 685

Graveyard for Lunatics, A (Bradbury), **Supp. IV Part 1:** 102, 114–116

Gravity's Rainbow (Pynchon), **Supp. II Part 2:** 617, 618–619, 621–625, 627, 630, 633–636; **Supp. IV Part 1:** 279; **Supp. V:** 44; **Supp. XIV:**49

Gray, Cecil, **Supp. I Part 1:** 258

Gray, Francine Du Plessix, **Supp. V:** 169

Gray, James, **III:** 207; **Supp. I Part 2:** 410

Gray, Jeffrey, **Supp. XV:** 27

Gray, Paul, **Supp. IV Part 1:** 305; **Supp. IV Part 2:** 639; **Supp. XVI:**74

Gray, Thomas, **I:** 68; **Supp. I Part 1:** 150; **Supp. I Part 2:** 422, 716

Gray, Thomas A., **Supp. I Part 2:** 710

"Gray Heron, The" (Kinnell), **Supp. III Part 1:** 250

"Gray Mills of Farley, The" (Jewett), **Retro. Supp. II:** 132, 144

"Gray Poem" (Everwine), **Supp. XV:** 81

Grayson, Charles, **Supp. XIII:** 171

"Gray Squirrel" (Francis), **Supp. IX:** 90

"Gray Wolf's H 'ant, The" (Chesnutt), **Supp. XIV:**60

Grealy, Lucy, **Supp. XII:** 310

Greasy Lake (Boyle), **Supp. VIII:** 14–15

"Greasy Lake" (Boyle), **Supp. VIII:** 15

"Great Adventure of Max Breuck, The" (Lowell), **II:** 522

Great American Novel, The (Roth), **Retro. Supp. II:** 283, 288–289; **Supp. III Part 2:** 414–416

Great American Short Novels (Phillips, ed.), **Supp. VIII:** 156

Great Battles of the World (Crane), **I:** 415

"Great Carousel, The" (Untermeyer), **Supp. XV:** 296

Great Christian Doctrine of Original Sin Defended, The . . . (Edwards), **I:** 549, 557, 559

Great Circle (Aiken), **I:** 53, 55, 57

"Great Class-Reunion Bazaar, The" (Theroux), **Supp. VIII:** 312

Great Day, The (Hurston), **Supp. VI:** 154

Great Days (Barthelme), **Supp. IV Part 1:** 39

Great Days, The (Dos Passos), **I:** 491

Great Digest (Pound, trans.), **III:** 472

"Great Elegy for John Donne" (Brodsky), **Supp. VIII:** 21, 23

Greater Inclination, The (Wharton), **Retro. Supp. I:** 363, 364–365, 366

"Greater Torment, The" (Blackmur), **Supp. II Part 1:** 92

Greatest Hits 1969–1996 (Salinas), **Supp. XIII:** 311

"Greatest Thing in the World, The"

(Mailer), **Retro. Supp. II:** 196

Great Expectations (Acker), **Supp. XII:** 5, 9–11

Great Expectations (Dickens), **III:** 247; **Supp. I Part 1:** 35; **Supp. XVI:**73

"Great Expectations, No Satisfaction" (D. Gates), **Supp. XVI:**73

"Great Figure, The" (W. C. Williams), **IV:** 414

"Great Fillmore Street Buffalo Drive, The" (Momaday), **Supp. IV Part 2:** 493

Great Gatsby, The (Fitzgerald), **I:** 107, 375, 514; **II:** 77, 79, 83, 84, 85, 87, 91–93, 94, 96, 98; **III:** 244, 260, 372, 572; **IV:** 124, 297; **Retro. Supp. I:** 98, 105, 105–108, 110, 114, 115, 335, 359; **Retro. Supp. II:** 107, 201; **Supp. II Part 2:** 626; **Supp. III Part 2:** 585; **Supp. IV Part 2:** 468, 475; **Supp. IX:** 57, 58; **Supp. X:** 175; **Supp. XI:** 65, 69, 334; **Supp. XVI:**64, 75

Great Gatsby, The (Fitzgerald) (Modern Library), **Retro. Supp. I:** 113

Great God Brown, The (O'Neill), **III:** 165, 391, 394–395

Great Goodness of Life: A Coon Show (Baraka), **Supp. II Part 1:** 47

Great Inclination, The (Wharton), **IV:** 310

"Great Infirmities" (Simic), **Supp. VIII:** 277

Great Jones Street (DeLillo), **Supp. VI:** 2, 3, 8–9, 11, 12

"Great Lawsuit, The: Man *versus* Men: Woman *versus* Women" (Fuller), **Retro. Supp. I:** 156; **Supp. II Part 1:** 292

"Great Men and Their Environment" (James), **II:** 347

"Great Mississippi Bubble, The" (Irving), **II:** 314

Great Railway Bazaar, The: By Train through Asia (Theroux), **Supp. VIII:** 318, 319, 320–321, 322

"Great Scott" (Conroy), **Supp. XVI:**75, 77

Great Stories of Suspense (Millar, ed.), **Supp. IV Part 2:** 474

Great Topics of the World (Goldbarth), **Supp. XII:** 187, 189, 191

Great Valley, The (Masters), **Supp. I Part 2:** 465

Great World and Timothy Colt, The (Auchincloss), **Supp. IV Part 1:** 25, 31, 32

Grédy, Jean-Pierre, **Supp. XVI:**194

"Greek Boy, The" (Bryant), **Supp. I**

Part 1: 168

Greek Mind/Jewish Soul: The Conflicted Art of Cynthia Ozick (Strandberg), **Supp. V:** 273

"Greek Partisan, The" (Bryant), **Supp. I Part 1:** 168

"Greeks, The" (McCarriston), **Supp. XIV:**271

Greeley, Horace, **II:** 7; **IV:** 197, 286–287

Green, Ashbel, **Supp. IV Part 2:** 474

Green, Henry, **IV:** 279; **Retro. Supp. I:** 354; **Supp. III Part 1:** 3; **Supp. XI:** 294–295, 296, 297; **Supp. XII:** 315

Green, Jack, **Supp. IV Part 1:** 284–285

Green, Martin, **Supp. I Part 1:** 299

Green, Michelle, **Supp. IV Part 1:** 95

"Green Automobile, The" (Ginsberg), **Supp. II Part 1:** 322

Greenberg, Clement, **Supp. XV:** 141, 143, 144, 145

Greenberg, Eliezer, **Supp. I Part 2:** 432

Greenberg, Jonathan, **Supp. XII:** 285

Greenberg, Samuel, **I:** 393

Green Bough, A (Faulkner), **Retro. Supp. I:** 84

Green Centuries (Gordon), **II:** 196, 197–207, 209

"Green Crab's Shell, A" (Doty), **Supp. XI:** 126

"Green Door, The" (O. Henry), **Supp. II Part 1:** 395

Greene, A. C., **Supp. V:** 223, 225

Greene, Graham, **I:** 480; **II:** 62, 320; **III:** 57, 556; **Retro. Supp. I:** 215; **Supp. I Part 1:** 280; **Supp. IV Part 1:** 341; **Supp. V:** 298; **Supp. IX:** 261; **Supp. XI:** 99,**Supp. XI:** 104; **Supp. XIII:** 233

Greene, Helga, **Supp. IV Part 1:** 134, 135

Greene, J. Lee, **Retro. Supp. II:** 121

Greene, Nathanael, **Supp. I Part 2:** 508

Greene, Richard Tobias, **III:** 76

Green Eggs and Ham (Geisel), **Supp. XVI:**108, 109

"Greene-ing of the Portables, The" (Cowley), **Supp. II Part 1:** 140

"Greenest Continent, The" (Stevens), **Retro. Supp. I:** 304

Greenfeld, Josh, **III:** 364

Green Hills of Africa (Hemingway), **II:** 253; **Retro. Supp. I:** 182, 186

"Green Lagoons, The" (Leopold), **Supp. XIV:**188

"Green Lampshade" (Simic), **Supp.**

VIII: 283

Greenlanders, The (Smiley), **Supp. VI:** 292, 296–298, 299, 305, 307

Greenlaw, Edwin A., **IV:** 453

"Greenleaf" (O'Connor), **III:** 350, 351; **Retro. Supp. II:** 233, 237

Greenman, Walter F., **I:** 217, 222

Green Memories (Mumford), **Supp. II Part 2:** 474, 475, 479, 480–481

"Green Pasture, The" (Leopold), **Supp. XIV:**184

Green Pastures, The (Connelly), **Supp. II Part 1:** 223

"Green Red Brown and White" (Swenson), **Supp. IV Part 2:** 639

"Green River" (Bryant), **Supp. I Part 1:** 155, 164

Green Shadows, White Whale (Bradbury), **Supp. IV Part 1:** 102, 103, 116

"Green Shirt, The" (Olds), **Supp. X:** 209

Greenslet, Ferris, **I:** 19; **Retro. Supp. I:** 9, 10, 11, 13; **Retro. Supp. II:** 41

Greenspan, Alan, **Supp. IV Part 2:** 526

Greenstreet, Sydney, **Supp. IV Part 1:** 356

"Green Thought, A" (L. Michaels), **Supp. XVI:**204

Greenwald, Ted, **Supp. IV Part 2:** 423

Green Wall, The (Wright), **Supp. III Part 2:** 591, 593, 595

Green Wave, The (Rukeyser), **Supp. VI:** 273, 280

"Green Ways" (Kunitz), **Supp. III Part 1:** 265

Green with Beasts (Merwin), **Supp. III Part 1:** 340, 344–346

Greenwood, Grace, **Supp. XIII:** 141

Gregerson, Linda, **Supp. IV Part 2:** 651; **Supp. X:** 204–205; **Supp. XI:** 142

"Gregorio Valdes" (Bishop), **Retro. Supp. II:** 51

Gregory, Alyse, **I:** 221, 226, 227, 231

Gregory, Horace, **II:** 512; **Supp. III Part 2:** 614, 615; **Supp. IX:** 229; **Supp. XV:** 143

Gregory, Lady Isabella Augusta, **III:** 458

Gregory, Sinda, **Supp. X:** 260, 268

Grendel (Gardner), **Supp. VI:** 63, 67, 68, 74

Grenstone Poems (Bynner), **Supp. XV:** 44

"Gretel in Darkness" (Glück), **Supp. V:** 82

Gretta (Caldwell), **I:** 301, 302

Greuze, Jean Baptiste, **Supp. I Part 2:** 714

Grey, Zane, **Supp. XIII:** 5

Grieg, Michael, **Supp. XV:** 133, 148

Griffin, Bartholomew, **Supp. I Part 1:** 369

Griffin, John Howard, **Supp. VIII:** 208

Griffin, Merv, **Supp. IV Part 2:** 526

Griffith, Albert J., **Supp. V:** 325

Griffith, D. W., **I:** 31, 481–482; **Retro. Supp. I:** 103, 325; **Supp. XI:** 45; **Supp. XVI:**183, 184

Griffiths, Clyde, **I:** 511

Grile, Dod (pseudonym). *See* Bierce, Ambrose

Grimm, Herman, **II:** 17

Grimm brothers, **II:** 378; **III:** 101, 491, 492; **IV:** 266; **Supp. I Part 2:** 596, 622; **Supp. X:** 78, 84, 86

Grinnell, George Bird, **Supp. XVI:**13

Gris, Juan, **I:** 442; **Retro. Supp. I:** 430

Griswold, Rufus Wilmot, **III:** 409, 429; **Retro. Supp. II:** 261, 262; **Supp. XV:** 277, 278; **Supp. XVI:**8, 10–11

Grogg, Sam, Jr., **Supp. IV Part 2:** 468, 471

Gromer, Crystal, **Supp. XII:** 297

Gronlund, Laurence, **II:** 276

Grooms, Red, **Supp. XV:** 178

"Groping for Trouts" (Gass), **Supp. VI:** 87

Grosholz, Emily, **Supp. XII:** 185

Gross, Terry, **Supp. XVI:**167

"*Grosse Fuge*" (Doty), **Supp. XI:** 126–127

Grossman, Allen, **Retro. Supp. II:** 83

Grosz, George, **III:** 172; **IV:** 438; **Retro. Supp. II:** 321; **Supp. X:** 137

"Grotesque in Modern Fiction, The" (E. Hoffman, Ph.D. dissertation), **Supp. XVI:**147

"Groundhog, The" (Eberhart), **I:** 523, 530–532, 533

"Ground on Which I Stand, The" (Wilson), **Supp. VIII:** 331

Group, The (McCarthy), **II:** 570, 574–578

"Group of Two, A" (Jarrell), **II:** 368

Group Therapy (Hearon), **Supp. VIII:** 64–65

"Grove" (Goldbarth), **Supp. XII:** 176

Groves of Academe, The (McCarthy), **II:** 568–571

Growing into Love (X. J. Kennedy), **Supp. XV:** 153, 158–160

Growing Pains (J. S. Untermeyer), **Supp. XV:** 303

"Growing Season, The" (Caldwell), **I:** 309

Growing Up Gay: A Literary Anthol-

ogy (Singer, ed.), **Supp. IV Part 1:** 330

"Growing Up Good in Maycomb" (Shaffer), **Supp. VIII:** 128

"Grown-Up" (Jewett), **Retro. Supp. II:** 134

"Growth" (Lowell), **II:** 554

"Growth and Decay in Recent Verse" (Untermeyer), **Supp. XV:** 299

Growth of the American Republic, The (Morison and Commager), **Supp. I Part 2:** 484

"Growtown Buggle, The" (Jewett), **Retro. Supp. II:** 132

Gruenberg, Louis, **III:** 392

Grumbach, Doris, **II:** 560

"Guacamaja" (Leopold), **Supp. XIV:**188–189

Guardian Angel, The (Holmes), **Supp. I Part 1:** 315–316

Guard of Honor (Cozzens), **I:** 370–372, 375, 376–377, 378, 379

Guardsman, The (Molnar), **Supp. XVI:**187

Guare, John, **Supp. XIII:** 196, 207

Gubar, Susan, **Retro. Supp. I:** 42; **Retro. Supp. II:** 324; **Supp. IX:** 66; **Supp. XV:** 270

Guerard, Albert, Jr., **Supp. X:** 79; **Supp. XIII:** 172

Guérin, Maurice de, **I:** 241

"Guerrilla Handbook, A" (Baraka), **Supp. II Part 1:** 36

Guess and Spell Coloring Book, The (Swenson), **Supp. IV Part 2:** 648

Guess Who's Coming to Dinner (film), **Supp. I Part 1:** 67

Guest, Judith, **Supp. XVI:**36

Guest, Val, **Supp. XI:** 307

Guest Book (Bynner), **Supp. XV:** 51

"Guests of Mrs. Timms, The" (Jewett), **II:** 408; **Retro. Supp. II:** 135

"Guevara . . .Guevara" (Salinas), **Supp. XIII:** 312–313, 315

Guevara, Martha, **Supp. VIII:** 74

Guided Tours of Hell (Prose), **Supp. XVI:**257, 261

"Guided Tours of Hell" (Prose), **Supp. XVI:**257

Guide in the Wilderness, A (Cooper), **I:** 337

"Guide to Dungeness Spit, A" (Wagoner), **Supp. IX:** 325–326, 329

Guide to Ezra Pound's Selected Cantos' (Kearns), **Retro. Supp. I:** 292

Guide to Kulchur (Pound), **III:** 475

Guide to the Ruins (Nemerov), **III:** 269, 270–271, 272

Guillén, Nicolás, **Retro. Supp. I:** 202; **Supp. I Part 1:** 345

Guillevic, Eugene, **Supp. III Part 1:** 283

"Guilty Man, The" (Kunitz), **Supp. II Part 1:** 263

Guilty of Everything: The Autobiography of Herbert Huncke (Huncke), **Supp. XIV:**138, 140, 141, 150

Guilty Pleasures (Barthelme), **Supp. IV Part 1:** 44, 45, 53

Guinness, Alec, **Retro. Supp. I:** 65

"Gulf, The" (Dunn), **Supp. XI:** 149

Gulistan (Saadi), **II:** 19

Gullible's Travels (Lardner), **II:** 426, 427

Gulliver's Travels (Swift), **I:** 209, 348, 366; **II:** 301; **Supp. I Part 2:** 656; **Supp. XI:** 209; **Supp. XVI:**110

"Gulls" (Hayden), **Supp. II Part 1:** 367

"Gulls, The" (Nemerov), **III:** 272

"Gun, The" (Dobyns), **Supp. XIII:** 88

Günderode: A Translation from the German (Fuller), **Supp. II Part 1:** 293

Gundy, Jeff, **Supp. XI:** 315; **Supp. XVI:**46, 265, 275

Gunn, Thom, **Supp. IX:** 269

Gunn, Thomas, **Supp. V:** 178

Gunn Allen, Paula, **Supp. IV Part 1:** 319–340, 404; **Supp. IV Part 2:** 499, 502, 557, 568; **Supp. XII:** 218

"Gunnar's Sword" (C. Bly), **Supp. XVI:**34, 35, 37, 42

"Guns as Keys; and the Great Gate Swings" (Lowell), **II:** 524

Gurdjieff, Georges, **Supp. V:** 199; **Supp. IX:** 320

Gurganus, Allan, **Supp. XII:** 308–309, 310

Gurko, Leo, **III:** 62

Gurney, A. R., **Supp. V:** 95–112; **Supp. IX:** 261

Gurney, Mary (Molly) Goodyear, **Supp. V:** 95

Gussow, Mel, **Supp. IX:** 93; **Supp. XII:** 325, 328, 341

Gustavus Vassa, the African (Vassa), **Supp. IV Part 1:** 11

Gusto, Thy Name Was Mrs. Hopkins: A Prose Rhapsody (Francis), **Supp. IX:** 89

Gute Mensch von Sezuan, Der (Brecht), **Supp. IX:** 138

Gutenberg, Johann, **Supp. I Part 2:** 392

Guthrie, A. B., **Supp. X:** 103

Gutman, Herbert, **Supp. I Part 1:** 47

Guttenplan, D. D., **Supp. XI:** 38

"Gutting of Couffignal, The" (Hammett), **Supp. IV Part 1:** 345

Guy Domville (James), **II:** 331; **Retro. Supp. I:** 228

"Gwendolyn" (Bishop), **Retro. Supp. II:** 51

Gypsy Ballads (Hughes, trans.), **Supp. I Part 1:** 345

Gypsy's Curse, The (Crews), **Supp. XI:** 110

"Gyroscope, The" (Rukeyser), **Supp. VI:** 271

Gysin, Brion, **Supp. XII:** 129

H

H. L. Mencken, a Portrait from Memory (Angoff), **III:** 107

H. L. Mencken: The American Scene (Cairns), **III:** 119

"H. L. Mencken Meets à Poet in the West Side Y.M.C.A." (White), **Supp. I Part 2:** 677

H. M. Pulham, Esquire (Marquand), **II:** 482–483; **III:** 58, 59, 65, 68–69

Haardt, Sara. *See* Mencken, Mrs. H. L. (Sara Haardt)

Habakkuk (biblical book), **III:** 200, 347

Habibi (Nye), **Supp. XIII:** 273, 279

"Habit" (James), **II:** 351

Habitations of the Word (Gass), **Supp. VI:** 88

Hacker, Marilyn, **Supp. XV:** 250

Hackett, David, **Supp. XII:** 236

Hadda, Janet, **Retro. Supp. II:** 317

Haeckel, Ernst Heinrich, **II:** 480

Haegert, John, **Supp. XVI:**69

Hafif, Marcia, **Supp. IV Part 2:** 423

Hagar's Daughter (P. Hopkins), **Supp. XVI:**143

Hagedorn, Jessica, **Supp. X:** 292

Hagen, Beulah, **Supp. I Part 2:** 679

Haggard, Rider, **III:** 189

Hagoromo (play), **III:** 466

Hagstrum, Jean, **Supp. XV:** 74

"Hail Mary" (Fante), **Supp. XI:** 160, 164

Haines, George, IV, **I:** 444

Haines, John, **Supp. XII:** 197–214

"Hair" (Corso), **Supp. XII:** 117, 126, 127

"Hair, The" (Carver), **Supp. III Part 1:** 137

"Haircut" (Lardner), **II:** 430, 436

"Hair Dressing" (Untermeyer), **Supp. XV:** 304, 305

Hairpiece: A Film for Nappy-Headed People (Chenzira; film), **Supp. XI:** 19–20

"Hairs" (Cisneros), **Supp. VII:** 59

Hairs/Pelitos (Cisneros), **Supp. VII:** 58

Hairy Ape, The (O'Neill), **III:** 391, 392, 393

"Haïta the Shepherd" (Bierce), **I:** 203

Haldeman, Anna, **Supp. I Part 1:** 2

Hale, Edward Everett, **Supp. I Part 2:** 584; **Supp. XI:** 193, 200

Hale, John Parker, **Supp. I Part 2:** 685

Hale, Nancy, **Supp. VIII:** 151, 171

Haley, Alex, **Supp. I Part 1:** 47, 66

Haley, J. Evetts, **Supp. V:** 226

"Half a Century Gone" (Lowell), **II:** 554

Half-a-Hundred: Tales by Great American Writers (Grayson, ed.), **Supp. XIII:** 171

Half Asleep in Frog Pajamas (Robbins), **Supp. X:** 259, 279–282

Half Breed, The (film), **Supp. XVI:**185

Half-Century of Conflict, A (Parkman), **Supp. II Part 2:** 600, 607, 610

"Half Deity" (Moore), **III:** 210, 214, 215

"Half Hour of August" (Ríos), **Supp. IV Part 2:** 552

Half-Lives (Jong), **Supp. V:** 115, 119

Half Moon Street: Two Short Novels (Theroux), **Supp. VIII:** 322, 323

Half of Paradise (Burke), **Supp. XIV:**22, 24

Half-Past Nation Time (Johnson), **Supp. VI:** 187

"Half-Skinned Steer, The" (Proulx), **Supp. VII:** 261–262

Half Sun Half Sleep (Swenson), **Supp. IV Part 2:** 645–646

Halfway (Kumin), **Supp. IV Part 2:** 441–442

"Halfway" (Rich), **Supp. I Part 2:** 553

Halfway Home (Monette), **Supp. X:** 154

Halfway to Silence (Sarton), **Supp. VIII:** 261

Half You Don't Know, The: Selected Stories (Cameron), **Supp. XII:** 79, 80, 81

Haliburton, Thomas Chandler, **II:** 301; **IV:** 193; **Supp. I Part 2:** 411

Halifax, Lord, **II:** 111

Hall, Daniel, **Supp. XII:** 258

Hall, Donald, **I:** 567; **III:** 194; **Supp. IV Part 1:** 63, 72; **Supp. IV Part 2:** 621; **Supp. IX:** 269; **Supp. XIV:**82, 126; **Supp. XV:** 21, 153, 176; **Supp. XVI:**39, 230, 235

Hall, James, **II:** 313; **Supp. I Part 2:** 584, 585

Hall, James Baker, **Supp. X:** 24

Hall, Timothy L., **Supp. VIII:** 127, 128

Halleck, Fitz-Greene, **Supp. I Part 1:** 156, 158

"Hallelujah: A Sestina" (Francis), **Supp. IX:** 82

"Hallelujah on the Bum" (Abbey), **Supp. XIII:** 2

"Haller's Second Home" (Maxwell), **Supp. VIII:** 169

Halliday, Mark, **Supp. XV:** 19, 20, 21, 23, 25, 27, 30

Hallock, Rev. Moses, **Supp. I Part 1:** 153

Hall of Mirrors, A (Stone), **Supp. V:** 295, 296–299, 300, 301

"Hallowe'en" (Huncke), **Supp. XIV:**145

"Halloween Party, The" (Chabon), **Supp. XI:** 72

Halloween Tree, The (Bradbury), **Supp. IV Part 1:** 102, 112–113

Hallwas, John E., **Supp. I Part 2:** 454

Halpern, Daniel, **Supp. IV Part 1:** 94–95, 95

Halsey, Theresa, **Supp. IV Part 1:** 330, 331

"Halt in the Desert, A" (Brodsky), **Supp. VIII:** 24

"Halves" (Dunn), **Supp. XI:** 149

Hamburg, Victoria, **Supp. XVI:**126

Hamerik, Asger, **Supp. I Part 1:** 356

Hamill, Sam, **Supp. X:** 112, 125, 126, 127

Hamilton, Alexander, **I:** 485; **Supp. I Part 2:** 456, 483, 509

Hamilton, Alice, **Supp. I Part 1:** 5

Hamilton, David, **Supp. IX:** 296

Hamilton, Edith, **Supp. XVI:**196

Hamilton, Lady Emma, **II:** 524

Hamilton, Hamish, **Supp. I Part 2:** 617

Hamilton, Walton, **Supp. I Part 2:** 632

Hamilton Stark (Banks), **Supp. V:** 8, 9–10, 11

"Hamlen Brook" (Wilbur), **Supp. III Part 2:** 564

"Hamlet" (Laforgue), **I:** 573; **III:** 11

Hamlet (Miller and Fraenkel), **III:** 178, 183

Hamlet (Shakespeare), **I:** 53, 183, 205, 377, 586–587; **II:** 158, 531; **III:** 7, 11, 12, 183; **IV:** 116, 131, 227; **Supp. I Part 1:** 369; **Supp. I Part 2:** 422, 457, 471; **Supp. IV Part 2:** 612; **Supp. IX:** 14

Hamlet, The (Faulkner), **II:** 69–71, 73, 74; **IV:** 131; **Retro. Supp. I:** 82, 91, 92; **Supp. VIII:** 178; **Supp. IX:** 103; **Supp. XI:** 247

"Hamlet and His Problems" (Eliot), **I:** 586–587

Hamlet of A. MacLeish, The (MacLeish), **III:** 11–12, 14, 15, 18

Hamlin, Eva, **Retro. Supp. II:** 115

"Hammer" (Bidart), **Supp. XV:** 35

Hammer, Adam, **Supp. XIII:** 112

Hammer, Langdon, **Retro. Supp. II:** 45, 53; **Supp. X:** 65

"Hammer Man, The" (Bambara), **Supp. XI:** 4–5

Hammett, Dashiell, **IV:** 286; **Retro. Supp. II:** 327; **Supp. I Part 1:** 286, 289, 291, 292, 293, 294, 295; **Supp. III Part 1:** 91; **Supp. IV Part 1:** 120, 121, 341–357; **Supp. IV Part 2:** 461, 464, 468, 469, 472, 473; **Supp. IX:** 200; **Supp. XI:** 228; **Supp. XIII:** 159; **Supp. XIV:**21

Hammond, Karla, **Supp. IV Part 2:** 439, 442, 448, 637, 640, 644, 648

Hampl, Patricia, **Supp. IX:** 291; **Supp. XI:** 126

Hampson, Alfred Leete, **Retro. Supp. I:** 35–36, 38

"Hamrick's Polar Bear" (Caldwell), **I:** 309–310

Hamsun, Knut, **Supp. VIII:** 40; **Supp. XI:** 161, 167; **Supp. XII:** 21, 128

Hancock, John, **Supp. I Part 2:** 524

Hancock, Wade, **Supp. XVI:**34

Handbook of North American Indians (Sando), **Supp. IV Part 2:** 510

Handcarved Coffins: A Nonfiction Account of an American Crime (Capote), **Supp. III Part 1:** 131

Handel, Georg Friedrich, **III:** 210; **IV:** 369

"Handfasting" (Wright), **Supp. XV:** 343

"Handfuls" (Sandburg), **III:** 584

"Handle with Care" (Fitzgerald), **Retro. Supp. I:** 114

Handmaid's Tale, The (Atwood), **Supp. XIII:** 19, 20, 27–29

"Hand of Emmagene, The" (Taylor), **Supp. V:** 314, 325–326

Hand of the Potter, The: A Tragedy in Four Acts (Dreiser), **Retro. Supp. II:** 104

"Hands" (Anderson), **I:** 106, 107

"Hands" (Mora), **Supp. XIII:** 215

Hand to Mouth (Auster), **Supp. XII:** 21

"Hand to Mouth" (Auster), **Supp. XII:** 31

Handy, Lowney, **Supp. XI:** 217, 220, 221, 225

Handy, W. C., **Supp. VIII:** 337

Handy Guide for Beggars, A (Lindsay), **Supp. I Part 2:** 376–378, 380, 382, 399

Hanging Garden, The (Wagoner), **Supp. IX:** 338–339

"Hanging Gardens of Tyburn, The" (Hecht), **Supp. X:** 58

"Hanging of the Crane, The" (Longfellow), **Retro. Supp. II:** 169, 171

Hanging On (Conroy), **Supp. XVI:**69

"Hanging Pictures in Nanny's Room" (Kenyon), **Supp. VII:** 164

"Hanging the Wash" (Alvarez), **Supp. VII:** 4

"Hangman, The" (Sexton), **Supp. II Part 2:** 680, 691

Hangover Mass (X. J. Kennedy), **Supp. XV:** 165

Hangsaman (Jackson), **Supp. IX:** 116, 123, 124

Hanh, Thich Nhat, **Supp. V:** 199

Hanks, Lucy, **III:** 587

Hanks, Nancy. *See* Lincoln, Mrs. Thomas (Nancy Hanks)

Hanley, Lynne T., **Supp. IV Part 1:** 208

Hanna, Mark, **Supp. I Part 2:** 395

Hannah, Barry, **Supp. X:** 285

Hannah and Her Sisters (film; Allen), **Supp. XV:** 9, 10–11

"Hannah Armstrong" (Masters), **Supp. I Part 2:** 461

"Hannah Binding Shoes" (Larcom), **Supp. XIII:** 141, 143

Hannah's House (Hearon), **Supp. VIII:** 58, 60–61

Hanneman, Audre, **II:** 259

Hannibal Lecter, My Father (Acker), **Supp. XII:** 6

Hanoi (McCarthy), **II:** 579

Hansberry, Lorraine, **Supp. IV Part 1:** 359–377; **Supp. VIII:** 329

Hanscom, Leslie, **Supp. XI:** 229

"Hansel and Gretel" (Prose), **Supp. XVI:**256, 258

Hansen, Erik, **Supp. V:** 241

Hansen, Harry, **IV:** 366

Han-shan, **Supp. VIII:** 292

Hanson, Curtis, **Supp. XI:** 67

Han Suyin, **Supp. X:** 291

Hanzlicek, C. G., **Supp. XV:** 73

"Happenings: An Art of Radical Juxtaposition" (Sontag), **Supp. III Part 2:** 456

"Happenstance" (Komunyakaa), **Supp. XIII:** 130

Happenstance (Shields), **Supp. VII:** 315–318, 320, 323, 324, 326

Happersberger, Lucien, **Supp. I Part 1:** 51

"Happiest I've Been, The" (Updike), **IV:** 219

"Happiness" (Oliver), **Supp. VII:** 236

"Happiness" (Sandburg), **III:** 582–583

Happiness of Getting It Down Right, The (Steinman, ed.), **Supp. VIII:** 172

"Happy Birthday" (Bambara), **Supp. XI:** 4

Happy Birthday (Loos), **Supp. XVI:**193

Happy Birthday, Wanda June (Vonnegut), **Supp. II Part 2:** 759, 776–777

Happy Birthday of Death, The (Corso), **Supp. XII:** 127–129

Happy Childhood, A (Matthews), **Supp. IX:** 155, 160, 161–163

Happy Days (Beckett), **Retro. Supp. I:** 206

Happy Days, 1880–1892 (Mencken), **III:** 100, 111, 120

"Happy End" (Simic), **Supp. VIII:** 276–277

"Happy Failure, The" (Melville), **III:** 90

Happy Families Are All Alike (Taylor), **Supp. V:** 322–323, 325

Happy Isles of Oceania, The: Paddling the Pacific (Theroux), **Supp. VIII:** 324

"Happy Journey to Trenton and Camden, The" (Wilder), **IV:** 366

"Happy Marriage, The" (MacLeish), **III:** 15–16

Happy Marriage and Other Poems, The (MacLeish), **III:** 4

Happy to Be Here (Keillor), **Supp. XVI:**165, 171

"Happy To Be Here" (Keillor), **Supp. XVI:**168

"Hapworth 16, 1924" (Salinger), **III:** 552, 571–572

"Harbor Lights" (Doty), **Supp. XI:** 122

Harcourt, Alfred, **II:** 191, 451–452; **III:** 587; **Retro. Supp. I:** 131; **Supp. XV:** 308

Harcourt, Brace, **Retro. Supp. I:** 83

Harcourt, T. A., **I:** 196

Hard Candy, a Book of Stories (T. Williams), **IV:** 383

"Hardcastle Crags" (Plath), **Supp. I Part 2:** 537

"Hard Daddy" (Hughes), **Retro. Supp. I:** 200

Harder They Fall, The (Schulberg), **Supp. XV:** 194, 201

Hard Facts (Baraka), **Supp. II Part 1:** 54, 55, 58

Hard Freight (Wright), **Supp. V:** 332, 339–340

Hard Hours, The (Hecht), **Supp. X:** 57, 59–62, 63, 64

Hardie, Kier, **Supp. I Part 1:** 5

Harding, Walter, **IV:** 177, 178

Harding, Warren G., **I:** 486; **II:** 253, 433; **Supp. I Part 1:** 24

"Hard Kind of Courage, The" (Baldwin), **Supp. I Part 1:** 52

"Hard Time Keeping Up, A" (Ellison), **Retro. Supp. II:** 124

Hard Times (Dickens), **Supp. I Part 2:** 675

"Hard Times in Elfland, The" (Lanier), **Supp. I Part 1:** 365

Hardwick, Elizabeth, **II:** 543, 554, 566; **Retro. Supp. II:** 179, 180, 183, 184, 190, 221, 228–229, 245; **Supp. I Part 1:** 196; **Supp. III Part 1:** 193–215; **Supp. IV Part 1:** 299; **Supp. V, 319; Supp. X, 171; Supp. XII:** 209; **Supp. XIV:**89

"Hard Work 1956" (Dunn), **Supp. XI:** 147

Hardy, Barbara, **Supp. I Part 2:** 527

Hardy, Oliver, **Supp. I Part 2:** 607; **Supp. IV Part 2:** 574

Hardy, René, **Supp. III Part 1:** 235

Hardy, Thomas, **I:** 59, 103, 292, 317, 377; **II:** 181, 184–185, 186, 191–192, 271, 275, 372, 523, 542; **III:** 32, 453, 485, 508, 524; **IV:** 83, 135, 136; **Retro. Supp. I:** 141, 377–378; **Supp. I Part 1:** 217; **Supp. I Part 2:** 429, 512; **Supp. II Part 1:** 4, 26; **Supp. VIII:** 32; **Supp. IX:** 40, 78, 85, 108, 211; **Supp. X:** 228; **Supp. XI:** 311; **Supp. XIII:** 294, **Supp. XIII:** 130; **Supp. XIV:**24; **Supp. XV:** 170

Harjo, Joy, **Supp. IV Part 1:** 325, 404; **Supp. IV Part 2:** 499, 507; **Supp. XII:** 215–234

"Harlem" (Hughes), **Retro. Supp. I:** 194, 204; **Supp. I Part 1:** 340; **Supp. VIII:** 213

Harlem, Mecca of the New Negro (Locke), **Supp. XIV:**201

Harlem: Negro Metropolis (McKay), **Supp. X:** 132, 141, 142

"Harlem Dancer, The" (McKay), **Supp. X:** 134

Harlem Gallery (Tolson), **Retro. Supp. I:** 208, 209, 210

Harlem Glory: A Fragment of Aframerican Life (McKay), **Supp. X:** 132, 141–142

"Harlem Runs Wild" (McKay), **Supp. X:** 140

Harlem Shadows (McKay), **Supp. X:** 131–132, 136

Harlem Underground (Lacy), **Supp. XV:** 206

"Harlequin of Dreams, The" (Lanier), **Supp. I Part 1:** 365

Harlot's Ghost (Mailer), **Retro. Supp. II:** 211–212

Harlow, Jean, **IV:** 256; **Retro. Supp. I:** 110

"Harm" (C. Frost), **Supp. XV:** 101

Harmon, William, **Retro. Supp. I:** 37; **Supp. XI:** 248

"Harmonic" (F. Barthelme), **Supp. XI:** 26

Harmonium (Stevens), **III:** 196; **IV:** 76, 77, 78, 82, 87, 89, 92; **Retro. Supp. I:** 296, 297, 299, 300–302, 301, 302

"Harmony of the Gospels" (Taylor), **IV:** 149

Harnett, Vincent, **Supp. XV:** 198

Harper (film), **Supp. IV Part 2:** 473

Harper, Donna, **Retro. Supp. I:** 194, 195, 209

Harper, Frances E. Watkins, **Supp. II Part 1:** 201–202

Harper, Gordon Lloyd, **Retro. Supp. II:** 23

Harper, Michael, **Supp. XV:** 74

Harper, Michael S., **Retro. Supp. II:** 116, 123

Harper, William Rainey, **Supp. I Part 2:** 631

Harper's Anthology of 20th Century Native American Poetry (Niatum, ed.), **Supp. IV Part 1:** 331

"Harriet" (Lowell), **II:** 554

Harrigan, Edward, **II:** 276; **III:** 14

Harrington, Michael, **I:** 306

Harrington, Ollie, **Supp. XVI:**142–143

Harris, Celia, **Retro. Supp. I:** 9

Harris, George, **II:** 70

Harris, Joel Chandler, **III:** 338; **Supp. I Part 1:** 352; **Supp. II Part 1:** 192, 201; **Supp. XIV:**61

Harris, Judith, **Supp. XIV:**269

Harris, Julie, **II:** 587, 601; **Supp. IX:** 125

Harris, Leonard, **Supp. XIV:**196, 211–212

Harris, MacDonald, **Supp. XI:** 65

Harris, Marie, **Supp. IX:** 153

Harris, Peter, **Supp. X:** 206, 207

Harris, Susan K., **Supp. XV:** 269

Harris, Thomas, **Supp. XIV:**26

Harris, Victoria Frenkel, **Supp. IV Part 1:** 68, 69

Harrison, Colin, **Supp. XIV:**26

Harrison, Hazel, **Retro. Supp. II:** 115

Harrison, Jim, **Supp. VIII:** 37–56

Harrison, Kathryn, **Supp. X:** 191

Harrison, Ken, **Supp. IX:** 101

Harrison, Oliver (pseudonym). *See*

Smith, Harrison Harryhausen, Ray, **Supp. IV Part 1:** 115

Harryman, Carla, **Supp. XV:** 344

"Harry of Nothingham" (Hugo), **Supp. VI:** 146–147

"Harry's Death" (Carver), **Supp. III Part 1:** 146

"Harsh Judgment, The" (Kunitz), **Supp. III Part 1:** 264

Hart, Albert Bushnell, **Supp. I Part 2:** 479, 480, 481

Hart, Bernard, **I:** 241, 242, 248–250, 256

Hart, Henry, **Retro. Supp. II:** 187; **Supp. XIV:**97

Hart, Lorenz, **III:** 361

Hart, Moss, **Supp. IV Part 2:** 574; **Supp. XV:** 329

Hart, Pearl, **Supp. X:** 103

"Hart Crane" (Tate), **I:** 381

"Hart Crane and Poetry: A Consideration of Crane's Intense Poetics with Reference to 'The Return'" (Grossman), **Retro. Supp. II:** 83

Harte, Anna Griswold, **Supp. II Part 1:** 341

Harte, Bret, **I:** 193, 195, 203; **II:** 289; **IV:** 196; **Retro. Supp. II:** 72; **Supp. II Part 1:** 335–359, 399; **Supp. XV:** 115

Harte, Walter Blackburn, **I:** 199

Harter, Carol C., **Supp. IV Part 1:** 217

Hartley, David, **III:** 77

Hartley, L. P., **Supp. I Part 1:** 293

Hartley, Lois, **Supp. I Part 2:** 459, 464–465

Hartley, Marsden, **IV:** 409, 413; **Retro. Supp. I:** 430; **Supp. X:** 137; **Supp. XV:** 298

Hartman, Geoffrey, **Supp. IV Part 1:** 119; **Supp. XII:** 130, 253

Harum, David, **II:** 102

"Harvard" (Lowell), **II:** 554

Harvard College in the Seventeenth Century (Morison), **Supp. I Part 2:** 485

"Harvesters of Night and Water" (Hogan), **Supp. IV Part 1:** 412

"Harvest Song" (Toomer), **Supp. III Part 2:** 483

Harvill Book of 20th Century Poetry in English, **Supp. X:** 55

"Harv Is Plowing Now" (Updike), **Retro. Supp. I:** 318

Haselden, Elizabeth Lee, **Supp. VIII:** 125

Hass, Robert, **Supp. VI:** 97–111; **Supp. VIII:** 24, 28; **Supp. XI:** 142, 270; **Supp. XIV:**83, 84

Hassam, Childe, **Retro. Supp. II:** 136

Hassan, Ihab, **IV:** 99–100, 115; **Supp. XI:** 221

Hasse, Henry, **Supp. IV Part 1:** 102

Hasty-Pudding, The (Barlow), **Supp. II Part 1:** 74, 77–80

Hatful of Rain, A (Gazzo), **III:** 155

Hatlen, Burton, **Supp. V:** 138, 139–140

"Hattie Bloom" (Oliver), **Supp. VII:** 232

Haunch, Paunch, and Jowl (Ornitz), **Supp. IX:** 227

"Haunted Landscape" (Ashbery), **Supp. III Part 1:** 22

"Haunted Mind" (Simic), **Supp. VIII:** 282

"Haunted Mind, The" (Hawthorne), **II:** 230–231

"Haunted Oak, The" (Dunbar), **Supp. II Part 1:** 207, 208

"Haunted Palace, The" (Poe), **III:** 421

"Haunted Valley, The" (Bierce), **I:** 200

Haunting, The (film), **Supp. IX:** 125

Haunting of Hill House, The (Jackson), **Supp. IX:** 117, 121, 126

Hauptmann, Gerhart, **III:** 472

Haussmann, Sonja, **Supp. XIII:** 331, **Supp. XIII:** 347

"Havanna vanities come to dust in Miami" (Didion), **Supp. IV Part 1:** 210

Haven, Cynthia, **Supp. XV:** 252, 264

Haven's End (Marquand), **III:** 55, 56, 63, 68

"Have You Ever Tried to Enter the Long Black Branches" (Oliver), **Supp. VII:** 247

"Having Been Interstellar" (Ammons), **Supp. VII:** 25

"Having It Out With Melancholy" (Kenyon), **Supp. VII:** 171

"Having Lost My Sons, I Confront the Wreckage of the Moon: Christmas, 1960" (Wright), **Supp. III Part 2:** 600

"Having Snow" (Schwartz), **Supp. II Part 2:** 652

Hawai'i One Summer (Kingston), **Supp. V:** 157, 160, 166, 169–170

"Hawk, The" (Francis), **Supp. IX:** 81

Hawke, David Freeman, **Supp. I Part 2:** 511, 516

Hawkes, John, **I:** 113; **Retro. Supp. II:** 234; **Supp. III Part 1:** 2; **Supp. V:** 40; **Supp. IX:** 212

Hawkins, William, **II:** 587

Hawk in the Rain, The (Hughes), **Retro. Supp. II:** 244; **Supp. I Part 2:** 537, 540

Hawk Is Dying, The (Crews), **Supp. XI:** 111

Hawk Moon (Shepard), **Supp. III Part 2:** 445

Hawks, Howard, **Supp. IV Part 1:** 130

"Hawk's Cry in Autumn, The" (Brodsky), **Supp. VIII:** 29

"Hawk's Shadow" (Glück), **Supp. V:** 85

Hawk's Well, The (Yeats), **III:** 459–460

Hawley, Adelaide, **Supp. XIV:**207

Hawley, Joseph, **I:** 546

Hawthorne (James), **II:** 372–378; **Retro. Supp. I:** 220, 223–224

"Hawthorne" (Longfellow), **Retro. Supp. II:** 169

"Hawthorne" (Lowell), **II:** 550

Hawthorne, Julian, **II:** 225; **Supp. I Part 1:** 38; **Supp. XV:** 274

Hawthorne, Mrs. Nathaniel (Sophia Peabody), **II:** 224, 244; **III:** 75, 86

Hawthorne, Nathaniel, **I:** 106, 204, 211, 340, 355, 363, 384, 413, 458, 561–562; **II:** 7, 8, 40, 60, 63, 74, 89, 127–128, 138, 142, 198, 223–246, 255, 259, 264, 267, 272, 274, 277, 281, 282, 295, 307, 309, 311, 313, 322, 324, 326, 402, 408, 446, 501, 545; **III:** 51, 81–82, 83, 84, 85, 87, 88, 91, 92, 113, 316, 359, 412, 415, 421, 438, 453, 454, 507, 565, 572; **IV:** 2, 4, 167, 172, 179, 194, 333, 345, 453; **Retro. Supp. I:** 1, 53, 59, 62, 63, 91, 145–167, 215, 218, 220, 223, 248–249, 252, 257, 258, 330, 331, 365; **Retro. Supp. II:** 136, 142, 153, 156–157, 158, 159, 187, 221; **Supp. I Part 1:** 38, 188, 197, 317, 372; **Supp. I Part 2:** 420, 421, 545, 579, 580, 582, 587, 595, 596; **Supp. III Part 2:** 501; **Supp. IV Part 1:** 80, 127, 297; **Supp. IV Part 2:** 463, 596; **Supp. V:** 152; **Supp. VIII:** 103, 105, 108, 153, 201; **Supp. IX:** 114; **Supp. X:** 78; **Supp. XI:** 51, 78; **Supp. XII:** 26; **Supp. XIII:** 102; **Supp. XIV:**48; **Supp. XV:** 269, 272, 282; **Supp. XVI:**83, 84, 157

Hawthorne, Rose, **II:** 225

Hawthorne, Una, **II:** 225

"Hawthorne and His Mosses" (Melville), **Retro. Supp. I:** 254; **Supp. XIV:**48

"Hawthorne Aspect [of Henry James], The" (Eliot), **Retro. Supp. I:** 63

"Hawthorne in Solitude" (Cowley), **Supp. II Part 1:** 143

Hay, John, **I:** 1, 10, 12, 14–15; **Supp. I Part 1:** 352

Hay, Mrs. John, **I:** 14

Hay, Sara Henderson, **Supp. XIV:**119–135

Hayakawa, S. I., **I:** 448; **Supp. I Part 1:** 315; **Supp. XV:** 176

Hayden, Robert, **Supp. II Part 1:** 361–383; **Supp. IV Part 1:** 169; **Supp. XIII:** 115, 127; **Supp. XIV:**119, 123

Hayden, Sterling, **Supp. XI:** 304

Haydn, Hiram, **IV:** 100, 358

Hayduke Lives! (Abbey), **Supp. XIII:** 16

Hayek, Friedrich A. von, **Supp. IV Part 2:** 524

Hayes, Helen, **Supp. XVI:**193, 195

Hayes, Ira, **Supp. IV Part 1:** 326

Hayes, Richard, **Supp. V:** 320

Hayes, Rutherford B., **Supp. I Part 2:** 419

Haygood, Wil, **Supp. VIII:** 79

Hayne, Paul Hamilton, **Supp. I Part 1:** 352, 354, 355, 360, 372

Hayward, Florence, **Retro. Supp. II:** 65

Hayward, John, **Retro. Supp. I:** 67

Haywood, "Big" Bill, **I:** 483; **Supp. V:** 286

Hazard, Grace, **II:** 530

Hazard of Fortunes, A (Howells), **Retro. Supp. II:** 288

Hazard of New Fortunes, A (Howells), **II:** 275, 276, 286–297, 290

Hazel, Robert, **Supp. VIII:** 137, 138

Hazen, General W. B., **I:** 192, 193

Hazlitt, Henry, **Supp. IV Part 2:** 524

Hazlitt, William, **I:** 58, 378; **II:** 315

Hazmat (McClatchy), **Supp. XII:** 265–270

Hazo, Samuel, **I:** 386; **Supp. XIV:**123, 124

Hazzard, Shirley, **Supp. VIII:** 151

H.D. *See* Doolittle, Hilda

"He" (Porter), **III:** 434, 435

"Head and Shoulders" (Fitzgerald), **Retro. Supp. I:** 101

"Head-Hunter, The" (O. Henry), **Supp. II Part 1:** 403

"Headless Hawk, The" (Capote), **Supp. III Part 1:** 124

Headlines (T. Williams), **IV:** 381

Headlong Hall (Peacock), **Supp. I Part 1:** 307

Headmaster, The (McPhee), **Supp. III Part 1:** 291, 294, 298

"Head of Joaquín Murrieta, The" (Rodriguez), **Supp. XIV:**303

Headsman, The (Cooper), **I:** 345–346

"Headwaters" (Momaday), **Supp. IV Part 2:** 486

Healy, Eloise Klein, **Supp. XI:** 121, 124, 126, 127, 129, 137

Healy, Tim, **II:** 129, 137

Heaney, Seamus, **Retro. Supp. II:** 245; **Supp. IX:** 41, 42; **Supp. X:** 67, 122; **Supp. XI:** 249; **Supp. XV:** 256

"Heard through the Walls of the Racetrack Glen Motel" (X. J. Kennedy), **Supp. XV:** 170

Hearn, Lafcadio, **I:** 211; **II:** 311

Hearon, Shelby, **Supp. VIII:** 57–72

Hearst, Patty, **Supp. IV Part 1:** 195

Hearst, William Randolph, **I:** 198, 207, 208; **IV:** 298

"Heart and the Lyre, The" (Bogan), **Supp. III Part 1:** 65

"Heartbeat" (Harjo), **Supp. XII:** 221–222

Heartbreak Kid, The (film), **Supp. IV Part 2:** 575, 589

Heart for the Gods of Mexico, A (Aiken), **I:** 54

"Hear the Nightingale Sing" (Gordon), **II:** 200

Hear the Wind Blow (Sanders), **Supp. XVI:**268

Heart is a Lonely Hunter, The (McCullers), **II:** 586, 588–593, 604, 605

Heart of a Woman, The (Angelou), **Supp. IV Part 1:** 2, 5, 7–9, 9, 14, 17

Heart of Darkness (Conrad), **Retro. Supp. II:** 292; **Supp. V:** 249, 311; **Supp. VIII:** 4, 316

"Heart of Darkness" (Conrad), **I:** 575, 578; **II:** 595; **Supp. XVI:**212

Heart of Darkness (Didion), **Supp. IV Part 1:** 207

Heart of Happy Hollow, The (Dunbar), **Supp. II Part 1:** 214

Heart of Knowledge, The: American Indians on the Bomb (Gunn Allen and Caputi, eds.), **Supp. IV Part 1:** 334–335

"Heart of Knowledge, The: Nuclear Themes in Native American Thought and Literature" (Caputi), **Supp. IV Part 1:** 335

"Heart of the Park, The " (O'Connor), **Retro. Supp. II:** 225

Heart of the West (O. Henry), **Supp. II Part 1:** 410

"Hearts, The" (Pinsky), **Supp. VI:** 245–247, 248

"'Hearts and Flowers'" (MacLeish), **III:** 8

"Hearts and Heads" (Ransom), **Supp. I Part 1:** 373

"Heart's Graveyard Shift, The" (Komunyakaa), **Supp. XIII:** 120

Heart-Shape in the Dust (Hayden), **Supp. II Part 1:** 365, 366

"Heart's Needle" (Snodgrass), **Supp. VI:** 311–313, 320

Heart's Needle (Snodgrass), **I:** 400

"Hearts of Oak" (Rowson), **Supp. XV:** 243

"Heart Songs" (Proulx), **Supp. VII:** 254

Heart Songs and Other Stories (Proulx), **Supp. VII:** 252–256, 261

Heart to Artemis, The (Bryher), **Supp. I Part 1:** 259

Heartwood (Burke), **Supp. XIV:**35

Heath Anthology of American Literature, The, **Supp. IX:** 4; **Supp. XV:** 270, 313

Heathcote, Anne. *See* De Lancey, Mrs. James

"Heathen Chinee, The" (Harte), **Supp. II Part 1:** 350–351, 352

Heathen Days, 1890–1936 (Mencken), **III:** 100, 111

Heath-Stubbs, John, **Supp. XV:** 153

Heat's On, The (C. Himes), **Supp. XVI:**143, 144

"Heaven" (Dunn), **Supp. XI:** 154

"Heaven" (Levine), **Supp. V:** 182

"Heaven" (Patchett), **Supp. XII:** 309

Heaven and Earth: A Cosmology (Goldbarth), **Supp. XII:** 187

"Heaven and Earth in Jest" (Dillard), **Supp. VI:** 24, 28

"Heaven as Anus" (Kumin), **Supp. IV Part 2:** 448

Heavenly Conversation, The (Mather), **Supp. II Part 2:** 460

"Heavenly Feast, The" (Schnackenberg), **Supp. XV:** 257, 259

Heavens (Untermeyer), **Supp. XV:** 306

Heavens and Earth (Benét), **Supp. XI:** 44

Heaven's Coast (Doty), **Supp. XI:** 119, 121, 129–130, 134

Heaven's Prisoners (Burke), **Supp. XIV:**23, 29

"Heavy Angel, The" (Everwine), **Supp. XV:** 80

"Heavy Bear Who Goes with Me, The" (Schwartz), **Supp. II Part 2:** 646

"He Came Also Still" (Zukofsky), **Supp. III Part 2:** 612

Hecht, Anthony, **IV:** 138; **Supp. III Part 2:** 541, 561; **Supp. X:** 55–75; **Supp. XII:** 269–270; **Supp. XV:** 251, 256

Hecht, Ben, **I:** 103; **II:** 42; **Supp. I**

Part 2: 646; **Supp. XI:** 307; **Supp. XIII:** 106

Hecht, S. Theodore, **Supp. III Part 2:** 614

Heckewelder, John, **II:** 503

"Hedge Island" (Lowell), **II:** 524

Hedges, William I., **II:** 311–312

"He 'Digesteth Harde Yron'" (Moore), **Supp. IV Part 2:** 454

Hedin, Robert, **Supp. XII:** 200, 202

Hedylus (Doolittle), **Supp. I Part 1:** 259, 270

"Heel & Toe To the End" (W. C. Williams), **Retro. Supp. I:** 430

Heffernan, Michael, **Supp. XII:** 177

"HEGEL" (Baraka), **Supp. II Part 1:** 53

Hegel, Georg Wilhelm Friedrich, **I:** 265; **II:** 358; **III:** 262, 308–309, 480, 481, 487, 607; **IV:** 86, 333, 453; **Supp. I Part 2:** 633, 635, 640, 645; **Supp. XVI:**289

"Hegemony of Race, The" (Du Bois), **Supp. II Part 1:** 181

Hegger, Grace Livingston. *See* Lewis, Mrs. Sinclair (Grace Livingston Hegger)

"He Had Spent His Youth Dreaming" (Dobyns), **Supp. XIII:** 90

Heidegger, Martin, **II:** 362, 363; **III:** 292; **IV:** 491; **Retro. Supp. II:** 87; **Supp. V:** 267; **Supp. VIII:** 9; **Supp. XVI:**283, 288

Heidenmauer, The (Cooper), **I:** 345–346

Heidi Chronicles, The (Wasserstein), **Supp. IV Part 1:** 309; **Supp. XV:** 319, 325–327

"Height of the Ridiculous, The" (Holmes), **Supp. I Part 1:** 302

Heilbroner, Robert, **Supp. I Part 2:** 644, 648, 650

Heilbrun, Carolyn G., **Supp. IX:** 66; **Supp. XI:** 208; **Supp. XIV:**161, 163

Heilman, Robert Bechtold, **Supp. XIV:**11, 12

Heilpern, John, **Supp. XIV:**242

Heim, Michael, **Supp. V:** 209

Heine, Heinrich, **II:** 272, 273, 277, 281, 282, 387, 544; **IV:** 5; **Supp. XV:** 293, 299; **Supp. XVI:**188

Heineman, Frank, **Supp. III Part 2:** 619

Heinlein, Robert, **Supp. IV Part 1:** 102; **Supp. XVI:**122

Heinz, Helen. *See* Tate, Mrs. Allen (Helen Heinz)

Heiress, The (film), **Retro. Supp. I:** 222

"Heirs" (Nye), **Supp. XIII:** 284

"He Is Not Worth the Trouble" (Rowson), **Supp. XV:** 240

"He Knew" (C. Himes), **Supp. XVI:**137

"Helas" (Creeley), **Supp. IV Part 1:** 150, 158

Helburn, Theresa, **IV:** 381

Heldreth, Leonard, **Supp. V:** 151

"Helen" (Lowell), **II:** 544

"Helen: A Courtship" (Faulkner), **Retro. Supp. I:** 81

"Helen, Thy Beauty Is to Me" (Fante), **Supp. XI:** 169

"Helen I Love You" (Farrell), **II:** 28, 45

Helen in Egypt (Doolittle), **Supp. I Part 1:** 260, 272, 273, 274

Helen in Egypt (H.D.), **Supp. XV:** 264

Helen Keller: Sketch for a Portrait (Brooks), **I:** 254

"Helen of Tyre" (Longfellow), **II:** 496

Heliodora (Doolittle), **Supp. I Part 1:** 266

"Helix" (Sobin), **Supp. XVI:**283

Hellbox (O'Hara), **III:** 361

Heller, Joseph, **III:** 2, 258; **IV:** 98; **Retro. Supp. II:** 324; **Supp. I Part 1:** 196; **Supp. IV Part 1:** 379–396; **Supp. V:** 244; **Supp. VIII:** 245; **Supp. XI:** 307; **Supp. XII:** 167–168; **Supp. XV:** 322

Hellman, Lillian, **I:** 28; **III:** 28; **Supp. I Part 1:** 276–298; **Supp. IV Part 1:** 1, 12, 83, 353, 355, 356; **Supp. VIII:** 243; **Supp. IX:** 196, 198, 200–201, 204

Hellmann, Lillian, **Retro. Supp. II:** 327

Hello (Creeley), **Supp. IV Part 1:** 155, 157

"Hello, Hello Henry" (Kumin), **Supp. IV Part 2:** 446

"Hello, Stranger" (Capote), **Supp. III Part 1:** 120

Hello Dolly! (musical play), **IV:** 357

Hellyer, John, **Supp. I Part 2:** 468

Helm, Bob, **Supp. XV:** 147

Helmets (Dickey), **Supp. IV Part 1:** 175, 178, 180

"Helmsman, The" (Doolittle), **Supp. I Part 1:** 266

"Help" (Barth), **I:** 139

"Help Her to Believe" (Olsen). *See* "I Stand There Ironing" (Olsen)

"Helsinki Window" (Creeley), **Supp. IV Part 1:** 158

Hemenway, Robert E., **Supp. IV Part 1:** 6

Hemingway, Dr. Clarence Edwards, **II:** 248, 259

Hemingway, Ernest, **I:** 28, 64, 97, 99, 105, 107, 117, 150, 162, 190, 211, 221, 288, 289, 295, 367, 374, 378, 421, 423, 445, 476, 477, 478, 482, 484–485, 487, 488, 489, 491, 495, 504, 517; **II:** 27, 44, 51, 58, 68–69, 78, 90, 97, 127, 206, 247–270, 289, 424, 431, 456, 457, 458–459, 482, 560, 600; **III:** 2, 18, 20, 35, 36, 37, 40, 61, 108, 220, 334, 363, 364, 382, 453, 454, 471–472, 476, 551, 575, 576, 584; **IV:** 27, 28, 33, 34, 35, 42, 49, 97, 108, 122, 126, 138, 190, 191, 201, 216, 217, 257, 297, 363, 404, 427, 433, 451; **Retro. Supp. I:** 74, 98, 108, 111, 112, 113, 115, 169–191, 215, 292, 359, 418; **Retro. Supp. II:** 19, 24, 30, 68, 115, 123; **Supp. I Part 2:** 621, 658, 678; **Supp. II Part 1:** 221; **Supp. III Part 1:** 146; **Supp. III Part 2:** 617; **Supp. IV Part 1:** 48, 102, 123, 197, 236, 342, 343, 344, 348, 350, 352, 380–381, 383; **Supp. IV Part 2:** 463, 468, 502, 607, 679, 680, 681, 689, 692; **Supp. V:** 237, 240, 244, 250, 336; **Supp. VIII:** 40, 101, 105, 179, 182, 183, 188, 189, 196; **Supp. IX:** 16, 57, 58, 94, 106, 260, 262; **Supp. X:** 137, 167, 223, 225; **Supp. XI:** 214, 221; **Supp. XIII:** 96, 255, 270; **Supp. XIV:**24, 83; **Supp. XV:** 69, 135; **Supp. XVI:**203, 205–206, 208, 210, 233, 236–237, 281–282

Hemingway, Mrs. Ernest (Hadley Richardson), **II:** 257, 260, 263

Hemingway, Mrs. Ernest (Martha Gellhorn), **II:** 260

Hemingway, Mrs. Ernest (Mary Welsh), **II:** 257, 260

Hemingway, Mrs. Ernest (Pauline Pfeiffer), **II:** 260

"Hemingway: The Old Lion" (Cowley), **Supp. II Part 1:** 143

"Hemingway in Paris" (Cowley), **Supp. II Part 1:** 144

"Hemingway Story, A" (Dubus), **Supp. VII:** 91

"Hemp, The" (Benét), **Supp. XI:** 44

"Henchman, The" (Whittier), **Supp. I Part 2:** 696

Henderson, Alice Corbin, **Supp. I Part 2:** 387; **Supp. XV:** 302–303

Henderson, Darwin L., **Supp. XIII:** 213, 221–222

Henderson, Jane, **Supp. VIII:** 87

Henderson, Katherine, **Supp. IV Part 1:** 203, 207

Henderson, Linda. *See* Hogan, Linda

Henderson, Robert W., **Supp. VIII:** 124

Henderson, Stephen, **Supp. IV Part 1:** 365

Henderson, the Rain King (Bellow), **I:** 144, 147, 148, 152, 153, 154, 155, 158, 160, 161, 162–163; **Retro. Supp. II:** 19, 24–25, 30

"Hen Flower, The" (Kinnell), **Supp. III Part 1:** 247–248

Henie, Sonja, **Supp. XII:** 165

Henle, James, **II:** 26, 30, 38, 41; **Supp. IX:** 2

Hennesy, Dale, **Supp. XV:** 5

Henri, Robert, **IV:** 411; **Supp. I Part 2:** 376

Henry, Arthur, **I:** 515; **Retro. Supp. II:** 97

Henry, DeWitt, **Supp. XI:** 342

Henry, O., **I:** 201; **III:** 5; **Supp. I Part 2:** 390, 462; **Supp. II Part 1:** 385–412; **Supp. XV:** 40

Henry, Robert, **Retro. Supp. II:** 103

Henry, William A., **III, Supp. IV Part 2:** 574

Henry and June (film), **Supp. X:** 186

Henry and June: From the Unexpurgated Diary of Anaïs Nin, **Supp. X:** 184, 185, 187, 194

Henry Holt and Company, **Retro. Supp. I:** 121, 131, 133, 136

Henry IV (Shakespeare), **III:** 166; **Supp. VIII:** 164

"Henry James, Jr." (Howells), **II:** 289; **Retro. Supp. I:** 220

"Henry James and the Art of Teaching" (Rowe), **Retro. Supp. I:** 216

"Henry Manley, Living Alone, Keeps Time" (Kumin), **Supp. IV Part 2:** 451

"Henry Manley Looks Back" (Kumin), **Supp. IV Part 2:** 451

"Henry Manley" poems (Kumin), **Supp. IV Part 2:** 446

Henry Miller Reader, The (Durrell, ed.), **III:** 175, 190

"Henry's Confession" (Berryman), **I:** 186

Henry VIII (Shakespeare), **Supp. IX:** 235

Henslee, **Supp. IV Part 1:** 217

Henson, Josiah, **Supp. I Part 2:** 589

Hentoff, Margot, **Supp. IV Part 1:** 205

Hentz, Caroline Lee, **Supp. I Part 2:** 584

Henze, Hans Werner, **Supp. II Part 1:** 24

"He of the Assembly" (Bowles), **Supp. IV Part 1:** 90

Hepburn, Katharine, **Supp. IX:** 189; **Supp. XI:** 17

Heraclitus, **II:** 1, 163; **IV:** 86

Herakles: A Play in Verse (MacLeish), **III:** 21, 22

Herald of the Autochthonic Spirit (Corso), **Supp. XII:** 134–136

Herberg, Will, **III:** 291

Herbert, Edward, **II:** 11

Herbert, Francis (pseudonym). *See* Bryant, William Cullen

Herbert, George, **II:** 12; **IV:** 141, 145, 146, 151, 153, 156, 165; **Retro. Supp. II:** 40; **Supp. I Part 1:** 80, 107, 108, 122; **Supp. IV Part 2:** 646; **Supp. XV:** 92, 212, 251

Herbert, Zbigniew, **Supp. VIII:** 20

Herbert Huncke Reader, The (Schafer, ed.), **Supp. XIV:** 137, 138, 139, 140, 145, 147, 150, 151–152

Herbert of Cherbury, Lord, **II:** 108

"Herbert White" (Bidart), **Supp. XV:** 24, 27

Herbst, Josephine, **Retro. Supp. II:** 325, 328; **Supp. XIII:** 295

"Her Choice" (Larcom), **Supp. XIII:** 144

"Her Dead Brother" (Lowell), **Retro. Supp. II:** 188

"Her Dream Is of the Sea" (Ríos), **Supp. IV Part 2:** 546

"Here" (Kenyon), **Supp. VII:** 164

Here and Beyond (Wharton), **Retro. Supp. I:** 382

Here and Now (Levertov), **Supp. III Part 1:** 275, 276

"Here and There" (Wallace), **Supp. X:** 305–306

Here Comes the Mystery Man (Sanders), **Supp. XVI:** 269

Heredia, Juanita, **Supp. XI:** 185, 190

Heredity and Variation (Lock), **Retro. Supp. I:** 375

Here Lies (Parker), **Supp. IX:** 192

Here on Earth (Hoffman), **Supp. X:** 77, 89

Heresy and the Ideal: On Contemporary Poetry (Baker), **Supp. XI:** 142

"Here to Learn" (Bowles), **Supp. IV Part 1:** 93

"Here to Yonder" (Hughes), **Retro. Supp. I:** 205

"Her Father's Letters" (Milburn), **Supp. XI:** 242

Herford, Reverend Brooke, **I:** 471

Hergesheimer, Joseph, **Supp. I Part 2:** 620; **Supp. XVI:** 187

"Heritage" (Cullen), **Supp. IV Part 1:** 164–165, 168, 170, 171

"Heritage" (Hogan), **Supp. IV Part 1:** 413

"Her Kind" (Sexton), **Supp. II Part 2:** 687

Herland (Gilman), **Supp. XI:** 208–209

Herman, Florence. *See* Williams, Mrs. William Carlos (Florence Herman)

Herman, Jan, **Supp. XIV:** 150–151

Herman, William (pseudonym). *See* Bierce, Ambrose

"Her Management" (Swenson), **Supp. IV Part 2:** 642

"Herman Melville" (Auden), **Supp. II Part 1:** 14

Herman Melville (Mumford), **Supp. II Part 2:** 471, 476, 489–491

"Hermes of the Ways" (Doolittle), **Supp. I Part 1:** 266

Hermetic Definition (Doolittle), **Supp. I Part 1:** 271, 272, 273, 274

"Hermitage, The" (Haines), **Supp. XII:** 205–206

Hermit and the Wild Woman, The (Wharton), **IV:** 315; **Retro. Supp. I:** 371

"Hermit and the Wild Woman, The" (Wharton), **Retro. Supp. I:** 372

"Hermit Meets the Skunk, The" (Kumin), **Supp. IV Part 2:** 447

"Hermit of Saba, The" (Freneau), **Supp. II Part 1:** 259

Hermit of 69th Street, The: The Working Papers or Norbert Kosky (Kosinski), **Supp. VII:** 215, 216, 223, 226–227

"Hermit Picks Berries, The" (Kumin), **Supp. IV Part 2:** 447

Hermit's Story, The (Bass), **Supp. XVI:** 23–24

"Hermit Thrush, A" (Clampitt), **Supp. IX:** 40

Hernández, Miguel, **Supp. V:** 194; **Supp. XIII:** 315, 323

Herne, James A., **II:** 276; **Supp. II Part 1:** 198

Hernton, Calvin, **Supp. X:** 240

"Hero, The" (Moore), **III:** 200, 211, 212

Hero, The (Raglan), **I:** 135

Hérodiade (Mallarmé), **I:** 66

Herodotus, **Supp. I Part 2:** 405

Heroes, The (Ashbery), **Supp. III Part 1:** 3

Hero in America, The (Van Doren), **II:** 103

"Heroines of Nature: Four Women Respond to the American Landscape" (Norwood), **Supp. IX:** 24

"Heron, The" (Roethke), **III:** 540–541

"Her One Bad Eye" (Karr), **Supp. XI:** 244

"Her Own People" (Warren), **IV:** 253

"Her Quaint Honour" (Gordon), **II:** 196, 199, 200

Herr, Michael, **Supp. XI:** 245

Herrick, Robert, **II:** 11, 18, 444; **III:** 463, 592; **IV:** 453; **Retro. Supp. I:** 319; **Retro. Supp. II:** 101; **Supp. I Part 2:** 646; **Supp. XIII:** 334; **Supp. XIV:** 8, 9; **Supp. XV:** 155

Herrmann, John, **Retro. Supp. II:** 328

Herron, George, **Supp. I Part 1:** 7

"Hers" (column, Prose), **Supp. XVI:** 254

Herschel, Sir John, **Supp. I Part 1:** 314

"Her Sense of Timing" (Elkin), **Supp. VI:** 56, 58

Hersey, John, **IV:** 4; **Supp. I Part 1:** 196; **Supp. XVI:** 105–106

"Her Sweet turn to leave the Homestead" (Dickinson), **Retro. Supp. I:** 44

Herzog (Bellow), **I:** 144, 147, 149, 150, 152, 153, 154, 155, 156, 157, 158, 159–160; **Retro. Supp. II:** 19, 26–27; **Supp. IV Part 1:** 30

Hesford, Walter A., **Supp. XV:** 215, 217, 218

"He/She" (Dunn), **Supp. XI:** 149

"Hesitation Blues" (Hughes), **Retro. Supp. I:** 211

Hesse, Hermann, **Supp. V:** 208

"Hetch Hetchy Valley" (Muir), **Supp. IX:** 185

He Who Gets Slapped (Andreyev), **II:** 425

"He Who Spits at the Sky" (Stegner), **Supp. IV Part 2:** 605

"He Will Not Leave a Note" (Ríos), **Supp. IV Part 2:** 548

Hewitt, James, **Supp. XV:** 240

Hewlett, Maurice, **I:** 359

Heyen, William, **Supp. XIII:** 285, 344; **Supp. XV:** 212

"Hey! Hey!" (Hughes), **Supp. I Part 1:** 327–328

Hey Rub-a-Dub-Dub (Dreiser), **I:** 515; **II:** 26; **Retro. Supp. II:** 104, 105, 108

"Hey Sailor, What Ship?" (Olsen), **Supp. XIII:** 293, 294, 298, 299

Hiawatha (Longfellow), **Supp. I Part 1:** 79; **Supp. III Part 2:** 609, 610

"Hibernaculum" (Ammons), **Supp. VII:** 26–27

Hichborn, Mrs. Philip. *See* Wylie, Elinor

Hichborn, Philip, **Supp. I Part 2:** 707, 708

"Hic Jacet" (W. C. Williams), **Retro. Supp. I:** 414

Hickok, James Butler ("Wild Bill"), **Supp. V:** 229, 230

Hicks, Granville, **I:** 254, 259, 374; **II:** 26; **III:** 342, 355, 452; **Supp. I Part 1:** 361; **Supp. I Part 2:** 609; **Supp. IV Part 1:** 22; **Supp. IV Part 2:** 526; **Supp. VIII:** 96, 124; **Supp. XII:** 250; **Supp. XIII:** 263

Hicok, Bethany, **Retro. Supp. II:** 39

"Hidden" (Nye), **Supp. XIII:** 283

"Hidden Gardens" (Capote), **Supp. III Part 1:** 125

Hidden Law, The (Hecht), **Supp. X:** 58

"Hidden Name and Complex Fate" (Ellison), **Supp. II Part 1:** 245

Hidden Wound, The (Berry), **Supp. X:** 23, 25, 26–27, 29, 34, 35

"Hide-and-Seek" (Francis), **Supp. IX:** 81

"Hiding" (Minot), **Supp. VI:** 203, 206

Hiding Place (Wideman), **Supp. X:** 320, 321, 327, 329, 331–332, 333

Hienger, Jorg, **Supp. IV Part 1:** 106

Higgins, George, **Supp. IV Part 1:** 356

Higginson, Thomas Wentworth, **I:** 451–452, 453, 454, 456, 458, 459, 463, 464, 465, 470; **Retro. Supp. I:** 26, 31, 33, 35, 39, 40; **Supp. I Part 1:** 307, 371; **Supp. IV Part 2:** 430

"High Bridge above the Tagus River at Toledo, The" (W. C. Williams), **Retro. Supp. I:** 429

"High Dive: A Variant" (Kumin), **Supp. IV Part 2:** 442

"High Diver" (Francis), **Supp. IX:** 82

"Higher Keys, The" (Merrill), **Supp. III Part 1:** 335–336

Higher Learning in America, The (Veblen), **Supp. I Part 2:** 630, 631, 641, 642

Highet, Gilbert, **Supp. I Part 1:** 268

High Noon (film), **Supp. V:** 46

"High on Sadness" (Komunyakaa), **Supp. XIII:** 114

"High School Senior" (Olds), **Supp. X:** 212

Highsmith, Patricia, **Supp. IV Part 1:** 79, 94, 132

"High Tide" (Marquand), **III:** 56

High Tide in Tucson: Essays from Now or Never (Kingsolver), **Supp. VII:** 198, 201, 209

"High-Toned Old Christian Woman, A" (Stevens), **Retro. Supp. I:** 301

"Highway, The" (Merwin), **Supp. III Part 1:** 346

"Highway 99E from Chico" (Carver), **Supp. III Part 1:** 136

High Window, The (Chandler), **Supp. IV Part 1:** 127–129, 130, 131

Hijuelos, Oscar, **Supp. IV Part 1:** 54; **Supp. VIII:** 73–91

Hike and the Aeroplane (Lewis), **II:** 440–441

Hilberg, Raul, **Supp. V:** 267

Hildebrand, Al, **III:** 118

Hiler, Hilaire, **Retro. Supp. II:** 327; **Supp. III Part 2:** 617

"Hill, A" (Hecht), **Supp. X:** 59–60, 63

Hill, Abram, **Supp. XV:** 194

Hill, Hamlin, **Retro. Supp. II:** 286

Hill, James J., **Supp. I Part 2:** 644

Hill, Joe, **I:** 493

Hill, Lee, **Supp. XI:** 293, 294, 297, 299, 301, 305, 307

Hill, Patti, **I:** 289

Hill, Peggy, **Supp. XIII:** 163

"Hill, The" (Strand), **Supp. IV Part 2:** 627

"Hill, The" (Toomer), **Supp. III Part 2:** 486

Hill, Vernon, **Supp. I Part 2:** 397

"Hillcrest" (Robinson), **III:** 504

Hill-Lubin, Mildred A., **Supp. IV Part 1:** 13

Hillman, Sidney, **Supp. I Part 1:** 5

Hillringhouse, Mark, **Supp. IX:** 286, 288, 299

Hills Beyond, The (Wolfe), **IV:** 450, 451, 460, 461

"Hills Beyond, The" (Wolfe), **IV:** 460

Hillside and Seaside in Poetry (Larcom, ed.), **Supp. XIII:** 142

"Hillside Thaw, A" (Frost), **Retro. Supp. I:** 133

"Hills Like White Elephants" (Hemingway), **Retro. Supp. I:** 170

"Hill-Top View, A" (Jeffers), **Supp. II Part 2:** 417

"Hill Wife, The" (Frost), **II:** 154; **Retro. Supp. I:** 131

Hillyer, Catherine, **Supp. XV:** 244

Hillyer, Robert, **I:** 475; **Supp. IX:** 75; **Supp. XIV:** 11

Hilton, James, **Supp. XIII:** 166

"Hiltons' Holiday, The" (Jewett), **II:** 391; **Retro. Supp. II:** 134

Him (Cummings), **I:** 429, 434–435

Himes, Chester, **Retro. Supp. II:** 117; **Supp. I Part 1:** 51, 325; **Supp. XIII:** 233

Himes, Chester Bomar, **Supp. XVI:** 135–146

Himes, Norman, **Supp. V:** 128

"Him with His Foot in His Mouth" (Bellow), **Retro. Supp. II:** 34

Him with His Foot in His Mouth and Other Stories (Bellow), **Retro. Supp. II:** 31

Hinchman, Sandra K., **Supp. IV Part 1:** 210

Hindemith, Paul, **IV:** 357; **Supp. IV Part 1:** 81

Hindsell, Oliver, **Supp. XIII:** 162

Hindus, Milton, **Supp. XIV:**288, 291, 292, 293

Hines, Suzanne, **Supp. XIV:**151

Hinge Picture (Howe), **Supp. IV Part 2:** 423–424

"Hinterlands" (W. Gibson), **Supp. XVI:**123, 128

"Hippies: Slouching towards Bethlehem" (Didion), **Supp. IV Part 1:** 200

Hippolytus (Euripides), **II:** 543; **Supp. I Part 1:** 270

Hippolytus Temporizes (Doolittle), **Supp. I Part 1:** 270

"Hips" (Cisneros), **Supp. VII:** 61, 62

"Hipster's Hipster" (Ginsberg), **Supp. XIV:**141

Hirsch, Edward, **Supp. XV:** 78, 225

Hirsch, Edward D., **Supp. V:** 177; **Supp. IX:** 262; **Supp. XIV:**15

Hirsch, Sidney, **Supp. XIV:**1. *See* Mttron-Hirsch, Sidney

Hirschorn, Clive, **Supp. IV Part 2:** 577, 579

Hirson, Roger, **Supp. XI:** 343

"His Bride of the Tomb" (Dunbar), **Supp. II Part 1:** 196

"His Chest of Drawers" (Anderson), **I:** 113, 114

"His Last Day" (C. Himes), **Supp. XVI:**137

"His Lover" (Dubus), **Supp. VII:** 86

"His Music" (Dunn), **Supp. XI:** 149

"His Own Key" (Ríos), **Supp. IV Part 2:** 543

His Picture in the Papers (film; Emerson), **Supp. XVI:**185

His Religion and Hers (Gilman), **Supp. XI:** 209

Hiss, Alger, **Supp. XV:** 143

"Hiss, Chambers, and the Age of Innocence" (Fiedler), **Supp. XIII:** 99

"His Shield" (Moore), **III:** 211

"His Story" (Cisneros), **Supp. VII:** 67

His Thought Made Pockets & the Plane Buckt (Berryman), **I:** 170

"His Three Women" (Gioia), **Supp. XV:** 119–120

Histoire comparée des systèmes de philosophie (Gérando), **II:** 10

Historical and Moral View of the Origin and Progress of the French Revolution (Wollstonecraft), **Supp. I Part 1:** 126

"Historical Conceptualization" (Huizinga), **I:** 255

Historical Evidence and the Reading of Seventeenth-Century Poetry (Brooks), **Supp. XIV:**11

"Historical Interpretation of Literature, The" (Wilson), **IV:** 431, 433, 445

Historical Jesus, The: The Life of a Mediterranean Jewish Peasant (Crossan), **Supp. V:** 251

"Historical Value of Crèvecoeur's *Voyage . . .,*" (Adams), **Supp. I Part 1:** 251

"History" (Emerson), **II:** 13, 15

"History" (Hughes), **Supp. I Part 1:** 344

History (Lowell), **Retro. Supp. II:** 183, 190

"History" (Simic), **Supp. VIII:** 279

"History, Myth, and the Western Writer" (Stegner), **Supp. IV Part 2:** 596, 601

"History among the Rocks" (Warren), **IV:** 252

History as a Literary Art (Morison), **Supp. I Part 2:** 493

"History as Fate in E. L. Doctorow's Tale of a Western Town" (Arnold), **Supp. IV Part 1:** 220

"History Is the Memory of Time" (Olson), **Supp. II Part 2:** 574

"History Lessons" (Komunyakaa), **Supp. XIII:** 126

"History of a Literary Movement" (Nemerov), **III:** 270

"History of a Literary Radical, The" (Bourne), **I:** 215, 235, 236

History of a Radical: Essays by Randolph Bourne (Brooks), **I:** 245

"History of Buttons, The" (Goldbarth), **Supp. XII:** 187

History of English Literature (Taine), **III:** 323

History of English Prosody (Saintsbury), **Supp. XV:** 181

History of Fortus, The (Emerson), **II:** 8

History of Henry Esmond, The (Thackeray), **II:** 91, 130

History of Modern Poetry, A (Perkins), **Supp. I Part 2:** 475; **Supp. XV:** 185

History of My Heart (Pinsky), **Supp. VI:** 243, 244, 245

History of New York, from the Beginning of the World to the End of the Dutch Dynasty, A (Irving), **II:** 300–303, 304, 310

History of Pendennis, The (Thackeray), **II:** 291

"History of Red, The" (Hogan), **Supp. IV Part 1:** 411

"History of Rodney, The" (Bass), **Supp. XVI:**20

History of Roxbury Town (Ellis), **Supp. I Part 1:** 99

History of the Conquest of Mexico (Prescott), **Retro. Supp. I:** 123

History of the Conquest of Peru (Morison, ed.), **Supp. I Part 2:** 494

History of the Dividing Line betwixt Virginia and North Carolina (Byrd), **Supp. IV Part 2:** 425

History of the Life and Voyages of Christopher Columbus, A (Irving), **II:** 310, 314

History of the Navy of the United States of America (Cooper), **I:** 347

History of the Rise and Fall of the Slavepower in America (Wilson), **Supp. XIV:**48, 49

History of the United States of America during the Administrations of Thomas Jefferson and James Madison (Adams), **I:** 6–9, 10, 20, 21

History of the Work of Redemption, A (Edwards), **I:** 560

History of United States Naval Operations in World War II (Morison), **Supp. I Part 2:** 490–492

History of Womankind in Western Europe, The, **Supp. XI:** 197

"History Through a Beard" (Morison), **Supp. I Part 2:** 490

His Toy, His Dream, His Rest (Berryman), **I:** 169, 170, 183, 184–186

"His Words" (Roethke), **III:** 544

Hitchcock, Ada. *See* MacLeish, Mrs. Archibald (Ada Hitchcock)

Hitchcock, Alfred, **IV:** 357; **Supp. IV Part 1:** 132; **Supp. VIII:** 177

Hitchcock, George, **Supp. X:** 127

"Hitch Haiku" (Snyder), **Supp. VIII:** 297

"Hitch-Hikers, The" (Welty), **IV:** 262

Hitchins, Christopher, **Supp. VIII:** 241

Hitler, Adolf, **I:** 261, 290, 492; **II:** 146, 454, 561, 565, 592; **III:** 2, 3, 110, 115, 140, 156, 246, 298, 446; **IV:** 5, 17, 18, 298, 372; **Supp. I Part 2:** 431, 436, 446, 664; **Supp. V:** 290

Hitler, Wendy, **III:** 404

Hitler Lives ? (film), **Supp. XVI:**102

Hix, H. L., **Supp. XV:** 114

Hnizdovsky, Jacques, **Supp. XIII:** 346

"Hoadley's Test Case in Indiana"

(Neugeboren), **Supp. XVI:**219

Hoagland, Edward, **Supp. XIV:**80; **Supp. XVI:**277

"Hoarder, The" (Sexton), **Supp. II Part 2:** 692

Hoban, Phoebe, **Supp. XV:** 319, 325

Hobb, Gormley, **I:** 203

Hobbes, Thomas, **I:** 277; **II:** 9, 10, 540; **III:** 306; **IV:** 88; **Supp. XII:** 33; **Supp. XIV:**5, 7

Hobson, Geary, **Supp. IV Part 1:** 321; **Supp. IV Part 2:** 502

Hobson, J. A., **I:** 232

Hobson, John A., **Supp. I Part 2:** 650

Hobson, Laura Z., **III:** 151

Hocking, Agnes, **Supp. VIII:** 251

Hocking, William Ernest, **III:** 303

Hodges, Campbell B., **Supp. XIV:**8

Hodgson, Captain Joseph, **III:** 328

Hoffa, Jimmy, **I:** 493

Hoffenberg, Mason, **Supp. XI:** 294, 297, 299, 305

Hoffer, Eric, **Supp. VIII:** 188

Hoffman, Abbie, **Supp. XIV:**150

Hoffman, Alice, **Supp. X:** 77–94; **Supp. XIII:** 13

Hoffman, Daniel, **Retro. Supp. II:** 265

Hoffman, Daniel G., **I:** 405; **II:** 307; **Supp. XI:** 152

Hoffman, Dustin, **Supp. IV Part 1:** 236

Hoffman, E. T. A., **Supp. XVI:**157

Hoffman, Eva, **Supp. XVI:**147–164

Hoffman, Frederick J., **I:** 60, 67; **II:** 443; **IV:** 113

Hoffman, Josiah Ogden, **II:** 297, 300

Hoffman, Matilda, **II:** 300, 314

Hoffman, Paul, **Supp. XV:** 141–142

Hoffman, William M., **Supp. X:** 153

Hoffmann, E. T. A., **III:** 415

Hofmann, Hans, **Supp. XV:** 144

Ho for a Hat (W. J. Smith), **Supp. XIII:** 346

Hofstadter, Richard, **Supp. VIII:** 98, 99, 108

Hogan, Linda, **Supp. IV Part 1:** 324, 325, 397–418

Hogan, Randolph, **Supp. XVI:**252–253

Hogarth, William, **Supp. XII:** 44

Hogg, James, **I:** 53; **Supp. I Part 1:** 349; **Supp. IX:** 275

Hoggart, Richard, **Supp. XIV:**299

Hohne, Karen, **Supp. V:** 147

Hojoki (Chomei), **IV:** 170

Holbrook, David, **Supp. I Part 2:** 526–527, 546

Holcroft, Thomas, **Supp. I Part 2:** 514

Holden, Jonathan, **Supp. XI:** 143

Holden, Raymond, **Supp. XIV:**121–122

Holden, William, **Supp. XI:** 307

Hölderlin, Friedrich, **Supp. XVI:**48

"Holding On" (Levine), **Supp. V:** 184

Holding the Line: Women in the Great Arizona Mine Strike of 1983 (Kingsolver), **Supp. VII:** 197, 201–202, 204

"Holding the Mirror Up to Nature" (Nemerov), **III:** 275, 276

"Hold Me" (Levine), **Supp. V:** 186

Hold the Press (film), **Supp. XIII:** 163

Hold with the Hares (Zinberg), **Supp. XV:** 197–198,**Supp. XV:** 203

"Hole in the Floor, A" (Wilbur), **Supp. III Part 2:** 556–557

Holiday (Barry), **Retro. Supp. I:** 104

"Holiday" (Porter), **III:** 454

Holiday, Billie, **Supp. I Part 1:** 80; **Supp. IV Part 1:** 2, 7

Holinshed, Raphael, **IV:** 370

Holland, Josiah, **Supp. I Part 2:** 420

Holland, Laurence Bedwell, **Retro. Supp. I:** 216

Holland, Mrs. Theodore, **I:** 453, 455, 465

Holland, Theodore, **I:** 453

Holland, William, **IV:** 381

Hollander, John, **Supp. III Part 2:** 541; **Supp. IV Part 2:** 642; **Supp. IX:** 50, 153, 155; **Supp. XII:** 254, 255, 260; **Supp. XV:** 256

Holley, Marietta, **Supp. XIII:** 152

Hollinghurst, Alan, **Supp. XIII:** 52

Hollis, Thomas Brand, **Supp. I Part 2:** 514

Hollow Men, The (Eliot), **I:** 574, 575, 578–579, 580, 585; **III:** 586; **Retro. Supp. I:** 63, 64

"Hollow Tree, A" (R. Bly), **Supp. IV Part 1:** 64, 66

Hollyberrys at the Shore, The, **Supp. X:** 42

"Hollywood!" (Vidal), **Supp. IV Part 2:** 688

Hollywood: American Movie-City (Rand, unauthorized), **Supp. IV Part 2:** 519

Hollywood: A Novel of America in the 1920s (Vidal), **Supp. IV Part 2:** 677, 684, 686, 688, 690, 691

Hollywood Ending (film; Allen), **Supp. XV:** 11

Hollywood on Trial (film), **Supp. I Part 1:** 295

Holmes, Abiel, **Supp. I Part 1:** 300, 301, 302, 310

Holmes, John, **I:** 169; **Supp. II Part 1:** 87; **Supp. IV Part 2:** 440–441; **Supp. XIV:**119

Holmes, John Clellon, **Supp. XII:** 118; **Supp. XIV:**144, 150

Holmes, Mrs. Abiel (Sarah Wendell), **Supp. I Part 1:** 300

Holmes, Mrs. Oliver Wendell (Amelia Jackson), **Supp. I Part 1:** 303

Holmes, Oliver Wendell, **I:** 487; **II:** 225, 273–274, 402, 403; **III:** 81–82, 590, 591–592; **IV:** 429, 436; **Retro. Supp. II:** 155; **Supp. I Part 1:** 103, 243, 254, 299–319; **Supp. I Part 2:** 405, 414, 415, 420, 593, 704, 705; **Supp. XI:** 194

Holmes, Oliver Wendell, Jr., **I:** 3, 19; **Supp. IV Part 2:** 422

Holmes, Steven J., **Supp. IX:** 172, 177

Holmes, Ted, **Supp. V:** 180

Holmes, William Henry, **Supp. IV Part 2:** 603–604

Holocaust (Reznikoff), **Supp. XIV:**281, 291–293

Holocaust in American Life, The (Novick), **Supp. XVI:**154

Holt, Edwin E., **I:** 59

Holt, Felix, **II:** 179

Holt, Henry, **II:** 348; **III:** 587

Holt, Patricia, **Supp. XIV:**89

Holtby, Winifred, **Supp. I Part 2:** 720

Holy Ghostly, The (Shepard), **Supp. III Part 2:** 437–438, 447

"Holy Innocents, The" (Lowell), **II:** 539

Holy Sonnets (Donne), **IV:** 145; **Supp. I Part 1:** 367; **Supp. III Part 2:** 619; **Supp. XIII:** 130–131

"Holy Terror, A" (Bierce), **I:** 203

"Holy Terror, The" (Maxwell), **Supp. VIII:** 169

Holy the Firm (Dillard), **Supp. VI:** 23, 29, 30, 31, 32

Holy War, The (Bunyan), **IV:** 156

"Homage to Arthur Rimbaud" (Wright), **Supp. V:** 339

Homage to Baudelaire (Duncan, ed.), **Supp. XV:** 75

"Homage to Che Guevara" (Banks), **Supp. V:** 5

Homage to Clio (Auden), **Supp. II Part 1:** 24

"Homage to Elizabeth Bishop" (Ivask, ed.), **Supp. I Part 1:** 96

"Homage to Ezra Pound" (Wright), **Supp. V:** 339

Homage to Frank O'Hara (Ashbery), **Supp. III Part 1:** 2–3

"Homage to Franz Joseph Haydn" (Hecht), **Supp. X:** 69

"Homage to Hemingway" (Bishop), **IV:** 35

Homage to Mistress Bradstreet (Berryman), **I:** 168, 169, 170–171,

172, 174, 175, 178–183, 184, 186
"Homage to Paul Cézanne" (Wright), **Supp. V:** 341–342
Homage to Sextus Propertius (Pound), **Retro. Supp. I:** 290
"Homage to Sextus Propertius" (Pound), **III:** 462, 476; **Supp. III Part 2:** 622
"Homage to Shakespeare" (Cheever), **Supp. I Part 1:** 180
"Homage to the Empress of the Blues" (Hayden), **Supp. II Part 1:** 379
"Homage to the Memory of Wallace Stevens" (Justice), **Supp. VII:** 126
Homage to Theodore Dreiser (Warren), **I:** 517
Homans, Margaret, **Supp. X:** 229
"Home" (Hughes), **Supp. I Part 1:** 329, 330
"Home" (Mora), **Supp. XIII:** 217
Home (Updike), **Retro. Supp. I:** 320
"Home, Home on the Strange" (J. D. Reed), **Supp. XVI:**174
Home: Social Essays (Baraka), **Supp. II Part 1:** 45, 61
"Home, Sweet Home" (Fante), **Supp. XI:** 164, 165
Home, The (Gilman), **Supp. XI:** 206–207
"Home after Three Months Away" (Lowell), **II:** 547
Home and Colonial Library (Murray), **Retro. Supp. I:** 246
Home as Found (Cooper), **I:** 348, 349, 350, 351
Home at the End of the World, A (Cunningham), **Supp. XV:** 59–62, 63
"Home Away from Home, A" (Humphrey), **Supp. IX:** 101
Home Book of Shakespeare Quotations (Stevenson), **Supp. XIV:**120
"Home Burial" (Frost), **Retro. Supp. I:** 124, 125, 128, 129–130; **Supp. VIII:** 31
"Home Burial" (R. Frost), **Supp. XV:** 159
Homecoming (Alvarez), **Supp. VII:** 1, 3–5, 9
"Homecoming" (Carruth), **Supp. XVI:**55
"Homecoming" (McGrath), **Supp. X:** 116
"Homecoming, The" (Gioia), **Supp. XV:** 123, 124
Homecoming, The (Wilson), **Supp. VIII:** 330
Homecoming Game, The (Nemerov), **III:** 268, 282, 284–285
"Home during a Tropical Snowstorm I

Feed My Father Lunch" (Karr), **Supp. XI:** 241–242, 248
Home Economics (Berry), **Supp. X:** 28, 31–32, 35, 36, 37
Home from the Hill (film), **Supp. IX:** 95
Home from the Hill (Humphrey), **Supp. IX:** 93, 95, 96–98, 104, 106, 109
"Home Grown" (Vital), **Supp. XVI:**160
"Homeland" (Merwin), **Supp. III Part 1:** 351
Homeland and Other Stories (Kingsolver), **Supp. VII:** 199, 202–204, 207
Home on the Range (Baraka), **Supp. II Part 1:** 47
Home Place, The (Morris), **III:** 221, 222, 232
Homer, **I:** 312, 433; **II:** 6, 8, 133, 302, 543, 544, 552; **III:** 14, 21, 278, 453, 457, 473, 567; **IV:** 54, 371; **Retro. Supp. I:** 59; **Supp. I Part 1:** 158, 283; **Supp. I Part 2:** 494; **Supp. X:** 36, 120, 122; **Supp. XIV:**21
Homer, Louise, **Retro. Supp. I:** 10
"Home Range" (Leopold), **Supp. XIV:**184, 185
"Homesick Blues" (Hughes), **Supp. I Part 1:** 327
Home to Harlem (McKay), **Supp. X:** 132, 137–138, 138–139
Homeward Bound (Cooper), **I:** 348
"Homeward Star, The" (Palmer), **Supp. XV:** 81–82
Homewood trilogy (Wideman), **Supp. X:** 319
"Homework" (Cameron), **Supp. XII:** 80, 83, 84
"Homily" (Tate), **IV:** 121–122
"Homme Moyen Sensuel, L'" (Pound), **III:** 462
Homme révolté, L' (Camus), **III:** 306
"Homoeopathy and Its Kindred Delusions" (Holmes), **Supp. I Part 1:** 303–304, 305
Homo Ludens (Huizinga), **II:** 416–417, 425
"Homosexual Villain, The" (Mailer), **III:** 36
"Homo Will Not Inherit" (Doty), **Supp. XI:** 128
Hone and Strong Diaries of Old Manhattan, The (Auchincloss, ed.), **Supp. IV Part 1:** 23
"Honey" (Beattie), **Supp. V:** 33
"Honey" (Wright), **Supp. III Part 2:** 589
"Honey, We'll Be Brave" (Farrell), **II:** 45

Honey and Salt (Sandburg), **III:** 594–596
"Honey and Salt" (Sandburg), **III:** 594
"Honey Babe" (Hughes), **Supp. I Part 1:** 334
"Honey Tree, The" (Oliver), **Supp. VII:** 236
Hong, Maxine. *See* Kingston, Maxine Hong
Hongo, Garrett, **Supp. X:** 292; **Supp. XIII:** 114
"Honkytonk" (Shapiro), **Supp. II Part 2:** 705
"Honky Tonk in Cleveland, Ohio" (Sandburg), **III:** 585
Honorable Men (Auchincloss), **Supp. IV Part 1:** 23
Hood, Tom, **I:** 195
"Hoodoo in America" (Hurston), **Supp. VI:** 153–154
"Hook" (Wright), **Supp. III Part 2:** 604
Hook, Sidney, **I:** 265; **Supp. IV Part 2:** 527; **Supp. VIII:** 96, 100; **Supp. XIV:**3
Hooker, Adelaide. *See* Marquand, Mrs. John P. (Adelaide Hooker)
Hooker, Isabella Beecher, **Supp. XI:** 193
Hooker, Samuel, **IV:** 162, 165
Hooker, Thomas, **II:** 15–16; **IV:** 162
Hooper, Marian. *See* Adams, Mrs. Henry (Marian Hooper)
Hoosier Holiday, A (Dreiser), **Retro. Supp. II:** 104
Hoover, Herbert, **Supp. I Part 2:** 638
Hoover, J. Edgar, **Supp. XIII:** 170
Hoover, Paul, **Supp. XV:** 179
"Hope" (Jarrell), **II:** 389
"Hope" (Matthews), **Supp. IX:** 163
Hope, A. D., **Supp. XIII:** 347
Hope, Lynn, **Supp. II Part 1:** 38
"Hope Atherton's Wanderings" (Howe), **Supp. IV Part 2:** 432
Hope of Heaven (O'Hara), **III:** 361
"Hop-Frog" (Poe), **Retro. Supp. II:** 264, 268, 269
Hopkin, Pauline, **Supp. XVI:**143
Hopkins, Anne Yale, **Supp. I Part 1:** 100, 102, 113
Hopkins, Gerard Manley, **I:** 171, 179, 397, 401, 522, 525, 533; **II:** 537; **III:** 197, 209, 523; **IV:** 129, 135, 141, 421; **Retro. Supp. II:** 40; **Supp. I Part 1:** 79, 81, 94; **Supp. III Part 2:** 551; **Supp. IV Part 1:** 178; **Supp. IV Part 2:** 637, 638, 639, 641, 643; **Supp. V:** 337; **Supp. IX:** 39, 42; **Supp. X:** 61, 115; **Supp.**

XIII: 294; **Supp. XIV:**83; **Supp. XV:** 250, 347; **Supp. XVI:**282

Hopkins, L. A., **I:** 502

Hopkins, Lemuel, **Supp. II Part 1:** 70

Hopkins, Miriam, **IV:** 381; **Supp. I Part 1:** 281

Hopkins, Samuel, **I:** 547, 549

Hopkins, Vivian, **II:** 20

Hopkinson, Francis, **Supp. I Part 2:** 504

Hopper (Strand), **Supp. IV Part 2:** 632

Hopper, Dennis, **Supp. XI:** 293, 308

Hopper, Edward, **IV:** 411, 413; **Supp. IV Part 2:** 619, 623, 631, 634

Hopwood, Avery, **Supp. IV Part 2:** 573

Horace, **II:** 8, 154, 169, 543, 552, 568; **III:** 15; **IV:** 89; **Supp. I Part 2:** 423; **Supp. IX:** 152; **Supp. X:** 65; **Supp. XII:** 258, 260, 262

Horae Canonicae (Auden), **Supp. II Part 1:** 21

"Horatian Ode" (Marvell), **IV:** 135

"Horatian Ode upon Cromwell's Return from Ireland" (Marvell), **Supp. XIV:**10

Horgan, Paul, **Supp. XV:** 46, 49, 52

Horkheimer, Max, **Supp. I Part 2:** 645; **Supp. IV Part 1:** 301

Horn, Mother, **Supp. I Part 1:** 49, 54

Hornby, Nick, **Supp. XII:** 286

"Horn of Plenty" (Hughes), **Retro. Supp. I:** 210; **Supp. I Part 1:** 342

Horovitz, Israel, **Supp. XV:** 321

Horowitz, James. *See* Salter, James

Horowitz, Mark, **Supp. V:** 219, 231

"Horse, The" (Levine), **Supp. V:** 182

"Horse, The" (Wright), **Supp. III Part 2:** 592, 601

Horse Eats Hay (play), **Supp. IV Part 1:** 82

Horse Feathers (film), **Supp. IV Part 1:** 384

Horse Has Six Legs, The (Simic), **Supp. VIII:** 272

"Horselaugh on Dibber Lannon" (Fante), **Supp. XI:** 164

Horseman, Pass By (McMurtry), **Supp. V:** 220–221, 224

"Horses" (Doty), **Supp. XI:** 122

Horses and Men (Anderson), **I:** 112–113, 114

"Horses and Men in Rain" (Sandburg), **III:** 584

"Horse Show, The" (W. C. Williams), **Retro. Supp. I:** 423

Horses Make a Landscape More Beautiful (Walker), **Supp. III Part 2:** 521, 533

"Horse Thief" (Caldwell), **I:** 310

"Horsie" (Parker), **Supp. IX:** 193

Horton, Philip, **I:** 383, 386, 387, 393, 441; **Supp. XV:** 138

Horton Hatches the Egg (Geisel), **Supp. XVI:**100, 112

Horton Hears a Who! (Geisel), **Supp. XVI:**102

Hosea (biblical book), **II:** 166

Hospers, John, **Supp. IV Part 2:** 528

Hospital, Janette Turner, **Supp. IV Part 1:** 311–302

Hospital Sketches (Alcott), **Supp. I Part 1:** 34, 35

Hostages to Fortune (Humphrey), **Supp. IX:** 96, 104–106, 109

"Hot Dog" (Stern), **Supp. IX:** 298–299

"Hotel Bar" (McClatchy), **Supp. XII:** 269

Hotel Dwellers, The (Lacy), **Supp. XV:** 205

Hotel Insomnia (Simic), **Supp. VIII:** 280, 281–282

Hotel Lambosa and Other Stories (Koch), **Supp. XV:** 186

Hotel New Hampshire, The (Irving), **Supp. VI:** 163, 164, 172–173, 177, 179

"Hot-Foot Hannibal" (Chesnutt), **Supp. XIV:**60

"Hot Night on Water Street" (Simpson), **Supp. IX:** 269, 270

"Hot Time, A" (Gunn Allen), **Supp. IV Part 1:** 333

Houdini, Harry, **IV:** 437

"Hound of Heaven" (Thompson), **Retro. Supp. I:** 55

"Hourglass, The" (Kees), **Supp. XV:** 147

"Hour in Chartres, An" (Bourne), **I:** 228

Hours, The (Cunningham), **Supp. XII:** 80; **Supp. XV:** 65–68

"Hours before Eternity" (Caldwell), **I:** 291

House, Bridge, Fountain, Gate (Kumin), **Supp. IV Part 2:** 448, 449, 451, 454

House, Edward, **Supp. I Part 2:** 643

"House, The" (Merrill), **Supp. III Part 1:** 323

House at Pooh Corner, The (Milne), **Supp. IX:** 189

House Behind the Cedars, The (Chesnutt), **Supp. XIV:**69–71

Houseboat Days (Ashbery), **Supp. III Part 1:** 18–20

Housebreaker of Shady Hill and Other Stories, The (Cheever), **Supp. I Part 1:** 184

"House by the Sea, The" (E. Stoddard), **Supp. XV:** 277

House by the Sea, The (Sarton), **Supp. VIII:** 264

House Divided, A (Buck), **Supp. II Part 1:** 118

"House Divided, The/La Casa Divida" (Kingsolver), **Supp. VII:** 207

"House Guest" (Bishop), **Retro. Supp. II:** 49; **Supp. I Part 1:** 93

Household Saints (film), **Supp. XVI:**256

Household Saints (Prose), **Supp. XVI:**252–253, 254, 261

"House in Athens, The" (Merrill), **Supp. III Part 1:** 323

House in the Uplands, A (Caldwell), **I:** 297, 301, 306

"House in Turk Street, The" (Hammett), **Supp. IV Part 1:** 344

"House in Winter, The" (Sarton), **Supp. VIII:** 259

"Housekeeping" (Alvarez), **Supp. VII:** 3–5, 10

"Housekeeping for Men" (Bourne), **I:** 231

House Made of Dawn (Momaday), **Supp. IV Part 1:** 274, 323, 326; **Supp. IV Part 2:** 479, 480, 481–484, 485, 486, 504, 562

Houseman, John, **Supp. IV Part 1:** 173

House of Dust, The: A Symphony (Aiken), **I:** 50

House of Earth trilogy (Buck), **Supp. II Part 1:** 118, 123

House of Five Talents, The (Auchincloss), **Supp. IV Part 1:** 21, 25–27

"House of Flowers" (Capote), **Supp. III Part 1:** 123

House of Games (Mamet), **Supp. XIV:**243

House of Houses (Mora), **Supp. XIII:** 213, 215, 218, 219, 223–224, 225–227, 228, 229

House of Incest (Nin), **Supp. III Part 1:** 43; **Supp. X:** 187, 190, 193

House of Life, The: Rachel Carson at Work (Brooks), **Supp. IX:** 26

House of Light (Oliver), **Supp. VII:** 238–240

House of Mirth, The (Wharton), **II:** 180, 193; **IV:** 311–313, 314, 316, 318, 323, 327; **Retro. Supp. I:** 360, 366, 367, 367–370, 373, 380

"House of Mist, The" (Rand), **Supp. IV Part 2:** 524

"House of My Own, A" (Cisneros), **Supp. VII:** 64

"House of Night, The" (Freneau),

Supp. II Part 1: 259, 260

"House of Representatives and Me, The" (Conroy), **Supp. XVI:**75

House of the Far and Lost, The (Wolfe), **IV:** 456

"House of the Injured, The" (Haines), **Supp. XII:** 203

House of the Prophet, The (Auchincloss), **Supp. IV Part 1:** 31

House of the Seven Gables (Hawthorne), **I:** 106; **II:** 60, 224, 225, 231, 237, 239, 240–241, 243, 244; **Retro. Supp. I:** 63, 149, 160–162, 163, 164; **Supp. I Part 2:** 579

House of the Solitary Maggot, The (Purdy), **Supp. VII:** 274–275

House on Mango Street, The (Cisneros), **Supp. VII:** 58, 59–64, 65, 66, 67, 68, 72

"House on Mango Street, The" (Cisneros), **Supp. VII:** 59

House on Marshland, The (Glück), **Supp. V:** 81–83, 84

"House on the Heights, A" (Capote), **Supp. III Part 1:** 120

"House on the Hill, The" (Robinson), **III:** 505, 524

"House on 15th S.W., The" (Hugo), **Supp. VI:** 140

"Houses" (Hogan), **Supp. IV Part 1:** 402

"Houses, The" (Merwin), **Supp. III Part 1:** 354

"Houses of the Spirit" (Karr), **Supp. XI:** 250

"House Sparrows" (Hecht), **Supp. X:** 68

House That Tai Maing Built, The (Lee), **Supp. X:** 291

"House Unroofed by the Gale" (Tu Fu), **II:** 526

"House Where Mark Twain Was Born, The" (Masters), **Supp. I Part 2:** 472

"Housewife" (Sexton), **Supp. II Part 2:** 682

Housman, A. E., **III:** 15, 136, 606; **Supp. II Part 1:** 4; **Supp. IV Part 1:** 165; **Supp. XV:** 40–41

Houston Trilogy (McMurtry), **Supp. V:** 223–225

How" (Ginsberg), **Supp. XIV:**142, 143

"How" (Moore), **Supp. X:** 167

"How About This?" (Carver), **Supp. III Part 1:** 141

"How Annandale Went Out" (Robinson), **III:** 513

Howard, Ben, **Supp. XVI:**54

Howard, Gerald, **Supp. XII:** 21

Howard, Jane, **Retro. Supp. I:** 334

Howard, June, **Retro. Supp. II:** 139

Howard, Leon, **Supp. I Part 2:** 408, 422, 423

Howard, Maureen, **Supp. XII:** 285

Howard, Richard, **Retro. Supp. II:** 43; **Supp. IV Part 2:** 624, 626, 640; **Supp. VIII:** 273; **Supp. IX:** 324, 326; **Supp. X:** 152; **Supp. XI:** 317; **Supp. XII:** 254; **Supp. XIII:** 76; **Supp. XV:** 23, 24

Howard, Vilma, **Retro. Supp. II:** 111, 112

Howards, J. Z., **Supp. VIII:** 178

Howards End (Forster), **Supp. XII:** 87

Howarth, Cora, **I:** 408, 409

Howbah Indians (Ortiz), **Supp. IV Part 2:** 513

"How Black Sees Green and Red" (McKay), **Supp. X:** 136

"How David Did Not Care" (R. Bly), **Supp. IV Part 1:** 73

Howe, E.W., **I:** 106

Howe, Florence, **Supp. XIII:** 295, 306

Howe, Harriet, **Supp. XI:** 200, 201

Howe, Irving, **IV:** 10; **Retro. Supp. I:** 369; **Retro. Supp. II:** 112, 286; **Supp. I Part 2:** 432; **Supp. II Part 1:** 99; **Supp. VI:** 113–129; **Supp. VIII:** 93, 232; **Supp. IX:** 227; **Supp. X:** 203, 245; **Supp. XII:** 160; **Supp. XIII:** 98

Howe, Irwing, **Supp. XIV:**103–104, 104

Howe, James Wong, **Supp. I Part 1:** 281; **Supp. V:** 223

Howe, Julia Ward, **III:** 505; **Retro. Supp. II:** 135

Howe, M. A. DeWolfe, **I:** 258; **II:** 406; **Supp. XIV:**54

Howe, Mary Manning, **Supp. IV Part 2:** 422

Howe, Samuel, **Supp. I Part 1:** 153

Howe, Susan, **Retro. Supp. I:** 33, 43; **Supp. IV Part 2:** 419–438; **Supp. XVI:**284

Howell, Chris, **Supp. XIII:** 112

Howell, James, **II:** 111

Howells: His Life and World (Brooks), **I:** 254

Howells, Margaret, **II:** 271

Howells, Mrs. William Dean (Elinor Mead), **II:** 273

Howells, William C., **II:** 273

Howells, William Dean, **I:** 109, 192, 204, 210, 211, 254, 355, 407, 411, 418, 459, 469; **II:** 127–128, 130, 131, 136, 137, 138, 140, 271–294, 322, 331–332, 338, 397–398, 400, 415, 444, 451, 556; **III:** 51, 118, 314, 327–328, 461, 576, 607; **IV:** 192, 202, 342, 349; **Retro. Supp. I:** 220, 334, 362, 378; **Retro. Supp. II:** 93, 101, 135, 288; **Supp. I Part 1:** 306, 318, 357, 360, 368; **Supp. I Part 2:** 414, 420, 645–646; **Supp. II Part 1:** 198, 352; **Supp. IV Part 2:** 678; **Supp. VIII:** 98, 101, 102; **Supp. XI:** 198, 200; **Supp. XIV:**45–46; **Supp. XV:** 269, 274, 285, 287

Howells, Winifred, **II:** 271

"Howells as Anti-Novelist" (Updike), **Retro. Supp. I:** 334

Hower, Edward, **Supp. XII:** 330, 343

Howes, Barbara, **Supp. XIII:** 331

How Good Is David Mamet, Anyway? (Heilpern), **Supp. XIV:**242

"How I Became a Shadow" (Purdy), **Supp. VII:** 269

"How I Came to Vedanta" (Isherwood), **Supp. XIV:**164

"How I Learned to Sweep" (Alvarez), **Supp. VII:** 4

"How I Spent My Forties" (Wasserstein), **Supp. XV:** 325, 330, 332

"How It Began" (Stafford), **Supp. XI:** 327

"How It Feels to Be Colored Me" (Hurston), **Supp. VI:** 152

"How It Is" (Everwine), **Supp. XV:** 79, 86

"How I Told My Child About Race" (Brooks), **Supp. III Part 1:** 78

"How I Went to the Mines" (Harte), **Supp. II Part 1:** 336

"How I Write" (Welty), **IV:** 279, 280

"How Jonah Did Not Care" (R. Bly), **Supp. IV Part 1:** 73

Howl (Ginsberg), **Retro. Supp. I:** 426; **Supp. III Part 1:** 92; **Supp. IV Part 1:** 90; **Supp. V:** 336; **Supp. VIII:** 290; **Supp. XIV:**15, 126, 157

Howl: Original Draft Facsimile, Transcript and Variant Versions (Gimsberg), **Supp. XIV:**142

Howl and Other Poems (Ginsberg), **Supp. II Part 1:** 308, 317–318, 319; **Supp. X:** 123

Howlett, William, **Retro. Supp. I:** 17

"How Many Midnights" (Bowles), **Supp. IV Part 1:** 86–87

"How Many Nights" (Kinnell), **Supp. III Part 1:** 245–246

How Much? (Blechman), **Supp. I Part 1:** 290

"How Much Are You Worth" (Salinas), **Supp. XIII:** 325–326

"How Much Earth" (Levine), **Supp. V:** 184

How Much Earth: The Fresno Poets (Buckley, Oliveira, and Williams,

eds.), **Supp. XIII:** 313

"How Not to Forget" (Bartov), **Supp. XVI:**153–154

"How Poetry Comes to Me" (Corso), **Supp. XII:** 122

"How Poetry Comes to Me" (Snyder), **Supp. VIII:** 305

"How She Came By Her Name: An Interview with Louis Massiah" (Bambara), **Supp. XI:** 20

"How Soon Hath Time" (Ransom), **IV:** 123

How Stella Got Her Groove Back (McMillan), **Supp. XIII:** 185, 190–191

How the Alligator Missed Breakfast (Kinney), **Supp. III Part 1:** 235, 253

"How the Devil Came Down Division Street" (Algren), **Supp. IX:** 3

How the García Girls Lost Their Accents (Alvarez), **Supp. VII:** 3, 5–9, 11, 15, 17, 18

How the Grinch Stole Christmas! (Geisel), **Supp. XVI:**102

How the Other Half Lives (Riis), **I:** 293

"How the Saint Did Not Care" (R. Bly), **Supp. IV Part 1:** 73

"How the Women Went from Dover" (Whittier), **Supp. I Part 2:** 694, 696, 697

"How To" (Carruth), **Supp. XVI:**51

"How to Be an Other Woman" (Moore), **Supp. X:** 165, 167, 168

"How to Become a Writer" (Moore), **Supp. X:** 167, 168

"How to Be Happy: Another Memo to Myself" (Dunn), **Supp. XI:** 145

How to Develop Your Personality (Shellow), **Supp. I Part 2:** 608

How to Know God: The Yoga Aphorisms of Patanjali (Isherwood and Prabhavananda)), **Supp. XIV:**164

"How To Like It" (Dobyns), **Supp. XIII:** 85–86

"How to Live. What to Do" (Stevens), **Retro. Supp. I:** 302

"How to Live on $36,000 a Year" (Fitzgerald), **Retro. Supp. I:** 105

"How Tom is Doin'" (Kees), **Supp. XV:** 143

How to Read (Pound), **Supp. VIII:** 291

How to Read a Novel (Gordon), **II:** 198

How to Save Your Own Life (Jong), **Supp. V:** 115, 123–125, 130

"How to Study Poetry" (Pound), **III:** 474

"How to Talk to Your Mother" (Moore), **Supp. X:** 167, 172

How to Win Friends and Influence

People (Carnegie), **Supp. I Part 2:** 608

How to Worry Successfully (Seabury), **Supp. I Part 2:** 608

How to Write (Stein), **IV:** 32, 34, 35

"How to Write a Blackwood Article" (Poe), **III:** 425; **Retro. Supp. II:** 273

"How to Write a Memoir Like This" (Oates), **Supp. III Part 2:** 509

"How to Write Like Somebody Else" (Roethke), **III:** 540

How to Write Short Stories (Lardner), **II:** 430, 431

"How Vincentine Did Not Care" (R. Bly), **Supp. IV Part 1:** 73

How We Became Human: New and Selected Poems (Harjo), **Supp. XII:** 230–232

"How We Danced" (Sexton), **Supp. II Part 2:** 692

"How You Sound??" (Baraka), **Supp. II Part 1:** 30

Hoy, Philip, **Supp. X:** 56, 58

Hoyer, Linda Grace (pseudonym). *See* Updike, Mrs. Wesley

Hoyt, Constance, **Supp. I Part 2:** 707

Hoyt, Elinor Morton. *See* Wylie, Elinor

Hoyt, Henry (father), **Supp. I Part 2:** 707

Hoyt, Henry (son), **Supp. I Part 2:** 708

Hoyt, Henry Martyn, **Supp. I Part 2:** 707

Hsu, Kai-yu, **Supp. X:** 292

Hsu, Ruth Y., **Supp. XV:** 212

Hubba City (Reed), **Supp. X:** 241

Hubbard, Elbert, **I:** 98, 383

Hubbell, Jay B., **Supp. I Part 1:** 372

"Hubbub, The" (Ammons), **Supp. VII:** 35

Huber, François, **II:** 6

Huckins, Olga, **Supp. IX:** 32

Huckleberry Finn (Twain). *See Adventures of Huckleberry Finn, The* (Twain)

Hud (film), **Supp. V:** 223, 226

Hudgins, Andrew, **Supp. X:** 206

Hudson, Henry, **I:** 230

"Hudsonian Curlew, The" (Snyder), **Supp. VIII:** 302

Hudson River Bracketed (Wharton), **IV:** 326–327; **Retro. Supp. I:** 382

Huebsch, B. W., **III:** 110

Hueffer, Ford Madox, **Supp. I Part 1:** 257, 262. *See also* Ford, Ford Madox

Hug Dancing (Hearon), **Supp. VIII:** 67–68

Huge Season, The (Morris), **III:** 225–226, 227, 230, 232, 233, 238

Hugging the Jukebox (Nye), **Supp. XIII:** 275–276, 277

"Hugging the Jukebox" (Nye), **Supp. XIII:** 276

Hughes, Brigid, **Supp. XVI:**247

Hughes, Carolyn, **Supp. XII:** 272, 285

Hughes, Frieda, **Supp. I Part 2:** 540, 541

Hughes, Glenn, **Supp. I Part 1:** 255

Hughes, H. Stuart, **Supp. VIII:** 240

Hughes, James Nathaniel, **Supp. I Part 1:** 321, 332

Hughes, Ken, **Supp. XI:** 307

Hughes, Langston, **Retro. Supp. I:** 193–214; **Retro. Supp. II:** 114, 115, 117, 120; **Supp. I Part 1:** 320–348; **Supp. II Part 1:** 31, 33, 61, 170, 173, 181, 227, 228, 233, 361; **Supp. III Part 1:** 72–77; **Supp. IV Part 1:** 15, 16, 164, 168, 169, 173, 243, 368; **Supp. VIII:** 213; **Supp. IX:** 306, 316; **Supp. X:** 131, 136, 139, 324; **Supp. XI:** 1; **Supp. XIII:** 75, 111, 132, 233; **Supp. XVI:**135, 138

Hughes, Nicholas, **Supp. I Part 2:** 541

Hughes, Robert, **Supp. X:** 73

Hughes, Ted, **IV:** 3; **Retro. Supp. II:** 244, 245, 247, 257; **Supp. I Part 2:** 536, 537, 538, 539, 540, 541; **Supp. XV:** 117, 347, 348

Hughes, Thomas, **Supp. I Part 2:** 406

"Hugh Harper" (Bowles), **Supp. IV Part 1:** 94

Hughie (O'Neill), **III:** 385, 401, 405

Hugh Selwyn Mauberley (Pound), **I:** 66, 476; **III:** 9, 462–463, 465, 468; **Retro. Supp. I:** 289–290, 291, 299; **Supp. XIV:**272

Hugo, Richard, **Supp. VI:** 131–148; **Supp. IX:** 296, 323, 324, 330; **Supp. XI:** 315, 317; **Supp. XII:** 178; **Supp. XIII:** 112, 113, 133

Hugo, Victor, **II:** 290, 490, 543; **Supp. IV Part 2:** 518; **Supp. IX:** 308

Hui-neng, **III:** 567

Huis Clos (Sartre), **Supp. IV Part 1:** 84

Huizinga, Johan, **I:** 225; **II:** 416–417, 418, 425

Hulbert, Ann, **Supp. XI:** 38–39

Hull, Lynda, **Supp. XI:** 131

Hulme, Thomas E., **I:** 68, 69, 475; **III:** 196, 209, 463–464, 465; **IV:** 122; **Supp. I Part 1:** 261, 262; **Supp. XV:** 43

Human, All Too Human (Nietzsche), **Supp. X:** 48

"Human Culture" (Emerson), **II:** 11–12

Human Factor, The (Greene), **Supp. V:** 298

"Human Figures" (Doty), **Supp. XI:** 123–124

"Human Immortality" (James), **II:** 353–354

"Human Life" (Emerson), **II:** 11–12

Human Rights, Human Wrongs: The Oxford Amnesty Lectures, 2001, **Supp. XVI:**155

Human Stain, The (Roth), **Retro. Supp. II:** 279, 289, 294–295

"Human Things" (Nemerov), **III:** 279

Human Universe (Olson), **Supp. II Part 2:** 571

"Human Universe" (Olson), **Supp. II Part 2:** 565, 567

Human Wishes (Hass), **Supp. VI:** 105–106, 107

Human Work (Gilman), **Supp. XI:** 206

Humbert, Humbert, **Supp. X:** 283

Humble Inquiry into the Rules of the Word of God, An, Concerning the Qualifications Requisite to a Complete Standing and Full Communion in the Visible Christian Church (Edwards), **I:** 548

Humboldt, Alexander von, **III:** 428

Humboldt's Gift (Bellow), **Retro. Supp. II:** 19, 28–29, 34; **Supp. XIII:** 320

Hume, David, **I:** 125; **II:** 349, 357, 480; **III:** 618

Humes, H. L. "Doc," **Supp. XI:** 294

Humes, Harold, **Supp. V:** 201; **Supp. XIV:**82

"Hummingbirds, The" (Welty), **IV:** 273

Humphrey, William, **Supp. IX:** 93–112; **Supp. XV:** 353

Humphreys, Christmas, **Supp. V:** 267

Humphreys, David, **Supp. II Part 1:** 65, 69, 70, 268

Humphreys, Josephine, **Supp. XII:** 311

Humphries, Rolfe, **III:** 124; **Retro. Supp. I:** 137

Hunchback of Notre Dame, The (film), **Supp. IV Part 1:** 101

Hunches in Bunches (Geisel), **Supp. XVI:**111

Huncke, Herbert, **Supp. XII:** 118; **Supp. XIV:**137–153

Huncke's Journal (Huncke), **Supp. XIV:**139, 144, 145, 146

Hundred Camels in the Courtyard, A (Bowles), **Supp. IV Part 1:** 90

"Hundred Collars, A" (Frost), **Retro. Supp. I:** 128; **Supp. XIII:** 147

Hundred Secret Senses, The (Tan), **Supp. X:** 289, 293, 295, 297, 298, 299

Hundred White Daffodils, A: Essays, Interviews, Newspaper Columns, *and One Poem* (Kenyon), **Supp. VII:** 160–162, 165, 166, 167, 174

Huneker, James, **III:** 102

Hunger (Hamsun), **Supp. XI:** 167

"Hunger" (Hogan), **Supp. IV Part 1:** 411

"Hunger . . ." (Rich), **Supp. I Part 2:** 571

"Hungerfield" (Jeffers), **Supp. II Part 2:** 416–417, 436

Hungerfield and Other Poems (Jeffers), **Supp. II Part 2:** 422

Hunger of Memory: The Education of Richard Rodriguez (Rodriguez), **Supp. XIV:**297, 298, 298–302, 310

Hungry Ghosts, The (Oates), **Supp. II Part 2:** 504, 510

Hungry Hearts (Prose), **Supp. XVI:**253

Hunnewell, Susannah, **Supp. VIII:** 83

Hunt, Harriot K., **Retro. Supp. II:** 146

Hunt, Leigh, **II:** 515–516; **Supp. XV:** 175

Hunt, Richard Morris, **IV:** 312

Hunt, Robert, **Supp. XV:** 42, 49, 52

Hunt, William, **II:** 343

Hunter, Dianna, **Supp. XVI:**38

Hunter, Dr. Joseph, **II:** 217

Hunter, J. Paul, **Supp. IV Part 1:** 332

Hunter, Kim, **Supp. I Part 1:** 286

"Hunter of Doves" (Herbst), **Retro. Supp. II:** 325

"Hunter of the West, The" (Bryant), **Supp. I Part 1:** 155

Hunters, The (film), **Supp. IX:** 250

Hunters, The (Salter), **Supp. IX:** 246, 249–250

Hunters and Gatherers (Prose), **Supp. XVI:**257

"Hunters in the Snow" (Brueghel), **I:** 174; **Retro. Supp. I:** 430

"Hunters in the Snow" (Wolff), **Supp. VII:** 339–340

"Hunter's Moon—Eating the Bear" (Oliver), **Supp. VII:** 234

"Hunter's Vision, The" (Bryant), **Supp. I Part 1:** 160

Hunting for Hope: A Father's Journey (Sanders), **Supp. XVI:**276–277, 278

"Hunting Is Not Those Heads on the Wall" (Baraka), **Supp. II Part 1:** 45

Huntington, Collis P., **I:** 198, 207

"Hunt in the Black Forest, The" (Jarrell), **II:** 379–380

Huntley, Jobe, **Supp. I Part 1:** 339

Hurray Home (Wideman), **Supp. X:** 320

"Hurricane, The" (Crane), **I:** 401

"Hurricane, The" (Freneau), **Supp. II Part 1:** 262

"Hurry Kane" (Lardner), **II:** 425, 426, 427

"Hurry up Please It's Time" (Sexton), **Supp. II Part 2:** 694, 695

Hurston, Zora Neale, **Retro. Supp. I:** 194, 198, 200, 201, 203; **Supp. I Part 1:** 325, 326, 332; **Supp. II Part 1:** 33; **Supp. IV Part 1:** 5, 11, 12, 164, 257; **Supp. VI:** 149–161; **Supp. VIII:** 214; **Supp. X:** 131, 139, 232, 242; **Supp. XI:** 85; **Supp. XIII:** 185, 233, 236, 295, 306

Hurt, John, **Supp. XIII:** 132

Husbands and Wives (film; Allen), **Supp. XV:** 12

Husband's Story, The (Shields), **Supp. VII:** 316. *See also* "Happenstance" (Shields)

Husserl, Edmund, **II:** 362, 363; **IV:** 491; **Supp. IV Part 1:** 42, 43

Hussey, Jo Ella, **Supp. XII:** 201

Hustler, The (film), **Supp. XI:** 306

Huston, John, **I:** 30, 31, 33, 35; **II:** 588; **III:** 161; **Supp. IV Part 1:** 102, 116, 355; **Supp. XI:** 307; **Supp. XIII:** 174

"Huswifery" (Taylor), **IV:** 161; **Supp. I Part 2:** 386

"Hut, The" (Sobin), **Supp. XVI:**284–285

Hutchens, John K., **Supp. IX:** 276

Hutcheson, Francis, **I:** 559

Hutchins, Patricia, **III:** 478

Hutchinson, Abigail, **I:** 562

Hutchinson, Anne, **Supp. I Part 1:** 100, 101, 113; **Supp. IV Part 2:** 434; **Supp. VIII:** 202, 205

Hutton, James, **Supp. IX:** 180

Huxley, Aldous, **II:** 454; **III:** 281, 428, 429–430; **IV:** 77, 435; **Supp. I Part 2:** 714; **Supp. XIV:**3, 164; **Supp. XVI:**189, 192

Huxley, Julian, **Supp. VIII:** 251; **Supp. X:** 108

Huxley, Juliette, **Supp. VIII:** 251, 265

Huxley, Thomas, **III:** 102, 108, 113, 281; **Retro. Supp. II:** 60, 65, 93

Huxley, Thomas Henry, **Supp. I Part 1:** 368

Huysmans, Joris Karl (Charles Marie Georges), **I:** 66; **III:** 315; **IV:** 286; **Retro. Supp. II:** 326

"Hwame, Koshkalaka, and the Rest: Lesbians in American Indian Cultures" (Gunn Allen), **Supp. IV Part 1:** 330

Hwang, David Henry, **Supp. X:** 292

"Hyacinth Drift" (Rawlings), **Supp. X:** 226–227

"Idiom of a Self, The" (Pinsky), **Supp. VI:** 240

"Idiot, The" (Crane), **I:** 401

Idiot, The (Dostoyevsky), **I:** 468

"Idiots First" (Malamud), **Supp. I Part 2:** 434–435, 437, 440–441

I Don't Need You Any More (A. Miller), **III:** 165

Idoru (W. Gibson), **Supp. XVI:**119, 124, 129–130

"I Dream I'm the Death of Orpheus" (Rich), **Supp. I Part 2:** 557–558

I Dreamt I Became a Nymphomaniac! Imagining (Acker), **Supp. XII:** 4, 6, 8, 11

Idylls of the King (Tennyson), **III:** 487; **Supp. I Part 2:** 410; **Supp. XIII:** 146

Idyl of Work, An (Larcom), **Supp. XIII:** 139, 142, 146–147, 150

"If" (Creeley), **Supp. IV Part 1:** 158

If Beale Street Could Talk (Baldwin), **Retro. Supp. II:** 13–14; **Supp. I Part 1:** 48, 59–60, 67

If Blessing Comes (Bambara), **Supp. XI:** 1

I Feel a Little Jumpy around You (Nye and Janeczko, eds.), **Supp. XIII:** 280

"I felt a Funeral, in my Brain" (Dickinson), **Retro. Supp. I:** 38

If He Hollers Let Him Go (C. Himes), **Supp. XVI:**135, 138–139, 142

"If I Could Be Like Wallace Stevens" (Stafford), **Supp. XI:** 327

"If I Could Only Live at the Pitch That Is Near Madness" (Eberhart), **I:** 523, 526–527

If I Die in a Combat Zone (O'Brien), **Supp. V:** 238, 239, 240, 245

"If I Had My Way" (Creeley), **Supp. IV Part 1:** 157

"If I Might Be" (Chopin), **Retro. Supp. II:** 61

"I Find the Real American Tragedy" (Dreiser), **Retro. Supp. II:** 105

If I Ran the Circus (Geisel), **Supp. XVI:**105

If I Ran the Zoo (Geisel), **Supp. XVI:**104–105

If It Die (Gide), **I:** 290

"If It Were Not for You" (Carruth), **Supp. XVI:**57

"If I Were a Man" (Gilman), **Supp. XI:** 207

"If I Were the Wind" (Leopold), **Supp. XIV:**184

If Morning Ever Comes (Tyler), **Supp. IV Part 2:** 658–659

If Mountains Die: A New Mexico Mem-

oir (Nichols), **Supp. XIII:** 255, 257, 267

I Forgot to Go to Spain (Harrison), **Supp. VIII:** 39, 52–53

If the River Was Whiskey (Boyle), **Supp. VIII:** 15–16

"If They Knew Yvonne" (Dubus), **Supp. VII:** 81

"If We Had Bacon" (H. Roth), **Supp. IX:** 232, 234

"If We Had Known" (Francis), **Supp. IX:** 78

"If We Must Die" (McKay), **Supp. IV Part 1:** 3; **Supp. X:** 132, 134

"If We Take All Gold" (Bogan), **Supp. III Part 1:** 52

If You Call This a Cry Song (Carruth), **Supp. XVI:**56

I Gaspiri (Lardner), **II:** 435

"I Gather the Limbs of Osiris" (Pound), **Retro. Supp. I:** 287

"I Give You Back" (Harjo), **Supp. XII:** 223

Ignatius of Loyola, **IV:** 151; **Supp. XI:** 162

Ignatow, David, **Supp. XIII:** 275

"Ignis Fatuus" (Tate), **IV:** 128

"I Go Back to May 1937" (Olds), **Supp. X:** 207

I Go Dreaming Serenades (Salinas), **Supp. XIII:** 316

I Got the Blues (Odets), **Supp. II Part 2:** 530

Iguana Killer, The (Ríos), **Supp. IV Part 2:** 542–544

"I Had Eight Birds Hatcht in One Nest" (Bradstreet), **Supp. I Part 1:** 102, 115, 117, 119

"I had no time to Hate" (Dickinson), **Retro. Supp. I:** 44–45, 46

I Had Trouble in Getting to Solla Sollew (Geisel), **Supp. XVI:**108, 109

"I Have a Rendezvous with Life" (Cullen), **Supp. IV Part 1:** 168

"I Have Increased Power" (Ginsberg), **Supp. II Part 1:** 313

"I Have Seen Black Hands" (Wright), **Supp. II Part 1:** 228

"I Hear an Army" (Joyce), **Supp. I Part 1:** 262

"I heard a Fly buzz when I died" (Dickinson), **Retro. Supp. I:** 38

"I Heard Immanuel Singing" (Lindsay), **Supp. I Part 2:** 379

"I Hear It Was Charged against Me" (Whitman), **IV:** 343

"I Held a Shelley Manuscript" (Corso), **Supp. XII:** 128

"I Held His Name" (Ríos), **Supp. IV**

Part 2: 547

I Knew a Phoenix (Sarton), **Supp. VIII:** 249, 251–252

"I Know a Man" (Creeley), **Supp. IV Part 1:** 147–148, 149

I Know Some Things: Stories about Childhood by Contemporary Writers (Moore, ed.), **Supp. X:** 175

"I Know Why the Caged Bird Cannot Read" (Prose), **Supp. XVI:**259

I Know Why the Caged Bird Sings (Angelou), **Supp. IV Part 1:** 2–4, 5, 7, 11, 12, 13, 14, 15, 17; **Supp. XVI:**259

"Ikon: The Harrowing of Hell" (Levertov), **Supp. III Part 1:** 284

Ile (O'Neill), **III:** 388

"I Let Him Take Me" (Cisneros), **Supp. VII:** 71

Iliad (Bryant, trans.), **Supp. I Part 1:** 158

Iliad (Homer), **II:** 470; **Supp. IV Part 2:** 631; **Supp. IX:** 211; **Supp. X:** 114

Iliad (Pope, trans.), **Supp. I Part 1:** 152

"I like to see it lap the Miles" (Dickinson), **Retro. Supp. I:** 37

"I Live Up Here" (Merwin), **Supp. III Part 1:** 349

"Illegal Alien" (Mora), **Supp. XIII:** 215

"Illegal Days, The" (Paley), **Supp. VI:** 222

Illig, Joyce, **Retro. Supp. II:** 20

"Illinois" (Masters), **Supp. I Part 2:** 458

Illinois Bus Ride (Leopold), **Supp. XIV:**189

Illinois Poems (Masters), **Supp. I Part 2:** 472

"Illinois Village, The" (Lindsay), **Supp. I Part 2:** 381

Illness as Metaphor (Sontag), **Supp. III Part 2:** 452, 461, 466

I'll Take My Stand ("Twelve Southerners"), **II:** 196; **III:** 496; **IV:** 125, 237; **Supp. X:** 25, 52–53; **Supp. XIV:**3

"I'll Take You to Tennessee" (Connell), **Supp. XIV:**82

Illumination (Frederic), **II:** 141

Illumination Night (Hoffman), **Supp. X:** 85, 86, 88, 89

Illusion comique, L' (Corneille), **Supp. IX:** 138

"Illusion of Eternity, The" (Eberhart), **I:** 541

"Illusion of Fiction in Frank Conroy's

Stop-Time, The" (R. Ramsey), **Supp. XVI:**69

Illusions (Dash; film), **Supp. XI:** 20

"Illusions" (Emerson), **II:** 2, 5, 14, 16

Illustrated Man, The (Bradbury), **Supp. IV Part 1:** 102, 103, 113

Illustrations of Political Economy (Martineau), **Supp. II Part 1:** 288

"I Look at My Hand" (Swenson), **Supp. IV Part 2:** 638, 647

I Love Myself When I Am Laughing . . . : A Zora Neale Hurston Reader (Walker), **Supp. III Part 2:** 531, 532

"I'm a Fool" (Anderson), **I:** 113, 114, 116; **Supp. I Part 2:** 430

Image and Idea (Rahv), **Supp. II Part 1:** 146

Image and the Law, The (Nemerov), **III:** 268, 269–271, 272

"Images" (Hass), **Supp. VI:** 103

"Images and 'Images'" (Simic), **Supp. VIII:** 274

"Images for Godard" (Rich), **Supp. I Part 2:** 558

"Images of Walt Whitman" (Fiedler), **IV:** 352

"Imaginary Friendships of Tom McGrath, The" (Cohen), **Supp. X:** 112

"Imaginary Iceberg, The" (Bishop), **Retro. Supp. II:** 42; **Supp. I Part 1:** 86, 88

"Imaginary Jew, The" (Berryman), **I:** 174–175

Imaginary Letters (Pound), **III:** 473–474

"Imaginary Prisons" (Schnackenberg), **Supp. XV:** 257, 258

Imagination and Fancy; or, Selections from the English Poets, illustrative of those first requisites of their art; with markings of the best passages, critical notices of the writers, and an essay in answer to the question- 'What is Poetry?' (Hunt), **II:** 515–516

"Imagination as Value" (Stevens), **Retro. Supp. I:** 298

"Imagination of Disaster, The" (Gordon), **Supp. IV Part 1:** 306

"Imagine a Day at the End of Your Life" (Beattie), **Supp. V:** 33

"Imagine Kissing Pete" (O'Hara), **III:** 372; **Supp. VIII:** 156

Imaging Robert: My Brother, Madness, and Survival (Neugeboren), **Supp. XVI:**225, 226–229

"Imagining How It Would Be to Be Dead" (Eberhart), **I:** 533

Imagining Los Angeles: A City in Fiction (Fine), **Supp. XI:** 160

"Imagining the Midwest" (Sanders), **Supp. XVI:**275–276

Imagining the Worst: Stephen King and the Representations of Women (Lant and Thompson), **Supp. V:** 141

"Imagisme" (Pound), **Retro. Supp. I:** 288

Imagistes, Des: An Anthology of the Imagists (Pound, ed.), **III:** 465, 471; **Retro. Supp. I:** 288

Imago (O. Butler), **Supp. XIII:** 63, 65–66

"Imago" (Stevens), **IV:** 74, 89

Imagoes (Coleman), **Supp. XI:** 89–90

I Married a Communist (Roth), **Retro. Supp. II:** 289, 293–294

I Married an Angel (film), **Supp. XVI:**193

"I May, I Might, I Must" (Moore), **III:** 215

"I'm Crazy" (Salinger), **III:** 553

"I'm Here" (Roethke), **III:** 547

Imitations (Lowell), **II:** 543, 544–545, 550, 555; **Retro. Supp. II:** 181, 187

"Imitations of Drowning" (Sexton), **Supp. II Part 2:** 684, 686

"Immaculate Man" (Gordon), **Supp. IV Part 1:** 311

"Immanence of Dostoevsky, The" (Bourne), **I:** 235

"Immigrants" (Mora), **Supp. XIII:** 216

"Immigrant Story, The" (Paley), **Supp. VI:** 230

Immobile Wind, The (Winters), **Supp. II Part 2:** 786

"Immobile Wind, The" (Winters), **Supp. II Part 2:** 788, 811

"Immolatus" (Komunyakaa), **Supp. XIII:** 126

"Immoral Proposition, The" (Creeley), **Supp. IV Part 1:** 144

"Immortal Autumn" (MacLeish), **III:** 13

Immortality Ode (Nemerov), **III:** 87

Immortality Ode (Wordsworth), **II:** 17; **Supp. I Part 2:** 673

"Immortal Woman, The" (Tate), **IV:** 130, 131, 137

"I'm Not Ready to Die Yet" (Harjo), **Supp. XII:** 231

"I'm on My Way" (Salinas), **Supp. XIII:** 320

"Impasse" (Hughes), **Supp. I Part 1:** 343

Imperative Duty, An, a Novel (Howells), **II:** 286

Imperial Eyes: Travel Writing and Transculturation (Pratt), **Retro.**

Supp. II: 48

Imperial Germany and the Industrial Revolution (Veblen), **Supp. I Part 2:** 642, 643

Imperial Way, The: By Rail from Peshawar to Chittagong (Theroux), **Supp. VIII:** 323

"Implosions" (Rich), **Supp. I Part 2:** 556

"Imp of the Perverse, The" (Poe), **III:** 414–415; **Retro. Supp. II:** 267

Impolite Interviews, **Supp. XI:** 293

"Importance of Artists' Biographies, The" (Goldbarth), **Supp. XII:** 183, 184, 191

Importance of Being Earnest, The (Wilde), **Supp. XIV:**324, 339

"Important Houses, The" (Gordon), **Supp. IV Part 1:** 315

"Impossible Indispensability of the Ars Poetica, The" (Carruth), **Supp. XVI:**57

"Impossible to Tell" (Pinsky), **Supp. VI:** 247, 248

"Imposter, The" (West), **Retro. Supp. II:** 322, 327

"Impressionism and Symbolism in *Heart of Darkness*" (Watt), **Supp. VIII:** 4

"Impressions of a European Tour" (Bourne), **I:** 225

"Impressions of a Plumber" (H. Roth), **Supp. IX:** 228, 234

"Impressions of Europe, 1913–1914" (Bourne), **I:** 225

"I'm Walking behind the Spanish" (Salinas), **Supp. XIII:** 323–324

"I/Myself" (Shields), **Supp. VII:** 311

"In Absence" (Lanier), **Supp. I Part 1:** 364

"In Absentia" (Bowles), **Supp. IV Part 1:** 94

"In a Cab" (Untermeyer), **Supp. XV:** 296

Inada, Lawson Fusao, **Supp. V:** 180

"In a Dark Room, Furniture" (Nye), **Supp. XIII:** 274

"In a Dark Time" (Roethke), **III:** 539, 547, 548

"In a Disused Graveyard" (Frost), **Retro. Supp. I:** 126, 133

In a Dusty Light (Haines), **Supp. XII:** 207

"In a Garden" (Lowell), **II:** 513

"In a Hard Intellectual Light" (Eberhart), **I:** 523

"In a Hollow of the Hills" (Harte), **Supp. II Part 1:** 354

In America (Sontag), **Supp. XIV:**95–96

"In Amicitia" (Ransom), **IV:** 141

In a Narrow Grave: Essays on Texas (McMurtry), **Supp. V:** 220, 223

"In Another Country" (Hemingway), **I:** 484–485; **II:** 249

In April Once (Percy), **Retro. Supp. I:** 341

"In a Prominent Bar in Secaucus One Day" (X. J. Kennedy), **Supp. XV:** 154, 155–156

In A Shallow Grave (Purdy), **Supp. VII:** 272

"In a Station of the Metro" (Pound), **Retro. Supp. I:** 288; **Supp. I Part 1:** 265; **Supp. XIV:**284–285

"In a Strange Town" (Anderson), **I:** 114, 115

"In Athens Once" (Rodriguez), **Supp. XIV:**303

In Battle for Peace: The Story of My 83rd Birthday (Du Bois), **Supp. II Part 1:** 185

In Bed One Night & Other Brief Encounters (Coover), **Supp. V:** 49, 50

"In Bertram's Garden" (Justice), **Supp. VII:** 117

"In Blackwater Woods" (Oliver), **Supp. VII:** 244, 246

In Black & Whitey (Lacy), **Supp. XV:** 206–207

In Broken Country (Wagoner), **Supp. IX:** 330

"In California" (Simpson), **Supp. IX:** 271

"In Camp" (Stafford), **Supp. XI:** 329

"Incant against Suicide" (Karr), **Supp. XI:** 249

"In Celebration of My Uterus" (Sexton), **Supp. II Part 2:** 689

"Incendiary, The" (Rowson), **Supp. XV:** 234

"In Certain Places and Certain Times There Can Be More of You" (Dunn), **Supp. XI:** 144

Incest: From "A Journal of Love," the Unexpurgated Diary of Anaïs Nin, 1932–1934 (Nin), **Supp. X:** 182, 184, 185, 187, 191

"In Chandler Country" (Gioia), **Supp. XV:** 119

Inchbald, Elizabeth, **II:** 8

"In Cheever Country" (Gioia), **Supp. XV:** 119

Inchiquin, the Jesuit's Letters (Ingersoll), **I:** 344

"Incident" (Cullen), **Supp. IV Part 1:** 165, 166

Incidental Numbers (Wylie), **Supp. I Part 2:** 708

Incidentals (Sandburg), **III:** 579

Incident at Vichy (A. Miller), **III:** 165, 166

Incidents in the Life of a Slave Girl (Brent), **Supp. IV Part 1:** 13

Incidents in the Life of a Slavegirl (Jacobs), **Supp. XVI:**85

"Incipience" (Rich), **Supp. I Part 2:** 559

"In Clare" (McCarriston), **Supp. XIV:**270–271

Including Horace (Untermeyer), **Supp. XV:** 301, 303–304

In Cold Blood: A True Account of a Multiple Murder and Its Consequences (Capote), **Retro. Supp. II:** 107–108; **Supp. I Part 1:** 292; **Supp. III Part 1:** 111, 117, 119, 122, 123, 125–131; **Supp. III Part 2:** 574; **Supp. IV Part 1:** 220; **Supp. XIV:**162

In Cold Hell, in Thicket (Olson), **Supp. II Part 2:** 571

"In Cold Hell, in Thicket" (Olson), **Supp. II Part 2:** 558, 563–564, 566, 572, 580

"Incomparable Light, The" (Eberhart), **I:** 541

Incorporative Consciousness of Robert Bly, The (Harris), **Supp. IV Part 1:** 68

In Country (Mason), **Supp. VIII:** 133, 142–143, 146

"Incredible Survival of Coyote, The" (Snyder), **Supp. VIII:** 297

"Increment" (Ammons), **Supp. VII:** 28

In Defense of Ignorance (Shapiro), **Supp. II Part 2:** 703, 704, 713–714

In Defense of Reason (Winters), **Supp. I Part 1:** 268

In Defense of Women (Mencken), **III:** 109

Independence Day (Ford), **Supp. V:** 57, 62–63, 67–68

Independence Day (film), **Supp. X:** 80

"Independent Candidate, The, a Story of Today" (Howells), **II:** 277

"Indestructible Mr. Gore, The" (Vidal), **Supp. IV Part 2:** 679

Index of American Design, **Supp. III Part 2:** 618

"India" (Rodriguez), **Supp. XIV:**302

"Indian at the Burial-Place of His Fathers, An" (Bryant), **Supp. I Part 1:** 155–156, 167–168

"Indian Burying Ground, The" (Freneau), **Supp. II Part 1:** 264, 266

"Indian Camp" (Hemingway), **II:** 247–248, 263; **Retro. Supp. I:** 174–175, 176, 177, 181; **Supp. XVI:**208

Indian Country (Matthiessen), **Supp. V:** 211

"Indian Country" (McCarriston), **Supp. XIV:**271

"Indian Country" (Simpson), **Supp. IX:** 274

Indian Earth (Bynner), **Supp. XV:** 46

"Indian Girls" (McCarriston), **Supp. XIV:**272–273

"Indian Manifesto" (Deloria), **Supp. IV Part 1:** 323

"Indian Names" (Sigourney), **Retro. Supp. II:** 47

"Indian Student, The" (Freneau), **Supp. II Part 1:** 264

"Indian Student, The" (Simpson), **Supp. IX:** 280

Indian Summer (Howells), **II:** 275, 279–281, 282

Indian Summer (Knowles), **Supp. XII:** 249, 250

"Indian Uprising, The" (Barthelme), **Supp. IV Part 1:** 44

Indifferent Children, The (Auchincloss), **Supp. IV Part 1:** 25

Indiscretions (Pound), **Retro. Supp. I:** 284

"Indispensability of the Eyes, The" (Olds), **Supp. X:** 202

"In Distrust of Merits" (Moore), **III:** 201, 214

"Individual and the State, The" (Emerson), **II:** 10

Individualism, Old and New (Dewey), **Supp. I Part 2:** 677

In Dreams Begin Responsibilities (Schwartz), **Supp. II Part 2:** 642, 645–650

"In Dreams Begin Responsibilities" (Schwartz), **Supp. II Part 2:** 641, 649, 654

In Dubious Battle (Steinbeck), **IV:** 51, 55–56, 59, 63

"In Durance" (Pound), **Retro. Supp. I:** 285

"Industry of Hard Kissing, The" (Ríos), **Supp. IV Part 2:** 547

"In Duty Bound" (Gilman), **Supp. XI:** 196–197

"I Need, I Need" (Roethke), **III:** 535–536

"I Need Help" (Stern), **Supp. IX:** 290

"Inés in the Kitchen" (García), **Supp. XI:** 190

"I never saw a Moor" (Dickinson), **Retro. Supp. I:** 37

I Never Told Anybody: Teaching Poetry Writing in a Nursing Home (Koch), **Supp. XV:** 190

"I Never Will Be Married, I'd Rather

Be Excus'd" (Rowson), **Supp. XV:** 240

Inevitable Exiles (Kielsky), **Supp. V:** 273

"Inevitable Trial, The" (Holmes), **Supp. I Part 1:** 318

"Inexhaustible Hat, The" (Wagoner), **Supp. IX:** 327

"In Extremis" (Berry), **Supp. X:** 23

"Infancy" (Wilder), **IV:** 375

"Infant Boy at Midcentury" (Warren), **IV:** 244–245, 252

Infante, Guillermo Cabrera, **Retro. Supp. I:** 278

Inferno (Dante), **IV:** 139; **Supp. V:** 338; **Supp. VIII:** 219–221

Inferno of Dante, The (Pinsky), **Supp. VI:** 235, 248

"Infidelity" (Komunyakaa), **Supp. XIII:** 130

"Infiltration of the Universe" (MacLeish), **III:** 19

Infinite Jest: A Novel (Wallace), **Supp. X:** 301, 310–314

"Infinite Reason, The" (MacLeish), **III:** 19

"Infirmity" (Lowell), **II:** 554

"Infirmity" (Roethke), **III:** 548

In Five Years Time (Haines), **Supp. XII:** 206

"In Flower" (Snodgrass), **Supp. VI:** 325

"Influence of Landscape upon the Poet, The" (Eliot), **Retro. Supp. I:** 67

"In Football Season" (Updike), **IV:** 219

Informer, The (film), **Supp. III Part 2:** 619

Ingersoll, Charles J., **I:** 344

Ingersoll, Robert Green, **Supp. II Part 1:** 198

Ingraham, Lloyd, **Supp. XVI:**184

Ingster, Boris, **Retro. Supp. II:** 330

Inhabitants, The (Morris), **III:** 221–222

"Inheritance and Invention in Li-Young Lee's Poetry" (Xiaojing), **Supp. XV:** 214

"Inheritance of Tools, The" (Sanders), **Supp. XVI:**273

Inheritors (Glaspell), **Supp. III Part 1:** 175, 179–181, 186, 189

"In Honor of David Anderson Brooks, My Father" (Brooks), **Supp. III Part 1:** 79

"Inhumanist, The" (Jeffers), **Supp. II Part 2:** 423, 426

"In Illo Tempore" (Karr), **Supp. XI:** 242

"In Interims: Outlyer" (Harrison), **Supp. VIII:** 38

"Injudicious Gardening" (Moore), **III:** 198

"Injustice" (Paley), **Supp. VI:** 220

Injustice Collectors, The (Auchincloss), **Supp. IV Part 1:** 25

Ink, Blood, Semen (Goldbarth), **Supp. XII:** 181, 183

Ink Truck, The (W. Kennedy), **Supp. VII:** 132, 133–138, 140, 141, 149, 152

In Life Sentences: Literary Essays (Epstein), **Supp. XIV:**112

"In Limbo" (Wilbur), **Supp. III Part 2:** 544, 561

In Limestone Country (Sanders), **Supp. XVI:**272

In Love and Trouble: Stories of Black Women (Walker), **Supp. III Part 2:** 520, 521, 530, 531, 532

In Mad Love and War (Harjo), **Supp. XII:** 224–226

"In Memoriam" (Emerson), **II:** 13

"In Memoriam" (Hay), **Supp. XIV:**122, 127

"In Memoriam" (Tennyson), **Retro. Supp. I:** 325; **Supp. I Part 2:** 416

In Memoriam: 1933 (Reznikoff), **Supp. XIV:**280, 285

In Memoriam to Identity (Acker), **Supp. XII:** 5, 16–18

"In Memory of Arthur Winslow" (Lowell), **II:** 541, 547, 550; **Retro. Supp. II:** 187

"In Memory of Congresswoman Barbara Jordan" (Pinsky), **Supp. VI:** 250

"In Memory of Joe Brainard" (Bidart), **Supp. XV:** 33

"In Memory of My Feelings" (O'Hara), **Supp. XV:** 215–216

"In Memory of W. B. Yeats" (Auden), **Supp. VIII:** 19, 30; **Supp. XI:** 243, 244

"In Memory of W. H. Auden" (Stern), **Supp. IX:** 288

"In Mercy on Broadway" (Doty), **Supp. XI:** 132

In Morocco (Wharton), **Retro. Supp. I:** 380; **Supp. IV Part 1:** 81

Inmost Leaf, The: A Selection of Essays (Kazin), **Supp. VIII:** 102, 103

In Motley (Bierce), **I:** 209

In My Father's Court (Singer), **IV:** 16–17; **Retro. Supp. II:** 301–302

"In My Life" (Dubus), **Supp. VII:** 81

Inner Landscape (Sarton), **Supp. VIII:** 259

Inner Room, The (Merrill), **Supp. III Part 1:** 336

"In Nine Sleep Valley" (Merrill), **Supp. III Part 1:** 328

Innocents, The: A Story for Lovers (Lewis), **II:** 441

Innocents Abroad, The; or, The New Pilgrim's Progress (Twain), **II:** 275, 434; **IV:** 191, 196, 197–198

Innocents at Cedro, The: A Memoir of Thorstein Veblen and Some Others (Duffus), **Supp. I Part 2:** 650

"In Off the Cliffs of Moher" (McCarriston), **Supp. XIV:**270

In Old Plantation Days (Dunbar), **Supp. II Part 1:** 214

In Ole Virginia (Page), **Supp. II Part 1:** 201

In Orbit (Morris), **III:** 236

In Other Words (Swenson), **Supp. IV Part 2:** 650–652

In Our Terribleness (Some elements and meaning in black style) (Baraka), **Supp. II Part 1:** 52, 53

In Our Time (Hemingway), **I:** 117; **II:** 68, 247, 252, 263; **IV:** 42; **Retro. Supp. I:** 170, 173, 174, 178, 180; **Supp. IX:** 106

"In Our Time" (Wolfe), **Supp. III Part 2:** 584

"Inpatient" (Kenyon), **Supp. VII:** 169

In Pharaoh's Army: Memories of the Lost War (Wolff), **Supp. VII:** 331–334, 335, 338

"In Plaster" (Plath), **Supp. I Part 2:** 540

"In Praise of Johnny Appleseed" (Lindsay), **Supp. I Part 2:** 397

"In Praise of Limestone" (Auden), **Supp. II Part 1:** 20–21; **Supp. VIII:** 23

In Pursuit of a Vanishing Star (Sobin), **Supp. XVI:**294

In Quest of the Ordinary (Cavell), **Retro. Supp. I:** 307

Inquiry into the Nature of Peace, An (Veblen), **Supp. I Part 2:** 642

Inquisitor, The (Rowson), **Supp. XV:** 232, 238

In Radical Pursuit (Snodgrass), **Supp. VI:** 312, 316, 318

In Reckless Ecstasy (Sandburg), **III:** 579

In Recognition of William Gaddis (Kuehl and Moore), **Supp. IV Part 1:** 279

"In Retirement" (Malamud), **Supp. I Part 2:** 437

"In Retrospect" (Angelou), **Supp. IV Part 1:** 15

In Russia (A. Miller), **III:** 165

"In Sabine" (Chopin), **Supp. I Part 1:** 213

"In School-Days" (Whittier), **Supp. I Part 2:** 699–700

"Inscription for the Entrance to a Wood" (Bryant), **Supp. I Part 1:** 154, 155, 161–162

Inscriptions, 1944–1956 (Reznikoff), **Supp. XIV:**281

In Search of Bisco (Caldwell), **I:** 296

"In Search of Our Mothers' Gardens" (Walker), **Supp. III Part 2:** 520–532, 524, 525, 527, 529, 532–533, 535, 536; **Supp. IX:** 306

"In Search of Thomas Merton" (Griffin), **Supp. VIII:** 208

"In Search of Yage" (Burroughs), **Supp. III Part 1:** 98

"Insertion of Self into a Space of Borderless Possibilities, The" (Fjellestad), **Supp. XVI:**150

"In Shadow" (Crane), **I:** 386

"In Sickness and in Health" (Auden), **Supp. II Part 1:** 15

"In Sickness and in Health" (Humphrey), **Supp. IX:** 94

Inside His Mind (A. Miller), **III:** 154

"Insider Baseball" (Didion), **Supp. IV Part 1:** 211

Inside Sports magazine, **Supp. V:** 58, 61

"In So Many Dark Rooms" (Hogan), **Supp. IV Part 1:** 400

"Insomnia" (Bishop), **Supp. I Part 1:** 92

"Insomniac" (Plath), **Supp. I Part 2:** 539

"Inspiration for Greatness" (Caldwell), **I:** 291

"Instability of Race Types, The" (Boas), **Supp. XIV:**209

"Installation #6" (Beattie), **Supp. V:** 33

Instinct of Workmanship and the State of the Industrial Arts, The (Veblen), **Supp. I Part 2:** 642

Instincts of the Herd in Peace and War, The (Trotter), **I:** 249

Institute (Calvin), **IV:** 158, 160

"Instruction Manual, The" (Ashbery), **Supp. III Part 1:** 6–7, 10, 12

"Instructions for the Afternoon" (Gioia), **Supp. XV:** 120

"Instruction to Myself" (Brooks), **Supp. III Part 1:** 87

Instrument, The (O'Hara), **III:** 362, 364

"In Such Times, Ties Must Bind" (Nye), **Supp. XIII:** 286

"Insurance and Social Change" (Stevens), **Retro. Supp. I:** 297

Insurgent Mexico (Reed), **I:** 476

In Suspect Terrain (McPhee), **Supp. III Part 1:** 309, 310

"In Tall Grass" (Sandburg), **III:** 585

"Integer Vitae" (Horace), **Supp. XV:** 304

Intellectual History, An (Senghor), **Supp. X:** 139

"Intellectual Pre-Eminence of Jews in Modern Europe, The" (Veblen), **Supp. I Part 2:** 643–644

Intellectual Things (Kunitz), **Supp. III Part 1:** 260, 262–264

Intellectual versus the City, The (White), **I:** 258

"In Temporary Pain" (Bynner), **Supp. XV:** 41–42

Intentions (Wilde), **Retro. Supp. I:** 56

"Interest in Life, An" (Paley), **Supp. VI:** 222, 224–225

Interest of Great Britain Considered, with Regard to Her Colonies and the Acquisition of Canada and Guadeloupe, The (Franklin), **II:** 119

Interior Landscapes (Vizenor), **Supp. IV Part 1:** 262

Interiors (film; Allen), **Supp. IV Part 1:** 205; **Supp. XV:** 1, 7, 10

Interlocking Lives (Koch), **Supp. XV:** 185

"Interlude" (A. Lowell), **Retro. Supp. II:** 46

Interlunar (Atwood), **Supp. XIII:** 35

"Intermezzo" (Schnackenberg), **Supp. XV:** 254

"In Terms of the Toenail: Fiction and the Figures of Life" (Gass), **Supp. VI:** 85

"International Episode, An" (James), **II:** 327

International Workers Order, **Retro. Supp. I:** 202

Interpretation of Christian Ethics, An (Niebuhr), **III:** 298–300, 301, 302

"Interpretation of Dreams, The" (Matthews), **Supp. IX:** 162–163

Interpretation of Music of the XVIIth and XVIIIth Centuries, The (Dolmetsch), **III:** 464

Interpretations and Forecasts: 1922–1972 (Mumford), **Supp. II Part 2:** 481

Interpretations of Poetry and Religion (Santayana), **III:** 611

Interpreters and Interpretations (Van Vechten), **Supp. II Part 2:** 729, 733–734

"Interrogate the Stones" (MacLeish), **III:** 9

Interrogations at Noon (Gioia), **Supp. XV:** 112, 125–127, 128, 129

"Interrupted Conversation, An" (Van Vechten), **Supp. II Part 2:** 735

Intersect: Poems (Shields), **Supp. VII:** 310–311

Interstate (Dixon), **Supp. XII:** 140, 152–153, 153, 156

"Interview" (Hay), **Supp. XIV:**132

"Interview, The" (Thurber), **Supp. I Part 2:** 616

"Interview With a Lemming" (Thurber), **Supp. I Part 2:** 603

"Interview with Peter Everwine, An" (Veinberg and Buckley), **Supp. XV:** 76–77

Interview with the Vampire (Rice), **Supp. VII:** 287, 288–291, 297–298, 303

"Interview with the Vampire" (Rice), **Supp. VII:** 288

Interzone (Burroughs), **Supp. IV Part 1:** 90

"In the Absence of Bliss" (Kumin), **Supp. IV Part 2:** 453

"In the Afternoon" (Dunn), **Supp. XI:** 146

"In the Alley" (Elkin), **Supp. VI:** 46–47

In the American Grain (W. C. Williams), **Retro. Supp. I:** 420–421

In the American Tree (Silliman), **Supp. IV Part 2:** 426

In the Bar of a Tokyo Hotel (T. Williams), **IV:** 382, 386, 387, 391, 393

In the Beauty of the Lilies (Updike), **Retro. Supp. I:** 322, 325, 326, 327, 333

"In the Beginning . . ." (Simic), **Supp. VIII:** 270, 271

In the Belly of the Beast: Letters from Prison (Abbott), **Retro. Supp. II:** 210

"In the Black Museum" (Nemerov), **III:** 275

"In the Bodies of Words" (Swenson), **Supp. IV Part 2:** 651

"In the Cage" (Gass), **Supp. VI:** 85

In the Cage (James), **Retro. Supp. I:** 229

"In the Cage" (James), **II:** 332; **Retro. Supp. I:** 231

"In the Cage" (Lowell), **Retro. Supp. II:** 187

"In the Cave at Lone Tree Meadow" (Haines), **Supp. XII:** 212

"In the City Ringed with Giants" (Kingsolver), **Supp. VII:** 209

"In the Clearing" (Brodsky), **Supp. VIII:** 32

In the Clearing (Frost), **II:** 153, 155,

164; **Retro. Supp. I:** 121, 122, 141

"In the Closet of the Soul" (Walker), **Supp. III Part 2:** 526

"In the Confidence of a Story-Writer" (Chopin), **Retro. Supp. II:** 66–67; **Supp. I Part 1:** 217

In the Country of Last Things (Auster), **Supp. XII:** 23, 29–30, 31, 32

"In the Courtyard of the Isleta Missions" (R. Bly), **Supp. IV Part 1:** 71

"In the Dark" (Levine), **Supp. V:** 194

"In the Dark New England Days" (Jewett), **Retro. Supp. II:** 139

"In the Days of Prismatic Colour" (Moore), **III:** 205, 213

In the Electric Mist with Confederate Dead (Burke), **Supp. XIV:**30, 31–32

"In the Field" (Wilbur), **Supp. III Part 2:** 558

"In the Fleeting Hand of Time" (Corso), **Supp. XII:** 122–123

"In the Footsteps of Gutenberg" (Mencken), **III:** 101

"In the Forest" (Simpson), **Supp. IX:** 270

"In the Forties" (Lowell), **II:** 554

In the Garden of the North American Martyrs (Wolff), **Supp. VII:** 341–342

In the Garret (Van Vechten), **Supp. II Part 2:** 735

"In the Grove: The Poet at Ten" (Kenyon), **Supp. VII:** 160

"In the Hall of Mirrors" (Merrill), **Supp. III Part 1:** 322

In the Harbor (Longfellow), **II:** 491

In the Heart of the Heart of the Country (Gass), **Supp. VI:** 82–83, 84, 85, 93

In the Heat of the Night (Ball), **Supp. XV:** 202

In the Heat of the Night (film), **Supp. I Part 1:** 67

In the Hollow of His Hand (Purdy), **Supp. VII:** 278–280

In the House of Light (Everwine, trans.), **Supp. XV:** 73, 75, 76–78, 82

In the Lake of the Woods (O'Brien), **Supp. V:** 240, 243, 250–252

"In the Last Days" (Everwine), **Supp. XV:** 88, 89

In the Loyal Mountains (Bass), **Supp. XVI:**19–20

"In the Loyal Mountains" (Bass), **Supp. XVI:**20

In the Mecca (Brooks), **Supp. III Part 1:** 74

"In the Mecca" (Brooks), **Supp. III Part 1:** 70, 83–84

In the Midst of Life (Bierce), **I:** 200–203, 204, 206, 208, 212

"In the Miro District" (Taylor), **Supp. V:** 323

In the Miro District and Other Stories (Taylor), **Supp. V:** 325–326

In the Money (W. C. Williams), **Retro. Supp. I:** 423

"In the Motel" (X. J. Kennedy), **Supp. XV:** 163

"In the Naked Bed, in Plato's Cave" (Schwartz), **Supp. II Part 2:** 646–649

In the Name of the Neither (Sobin), **Supp. XVI:**291

"In the Night" (Kincaid), **Supp. VII:** 183

In the Night Season: A Novel (Bausch), **Supp. VII:** 52–53

"In the Old Neighborhood" (Dove), **Supp. IV Part 1:** 241, 257

"In the Old World" (Oates), **Supp. II Part 2:** 503, 504

"In the Park" (Huncke), **Supp. XIV:**139

"In the Pit" (Proulx), **Supp. VII:** 255, 261

In the Presence of the Sun (Momaday), **Supp. IV Part 2:** 489, 490, 491–493, 493

"In the Quiet Night" (Li Po), **Supp. XV:** 47

"In the Realm of the Fisher King" (Didion), **Supp. IV Part 1:** 211

"In the Red Room" (Bowles), **Supp. IV Part 1:** 93

"In the Region of Ice" (Oates), **Supp. II Part 2:** 520

In the Room We Share (Simpson), **Supp. IX:** 279

"In These Dissenting Times" (Walker), **Supp. III Part 2:** 522

"In the Shadow of Gabriel, A.D.1550" (Frederic), **II:** 139

In the Spirit of Crazy Horse (Matthiessen), **Supp. V:** 211

"In the Subway" (Untermeyer), **Supp. XV:** 296

In the Summer House (Jane Bowles), **Supp. IV Part 1:** 83, 89

In the Tennessee Country (Taylor), **Supp. V:** 328

"In the Thick of Darkness" (Salinas), **Supp. XIII:** 325

"In the Time of the Blossoms" (Mervin), **Supp. III Part 1:** 352

In the Time of the Butterflies (Alvarez), **Supp. VII:** 1, 12–15, 18

"In the Tunnel Bone of Cambridge" (Corso), **Supp. XII:** 120–121

"In the Upper Pastures" (Kumin), **Supp. IV Part 2:** 453

In the Valley (Frederic), **II:** 133–134, 136, 137

"In the Village" (Bishop), **Retro. Supp. II:** 38; **Supp. I Part 1:** 73, 74–75, 76, 77, 78, 88

"In the Waiting Room" (Bishop), **Retro. Supp. II:** 50; **Supp. I Part 1:** 81, 94, 95; **Supp. IV Part 1:** 249

"In the Ward: The Sacred Wood" (Jarrell), **II:** 376, 377

In the Western Night: Collected Poems 1965–90 (Bidart), **Supp. XV:** 19, 30–32

"In the White Night" (Beattie), **Supp. V:** 30–31

"In the Wind My Rescue Is" (Ammons), **Supp. VII:** 25

In the Winter of Cities (T. Williams), **IV:** 383

"In the X-Ray of the Sarcophagus of Ta-pero" (Goldbarth), **Supp. XII:** 191

"In the Yard" (Swenson), **Supp. IV Part 2:** 647

In the Zone (O'Neill), **III:** 388

In This, Our Life (film), **Supp. I Part 1:** 67

"In This Country, but in Another Language, My Aunt Refuses to Marry the Men Everyone Wants Her To" (Paley), **Supp. VI:** 225

In This Hung-up Age (Corso), **Supp. XII:** 119–120, 129

In This Our Life (Glasgow), **II:** 175, 178, 189

In This Our World (Gilman), **Supp. XI:** 196, 200, 202

"In Those Days" (Jarrell), **II:** 387–388

"In Time of War" (Auden), **Supp. II Part 1:** 8, 13

"Into Egypt" (Benét), **Supp. XI:** 56, 57–58

Intolerance (film; Griffith), **Supp. XVI:**184

"Into My Own" (Frost), **II:** 153; **Retro. Supp. I:** 127

"Into the Night Life . . ." (H. Miller), **III:** 180, 184

"Into the Nowhere" (Rawlings), **Supp. X:** 220

Into the Stone (Dickey), **Supp. IV Part 1:** 178

"Into the Stone" (Dickey), **Supp. IV Part 1:** 179

Into the Stone and Other Poems (Dickey), **Supp. IV Part 1:** 176

In Touch: The Letters of Paul Bowles (J. Miller, ed.), **Supp. IV Part 1:** 95

"Intoxicated, The" (Jackson), **Supp. IX:** 116

"Intrigue" (Crane), **I:** 419

"Introducing the Fathers" (Kumin), **Supp. IV Part 2:** 452

Introductio ad Prudentiam (Fuller), **II:** 111

"Introduction to a Haggadah" (Paley), **Supp. VI:** 219

Introduction to Objectivist Epistemology (Rand), **Supp. IV Part 2:** 527, 528–529

Introduction to Objectivist Epistemology 2nd ed. (Rand), **Supp. IV Part 2:** 529

Introduction to Poetry, An (Gioia and X. J. Kennedy), **Supp. XV:** 113, 153

"Introduction to Some Poems, An" (Stafford), **Supp. XI:** 311, 324

Introduction to the Geography of Iowa, The (Doty), **Supp. XI:** 120

"Introduction to the Hoh" (Hugo), **Supp. VI:** 136–137

"Introduction to *The New Writing in the USA*" (Creeley), **Supp. IV Part 1:** 153–154

"Introduction to William Blake, An" (Kazin), **Supp. VIII:** 103

Introitus (Longfellow), **II:** 505, 506–507

"Intruder, The" (Dubus), **Supp. VII:** 76–78, 91

Intruder, The (Maeterlinck), **I:** 91

Intruder in the Dust (Faulkner), **II:** 71, 72; **Supp. XVI:**148

"Invaders, The" (Haines), **Supp. XII:** 205

Invasion of Privacy: The Cross Creek Trial of Marjorie Kinnan Rawlings (Acton), **Supp. X:** 233

Inventing Memory: A Novel of Mothers and Daughters (Jong), **Supp. V:** 115, 129

Inventing the Abbotts (Miller), **Supp. XII:** 294–295

"Invention of God in a Mouthful of Milk, The" (Karr), **Supp. XI:** 250

Invention of Solitude, The (Auster), **Supp. XII:** 21–22

Inventions of the March Hare (Eliot), **Retro. Supp. I:** 55–56, 58

"Inventions of the March Hare" (Eliot), **Retro. Supp. I:** 55

"Inventory" (Parker), **Supp. IX:** 192

"Inverted Forest, The" (Salinger), **III:** 552, 572

"Investigations of a Dog" (Kafka), **IV:** 438

"Investiture, The" (Banks), **Supp. V:** 7

"Investiture at Cecconi's" (Merrill),

Supp. III Part 1: 336

Invisible: Poems (Nye), **Supp. XIII:** 277

Invisible Company, The (Sanders), **Supp. XVI:**270–271

Invisible Man (Ellison), **IV:** 493; **Retro. Supp. II:** 3, 12, 111, 112, 113, 117, 119, 120–123, 125; **Supp. II Part 1:** 40, 170, 221, 224, 226, 227, 230, 231–232, 235, 236, 241–245; **Supp. IX:** 306; **Supp. X:** 242; **Supp. XI:** 18, 92

Invisible Spectator, An (Sawyer-Lauçanno), **Supp. IV Part 1:** 95

Invisible Swords (Farrell), **II:** 27, 46, 48–49

Invisible Worm, The (Millar), **Supp. IV Part 2:** 465

Invitation to a Beheading (Nabokov), **III:** 252–253, 254, 257–258; **Retro. Supp. I:** 265, 270, 273

"Invitation to the Country, An" (Bryant), **Supp. I Part 1:** 160

"Invocation" (McKay), **Supp. X:** 134

"Invocation" (Untermeyer), **Supp. XV:** 296

"Invocation to Kali" (Sarton), **Supp. VIII:** 260

"Invocation to the Social Muse" (MacLeish), **III:** 15

"In Weather" (Hass), **Supp. VI:** 102–103

"In Your Fugitive Dream" (Hugo), **Supp. VI:** 143

"In Your Good Dream" (Hugo), **Supp. VI:** 143–144

"Iola, Kansas" (Clampitt), **Supp. IX:** 45–46

Ion (Doolittle, trans.), **Supp. I Part 1:** 269, 274

Ion (Plato), **I:** 523

"Ione" (Dunbar), **Supp. II Part 1:** 199

Ionesco, Eugène, **I:** 71, 74, 75, 84, 295; **II:** 435; **Supp. VIII:** 201

"I Only Am Escaped Alone to Tell Thee" (Nemerov), **III:** 272, 273–274

"I Opened All the Portals Wide" (Chopin), **Retro. Supp. II:** 71

I Ought to Be in Pictures (Simon), **Supp. IV Part 2:** 584

Iphigenia in Tauris (Euripedes), **Supp. XV:** 42, 50

I Promessi Sposi (Manzoni), **II:** 291

"Irascibles, The" (Kees), **Supp. XV:** 145–146

"I Remember" (Sexton), **Supp. II Part 2:** 680

"Irenicon" (Shapiro), **Supp. II Part 2:** 704

Irigaray, Luce, **Supp. XII:** 6

"Iris by Night" (Frost), **Retro. Supp. I:** 132

"Irises" (L.-Y. Lee), **Supp. XV:** 214–215

Irish Stories of Sarah Orne Jewett, The (Jewett), **Retro. Supp. II:** 142

Irish Triangle, An (Barnes), **Supp. III Part 1:** 34

"Iron Characters, The" (Nemerov), **III:** 279, 282

"Iron Hans" (Sexton), **Supp. II Part 2:** 691

Iron Heel, The (London), **II:** 466, 480

Iron John: A Book about Men (R. Bly), **Supp. IV Part 1:** 59, 67; **Supp. XVI:**177

"Iron Table, The" (Jane Bowles), **Supp. IV Part 1:** 82–83

"Iron Throat, The" (Olsen), **Supp. XIII:** 292, 297, 299

Ironweed (W. Kennedy), **Supp. VII:** 132, 133, 134, 135, 142, 144, 145–147, 148, 150, 153

"Irony as Art: The Short Fiction of William Humphrey" (Tebeaux), **Supp. IX:** 109

"Irony Is Not Enough: Essay on My Life as Catherine Deneuve" (Carson), **Supp. XII:** 112–113

Irony of American History, The (Niebuhr), **III:** 292, 306–307, 308

"Irrational Element in Poetry, The" (Stevens), **Retro. Supp. I:** 298, 301

"Irrevocable Diameter, An" (Paley), **Supp. VI:** 231–232

Irvine, Lorna, **Supp. XIII:** 26

Irving, Ebenezer, **II:** 296

Irving, John, **Supp. VI:** 163–183; **Supp. X:** 77, 85

Irving, John Treat, **II:** 296

Irving, Peter, **II:** 296, 297, 298, 299, 300, 303

Irving, Sir Henry, **IV:** 350

Irving, Washington, **I:** 211, 335, 336, 339, 343; **II:** 295–318, 488, 495; **III:** 113; **IV:** 309; **Retro. Supp. I:** 246; **Supp. I Part 1:** 155, 157, 158, 317; **Supp. I Part 2:** 377, 487, 585; **Supp. II Part 1:** 335; **Supp. IV Part 1:** 380

Irving, William, **II:** 296

Irving, William, Jr., **II:** 296, 297, 298, 299, 303

Irwin, Mark, **Supp. XII:** 21, 22, 24, 29

Irwin, William Henry, **Supp. II Part 1:** 192

Is 5 (Cummings), **I:** 429, 430, 434, 435, 440, 445, 446, 447

"Isaac and Abraham" (Brodsky), **Supp. VIII:** 21

"Isaac and Archibald" (Robinson), **III:** 511, 521, 523

"Isabel Sparrow" (Oliver), **Supp. VII:** 232

Isaiah (biblical book), **Supp. I Part 1:** 236; **Supp. I Part 2:** 516

"Isaiah Beethoven" (Masters), **Supp. I Part 2:** 461

"I Saw in Louisiana a Live-Oak Growing" (Whitman), **I:** 220

"I Shall Be Released" (Dylan), **Supp. XV:** 349

I Shall Spit on Your Graves (film), **Supp. I Part 1:** 67

Isherwood, Christopher, **II:** 586; **Supp. II Part 1:** 10, 11, 13; **Supp. IV Part 1:** 79, 82, 102; **Supp. XI:** 305; **Supp. XIV:**155–175; **Supp. XVI:**194

Isherwood Century, The (Berg and Freeman), **Supp. XIV:**157, 159

Isherwood's Fiction (Schwerdt), **Supp. XIV:**155

Ishiguro, Kazuo, **Supp. VIII:** 15

Ishi Means Man (Merton), **Supp. VIII:** 208

"Ishmael's Dream" (Stern), **Supp. IX:** 287

I Should Have Stayed Home (McCoy), **Supp. XIII:** 167, 168–170, 171

"I Should Worry" (Kees), **Supp. XV:** 140

"I Sigh in the Afternoon" (Salinas), **Supp. XIII:** 318

"I Sing the Body Electric" (Whitman), **Retro. Supp. I:** 394, 395

"Isis: Dorothy Eady, 1924" (Doty), **Supp. XI:** 122

"Is It O.K. to Be a Luddite?" (Pynchon), **Supp. XVI:**128

"Is It True?" (Hughes), **Supp. I Part 1:** 342

"Island" (Hughes), **Supp. I Part 1:** 340

Island Garden, An (Thaxter), **Retro. Supp. II:** 136; **Supp. XIII:** 152

Island Holiday, An (Henry), **I:** 515

"Island of the Fay, The" (Poe), **III:** 412, 417

"Islands, The" (Hayden), **Supp. II Part 1:** 373

"Island Sheaf, An" (Doty), **Supp. XI:** 136

Islands in the Stream (Hemingway), **II:** 258; **Retro. Supp. I:** 186

Isn't It Romantic (Wasserstein), **Supp. XV:** 323–325, 327

Is Objectivism a Religion? (Ellis), **Supp. IV Part 2:** 527

"Isolation of Modern Poetry, The" (Schwartz), **Supp. II Part 2:** 644

"Israel" (Reznikoff), **Supp. XIV:**283

Israel Potter, or Fifty Years of Exile (Melville), **III:** 90

"Israfel" (Poe), **III:** 411

Is Sex Necessary? (Thurber and White), **Supp. I Part 2:** 607, 612, 614, 653

"Issues, The" (Olds), **Supp. X:** 205

"I Stand Here Ironing" (Olsen), **Supp. XIII:** 292, 294, 296, 298, 300, 305

I Stole a Million (West), **IV:** 287

"Is Verse a Dying Technique?" (Wilson), **IV:** 431

It (Creeley), **Supp. IV Part 1:** 157, 158

IT (King), **Supp. V:** 139, 140, 141, 146–147, 151, 152

"It" (Olds), **Supp. X:** 208

Italian American Reconciliation: A Folktale (Shanley), **Supp. XIV:**315, 324–326, 328, 330

Italian Backgrounds (Wharton), **Retro. Supp. I:** 370

Italian Hours (James), **I:** 12; **II:** 337; **Retro. Supp. I:** 235

Italian Journeys (Howells), **II:** 274

"Italian Morning" (Bogan), **Supp. III Part 1:** 58

Italian Villas and Their Gardens (Wharton), **IV:** 308; **Retro. Supp. I:** 361, 367

Italie, Hillel, **Supp. XV:** 128

It All Adds Up: From the Dim Past to the Uncertain Future (Bellow), **Retro. Supp. II:** 32

"It Always Breaks Out" (Ellison), **Retro. Supp. II:** 126; **Supp. II Part 1:** 248

Itard, Jean-Marc Gaspard, **Supp. I Part 2:** 564

"I taste a liquor never brewed" (Dickinson), **Retro. Supp. I:** 30, 37

It Came from Outer Space (film), **Supp. IV Part 1:** 102

It Can't Happen Here (Lewis), **II:** 454

"It Don't Mean a Thing If It Ain't Got That Swing" (Matthews), **Supp. IX:** 164–165

I Tell You Now (Ortiz), **Supp. IV Part 2:** 500

"Ithaca" (Glück), **Supp. V:** 89

It Happened One Night (Capra), **Supp. XV:** 197

It Has Come to Pass (Farrell), **II:** 26

"I think to live May be a Bliss" (Dickinson), **Retro. Supp. I:** 44

I Thought of Daisy (Wilson), **IV:** 428, 434, 435

"Itinerary of an Obsession" (Kumin),

Supp. IV Part 2: 450

"It Is a Strange Country" (Ellison), **Supp. II Part 1:** 238

"It Is Dangerous to Read Newspapers" (Atwood), **Supp. XIII:** 33

"It Must Be Abstract" (Stevens), **IV:** 95; **Retro. Supp. I:** 307

"It Must Change" (Stevens), **Retro. Supp. I:** 300, 307, 308

"It Must Give Pleasure" (Stevens), **Retro. Supp. I:** 307, 308, 309

"'It Out-Herods Herod. Pray You, Avoid It'" (Hecht), **Supp. X:** 62, 64

It's Loaded, Mr. Bauer (Marquand), **III:** 59

"It's Nation Time" (Baraka), **Supp. II Part 1:** 53

It's Nation Time (Baraka), **Supp. II Part 1:** 52, 53

It's Only a Play (McNally), **Supp. XIII:** 198

It Was (Zukofsky), **Supp. III Part 2:** 630

It Was the Nightingale (Ford), **III:** 470–471

"It Was When" (Snyder), **Supp. VIII:** 300

Ivanhoe (Scott), **I:** 216; **Supp. I Part 2:** 410

Ivens, Bryna, **Supp. XV:** 311, 312

Ivens, Joris, **I:** 488; **Retro. Supp. I:** 184

"Iverson Boy, The" (Simpson), **Supp. IX:** 280

"Ives" (Rukeyser), **Supp. VI:** 273, 283

Ives, George H., **Supp. I Part 1:** 153

Ivory Grin, The (Macdonald), **Supp. IV Part 2:** 471, 472

Ivory Tower, The (James), **II:** 337–338

"Ivory Tower, The: Louis Untermeyer as Critic" (Aiken), **Supp. XV:** 298

"Ivy Winding" (Ammons), **Supp. VII:** 33

"I Wandered Lonely as a Cloud" (Wordsworth), **Retro. Supp. I:** 121–122; **Supp. X:** 73; **Supp. XIV:**184

"I want, I want" (Plath), **Retro. Supp. II:** 246

"I Wanted to Be There When My Father Died" (Olds), **Supp. X:** 210

"I Want to Be a Father Like the Men" (Cisneros), **Supp. VII:** 71

"I Want to Be Miss America" (Alvarez), **Supp. VII:** 18

"I Want to Know Why" (Anderson), **I:** 114, 115, 116; **II:** 263

"I Want You Women Up North To Know" (Olsen), **Supp. XIII:** 292, 297

"I Was Born in Lucerne" (Levine),

Supp. V: 181, 189

"I Went into the Maverick Bar" (Snyder), **Supp. VIII:** 301

"I Will Lie Down" (Swenson), **Supp. IV Part 2:** 640

I Will Say Beauty (C. Frost), **Supp. XV:** 96, 105–107

I Wonder As I Wander (Hughes), **Retro. Supp. I:** 196, 203; **Supp. I Part 1:** 329, 332–333

I Would Have Saved Them If I Could (L. Michaels), **Supp. XVI:**203, 205, 206–210

"Iyani: It goes this Way" (Gunn Allen), **Supp. IV Part 1:** 321

"I years had been from home" (Dickinson), **I:** 471

Iyer, Pico, **Supp. V:** 215

Izzo, David Garrett, **Supp. XIV:**155, 156, 159, 160, 161, 163, 169, 171

J

J. B.: A Play in Verse (MacLeish), **II:** 163, 228; **III:** 3, 21–22, 23; **Supp. IV Part 2:** 586

"Jachid and Jechidah" (Singer), **IV:** 15

Jack and Jill (Alcott), **Supp. I Part 1:** 42

"Jack and the Beanstalk" (Hay), **Supp. XIV:**124

Jack Kelso (Masters), **Supp. I Part 2:** 456, 471–472

Jacklight (Erdrich), **Supp. IV Part 1:** 259, 270

Jack London, Hemingway, and the Constitution (Doctorow), **Supp. IV Part 1:** 220, 222, 224, 232, 235

Jackpot (Caldwell), **I:** 304

"Jack Schmidt, Arts Administrator" (Keillor), **Supp. XVI:**171

"Jack Schmidt on the Burning Sands" (Keillor), **Supp. XVI:**171

Jackson, Amelia. *See* Holmes, Mrs. Oliver Wendell (Amelia Jackson)

Jackson, Andrew, **I:** 7, 20; **III:** 473; **IV:** 192, 248, 298, 334, 348; **Supp. I Part 2:** 456, 461, 473, 474, 493, 695

Jackson, Blyden, **Supp. I Part 1:** 337

Jackson, Charles, **Supp. I Part 1:** 303

Jackson, George, **Supp. I Part 1:** 66

Jackson, Helen Hunt, **I:** 459, 470; **Retro. Supp. I:** 26, 27, 30–31, 32, 33

Jackson, J. O., **III:** 213

Jackson, James, **Supp. I Part 1:** 302, 303

Jackson, Joe, **Supp. I Part 2:** 441

Jackson, Katherine Gauss, **Supp. VIII:** 124

Jackson, Lawrence, **Retro. Supp. II:** 113, 115

Jackson, Melanie, **Supp. X:** 166

Jackson, Michael, **Supp. VIII:** 146

Jackson, Richard, **II:** 119; **Supp. IX:** 165

Jackson, Shirley, **Supp. IX:** 113–130

Jackson, Thomas J. ("Stonewall"), **IV:** 125, 126

"Jackson Square" (Levertov), **Supp. III Part 1:** 276

Jackstraws (Simic), **Supp. VIII:** 280, 282–283

"Jackstraws" (Simic), **Supp. VIII:** 283

Jack Tier (Cooper), **I:** 354, 355

"Jacob" (Garrett), **Supp. VII:** 109–110

"Jacob" (Schwartz), **Supp. II Part 2:** 663

Jacob, Max, **Supp. XV:** 178, 182

"Jacob and the Indians" (Benét), **Supp. XI:** 47–48

Jacobs, Harriet, **Supp. XVI:**85

Jacobs, Rita D., **Supp. XII:** 339

Jacobsen, Josephine, **Supp. XIII:** 346; **Supp. XIV:**260

"Jacob's Ladder" (Rawlings), **Supp. X:** 224, 228

"Jacob's Ladder, The" (Levertov), **Supp. III Part 1:** 278

Jacob's Ladder, The (Levertov), **Supp. III Part 1:** 272, 276–278, 281

Jacobson, Dale, **Supp. X:** 112

Jacobson, Leslie, **Supp. XV:** 323

Jacoby, Russell, **Supp. IV Part 2:** 692

"Jacquerie, The" (Lanier), **Supp. I Part 1:** 355, 356, 360, 364, 370

Jade Mountain, The: A Chinese Anthology, Being Three Hundred Poems of the T'ang Dynasty (Bynner, trans.), **II:** 527; **Supp. XV:** 46, 47, 48

Jafsie and John Henry: Essays on Hollywood, Bad Boys, and Six Hours of Perfect Poker (Mamet), **Supp. XIV:**252

Jaguar Totem (LaBastille), **Supp. X:** 99, 106, 107–109

Jailbird (Vonnegut), **Supp. II Part 2:** 760, 779–780

Jaimes, M. Annette, **Supp. IV Part 1:** 330, 331

Jain, Manju, **Retro. Supp. I:** 53, 58

Jake's Women (Simon), **Supp. IV Part 2:** 576, 588

"Jakie's Mother" (Fante), **Supp. XI:** 164

Jakobson, Roman, **Supp. IV Part 1:** 155

"Jamaica Kincaid's New York" (Kincaid), **Supp. VII:** 181

James, A. Lloyd, **Supp. XIV:**343

James, Alice, **I:** 454; **Retro. Supp. I:** 228, 235

James, Caryn, **Supp. X:** 302, 303

James, Etta, **Supp. X:** 242

James, Henry, **I:** 4, 5, 9, 10, 12, 15, 16, 20, 52, 93, 109, 211, 226, 228, 244, 246, 251, 255, 258, 259, 336, 363, 374, 375, 379, 384, 409, 429, 436, 439, 452, 454, 459, 461–462, 463, 464, 485, 500, 504, 513, 514, 517–518, 571; **II:** 38, 58, 60, 73, 74, 95, 138, 140, 144, 147, 196, 198, 199, 228, 230, 234, 243, 259, 267, 271, 272, 275, 276, 278, 281, 282, 283, 284, 285, 286, 287, 288, 290, 306, 309, 316, 319–341, 398, 404, 410, 415, 427, 444, 542, 544, 547–548, 556, 600; **III:** 44, 51, 136, 194–195, 199, 206, 208, 218, 228–229, 237, 281, 319, 325, 326, 334, 409, 453, 454, 457, 460, 461, 464, 511, 522, 576, 607; **IV:** 8, 27, 34, 37, 40, 53, 58, 73, 74, 134, 168, 172, 182, 198, 202, 285, 308, 309, 310, 311, 314, 316, 317, 318, 319, 321, 322, 323, 324, 328, 347, 352, 359, 433, 439, 476; **Retro. Supp. I:** 1, 8, 53, 56, 59, 108, 112, 215–242, 272, 283, 284, 362, 366, 367, 368, 371, 373, 374, 375, 376, 377, 378, 379; **Retro. Supp. II:** 93, 135, 136, 203, 223; **Supp. I Part 1:** 35, 38, 43; **Supp. I Part 2:** 414, 454, 608, 609, 612–613, 618, 620, 646; **Supp. II Part 1:** 94–95; **Supp. III Part 1:** 14, 200; **Supp. III Part 2:** 410, 412; **Supp. IV Part 1:** 31, 35, 80, 127, 197, 349, 353; **Supp. IV Part 2:** 613, 677, 678, 682, 689, 693; **Supp. V:** 97, 101, 103, 258, 261, 263, 313; **Supp. VIII:** 98, 102, 156, 166, 168; **Supp. IX:** 121; **Supp. XI:** 153; **Supp. XIII:** 102; **Supp. XIV:**40, 110, 112, 335, 336, 348, 349; **Supp. XV:** 41

James, Henry (father), **II:** 7, 275, 321, 337, 342–344, 364; **IV:** 174; **Supp. I Part 1:** 300

James, Henry (nephew), **II:** 360

James, Horace, **Supp. XIV:**57

James, William, **I:** 104, 220, 224, 227, 228, 255, 454; **II:** 20, 27, 165, 166, 276, 321, 337, 342–366, 411; **III:** 303, 309, 509, 599, 600, 605, 606, 612; **IV:** 26, 27, 28–29, 31, 32, 34, 36, 37, 43, 46, 291, 486; **Retro. Supp. I:** 57, 216, 227, 228, 235, 295, 300, 306; **Supp. I Part 1:** 3, 7, 11, 20; **Supp. XIV:**40, 50, 197, 199, 212, 335

James, William (grandfather), **II:** 342
James Baldwin: The Legacy (Troupe, ed.), **Retro. Supp. II:** 15
James Baldwin—The Price of the Ticket (film), **Retro. Supp. II:** 2
James Dickey and the Politics of Canon (Suarez), **Supp. IV Part 1:** 175
"James Dickey on Yeats: An Interview" (Dickey), **Supp. IV Part 1:** 177
James Hogg: A Critical Study (Simpson), **Supp. IX:** 269, 276
James Jones: A Friendship (Morris), **Supp. XI:** 234
James Jones: An American Literary Orientalist Master (Carter), **Supp. XI:** 220
James Jones: Reveille to Taps (television documentary), **Supp. XI:** 234
"James Jones and Jack Kerouac: Novelists of Disjunction" (Stevenson), **Supp. XI:** 230
Jameson, F. R., **Supp. IV Part 1:** 119
Jameson, Sir Leander Starr, **III:** 327
James Shore's Daughter (Benét), **Supp. XI:** 48
"James Thurber" (Pollard), **Supp. I Part 2:** 468
"James Whitcomb Riley (From a Westerner's Point of View)" (Dunbar), **Supp. II Part 1:** 198
Jammes, Francis, **II:** 528; **Retro. Supp. I:** 55
Jan. 31 (Goldbarth), **Supp. XII:** 177, 178–179, 180
"Jan, the Son of Thomas" (Sandburg), **III:** 593–594
Janeczko, Paul, **Supp. XIII:** 280
Jane Eyre (Brontë), **Supp. XVI:**158
Janet, Pierre, **I:** 248, 249, 252; **Retro. Supp. I:** 55, 57
Jane Talbot: A Novel (Brown), **Supp. I Part 1:** 145–146
"Janet Waking" (Ransom), **III:** 490, 491
"Janice" (Jackson), **Supp. IX:** 117
Janowitz, Tama, **Supp. X:** 7
Jantz, Harold S., **Supp. I Part 1:** 112
"January" (Barthelme), **Supp. IV Part 1:** 54
January Man, The (screenplay, Shanley), **Supp. XIV:**316
"January Thaw" (Leopold), **Supp. XIV:**183–184
"Janus" (Beattie), **Supp. V:** 31
Janzen, Jean, **Supp. V:** 180
"Japanese Beetles" (X. J. Kennedy), **Supp. XV:** 161, 165
Japanese by Spring (Reed), **Supp. X:** 241, 253–255

"Japan's Young Dreams" (Geisel), **Supp. XVI:**102
Jara, Victor, **Supp. IV Part 2:** 549
Jarman, Mark, **Supp. IV Part 1:** 68; **Supp. IX:** 266, 270, 276; **Supp. XII:** 209; **Supp. XV:** 251
Jarrell, Mrs. Randall (Mary von Schrader), **II:** 368, 385
Jarrell, Randall, **I:** 167, 169, 173, 180; **II:** 367–390, 539–540; **III:** 134, 194, 213, 268, 527; **IV:** 352, 411, 422; **Retro. Supp. I:** 52, 121, 135, 140; **Retro. Supp. II:** 44, 177, 178, 182; **Supp. I Part 1:** 89; **Supp. I Part 2:** 552; **Supp. II Part 1:** 109, 135; **Supp. III Part 1:** 64; **Supp. III Part 2:** 541, 550; **Supp. IV Part 2:** 440; **Supp. V:** 315, 318, 323; **Supp. VIII:** 31, 100, 271; **Supp. IX:** 94, 268; **Supp. XI:** 311, 315; **Supp. XII:** 121, 260, 297; **Supp. XV:** 93, 153
Jarry, Alfred, **Retro. Supp. II:** 326; **Supp. XV:** 177–178, 182, 188
Jarvis, John Wesley, **Supp. I Part 2:** 501, 520
Jaskoski, Helen, **Supp. IV Part 1:** 325
"Jasmine" (Komunyakaa), **Supp. XIII:** 132
"Jason" (Hecht), **Supp. X:** 62
"Jason" (MacLeish), **III:** 4
Jason and Medeia (Gardner), **Supp. VI:** 63, 68–69
Jaspers, Karl, **III:** 292; **IV:** 491
Jay, William, **I:** 338
Jayber Crow (Berry), **Supp. X:** 28, 34
"Jaz Fantasia" (Sandburg), **III:** 585
"Jazz Age Clerk, A" (Farrell), **II:** 45
Jazz Country: Ralph Ellison in America (Porter), **Retro. Supp. II:** 127
"Jazzonia" (Hughes), **Supp. I Part 1:** 324
Jazz Poetry Anthology, The (Komunyakaa and Feinstein, eds.), **Supp. XIII:** 125
"Jazztet Muted" (Hughes), **Supp. I Part 1:** 342
"Jealous" (Ford), **Supp. V:** 71
Jealousies, The: A Faery Tale, by Lucy Vaughan Lloyd of China Walk, Lambeth (Keats), **Supp. XII:** 113
"Jean Harlow's Wedding Night" (Wasserstein), **Supp. XV:** 328
Jean Huguenot (Benét), **Supp. XI:** 44
"Jeff Briggs's Love Story" (Harte), **Supp. II Part 1:** 355
Jeffers, Robinson, **I:** 66; **III:** 134; **Retro. Supp. I:** 202; **Supp. II Part 2:** 413–440; **Supp. VIII:** 33, 292; **Supp. IX:** 77; **Supp. X:** 112; **Supp.**

XI: 312; **Supp. XV:** 113, 114, 115
Jeffers, Una Call Kuster (Mrs. Robinson Jeffers), **Supp. II Part 2:** 414
Jefferson, Blind Lemon, **Supp. VIII:** 349
Jefferson, Thomas, **I:** 1, 2, 5, 6–8, 14, 485; **II:** 5, 6, 34, 217, 300, 301, 437; **III:** 3, 17, 18, 294–295, 306, 310, 473, 608; **IV:** 133, 243, 249, 334, 348; **Supp. I Part 1:** 146, 152, 153, 229, 230, 234, 235; **Supp. I Part 2:** 389, 399, 456, 474, 475, 482, 507, 509, 510, 511, 516, 518–519, 520, 522; **Supp. X:** 26; **Supp. XIV:**191
Jefferson and/or Mussolini (Pound), **Retro. Supp. I:** 292
"Jefferson Davis as a Representative American" (Du Bois), **Supp. II Part 1:** 161
J-E-L-L-O (Baraka), **Supp. II Part 1:** 47
"Jelly-Bean, The" (Fitzgerald), **II:** 88
"Jellyfish, A" (Moore), **III:** 215
Jemie, Onwuchekwa, **Supp. I Part 1:** 343
Jenkins, J. L., **I:** 456
Jenkins, Kathleen, **III:** 403
Jenkins, Susan, **IV:** 123
Jenks, Deneen, **Supp. IV Part 2:** 550, 554
Jennie Gerhardt (Dreiser), **I:** 497, 499, 500, 501, 504–505, 506, 507, 519; **Retro. Supp. II:** 94, 99–101
"Jennie M'Grew" (Masters), **Supp. I Part 2:** 468
Jennifer Lorn (Wylie), **Supp. I Part 2:** 709, 714–717, 718, 721, 724
"Jenny Garrow's Lover" (Jewett), **II:** 397
"Jerboa, The" (Moore), **III:** 203, 207, 209, 211–212
Jeremiah, **Supp. X:** 35
Jeremy's Version (Purdy), **Supp. VII:** 274
"Jericho" (Lowell), **II:** 536
"Jersey City Gendarmerie, Je T'aime" (Lardner), **II:** 433
Jersey Rain (Pinsky), **Supp. VI:** 235, 247–250
"Jerusalem" (Nye), **Supp. XIII:** 287
Jerusalem the Golden (Reznikoff), **Supp. XIV:**280, 285, 286
Jessup, Richard, **Supp. XI:** 306
"Je Suis Perdu" (Taylor), **Supp. V:** 314, 321–322
Jesuits in North America in the Seventeenth Century, The (Parkman), **Supp. II Part 2:** 597, 603–605
Jesus, **I:** 27, 34, 68, 89, 136, 552, 560; **II:** 1, 16, 197, 198, 214, 215, 216,

218, 219, 239, 373, 377, 379, 537, 538, 539, 549, 569, 585, 591, 592; **III:** 39, 173, 179, 270, 291, 296–297, 300, 303, 305, 307, 311, 339, 340, 341, 342, 344, 345, 346, 347, 348, 352, 353, 354, 355, 436, 451, 489, 534, 564, 566, 567, 582; **IV:** 51, 69, 86, 107, 109, 117, 137, 138, 141, 144, 147, 149, 150, 151, 152, 155, 156, 157, 158, 159, 163, 164, 232, 241, 289, 293, 294, 296, 331, 364, 392, 396, 418, 430; **Supp. I Part 1:** 2, 54, 104, 107, 108, 109, 121, 267, 371; **Supp. I Part 2:** 379, 386, 458, 515, 580, 582, 583, 587, 588, 683; **Supp. V:** 280

"Jesus Asleep" (Sexton), **Supp. II Part 2:** 693

"Jesus of Nazareth, Then and Now" (Price), **Supp. VI:** 268

"Jesus Papers, The" (Sexton), **Supp. II Part 2:** 693

"Jesus Raises Up the Harlot" (Sexton), **Supp. II Part 2:** 693

Jetée, La (film), **Supp. IV Part 2:** 436

"Jeune Parque, La" (Valéry), **IV:** 92

"Jewbird, The" (Malamud), **Supp. I Part 2:** 435

"Jewboy, The" (Roth), **Supp. III Part 2:** 412

Jewett, Caroline, **II:** 396

Jewett, Dr. Theodore Herman, **II:** 396–397, 402

Jewett, Katharine, **Retro. Supp. II:** 46

Jewett, Mary, **II:** 396, 403

Jewett, Rutger, **Retro. Supp. I:** 381

Jewett, Sarah Orne, **I:** 313; **II:** 391–414; **Retro. Supp. I:** 6, 7, 19; **Retro. Supp. II:** 51, 52, 131–151, 156; **Supp. I Part 2:** 495; **Supp. VIII:** 126; **Supp. IX:** 79; **Supp. XIII:** 153

Jewett, Theodore Furber, **II:** 395

"Jew for Export, The" (Mamet), **Supp. XIV:**251–252

Jew in the American Novel, The (Fiedler), **Supp. XIII:** 106

"Jewish Graveyards, Italy" (Levine), **Supp. V:** 190

"Jewish Hunter, The" (Moore), **Supp. X:** 163, 165, 174

Jewison, Norman, **Supp. XI:** 306; **Supp. XIV:**316

Jews of Shklov (Schneour), **IV:** 11

Jews without Money (Gold), **Supp. XIV:**288–289

JFK (film), **Supp. XIV:**48

Jig of Forslin, The: A Symphony (Aiken), **I:** 50, 51, 57, 62, 66

"Jig Tune: Not for Love" (McGrath), **Supp. X:** 116

"Jihad" (McClatchy), **Supp. XII:** 266

"Jilting of Granny Weatherall, The" (Porter), **III:** 434, 435, 438

Jim Crow's Last Stand (Hughes), **Retro. Supp. I:** 205

Jiménez, Juan Ramón, **Supp. XIII:** 315, 323

Jimmie Higgins (Sinclair), **Supp. V:** 288

"Jimmy Harlow" (X. J. Kennedy), **Supp. XV:** 170

Jimmy's Blues (Baldwin), **Retro. Supp. II:** 8, 9, 15

Jim's Book: A Collection of Poems and Short Stories (Merrill), **Supp. III Part 1:** 319

Jitney (Wilson), **Supp. VIII:** 330, 331, 351

Jitterbug Perfume (Robbins), **Supp. X:** 273, 274–276, 279

Joachim, Harold, **Retro. Supp. I:** 58

Joan, Pope, **IV:** 165

Joanna and Ulysses (Sarton), **Supp. VIII:** 254–255

Joan of Arc, **IV:** 241; **Supp. I Part 1:** 286–288; **Supp. I Part 2:** 469

Joans, Ted, **Supp. IV Part 1:** 169

Job (biblical book), **II:** 165, 166–167, 168; **III:** 21, 199, 512; **IV:** 13, 158; **Supp. I Part 1:** 125

Job, The (Burroughs and Odier), **Supp. III Part 1:** 97, 103

Job, The: An American Novel (Lewis), **II:** 441

"Job History" (Proulx), **Supp. VII:** 262

Jobim, Antonio Carlos, **Supp. IV Part 2:** 549

"Job of the Plains, A" (Humphrey), **Supp. IX:** 101

"Jody Rolled the Bones" (Yates), **Supp. XI:** 335, 341

"Joe" (Alvarez), **Supp. VII:** 7–8

Joe Hill: A Biographical Novel (Stegner), **Supp. IV Part 2:** 599

Joe Turner's Come and Gone (Wilson), **Supp. VIII:** 334, 337–342, 345

Joe versus the Volcano (screenplay, Shanley), **Supp. XIV:**316

"Joey Martiney" (Huncke), **Supp. XIV:**149

Johannes in Eremo (Mather), **Supp. II Part 2:** 453

John (biblical book), **I:** 68; **Supp. XV:** 222, 224

"John" (Shields), **Supp. VII:** 310–311

"John, John Chinaman" (Buck), **Supp. II Part 1:** 128

John Addington Symonds: A Biographical Study (Brooks), **I:** 240, 241

John Barleycorn (London), **II:** 467, 481

John Brown (Du Bois), **Supp. II Part 1:** 171–172

"John Brown" (Emerson), **II:** 13

"John Brown" (Lindsay), **Supp. I Part 2:** 393

John Brown: The Making of a Martyr (Warren), **IV:** 236

John Brown's Body (Benét), **II:** 177; **Supp. XI:** 45, 46, 47, 56–57

John Bull in America; or, The New Munchausen (Paulding), **I:** 344

"John Burke" (Olson), **Supp. II Part 2:** 579, 580

"John Burns of Gettysburg" (Harte), **Supp. II Part 1:** 343

"John Carter" (Agee), **I:** 27

"John Coltrane: Where Does Art Come From?" (Baraka), **Supp. II Part 1:** 60

John Deth: A Metaphysical Legend and Other Poems (Aiken), **I:** 61

"John Endicott" (Longfellow), **II:** 505, 506; **Retro. Supp. II:** 165–166, 167

"John Evereldown" (Robinson), **III:** 524

John Fante: Selected Letters, 1932–1981 (Cooney, ed.), **Supp. XI:** 170

John Fante Reader, The (Cooper, ed.), **Supp. XI:** 174

"John Gardner: The Writer As Teacher" (Carver), **Supp. III Part 1:** 136, 146–147

John Gaunt (Davis), **Supp. XVI:**89

John Jay Chapman and His Letters (Howe), **Supp. XIV:**54

John Keats (Lowell), **II:** 530–531

"John L. Sullivan" (Lindsay), **Supp. I Part 2:** 394, 395

"John Lamar" (Davis), **Supp. XVI:**89–90

John Lane, **Retro. Supp. I:** 59

"John Marr" (Melville), **III:** 93

John Marr and Other Sailors (Melville), **III:** 93; **Retro. Supp. I:** 257

John Muir: A Reading Bibliography (Kimes and Kimes), **Supp. IX:** 178

Johnny Appleseed and Other Poems (Lindsay), **Supp. I Part 2:** 397

"Johnny Bear" (Steinbeck), **IV:** 67

"Johnny Mnemonic" (W. Gibson), **Supp. XVI:**122, 123–125, 128, 131

"Johnny Panic and the Bible of Dreams" (Plath), **Retro. Supp. II:** 245

"Johnny Ray" (Ríos), **Supp. IV Part 2:** 543

John of the Cross (Saint), **I:** 585; **Supp.**

IV Part 1: 284; **Supp. XV:** 223

John Paul Jones: A Sailor's Biography (Morison), **Supp. I Part 2:** 494–495

"John Redding Goes to Sea" (Hurston), **Supp. VI:** 150

Johns, George Sibley, **Retro. Supp. II:** 65

Johns, Orrick, **Retro. Supp. II:** 71

John Sloan: A Painter's Life (Brooks), **I:** 254

"John Smith Liberator" (Bierce), **I:** 209

Johnson, Alexandra, **Supp. X:** 86

Johnson, Alvin, **I:** 236; **Supp. XV:** 304

Johnson, Ben, **Retro. Supp. I:** 56

Johnson, Buffie, **Supp. IV Part 1:** 94

Johnson, Charles, **Supp. I Part 1:** 325; **Supp. V:** 128; **Supp. VI:** 185–201; **Supp. X:** 239; **Supp. XIII:** 182

Johnson, Charles S., **Supp. IX:** 309

Johnson, Claudia Durst, **Supp. VIII:** 126–127

Johnson, Diane, **Supp. XIII:** 127

Johnson, Dianne, **Retro. Supp. I:** 196

Johnson, Eastman, **IV:** 321

Johnson, Edward, **IV:** 157; **Supp. I Part 1:** 110, 115

Johnson, Fenton, **Supp. XI:** 129

Johnson, Georgia Douglas, **Supp. IV Part 1:** 164

Johnson, James Weldon, **Retro. Supp. II:** 114; **Supp. I Part 1:** 324, 325; **Supp. II Part 1:** 33, 194, 200, 202–203, 206–207; **Supp. III Part 1:** 73; **Supp. IV Part 1:** 7, 11, 15, 16, 164, 165, 166, 169; **Supp. X:** 42, 136, 246

Johnson, Joyce, **Supp. XIV:**150

Johnson, Kent, **Supp. XV:** 347

Johnson, Lady Bird, **Supp. IV Part 1:** 22

Johnson, Lyndon B., **I:** 254; **II:** 553, 582; **Retro. Supp. II:** 27

Johnson, Marguerite. *See* Angelou, Maya

Johnson, Maurice, **Supp. XV:** 136, 137, 138

Johnson, Mordecai, **Supp. XIV:**202

Johnson, Nunnally, **Supp. IV Part 1:** 355

Johnson, Pamela Hansford, **IV:** 469

Johnson, Rafer, **Supp. I Part 1:** 271

Johnson, Reed, **Supp. IV Part 2:** 589

Johnson, Richard, **Supp. XIII:** 132

Johnson, Robert, **Supp. IV Part 1:** 146; **Supp. VIII:** 15, 134

Johnson, Robert K., **Supp. IV Part 2:** 573, 584

Johnson, Robert Underwood, **Supp. IX:** 182, 184, 185

Johnson, Samuel, **II:** 295; **III:** 491, 503; **IV:** 452; **Retro. Supp. I:** 56, 65; **Supp. I Part 1:** 33; **Supp. I Part 2:** 422, 498, 503, 523, 656; **Supp. IV Part 1:** 34, 124; **Supp. XI:** 209; **Supp. XII:** 159; **Supp. XIII:** 55, 347; **Supp. XVI:**204

Johnson, Steve, **Supp. XVI:**177

Johnson, Thomas H., **I:** 470–471; **IV:** 144, 158; **Retro. Supp. I:** 26, 28, 36, 39, 40, 41, 43

Johnson, Walter, **II:** 422

Johnson, Willard "Spud," **Supp. XV:** 42, 46

"Johnson Girls, The" (Bambara), **Supp. XI:** 7

Johnsrud, Harold, **II:** 562

Johnston, Basil, **Supp. IV Part 1:** 269

Johnston, Mary, **II:** 194

Johnston, Robert M., **Supp. I Part 1:** 369

"John Sutter" (Winters), **Supp. II Part 2:** 810

John's Wife (Coover), **Supp. V:** 51–52

John the Baptist, **I:** 389; **II:** 537, 591

John XXIII, Pope, **Supp. I Part 2:** 492

Jolas, Eugène, **Retro. Supp. II:** 85, 328; **Supp. IV Part 1:** 80

Jolie Blon's Bounce (Burke), **Supp. XIV:**26, 33–34

Jolly (Mamet), **Supp. XIV:**240, 254

"Jolly Corner, The" (James), **I:** 571; **Retro. Supp. I:** 235

"Jonah" (Lowell), **II:** 536

Jonah's Gourd Vine (Hurston), **Supp. VI:** 149, 155

"Jonathan Edwards" (Holmes), **Supp. I Part 1:** 302, 315

"Jonathan Edwards in Western Massachusetts" (Lowell), **II:** 550

Jonathan Troy (Abbey), **Supp. XIII:** 4, 13

Jones, Anne, **Supp. X:** 8

Jones, Carolyn, **Supp. VIII:** 128

Jones, Chuck, **Supp. XVI:**102

Jones, E. Stanley, **III:** 297

Jones, Edith Newbold. *See* Wharton, Edith

Jones, Everett LeRoi. *See* Baraka, Imamu Amiri

Jones, George Frederic, **IV:** 309

Jones, Grover, **Supp. XIII:** 166

Jones, Harry, **Supp. I Part 1:** 337

Jones, Howard Mumford, **I:** 353; **Supp. IV Part 2:** 606; **Supp. XIV:**11

Jones, James, **III:** 40; **IV:** 98; **Supp. XI:** 213–237

Jones, James Earl, **Supp. VIII:** 334; **Supp. XI:** 309

Jones, Jennifer, **Supp. IV Part 2:** 524

Jones, John Paul, **II:** 405–406; **Supp. I Part 2:** 479, 480, 494–495

Jones, LeRoi. *See* Baraka, Imamu Amiri

Jones, Louis B., **Supp. XVI:**41

Jones, Lucretia Stevens Rhinelander, **IV:** 309

Jones, Madison, **Retro. Supp. II:** 235; **Supp. X:** 1

Jones, Major (pseudonym). *See* Thompson, William T.

Jones, Malcolm, **Supp. V:** 219

Jones, Robert Edmond, **III:** 387, 391, 394, 399

Jones, Tommy Lee, **Supp. V:** 227

"Jones's Private Argyment" (Lanier), **Supp. I Part 1:** 352

"Jones's *The Thin Red Line:* The End of Innocence" (Michel-Michot), **Supp. XI:** 224–225

Jong, Allan, **Supp. V:** 115

Jong, Erica, **Supp. V:** 113–135

Jong-Fast, Molly Miranda, **Supp. V:** 115

Jonson, Ben, **I:** 58, 358; **II:** 11, 16, 17, 18, 436, 556; **III:** 3, 463, 575–576; **IV:** 395, 453; **Retro. Supp. II:** 76; **Supp. I Part 2:** 423; **Supp. IV Part 2:** 585

Jonsson, Thorsten, **Retro. Supp. I:** 73

Joplin, Janis, **Supp. IV Part 1:** 206; **Supp. XI:** 239

Joplin, Scott, **Supp. IV Part 1:** 223

Jordan, Barbara, **Supp. VIII:** 63; **Supp. XI:** 249

Jordan, June, **Supp. XII:** 217

Jordan, Marie, **Supp. XV:** 224

Jo's Boys (Alcott), **Supp. I Part 1:** 32, 35, 40–41, 42

Joseph Heller (Ruderman), **Supp. IV Part 1:** 380

"Josephine Has Her Day" (Thurber), **Supp. I Part 2:** 606

Josephine Stories, The (Fitzgerald), **Retro. Supp. I:** 109

"Joseph Martinez" (Huncke), **Supp. XIV:**149

"Joseph Pockets" (Stern), **Supp. IX:** 292

Josephson, Matthew, **I:** 259

"José's Country" (Winters), **Supp. II Part 2:** 789, 790

Joshua (biblical book), **Supp. I Part 2:** 515

Joslin, Katherine, **Retro. Supp. I:** 376

Journal (Emerson), **Supp. I Part 1:** 309

"Journal" (L. Michaels), **Supp. XVI:**213

Journal (Thoreau), **IV:** 175

Journal (Woolman), **Supp. VIII:** 202

"Journal for My Daughter" (Kunitz), **Supp. III Part 1:** 268

Journal of Arthur Stirling, The (Sinclair), **Supp. V:** 280

"Journal of a Solitary Man, The" (Hawthorne), **II:** 226

Journal of a Solitude (Sarton), **Supp. VIII:** 256, 262–263

Journal of My Other Self (Rilke), **Retro. Supp. II:** 20

Journal of the Fictive Life (Nemerov), **III:** 267, 268, 269, 272, 273, 274, 280–281, 284–285, 286, 287

Journal of the Plague Year, A (Defoe), **III:** 423

"Journal of the Year of the Ox, A" (Wright), **Supp. V:** 343

Journals (Thoreau), **Supp. I Part 1:** 299

Journals and Other Documents on the Life and Voyages of Christopher Columbus (Morison, ed.), **Supp. I Part 2:** 494

Journals of Ralph Waldo Emerson, The (Emerson), **II:** 8, 17, 21

Journals of Susanna Moodie, The: Poems (Atwood), **Supp. XIII:** 33

"Journey, A" (Wharton), **Retro. Supp. I:** 364

"Journey, The" (Winters), **Supp. II Part 2:** 795

"Journey, The" (Wright), **Supp. III Part 2:** 605–606

"Journey, The: For Jane at Thirteen" (Kumin), **Supp. IV Part 2:** 442

"Journey, the Arrival and the Dream, The" (Gioia), **Supp. XV:** 120

Journey and Other Poems, The (Winters), **Supp. II Part 2:** 786, 794, 795, 796, 799, 800, 801

Journey Around My Room: The Autobiography of Louise Bogan—A Mosaic (Bogan), **Supp. III Part 1:** 47, 48, 52, 53

Journey Down, The (Bernstein), **IV:** 455

Journey Home, The (Abbey), **Supp. XIII:** 2, 12

Journeyman (Caldwell), **I:** 297, 302–304, 307, 309

Journey of Tai-me, The (Momaday), **Supp. IV Part 2:** 485

"Journey of the Magi" (Eliot), **Retro. Supp. I:** 64

Journey to a War (Auden and Isherwood), **Supp. II Part 1:** 13; **Supp. XIV:** 156, 158, 162

Journey to Love (W. C. Williams), **IV:** 422; **Retro. Supp. I:** 429

Journey to My Father; Isaac Bashevis Singer (Zamir), **Retro. Supp. II:** 317

"Journey to Nine Miles" (Walker), **Supp. III Part 2:** 527

"Journey to the Interior" (W. J. Smith), **Supp. XIII:** 339, 340

Journey with Genius: Recollections and Reflections Concerning the D. H. Lawrences (Bynner), **Supp. XV:** 46

Jowett, Benjamin, **Supp. XIV:** 335

"Joy" (Moore), **Supp. X:** 174

"Joy" (Singer), **IV:** 9; **Retro. Supp. II:** 307

Joyce, Cynthia, **Supp. X:** 194, 195, 196

Joyce, James, **I:** 53, 105, 108, 130, 174, 256, 285, 377, 395, 475–476, 478, 480, 483, 576; **II:** 27, 42, 58, 73, 74, 198, 209, 264, 320, 569; **III:** 7, 16, 26–27, 45, 174, 181, 184, 261, 273, 277, 343, 396, 398, 465, 471, 474; **IV:** 32, 73, 85, 95, 103, 171, 182, 211, 286, 370, 412, 418, 419, 428, 434, 456; **Retro. Supp. I:** 59, 63, 75, 80, 89, 91, 108, 109, 127, 287, 290, 292, 334, 335, 420; **Retro. Supp. II:** 221, 326; **Supp. I Part 1:** 257, 262, 270; **Supp. I Part 2:** 437, 546, 613, 620; **Supp. II Part 1:** 136; **Supp. III Part 1:** 35, 36, 65, 225, 229; **Supp. III Part 2:** 611, 617, 618; **Supp. IV Part 1:** 40, 47, 80, 227, 300, 310; **Supp. IV Part 2:** 424, 677; **Supp. V:** 261, 331; **Supp. VIII:** 14, 40, 103; **Supp. IX:** 211, 229, 235, 308; **Supp. X:** 115, 137, 194, 324; **Supp. XI:** 66; **Supp. XII:** 139, 151, 165, 191, 289; **Supp. XIV:** 83; **Supp. XVI:** 41, 189, 282

Joy Luck Club, The (Tan), **Supp. X:** 289, 291, 293, 294, 296, 297, 298, 299

"Joy of Sales Resistance, The" (Berry), **Supp. X:** 36

J R (Gaddis), **Supp. IV Part 1:** 279, 280, 285–289, 291, 294; **Supp. IV Part 2:** 484

"Juan's Song" (Bogan), **Supp. III Part 1:** 50

Jubilate Agno (Smart), **Supp. IV Part 2:** 626

Judah, Hettie, **Supp. XIII:** 246

Judah the Pious (Prose), **Supp. XVI:** 249, 250, 262

"Judas Maccabaeus" (Longfellow), **II:** 506; **Retro. Supp. II:** 165, 167

Judd, Sylvester, **II:** 290; **Supp. I Part 2:** 420

Judd Rankin's Daughter (Glaspell), **Supp. III Part 1:** 186–188

Jude the Obscure (Hardy), **Supp. I Part 1:** 217

"Judgement Day" (O'Connor), **III:** 349, 350; **Retro. Supp. II:** 236

Judgment Day (Farrell), **II:** 29, 31, 32, 34, 39

"Judgment of Paris, The" (Merwin), **Supp. III Part 1:** 350

Judgment of Paris, The (Vidal), **Supp. IV Part 2:** 680, 682

"Judgment of the Sage, The" (Crane), **I:** 420

Judith (Farrell), **II:** 46, 48

"Judith" (Garrett), **Supp. VII:** 109–110

"Juggernaut" (Bass), **Supp. XVI:** 16–17

"Jug of Sirup, A" (Bierce), **I:** 206

"Jugurtha" (Longfellow), **II:** 499

"Juice or Gravy" (Roth), **Retro. Supp. II:** 279

"Juke Box Love Song" (Hughes), **Retro. Supp. I:** 209

"Julia" (Hellman), **Supp. I Part 1:** 280, 293

"Julia Miller" (Masters), **Supp. I Part 2:** 461

Julian (Vidal), **Supp. IV Part 2:** 677, 684–685, 685, 689

Julian the Apostate, **Retro. Supp. I:** 247

"Julian Vreden" (Bowles), **Supp. IV Part 1:** 94

Julie; ou, La nouvelle Héloïse (Rousseau), **Supp. XVI:** 184

Julie and Romeo (Ray), **Supp. XII:** 308, 310

Julien, Isaac, **Supp. XI:** 19

Julier, Laura, **Supp. IV Part 1:** 211

Julip (Harrison), **Supp. VIII:** 51

Julius Caesar (Shakespeare), **I:** 284

"July Midnight" (Lowell), **II:** 521

Jumel, Madame, **Supp. I Part 2:** 461

Jumping Out of Bed (R. Bly), **Supp. IV Part 1:** 71

"Jump-Up Day" (Kingsolver), **Supp. VII:** 203

"June 1940" (Kees), **Supp. XV:** 141

"June Light" (Wilbur), **Supp. III Part 2:** 545

June Moon (Lardner and Kaufman), **II:** 427

"June Recital" (Welty), **IV:** 272–273

Juneteenth (Ellison), **Retro. Supp. II:** 119, 124, 126–128

"Juneteenth" (Ellison), **Retro. Supp. II:** 119, 126; **Supp. II Part 1:** 248

"June the Third" (Gander), **Supp. XV:** 340

Jung, Carl, **I:** 58, 135, 241, 248, 252, 402; **III:** 400, 534, 543; **Supp. I**

Part 2: 439; **Supp. IV Part 1:** 68, 69; **Supp. VIII:** 45; **Supp. X:** 193; **Supp. XV:** 214

Junger, Ernst, **Supp. III Part 1:** 63

Jungle, The (Sinclair), **III:** 580; **Supp. V:** 281–284, 285, 289

Jungle Lovers (Theroux), **Supp. VIII:** 314, 315, 316, 317

"Junior Addict" (Hughes), **Supp. I Part 1:** 343

"Juniper" (Francis), **Supp. IX:** 79

"Junk" (Wilbur), **Supp. III Part 2:** 556

Junker, Howard, **Supp. XV:** 116

Junkie: Confessions of an Unredeemed Drug Addict (Burroughs), **Supp. III Part 1:** 92, 94–96, 101

Junky (Burroughs), **Supp. XIV:** 143

Juno and the Paycock (O'Casey), **Supp. IV Part 1:** 361

"Jupiter Doke, Brigadier General" (Bierce), **I:** 204

Jurgen (Cabell), **III:** 394; **IV:** 286; **Retro. Supp. I:** 80; **Supp. I Part 2:** 718

Jusserand, Jules, **II:** 338

Just above My Head (Baldwin), **Retro. Supp. II:** 14–15

"Just a Little One" (Parker), **Supp. IX:** 191

Just and the Unjust, The (Cozzens), **I:** 367–370, 372, 375, 377, 378, 379

Just an Ordinary Day (Jackson), **Supp. IX:** 120

Just Before Dark: Collected Nonfiction (Harrison), **Supp. VIII:** 41, 45, 46, 53

"Just Before the War with the Eskimos" (Salinger), **III:** 559

"Just Boys" (Farrell), **II:** 45

"Just for the Thrill: An Essay on the Difference Between Women and Men" (Carson), **Supp. XII:** 103–104

"Justice" (Hughes), **Supp. I Part 1:** 331

"Justice, A" (Faulkner), **Retro. Supp. I:** 83

Justice, Donald, **Retro. Supp. I:** 313; **Supp. III Part 2:** 541; **Supp. V:** 180, 337, 338, 341; **Supp. VII:** 115–130; **Supp. XI:** 141, 315; **Supp. XIII:** 76, 312; **Supp. XV:** 74, 93, 118, 119, 134

Justice and Expediency (Whitter), **Supp. I Part 2:** 686

"Justice Denied in Massachusetts" (Millay), **III:** 140

Justice of Gold in the Damnation of Sinners, The (Edwards), **I:** 559

"Justice to Feminism" (Ozick), **Supp. V:** 272

"Just Like a Woman" (Dylan), **Supp. XV:** 350

"Just Like Job" (Angelou), **Supp. IV Part 1:** 15

Just Whistle: A Valentine (Wright), **Supp. XV:** 346–348

Just Wild About Harry (H. Miller), **III:** 190

Juvenal, **II:** 8, 169, 552

K

"K, The" (Olson), **Supp. II Part 2:** 558, 563, 569

Kabir, **Supp. IV Part 1:** 74

"Kabnis" (Toomer), **Supp. III Part 2:** 481, 484; **Supp. IX:** 309, 310, 319–320

Kachel, Elsie. *See* Stevens, Mrs. Wallace (Elsie Kachel)

"Kaddish" (Ginsberg), **Supp. II Part 1:** 319, 327

Kaddish and Other Poems, 1958–1960 (Ginsberg), **Supp. II Part 1:** 309, 319–320; **Supp. XIV:** 269

Kael, Pauline, **Supp. IX:** 253; **Supp. XV:** 147, 148

Kafka, Franz, **II:** 244, 565, 569; **III:** 51, 253, 418, 566, 572; **IV:** 2, 113, 218, 437–439, 442; **Retro. Supp. II:** 20, 221, 282; **Supp. I Part 1:** 197; **Supp. III Part 1:** 105; **Supp. III Part 2:** 413; **Supp. IV Part 1:** 379; **Supp. IV Part 2:** 623; **Supp. VIII:** 14, 15, 103; **Supp. XII:** 21, 37, 98, 168; **Supp. XIII:** 305; **Supp. XVI:** 17, 201, 206, 209

Kaganoff, Penny, **Supp. XI:** 122

Kahane, Jack, **III:** 171, 178

Kahn, Otto, **I:** 385; **IV:** 123; **Retro. Supp. II:** 81, 84, 85

Kahn, R. T., **Supp. XI:** 216

"Kai, Today" (Snyder), **Supp. VIII:** 300

Kaiser, Georg, **I:** 479

Kaiser, Henry, **Supp. I Part 2:** 644

Kakutani, Michiko, **Supp. IV Part 1:** 196, 201, 205, 211, 212; **Supp. V:** 63; **Supp. VIII:** 81, 84, 86, 88, 141; **Supp. X:** 171, 301, 302, 310, 314; **Supp. XI:** 38, 179; **Supp. XII:** 165, 171, 172, 299; **Supp. XVI:** 71

Kalem, T. E., **Supp. IV Part 2:** 585

Kalevala (Finnish epic), **II:** 503, 504; **Retro. Supp. II:** 155

Kalevala (Lönnrot), **Retro. Supp. II:** 159, 160

Kalki: A Novel (Vidal), **Supp. IV Part 2:** 677, 682, 685, 691, 692

Kallen, Horace, **I:** 229; **Supp. I Part 2:** 643; **Supp. XIV:** 195, 197, 198

Kallman, Chester, **II:** 586; **Supp. II Part 1:** 15, 17, 24, 26

"Kallundborg Church" (Whittier), **Supp. I Part 2:** 696

Kalstone, David, **Retro. Supp. II:** 40

Kamel, Rose, **Supp. XIII:** 306

Kamera Obskura (Nabokov), **III:** 255

Kamhi, Michelle Moarder, **Supp. IV Part 2:** 529, 530

Kandy-Kolored Tangerine-Flake Streamline Baby, The (Wolfe), **Supp. III Part 2:** 569, 573–576, 580, 581

Kane, Lesley, **Supp. XIV:** 250

Kanellos, Nicolás, **Supp. VIII:** 82; **Supp. XIII:** 213

Kanin, Garson, **Supp. IV Part 2:** 574

"Kansas City Coyote" (Harjo), **Supp. XII:** 219, 222

"Kansas Emigrants, The" (Whittier), **Supp. I Part 2:** 687

Kant, Immanuel, **I:** 61, 277, 278; **II:** 10–11, 362, 480, 580–581, 582, 583; **III:** 300, 480, 481, 488, 612; **IV:** 90; **Supp. I Part 2:** 640; **Supp. IV Part 2:** 527; **Supp. XIV:** 198, 199; **Supp. XVI:** 184

Kanter, Hal, **IV:** 383

Kapital, Das (Marx), **III:** 580

Kaplan, Abraham, **I:** 277

Kaplan, Justin, **I:** 247–248; **Retro. Supp. I:** 392

Kaplan, Steven, **Supp. V:** 238, 241, 243, 248

Karate Is a Thing of the Spirit (Crews), **Supp. XI:** 112–113

Karbo, Karen, **Supp. X:** 259, 262

"Karintha" (Toomer), **Supp. IX:** 311

Karl, Frederick R., **Supp. IV Part 1:** 384

Karl Shapiro's America (film), **Supp. II Part 2:** 703

Karmi, T., **Supp. XV:** 78, 88

Karr, Mary, **Supp. XI:** 239–256; **Supp. XIII:** 285; **Supp. XV:** 223; **Supp. XVI:** 63, 70, 77

Kasabian, Linda, **Supp. IV Part 1:** 206

Kasper, Catherine, **Supp. XVI:** 294–295

Kate Chopin (Toth), **Retro. Supp. II:** 71

Kate Chopin: A Critical Biography (Seyersted), **Retro. Supp. II:** 65; **Supp. I Part 1:** 225

Kate Chopin and Edith Wharton: An Annotated Bibliographical Guide to Secondary Sources (Springer), **Supp. I Part 1:** 225

Kate Chopin and Her Creole Stories

(Rankin), **Retro. Supp. II:** 57; **Supp. I Part 1:** 200, 225

"Kate Chopin's *The Awakening* in the Perspective of Her Literary Career" (Arms), **Supp. I Part 1:** 225

Kate Vaiden (Price), **Supp. VI:** 264, 265

"Käthe Kollwitz" (Rukeyser), **Supp. VI:** 283, 284

Katherine and Jean (Rice), **Supp. VII:** 288

"Kathleen" (Whittier), **Supp. I Part 2:** 693

Kathleen and Frank: The Autobiography of a Family (Isherwood), **Supp. XIV:**158, 171

Kathy Goes to Haiti (Acker), **Supp. XII:** 5

Katz, Alex, **Supp. XV:** 185

Katz, Jonathan, **Supp. XII:** 179

Katz, Steve, **Supp. V:** 44

Katz, Steven T., **Supp. XVI:**154

Kauffman, Carol, **Supp. XI:** 295

Kauffmann, Stanley, **III:** 452; **Supp. I Part 2:** 391; **Supp. XVI:**74

Kaufman, Charlie, **Supp. XV:** 16

Kaufman, George S., **II:** 427, 435, 437; **III:** 62, 71–72, 394; **Retro. Supp. II:** 327; **Supp. IV Part 2:** 574; **Supp. IX:** 190; **Supp. XV:** 329

Kaufmann, James, **Supp. XI:** 39

Kauvar, Elaine M., **Supp. V:** 273

Kavanaugh (Longfellow), **I:** 458; **II:** 489, 491; **Retro. Supp. II:** 156; **Supp. I Part 2:** 420

Kaveney, Roz, **Supp. XI:** 39

Kawabata, Yasunari, **Supp. XV:** 186

Kazan, Elia, **III:** 153, 163; **IV:** 383; **Supp. I Part 1:** 66, 295; **Supp. XVI:**193

Kazin, Alfred, **I:** 248, 417, 419, 517; **II:** 177, 459; **IV:** 236; **Retro. Supp. II:** 206, 243, 246, 286; **Supp. I Part 1:** 195, 196, 294, 295, 296; **Supp. I Part 2:** 536, 631, 647, 650, 678, 679, 719; **Supp. II Part 1:** 143; **Supp. IV Part 1:** 200, 382; **Supp. V:** 122; **Supp. VIII:** 93–111; **Supp. IX:** 3, 227; **Supp. XIII:** 98, 106; **Supp. XIV:**11; **Supp. XV:** 142

Keach, Stacey, **Supp. XI:** 309

Keane, Sarah, **Supp. I Part 1:** 100

Kearns, Cleo McNelly, **Retro. Supp. I:** 57

Kearns, George, **Retro. Supp. I:** 292

Keating, AnnLouise, **Supp. IV Part 1:** 330

Keaton, Buster, **I:** 31; **Supp. I Part 2:** 607; **Supp. IV Part 2:** 574

Keaton, Diane, **Supp. XV:** 5

Keats, John, **I:** 34, 103, 284, 314, 317–318, 385, 401, 448; **II:** 82, 88, 97, 214, 368, 512, 516, 530–531, 540, 593; **III:** 4, 10, 45, 122, 133–134, 179, 214, 237, 272, 275, 469, 485, 523; **IV:** 360, 405, 416; **Retro. Supp. I:** 91, 301, 313, 360, 395, 412; **Supp. I Part 1:** 82, 183, 266, 267, 312, 349, 362, 363, 365; **Supp. I Part 2:** 410, 422, 424, 539, 552, 675, 719, 720; **Supp. III Part 1:** 73; **Supp. IV Part 1:** 123, 168, 325; **Supp. IV Part 2:** 455; **Supp. VIII:** 41, 273; **Supp. IX:** 38, 39, 45; **Supp. XI:** 43, 320; **Supp. XII:** 9, 113, 255; **Supp. XIII:** 131, 281; **Supp. XIV:**274; **Supp. XV:** 92

Keats, John (other), **Supp. IX:** 190, 195, 200

"Keela, the Outcast Indian Maiden" (Welty), **IV:** 263

Keeley, Mary Paxton, **Supp. XV:** 136

"Keen Scalpel on Racial Ills" (Bruell), **Supp. VIII:** 126

"Keep A-Inchin' Along" (Van Vechten), **Supp. III Part 2:** 744

Keeping (Goldbarth), **Supp. XII:** 179–180, 180

"Keeping Informed in D.C." (Nemerov), **III:** 287

Keeping Slug Woman Alive: A Holistic Approach to American Indian Texts (Sarris), **Supp. IV Part 1:** 329

"'Keeping Their World Large'" (Moore), **III:** 201–202

Keeping the Night (Everwine), **Supp. XV:** 75, 81–85, 86

"Keeping Things Whole" (Strand), **Supp. IV Part 2:** 624

Keep It Simple: A Defense of the Earth (Nichols), **Supp. XIII:** 268

Kees, Weldon, **Supp. X:** 118; **Supp. XII:** 198; **Supp. XV:** 113, 114, 115, 133–149

Keillor, Garrison, **Supp. XII:** 343; **Supp. XIII:** 274; **Supp. XVI:**165–179

Keillor, Gary Edward. See Keiller, Garrison

Keith, Brian, **Supp. IV Part 2:** 474

Keith, Minor C., **I:** 483

Keller, A. G., **III:** 108

Keller, Helen, **I:** 254, 258

Keller, Lynn, **Supp. IV Part 2:** 423; **Supp. V:** 78, 80

Kelley, David, **Supp. IV Part 2:** 528, 529

Kelley, Florence, **Supp. I Part 1:** 5, 7

Kellogg, Paul U., **Supp. I Part 1:** 5, 7, 12

Kellogg, Reverend Edwin H., **III:** 200

Kelly, **II:** 464

Kelly, Emmett, **Supp. XI:** 99, 106

Kelly, Walt, **Supp. XI:** 105

Kelly, William, **Supp. XV:** 75, 88

Kemble, Fanny, **Retro. Supp. I:** 228

Kemble, Gouverneur, **II:** 298

Kemble, Peter, **II:** 298

Kempton, Murray, **Supp. VIII:** 104

Kempton-Wace Letters, The (London and Strunsky), **II:** 465

Kennan, George F., **Supp. VIII:** 241

Kennedy, Albert J., **Supp. I Part 1:** 19

Kennedy, Arthur, **III:** 153

Kennedy, Burt, **Supp. IV Part 1:** 236

Kennedy, J. Gerald, **Retro. Supp. II:** 271

Kennedy, John F., **I:** 136, 170; **II:** 49, 152–153; **III:** 38, 41, 42, 234, 411, 415, 581; **IV:** 229; **Supp. I Part 1:** 291; **Supp. I Part 2:** 496; **Supp. VIII:** 98, 104, 203; **Supp. XII:** 132

Kennedy, John Pendleton, **II:** 313

Kennedy, Mrs. John F., **I:** 136

Kennedy, Robert, **Supp. V:** 291

Kennedy, Robert F., **I:** 294; **Supp. I Part 1:** 52; **Supp. XI:** 343

Kennedy, William, **Supp. VII:** 131–157

Kennedy, X. J., **Supp. V:** 178, 182; **Supp. XV:** 113, 151–173

Kenner, Hugh, **III:** 475, 478; **IV:** 412; **Supp. I Part 1:** 255; **Supp. IV Part 2:** 474; **Supp. XV:** 147

"Kenneth Koch's 'Serious Moment'" (Spurr), **Supp. XV:** 183

Kenneth Millar/Ross Macdonald: A Checklist (Bruccoli), **Supp. IV Part 2:** 464, 469, 471

Kenny, Maurice, **Supp. IV Part 2:** 502

Kent, George, **Supp. IV Part 1:** 11

Kent, Rockwell, **Supp. XV:** 41

Kenton, Maxwell. *See* Burnett, David; Hoffenberg, Mason; Southern, Terry

"Kent State, May 1970" (Haines), **Supp. XII:** 211

Kenyatta, Jomo, **Supp. X:** 135

Kenyon, Jane, **Supp. VII:** 159–177; **Supp. VIII:** 272

Keogh, Tom, **Supp. XVI:**230

Kepler, Johannes, **III:** 484; **IV:** 18

Keppel, Frederick P., **I:** 214

"Kéramos" (Longfellow), **II:** 494; **Retro. Supp. II:** 167, 169

Kéramos and Other Poems (Longfellow), **II:** 490

Kerim, Ussin, **Supp. IX:** 152

Kermode, Frank, **IV:** 133; **Retro. Supp. I:** 301

Kern, Jerome, **II:** 427

Kerouac, Jack, **III:** 174; **Retro. Supp. I:** 102; **Supp. II Part 1:** 31, 307, 309, 318, 328; **Supp. III Part 1:** 91–94, 96, 100, 217–234; **Supp. IV Part 1:** 90, 146; **Supp. V:** 336; **Supp. VIII:** 42, 138, 289, 305; **Supp. IX:** 246; **Supp. XII:** 118, 121, 122, 123, 126, 131, 132; **Supp. XIII:** 275, 284; **Supp. XIV:**137, 138, 141, 142, 143–144; **Supp. XV:** 134, 221; **Supp. XVI:**123

Kerr, Deborah, **Supp. XI:** 307

Kerr, Orpheus C. (pseudonym). *See* Newell, Henry

Kerr, Walter, **Supp. IV Part 2:** 575, 579

Kerridge, Richard, **Supp. XVI:**26

Kesey, Ken, **III:** 558; **Supp. III Part 1:** 217; **Supp. V:** 220, 295; **Supp. X:** 24, 265; **Supp. XI:** 104

Kesten, Stephen, **Supp. XI:** 309

Ketchup (Shanley), **Supp. XIV:**315

Kevane, Bridget, **Supp. XI:** 185, 190

"Key, The" (Welty), **IV:** 262

"Keys" (Nye), **Supp. XIII:** 281

Key to Uncle Tom's Cabin, A (Stowe), **Supp. I Part 2:** 580

Key West (H. Crane), **Retro. Supp. II:** 84

"Key West" (H. Crane), **I:** 400

Key West: An Island Sheaf (Crane), **I:** 385, 399–402

Khrushchev, Nikita, **I:** 136

Kiang Kang-hu, **Supp. XV:** 45, 47

Kick for a Bite, A (Cobbett), **Supp. XV:** 237

Kid, The (Aiken), **I:** 61

Kid, The (Chaplin), **I:** 386

Kidder, Tracy, **Supp. III Part 1:** 302

Kidman, Nicole, **Supp. X:** 80

"Kidnapping in the Family, A" (Fante), **Supp. XI:** 164

"Kid's Guide to Divorce, The" (Moore), **Supp. X:** 167, 172

Kidwell, Clara Sue, **Supp. IV Part 1:** 333

Kielsky, Vera Emuma, **Supp. V:** 273

Kieran, John, **II:** 417

Kierkegaard, Søren Aabye, **II:** 229; **III:** 292, 305, 309, 572; **IV:** 438, 491; **Retro. Supp. I:** 326; **Retro. Supp. II:** 222; **Supp. V:** 9; **Supp. VIII:** 7–8

Kiernan, Robert F., **Supp. IV Part 2:** 684

Kieseritsky, L., **III:** 252

"Kilim" (McClatchy), **Supp. XII:** 258

"Killed at Resaca" (Bierce), **I:** 202

"Killed at the Ford" (Longfellow), **Retro. Supp. II:** 170–171

Killens, John Oliver, **Supp. IV Part 1:** 8, 369

"Killer in the Rain" (Chandler), **Supp. IV Part 1:** 122

"Killers, The" (Hemingway), **II:** 249; **Retro. Supp. I:** 188, 189

Killing Mister Watson (Matthiessen), **Supp. V:** 212, 214

"Killing of a State Cop, The" (Ortiz), **Supp. IV Part 2:** 499

Killing of Sister George, The (Marcus), **Supp. I Part 1:** 277

"Killings" (Dubus), **Supp. VII:** 85–86

"Killing the Plants" (Kenyon), **Supp. VII:** 167, 168

Kilmer, Joyce, **Supp. I Part 2:** 387; **Supp. XV:** 294

Kilpatrick, James K., **Supp. X:** 145

Kilvert, Francis, **Supp. VIII:** 172

Kim (Kipling), **Supp. X:** 230

Kim, Alfred, **Supp. XI:** 140

Kimball, J. Golden, **Supp. IV Part 2:** 602

Kimbrough, Mary Craig. *See* Sinclair, Mary Craig (Mary Craig Kimbrough)

Kimes, Maymie B., **Supp. IX:** 178

Kimes, William F., **Supp. IX:** 178

"Kin" (Welty), **IV:** 277; **Retro. Supp. I:** 353

Kinard, Agnes Dodds, **Supp. XIV:**122, 123, 127

Kincaid, Jamaica, **Supp. VII:** 179–196

"Kindness" (Dunn), **Supp. XI:** 149, 150

"Kindness" (Nye), **Supp. XIII:** 285

"Kindness" (Plath), **Retro. Supp. II:** 256

Kind of Order, A Kind of Folly, A: Essays and Conversations (Kunitz), **Supp. III Part 1:** 262, 268

Kindred (O. Butler), **Supp. XIII:** 59–60, 69

"Kind Sir: These Woods" (Sexton), **Supp. II Part 2:** 673

Kinds of Love (Sarton), **Supp. VIII:** 253–254, 256

Kinfolk (Buck), **Supp. II Part 1:** 126

King, Alexander, **IV:** 287

King, Carole, **Supp. XII:** 308

King, Clarence, **I:** 1

King, Ernest, **Supp. I Part 2:** 491

King, Fisher, **II:** 425

King, Francis, **Supp. XIV:**155, 156, 166, 169

King, Grace, **Retro. Supp. II:** 136

King, Martin Luther, Jr., **Retro. Supp. II:** 12, 13

King, Michael, **Supp. XII:** 182

King, Queen, Knave (Nabokov), **III:** 251; **Retro. Supp. I:** 270

King, Starr, **Supp. II Part 1:** 341, 342

King, Stephen, **Supp. IV Part 1:** 102, 104; **Supp. IV Part 2:** 467; **Supp. V:** 137–155; **Supp. IX:** 114; **Supp. XIII:** 53

King, Tabitha (Mrs. Stephen King), **Supp. V:** 137

King, The (Barthelme), **Supp. IV Part 1:** 47, 52

King Coffin (Aiken), **I:** 53–54, 57

"King David" (Benét), **Supp. XI:** 44

"King David" (Reznikoff), **Supp. XIV:**283

Kingdom by the Sea, The: A Journey around Great Britain (Theroux), **Supp. VIII:** 323

Kingdom of Earth (T. Williams), **IV:** 382, 386, 387, 388, 391, 393, 398

"Kingdom of Earth, The" (T. Williams), **IV:** 384

Kingfisher, The (Clampitt), **Supp. IX:** 38

"Kingfishers, The" (Olson), **Supp. II Part 2:** 557, 558–563, 582

King Jasper (Robinson), **III:** 523

King Kong (film), **Supp. IV Part 1:** 104

King Lear (Shakespeare), **I:** 538; **II:** 540, 551; **Retro. Supp. I:** 248; **Supp. IV Part 1:** 31, 36; **Supp. IX:** 14; **Supp. XI:** 172; **Supp. XV:** 349

King Leopold's Soliloquy (Twain), **IV:** 208

King My Father's Wreck, The (Simpson), **Supp. IX:** 266, 267, 270, 275, 276

King of Babylon Shall Not Come Against You, The (Garrett), **Supp. VII:** 110–111; **Supp. X:** 3

"King of Folly Island, The" (Jewett), **II:** 394; **Retro. Supp. II:** 132, 133

King of Kings (film), **Supp. IV Part 2:** 520

"King of the Bingo Game" (Ellison), **Retro. Supp. II:** 117, 125; **Supp. II Part 1:** 235, 238, 240–241

"King of the Cats, The" (Benét), **Supp. XI:** 49–50

"King of the Clock Tower" (Yeats), **III:** 473

"King of the Desert, The" (O'Hara), **III:** 369

King of the Fields, The (Singer), **Retro. Supp. II:** 317

King of the Jews (Epstein), **Supp. XII:** 161, 166–170, 172

King of the Mountain (Garrett), **Supp. VII:** 96, 97

"King of the River" (Kunitz), **Supp.**

III Part 1: 263, 267–268

"King of the Sea" (Marquand), **III:** 60

"King over the Water" (Blackmur), **Supp. II Part 1:** 107

"King Pandar" (Blackmur), **Supp. II Part 1:** 92, 102

"King Pest" (Poe), **Retro. Supp. II:** 273

Kingsblood Royal (Lewis), **II:** 456

Kingsbury, John, **Supp. I Part 1:** 8

"King's Daughters, Home for Unwed Mothers, 1948" (Stanford), **Supp. XV:** 345

King's Henchman, The (Millay), **III:** 138–139

Kingsley, Sidney, **Supp. I Part 1:** 277, 281

King's Mare, The (Canolle; Loos, trans.), **Supp. XVI:**194

"King's Missive, The" (Whittier), **Supp. I Part 2:** 694

Kingsolver, Barbara, **Supp. VII:** 197–214; **Supp. XIII:** 16

King's Stilts, The (Geisel), **Supp. XVI:**100, 104

Kingston, Earll, **Supp. V:** 160

Kingston, Maxine Hong, **Supp. IV Part 1:** 1, 12; **Supp. V:** 157–175, 250; **Supp. X:** 291–292; **Supp. XI:** 18, 245

"King Volmer and Elsie" (Whittier), **Supp. I Part 2:** 696

Kinmont, Alexander, **Supp. I Part 2:** 588–589

Kinnaird, John, **Retro. Supp. I:** 399

Kinnell, Galway, **Supp. III Part 1:** 235–256; **Supp. III Part 2:** 541; **Supp. IV Part 2:** 623; **Supp. V:** 332; **Supp. VIII:** 39; **Supp. XI:** 139; **Supp. XII:** 241; **Supp. XV:** 212; **Supp. XVI:**53

Kinsey, Alfred, **IV:** 230; **Supp. XIV:**140

Kinsgton, Maxine Hong, **Supp. XV:** 220, 223

Kinzie, Mary, **Supp. XII:** 181

"Kipling" (Trilling), **Supp. III Part 2:** 495

Kipling, Rudyard, **I:** 421, 587–588; **II:** 271, 338, 404, 439; **III:** 55, 328, 508, 511, 521, 524, 579; **IV:** 429; **Supp. IV Part 2:** 603; **Supp. X:** 255

Kirby, David, **Supp. XIII:** 89

Kirkland, David, **Supp. XVI:**186

Kirkland, Jack, **I:** 297

Kirkpatrick, Jeane, **Supp. VIII:** 241

Kirkus, Virginia, **Supp. XV:** 198

Kirkwood, Cynthia A., **Supp. XI:** 177, 178, 179

Kirp, David L., **Supp. XI:** 129

Kirsch, Adam, **Supp. XV:** 251, 260, 264, 266, 341, 347, 350–351

Kirstein, Lincoln, **Supp. II Part 1:** 90, 97; **Supp. IV Part 1:** 82, 83

Kiss, The (Harrison), **Supp. X:** 191

"Kiss, The" (Sexton), **Supp. II Part 2:** 687

Kissel, Howard, **Supp. IV Part 2:** 580

Kiss Hollywood Good-by (Loos), **Supp. XVI:**190, 195

Kissinger, Henry, **Supp. IV Part 1:** 388; **Supp. XII:** 9, 14

Kiss of the Spider Woman, the Musical (McNally), **Supp. XIII:** 207, **Supp. XIII:** 208

Kiss Tomorrow Good-bye (McCoy), **Supp. XIII:** 170, 172–173, 174

"Kit and Caboodle" (Komunyakaa), **Supp. XIII:** 115

Kit Brandon: A Portrait (Anderson), **I:** 111

Kitchen, Judith, **Supp. IV Part 1:** 242, 245, 252; **Supp. IX:** 163; **Supp. XI:** 312, 313, 315, 317, 319, 320, 326, 329; **Supp. XV:** 215, 219

"Kitchenette" (Brooks), **Retro. Supp. I:** 208

Kitchen God's Wife, The (Tan), **Supp. X:** 289, 292, 293, 294–295, 296–297, 298–299

"Kitchen Terrarium: 1983" (McCarriston), **Supp. XIV:**270

Kit O'Brien (Masters), **Supp. I Part 2:** 471

Kittel, Frederick August. *See* Wilson, August

Kittredge, Charmian. *See* London, Mrs. Jack (Charmian Kittredge)

Kittredge, William, **Supp. VIII:** 39; **Supp. XI:** 316; **Supp. XII:** 209; **Supp. XIII:** 16

"Kitty Hawk" (Frost), **II:** 164; **Retro. Supp. I:** 124, 141

Klein, Joe, **Supp. XII:** 67–68

Klein, Marcus, **Supp. I Part 2:** 432; **Supp. XI:** 233

Kleist, Heinrich von, **Supp. IV Part 1:** 224

Kline, Franz, **Supp. XII:** 198

Kline, George, **Supp. VIII:** 22, 28

Klinghoffer, David, **Supp. XVI:**74

Klinkowitz, Jerome, **Supp. IV Part 1:** 40; **Supp. X:** 263; **Supp. XI:** 347

Knapp, Adeline, **Supp. XI:** 200

Knapp, Friedrich, **III:** 100

Knapp, Samuel, **I:** 336

Knapp, Samuel Lorenzo, **Supp. XV:** 246

Kneel to the Rising Sun (Caldwell), **I:** 304, 309

"Knees/Dura-Europos" (Goldbarth), **Supp. XII:** 185

"Knife" (Simic), **Supp. VIII:** 275

Knight, Arthur, **Supp. XIV:**144

Knight, Etheridge, **Supp. XI:** 239

"Knight in Disguise, The" (Lindsay), **Supp. I Part 2:** 390

Knightly Quest, The (T. Williams), **IV:** 383

Knight's Gambit (Faulkner), **II:** 72

Knish, Anne. *See* Ficke, Arthur Davison

"Knit One, Purl Two" (K. Snodgrass), **Supp. XVI:**42

"Knock" (Dickey), **Supp. IV Part 1:** 182

"Knocking Around" (Ashbery), **Supp. III Part 1:** 22

"Knocking on Three, Winston" (Epstein), **Supp. XIV:**109

Knockout Artist, The (Crews), **Supp. XI:** 113–114

Knoll, Robert E., **Supp. XV:** 118

Knopf, Alfred A., **III:** 99, 105, 106, 107; **Retro. Supp. I:** 13, 19, 317; **Supp. I Part 1:** 324, 325, 327; **Supp. IV Part 1:** 125, 354; **Supp. XIII:** 172

Knopf, Blanche, **Supp. I Part 1:** 324, 325, 327, 328, 332, 341; **Supp. IV Part 1:** 128, 346, 348; **Supp. XIII:** 169

"Knot, The" (Rich), **Supp. I Part 2:** 555

Knotts, Kristina, **Supp. XIII:** 238

"Knowing, The" (Olds), **Supp. X:** 215

"Knowledge Forwards and Backwards" (Stern), **Supp. IX:** 296

Knowles, John, **Supp. IV Part 2:** 679; **Supp. XII:** 235–250

Knox, Frank, **Supp. I Part 2:** 488, 489

Knox, Israel, **Supp. X:** 70

Knox, Vicesimus, **II:** 8

Knoxville: Summer of 1915 (Agee), **I:** 42–46

Knudson, R. Rozanne, **Supp. IV Part 2:** 648

Ko; or, A Season on Earth (Koch), **Supp. XV:** 175, 180, 181, 183, 186

Kober, Arthur, **Supp. I Part 1:** 292

Koch, Frederick, **IV:** 453

Koch, John, **Supp. VIII:** 88

Koch, Kenneth, **Supp. XV:** 175–192

Koch, Vivienne, **III:** 194; **IV:** 136, 140; **Retro. Supp. I:** 428, 430

"Kochinnenako in Academe: Three Approaches to Interpreting a Keres Indian Tale" (Gunn Allen), **Supp.**

IV Part 1: 329

"Kodachromes of the Island" (Hayden), **Supp. II Part 1:** 367, 380

Koestler, Arthur, **I:** 258; **Supp. I Part 2:** 671

Kokkinen, Eila, **Supp. XIV:**146, 148

Kolbenheyer, Dr. Frederick, **Supp. I Part 1:** 207

Kolodny, Annette, **Supp. X:** 97, 103, 229

"Komodo" (C. Frost), **Supp. XV:** 95

Komunyakaa, Yusef, **Supp. XIII:** 111–136

Konigsberg, Allan Stewart. See Allen, Woody

Kon-Tiki (Heyerdahl), **II:** 477

Koopman, Harry Lyman, **Retro. Supp. I:** 40

Kooser, Ted, **Supp. XV:** 113, 115

Kootz, Samuel, **Supp. XV:** 144

Kora and Ka (Doolittle), **Supp. I Part 1:** 270

Kora in Hell (W. C. Williams), **Retro. Supp. I:** 416, 417–418, 419, 430, 431

Korb, Rena, **Supp. XI:** 2

Korczak, Janosz, **Supp. X:** 70

Kornblatt, Joyce Reiser, **Supp. XV:** 62

Kort, Amy, **Supp. XIII:** 148

Kosinski, Jerzy, **Supp. VII:** 215–228; **Supp. XII:** 21

"Kostas Tympakianakis" (Merrill), **Supp. III Part 1:** 326

Koteliansky, S. S., **Supp. VIII:** 251, 265

Kowloon Tong (Theroux), **Supp. VIII:** 325

Kozlenko, William, **IV:** 378, 381

Kraft, James, **Supp. XV:** 40, 41, 42, 43, 52

Kramer, Dale, **Supp. I Part 2:** 669

Kramer, Hilton, **III:** 537; **Supp. I Part 1:** 295, 296; **Supp. VIII:** 239; **Supp. XV:** 113

Kramer, Lawrence, **Supp. IV Part 1:** 61, 65, 66; **Supp. IX:** 291

Kramer, Peter D., **Supp. XVI:**229

Kramer, Stanley, **II:** 421, 587

Krapp's Last Tape (Beckett), **I:** 71; **III:** 387; **Retro. Supp. I:** 206

Krassner, Paul, **Supp. IV Part 1:** 385; **Supp. XI:** 293

Kreisler, Harry, **Supp. XVI:**155

Kreitman, Esther, **IV:** 2

"Kremlin of Smoke" (Schnackenberg), **Supp. XV:** 257–258

Kreymborg, Alfred, **II:** 530; **III:** 465; **IV:** 76; **Retro. Supp. I:** 417; **Supp. XV:** 301, 306

Krim, Seymour, **Supp. XV:** 338; **Supp. XVI:**217

Kristeva, Julia, **Supp. XII:** 6

Kristofferson, Kris, **Supp. XIII:** 119

Kristol, Irving, **Supp. VIII:** 93, 244; **Supp. XIII:** 98

Kroll, Jack, **Supp. IV Part 2:** 590

Kroll, Judith, **Supp. I Part 2:** 541–543, 544, 546

Kroll Ring, Frances. *See* Ring, Frances Kroll

Krondorfer, Björn, **Supp. XVI:**160

Krook, Dorothea, **Retro. Supp. II:** 243

Kropotkin, Peter, **I:** 493; **Supp. I Part 1:** 5; **Supp. IV Part 2:** 521

Kruif, Paul de, **II:** 446

Krupat, Arnold, **Supp. IV Part 2:** 500

Krupnick, Mark, **Supp. XVI:**153

Krutch, Joseph Wood, **II:** 459; **III:** 425; **IV:** 70, 175

Kublai Khan, **III:** 395

"Kubla Khan" (Coleridge), **Supp. XIII:** 131, 283

Kubrick, Stanley, **Supp. IV Part 1:** 392; **Supp. XI:** 293,**Supp. XI:** 301, 302–303

Kuehl, John, **Supp. IV Part 1:** 279, 284, 285, 287

Kuehl, Linda, **Supp. IV Part 1:** 199

"Kugelmass Episode, The" (Allen), **Supp. XV:** 15, 16

Kukachin, Princess, **III:** 395

"Ku Klux" (Hughes), **Retro. Supp. I:** 205

Kulshrestha, Chirantan, **Retro. Supp. II:** 21

Kumin, Maxine, **Supp. IV Part 2:** 439–457; **Supp. XIII:** 294

Kundera, Milan, **Supp. VIII:** 241

Kunitz, Stanley, **I:** 179, 180, 181, 182, 521; **II:** 545; **Supp. III Part 1:** 257–270; **Supp. V:** 79; **Supp. XI:** 259; **Supp. XIII:** 341

Kuo, Helena, **Supp. X:** 291

Kuropatkin, General Aleksei Nikolaevich, **III:** 247–248

Kurzy of the Sea (Barnes), **Supp. III Part 1:** 34

Kushner, Tony, **Supp. IX:** 131–149

Kussy, Bella, **IV:** 468

Kuttner, Henry, **Supp. IV Part 1:** 102

Kuzma, Greg, **Supp. XV:** 118

L

LaBastille, Anne, **Supp. X:** 95–110

"Labours of Hercules, The" (Moore), **III:** 201

La Bruyère, Jean de, **I:** 58

La Bufera e Altro (Montale), **Supp. V:** 337

Labyrinth of Love (Untermeyer), **Supp. XV:** 312

Labyrinth of Solitude, The (Paz), **Supp. XIII:** 223

Lacan, Jacques, **Supp. IV Part 1:** 45; **Supp. VIII:** 5; **Supp. XII:** 98

La Casa en Mango Street (Cisneros), **Supp. VII:** 58–59

Lachaise, Gaston, **I:** 434

"Lackawanna" (Merwin), **Supp. III Part 1:** 350

Lackawanna Elegy (Goll; Kinnell, trans.), **Supp. III Part 1:** 235, 243–244

Laclède, Pierre, **Supp. I Part 1:** 205

"Lacquer Prints" (Lowell), **II:** 524–525

Lacy, Ed, **Supp. XV:** 193–210

Ladder of Years (Tyler), **Supp. IV Part 2:** 657, 671–672

Ladders to Fire (Nin), **Supp. X:** 185

"Ladies" (Coleman), **Supp. XI:** 93

Ladies Almanack (Barnes), **Supp. III Part 1:** 37–39, 42

"Ladies in Spring" (Welty), **IV:** 276–277; **Retro. Supp. I:** 353

Lady Audley's Secret (Braddon), **Supp. I Part 1:** 35, 36

"Lady Barberina" (James), **Retro. Supp. I:** 227

"Lady Bates" (Jarrell), **II:** 380–381

Lady Chatterley's Lover (Lawrence), **III:** 170; **IV:** 434; **Supp. XVI:**267

"Lady from Redhorse, A" (Bierce), **I:** 203

Lady in Kicking Horse Reservoir, The (Hugo), **Supp. VI:** 134, 138–139

Lady in the Lake, The (Chandler), **Supp. IV Part 1:** 127, 129–130

"Lady in the Lake, The" (Chandler), **Supp. IV Part 1:** 129

Lady in the Lake, The (film), **Supp. IV Part 1:** 130

"Lady in the Pink Mustang, The" (Erdrich), **Supp. IV Part 1:** 270

"Lady Is Civilized, The" (Taylor), **Supp. V:** 315

Lady Is Cold, The (White), **Supp. I Part 2:** 653

"Lady Lazarus" (Plath), **Retro. Supp. II:** 250, 251, 255; **Supp. I Part 2:** 529, 535, 542, 545

Lady of Aroostook, The (Howells), **II:** 280

"Lady of Bayou St. John, A" (Chopin), **Retro. Supp. II:** 58

"Lady of the Lake, The" (Malamud), **Supp. I Part 2:** 437

Lady Oracle (Atwood), **Supp. XIII:** 21, 23–24

Lady Sings the Blues (film), **Supp. I**

Part 1: 67

"Lady's Maid's Bell, The" (Wharton), **IV:** 316

"Lady Wentworth" (Longfellow), **II:** 505

"Lady with a Lamp" (Parker), **Supp. IX:** 193

"Lady with the Heron, The" (Merwin), **Supp. III Part 1:** 343

La Farge, John, **I:** 1, 2, 20; **II:** 322, 338; **Retro. Supp. I:** 217

La Farge, Oliver, **Supp. IV Part 2:** 503

Lafayette, Marquis de, **I:** 344, 345; **II:** 405–406; **Supp. I Part 2:** 510, 511, 683

"La Figlia che Piange" (Eliot), **Retro. Supp. I:** 63

La Follette, Robert, **I:** 483, 485, 492; **III:** 580

La Fontaine, Jean de, **II:** 154; **III:** 194; **IV:** 80

Laforgue, Jules, **I:** 386, 569, 570, 572–573, 575, 576; **II:** 528; **III:** 8, 11, 466; **IV:** 37, 79, 80, 122; **Retro. Supp. I:** 55, 56; **Supp. XIII:** 332, 335, 346; **Supp. XV:** 165

La Gallienne, Eva, **Supp. VIII:** 251

"Lager Beer" (Dunbar), **Supp. II Part 1:** 193

"La Gringuita: On Losing a Native Language" (Alvarez), **Supp. VII:** 18

Laguna Woman (Silko), **Supp. IV Part 2:** 557, 560–561

Laing, R. D., **Supp. I Part 2:** 527

La kabbale pratique (Ambelain), **Supp. I Part 1:** 273

"Lake, The" (Bradbury), **Supp. IV Part 1:** 101

Lake, The (play), **Supp. IX:** 189

Lakeboat (Mamet), **Supp. XIV:**240–241

"Lake Chelan" (Stafford), **Supp. XI:** 321

Lake Effect Country (Ammons), **Supp. VII:** 34, 35

"Lake Isle of Innisfree" (Yeats), **Retro. Supp. I:** 413

"Lake Return" (Wright), **Supp. XV:** 345

Lake Wobegon Days (Keillor), **Supp. XVI:**165, 166, 173–174

Lake Wobegon Summer 1956 (Keillor), **Supp. XVI:**178

Lalic, Ivan V., **Supp. VIII:** 272

L'Alouette (Anouilh), **Supp. I Part 1:** 286–288

Lamantia, Philip, **Supp. VIII:** 289

Lamb, Charles, **III:** 111, 207; **Supp. VIII:** 125

Lamb, Wendy, **Supp. IV Part 2:** 658

Lambardi, Marilyn May, **Retro. Supp. II:** 45–46

"Lament" (Wilbur), **Supp. III Part 2:** 550

"Lamentations" (Glück), **Supp. V:** 83, 84

"Lament for Dark Peoples" (Hughes), **Retro. Supp. I:** 199

"Lament for Saul and Jonathan" (Bradstreet), **Supp. I Part 1:** 111

"Lament-Heaven" (Doty), **Supp. XI:** 125

"Lament of a New England Mother, The" (Eberhart), **I:** 539

Laments for the Living (Parker), **Supp. IX:** 192

"Lame Shall Enter First, The" (O'Connor), **III:** 348, 351, 352, 355, 356–357, 358; **Retro. Supp. II:** 237

Lamia (Keats), **II:** 512; **III:** 523

La Motte-Fouqué, Friedrich Heinrich Karl, **III:** 77, 78

L'Amour, Louis, **Supp. XIII:** 5

Lamp for Nightfall, A (Caldwell), **I:** 297

Lamplit Answer, The (Schnackenberg), **Supp. XV:** 251, 254, 256–260

"Lance" (Nabokov), **Retro. Supp. I:** 266

Lancelot (Percy), **Supp. III Part 1:** 384, 395–396

Lancelot (Robinson), **III:** 513, 522

Lanchester, John, **Retro. Supp. I:** 278

"Land" (Emerson), **II:** 6

"Land Aesthetic, The" (Callicott), **Supp. XIV:**184

Landau, Deborah, **Supp. XI:** 122, 123

"Land beyond the Blow, The" (Bierce), **I:** 209

"Land Ethic, The" (Leopold), **Supp. XIV:**179, 180, 183, 191, 192

Landfall (Wagoner), **Supp. IX:** 330

"Landing in Luck" (Faulkner), **Retro. Supp. I:** 85

"Landing on the Moon" (Swenson), **Supp. IV Part 2:** 643

Landlord at Lion's Head, The (Howells), **II:** 276, 287–288

Landmarks of Healing: A Study of House Made of Dawn (Scarberry-García), **Supp. IV Part 2:** 486

Land of Little Rain, The (Dillard), **Supp. VI:** 27–28

Land of the Free U.S.A. (MacLeish), **I:** 293; **III:** 16–17

Land of Unlikeness (Lowell), **II:** 537–538, 539, 547; **Retro. Supp. II:** 177, 178, 184–185

Landor, Walter Savage, **III:** 15, 469; **Supp. I Part 2:** 422

"Landscape" (Sarton), **Supp. VIII:** 259

"Landscape: The Eastern Shore" (Barth), **I:** 122

"Landscape as a Nude" (MacLeish), **III:** 14

Landscape at the End of the Century (Dunn), **Supp. XI:** 139, 143, 150–151

"Landscape Chamber, The" (Jewett), **II:** 408–409

"Landscape for the Disappeared" (Komunyakaa), **Supp. XIII:** 120, 126

Landscape in American Poetry (Larcom), **Supp. XIII:** 142

"Landscape Painter, A" (James), **II:** 322; **Retro. Supp. I:** 219

"Landscape Symbolism in Kate Chopin's *At Fault*" (Arner), **Retro. Supp. II:** 62

"Landscape with Boat" (Stevens), **Retro. Supp. I:** 306

"Landscape with the Fall of Icarus" (Brueghel), **Retro. Supp. I:** 430

Land's End: A Walk through Provincetown (Cunningham), **Supp. XV:** 69

"Land Where There Is No Death, The" (Benét), **Supp. XI:** 56

Lane, Ann, **Supp. XI:** 195, 208

Lane, Cornelia. *See* Anderson, Mrs. Sherwood

Lane, Homer, **Supp. II Part 1:** 6; **Supp. XIV:**160

Lane, Nathan, **Supp. XIII:** 207

Lane, Rose Wilder, **Supp. IV Part 2:** 524

Lanes, Selma G., **Supp. XVI:**104, 107

Lang, Andrew, **Retro. Supp. I:** 127

Lang, Violet, **Supp. XII:** 119

Langdon, Olivia. *See* Clemens, Mrs. Samuel Langhorne (Olivia Langdon)

Lange, Carl Georg, **II:** 350

Lange, Dorothea, **I:** 293; **Supp. XIV:**181

Langland, Joseph, **III:** 542

Langston Hughes, American Poet (Walker), **Supp. III Part 2:** 530–531

Langston Hughes: Modern Critical Views (Bloom, ed.), **Retro. Supp. I:** 193

Langston Hughes: The Poet and His Critics (Barksdale), **Retro. Supp. I:** 202

Langston Hughes and the "Chicago Defender": Essays on Race, Politics, and Culture (De Santis, ed.), **Retro. Supp. I:** 194

Langston Hughes Reader, The (Hughes), **Retro. Supp. I:** 202;

Supp. I Part 1: 345

"Language, Visualization and the Inner Library" (Shepard), **Supp. III Part 2:** 436, 438, 449

"Language and the Writer" (Bambara), **Supp. XI:** 18

Language As Gesture (Blackmur), **Supp. II Part 1:** 108

Language as Symbolic Action (Burke), **I:** 275, 282, 285

Language Book, The (Andrews and Bernstein), **Supp. IV Part 2:** 426

Language in Thought and Action (Hayakawa), **I:** 448

"Language of Being and Dying, The" (Gass), **Supp. VI:** 91

"Language of Home, The" (Wideman), **Supp. X:** 320, 323–324

Language of Life, The (Moyers, television series), **Supp. XIII:** 274, 276

Language of the American South, The (Brooks), **Supp. XIV:**14

"Language of the Brag, The" (Olds), **Supp. X:** 204

"Language We Know, The" (Ortiz), **Supp. IV Part 2:** 500

Lanier, Clifford, **Supp. I Part 1:** 349, 350, 353, 355, 356, 371

Lanier, James F. D., **Supp. I Part 1:** 350

Lanier, Lyle H., **Supp. X:** 25

Lanier, Mrs. Robert Sampson (Mary Jane Anderson), **Supp. I Part 1:** 349

Lanier, Mrs. Sidney (Mary Day), **Supp. I Part 1:** 351, 355, 357, 361, 362, 364, 370, 371

Lanier, Robert Sampson, **Supp. I Part 1:** 349, 351, 355, 356, 361

Lanier, Sidney, **IV:** 444; **Supp. I Part 1:** 349–373; **Supp. I Part 2:** 416; **Supp. IV Part 1:** 165

"Lanier as Poet" (Parks), **Supp. I Part 1:** 373

"Lanier's Reading" (P. Graham), **Supp. I Part 1:** 373

"Lanier's Use of Science for Poetic Imagery" (Beaver), **Supp. I Part 1:** 373

Lannegan, Helen. *See* Caldwell, Mrs. Erskine

Lannin, Paul, **II:** 427

Lanny Budd novels (Sinclair), **Supp. V:** 290

Lant, Kathleen Margaret, **Supp. V:** 141

Lanthenas, François, **Supp. I Part 2:** 515

Laotzu, **III:** 173, 189, 567; **Supp. XV:** 39, 46, 48

"Lapis Lazuli" (Yeats), **I:** 532; **III:** 40

Laplace, Pierre Simon de, **III:** 428

Lapouge, M. G., **Supp. I Part 2:** 633

Lappa, Katherine, **Supp. XV:** 176

Laqueur, Thomas, **Supp. XVI:**154

Larbaud, Valery, **IV:** 404; **Supp. XIII:** 332; **Supp. XIV:**338

Larcom, Lucy, **Retro. Supp. II:** 145; **Supp. XIII:** 137–157

Larcom's Poetical Works (Larcom), **Supp. XIII:** 142

Lardner, John, **II:** 437

Lardner, Ring, **I:** 487; **II:** 44, 91, 259, 263, 415–438; **III:** 566, 572; **IV:** 433; **Retro. Supp. I:** 105; **Retro. Supp. II:** 222; **Supp. I Part 2:** 609; **Supp. IX:** 200; **Supp. XVI:**189

Lardner, Ring, Jr., **Supp. XI:** 306

"Lardner, Shakespeare and Chekhov" (Matthews), **II:** 430

"Large Bad Picture" (Bishop), **Retro. Supp. II:** 43; **Supp. I Part 1:** 73, 80–82, 85, 86, 89, 90

"Large Coffee" (Lardner), **II:** 437

Large Glass, or The Bride Stripped Bare by Her Bachelors, Even (Duchamp), **Supp. IV Part 2:** 423, 424

Largo (Handel), **IV:** 369

Lark, The (Hellman), **Supp. I Part 1:** 286–288, 297

Larkin, Philip, **Supp. I Part 2:** 536; **Supp. XI:** 243, 249; **Supp. XIII:** 76, 85; **Supp. XV:** 117, 251

Larkin, Sharon Alile, **Supp. XI:** 20

Larmore, Phoebe, **Supp. X:** 266

Larner, Jeremy, **Supp. XVI:**220

La Rochefoucauld, François de, **I:** 279; **II:** 111; **Supp. XIV:**130

"La Rose des Vents" (Wilbur), **Supp. III Part 2:** 550

Larry's Party (Shields), **Supp. VII:** 324, 326–327

Larsen, Nella, **Supp. I Part 1:** 325, 326; **Supp. IV Part 1:** 164

Larson, Charles, **Supp. IV Part 1:** 331

Larson, Clinton, **Supp. XI:** 328

"Larval Stage of a Bookworm" (Mencken), **III:** 101

La Salle and the Discovery of the Great West (Parkman), **Supp. II Part 2:** 595, 598, 605–607

Lasch, Christopher, **I:** 259

Lasher (Rice), **Supp. VII:** 299–300

Lask, Thomas, **III:** 576; **Supp. XVI:**250

Laski, Harold, **Supp. I Part 2:** 632, 643

Lassalle, Ferdinand, **IV:** 429

Lasser, Louise, **Supp. XV:** 4

"Last Acts" (Olds), **Supp. X:** 210

Last Adam, The (Cozzens), **I:** 362–363, 364, 368, 375, 377, 378, 379

Last Analysis, The (Bellow), **I:** 152, 160, 161; **Retro. Supp. II:** 26

Last and Lost Poems of Delmore Schwartz (Phillips, ed.), **Supp. II Part 2:** 661, 665

Last Avant-Garde, The: The Making of the New York School of Poets (Lehman), **Supp. XV:** 178–179, 187

Last Beautiful Days of Autumn, The (Nichols), **Supp. XIII:** 254, 255, 267, 269

Last Blue (Stern), **Supp. IX:** 299–300

Last Carousel, The (Algren), **Supp. IX:** 16

"Last Child" (X. J. Kennedy), **Supp. XV:** 162, 165

"Last Day in the Field, The" (Gordon), **II:** 200

"Last Day of the Last Furlough" (Salinger), **III:** 552–553

"Last Days of Alice" (Tate), **IV:** 129

"Last Days of August, The" (Nye), **Supp. XIII:** 284

"Last Days of John Brown, The" (Thoreau), **IV:** 185

Last Days of Louisiana Red, The (Reed), **Supp. X:** 240, 248–249

Last Decade, The (Trilling), **Supp. III Part 2:** 493, 499

"Last Demon, The" (Singer), **IV:** 15, 21

Last Exit to Brooklyn (Selby), **Supp. III Part 1:** 125

Last Flower, The (Thurber), **Supp. I Part 2:** 610

"Last Frontier" (McCarriston), **Supp. XIV:**272

Last Gentleman, The (Percy), **Supp. III Part 1:** 383–388, 392–393

"Last Good Country, The" (Hemingway), **II:** 258–259

Last Good Time, The (Bausch), **Supp. VII:** 45–46

"Last Hiding Places of Snow, The" (Kinnell), **Supp. III Part 1:** 252

"Last Hours, The" (Dunn), **Supp. XI:** 141

Last Husband and Other Stories, The (Humphrey), **Supp. IX:** 94

Last Jew in America, The (Fiedler), **Supp. XIII:** 103

"Last Jew in America, The" (Fiedler), **Supp. XIII:** 103

Last Laugh, Mr. Moto (Marquand), **III:** 57

"Last Leaf, The" (Holmes), **Supp. I Part 1:** 302, 309

"Last Leaf, The" (Porter), **III:** 444

"Last Look at the Lilacs" (Stevens), **IV:** 74

Last Man, The (Kees), **Supp. XV:** 142, 143, 145

"Last May" (Dixon), **Supp. XII:** 143

"Last Mohican, The" (Malamud), **Supp. I Part 2:** 437–438, 450, 451

"Lastness" (Kinnell), **Supp. III Part 1:** 248–249

"Last Night" (Olds), **Supp. X:** 212

"Last Night at Tía's" (Alvarez), **Supp. VII:** 5

Last Night of Summer, The (Caldwell), **I:** 292–293

Last of Mr. Norris, The (Isherwood), **Supp. XIV:**161

"Last of the Brooding Miserables, The" (Karr), **Supp. XI:** 250

"Last of the Caddoes, The" (Humphrey), **Supp. IX:** 101

"Last of the Gold Star Mothers, The" (C. Bly), **Supp. XVI:**34, 35, 36

"Last of the Legions, The" (Benét), **Supp. XI:** 56, 57

Last of the Mohicans, The (Cooper), **I:** 341, 342, 349

Last of the Red Hot Lovers (Simon), **Supp. IV Part 2:** 575, 583, 589

"Last of the Valerii, The" (James), **II:** 327; **Retro. Supp. I:** 218

"Last One, The" (Merwin), **Supp. III Part 1:** 355

Last Picture Show, The (film), **Supp. V:** 223, 226

Last Picture Show, The (McMurtry), **Supp. V:** 220, 222–223, 233

Last Puritan, The (Santayana), **III:** 64, 600, 604, 607, 612, 615–617

"Last Ride Together, The" (Browning), **I:** 468

"Last River, The" (Kinnell), **Supp. III Part 1:** 236

Last Song, The (Harjo), **Supp. XII:** 218

"Last Song for the Mend-It Shop" (Nye), **Supp. XIII:** 283

"Last Tango in Fresno" (Salinas), **Supp. XIII:** 318

Last Tycoon, The: An Unfinished Novel (Fitzgerald), **II:** 84, 98; **Retro. Supp. I:** 109, 114, 114–115; **Retro. Supp. II:** 337; **Supp. IV Part 1:** 203; **Supp. IX:** 63; **Supp. XII:** 173; **Supp. XIII:** 170

"Last WASP in the World, The" (Fiedler), **Supp. XIII:** 103

Last Watch of the Night: Essays Too Personal and Otherwise (Monette), **Supp. X:** 147, 148, 153, 157–159

Last Word, The: Letters between Mar-cia Nardi and William Carlos Williams (O'Neil, ed.), **Retro. Supp. I:** 427

"Last Words" (Levine), **Supp. V:** 190

"Last Words" (Olds), **Supp. X:** 210

Last Worthless Evening, The (Dubus), **Supp. VII:** 87–88

"Las Vegas (What?) Las Vegas (Can't Hear You! Too Noisy) Las Vegas! ! ! !" (Wolfe), **Supp. III Part 2:** 572

"Late" (Bogan), **Supp. III Part 1:** 53

"Late Air" (Bishop), **Supp. I Part 1:** 89

"Late Autumn" (Sarton), **Supp. VIII:** 261

"Late Bronze, Early Iron: A Journey Book" (Sobin), **Supp. XVI:**290

Late Child, The (McMurtry), **Supp. V:** 231

"Late Conversation" (Doty), **Supp. XI:** 122

"Late Encounter with the Enemy, A" (O'Connor), **III:** 345; **Retro. Supp. II:** 232

Late Fire, Late Snow (Francis), **Supp. IX:** 89–90

Late George Apley, The (Marquand), **II:** 482–483; **III:** 50, 51, 52, 56–57, 58, 62–64, 65, 66

Late George Apley, The (Marquand and Kaufman), **III:** 62

"Late Hour" (Everwine), **Supp. XV:** 85

Late Hour, The (Strand), **Supp. IV Part 2:** 620, 629–630

"Lately, at Night" (Kumin), **Supp. IV Part 2:** 442

"Late Moon" (Levine), **Supp. V:** 186

"Late Night Ode" (McClatchy), **Supp. XII:** 262–263

Later (Creeley), **Supp. IV Part 1:** 153, 156, 157

Later Life (Gurney), **Supp. V:** 103, 105

La Terre (Zola), **III:** 316, 322

Later the Same Day (Paley), **Supp. VI:** 218

Late Settings (Merrill), **Supp. III Part 1:** 336

"Late Sidney Lanier, The" (Stedman), **Supp. I Part 1:** 373

"Late Snow & Lumber Strike of the Summer of Fifty-Four, The" (Snyder), **Supp. VIII:** 294

"Latest Freed Man, The" (Stevens), **Retro. Supp. I:** 306

"Latest Injury, The" (Olds), **Supp. X:** 209

Latest Literary Essays and Addresses (Lowell), **Supp. I Part 2:** 407

"Late Subterfuge" (Warren), **IV:** 257

"Late Supper, A" (Jewett), **Retro. Supp. II:** 137

"Late Victorians" (Rodriguez), **Supp. XIV:**303–304

"Late Walk, A" (Frost), **II:** 153; **Retro. Supp. I:** 127

Latham, Edyth, **I:** 289

Lathrop, George Parsons, **Supp. I Part 1:** 365

Lathrop, H. B., **Supp. III Part 2:** 612

Lathrop, Julia, **Supp. I Part 1:** 5

Latière de Trianon, La (Wekerlin), **II:** 515

"La Tigresse" (Van Vechten), **Supp. II Part 2:** 735, 738

Latimer, Hugh, **II:** 15

Latimer, Margery, **Supp. IX:** 320

La Traviata (Verdi), **III:** 139

"Latter-Day Warnings" (Holmes), **Supp. I Part 1:** 307

La Turista (Shepard), **Supp. III Part 2:** 440

Lauber, John, **Supp. XIII:** 21

Laud, Archbishop, **II:** 158

"Lauds" (Auden), **Supp. II Part 1:** 23

"Laughing Man, The" (Salinger), **III:** 559

Laughing to Keep From Crying (Hughes), **Supp. I Part 1:** 329–330

"Laughing with One Eye" (Schnackenberg), **Supp. XV:** 253

Laughlin, J. Laurence, **Supp. I Part 2:** 641

Laughlin, James, **III:** 171; **Retro. Supp. I:** 423, 424, 428, 430, 431; **Supp. VIII:** 195; **Supp. XV:** 140; **Supp. XVI:**284

Laughlin, Jay, **Supp. II Part 1:** 94

Laughter in the Dark (Nabokov), **III:** 255–258; **Retro. Supp. I:** 270

Laughter on the 23rd Floor (Simon), **Supp. IV Part 2:** 575, 576, 588, 591–592

"Launcelot" (Lewis), **II:** 439–440

"Laura Dailey's Story" (Bogan), **Supp. III Part 1:** 52

Laurel, Stan, **Supp. I Part 2:** 607; **Supp. IV Part 2:** 574

Laurel and Hardy Go to Heaven (Auster), **Supp. XII:** 21

Laurence, Dan H., **II:** 338–339

Laurens, John, **Supp. I Part 2:** 509

Lauter, Paul, **Supp. XV:** 313

Lautréamont, Comte de, **III:** 174

Law, John, **Supp. XI:** 307

Lawd Today (Wright), **IV:** 478, 492

Law for the Lion, A (Auchincloss), **Supp. IV Part 1:** 25

"Law Lane" (Jewett), **II:** 407

"Law of Nature and the Dream of Man,

The: Ruminations of the Art of Fiction" (Stegner), **Supp. IV Part 2:** 604

Lawrence, D. H., **I:** 291, 336, 377, 522, 523; **II:** 78, 84, 98, 102, 264, 517, 523, 532, 594, 595; **III:** 27, 33, 40, 44, 46, 172, 173, 174, 178, 184, 229, 261, 423, 429, 458, 546–547; **IV:** 138, 339, 342, 351, 380; **Retro. Supp. I:** 7, 18, 203, 204, 421; **Retro. Supp. II:** 68; **Supp. I Part 1:** 227, 230, 243, 255, 257, 258, 263, 329; **Supp. I Part 2:** 546, 613, 728; **Supp. II Part 1:** 1, 9, 20, 89; **Supp. IV Part 1:** 81; **Supp. VIII:** 237; **Supp. X:** 137, 193, 194; **Supp. XII:** 172; **Supp. XIV:**310; **Supp. XV:** 45, 46, 158, 254; **Supp. XVI:**267

Lawrence, Frieda, **Supp. XV:** 46

Lawrence, Rhoda, **Supp. I Part 1:** 45

Lawrence, Seymour, **Supp. IX:** 107; **Supp. XI:** 335, 346, 348

Lawrence, T. E., **Supp. XIV:**159

Lawrence of Arabia (Aldington), **Supp. I Part 1:** 259

Lawrence of Arabia (film), **Supp. I Part 1:** 67

Laws (Plato), **Supp. IV Part 1:** 391

Laws of Ice, The (Price), **Supp. VI:** 264

Lawson, John Howard, **I:** 479, 482

Lawton Girl, The (Frederic), **II:** 132–133, 144

Layachi, Larbi (Driss ben Hamed Charhadi), **Supp. IV Part 1:** 92, 93

Layard, John, **Supp. XIV:**160

Lay Down My Sword and Shield (Burke), **Supp. XIV:**22, 25, 34

"Layers, The" (Kunitz), **Supp. III Part 1:** 260, 266–267

"Layers, The: Some Notes on 'The Abduction'" (Kunitz), **Supp. III Part 1:** 266

"Lay-mans Lamentation, The" (Taylor), **IV:** 162–163

Lay of the Land, The: Metaphor as Experience and History in American Life and Letters (Kolodny), **Supp. X:** 97

"Layover" (Hass), **Supp. VI:** 109

"Lay Preacher" (Dennie), **Supp. I Part 1:** 125

Layton, Irving, **Supp. XII:** 121

Lazarillo de Tormes (Mendoza), **III:** 182

Lazarus Laughed (O'Neill), **III:** 391, 395–396

Lazer, Hank, **Supp. IX:** 265

Lea, Luke, **IV:** 248

Leacock, Stephen, **Supp. IV Part 2:** 464

"LEADBELLY GIVES AN AUTO-GRAPH" (Baraka), **Supp. II Part 1:** 49

Leaflets: Poems, 1965–1968 (Rich), **Supp. I Part 2:** 551, 556–557

"League of American Writers, The: Communist Organizational Activity among American Writers 1929–1942" (Wolfe), **Supp. III Part 2:** 568

League of Brightened Philistines and Other Papers, The (Farrell), **II:** 49

Leaning Forward (Paley), **Supp. VI:** 221

"Leaning Tower, The" (Porter), **III:** 442, 443, 446–447

Leaning Tower and Other Stories, The (Porter), **III:** 433, 442, 443–447

"Leap, The" (Dickey), **Supp. IV Part 1:** 182

"Leaping Up into Political Poetry" (R. Bly), **Supp. IV Part 1:** 61, 63

Leap Year (Cameron), **Supp. XII:** 79–80, 81, 85–86, 88

Lear, Edward, **III:** 428, 536; **Supp. XVI:**103

Lear, Linda, **Supp. IX:** 19, 22, 25, 26

Learned Ladies, The (Molière; Wilbur, trans.), **Supp. III Part 2:** 560

"Learning a Dead Language" (Merwin), **Supp. III Part 1:** 345

Learning a Trade: A Craftsman's Notebooks, 1955–1997 (Price), **Supp. VI:** 254, 255, 267

Learning to Love: Exploring Solitude and Freedom (Merton), **Supp. VIII:** 200

"Learning to Read" (Harper), **Supp. II Part 1:** 201–202

"Learning to Speak" (Everwine), **Supp. XV:** 79

Leary, Lewis, **III:** 478

Leary, Paris, **Supp. IV Part 1:** 176

Leary, Timothy, **Supp. X:** 265; **Supp. XIV:**150

Least Heat Moon, William, **Supp. V:** 169

Leather-Stocking Tales, The (Cooper), **I:** 335

Leatherwood God, The (Howells), **II:** 276, 277, 288

"Leaves" (Updike), **Retro. Supp. I:** 323, 329, 335

Leaves and Ashes (Haines), **Supp. XII:** 206

Leaves from the Notebook of a Tamed Cynic (Niebuhr), **III:** 293

Leaves of Grass (Whitman), **II:** 8; **IV:** 331, 332, 333, 334, 335, 336, 340, 341–342, 348, 350, 405, 464; **Retro. Supp. I:** 387, 388, 389, 390, 392–395, 406, 407, 408; **Retro. Supp. II:** 93; **Supp. I Part 1:** 365; **Supp. I Part 2:** 416, 579; **Supp. III Part 1:** 156; **Supp. V:** 170; **Supp. VIII:** 275; **Supp. IX:** 265; **Supp. X:** 120; **Supp. XIV:**334; **Supp. XV:** 218

"Leaves of Grass" (Whitman), **IV:** 463

Leaves of Grass (1856) (Whitman), **Retro. Supp. I:** 399–402

Leaves of Grass (1860) (Whitman), **Retro. Supp. I:** 402–405

Leaves of the Tree, The (Masters), **Supp. I Part 2:** 460

"Leaving" (Hogan), **Supp. IV Part 1:** 400

"Leaving" (Wilbur), **Supp. III Part 2:** 563

Leaving a Doll's House: A Memoir (C. Bloom), **Retro. Supp. II:** 281

Leaving Another Kingdom: Selected Poems (Stern), **Supp. IX:** 296

"Leaving Brooklyn" (Neugeboren), **Supp. XVI:**226

Leaving Cheyenne (McMurtry), **Supp. V:** 220, 221–222, 224, 229

Leaving Home (Keillor), **Supp. XVI:**175

"Leaving the Island" (Olds), **Supp. X:** 214

"Leaving the Yellow House" (Bellow), **Retro. Supp. II:** 27, 32

"Leaving Town" (Kenyon), **Supp. VII:** 163

Leavis, F. R., **I:** 522; **III:** 462–463, 475, 478; **Retro. Supp. I:** 67; **Retro. Supp. II:** 243; **Supp. I Part 2:** 536; **Supp. VIII:** 234, 236, 245

"Leavis-Snow Controversy, The" (Trilling), **Supp. III Part 2:** 512

Leavitt, David, **Supp. VIII:** 88

Le Braz, Anatole, **Supp. XIII:** 253

Lecker, Robert, **Supp. XIII:** 21

LeClair, Thomas, **Supp. IV Part 1:** 286

LeClair, Tom, **Supp. V:** 53; **Supp. XII:** 152

Le Conte, Joseph, **II:** 479; **III:** 227–228

"Lecture, The" (Singer), **IV:** 21

"LECTURE PAST DEAD CATS" (Baraka), **Supp. II Part 1:** 52

Lectures in America (Stein), **IV:** 27, 32, 33, 35, 36, 41, 42

"Lectures on Poetry" (Bryant), **Supp. I Part 1:** 159, 161

Lectures on Rhetoric (Blair), **II:** 8

"Leda and the Swan" (Yeats), **III:** 347;

Supp. IX: 52

Ledger (Fitzgerald), **Retro. Supp. I:** 109, 110

Lee (Masters), **Supp. I Part 2:** 471

Lee, Don, **Supp. XII:** 295

Lee, Don L. *See* Madhubuti, Haki R.

Lee, Gypsy Rose, **II:** 586; **III:** 161; **Supp. IV Part 1:** 84

Lee, Harper, **Supp. VIII:** 113–131

Lee, Harriett, **Supp. XV:** 230

Lee, James Kyun-Jin, **Supp. XV:** 213

Lee, James W., **Supp. IX:** 94, 97, 109

Lee, James Ward, **Supp. VIII:** 57

Lee, Li Lin, **Supp. XV:** 211, 212

Lee, Li-Young, **Supp. XV:** 211–228

Lee, Robert E., **II:** 150, 206; **IV:** 126; **Supp. I Part 2:** 471, 486

Lee, Samuel, **IV:** 158

Lee, Spike, **Retro. Supp. II:** 12; **Supp. XI:** 19; **Supp. XIII:** 179, 186; **Supp. XVI:**144

Lee, Virginia Chin-lan, **Supp. X:** 291

Leeds, Barry, **Retro. Supp. II:** 204

Leeds, Daniel, **II:** 110

Leeds, Titan, **II:** 110, 111

Leeming, David, **Retro. Supp. II:** 4, 10

"Lees of Happiness, The" (Fitzgerald), **II:** 88

Left Out in the Rain: New Poems 1947–1985 (Snyder), **Supp. VIII:** 305

"Legacy" (Dunn), **Supp. XI:** 148

"Legacy" (Komunyakaa), **Supp. XIII:** 132

"Legacy of Aldo Leopold, The" (Stegner), **Supp. XIV:**193

Legacy of Fear, A (Farrell), **II:** 39

"Legacy of the Ancestral Arts, The" (Locke), **Supp. XIV:**201

Legacy of the Civil War, The: Meditations on the Centennial (Warren), **IV:** 236

"Legal Alien" (Mora), **Supp. XIII:** 215

"Legal Tender Act, The" (Adams), **I:** 5

Légende de la mort, La (Le Braz), **Supp. XIII:** 253

"Legend of Duluoz, The" (Kerouac), **Supp. III Part 1:** 218, 226, 227, 229

"Legend of Lillian Hellman, The" (Kazin), **Supp. I Part 1:** 297

"Legend of Monte del Diablo, The" (Harte), **Supp. II Part 1:** 339

"Legend of Paper Plates, The" (Haines), **Supp. XII:** 204

"Legend of Sammtstadt, A" (Harte), **Supp. II Part 1:** 355

"Legend of Sleepy Hollow, The" (Irving), **II:** 306–308

Legends (Lowell), **II:** 525–526

Legends of New England (Whittier), **Supp. I Part 2:** 684, 692

Legends of the Fall (Harrison), **Supp. VIII:** 38, 39, 45–46, 48

Legends of the West (Hall), **II:** 313

Léger, Fernand, **Retro. Supp. I:** 292

Legge, James, **III:** 472

Leggett, William, **Supp. I Part 1:** 157

"Legion, The" (Karr), **Supp. XI:** 243

Legs (W. Kennedy), **Supp. VII:** 133, 134, 138–142, 143, 151

Le Guin, Ursula K., **Supp. IV Part 1:** 333

Lehan, Richard, **Retro. Supp. II:** 104

Lehman, David, **Supp. IX:** 161; **Supp. XIII:** 130; **Supp. XV:** 178–179, 180, 187, 190

Lehmann, John, **Retro. Supp. II:** 243; **Supp. XIV:**158, 159

Lehmann, Paul, **III:** 311

Lehmann-Haupt, Christopher, **Retro. Supp. II:** 291; **Supp. IV Part 1:** 205, 209, 306; **Supp. IX:** 95, 103; **Supp. XVI:**73, 210, 294, 295

Leiber, Fritz, **Supp. XVI:**123

Leibling, A. J., **Supp. XIV:**112

Leibniz, Gottfried Wilhelm von, **II:** 103; **III:** 428

Leibowitz, Herbert A., **I:** 386; **Supp. XV:** 78

Leich, Roland, **Supp. XIV:**123

Leithauser, Brad, **Retro. Supp. I:** 133; **Supp. XV:** 250

Leitz, Robert, **Supp. XIV:**62

Leivick, H., **IV:** 6

Lekachman, Robert, **Supp. I Part 2:** 648

Leland, Charles, **Supp. II Part 1:** 193

Leland, Charles Godfrey, **I:** 257

Leland, John, **Supp. XV:** 69

Lem, Stanislaw, **Supp. IV Part 1:** 103

"Le marais du cygne" (Whittier), **Supp. I Part 2:** 687

Lemay, Harding, **Supp. VIII:** 125; **Supp. IX:** 98

Lemercier, Eugène, **Retro. Supp. I:** 299

"Lemorne *versus* Huell" (E. Stoddard), **Supp. XV:** 270, 273, 283

Le Morte D'Arthur Notes (Gardner), **Supp. VI:** 65, 66

Lenin, V. I., **I:** 366, 439, 440; **III:** 14–15, 262, 475; **IV:** 429, 436, 443–444; **Supp. I Part 2:** 647

"Lenore" (Poe), **III:** 411

"Lenox Avenue: Midnight" (Hughes), **Retro. Supp. I:** 198

Leonard, Elmore, **Supp. IV Part 1:** 356; **Supp. X:** 5; **Supp. XIV:**26

Leonard, John, **Supp. IV Part 1:** 24; **Supp. IV Part 2:** 474; **Supp. V:** 164, 223–224; **Supp. XI:** 13

Leonardo da Vinci, **Supp. XII:** 44

León-Portilla, Miguel, **Supp. XV:** 77

Leontiev, Constantine, **Supp. XIV:**98

Leopard, The (Lampedusa), **Supp. XII:** 13–14

Leopardi, Giacomo, **II:** 543

"Leopard Man's Story, The" (London), **II:** 475

Leopard's Mouth Is Dry and Cold Inside, The (Levis), **Supp. XI:** 258

Leopold, Aldo, **Supp. V:** 202; **Supp. X:** 108; **Supp. XIV:**177–194

"Leper's Bell, the" (Komunyakaa), **Supp. XIII:** 118

Lerman, Leo, **Supp. X:** 188; **Supp. XVI:**194

Lerner, Max, **III:** 60; **Supp. I Part 2:** 629, 630, 631, 647, 650, 654

"Lesbos" (Plath), **Retro. Supp. II:** 254

Lesesne, Teri, **Supp. XIII:** 277

LeSieg, Theo (pseudo.). See Geisel, Theodor Seuss (Dr. Seuss)

Leskov, Nikolai, **IV:** 299

Leslie, Alfred, **Supp. XII:** 127

Les Misérables (Hugo), **II:** 179; **Supp. I Part 1:** 280

"Less and Less Human, O Savage Spirit" (W. Stevens), **Supp. XVI:**64

Lesser, Wendy, **Supp. IV Part 2:** 453; **Supp. X:** 297; **Supp. XVI:**201

Lessing, Gotthold, **Supp. I Part 2:** 422

"Lesson, The" (Bambara), **Supp. XI:** 5–6

"Lesson, The" (Dunbar), **Supp. II Part 1:** 199

"Lesson, The" (Olsen), **Supp. XIII:** 297

"Lesson of the Master, The" (James), **Retro. Supp. I:** 227

Lesson of the Masters: An Anthology of the Novel from Cervantes to Hemingway (Cowley-Hugo, ed.), **Supp. II Part 1:** 140

"Lesson on Concealment, A" (Brown), **Supp. I Part 1:** 133

"Lessons" (Epstein), **Supp. XII:** 163

"Lessons of the Body" (Simpson), **Supp. IX:** 267

Less than One (Brodsky), **Supp. VIII:** 22, 29–31

Lester, Jerry, **Supp. IV Part 2:** 574

Lester, Ketty, **Supp. XV:** 133, 147

Le Style Apollinaire (Zukofsky), **Supp. III Part 2:** 616

Le Sueur, Meridel, **Supp. V:** 113, 130; **Supp. XII:** 217

"Let America Be America Again"

(Hughes), **Retro. Supp. I:** 202; **Supp. I Part 1:** 331

Let Evening Come (Kenyon), **Supp. VII:** 160, 169–171

Lethem, Jonathan, **Supp. IX:** 122

Let It Come Down (Bowles), **Supp. IV Part 1:** 87

"Let Me Be" (Levine), **Supp. V:** 181, 189

"Let Me Begin Again" (Levine), **Supp. V:** 181, 189

"Let No Charitable Hope" (Wylie), **Supp. I Part 2:** 713–714, 729

Letofsky, Irv, **Supp. XVI:**167

"Let one Eye his watches keep/While the Other Eye doth sleep" (Fletcher), **Supp. IV Part 2:** 621

Let's Balance the Books (radio show; Untermeyer), **Supp. XV:** 311

"Letter . . ." (Whittier), **Supp. I Part 2:** 687

"Letter, A" (Bogan), **Supp. III Part 1:** 54

"Letter, May 2, 1959" (Olson), **Supp. II Part 2:** 579, 580

"Letter, Much Too Late" (Stegner), **Supp. IV Part 2:** 613

"Letter, The" (Gioia), **Supp. XV:** 120

"Letter, The" (Malamud), **Supp. I Part 2:** 435–436

"Letter about Money, Love, or Other Comfort, If Any, The" (Warren), **IV:** 245

Letter Addressed to the People of Piedmont, on the Advantages of the French Revolution, and the Necessity of Adopting Its Principles in Italy, A (Barlow), **Supp. II Part 1:** 80, 81

"Letter for Marion, A" (McGrath), **Supp. X:** 116

"Letter from Aldermaston" (Merwin), **Supp. III Part 1:** 347

"Letter from a Region in My Mind" (Baldwin). *See* "Down at the Cross"

Letter from Li Po, A (Aiken), **I:** 68

"Letter from 'Manhattan'" (Didion), **Supp. IV Part 1:** 205

"Letter from the Country" (column, C. Bly), **Supp. XVI:**33

Letter from the End of the Twentieth Century (Harjo), **Supp. XII:** 223

"Letter from the End of the Twentieth Century" (Harjo), **Supp. XII:** 227

"Letter on Céline" (Kerouac), **Supp. III Part 1:** 232

Letters (Cato), **II:** 114

Letters (Landor), **Supp. I Part 2:** 422

Letters (White), **Supp. I Part 2:** 651, 653, 675, 680

Letters (Wolfe), **IV:** 462

Letters and Leadership (Brooks), **I:** 228, 240, 245, 246

"Letters for the Dead" (Levine), **Supp. V:** 186

Letters from an American Farmer (Crèvecoeur), **Supp. I Part 1:** 227–251

Letters from Maine (Sarton), **Supp. VIII:** 261

"Letters from Maine" (Sarton), **Supp. VIII:** 261

"Letters from My Father" (R. O. Butler), **Supp. XII:** 71

Letters from the Country (C. Bly), **Supp. XVI:**33–34, 35, 37

Letters from the Earth (Twain), **IV:** 209

Letters from the East (Bryant), **Supp. I Part 1:** 158

"Letters from the Ming Dynasty" (Brodsky), **Supp. VIII:** 28

Letters of a Traveller (Bryant), **Supp. I Part 1:** 158

Letters of a Traveller, Second Series (Bryant), **Supp. I Part 1:** 158

Letters of Emily Dickinson, The (Johnson and Ward, eds.), **I:** 470; **Retro. Supp. I:** 28

Letters of William James (Henry James, ed.), **II:** 362

Letters on Various Interesting and Important Subjects . . . (Freneau), **Supp. II Part 1:** 272

Letters to a Niece (Adams), **I:** 22

Letters to a Young Poet (Rilke), **Supp. XIII:** 74; **Supp. XV:** 93

"Letters to Dead Imagists" (Sandburg), **I:** 421

"Letters Written on a Ferry While Crossing Long Island Sound" (Sexton), **Supp. II Part 2:** 683

"Letter to Abbé Raynal" (Paine), **Supp. I Part 2:** 510

Letter to a Man in the Fire: Does God Exist or Does He Care? (Price), **Supp. VI:** 267–268

"Letter to American Teachers of History, A" (Adams), **I:** 19

Letter to an Imaginary Friend (McGrath), **Supp. X:** 111, 112–113, 116, 119–125

"Letter to a Reader" (Sanders), **Supp. XVI:**266, 267, 268, 269, 275

"Letter to a Young Contributor" (Higginson), **Retro. Supp. I:** 31

"Letter to a Young Writer" (Price), **Supp. VI:** 267

"Letter to Bell from Missoula" (Hugo), **Supp. VI:** 142–143

"Letter to E. Franklin Frazier" (Baraka), **Supp. II Part 1:** 49

"Letter to Elaine Feinstein" (Olson), **Supp. II Part 2:** 561

"Letter to Freddy" (music) (Bowles), **Supp. IV Part 1:** 82

"Letter to Garber from Skye" (Hugo), **Supp. VI:** 146

"Letter to George Washington" (Paine), **Supp. I Part 2:** 517

"Letter to His Brother" (Berryman), **I:** 172, 173

Letter to His Countrymen, A (Cooper), **I:** 346, 347, 349

"Letter to Kizer from Seattle" (Hugo), **Supp. VI:** 142

Letter to Lord Byron (Auden), **Supp. II Part 1:** 11

"Letter to Lord Byron" (Mumford), **Supp. II Part 2:** 494

"Letter to Matthews from Barton Street Flats" (Hugo), **Supp. VI:** 133

"Letter to Minnesota" (Dunn), **Supp. XI:** 146

"Letter to Mr." (Poe), **III:** 411

"Letter Too Late to Vallejo" (Salinas), **Supp. XIII:** 313, 324

"Letter to Sister Madeline from Iowa City" (Hugo), **Supp. VI:** 142–143

"Letter to Soto" (Salinas), **Supp. XIII:** 325

"Letter to the Lady of the House" (Bausch), **Supp. VII:** 48

"Letter to the Rising Generation, A" (Comer), **I:** 214

"Letter to Walt Whitman" (Doty), **Supp. XI:** 135–136

"Letter to Wendell Berry, A" (Stegner), **Supp. IV Part 2:** 600

"Letter Writer, The" (Singer), **IV:** 20–21

"Let the Air Circulate" (Clampitt), **Supp. IX:** 45

"Letting Down of the Hair, The" (Sexton), **Supp. II Part 2:** 692

Letting Go (Roth), **Retro. Supp. II:** 282, 283; **Supp. III Part 2:** 403, 404, 409–412

"Letting the Puma Go" (Dunn), **Supp. XI:** 149

"Lettres d'un Soldat" (Stevens), **Retro. Supp. I:** 299

Let Us Go into the Starry Night (Shanley), **Supp. XIV:**317

Let Us Now Praise Famous Men (Agee and Evans), **I:** 25, 27, 35, 36–39, 42, 45, 293

Let Your Mind Alone! (Thurber), **Supp. I Part 2:** 608

Leutze, Emanuel, **Supp. X:** 307

Levels of the Game (McPhee), **Supp.**

III Part 1: 292, 294, 301
Levertov, Denise, **Retro. Supp. I:** 411; **Supp. III Part 1:** 271–287; **Supp. III Part 2:** 541; **Supp. IV Part 1:** 325; **Supp. VIII:** 38, 39; **Supp. XVI:** 39, 40
Levi, Primo, **Supp. X:** 149
Leviathan (Auster), **Supp. XII:** 27, 33–34
"Leviathan" (Lowell), **II:** 537, 538
"Leviathan" (Merwin), **Supp. III Part 1:** 345
Levin, Harry, **Supp. I Part 2:** 647
Levin, Jennifer, **Supp. X:** 305
Lévinas, Emmanuel, **Supp. XVI:** 290, 291
Levine, Ellen, **Supp. V:** 4; **Supp. XI:** 178
Levine, Paul, **Supp. IV Part 1:** 221, 224
Levine, Philip, **Supp. III Part 2:** 541; **Supp. V:** 177–197, 337; **Supp. IX:** 293; **Supp. XI:** 123, 257, 259, 267, 271, 315; **Supp. XIII:** 312; **Supp. XV:** 73, 74, 212
Levine, Rosalind, **Supp. XII:** 123
Levine, Sherry, **Supp. XII:** 4
Le Violde Lucréce (Obey), **IV:** 356
Levis, Larry, **Supp. V:** 180; **Supp. IX:** 299; **Supp. XI:** 257–274; **Supp. XIII:** 312; **Supp. XV:** 73
Lévi-Strauss, Claude, **Supp. I Part 2:** 636; **Supp. IV Part 1:** 45; **Supp. IV Part 2:** 490
Levitation: Five Fictions (Ozick), **Supp. V:** 268–270
Levitt, Saul, **Supp. XV:** 197
Levy, Alan, **Supp. IV Part 2:** 574, 589
Levy, G. Rachel, **Supp. I Part 2:** 567
Lévy-Bruhl, Lucien, **Retro. Supp. I:** 57
Levy Mayer and the New Industrial Era (Masters), **Supp. I Part 2:** 473
Lewes, George Henry, **II:** 569
Lewin, Albert, **Supp. XIV:** 279, 293
Lewis, C. Day, **III:** 527
Lewis, Dr. Claude, **II:** 442
Lewis, Edith, **I:** 313; **Retro. Supp. I:** 19, 21, 22
Lewis, Edwin, J., **II:** 439, 442
Lewis, Jerry, **Supp. IV Part 2:** 575; **Supp. X:** 172
Lewis, John L., **I:** 493
Lewis, Lilburn, **IV:** 243
Lewis, Lorene, **Supp. IV Part 2:** 596, 597
Lewis, Lucy, **IV:** 243
Lewis, Maggie, **Supp. V:** 23
Lewis, Meriwether, **II:** 217; **III:** 14; **IV:** 179, 243, 283

Lewis, Merrill, **Supp. IV Part 2:** 596, 597
Lewis, Michael, **II:** 451, 452
Lewis, Mrs. Sinclair (Dorothy Thompson), **II:** 449–450, 451, 453
Lewis, Mrs. Sinclair (Grace Livingston Hegger), **II:** 441
Lewis, R. W. B., **I:** 386, 561; **II:** 457–458; **Retro. Supp. I:** 362, 367; **Supp. I Part 1:** 233; **Supp. XIII:** 93
Lewis, Robert Q., **Supp. IV Part 2:** 574
Lewis, Sinclair, **I:** 116, 212, 348, 355, 362, 374, 378, 487, 495; **II:** 27, 34, 74, 79, 271, 277, 306, 439–461, 474; **III:** 28, 40, 51, 60, 61, 63–64, 66, 70, 71, 106, 394, 462, 572, 606; **IV:** 53, 326, 366, 455, 468, 475, 482; **Retro. Supp. I:** 332; **Retro. Supp. II:** 95, 108, 197, 322; **Supp. I Part 2:** 378, 613, 709; **Supp. IV Part 2:** 678; **Supp. V:** 278; **Supp. IX:** 308; **Supp. X:** 137
Lewis, Wyndham, **III:** 458, 462, 465, 470; **Retro. Supp. I:** 59, 170, 292; **Supp. III Part 2:** 617
Lexicon Tetraglotton (Howell), **II:** 111
"Leyenda" (Mora), **Supp. XIII:** 214
Leyte (Morison), **Supp. I Part 2:** 491
"Liar, The" (Baraka), **Supp. II Part 1:** 36
"Liars, The" (Sandburg), **III:** 586
Liars' Club, The: A Memoir (Karr), **Supp. XI:** 239, 240, 241, 242, 244–248, 252, 254; **Supp. XVI:** 70
"Liar's Dice" (C. Frost), **Supp. XV:** 94, 107
Liar's Dice (C. Frost), **Supp. XV:** 93, 96
Liars in Love (Yates), **Supp. XI:** 348, 349
Libation Bearers, The (Aeschylus), **III:** 398; **Supp. IX:** 103
Li Bay. See Li Po
Libby, Anthony, **Supp. XIII:** 87
Libera, Padre, **II:** 278
Liberal Imagination, The (Trilling), **III:** 308; **Retro. Supp. I:** 97, 216; **Supp. II Part 1:** 146; **Supp. III Part 2:** 495, 498, 501–504
"Liberation" (Winters), **Supp. II Part 2:** 791
Liber Brunenesis (yearbook), **IV:** 286
Liberties, The (Howe), **Supp. IV Part 2:** 426–428, 430, 432
Liberty Jones (play), **Supp. IV Part 1:** 83
"Liberty Tree" (Paine), **Supp. I Part 2:** 505

Libra (DeLillo), **Supp. VI:** 2, 4, 5, 6, 7, 9, 10, 12, 13, 14, 16
Library for Juana, A (Mora), **Supp. XIII:** 218
Library of America, **Retro. Supp. I:** 2
"Library of Law, A" (MacLeish), **III:** 4
"Librettos for Eros" (Gander), **Supp. XV:** 340
Lice, The (Merwin), **Supp. III Part 1:** 339, 341–342, 346, 348, 349, 355
Lichtenberg, Georg Christoph, **Supp. XIV:** 339
Lichtenstein, Roy, **Supp. I Part 2:** 665; **Supp. XV:** 186
"Liddy's Orange" (Olds), **Supp. X:** 209
Lieberman, Laurence, **Supp. XI:** 323–324
Liebestod (Wagner), **I:** 284, 395
Liebling, A. J., **IV:** 290; **Supp. VIII:** 151; **Supp. XVI:** 167
Lie Down in Darkness (Styron), **IV:** 98, 99, 100–104, 105, 111; **Supp. XI:** 343
Lie of the Mind, A (Shepard), **Supp. III Part 2:** 433, 435, 441, 447–449
"Lies" (Haines), **Supp. XII:** 204
Lies Like Truth (Clurman), **IV:** 385
Lieutenant, The (Dubus), **Supp. VII:** 78
"Life" (Wharton), **Retro. Supp. I:** 372
Life along the Passaic River (W. C. Williams), **Retro. Supp. I:** 423
Life Among the Savages (Jackson), **Supp. IX:** 115, 125
Life and Gabriella (Glasgow), **II:** 175, 176, 182–183, 184, 189
"Life and I" (Wharton), **Retro. Supp. I:** 360, 361, 362
"Life and Letters" (Epstein), **Supp. XIV:** 104–105
Life and Letters of Harrison Gray Otis, Federalist, 1765–1848, The (Morison), **Supp. I Part 2:** 480–481
Life and Letters of Sir Henry Wotton (L. P. Smith), **Supp. XIV:** 340–341
Life and Times of Frederick Douglass, Written by Himself, The (Douglass), **Supp. III Part 1:** 155, 159–163
Life and Writings of Horace McCoy, The (Wolfson), **Supp. XIII:** 172, 174
"Life as a Visionary Spirit" (Eberhart), **I:** 540, 541
"Life at Angelo's, A" (Benét), **Supp. XI:** 53
Life at Happy Knoll (Marquand), **III:** 50, 61
Life Before Man (Atwood), **Supp.**

XIII: 24–25

"Life Cycle of Common Man" (Nemerov), **III:** 278

"Lifecycle Stairmaster" (Karr), **Supp. XI:** 250

Life Estates (Hearon), **Supp. VIII:** 68–69

Life for Life's Sake (Aldington), **Supp. I Part 1:** 256

Life Full of Holes, A (Layachi), **Supp. IV Part 1:** 92

"Lifeguard" (Updike), **IV:** 226; **Retro. Supp. I:** 325

"Lifeguard, The" (Dickey), **Supp. IV Part 1:** 179–180

Life in the Clearings (Shields), **Supp. VII:** 313

"Life in the Country: A City Friend Asks, 'Is It Boring?'" (Paley), **Supp. VI:** 231

Life in the Forest (Levertov), **Supp. III Part 1:** 282–283

Life in the Iron Mills (Davis), **Supp. XIII:** 292, 295, 299, 305; **Supp. XVI:**79–82, 85–88, 91

Life in the Iron Mills and Other Stories (T. Olson, ed.), **Supp. XVI:**83

Life in the Theatre, A (Mamet), **Supp. XIV:**241, 255

Life Is a Miracle: An Essay Against Modern Superstition (Berry), **Supp. X:** 35

"Life Is Fine" (Hughes), **Supp. I Part 1:** 334, 338

"Life Is Motion" (Stevens), **IV:** 74

Life of Albert Gallatin, The (Adams), **I:** 6, 14

Life of an Ordinary Woman, The: Anne Ellis (A. Ellis), **Supp. XVI:**38

Life of Dryden (Johnson), **Retro. Supp. II:** 223

Life of Emily Dickinson, The (Sewall), **Retro. Supp. I:** 25

Life of Forms, The (Focillon), **IV:** 90

Life of Franklin Pierce (Hawthorne), **Retro. Supp. I:** 163

Life of George Cabot Lodge, The (Adams), **I:** 21

Life of George Washington (Irving), **II:** 314, 315–316

Life of Henry James (Edel), **Retro. Supp. I:** 224

"Life of Irony, The" (Bourne), **I:** 219

"Life of Lincoln West, The" (Brooks), **Supp. III Part 1:** 86

Life of Michelangelo (Grimm), **II:** 17

"Life of Nancy, The" (Jewett), **Retro. Supp. II:** 133, 144

Life of Oliver Goldsmith, The, with Selections from His Writings (Irving), **II:** 315

Life of Phips (Mather), **Supp. II Part 2:** 451, 452, 459

Life of Poetry, The (Rukeyser), **Supp. VI:** 271, 273, 275–276, 282, 283, 286

Life of Samuel Johnson (Boswell), **Supp. I Part 2:** 656

Life of Savage (Johnson), **Supp. I Part 2:** 523

Life of the Drama, The (Bentley), **IV:** 396

"Life of the Mind, The" (Kees), **Supp. XV:** 140

Life of the Right Reverend Joseph P. Machebeuf, The (Howlett), **Retro. Supp. I:** 17

Life of Thomas Paine, author of Rights of Men, With a Defence of his Writings (Chalmers), **Supp. I Part 2:** 514

Life of Thomas Paine, The (Cobbett), **Supp. I Part 2:** 517

"Life of Towne, The" (Carson), **Supp. XII:** 102

"Life on Beekman Place, A" (Naylor), **Supp. VIII:** 214

Life on the Hyphen: The Cuban-American Way (Firmat), **Supp. VIII:** 76; **Supp. XI:** 184

Life on the Mississippi (Twain), **I:** 209; **IV:** 198, 199; **Supp. I Part 2:** 440

"Life on the Rocks: The Galápagos" (Dillard), **Supp. VI:** 32

"Life Stories, East and West" (E. Hoffman), **Supp. XVI:**157

Life Story (Baker), **II:** 259

Life Studies (Lowell), **I:** 400; **II:** 384, 386, 543, 546–550, 551, 555; **Retro. Supp. II:** 180, 185, 186, 188, 189, 191; **Supp. I Part 2:** 543; **Supp. XI:** 240, 244, 250, 317; **Supp. XII:** 255; **Supp. XIV:**15; **Supp. XV:** 252

"Life Studies" (Lowell), **Retro. Supp. II:** 188

"Life Styles in the Golden Land" (Didion), **Supp. IV Part 1:** 200

"Life That Is, The" (Bryant), **Supp. I Part 1:** 169

"Life Work" (Stafford), **Supp. XI:** 329–330

"Life You Save May Be Your Own, The" (O'Connor), **III:** 344, 350, 354; **Retro. Supp. II:** 229, 230, 233

Lifshin, Lyn, **Supp. XVI:**37

"Lifting, The" (Olds), **Supp. X:** 210

"Ligeia" (Poe), **III:** 412, 414; **Retro. Supp. II:** 261, 270, 271, 275

Liggett, Walter W., **Supp. XIII:** 168

Light, James F., **IV:** 290; **Retro. Supp. II:** 325

Light around the Body, The (R. Bly), **Supp. IV Part 1:** 61–62, 62

"Light Comes Brighter, The" (Roethke), **III:** 529–530

"Light from Above" (Eberhart), **I:** 541

Light in August (Faulkner), **II:** 63–64, 65, 74; **IV:** 207; **Retro. Supp. I:** 82, 84, 85, 86, 89, 92; **Supp. XIV:**12

"Light Man, A" (James), **II:** 322; **Retro. Supp. I:** 219

"Lightning" (Barthelme), **Supp. IV Part 1:** 53

"Lightning" (Bynner), **Supp. XV:** 44

"Lightning" (Oliver), **Supp. VII:** 235

"Lightning, The" (Swenson), **Supp. IV Part 2:** 645

"Lightning Rod Man, The" (Melville), **III:** 90

"Light of the World, The" (Hemingway), **II:** 249

"Lights in the Windows" (Nye), **Supp. XIII:** 280

Light Verse and Satires (Bynner), **Supp. XV:** 52

Light Years (Salter), **Supp. IX:** 257–259

"LIKE, THIS IS WHAT I MEANT!" (Baraka), **Supp. II Part 1:** 59

"Like All the Other Nations" (Paley), **Supp. VI:** 220

"Like Decorations in a Nigger Cemetery" (Stevens), **IV:** 74, 79; **Retro. Supp. I:** 305

Like Ghosts of Eagles (Francis), **Supp. IX:** 86

"Like Life" (Moore), **Supp. X:** 163, 165, 172–173

Like Life: Stories (Moore), **Supp. X:** 163, 171–175, 177, 178

"Like Talk" (Mills), **Supp. XI:** 311

"Like the New Moon I Will Live My Life" (R. Bly), **Supp. IV Part 1:** 71

Li'l Abner (Capp), **IV:** 198

"Lilacs" (Lowell), **II:** 527

"Lilacs, The" (Wilbur), **Supp. III Part 2:** 557–558

"Lilacs for Ginsberg" (Stern), **Supp. IX:** 299

Liliom (Molnar), **Supp. XVI:**187

Lilith's Brood (O. Butler), **Supp. XIII:** 63

Lillabulero Press, **Supp. V:** 4, 5

Lillian Hellman (Adler), **Supp. I Part 1:** 297

Lillian Hellman (Falk), **Supp. I Part 1:** 297

Lillian Hellman: Playwright (Moody), **Supp. I Part 1:** 280

Lillo, George, **II:** 111, 112
"Lily Daw and the Three Ladies" (Welty), **IV:** 262
Lima, Agnes de, **I:** 231, 232
"Limbo: Altered States" (Karr), **Supp. XI:** 249–250
Lime Orchard Woman, The (Ríos), **Supp. IV Part 2:** 538, 547–550, 553
"Lime Orchard Woman, The" (Ríos), **Supp. IV Part 2:** 548
"Limits" (Emerson), **II:** 19
Lincoln, Abraham, **I:** 1, 4, 30; **II:** 8, 13, 135, 273, 555, 576; **III:** 576, 577, 580, 584, 587–590, 591; **IV:** 192, 195, 298, 347, 350, 444; **Supp. I Part 1:** 2, 8, 26, 309, 321; **Supp. I Part 2:** 379, 380, 382, 385, 390, 397, 399, 418, 424, 454, 456, 471, 472, 473, 474, 483, 579, 687; **Supp. VIII:** 108; **Supp. IX:** 15; **Supp. XIV:**73
Lincoln: A Novel (Vidal), **Supp. IV Part 2:** 677, 684, 685, 688, 689–690, 691, 692
Lincoln, Kenneth, **Supp. IV Part 1:** 329; **Supp. IV Part 2:** 507
Lincoln, Mrs. Thomas (Nancy Hanks), **III:** 587
Lincoln: The Man (Masters), **Supp. I Part 2:** 471, 473–474
Lincoln, Thomas, **III:** 587
"Lincoln Relics, The" (Kunitz), **Supp. III Part 1:** 269
Lindbergh, Charles A., **I:** 482
"Linden Branch, The" (MacLeish), **III:** 19, 20
Linden Hills (Naylor), **Supp. VIII:** 214, 218, 219–223
Linderman, Lawrence, **Supp. IV Part 2:** 579, 583, 585, 589
Lindner, April, **Supp. XV:** 111, 119
Lindsay, Howard, **III:** 284
Lindsay, John, **Supp. I Part 2:** 374
Lindsay, Mrs. Vachel (Elizabeth Connors), **Supp. I Part 2:** 398, 399, 473
Lindsay, Mrs. Vachel Thomas (Esther Catherine Frazee), **Supp. I Part 2:** 374, 375, 384–385, 398
Lindsay, Olive, **Supp. I Part 2:** 374, 375, 392
Lindsay, Vachel, **I:** 384; **II:** 263, 276, 530; **III:** 5, 505; **Retro. Supp. I:** 133; **Supp. I Part 1:** 324; **Supp. I Part 2:** 374–403, 454, 473, 474; **Supp. III Part 1:** 63, 71; **Supp. XV:** 293, 297, 299, 301, 306; **Supp. XVI:**184–185
Lindsay, Vachel Thomas, **Supp. I Part 2:** 374, 375

Lindsey, David, **Supp. XIV:**26
"Line, The" (Olds), **Supp. X:** 206
Lineage of Ragpickers, Songpluckers, Elegiasts, and Jewelers, A (Goldbarth), **Supp. XII:** 191
"Line of Least Resistance, The" (Wharton), **Retro. Supp. I:** 366
Line Out for a Walk, A: Familiar Essays (Epstein), **Supp. XIV:**107
"Liner Notes for the Poetically Unhep" (Hughes), **Retro. Supp. I:** 210
"Lines After Rereading T. S. Eliot" (Wright), **Supp. V:** 343
"Lines Composed a Few Miles Above Tintern Abbey" (Wordsworth), **Supp. III Part 1:** 12
"Lines for an Interment" (MacLeish), **III:** 15
"Lines for My Father" (Cullen), **Supp. IV Part 1:** 167
"Lines from Israel" (Lowell), **II:** 554
"Lines from Pietro Longhi" (Sobin), **Supp. XVI:**289
"Lines on Revisiting the Country" (Bryant), **Supp. I Part 1:** 164
"Lines Suggested by a Tennessee Song" (Agee), **I:** 28
"Line-Storm Song, A" (Frost), **Retro. Supp. I:** 127
"Lines Written at Port Royal" (Freneau), **Supp. II Part 1:** 264
"Lines Written in an Asylum" (Carruth), **Supp. XVI:**48
"Lines Written in Manassas," **Supp. XV:** 99–100
Lingeman, Richard, **Supp. X:** 82
Linn, Elizabeth. *See* Brown, Mrs. Charles Brockden (Elizabeth Linn)
Linn, John Blair, **Supp. I Part 1:** 145
Linnaeus, Carolus, **II:** 6; **Supp. I Part 1:** 245
"Linnets" (Levis), **Supp. XI:** 260, 261
"Linoleum Roses" (Cisneros), **Supp. VII:** 63, 66
Linotte: 1914–1920 (Nin), **Supp. X:** 193, 196, 197
Linschoten, Hans, **II:** 362, 363, 364
"Lion and Honeycomb" (Nemerov), **III:** 275, 278, 280
Lion and the Archer, The (Hayden), **Supp. II Part 1:** 366, 367
Lion and the Honeycomb, The (Blackmur), **Supp. II Part 1:** 91
Lion Country (Buechner), **Supp. XII:** 52, 53
Lionel Lincoln (Cooper), **I:** 339, 342
"Lion for Real, The" (Ginsberg), **Supp. II Part 1:** 320

Lionhearted, The: A Story about the Jews of Medieval England (Reznikoff), **Supp. XIV:**280, 289
Lion in the Garden (Meriweather and Millgate), **Retro. Supp. I:** 91
"Lionizing" (Poe), **III:** 411, 425
"Lions, Harts, and Leaping Does" (Powers), **III:** 356
Lions and Shadows: An Education in the Twenties (Isherwood), **Supp. XIV:**158, 159, 160, 162
"Lions in Sweden" (Stevens), **IV:** 79–80
Lipman, William R., **Supp. XIII:** 170
Li Po, **Supp. XI:** 241; **Supp. XII:** 218; **Supp. XV:** 47, 217
Lippmann, Walter, **I:** 48, 222–223, 225; **III:** 291, 600; **IV:** 429; **Supp. I Part 2:** 609, 643; **Supp. VIII:** 104
Lips Together, Teeth Apart (McNally), **Supp. XIII:** 201–202, 208, 209
Lipsyte, Robert, **Supp. XVI:**220
Lipton, James, **Supp. IV Part 2:** 576, 577, 579, 583, 586, 588
Lipton, Lawrence, **Supp. IX:** 3
Lisbon Traviata, The (McNally), **Supp. XIII:** 198, 199–200, 201, 204, 208
Lisicky, Paul, **Supp. XI:** 120, 131, 135
"Lisp, The" (Olds), **Supp. X:** 211
Listen, Ruben Fontanez (Neugeboren), **Supp. XVI:**220–221
"Listeners and Readers: The Unforgetting of Vachel Lindsay" (Trombly), **Supp. I Part 2:** 403
"Listening" (Paley), **Supp. VI:** 218, 231, 232
"Listening" (Stafford), **Supp. XI:** 321, 322
Listening to Prozac (P. Kramer), **Supp. XVI:**229
"Listening to the Desert" (Henderson), **Supp. XIII:** 221–222
"Listening to the Mockingbird" (Woodard), **Supp. VIII:** 128
Listening to Your Life: Daily Meditations with Frederick Buechner (Buechner), **Supp. XII:** 53
Listen to the Desert/Oye al desierto (Mora), **Supp. XIII:** 221
"Listen to the People" (Benét), **Supp. XI:** 51–52
Liston, Sonny, **III:** 38, 42
Li T'ai-po, **II:** 526
"Litany" (Ashbery), **Supp. III Part 1:** 21–22, 25, 26
"Litany" (Sandburg), **III:** 593
"Litany, The" (Gioia), **Supp. XV:** 125, 126
"Litany for Dictatorships" (Benét), **Supp. XI:** 46, 58

"Litany for Survival, A" (Lorde), **Supp. XII:** 220

"Litany of the Dark People, The" (Cullen), **Supp. IV Part 1:** 170, 171

"Litany of the Heroes" (Lindsay), **Supp. I Part 2:** 397

"Litany of Washington Street, The" (Lindsay), **Supp. I Part 2:** 376, 398–399

Literary Anthropology (Trumpener and Nyce), **Retro. Supp. I:** 380

Literary Art and Activism of Rick Bass, The (Weltzien), **Supp. XVI:**20–21

"Literary Blacks and Jews" (Ozick), **Supp. V:** 272

"Literary Career of Elizabeth Barstow Stoddard, The" (Matlack), **Supp. XV:** 269

Literary Criticism: A Short History (Brooks and Wimsatt), **Supp. XIV:**12

"Literary Criticism of Georg Lukács, The" (Sontag), **Supp. III Part 2:** 453

Literary Essays of Thomas Merton, The, **Supp. VIII:** 207

"Literary Folk As They Came and Went with Ourselves" (E. Stoddard), **Supp. XV:** 274

Literary Friends and Acquaintance (Howells), **Supp. I Part 1:** 318; **Supp. XV:** 287

"Literary Heritage of Tennyson, The" (Locke), **Supp. XIV:**197

Literary History of the United States (Spiller et al., ed.), **Supp. I Part 1:** 104; **Supp. II Part 1:** 95

"Literary Importation" (Freneau), **Supp. II Part 1:** 264

"Literary Life of America, The" (Brooks), **I:** 245

Literary Outlaw: The Life and Times of William S. Burroughs (Morgan), **Supp. XIV:**141

Literary Situation, The (Cowley), **Supp. II Part 1:** 135, 140, 144, 146, 147, 148

"Literary Worker's Polonius, The" (Wilson), **IV:** 431, 432

"Literature" (Emerson), **II:** 6

Literature (X. J. Kennedy), **Supp. XV:** 153

Literature and American Life (Boynton), **Supp. I Part 2:** 415

Literature and Life (Howells), **Supp. XIV:**45–46

Literature and Morality (Farrell), **II:** 49

"Literature and Place: Varieties of Regional Experience" (Erisman),

Supp. VIII: 126

"Literature as a Symptom" (Warren), **IV:** 237

"Literature of Exhaustion, The" (Barth), **Supp. IV Part 1:** 48

"Lithuanian Nocturne" (Brodsky), **Supp. VIII:** 29

"Lit Instructor" (Stafford), **Supp. XI:** 321

Littauer, Kenneth, **Retro. Supp. I:** 114

Little Big Man (Berger), **Supp. XII:** 171

Little Big Man (film), **Supp. X:** 124

Littlebird, Harold, **Supp. IV Part 2:** 499

Littlebird, Larry, **Supp. IV Part 2:** 499, 505

Little Birds: Erotica (Nin), **Supp. X:** 192, 195

"Little Brown Baby" (Dunbar), **Supp. II Part 1:** 206

"Little Brown Jug" (Baraka), **Supp. II Part 1:** 51

"Little Clown, My Heart" (Cisneros), **Supp. VII:** 71

"Little Cosmic Dust Poem" (Haines), **Supp. XII:** 209–210

"Little Country Girl, A" (Chopin), **Retro. Supp. II:** 71

"Little Curtis" (Parker), **Supp. IX:** 193

Little Disturbances of Man, The (Paley), **Supp. VI:** 218

"Little Dog" (Hughes), **Supp. I Part 1:** 329

Little Dorrit (Dickens), **Supp. I Part 1:** 35

"Little Edward" (Stowe), **Supp. I Part 2:** 587

"Little Elegy" (X. J. Kennedy), **Supp. XV:** 155

Little Essays Drawn from the Writings of George Santayana (L. P. Smith), **Supp. XIV:**342

"Little Expressionless Animals" (Wallace), **Supp. X:** 305

"Little Fable" (Hay), **Supp. XIV:**131

Littlefield, Catherine, **Supp. IX:** 58

Little Foxes, The (Hellman), **Supp. I Part 1:** 276, 278–279, 281, 283, 297

"Little Fred, the Canal Boy" (Stowe), **Supp. I Part 2:** 587

"Little French Mary" (Jewett), **II:** 400

Little Friend, Little Friend (Jarrell), **II:** 367, 372, 375–376

"Little Gidding" (Eliot), **I:** 582, 588; **II:** 539; **Retro. Supp. I:** 66

"Little Girl, My Stringbean, My Lovely Woman" (Sexton), **Supp. II Part 2:** 686

"Little Girl, The" (Paley), **Supp. VI:**

222, 228–229

"Little Girl Tells a Story to a Lady, A" (Barnes), **Supp. III Part 1:** 36

"Little Goose Girl, The" (Grimm), **IV:** 266

Little Ham (Hughes), **Retro. Supp. I:** 203; **Supp. I Part 1:** 328, 339

Little King, The (Bynner), **Supp. XV:** 42, 50

Little Lady of the Big House, The (London), **II:** 481–482

Little Liar, The (film; Ingraham), **Supp. XVI:**184–185

"Little Lion Face" (Swenson), **Supp. IV Part 2:** 651

"Little Lobelia's Song" (Bogan), **Supp. III Part 1:** 66

"Little Local Color, A" (Henry), **Supp. II Part 1:** 399

Little Lord Fauntleroy (Burnett), **Retro. Supp. I:** 188; **Supp. XVI:**182

"Little Lyric" (Hughes), **Supp. I Part 1:** 334

Little Man, Little Man (Baldwin), **Supp. I Part 1:** 67

"Little Man at Chehaw Station, The" (Ellison), **Retro. Supp. II:** 123

Little Me (musical), **Supp. IV Part 2:** 575

Little Men (Alcott), **Supp. I Part 1:** 32, 39, 40

"Little Morning Music, A" (Schwartz), **Supp. II Part 2:** 662–663

Little Ocean (Shepard), **Supp. III Part 2:** 447

"Little Old Girl, A" (Larcom), **Supp. XIII:** 144

"Little Old Spy" (Hughes), **Supp. I Part 1:** 329

"Little Owl Who Lives in the Orchard" (Oliver), **Supp. VII:** 239

"Little Peasant, The" (Sexton), **Supp. II Part 2:** 690

"Little Rapids, The" (Swenson), **Supp. IV Part 2:** 645

Little Regiment and Other Episodes of the American Civil War, The (Crane), **I:** 408

Little River: New and Selected Poems (McCarriston), **Supp. XIV:**269–272

"Little Road not made of Man , A" (Dickinson), **Retro. Supp. I:** 44

Little Sister, The (Chandler), **Supp. IV Part 1:** 122, 130, 131–132

"Little Sleep's-Head Sprouting Hair in the Moonlight" (Kinnell), **Supp. III Part 1:** 247

"Little Snow White" (Grimm), **IV:** 266

"Little Testament of Bernard Martin,

Aet. 30" (Mumford), **Supp. II Part 2:** 472, 473, 474

"Little Things" (Olds), **Supp. X:** 208

Little Tour in France (James), **II:** 337

Little Women (Alcott), **Supp. I Part 1:** 28, 29, 32, 35, 37, 38, 39–40, 41, 43, 44; **Supp. IX:** 128

Little Yellow Dog, A (Mosley), **Supp. XIII:** 237, 241

"Liturgy and Spiritual Personalism" (Merton), **Supp. VIII:** 199

Litz, A. Walton, **Retro. Supp. I:** 306

"Liu Ch'e" (Pound), **III:** 466

"Live" (Sexton), **Supp. II Part 2:** 684, 686

Live from Baghdad (screenplay, Shanley), **Supp. XIV:**316

Live from Golgotha (Vidal), **Supp. IV Part 2:** 677, 682, 691, 692

Live Now and Pay Later (Garrett), **Supp. VII:** 111

"Live-Oak with Moss" (Whitman), **Retro. Supp. I:** 403

Live or Die (Sexton), **Supp. II Part 2:** 670, 683–687

Liveright, Horace, **Retro. Supp. I:** 80, 81, 83; **Supp. I Part 2:** 464

Lives (Plutarch), **II:** 5, 104

Lives of a Cell, The (L. Thomas), **Retro. Supp. I:** 322, 323

Lives of Distinguished American Naval Officers (Cooper), **I:** 347

"Lives of Gulls and Children, The" (Nemerov), **III:** 271, 272

Lives of the Artists (Vasari), **Supp. I Part 2:** 450

Lives of the Muses, The: Nine Women and the Artists They Inspired (Prose), **Supp. XVI:**250, 260

Lives of the Poets (Doctorow), **Supp. IV Part 1:** 234

"Lives of the Poets" (Doctorow), **Supp. IV Part 1:** 234

"Lives of the—Wha'?, The" (Goldbarth), **Supp. XII:** 191

"Living" (Wright), **Supp. XV:** 345

Living, The (Dillard), **Supp. VI:** 23

"Living at Home" (Gordon), **Supp. IV Part 1:** 311

Living by Fiction (Dillard), **Supp. VI:** 23, 31, 32, 33

Living by the Word (Walker), **Supp. III Part 2:** 521, 522, 526, 527, 535

Living End, The (Elkin), **Supp. VI:** 54, 58

"Living in the Flatlands" (Carruth), **Supp. XVI:**54

"Living Like Weasels" (Dillard), **Supp. VI:** 26, 33

Living Novel, The (Hicks), **III:** 342

Living of Charlotte Perkins Gilman, The (Gilman), **Supp. XI:** 193, 209

Living off the Country: Essays on Poetry and Place (Haines), **Supp. XII:** 199, 203, 207

"Living on a Giant" (X. J. Kennedy), **Supp. XV:** 163

Living Reed, The (Buck), **Supp. II Part 1:** 129–130

Livingston, Myra Cohn, **Supp. XV:** 153, 162

Living Theater, **Retro. Supp. I:** 424

"Living There" (Dickey), **Supp. IV Part 1:** 182–183

Living the Spirit: A Gay American Indian Anthology (Roscoe, ed.), **Supp. IV Part 1:** 330

"Living with a Peacock" (O'Connor), **III:** 350

"Livvie" (Welty), **IV:** 265; **Retro. Supp. I:** 348–349

"Livvie Is Back" (Welty), **Retro. Supp. I:** 351

Livy, **II:** 8

Lizzie (film), **Supp. IX:** 125

"Llantos de La Llorona: Warnings from the Wailer" (Mora), **Supp. XIII:** 217, 224

"L'Lapse" (Barthelme), **Supp. IV Part 1:** 45–47, 48

Lloyd, Henry Demarest, **Supp. I Part 1:** 5

Lloyd George, Harold, **I:** 490

"LMFBR" (Snyder), **Supp. VIII:** 302

"Loam" (Sandburg), **III:** 584–585

"Loan, The" (Malamud), **Supp. I Part 2:** 427, 428, 431, 437

Loberer, Eric, **Supp. XV:** 339

"Local" (McCarriston), **Supp. XIV:**270

Local Color (Capote), **Supp. III Part 1:** 120

"Local Color" (London), **II:** 475

"Local Family Keeps Son Happy" (Keillor), **Supp. XVI:**168, 169

Local Girls (Hoffman), **Supp. X:** 77, 90–91, 92

"Local Girls" (Hoffman), **Supp. X:** 90

Local Men (Whitehead), **Supp. XV:** 339

Local Time (Dunn), **Supp. XI:** 143, 148–149

Lock, Helen, **Supp. XIII:** 233, 237–238

Lock, Robert H., **IV:** 319; **Retro. Supp. I:** 375

Locke, Alain, **Retro. Supp. II:** 115; **Supp. I Part 1:** 323, 325, 341; **Supp. II Part 1:** 53, 176, 182, 228, 247; **Supp. IV Part 1:** 170; **Supp. IX:** 306, 309; **Supp. X:** 134, 137, 139; **Supp. XIV:**195–219

Locke, Duane, **Supp. IX:** 273

Locke, John, **I:** 554–555, 557; **II:** 15–16, 113–114, 348–349, 480; **III:** 294–295; **IV:** 149; **Supp. I Part 1:** 130, 229, 230; **Supp. I Part 2:** 523

Locke, Sondra, **II:** 588

"Locked House, A" (Snodgrass), **Supp. VI:** 323

Locked Room, The (Auster), **Supp. XII:** 22, 24, 27–28

Locket, The (Masters), **Supp. I Part 2:** 460

"Locksley Hall" (Tennyson), **Supp. IX:** 19

Lockwood Concern, The (O'Hara), **III:** 362, 364, 377–382

"Locus" (Ammons), **Supp. VII:** 28

"Locus" (Hayden), **Supp. II Part 1:** 361–362, 381

"Locusts, the Plaza, the Room, The" (Kees), **Supp. XV:** 141

Loden, Barbara, **III:** 163

Lodge, Henry Cabot, **I:** 11–12, 21

Lodge, Mrs. Henry Cabot, **I:** 11–12, 19

Lodge, Thomas, **IV:** 370

Loeb, Gerald, **Supp. IV Part 2:** 523

Loeb, Jacques, **I:** 513; **Retro. Supp. II:** 104; **Supp. I Part 2:** 641

Loeffler, Jack, **Supp. XIII:** 1, 3, 12, 14, 16

"Log" (Merrlll), **Supp. III Part 1:** 328

Logan, Rayford W., **Supp. II Part 1:** 171, 194; **Supp. XIV:**73

Logan, William, **Supp. X:** 201, 213; **Supp. XI:** 131, 132; **Supp. XII:** 98, 107, 113, 184; **Supp. XV:** 212, 226, 251, 257, 260–261, 262,**Supp. XV:** 263, 266

Log Book of "The Loved One," The, **Supp. XI:** 306

"Logging and Pimping and 'Your Pal, Jim' " (Maclean), **Supp. XIV:**229

Logue, Christopher, **Supp. XIV:**82

Lohengrin (Wagner), **I:** 216

Lohrfinck, Rosalind, **III:** 107, 117

Lolita (Nabokov), **III:** 246, 247, 255, 258–261; **Retro. Supp. I:** 263, 264, 265, 266, 269, 270, 272–274, 275; **Supp. V:** 127, 252; **Supp. VIII:** 133; **Supp. XVI:**294

"Lolita" (Parker), **Supp. IX:** 193

Lolly Dinks' Doings (E. Stoddard), **Supp. XV:** 273,**Supp. XV:** 286

Lombardi, Marilyn May, **Retro. Supp. II:** 40

London, Eliza, **II:** 465

London, Jack, **I:** 209; **II:** 264, 440, 444, 451, 462–485; **III:** 314, 580;

Supp. IV Part 1: 236; **Supp. V:** 281; **Supp. IX:** 1, 14; **Supp. XIII:** 312; **Supp. XIV:**227; **Supp. XV:** 115; **Supp. XVI:**181

London, John, **II:** 464, 465

London, Mrs. Jack (Bessie Maddern), **II:** 465, 466, 473, 478

London, Mrs. Jack (Charmian Kittredge), **II:** 466, 468, 473, 476, 478, 481

London, Scott, **Supp. XIV:**301, 307, 311

London Embassy, The (Theroux), **Supp. VIII:** 323

London Fields (Amis), **Retro. Supp. I:** 278

"London Letter" (column; Eliot), **Supp. XV:** 306

London Magazine (Plath), **Supp. I Part 2:** 541

London Snow: A Christmas Story (Theroux), **Supp. VIII:** 322

London Suite (Simon), **Supp. IV Part 2:** 576, 581, 582, 588

Lonely Are the Brave (film), **Supp. XIII:** 6

"Lonely Coast, A" (Proulx), **Supp. VII:** 264

Lonely Crusade (C. Himes), **Supp. XVI:**135, 139–140

Lonely for the Future (Farrell), **II:** 46, 47

Lonely Impulse of Delight, A (Shanley), **Supp. XIV:**317–318

"Lonely Street, The" (W. C. Williams), **IV:** 413

"Lonely Worker, A" (Jewett), **Retro. Supp. II:** 132

Lonergan, Wayne, **Supp. I Part 1:** 51

Lonesome Dove (McMurtry), **Supp. V:** 226–228, 231, 232, 233

Lonesome Traveler (Kerouac), **Supp. III Part 1:** 219, 225

"Lonesome Whistle Blowing" (Skow), **Supp. XVI:**174

"Lone Striker, A" (Frost), **Retro. Supp. I:** 136, 137

Long, Ada, **Supp. V:** 178

Long, Haniel, **Supp. XV:** 46, 49

Long, Huey, **I:** 489; **II:** 454; **IV:** 249; **Supp. IV Part 2:** 679; **Supp. XIV:**14

Long, Ray, **II:** 430; **III:** 54

Long after Midnight (Bradbury), **Supp. IV Part 1:** 102

Long and Happy Life, A (Price), **Supp. VI:** 258, 259–260, 262, 264, 265

Long Approach, The (Kumin), **Supp. IV Part 2:** 452–453, 453

Long Christmas Dinner, The (Wilder), **IV:** 357, 365; **Supp. V:** 105

Long Christmas Dinner and Other Plays (Wilder), **IV:** 365–366

Long Day's Dying, A (Buechner), **Supp. XII:** 45–47

Long Day's Journey into Night (O'Neill), **III:** 385, 401, 403–404; **Supp. IV Part 1:** 359; **Supp. XIV:**327

Long Desire, A (Connell), **Supp. XIV:**79, 80, 97

"Long Distance" (Stafford), **Supp. XI:** 329

"Long-Distance Runner, The" (Paley), **Supp. VI:** 221–222, 228, 230

Long Dream, The (Wright), **IV:** 478, 488, 494

"Long Embrace, The" (Levine), **Supp. V:** 187

"Long Enough" (Rukeyser), **Supp. VI:** 274

"Longest Night of My Life, The " (Nichols), **Supp. XIII:** 269

Longfellow, Henry Wadsworth, **I:** 458, 471; **II:** 274, 277, 295–296, 310, 313, 402, 486–510; **III:** 269, 412, 421, 422, 577; **IV:** 309, 371; **Retro. Supp. I:** 54, 123, 150, 155, 362; **Retro. Supp. II:** 153–174; **Supp. I Part 1:** 158, 299, 306, 317, 362, 368; **Supp. I Part 2:** 405, 406, 408, 409, 414, 416, 420, 586, 587, 602, 699, 704; **Supp. II Part 1:** 291, 353; **Supp. III Part 2:** 609; **Supp. IV Part 1:** 165; **Supp. IV Part 2:** 503; **Supp. XII:** 260; **Supp. XIII:** 141; **Supp. XIV:**120

"Long Feud" (Untermeyer), **Supp. XV:** 309

Long Feud: Selected Poems (Untermeyer), **Supp. XV:** 312

"Long Fourth, A" (Taylor), **Supp. V:** 313

Long Fourth and Other Stories, A (Taylor), **Supp. V:** 318–319

Long Gay Book, A (Stein), **IV:** 42

Long Goodbye, The (Chandler), **Supp. IV Part 1:** 120, 122, 132–134, 135

Long Goodbye, The (T. Williams), **IV:** 381

"Long Hair" (Snyder), **Supp. VIII:** 300

Longing for Home, The: Recollections and Reflections (Buechner), **Supp. XII:** 53

Longinus, Dionysius Cassius, **I:** 279

"Long-Legged House, The" (Berry), **Supp. X:** 21, 24–25, 27, 31

Long Live Man (Corso), **Supp. XII:** 129–130, 132

Long Love, The (Sedges), **Supp. II Part 1:** 125

Long Made Short (Dixon), **Supp. XII:** 152

Long March, The (Styron), **IV:** 97, 99, 104–107, 111, 113, 117

"Long Night, The" (Bambara), **Supp. XI:** 9

"Long Novel, A" (Ashbery), **Supp. III Part 1:** 6

Longo, Robert, **Supp. XVI:**124

Long Patrol, The (Mailer), **III:** 46

"Long Point Light" (Doty), **Supp. XI:** 127

Long Road of Woman's Memory, The (Addams), **Supp. I Part 1:** 17–18

"Long Run, The" (Wharton), **IV:** 314

Long Season, The (Brosnan), **II:** 424, 425

"Long Shadow of Lincoln, The: A Litany" (Sandburg), **III:** 591, 593

Longshot O'Leary (McGrath), **Supp. X:** 117

"Long Shower, The" (Francis), **Supp. IX:** 90

Longstreet, Augustus B., **II:** 70, 313; **Supp. I Part 1:** 352; **Supp. V:** 44; **Supp. X:** 227

"Long Summer" (Lowell), **II:** 553–554

"Long Term" (Dunn), **Supp. XI:** 149

Longtime Companion (film), **Supp. X:** 146, 152

Long Valley, The (Steinbeck), **IV:** 51

Long Voyage Home, The (O'Neill), **III:** 388

"Long Wail, A" (Crews), **Supp. XI:** 101

"Long Walk, The" (Bogan), **Supp. III Part 1:** 61

Long Walks and Intimate Talks (Paley), **Supp. VI:** 221

Long Way from Home, A (McKay), **Supp. X:** 132, 140

Lönnrot, Elias, **Retro. Supp. II:** 159

Looby, Christopher, **Supp. XIII:** 96

Look, Stranger! (Auden), **Supp. II Part 1:** 11

"Look, The" (Olds), **Supp. X:** 210

Look at the Harlequins (Nabokov), **Retro. Supp. I:** 266, 270

"Look for My White Self" (Ammons), **Supp. VII:** 25

Look Homeward, Angel (Wolfe), **II:** 457; **IV:** 450, 452, 453, 454, 455–456, 461, 462, 463, 464, 468, 471; **Supp. XI:** 216

"Looking" (Sanders), **Supp. XVI:**277

"Looking a Mad Dog Dead in the Eyes" (Komunyakaa), **Supp. XIII:** 114

"Looking at Each Other" (Rukeyser), **Supp. VI:** 280, 285–286

"Looking at Kafka" (Roth), **Supp. III Part 2:** 402

"Looking at Women" (Sanders), **Supp. XVI:** 274

"Looking Back" (Harjo), **Supp. XII:** 218

"Looking Back" (Merwin), **Supp. III Part 1:** 352

"Looking Back at Girlhood" (Jewett), **Retro. Supp. II:** 131, 133

Looking Backward (Bellamy), **II:** 276; **Supp. I Part 2:** 641; **Supp. XI:** 200

"Looking for a Ship" (McPhee), **Supp. III Part 1:** 312–313

"Looking for Dragon Smoke" (R. Bly), **Supp. IV Part 1:** 60

Looking for Holes in the Ceiling (Dunn), **Supp. XI:** 139, 143–145

Looking for Langston (Julien; film), **Supp. XI:** 19, 20

Looking for Luck (Kumin), **Supp. IV Part 2:** 453, 454–455

"Looking for Mr. Green" (Bellow), **Retro. Supp. II:** 27

"Looking for the Buckhead Boys" (Dickey), **Supp. IV Part 1:** 182, 183

"Looking Forward to Age" (Harrison), **Supp. VIII:** 49

"Looking from Inside My Body" (R. Bly), **Supp. IV Part 1:** 71

"Looking Glass, The" (Wharton), **Retro. Supp. I:** 382

"Lookout's Journal" (Snyder), **Supp. VIII:** 291

"Looks Like They'll Never Learn" (McCoy), **Supp. XIII:** 166

"Look to Thy Heart . . ." (Hay), **Supp. XIV:** 130

Loon, Hendrik Willem van, **Supp. XVI:** 185

Loon Lake (Doctorow), **Supp. IV Part 1:** 219, 222, 224–227, 230, 231, 232, 233

"Loon Point" (O'Brien), **Supp. V:** 237

Loos, Adolf, **Supp. XVI:** 187

Loos, Anita, **Supp. XVI:** 181–199

Loos, Mary Anita, **Supp. XVI:** 196

Loosestrife (Dunn), **Supp. XI:** 152–154

"Loosestrife" (Dunn), **Supp. XI:** 154

"Loose Woman" (X. J. Kennedy), **Supp. XV:** 159

Loose Woman: Poems (Cisneros), **Supp. VII:** 58, 71–72

Lopate, Edward, **Supp. XVI:** 266

Lopate, Philip, **Supp. XII:** 184; **Supp. XIII:** 280–281; **Supp. XVI:** 230

Lopatnikoff, Nikolai, **Supp. XIV:** 123

Lopez, Barry, **Supp. IV Part 1:** 416; **Supp. V:** 211; **Supp. X:** 29, 31; **Supp. XIII:** 16; **Supp. XIV:** 227

Lopez, Rafael, **Supp. IV Part 2:** 602

Lorax, The (Geisel), **Supp. XVI:** 109–110

Lorca, Federico García, **IV:** 380; **Supp. I Part 1:** 345; **Supp. IV Part 1:** 83; **Supp. VIII:** 38, 39; **Supp. XIII:** 315, 323, 324; **Supp. XV:** 186

Lord, Judge Otis P., **I:** 454, 457, 458, 470

Lorde, Audre, **Supp. I Part 2:** 550, 571; **Supp. IV Part 1:** 325; **Supp. XI:** 20; **Supp. XII:** 217, 220; **Supp. XIII:** 295

Lord Jim (Conrad), **I:** 422; **II:** 26; **Retro. Supp. II:** 292; **Supp. I Part 2:** 623; **Supp. IV Part 2:** 680; **Supp. V:** 251

"Lord of Hosts" (Pinsky), **Supp. VI:** 244

Lord of the Flies (W. Golding), **Supp. XVI:** 65

Lord of the Rings (Tolkien), **Supp. V:** 140

Lords of Misrule, The (X. J. Kennedy), **Supp. XV:** 154, 170–171

Lords of the Housetops (Van Vechten), **Supp. II Part 2:** 736

Lord's Prayer, **I:** 579

Lord Timothy Dexter of Newburyport, Mass. (Marquand), **III:** 55

Lord Weary's Castle (Lowell), **II:** 538, 542–551; **Retro. Supp. II:** 178, 186–187, 188; **Supp. XV:** 252

"Lorelei" (Plath), **Retro. Supp. II:** 246; **Supp. I Part 2:** 538

"Lorenzo" (Bynner), **Supp. XV:** 46, 50

Lorimer, George Horace, **II:** 430; **Retro. Supp. I:** 101, 113

Lorre, Peter, **Supp. IV Part 1:** 356

"Los Alamos" (Momaday), **Supp. IV Part 2:** 482

"Los Angeles, 1980" (Gunn Allen), **Supp. IV Part 1:** 325

"Los Angeles Days" (Didion), **Supp. IV Part 1:** 211

Losey, Joseph, **IV:** 383

"Losing a Language" (Merwin), **Supp. III Part 1:** 356

Losing Battles (Welty), **IV:** 261, 281–282; **Retro. Supp. I:** 341, 352, 353–354

"Losing the Marbles" (Merrill), **Supp. III Part 1:** 337

"Losing Track of Language" (Clampitt), **Supp. IX:** 38, 40

Losses (Jarrell), **II:** 367, 372, 373–375, 376, 377, 380–381

"Losses" (Jarrell), **II:** 375–376

Lossky, N. O., **Supp. IV Part 2:** 519

"Loss of Breath" (Poe), **III:** 425–426

"Loss of My Arms and Legs, The" (Kingsolver), **Supp. VII:** 208

"Loss of the Creature, The" (Percy), **Supp. III Part 1:** 387

"Lost" (Wagoner), **Supp. IX:** 328

"Lost, The/Los Perdidos" (Kingsolver), **Supp. VII:** 208

"Lost and Found" (Levine), **Supp. V:** 188

"Lost Bodies" (Wright), **Supp. V:** 342

"Lost Boy, The" (Wolfe), **IV:** 451, 460, 466–467

"Lost Decade, The" (Fitzgerald), **II:** 98

Lost Galleon and Other Tales, The (Harte), **Supp. II Part 1:** 344

Lost Get-Back Boogie, The (Burke), **Supp. XIV:** 22, 25

"Lost Girls, The" (Hogan), **Supp. IV Part 1:** 406–407

Lost Grizzlies, The: A Search for Survivors in the Wilderness of Colorado (Bass), **Supp. XVI:** 25, 26

Lost Highway (film), **Supp. X:** 314

Lost Illusions (Balzac), **I:** 500

"Lost in Nostalgia: The Autobiographies of Eva Hoffman and Richard Rodriguez" (Fachinger), **Supp. XVI:** 153

Lost in the Bonewheel Factory (Komunyakaa), **Supp. XIII:** 114–115, 116

Lost in the Cosmos: The Last Self-Help Book (Percy), **Supp. III Part 1:** 397

Lost in the Funhouse (Barth), **I:** 122, 135, 139; **Supp. X:** 307

"Lost in the Whichy Thicket" (Wolfe), **Supp. III Part 2:** 573, 574

Lost in Translation (E. Hoffman), **Supp. XVI:** 147, 148–151, 153, 154, 159

"Lost in Translation" (Hass), **Supp. VIII:** 28

"Lost in Translation" (Merrill), **Supp. III Part 1:** 324, 329–330

Lost in Yonkers (film), **Supp. IV Part 2:** 588

Lost in Yonkers (Simon), **Supp. IV Part 2:** 576, 577, 584, 587–588, 590–591

"Lost Jerusalem" (Untermeyer), **Supp. XV:** 307

Lost Lady, A (Cather), **I:** 323–325, 327; **Retro. Supp. I:** 15–16, 20, 21, 382

"Lost Lover, A" (Jewett), **II:** 400–401, 402; **Retro. Supp. II:** 137

"Lost Loves" (Kinnell), **Supp. III Part 1:** 237, 245

Lost Man's River (Matthiessen), **Supp. V:** 212, 213, 214, 215

"Lost on September Trail, 1967" (Ríos), **Supp. IV Part 2:** 540

Lost Puritan (Mariani), **Retro. Supp. II:** 189

Lost Roads Project, The: A Walk-In Book of Arkansas (exhibition; Wright and Luster), **Supp. XV:** 337, 348

"Lost Sailor, The" (Freneau), **Supp. II Part 1:** 264

Lost Son, The (Roethke), **III:** 529, 530–532, 533

"Lost Son, The" (Roethke), **III:** 536, 537–539, 542

"Lost Sons" (Salter), **Supp. IX:** 260

Lost Souls (Singer). *See* Meshugah (Singer)

Lost Weekend, The (Jackson), **Supp. XIII:** 262

"Lost World, A" (Ashbery), **Supp. III Part 1:** 9

"Lost World, The" (Chabon), **Supp. XI:** 72–73

Lost World, The (Jarrell), **II:** 367, 368, 371, 379–380, 386, 387

"Lost World, The" cycle (Chabon), **Supp. XI:** 71–73

"Lost World of Richard Yates, The: How the Great Writer of the Age of Anxiety Disappeared from Print" (O'Nan), **Supp. XI:** 348

"Lost Young Intellectual, The" (Howe), **Supp. VI:** 113, 115–116

Lost Zoo, The: (A Rhyme for the Young, But Not Too Young) (Cullen), **Supp. IV Part 1:** 173

Loti, Pierre, **II:** 311, 325; **Supp. IV Part 1:** 81

"Lot of People Bathing in a Stream, A" (Stevens), **IV:** 93

Lotringer, Sylvère, **Supp. XII:** 4

"Lot's Wife" (Nemerov), **III:** 270

"Lottery, The" (Jackson), **Supp. IX:** 113, 114, 118, 120, 122–123

Lottery, The; or, The Adventures of James Harris (Jackson), **Supp. IX:** 113, 115, 116, 124, 125

Lotze, Hermann, **III:** 600

"Louie, His Cousin & His Other Cousin" (Cisneros), **Supp. VII:** 60

Louis, Joe, **II:** 589; **Supp. IV Part 1:** 360

Louis, Pierre Charles Alexandre, **Supp. I Part 1:** 302, 303

"Louisa, Please Come Home"

(Jackson), **Supp. IX:** 122

Louis Lambert (Balzac), **I:** 499

"Louis Simpson and Walt Whitman: Destroying the Teacher" (Lazer), **Supp. IX:** 265

"*Louis Zukofsky: All: The Collected Short Poems, 1923–1958*" (Creeley), **Supp. IV Part 1:** 154

"Lounge" (Francis), **Supp. IX:** 83

Lounsbury, Thomas R., **I:** 335

Louter, Jan, **Supp. XI:** 173

"Love" (Olson), **Supp. II Part 2:** 571

"Love" (Paley), **Supp. VI:** 219, 222, 230

Love, Deborah, **Supp. V:** 208, 210

Love Alone: 18 Elegies for Rog (Monette), **Supp. X:** 146, 154

Love Always (Beattie), **Supp. V:** 29, 30, 35

Love among the Cannibals (Morris), **III:** 228, 230–231

"Love Among the Ruins" (Mosley), **Supp. XIII:** 247

Love and Death (film; Allen), **Supp. XV:** 2, 5–6, 7, 11

Love and Death in the American Novel (Fiedler), **Supp. XIII:** 93, 96, 99–101, 104

Love and Exile (Singer), **Retro. Supp. II:** 302–304, 315

Love and Fame (Berryman), **I:** 170

Love and Friendship (Bloom), **Retro. Supp. II:** 31, 33–34

"Love and How to Cure It" (Wilder), **IV:** 365

Love and Scorn: New and Selected Poems (C. Frost), **Supp. XV:** 95, 96, 100, 103–105, 106

"Love and the Hate, The" (Jeffers), **Supp. II Part 2:** 434–435

Love and Will (Dixon), **Supp. XII:** 148, 149

Love and Work (Price), **Supp. VI:** 261

"Love Calls Us to the Things of This World" (Wilbur), **Supp. III Part 2:** 544, 552–553

Love Course, The (Gurney), **Supp. V:** 98

Loved One, The (film), **Supp. XI:** 305–306, 307

Loved One, The (Waugh), **Supp. XI:** 305

Love Expert, The (film; Kirkland), **Supp. XVI:** 186

Love Feast (Buechner), **Supp. XII:** 52

"Love Fossil" (Olds), **Supp. X:** 203

Love in Buffalo (Gurney), **Supp. V:** 96

"Love—In Other Words" (Lee), **Supp. VIII:** 113

"Love in the Morning" (Dubus), **Supp. VII:** 91

Love in the Ruins: The Adventures of a Bad Catholic at a Time near the End of the World (Percy), **Supp. III Part 1:** 385, 387, 393–394, 397–398

Love in the Western World (de Rougemont), **Retro. Supp. I:** 328

"Love Is a Deep and a Dark and a Lonely" (Sandburg), **III:** 595

Lovejoy, Elijah P., **Supp. I Part 2:** 588

Lovejoy, Owen R., **Supp. I Part 1:** 8

Lovejoy, Thomas, **Supp. X:** 108

Lovelace, Richard, **II:** 590

"Love Letter (Schnackenberg), **Supp. XV:** 258–259

Love Letters (film), **Supp. IV Part 2:** 524

Love Letters (Gurney), **Supp. V:** 105, 108–109

Love Letters, The (Massie), **Supp. IV Part 2:** 524

Love Letters and Two Other Plays: The Golden Age and What I Did Last Summer (Gurney), **Supp. V:** 100

"Love Lies Sleeping" (Bishop), **Retro. Supp. II:** 42

Love Life (Mason), **Supp. VIII:** 145–146

"Love Life" (Mason), **Supp. VIII:** 145–146

Lovely Lady, The (Lawrence), **Retro. Supp. I:** 203

"Lovely Lady, The" (Lawrence), **Supp. I Part 1:** 329

Love Me (Keillor), **Supp. XVI:** 178

Love Medicine (Erdrich), **Supp. IV Part 1:** 259, 260, 261, 263, 265, 266, 267–268, 270, 271, 274–275; **Supp. X:** 290

Love Medicine (expanded version) (Erdrich), **Supp. IV Part 1:** 263, 273, 274, 275

"Love Nest, The" (Lardner), **II:** 427, 429

Love Nest, The, and Other Stories (Lardner), **II:** 430–431, 436

Lovenheim, Barbara, **Supp. X:** 169

"Love of Elsie Barton: A Chronicle, The" (Warren), **IV:** 253

Love of Landry, The (Dunbar), **Supp. II Part 1:** 212

"Love of Morning, The" (Levertov), **Supp. III Part 1:** 284

Love of the Last Tycoon, The: A Western. See Last Tycoon, The

"Love on the Bon Dieu" (Chopin), **Supp. I Part 1:** 213

Love Poems (Sexton), **Supp. II Part 2:** 687–689

Love Poems of May Swenson, The (Swenson), **Supp. IV Part 2:** 652, 653

"Love Poet" (Agee), **I:** 28

"Love Ritual" (Mora), **Supp. XIII:** 215

Loveroot (Jong), **Supp. V:** 115, 130

"Lovers, The" (Berryman), **I:** 174

"Lovers, The" (Buck), **Supp. II Part 1:** 128

"Lover's Garden, A" (Ginsberg), **Supp. II Part 1:** 311

"Lovers of the Poor, The" (Brooks), **Supp. III Part 1:** 81, 85

Lovers Should Marry (Martin), **Supp. IV Part 1:** 351

"Lover's Song" (Yeats), **Supp. I Part 1:** 80

"Love Rushes By" (Salinas), **Supp. XIII:** 326–327

Lovesick (Stern), **Supp. IX:** 295–296

Love's Labour's Lost (Shakespeare), **III:** 263

Love's Old Sweet Song (Saroyan), **Supp. IV Part 1:** 83

"Love Song of J. Alfred Prufrock, The" (Eliot), **I:** 52, 66, 569–570; **III:** 460; **Retro. Supp. I:** 55, 56, 57, 60; **Supp. II Part 1:** 5; **Supp. XIII:** 346

"Lovesong of J. Alfred Prufrock, The" (T. S. Eliot), **Supp. XVI:** 150

"Love Song of St. Sebastian" (Eliot), **Retro. Supp. I:** 57

Love's Pilgrimage (Sinclair), **Supp. V:** 286

"Love the Wild Swan" (Jeffers), **Supp. VIII:** 33

Love to Mamá: A Tribute to Mothers (Mora, ed.), **Supp. XIII:** 221

Lovett, Robert Morss, **II:** 43

"Love-Unknown" (Herbert), **Supp. I Part 1:** 80

Love! Valor! Compassion! (film), **Supp. XIII:** 206

Love! Valour! Compassion! (McNally), **Supp. XIII:** 199, 203–204, 208, 209

"Love *versus* Law" (Stowe), **Supp. I Part 2:** 585–586

Love with a Few Hairs (Mrabet), **Supp. IV Part 1:** 92

Loving a Woman in Two Worlds (R. Bly), **Supp. IV Part 1:** 66, 67, 68–69, 71, 72

"Loving Shepherdess, The" (Jeffers), **Supp. II Part 2:** 432

"Loving the Killer" (Sexton), **Supp. II Part 2:** 688

Lovin' Molly (film), **Supp. V:** 223, 226

Lowe, John, **Supp. XIII:** 238

Lowe, Pardee, **Supp. X:** 291

Lowell, Abbott Lawrence, **I:** 487; **II:** 513; **Supp. I Part 2:** 483

Lowell, Amy, **I:** 231, 384, 405, 475, 487; **II:** 174, 511–533, 534; **III:** 465, 581, 586; **Retro. Supp. I:** 131, 133, 288; **Retro. Supp. II:** 46, 175; **Supp. I Part 1:** 257–259, 261–263, 265, 266; **Supp. I Part 2:** 465, 466, 707, 714, 729; **Supp. XIV:** 128; **Supp. XV:** 43, 293, 295, 297, 298, 299, 300, 301, 303, 306

Lowell, Blanche, **Supp. I Part 2:** 409

Lowell, Harriet, **II:** 553, 554

Lowell, James Russell, **I:** 216, 458; **II:** 273, 274, 289, 302, 320, 402, 529, 530, 532, 534, 551; **III:** 409; **IV:** 129, 171, 175, 180, 182–183, 186; **Retro. Supp. I:** 228; **Retro. Supp. II:** 155, 175, 326; **Supp. I Part 1:** 168, 299, 300, 303, 306, 311, 312, 317, 318, 362; **Supp. I Part 2:** 404–426; **Supp. II Part 1:** 197, 291, 352; **Supp. XV:** 278, 279; **Supp. XVI:** 84

Lowell, Mrs. James Russell (Maria White), **Supp. I Part 2:** 405, 406, 414, 424

Lowell, Percival, **II:** 513, 525, 534

Lowell, Robert, **I:** 172, 381, 382, 400, 442, 521, 544–545, 550; **II:** 371, 376, 377, 384, 386–387, 532, 534–557; **III:** 39, 44, 142, 508, 527, 528–529, 606; **IV:** 120, 138, 402, 430; **Retro. Supp. I:** 67, 140, 411; **Retro. Supp. II:** 27, 40, 44, 46, 48, 50, 175–193, 221, 228–229, 235, 245; **Supp. I Part 1:** 89; **Supp. I Part 2:** 538, 543, 554; **Supp. III Part 1:** 6, 64, 84, 138, 147, 193, 194, 197–202, 205–208; **Supp. III Part 2:** 541, 543, 555, 561, 599; **Supp. IV Part 2:** 439, 620, 637; **Supp. V:** 81, 179, 180, 315–316, 337, 344; **Supp. VIII:** 27, 100, 271; **Supp. IX:** 325; **Supp. X:** 53, 58; **Supp. XI:** 146, 240, 244, 250, 317; **Supp. XII:** 253–254, 255; **Supp. XIII:** 76; **Supp. XIV:** 15, 126, 269; **Supp. XV:** 20, 22, 93, 184, 249, 251, 253, 340

Lowell, Rose, **Supp. I Part 2:** 409

"Lowell in the Classrom" (Vendler), **Retro. Supp. II:** 191

Lowenthal, Michael, **Supp. XII:** 82

Lower Depths, The (Gorki), **III:** 402

"Lower the Standard" (Shapiro), **Supp. II Part 2:** 715

Lowes, John Livingston, **II:** 512, 516, 532; **IV:** 453, 455

Lowin, Joseph, **Supp. V:** 273

"Low-Lands" (Pynchon), **Supp. II Part 2:** 620, 624

Lowle, Percival, **Supp. I Part 2:** 404

Lownsbrough, John, **Supp. IV Part 1:** 209, 211

Lowth, Richard, **II:** 8

Loy, Mina, **III:** 194

Loy, Myrna, **Supp. IV Part 1:** 355

"Loyal Woman's No, A" (Larcom), **Supp. XIII:** 142, 143–144

"Luani of the Jungle" (Hughes), **Supp. I Part 1:** 328

Lubbock, Percy, **I:** 504; **II:** 337; **IV:** 308, 314, 319, 322; **Retro. Supp. I:** 366, 367, 373; **Supp. VIII:** 165

Lubin, Isidor, **Supp. I Part 2:** 632

Lubow, Arthur, **Supp. VIII:** 310

Lucas, Victoria (pseudonym). *See* Plath, Sylvia

Luce, Dianne C., **Supp. VIII:** 189

Lucid, Robert F., **Retro. Supp. II:** 195, 204

"Lucid Eye in Silver Town, The" (Updike), **IV:** 218

"Lucinda Matlock" (Masters), **Supp. I Part 2:** 461, 465

"Luck" (Dunn), **Supp. XI:** 149

Luck of Barry Lyndon, The (Thackeray), **II:** 290

"Luck of Roaring Camp, The" (Harte), **Supp. II Part 1:** 335, 344, 345–347

"Luck of the Bogans, The" (Jewett), **Retro. Supp. II:** 142

Lucky Life (Stern), **Supp. IX:** 290–291

Lucretius, **I:** 59; **II:** 162, 163; **III:** 600, 610–611, 612; **Supp. I Part 1:** 363

Lucy (Kincaid), **Supp. VII:** 180, 185, 186, 187–188, 194

Lucy, Saint, **II:** 211

Lucy Gayheart (Cather), **I:** 331; **Retro. Supp. I:** 19

"Lucy Tavish's Journey" (E. Stoddard), **Supp. XV:** 286

Lucy Temple (Rowson). See *Charlotte's Daughter; or, The Three Orphans*

Ludvigson, Susan, **Supp. IV Part 2:** 442, 446, 447, 448, 451

Lueders, Edward, **Supp. XVI:** 265

"Luggage" (Bidart), **Supp. XV:** 35

Luhan, Mabel Dodge, **Retro. Supp. I:** 7; **Supp. XV:** 46, 50

Lu Ji, **Supp. VIII:** 303

Luke (biblical book), **III:** 606

"Luke Havergal" (Robinson), **III:** 524

Lukeman, Gary, **Supp. XV:** 221

Luks, George, **IV:** 411; **Retro. Supp. II:** 103

"Lullaby" (Auden), **Supp. II Part 1:** 9

"Lullaby" (Bishop), **Supp. I Part 1:** 85

"Lullaby" (Everwine), **Supp. XV:** 89

"Lullaby" (Silko), **Supp. IV Part 2:** 560, 568–569

Lullaby: The Comforting of Cock Robin (Snodgrass), **Supp. VI:** 324

"Lullaby of Cape Cod" (Brodsky), **Supp. VIII:** 27–28

Lullaby Raft (Nye), **Supp. XIII:** 278

Lullaby Raft (Nye, album), **Supp. XIII:** 274

"Lulls" (Walker), **Supp. III Part 2:** 525

"Lulu" (Wedekind), **Supp. XII:** 14

Lulu on the Bridge (film), **Supp. XII:** 21

Lulu's Library (Alcott), **Supp. I Part 1:** 43

"Lumber" (Baker), **Supp. XIII:** 55, 56

"Lumens, The" (Olds), **Supp. X:** 209

Lume Spento, A (Pound), **III:** 470

Lumet, Sidney, **Supp. IV Part 1:** 236; **Supp. IX:** 253

Luminous Debris: Reflecting on Vestige in Provence and Languedoc (Sobin), **Supp. XVI:**291–293, 293–294

"Lumumba's Grave" (Hughes), **Supp. I Part 1:** 344

"Luna, Luna" (Mora), **Supp. XIII:** 217

Lupercal (Hughes), **Retro. Supp. II:** 245; **Supp. I Part 2:** 540

Lupton, Mary Jane, **Supp. IV Part 1:** 7

Luria, Isaac, **IV:** 7

Lurie, Alison, **Supp. X:** 166; **Supp. XVI:**103, 111–112

Lust and Other Stories (Minot), **Supp. VI:** 205

Luster, Deborah, **Supp. XV:** 337,**Supp. XV:** 353, 348, 349, 350

Lustgarten, Edith, **III:** 107

Lustra (Pound), **Retro. Supp. I:** 289, 290

Luther, Martin, **II:** 11–12, 506; **III:** 306, 607; **IV:** 490

"Luther on Sweet Auburn" (Bambara), **Supp. XI:** 16–17

Lux, Thomas, **Supp. XI:** 270

Luxury Girl, The (McCoy), **Supp. XIII:** 163

Lyall, Sarah, **Supp. XIII:** 247

Lycidas (Milton), **II:** 540; **IV:** 347; **Retro. Supp. I:** 60; **Retro. Supp. II:** 186; **Supp. I Part 1:** 370; **Supp. IX:** 41

"Lydia and Marian" (Rowson), **Supp. XV:** 234

Lydon, Susan, **Supp. XII:** 170

Lyell, Charles, **Supp. IX:** 180

Lyell, Frank H., **Supp. VIII:** 125

Lyford, Harry, **Supp. I Part 2:** 679

"Lying" (Wilbur), **Supp. III Part 2:** 547, 562

"Lying and Looking" (Swenson), **Supp. IV Part 2:** 652

"Lying in a Hammock at William Duffy's Farm in Pine Island, Minnesota" (Wright), **Supp. III Part 2:** 589, 599, 600

"Lying in the Pollen and Water" (C. Frost), **Supp. XV:** 96

Lyles, Lois F., **Supp. XI:** 7, 8

Lyly, John, **III:** 536; **Supp. I Part 1:** 369

Lynch, Anne, **Supp. XV:** 273

Lynch, Doris, **Supp. XVI:**294

Lynchburg (Gander), **Supp. XV:** 340

"Lynched Man, The" (Karr), **Supp. XI:** 241

Lynchers, The (Wideman), **Supp. X:** 320

"Lynching, The" (McKay), **Supp. I Part 1:** 63

"Lynching of Jube Benson, The" (Dunbar), **Supp. II Part 1:** 214

"Lynching Song" (Hughes), **Supp. I Part 1:** 331

Lynd, Staughton, **Supp. VIII:** 240

Lynn, Kenneth, **Supp. XIII:** 96–97

Lynn, Kenneth S., **Supp. XIV:**103

Lynn, Vera, **Supp. XI:** 304

Lyon, Kate, **I:** 409; **II:** 138, 143, 144

Lyon, Thomas, **Supp. IX:** 175

"Lyonnesse" (Plath), **Supp. I Part 2:** 541

Lyons, Bonnie, **Supp. V:** 58; **Supp. VIII:** 138

Lyotard, Jean-François, **Supp. IV Part 1:** 54

Lyrical Ballads (Wordsworth), **III:** 583; **IV:** 120; **Supp. IX:** 274; **Supp. XI:** 243; **Supp. XV:** 21

Lyrics of Love and Laughter (Dunbar), **Supp. II Part 1:** 207

Lyrics of Lowly Life (Dunbar), **Supp. II Part 1:** 197, 199, 200, 207

Lyrics of the Hearthside (Dunbar), **Supp. II Part 1:** 206

Lytal, Tammy, **Supp. XI:** 102

Lytle, Andrew, **IV:** 125; **Retro. Supp. II:** 220, 221, 235; **Supp. II Part 1:** 139; **Supp. X:** 1, 25; **Supp. XI:** 101

Lytton of Knebworth. *See* Bulwer-Lytton, Edward George

M

"M. Degas Teaches Art & Science at Durfee Intermediate School, Detroit, 1942" (Levine), **Supp. V:** 181, 193

McAlexander, Hubert H., **Supp. V:** 314, 319, 320, 323

McAlmon, Mrs. Robert (Winifred Ellerman), **III:** 194. *See also* Ellerman, Winifred

McAlmon, Robert, **IV:** 404; **Retro. Supp. I:** 418, 419, 420; **Retro. Supp. II:** 328; **Supp. I Part 1:** 259; **Supp. III Part 2:** 614

McAninch, Jerry, **Supp. XI:** 297, 298

Macaulay, Catherine, **Supp. I Part 2:** 522

Macaulay, Rose, **Supp. XII:** 88; **Supp. XIV:**348

Macaulay, Thomas, **II:** 15–16; **III:** 113, 591–592

Macauley, Robie, **Retro. Supp. II:** 228; **Supp. X:** 56

Macbeth (Shakespeare), **I:** 271; **IV:** 227; **Retro. Supp. I:** 131; **Supp. I Part 1:** 67; **Supp. I Part 2:** 457; **Supp. IV Part 1:** 87; **Supp. XIV:**8

Macbeth (silent film), **Supp. XVI:**184

MacBeth, George, **Retro. Supp. II:** 250

McCaffery, Larry, **Supp. IV Part 1:** 217, 227, 234; **Supp. V:** 53, 238; **Supp. VIII:** 13, 14; **Supp. X:** 260, 268, 301, 303, 307; **Supp. XVI:**117

McCarriston, Linda, **Supp. X:** 204; **Supp. XIV:**259–275

McCarthy, Charles Joseph, Jr. *See* McCarthy, Cormac

McCarthy, Cormac, **Supp. VIII:** 175–192; **Supp. XII:** 310

McCarthy, Eugene, **Retro. Supp. II:** 182

McCarthy, Joseph, **I:** 31, 492; **II:** 562, 568; **Supp. I Part 1:** 294, 295; **Supp. I Part 2:** 444, 611, 612, 620; **Supp. XV:** 198, 311–312

McCarthy, Mary, **II:** 558–584; **Supp. I Part 1:** 84; **Supp. IV Part 1:** 209, 297, 310; **Supp. VIII:** 96, 99, 100; **Supp. X:** 177; **Supp. XI:** 246; **Supp. XIV:**3; **Supp. XV:** 142; **Supp. XVI:**64, 70

McCay, Maura, **Supp. XII:** 271, 276

McClanahan, Ed, **Supp. X:** 24

McClanahan, Thomas, **Supp. XII:** 125–126

McClatchy, J. D., **Supp. XII:** 253–270; **Supp. XV:** 185, 257, 258

McClellan, John L., **I:** 493

McClung, Isabelle, **Retro. Supp. I:** 5

McClure, John, **Retro. Supp. I:** 80

McClure, Michael, **Supp. II Part 1:** 32; **Supp. VIII:** 289; **Supp. XVI:**283

McClure, S. S., **I:** 313; **II:** 465; **III:** 327; **Retro. Supp. I:** 5, 6, 9; **Supp. XV:** 40

McCombs, Judith, **Supp. XIII:** 33

McConagha, Alan, **Supp. XVI:**166
McConnell, Frank, **Supp. X:** 260, 274
McCorkle, Jill, **Supp. X:** 6
McCourt, Frank, **Supp. XII:** 271–287
McCoy, Horace, **Supp. XIII:** 159–177
McCracken, Elizabeth, **Supp. X:** 86;
  Supp. XII: 310, 315–316, 321
McCullers, Carson, **I:** 113, 190, 211;
  II: 585–608; **IV:** 282, 384, 385, 386;
  Retro. Supp. II: 324; **Supp. II Part
  1:** 17; **Supp. IV Part 1:** 31, 84;
  Supp. IV Part 2: 502; **Supp. VIII:**
  124; **Supp. XII:** 309; **Supp.
  XIV:**120; **Supp. XV:** 338
McCullers, Reeves, **III:** 585, 586, 587
McDavid, Raven I., **III:** 120; **Supp.
  XIV:**14
McDermott, Alice, **Supp. XII:** 311
McDermott, John J., **II:** 364
MacDiarmid, Hugh, **Supp. X:** 112
Macdonald, Dwight, **I:** 233, 372, 379;
  III: 39; **Supp. V:** 265; **Supp.
  XIV:**340; **Supp. XV:** 140
McDonald, E. J., **Supp. I Part 2:** 670
Macdonald, George, **Supp. XIII:** 75
MacDonald, Jeanette, **II:** 589
Macdonald, Ross, **Supp. IV Part 1:**
  116, 136; **Supp. IV Part 2:** 459–
  477; **Supp. XIII:** 233
MacDonald, Ruth K., **Supp. XVI:**102
MacDougall, Ruth Doan, **Supp. XV:**
  58; **Supp. XVI:**174
MacDowell, Edward, **I:** 228; **III:** 504,
  508, 524
McDowell, Frederick P. W., **II:** 194
McDowell, Mary, **Supp. I Part 1:** 5
McDowell, Robert, **Supp. IX:** 266,
  270, 276, 279
MacDowell, Robert, **Supp. XI:** 249
McElderry, Margaret K., **Supp. XV:**
  162
McElrath, Joseph, **Supp. XIV:**62
McElroy, Joseph, **Supp. IV Part 1:**
  279, 285
McEuen, Kathryn, **II:** 20
McEwen, Arthur, **I:** 206
McFarland, Ron, **Supp. IX:** 323, 327,
  328, 333
McGann, Jerome, **Retro. Supp. I:** 47
MacGillivray, William, **Supp. XVI:**8
McGovern, Edythe M., **Supp. IV Part
  2:** 573, 582, 585
McGovern, George, **III:** 46
MacGowan, Christopher, **Retro. Supp.
  I:** 430
MacGowan, Kenneth, **III:** 387, 391
McGrath, Douglas, **Supp. XV:** 12
McGrath, Joseph, **Supp. XI:** 307, 309
McGrath, Patrick, **Supp. IX:** 113
McGrath, Thomas, **Supp. X:** 111–130

"McGrath on McGrath" (McGrath),
  Supp. X: 119, 120
McGuane, Thomas, **Supp. V:** 53, 220;
  Supp. VIII: 39, 40, 42, 43
MacGuffin, The (Elkin), **Supp. VI:**
  55–56
McGuiness, Daniel, **Supp. XV:** 261
Machado y Ruiz, Antonio, **Supp. XIII:**
  315, 323
Machan, Tibor, **Supp. IV Part 2:** 528
Machen, Arthur, **IV:** 286
Machiavelli, Niccolò, **I:** 485
"Machine-Gun, The" (Jarrell), **II:** 371
"Machine Song" (Anderson), **I:** 114
McHugh, Vincent, **Supp. XV:** 147
McInerney, Jay, **Supp. X:** 7, 166;
  Supp. XI: 65; **Supp. XII:** 81
"Mac in Love" (Dixon), **Supp. XII:**
  142
McIntire, Holly, **Supp. V:** 338
McIntosh, Maria, **Retro. Supp. I:** 246
Mack, Maynard, **Supp. XIV:**12
Mackail, John William, **Supp. I Part
  1:** 268; **Supp. I Part 2:** 461
McKay, Claude, **Supp. I Part 1:** 63;
  Supp. III Part 1: 75, 76; **Supp. IV
  Part 1:** 3, 79, 164; **Supp. IX:** 306;
  Supp. X: 131–144; **Supp. XI:** 91
McKay, Donald, **Supp. I Part 2:** 482
McKee, Elizabeth, **Retro. Supp. II:**
  221, 222
McKee, Ellen, **Retro. Supp. II:** 67
McKenney, Eileen, **IV:** 288; **Retro.
  Supp. II:** 321, 330
McKenney, Ruth, **IV:** 288; **Retro.
  Supp. II:** 321
MacKenzie, Agnes, **I:** 199
Mackenzie, Captain Alexander, **III:** 94
Mackenzie, Compton, **II:** 82; **Retro.
  Supp. I:** 100, 102
McKenzie, Geraldine, **Supp. XII:** 107
MacKenzie, Margaret, **I:** 199
McKinley, William, **I:** 474; **III:** 506;
  Supp. I Part 2: 395–396, 707
MacKinnon, Catharine, **Supp. XII:** 6
MacLachlan, Suzanne L., **Supp. XII:**
  300,**Supp. XII:** 299
McLaverty, Michael, **Supp. X:** 67
McLay, Catherine, **Supp. XIII:** 21
Maclean, Alasdair, **Supp. V:** 244
Maclean, Norman, **Supp. XIV:**221–
  237; **Supp. XVI:**98
MacLeish, Archibald, **I:** 283, 293, 429;
  II: 165, 228; **III:** 1–25, 427; **Supp.
  I Part 1:** 261; **Supp. I Part 2:** 654;
  Supp. IV Part 1: 359; **Supp. IV
  Part 2:** 586; **Supp. X:** 120; **Supp.
  XIV:**11
MacLeish, Kenneth, **III:** 1
MacLeish, Mrs. Archibald (Ada

Hitchcock), **III:** 1
McLennan, Gordon Lawson, **Supp. IX:**
  89
McLeod, A. W., **Supp. I Part 1:** 257
McLuhan, Marshall, **Supp. IV Part 2:**
  474
McLure, Michael, **Supp. XIV:**150
Macmahon, Arthur, **I:** 226
McMahon, Helen, **Supp. IV Part 2:**
  579
McMichael, George, **Supp. VIII:** 124
McMichael, Morton, **Supp. I Part 2:**
  707
McMichaels, James, **Supp. XIII:** 114
McMillan, James B., **Supp. VIII:** 124
McMillan, Terry, **Supp. XIII:** 179–193
McMullan, Jim, **Supp. XIV:**124
McMurtry, Josephine, **Supp. V:** 220
McMurtry, Larry, **Supp. V:** 219–235;
  Supp. X: 24; **Supp. XI:** 172
McNally, Terrence, **Supp. XIII:** 195–
  211
McNamer, Deirdre, **Supp. XI:** 190
McNeese, Gretchen, **Supp. V:** 123
MacNeice, Louis, **II:** 586; **III:** 527;
  Supp. II Part 1: 17, 24; **Supp. IV
  Part 2:** 440; **Supp. X:** 116; **Supp.
  XIII:** 347
McNeil, Claudia, **Supp. IV Part 1:**
  360, 362
McPhee, John, **Supp. III Part 1:** 289–
  316; **Supp. X:** 29, 30
MacPherson, Aimee Semple, **Supp. V:**
  278
McPherson, Dolly, **Supp. IV Part 1:**
  2, 3, 4, 6, 8, 11, 12
McPherson, James Allen, **Retro. Supp.
  II:** 126
Macpherson, Jay, **Supp. XIII:** 19
MacPherson, Kenneth, **Supp. I Part 1:**
  259
McPhillips, Robert, **Supp. XV:** 119,
  250, 251, 252, 264, 266
McQuade, Molly, **Supp. VIII:** 277,
  281; **Supp. IX:** 151, 163
McQueen, Steve, **Supp. XI:** 306
Macrae, John, **I:** 252–253
McRobbie, Angela, **Supp. IV Part 2:**
  691
MacShane, Frank, **Supp. IV Part 2:**
  557; **Supp. XI:** 214, 216
"MacSwiggen" (Freneau), **Supp. II
  Part 1:** 259
McTaggart, John, **I:** 59
McTeague (Norris), **III:** 314, 315, 316–
  320, 322, 325, 327–328, 330, 331,
  333, 335; **Retro. Supp. II:** 96;
  Supp. IX: 332
McWilliams, Carey, **Supp. XI:** 169
Madama Butterfly (Puccini), **III:** 139

"Madam and the Minister" (Hughes), **Supp. I Part 1:** 335

"Madam and the Wrong Visitor" (Hughes), **Supp. I Part 1:** 335

"Madame and Ahmad" (Bowles), **Supp. IV Part 1:** 93

"Madame Bai and the Taking of Stone Mountain" (Bambara), **Supp. XI:** 14–15

Madame Bovary (Flaubert), **II:** 185; **Retro. Supp. I:** 225; **Retro. Supp. II:** 70; **Supp. XI:** 334

"Madame Célestin's Divorce" (Chopin), **Supp. I Part 1:** 213

Madame Curie (film), **Retro. Supp. I:** 113

"Madame de Mauves" (James), **II:** 327; **Retro. Supp. I:** 218, 220

Madame de Treymes (Wharton), **IV:** 314, 323; **Retro. Supp. I:** 376

"Madam's Calling Cards" (Hughes), **Retro. Supp. I:** 206

Madden, David, **Supp. IV Part 1:** 285

Maddern, Bessie. *See* London, Mrs. Jack (Bessie Maddern)

Mad Dog Black Lady (Coleman), **Supp. XI:** 85–89, 90

Mad Dog Blues (Shepard), **Supp. III Part 2:** 437, 438, 441

Maddox, Lucy, **Supp. IV Part 1:** 323, 325

Mad Ducks and Bears: Football Revisited (Plimpton), **Supp. XVI:**243

Mademoiselle Coeur-Brisé (Sibon, trans.), **IV:** 288

Mademoiselle de Maupin (Gautier), **Supp. I Part 1:** 277

"Mad Farmer, Flying the Flag of Rough Branch, Secedes from the Union, The" (Berry), **Supp. X:** 35

"Mad Farmer Manifesto, The: The First Amendment" (Berry), **Supp. X:** 35

"Mad Farmer's Love Song, The" (Berry), **Supp. X:** 35

Madheart (Baraka), **Supp. II Part 1:** 47

Madhouse, The (Farrell), **II:** 41

Madhubuti, Haki R. (Don L. Lee), **Supp. II Part 1:** 34, 247; **Supp. IV Part 1:** 244

Madison, Dolley, **II:** 303

Madison, James, **I:** 1, 2, 6–9; **II:** 301; **Supp. I Part 2:** 509, 524

"Madison Smartt Bell: *The Year of Silence*" (Garrett), **Supp. X:** 7

"Madman, A" (Updike), **Retro. Supp. I:** 320

"Madman's Song" (Wylie), **Supp. I Part 2:** 711, 729

"Madonna" (Lowell), **II:** 535–536

"Madonna of the Evening Flowers" (Lowell), **II:** 524

"Madonna of the Future, The" (James), **Retro. Supp. I:** 219

"Mad Song" (Gioia), **Supp. XV:** 128

Madwoman in the Attic, The (Gilbert and Gubar), **Retro. Supp. I:** 42; **Supp. IX:** 66

"Maelzel's Chess-Player" (Poe), **III:** 419, 420

"Maestria" (Nemerov), **III:** 275, 278–279

Maeterlinck, Maurice, **I:** 91, 220

"Magazine-Writing Peter Snook" (Poe), **III:** 421

Magdeburg Centuries (Flacius), **IV:** 163

Magellan, Ferdinand, **Supp. I Part 2:** 497

Maggie: A Girl of the Streets (S. Crane), **I:** 407, 408, 410–411, 416; **IV:** 208; **Retro. Supp. II:** 97, 107

Maggie Cassidy (Kerouac), **Supp. III Part 1:** 220–221, 225, 227, 229, 232

"Maggie of the Green Bottles" (Bambara), **Supp. XI:** 2–3

"Magi" (Plath), **Supp. I Part 2:** 544–545

"Magi, The" (Garrett), **Supp. VII:** 97

"Magic" (Porter), **III:** 434, 435

Magic Barrel, The (Malamud), **Supp. I Part 2:** 427, 428, 430–434

"Magic Barrel, The" (Malamud), **Supp. I Part 2:** 427, 428, 431, 432–433

Magic Christian, The (film), **Supp. XI:** 309

Magic Christian, The (Southern), **Supp. XI:** 297, 299–301, 309

Magic City (Komunyakaa), **Supp. XIII:** 125–127, 128, 131

"Magic Flute, The" (Epstein), **Supp. XII:** 165

Magic Flute, The (Mozart), **III:** 164

Magician of Lublin, The (Singer), **IV:** 6, 9–10; **Retro. Supp. II:** 308–309

Magician's Assistant, The (Patchett), **Supp. XII:** 307, 310, 317–320, 322

"Magician's Wife, The" (Gordon), **Supp. IV Part 1:** 306

Magic Journey, The (Nichols), **Supp. XIII:** 266–267

Magic Kingdom, The (Elkin), **Supp. VI:** 42, 54–55, 56, 58

"Magic Mirror, The: A Study of the Double in Two of Doestoevsky's Novels" (Plath), **Supp. I Part 2:** 536

Magic Mountain, The (Mann), **III:** 281–282; **Supp. IV Part 2:** 522;

Supp. XII: 321

Magic Tower, The (Willams), **IV:** 380

Magnaghi, Ambrogio, **Supp. XVI:**286

Magnalia Christi Americana (Mather), **II:** 302; **Supp. I Part 1:** 102; **Supp. I Part 2:** 584; **Supp. II Part 2:** 441, 442, 452–455, 460, 467, 468; **Supp. IV Part 2:** 434

"Magnificent Little Gift" (Salinas), **Supp. XIII:** 318

"Magnifying Mirror" (Karr), **Supp. XI:** 240

Magpie, The (Baldwin, ed.), **Supp. I Part 1:** 49

Magpie's Shadow, The (Winters), **Supp. II Part 2:** 786, 788

"Magpie's Song" (Snyder), **Supp. VIII:** 302

Magritte, René, **Supp. IV Part 2:** 623

Mahan, Albert Thayer, **Supp. I Part 2:** 491

"Mahatma Joe" (Bass), **Supp. XVI:**19

Mahomet and His Successors (Irving), **II:** 314

Mahoney, Jeremiah, **IV:** 285

Mahoney, Lynn, **Supp. XV:** 270

"Maiden in a Tower" (Stegner), **Supp. IV Part 2:** 613

"Maiden Without Hands" (Sexton), **Supp. II Part 2:** 691

"Maid of St. Philippe, The" (Chopin), **Retro. Supp. II:** 63

"Maid's Shoes, The" (Malamud), **Supp. I Part 2:** 437

Mailer, Fanny, **III:** 28

Mailer, Isaac, **III:** 28

Mailer, Norman, **I:** 261, 292, 477; **III:** 26–49, 174; **IV:** 98, 216; **Retro. Supp. II:** 182, 195–217, 279; **Supp. I Part 1:** 291, 294; **Supp. III Part 1:** 302; **Supp. IV Part 1:** 90, 198, 207, 236, 284, 381; **Supp. IV Part 2:** 689; **Supp. VIII:** 236; **Supp. XI:** 104, 218, 222, 229; **Supp. XIV:**49, 53, 54, 111, 162

"Maimed Man, The" (Tate), **IV:** 136

Main Currents in American Thought: The Colonial Mind, 1625–1800 (Parrington), **I:** 517; **Supp. I Part 2:** 484

"Maine Roustabout, A" (Eberhart), **I:** 539

"Maine Speech" (White), **Supp. I Part 2:** 669–670

Maine Woods, The (Thoreau), **IV:** 188

Main Street (Lewis), **I:** 362; **II:** 271, 440, 441–442, 447, 449, 453; **III:** 394

Maitland, Margaret Todd, **Supp. XVI:**292

"Majorat, Das" (Hoffman), **III:** 415

Major Barbara (Shaw), **III:** 69

"Major Chord, The" (Bourne), **I:** 221

Majors and Minors (Dunbar), **Supp. II Part 1:** 197, 198

"Major's Tale, The" (Bierce), **I:** 205

Make-Believe Town: Essays and Remembrances (Mamet), **Supp. XIV:**240, 251

Make It New (Pound), **III:** 470

Makers and Finders (Brooks), **I:** 253, 254, 255, 257, 258

Makers of the Modern World (Untermeyer), **Supp. XV:** 312

"Making a Change" (Gilman), **Supp. XI:** 207

"Making a Living" (Sexton), **Supp. II Part 2:** 695

"Making Changes" (L. Michaels), **Supp. XVI:**204

"Making Do" (Hogan), **Supp. IV Part 1:** 406

Making Face, Making Soul: Haciendo Caras, Creative and Critical Perspectives by Feminists of Color (Anzaldúa, ed.), **Supp. IV Part 1:** 330

Making It (Podhoretz), **Supp. VIII:** 231, 232, 233, 237–238, 239, 244

"Making Light of Auntie" (X. J. Kennedy), **Supp. XV:** 163

"Making of a Marginal Farm, The" (Berry), **Supp. X:** 22

Making of Americans, The (Stein), **IV:** 35, 37, 40–42, 45, 46; **Supp. III Part 1:** 37

"Making of Ashenden, The" (Elkin), **Supp. VI:** 49, 50

"Making of a Soldier USA, The" (Simpson), **Supp. IX:** 270

"Making of Garrison Keillor, The" (McConagha), **Supp. XVI:**166"

"Making of Paths, The" (Stegner), **Supp. IV Part 2:** 614

"Making of Poems, The" (W. J. Smith), **Supp. XIII:** 348

Making of the Modern Mind (Randall), **III:** 605

Making the Light Come: The Poetry of Gerald Stern (Somerville), **Supp. IX:** 296–297

"Making Up Stories" (Didion), **Supp. IV Part 1:** 196, 203, 205

Making Your Own Days: The Pleasures of Reading and Writing Poetry (Koch), **Supp. XV:** 188

Malady of the Ideal, The: Oberman, Maurice de Guérin, and Amiel (Brooks), **I:** 240, 241, 242

Malamud, Bernard, **I:** 144, 375; **II:** 424, 425; **III:** 40, 272; **IV:** 216; **Retro. Supp. II:** 22, 279, 281; **Supp. I Part 2:** 427–453; **Supp. IV Part 1:** 297, 382; **Supp. V:** 257, 266; **Supp. IX:** 114, 227; **Supp. XIII:** 106, 264, 265, 294; **Supp. XVI:**220

Malamud, Mrs. Bernard (Ann de Chiara), **Supp. I Part 2:** 451

Malanga, Gerard, **Supp. III Part 2:** 629

Malaquais, Jean, **Retro. Supp. II:** 199

Malatesta, Sigismondo de, **III:** 472, 473

Malcolm (Purdy), **Supp. VII:** 270–273, 277

"Malcolm Cowley and the American Writer" (Simpson), **Supp. II Part 1:** 147

"MALCOLM REMEMBERED (FEB. 77)" (Baraka), **Supp. II Part 1:** 60

Malcolm X, **Retro. Supp. II:** 12, 13; **Supp. I Part 1:** 52, 63, 65, 66; **Supp. IV Part 1:** 2, 10; **Supp. VIII:** 330, 345; **Supp. X:** 240; **Supp. XIV:**306

Malcolm X (film), **Retro. Supp. II:** 12

"Maldrove" (Jeffers), **Supp. II Part 2:** 418

Male, Roy, **II:** 239

Male Animal, The (Thurber), **Supp. I Part 2:** 605, 606, 610–611

"Malediction upon Myself" (Wylie), **Supp. I Part 2:** 722

Malefactors, The (Gordon), **II:** 186, 199, 213–216; **IV:** 139

"Malest Cornifici Tuo Catullo" (Ginsberg), **Supp. II Part 1:** 315

Malick, Terrence, **Supp. XI:** 234; **Supp. XV:** 351

Malin, Irving, **I:** 147; **Supp. XVI:**71–72

"Malinche's Tips: Pique from Mexico's Mother" (Mora), **Supp. XIII:** 223

"Mallard" (C. Frost), **Supp. XV:** 98, 99

Mallarmé, Stéphane, **I:** 66, 569; **II:** 529, 543; **III:** 8, 409, 428; **IV:** 80, 86; **Retro. Supp. I:** 56; **Supp. I Part 1:** 261; **Supp. II Part 1:** 1; **Supp. III Part 1:** 319–320; **Supp. III Part 2:** 630; **Supp. XIII:** 114; **Supp. XV:** 158; **Supp. XVI:**282, 285

Mallia, Joseph, **Supp. XII:** 26, 29, 37

Mallon, Thomas, **Supp. IV Part 1:** 200, 209

Maloff, Saul, **Supp. VIII:** 238

Malory, Thomas, **II:** 302; **III:** 486; **IV:** 50, 61; **Supp. IV Part 1:** 47

"Mal Paso Bridge" (Jeffers), **Supp. II Part 2:** 415, 420

Malraux, André, **I:** 33–34, 127, 509; **II:** 57, 376; **III:** 35, 310; **IV:** 236, 247, 434; **Retro. Supp. I:** 73; **Retro. Supp. II:** 115–116, 119; **Supp. II Part 1:** 221, 232

Maltese Falcon, The (film), **Supp. IV Part 1:** 342, 353, 355

Maltese Falcon, The (Hammett), **IV:** 286; **Supp. IV Part 1:** 345, 348–351

Mama (McMillan), **Supp. XIII:** 182, 187–188

"Mama and Daughter" (Hughes), **Supp. I Part 1:** 334

Mama Day (Naylor), **Supp. VIII:** 223–226, 230

Mama Poc: An Ecologist's Account of the Extinction of a Species (LaBastille), **Supp. X:** 99, 104–105, 106

"Mama Still Loves You" (Naylor), **Supp. VIII:** 214

Mambo Hips and Make Believe (Coleman), **Supp. XI:** 94–96

Mambo Kings, The (film), **Supp. VIII:** 73, 74

Mambo Kings Play Songs of Love, The (Hijuelos), **Supp. VIII:** 73–74, 79–82

"Ma'me Pélagie" (Chopin), **Retro. Supp. II:** 64

Mamet, David, **Supp. XIV:**239–258, 315

"Mamie" (Sandburg), **III:** 582

Mammedaty, Novarro Scott. *See* Momaday, N. Scott

"Mammon and the Archer" (O. Henry), **Supp. II Part 1:** 394, 408

Mammonart (Sinclair), **Supp. V:** 276–277

"Mamouche" (Chopin), **Retro. Supp. II:** 66

"Man" (Corso), **Supp. XII:** 130

"Man" (Herbert), **II:** 12

"Man Against the Sky, The" (Robinson), **III:** 509, 523

"Man and a Woman Sit Near Each Other, A" (R. Bly), **Supp. IV Part 1:** 71

Man and Boy (Morris), **III:** 223, 224, 225

"Man and the Snake, The" (Bierce), **I:** 203

"Man and Woman" (Caldwell), **I:** 310

Manassas (Sinclair), **Supp. V:** 280, 281, 285

"Man Bring This Up Road" (T.

Williams), **IV:** 383–384

"Man Carrying Thing" (Stevens), **IV:** 90

Manchester, William, **III:** 103

"Man Child, The" (Baldwin), **Supp. I Part 1:** 63

Man Could Stand Up, A (Ford), **I:** 423

"Mandarin's Jade" (Chandler), **Supp. IV Part 1:** 125

Mandel, Charlotte, **Supp. XVI:**57

Mandelbaum, Maurice, **I:** 61

Mandelstam, Osip, **Retro. Supp. I:** 278; **Supp. III Part 1:** 268; **Supp. VIII:** 21, 22, 23, 27; **Supp. XIII:** 77; **Supp. XV:** 254, 261, 263

"Mandelstam: The Poem as Event" (Dobyns), **Supp. XIII:** 78

"Mandolin" (Dove), **Supp. IV Part 1:** 247

"Mandoline" (Verlaine), **IV:** 79

"Man Eating" (Kenyon), **Supp. VII:** 173

"Man Feeding Pigeons" (Clampitt), **Supp. IX:** 49–50, 52

Manfred, Frederick, **Supp. X:** 126

"Mango Says Goodbye Sometimes" (Cisneros), **Supp. VII:** 64

Manhattan (film; Allen), **Supp. IV Part 1:** 205; **Supp. XV:** 5, 7–8, 13

"Manhattan: Luminism" (Doty), **Supp. XI:** 135

"Manhattan Dawn" (Justice), **Supp. VII:** 117

Manhattan Murder Mystery (film; Allen), **Supp. XV:** 5, 11

Manhattan Transfer (Dos Passos), **I:** 26, 475, 478, 479, 480, 481, 482–484, 487; **II:** 286; **Supp. I Part 1:** 57

"Mania" (Lowell), **II:** 554

"Manic in the Moon, The" (Thurber), **Supp. I Part 2:** 620

"Man in Black" (Plath), **Supp. I Part 2:** 538

Man in Prehistory (Chard), **Supp. XII:** 177–178

Man in the Black Coat Turns, The (R. Bly), **Supp. IV Part 1:** 66–68, 71, 73

"Man in the Brooks Brothers Shirt, The" (McCarthy), **II:** 563–564

"Man in the Drawer, The" (Malamud), **Supp. I Part 2:** 437

Man in the Flying Lawn Chair and Other Excursions and Observations, The (Plimpton), **Supp. XVI:**234

Man in the Gray Flannel Suit, The (Wilson), **Supp. IV Part 1:** 387

Man in the Middle, The (Wagoner), **Supp. IX:** 324, 332–333

Mankiewicz, Herman, **Supp. XVI:**189

Mankiewicz, Joseph, **Retro. Supp. I:** 113

Mankowitz, Wolf, **Supp. XI:** 307

"Man Made of Words, The" (Momaday), **Supp. IV Part 2:** 481, 484–485, 486, 487, 488

Man-Made World, The (Gilman), **Supp. XI:** 207

"Man-Moth, The" (Bishop), **Retro. Supp. II:** 42; **Supp. I Part 1:** 85–87, 88

Mann, Charles, **Retro. Supp. II:** 40

Mann, Erika, **Supp. II Part 1:** 11

Mann, Seymour (Samuel Weisman), **Supp. V:** 113

Mann, Thomas, **I:** 271, 490; **II:** 42, 539; **III:** 231, 281–282, 283; **IV:** 70, 73, 85; **Supp. IV Part 1:** 392; **Supp. IV Part 2:** 522; **Supp. V:** 51; **Supp. IX:** 21; **Supp. XI:** 275; **Supp. XII:** 173, 310, 321; **Supp. XIV:**87

Mannerhouse (Wolfe), **IV:** 460

Manner Music, The (Reznikoff), **Supp. XIV:**293–295

"Manners" (Bishop), **Supp. I Part 1:** 73

"Manners" (Emerson), **II:** 4, 6

"Manners, Morals, and the Novel" (Trilling), **Supp. III Part 2:** 502, 503

Mannheim, Karl, **I:** 279; **Supp. I Part 2:** 644

Manning, Frederic, **III:** 459

Manning, Robert, **Supp. IX:** 236

Mannix, Daniel P., **Supp. II Part 1:** 140

Man Nobody Knows, The (B. Barton), **Retro. Supp. I:** 179

Mano, D. Keith, **Supp. XVI:**250

Mano, Guy Levis, **Supp. XVI:**282

"Man of Letters as a Man of Business, The" (Howells), **Supp. XIV:**45–46

"Man of No Account, The" (Harte), **Supp. II Part 1:** 339

"Man of the Crowd, The" (Poe), **III:** 412, 417; **Retro. Supp. I:** 154

Man on Spikes (Asinof), **II:** 424

Man on Stage (Dixon), **Supp. XII:** 141, 154–155

"Man on the Dump, The" (Stevens), **IV:** 74; **Retro. Supp. I:** 306

"Man on the Train, The" (Percy), **Supp. III Part 1:** 387

Manor, The (Singer), **IV:** 6, 17–19

Manrique, Jorge, **Retro. Supp. II:** 154

Mansart Builds a School (Du Bois), **Supp. II Part 1:** 185–186

Man's Fate (Malraux), **I:** 127; **Retro. Supp. II:** 121

"Man's Fate A Film Treatment of the Malraux Novel" (Agee), **I:** 33–34

Mansfield, June, **Supp. X:** 183, 194

Mansfield, Katherine, **III:** 362, 453

Mansfield, Stephanie, **Supp. IV Part 1:** 227

Man's Hope (Malraux), **IV:** 247

Mansion, The (Faulkner), **II:** 73; **Retro. Supp. I:** 74, 82

Man's Nature and His Communities (Niebuhr), **III:** 308

Manson, Charles, **Supp. IV Part 1:** 205

"Man Splitting Wood in the Daybreak, The" (Kinnell), **Supp. III Part 1:** 254

"Man's Pride" (Jeffers), **Supp. II Part 2:** 417

"Man's Story, The" (Anderson), **I:** 114

Man's Woman, A (Norris), **III:** 314, 322, 328, 329, 330, 332, 333

Man That Corrupted Hadleyburg, The (Twain), **I:** 204; **IV:** 208

"Man That Was Used Up, The" (Poe), **III:** 412, 425

"Mantis" (Zukofsky), **Supp. III Part 2:** 617

"'Mantis': An Interpretation" (Zukofsky), **Supp. III Part 2:** 617–618

Man to Send Rain Clouds, The (Rosen, ed.), **Supp. IV Part 2:** 499, 505, 513

"Man to Send Rain Clouds, The" (Silko), **Supp. IV Part 2:** 559

Mantrap (Lewis), **II:** 447

Manuductio Ad Ministerium (Mather), **Supp. II Part 2:** 465–467

"Manuelzinho" (Bishop), **Retro. Supp. II:** 47–48

Manuscript Books of Emily Dickinson, The (Franklin, ed.), **Retro. Supp. I:** 29, 41

"Man Waiting for It to Stop, A" (Dunn), **Supp. XI:** 144

"Man Who Became a Woman, The" (Anderson), **I:** 114

"Man Who Carries the Desert Around Inside Himself, The: For Wally" (Komunyakaa), **Supp. XIII:** 125

"Man Who Closed Shop, The" (Dunn), **Supp. XI:** 149

Man Who Gave Up His Name, The (Harrison), **Supp. VIII:** 45, 52

Man Who Had All the Luck, The (A. Miller), **III:** 148, 149, 164, 166

"Man Who Knew Belle Star, The" (Bausch), **Supp. VII:** 46

"Man Who Knew Coolidge, The" (Lewis), **II:** 449

Man Who Knew Coolidge, The: Being the Soul of Lowell Schmaltz, Constructive and Nordic Citizen (Lewis), **II:** 450

Man Who Lived Underground, The (Wright), **Supp. II Part 1:** 40

"Man Who Lived Underground, The" (Wright), **IV:** 479, 485–487, 492; **Retro. Supp. II:** 121

"Man Who Makes Brooms, The" (Nye), **Supp. XIII:** 276

"Man Who Studied Yoga, The" (Mailer), **III:** 35–36; **Retro. Supp. II:** 200

"Man Who Wanted to Win, The" (McCoy), **Supp. XIII:** 161

Man Who Was There, The (Morris), **III:** 220–221

"Man Who Writes Ants, The" (Merwin), **Supp. III Part 1:** 348

"Man with a Family" (Humphrey), **Supp. IX:** 94

Man without a Country, The (Hale), **I:** 488

"Man with the Blue Guitar, The" (Stevens), **I:** 266; **IV:** 85–87; **Retro. Supp. I:** 303–305, 306, 307, 309

Man with the Blue Guitar and Other Poems, The (Stevens), **IV:** 76; **Retro. Supp. I:** 303, 422

Man with the Golden Arm, The (Algren), **Supp. V:** 4; **Supp. IX:** 1, 3, 9–11, 14, 15

Man with the Golden Arm, The (film), **Supp. IX:** 3

"Man with the Golden Beef, The" (Podhoretz), **Supp. IX:** 3

"Man with the Hoe, The" (Markham), **Supp. XV:** 115

Manyan Letters (Olson), **Supp. II Part 2:** 571

Many Circles (Goldbarth), **Supp. XII:** 193

"Many Handles" (Sandburg), **III:** 594

"Many Happy Returns" (Auden), **Supp. II Part 1:** 15

Many Loves (W. C. Williams), **Retro. Supp. I:** 424

"Many Mansions" (H. Roth), **Supp. IX:** 233, 234

Many Marriages (Anderson), **I:** 104, 111, 113

"Many of Our Waters: Variations on a Poem by a Black Child" (Wright), **Supp. III Part 2:** 602

"Many Swans" (Lowell), **II:** 526

"Many Thousands Gone" (Baldwin), **Retro. Supp. II:** 4; **Supp. I Part 1:** 51

"Many Wagons Ago" (Ashbery), **Supp.**

III Part 1: 22

"Many-Windowed House, A" (Cowley), **Supp. II Part 1:** 137

Many-Windowed House, A (Cowley), **Supp. II Part 1:** 141, 143

Mao II (DeLillo), **Supp. VI:** 2, 4, 5, 6, 7, 8, 9, 14, 16

"Map, The" (Bishop), **Retro. Supp. II:** 41; **Supp. I Part 1:** 72, 82, 85–88, 93

"Map, The" (Strand), **Supp. IV Part 2:** 623–624

"Maple Leaf, The" (Joplin), **Supp. IV Part 1:** 223

"Map of Montana in Italy, A" (Hugo), **Supp. VI:** 139

"Maps" (Hass), **Supp. VI:** 103–104

Mapson, Jo-Ann, **Supp. IV Part 2:** 440, 454

Map to the Next World, A: Poems and Tales (Harjo), **Supp. XII:** 228–230

"Mara" (Jeffers), **Supp. II Part 2:** 434

Ma Rainey's Black Bottom (Wilson), **Supp. VIII:** 331, 332–334, 346, 349, 350

Marat, Jean Paul, **IV:** 117; **Supp. I Part 2:** 514, 515, 521

"Marathon" (Glück), **Supp. V:** 85

Marble Faun, The (Faulkner), **II:** 55, 56; **Retro. Supp. I:** 79

Marble Faun, The; or, The Romance of Monte Beni (Hawthorne), **II:** 225, 239, 242–243, 290, 324; **IV:** 167; **Retro. Supp. I:** 63, 149, 163, 164–165; **Supp. I Part 1:** 38; **Supp. I Part 2:** 421, 596; **Supp. XIII:** 102

Marbles (Brodsky), **Supp. VIII:** 26–27

"March" (W. C. Williams), **Retro. Supp. I:** 418

March, Alan, **Supp. XVI:**242

March, Fredric, **III:** 154, 403; **IV:** 357; **Supp. X:** 220

Marchalonis, Shirley, **Supp. XIII:** 138, 140, 141, 143, 147–148

"Marché aux Oiseaux" (Wilbur), **Supp. III Part 2:** 550

"Märchen, The" (Jarrell), **II:** 378–379

March Hares (Frederic), **II:** 143–144

Marching Men (Anderson), **I:** 99, 101, 103–105, 111

"Marching Music" (Simic), **Supp. VIII:** 281

"Marcia" (Davis), **Supp. XVI:**91–92

Marco Millions (O'Neill), **III:** 391, 395

Marcosson, Isaac, **III:** 322

Marcus, Steven, **Retro. Supp. II:** 196, 200

Marcus Aurelius, **II:** 1; **III:** 566

Marcuse, Herbert, **Supp. I Part 2:** 645;

Supp. VIII: 196; **Supp. XII:** 2

Mardi and a Voyage Thither (Melville), **I:** 384; **II:** 281; **III:** 77–79, 84, 87, 89; **Retro. Supp. I:** 247, 254, 256

Margaret (Judd), **II:** 290

"Margaret Fuller, 1847" (Clampitt), **Supp. IX:** 43

"Marginalia" (Wilbur), **Supp. III Part 2:** 544

Margin of Hope, A: An Intellectual Autobiography (Howe), **Supp. VI:** 113–114, 117, 125, 128

"Margins of Maycomb, The: A Rereading of *To Kill a Mockingbird*" (Phelps), **Supp. VIII:** 128

Margoshes, Samuel, **Supp. X:** 70

"Margrave" (Jeffers), **Supp. II Part 2:** 426

Margret Howth (Davis), **Supp. XVI:**81, 83, 84, 88–89

Margret Howth: A Story of Today (J. Yellin, ed.), **Supp. XVI:**88

"Maria Concepción" (Porter), **III:** 434–435, 451

Mariani, Paul L., **Retro. Supp. I:** 412, 419; **Retro. Supp. II:** 189

Marianne Moore Reader, (Moore), **III:** 199

Marie Antoinette (film), **Retro. Supp. I:** 113

Marie Laveau (Prose), **Supp. XVI:**251

Mariella Gable, Sister, **III:** 339, 355

"Marijuana and a Pistol" (C. Himes), **Supp. XVI:**137

"Marijuana Notation" (Ginsberg), **Supp. II Part 1:** 313

Marilyn: A Biography (Mailer), **Retro. Supp. II:** 208

"Marin" (Cisneros), **Supp. VII:** 60, 61

Marin, Jay, **Retro. Supp. II:** 325

"Marina" (Eliot), **I:** 584, 585; **Retro. Supp. I:** 64

"Marine Surface, Low Overcast" (Clampitt), **Supp. IX:** 47–48

Marinetti, Tommaso, **Retro. Supp. I:** 59

Marionettes, The (Faulkner), **Retro. Supp. I:** 79

Maritain, Jacques, **I:** 402

Maritime Compact (Paine), **Supp. I Part 2:** 519

Maritime History of Massachusetts, 1783–1860, The (Morison), **Supp. I Part 2:** 481–483

Marjolin, Jean-Nicolas, **Supp. I Part 1:** 302

Marjorie Kinnan Rawlings: Sojourner at Cross Creek (Silverthorne), **Supp. X:** 220, 234

"Mark, The" (Bogan), **Supp. III Part 1:** 52

Marker, Chris, **Supp. IV Part 2:** 434, 436

"Market" (Hayden), **Supp. II Part 1:** 368, 369

Marketplace, The (Frederic), **II:** 145–146

Markham, Edwin, **I:** 199, 207; **Supp. XV:** 115

Markings (Hammarskjold), **Supp. II Part 1:** 26

Markopoulos, Gregory, **Supp. XII:** 2

Markowick-Olczakova, Hanna, **Supp. X:** 70

Marks, Alison, **Supp. I Part 2:** 660

Marks, Barry A., **I:** 435, 438, 442, 446

Mark Twain in Eruption (Twain), **IV:** 209

Mark Twain's America (De Voto), **I:** 248

Mark Twain's Autobiography (Twain), **IV:** 209

Marley, Bob, **Supp. IX:** 152

Marlowe, Christopher, **I:** 68, 368, 384; **II:** 590; **III:** 259, 491; **Retro. Supp. I:** 127; **Retro. Supp. II:** 76; **Supp. I Part 2:** 422

"Marlowe Takes on the Syndicate" (Chandler), **Supp. IV Part 1:** 135

Marne, The (Wharton), **IV:** 319, 320; **Retro. Supp. I:** 378

Marquand, J. P., **I:** 362, 375; **II:** 459, 482–483; **III:** 50–73, 383; **Supp. I Part 1:** 196; **Supp. IV Part 1:** 31; **Supp. V:** 95

Marquand, John, **Supp. XI:** 301

Marquand, Mrs. John P. (Adelaide Hooker), **III:** 57, 61

Marquand, Mrs. John P. (Christina Sedgwick), **III:** 54, 57

Marquand, Philip, **III:** 52

Marquis, Don, **Supp. I Part 2:** 668

"Marriage" (Corso), **Supp. XII:** 117, 124, 127–128

Marriage (Moore), **III:** 194

"Marriage" (Moore), **III:** 198–199, 213

"Marriage, A" (Untermeyer), **Supp. XV:** 305

Marriage A-la-Mode (Dryden), **Supp. IX:** 68

Marriage and Other Science Fiction (Goldbarth), **Supp. XII:** 189, 190

"Marriage in the Sixties, A" (Rich), **Supp. I Part 2:** 554

"Marriage of Heaven and Hell, The" (Blake), **III:** 544–545; **Supp. VIII:** 99

"Marriage of Phaedra, The" (Cather), **Retro. Supp. I:** 5

Marrow of Tradition, The (Chesnutt), **Supp. XIV:**63, 71–75, 76

Marryat, Captain Frederick, **III:** 423

"Marrying Absurd" (Didion), **Supp. IV Part 1:** 200

"Marrying Iseult?" (Updike), **Retro. Supp. I:** 329

Marrying Man (Simon), **Supp. IV Part 2:** 588

"Marrying the Hangman" (Atwood), **Supp. XIII:** 34

Marry Me: A Romance (Updike), **Retro. Supp. I:** 329, 330, 332

"Mars and Hymen" (Freneau), **Supp. II Part 1:** 258

Marsden, Dora, **III:** 471; **Retro. Supp. I:** 416

Marsena (Frederic), **II:** 135, 136–137

Marsh, Edward, **Supp. I Part 1:** 257, 263

Marsh, Fred T., **Supp. IX:** 232

Marsh, Mae, **Supp. I Part 2:** 391

Marshall, George, **III:** 3

Marshall, John, **Supp. I Part 2:** 455; **Supp. XVI:**117

Marshall, Paule, **Supp. IV Part 1:** 8, 14, 369; **Supp. XI:** 18, 275–292; **Supp. XIII:** 295

Marshall, Tod, **Supp. XV:** 224

"Marshall Carpenter" (Masters), **Supp. I Part 2:** 463

"Marshes of Glynn, The" (Lanier), **Supp. I Part 1:** 364, 365–368, 370, 373

"'Marshes of Glynn, The': A Study in Symbolic Obscurity" (Ross), **Supp. I Part 1:** 373

Marsh Island, A (Jewett), **II:** 405; **Retro. Supp. II:** 134

"Marshland Elegy" (Leopold), **Supp. XIV:**187, 189

"Mars Is Heaven!" (Bradbury), **Supp. IV Part 1:** 103, 106

Marsman, Henrik, **Supp. IV Part 1:** 183

Marston, Ed, **Supp. IV Part 2:** 492

Marta y Maria (Valdes), **II:** 290

"Martha's Lady" (Jewett), **Retro. Supp. II:** 140, 143

Marthe, Saint, **II:** 213

Martial, **II:** 1, 169; **Supp. IX:** 152

Martian Chronicles, The (Bradbury), **Supp. IV Part 1:** 102, 103, 106–107

Martin, Benjamin, **Supp. I Part 2:** 503

Martin, Dick, **Supp. XII:** 44

Martin, Jay, **I:** 55, 58, 60, 61, 67; **III:** 307; **Retro. Supp. II:** 326, 327, 329; **Supp. XI:** 162

Martin, John, **Supp. XI:** 172

Martin, Judith, **Supp. V:** 128

Martin, Nell, **Supp. IV Part 1:** 351, 353

Martin, Reginald, **Supp. X:** 247, 249

Martin, Stephen-Paul, **Supp. IV Part 2:** 430

Martin, Tom, **Supp. X:** 79

Martin du Gard, Roger, **Supp. I Part 1:** 51

Martineau, Harriet, **Supp. II Part 1:** 282, 288, 294

Martin Eden (London), **II:** 466, 477–481

Martinelli, Sheri, **Supp. IV Part 1:** 280

Martínez, Guillermo, **Supp. XIII:** 313

Mart'nez, Rafael, **Retro. Supp. I:** 423

Martone, John, **Supp. V:** 179

Marty (Chayefsky), **Supp. XV:** 205

"Martyr, The" (Porter), **III:** 454

Martz, Louis L., **IV:** 151, 156, 165; **Supp. I Part 1:** 107; **Supp. XIV:**12

Marvell, Andrew, **IV:** 135, 151, 156, 161, 253; **Retro. Supp. I:** 62, 127; **Retro. Supp. II:** 186, 189; **Supp. I Part 1:** 80; **Supp. XII:** 159; **Supp. XIV:**10; **Supp. XVI:**204

"Marvella, for Borrowing" (Ríos), **Supp. IV Part 2:** 551

Marx, Eleanor, **Supp. XVI:**85

Marx, Karl, **I:** 60, 267, 279, 283, 588; **II:** 376, 462, 463, 483, 577; **IV:** 429, 436, 443–444, 469; **Retro. Supp. I:** 254; **Supp. I Part 2:** 518, 628, 632, 633, 634, 635, 639, 643, 645, 646; **Supp. III Part 2:** 619; **Supp. IV Part 1:** 355; **Supp. VIII:** 196; **Supp. IX:** 133; **Supp. X:** 119, 134; **Supp. XIII:** 75

Marx, Leo, **Supp. I Part 1:** 233

"Marxism and Monastic Perpectives" (Merton), **Supp. VIII:** 196

Mary (Nabokov), **Retro. Supp. I:** 267–268, 270, 277

Mary; or, The Test of Honour (Rowson), **Supp. XV:** 233, 236

"Mary Karr, Mary Karr, Mary Karr, Mary Karr" (Harmon), **Supp. XI:** 248

Maryles, Daisy, **Supp. XII:** 271

Mary Magdalene, **I:** 303

"Mary O'Reilly" (Anderson), **II:** 44

"Mary Osaka , I Love You" (Fante), **Supp. XI:** 169

"Mary's Song" (Plath), **Supp. I Part 2:** 541

"Mary Winslow" (Lowell), **Retro. Supp. II:** 187

Marzynski, Marian, **Supp. XVI:**153

Masefield, John, **II:** 552; **III:** 523

Mask for Janus, A (Merwin), **Supp. III**

Part 1: 339, 341, 342

Maslin, Janet, **Supp. XVI:**213

Maslow, Abraham, **Supp. I Part 2:** 540

Mason, Bobbie Ann, **Supp. VIII:** 133–149; **Supp. XI:** 26; **Supp. XII:** 294, 298, 311

Mason, Charlotte, **Supp. XIV:**201

Mason, David, **Supp. V:** 344; **Supp. XV:** 116, 251

Mason, Lowell, **I:** 458

Mason, Marsha, **Supp. IV Part 2:** 575, 586

Mason, Otis Tufton, **Supp. I Part 1:** 18

Mason, Walt, **Supp. XV:** 298

"Mason Jars by the Window" (Ríos), **Supp. IV Part 2:** 548

Masque of Mercy, A (Frost), **II:** 155, 165, 167–168; **Retro. Supp. I:** 131, 140

"Masque of Mummers, The" (MacLeish), **III:** 18

"Masque of Pandora, The" (Longfellow), **Retro. Supp. II:** 167

Masque of Pandora, The, and Other Poems (Longfellow), **II:** 490, 494, 506; **Retro. Supp. II:** 169

Masque of Poets, A (Lathrop, ed.), **Retro. Supp. I:** 31; **Supp. I Part 1:** 365, 368

Masque of Reason, A (Frost), **II:** 155, 162, 165–167; **Retro. Supp. I:** 131, 140; **Retro. Supp. II:** 42

"Masque of the Red Death, The" (Poe), **III:** 412, 419, 424; **Retro. Supp. II:** 262, 268–269

"Masquerade" (Banks), **Supp. V:** 7

"Massachusetts 1932" (Bowles), **Supp. IV Part 1:** 94

Massachusetts, Its Historians and Its History (Adams), **Supp. I Part 2:** 484

"Massachusetts to Virginia" (Whittier), **Supp. I Part 2:** 688–689

"Massacre and the Mastermind, The" (Bausch), **Supp. VII:** 49

"Massacre at Scio, The" (Bryant), **Supp. I Part 1:** 168

"Massacre of the Innocents, The" (Simic), **Supp. VIII:** 282

Masses and Man (Toller), **I:** 479

"Masseur de Ma Soeur, Le" (Hecht), **Supp. X:** 58

Massey, Raymond, **Supp. IV Part 2:** 524

"Mass Eye and Ear: The Ward" (Karr), **Supp. XI:** 244

"Mass for the Day of St. Thomas Didymus" (Levertov), **Supp. III Part 1:** 283

Massie, Chris, **Supp. IV Part 2:** 524

Massing, Michael, **Supp. IV Part 1:** 208

Massinger, Philip, **Supp. I Part 2:** 422; **Supp. XV:** 238

Master Builder, The (Ibsen), **Supp. IV Part 2:** 522

Master Class (McNally), **Supp. XIII:** 204–205, 208

"Masterful" (Matthews), **Supp. IX:** 161–162

"Master Misery" (Capote), **Supp. III Part 1:** 117

Master of Dreams: A Memoir of Isaac Bashevis Singer (Telushkin), **Retro. Supp. II:** 317

"Master of Secret Revenges, The" (Gass), **Supp. VI:** 93

Master of the Crossroads (Bell), **Supp. X:** 16–17

"'Masterpiece of Filth, A': Portrait of Knoxville Forgets to Be Fair" (Howards), **Supp. VIII:** 178

Masterpieces of American Fiction, **Supp. XI:** 198

"Master Player, The" (Dunbar), **Supp. II Part 1:** 200

Masters, Edgar Lee, **I:** 106, 384, 475, 480, 518; **II:** 276, 529; **III:** 505, 576, 579; **IV:** 352; **Retro. Supp. I:** 131; **Supp. I Part 2:** 378, 386, 387, 454–478; **Supp. III Part 1:** 63, 71, 73, 75; **Supp. IV Part 2:** 502; **Supp. IX:** 308; **Supp. XIV:**282–283; **Supp. XV:** 256, 293, 297, 301, 306

Masters, Hardin W., **Supp. I Part 2:** 468

Masters, Hilary, **Supp. IX:** 96

Masters of Sociological Thought (Coser), **Supp. I Part 2:** 650

Masters of the Dew (Roumain), **Supp. IV Part 1:** 367

Matchmaker, The (Wilder), **IV:** 357, 369, 370, 374

Mate of the Daylight, The, and Friends Ashore (Jewett), **II:** 404; **Retro. Supp. II:** 146–147

Materassi, Mario, **Supp. IX:** 233

Mather, Cotton, **II:** 10, 104, 302, 506, 536; **III:** 442; **IV:** 144, 152–153, 157; **Supp. I Part 1:** 102, 117, 174, 271; **Supp. I Part 2:** 584, 599, 698; **Supp. II Part 2:** 441–470; **Supp. IV Part 2:** 430, 434

Mather, Increase, **II:** 10; **IV:** 147, 157; **Supp. I Part 1:** 100

Mathews, Cornelius, **III:** 81; **Supp. I Part 1:** 317

Mathews, Shailer, **III:** 293

"Matinees" (Merrill), **Supp. III Part 1:** 319, 327

"Matins" (C. Frost), **Supp. XV:** 105

"Matins" (Glück), **Supp. V:** 88

"Matisse: Blue Interior with Two Girls–1947" (Hecht), **Supp. X:** 73–74

Matisse, Henri, **III:** 180; **IV:** 90, 407; **Supp. I Part 2:** 619; **Supp. VIII:** 168; **Supp. IX:** 66; **Supp. X:** 73, 74

"Matisse: The Red Studio" (Snodgrass), **Supp. VI:** 316–317

Matlack, James, **Supp. XV:** 269, 271, 286

Matlock, Lucinda, **Supp. I Part 2:** 462

Matrimaniac, The (film), **Supp. XVI:**185, 186

Matrix Trilogy, The (film), **Supp. XVI:**271

Matson, Harold, **Supp. XIII:** 164, 166, 167, 169, 172

Matson, Peter, **Supp. IV Part 1:** 299

Matson, Suzanne, **Supp. VIII:** 281

Matters of Fact and Fiction: Essays 1973–1976 (Vidal), **Supp. IV Part 2:** 687

Matthew (biblical book), **IV:** 164; **Supp. XV:** 222

Matthew Arnold (Trilling), **Supp. III Part 2:** 500–501

Matthews, Jackson, **Supp. XVI:**282

Matthews, T. S., **II:** 430; **Supp. XV:** 142

Matthews, William, **Supp. V:** 4, 5; **Supp. IX:** 151–170; **Supp. XIII:** 112

Matthiessen, F. O., **I:** 254, 259–260, 517; **II:** 41, 554; **III:** 310, 453; **IV:** 181; **Retro. Supp. I:** 40, 217; **Retro. Supp. II:** 137; **Supp. IV Part 2:** 422; **Supp. XIII:** 93; **Supp. XIV:**3

Matthiessen, Peter, **Supp. V:** 199–217, 332; **Supp. XI:** 231, 294; **Supp. XIV:**82; **Supp. XVI:**230

Mattingly, Garrett, **Supp. IV Part 2:** 601

Mattu, Ravi, **Supp. XVI:**124

"Maud Island" (Caldwell), **I:** 310

Maud Martha (Brooks), **Supp. III Part 1:** 74, 78–79, 87; **Supp. XI:** 278

"Maud Muller" (Whittier), **Supp. I Part 2:** 698

Maugham, W. Somerset, **III:** 57, 64; **Supp. IV Part 1:** 209; **Supp. X:** 58; **Supp. XIV:**161

Maule's Curse: Seven Studies in the History of American Obscurantism (Winters), **Supp. II Part 2:** 807–808, 812

"Mau-mauing the Flak Catchers"

(Wolfe), **Supp. III Part 2:** 577

Maupassant, Guy de, **I:** 309, 421; **II:** 191–192, 291, 325, 591; **IV:** 17; **Retro. Supp. II:** 65, 66, 67, 299; **Supp. I Part 1:** 207, 217, 223, 320; **Supp. XIV:**336

"Maurice Barrès and the Youth of France" (Bourne), **I:** 228

Maurier, George du, **II:** 338

Maurras, Charles, **Retro. Supp. I:** 55

Mauve Gloves & Madmen, Clutter & Vine (Wolfe), **Supp. III Part 2:** 581

Maverick in Mauve (Auchincloss), **Supp. IV Part 1:** 26

"Mavericks, The" (play) (Auchincloss), **Supp. IV Part 1:** 34

"Mavericks, The" (story) (Auchincloss), **Supp. IV Part 1:** 32

"Max" (H. Miller), **III:** 183

Max and the White Phagocytes (H. Miller), **III:** 178, 183–184

Maximilian (emperor of Mexico), **Supp. I Part 2:** 457–458

Maximilian: A Play in Five Acts (Masters), **Supp. I Part 2:** 456, 457–458

"Maximus, to Gloucester" (Olson), **Supp. II Part 2:** 574

"Maximus, to himself" (Olson), **Supp. II Part 2:** 565, 566, 567, 569, 570, 572

Maximus Poems, The (Olson), **Retro. Supp. I:** 209; **Supp. II Part 2:** 555, 556, 563, 564–580, 584; **Supp. VIII:** 305; **Supp. XV:** 170, 264, 349; **Supp. XVI:**287

Maximus Poems 1–10, The (Olson), **Supp. II Part 2:** 571

Maximus Poems IV, V, VI (Olson), **Supp. II Part 2:** 555, 580, 582–584

Maximus Poems Volume Three, The (Olson), **Supp. II Part 2:** 555, 582, 584–585

"Maximus to Gloucester, Letter 19 (A Pastoral Letter)" (Olson), **Supp. II Part 2:** 567

"Maximus to Gloucester, Sunday July 19" (Olson), **Supp. II Part 2:** 580

"Maximus to himself June 1964" (Olson), **Supp. II Part 2:** 584

Maxwell, Glyn, **Supp. XV:** 252, 253, 260, 261, 263, 264

Maxwell, William, **Supp. I Part 1:** 175; **Supp. III Part 1:** 62; **Supp. VIII:** 151–174

"May 1968" (Olds), **Supp. X:** 211–212

May, Abigail (Abba). *See* Alcott, Mrs. Amos Bronson (Abigail May)

May, Jill, **Supp. VIII:** 126

"May 24, 1980" (Brodsky), **Supp. VIII:** 28

"Mayan Warning" (Mora), **Supp. XIII:** 214

Maybe (Hellman), **Supp. IV Part 1:** 12

"Maybe" (Oliver), **Supp. VII:** 239

"Maybe, Someday" (Ritsos), **Supp. XIII:** 78

May Blossom (Belasco), **Supp. XVI:**182

"Mayday" (Faulkner), **Retro. Supp. I:** 80

"May Day" (Fitzgerald), **II:** 88–89; **Retro. Supp. I:** 103

"May Day Dancing, The" (Nemerov), **III:** 275

"May Day Sermon to the Women of Gilmer County, Georgia, by a Woman Preacher Leaving the Baptist Church" (Dickey), **Supp. IV Part 1:** 182

Mayer, Elizabeth, **Supp. II Part 1:** 16; **Supp. III Part 1:** 63

Mayer, John, **Retro. Supp. I:** 58

Mayer, Louis B., **Supp. XII:** 160

Mayes, Wendell, **Supp. IX:** 250

Mayfield, Sara, **Supp. IX:** 65

Mayflower, The (Stowe), **Supp. I Part 2:** 585, 586

Mayle, Peter, **Supp. XVI:**295

Maynard, Joyce, **Supp. V:** 23

Maynard, Tony, **Supp. I Part 1:** 65

Mayo, Robert, **III:** 478

Mayorga, Margaret, **IV:** 381

"Maypole of Merrymount, The" (Hawthorne), **II:** 229

May Sarton: Selected Letters 1916–1954, **Supp. VIII:** 265

"May Sun Sheds an Amber Light, The" (Bryant), **Supp. I Part 1:** 170

"May Swenson: The Art of Perceiving" (Stanford), **Supp. IV Part 2:** 637

"Maze" (Eberhart), **I:** 523, 525–526, 527

Mazurkiewicz, Margaret, **Supp. XI:** 2

Mazzini, Giuseppe, **Supp. I Part 1:** 2, 8; **Supp. II Part 1:** 299

M Butterfly (Hwang), **Supp. X:** 292

Mc. Names starting with Mc are alphabetized as if spelled Mac.

McElligot's Pool (Geisel), **Supp. XVI:**104

McLean, Carolyn (pseudo.). See Bly, Carol

"Me, Boy Scout" (Lardner), **II:** 433

Me: By Jimmy (Big Boy) Valente (Keillor), **Supp. XVI:**177

Me, Vashya! (T. Williams), **IV:** 381

Mead, Elinor. *See* Howells, Mrs. William Dean (Elinor Mead)

Mead, George Herbert, **II:** 27, 34; **Supp. I Part 1:** 5; **Supp. I Part 2:** 641

Mead, Margaret, **Supp. I Part 1:** 49, 52, 66; **Supp. IX:** 229

Mead, Taylor, **Supp. XV:** 187

Meade, Frank, **Retro. Supp. II:** 114

Meade, Marion, **Supp. IX:** 191, 193, 194, 195

Meadow, Lynne, **Supp. XIII:** 198

"Meadow House" (Carruth), **Supp. XVI:**48

Meadowlands (Glück), **Supp. V:** 88–90

"Mean, Mrs." (Gass), **Supp. VI:** 83

"Me and the Mule" (Hughes), **Supp. I Part 1:** 334

"Meaningless Institution, A" (Ginsberg), **Supp. II Part 1:** 313

"Meaning of a Literary Idea, The" (Trilling), **Supp. III Part 2:** 498

"Meaning of Birds, The" (C. Smith), **Supp. X:** 177

"Meaning of Death, The, An After Dinner Speech" (Tate), **IV:** 128, 129

"Meaning of Life, The" (Tate), **IV:** 137

"Meaning of Simplicity, The" (Ritsos), **Supp. XIII:** 78

Mean Spirit (Hogan), **Supp. IV Part 1:** 397, 404, 407–410, 415, 416–417

Mearns, Hughes, **III:** 220

"Measure" (Hass), **Supp. VI:** 99–100, 101

"Measuring My Blood" (Vizenor), **Supp. IV Part 1:** 262

Meatyard, Gene, **Supp. X:** 30

Mechan, Dennis B., **Supp. XVI:**267–268

Mechanic, The (Bynner and DeMille), **Supp. XV:** 42, 50

"Mechanism" (Ammons), **Supp. VII:** 28

"Mechanism in Thought and Morals" (Holmes), **Supp. I Part 1:** 314

Mecom, Mrs. Jane, **II:** 122

"Meddlesome Jack" (Caldwell), **I:** 309

Medea (Jeffers), **Supp. II Part 2:** 435

Medea and Some Poems, The (Cullen), **Supp. IV Part 1:** 169, 173

"Me Decade and the Third Great Awakening, The" (Wolfe), **Supp. III Part 2:** 581

"Médecin Malgré Lui, Le" (W. C. Williams), **IV:** 407–408

"Medfield" (Bryant), **Supp. I Part 1:** 157

Medical History of Contraception, A

(Himes), **Supp. V:** 128

"Medicine Song" (Gunn Allen), **Supp. IV Part 1:** 326

Médicis, Marie de, **II:** 548

Medina (McCarthy), **II:** 579

"Meditation 1.6" (Taylor), **IV:** 165

"Meditation 1.20" (Taylor), **IV:** 165

"Meditation 2.102" (Taylor), **IV:** 150

"Meditation 2.112" (Taylor), **IV:** 165

"Meditation 20" (Taylor), **IV:** 154–155

"Meditation 40" (Second Series) (Taylor), **IV:** 147

"Meditation, A" (Eberhart), **I:** 533–535

"Meditation 2.68A" (Taylor), **IV:** 165

"Meditation at Lagunitas" (Hass), **Supp. VI:** 104–105

"Meditation at Oyster River" (Roethke), **III:** 537, 549

Meditations (Descartes), **III:** 618

"Meditations for a Savage Child" (Rich), **Supp. I Part 2:** 564–565

Meditations from a Movable Chair (Dubus), **Supp. VII:** 91

"Meditations in a Swine Yard" (Komunyakaa), **Supp. XIII:** 131

"Meditations of an Old Woman" (Roethke), **III:** 529, 540, 542, 543, 545–547, 548

Meditations on the Insatiable Soul (R. Bly), **Supp. IV Part 1:** 72–73

Meditative Poems, The (Martz), **IV:** 151

"Mediterranean, The" (Tate), **IV:** 129

"Medium of Fiction, The" (Gass), **Supp. VI:** 85–86

"Medley" (Bambara), **Supp. XI:** 9

"Medusa" (Bogan), **Supp. III Part 1:** 50, 51

Meehan, Thomas, **Supp. IV Part 2:** 577–578, 586, 590

Meek, Martha, **Supp. IV Part 2:** 439, 440, 441, 442, 445, 447, 448

Meeker, Richard K., **II:** 190

Meese, Elizabeth, **Supp. XIII:** 297

"Meeting and Greeting Area, The" (Cameron), **Supp. XII:** 84–85

Meeting by the River, A (Isherwood), **Supp. XIV:**164, 170–171, 172

"Meeting-House Hill" (Lowell), **II:** 522, 527

"Meeting in the Kitchen, The" (Schnackenberg), **Supp. XV:** 256

"Meeting South, A" (Anderson), **I:** 115

"Meeting the Mountains" (Snyder), **Supp. VIII:** 300

Meeting Trees (Sanders), **Supp. XVI:**269

Meet Me at the Morgue (Macdonald), **Supp. IV Part 2:** 472

Mehta, Sonny, **Supp. XI:** 178

Meine, Curt, **Supp. XIV:**179

Meiners, R. K., **IV:** 136, 137, 138, 140

Meinong, Alexius, **Supp. XIV:**198, 199

Meisner, Sanford, **Supp. XIV:**240, 242

Meister, Charles W., **II:** 112

"Melancholia" (Dunbar), **Supp. II Part 1:** 194

"Melanctha" (Stein), **IV:** 30, 34, 35, 37, 38–40, 45

"Melancthon" (Moore), **III:** 212, 215

Meliboeus Hipponax (Lowell). *See Bigelow Papers, The* (Lowell)

Melinda and Melinda (Allen), **Supp. XV:** 16

Mellaart, James, **Supp. I Part 2:** 567

Mellard, James, **Supp. IV Part 1:** 387

Mellon, Andrew, **III:** 14

Melnick, Jeffrey, **Supp. X:** 252

Melnyczuk, Askold, **Supp. IV Part 1:** 70

Melodrama Play (Shepard), **Supp. III Part 2:** 440–441, 443, 445

Melodramatists, The (Nemerov), **III:** 268, 281–283, 284

Melting-Pot, The (Zangwill), **I:** 229

Melville, Allan, **III:** 74, 77

Melville, Gansevoort, **III:** 76

Melville, Herman, **I:** 104, 106, 211, 288, 340, 343, 348, 354, 355, 561–562; **II:** 27, 74, 224–225, 228, 230, 232, 236, 255, 259, 271, 272, 277, 281, 295, 307, 311, 319, 320, 321, 418, 477, 497, 539–540, 545; **III:** 29, 45, 70, 74–98, 359, 438, 453, 454, 507, 562–563, 572, 576; **IV:** 57, 105, 194, 199, 202, 250, 309, 333, 345, 350, 380, 444, 453; **Retro. Supp. I:** 54, 91, 160, 215, 220, 243–262; **Retro. Supp. II:** 76; **Supp. I Part 1:** 147, 238, 242, 249, 309, 317, 372; **Supp. I Part 2:** 383, 495, 579, 580, 582, 602; **Supp. IV Part 2:** 463, 613; **Supp. V:** 279, 281, 298, 308; **Supp. VIII:** 48, 103, 104, 105, 106, 108, 156, 175, 181, 188; **Supp. XI:** 83; **Supp. XII:** 282; **Supp. XIII:** 294, 305; **Supp. XIV:**48, 227; **Supp. XV:** 287

Melville, Maria Gansevoort, **III:** 74, 77, 85

Melville, Mrs. Herman (Elizabeth Shaw), **III:** 77, 91, 92

Melville, Thomas, **III:** 77, 79, 92; **Supp. I Part 1:** 309

Melville, Whyte, **IV:** 309

Melville Goodwin, USA (Marquand), **III:** 60, 65–66

Melville's Marginalia (Cowen), **Supp.**

IV Part 2: 435

"Melville's Marginalia" (Howe), **Supp. IV Part 2:** 435

Member of the Wedding, The (McCullers), **II:** 587, 592, 600–604, 605, 606; **Supp. VIII:** 124

"Meme Ortiz" (Cisneros), **Supp. VII:** 60

Memmon (song cycle) (Bowles), **Supp. IV Part 1:** 82

Memnoch the Devil (Rice), **Supp. VII:** 289, 290, 294, 296–299

"Memoir" (Untermeyer), **II:** 516–517

"Memoir, A" (Koch), **Supp. XV:** 184

"Memoirist's Apology, A" (Karr), **Supp. XI:** 245, 246

Memoir of Mary Ann, A (O'Connor), **III:** 357

Memoir of Thomas McGrath, A (Beeching), **Supp. X:** 114, 118

Memoirs of Arii Taimai (Adams), **I:** 2–3

"Memoirs of Carwin, the Biloquist" (Brown), **Supp. I Part 1:** 132

Memoirs of Hecate County (Wilson), **IV:** 429

Memoirs of Margaret Fuller Ossoli (Fuller), **Supp. II Part 1:** 280, 283, 285

"Memoirs of Stephen Calvert" (Brown), **Supp. I Part 1:** 133, 144

Memorabilia (Xenophon), **II:** 105

Memorable Providences (Mather), **Supp. II Part 2:** 458

Memorial, The: Portrait of a Family (Isherwood), **Supp. XIV:**156, 159, 160–161

"Memorial Day" (Cameron), **Supp. XII:** 80, 82–83

"Memorial for the City" (Auden), **Supp. II Part 1:** 20

"Memorial Rain" (MacLeish), **III:** 15

"Memorial to Ed Bland" (Brooks), **Supp. III Part 1:** 77

"Memorial Tribute" (Wilbur), **Supp. IV Part 2:** 642

"Memories" (Whittier), **Supp. I Part 2:** 699

Memories of a Catholic Girlhood (McCarthy), **II:** 560–561, 566; **Supp. XI:** 246; **Supp. XVI:**64, 70

"Memories of East Texas" (Karr), **Supp. XI:** 239

"Memories of Uncle Neddy" (Bishop), **Retro. Supp. II:** 38; **Supp. I Part 1:** 73, 93

"Memories of West Street and Lepke" (Lowell), **II:** 550

"Memory" (Epstein), **Supp. XII:** 163

"Memory" (Everwine), **Supp. XV:** 82

"Memory, A" (Welty), **IV:** 261–262; **Retro. Supp. I:** 344–345

"Memory, The" (Gioia), **Supp. XV:** 119

Memory Gardens (Creeley), **Supp. IV Part 1:** 141, 157

Memory of Murder, A (Bradbury), **Supp. IV Part 1:** 103

Memory of Old Jack, The (Berry), **Supp. X:** 34

Memory of Two Mondays, A (A. Miller), **III:** 153, 156, 158–159, 160, 166

"Memo to Non-White Peoples" (Hughes), **Retro. Supp. I:** 209

Men, Women and Ghosts (Lowell), **II:** 523–524

Menaker, Daniel, **Supp. VIII:** 151

Menand, Louis, **Supp. XIV:**40, 197; **Supp. XVI:**106, 107

Men and Angels (Gordon), **Supp. IV Part 1:** 304–305, 306, 308

Men and Brethen (Cozzens), **I:** 363–365, 368, 375, 378, 379

"Men and Women" (R. Bly), **Supp. IV Part 1:** 72

"Men at Forty" (Justice), **Supp. VII:** 126–127

Mencius (Meng-tzu), **IV:** 183

Mencken, August, **III:** 100, 108

Mencken, August, Jr., **III:** 99, 109, 118–119

Mencken, Burkhardt, **III:** 100, 108

Mencken, Charles, **III:** 99

Mencken, Gertrude, **III:** 99

Mencken, H. L., **I:** 199, 210, 212, 235, 245, 261, 405, 514, 515, 517; **II:** 25, 27, 42, 89, 90, 91, 271, 289, 430, 443, 449; **III:** 99–121, 394, 482; **IV:** 76, 432, 440, 475, 482; **Retro. Supp. I:** 1, 101; **Retro. Supp. II:** 97, 98, 102, 265; **Supp. I Part 2:** 484, 629–630, 631, 647, 651, 653, 659, 673; **Supp. II Part 1:** 136; **Supp. IV Part 1:** 201, 314, 343; **Supp. IV Part 2:** 521, 692, 693; **Supp. XI:** 163–164, 166; **Supp. XIII:** 161; **Supp. XIV:**111; **Supp. XV:** 297, 301, 303; **Supp. XVI:**187–188, 189

Mencken, Mrs. August (Anna Abhau), **III:** 100, 109

Mencken, Mrs. H. L. (Sara Haardt), **III:** 109, 111

"Men Deified Because of Their Cruelty" (Simic), **Supp. VIII:** 282

Mendelbaum, Paul, **Supp. V:** 159

Mendele, **IV:** 3, 10

Mendelief, Dmitri Ivanovich, **IV:** 421

Mendelsohn, Daniel, **Supp. X:** 153, 154; **Supp. XV:** 257, 258, 261, 266

"Mending Wall" (Frost), **II:** 153–154; **Retro. Supp. I:** 128, 130; **Supp. X:** 64

Men from the Boys, The (Lacy), **Supp. XV:** 202, 205

Men in the Off Hours (Carson), **Supp. XII:** 111–113

"Men in the Storm, The" (Crane), **I:** 411

"Men Loved Wholly Beyond Wisdom" (Bogan), **Supp. III Part 1:** 50

"Men Made Out of Words" (Stevens), **IV:** 88

Men Must Act (Mumford), **Supp. II Part 2:** 479

Mennes, John, **II:** 111

Mennoti, Gian Carlo, **Supp. IV Part 1:** 84

Men of Brewster Place, The (Naylor), **Supp. VIII:** 213, 228–230

"Men of Color, to Arms!" (Douglass), **Supp. III Part 1:** 171

Men of Good Hope: A Story of American Progressives (Aaron), **Supp. I Part 2:** 650

Mens' Club, The (film), **Supp. XVI:**212–213

Men's Club, The (L. Michaels), **Supp. XVI:**206, 210–212

"Menstruation at Forty" (Sexton), **Supp. II Part 2:** 686

Mental Hospital Garden, The (W. C. Williams), **Retro. Supp. I:** 428

Mental Radio (Sinclair), **Supp. V:** 289

Mentoria; or, The Young Lady's Friend (Rowson), **Supp. XV:** 233–234, 238

"Men We Carry in Our Minds, The" (Sanders), **Supp. XVI:**273

Men Who Made the Nation, The (Dos Passos), **I:** 485

Men Without Women (Hemingway), **II:** 249; **Retro. Supp. I:** 170, 176; **Supp. IX:** 202

"Merced" (Rich), **Supp. I Part 2:** 563

"Mercedes" (E. Stoddard), **Supp. XV:** 278

"Mercedes Hospital" (Bishop), **Retro. Supp. II:** 51

"Mercenary, A" (Ozick), **Supp. V:** 267

Merchant of Venice, The (Shakespeare), **IV:** 227; **Supp. XIV:**325

Mercury Theatre, **Retro. Supp. I:** 65

Mercy, Pity, Peace, and Love (Ozick), **Supp. V:** 257, 258

Mercy, The (Levine), **Supp. V:** 194–195

Mercy of a Rude Stream (H. Roth), **Supp. IX:** 231, 234, 235–242

Mercy Philbrick's Choice (Jackson),

Retro. Supp. I: 26, 27, 33

Mercy Street (Sexton), **Supp. II Part 2:** 683, 689

Meredith, George, **II:** 175, 186; **Supp. IV Part 1:** 300

Meredith, Mary. *See* Webb, Mary

Meredith, William, **II:** 545; **Retro. Supp. II:** 181

"Merely to Know" (Rich), **Supp. I Part 2:** 554

"Mère Pochette" (Jewett), **II:** 400

"Merger II, The" (Auchincloss), **Supp. IV Part 1:** 34

"Mericans" (Cisneros), **Supp. VII:** 69

"Merida, 1969" (Matthews), **Supp. IX:** 151

"Meridian" (Clampitt), **Supp. IX:** 48–49

Meridian (Walker), **Supp. III Part 2:** 520, 524, 527, 528, 531–537

Mérimée, Prosper, **II:** 322

Meriweather, James B., **Retro. Supp. I:** 77, 91

Meriwether, James B., Retro **Supp. I:** 77, 91

"Meriwether Connection, The" (Cowley), **Supp. II Part 1:** 142

Merker, Kim K., **Supp. XI:** 261; **Supp. XV:** 75, 77

"Merlin" (Emerson), **II:** 19, 20

Merlin (Robinson), **III:** 522

"Merlin Enthralled" (Wilbur), **Supp. III Part 2:** 544, 554

Merril, Judith, **Supp. XVI:**123

Merrill, Christopher, **Supp. XI:** 329

Merrill, James, **Retro. Supp. I:** 296; **Retro. Supp. II:** 53; **Supp. III Part 1:** 317–338; **Supp. III Part 2:** 541, 561; **Supp. IX:** 40, 42, 48, 52; **Supp. X:** 73; **Supp. XI:** 123, 131, 249; **Supp. XII:** 44, 254, 255, 256, 261–262, 269–270; **Supp. XIII:** 76, 85; **Supp. XV:** 249, 250, 253

Merrill, Robert, **Retro. Supp. II:** 201

Merrill, Ronald, **Supp. IV Part 2:** 521

Merritt, Theresa, **Supp. VIII:** 332

"Merry-Go-Round" (Hughes), **Retro. Supp. I:** 194, 205; **Supp. I Part 1:** 333

Merry-Go-Round, The (Van Vechten), **Supp. II Part 2:** 734, 735

Merry Month of May, The (Jones), **Supp. XI:** 227–228

Merry Widow, The (Lehar), **III:** 183

Merton, Thomas, **III:** 357; **Supp. VIII:** 193–212

Merwin, W. S., **Supp. III Part 1:** 339–360; **Supp. III Part 2:** 541; **Supp. IV Part 2:** 620, 623, 626; **Supp. V:** 332; **Supp. IX:** 152, 155, 290;

Supp. XIII: 274, 277; **Supp. XV:** 222, 342

Meryman, Richard, **Supp. IV Part 2:** 579, 583

Meshugah (Singer), **Retro. Supp. II:** 315–316

Mesic, Michael, **Supp. IV Part 1:** 175

Mesic, Penelope, **Supp. X:** 15

Message in the Bottle, The (Percy), **Supp. III Part 1:** 387–388, 393, 397

"Message in the Bottle, The" (Percy), **Supp. III Part 1:** 388

"Message of Flowers and Fire and Flowers, The" (Brooks), **Supp. III Part 1:** 69

Messengers Will Come No More, The (Fiedler), **Supp. XIII:** 103

Messerli, Douglas, **Supp. XVI:** 293

Messiah (Vidal), **Supp. IV Part 2:** 677, 680, 681–682, 685, 691, 692

"Messiah, The" (Wasserstein), **Supp. XV:** 328

Messiah of Stockholm, The (Ozick), **Supp. V:** 270–271

Metamorphic Tradition in Modern Poetry (Quinn), **IV:** 421

Metamorphoses (Ovid), **II:** 542–543; **III:** 467, 468

Metamorphoses (Pound, trans.), **III:** 468–469

Metamorphosis (Ovid), **Supp. XV:** 33; **Supp. XVI:** 20

Metamorphosis, The (Kafka), **IV:** 438; **Retro. Supp. II:** 287–288; **Supp. VIII:** 3

"Metamorphosis and Survival" (Woodcock), **Supp. XIII:** 33

"Metaphor as Mistake" (Percy), **Supp. III Part 1:** 387–388

Metaphor & Memory: Essays (Ozick), **Supp. V:** 272

"Metaphors of a Magnifico" (Stevens), **IV:** 92

Metaphysical Club, The (Menand), **Supp. XIV:** 40, 197

"Metaphysical Poets, The" (Eliot), **I:** 527, 586

"Metaphysics" (Ginsberg), **Supp. II Part 1:** 313

Metcalf, Paul, **Supp. XIV:** 96

"Meteor, The" (Bradbury), **Supp. IV Part 1:** 102

Metress, Christopher P., **Supp. V:** 314

Metrical History of Christianity, The (Taylor), **IV:** 163

Metropolis, The (Sinclair), **Supp. V:** 285

"Metterling Lists, The" (Allen), **Supp. XV:** 15

"Metzengerstein" (Poe), **III:** 411, 417

Mew, Charlotte, **Retro. Supp. II:** 247

Mewshaw, Michael, **Supp. V:** 57; **Supp. X:** 82

"Mexico" (Lowell), **II:** 553, 554

"Mexico, Age Four" (Salinas), **Supp. XIII:** 315

Mexico City Blues (Kerouac), **Supp. III Part 1:** 225, 229

"Mexico Is a Foreign Country: Five Studies in Naturalism" (Warren), **IV:** 241, 252

"Mexico's Children" (Rodriguez), **Supp. XIV:** 302

Meyer, Donald B., **III:** 298

Meyer, Ellen Hope, **Supp. V:** 123

Meyers, Jeffrey, **Retro. Supp. I:** 124, 138; **Retro. Supp. II:** 191

Meynell, Alice, **Supp. I Part 1:** 220

Mezey, Robert, **Supp. IV Part 1:** 60; **Supp. V:** 180; **Supp. XIII:** 312; **Supp. XV:** 74

Mezzanine, The (Baker), **Supp. XIII:** 41–43, 44, 45, 48, 55

"Mezzo Cammin" (Longfellow), **II:** 490

"Mi Abuelo" (Ríos), **Supp. IV Part 2:** 541

Miami (Didion), **Supp. IV Part 1:** 199, 210

Miami and the Siege of Chicago (Mailer), **Retro. Supp. II:** 206

"Michael" (Wordsworth), **III:** 523

Michael, Magali Cornier, **Supp. XIII:** 32

"Michael Angelo: A Fragment" (Longfellow), **II:** 490, 494, 495, 506; **Retro. Supp. II:** 167

"Michael Egerton" (Price), **Supp. VI:** 257–258, 260

Michael Kohlhaas (Kleist), **Supp. IV Part 1:** 224

Michaels, Leonard, **Supp. XVI:** 201–215

Michaels, Walter Benn, **Retro. Supp. I:** 115, 369, 379

Michael Scarlett (Cozens), **I:** 358–359, 378

Michaux, Henri, **Supp. XVI:** 288

Michelangelo, **I:** 18; **II:** 11–12; **III:** 124; **Supp. I Part 1:** 363

Michel-Michot, Paulette, **Supp. XI:** 224–225

Michelson, Albert, **IV:** 27

Mickelsson's Ghosts (Gardner), **Supp. VI:** 63, 73–74

Mickiewicz, Adam, **Supp. II Part 1:** 299

Midair (Conroy), **Supp. XVI:** 63, 71–72

"Mid-Air" (Conroy), **Supp. XVI:** 69, 71

Mid-American Chants (Anderson), **I:** 109, 114

"Midas" (Winters), **Supp. II Part 2:** 801

"Mid-August at Sourdough Mountain Lookout" (Snyder), **Supp. VIII:** 292–293

Midcentury (Dos Passos), **I:** 474, 475, 478, 490, 492–494; **Supp. I Part 2:** 646

Mid-Century American Poets, **III:** 532

"Mid-Day" (Doolittle), **Supp. I Part 1:** 266–267

"Middle Age" (Lowell), **II:** 550

"Middleaged Man, The" (Simpson), **Supp. IX:** 274–275

Middle Ages, The (Gurney), **Supp. V:** 96, 105, 108

Middlebrook, Diane Wood, **Supp. IV Part 2:** 444, 451

"Middle Daughter, The" (Kingsolver), **Supp. VII:** 209

Middlemarch (Eliot), **I:** 457, 459; **II:** 290, 291; **Retro. Supp. I:** 225; **Supp. I Part 1:** 174; **Supp. IX:** 43; **Supp. XI:** 68; **Supp. XII:** 335

Middle of My Tether, The: Familiar Essays (Epstein), **Supp. XIV:** 106–107

"Middle of Nowhere, The" (Wagoner), **Supp. IX:** 327–328

Middle of the Journey, The (Trilling), **Supp. III Part 2:** 495, 504–506

"Middle of the Way" (Kinnell), **Supp. III Part 1:** 242

"Middle Passage" (Hayden), **Supp. II Part 1:** 363, 375–376

Middle Passage (Johnson), **Supp. VI:** 194–196, 198, 199; **Supp. XIII:** 182

"Middle Toe of the Right Foot, The" (Bierce), **I:** 203

Middleton, Thomas, **Retro. Supp. I:** 62

Middle Years, The (James), **II:** 337–338; **Retro. Supp. I:** 235

"Middle Years, The" (James), **Retro. Supp. I:** 228, 272

"Midnight" (Dunn), **Supp. XI:** 147

"Midnight Consultations, The" (Freneau), **Supp. II Part 1:** 257

Midnight Cry, A (Mather), **Supp. II Part 2:** 460

"Midnight Gladness" (Levertov), **Supp. III Part 1:** 284–285

"Midnight Magic" (Mason), **Supp. VIII:** 146

Midnight Magic: Selected Stories of Bobbie Ann Mason (Mason), **Supp. VIII:** 148

Midnight Mass (Bowles), **Supp. IV Part 1:** 93

"Midnight Show" (Shapiro), **Supp. II Part 2:** 705

"Midpoint" (Updike), **Retro. Supp. I:** 321, 323, 327, 330, 335

Midpoint and Other Poems (Updike), **IV:** 214

"Midrash on Happiness" (Paley), **Supp. VI:** 217

"Midsummer in the Blueberry Barrens" (Clampitt), **Supp. IX:** 40–41

"Midsummer Letter" (Carruth), **Supp. XVI:**47

Midsummer Night's Dream, A (Shakespeare), **Supp. I Part 1:** 369–370; **Supp. X:** 69

Midsummer Night's Sex Comedy, A (film; Allen), **Supp. XV:** 8

"Midwest" (Stafford), **Supp. XI:** 317

Mieder, Wolfgang, **Supp. XIV:**126

Mies van der Rohe, Ludwig, **Supp. IV Part 1:** 40

Mighty Aphrodite (film; Allen), **Supp. XV:** 11

"Mighty Fortress, A" (Leopold), **Supp. XIV:**185

"Mighty Lord, The (Rowson), **Supp. XV:** 243

"Migration, The" (Tate), **IV:** 130

Mihailovitch, Bata, **Supp. VIII:** 272

Miklitsch, Robert, **Supp. IV Part 2:** 628, 629

Mila 18 (Uris), **Supp. IV Part 1:** 379

Milagro Beanfield War, The (film), **Supp. XIII:** 267

Milagro Beanfield War, The (Nichols), **Supp. XIII:** 253, 265–266

Milburn, Michael, **Supp. XI:** 239, 242

Milch, David, **Supp. XI:** 348

Miles, Barry, **Supp. XII:** 123

Miles, Jack, **Supp. VIII:** 86

Miles, Josephine, **Supp. XIII:** 275

Miles, Julie, **I:** 199

Miles, Kitty, **I:** 199

Milestone, Lewis, **Supp. I Part 1:** 281

Miles Wallingford (Cooper). *See Afloat and Ashore* (Cooper)

Milford, Nancy, **II:** 83; **Supp. IX:** 60

Milhaud, Darius, **Supp. IV Part 1:** 81

Miligate, Michael, **IV:** 123, 130, 132

"Militant Nudes" (Hardwick), **Supp. III Part 1:** 210–211

"Milk Bottles" (Anderson), **I:** 114

Milk Train Doesn't Stop Here Anymore, The (T. Williams), **IV:** 382, 383, 384, 386, 390, 391, 392, 393, 394, 395, 398

Mill, James, **II:** 357

Mill, John Stuart, **III:** 294–295; **Supp. XI:** 196; **Supp. XIV:**22

Millar, Kenneth. *See* Macdonald, Ross

Millar, Margaret (Margaret Sturm), **Supp. IV Part 2:** 464, 465

Millay, Cora, **III:** 123, 133–134, 135–136

Millay, Edna St. Vincent, **I:** 482; **II:** 530; **III:** 122–144; **IV:** 433, 436; **Retro. Supp. II:** 48; **Supp. I Part 2:** 707, 714, 726; **Supp. IV Part 1:** 168; **Supp. IV Part 2:** 607; **Supp. V:** 113; **Supp. IX:** 20; **Supp. XIV:**120, 121, 122, 127; **Supp. XV:** 42, 46, 51, 250, 293, 307

Millennium Approaches (Kushner), **Supp. IX:** 141, 142, 145

Miller, Arthur, **I:** 81, 94; **III:** 145–169; **Supp. IV Part 1:** 359; **Supp. IV Part 2:** 574; **Supp. VIII:** 334; **Supp. XIII:** 127; **Supp. XIV:**102, 239; **Supp. XVI:**194

Miller, Brown, **Supp. IV Part 1:** 67

Miller, Carol, **Supp. IV Part 1:** 400, 405, 409, 410, 411

Miller, Henry, **I:** 97, 157; **III:** 40, 170–192; **IV:** 138; **Retro. Supp. II:** 327; **Supp. I Part 2:** 546; **Supp. V:** 119, 131; **Supp. X:** 183, 185, 187, 194, 195; **Supp. XIII:** 1, 17

Miller, Henry (actor), **Supp. XVI:**182

Miller, Herman, **Supp. I Part 2:** 614, 617

Miller, J. Hillis, **Supp. IV Part 1:** 387

Miller, James E., Jr., **IV:** 352

Miller, Jeffrey, **Supp. IV Part 1:** 95

Miller, Joaquin, **I:** 193, 195, 459; **Supp. II Part 1:** 351

Miller, John Duncan, **Supp. I Part 2:** 604

Miller, Jonathan, **Retro. Supp. II:** 181

Miller, Laura, **Supp. XIII:** 48

Miller, Marilyn, **Supp. XVI:**187

Miller, Matt, **Supp. XV:** 211

Miller, Matthew, **Supp. XVI:**47, 51

Miller, Mrs. Arthur (Ingeborg Morath), **III:** 162–163

Miller, Mrs. Arthur (Marilyn Monroe), **III:** 161, 162–163

Miller, Mrs. Arthur (Mary Grace Slattery), **III:** 146, 161

Miller, Orilla, **Supp. I Part 1:** 48

Miller, Perry, **I:** 546, 547, 549, 550, 560; **IV:** 186; **Supp. I Part 1:** 31, 104; **Supp. I Part 2:** 484; **Supp. IV Part 2:** 422; **Supp. VIII:** 101

Miller, R. Baxter, **Retro. Supp. I:** 195, 207

Miller, Robert Ellis, **II:** 588

Miller, Ruth, **Supp. X:** 324

Miller, Stuart, **Supp. XVI:**242

Miller, Sue, **Supp. X:** 77, 85; **Supp. XI:** 190; **Supp. XII:** 289–305

Miller of Old Church, The (Glasgow), **II:** 175, 181

"Miller's Tale" (Chaucer), **III:** 283

Miller Williams and the Poetry of the Particular (Burns), **Supp. XV:** 339

Millett, Kate, **Supp. X:** 193, 196

Millgate, Michael, **Retro. Supp. I:** 91

Mill Hand's Lunch Bucket (Bearden), **Supp. VIII:** 337

Millier, Brett C., **Retro. Supp. II:** 39

Milligan, Bryce, **Supp. XIII:** 274, 275, 277

Millions of Strange Shadows (Hecht), **Supp. X:** 57, 62–65

"Million Young Workmen, 1915, A" (Sandburg), **III:** 585

Millroy the Magician (Theroux), **Supp. VIII:** 325

Mills, Alice, **Supp. XIII:** 233

Mills, Benjamin Fay, **III:** 176

Mills, C. Wright, **Supp. I Part 2:** 648, 650

Mills, Florence, **Supp. I Part 1:** 322

Mills, Ralph J., Jr., **III:** 530; **Supp. IV Part 1:** 64; **Supp. XI:** 311

Mills, Tedi López, **Supp. XVI:**281

Mills of the Kavanaughs, The (Lowell), **II:** 542–543, 546, 550; **III:** 508; **Retro. Supp. II:** 178, 179, 188

"Mills of the Kavanaughs, The" (Lowell), **II:** 542–543

Milne, A. A., **Supp. IX:** 189

Milne, A. J. M., **I:** 278

Milosz, Czeslaw, **Supp. III Part 2:** 630; **Supp. VIII:** 20, 22; **Supp. XI:** 267, 312

Miltner, Robert, **Supp. XI:** 142

Milton, Edith, **Supp. VIII:** 79; **Supp. X:** 82

Milton, John, **I:** 6, 138, 273, 587–588; **II:** 11, 15, 113, 130, 411, 540, 542; **III:** 40, 124, 201, 225, 274, 468, 471, 486, 487, 503, 511; **IV:** 50, 82, 126, 137, 155, 157, 241, 279, 347, 422, 461, 494; **Retro. Supp. I:** 60, 67, 127, 360; **Retro. Supp. II:** 161, 295; **Supp. I Part 1:** 124, 150, 370; **Supp. I Part 2:** 412, 422, 491, 501, 522, 622, 722, 724; **Supp. IV Part 2:** 430, 634; **Supp. VIII:** 294; **Supp. X:** 22, 23, 36; **Supp. XII:** 180; **Supp. XIV:**5, 7

Milton, John R., **Supp. IV Part 2:** 503

Milton and His Modern Critics (L. P. Smith), **Supp. XIV:**347

"Milton by Firelight" (Snyder), **Supp.**

II Part 1: 314; **Supp. VIII:** 294

"Miltonic Sonnet, A" (Wilbur), **Supp. III Part 2:** 558

Mimesis (Auerbach), **III:** 453

"Mimnermos and the Motions of Hedonism" (Carson), **Supp. XII:** 99–100

"Mimnermos Interviews, The" (Carson), **Supp. XII:** 100–101

Mims, Edwin, **Supp. I Part 1:** 362, 364, 365, 371

"Mind" (Wilbur), **Supp. III Part 2:** 554

"Mind, The" (Kinnell), **Supp. III Part 1:** 245

Mind Breaths: Poems 1972–1977 (Ginsberg), **Supp. II Part 1:** 326

Mindfield: New and Selected Poems (Corso), **Supp. XII:** 136

"Mind in the Modern World" (Trilling), **Supp. III Part 2:** 512

"Mind Is Shapely, Art Is Shapely" (Ginsberg), **Supp. II Part 1:** 327

Mindlin, Henrique, **Supp. I Part 1:** 92

Mind of My Mind (O. Butler), **Supp. XIII:** 62, 63

Mind of Primitive Man, The (Boas), **Supp. XIV:**209

"Mind-Reader, The" (Wilbur), **Supp. III Part 2:** 561–562

Mind-Reader, The (Wilbur), **Supp. III Part 2:** 560–562

Mindwheel (Pinsky), **Supp. VI:** 235

Minear, Richard H., **Supp. XVI:**101, 102

"Mined Country" (Wilbur), **Supp. III Part 2:** 546–548

"Mine Own John Berryman" (Levine), **Supp. V:** 179–180

Miner, Bob, **Supp. V:** 23

Miner, Earl, **III:** 466, 479

Miner, Madonne, **Supp. XIII:** 29

"Minerva Writes Poems" (Cisneros), **Supp. VII:** 63–64, 66

Mingus, Charles, **Supp. IX:** 152

"Mingus in Diaspora" (Matthews), **Supp. IX:** 166

"Mingus in Shadow" (Matthews), **Supp. IX:** 168–169

Ming Yellow (Marquand), **III:** 56

"Minimal, The" (Roethke), **III:** 531–532

Minimus Poems, The (X. J. Kennedy), **Supp. XV:** 169–170

"Mini-novela: *Rosa y sus espinas*" (Mora), **Supp. XIII:** 218

"Minions of Midas, The" (London), **II:** 474–475

Minister's Charge, The, or The Apprenticeship of Lemuel Barber (Howells), **II:** 285–286, 287

"Minister's Wooing, The" (Stowe), **Supp. I Part 2:** 592–595

Minister's Wooing, The (Stowe), **II:** 541

"Ministration of Our Departed Friends, The" (Stowe), **Supp. I Part 2:** 586–587

"Minneapolis Poem, The" (Wright), **Supp. III Part 2:** 601–602

Minnesota Grain Show, The (radio, Keillor), **Supp. XVI:**170

"Minnesota Transcendentalist" (Peseroff), **Supp. IV Part 1:** 71

Minnie, Temple, **II:** 344

Minority Report: H. L. Mencken's Notebooks (Mencken), **III:** 112

Minor Pleasures of Life, The (Macaulay), **Supp. XIV:**348

"Minor Poems" (Eliot), **I:** 579

"Minor Poet" (Hay), **Supp. XIV:**127

"Minor Topics" (Howells), **II:** 274

Minot, Susan, **Supp. VI:** 203–215

"Minotaur Loves His Labyrinth, The" (Simic), **Supp. VIII:** 270, 279, 281

"Minstrel Man" (Hughes), **Supp. I Part 1:** 325

Mint (Nye), **Supp. XIII:** 277

"Minting Time" (Sarton), **Supp. VIII:** 259

Mint Snowball (Nye), **Supp. XIII:** 277–278, 284–285

"Mint Snowball" (Nye), **Supp. XIII:** 278, 284

"Mint Snowball II" (Nye), **Supp. XIII:** 284, 285

Mintzlaff, Dorothy, **Supp. XV:** 153

Minutes to Go (Corso, Gysin, Beiles and Burroughs), **Supp. XII:** 129

Mirabell: Books of Number (Merrill), **Supp. III Part 1:** 332–334

"Miracle" (Carver), **Supp. III Part 1:** 139–140

"Miracle for Breakfast, A" (Bishop), **Retro. Supp. II:** 43

"Miracle of Lava Canyon, The" (Henry), **Supp. II Part 1:** 389, 390

Miracle of Mindfulness, The: A Manual on Meditation (Thich Nhat Hanh), **Supp. V:** 199–200

Mirage (Masters), **Supp. I Part 2:** 459, 470, 471

"Mirages, The" (Hayden), **Supp. II Part 1:** 373

"Miranda" (Buck), **Supp. II Part 1:** 128

Miranda, Carmen, **Supp. XII:** 165

Miranda, Francisco de, **Supp. I Part 2:** 522

"Miranda Over the Valley" (Dubus), **Supp. VII:** 81–83

"Miriam" (Capote), **Supp. III Part 1:** 117, 120, 122

"Miriam" (Whittier), **Supp. I Part 2:** 691, 703

"Miriam Tazewell" (Ransom), **Supp. X:** 58

"Mirror" (Merrill), **Supp. III Part 1:** 322

"Mirror" (Plath), **Retro. Supp. II:** 248–249, 257

"Mirror, The" (Glück), **Supp. V:** 83

"Mirroring Evil: Nazi Images/Recent Art" (Epstein), **Supp. XII:** 166

Mirrors (Creeley), **Supp. IV Part 1:** 156

Mirrors and Windows (Nemerov), **III:** 269, 275–277

"Mirrors of Chartres Street" (Faulkner), **II:** 56

Misanthrope, The (Molière; Wilbur, trans.), **Supp. III Part 2:** 552, 560

Miscellaneous Poems (Rowson), **Supp. XV:** 243

Miscellaneous Works of Mr. Philip Freneau, Containing His Essays and Additional Poems (Freneau), **Supp. II Part 1:** 263, 264, 266

Miscellany of American Poetry, A (Untermeyer, ed.), **Supp. XV:** 305, 310

Misery (King), **Supp. V:** 140, 141, 142, 147–148, 151, 152

Mises, Ludwig von, **Supp. IV Part 2:** 524

Misfits, The (A. Miller), **III:** 147, 149, 156, 161–162, 163

"Misogamist, The" (Dubus), **Supp. VII:** 86–87

Misread City, The: New Literary Los Angeles (Gioia and Timberg, eds.), **Supp. XV:** 116

Misrepresentations Corrected, and Truth Vindicated, in a Reply to the Rev. Mr. Solomon Williams's Book (Edwards), **I:** 549

"Miss Ella" (Z. Fitzgerald), **Supp. IX:** 57, 59, 71–72

"Miss Emily and the Bibliographer" (Tate), **Supp. II Part 1:** 103

"Miss Furr and Miss Skeene" (Stein), **IV:** 29–30

"Missing Child" (Simic), **Supp. VIII:** 282

"Missing in Action" (Komunyakaa), **Supp. XIII:** 123, 124

Missing/Kissing: Missing Marisa, Kissing Christine (Shanley), **Supp. XIV:**316

Missing Link (X. J. Kennedy), **Supp. XV:** 165

"Mission of Jane, The" (Wharton), **Retro. Supp. I:** 367

"Missions, The" (Rodriguez), **Supp. XIV:**303

Mission to Moscow (film), **Supp. I Part 1:** 281

"Mississippi" (Bass), **Supp. XVI:**17

"Mississippi" (Faulkner), **Retro. Supp. I:** 77

"Mississippi" (Simpson), **Supp. IX:** 271

"Miss Kate in H-1" (Twain), **IV:** 193

Miss Leonora When Last Seen (Taylor), **Supp. V:** 323

Miss Lonelyhearts (West), **I:** 107; **II:** 436; **III:** 357; **IV:** 287, 288, 290–297, 300, 301, 305, 306; **Retro. Supp. II:** 321, 322, 325, 328, 332–335

Miss Mamma Aimee (Caldwell), **I:** 308, 309, 310

"Miss Mary Pask" (Wharton), **IV:** 316; **Retro. Supp. I:** 382

"Miss McEnders" (Chopin), **Retro. Supp. II:** 67

"Missoula Softball Tournament" (Hugo), **Supp. VI:** 132

Miss Ravenel's Conversion from Secession to Loyalty (De Forest), **IV:** 350

"Miss Tempy's Watchers" (Jewett), **II:** 401; **Retro. Supp. II:** 139

"Miss Terriberry to Wed in Suburbs" (Updike), **Retro. Supp. I:** 335

"Mist, The" (King), **Supp. V:** 144

"Mistaken Charity, A" (Freeman), **Retro. Supp. II:** 138

"Mister Brother" (Cunningham), **Supp. XV:** 68

"Mister Toussan" (Ellison), **Retro. Supp. II:** 124–125; **Supp. II Part 1:** 238

"Mistress of Sydenham Plantation, The" (Jewett), **Retro. Supp. II:** 141

Mitchell, Burroughs, **Supp. XI:** 218, 222, 227

Mitchell, Dr. S. Weir, **IV:** 310

Mitchell, Margaret, **II:** 177

Mitchell, Roger, **Supp. IV Part 1:** 70; **Supp. XV:** 213, 215

Mitchell, Tennessee. *See* Anderson, Mrs. Sherwood (Tennessee Mitchell)

Mitchell, Wesley C., **Supp. I Part 2:** 632, 643

Mitch Miller (Masters), **Supp. I Part 2:** 456, 466, 469–471, 474, 475, 476

Mitchum, Robert, **Supp. IX:** 95, 250

Mitgang, Herbert, **Supp. IV Part 1:** 220, 226, 307; **Supp. VIII:** 124

"Mixed Sequence" (Roethke), **III:** 547

Miyazawa Kenji, **Supp. VIII:** 292

Mizener, Arthur, **II:** 77, 81, 84, 94; **IV:** 132

Mizner, Addison, **Supp. XVI:**191

Mizner, Wilson, **Supp. XVI:**191, 195

Mladenoff, Nancy, **Supp. X:** 176

"M'liss: An Idyl of Red Mountain" (Harte), **Supp. II Part 1:** 339

"Mnemonic Devices" (Goldbarth), **Supp. XII:** 183

"Mobile in Back of the Smithsonian, The" (Swenson), **Supp. IV Part 2:** 646

Mobilio, Albert, **Supp. VIII:** 3

Moby Dick (film), **Supp. IV Part 1:** 102, 116

Moby Dick; or, The Whale (Melville), **I:** 106, 354; **II:** 33, 224–225, 236, 539–540; **III:** 28–29, 74, 75, 77, 81, 82, 83–86, 87, 89, 90, 91, 93, 94, 95, 359, 453, 556; **IV:** 57, 199, 201, 202; **Retro. Supp. I:** 160, 220, 243, 244, 248, 249–253, 254, 256, 257, 335; **Retro. Supp. II:** 121, 186, 275; **Supp. I Part 1:** 249; **Supp. I Part 2:** 579; **Supp. IV Part 2:** 613; **Supp. V:** 281; **Supp. VIII:** 106, 188, 198

Mock, John, **Supp. XIII:** 174

"Mocking-Bird, The" (Bierce), **I:** 202

"Mock Orange" (Glück), **Supp. V:** 84–85

Modarressi, Mitra, **Supp. IV Part 2:** 657

Models of Misrepresentation: On the Fiction of E. L. Doctorow (Morris), **Supp. IV Part 1:** 231

Model World and Other Stories, A (Chabon), **Supp. XI:** 66

Modern American and British Poetry (Untermeyer, ed.), **Supp. XV:** 306

Modern American Poetry (Untermeyer, ed.), **Supp. XV:** 293, 303, 306, 312

Modern American Verse (Untermeyer), **Supp. XV:** 301

Modern Brazilian Architecture (Bishop, trans.), **Supp. I Part 1:** 92

Modern British Poetry (Untermeyer, ed.), **Supp. XV:** 305, 308, 312

Modern Fiction Studies, **Supp. V:** 238

Modern Fiction Studies (Haegert), **Supp. XVI:**69

Modern Instance a Novel, A (Howells), **II:** 275, 279, 282–283, 285

Modern Library, The, **Retro. Supp. I:** 112, 113

Modern Mephistopheles, A (Alcott), **Supp. I Part 1:** 37–38

Modern Poetic Sequence, The (Rosenthal), **Supp. V:** 333

"Modern Poetry" (Crane), **I:** 390

Modern Poetry and the Tradition (Brooks), **Supp. XIV:**5–7

"Modern Race Creeds and Their Fallacies" (Locke), **Supp. XIV:**210

Modern Rhetoric, with Readings (Brooks and Warren), **Supp. XIV:**11

"Modern Sorcery" (Simic), **Supp. VIII:** 283

"Modern Times" (Zukofsky), **Supp. III Part 2:** 624

Modern Writer, The (Anderson), **I:** 117

Modersohn, Mrs. Otto (Paula Becker), **Supp. I Part 2:** 573–574

Modersohn, Otto, **Supp. I Part 2:** 573

"Modes of Being" (Levertov), **Supp. III Part 1:** 282

Modest Enquiry into the Nature and Necessity of a Paper-Currency, A (Franklin), **II:** 108–109

"Modest Proposal, A" (Swift), **I:** 295; **Retro. Supp. II:** 287

"Modest Proposal with Feline Feeling, A" (Neugeboren), **Supp. XVI:**219

"Modest Self-Tribute, A" (Wilson), **IV:** 431, 432

Moeller, Philip, **III:** 398, 399

"Moench von Berchtesgaden, Der" (Voss), **I:** 199–200

Moers, Ellen, **Retro. Supp. II:** 99

Moe's Villa and Other Stories (Purdy), **Supp. VII:** 270, 280

Mogen, David, **Supp. IV Part 1:** 106

Mohammed, **I:** 480; **II:** 1

Mohawk (Russo), **Supp. XII:** 326–328

Moir, William Wilmerding, **Supp. V:** 279

Moldaw, Carol, **Supp. XV:** 264

"Moles" (Oliver), **Supp. VII:** 235

Molesworth, Charles, **Supp. IV Part 1:** 39; **Supp. VIII:** 292, 306

Molière (Jean-Baptiste Poquelin), **III:** 113; **Supp. I Part 2:** 406; **Supp. III Part 2:** 552, 560; **Supp. IV Part 2:** 585; **Supp. V:** 101

"Molino Rojo, El" (Ríos), **Supp. IV Part 2:** 544

Moll Flanders (Defoe), **Supp. V:** 127; **Supp. XIII:** 43

"Molloch in State Street" (Whittier), **Supp. I Part 2:** 687

"Moll Pitcher" (Whittier), **Supp. I Part 2:** 684

"Molly Brant, Iroquois Matron" (Gunn Allen), **Supp. IV Part 1:** 331

Molnar, Ferenc, **Supp. XVI:**187

"Moloch" (H. Miller), **III:** 177

Momaday, N. Scott, **Supp. IV Part 1:** 274, 323, 324, 404; **Supp. IV Part**

2: 479–496, 504, 557, 562; **Supp. XII:** 209

" 'Momentary Stay against Confusion,' A: Frank Conroy's *Stop-Time*" (T. Adams), **Supp. XVI:**69

Moment of Untruth (Lacy), **Supp. XV:** 206, 207

Moments of the Italian Summer (Wright), **Supp. III Part 2:** 602

"Momus" (Robinson), **III:** 508

Monaghan, Pat, **Supp. XI:** 121

Mona Lisa Overdrive (W. Gibson), **Supp. XVI:**119, 120, 127–128

"Mon Ami" (Bourne), **I:** 227

Monet, Claude, **Retro. Supp. I:** 378

"Monet's 'Waterlilies'" (Hayden), **Supp. II Part 1:** 361–362

Monette, Paul, **Supp. X:** 145–161

Money (Amis), **Retro. Supp. I:** 278

"Money" (Matthews), **Supp. IX:** 166

"Money" (Nemerov), **III:** 287

Money, Money, Money (Wagoner), **Supp. IX:** 324, 333–334

Moneychangers, The (Sinclair), **Supp. V:** 285

Money Writes! (Sinclair), **Supp. V:** 277

Monica, Saint, **IV:** 140

Monikins, The (Cooper), **I:** 348, 354

Monk and the Hangman's Daughter, The (Bierce), **I:** 199–200, 209

"Monkey Garden, The" (Cisneros), **Supp. VII:** 63

"Monkey Puzzle, The" (Moore), **III:** 194, 207, 211

Monkeys (Minot), **Supp. VI:** 203–205, 206–210

"Monkeys, The" (Moore), **III:** 201, 202

Monkey Wrench Gang, The (Abbey), **Supp. VIII:** 42; **Supp. XIII:** 9–11, 16

"Monk of Casal-Maggiore, The" (Longfellow), **II:** 505

"Monocle de Mon Oncle, Le" (Stevens), **IV:** 78, 84; **Retro. Supp. I:** 301; **Supp. III Part 1:** 20; **Supp. X:** 58

"Monolog from a Mattress" (Untermeyer), **Supp. XV:** 307

Monro, Harold, **III:** 465; **Retro. Supp. I:** 127; **Supp. XV:** 296

Monroe, Harriet, **I:** 235, 384, 390, 393; **III:** 458, 581, 586; **IV:** 74; **Retro. Supp. I:** 58, 131; **Retro. Supp. II:** 82, 83; **Supp. I Part 1:** 256, 257, 258, 262, 263, 267; **Supp. I Part 2:** 374, 387, 388, 464, 610, 611, 613, 614, 615, 616; **Supp. XIV:**286; **Supp. XV:** 43, 299, 302

Monroe, James, **Supp. I Part 2:** 515, 517

Monroe, Lucy, **Retro. Supp. II:** 70

Monroe, Marilyn, **III:** 161, 162–163

Monroe's Embassy; or, the Conduct of the Government in Relation to Our Claims to the Navigation of the Mississippi (Brown), **Supp. I Part 1:** 146

"Monsoon Season" (Komunyakaa), **Supp. XIII:** 122

Monsour, Leslie, **Supp. XV:** 125

"Monster, The" (Crane), **I:** 418

Monster, The, and Other Stories (Crane), **I:** 409

Montage of a Dream Deferred (Hughes), **Retro. Supp. I:** 194, 208–209; **Supp. I Part 1:** 333, 339–341

Montagu, Ashley, **Supp. I Part 1:** 314

"Montaigne" (Emerson), **II:** 6

Montaigne, Michel de, **II:** 1, 5, 6, 8, 14–15, 16, 535; **III:** 600; **Retro. Supp. I:** 247; **Supp. XIV:**105

Montale, Eugenio, **Supp. III Part 1:** 320; **Supp. V:** 337–338; **Supp. VIII:** 30; **Supp. XV:** 112

Montalembert, Hughes de, **Supp. XV:** 349

"Montana; or the End of Jean-Jacques Rousseau" (Fiedler), **Supp. XIII:** 97–98

"Montana Memory" (Maclean), **Supp. XIV:**221

"Montana Ranch Abandoned" (Hugo), **Supp. VI:** 139

"Mont Blanc" (Shelley), **Supp. IX:** 52

Montcalm, Louis Joseph de, **Supp. I Part 2:** 498

Montcalm and Wolfe (Parkman), **Supp. II Part 2:** 596, 609, 610, 611–613

Montemarano, Nicholas, **Supp. XVI:**227

Montgomery, Benilde, **Supp. XIII:** 202

Montgomery, Robert, **Supp. I Part 2:** 611; **Supp. IV Part 1:** 130

Month of Sundays, A (Updike), **Retro. Supp. I:** 325, 327, 329, 330, 331, 333, 335

Monti, Luigi, **II:** 504

Montoya, José, **Supp. IV Part 2:** 545

"Montrachet-le-Jardin" (Stevens), **IV:** 82

Mont-Saint-Michel and Chartres (Adams), **I:** 1, 9, 12–14, 18, 19, 21; **Supp. I Part 2:** 417

Montserrat (Hellman), **Supp. I Part 1:** 283–285

Montserrat (Robles), **Supp. I Part 1:** 283–285

"Monument, The" (Bishop), **Supp. I Part 1:** 89

Monument, The (Strand), **Supp. IV Part 2:** 629, 630

"Monument in Utopia, A" (Schnackenberg), **Supp. XV:** 261, 263

"Monument Mountain" (Bryant), **Supp. I Part 1:** 156, 162

"Monument to After-Thought Unveiled, A" (Frost), **Retro. Supp. I:** 124

Moo (Smiley), **Supp. VI:** 292, 303–305

Moods (Alcott), **Supp. I Part 1:** 33, 34–35, 43

Moody, Anne, **Supp. IV Part 1:** 11

Moody, Mrs. William Vaughn, **I:** 384; **Supp. I Part 2:** 394

Moody, Richard, **Supp. I Part 1:** 280

Moody, William Vaughn, **III:** 507; **IV:** 26

"Moon and the Night and the Men, The" (Berryman), **I:** 172

"Moon Deluxe" (F. Barthelme), **Supp. XI:** 26, 27, 33, 36

Mooney, Tom, **I:** 505

"Moon-Face" (London), **II:** 475

Moon-Face and Other Stories (London), **II:** 483

"Moon Flock" (Dickey), **Supp. IV Part 1:** 186

Moon for the Misbegotten, A (O'Neill), **III:** 385, 401, 403, 404

Moon Is a Gong, The (Dos Passos). See *Garbage Man, The* (Dos Passos)

Moon Is Down, The (Steinbeck), **IV:** 51

Moon Lady, The (Tan), **Supp. X:** 289

"Moonlight Alert" (Winters), **Supp. II Part 2:** 801, 811, 815

"Moonlit Night" (Reznikoff), **Supp. XIV:**285–286

Moon of the Caribbees, The (O'Neill), **III:** 388

Moon Palace (Auster), **Supp. XII:** 22, 27, 30–32

"Moonshine" (Komunyakaa), **Supp. XIII:** 127, 128

"Moon Solo" (Laforgue), **Supp. XIII:** 346

Moonstruck (screenplay, Shanley), **Supp. XIV:**315, 316, 321–324

"Moon upon her fluent Route, The" (Dickinson), **I:** 471

Moony's Kid Don't Cry (T. Williams), **IV:** 381

Moore, Arthur, **Supp. I Part 1:** 49
Moore, Dr. Merrill, **III:** 506
Moore, George, **I:** 103
Moore, Hannah, **Supp. XV:** 231
Moore, John Milton, **III:** 193
Moore, Lorrie, **Supp. VIII:** 145; **Supp. X:** 163–180
Moore, Marianne, **I:** 58, 285, 401, 428; **III:** 193–217, 514, 592–593; **IV:** 74, 75, 76, 91, 402; **Retro. Supp. I:** 416, 417; **Retro. Supp. II:** 39, 44, 48, 50, 82, 178, 179, 243, 244; **Supp. I Part 1:** 84, 89, 255, 257; **Supp. I Part 2:** 707; **Supp. II Part 1:** 21; **Supp. III Part 1:** 58, 60, 63; **Supp. III Part 2:** 612, 626, 627; **Supp. IV Part 1:** 242, 246, 257; **Supp. IV Part 2:** 454, 640, 641; **Supp. XIV:**124, 130; **Supp. XV:** 306, 307
Moore, Marie Lorena. *See* Moore, Lorrie
Moore, Mary Tyler, **Supp. V:** 107
Moore, Mary Warner, **III:** 193
Moore, Steven, **Supp. IV Part 1:** 279, 283, 284, 285, 287; **Supp. XII:** 151
Moore, Sturge, **III:** 459
Moore, Thomas, **II:** 296, 299, 303; **Supp. IX:** 104; **Supp. X:** 114
Moore, Virginia, **Supp. XV:** 308
Moorehead, Caroline, **Supp. XIV:**337
Moorepack, Howard, **Supp. XV:** 199
Moos, Malcolm, **III:** 116, 119
"Moose, The" (Bishop), **Retro. Supp. II:** 50; **Supp. I Part 1:** 73, 93, 94, 95; **Supp. IX:** 45, 46
"Moose Wallow, The" (Hayden), **Supp. II Part 1:** 367
"Moquihuitzin's Answer" (Everwine), **Supp. XV:** 78
Mora, Pat, **Supp. XIII:** 213–232
"Moral Bully, The" (Holmes), **Supp. I Part 1:** 302
"Moral Character, the Practice of Law, and Legal Education" (Hall), **Supp. VIII:** 127
"Moral Equivalent for Military Service, A" (Bourne), **I:** 230
"Moral Equivalent of War, The" (James), **II:** 361; **Supp. I Part 1:** 20
"Moral Imperatives for World Order" (Locke), **Supp. XIV:**207, 213
Moralités Légendaires (Laforgue), **I:** 573
"Morality and Mercy in Vienna" (Pynchon), **Supp. II Part 2:** 620, 624
"Morality of Indian Hating, The" (Momaday), **Supp. IV Part 2:** 484

"Morality of Poetry, The" (Wright), **Supp. III Part 2:** 596–597, 599
Moral Man and Immoral Society (Niebuhr), **III:** 292, 295–297
"Morals Is Her Middle Name" (Hughes), **Supp. I Part 1:** 338
"Morals of Chess, The" (Franklin), **II:** 121
"Moral Substitute for War, A" (Addams), **Supp. I Part 1:** 20
"Moral Theology of Atticus Finch, The" (Shaffer), **Supp. VIII:** 127
"Moral Thought, A" (Freneau), **Supp. II Part 1:** 262
Moran, Thomas, **Supp. IV Part 2:** 603–604
Moran of the Lady Letty (Norris), **II:** 264; **III:** 314, 322, 327, 328, 329, 330, 331, 332, 333
Morath, Ingeborg. *See* Miller, Mrs. Arthur (Ingeborg Morath)
Moravia, Alberto, **I:** 301
Moré, Gonzalo, **Supp. X:** 185
More, Henry, **I:** 132
More, Paul Elmer, **I:** 223–224, 247; **Supp. I Part 2:** 423
Moreau, Gustave, **I:** 66
"More Blues and the Abstract Truth" (Wright), **Supp. XV:** 345
More Boners (Abingdon), **Supp. XVI:**99
More Conversations with Eudora Welty (Prenshaw, ed.), **Retro. Supp. I:** 340, 341, 342, 343, 344, 352, 353, 354
More Die of Heartbreak (Bellow), **Retro. Supp. II:** 31, 33, 34
"More Girl Than Boy" (Komunyakaa), **Supp. XIII:** 117
"More Light! More Light!" (Hecht), **Supp. X:** 60
"Morella" (Poe), **III:** 412; **Retro. Supp. II:** 270
"More Love in the Western World" (Updike), **Retro. Supp. I:** 327–328, 329
"Morels" (W. J. Smith), **Supp. XIII:** 336–339
Moreno, Gary, **Supp. XV:** 5
"More Observations Now" (Conroy), **Supp. XVI:**75
"More of a Corpse Than a Woman" (Rukeyser), **Supp. VI:** 280
"More Pleasant Adventures" (Ashbery), **Supp. III Part 1:** 1
More Poems to Solve (Swenson), **Supp. IV Part 2:** 640, 642, 648
More Stately Mansions (O'Neill), **III:** 385, 401, 404–405
"More Than Human" (Chabon), **Supp.**

XI: 71–72
More Triva (L. P. Smith), **Supp. XIV:**339
Morgan, Edmund S., **IV:** 149; **Supp. I Part 1:** 101, 102; **Supp. I Part 2:** 484
Morgan, Edwin, **Supp. IV Part 2:** 688
Morgan, Emanuel. *See* Bynner, Witter
Morgan, Henry, **II:** 432; **IV:** 63
Morgan, J. P., **I:** 494; **III:** 14, 15
Morgan, Jack, **Retro. Supp. II:** 142
Morgan, Judith, **Supp. XVI:**103
Morgan, Neil, **Supp. XVI:**103
Morgan, Robert, **Supp. V:** 5
Morgan, Robin, **Supp. I Part 2:** 569
Morgan, Ted, **Supp. XIV:**141
Morgan's Passing (Tyler), **Supp. IV Part 2:** 666–667, 668, 669
Morgenthau, Hans, **III:** 291, 309
Morgesons, The (E. Stoddard), **Supp. XV:** 270, 273, 274, 278, 279–282, 283
Morgesons and Other Writings, Published and Unpublished, The (Buell and Zagarell), **Supp. XV:** 269
Moricand, Conrad, **III:** 190
Morison, Mrs. Samuel Eliot (Elizabeth Shaw Greene), **Supp. I Part 2:** 483
Morison, Mrs. Samuel Eliot (Priscilla Barton), **Supp. I Part 2:** 493, 496, 497
Morison, Samuel Eliot, **Supp. I Part 2:** 479–500
"Morituri Salutamus" (Longfellow), **II:** 499, 500; **Retro. Supp. II:** 169; **Supp. I Part 2:** 416
"Moriturus" (Millay), **III:** 126, 131–132
Morley, Christopher, **III:** 481, 483, 484; **Supp. I Part 2:** 653; **Supp. IX:** 124
Morley, Edward, **IV:** 27
Morley, Lord John, **I:** 7
Mormon Country (Stegner), **Supp. IV Part 2:** 598, 601–602
"Morning, The" (Updike), **Retro. Supp. I:** 329
"Morning after My Death, The" (Levis), **Supp. XI:** 260, 263–264
Morning for Flamingos, A (Burke), **Supp. XIV:**30, 31, 32
"Morning Glory" (Merrill), **Supp. III Part 1:** 337
Morning Glory, The (R. Bly), **Supp. IV Part 1:** 63–65, 66, 71
"Morning Imagination of Russia, A" (W. C. Williams), **Retro. Supp. I:** 428
Morning in Antibes (Knowles), **Supp. XII:** 249

Morning in the Burned House (Atwood), **Supp. XIII:** 20, 35

Morning Is Near Us, The (Glaspell), **Supp. III Part 1:** 184–185

Morning Noon and Night (Cozzens), **I:** 374, 375, 376, 377, 379, 380

"Morning of the Day They Did It, The" (White), **Supp. I Part 2:** 663

"Morning Prayers" (Harjo), **Supp. XII:** 231

"Morning Roll Call" (Anderson), **I:** 116

"Mornings in a New House" (Merrill), **Supp. III Part 1:** 327

Mornings Like This (Dillard), **Supp. VI:** 23, 34

"Morning Song" (Plath), **Retro. Supp. II:** 252

Morning Watch, The (Agee), **I:** 25, 39–42

"Morning with Broken Window" (Hogan), **Supp. IV Part 1:** 405

Morrell, Ottoline, **Retro. Supp. I:** 60

Morris, Bernard E., **Supp. XV:** 154, 169

Morris, Christopher D., **Supp. IV Part 1:** 231, 236

Morris, George Sylvester, **Supp. I Part 2:** 640

Morris, Gouverneur, **Supp. I Part 2:** 512, 517, 518

Morris, Lloyd, **III:** 458

Morris, Robert, **Supp. I Part 2:** 510

Morris, Timothy, **Retro. Supp. I:** 40

Morris, William, **II:** 323, 338, 523; **IV:** 349; **Supp. I Part 1:** 260, 356; **Supp. XI:** 202

Morris, Willie, **Supp. XI:** 216, 231, 234

Morris, Wright, **I:** 305; **III:** 218–243, 558, 572; **IV:** 211

Morrison, Charles Clayton, **III:** 297

Morrison, Jim, **Supp. IV Part 1:** 206

Morrison, Toni, **Retro. Supp. II:** 15, 118; **Supp. III Part 1:** 361–381; **Supp. IV Part 1:** 2, 13, 14, 250, 253, 257; **Supp. V:** 169, 259; **Supp. VIII:** 213, 214; **Supp. X:** 85, 239, 250, 325; **Supp. XI:** 4, 14, 20, 91; **Supp. XII:** 289, 310; **Supp. XIII:** 60, 185; **Supp. XVI:**143

"Morro Bay" (Jeffers), **Supp. II Part 2:** 422

Morrow, W. C., **I:** 199

Morse, Jedidiah, **Supp. XV:** 243

Morse, Robert, **Supp. XI:** 305

Morse, Samuel F. B., **Supp. I Part 1:** 156

Mortal Acts, Mortal Words (Kinnell),

Supp. III Part 1: 235, 236, 237, 249–254

Mortal Antipathy, A (Holmes), **Supp. I Part 1:** 315–316

"Mortal Enemies" (Humphrey), **Supp. IX:** 109

"Mortal Eternal" (Olds), **Supp. X:** 214

Mortal No, The (Hoffman), **IV:** 113

Morte D'Arthur, Le (Malory), **Supp. IV Part 1:** 47

Mortmere Stories, The (Isherwood and Upward), **Supp. XIV:**159

Morton, David, **Supp. IX:** 76

Morton, Jelly Roll, **Supp. X:** 242

"Mosaic of the Nativity: Serbia, Winter 1993" (Kenyon), **Supp. VII:** 173

Mosby's Memoirs and Other Stories (Bellow), **Retro. Supp. II:** 27

Moscow under Fire (Caldwell), **I:** 296

Moser, Barry, **Supp. XIV:**223

Moses (Untermeyer), **Supp. XV:** 309

Moses, Man of the Mountain (Hurston), **Supp. VI:** 149, 158, 160

"Moses on Sinai" (Untermeyer), **Supp. XV:** 300

Mosle, Sara, **Supp. XI:** 254

Mosley, Walter, **Supp. XIII:** 233–252; **Supp. XVI:**143

Mosquito Coast, The (film), **Supp. VIII:** 323

Mosquito Coast, The (Theroux), **Supp. VIII:** 321, 322–323

Mosquitos (Faulkner), **II:** 56; **Retro. Supp. I:** 79, 81

Moss, Howard, **III:** 452; **Supp. IV Part 2:** 642; **Supp. IX:** 39; **Supp. XIII:** 114; **Supp. XV:** 143, 152

Moss, Stanley, **Supp. XI:** 321

Moss, Thylias, **Supp. XI:** 248

Mosses from an Old Manse (Hawthorne), **I:** 562; **II:** 224; **III:** 82, 83; **Retro. Supp. I:** 157, 248

"Moss of His Skin" (Sexton), **Supp. II Part 2:** 676

"Most Extraordinary Case, A" (James), **II:** 322; **Retro. Supp. I:** 218

Most Likely to Succeed (Dos Passos), **I:** 491

"Most of It, The" (Frost), **Retro. Supp. I:** 121, 125, 129, 139

Motel Chronicles (Shepard), **Supp. III Part 2:** 445

"Mother" (Paley), **Supp. VI:** 222–223

"Mother" (Snyder), **Supp. VIII:** 298

Mother (Whistler), **IV:** 369

Mother, The (Buck), **Supp. II Part 1:** 118–119

"Mother and Jack and the Rain" (Sexton), **Supp. II Part 2:** 686

"Mother and Son" (Tate), **IV:** 128, 137–138

Mother Courage and Her Children (Brecht), **III:** 160; **Supp. IX:** 140; **Supp. XII:** 249

"Mother Earth: Her Whales" (Snyder), **Supp. VIII:** 302

"Motherhood" (Swenson), **Supp. IV Part 2:** 645

Mother Hubbard (Reed), **Supp. X:** 241

Mother Love (Dove), **Supp. IV Part 1:** 250–251, 254

"Mother Marie Therese" (Lowell), **Retro. Supp. II:** 188

Mother Night (Vonnegut), **Supp. II Part 2:** 757, 758, 767, 770, 771

"Mother Rosarine" (Kumin), **Supp. IV Part 2:** 442

"Mothers and Daughters in the Fiction of the New Republic" (Davidson), **Supp. XV:** 238

Mother's Recompense, The (Wharton), **IV:** 321, 324; **Retro. Supp. I:** 382

"Mother's Tale, A" (Agee), **I:** 29–30

"Mother's Things" (Creeley), **Supp. IV Part 1:** 141

"Mother's Voice" (Creeley), **Supp. IV Part 1:** 156

Mother to Daughter, Daughter to Mother (Olsen, ed.), **Supp. XIII:** 295

"Mother Tongue" (Simic), **Supp. VIII:** 283

"Mother to Son" (Hughes), **Retro. Supp. I:** 199, 203; **Supp. I Part 1:** 321–322, 323

Motherwell, Robert, **Supp. XV:** 145

"Mother Writes to the Murderer, The: A Letter" (Nye), **Supp. XIII:** 276

"Motion, The" (Olson), **Supp. II Part 2:** 571

Motion of History, The (Baraka), **Supp. II Part 1:** 55, 56

"Motive for Metaphor, The" (Stevens), **IV:** 89; **Retro. Supp. I:** 310

Motiveless Malignity (Auchincloss), **Supp. IV Part 1:** 31

Motley, John Lothrop, **Supp. I Part 1:** 299; **Supp. I Part 2:** 479

"Motor Car, The" (White), **Supp. I Part 2:** 661

Motor-Flight Through France (Wharton), **I:** 12; **Retro. Supp. I:** 372

Mott, Michael, **Supp. VIII:** 204, 208

Mottetti: Poems of Love: The Motets of Eugenio Montale (Montale; Gioia, trans.), **Supp. XV:** 112, 127–128

"Mountain, The" (Frost), **Retro. Supp. I:** 121

"Mountain Hermitage, The: Pages from a Japanese Notebook" (Passin), **Supp. XIII:** 337

Mountain Interval (Frost), **II:** 154; **Retro. Supp. I:** 131, 132, 133

"Mountain Lion" (Hogan), **Supp. IV Part 1:** 412

"Mountain Music" essays (Sanders), **Supp. XVI:**276–277

Mountainous Journey, A (Tuqan), **Supp. XIII:** 278

Mountains, The (Wolfe), **IV:** 461

Mountains and Rivers without End (Snyder), **Supp. VIII:** 295, 305–306

"Mountains grow unnoticed, The" (Dickinson), **Retro. Supp. I:** 46

Mountains of California, The (Muir), **Supp. IX:** 183

"Mountain Whippoorwill, The" (Benét), **Supp. XI:** 44–45, 46, 47

"Mount-Joy: or Some Passages Out of the Life of a Castle-Builder" (Irving), **II:** 314

"Mount Venus" (Wright), **Supp. XV:** 346

"Mourners, The" (Malamud), **Supp. I Part 2:** 431, 435, 436–437

Mourners Below (Purdy), **Supp. VII:** 274, 280

"Mourning and Melancholia" (Freud), **Supp. IV Part 2:** 450; **Supp. XVI:**161

Mourning Becomes Electra (O'Neill), **III:** 391, 394, 398–400

"Mourning Poem for the Queen of Sunday" (Hayden), **Supp. II Part 1:** 379–380

"Mouse Elegy" (Olds), **Supp. X:** 209

Mouse Is Born, A (Loos), **Supp. XVI:**193

"Mouse Roulette Wheel, The" (C. Bly), **Supp. XVI:**34

"Mouth of Brass" (Humphrey), **Supp. IX:** 101

Moveable Feast, A (Hemingway), **II:** 257; **Retro. Supp. I:** 108, 171, 186–187

Movement, The: Documentary of a Struggle for Equality (Student Nonviolent Coordinating Committee), **Supp. IV Part 1:** 369

"Move over Macho, Here Comes Feminismo" (Robbins), **Supp. X:** 272

"Move to California, The" (Stafford), **Supp. XI:** 318, 321

"Movie" (Shapiro), **Supp. II Part 2:** 707

Movie at the End of the World, The (McGrath), **Supp. X:** 127

Moviegoer, The (Percy), **Supp. III Part 1:** 383–385, 387, 389–392, 394, 397

"Movie Magazine, The: A Low 'Slick'" (Percy), **Supp. III Part 1:** 385

Movies (Dixon), **Supp. XII:** 147

"Moving Around" (Matthews), **Supp. IX:** 155

"Moving Finger, The" (Wharton), **Retro. Supp. I:** 365

Moving On (McMurtry), **Supp. V:** 223–224

Moving Target, The (Macdonald), **Supp. IV Part 2:** 462, 463, 467, 470, 471, 473, 474

Moving Target, The (Merwin), **Supp. III Part 1:** 346, 347–348, 352, 357

"Mowbray Family, The" (Farrell and Alden), **II:** 45

"Mowing" (Frost), **II:** 169–170; **Retro. Supp. I:** 127, 128

"Moxan's Master" (Bierce), **I:** 206

Moyers, Bill, **Supp. IV Part 1:** 267; **Supp. VIII:** 331; **Supp. XI:** 126, 132; **Supp. XII:** 217; **Supp. XIII:** 274, 276; **Supp. XV:** 212

Moynihan, Daniel Patrick, **Retro. Supp. II:** 123; **Supp. VIII:** 241

"Mozart" (C. Frost), **Supp. XV:** 94

Mozart, Wolfgang Amadeus, **I:** 479, 588; **IV:** 74, 358; **Supp. IV Part 1:** 284

"Mozart and the Gray Steward" (Wilder), **IV:** 358

Mr. and Mrs. Baby and Other Stories (Strand), **Supp. IV Part 2:** 631

"Mr. and Mrs. Fix-It" (Lardner), **II:** 431

Mr. Arcularis (Aiken), **I:** 54, 56

"Mr. Big" (Allen), **Supp. XV:** 15

Mr. Bridge (Connell), **Supp. XIV:**80, 82, 93

Mr. Brown Can Moo! Can You? (Geisel), **Supp. XVI:**104

"Mr. Bruce" (Jewett), **II:** 397; **Retro. Supp. II:** 134, 143

"Mr. Burnshaw and the Statue" (Stevens), **Retro. Supp. I:** 298, 303

"Mr. Carson Death on His Nights Out" (McGrath), **Supp. X:** 118

Mr. Clemens and Mark Twain (Kaplan), **I:** 247–248

"Mr. Coffee and Mr. Fixit" (Carver), **Supp. III Part 1:** 145

"Mr. Cornelius Johnson, Office-Seeker" (Dunbar), **Supp. II Part 1:** 211, 213

"Mr. Costyve Duditch" (Toomer), **Supp. III Part 2:** 486

"Mr. Dajani, Calling from Jericho" (Nye), **Supp. XIII:** 286–287

"Mr. Edwards and the Spider" (Lowell), **I:** 544; **II:** 550; **Retro. Supp. II:** 187

Mr. Field's Daughter (Bausch), **Supp. VII:** 47–48, 51–52

"Mr. Flood's Party" (Robinson), **III:** 512

"Mr. Forster's Pageant" (Maxwell), **Supp. VIII:** 172

"Mr. Frost's Chickens" (Oliver), **Supp. VII:** 232–233

Mr. Hodge and Mr. Hazard (Wylie), **Supp. I Part 2:** 708, 709, 714, 721–724

"Mr. Hueffer and the Prose Tradition" (Pound), **III:** 465

Mr. Ives' Christmas (Hijuelos), **Supp. VIII:** 85–86

"Mr. Longfellow and His Boy" (Sandburg), **III:** 591

"Mr. Luna and History" (Ríos), **Supp. IV Part 2:** 551

Mr. Moto Is So Sorry (Marquand), **III:** 57, 58

Mr. Norris Changes Trains (Isherwood), **Supp. XIV:**161

"Mr. Preble Gets Rid of His Wife" (Thurber), **Supp. I Part 2:** 615

"Mr. Rolfe" (Wilson), **IV:** 436

Mr. Sammler's Planet (Bellow), **I:** 144, 147, 150, 151, 152, 158; **Retro. Supp. II:** 19, 28, 30

"Mr. Shelley Speaking" (Wylie), **Supp. I Part 2:** 719

Mr. Spaceman (R. O. Butler), **Supp. XII:** 62, 74–75

"Mr. Thompson's Prodigal" (Harte), **Supp. II Part 1:** 354

Mr. Vertigo (Auster), **Supp. XII:** 34–35, 36

"Mr. Whittier" (Scott), **Supp. I Part 2:** 705

Mr. Wilson's War (Dos Passos), **I:** 485

Mrabet, Mohammed, **Supp. IV Part 1:** 92, 93

Mrs. Albert Grundy: Observations in Philistia (Frederic), **II:** 138–139

"Mrs. Bilingsby's Wine" (Taylor), **Supp. V:** 323

Mrs. Bridge: A Novel (Connell), **Supp. XIV:**79, 80, 81, 82, 89–94, 95

"Mrs. Cassidy's Last Year" (Gordon), **Supp. IV Part 1:** 306

Mrs. Dalloway (Woolf), **Supp. IV Part 1:** 299; **Supp. VIII:** 5; **Supp. XV:** 55, 65–66

"Mrs. Jellison" (Hay), **Supp. XIV:**123

"Mrs. Krikorian" (Olds), **Supp. X:** 211

"Mrs. Maecenas" (Burke), **I:** 271

"Mrs. Mandrill" (Nemerov), **III:** 278

"Mrs. Manstey's View" (Wharton),

Retro. Supp. I: 362, 363
"Mrs. Mobry's Reason" (Chopin), **Retro. Supp. II:** 61
Mrs. Reynolds (Stein), **IV:** 43
Mrs. Stevens Hears the Mermaids Singing (Sarton), **Supp. VIII:** 252–253, 256–257
Mrs. Ted Bliss (Elkin), **Supp. VI:** 56, 58
"Mrs. Turner Cutting the Grass" (Shields), **Supp. VII:** 319–320
"Mrs. Walpurga" (Rukeyser), **Supp. VI:** 273
"MS. Found in a Bottle" (Poe), **III:** 411, 416; **Retro. Supp. II:** 274
"Ms. Lot" (Rukeyser), **Supp. VI:** 281
Ms. Magazine, **Supp. V:** 259
Mttron-Hirsch, Sidney, **III:** 484–485
"Muchas Gracias Por Todo" (Nye), **Supp. XIII:** 282–283
"Much Madness is divinest Sense" (Dickinson), **Retro. Supp. I:** 37–38
"Muck-A-Muck" (Harte), **Supp. II Part 1:** 342
"Mud Below, The" (Proulx), **Supp. VII:** 262
Mudge, Alden, **Supp. XIV:**35
Mudrick, Marvin, **Retro. Supp. II:** 289
"Mud Season" (Kenyon), **Supp. VII:** 167–168
Mueller, Lisel, **Supp. I Part 1:** 83, 88; **Supp. XIV:**268
Muggli, Mark, **Supp. IV Part 1:** 207
Muhammad, Elijah, **Supp. I Part 1:** 60
Muir, Edwin, **I:** 527; **II:** 368; **III:** 20
Muir, John, **Supp. VIII:** 296; **Supp. IX:** 33, 171–188; **Supp. X:** 29; **Supp. XIV:**177, 178, 181
Mujica, Barbara, **Supp. VIII:** 89
Mulatto (Hughes), **Retro. Supp. I:** 197, 203; **Supp. I Part 1:** 328, 339
Mulching of America, The (Crews), **Supp. XI:** 107
Muldoon, William, **I:** 500–501
Mule Bone (Hughes and Hurston), **Retro. Supp. I:** 194, 203; **Supp. VI:** 154
Mules and Men (Hurston), **Supp. VI:** 149, 153, 154, 160
Mulford, Prentice, **I:** 193
Mulligan, Robert, **Supp. VIII:** 128, 129
Mulligan Stew (Sorrentino), **Supp. XII:** 139
Mullins, Eustace, **III:** 479
Mullins, Priscilla, **II:** 502–503
"Multiplication of Wool, The" (Sanders), **Supp. XVI:**268
Multitudes, Multitudes (Clampitt),

Supp. IX: 39
Mumbo Jumbo (Reed), **Supp. X:** 240, 242, 245–248, 251
Mumford, Lewis, **I:** 245, 250, 251, 252, 259, 261; **II:** 271, 473–474; **Supp. I Part 2:** 632, 638; **Supp. II Part 2:** 471–501
Mumford, Sophia Wittenberg (Mrs. Lewis Mumford), **Supp. II Part 2:** 474, 475
Mummy, The (film), **Supp. IV Part 1:** 104
"Mundus et Infans" (Auden), **Supp. II Part 1:** 15
"Munich, 1938" (Lowell), **II:** 554
"Munich Mannequins, The" (Plath), **Retro. Supp. II:** 256
"Municipal Report, A" (Henry), **Supp. II Part 1:** 406–407
Munro, Alice, **Supp. IX:** 212; **Supp. X:** 290; **Supp. XII:** 289–290, 310
Munsey, Frank, **I:** 501
Munson, Gorham, **I:** 252, 388, 432; **Retro. Supp. II:** 77, 78, 79, 82, 83; **Supp. I Part 2:** 454
Münsterberg, Hugo, **Supp. XIV:**197
Murakami, Haruki, **Supp. XVI:**124
"Murano" (Doty), **Supp. XI:** 131
Murasaki, Lady, **II:** 577
Muratori, Fred, **Supp. XVI:**281
Muray, Nicholas, **Supp. I Part 2:** 708
Murder, My Sweet (film), **Supp. IV Part 1:** 130
"Murderer Guest, The" (Gordon), **Supp. IV Part 1:** 306
"Murderers" (L. Michaels), **Supp. XVI:**207–208
Murder in Mount Holly (Theroux), **Supp. VIII:** 315–316
Murder in the Cathedral (Eliot), **I:** 571, 573, 580, 581; **II:** 20; **Retro. Supp. I:** 65; **Retro. Supp. II:** 222
Murder of Lidice, The (Millay), **III:** 140
"Murders in the Rue Morgue, The" (Poe), **III:** 412, 416, 419–420; **Retro. Supp. II:** 271, 272
Murdoch, Iris, **Supp. VIII:** 167
Murnau, F. W., **Supp. XV:** 128
Murphy, Jacqueline Shea, **Retro. Supp. II:** 143
Murphy, Patrick, **Supp. XIII:** 214
Murphy, Richard, **Retro. Supp. II:** 250
Murray, Albert, **Retro. Supp. II:** 119, 120
Murray, Edward, **I:** 229
Murray, G. E., **Supp. X:** 201; **Supp. XI:** 143, 155
Murray, Gilbert, **III:** 468–469
Murray, Jan, **Supp. IV Part 2:** 574

Murray, John, **II:** 304; **III:** 76, 79; **Retro. Supp. I:** 246
Murray, Judith Sargent, **Supp. XV:** 236–237
Murray, Margaret A., **Supp. V:** 128
Murrell, John A., **IV:** 265
Mursell, James L., **Supp. I Part 2:** 608
"Muse" (Ammons), **Supp. VII:** 29
"Muse, Postmodern and Homeless, The" (Ozick), **Supp. V:** 272
"Musée des Beaux Arts" (Auden), **Retro. Supp. I:** 430; **Supp. II Part 1:** 14
"Muse of Aboutness, The" (Baker), **Supp. XVI:**288
Muses Are Heard, The (Capote), **Supp. III Part 1:** 126
"Muses of Terrence McNally, The" (Zinman), **Supp. XIII:** 207–208
"Muse's Tragedy, The" (Wharton), **Retro. Supp. I:** 364
Museum (Dove), **Supp. IV Part 1:** 245–247, 248
"Museum" (Hass), **Supp. VI:** 107
Museums and Women (Updike), **Retro. Supp. I:** 321
"Museum Vase" (Francis), **Supp. IX:** 83
"Mushrooms" (Plath), **Retro. Supp. II:** 246; **Supp. I Part 2:** 539
"Music" (Oliver), **Supp. VII:** 236
Music After the Great War (Van Vechten), **Supp. II Part 2:** 732
Music and Bad Manners (Van Vechten), **Supp. II Part 2:** 733
"Music for a Farce" (Bowles), **Supp. IV Part 1:** 83
Music for Chameleons (Capote), **Supp. III Part 1:** 120, 125–127, 131, 132
"Music for Museums?" (Van Vechten), **Supp. II Part 2:** 732
"Music for the Movies" (Van Vechten), **Supp. II Part 2:** 733
"Music from Spain" (Welty), **IV:** 272
Music Like Dirt (Bidart), **Supp. XV:** 35
"Music Like Dirt" (Bidart), **Supp. XV:** 35
Music of Chance, The (Auster), **Supp. XII:** 21, 23, 32–33
"Music of Prose, The" (Gass), **Supp. VI:** 92
Music of Spain, The (Van Vechten), **Supp. II Part 2:** 734, 735
"Music of the Spheres" (Epstein), **Supp. XII:** 165
Music School, The (Updike), **IV:** 214, 215, 219, 226, 227; **Retro. Supp. I:** 320, 328, 329, 330
"Music School, The" (Updike), **Retro.**

Supp. I: 326, 329, 335

"Music Swims Back to Me" (Sexton), **Supp. II Part 2:** 673

Muske, Carol, **Supp. IV Part 2:** 453–454

"Mussel Hunter at Rock Harbor" (Plath), **Supp. I Part 2:** 529, 537

Musset, Alfred de, **I:** 474; **II:** 543

Mussolini, Benito, **III:** 115, 473, 608; **IV:** 372, 373; **Supp. I Part 1:** 281, 282; **Supp. I Part 2:** 618; **Supp. V:** 290; **Supp. XVI:**191

"Mustafa Ferrari" (X. J. Kennedy), **Supp. XV:** 170–171

"Must the Novelist Crusade?" (Welty), **IV:** 280

"Mutability of Literature, The" (Irving), **II:** 308

"Mutation of the Spirit" (Corso), **Supp. XII:** 132, 133

Mute, The (McCullers), **II:** 586

Mutilated, The (T. Williams), **IV:** 382, 386, 393

Mutiny of the Elsinore, The (London), **II:** 467

"My Adventures as a Social Poet" (Hughes), **Retro. Supp. I:** 194, 207

"My Alba" (Ginsberg), **Supp. II Part 1:** 320, 321

My Alexandria (Doty), **Supp. XI:** 119, 120, 121, 123–125, 130

My Ántonia (Cather), **I:** 321–322; **Retro. Supp. I:** 1, 3, 4, 11–13, 14, 17, 18, 22; **Supp. IV Part 2:** 608; **Supp. XVI:**226

"My Appearance" (Wallace), **Supp. X:** 306–307

My Argument with the Gestapo: A Macaronic Journal (Merton), **Supp. VIII:** 207; **Supp. XV:** 344

"My Arkansas" (Angelou), **Supp. IV Part 1:** 15

"My Aunt" (Holmes), **Supp. I Part 1:** 302, 310

"My Beginnings" (Simpson), **Supp. IX:** 273

My Bondage and My Freedom (Douglass), **Supp. III Part 1:** 155, 173

My Brother (Kincaid), **Supp. VII:** 191–193

"My Brother Paul" (Dreiser), **Retro. Supp. II:** 94

"My Brothers the Silent" (Merwin), **Supp. III Part 1:** 349–350

"My Brother's Work" (Dunn), **Supp. XI:** 147

"My Butterfly" (Frost), **II:** 151; **Retro. Supp. I:** 124

"My Children, and a Prayer for Us"

(Ortiz), **Supp. IV Part 2:** 507

"My Confession" (McCarthy), **II:** 562

"My Confessional Sestina" (Gioia), **Supp. XV:** 123

My Country and My People (Yutang), **Supp. X:** 291

"My Country 'Tis of Thee" (Reznikoff), **Supp. III Part 2:** 616

My Days of Anger (Farrell), **II:** 34, 35–36, 43

"My Dear Republican Mother" (C. Bly), **Supp. XVI:**31–32

My Death My Life by Pier Paolo Pasolini (Acker), **Supp. XII:** 7

My Dog Stupid (Fante), **Supp. XI:** 160, 170–171

My Emily Dickinson (Howe), **Retro. Supp. I:** 33, 43; **Supp. IV Part 2:** 430–431

"My English" (Alvarez), **Supp. VII:** 2

Myers, Linda A., **Supp. IV Part 1:** 10

"My Extended Family" (Theroux), **Supp. VIII:** 311

"My Father" (L. Michaels), **Supp. XVI:**214

"My Father" (Sterne), **IV:** 466

"My Father: October 1942" (Stafford), **Supp. XI:** 323

"My Father at Eighty-Five" (R. Bly), **Supp. IV Part 1:** 73

"My Father Is a Simple Man" (Salinas), **Supp. XIII:** 324

"My Fathers Came From Kentucky" (Lindsay), **Supp. I Part 2:** 395

"My Father's Friends" (Maxwell), **Supp. VIII:** 171

"My Father's Ghost" (Wagoner), **Supp. IX:** 330

"My Father's God" (Fante), **Supp. XI:** 160, 174

"My Father's House" (L.-Y. Lee), **Supp. XV:** 225

"My Father's Love Letters" (Komunyakaa), **Supp. XIII:** 127

"My Father Speaks to me from the Dead" (Olds), **Supp. X:** 210

"My Father's Telescope" (Dove), **Supp. IV Part 1:** 246, 248

"My Father with Cigarette Twelve Years Before the Nazis Could Break His Heart" (Levine), **Supp. V:** 194

"My Favorite Murder" (Bierce), **I:** 205

My Favorite Plant: Writers and Gardeners on the Plants They Love (Kincaid), **Supp. VII:** 193–194

"My Fifty-Plus Years Celebrate Spring" (Salinas), **Supp. XIII:** 327

"My First Book" (Harte), **Supp. II Part 1:** 343

My First Summer in the Sierra (Muir),

Supp. IX: 172, 173, 178–181, 183, 185; **Supp. XIV:**177

"My Fountain Pen" (McClatchy), **Supp. XII:** 254, 260

My Friend, Henry Miller (Perlès), **III:** 189

My Friend, Julia Lathrop (Addams), **Supp. I Part 1:** 25

"My Friend, Walt Whitman" (Oliver), **Supp. VII:** 245

"My Garden Acquaintance" (Lowell), **Supp. I Part 2:** 420

My Garden [Book]: (Kincaid), **Supp. VII:** 193–194

"My Grandfather" (Lowell), **II:** 554

"My Grandmother's Love Letters" (H. Crane), **Retro. Supp. II:** 78

"My Grandson, Home at Last" (Angelou), **Supp. IV Part 1:** 13

My Green Hills of Jamaica (McKay), **Supp. X:** 132, 142

My Guru and His Disciple (Isherwood), **Supp. XIV:**157, 164, 172

My Heart's in the Highlands (Saroyan), **Supp. IV Part 1:** 83

"My High School Reunion" (Kingston), **Supp. V:** 169

"My Indigo" (L.-Y. Lee), **Supp. XV:** 214

"My Kinsman, Major Molineux" (Hawthorne), **II:** 228, 229, 237–239, 243; **Retro. Supp. I:** 153–154, 158, 160, 161; **Retro. Supp. II:** 181, 187; **Supp. XVI:**157

My Kinsman, Major Molineux (Lowell), **II:** 545–546

"My Last Afternoon with Uncle Devereux Winslow" (Lowell), **II:** 547–548; **Retro. Supp. II:** 189

"My Last Drive" (Hardy), **Supp. VIII:** 32

"My Last Duchess" (Browning), **Supp. XV:** 121

"My Life" (Strand), **Supp. IV Part 2:** 627

My Life, Starring Dara Falcon (Beattie), **Supp. V:** 31, 34–35

My Life a Loaded Gun: Dickinson, Plath, Rich, and Female Creativity (Bennett), **Retro. Supp. I:** 29

My Life and Hard Times (Thurber), **Supp. I Part 2:** 607, 609

My Life as a Man (Roth), **Retro. Supp. II:** 281, 286, 289; **Supp. III Part 2:** 401, 404, 405, 417–418

"My Life as a P.I.G., or the True Adventures of Smokey the Cop" (Abbey), **Supp. XIII:** 3

"My life closed twice before its close" (Dickinson), **Retro. Supp. I:** 38

"My Life had stood a Loaded Gun" (Dickinson), **Retro. Supp. I:** 42, 43, 45, 46; **Supp. IV Part 2:** 430

My Life of Absurdity (C. Himes), **Supp. XVI:**145

"My Life with Medicine" (Nye), **Supp. XIII:** 282

"My Life with *Playboy*" (Plimpton), **Supp. XVI:**246

"My Life with R. H. Macy" (Jackson), **Supp. IX:** 118

"My Little Utopia" (Simic), **Supp. VIII:** 283

My Lives and How I Lost Them (Cullen), **Supp. IV Part 1:** 173

"My Lord Bag of Rice" (C. Bly), **Supp. XVI:**40

My Lord Bag of Rice: New and Selected Stories (C. Bly), **Supp. XVI:**41

"My Lost City" (Fitzgerald), **Retro. Supp. I:** 102

"My Lost Youth" (Longfellow), **II:** 487, 499; **Retro. Supp. II:** 168

My Love Affair with America: The Cautionary Tale of a Cheerful Conservative (Podhoretz), **Supp. VIII:** 232, 233, 237, 244–246

"My Lover Has Dirty Fingernails" (Updike), **Retro. Supp. I:** 332, 333

"My Lucy Friend Who Smells Like Corn" (Cisneros), **Supp. VII:** 68–69

"My Mammogram" (McClatchy), **Supp. XII:** 263–264

"My Man Bovanne" (Bambara), **Supp. XI:** 2

"My Mariner" (Larcom), **Supp. XIII:** 147

My Mark Twain (Howells), **II:** 276

"My Metamorphosis" (Harte), **Supp. II Part 1:** 339

"My Moby Dick" (Humphrey), **Supp. IX:** 95

My Mortal Enemy (Cather), **I:** 327–328; **Retro. Supp. I:** 16–17; **Supp. I Part 2:** 719

My Mother: Demonology (Acker), **Supp. XII:** 6

My Mother, My Father and Me (Hellman), **Supp. I Part 1:** 290–291

"My Mother and My Sisters" (Ortiz), **Supp. IV Part 2:** 499

"My Mother Is Speaking from the Desert" (Gordon), **Supp. IV Part 1:** 309, 314

"My Mother's Goofy Song" (Fante), **Supp. XI:** 164

"My Mother's Memoirs, My Father's Lie, and Other True Stories" (Banks), **Supp. V:** 15

"My Mother's Nipples" (Hass), **Supp. VI:** 109

"My Mother's Story" (Kunitz), **Supp. III Part 1:** 259

"My Mother Then and Now" (Wasserstein), **Supp. XV:** 327

"My Mother with Purse the Summer They Murdered the Spanish Poet" (Levine), **Supp. V:** 194

My Movie Business: A Memoir (Irving), **Supp. VI:** 164

"My Name" (Cisneros), **Supp. VII:** 60

"My Negro Problem—And Ours" (Podhoretz), **Supp. VIII:** 234–236

"My New Diet" (Karr), **Supp. XI:** 241

"My Old Man" (Hemingway), **II:** 263

My Other Life (Theroux), **Supp. VIII:** 310, 324

"My Own Story" (E. Stoddard), **Supp. XV:** 273, 279, 283

My Own True Name: New and Selected Poems for Young Adults, 1984–1999 (Mora), **Supp. XIII:** 222

"My Passion for Ferries" (Whitman), **IV:** 350

"My People" (Hughes), **Retro. Supp. I:** 197; **Supp. I Part 1:** 321–322, 323

"My Philosophy" (Allen), **Supp. XV:** 15

"My Playmate" (Whittier), **Supp. I Part 2:** 699–700

"My Priests" (Monette), **Supp. X:** 159

Myra Breckinridge (Vidal), **Supp. IV Part 2:** 677, 685–686, 689, 691

"My Recollections of S. B. Fairchild" (Jackson), **Supp. IX:** 118–119

"My Religion" (Carson), **Supp. XII:** 105–106

"My Road to Hell Was Paved" (Patchett), **Supp. XII:** 310–311

Myron (Vidal), **Supp. IV Part 2:** 677, 685, 686, 691

"My Roomy" (Lardner), **II:** 420, 421, 428, 430

"My Sad Self" (Ginsberg), **Supp. II Part 1:** 320

My Secret History (Theroux), **Supp. VIII:** 310, 324

"Myself" (Audubon), **Supp. XVI:**1–2, 5, 12

"My Shoes" (Simic), **Supp. VIII:** 275

"My Side of the Matter" (Capote), **Supp. III Part 1:** 114, 115

My Silk Purse and Yours: The Publishing Scene and American Literary Art (Garrett), **Supp. VII:** 111; **Supp. X:** 7

My Sister Eileen (McKenney), **IV:** 288; **Retro. Supp. II:** 321

My Sister's Hand in Mine: The Collected Works of Jane Bowles, **Supp. IV Part 1:** 82–83

"My Son" (Strand), **Supp. IV Part 2:** 629

My Son, John (film), **Supp. I Part 1:** 67

"My Son, the Murderer" (Malamud), **Supp. I Part 2:** 437

"My Son the Man" (Olds), **Supp. X:** 212

"My Speech to the Graduates" (Allen), **Supp. XV:** 16

"Mysteries of Caesar, The" (Hecht), **Supp. X:** 73

"Mysteries of Eleusis, The" (Hardwick), **Supp. III Part 1:** 195

Mysteries of Pittsburgh, The (Chabon), **Supp. XI:** 65, 68, 69–71

"Mysterious Case of R, The" (Conroy), **Supp. XVI:**72

Mysterious Stranger, The (Twain), **IV:** 190–191, 210

Mystery, A (Shields). *See Swann* (Shields)

"Mystery, The" (Dunbar), **Supp. II Part 1:** 199, 210

"Mystery, The" (Glück), **Supp. V:** 91

Mystery and Manners (O'Connor), **Retro. Supp. II:** 230

"'Mystery Boy' Looks for Kin in Nashville" (Hayden), **Supp. II Part 1:** 366, 372

"Mystery of Coincidence, The" (Conroy), **Supp. XVI:**74

"Mystery of Heroism, A" (Crane), **I:** 414

"Mystery of Marie Rogêt, The" (Poe), **III:** 413, 419; **Retro. Supp. II:** 271

"Mystic" (Plath), **Retro. Supp. II:** 257; **Supp. I Part 2:** 539, 541

"Mystical Poet, A" (Bogan), **Retro. Supp. I:** 36

"Mystic of Sex, The—A First Look at D. H. Lawrence" (Nin), **Supp. X:** 188

"Mystic Vision in 'The Marshes of Glynn'" (Warfel), **Supp. I Part 1:** 366, 373

"Mystification" (Poe), **III:** 425

My Study Windows (Lowell), **Supp. I Part 2:** 407

"My Teacher" (Conroy), **Supp. XVI:**75

"Myth" (Rukeyser), **Supp. VI:** 281–282

Myth of Sisyphus, The (Camus), **I:** 294; **Supp. XIII:** 165

"Myth of the Isolated Artist, The" (Oates), **Supp. II Part 2:** 520

Myth of the Machine, The (Mumford), **Supp. II Part 2:** 476, 478, 482, 483, 493, 497

Mythology and the Romantic Tradition in English Poetry (Bush), **Supp. I Part 1:** 268

Myths and Texts (Snyder), **Supp. VIII:** 295–296

"Myths of Bears, The" (Bass), **Supp. XVI:**19, 20

"My *Tocaya*" (Cisneros), **Supp. VII:** 69

My Uncle Dudley (Morris), **I:** 305; **III:** 219–220

"My Uncle's Favorite Coffee Shop" (Nye), **Supp. XIII:** 283

"My Weariness of Epic Proportions" (Simic), **Supp. VIII:** 276

My Wicked Wicked Ways (Cisneros), **Supp. VII:** 58, 64–68, 71

"My Wicked Wicked Ways" (Cisneros), **Supp. VII:** 58, 64–66

"My Word-house" (Mora), **Supp. XIII:** 219, 225

My Works and Days (Mumford), **Supp. II Part 2:** 475, 477, 481

My World and Welcome to It (Thurber), **Supp. I Part 2:** 610

N

Nabokov, Peter, **Supp. IV Part 2:** 490

Nabokov, Véra, **Retro. Supp. I:** 266, 270

Nabokov, Vladimir, **I:** 135; **III:** 244–266, 283, 286; **Retro. Supp. I:** 263–281, 317, 335; **Supp. I Part 1:** 196; **Supp. II Part 1:** 2; **Supp. IV Part 1:** 135; **Supp. V:** 127, 237, 251, 252, 253; **Supp. VIII:** 105, 133, 138; **Supp. IX:** 152, 212, 261; **Supp. X:** 283; **Supp. XI:** 66; **Supp. XII:** 310; **Supp. XIII:** 46, 52; **Supp. XVI:**148, 294

Nabokov's Dozen (Nabokov), **Retro. Supp. I:** 266

Nabokov's Garden: A Guide to Ada (Mason), **Supp. VIII:** 138

Naca, Kristin, **Supp. XIII:** 133

Nadeau, Robert, **Supp. X:** 261, 270

Nadel, Alan, **Supp. IV Part 1:** 209

Naipaul, V. S., **Supp. IV Part 1:** 297; **Supp. VIII:** 314; **Supp. X:** 131; **Supp. XIV:**111

Naked and the Dead, The (Mailer), **I:** 477; **III:** 26, 27, 28–30, 31, 33, 35, 36, 44; **Retro. Supp. II:** 197–199; **Supp. IV Part 1:** 381; **Supp. XI:** 218

Naked in Garden Hills (Crews), **Supp. XI:** 102, 110

Naked Lunch (Burroughs), **Supp. III**

Part 1: 92–95, 97–105; **Supp. IV Part 1:** 90

"Naked Nude" (Malamud), **Supp. I Part 2:** 450

Naked Poetry (Berg and Mezey, eds.), **Supp. IV Part 1:** 60

Naked Poetry (Levine), **Supp. V:** 180

Namedropping: Mostly Literary Memoirs (Coover), **Supp. V:** 40

"Name in the Papers" (Hughes), **Supp. I Part 1:** 330

Name Is Archer, The (Macdonald, under Millar), **Supp. IV Part 2:** 466

"Name Is Burroughs, The" (Burroughs), **Supp. III Part 1:** 93

Name Is Fogarty, The: Private Papers on Public Matters (Farrell), **II:** 49

"Names" (Carruth), **Supp. XVI:**54, 56

Names, The (DeLillo), **Supp. VI:** 3, 10, 13, 14

Names, The (Momaday), **Supp. IV Part 2:** 479, 480, 483, 486, 487, 488, 489

Names and Faces of Heroes, The (Price), **Supp. VI:** 258, 260

Names of the Lost, The (Levine), **Supp. V:** 177–178, 179, 187–188

"Naming for Love" (Carruth), **Supp. XVI:**48

"Naming Myself" (Kingsolver), **Supp. VII:** 208

"Naming of Names, The" (Sanders), **Supp. XVI:**268

Naming of the Beasts, The (Stern). *See Rejoicings: Selected Poems, 1966–1972* (Stern)

Nana (Zola), **III:** 321

"Nancy Culpepper" (Mason), **Supp. VIII:** 141

Nancy Drew stories, **Supp. VIII:** 133, 135, 137, 142

"Nancy Knapp" (Masters), **Supp. I Part 2:** 461

"Naomi Shihab Nye: U.S. Mideast-History a Harbinger of 9-11?" (Nye), **Supp. XIII:** 286

"Naomi Trimmer" (X. J. Kennedy), **Supp. XV:** 170

"Nap, The" (Banks), **Supp. V:** 7

"Napoleon" (Emerson), **II:** 6

Napoleon I, **I:** 6, 7, 8, 474; **II:** 5, 309, 315, 321, 523; **Supp. I Part 1:** 153; **Supp. I Part 2:** 518, 519

Narcissa and Other Fables (Auchincloss), **Supp. IV Part 1:** 21, 34

"Narcissus as Narcissus" (Tate), **IV:** 124

"Narcissus Leaves the Pool" (Epstein), **Supp. XIV:**110

Narcissus Leaves the Pool: Familiar Essays (Epstein), **Supp. XIV:**110

Nardal, Paulette, **Supp. X:** 139

Nardi, Marcia, **Retro. Supp. I:** 426, 427

Narration (Stein), **IV:** 27, 30, 32, 33, 36

Narrative of a Four Months' Residence among the Natives of a Valley of the Marquesas Islands (Melville), **III:** 76

Narrative of Arthur Gordon Pym, The (Poe), **III:** 412, 416; **Retro. Supp. II:** 265, 273–275; **Supp. XI:** 293

Narrative of the Life of Frederick Douglass, an American Slave, Written by Himself (Douglass), **Supp. III Part 1:** 154–159, 162, 165; **Supp. IV Part 1:** 13; **Supp. VIII:** 202

"Narrativity Scenes" (Wright), **Supp. XV:** 345

Narrenschiff, Das (Brant), **III:** 447

"Narrow Fellow in the Grass, A" (Dickinson), **Retro. Supp. I:** 30, 37

Narrow Heart, A: Portrait of a Woman (Gordon), **II:** 197, 217

Narrow Rooms (Purdy), **Supp. VII:** 274

Nash, Roderick, **Supp. IX:** 185; **Supp. XIV:**191–192

Nash, Susan Smith, **Supp. XVI:**274

Nash, Thomas, **Supp. III Part 1:** 387–388

Nashe, Thomas, **I:** 358

Nashville (film), **Supp. IX:** 143

Nason, Elias, **Supp. XV:** 242

Nasser, Gamal Abdel, **IV:** 490

Natalie Mann (Toomer), **Supp. III Part 2:** 484–486

Nathan, George Jean, **II:** 91; **III:** 103, 104, 106, 107; **IV:** 432; **Supp. IV Part 1:** 343; **Supp. IX:** 56–57; **Supp. XIII:** 161

"Nathanael West" (Herbst), **Retro. Supp. II:** 325

Nathanael West: The Art of His Life (Martin), **Retro. Supp. II:** 325

Nathan Coulter (Berry), **Supp. X:** 24, 33

"Nationalist, The" (Anderson), **I:** 115

"Nation Is Like Ourselves, The" (Baraka), **Supp. II Part 1:** 53

"Native, The" (Olds), **Supp. X:** 215

"Native American Attitudes to the Environment" (Momaday), **Supp. IV Part 2:** 481, 491

Native American Renaissance (Lincoln), **Supp. IV Part 2:** 507

Native American Testimony (Nabokov, ed.), **Supp. IV Part 2:** 490

"Native Hill, A" (Berry), **Supp. X:** 21

Native in a Strange Land: Trials & Tremors (Coleman), **Supp. XI:** 84–85, 87

Native of Winby and Other Tales, A (Jewett), **II:** 396; **Retro. Supp. II:** 138

Native Son (Wright), **IV:** 476, 477, 478, 479, 481, 482–484, 485, 487, 488, 491, 495; **Retro. Supp. II:** 107, 116; **Supp. I Part 1:** 51, 64, 67, 337; **Supp. II Part 1:** 170, 235–236; **Supp. IX:** 306; **Supp. XIV:**73

"Native Trees" (Merwin), **Supp. III Part 1:** 355

Natorp, Paul, **Supp. XIV:**198

Natural, The (Malamud), **II:** 424, 425; **Retro. Supp. II:** 288; **Supp. I Part 2:** 438–441, 443

"*Natural, The:* Malamud's World Ceres" (Wasserman), **Supp. I Part 2:** 439

"Natural History" (Olds), **Supp. X:** 210

"Natural History Note" (Hay), **Supp. XIV:**124, 130

"Natural History of Some Poems, A" (Harrison), **Supp. VIII:** 53

"Natural History of the Dead" (Hemingway), **II:** 206; **Retro. Supp. I:** 176

"Naturally Superior School, A" (Knowles), **Supp. XII:** 235, 240–241

"Natural Method of Mental Philosophy" (Emerson), **II:** 14

"Natural Resources" (Rich), **Supp. I Part 2:** 575

Natural Selection (F. Barthelme), **Supp. XI:** 2, 28, 32, 33

Nature (Emerson), **I:** 463; **II:** 1, 8, 12, 16; **IV:** 171, 172–173

"Nature" (Emerson), **Retro. Supp. I:** 250; **Supp. I Part 2:** 383; **Supp. III Part 1:** 387; **Supp. IX:** 178

"Nature, Inc." (Lewis), **II:** 441

Nature: Poems Old and New (Swenson), **Supp. IV Part 2:** 652

Nature and Destiny of Man, The (Niebuhr), **III:** 292, 303–306, 310

"Nature and Life" (Emerson), **II:** 19

"Nature and Nurture: When It Comes to Twins, Sometimes It's Hard to Tell the Two Apart" (Bausch), **Supp. VII:** 40

"Nature-Metaphors" (Lanier), **Supp. I Part 1:** 352

Nature Morte (Brodsky), **Supp. VIII:** 25

Nature of Evil, The (James), **II:** 343

Nature of Peace, The (Veblen), **Supp. I Part 2:** 642

Nature of True Virtue, The (Edwards), **I:** 549, 557–558, 559

Nature's Economy: A History of Ecological Ideas (Worster), **Supp. IX:** 19

Nausea (Sartre), **Supp. VIII:** 7

"Navajo Blanket, A" (Swenson), **Supp. IV Part 2:** 649

Navarette, Don Martín de, **II:** 310

Navarro, Ramon, **Supp. IV Part 1:** 206

Navigator, The (film), **I:** 31

Naylor, Gloria, **Supp. VIII:** 213–230

Naylor, Paul Kenneth, **Supp. IV Part 2:** 420

Nazimova, **III:** 399

Neal, Larry, **Retro. Supp. II:** 112, 128; **Supp. X:** 324, 328

Neal, Lawrence P., **Supp. II Part 1:** 53

Neal, Patricia, **Supp. I Part 1:** 286; **Supp. IV Part 2:** 524; **Supp. V:** 223

Neale, Walter, **I:** 192, 208

Nearer the Moon: From "A Journal of Love," the Unexpurgated Diary of Anaïs Nin, 1937–1939, **Supp. X:** 184, 185

Near-Johannesburg Boy and Other Poems, The (Brooks), **Supp. III Part 1:** 86

Near Klamath (Carver), **Supp. III Part 1:** 137

"Near Perigord" (Pound), **Retro. Supp. I:** 289, 290

Near the Ocean (Lowell), **II:** 543, 550, 551–553, 554, 555; **Retro. Supp. II:** 182, 186, 189–190

"Near View of the High Sierra, A" (Muir), **Supp. IX:** 183

Nebeker, Helen, **Supp. IX:** 122

Necessary Angel, The (Stevens), **IV:** 76, 79, 89, 90

Necessities of Life: Poems, 1962–1965 (Rich), **Supp. I Part 2:** 553, 555

"Necrological" (Ransom), **III:** 486–489, 490, 492

Ned Christie's War (Conley), **Supp. V:** 232

"Need for a Cultural Base to Civil Rites & Bpower Mooments, The" (Baraka), **Supp. II Part 1:** 48

"Need for Christian Preaching, The" (Buechner), **Supp. XII:** 49

Needful Things (King), **Supp. V:** 139, 146

"Needle" (Simic), **Supp. VIII:** 275

"Needle Trade" (Reznikoff), **Supp. XIV:**277, 289

"Need of Being Versed in Country Things, The" (Frost), **II:** 154; **Retro. Supp. I:** 133, 135

Neel, Philippe, **Supp. XIV:**338

Neelakantappa, Tara, **Supp. XV:** 104–105

Neeley, Barbara, **Supp. XVI:**143

"Negative Capability" (Komunyakaa), **Supp. XIII:** 131

Negligible Tales (Bierce), **I:** 209

"Negotiating the Darkness, Fortified by Poets' Strength" (Karr), **Supp. XI:** 254; **Supp. XIII:** 285

Negotiating with the Dead (Atwood), **Supp. XIII:** 20, 35

Negritude movement, **Supp. X:** 131, 139

"Negro" (Hughes), **Supp. I Part 1:** 321–322

Negro, The (Du Bois), **Supp. II Part 1:** 178, 179, 185

Negro, The: The Southerner's Problem (Page), **Supp. II Part 1:** 168

Negro and His Music, The (Locke), **Supp. XIV:**202

Negro Art: Past and Present (Locke), **Supp. XIV:**202

"Negro Artisan, The" (Du Bois), **Supp. II Part 1:** 166

"Negro Artist and the Racial Mountain, The" (Hughes), **Retro. Supp. I:** 200, 207; **Supp. I Part 1:** 323, 325; **Supp. IV Part 1:** 169

"Negro Assays the Negro Mood, A" (Baldwin), **Supp. I Part 1:** 52

"Negro Citizen, The" (Du Bois), **Supp. II Part 1:** 179

"Negro Dancers" (Hughes), **Retro. Supp. I:** 199; **Supp. I Part 1:** 324

Negroes in America, The (McKay), **Supp. X:** 132, 136

"Negroes of Farmville, Virginia, The: A Social Study" (Du Bois), **Supp. II Part 1:** 166

Negro Family, The: The Case for National Action (Moynihan), **Retro. Supp. II:** 123

"Negro Farmer, The" (Du Bois), **Supp. II Part 1:** 167

"Negro Ghetto" (Hughes), **Supp. I Part 1:** 331

Negro in America, The (Locke), **Supp. XIV:**208

Negro in American Civilization, The (Du Bois), **Supp. II Part 1:** 179

Negro in American Culture, The (Locke and Butcher), **Supp. XIV:**202–203

Negro in Art, The: A Pictorial Record of the Negro Artist and of the Negro

Theme in Art (Locke), **Supp. XIV:**202

"Negro in Large Cities, The" (Du Bois), **Supp. II Part 1:** 169

"Negro in Literature and Art, The" (Du Bois), **Supp. II Part 1:** 174

Negro in New York, The (Ellison), **Supp. II Part 1:** 230

"Negro in the Black Belt, The: Some Social Sketches" (Du Bois), **Supp. II Part 1:** 166

"Negro in the Three Americas, The" (Locke), **Supp. XIV:**211

"Negro in the Well, The" (Caldwell), **I:** 309

"Negro Love Song, A" (Dunbar), **Supp. II Part 1:** 204

"Negro Martyrs Are Needed" (C. Himes), **Supp. XVI:**138

Negro Mother, The (Hughes), **Supp. I Part 1:** 328

Negro Mother and Other Dramatic Recitations, The (Hughes), **Retro. Supp. I:** 203

Negro Novel in America, The (Bone), **Supp. IX:** 318–319

Negro Publication Society of America, **Retro. Supp. I:** 205

"Negro Renaissance, The: Jean Toomer and the Harlem of the 1920s" (Bontemps), **Supp. IX:** 306

"Negro Schoolmaster in the New South, A" (Du Bois), **Supp. II Part 1:** 168

"Negro's Contribution to American Culture, The" (Locke), **Supp. XIV:**210, 211

"Negro Sermon, A: Simon Legree" (Lindsay), **Supp. I Part 2:** 393

"Negro Sings of Rivers, The" (Hughes), **Supp. IV Part 1:** 16

"Negro Speaks of Rivers, The" (Hughes), **Retro. Supp. I:** 199; **Supp. I Part 1:** 321

"Negro Spirituals, The (Locke), **Supp. XIV:**201

"Negro Takes Stock, The" (Du Bois), **Supp. II Part 1:** 180

"Negro Theatre, The" (Van Vechten), **Supp. II Part 2:** 735

"Negro Voter Sizes Up Taft, A" (Hurston), **Supp. VI:** 160

"Negro Writer and His Roots, The: Toward a New Romanticism" (Hansberry), **Supp. IV Part 1:** 364

"Negro Youth Speaks" (Locke), **Supp. XIV:**201

"Nehemias Americanus" (Mather), **Supp. II Part 2:** 453

Nehru, Jawaharlal, **IV:** 490

"Neighbor" (Hugo), **Supp. VI:** 135–136

"Neighbors" (Carver), **Supp. III Part 1:** 135, 139, 141; **Supp. XI:** 153

"Neighbors" (Hogan), **Supp. IV Part 1:** 405

"Neighbors, The" (Hay), **Supp. XIV:**126

"Neighbour Rosicky" (Cather), **I:** 331–332

Neil Simon (Johnson), **Supp. IV Part 2:** 573

"Neil Simon: Toward Act III?" (Walden), **Supp. IV Part 2:** 591

"Neil Simon's Jewish-Style Comedies" (Walden), **Supp. IV Part 2:** 584, 591

Neilson, Heather, **Supp. IV Part 2:** 681

Neiman, Gilbert, **Supp. XV:** 140

"Neither Out Far Nor In Deep" (Frost), **I:** 303; **Retro. Supp. I:** 121, 138

"Nellie Clark" (Masters), **Supp. I Part 2:** 461

Nelson, Ernest, **I:** 388

Nelson, Howard, **Supp. IV Part 1:** 66, 68

Nelson, Lord Horatio, **II:** 524

Nelson, Shirley, **Supp. XII:** 293

Nelson Algren (Cox and Chatterton), **Supp. IX:** 11–12

Nelson Algren: A Life on the Wild Side (Drew), **Supp. IX:** 2

Nemerov, David, **II:** 268

Nemerov, Howard, **III:** 267–289; **IV:** 137, 140; **Supp. III Part 2:** 541; **Supp. IV Part 2:** 455, 650; **Supp. IX:** 114

Nemiroff, Robert Barron, **Supp. IV Part 1:** 360, 361, 365, 369, 370, 374

Neoconservative Criticism: Norman Podhoretz, Kenneth S. Lynn, and Joseph Epstein (Winchell), **Supp. VIII:** 241; **Supp. XIV:**103

"Neo-Hoodoo Manifesto, The" (Reed), **Supp. X:** 242

Neon Rain, The (Burke), **Supp. XIV:**22, 24, 26–27, 28–29, 30

Neon Vernacular (Komunyakaa), **Supp. XIII:** 121, 127–128, 131

Neon Wilderness, The (Algren), **Supp. IX:** 3, 4

Neo-Slave Narratives (Rushdy), **Supp. X:** 250

Nepantla: Essays from the Land in the Middle (Mora), **Supp. XIII:** 213, 219–221, 227

Nephew, The (Purdy), **Supp. VII:** 271, 273, 282

"Nereids of Seriphos, The" (Clampitt),

Supp. IX: 41

Nericcio, William, **Supp. XIV:**304–305

Neruda, Pablo, **Supp. I Part 1:** 89; **Supp. IV Part 2:** 537; **Supp. V:** 332; **Supp. VIII:** 272, 274; **Supp. IX:** 157, 271; **Supp. X:** 112; **Supp. XI:** 191; **Supp. XII:** 217; **Supp. XIII:** 114, 315, 323

Nesbit, Edith, **Supp. VIII:** 171

Nesbitt, Robin, **Supp. VIII:** 89

Nesting Ground, The (Wagoner), **Supp. IX:** 324, 325–326

Nest of Ninnies, A (Ashbery and Schuyler), **Supp. III Part 1:** 3; **Supp. XV:** 178

Nets to Catch the Wind (Wylie), **Supp. I Part 2:** 709, 710–712, 714

Nettleton, Asahel, **I:** 458

"Net to Snare the Moonlight, A" (Lindsay), **Supp. I Part 2:** 387

Neubauer, Carol E., **Supp. IV Part 1:** 9

Neugeboren, Jacob Mordecai. See Neugeboren, Jay

Neugeboren, Jay, **Supp. XVI:**217–231

Neugroschel, Joachim, **Supp. IX:** 138

Neuhaus, Richard John, **Supp. VIII:** 245

Neumann, Erich, **Supp. I Part 2:** 567; **Supp. IV Part 1:** 68, 69

Neuromancer (W. Gibson), **Supp. XII:** 15; **Supp. XVI:**117, 119–120, 122, 124, 125–126, 127, 129, 131

"Neurotic America and the Sex Impulse" (Dreiser), **Retro. Supp. II:** 105

Neutra, Richard, **Supp. XVI:**192

"Never Bet the Devil Your Head" (Poe), **III:** 425; **Retro. Supp. II:** 273

Never Come Morning (Algren), **Supp. IX:** 3, 7–9

Never in a Hurry: Essays on People and Places (Nye), **Supp. XIII:** 273, 280–282, 286

"Never Marry a Mexican" (Cisneros), **Supp. VII:** 70

"Never Room with a Couple" (Hughes), **Supp. I Part 1:** 330

"Nevertheless" (Moore), **III:** 214

Nevins, Allan, **I:** 253; **Supp. I Part 2:** 486, 493

"Nevsky Prospekt" (Olds), **Supp. X:** 205

New Adam, The (Untermeyer), **Supp. XV:** 304, 305

New Addresses (Koch), **Supp. XV:** 177, 184

"New Age of the Rhetoricians, The"

(Cowley), **Supp. II Part 1:** 135

New American Literature, The (Pattee), **II:** 456

New American Novel of Manners, The (Klinkowitz), **Supp. XI:** 347

"New American Ode, The" (Wright), **Supp. XV:** 346

New American Poetry, 1945–1960 (Allen, ed.), **Supp. XIII:** 112

New American Poetry, The (Allen, ed.), **Supp. VIII:** 291, 292

"New American Writer, A" (W. C. Williams), **Retro. Supp. II:** 335

New and Collected Poems (Reed), **Supp. X:** 241

New and Collected Poems (Wilbur), **Supp. III Part 2:** 562–564

New and Selected Poems (Nemerov), **III:** 269, 275, 277–279

New and Selected Poems (Oliver), **Supp. VII:** 240–241, 245

New and Selected Poems (Wagoner), **Supp. IX:** 326–327

New and Selected Poems (W. J. Smith), **Supp. XIII:** 332

New and Selected Poems: 1974–1994 (Dunn), **Supp. XI:** 151–152

New and Selected Things Taking Place (Swenson), **Supp. IV Part 2:** 648–650, 651

"New Art Gallery Society, The" (Wolfe), **Supp. III Part 2:** 580

"New Capitalist Tool, The" (Wasserstein), **Supp. XV:** 328

Newcomb, Ralph, **Supp. XIII:** 12

Newcomb, Robert, **II:** 111

New Conscience and an Ancient Evil, A (Addams), **Supp. I Part 1:** 14–15, 16

"New Conservatives, The: Intellectuals in Retreat" (Epstein), **Supp. XIV:**103

New Criticism, The (Ransom), **III:** 497–498, 499, 501

"New Day, A" (Levine), **Supp. V:** 182

Newdick, Robert Spangler, **Retro. Supp. I:** 138

Newdick's Season of Frost (Newdick), **Retro. Supp. I:** 138

New Dictionary of Quotations, A (Mencken), **III:** 111

New Directions Anthology in Prose and Poetry (Laughlin, ed.), **Supp. XVI:**284

"New Directions in Poetry" (D. Locke), **Supp. IX:** 273

"New Dog, The: Variations on a Text by Jules Laforgue" (C. Frost), **Supp. XV:** 98

Newell, Henry, **IV:** 193

"New England" (Lowell), **II:** 536

"New England" (Robinson), **III:** 510, 524

New England: Indian Summer (Brooks), **I:** 253, 256

"New England Bachelor, A" (Eberhart), **I:** 539

"New Englander, The" (Anderson), **I:** 114

New England Girlhood, A (Larcom), **Supp. XIII:** 137, 142, 143, 144, 147–154

New England Local Color Literature (Donovan), **Retro. Supp. II:** 138

"New England Sabbath-Day Chace, The" (Freneau), **Supp. II Part 1:** 273

New-England Tale, A (Sedgwick), **I:** 341

New England Tragedies, The (Longfellow), **II:** 490, 505, 506; **Retro. Supp. II:** 165, 167

New Era in American Poetry, The (Untermeyer, ed.), **Supp. XV:** 301, 303, 306

Newer Ideals of Peace (Addams), **Supp. I Part 1:** 11–12, 15, 16–17, 19, 20–21

New Feminist Criticism, The: Essays on Women, Literature, and Theory (Showalter), **Supp. X:** 97

"New Folsom Prison" (Matthews), **Supp. IX:** 165

New Formalism, The: A Critical Introduction (McPhillips), **Supp. XV:** 250, 251, 252, 264

New Found Land: Fourteen Poems (MacLeish), **III:** 12–13

New Hampshire: A Poem with Notes and Grace Notes (Frost), **II:** 154–155; **Retro. Supp. I:** 132, 133, 135

"New Hampshire, February" (Eberhart), **I:** 536

New Hard-Boiled Writers (Panek), **Supp. XIV:**27

New Industrial State, The (Galbraith), **Supp. I Part 2:** 648

"New Journalism, The" (Wolfe), **Supp. III Part 2:** 571

New Journalism, The (Wolfe and Johnson, eds.), **Supp. III Part 2:** 570, 579–581, 583, 586

New Left, The: The Anti-Industrial Revolution (Rand), **Supp. IV Part 2:** 527

"New Letters from Thomas Jefferson" (Stafford), **Supp. XI:** 324

New Letters on the Air: Contemporary Writers on Radio, **Supp. X:** 165, 169, 173

"New Life" (Glück), **Supp. V:** 90

New Life, A (Malamud), **Supp. I Part 2:** 429–466

"New Life, The" (Bynner), **Supp. XV:** 44

"New Life at Kyerefaso" (Sutherland), **Supp. IV Part 1:** 9

"New Light on Veblen" (Dorfman), **Supp. I Part 2:** 650

Newman, Charles, **Supp. I Part 2:** 527, 546–548

Newman, Edwin, **Supp. IV Part 2:** 526

Newman, Judie, **Supp. IV Part 1:** 304, 305

Newman, Paul, **Supp. IV Part 2:** 473, 474

New Man, The (Merton), **Supp. VIII:** 208

"New Medea, The" (Howells), **II:** 282

New Mexico trilogy (Nichols), **Supp. XIII:** 269

"New Mother" (Olds), **Supp. X:** 206

"New Mothers, The" (Shields), **Supp. VII:** 310

New Music (Price), **Supp. VI:** 264, 265

"New Mutants, The" (Fiedler), **Supp. XIII:** 104

"New Name for Some Old Ways of Thinking, A" (James), **II:** 353

New Native American Novel, The: Works in Progress (Bartlett), **Supp. IV Part 1:** 335

"New Natural History, A" (Thurber), **Supp. I Part 2:** 619

"New Negro, The" (Locke), **Supp. XIV:**201

New Negro, The (Locke, ed.), **Supp. II Part 1:** 176; **Supp. IX:** 309; **Supp. X:** 137

New Negro, The: An Interpretation (Locke, ed.), **Retro. Supp. I:** 199; **Supp. IV Part 1:** 170; **Supp. XIV:**195, 201–202

New Negro for a New Century, A (Washington, Wood, and Williams), **Supp. XIV:**201

"New Nomads, The" (E. Hoffman), **Supp. XVI:**161

"New Orleans" (Carruth), **Supp. XVI:**50

New Orleans Sketches (Faulkner), **Retro. Supp. I:** 80

New Path to the Waterfall, A (Carver), **Supp. III Part 1:** 138–140, 147, 149

"New Poem, The" (Wright), **Supp. V:** 339, 340

"New Poems" (MacLeish), **III:** 19

"New Poems" (Oliver), **Supp. VII:** 240

New Poems 1960 (Bynner), **Supp. XV:** 51

New Poems: 1980–88 (Haines), **Supp. XII:** 209–210

New Poetry, The (Monroe and Henderson, eds.), **Supp. I Part 2:** 387

"New Poetry Handbook, The" (Strand), **Supp. IV Part 2:** 626

New Poetry of Mexico (Strand, trans.), **Supp. IV Part 2:** 630

New Poets of England and America (Hall, Pack, and Simpson, eds.), **Supp. IV Part 2:** 621

"Newport of Anchuria" (Henry), **Supp. II Part 1:** 409

New Princeton Encyclopedia of Poetry and Poetics (Preminger and Brogan, eds.), **Supp. XV:** 250

"*New Republic* Moves Uptown, The" (Cowley), **Supp. II Part 1:** 142

"New Rose Hotel" (W. Gibson), **Supp. XVI:** 120, 122, 124

"News, The" (McClatchy), **Supp. XII:** 269

New Season" (Levine), **Supp. V:** 188

New Seeds of Contemplation (Merton), **Supp. VIII:** 200, 208

News from the Glacier: Selected Poems 1960–1980 (Haines), **Supp. XII:** 207, 208–209

"News Item" (Parker), **Supp. IX:** 190

New Song, A (Hughes), **Retro. Supp. I:** 202; **Supp. I Part 1:** 328, 331–332

"New South, The" (Lanier), **Supp. I Part 1:** 352, 354, 370

Newspaper Days, 1899–1906 (Mencken), **III:** 100, 102, 120

"New Spirit, The" (Ashbery), **Supp. III Part 1:** 14, 15

New Spoon River, The (Masters), **Supp. I Part 2:** 461–465, 473

New Star Chamber and Other Essays, The (Masters), **Supp. I Part 2:** 455–456, 459

New Tales of the Vampires (Rice), **Supp. VII:** 290

New Testament, **I:** 303, 457, 458; **II:** 167; **III:** 305; **IV:** 114, 134, 152; **Retro. Supp. I:** 58, 140, 360; **Supp. I Part 1:** 104, 106; **Supp. I Part 2:** 516. *See also* names of New Testament books

New Testament, A (Anderson), **I:** 101, 114

"New Theory of Thorstein Veblen, A" (Galbraith), **Supp. I Part 2:** 650

Newton, Benjamin Franklin, **I:** 454

Newton, Huey P., **Supp. I Part 1:** 66; **Supp. IV Part 1:** 206

Newton, Isaac, **I:** 132, 557; **II:** 6, 103, 348–349; **III:** 428; **IV:** 18, 149

Newton, Sarah Emily, **Supp. XV:** 234

"New-Wave Format, A" (Mason), **Supp. VIII:** 141, 143, 147

New West of Edward Abbey, The (Ronald), **Supp. XIII:** 4

New Wolves, The: The Return of the Mexican Wolf to the American Southwest (Bass), **Supp. XVI:**26–27

New Woman's Survival Sourcebook, The (Rennie and Grimstead, eds.), **Supp. I Part 2:** 569

New World, The (Bynner), **Supp. XV:** 41, 42

New World, The: Tales (Banks), **Supp. V:** 8, 9, 10

New World Naked, A (Mariani), **Retro. Supp. I:** 419

New Worlds of Literature (Beaty and Hunter, eds.), **Supp. IV Part 1:** 331

New World Writing (Updike), **IV:** 217

New Year Letter (Auden), **Supp. II Part 1:** 14, 16

"New Year's Day" (Wharton), **Retro. Supp. I:** 381

"New Year's Eve" (Schwartz), **Supp. II Part 2:** 640, 656–657

New Year's Eve/1929 (Farrell), **II:** 43

"New Year's Eve 1968" (Lowell), **II:** 554

"New Year's Gift, The" (Stowe), **Supp. I Part 2:** 587

"New York" (Capote), **Supp. III Part 1:** 122

"New York" (Moore), **III:** 196, 198, 202, 206

"New York 1965" (Bowles), **Supp. IV Part 1:** 94

New York City Arts Project, **Supp. III Part 2:** 618

"New York City in 1979"(Acker), **Supp. XII:** 5

New York Edition, **Retro. Supp. I:** 235

"New York Edition" (James), **II:** 336, 337

"New York Gold Conspiracy, The" (Adams), **I:** 4

New York Hat, The (film; Griffith), **Supp. XVI:**183

New York Intellectuals, **Supp. VIII:** 93

"New York Intellectuals, The" (Howe), **Supp. VI:** 120

New York Jew (Kazin), **Supp. VIII:** 95, 97–100

"New York Theater: Isn't It Romantic" (Wasserstein), **Supp. XV:** 320

New York Trilogy, The (Auster), **Supp. XII:** 21, 24–28

Next (McNally), **Supp. XIII:** 197

"Next in Line, The" (Bradbury), **Supp. IV Part 1:** 102

Next Room of the Dream, The (Nemerov), **III:** 269, 275, 278, 279–280, 284

"Next Time I Crossed the Line into Oklahoma, The" (Wright), **Supp. XV:** 345

Next-to-Last Things: New Poems and Essays (Kunitz), **Supp. III Part 1:** 257–259, 261, 262, 265, 266, 268

"'Next to Reading Matter'" (Henry), **Supp. II Part 1:** 399

Nexus (H. Miller), **III:** 170, 187, 188, 189

Niatum, Duane, **Supp. IV Part 1:** 331; **Supp. IV Part 2:** 505

Nice and Noir (Schwartz), **Supp. XIV:**23

Nice Jewish Boy, The (Roth), **Supp. III Part 2:** 412

Nicholas II, Tsar, **Supp. I Part 2:** 447

Nichols, Charles, **Retro. Supp. I:** 194

Nichols, John Treadwell, **Supp. XIII:** 253–272

Nichols, Luther, **Supp. X:** 265

Nichols, Mike, **Supp. IV Part 1:** 234; **Supp. IV Part 2:** 577

Nicholson, Colin, **Supp. VIII:** 129

Nicholson, Harold, **Supp. XIV:**163

Nicholson, Jack, **Supp. V:** 26; **Supp. VIII:** 45; **Supp. XI:** 308

Nicholson, John, **Supp. XVI:**293

Nick Adams Stories, The (Hemingway), **II:** 258; **Retro. Supp. I:** 174

"Nick and the Candlestick" (Plath), **Supp. I Part 2:** 544

Nickel Mountain: A Pastoral Novel (Gardner), **Supp. VI:** 63, 64, 68, 69

"Nicodemus" (Keillor), **Supp. XVI:**167

Nicoll, Allardyce, **III:** 400

Nicoloff, Philip, **II:** 7

Niebuhr, Gustav, **III:** 292

Niebuhr, H. Richard, **I:** 494

Niebuhr, Lydia, **III:** 292

Niebuhr, Reinhold, **III:** 290–313; **Supp. I Part 2:** 654

Niedecker, Lorine, **Supp. III Part 2:** 616, 623; **Supp. XIV:**287

Nielsen, Ed, **Supp. IX:** 254

Nielson, Dorothy, **Supp. I Part 2:** 659

Nietzsche, Friedrich Wilhelm, **I:** 227, 283, 383, 389, 396, 397, 402, 509; **II:** 7, 20, 27, 42, 90, 145, 262, 462, 463, 577, 583, 585; **III:** 102–103, 113, 156, 176; **IV:** 286, 491; **Supp.**

I Part 1: 254, 299, 320; **Supp. I Part 2:** 646; **Supp. IV Part 1:** 104, 105–106, 107, 110, 284; **Supp. IV Part 2:** 519; **Supp. V:** 277, 280; **Supp. VIII:** 11, 181, 189; **Supp. X:** 48; **Supp. XII:** 98; **Supp. XIV:**339

Niflis, N. Michael, **Supp. IV Part 1:** 175

Nigger Heaven (Van Vechten), **Supp. II Part 2:** 739, 744–746

"Nigger Jeff" (Dreiser), **Retro. Supp. II:** 97

Nigger of the "Narcissus," The (Conrad), **II:** 91; **Retro. Supp. I:** 106

"NIGGY THE HO" (Baraka), **Supp. II Part 1:** 54

"Night, Death, Mississippi" (Hayden), **Supp. II Part 1:** 369

'Night, Mother (Norman), **Supp. VIII:** 141

"Night above the Avenue" (Merwin), **Supp. III Part 1:** 355

"Night among the Horses, A" (Barnes), **Supp. III Part 1:** 33–34, 39, 44

Night at the Movies, A, or, You Must Remember This: Fictions (Coover), **Supp. V:** 50–51

"Night at the Opera, A" (Matthews), **Supp. IX:** 167

"Night before the Sentence Is Carried Out, The" (Wright), **Supp. XV:** 341

"Nightbird" (Komunyakaa), **Supp. XIII:** 132

"Night-Blooming Cereus, The" (Hayden), **Supp. II Part 1:** 367

Night-Blooming Cereus, The (Hayden), **Supp. II Part 1:** 367, 373

Night-Born, The (London), **II:** 467

"Nightbreak" (Rich), **Supp. I Part 2:** 556

Night Dance (Price), **Supp. VI:** 264

"Night Dances, The" (Plath), **Supp. I Part 2:** 544

"Night Dream, The" (MacLeish), **III:** 15

"Night Ferry" (Doty), **Supp. XI:** 124

"Nightfishing" (Schnackenberg), **Supp. XV:** 254

"Night I Met Little Floyd, The" (Wright), **Supp. XV:** 345–346

Night in Acadie, A (Chopin), **Retro. Supp. II:** 66–67, 73; **Supp. I Part 1:** 200, 219, 220, 224

"Night in Acadie, A" (Chopin), **Retro. Supp. II:** 66

"Night in June, A" (W. C. Williams), **Retro. Supp. I:** 424

"Night in New Arabia, A" (Henry), **Supp. II Part 1:** 402

Night in Question, The: Stories (Wolff), **Supp. VII:** 342–344

"Night Journey" (Roethke), **Supp. III Part 1:** 260

Night Light (Justice), **Supp. VII:** 126–127

"Nightmare" (Kumin), **Supp. IV Part 2:** 442

Nightmare Factory, The (Kumin), **Supp. IV Part 2:** 444–447, 451

"Nightmare Factory, The" (Kumin), **Supp. IV Part 2:** 445, 453

Nightmare on Main Street (Poe), **Retro. Supp. II:** 262

"Nightmare" poems (Benét), **Supp. XI:** 46, 58

"Night Mirror" (L.-Y. Lee), **Supp. XV:** 225

Night Music (Odets), **Supp. II Part 2:** 541, 543, 544

"Night of First Snow" (R. Bly), **Supp. IV Part 1:** 71

Night of January 16th (Rand), **Supp. IV Part 2:** 527

Night of the Iguana, The (T. Williams), **IV:** 382, 383, 384, 385, 386, 387, 388, 391, 392, 393, 394, 395, 397, 398

"Night of the Iguana, The" (T. Williams), **IV:** 384

"Night of the Living Beanfield: How an Unsuccessful Cult Novel Became an Unsuccessful Cult Film in Only Fourteen Years, Eleven Nervous Breakdowns, and $20 Million" (Nichols), **Supp. XIII:** 267

Night Rider (Warren), **IV:** 243, 246–247

Nights (Doolittle), **Supp. I Part 1:** 270, 271

Nights and Days (Merrill), **Supp. III Part 1:** 319, 320, 322–325

"Nights and Days" (Rich), **Supp. I Part 2:** 574

"Night's for Cryin,' The" (C. Himes), **Supp. XVI:**137

"Night Shift" (Plath), **Supp. I Part 2:** 538

"Night-Side" (Oates), **Supp. II Part 2:** 523

Night-Side (Oates), **Supp. II Part 2:** 522

"Night Sketches: Beneath an Umbrella" (Hawthorne), **II:** 235–237, 238, 239, 242

"Night-Sweat" (Lowell), **II:** 554

"Night-Talk" (Ellison), **Retro. Supp. II:** 126; **Supp. II Part 1:** 248

Night Thoughts (Young), **III:** 415

Night Traveler, The (Oliver), **Supp. VII:** 233

"Night Watch" (Gioia), **Supp. XV:** 117

"Night Watch, The" (Wright), **Supp. V:** 339

"Night We All Had Grippe, The" (Jackson), **Supp. IX:** 118

Nightwood (Barnes), **Supp. III Part 1:** 31, 32, 35–37, 39–43

"Nihilist as Hero, The" (Lowell), **II:** 554; **Retro. Supp. II:** 190

Nijinsky, Vaslav, **Supp. XV:** 28–29

Nikolai Gogol (Nabokov), **Retro. Supp. I:** 266

Niles, Thomas, **Retro. Supp. I:** 35

Niles, Thomas, Jr., **Supp. I Part 1:** 39

Nilsson, Christine, **Supp. I Part 1:** 355

Nilsson, Harry, **Supp. XI:** 309

Nilsson, Jenny Lind, **Supp. XVI:**177

Nimitz, Chester, **Supp. I Part 2:** 491

"Nimram" (Gardner), **Supp. VI:** 73

Nims, John Frederick, **III:** 527

Nin, Anaïs, **III:** 182, 184, 190; **Supp. III Part 1:** 43; **Supp. IV Part 2:** 680; **Supp. X:** 181–200

"9" (Oliver), **Supp. VII:** 244

"Nine from Eight" (Lanier), **Supp. I Part 1:** 352–354

Nine Headed Dragon River: Zen Journals 1969–1982 (Matthiessen), **Supp. V:** 199

Ninemile Wolves,The (Bass), **Supp. XVI:**24–25, 26

"Nine Nectarines" (Moore), **III:** 203, 209, 215

Nine Plays (Reznikoff), **Supp. XIV:**288

"Nine Poems for the Unborn Child" (Rukeyser), **Supp. VI:** 280–281, 284

Nine Stories (Nabokov), **Retro. Supp. I:** 266

Nine Stories (Salinger), **III:** 552, 558–564

1984 (Orwell), **Supp. XIII:** 29

"1940" (Stafford), **Supp. XI:** 328–329

"1945–1985: Poem for the Anniversary" (Oliver), **Supp. VII:** 237

"19 Hadley Street" (Schnackenberg), **Supp. XV:** 253

19 Necromancers from Now (Reed), **Supp. X:** 240

1919 (Dos Passos), **I:** 482, 485–486, 487, 489, 490, 492

"1975" (Wright), **Supp. V:** 341

"1910" (Mora), **Supp. XIII:** 215

"1938" (Komunyakaa), **Supp. XIII:** 114

"1939" (Taylor), **Supp. V:** 316

1933 (Levine), **Supp. V:** 185–187

"1933" (Levine), **Supp. V:** 188
"Nineteenth New York, The" (Doctorow), **Supp. IV Part 1:** 232
"1929" (Auden), **Supp. II Part 1:** 6
"1926" (Kees), **Supp. XV:** 135
19 Varieties of Gazelle (Nye), **Supp. XIII:** 275, 286–288
"19 Varieties of Gazelle" (Nye), **Supp. XIII:** 286
95 Poems (Cummings), **I:** 430, 433, 435, 439, 446, 447
"90 North" (Jarrell), **II:** 370, 371
"91 Revere Street" (Lowell), **II:** 547; **Retro. Supp. II:** 188; **Supp. XI:** 240
90 Trees (Zukofsky), **Supp. III Part 2:** 631
"Nine Years Later" (Brodsky), **Supp. VIII:** 32
"Nirvana" (Lanier), **Supp. I Part 1:** 352
Nirvana Blues, The (Nichols), **Supp. XIII:** 266, 267
Nishikigi (play), **III:** 466
Niven, David, **Supp. XI:** 307
Nixon (film), **Supp. XIV:**48
Nixon, Richard M., **I:** 376; **III:** 38, 46; **Supp. I Part 1:** 294, 295; **Supp. V:** 45, 46, 51; **Supp. XII:** 14; **Supp. XIV:**306
"NJ Transit" (Komunyakaa), **Supp. XIII:** 132
Nketia, J. H., **Supp. IV Part 1:** 10
Nketsia, Nana, **Supp. IV Part 1:** 2, 10
Nkize, Julius, **Supp. IV Part 1:** 361
Nkrumah, Kwame, **I:** 490, 494; **Supp. IV Part 1:** 361; **Supp. X:** 135
Noailles, Anna de, **IV:** 328
Noa Noa (Gauguin), **I:** 34
Nobel Lecture (Singer), **Retro. Supp. II:** 300
"No Better Than a 'Withered Daffodil'" (Moore), **III:** 216
Noble, David W., **Supp. I Part 2:** 650
"Noble Rider and the Sound of Words, The" (Stevens), **Retro. Supp. I:** 299
Noble Savage, The (Coover), **Supp. V:** 40
"No Bobolink reverse His Singing" (Dickinson), **Retro. Supp. I:** 45
Nobodaddy (MacLeish), **III:** 5–6, 8, 10, 11, 18, 19, 20
"Nobody in Hollywood" (Bausch), **Supp. VII:** 54
Nobody Knows My Name (Baldwin), **Supp. XIII:** 111
"Nobody Knows My Name" (Baldwin), **Retro. Supp. II:** 8; **Supp. I Part 1:** 52
Nobody Knows My Name: More Notes

of a Native Son (Baldwin), **Retro. Supp. II:** 6, 8; **Supp. I Part 1:** 47, 52, 55
"Nobody knows this little Rose" (Dickinson), **Retro. Supp. I:** 30
"Nobody Said Anything" (Carver), **Supp. III Part 1:** 141
Nobody's Fool (Russo), **Supp. XII:** 326, 331–335, 340
"No Change of Place" (Auden), **Supp. II Part 1:** 5
"Noche Triste, La" (Frost), **Retro. Supp. I:** 123
Nock, Albert Jay, **I:** 245; **Supp. IV Part 2:** 521, 524
"No Coward Soul Is Mine" (Brontë), **I:** 458
"No Crime in the Mountains" (Chandler), **Supp. IV Part 1:** 129
"Nocturne" (Komunyakaa), **Supp. XIII:** 126
"Nocturne" (MacLeish), **III:** 8
"Nocturne in a Deserted Brickyard" (Sandburg), **III:** 586
Nocturne of Remembered Spring (Aiken), **I:** 50
No Door (Wolfe), **IV:** 451–452, 456
"No Door" (Wolfe), **IV:** 456
"No Epitaph" (Carson), **Supp. XII:** 111
No Exit (Sartre), **I:** 82, 130; **Supp. XIV:**320
No Exit (Sartre; Bowles, trans.), **Supp. IV Part 1:** 84
No Gifts from Chance (Benstock), **Retro. Supp. I:** 361
"No-Good Blues" (Komunyakaa), **Supp. XIII:** 130
No Hero (Marquand), **III:** 57
No! In Thunder (Fiedler), **Supp. XIII:** 101
"Noiseless Patient Spider" (Whitman), **III:** 555; **IV:** 348; **Supp. IV Part 1:** 325
Noises Off (Frayn), **Supp. IV Part 2:** 582
Noi vivi. See We the Living (film)
"No Lamp Has Ever Shown Us Where to Look" (MacLeish), **III:** 9
Nolan, Sidney, **Retro. Supp. II:** 189
No Laughing Matter (Heller and Vogel), **Supp. IV Part 1:** 384, 389
No Love Lost, a Romance of Travel (Howells), **II:** 277
No Man Is an Island (Merton), **Supp. VIII:** 207
No Mother to Guide Her (Loos), **Supp. XVI:**194

No Name in the Street (Baldwin), **Retro. Supp. II:** 13, 14; **Supp. I Part 1:** 47, 48, 52, 65–66, 67
No Nature: New and Selected Poems (Snyder), **Supp. VIII:** 305
Nonconformist's Memorial, The (Howe), **Supp. IV Part 2:** 434, 435–436
Nonconformity (Algren), **Supp. IX:** 15
None but the Lonely Heart (film), **Supp. II Part 2:** 546
Nones (Auden), **Supp. II Part 1:** 21
"Nones" (Auden), **Supp. II Part 1:** 22–23
None Shall Look Back (Gordon), **II:** 205–207, 208
Nonverbal Communication: Notes on the Visual Perception of Human Relations (Kees and Ruesch), **Supp. XV:** 147
"Noon" (Bryant), **Supp. I Part 1:** 157
"No One Remembers" (Levine), **Supp. V:** 187
"Noon Walk on the Asylum Lawn" (Sexton), **Supp. II Part 2:** 673
"Noon Wine" (Porter), **III:** 436, 437–438, 442, 446
"No Pain Whatsoever" (Yates), **Supp. XI:** 341
"No Place for You, My Love" (Welty), **IV:** 278, 279; **Retro. Supp. I:** 353
No Plays of Japan, The (Waley), **III:** 466
No Pockets in a Shroud (McCoy), **Supp. XIII:** 166–168, 171, 172, 173, 174
"No Poem So Fine" (Francis), **Supp. IX:** 83
Norcross, Frances, **I:** 456, 462
Norcross, Louise, **I:** 456, 462
Nordyke, Lewis, **Supp. XIII:** 5
No Relief (Dixon), **Supp. XII:** 139, 142–143
No Resting Place (Humphrey), **Supp. IX:** 94, 106–108
Norfolk Poems, The (Carruth), **Supp. XVI:**47, 48
Norma (Bellini), **IV:** 309
Norma Ashe (Glaspell), **Supp. III Part 1:** 175, 186–187
"Normal Motor Adjustments" (Stein and Solomons), **IV:** 26
Norman, Charles, **III:** 479
Norman, Gurney, **Supp. X:** 24
Norman, Marsha, **Supp. VIII:** 141
Norman Mailer (Poirier), **Retro. Supp. II:** 207–208
Norman Mailer: Modern Critical Views (Bloom), **Retro. Supp. II:** 205
Norman Mailer Revisited (Merrill),

Retro. Supp. II: 201

Norna; or, The Witch's Curse (Alcott), **Supp. I Part 1:** 33

Norris, Charles, **III:** 320; **Retro. Supp. I:** 100

Norris, Frank, **I:** 211, 355, 500, 506, 517, 518, 519; **II:** 89, 264, 276, 289, 307; **III:** 227, 314–336, 596; **IV:** 29; **Retro. Supp. I:** 100, 325; **Retro. Supp. II:** 96, 101; **Supp. III Part 2:** 412; **Supp. VIII:** 101, 102; **Supp. IX:** 14, 15; **Supp. XV:** 115

"North" (Hugo), **Supp. VI:** 135

North, Milou (pseudonym), **Supp. IV Part 1:** 260. *See also* Dorris, Michael; Erdrich, Louise

North, Sir Thomas, **IV:** 370

"North American Sequence" (Roethke), **I:** 171–172, 183; **III:** 529, 545, 547, 548

"North Beach" (Snyder), **Supp. VIII:** 289

"North Country Sketches" (McClatchy), **Supp. XII:** 256

"Northeast Playground" (Paley), **Supp. VI:** 226–227, 229

Northern Lights (O'Brien), **Supp. V:** 237, 239, 241–244, 250

"Northern Motive" (Levine), **Supp. V:** 195

Northfield Poems (Ammons), **Supp. VII:** 29

"Northhanger Ridge" (Wright), **Supp. V:** 335, 340

"North Haven" (Bishop), **Retro. Supp. II:** 50

"North Labrador" (Crane), **I:** 386

North of Boston (Frost), **II:** 152, 153–154, 527; **Retro. Supp. I:** 121, 125, 127, 128–130, 131; **Supp. I Part 1:** 263; **Supp. XIII:** 146

North of Jamaica (Simpson), **Supp. IV Part 2:** 448; **Supp. IX:** 275, 276

North of the Danube (Caldwell), **I:** 288, 290, 293, 294, 309, 310

Northrup, Cyrus, **Supp. I Part 1:** 350

"North Sea Undertaker's Complaint, The" (Lowell), **II:** 550

North & South (Bishop), **Retro. Supp. II:** 41–43; **Supp. I Part 1:** 72, 84, 85, 89

North Star, The (Hellman), **Supp. I Part 1:** 281

Northup, Solomon, **Supp. XIV:**32

"North Winter" (Carruth), **Supp. XVI:**53

Norton, Charles Eliot, **I:** 223, 568; **II:** 279, 322–323, 338; **Retro. Supp. I:** 371; **Retro. Supp. II:** 135; **Supp. I**

Part 1: 103; **Supp. I Part 2:** 406, 479

Norton, Jody, **Supp. VIII:** 297

Norton, John, **Supp. I Part 1:** 99, 110, 112, 114

Norton Anthology of African American Literature, The, **Supp. X:** 325

Norton Anthology of American Literature, **Supp. X:** 325; **Supp. XV:** 270

Norton Anthology of Literature by Women (Gilbert and Gubar, eds.), **Supp. XV:** 270

Norton Anthology of Modern Poetry, The, **Supp. XI:** 259; **Supp. XV:** 258

Norton Anthology of Short Fiction, The, **Supp. IX:** 4

Norton Book of Personal Essays, The, **Supp. XIV:**105

Norton Lectures, **Retro. Supp. I:** 65

Norwood, Vera, **Supp. IX:** 24

No Safe Harbour (Porter), **III:** 447

Nosferatu: An Opera Libretto (Gioia), **Supp. XV:** 112, 128

"Nosferatu's Serenade" (Gioia), **Supp. XV:** 128

"No Speak English" (Cisneros), **Supp. VII:** 63

"Nostalgia of the Lakefronts" (Justice), **Supp. VII:** 118, 119, 120

"Nostalgic Mood" (Farrell), **II:** 45

No Star Is Lost (Farrell), **II:** 34, 35, 44

Nostromo (Conrad), **II:** 600; **IV:** 245

"Nosty Fright, A" (Swenson), **Supp. IV Part 2:** 651

Not about Nightingales (T. Williams), **IV:** 381

Not Dancing (Dunn), **Supp. XI:** 143, 148

"Note about *Iconographs,* A" (Swenson), **Supp. IV Part 2:** 646

Notebook (Lowell), **Retro. Supp. II:** 186, 190; **Supp. V:** 343

Notebook 1967–68 (Lowell), **II:** 553–555; **Retro. Supp. II:** 182, 186, 190

Notebook of Malte Laurids Brigge, The (Rilke), **III:** 571

Notebooks (Fitzgerald), **Retro. Supp. I:** 110

"Note on Abraham Lincoln" (Vidal), **Supp. IV Part 2:** 688

"Note on Commercial Theatre" (Hughes), **Retro. Supp. I:** 207

"Note on Ezra Pound, A" (Eliot), **Retro. Supp. I:** 290

"Note on Lanier's Music, A" (P. Graham), **Supp. I Part 1:** 373

Note on Literary Criticism, A (Farrell), **II:** 26, 49

"Note on Poetry, A" (Doolittle), **Supp. I Part 1:** 254, 267–268

"Note on Realism, A" (Anderson), **I:** 110

"Note on the Limits of 'History' and the Limits of 'Criticism,' A" (Brooks), **Supp. XIV:**11

"Note on the Poetry of Love, A" (Untermeyer), **Supp. XV:** 304

"Notes" (Dove), **Supp. IV Part 1:** 246

"Notes for a Moving Picture: The House" (Agee), **I:** 33, 34

"Notes for an Autobiography" (Van Vechten), **Supp. II Part 2:** 749

"Notes for a Novel About the End of the World" (Percy), **Supp. III Part 1:** 393

"Notes for a Preface" (Sandburg), **III:** 591, 596–597

"NOTES FOR A SPEECH" (Baraka), **Supp. II Part 1:** 33

Notes for the Green Box (Duchamp), **Supp. IV Part 2:** 423

Notes from a Bottle Found on the Beach at Carmel (Connell), **Supp. XIV:**80, 87, 96, 97

Notes from a Sea Diary: Hemingway All the Way (Algren), **Supp. IX:** 16

"Notes from the Childhood and Girlhood" (Brooks), **Supp. III Part 1:** 77

"Notes from the River" (Stern), **Supp. IX:** 285, 287, 294, 295

Notes from Underground (Dostoyevsky), **III:** 571; **IV:** 485; **Retro. Supp. II:** 121

"Notes of a Faculty Wife" (Jackson), **Supp. IX:** 126

"Notes of a Native Daughter" (Didion), **Supp. IV Part 1:** 196, 197, 200, 201

Notes of a Native Son (Baldwin), **Retro. Supp. II:** 1, 2, 3, 5, 6; **Supp. I Part 1:** 50, 52, 54; **Supp. IV Part 1:** 163

"Notes of a Native Son" (Baldwin), **Supp. I Part 1:** 50, 54

Notes of a Son and Brother (James), **II:** 337; **Retro. Supp. I:** 235

"Notes on a Departure" (Trilling), **Supp. III Part 2:** 498

"Notes on Babbitt and More" (Wilson), **IV:** 435

"Notes on Camp" (Sontag), **Supp. XIV:**167

"Notes on 'Camp'" (Sontag), **Supp. III Part 2:** 455–456

Notes on Democracy (Mencken), **III:** 104, 107–108, 109, 116, 119

"Notes on Free Verse" (Dobyns), **Supp. XIII:** 77

"Notes on 'Layover'" (Hass), **Supp. VI:** 109

Notes on Novelists (James), **II:** 336, 337; **Retro. Supp. I:** 235

"Notes on Nukes, Nookie, and Neo-Romanticism" (Robbins), **Supp. X:** 272

"Notes on Poetry" (Eberhart), **I:** 524, 527–528, 529

"Notes on the Craft of Poetry" (Strand), **Supp. IV Part 2:** 626

"Notes on the Decline of Outrage" (Dickey), **Supp. IV Part 1:** 181

"Notes on the New Formalism" (Gioia), **Supp. XV:** 113, 114–115

"Notes on the Novel-as-Autobiography" (P. Bailey), **Supp. XVI:**69

Notes on the State of Virginia (1781–1782) (Jefferson), **Supp. XIV:**191

"Notes to Be Left in a Cornerstone" (Benét), **Supp. XI:** 46, 58

"Notes toward a Supreme Fiction" (Stevens), **IV:** 87–89; **Retro. Supp. I:** 300, 306, 306–309, 311; **Supp. I Part 1:** 80

"Notes towards a Poem That Can Never Be Written" (Atwood), **Supp. XIII:** 34–35

No Thanks (Cummings), **I:** 430, 431, 432, 436, 437, 441, 443, 446

"Nothing" (C. Frost), **Supp. XV:** 94

"Nothing Big" (Komunyakaa), **Supp. XIII:** 121

Nothing for Tigers (Carruth), **Supp. XVI:**47, 48, 50

"Nothing Gold Can Stay" (Frost), **Retro. Supp. I:** 133

"Nothing in Heaven Functions as It Ought" (X. J. Kennedy), **Supp. XV:** 158–159

"Nothing Missing" (O'Hara), **III:** 369

Nothing Personal (Baldwin), **Supp. I Part 1:** 58, 60

"Nothing Song, The" (Snodgrass), **Supp. VI:** 326

"Nothing Stays Put" (Clampitt), **Supp. IX:** 42

"Nothing Will Yield" (Nemerov), **III:** 279

No Third Path (Kosinski), **Supp. VII:** 215

"Not Ideas About the Thing but the Thing Itself" (Stevens), **IV:** 87

Notions of the Americans: Picked up by a Travelling Bachelor (Cooper), **I:** 343–345, 346

"Not-Knowing" (Barthelme), **Supp. IV Part 1:** 48

"Not Leaving the House" (Snyder), **Supp. VIII:** 300

"'Not Marble nor the Gilded Monument'" (MacLeish), **III:** 12

"Not Quite Social" (Frost), **II:** 156

"Not Sappho, Sacco" (Rukeyser), **Supp. VI:** 277

"Not Sixteen" (Anderson), **I:** 114

"Not Slightly" (Stein), **IV:** 44

Not So Deep as a Well (Parker), **Supp. IX:** 192

"Not Somewhere Else, but Here" (Rich), **Supp. I Part 2:** 552, 573

Not So Simple: The "Simple" Stories by Langston Hughes (Harper), **Retro. Supp. I:** 194, 209

Not-So-Simple Neil Simon (McGovern), **Supp. IV Part 2:** 573

"Not the Point" (Cameron), **Supp. XII:** 83

"Not They Who Soar" (Dunbar), **Supp. II Part 1:** 199

Not This Pig (Levine), **Supp. V:** 178, 181, 182–183

Not to Eat; Not for Love (Weller), **III:** 322

Not Without Laughter (Hughes), **Retro. Supp. I:** 197, 198, 201; **Supp. I Part 1:** 328, 332

Nouvelle Héloïse, La (Rousseau), **Supp. XV:** 232

Nova Express (Burroughs), **Supp. III Part 1:** 93, 103, 104

Novel, The (Bulwer), **Retro. Supp. II:** 58

"Novel as a Function of American Democracy, The" (Ellison), **Retro. Supp. II:** 124

"Novel Démeublé, The" (Cather), **Retro. Supp. I:** 15

Novel History: Historians and Novelists Confront America's Past (and Each Other) (Carnes), **Supp. X:** 14

Novella (Goethe; Bogan and Mayer, trans.), **Supp. III Part 1:** 63

Novellas and Other Writings (Wharton), **Retro. Supp. I:** 360

"Novel of the Thirties, A" (Trilling), **Supp. III Part 2:** 499

Novels and Other Writings (Bercovitch), **Retro. Supp. II:** 325

Novels and Tales of Henry James, The (James), **Retro. Supp. I:** 232

"Novel-Writing and Novel-Reading" (Howells), **II:** 276, 290

"November" (Larcom), **Supp. XIII:** 143

"November Cotton Flower" (Toomer), **Supp. IX:** 312

November Twenty Six Nineteen Sixty Three (Berry), **Supp. X:** 24

"Novices" (Moore), **III:** 200–201, 202, 213

Novick, Peter, **Supp. XVI:**154–155

"Novogodnee" ("New Year's Greetings") (Tsvetayeva), **Supp. VIII:** 30

"Novotny's Pain" (Roth), **Supp. III Part 2:** 403

"No Voyage" (Oliver), **Supp. VII:** 231

No Voyage and Other Poems (Oliver), **Supp. VII:** 230–231, 232

Now and Another Time (Hearon), **Supp. VIII:** 58, 61–62

Now and Then (Buechner), **Supp. XII:** 49, 53

"Now and Then, America" (Mora), **Supp. XIII:** 217

Nowhere Is a Place: Travels in Patagonia (Theroux and Chatwin), **Supp. VIII:** 322

"Now I Am Married" (Gordon), **Supp. IV Part 1:** 299

"Now I Lay Me" (Hemingway), **II:** 249; **Retro. Supp. I:** 175

"Now I Lay Me" (Olds), **Supp. X:** 208

"Now Is the Air Made of Chiming Balls" (Eberhart), **I:** 523

"No Word" (Kunitz), **Supp. III Part 1:** 263

Now Sheba Sings the Song (Angelou), **Supp. IV Part 1:** 16

"Now That We Live" (Kenyon), **Supp. VII:** 165

"Now the Servant's Name Was Malchus" (Wilder), **IV:** 358

"Now We Know" (O'Hara), **III:** 368–369

NOW with Bill Moyers (television), **Supp. XIII:** 286

Noyes, Alfred, **IV:** 434

Nuamah, Grace, **Supp. IV Part 1:** 10

"Nuances of a Theme by Williams" (Stevens), **Retro. Supp. I:** 422

Nuclear Age, The (O'Brien), **Supp. V:** 238, 243, 244, 246–248, 249, 251

"Nuclear Arms and Morality" (Sanders), **Supp. XVI:**266

Nude Croquet (Fiedler), **Supp. XIII:** 103

"Nude Descendig a Staircase" (X. J. Kennedy), **Supp. XV:** 168

"Nude Descending a Staircase" (Duchamp), **IV:** 408; **Retro. Supp. I:** 416

Nude Descending a Staircase (X. J. Kennedy), **Supp. XV:** 153, 154–157

Nugent, Bruce, **Retro. Supp. I:** 200

Nugent, Elliot, **Supp. I Part 2:** 606, 611, 613

Nuggets and Dust (Bierce), **I:** 195

"Nullipara" (Olds), **Supp. X:** 209

Number One (Dos Passos), **I:** 489

"Numbers, Letters" (Baraka), **Supp. II Part 1:** 50

Nunc Dimittis (Brodsky), **Supp. VIII:** 25–26, 28

"Nun No More, A" (Fante), **Supp. XI:** 160

"Nun's Priest's Tale" (Chaucer), **III:** 492

Nunzio, Nanzia, **IV:** 89

Nuptial Flight, The (Masters), **Supp. I Part 2:** 460, 471

"Nuptials" (Tate), **IV:** 122

"Nurse Whitman" (Olds), **Supp. X:** 203

Nurture (Kumin), **Supp. IV Part 2:** 453–454, 455

Nussbaum, Emily, **Supp. XI:** 143

Nussbaum, Felicity A., **Supp. X:** 189

Nutcracker, The (Tchaikovsky), **Retro. Supp. I:** 196

"Nux Postcoenatica" (Holmes), **Supp. I Part 1:** 303

Nyce, James M., **Retro. Supp. I:** 380

Nye, Naomi Shihab, **Supp. XI:** 316; **Supp. XIII:** 273–290

Nyerere, Julius, **Supp. X:** 135

"Nympholepsy" (Faulkner), **Retro. Supp. I:** 81

O

"Ö" (Dove), **Supp. IV Part 1:** 245

O. Henry Biography (C. A. Smith), **Supp. II Part 1:** 395

Oak and Ivy (Dunbar), **Supp. II Part 1:** 98

Oak Openings, The (Cooper), **I:** 354, 355

Oandasan, Bill, **Supp. IV Part 2:** 499

Oasis, The (McCarthy), **II:** 566–568

Oates, Joyce Carol, **Supp. II Part 2:** 503–527; **Supp. IV Part 1:** 205; **Supp. IV Part 2:** 447, 689; **Supp. V:** 323; **Supp. XI:** 239; **Supp. XII:** 343; **Supp. XIII:** 306; **Supp. XIV:** 26, 109

"Oath, The" (Tate), **IV:** 127

Obbligati (Hecht), **Supp. X:** 57

Ober, Harold, **Retro. Supp. I:** 101, 103, 105, 110, 113

Oberndorf, Clarence P., **Supp. I Part 1:** 315

Obey, André, **IV:** 356, 375

"Obit" (Lowell), **II:** 554

"Objective Value of a Social Settlement, The" (Addams), **Supp. I Part 1:** 4

"Objective Woman, The" (Jong), **Supp. V:** 119

Objectivist Anthology, An, **Supp. XIV:** 287

"Objectivist Ethics, The" (Rand), **Supp. IV Part 2:** 530–532

"Objectivists" Anthology, An (Zukofsky), **Supp. III Part 2:** 613, 615

"Objects" (Wilbur), **Supp. III Part 2:** 545–547

Oblique Prayers (Levertov), **Supp. III Part 1:** 283

"Oblivion" (Justice), **Supp. VII:** 121

Oblivion Seekers, The (Eberhardt), **Supp. IV Part 1:** 92

"Oblong Box, The" (Poe), **III:** 416

Obregon, Maurice, **Supp. I Part 2:** 488

O'Briant, Don, **Supp. X:** 8

O'Brien, Edward, **Supp. XV:** 140

O'Brien, Edward J., **I:** 289; **III:** 56

O'Brien, Fitzjames, **I:** 211

O'Brien, Geoffrey, **Supp. IV Part 2:** 471, 473

O'Brien, John, **Supp. V:** 48, 49; **Supp. X:** 239, 244

O'Brien, Tim, **Supp. V:** 237–255; **Supp. XI:** 234

"Obscene Poem, An" (Creeley), **Supp. IV Part 1:** 150

Obscure Destinies (Cather), **I:** 331–332; **Retro. Supp. I:** 19

"Observation Relative to the Intentions of the Original Founders of the Academy in Philadelphia" (Franklin), **II:** 114

"Observations" (Dillard), **Supp. VI:** 34

Observations (Moore), **III:** 194, 195–196, 197, 199, 203, 205, 215

Observations: Photographs by Richard Avedon: Comments by Truman Capote, **Supp. III Part 1:** 125–126

"Observations Now" (Conroy), **Supp. XVI:** 75

O Canada: An American's Notes on Canadian Culture (Wilson), **IV:** 429–430

"O Carib Isle!" (Crane), **I:** 400–401

O'Casey, Sean, **III:** 145; **Supp. IV Part 1:** 359, 361, 364

"Occidentals" (Ford), **Supp. V:** 71–72

"Occultation of Orion, The" (Longfellow), **Retro. Supp. II:** 168

"Occurrence at Owl Creek Bridge, An" (Bierce), **I:** 200–201; **II:** 264

"Ocean 1212-W" (Plath), **Supp. I Part 2:** 528

O'Connell, Nicholas, **Supp. IX:** 323, 325, 334

O'Connor, Edward F., Jr., **III:** 337

O'Connor, Flannery, **I:** 113, 190, 211, 298; **II:** 606; **III:** 337–360; **IV:** 4, 217, 282; **Retro. Supp. II:** 179, 219–239, 272, 324; **Supp. I Part 1:** 290; **Supp. III Part 1:** 146; **Supp. V:** 59, 337; **Supp. VIII:** 13, 14, 158; **Supp. X:** 1, 26, 69, 228, 290; **Supp. XI:** 104; **Supp. XIII:** 294; **Supp. XIV:** 93; **Supp. XV:** 338; **Supp. XVI:** 219

O'Connor, Frank, **III:** 158; **Retro. Supp. II:** 242; **Supp. I Part 2:** 531; **Supp. VIII:** 151, 157, 165, 167, 171; **Supp. XV:** 74

O'Connor, Richard, **II:** 467

O'Connor, T. P., **II:** 129

O'Connor, William, **IV:** 346; **Retro. Supp. I:** 392, 407

O'Connor, William Van, **III:** 479; **Supp. I Part 1:** 195

"Octascope" (Beattie), **Supp. V:** 27, 28

"Octaves" (Robinson), **Supp. III Part 2:** 593

"Octet" (Wallace), **Supp. X:** 309

October (Isherwood), **Supp. XIV:** 157, 164

"October" (Oliver), **Supp. VII:** 241

"October" (Swenson), **Supp. IV Part 2:** 649

"October 1913" (McCarriston), **Supp. XIV:** 266

"October, 1866" (Bryant), **Supp. I Part 1:** 169

"October and November" (Lowell), **II:** 554

"October in the Railroad Earth" (Kerouac), **Supp. III Part 1:** 225, 227, 229

October Light (Gardner), **Supp. VI:** 63, 69–71, 72

"October Maples, Portland" (Wilbur), **Supp. III Part 2:** 556

"Octopus, An" (Moore), **III:** 202, 207–208, 214

"Octopus, The" (Merrill), **Supp. III Part 1:** 321

Octopus, The (Norris), **I:** 518; **III:** 314, 316, 322–326, 327, 331–333, 334, 335

"O Daedalus, Fly Away Home" (Hayden), **Supp. II Part 1:** 377–378

"OD and Hepatitis Railroad or Bust, The" (Boyle), **Supp. VIII:** 1

Odd Couple, The (film), **Supp. IV Part 2:** 589

Odd Couple, The (Simon), **Supp. IV Part 2:** 575, 579–580, 585, 586

Odd Couple, The (1985 version, Simon), **Supp. IV Part 2:** 580

Odd Jobs (Updike), **Retro. Supp. I:** 334

Odd Mercy (Stern), **Supp. IX:** 298–299

"Odds, The" (Hecht), **Supp. X:** 64–65

"Odds, The" (Salinas), **Supp. XIII:** 321

"Ode" (Emerson), **II:** 13

"Ode (Intimations of Immortality)" (Matthews), **Supp. IX:** 162

"Ode" (Sobin), **Supp. XVI:**284–285

"Ode" (X. J. Kennedy), **Supp. XV:** 160

"Ode: For the Budding of Islands" (Sobin), **Supp. XVI:**287

"Ode: Intimations of Immortality" (Wordsworth), **Supp. I Part 2:** 729; **Supp. III Part 1:** 12; **Supp. XIV:**8

"Ode: My 24th Year" (Ginsberg), **Supp. II Part 1:** 312

"Ode for Memorial Day" (Dunbar), **Supp. II Part 1:** 199

"Ode for the American Dead in Asia" (McGrath), **Supp. X:** 119

"Ode Inscribed to W. H. Channing" (Emerson), **Supp. XIV:**46

"Ode on a Grecian Urn" (Keats), **I:** 284; **III:** 472; **Supp. XII:** 113; **Supp. XIV:**8, 9–10; **Supp. XV:** 100

"Ode on Human Destinies" (Jeffers), **Supp. II Part 2:** 419

"Ode on Indolence" (Keats), **Supp. XII:** 113

"Ode on Melancholy" (Keats), **Retro. Supp. I:** 301

Ode Recited at the Harvard Commemoration (Lowell), **Supp. I Part 2:** 416–418, 424

"Ode Recited at the Harvard Commemoration" (Lowell), **II:** 551

"Ode Secrète" (Valéry), **III:** 609

"Odes of Estrangement" (Sobin), **Supp. XVI:**289

"Odes to Natural Processes" (Updike), **Retro. Supp. I:** 323

"Ode to a Nightingale" (Keats), **II:** 368; **Retro. Supp. II:** 261; **Supp. IX:** 52

"Ode to Autumn" (Masters), **Supp. I Part 2:** 458

"Ode to Cervantes" (Salinas), **Supp. XIII:** 324

"Ode to Coit Tower" (Corso), **Supp. XII:** 122

"Ode to Ethiopia" (Dunbar), **Supp. II Part 1:** 199, 207, 208, 209

"Ode to Fear" (Tate), **IV:** 128

Ode to Harvard and Other Poems, An (Bynner), **Supp. XV:** 41, 44

"Ode to Meaning" (Pinsky), **Supp. VI:** 249–250, 251

"Ode to Night" (Masters), **Supp. I Part 2:** 458

"Ode to Our Young Pro-Consuls of the Air" (Tate), **IV:** 135

"Ode to the Austrian Socialists" (Benét), **Supp. XI:** 46, 58

"Ode to the Confederate Dead" (Tate), **II:** 551; **IV:** 124, 133, 137; **Supp. X:** 52

"Ode to the Johns Hopkins University" (Lanier), **Supp. I Part 1:** 370

"Ode to the Maggot" (Komunyakaa), **Supp. XIII:** 130

"Ode to the Mexican Experience" (Salinas), **Supp. XIII:** 316–317

"Ode to the Virginian Voyage" (Drayton), **IV:** 135

"Ode to the West Wind" (Shelley), **Retro. Supp. I:** 308; **Supp. I Part 2:** 728; **Supp. IX:** 52; **Supp. XII:** 117; **Supp. XIV:**271–272; **Supp. XV:** 221

"Ode to Walt Whitman" (Benét), **Supp. XI:** 52

Odets, Clifford, **Supp. I Part 1:** 277, 295; **Supp. I Part 2:** 679; **Supp. II Part 2:** 529–554; **Supp. IV Part 2:** 587; **Supp. V:** 109; **Supp. VIII:** 96

Odier, Daniel, **Supp. III Part 1:** 97

"Odi et Amo" (Catullus), **Supp. XV:** 27, 32, 35

O'Donnell, George Marion, **II:** 67

O'Donnell, Thomas F., **II:** 131

"Odor of Verbena" (Faulkner), **II:** 66

O'Doul, Lefty, **II:** 425

"Odysseus to Telemachus" (Brodsky), **Supp. VIII:** 25

Odyssey (Bryant, trans.), **Supp. I Part 1:** 158

Odyssey (Homer), **III:** 14, 470; **Retro. Supp. I:** 286, 290; **Retro. Supp. II:** 121; **Supp. I Part 1:** 185; **Supp. IV Part 2:** 631; **Supp. IX:** 211; **Supp. X:** 114; **Supp. XIV:**191

"Odyssey of a Wop, The" (Fante), **Supp. XI:** 164, 165

Oedipus Rex (Sophocles), **I:** 137; **III:** 145, 151, 152, 332; **Supp. I Part 2:** 428

Oedipus Tyrannus (Sophocles), **II:** 203; **Supp. XV:** 265

Oehlschlaeger, Fritz, **Supp. IX:** 123

"Of Alexander Crummell" (Du Bois), **Supp. II Part 1:** 170

O'Faoláin, Seán, **Supp. II Part 1:** 101

Of a World That Is No More (Singer), **IV:** 16

"Of Booker T. Washington and Others" (Du Bois), **Supp. II Part 1:** 168

"Of Bright & Blue Birds & the Gala Sun" (Stevens), **IV:** 93

"Of Christian Heroism" (Ozick), **Supp. V:** 272

"Of Dying Beauty" (Zukofsky), **Supp. III Part 2:** 610

"Of 'Father and Son'" (Kunitz), **Supp. III Part 1:** 262

Offenbach, Jacques, **II:** 427

"Offering for Mr. Bluehart, An" (Wright), **Supp. III Part 2:** 596, 601

"Offerings" (Mason), **Supp. VIII:** 141

"Official Piety" (Whittier), **Supp. I Part 2:** 687

"Off-Shore Pirates, The" (Fitzgerald), **II:** 88

Off the Beaten Path (Proulx), **Supp. VII:** 261

Off the Beaten Path: Stories of Place, **Supp. XVI:**22

"Off the Cuff" (Simpson), **Supp. IX:** 278

Off the Map (Levine), **Supp. V:** 178

O'Flaherty, George, **Supp. I Part 1:** 202, 205–206

O'Flaherty, Kate. *See* Chopin, Kate

O'Flaherty, Thomas, **Supp. I Part 1:** 202, 203–204, 205

O'Flaherty, Thomas, Jr., **Supp. I Part 1:** 202

"Of Maids and Other Muses" (Alvarez), **Supp. VII:** 11

"Of Margaret" (Ransom), **III:** 491

Of Mice and Men (Steinbeck), **IV:** 51, 57–58

"Of Modern Poetry" (Stevens), **IV:** 92

Of Plymouth Plantation (Bradford), **Retro. Supp. II:** 161, 162

Of Plymouth Plantation (Morison, ed.), **Supp. I Part 2:** 494

"Ofrenda for Lobo" (Mora), **Supp. XIII:** 224

"Often" (Kenyon), **Supp. VII:** 171

"Often, in Dreams, He Moved through a City" (Dobyns), **Supp. XIII:** 90

"Of the Coming of John" (Du Bois), **Supp. II Part 1:** 170

"Of the Culture of White Folk" (Du Bois), **Supp. II Part 1:** 175

Of the Farm (Updike), **IV:** 214, 217, 223–225, 233; **Retro. Supp. I:** 318, 329, 332

"Of the Four-Winged Cherubim as Signature" (Sobin), **Supp. XVI:**287

"Of 'The Frill'" (McCarriston), **Supp. XIV:**274

"Of the Passing of the First-Born" (Du Bois), **Supp. II Part 1:** 170

"Of the Sorrow Songs" (Du Bois), **Supp. II Part 1:** 170

"Of the Wings of Atlanta" (Du Bois), **Supp. II Part 1:** 170

Of This Time, Of This Place (Trilling), **Supp. III Part 2:** 498, 504

Of Time and the River (Wolfe), **IV:** 450, 451, 452, 455, 456, 457, 458, 459, 462, 464–465, 467, 468, 469

Of Woman Born: Motherhood as Experience and Institution (Rich), **Supp. I Part 2:** 554, 567–569

Of Women and Their Elegance (Mailer), **Retro. Supp. II:** 209

Ogden, Archie, **Supp. XIII:** 174

Ogden, Henry, **II:** 298

Ogden, Uzal, **Supp. I Part 2:** 516

"Oh, Fairest of the Rural Maids" (Bryant), **Supp. I Part 1:** 169

"Oh, Immobility, Death's Vast Associate" (Dobyns), **Supp. XIII:** 89

"Oh, Joseph, I'm So Tired" (Yates), **Supp. XI:** 348

Oh, the Places You'll Go! (Geisel), **Supp. XVI:**111

Oh, the Thinks You can Think! (Geisel), **Supp. XVI:**111

"O'Halloran's Luck" (Benét), **Supp. XI:** 47

O'Hara, Frank, **Supp. XII:** 121; **Supp. XV:** 93, 176, 177, 178, 179–180, 182, 186, 187, 215–216

O'Hara, J. D., **Supp. IV Part 1:** 43; **Supp. V:** 22; **Supp. XVI:**221

O'Hara, John, **I:** 375, 495; **II:** 444, 459; **III:** 66, 361–384; **IV:** 59; **Retro. Supp. I:** 99, 112; **Supp. I Part 1:** 196; **Supp. II Part 1:** 109; **Supp. IV Part 1:** 31, 383; **Supp. IV Part 2:** 678; **Supp. V:** 95; **Supp. VIII:** 151, 156; **Supp. IX:** 208

O'Hehir, Andrew, **Supp. XII:** 280

"Ohio Pagan, An" (Anderson), **I:** 112, 113

Oh Say Can You Say? (Geisel), **Supp. XVI:**111

Oil! (Sinclair), **Supp. V:** 276, 277–279, 282, 288, 289

Oil Notes (Bass), **Supp. XVI:**17

"Oil Painting of the Artist as the Artist" (MacLeish), **III:** 14

O'Keeffe, Georgia, **Supp. IX:** 62, 66

"Oklahoma" (Levis), **Supp. XI:** 267

"Old, Old, Old, Old Andrew Jackson" (Lindsay), **Supp. I Part 2:** 398

"Old Amusement Park, An" (Moore), **III:** 216

"Old Angel Midnight" (Kerouac), **Supp. III Part 1:** 229–230

"Old Apple Dealer, The" (Hawthorne), **II:** 227, 233–235, 237, 238

"Old Apple-Tree, The" (Dunbar),

Supp. II Part 1: 198

"Old Army Game, The" (Garrett), **Supp. VII:** 100–101

"Old Aunt Peggy" (Chopin), **Retro. Supp. II:** 64

"Old Barn at the Bottom of the Fogs, The" (Frost), **Retro. Supp. I:** 138

Old Beauty and Others, The (Cather), **I:** 331

Old Bruin: Commodore Matthew C. Perry, 1794–1858 (Morison), **Supp. I Part 2:** 494–495

"Old Cracked Tune, An" (Kunitz), **Supp. III Part 1:** 264

Old Curiosity Shop, The (Dickens), **I:** 458; **Supp. I Part 2:** 409

Oldest Killed Lake in North America, The (Carruth), **Supp. XVI:**51

"Old Farmer, The" (Jeffers), **Supp. II Part 2:** 418

Old-Fashioned Girl, An (Alcott), **Supp. I Part 1:** 29, 41, 42

"Old Father Morris" (Stowe), **Supp. I Part 2:** 586

"Old Flame, The" (Lowell), **II:** 550

"Old Florist" (Roethke), **III:** 531

"Old Folsom Prison" (Matthews), **Supp. IX:** 165

Old Forest, The (Taylor), **Supp. V:** 320, 321, 326, 327

"Old Forest, The" (Taylor), **Supp. V:** 313, 321, 323, 326

Old Forest and Other Stories (Taylor), **Supp. V:** 326

Old Friends and New (Jewett), **II:** 402; **Retro. Supp. II:** 137, 140

Old Glory, The (Lowell), **II:** 543, 545–546, 555; **Retro. Supp. II:** 188

"Old Homestead, The" (Dunbar), **Supp. II Part 1:** 198

"Old Iron" (Nye), **Supp. XIII:** 276

"Old Ironsides" (Holmes), **Supp. I Part 1:** 302

"Old Lady We Saw, An" (Shields), **Supp. VII:** 310–311

"Old Love" (Singer), **Retro. Supp. II:** 307

"Old McGrath Place, The" (McGrath), **Supp. X:** 114

"Old Maid, The" (Wharton), **Retro. Supp. I:** 381, 382

"Old Man" (Faulkner), **II:** 68, 69

Old Man and the Sea, The (Hemingway), **II:** 250, 256–257, 258, 265; **III:** 40; **Retro. Supp. I:** 180, 185, 186

"Old Man Drunk" (Wright), **Supp. III Part 2:** 595

"Old Man Feeding Hens" (Francis), **Supp. IX:** 78

"Old Man on the Hospital Porch" (Ríos), **Supp. IV Part 2:** 546–547

Old Man Rubbing His Eyes (R. Bly), **Supp. IV Part 1:** 65

"Old Manse, The" (Hawthorne), **II:** 224

"Old Man's Winter Night, An" (Frost), **Retro. Supp. I:** 126, 131

Old Man Who Love Cheese, The (Keillor), **Supp. XVI:**177

"Old Man with a Dog" (Wright), **Supp. XV:** 346

"Old Meeting House, The" (Stowe), **Supp. I Part 2:** 586

"Old Memory, An" (Dunbar), **Supp. II Part 1:** 198

"Old Men, The" (McCarthy), **II:** 566

"Old Men Pitching Horseshoes" (X. J. Kennedy), **Supp. XV:** 166

Old Money (Wasserstein), **Supp. XV:** 333–334

"Old Morgue, The" (Prose), **Supp. XVI:**250

Old Morning Program, The (radio show, Keillor). See *Prairie Home Companion, A* (radio show, Keillor)

"Old Mortality" (Porter), **III:** 436, 438–441, 442, 445, 446

"Old Mrs. Harris" (Cather), **I:** 332; **Retro. Supp. I:** 19

Old Neighborhood, The (Mamet), **Supp. XIV:**240, 241, 242, 249–250, 251, 252, 254

Old New York (Wharton), **IV:** 322; **Retro. Supp. I:** 381

"Ol' Doc Hyar" (Campbell), **Supp. II Part 1:** 202

Old One-Two, The (Gurney), **Supp. V:** 98

"Old Order, The" (Porter), **III:** 443, 444–445, 451

"Old Osawatomie" (Sandburg), **III:** 584

Old Patagonia Express, The: By Train through the Americas (Theroux), **Supp. VIII:** 322

"Old People, The" (Faulkner), **II:** 71–72

"Old Poet Moves to a New Apartment 14 Times, The" (Zukofsky), **Supp. III Part 2:** 628

Old Possum's Book of Practical Cats (Eliot), **Supp. XIII:** 228, 344

"Old Red" (Gordon), **II:** 199, 200, 203

Old Red and Other Stories (Gordon), **II:** 157

Old Régime in Canada, The (Parkman), **Supp. II Part 2:** 600, 607, 608–609, 612

Old Religion, The (Mamet), **Supp. XIV:**253

Olds, Sharon, **Supp. X:** 201–217; **Supp. XI:** 139, 142, 244; **Supp. XII:** 229; **Supp. XIV:**265

"Old Saws" (Garrett), **Supp. VII:** 96–97

Old Testament, **I:** 109, 181, 300, 328, 401, 410, 419, 431, 457, 458; **II:** 166, 167, 219; **III:** 270, 272, 348, 390, 396; **IV:** 41, 114, 152, 309; **Retro. Supp. I:** 122, 140, 249, 311, 360; **Retro. Supp. II:** 299; **Supp. I Part 1:** 60, 104, 106, 151; **Supp. I Part 2:** 427, 515, 516; **Supp. IX:** 14. *See also* names of Old Testament books

"Old Things, The" (James), **Retro. Supp. I:** 229

"Old Times on the Mississippi" (Twain), **IV:** 199

Oldtown Folks (Stowe), **Supp. I Part 2:** 587, 596–598

"Old Town of Berwick, The" (Jewett), **Retro. Supp. II:** 132

"Old Trails" (Robinson), **III:** 513, 517

"Old Tyrannies" (Bourne), **I:** 233

"Old West" (Bausch), **Supp. VII:** 48

"Old Whorehouse, An" (Oliver), **Supp. VII:** 235

"Old Woman" (Pinsky), **Supp. VI:** 238

"Old Woman of Beare, The" (X. J. Kennedy), **Supp. XV:** 156

"Old Word, The" (Simic), **Supp. VIII:** 282

"Old-World Landowners" (Gogol), **Supp. XV:** 262

Oldys, Francis. *See* Chalmers, George

Oleanna (Mamet), **Supp. XIV:**239, 241, 245, 248, 250

Olendorf, Donna, **Supp. IV Part 1:** 196

"Olga Poems, The" (Levertov), **Supp. III Part 1:** 279–281

"Olive Groves of Thasos, The" (Clampitt), **Supp. IX:** 51–52

Oliver, Bill, **Supp. VIII:** 138

Oliver, Mary, **Supp. VII:** 229–248; **Supp. X:** 31; **Supp. XVI:**39

Oliver, Sydney, **I:** 409

Oliver Goldsmith: A Biography (Irving), **II:** 315

Oliver Twist (Dickens), **I:** 354; **Supp. IV Part 2:** 464

"Olivia" (Salinas), **Supp. XIII:** 316

Olivieri, David (pseudonym), **Retro. Supp. I:** 361. *See also* Wharton, Edith

Ollive, Samuel, **Supp. I Part 2:** 503

Olmsted, Frederick Law, **Supp. I Part 1:** 355

Olsen, Lance, **Supp. IV Part 1:** 54; **Supp. IV Part 2:** 623

Olsen, Tillie, **Supp. V:** 114, 220; **Supp. XIII:** 291–309; **Supp. XVI:**83, 90

Olson, Charles, **Retro. Supp. I:** 209; **Supp. II Part 1:** 30, 328; **Supp. II Part 2:** 555–587; **Supp. III Part 1:** 9, 271; **Supp. III Part 2:** 542, 624; **Supp. IV Part 1:** 139, 144, 146, 153, 154, 322; **Supp. IV Part 2:** 420, 421, 423, 426; **Supp. VIII:** 290, 291; **Supp. XII:** 2, 198; **Supp. XIII:** 104; **Supp. XIV:**96; **Supp. XV:** 177

"Ol' Tunes, The" (Dunbar), **Supp. II Part 1:** 197

"O Lull Me, Lull Me" (Roethke), **III:** 536–537

Omar Khayyam, **Supp. I Part 1:** 363

O'Meally, Robert, **Retro. Supp. II:** 112

"Omen" (Komunyakaa), **Supp. XIII:** 126, 127

Omensetter's Luck (Gass), **Supp. VI:** 80–82, 87

Omeros (Walcott), **Supp. XV:** 264

"Ominous Baby, An" (Crane), **I:** 411

Ommateum, with Doxology (Ammons), **Supp. VII:** 24–26, 27, 28, 36

"Omnibus Jaunts and Drivers" (Whitman), **IV:** 350

Omoo: A Narrative of Adventures in the South Seas (Melville), **III:** 76–77, 79, 84; **Retro. Supp. I:** 247

O My Land, My Friends (H. Crane), **Retro. Supp. II:** 76

"On a Certain Condescension in Foreigners" (Lowell), **Supp. I Part 2:** 419

"On a Certain Engagement South of Seoul" (Carruth), **Supp. XVI:**47

"On a Child Who Lived One Minute" (X. J. Kennedy), **Supp. XV:** 152, 155

"On Acquiring Riches" (Banks), **Supp. V:** 5

On a Darkling Plain (Stegner), **Supp. IV Part 2:** 598, 607

On a Fire on the Moon (Mailer), **Retro. Supp. II:** 206

"On a Hill Far Away" (Dillard), **Supp. VI:** 28

"On a Honey Bee, Drinking from a Glass and Drowned Therein" (Freneau), **Supp. II Part 1:** 273

"On a Monument to a Pigeon" (Leopold), **Supp. XIV:**187–188

"On a Mountainside" (Wagoner),

Supp. IX: 332

O'Nan, Stewart, **Supp. XI:** 348

"On an Old Photograph of My Son" (Carver), **Supp. III Part 1:** 140

"Onan's Soliloquy" (X. J. Kennedy), **Supp. XV:** 165

"On a Proposed Trip South" (W. C. Williams), **Retro. Supp. I:** 413

"On a Tree Fallen across the Road" (Frost), **Retro. Supp. I:** 134

"On a View of Pasadena from the Hills" (Winters), **Supp. II Part 2:** 795, 796–799, 814

"On a Visit to a Halfway House after a Long Absence" (Salinas), **Supp. XIII:** 325

"On a Windy Night" (Dixon), **Supp. XII:** 155

On Becoming a Novelist (Gardner), **Supp. VI:** 64

"On Being an American" (Toomer), **Supp. III Part 2:** 479

"On Being Asked to Write a Poem against the War in Vietnam" (Carruth), **Supp. XVI:**55–56

"On Being a Woman" (Parker), **Supp. IX:** 201

On Being Blue (Gass), **Supp. VI:** 77, 78, 86, 94; **Supp. XIV:**305

"On Being Too Inhibited" (Hay), **Supp. XIV:**130

On Beyond Zebra! (Geisel), **Supp. XVI:**105

"On Burroughs' Work" (Ginsberg), **Supp. II Part 1:** 320

Once (Walker), **Supp. III Part 2:** 519, 522, 530

Once at Antietam (Gaddis), **Supp. IV Part 1:** 285

"Once by the Pacific" (Frost), **II:** 155; **Retro. Supp. I:** 122, 137

"Once More, the Round" (Roethke), **III:** 529

Once More around the Block: Familiar Essays (Epstein), **Supp. XIV:**107

"Once More to the Lake" (White), **Supp. I Part 2:** 658, 668, 673–675

"On Certain Political Measures Proposed to Their Consideration" (Barlow), **Supp. II Part 1:** 82

"Once There Was Light" (Kenyon), **Supp. VII:** 171–172

Ondaatje, Michael, **Supp. IV Part 1:** 252

On Distant Ground (R. O. Butler), **Supp. XII:** 62, 66–68, 69, 74

O'Neale, Sondra, **Supp. IV Part 1:** 2

"One A.M. with Voices" (X. J. Kennedy), **Supp. XV:** 157

"One Arm" (T. Williams), **IV:** 383

One Arm, and Other Stories (T. Williams), **IV:** 383

"One Art" (Bell), **Supp. X:** 2

One Art (Bishop), **Retro. Supp. II:** 51

"One Art" (Bishop), **Retro. Supp. II:** 50; **Supp. I Part 1:** 72, 73, 82, 93, 94–95, 96; **Supp. XV:** 126

"One Art: The Poetry of Elizabeth Bishop, 1971–1976" (Schwartz), **Supp. I Part 1:** 81

One Big Self: Prisoners of Louisiana (Wright and Luster), **Supp. XV:** 337, 344, 350, 351–353

"One Blessing had I than the rest" (Dickinson), **Retro. Supp. I:** 45

"One Body" (Hass), **Supp. VI:** 106

One Boy's Boston, 1887–1901 (Morison), **Supp. I Part 2:** 494

"One Coat of Paint" (Ashbery), **Supp. III Part 1:** 26

"One Dash-Horses" (Crane), **I:** 416

One Day (Morris), **III:** 233–236

One Day, When I Was Lost (Baldwin), **Retro. Supp. II:** 13; **Supp. I Part 1:** 48, 66, 67

"One Dead Friend" (Kumin), **Supp. IV Part 2:** 441

One Fish Two Fish Red Fish Blue Fish (Geisel), **Supp. XVI:**108

One Flew Over the Cuckoo's Nest (Kesey), **III:** 558

One for the Rose (Levine), **Supp. V:** 178, 179, 181, 187, 189–191

"One for the Rose" (Levine), **Supp. V:** 181, 190

"One Friday Morning" (Hughes), **Supp. I Part 1:** 330

"One Holy Night" (Cisneros), **Supp. VII:** 69–70

"One Home" (Stafford), **Supp. XI:** 321

"$106,000 Blood Money" (Hammett), **Supp. IV Part 1:** 345, 346

$106,000 Blood Money (Hammett), **Supp. IV Part 1:** 345

One Hundred Days in Europe (Holmes), **Supp. I Part 1:** 317

100 Faces of Death, The, Part IV (Boyle), **Supp. VIII:** 16

158-Pound Marriage, The (Irving), **Supp. VI:** 163, 164, 167–170

O'Neil, Elizabeth Murrie, **Retro. Supp. I:** 427

O'Neill, Brendan, **Supp. XII:** 286

O'Neill, Eugene, **I:** 66, 71, 81, 94, 393, 445; **II:** 278, 391, 427, 585; **III:** 151, 165, 385–408; **IV:** 61, 383; **Retro. Supp. II:** 82, 104; **Supp. III Part 1:** 177–180, 189; **Supp. IV Part 1:** 359; **Supp. IV Part 2:** 587, 607; **Supp. V:** 277; **Supp. VIII:** 332, 334; **Supp. XIV:**239, 320, 328; **Supp. XVI:**193

"One Is a Wanderer" (Thurber), **Supp. I Part 2:** 616

"1 January 1965" (Brodsky), **Supp. VIII:** 23–24

"One Last Look at the Adige: Verona in the Rain" (Wright), **Supp. III Part 2:** 603

One Life (Rukeyser), **Supp. VI:** 273, 281, 283

One Life at a Time, Please (Abbey), **Supp. XIII:** 13

One Man in His Time (Glasgow), **II:** 178, 184

"One Man's Fortunes" (Dunbar), **Supp. II Part 1:** 211, 212–213

One Man's Initiation (Dos Passos), **I:** 476–477, 479, 488

"One Man's Meat" (White), **Supp. I Part 2:** 655

One Man's Meat (White), **Supp. I Part 2:** 654, 669, 676

"One Moment on Top of the Earth" (Nye), **Supp. XIII:** 282

One More July: A Football Dialogue with Bill Curry (Plimpton), **Supp. XVI:**243

"One More Song" (Lindsay), **Supp. I Part 2:** 400–401

"One More Thing" (Carver), **Supp. III Part 1:** 138, 144

"One More Time" (Gordon), **II:** 200

One Nation (Stegner), **Supp. IV Part 2:** 599, 608

"One-Night Homecoming" (X. J. Kennedy), **Supp. XV:** 167

"ONE NIGHT STAND" (Baraka), **Supp. II Part 1:** 32

"One of Our Conquerors" (Bourne), **I:** 223

One of Ours (Cather), **I:** 322–323; **Retro. Supp. I:** 1, 3, 13–15, 20

"One of the Missing" (Bierce), **I:** 201–202

"One of the Rooming Houses of Heaven" (Doty), **Supp. XI:** 131

"One of the Smallest" (Stern), **Supp. IX:** 299–300

"One of Us" (Fante), **Supp. XI:** 165

"One Out of Twelve: Writers Who Are Women in Our Century" (Olsen), **Supp. XIII:** 294

"One Part Humor, 2 Parts Whining" (Kakutani), **Supp. XI:** 38

"One Person" (Wylie), **Supp. I Part 2:** 709, 724–727

"One Sister have I in our house" (Dickinson), **Retro. Supp. I:** 34

"One Song, The" (Strand), **Supp. IV Part 2:** 619

"One Summer in Spain" (Coover), **Supp. V:** 40

One Thousand Avant-Garde Plays (Koch), **Supp. XV:** 187

One Time, One Place: Mississippi in the Depression, a Snapshot Album (Welty), **Retro. Supp. I:** 339, 343, 344

1 x 1 (One Times One) (Cummings), **I:** 430, 436, 438–439, 441, 446, 447, 448

"One Touch of Nature" (McCarthy), **II:** 580

One Train (Koch), **Supp. XV:** 177, 184

"One Trip Abroad" (Fitzgerald), **II:** 95

"One Way" (Creeley), **Supp. IV Part 1:** 150–151

One Way or Another (Cameron), **Supp. XII:** 81

One-Way Ticket (Hughes), **Retro. Supp. I:** 206, 207, 208; **Supp. I Part 1:** 333–334

One Way to Heaven (Cullen), **Supp. IV Part 1:** 170, 172

One Way to Spell Man (Stegner), **Supp. IV Part 2:** 595, 598, 601, 609

"One Way to Spell Man" (Stegner), **Supp. IV Part 2:** 601

"One Who Skins Cats, The" (Gunn Allen), **Supp. IV Part 1:** 331

"One Who Went Forth to Feel Fear" (Grimms), **Supp. X:** 86

"One Winter I Devise a Plan of My Own" (Ríos), **Supp. IV Part 2:** 549

One Winter Night in August (X. J. Kennedy), **Supp. XV:** 154, 162

One Writer's Beginnings (Welty), **Retro. Supp. I:** 339, 340, 341, 343, 344, 355–356

"One Year" (Olds), **Supp. X:** 210

"On First Looking Out through Juan de la Cosa's Eyes" (Olson), **Supp. II Part 2:** 565, 566, 570, 579

"On First Opening *The Lyric Year*" (W. C. Williams), **Retro. Supp. I:** 414

"On Freedom's Ground" (Wilbur), **Supp. III Part 2:** 562

On Glory's Course (Purdy), **Supp. VII:** 275–276, 279, 280

On Grief and Reason (Brodsky), **Supp. VIII:** 31–32

"On Hearing a Symphony of Beethoven" (Millay), **III:** 132–133

"On Hearing the Airlines Will Use a Psychological Profile to Catch Potential Skyjackers" (Dunn), **Supp. XI:** 144–145

On Human Finery (Bell), **Supp. I Part 2:** 636

"On *Imagerie:* Esther Williams, 1944" (Sobin), **Supp. XVI:**294

"On Imminence: An Essay" (Sobin), **Supp. XVI:**291

On Liberty (Mill), **Supp. XI:** 196

"On Looking at a Copy of Alice Meynell's Poems, Given Me, Years Ago, by a Friend" (Lowell), **II:** 527–528

"On Lookout Mountain" (Hayden), **Supp. II Part 1:** 380

Only a Few of Us Left (Marquand), **III:** 55

"Only Bar in Dixon, The" (Hugo), **Supp. VI:** 140, 141

Only Dark Spot in the Sky, The (Dove), **Supp. IV Part 1:** 244

"Only Good Indian, The" (Humphrey), **Supp. IX:** 101

Only in America (Golden), **Supp. VIII:** 244

"Only in the Dream" (Eberhart), **I:** 523

"Only Path to Tomorrow, The" (Rand), **Supp. IV Part 2:** 524

"Only Rose, The" (Jewett), **II:** 408

"Only Son of the Doctor, The" (Gordon), **Supp. IV Part 1:** 305, 306

"Only the Cat Escapes," **Supp. XII:** 150–151

"Only the Dead Know Brooklyn" (Wolfe), **IV:** 451

Only When I Laugh (Simon), **Supp. IV Part 2:** 575

On Moral Fiction (Gardner), **Supp. VI:** 61, 71, 72, 73

"On Morality" (Didion), **Supp. IV Part 1:** 196

"On My Own" (Levine), **Supp. V:** 181, 189–190

"On My Own Work" (Wilbur), **Supp. III Part 2:** 541–542

On Native Grounds: An Interpretation of Modern American Prose Literature (Kazin), **I:** 517; **Supp. I Part 2:** 650; **Supp. VIII:** 93, 96–97, 98, 100–102

"On Not Being a Dove" (Updike), **Retro. Supp. I:** 323

"On Open Form" (Merwin), **Supp. III Part 1:** 347–348, 353

On Photography (Sontag), **Supp. III Part 2:** 451, 458, 462–465

"On Political Poetry" (R. Bly), **Supp. IV Part 1:** 61

On Politics: A Carnival of Buncombe (Moos, ed.), **III:** 116

"On Pretentiousness" (Kushner), **Supp. IX:** 131–132

"On Quitting a Little College" (Stafford), **Supp. XI:** 321

"On Reading Eckerman's Conversations with Goethe" (Masters), **Supp. I Part 2:** 458

On Reading Shakespeare (L. P. Smith), **Supp. XIV:**345–346

"On Reading to Oneself" (Gass), **Supp. VI:** 88, 89

On Revolution (Arendt), **Retro. Supp. I:** 87

"On Seeing Larry Rivers' *Washington Crossing the Delaware* at the Museum of Modern Art" (O'Hara), **Supp. XV:** 186

"On Seeing Red" (Walker), **Supp. III Part 2:** 527

"On Social Plays" (A. Miller), **III:** 147, 148, 159

"On Steinbeck's Story 'Flight'" (Stegner), **Supp. IV Part 2:** 596

"On Style" (Sontag), **Supp. III Part 2:** 456–459, 465–466

"On Suicide" (Hay), **Supp. XIV:**130, 132

"On Teaching the Young Laurel to Shoot" (Bynner), **Supp. XV:** 50

"On the Antler" (Proulx), **Supp. VII:** 252–253

"On the Banks of the Wabash" (Paul Dresser), **Retro. Supp. II:** 94

"On the Beach, at Night" (Whitman), **IV:** 348

On the Boundary (Tillich), **Retro. Supp. I:** 326

"On the Building of Springfield" (Lindsay), **Supp. I Part 2:** 381

"On the Coast of Maine" (Hayden), **Supp. II Part 1:** 381

On the Contrary: Articles of Belief (McCarthy), **II:** 559, 562

"On the Death of a Friend's Child" (Lowell), **Supp. I Part 2:** 409

"On the Death of Senator Thomas J. Walsh" (Winters), **Supp. II Part 2:** 802, 806

"On the Death of Yeats" (Bogan), **Supp. III Part 1:** 59

"On the Death of Zhukov" (Brodsky), **Supp. VIII:** 27

"On the Disadvantages of Central Heating" (Clampitt), **Supp. IX:** 41, 47, 52

"On the Edge" (Levine), **Supp. V:** 181–182

On the Edge and Over (Levine), **Supp. V:** 178, 180–182, 186

On the Edge of the Great Rift: Three Novels of Africa (Theroux), **Supp. VIII:** 316

"On the Eve of the Feast of the Immaculate Conception, 1942"

(Lowell), **II:** 538; **Retro. Supp. II:** 185

"On the Eyes of an SS Officer" (Wilbur), **Supp. III Part 2:** 548

"On the Fall of General Earl Cornwallis" (Freneau), **Supp. II Part 1:** 261

"On the Folly of Writing Poetry" (Freneau), **Supp. II Part 1:** 263

On the Frontier (Auden and Isherwood), **Supp. II Part 1:** 13; **Supp. XIV:**163

On the Great Atlantic Rainway: Selected Poems, 1950–1988 (Koch), **Supp. XV:** 177

"On the Island" (Stern), **Supp. IX:** 290

"On the Late Eclipse" (Bryant), **Supp. I Part 1:** 152

On the Laws of the Poetic Art (Hecht), **Supp. X:** 58

"On the Marginal Way" (Wilbur), **Supp. III Part 2:** 558, 559

On the Mesa (Nichols), **Supp. XIII:** 268

"On the Moon and Matriarchal Consciousness" (Neumann), **Supp. IV Part 1:** 68

"On the Morning after the Sixties" (Didion), **Supp. IV Part 1:** 205, 206

On the Motion and Immobility of Douve (Bonnefoy; Kinnell, trans.), **Supp. III Part 1:** 235

"On the Murder of Lieutenant José del Castillo by the Falangist Bravo Martinez, July 12, 1936" (Levine), **Supp. V:** 187

"On the Night of a Friend's Wedding" (Robinson), **III:** 524

"On the Occasion of a Poem: Richard Hugo" (Wright), **Supp. III Part 2:** 596

On the Occasion of My Last Afternoon (Gibbons), **Supp. X:** 46, 50–53

On the Origin of Species (Darwin), **Supp. XIV:**192

"On the Parapet" (Tanner), **Retro. Supp. II:** 205

"On the Platform" (Nemerov), **III:** 287

On the Poetry of Philip Levine: Stranger to Nothing (Levis), **Supp. XI:** 257

"On the Powers of the Human Understanding" (Freneau), **Supp. II Part 1:** 274

On the Prejudices, Predilections, and Firm Beliefs of William Faulkner (Brooks), **Supp. XIV:**13

"On the Pulse of Morning" (Angelou), **Supp. IV Part 1:** 15–17

"On the Railway Platform" (Jarrell), **II:** 370

"On the Rainy River" (O'Brien), **Supp. V:** 250

On the Rebound: A Story and Nine Poems (Purdy), **Supp. VII:** 276–277

"On the Religion of Nature" (Freneau), **Supp. II Part 1:** 275

"On the River" (Dunbar), **Supp. II Part 1:** 193

"On the River" (Levine), **Supp. V:** 193

On the River Styx and Other Stories (Matthiessen), **Supp. V:** 212

On the Road (Kerouac), **Retro. Supp. I:** 102; **Supp. III Part 1:** 92, 218, 222–224, 226, 230–231; **Supp. V:** 336; **Supp. X:** 269; **Supp. XIII:** 275; **Supp. XIV:**138, 150; **Supp. XV:** 221

"On the Road Home" (Stevens), **Retro. Supp. I:** 306

On the Road with the Archangel (Buechner), **Supp. XII:** 54

On These I Stand: An Anthology of the Best Poems of Countee Cullen (Cullen), **Supp. IV Part 1:** 173

"On the Skeleton of a Hound" (Wright), **Supp. III Part 2:** 593

"On the Street: Monument" (Gunn Allen), **Supp. IV Part 1:** 326

"On the Subway" (Olds), **Supp. X:** 207

"On the System of Policy Hitherto Pursued by Their Government" (Barlow), **Supp. II Part 1:** 82

"On the Teaching of Modern Literature" (Trilling), **Supp. III Part 2:** 509–510

"On the Uniformity and Perfection of Nature" (Freneau), **Supp. II Part 1:** 275

"On the Universality and Other Attributes of the God of Nature" (Freneau), **Supp. II Part 1:** 275

"On the Use of Trisyllabic Feet in Iambic Verse" (Bryant), **Supp. I Part 1:** 156

On the Way toward a Phenomenological Psychology: The Psychology of William James (Linschoten), **II:** 362

"On the Way to Work" (Dunn), **Supp. XI:** 149–150

"On the Wide Heath" (Millay), **III:** 130

"On the Writing of Novels" (Buck), **Supp. II Part 1:** 121

On This Island (Auden), **Supp. II Part 1:** 11

"On Time" (O'Hara), **III:** 369–370

"Ontological Episode of the Asylum" (Carruth), **Supp. XVI:**48, 50

"Ontology of the Sentence, The" (Gass), **Supp. VI:** 77

"On Top" (Leopold), **Supp. XIV:**188

"On Top" (Snyder), **Supp. VIII:** 304

"On Translating Akhmatova" (Kunitz), **Supp. III Part 1:** 268

"On Waking to Old Debts" (Keillor), **Supp. XVI:**167

On William Stafford: The Worth of Local Things (Andrews, ed.), **Supp. XI:** 311, 312, 317, 321, 324, 326

"On Writing" (Carver), **Supp. III Part 1:** 142–143

"On Writing" (Nin), **Supp. X:** 182

Opatoshu, Joseph, **IV:** 9

"Open Boat, The" (Crane), **I:** 408, 415, 416–417, 423; **Retro. Supp. I:** 325; **Supp. XIV:**51

Open Boat and Other Stories (Crane), **I:** 408

Open Heart: A Patient's Story of Life-Saving Medicine and Life-Giving Friendship (Neugeboren), **Supp. XVI:**217, 229–230

Open House (Roethke), **III:** 529–530, 540

"Open House" (Roethke), **III:** 529

"Opening, An" (Swenson), **Supp. IV Part 2:** 639

Opening of the Field, The (Duncan), **Supp. III Part 2:** 625

Opening the Hand (Merwin), **Supp. III Part 1:** 341, 353, 355

"Open Letter" (Roethke), **III:** 532, 534

"Open Letter to Surrealists Everywhere, An" (H. Miller), **III:** 184

Open Meeting, The (Gurney), **Supp. V:** 98

Open Net (Plimpton), **Supp. XVI:**241

"Open Road, The" (Dreiser), **II:** 44

Open Sea, The (Masters), **Supp. I Part 2:** 471

Open Season: Sporting Adventures (Humphrey), **Supp. IX:** 95

"Open the Gates" (Kunitz), **Supp. III Part 1:** 264–265, 267

"Opera Company, The" (Merrill), **Supp. III Part 1:** 326

"Operation, The" (Sanders), **Supp. XVI:**266

"Operation, The" (Sexton), **Supp. II Part 2:** 675, 679

Operation Shylock: A Confession (Roth), **Retro. Supp. II:** 279, 280, 291

Operation Sidewinder (Shepard), **Supp. III Part 2:** 434–435, 439, 446–447

Operations in North African Waters (Morison), **Supp. I Part 2:** 490

Operation Wandering Soul (Powers), **Supp. IX:** 212, 217–219

Opffer, Emil, **Retro. Supp. II:** 80

"Opinion" (Du Bois), **Supp. II Part 1:** 173

Opinionator, The (Bierce), **I:** 209

Opinions of Oliver Allston (Brooks), **I:** 254, 255, 256

O Pioneers! (Cather), **I:** 314, 317–319, 320; **Retro. Supp. I:** 1, 5, 6, 7–9, 10, 13, 20; **Retro. Supp. II:** 136

Oppen, George, **IV:** 415; **Supp. III Part 2:** 614, 615, 616, 626, 628; **Supp. XIV:**285, 286, 287; **Supp. XVI:**282, 283

Oppenheim, James, **I:** 106, 109, 239, 245; **Supp. XV:** 294, 296, 298, 299, 301, 302, 307, 313

Oppenheimer, J. Robert, **I:** 137, 492

Oppenheimer, Judy, **Supp. IX:** 115, 116, 118, 120, 126

"Opportunity for American Fiction, An" (Howells), **Supp. I Part 2:** 645–646

Opposing Self, The (Trilling), **Supp. III Part 2:** 506–507

"Opposition" (Lanier), **Supp. I Part 1:** 368, 373

Opticks: A Poem in Seven Sections (Goldbarth), **Supp. XII:** 177, 178

"Optimist's Daughter, The" (Welty), **IV:** 280–281

Optimist's Daughter, The (Welty), **IV:** 261, 280; **Retro. Supp. I:** 339, 355

Options (O. Henry), **Supp. II Part 1:** 410

Opus Posthumous (Stevens), **IV:** 76, 78

Oracle at Stoneleigh Court, The (Taylor), **Supp. V:** 328

Orage, Alfred, **III:** 473

Orange, Max (pseudonym). *See* Heller, Joseph

Orange Fish, The (Shields), **Supp. VII:** 318, 320, 323, 328

Oranges (McPhee), **Supp. III Part 1:** 298–299, 301, 309

Oration Delivered at Washington, July Fourth, 1809 (Barlow), **Supp. II Part 1:** 80, 83

Orations and Addresses (Bryant), **Supp. I Part 1:** 158

Orators, The (Auden), **Supp. II Part 1:** 6, 7, 11, 18–19

Orb Weaver, The (Francis), **Supp. IX:** 81–82

"Orchard" (Doolittle), **Supp. I Part 1:** 263–264, 265, 266

"Orchard" (Eberhart), **I:** 539

Orchard Keeper, The (McCarthy), **Supp. VIII:** 175–176

Orchestra (Davies), **III:** 541

"Orchids" (Roethke), **III:** 530–531
"Or Consider Prometheus" (Clampitt), **Supp. IX:** 44
Ordeal of Mansart, The (Du Bois), **Supp. II Part 1:** 185–186
Ordeal of Mark Twain, The (Brooks), **I:** 240, 247, 248; **II:** 482
"Order of Insects" (Gass), **Supp. VI:** 83
Order Out of Chaos (McPherson), **Supp. IV Part 1:** 2, 12
"Ordinary Afternoon in Charlottesville, An" (Wright), **Supp. V:** 344
"Ordinary Days" (Dunn), **Supp. XI:** 151
"Ordinary Evening in New Haven, An" (Stevens), **IV:** 91–92; **Retro. Supp. I:** 297, 300, 311, 312
Ordinary Love (Smiley), **Supp. VI:** 292, 299–300
Ordinary Love; and Good Will: Two Novellas (Smiley), **Supp. VI:** 292, 299–300
Ordinary Miracles (Jong), **Supp. V:** 115, 130–131
"Ordinary Time: Virginia Woolf and Thucydides on War" (Carson), **Supp. XII:** 111
"Ordinary Women, The" (Stevens), **IV:** 81
Ordways, The (Humphrey), **Supp. IX:** 95, 98–100, 109; **Supp. XV:** 353
"Oread" (Doolittle), **II:** 520–521; **Supp. I Part 1:** 265–266
Oregon Message, An (Stafford), **Supp. XI:** 328–329
Oregon Trail, The (Parkman), **II:** 312; **Supp. II Part 2:** 592, 595–596, 598, 606
Oresteia (Aeschylus), **Supp. IX:** 103
"Orestes at Tauris" (Jarrell), **II:** 376, 377
Orfalea, Gregory, **Supp. XIII:** 278
Orfeo ed Euridice (Gluck), **II:** 210, 211
Orff, Carl, **Supp. X:** 63
"Organizer's Wife, The" (Bambara), **Supp. XI:** 8–9
"Orgy" (Rukeyser), **Supp. VI:** 280
Orgy, The (Rukeyser), **Supp. VI:** 274, 283
"Orientation of Hope, The" (Locke), **Supp. XIV:** 212–213
Orient Express (Dos Passos), **I:** 480
"Orient Express, The" (Jarrell), **II:** 382, 383–384
Origen, Adamantius, **IV:** 153
"Origin" (Harjo), **Supp. XII:** 219
Original Child Bomb: Points for Meditation to Be Scratched on the Walls of a Cave (Merton), **Supp. VIII:** 203
Original Essays on the Poetry of Anne Sexton (George), **Supp. IV Part 2:** 450
"Original Follies Girl, The" (Z. Fitzgerald), **Supp. IX:** 71
Original Light (Goldbarth), **Supp. XII:** 181, 183–184, 188
Original of Laura, The (Nabokov), **Retro. Supp. I:** 266
"Original Sin" (Jeffers), **Supp. II Part 2:** 426
"Original Sin" (Warren), **IV:** 245
"Origin of Extermination in the Imagination, The" (Gass), **Supp. VI:** 89
Origin of Species, The (Darwin), **II:** 173, 462; **Supp. XVI:** 13
Origin of the Brunists, The (Coover), **Supp. V:** 39, 41, 52
"Origins and History of Consciousness" (Rich), **Supp. I Part 2:** 570
"Origins of a Poem" (Levertov), **Supp. III Part 1:** 273
"Origins of the Beat Generation, The" (Kerouac), **Supp. III Part 1:** 231
Origo, Iris, **IV:** 328
"O'Riley's Late-Bloomed Little Son" (X. J. Kennedy), **Supp. XV:** 159
"Orion" (Rich), **Supp. I Part 2:** 557
O'Riordan, Conal Holmes O'Connell, **III:** 465
Orlando (Woolf), **Supp. I Part 2:** 718; **Supp. VIII:** 263; **Supp. XII:** 9
Orlando Furioso (Ariosto), **Supp. XV:** 175
Orlovsky, Peter, **Supp. XII:** 121, 126; **Supp. XIV:** 150
Ormond; or, The Secret Witness (Brown), **Supp. I Part 1:** 133–137
Ormonde, Czenzi, **Supp. IV Part 1:** 132
Ornament and Crime (Loos), **Supp. XVI:** 187
Orne, Sarah. *See* Jewett, Sarah Orne
Ornithological Biography; or, An Account of the Habits of the Birds of the United States of America, and Interspersed with Delineations of American Scenery and Manners (Audubon), 7–10; **Supp. XVI:** 13
Ornitz, Samuel, **Supp. IX:** 227; **Supp. XIII:** 166
Orphan Angel, The (Wylie), **Supp. I Part 2:** 707, 709, 714, 717, 719–721, 722, 724
Orphan's Tale, An (Neugeboren), **Supp. XVI:** 222, 223
Orpheus (Rukeyser), **Supp. VI:** 273
"Orpheus" (Winters), **Supp. II Part 2:** 801
"Orpheus (1)" (Atwood), **Supp. XIII:** 35
"Orpheus (2)" (Atwood), **Supp. XIII:** 35
"Orpheus, Eurydice, Hermes" (Rilke), **Supp. VIII:** 31, 32
"Orpheus Alone" (Strand), **Supp. IV Part 2:** 632
Orpheus Descending (T. Williams), **IV:** 380, 381, 382, 385, 386, 387, 389, 391–392, 395, 396, 398
Orr, Peter, **Supp. I Part 2:** 538, 540, 543
Ortega y Gasset, José, **I:** 218, 222; **Supp. IV Part 2:** 521
Ortiz, Simon J., **Supp. IV Part 1:** 319, 404; **Supp. IV Part 2:** 497–515, 557; **Supp. XII:** 217, 218
O'Ruddy, The (Crane), **I:** 409, 424
Orwell, George, **I:** 489; **II:** 454, 580; **Supp. I Part 2:** 523, 620; **Supp. II Part 1:** 143; **Supp. IV Part 1:** 236; **Supp. V:** 250; **Supp. VIII:** 241; **Supp. XIV:** 112, 158
Osborn, Dwight, **III:** 218–219, 223
"Osborn Look, The" (Morris), **III:** 221
Osgood, J. R., **II:** 283
O'Shea, Kitty, **II:** 137
O'Shea, Milo, **Supp. XI:** 308
"Oshkikwe's Baby" (traditional Chippewa story), **Supp. IV Part 1:** 333
Oshogay, Delia, **Supp. IV Part 1:** 333
Ossana, Diana, **Supp. V:** 230–231, 232
Ossian, **Supp. I Part 2:** 491
Ossip, Kathleen, **Supp. X:** 201
Ostanovka v Pustyne (A halt in the wilderness) (Brodsky), **Supp. VIII:** 21
Oster, Judith, **Supp. XVI:** 151
Ostriker, Alicia, **Supp. I Part 2:** 540; **Supp. IV Part 2:** 439, 447, 449; **Supp. X:** 207, 208; **Supp. XI:** 143; **Supp. XV:** 251
Ostrom, Hans, **Retro. Supp. I:** 195
Oswald, Lee Harvey, **III:** 234, 235
Oswald II (DeLillo), **Supp. VI:** 16
Oswald's Tale (Mailer), **Retro. Supp. II:** 212–213
O Taste and See (Levertov), **Supp. III Part 1:** 278–279, 281
Othello (Shakespeare), **I:** 284–285
"Other, The" (Sexton), **Supp. II Part 2:** 692
Other America, The (Harrington), **I:** 306
Other Destinies: Understanding the American Indian Novel (Owens),

Supp. IV Part 1: 404

"Other Frost, The" (Jarrell), **Retro. Supp. I:** 121

Other Gods: An American Legend (Buck), **Supp. II Part 1:** 123, 130–131

Other House, The (James), **Retro. Supp. I:** 229

"Other League of Nations, The" (Ríos), **Supp. IV Part 2:** 552

"Other Margaret, The" (Trilling), **Supp. III Part 2:** 504–505

"Other Miller, The" (Wolff), **Supp. VII:** 343–344

"Other Mothers" (Paley), **Supp. VI:** 225

"Other Night at Columbia, The" (Trilling), **Supp. XII:** 126

"Other Robert Frost, The" (Jarrell), **Retro. Supp. I:** 135

Others (Shields), **Supp. VII:** 310

Other Side, The (Gordon), **Supp. IV Part 1:** 299, 306, 307–309, 310–311

Other Side, The/El Otro Lado (Alvarez), **Supp. VII:** 9–12

Other Side of the River, The (Wright), **Supp. V:** 332–333, 342

"Other Side of the River, The" (Wright), **Supp. V:** 335

"Other Tradition, The" (Ashbery), **Supp. III Part 1:** 15, 18

"Other Two, The" (Wharton), **Retro. Supp. I:** 367

Other Voices, Other Rooms (Capote), **Supp. III Part 1:** 113–118, 121, 123–124

"Other War, The" (Cowley), **Supp. II Part 1:** 144

"Otherwise" (Kenyon), **Supp. VII:** 172, 174

Otherwise: New and Selected Poems (Kenyon), **Supp. VII:** 167, 172–174

Otherwise Than Being; or, Beyond Essence (Lévinas), **Supp. XVI:** 290, 291

"Other Woman, The" (Anderson), **I:** 114

Otho the Great: A Tragedy in Five Acts (Keats), **Supp. XII:** 113

Otis, Harrison Gray, **Supp. I Part 2:** 479–481, 483, 486, 488

Otis, James, **III:** 577; **Supp. I Part 2:** 486; **Supp. XV:** 229

O to Be a Dragon (Moore), **III:** 215

"Ouija" (McClatchy), **Supp. XII:** 269–270

Oupensky, Peter, **Supp. XIV:** 188

Our America (Frank), **I:** 229; **Supp. IX:** 308

Our America (Michaels), **Retro. Supp. I:** 379

"Our Assistant's Column" (Twain), **IV:** 193

"Our Bourgeois Literature" (Sinclair), **Supp. V:** 281

Our Brains and What Ails Them (Gilman), **Supp. XI:** 207

Our Century (Wilder), **IV:** 374

"Our Christmas Party" (E. Stoddard), **Supp. XV:** 273, 278

Our Country (Strong), **Supp. XIV:** 64

"Our Countrymen in Chains!" (Whittier), **Supp. I Part 2:** 688

"Our Cultural Humility" (Bourne), **I:** 223, 228

Our Depleted Society (Seymour), **Supp. XIII:** 264

"Our Dust" (Wright), **Supp. XV:** 345, 346

"Our Father Who Drowns the Birds" (Kingsolver), **Supp. VII:** 208–209

"Our First House" (Kingston), **Supp. V:** 169

Our Gang (Roth), **Retro. Supp. II:** 287; **Supp. III Part 2:** 414; **Supp. IV Part 1:** 388

"Our Good Day" (Cisneros), **Supp. VII:** 60

Our Ground Time Here Will Be Brief (Kumin), **Supp. IV Part 2:** 450–452

Our House in the Last World (Hijuelos), **Supp. VIII:** 73, 76–79, 87, 88

"Our Lady of the Annunciation/Nuestra Señora de Anunciación" (Mora), **Supp. XIII:** 217, 224, 228

"Our Lady of Troy" (MacLeish), **III:** 3, 20

"Our Limitations" (Holmes), **Supp. I Part 1:** 314

"Our Martyred Soldiers" (Dunbar), **Supp. II Part 1:** 193

"Our Master" (Whittier), **Supp. I Part 2:** 704

"Our Mother Pocahontas" (Lindsay), **Supp. I Part 2:** 393

Our Mr. Wrenn: The Romantic Adventures of a Gentle Man (Lewis), **II:** 441

Our National Parks (Muir), **Supp. IX:** 181, 184

Our New York: A Personal Vision in Words and Photographs (Kazin), **Supp. VIII:** 106–107

"Our Old Aunt Who Is Now in a Retirement Home" (Shields), **Supp. VII:** 310

Our Old Home: A Series of English Sketches (Hawthorne), **II:** 225;

Retro. Supp. I: 163

"Our Own Movie Queen" (Z. Fitzgerald), **Supp. IX:** 71

"Our River Now" (L.-Y. Lee), **Supp. XV:** 224, 225

Ourselves to Know (O'Hara), **III:** 362, 365

"Our Story Begins" (Wolff), **Supp. VII:** 345

Our Town (Wilder), **IV:** 357, 364, 365, 366, 368–369

"Our Unplanned Cities" (Bourne), **I:** 229, 230

Our Wonder World, **Retro. Supp. I:** 341

Ouspensky, P. D., **I:** 383

"Out" (Harjo), **Supp. XII:** 219

"'Out, Out'" (Frost), **Retro. Supp. I:** 131

"Outcast" (McKay), **Supp. X:** 135

"Outcasts of Poker Flats, The" (Harte), **Supp. II Part 1:** 345, 347–348

Outcroppings (Harte), **Supp. II Part 1:** 343

Out Cry (T. Williams), **IV:** 383, 393

Outcry, The (James), **Retro. Supp. I:** 235

"Outdoor Shower" (Olds), **Supp. X:** 214

Outerbridge Reach (Stone), **Supp. V:** 306–308

Outer Dark (McCarthy), **Supp. VIII:** 176–177

Outermost Dream, The: Essays and Reviews (Maxwell), **Supp. VIII:** 171–172

"Outing, The" (Baldwin), **Supp. I Part 1:** 63

"Out Like a Lamb" (Dubus), **Supp. VII:** 91

"Outline of an Autobiography" (Toomer), **Supp. III Part 2:** 478

Outlyer and Ghazals (Harrison), **Supp. VIII:** 41

"Out of Business" (Mora), **Supp. XIII:** 217

Out of My League (Plimpton), **Supp. XVI:** 233, 239

"Out of Nowhere into Nothing" (Anderson), **I:** 113

"Out of Season" (Hemingway), **II:** 263

"Out of the Cradle Endlessly Rocking" (Whitman), **IV:** 342, 343–345, 346, 351; **Retro. Supp. I:** 404, 406

"Out of the Deeps" (E. Stoddard), **Supp. XV:** 286

"Out of the Hospital and Under the Bar" (Ellison), **Retro. Supp. II:** 118–119; **Supp. II Part 1:** 246

"Out of the Rainbow End" (Sandburg),

III: 594–595

"Out of the Sea, Early" (Swenson), **Supp. IV Part 2:** 645

"Out of the Snow" (Dubus), **Supp. VII:** 91

Out of the Stars (Purdy), **Supp. VII:** 281–282

Outre-Mer: A Pilgrimage beyond the Sea (Longfellow), **II:** 313, 491; **Retro. Supp. II:** 155, 165

"Outside" (Stafford), **Supp. XI:** 318

Outside, The (Glaspell), **Supp. III Part 1:** 179, 187

Outsider, The (Wright), **IV:** 478, 481, 488, 491–494, 495

Out West (Shanley), **Supp. XIV:**317

"Out with the Old" (Yates), **Supp. XI:** 342

"Ouzo for Robin" (Merrill), **Supp. III Part 1:** 326

"Oval Portrait, The" (Poe), **III:** 412, 415; **Retro. Supp. II:** 270

"Oven Bird, The" (Frost), **Retro. Supp. I:** 131; **Supp. XI:** 153

"Over by the River" (Maxwell), **Supp. VIII:** 169, 170

"Overgrown Pasture, The" (Lowell), **II:** 523

"Overheard through the Walls of the Invisible City" (Bidart), **Supp. XV:** 32

"Over 2,000 Illustrations and a Complete Concordance" (Bishop), **Retro. Supp. II:** 45; **Supp. I Part 1:** 90–91

"Over Kansas" (Ginsberg), **Supp. II Part 1:** 320

Overland to the Islands (Levertov), **Supp. III Part 1:** 275, 276

"Overnight Pass" (X. J. Kennedy), **Supp. XV:** 168

"Over-Soul, The" (Emerson), **II:** 7

"Over the Hill" (Dubus), **Supp. VII:** 76, 79–80

Overtime (Gurney), **Supp. V:** 104

"Overwhelming Question, An" (Taylor), **Supp. V:** 323

Ovid, **I:** 62; **II:** 542–543; **III:** 457, 467, 468, 470; **Retro. Supp. I:** 63; **Supp. IV Part 2:** 634; **Supp. XII:** 264

"Ovid's Farewell" (McClatchy), **Supp. XII:** 257–258

Owen, David, **II:** 34

Owen, Maureen, **Supp. IV Part 2:** 423

Owen, Wilfred, **II:** 367, 372; **III:** 524; **Supp. X:** 146

Owens, Hamilton, **III:** 99, 109

Owens, Louis, **Supp. IV Part 1:** 404

"O Where Are You Going?" (Auden), **Supp. X:** 116

Owl in the Attic, The (Thurber), **Supp.**

I Part 2: 614

Owl in the Mask of the Dreamer, The: Collected Poems (Haines), **Supp. XII:** 211

"Owl in the Sarcophagus, The" (Stevens), **Retro. Supp. I:** 300

"Owl's Clover" (Stevens), **IV:** 75

Owl's Clover (Stevens), **Retro. Supp. I:** 298, 303–304

Owl's Insomnia, Poems by Rafael Alberti, The (Strand, trans.), **Supp. IV Part 2:** 630

Owlstone Crown, The (X. J. Kennedy), **Supp. XV:** 162, 164

"Owl Who Was God, The" (Thurber), **Supp. I Part 2:** 610

Owning Jolene (Hearon), **Supp. VIII:** 66–67

Oxford Anthology of American Literature, The, **III:** 197; **Supp. I Part 1:** 254

Oxford Book of American Verse (Matthiessen, ed.), **Retro. Supp. I:** 40

Oxford Book of Children's Verse in America, The (Hall, ed.), **Supp. XIV:**126

Oxford History of the American People, The (Morison), **Supp. I Part 2:** 495–496

Oxford History of the United States, 1783–1917, The (Morison), **Supp. I Part 2:** 483–484

Oxherding Tale (Johnson), **Supp. VI:** 190–192, 193, 194, 196

Oxley, William, **Supp. XV:** 125

"O Yes" (Olsen), **Supp. XIII:** 294, 298, 299–300, 301

"O Youth and Beauty!" (Cheever), **Retro. Supp. I:** 335

"Oysters" (Sexton), **Supp. II Part 2:** 692

"Ozark Odes" (Wright), **Supp. XV:** 346

Ozick, Cynthia, **Supp. V:** 257–274; **Supp. VIII:** 141; **Supp. X:** 192

O-Zone (Theroux), **Supp. VIII:** 323–324

P

P. D. Kimerakov (Epstein), **Supp. XII:** 160, 162

Pace, Patricia, **Supp. XI:** 245

Pacernik, Gary, **Supp. IX:** 287, 291

"Pacific Distances" (Didion), **Supp. IV Part 1:** 211

Pack, Robert, **Supp. IV Part 2:** 621

"Packed Dirt, Churchgoing, a Dying Cat, a Traded Cat" (Updike), **IV:** 219

"Packing Mother's Things" (C. Frost),

Supp. XV: 97

Paddock, Joe, **Supp. XVI:**36

Paddock, Nancy, **Supp. XVI:**36

Padel, Ruth, **Supp. XII:** 107

Padgett, Ron, **Supp. XV:** 190

Pafko at the Wall (DeLillo), **Supp. VI:** 4

"Pagan Prayer" (Cullen), **Supp. IV Part 1:** 170

"Pagan Rabbi, The" (Ozick), **Supp. V:** 262, 264, 265

Pagan Rabbi and Other Stories, The (Ozick), **Supp. V:** 260, 261, 263–265

Pagan Spain (Wright), **IV:** 478, 488, 495

Page, Geraldine, **Supp. XV:** 7

Page, Kirby, **III:** 297

Page, Thomas Nelson, **II:** 174, 176, 194; **Supp. XIV:**61

Page, Walter Hines, **II:** 174, 175; **Supp. I Part 1:** 370

"Pages from Cold Point" (Bowles), **Supp. IV Part 1:** 85, 86, 87

Paid on Both Sides: A Charade (Auden), **Supp. II Part 1:** 6, 18–19

Paige, Satchel, **Supp. I Part 1:** 234

Paige, T. D. D., **III:** 475

Pain, Joseph, **Supp. I Part 2:** 502

Paine, Albert Bigelow, **I:** 249

Paine, Thomas, **I:** 490; **II:** 117, 302; **III:** 17, 148, 219; **Retro. Supp. I:** 390; **Supp. I Part 1:** 231; **Supp. I Part 2:** 501–525; **Supp. XI:** 55

"Pain has an Element of Blank" (Dickinson), **Retro. Supp. I:** 44

"Paint and Powder" (Z. Fitzgerald), **Supp. IX:** 71

Painted Bird, The (Kosinski), **Supp. VII:** 215–217, 219–221, 222, 227

Painted Desert (F. Barthelme), **Supp. XI:** 28–29, 32

Painted Dresses (Hearon), **Supp. VIII:** 63

"Painted Head" (Ransom), **III:** 491, 494; **Supp. II Part 1:** 103, 314

Painted Word, The (Wolfe), **Supp. III Part 2:** 580–581, 584; **Supp. XV:** 143

"Painter, The" (Ashbery), **Supp. III Part 1:** 5–6, 13

Painter Dreaming in the Scholar's House, The (Nemerov), **III:** 269

"Painters" (Rukeyser), **Supp. VI:** 281

"Painting a Mountain Stream" (Nemerov), **III:** 275

"Pair a Spurs" (Proulx), **Supp. VII:** 263–264

"Pair of Bright Blue Eyes, A" (Taylor), **Supp. V:** 321

"Pajamas" (Olds), **Supp. X:** 206

Pakula, Alan, **Supp. XIII:** 264

Palace at 4 A.M. (Giacometti), **Supp. VIII:** 169

"Palantine, The" (Whittier), **Supp. I Part 2:** 694, 696

Palatella, John, **Retro. Supp. II:** 48

Pale Fire (Nabokov), **III:** 244, 246, 252, 263–265; **Retro. Supp. I:** 264, 265, 266, 270, 271, 272, 276, 278, 335; **Supp. V:** 251, 253

"Pale Horse, Pale Rider" (Porter), **III:** 436, 437, 441–442, 445, 446, 449

Pale Horse, Pale Rider: Three Short Novels (Porter), **III:** 433, 436–442; **Supp. VIII:** 157

"Pale Pink Roast, The" (Paley), **Supp. VI:** 217

Paley, Grace, **Supp. VI:** 217–233; **Supp. IX:** 212; **Supp. X:** 79, 164; **Supp. XII:** 309

Paley, William, **II:** 9

Palgrave, Francis Turner, **Retro. Supp. I:** 124; **Supp. XIV:**340

Palgrave's Golden Treasury (Palgrave), **IV:** 405

Palimpsest (Doolittle), **Supp. I Part 1:** 259, 268, 269, 270–271

Palimpsest (Vidal), **Supp. X:** 186

"Palingenesis" (Longfellow), **II:** 498

Pal Joey (O'Hara), **III:** 361, 367–368

"Pal Joey" stories (O'Hara), **III:** 361

Pallbearers Envying the One Who Rides (Dobyns), **Supp. XIII:** 89

"Palm, The" (Merwin), **Supp. III Part 1:** 355

Palmer, Charles, **II:** 111

Palmer, Elihu, **Supp. I Part 2:** 520

Palmer, George Herbert, **Supp. XIV:**197

Palmer, Michael, **Supp. IV Part 2:** 421; **Supp. XVI:**284

Palmer, Samuel, **Supp. XV:** 81

Palmerston, Lord, **I:** 15

Palm-of-the-Hand-Stories (Kawabata), **Supp. XV:** 186

"Palo Alto: The Marshes" (Hass), **Supp. VI:** 100

Palpable God, A: Thirty Stories Translated from the Bible with an Essay on the Origins and Life of Narrative (Price), **Supp. VI:** 262, 267

Palubinskas, Helen, **Supp. X:** 292

Pamela (Richardson), **Supp. V:** 127

Pamela's First Musical (Wasserstein), **Supp. XV:** 333

Panache de bouquets (Komunyakaa; Cadieux, trans.), **Supp. XIII:** 127

Pan-African movement, **Supp. II Part 1:** 172, 175

Pandaemonium (Epstein), **Supp. XII:** 161, 172–173

"Pandora" (Adams), **I:** 5

Pandora: New Tales of Vampires (Rice), **Supp. VII:** 295

Panek, LeRoy, **Supp. XIV:**27

"Pangolin, The" (Moore), **III:** 210

Panic: A Play in Verse (MacLeish), **III:** 2, 20

Panic in Needle Park (film), **Supp. IV Part 1:** 198

Pantagruel (Rabelais), **II:** 112

"Pantaloon in Black" (Faulkner), **II:** 71

Panther and the Lash, The (Hughes), **Retro. Supp. I:** 204, 211; **Supp. I Part 1:** 342–344, 345–346

"Panthers, The" (Southern), **Supp. XI:** 295

"Pan *versus* Moses" (Ozick), **Supp. V:** 262

"Paolo Castelnuovo" (Everwine), **Supp. XV:** 83–84

"Papa and Mama Dance, The" (Sexton), **Supp. II Part 2:** 688

"Papa Who Wakes Up Tired in the Dark" (Cisneros), **Supp. VII:** 62

Pape, Greg, **Supp. V:** 180; **Supp. XIII:** 312; **Supp. XV:** 73

"Paper Dolls Cut Out of a Newspaper" (Simic), **Supp. VIII:** 282

"Paper House, The" (Mailer), **III:** 42–43

Paper Lion (film, March), **Supp. XVI:**242

Paper Lion: Confessions of a Last-String Quarterback (Plimpton), **Supp. XVI:**242–243

Papers on Literature and Art (Fuller), **Supp. II Part 1:** 292, 299

Papini, Giovanni, **Supp. XVI:**195

Papp, Joseph, **Supp. IV Part 1:** 234

"Paprika Johnson" (Barnes), **Supp. III Part 1:** 33

"Par" (Bausch), **Supp. VII:** 54

"Parable in the Later Novels of Henry James" (Ozick), **Supp. V:** 257

"Parable of the Gift" (Glück), **Supp. V:** 89

"Parable of the Hostages" (Glück), **Supp. V:** 89

"Parable of the King" (Glück), **Supp. V:** 89

Parable of the Sower (O. Butler), **Supp. XIII:** 66–67, 69

Parable of the Talents (O. Butler), **Supp. XIII:** 61,**Supp. XIII:** 66, 67–69

"Parable of the Trellis" (Glück), **Supp. V:** 89

Parachutes & Kisses (Jong), **Supp. V:** 115, 123, 125–126, 129

"Parade of Painters" (Swenson), **Supp. IV Part 2:** 645

"Paradigm, The" (Tate), **IV:** 128

Paradise (Barthelme), **Supp. IV Part 1:** 52

"Paradise" (Doty), **Supp. XI:** 123

Paradise Lost (Milton), **I:** 137; **II:** 168, 549; **IV:** 126; **Supp. XII:** 173, 297; **Supp. XV:** 181

Paradise Lost (Odets), **Supp. II Part 2:** 530, 531, 538–539, 550

"Paradise of Bachelors and the Tartarus of Maids, The" (Melville), **III:** 91

Paradise of Bombs, The (Sanders), **Supp. XVI:**265, 272–273

Paradise Poems (Stern), **Supp. IX:** 293–294, 295

Paradiso (Dante), **Supp. IX:** 50

"Paradoxes and Oxymorons" (Ashbery), **Supp. III Part 1:** 23–24

Paradox of Progressive Thought, The (Noble), **Supp. I Part 2:** 650

Paragon, The (Knowles), **Supp. XII:** 249

"Paragraphs" (Carruth), **Supp. XVI:**52–53

"Parameters" (Dunn), **Supp. XI:** 154

"Paraphrase" (Crane), **I:** 391–392, 393

"Pardon, The" (Wilbur), **Supp. III Part 2:** 544, 550

Paredes, Américo, **Supp. XIII:** 225

Paredes, Raymund A., **Supp. XIII:** 320, 321

"Parentage" (Stafford), **Supp. XI:** 321, 322

Parentheses: An Autobiographical Journey (Neugeboren), **Supp. XVI:**217, 218, 219, 221, 226

"Parents" (F. Barthelme), **Supp. XI:** 34

"Parents Taking Shape" (Karr), **Supp. XI:** 243

"Parents' Weekend: Camp Kenwood" (Kenyon), **Supp. VII:** 169

Pareto, Vilfredo, **II:** 577

Paretsky, Sara, **Supp. XIV:**26

Paretsky, Sarah, **Supp. IV Part 2:** 462

Parini, Jay, **Supp. X:** 17

"Paris" (Stern), **Supp. IX:** 300

"Paris, 7 A.M." (Bishop), **Retro. Supp. II:** 41, 42; **Supp. I Part 1:** 85, 89

Paris France (Stein), **IV:** 45

Park, Robert, **IV:** 475

"Park Bench" (Hughes), **Supp. I Part 1:** 331–332

Park City (Beattie), **Supp. V:** 24, 35–36

"Park City" (Beattie), **Supp. V:** 35

Parker, Charlie, **Supp. I Part 1:** 59; **Supp. X:** 240, 242, 246; **Supp. XIII:** 129

Parker, Dorothy, **Retro. Supp. II:** 327; **Supp. IV Part 1:** 353; **Supp. IX:** 62, 114, 189–206; **Supp. X:** 164; **Supp. XI:** 28

Parker, Idella, **Supp. X:** 232, 234–235

Parker, Muriel, **Supp. IX:** 232

Parker, Patricia, **Supp. XV:** 242

Parker, Robert B., **Supp. IV Part 1:** 135, 136

Parker, Theodore, **Supp. I Part 1:** 38; **Supp. I Part 2:** 518

Parker, Thomas, **Supp. I Part 1:** 102

"Parker's Back" (O'Connor), **III:** 348, 352, 358

Parkes, Henry Bamford, **Supp. I Part 2:** 617

Park-Fuller, Linda, **Supp. XIII:** 297

Parkman, Francis, **II:** 278, 310, 312; **IV:** 179, 309; **Supp. I Part 2:** 420, 479, 481–482, 486, 487, 493, 498; **Supp. II Part 2:** 589–616

Parkman Reader, The (Morison, ed.), **Supp. I Part 2:** 494

Parks, Gordon, Sr., **Supp. XI:** 17

Parks, Larry, **Supp. I Part 1:** 295

Parks, Rosa, **Supp. I Part 1:** 342

"Park Street Cemetery, The" (Lowell), **II:** 537, 538

Par le Détroit (cantata) (Bowles), **Supp. IV Part 1:** 82

Parliament of Fowls, The (Chaucer), **III:** 492

Parmenides (Plato), **II:** 10

Parnassus (Emerson), **II:** 8, 18

Parnell, Charles Stewart, **II:** 129, 137

Parole (film), **Supp. XIII:** 166

Parole Fixer (film), **Supp. XIII:** 170

Parrington, Vernon Louis, **I:** 254, 517, 561; **III:** 335, 606; **IV:** 173; **Supp. I Part 2:** 484, 640

Parrish, Robert, **Supp. XI:** 307

"Parrot, The" (Merrill), **Supp. III Part 1:** 320

"Parsley" (Dove), **Supp. IV Part 1:** 245, 246

Parson, Annie, **Supp. I Part 2:** 655

Parsons, Elsie Clews, **I:** 231, 235

Parsons, Ian, **Supp. IX:** 95

Parsons, Louella, **Supp. XII:** 173

Parsons, Talcott, **Supp. I Part 2:** 648

Parsons, Theophilus, **II:** 396, 504; **Retro. Supp. II:** 134; **Supp. I Part 1:** 155

"Parthian Shot, The" (Hammett), **Supp. IV Part 1:** 343

Partial Payments: Essays on Writers and Their Lives (Epstein), **Supp. XIV:**111

Partial Portraits (James), **II:** 336

Parties (Van Vechten), **Supp. II Part 2:** 739, 747–749

"Parting" (Kunitz), **Supp. III Part 1:** 263

"Parting Gift" (Wylie), **Supp. I Part 2:** 714

"Parting Glass, The" (Freneau), **Supp. II Part 1:** 273

"Partings" (Hogan), **Supp. IV Part 1:** 413

Partington, Blanche, **I:** 199

Partisans (Matthiessen), **Supp. V:** 201

"Partner, The" (Roethke), **III:** 541–542

Partners, The (Auchincloss), **Supp. IV Part 1:** 31, 34

"Part of a Letter" (Wilbur), **Supp. III Part 2:** 551

Part of Speech, A (Brodsky), **Supp. VIII:** 22

"Part of the Bee's Body Embedded in the Flesh, The" (C. Frost), **Supp. XV:** 105, 107

"Part of the Story" (Dobyns), **Supp. XIII:** 79

Parton, Sara, **Retro. Supp. I:** 246

Partridge, Jeffrey F., **Supp. XV:** 219

Partridge, John, **II:** 110, 111

"Parts of a Journal" (Gordon), **Supp. IV Part 1:** 310

Parts of a World (Stevens), **Retro. Supp. I:** 305–306, 307, 309, 313

"Party, The" (Dunbar), **Supp. II Part 1:** 198, 205–206

"Party, The" (Taylor), **Supp. V:** 315

Party at Jack's, The (Wolfe), **IV:** 451–452, 469

"Party Down at the Square, A" (Ellison), **Retro. Supp. II:** 124

Pascal, Blaise, **II:** 8, 159; **III:** 292, 301, 304, 428; **Retro. Supp. I:** 326, 330

"Pass, The" (Neugeboren), **Supp. XVI:**225

"Passage" (Crane), **I:** 391

"Passage in the Life of Mr. John Oakhurst, A" (Harte), **Supp. II Part 1:** 353–354

"Passages" (Duncan), **Supp. XVI:**287

"Passages from a Relinquished Work" (Hawthorne), **Retro. Supp. I:** 150

Passages toward the Dark (McGrath), **Supp. X:** 126, 127

"Passage to India" (Whitman), **IV:** 348

Passage to India, A (Forster), **II:** 600

Passaro, Vince, **Supp. X:** 167, 302, 309, 310

"Passenger Pigeons" (Jeffers), **Supp. II Part 2:** 437

Passin, Herbert, **Supp. XIII:** 337

"Passing Beauty" (C. Frost), **Supp. XV:** 97

"Passing of Grandison, The" (Chesnutt), **Supp. XIV:**62, 66–69

"Passing of Sister Barsett, The" (Jewett), **Retro. Supp. II:** 138–139, 143

"Passing Show, The" (Bierce), **I:** 208

"Passing Through" (Kunitz), **Supp. III Part 1:** 265

"Passion, The" (Barnes), **Supp. III Part 1:** 36

"Passion, The" (Merwin), **Supp. III Part 1:** 343

Passionate, Accurate Story, The: Making Your Heart's Truth into Literature (C. Bly), **Supp. XVI:**41–42

Passionate Pilgrim, A (James), **II:** 324; **Retro. Supp. I:** 219

"Passionate Pilgrim, A" (James), **II:** 322, 323–324; **Retro. Supp. I:** 218

Passion Play (Kosinski), **Supp. VII:** 215, 225–226

Passions of Uxport, The (Kumin), **Supp. IV Part 2:** 444

"Passive Resistance" (McKay), **Supp. X:** 133

Passport to the War (Kunitz), **Supp. III Part 1:** 261–264

Passwords (Stafford), **Supp. XI:** 329–330

"Past, The" (Bryant), **Supp. I Part 1:** 157, 170

Past, The (Kinnell), **Supp. III Part 1:** 235, 253–254

"Past, The" (Kinnell), **Supp. III Part 1:** 254

Past and Present (Carlyle), **Supp. I Part 2:** 410

Pasternak, Boris, **II:** 544

"Pastiches et Pistaches" (Van Vechten), **Supp. II Part 2:** 732

"Past Is the Present, The" (Moore), **III:** 199–200

"Pastoral" (Carver), **Supp. III Part 1:** 137, 146

"Pastoral" (Dove), **Supp. IV Part 1:** 249

"Pastoral Hat, A" (Stevens), **IV:** 91

"Pastor Dowe at Tacaté" (Bowles), **Supp. IV Part 1:** 87

Pastorela (ballet) (Kirstein), **Supp. IV Part 1:** 83

Pastorius, Francis Daniel, **Supp. I Part 2:** 700

"Pasture Poems" (Kumin), **Supp. IV Part 2:** 446

Pastures of Heaven, The (Steinbeck), **IV:** 51

Patchen, Kenneth, **Supp. III Part 2:** 625

Patchett, Ann, **Supp. XII:** 307–324

Pater, Walter, **I:** 51, 272, 476; **II:** 27, 338; **III:** 604; **IV:** 74; **Retro. Supp. I:** 56, 79; **Retro. Supp. II:** 326; **Supp. I Part 2:** 552; **Supp. IX:** 66

Paterna (Mather), **Supp. II Part 2:** 451

"Paterson" (Ginsberg), **Supp. II Part 1:** 314–315, 321, 329

Paterson (W. C. Williams), **I:** 62, 446; **IV:** 418–423; **Retro. Supp. I:** 209, 284, 413, 419, 421, 424–428, 428, 429, 430; **Retro. Supp. II:** 321, 328; **Supp. II Part 2:** 557, 564, 625; **Supp. VIII:** 275, 305; **Supp. XIV:**96; **Supp. XV:** 264, 349

Paterson, Book Five (W. C. Williams), **IV:** 422–423

Paterson, Book One (W. C. Williams), **IV:** 421–422

Paterson, Isabel, **Supp. IV Part 2:** 524

Paterson, Part Three (W. C. Williams), **IV:** 420–421

"Path, The" (Bryant), **Supp. I Part 1:** 169

Pathfinder, The (Cooper), **I:** 349, 350, 355

Pat Hobby Stories, The (Fitzgerald), **Retro. Supp. I:** 114

"Patience of a Saint, The" (Humphrey), **Supp. IX:** 106

Patinkin, Mandy, **Supp. IV Part 1:** 236

Paton, Alan, **Supp. VIII:** 126

Patria Mia (Pound), **III:** 460–461; **Retro. Supp. I:** 284

"Patria Mia" (Pound), **Retro. Supp. I:** 284

"Patriarch, The" (Alvares), **Supp. V:** 11

Patrimony: A True Story (Roth), **Retro. Supp. II:** 279, 280, 291; **Supp. III Part 2:** 427

Patriot, The (Buck), **Supp. II Part 1:** 122–123

Patriot, The (Connell), **Supp. XIV:**94–95

Patriotic Gore: Studies in the Literature of the American Civil War (Wilson), **III:** 588; **IV:** 430, 438, 443, 445–445, 446; **Supp. VIII:** 100

"Patriots, The/Los Patriotas" (Kingsolver), **Supp. VII:** 209

Patron Saint of Liars, The (Patchett), **Supp. XII:** 307, 310, 311–314, 317

Pattee, Fred L., **II:** 456

Patten, Gilbert, **II:** 423

Patten, Simon, **Supp. I Part 2:** 640

Patternmaster (O. Butler), **Supp. XIII:** 61, 62, 63

Patternmaster Series (O. Butler), **Supp. XIII:** 62–63

Pattern Recognition (W. Gibson), **Supp. XVI:**124, 130–131

"Patterns" (Lowell), **II:** 524

Patterson, Floyd, **III:** 38

Patterson, William M., **Supp. I Part 1:** 265

Patton, General George, **III:** 575; **Supp. I Part 2:** 664

Paul, Saint, **I:** 365; **II:** 15, 494; **IV:** 122, 154, 164, 335; **Retro. Supp. I:** 247; **Supp. I Part 1:** 188

Paul, Sherman, **I:** 244; **IV:** 179

"Paula Becker to Clara Westhoff" (Rich), **Supp. I Part 2:** 573–574

"Paula Gunn Allen" (Ruppert), **Supp. IV Part 1:** 321

Paul Bowles: Romantic Savage (Caponi), **Supp. IV Part 1:** 95

Paulding, James Kirke, **I:** 344; **II:** 298, 299, 303; **Supp. I Part 1:** 157

Paul Marchand, F.M.C. (Chesnutt), **Supp. XIV:**76

"Paul Monette: The Brink of Summer's End" (film), **Supp. X:** 152

"Paul Revere" (Longfellow), **II:** 489, 501

"Paul Revere's Ride" (Longfellow), **Retro. Supp. II:** 163

"Paul's Case" (Cather), **I:** 314–315; **Retro. Supp. I:** 3, 5

Paulsen, Friedrich, **III:** 600

"Pauper Witch of Grafton, The" (Frost), **Retro. Supp. II:** 42

"Pause by the Water, A" (Merwin), **Supp. III Part 1:** 354

"Pavane for the Nursery, A" (W. J. Smith), **Supp. XIII:** 335

"Pavement, The" (Olson), **Supp. II Part 2:** 571

Pavilion of Women (Buck), **Supp. II Part 1:** 125–126

"Pawnbroker, The" (Kumin), **Supp. IV Part 2:** 442, 443–444, 451

Pawnbroker, The (Wallant), **Supp. XVI:**220

"Paying Dues" (Bass), **Supp. XVI:**16

Payne, Daniel, **Supp. V:** 202

Payne, John Howard, **II:** 309

Paz, Octavio, **Supp. III Part 2:** 630; **Supp. VIII:** 272; **Supp. XI:** 191; **Supp. XIII:** 223

Peabody, Elizabeth, **Retro. Supp. I:** 155–156, 225

Peabody, Francis G., **III:** 293; **Supp. I Part 1:** 5

Peabody, Josephine Preston, **III:** 507

Peaceable Kingdom, The (Prose), **Supp. XVI:**256–257

Peace and Bread in Time of War (Addams), **Supp. I Part 1:** 21, 22–23

"Peace Between Black and White in the United States" (Locke), **Supp. XIV:**205

Peace Breaks Out (Knowles), **Supp. XII:** 249

"Peace March, The" (Simpson), **Supp. IX:** 279

"Peace of Cities, The" (Wilbur), **Supp. III Part 2:** 545

"Peaches—Six in a Tin Box, Sarajevo" (Cisneros), **Supp. VII:** 67

Peacock, Doug, **Supp. VIII:** 38; **Supp. XIII:** 12

Peacock, Gibson, **Supp. I Part 1:** 360

"Peacock, The" (Merrill), **Supp. III Part 1:** 320

Peacock, Thomas Love, **Supp. I Part 1:** 307; **Supp. VIII:** 125

"Peacock Room, The" (Hayden), **Supp. II Part 1:** 374–375

Pearce, Richard, **Supp. IX:** 254

Pearce, Roy Harvey, **II:** 244; **Supp. I Part 1:** 111, 114; **Supp. I Part 2:** 475

Pearl, The (Steinbeck), **IV:** 51, 62–63

Pearlman, Daniel, **III:** 479

Pearlman, Mickey, **Supp. XIII:** 293, 306

Pearl of Orr's Island, The (Stowe), **Supp. I Part 2:** 592–593, 595

Pears, Peter, **II:** 586; **Supp. IV Part 1:** 84

Pearson, Drew, **Supp. XIV:**126

Pearson, Norman Holmes, **Supp. I Part 1:** 259, 260, 273

"Pear Tree" (C. Frost), **Supp. XV:** 105

"Peasants' Way O' Thinkin'" (McKay), **Supp. X:** 133

Pease, Donald E., **Supp. IV Part 2:** 687

Peck, Gregory, **Supp. VIII:** 128, 129; **Supp. XII:** 160, 173

Peckinpah, Sam, **Supp. XI:** 306

"Peck of Gold, A" (Frost), **II:** 155

Peculiar Treasures: A Biblical Who's Who (Buechner), **Supp. XII:** 53

"Pedal Point" (Francis), **Supp. IX:** 87

"Pedersen Kid, The" (Gass), **Supp. VI:** 83

"Pedigree, The" (Creeley), **Supp. IV Part 1:** 150

Peebles, Melvin Van, **Supp. XI:** 17; **Supp. XVI:**144

"Peed Onk" (Moore). *See* "People Like

That Are the Only People Here: Canonical Babbling in Peed Onk" (Moore)

"Peeler, The" (O'Connor), **Retro. Supp. II:** 225

Peich, Michael, **Supp. XV:** 113, 117

Peikoff, Leonard, **Supp. IV Part 2:** 520, 526, 529

Peirce, Charles Sanders, **II:** 20, 352–353; **III:** 599; **Supp. I Part 2:** 640; **Supp. III Part 2:** 626

Pelagius, **III:** 295

"Pelican, The" (Merrill), **Supp. III Part 1:** 320

"Pelican, The" (Wharton), **IV:** 310; **Retro. Supp. I:** 364

Pellacchia, Michael, **Supp. XIII:** 16

Peltier, Leonard, **Supp. V:** 212

"Pen and Paper and a Breath of Air" (Oliver), **Supp. VII:** 245

Pence, Amy, **Supp. XV:** 211, 223

"Pencil, The" (Chandler), **Supp. IV Part 1:** 135

Pencillings by the Way (Willis), **II:** 313

"Pencils" (Sandburg), **III:** 592

"Pendulum" (Bradbury and Hasse), **Supp. IV Part 1:** 102

"Penelope's Song" (Glück), **Supp. V:** 89

Penhally (Gordon), **II:** 197, 199, 201–203, 204

"Penis" (McClatchy), **Supp. XII:** 266–267

Penitent, The (Singer), **Retro. Supp. II:** 309–310, 313

Penn, Robert, **I:** 489

Penn, Sean, **Supp. XI:** 107

Penn, Thomas, **II:** 118

Penn, William, **Supp. I Part 2:** 683

"Pennsylvania Pilgrim, The" (Whittier), **Supp. I Part 2:** 700

"Pennsylvania Planter, The" (Freneau), **Supp. II Part 1:** 268

Penny, Rob, **Supp. VIII:** 330

Penrod (Tarkington), **III:** 223

"Penseroso, Il" (Milton), **Supp. XIV:**8

Pentagon of Power, The (Mumford), **Supp. II Part 2:** 498

Pentimento (Hellman), **Supp. I Part 1:** 280, 292–294, 296; **Supp. IV Part 1:** 12; **Supp. VIII:** 243

"Peonies at Dusk" (Kenyon), **Supp. VII:** 171

People, The (Glaspell), **Supp. III Part 1:** 179

People, Yes, The (Sandburg), **III:** 575, 589, 590, 591

"PEOPLE BURNING, THE" (Baraka), **Supp. II Part 1:** 49

"People in Hell Just Want a Drink of Water" (Proulx), **Supp. VII:** 263

"People Like That Are the Only People Here: Canonical Babbling in Peed Onk" (Moore), **Supp. X:** 168, 178–179

People Live Here: Selected Poems 1949–1983 (Simpson), **Supp. IX:** 269, 277

"People Next Door, The" (Simpson), **Supp. IX:** 279

People of the Abyss, The (London), **II:** 465–466

"People on the Roller Coaster, The" (Hardwick), **Supp. III Part 1:** 196

People Shall Continue, The (Ortiz), **Supp. IV Part 2:** 510

"People's Surroundings" (Moore), **III:** 201, 202, 203

"People v. Abe Lathan, Colored, The" (Caldwell), **I:** 309

"Peppermint Lounge Revisited, The" (Wolfe), **Supp. III Part 2:** 571

Pepys, Samuel, **Supp. I Part 2:** 653

"Perch'io non spero di tornar giammai" (Cavalcanti), **Supp. III Part 2:** 623

Percy, Thomas, **Supp. XIV:**2

Percy, Walker, **Supp. III Part 1:** 383–400; **Supp. IV Part 1:** 297; **Supp. V:** 334; **Supp. X:** 42; **Supp. XIV:**21

Percy, William, **Supp. V:** 334

Percy, William Alexander, **Retro. Supp. I:** 341

Peregrin, Tony, **Supp. XV:** 69

"Peregrine" (Wylie), **Supp. I Part 2:** 712–713, 714

Perelman, Bob, **Supp. XII:** 23

Perelman, S. J., **IV:** 286; **Retro. Supp. I:** 342; **Retro. Supp. II:** 321, 322, 325, 326, 327, 336; **Supp. IV Part 1:** 353; **Supp. XI:** 66

Perestroika (Kushner), **Supp. IX:** 141, 142, 145

Péret, Benjamin, **Supp. VIII:** 272

Peretz, Isaac Loeb, **IV:** 1, 3; **Retro. Supp. II:** 299

Pérez Galdós, Benito, **II:** 275

Perfect Analysis Given by a Parrot, A (T. Williams), **IV:** 395

"Perfect Day for Bananafish, A" (Salinger), **III:** 563–564, 571

Perfect Ganesh, A (McNally), **Supp. XIII:** 202–203, 208, 209

"Perfect Knight, The" (Chandler), **Supp. IV Part 1:** 120

Perfect Party, The (Gurney), **Supp. V:** 100, 105, 106–107

"Perfect Things" (F. Barthelme), **Supp. XI:** 30, 33–34

"Performance, The" (Dickey), **Supp.**

IV Part 1: 178–179, 181

"Perfume" (Mora), **Supp. XIII:** 218

"Perhaps the World Ends Here" (Harjo), **Supp. XII:** 228, 231

Perhaps Women (Anderson), **I:** 114

Pericles (Shakespeare), **I:** 585; **Supp. III Part 2:** 624, 627, 629

Period of Adjustment (T. Williams), **IV:** 382, 386, 387, 388, 389, 390, 392, 393, 394, 397

"Period Pieces from the Mid-Thirties" (Agee), **I:** 28

"Periphery" (Ammons), **Supp. VII:** 28

Perkins, David, **Supp. I Part 2:** 459, 475; **Supp. XV:** 185

Perkins, Maxwell, **I:** 252, 289, 290; **II:** 87, 93, 95, 252; **IV:** 452, 455, 457, 458, 461, 462, 463, 469; **Retro. Supp. I:** 101, 105, 108, 109, 110, 113, 114, 178; **Supp. IX:** 57, 58, 60, 232; **Supp. X:** 219, 224, 225, 229, 230, 233; **Supp. XI:** 218, 227

Perlès, Alfred, **III:** 177, 183, 187, 189

Perloff, Marjorie, **Supp. I Part 2:** 539, 542; **Supp. IV Part 1:** 68; **Supp. IV Part 2:** 420, 424, 432

Permanence and Change (Burke), **I:** 274

Permanent Errors (Price), **Supp. VI:** 261

"Permanent Traits of the English National Genius" (Emerson), **II:** 18

Permit Me Voyage (Agee), **I:** 25, 27

"Perosa Canavese" (Everwine), **Supp. XV:** 84

Perrault, Charles, **IV:** 266; **Supp. I Part 2:** 622

Perrin, Noel, **Supp. XVI:**34

Perrins, Carol. See Frost, Carol

Perry, Anne, **Supp. V:** 335

Perry, Bliss, **I:** 243

Perry, Donna, **Supp. IV Part 1:** 322, 327, 335

Perry, Dr. William, **II:** 395, 396

Perry, Edgar A., **III:** 410

Perry, Lincoln, **Supp. V:** 24, 33

Perry, Matthew C., **Supp. I Part 2:** 494–495

Perry, Patsy Brewington, **Supp. I Part 1:** 66

Perry, Ralph Barton, **I:** 224; **II:** 356, 362, 364; **Supp. XIV:**197

Perse, St.-John, **III:** 12, 13, 14, 17; **Supp. III Part 1:** 14; **Supp. IV Part 1:** 82; **Supp. XIII:** 344; **Supp. XV:** 178

"Persephone in Hell" (Dove), **Supp. IV Part 1:** 250, 251

"Persimmons" (L.-Y. Lee), **Supp. XV:** 211, 213

"Persistence of Desire, The" (Updike), **IV:** 222–223, 228

"Persistence of Poetry, The" (Bynner), **Supp. XV:** 49

"Persistences" (Hecht), **Supp. X:** 68–69

Person, Place, and Thing (Shapiro), **Supp. II Part 2:** 702, 705

Personae: The Collected Poems (Pound), **Retro. Supp. I:** 285, 286; **Supp. I Part 1:** 255

Personae of Ezra Pound (Pound), **III:** 458

"Personal" (Stern), **Supp. IX:** 299

"Personal and Occasional Pieces" (Welty), **Retro. Supp. I:** 355

"Personal and the Individual, The" (L. Michaels), **Supp. XVI:**201

Personal Narrative (Edwards), **I:** 545, 552, 553, 561, 562; **Supp. I Part 2:** 700

Personal Recollection of Joan of Arc (Twain), **IV:** 208

"Personals" (Didion), **Supp. IV Part 1:** 200

"Personism" (O'Hara), **Supp. XV:** 181

Persons and Places (Santayana), **III:** 615

Persons in Hiding (film), **Supp. XIII:** 170

Persons in Hiding (Hoover), **Supp. XIII:** 170

Person Sitting in Darkness, A (Twain), **IV:** 208

"Perspective" (Francis), **Supp. IX:** 78

"Perspective: Anniversary D-Day" (Karr), **Supp. XI:** 241

"Perspectives: Is It Out of Control?" (Gleason), **Supp. IX:** 16

Perspectives by Incongruity (Burke), **I:** 284–285

Perspectives on Cormac McCarthy (Arnold and Luce, eds.), **Supp. VIII:** 189

Pertes et Fracas (McCoy), **Supp. XIII:** 175

"Peruvian Child" (Mora), **Supp. XIII:** 218

Peseroff, Joyce, **Supp. IV Part 1:** 71

"Peter" (Cather), **Retro. Supp. I:** 4

"Peter" (Moore), **III:** 210, 212

Peter, Saint, **III:** 341, 346; **IV:** 86, 294

Peterkin, Julia, **Supp. I Part 1:** 328

"Peter Klaus" (German tale), **II:** 306

Peter Pan (Barrie), **Supp. XV:** 319

"Peter Parley" works (Goodrich), **Supp. I Part 1:** 38

"Peter Pendulum" (Poe), **III:** 425

"Peter Quince at the Clavier" (Stevens), **IV:** 81, 82

Peter Rabbit tales, **Retro. Supp. I:** 335

Peters, Cora, **Supp. I Part 2:** 468

Peters, Jacqueline, **Supp. XII:** 225

Peters, Margot, **Supp. VIII:** 252

Peters, Robert, **Supp. XIII:** 114

Peters, S. H. (pseudonym). *See* Henry, O.

Peters, Timothy, **Supp. XI:** 39

"Peter's Avocado" (Rodriguez), **Supp. XIV:**308–309

Petersen, David, **Supp. XIII:** 2

Petersen, Donald, **Supp. V:** 180; **Supp. XV:** 74, 92

Peterson, Houston, **I:** 60

Peterson, Roger Tory, **Supp. V:** 202

Peterson, Virgilia, **Supp. IV Part 1:** 30

Peter Whiffle: His Life and Works (Van Vechten), **Supp. II Part 2:** 728–729, 731, 735, 738–741, 749

"Petey and Yotsee and Mario" (H. Roth), **Supp. IX:** 234

"Petition, A" (Winters), **Supp. II Part 2:** 785

"'Pet Negro' System, The" (Hurston), **Supp. VI:** 159

"Petra and Its Surroundings" (Frost), **Retro. Supp. I:** 124

Petrarch, **I:** 176; **II:** 590; **III:** 4

"Petrarch, Shakespeare, and the Blues" (C. Frost), **Supp. XV:** 92, 104, 105

"Petrified Man" (Welty), **IV:** 262; **Retro. Supp. I:** 345, 351

"Petrified Man, The" (Twain), **IV:** 195

"Petrified Woman, The" (Gordon), **II:** 199

Petronius, **III:** 174, 179

Petry, Ann, **Supp. VIII:** 214; **Supp. XI:** 6, 85

Pet Sematary (King), **Supp. V:** 138, 143, 152

Pettengill, Richard, **Supp. VIII:** 341, 345, 348

Pettingell, Phoebe, **Supp. XV:** 251, 256–257, 262

Pettis, Joyce, **Supp. XI:** 276, 277, 278, 281

Pfaelzer, Jean, **Supp. XVI:**88, 90

Pfaff, Timothy, **Supp. V:** 166

Pfeil, Fred, **Supp. XIV:**36

Pfister, Karin, **IV:** 467, 475

Phaedo (Plato), **II:** 10

Phaedra (Lowell and Barzun, trans.), **II:** 543–544

"Phantasia for Elvira Shatayev" (Rich), **Supp. I Part 2:** 570

Phantasms of War (Lowell), **II:** 512

"Phantom of the Movie Palace, The" (Coover), **Supp. V:** 50–51

"Pharaoh, The" (Kenyon), **Supp. VII:** 172

Pharr, Mary, **Supp. V:** 147

"Phases" (E. Stoddard), **Supp. XV:** 273

"Phases" (Stevens), **Retro. Supp. I:** 299

Phases of an Inferior Planet (Glasgow), **II:** 174–175

"Pheasant, The" (Carver), **Supp. III Part 1:** 146

Pheloung, Grant, **Supp. XI:** 39

Phelps, Elizabeth Stuart, **Retro. Supp. II:** 146; **Supp. XIII:** 141; **Supp. XVI:**80

Phelps, Teresa Godwin, **Supp. VIII:** 128

"Phenomena and Laws of Race Contacts, The" (Locke), **Supp. XIV:**210

"Phenomenology of Anger, The" (Rich), **Supp. I Part 2:** 562–563, 571

Phenomenology of Moral Experience, The (Mandelbaum), **I:** 61

"Phenomenology of *On Moral Fiction*" (Johnson), **Supp. VI:** 188

Phidias, **Supp. I Part 2:** 482

Philadelphia Fire (Wideman), **Supp. X:** 320, 334

Philadelphia Negro, The (Du Bois), **Supp. II Part 1:** 158, 163–164, 166

Philbrick, Thomas, **I:** 343

Philip, Jim, **Supp. XII:** 136

Philip, Prince, **Supp. X:** 108

"Philip of Pokanoket" (Irving), **II:** 303

Philippians (biblical book), **IV:** 154

"Philippine Conquest, The" (Masters), **Supp. I Part 2:** 456

"Philip Roth Reconsidered" (Howe), **Retro. Supp. II:** 286

"Philistinism and the Negro Writer" (Baraka), **Supp. II Part 1:** 39, 44

Phillips, Adam, **Supp. XII:** 97–98

Phillips, David Graham, **II:** 444; **Retro. Supp. II:** 101

Phillips, Gene D., **Supp. XI:** 306

Phillips, J. O. C., **Supp. I Part 1:** 19

Phillips, Jayne Anne, **Supp. XIV:**21

Phillips, Robert, **Supp. XIII:** 335, 344

Phillips, Wendell, **Supp. I Part 1:** 103; **Supp. I Part 2:** 524

Phillips, Willard, **Supp. I Part 1:** 154, 155

Phillips, William, **Supp. VIII:** 156

Phillips, William L., **I:** 106

"Philosopher, The" (Farrell), **II:** 45

Philosopher of the Forest (pseudonym). *See* Freneau, Philip

Philosophes classiques, Les (Taine), **III:** 323

"Philosophical Cobbler, The"

(Sanders), **Supp. XVI:**268

"Philosophical Concepts and Practical Results" (James), **II:** 352

"Philosophical Investigation of Metaphor, A" (Gass), **Supp. VI:** 79

Philosophical Transactions (Watson), **II:** 114

"Philosophy, Or Something Like That" (Roth), **Supp. III Part 2:** 403

Philosophy: Who Needs It (Rand), **Supp. IV Part 2:** 517, 518, 527, 533

"Philosophy and Its Critics" (James), **II:** 360

"Philosophy and the Form of Fiction" (Gass), **Supp. VI:** 85

"Philosophy for People" (Emerson), **II:** 14

"Philosophy in Warm Weather" (Kenyon), **Supp. VII:** 168

"Philosophy Lesson" (Levine), **Supp. V:** 195

Philosophy of Alain Locke, The: Harlem Renaissance and Beyond (Harris, ed.), **Supp. XIV:**196, 211–212

"Philosophy of Composition, The" (Poe), **III:** 416, 421; **Retro. Supp. II:** 266, 267, 271

Philosophy of Friedrich Nietzsche, The (Mencken), **III:** 102–103

"Philosophy of Handicap, A" (Bourne), **I:** 216, 218

"Philosophy of History" (Emerson), **II:** 11–12

Philosophy of Literary Form, The (Burke), **I:** 275, 281, 283, 291

Philosophy of the Human Mind, The (Stewart), **II:** 8

Philoxenes, **Supp. VIII:** 201

"Phineas" (Knowles), **Supp. XII:** 238–240

Phineas: Six Stories (Knowles), **Supp. XII:** 249

"Phocion" (Lowell), **II:** 536

Phoenix and the Turtle, The (Shakespeare), **I:** 284

"Phoenix Lyrics" (Schwartz), **Supp. II Part 2:** 665

"Phony War Films" (Jones), **Supp. XI:** 217, 232

"Photograph: Migrant Worker, Parlier, California, 1967" (Levis), **Supp. XI:** 272

"Photograph of a Child on a Vermont Hillside" (Kenyon), **Supp. VII:** 168

"Photograph of My Mother as a Young Girl" (Gioia), **Supp. XV:** 119

"Photograph of the Girl" (Olds), **Supp. X:** 205

"Photograph of the Unmade Bed" (Rich), **Supp. I Part 2:** 558

Photographs (Welty), **Retro. Supp. I:** 343

"Photographs, The" (Barthelme), **Supp. IV Part 1:** 53

"Photography" (Levine), **Supp. V:** 194

Phyrrho, **Retro. Supp. I:** 247

"Physical Universe" (Simpson), **Supp. IX:** 278

"Physicist We Know, A" (Shields), **Supp. VII:** 310

"Physics and Cosmology in the Fiction of Tom Robbins" (Nadeau), **Supp. X:** 270

"Physiology of Versification, The: Harmonies of Organic and Animal Life" (Holmes), **Supp. I Part 1:** 311

Physique de l'Amour (Gourmont), **III:** 467–468

Piaf, Edith, **Supp. IV Part 2:** 549

"Piano" (Lawrence), **Supp. XV:** 254

"Piano Fingers" (Mason), **Supp. VIII:** 146

Piano Lesson, The (Bearden), **Supp. VIII:** 342

Piano Lesson, The (Wilson), **Supp. VIII:** 342–345

Piatt, James, **Supp. I Part 2:** 420

Piatt, John J., **II:** 273

Piazza, Ben, **Supp. XIII:** 163

Piazza, Paul, **Supp. XIV:**157, 160, 171

"Piazza de Spagna, Early Morning" (Wilbur), **Supp. III Part 2:** 553

Piazza Tales (Melville), **III:** 91

Picabia, Francis, **Retro. Supp. I:** 416; **Retro. Supp. II:** 331

Picasso (Stein), **IV:** 28, 32, 45

Picasso, Pablo, **I:** 429, 432, 440, 442, 445; **II:** 602; **III:** 197, 201, 470; **IV:** 26, 31, 32, 46, 87, 407, 436; **Retro. Supp. I:** 55, 63; **Supp. IV Part 1:** 81; **Supp. IX:** 66

Piccione, Anthony, **Supp. XV:** 212

"Piccola Comedia" (Wilbur), **Supp. III Part 2:** 561

Pickard, Samuel T., **Supp. I Part 2:** 682

Picked-Up Pieces (Updike), **Retro. Supp. I:** 320, 322, 323, 335

Picker, Lauren, **Supp. VIII:** 78, 83

Picker, Tobias, **Supp. XII:** 253

Pickford, Mary, **Retro. Supp. I:** 325; **Supp. I Part 2:** 391

"Picking and Choosing" (Moore), **III:** 205

Picnic Cantata (music) (Bowles), **Supp. IV Part 1:** 89

"Picnic Remembered" (Warren), **IV:** 240

Pictorial History of the Negro in America, A (Hughes), **Supp. I Part 1:** 345

"Picture, The" (Olson), **Supp. II Part 2:** 574

Picture Bride (Son), **Supp. X:** 292

"Picture I Want, The" (Olds), **Supp. X:** 209

Picture of Dorian Gray, The (Wilde), **Supp. IX:** 105

"Picture of Little J. A. in a Prospect of Flowers, A" (Ashbery), **Supp. III Part 1:** 3

Picture Palace (Theroux), **Supp. VIII:** 322

"Pictures at an Extermination" (Epstein), **Supp. XII:** 161

"Pictures from an Expedition" (Duffy), **Supp. IV Part 1:** 207

Pictures from an Institution (Jarrell), **II:** 367, 385

Pictures from Brueghel (W. C. Williams), **Retro. Supp. I:** 429–431

"Pictures from Brueghel" (W. C. Williams), **Retro. Supp. I:** 419

"Pictures of Columbus, the Genoese, The" (Freneau), **Supp. II Part 1:** 258

Pictures of Fidelman: An Exhibition (Malamud), **Supp. I Part 2:** 450–451

"Pictures of the Artist" (Malamud), **Supp. I Part 2:** 450

Pictures of the Floating World (Lowell), **II:** 521, 524–525

Pictures of Travel (Heine), **II:** 281

"Picturesque: San Cristóbal de las Casas" (Mora), **Supp. XIII:** 218

Picturesque America; or, the Land We Live In (Bryant, ed.), **Supp. I Part 1:** 158

Picture This (Heller), **Supp. IV Part 1:** 386, 388, 390–391

Picturing Will (Beattie), **Supp. V:** 29, 31–32, 34

"Pie" (X. J. Kennedy), **Supp. XV:** 170

"Piece, A" (Creeley), **Supp. IV Part 1:** 155, 156

"Piece of Moon, A" (Hogan), **Supp. IV Part 1:** 407

Piece of My Heart, A (Ford), **Supp. V:** 57, 58–61, 62

Piece of My Mind, A: Reflections at Sixty (Wilson), **IV:** 426, 430, 438, 441

"Piece of News, A" (Welty), **IV:** 263; **Retro. Supp. I:** 345, 346

Pieces (Creeley), **Supp. IV Part 1:** 155

Pieces and Pontifications (Mailer), **Retro. Supp. II:** 209–210

Pieces of the Frame (McPhee), **Supp. III Part 1:** 293

Pierce, Franklin, **II:** 225, 226, 227; **III:** 88; **Retro. Supp. I:** 150, 163, 164, 165

Pierce, Frederick, **Retro. Supp. I:** 136

Piercy, Josephine K., **Supp. I Part 1:** 103

"Pierian Handsprings" (column, Untermeyer), **Supp. XV:** 294

Pierpont, Claudia Roth, **Supp. X:** 192, 193, 196

Pierre: or The Ambiguities (Melville), **III:** 86–88, 89; **IV:** 194; **Retro. Supp. I:** 249, 253–254, 256; **Supp. I Part 2:** 579

Pierre et Jean (Maupassant), **I:** 421

Pierrepont, Sarah. *See* Edwards, Sarah

Pierrot qui pleure et Pierrot qui rit (Rostand), **II:** 515

Pig Cookies (Ríos), **Supp. IV Part 2:** 537, 550, 552–554

Pigeon Feathers (Updike), **IV:** 214, 218, 219, 221–223, 226

"Pigeon Feathers" (Updike), **Retro. Supp. I:** 318, 322, 323

"Pigeons" (Rilke), **II:** 544

"Pigeon Woman" (Swenson), **Supp. IV Part 2:** 644

Pigs in Heaven (Kingsolver), **Supp. VII:** 197, 199, 209–210

Pike County Ballads, The (Hay), **Supp. I Part 1:** 352

Piket, Vincent, **Supp. IV Part 1:** 24

Pilar San-Mallafre, Maria del, **Supp. V:** 40

"Pilgrim" (Freneau), **Supp. I Part 1:** 125

"Pilgrimage" (Sontag), **Supp. III Part 2:** 454–455

"Pilgrimage, The" (Maxwell), **Supp. VIII:** 169, 171

Pilgrimage of Festus, The (Aiken), **I:** 50, 55, 57

Pilgrimage of Henry James, The (Brooks), **I:** 240, 248, 250; **IV:** 433

Pilgrim at Tinker Creek (Dillard), **Supp. VI:** 22, 23–26, 28, 29, 30–31, 34

"Pilgrim Makers" (Lowell), **II:** 541

Pilgrim's Progress (Bunyan), **I:** 92; **II:** 15, 168, 572; **Supp. I Part 1:** 32, 38; **Supp. I Part 2:** 599

Pili's Wall (Levine), **Supp. V:** 178, 183–184

"Pillar of Fire" (Bradbury), **Supp. IV**

Part 1: 113–114

Pillars of Hercules, The: A Grand Tour of the Mediterranean (Theroux), **Supp. VIII:** 325

"Pillow" (L.-Y. Lee), **Supp. XV:** 224

Pilot, The (Cooper), **I:** 335, 337, 339, 342–343, 350

"Pilot from the Carrier, A" (Jarrell), **II:** 374

"Pilots, Man Your Planes" (Jarrell), **II:** 374–375

"Pilots, The" (Levertov), **Supp. III Part 1:** 282

"Pimp's Revenge, A" (Malamud), **Supp. I Part 2:** 435, 450, 451

Pinball (Kosinski), **Supp. VII:** 215, 226

Pinchot, Gifford, **Supp. IX:** 184; **Supp. XIV:**178

Pindar, **I:** 381; **II:** 543; **III:** 610

"Pine" (Dickey), **Supp. IV Part 1:** 183

Pine Barrens, The (McPhee), **Supp. III Part 1:** 298–301, 309

"Pineys, The" (Stern), **Supp. IX:** 288, 296

Pinget, Robert, **Supp. V:** 39

"Pink Dog" (Bishop), **Retro. Supp. II:** 48

Pinker, James B., **I:** 409; **Retro. Supp. I:** 231

Pinkerton, Jan, **Supp. V:** 323–324

"Pink Moon—The Pond" (Oliver), **Supp. VII:** 234

Pinktoes (C. Himes), **Supp. XVI:**142

Pinocchio in Venice (Coover), **Supp. V:** 40, 51

Pinsker, Sanford, **Retro. Supp. II:** 23; **Supp. V:** 272; **Supp. IX:** 293, 327; **Supp. XI:** 251, 254, 317

Pinsky, Robert, **Retro. Supp. II:** 50; **Supp. VI:** 235–251; **Supp. IX:** 155, 158; **Supp. XIII:** 277, 285

Pinter, Harold, **I:** 71; **Supp. XIII:** 20, 196; **Supp. XIV:**239; **Supp. XVI:**207

Pinto and Sons (Epstein), **Supp. XII:** 170, 171–172

Pioneers, The (Cooper), **I:** 336, 337, 339, 340–341, 342, 348; **II:** 313

Pioneers of France in the New World (Parkman), **Supp. III Part 2:** 599, 602

"Pioneers! O Pioneers!" (Whitman), **Retro. Supp. I:** 8

"Pioneer's Vision, The" (Larcom), **Supp. XIII:** 140

Pious and Secular America (Niebuhr), **III:** 308

Pipe Night (O'Hara), **III:** 361, 368

Piper, Dan, **Supp. IX:** 65

Pipers at the Gates of Dawn: The Wisdom of Children's Literature (Cott), **Supp. XVI:**104

"Piper's Rocks" (Olson), **Supp. IV Part 1:** 153

Pipkin, Charles W., **Supp. XIV:**3

Pippa Passes (Browning), **IV:** 128

Piquion, René, **Supp. I Part 1:** 346

Pirandello, Luigi, **Supp. IV Part 2:** 576, 588

Piranesi, Giovanni Battista, **Supp. XV:** 258

Pirate, The (Robbins), **Supp. XII:** 6

Pirate, The (Scott), **I:** 339

Pirates of Penzance, The (Gilbert and Sullivan), **IV:** 386

Pisan Cantos, The (Pound), **III:** 476; **Retro. Supp. I:** 140, 283, 285, 293; **Supp. III Part 1:** 63; **Supp. V:** 331, 337; **Supp. XIV:**11; **Supp. XV:** 351

Piscator, Erwin, **IV:** 394

Pissarro, Camille, **I:** 478

"Pissing off the Back of the Boat into the Nevernais Canal" (Matthews), **Supp. IX:** 160–161

Pistol, The (Jones), **Supp. XI:** 219, 223–224, 227, 234

Pit, The (Norris), **III:** 314, 322, 326–327, 333, 334

"Pit, The" (Roethke), **III:** 538

"Pit and the Pendulum, The" (Poe), **III:** 413, 416; **Retro. Supp. II:** 264, 269–270, 273

"Pitcher" (Francis), **Supp. IX:** 82

"Pitcher, The" (Dubus), **Supp. VII:** 87

Pitchford, Nicola, **Supp. XII:** 13

"Pits, The" (D. Graham), **Supp. XI:** 252, 254

Pitt, William, **Supp. I Part 2:** 510, 518

"Pittsburgh" (Carruth), **Supp. XVI:**58

"Pity Me" (Wylie), **Supp. I Part 2:** 729

Pity the Monsters (Williamson), **Retro. Supp. II:** 185

Pius II, Pope, **III:** 472

Pius IX, Pope, **II:** 79

"Piute Creek" (Snyder), **Supp. VIII:** 293

Pixley, Frank, **I:** 196

Pizer, Donald, **III:** 321; **Retro. Supp. II:** 100, 199

"Place at the Outskirts" (Simic), **Supp. VIII:** 282

Place Called Estherville, A (Caldwell), **I:** 297, 307

Place Called Freedom, A (Sanders), **Supp. XVI:**269

"Place in Fiction" (Welty), **IV:** 260, 279

Place of Dead Roads, The (Burroughs),

Supp. III Part 1: 196

Place of Love, The (Shapiro), **Supp. II Part 2:** 702, 706

"Place of Poetry, The" (Stevens), **Retro. Supp. I:** 304

Place of Science in Modern Civilization and Other Essays, The (Veblen), **Supp. I Part 2:** 629, 642

Place on Earth, A (Berry), **Supp. X:** 33–34, 36

Places Left Unfinished at the Time of Creation (Santos), **Supp. XIII:** 274

"Places to Look for Your Mind" (Moore), **Supp. X:** 174–175

"Place They'd Never Seen, A: The Theater" (Wasserstein), **Supp. XV:** 332

"Place to Live, A" (Levertov), **Supp. III Part 1:** 281

"Place to Stand, A" (Price), **Supp. VI:** 258

Place to Stand, A (Wagoner), **Supp. IX:** 324

"Place (Any Place) to Transcend All Places, A" (W. C. Williams), **Retro. Supp. I:** 422

Placi, Carlo, **IV:** 328

"Plagiarist, The" (Singer), **IV:** 19

"Plain Language from Truthful James" (Harte). *See* "Heathen Chinee, The"

"Plain Sense of Things, The" (Stevens), **Retro. Supp. I:** 298, 299, 307, 312

"Plain Song" (Carruth), **Supp. XVI:**54

Plain Song (Harrison), **Supp. VIII:** 38–39

"Plain Song for Comadre, A" (Wilbur), **Supp. III Part 2:** 554

"Plain Talk." *See Common Sense* (Paine)

Plaint of a Rose, The (Sandburg), **III:** 579

Plain Truth: Or, Serious Considerations on the Present State of the City of Philadelphia, and Province of Pennsylvania (Franklin), **II:** 117–119

Plainwater: Essays and Poetry (Carson), **Supp. XII:** 97, 99–104

Plan B (C. Himes), **Supp. XVI:**143, 144

"Planchette" (London), **II:** 475–476

"Planetarium" (Rich), **Supp. I Part 2:** 557

Planet News: 1961–1967 (Ginsberg), **Supp. II Part 1:** 321

"Plantation a beginning, a" (Olson), **Supp. II Part 2:** 573

Plant Dreaming Deep (Sarton), **Supp. VIII:** 250, 263

Plante, David, **Supp. IV Part 1:** 310

Planting a Sequoia (Gioia), **Supp. XV:** 117

"Planting a Sequoia" (Gioia), **Supp. XV:** 111, 112, 117, 121–122

Plarr, Victor, **III:** 459, 477

Plath, James, **Retro. Supp. I:** 334

Plath, Sylvia, **Retro. Supp. II:** 181, 241–260; **Supp. I Part 2:** 526–549, 554, 571; **Supp. III Part 2:** 543, 561; **Supp. IV Part 2:** 439; **Supp. V:** 79, 81, 113, 117, 118, 119, 344; **Supp. X:** 201, 202, 203, 215; **Supp. XI:** 146, 240, 241, 317; **Supp. XII:** 217, 308; **Supp. XIII:** 35, 76, 312; **Supp. XIV:**269; **Supp. XV:** 123, 148, 184, 252, 253, 340

Plath, Warren, **Supp. I Part 2:** 528

Plato, **I:** 224, 279, 383, 389, 485, 523; **II:** 5, 8, 10, 15, 233, 346, 391–392, 591; **III:** 115, 480, 600, 606, 609, 619–620; **IV:** 74, 140, 333, 363, 364; **Retro. Supp. I:** 247; **Retro. Supp. II:** 31; **Supp. I Part 2:** 595, 631; **Supp. IV Part 1:** 391; **Supp. IV Part 2:** 526; **Supp. X:** 78

"Plato" (Emerson), **II:** 6

"Platonic Relationship, A" (Beattie), **Supp. V:** 22

Platonic Scripts (Justice), **Supp. VII:** 115

Platonov, Dmitri, **Supp. VIII:** 30

Platt, Anthony M., **Supp. I Part 1:** 13–14

Platte River (Bass), **Supp. XVI:**19

"Platte River" (Bass), **Supp. XVI:**20

Plausible Prejudices: Essays on American Writing (Epstein), **Supp. XIV:**111

Plautus, Titus Maccius, **IV:** 155; **Supp. III Part 2:** 630

Play and Other Stories, The (Dixon), **Supp. XII:** 148, 149

Playback (Chandler), **Supp. IV Part 1:** 134–135

Playback (script) (Chandler), **Supp. IV Part 1:** 131

"Play Ball!" (Francis), **Supp. IX:** 89

Playboy of the Western World, The (Synge), **Supp. III Part 1:** 34

Play Days (Jewett), **Retro. Supp. II:** 135

Play Days: A Book of Stories for Children (Jewett), **II:** 401–402

Player Piano (Vonnegut), **Supp. II Part 2:** 756, 757, 760–765

Players (DeLillo), **Supp. VI:** 3, 6, 8, 14

"Players, The" (W. J. Smith), **Supp. XIII:** 340, 343

"Playground, The" (Bradbury), **Supp. IV Part 1:** 104

Playing in the Dark (Morrison), **Retro. Supp. II:** 118; **Supp. XIII:** 185–186

Play in Poetry (Untermeyer), **Supp. XV:** 310

"Playin with Punjab" (Bambara), **Supp. XI:** 6

Play It Again Sam (Allen), **Supp. XV:** 2, 3, 14

Play It as It Lays (Didion), **Supp. IV Part 1:** 198, 201–203, 203, 211

Play It as It Lays (film), **Supp. IV Part 1:** 198

Plays: Winesburg and Others (Anderson), **I:** 113

"Plays and Operas Too" (Whitman), **IV:** 350

Plays of Negro Life: A Source-Book of Native American Drama (Locke and Gregory), **Supp. XIV:**202

"Playthings" (Komunyakaa), **Supp. XIII:** 126

Playwright's Voice, The (Savran), **Supp. XIII:** 209; **Supp. XV:** 321

Plaza Suite (Simon), **Supp. IV Part 2:** 575, 581–582, 583, 589

"Plea for Captain Brown, A" (Thoreau), **IV:** 185

"Please" (Komunyakaa), **Supp. XIII:** 122

"Please Don't Kill Anything" (A. Miller), **III:** 161

"Please Don't Take My Sunshine Away" (Conroy), **Supp. XVI:**69

Pleasure Dome (Frankenberg), **I:** 436

Pleasure Dome (Komunyakaa), **Supp. XIII:** 113, 121, 131–133

Pleasure of Hope, The (Emerson), **II:** 8

"Pleasure of Ruins, The" (McClatchy), **Supp. XII:** 256

"Pleasures of Formal Poetry, The" (Bogan), **Supp. III Part 1:** 51

"Pleasures of Peace, The" (Koch), **Supp. XV:** 180

"Plea to the Protestant Churches, A" (Brooks), **Supp. XIV:**4

Plimpton, George, **Supp. IV Part 1:** 386; **Supp. V:** 201; **Supp. VIII:** 82, 157; **Supp. IX:** 256; **Supp. XI:** 294; **Supp. XIV:**82; **Supp. XVI:**233–248

Pliny the Elder, **Supp. XVI:**292

Pliny the Younger, **II:** 113

"Ploesti Isn't Long Island" (Zinberg), **Supp. XV:** 195

"Plot against the Giant, The" (Stevens), **IV:** 81

Plotinus, **Supp. XV:** 33; **Supp. XVI:**291

Plough and the Stars, The (O'Casey), **III:** 159

"Ploughing on Sunday" (Stevens), **IV:** 74

Plowing the Dark (Powers), **Supp. IX:** 212–213, 221–224

Plumed Serpent, The (Lawrence), **Supp. XV:** 46

"Plumet Basilisk, The" (Moore), **III:** 203, 208, 215

Plumly, Stanley, **Supp. IV Part 2:** 625

Plummer, Amanda, **Supp. IV Part 1:** 236

Plunder (serial movie), **Supp. IV Part 2:** 464

Plunket, Robert, **Supp. XV:** 68

"Plunkville Patriot" (O'Henry), **Supp. II Part 1:** 389

"Pluralism and Ideological Peace" (Locke), **Supp. XIV:**202, 212

"Pluralism and Intellectual Democracy" (Locke), **Supp. XIV:**202, 208, 212

Pluralistic Universe, A (James), **II:** 342, 348, 357–358

Plutarch, **II:** 5, 8, 16, 555; **Retro. Supp. I:** 360; **Supp. XVI:**292

Plymell, Charles, **Supp. XIV:**149

Plymell, Pam, **Supp. XIV:**149

Pnin (Nabokov), **III:** 246; **Retro. Supp. I:** 263, 265, 266, 275, 335

"Po' Boy Blues" (Hughes), **Supp. I Part 1:** 327

Pocahontas, **I:** 4; **II:** 296; **III:** 584

"Pocahontas to Her English Husband, John Rolfe" (Gunn Allen), **Supp. IV Part 1:** 331

Podhoretz, Norman, **IV:** 441; **Retro. Supp. II:** 323; **Supp. IV Part 1:** 382; **Supp. VIII:** 93, 231–247; **Supp. IX:** 3; **Supp. XIV:**103

Podnieks, Elizabeth, **Supp. X:** 189, 190, 191, 192

"Pod of the Milkweed" (Frost), **Retro. Supp. I:** 141

Poe, Edgar Allan, **I:** 48, 53, 103, 190, 194, 200, 210, 211, 261, 340, 459; **II:** 74, 77, 194, 255, 273, 295, 308, 311, 313, 421, 475, 482, 530, 595; **III:** 259, 409–432, 485, 507, 593; **IV:** 123, 129, 133, 141, 187, 261, 345, 350, 432, 438, 439, 453; **Retro. Supp. I:** 41, 273, 365, 421; **Retro. Supp. II:** 102, 104, 160, 164, 220, 261–277, 322; **Supp. I Part 1:** 36, 309; **Supp. I Part 2:** 376, 384, 385, 388, 393, 405, 413, 421, 474, 682; **Supp. II Part 1:** 385, 410; **Supp. III Part 2:** 544, 549–550; **Supp. IV Part 1:** 80, 81, 101, 128, 341, 349;

Supp. IV Part 2: 464, 469; **Supp. VIII:** 105; **Supp. IX:** 115; **Supp. X:** 42, 78; **Supp. XI:** 85, 293; **Supp. XIII:** 100, 111; **Supp. XVI:**294

Poe, Edgar Allen, **Supp. XV:** 275

Poe Abroad: Influence, Reputation, Affinities (Vines), **Retro. Supp. II:** 261

"Poem" (Bishop), **Retro. Supp. II:** 40; **Supp. I Part 1:** 73, 76–79, 82, 95

"Poem" (Harrison), **Supp. VIII:** 38

"Poem" (Justice), **Supp. VII:** 125

"Poem" (Kunitz), **Supp. III Part 1:** 263

"Poem" (Wright), **Supp. III Part 2:** 590

"Poem About George Doty in the Death House, A" (Wright), **Supp. III Part 2:** 594–595, 597–598

"Poem about People" (Pinsky), **Supp. VI:** 240–241, 244, 248

"Poem as Mask, The" (Rukeyser), **Supp. VI:** 281, 285

"Poem Beginning 'The'" (Zukofsky), **Supp. III Part 2:** 610, 611, 614

"Poem Catching Up with an Idea" (Carruth), **Supp. XVI:**56

"Poem for a Birthday" (Plath), **Supp. I Part 2:** 539

"POEM FOR ANNA RUSS AND FANNY JONES, A" (Baraka), **Supp. II Part 1:** 58

"Poem for Black Hearts, A" (Baraka), **Supp. II Part 1:** 50

"Poem for D. H. Lawrence" (Creeley), **Supp. IV Part 1:** 141

"POEM FOR DEEP THINKERS, A" (Baraka), **Supp. II Part 1:** 55

"Poem for Dorothy, A" (Merwin), **Supp. III Part 1:** 342

"Poem for Hemingway and W. C. Williams" (Carver), **Supp. III Part 1:** 147

"Poem for my Son" (Kumin), **Supp. IV Part 2:** 442

"Poem for People Who Are Understandably Too Busy to Read Poetry" (Dunn), **Supp. XI:** 147

"Poem for Someone Killed in Spain, A" (Jarrell), **II:** 371

"Poem for the Blue Heron, A" (Oliver), **Supp. VII:** 235–236

"Poem for Two Voices" (Everwine), **Supp. XV:** 89

"Poem For Willie Best, A" (Baraka), **Supp. II Part 1:** 36

"Poem in Prose" (Bogan), **Supp. III Part 1:** 58

"Poem in Which I Refuse Contemplation" (Dove), **Supp. IV Part 1:** 249

"Poem Is a Walk, A" (Ammons), **Supp. VII:** 36

"Poem Like a Grenade, A" (Haines), **Supp. XII:** 204

"Poem of Flight, The" (Levine), **Supp. V:** 189

"Poem of Liberation, The" (Stern), **Supp. IX:** 292

Poem of the Cid (Merwin, trans.), **Supp. III Part 1:** 347

"Poem of the Forgotten" (Haines), **Supp. XII:** 202–203

"Poem on the Memorable Victory Obtained by the Gallant Captain Paul Jones" (Freneau), **Supp. II Part 1:** 261

"Poem out of Childhood" (Rukeyser), **Supp. VI:** 272, 277

"Poem Read at the Dinner Given to the Author by the Medical Profession" (Holmes), **Supp. I Part 1:** 310–311

Poems (Auden), **Supp. II Part 1:** 6

Poems (Berryman), **I:** 170

Poems (Bryant), **II:** 311; **Supp. I Part 1:** 155, 157

Poems (Cummings), **I:** 430, 447

Poems (Eliot), **I:** 580, 588; **IV:** 122; **Retro. Supp. I:** 59, 291

Poems (Emerson), **II:** 7, 8, 12–13, 17

Poems (E. Stoddard), **Supp. XV:** 274

Poems (Holmes), **Supp. I Part 1:** 303

Poems (Koch), **Supp. XV:** 179

Poems (Lowell), **Supp. I Part 2:** 405

Poems (Moore), **III:** 194, 205, 215

Poems (Poe), **III:** 411

Poems (Reznikoff), **Supp. XIV:**282, 283, 284, 285

Poems (Tate), **IV:** 121

Poems (Winters), **Supp. II Part 2:** 809, 810

Poems (Wordsworth), **I:** 468

Poems (W. C. Williams), **Retro. Supp. I:** 412–413, 416, 424

Poems (W. J. Smith), **Supp. XIII:** 332

Poems 1940–1953 (Shapiro), **Supp. II Part 2:** 703, 711

Poems 1947–1954 (Kees), **Supp. XV:** 147

Poems 1957–1967 (Dickey), **Supp. IV Part 1:** 178, 181

Poems, 1909–1925 (Eliot), **Retro. Supp. I:** 64

Poems, 1924–1933 (MacLeish), **III:** 7, 15

Poems, 1943–1956 (Wilbur), **Supp. III Part 2:** 554

Poems: 1947–1957 (W. J. Smith), **Supp. XIII:** 333

Poems: North & South–A Cold Spring,

(Bishop), **Supp. I Part 1:** 83, 89

Poems, The (Freneau), **Supp. II Part 1:** 263

Poems 1918–1975 : The Complete Poems of Charles Reznikoff (Cooney, ed.), **Supp. XIV:**289

Poems about God (Ransom), **III:** 484, 486, 491; **IV:** 121

"Poems about Painting" (Snodgrass), **Supp. VI:** 316

Poems and Essays (Ransom), **III:** 486, 490, 492

Poems and New Poems (Bogan), **Supp. III Part 1:** 60–62

"Poems and Places" (Haines), **Supp. XII:** 203

Poems and Poetry of Europe, The (Longfellow, ed.), **Retro. Supp. II:** 155

Poems by Emily Dickinson (Todd and Higginson, eds.), **I:** 469, 470; **Retro. Supp. I:** 35, 39

Poems by Emily Dickinson, Second Series (Todd and Higginson, eds.), **I:** 454; **Retro. Supp. I:** 35

Poems by Emily Dickinson, The (Bianchi and Hampson, eds.), **Retro. Supp. I:** 35

Poems by Emily Dickinson, Third Series (Todd, ed.), **Retro. Supp. I:** 35

Poems by James Russell Lowell, Second Series (Lowell), **Supp. I Part 2:** 406, 409

Poems by Sidney Lanier, (Lanier), **Supp. I Part 1:** 364

Poems from Black Africa (Hughes, ed.), **Supp. I Part 1:** 344

"Poems I Have Lost, The" (Ortiz), **Supp. IV Part 2:** 507

Poems of a Jew (Shapiro), **Supp. II Part 2:** 703, 712–713

Poems of Anna Akhmatova, The (Kunitz and Hayward, trans.), **Supp. III Part 1:** 269

Poems of Emily Dickinson, The (Bianchi and Hampson, eds.), **Retro. Supp. I:** 35

Poems of Emily Dickinson, The (Johnson, ed.), **I:** 470

Poems of François Villon (Kinnell, trans.), **Supp. III Part 1:** 235, 243, 249

"Poems of Our Climate, The" (Stevens), **Retro. Supp. I:** 313

Poems of Philip Freneau, Written Chiefly during the Late War (Freneau), **Supp. II Part 1:** 261

Poems of Places (Longfellow, ed.), **II:** 490; **Retro. Supp. II:** 155; **Supp. I Part 1:** 368

Poems of Stanley Kunitz, The (Kunitz), **Supp. III Part 1:** 258, 263, 264, 266, 268

"Poems of These States" (Ginsberg), **Supp. II Part 1:** 323, 325

Poems of Two Friends (Howells and Piatt), **II:** 273, 277

"POEM SOME PEOPLE WILL HAVE TO UNDERSTAND, A" (Baraka), **Supp. II Part 1:** 49

Poems on Slavery (Longfellow), **II:** 489; **Retro. Supp. II:** 157, 168; **Supp. I Part 2:** 406

Poems on Various Subjects (Rowson), **Supp. XV:** 232

Poem Spoken at the Public Commencement at Yale College, in New Haven; September 1, 1781, A (Barlow), **Supp. II Part 1:** 67–68, 74, 75

Poems to Solve (Swenson), **Supp. IV Part 2:** 642

Poems Written and Published during the American Revolutionary War (Freneau), **Supp. II Part 1:** 273, 274

Poems Written between the Years 1768 and 1794 (Freneau), **Supp. II Part 1:** 269

"Poem That Took the Place of a Mountain" (Olson), **Supp. II Part 2:** 582

"Poem to My First Lover" (Olds), **Supp. X:** 206

"Poem to the Reader" (Olds), **Supp. X:** 213

"Poem with No Ending, A" (Levine), **Supp. V:** 186, 190

"Poem You Asked For, The" (Levis), **Supp. XI:** 259–260

Poe Poe Poe Poe Poe Poe Poe (Hoffman), **Retro. Supp. II:** 265

Poesía Náhuatl, **Supp. XV:** 77

Poésies 1917–1920 (Cocteau), **Retro. Supp. I:** 82

"Poesis: A Conceit" (Sobin), **Supp. XVI:**288

"Poet, The" (Dunbar), **Supp. II Part 1:** 207, 209–210

"Poet, The" (Emerson), **II:** 13, 19, 20, 170

"Poet, The" (Ortiz), **Supp. IV Part 2:** 505

"Poet and His Book, The" (Millay), **III:** 126, 138

"Poet and His Public, The" (Jarrell), **Supp. I Part 1:** 96

"Poet and His Song, The" (Dunbar), **Supp. II Part 1:** 199

"Poet and the Person, The" (Kinard), **Supp. XIV:**127

"Poet and the World, The" (Cowley),

Supp. II Part 1: 145

"Poet as Anti-Specialist, The" (Swenson), **Supp. IV Part 2:** 638, 643

"Poet as *Curandera*" (Mora), **Supp. XIII:** 214, 220

"Poet as Hero, The: Keats in His Letters" (Trilling), **Supp. III Part 2:** 506–507

"Poet as Religious Moralist, The" (Larson), **Supp. XI:** 328

"Poet at Seven, The" (Rimbaud), **II:** 545

Poet at the Breakfast-Table, The (Holmes), **Supp. I Part 1:** 313–314

"Poète contumace, Le" (Corbiere), **II:** 384–385

"Poet for President, A" (Mora), **Supp. XIII:** 220–221

Poetic Achievement of Ezra Pound, The (Alexander), **Retro. Supp. I:** 293

Poetic Diction: A Study in Meaning (Barfield), **III:** 274, 279

"Poetic Principle, The" (Poe), **III:** 421, 426; **Retro. Supp. II:** 266

"Poetics" (Ammons), **Supp. VII:** 29–30

Poetics (Aristotle), **III:** 422; **Supp. XI:** 249; **Supp. XIII:** 75; **Supp. XIV:**243; **Supp. XV:** 265

Poetics of Space, The (Bachelard), **Supp. XIII:** 225; **Supp. XVI:**292

"Poetics of the Periphery: Literary Experimentalism in Kathy Acker's *In Memoriam to Identity*" (Acker), **Supp. XII:** 17

"Poetics of the Physical World, The" (Kinnell), **Supp. III Part 1:** 239

Poet in the World, The (Levertov), **Supp. III Part 1:** 271, 273, 278, 282

"Poet or the Growth of a Lit'ry Figure" (White), **Supp. I Part 2:** 676

Poetry (Barber), **Supp. IV Part 2:** 550

"Poetry" (Moore), **III:** 204–205, 215

"Poetry" (Nye), **Supp. XIII:** 282

"Poetry: A Metrical Essay" (Holmes), **Supp. I Part 1:** 310

"Poetry, Community and Climax" (Snyder), **Supp. VIII:** 290

"Poetry and Belief in Thomas Hardy" (Schwartz), **Supp. II Part 2:** 666

Poetry and Criticism (Nemerov, ed.), **III:** 269

"Poetry and Drama" (Eliot), **I:** 588

Poetry and Fiction: Essays (Nemerov), **III:** 269, 281

"Poetry and Place" (Berry), **Supp. X:** 22, 28, 31, 32

Poetry and Poets (Lowell), **II:** 512

Poetry and the Age (Jarrell), **IV:** 352; **Retro. Supp. I:** 121; **Supp. II Part 1:** 135

"Poetry and the Primitive: Notes on Poetry as an Ecological Survival Technique" (Snyder), **Supp. VIII:** 291, 292, 299, 300

"Poetry and the Public World" (MacLeish), **III:** 11

Poetry and the World (Pinsky), **Supp. VI:** 236, 239, 244, 247

Poetry and Truth (Olson), **Supp. II Part 2:** 583

"Poetry As a Way of Life" (Bishop interview), **Retro. Supp. II:** 53

"Poetry as Survival" (Harrison), **Supp. VIII:** 45

Poetry for Students (Taibl), **Supp. XV:** 255

"Poetry for the Advanced" (Baraka), **Supp. II Part 1:** 58

Poetry Handbook, A (Oliver), **Supp. VII:** 229, 245

"Poetry of Barbarism, The" (Santayana), **IV:** 353

Poetry of Chaucer, The (Gardner), **Supp. VI:** 63

Poetry of Meditation, The (Martz), **IV:** 151; **Supp. I Part 1:** 107

Poetry of Mourning: The Modern Elegy from Hardy to Heaney (Ramazani), **Supp. IV Part 2:** 450

Poetry of Stephen Crane, The (Hoffman), **I:** 405

Poetry of the Negro 1746–1949, The (Hughes, ed.), **Supp. I Part 1:** 345

Poetry Reading against the Vietnam War, A (Bly and Ray, eds.), **Supp. IV Part 1:** 61, 63

"Poetry Wreck, The" (Shapiro), **Supp. II Part 2:** 717

Poetry Wreck, The: Selected Essays (Shapiro), **Supp. II Part 2:** 703, 704, 717

"Poets" (X. J. Kennedy), **Supp. XV:** 158

Poet's Alphabet, A: Reflections on the Literary Art and Vocation (Bogan), **Supp. III Part 1:** 55, 64

Poets and Poetry of America (Griswold), **Supp. XV:** 277

Poet's Choice (Engle and Langland, eds.), **III:** 277, 542

Poets of the Old Testament, The (Gordon), **III:** 199

Poets of Today (Wheelock, ed.), **Supp. IV Part 2:** 639

Poets on Poetry (Nemerov, ed.), **III:** 269

"Poet's Tact, and a Necessary Tactless-

ness, The" (C. Frost), **Supp. XV:** 94–95

"Poet's View, A" (Levertov), **Supp. III Part 1:** 284

"Poet's Voice, The" (Oliver), **Supp. VII:** 245

"Poet Turns on Himself, The" (Dickey), **Supp. IV Part 1:** 177, 181, 185

Poganuc People (Stowe), **Supp. I Part 2:** 581, 596, 599–600

Pogo (comic strip), **Supp. XI:** 105

Poincaré, Raymond, **IV:** 320

"Point, The" (Hayden), **Supp. II Part 1:** 373

"Point at Issue!, A" (Chopin), **Retro. Supp. II:** 61; **Supp. I Part 1:** 208

Point of No Return (Marquand), **III:** 56, 59–60, 65, 67, 69

Point Reyes Poems (R. Bly), **Supp. IV Part 1:** 71

Points for a Compass Rose (Connell), **Supp. XIV:** 79, 80, 96

"Point Shirley" (Plath), **Supp. I Part 2:** 529, 538

Points in Time (Bowles), **Supp. IV Part 1:** 93

"Points West" (column), **Supp. IV Part 1:** 198

Poirier, Richard, **I:** 136, 239; **III:** 34; **Retro. Supp. I:** 134; **Retro. Supp. II:** 207–208; **Supp. I Part 2:** 660, 665; **Supp. IV Part 2:** 690

Poison Pen (Garrett), **Supp. VII:** 111

Poisonwood Bible, The (Kingsolver), **Supp. VII:** 197–198, 202, 210–213

Poitier, Sidney, **Supp. IV Part 1:** 360, 362

"Polar Bear" (Heller), **Supp. IV Part 1:** 383

Pole, Rupert, **Supp. X:** 185

"Pole Star" (MacLeish), **III:** 16

Po Li, **Supp. I Part 1:** 262

Police (Baraka), **Supp. II Part 1:** 47

"Police" (Corso), **Supp. XII:** 117, 127

"Police Court Saturday Morning" (X. J. Kennedy), **Supp. XV:** 170

"Police Dreams" (Bausch), **Supp. VII:** 47

Politian (Poe), **III:** 412

"Political and Practical Conceptions of Race, The" (Locke), **Supp. XIV:** 209–210

Political Essays (Lowell), **Supp. I Part 2:** 407

Political Fable, A (Coover), **Supp. V:** 44, 46, 47, 49, 51

"Political Fables" (Mather), **Supp. II Part 2:** 450

"Political Interests" (Stevens), **Retro. Supp. I:** 295

"Political Litany, A" (Freneau), **Supp. II Part 1:** 257

"Political Pastoral" (Frost), **Retro. Supp. I:** 139

"Political Poem" (Baraka), **Supp. II Part 1:** 36

Politics (Acker), **Supp. XII:** 3, 4

Politics (Macdonald), **I:** 233–234

"Politics" (Paley), **Supp. VI:** 217

"Politics, Structure, and Poetic Development" (McCombs), **Supp. XIII:** 33

"Politics and the English Language" (Orwell), **Retro. Supp. II:** 287; **Supp. I Part 2:** 620

Politics and the Novel (Howe), **Supp. VI:** 113

"Politics and the Personal Lyric in the Poetry of Joy Harjo and C. D. Wright" (Goodman), **Supp. XV:** 344

"Politics of Ethnic Authorship, The: Li-Young Lee, Emerson, and Whitman at the Banquet Table" (Partridge), **Supp. XV:** 219

"Politics of Silence, The" (Monette), **Supp. X:** 148

Politt, Katha, **Supp. XII:** 159

Polk, James, **Supp. XIII:** 20

Polk, James K., **I:** 17; **II:** 433–434

Pollack, Sydney, **Supp. XIII:** 159

"Pollen" (Nye), **Supp. XIII:** 284

Pollitt, Katha, **Supp. X:** 186, 191, 193; **Supp. XVI:** 39

Pollock, Jackson, **IV:** 411, 420; **Supp. XV:** 145, 177, 178

"Polly" (Chopin), **Retro. Supp. II:** 72

Polo, Marco, **III:** 395

Polybius, **Supp. I Part 2:** 491

"Polydore" (Chopin), **Retro. Supp. II:** 66

"Pomegranate" (Glück), **Supp. V:** 82

"Pomegranate Seed" (Wharton), **IV:** 316; **Retro. Supp. I:** 382

Ponce de Leon, Luis, **III:** 391

"Pond, The" (Nemerov), **III:** 272

"Pond at Dusk, The" (Kenyon), **Supp. VII:** 168

Ponder Heart, The (Welty), **IV:** 261, 274–275, 281; **Retro. Supp. I:** 351–352

"Ponderosa Pine" (Huncke), **Supp. XIV:** 146

"Pony" (Sanders), **Supp. XVI:** 277

Poodle Springs (Parker and Chandler), **Supp. IV Part 1:** 135

Poodle Springs Story, The (Chandler), **Supp. IV Part 1:** 135

"Pool, The" (Doolittle), **Supp. I Part

1: 264–265

Poole, Ernest, **II:** 444

"Pool Lights" (F. Barthelme), **Supp. XI:** 25, 26–27, 36

"Pool Room in the Lions Club" (Merwin), **Supp. III Part 1:** 346

"Poor Black Fellow" (Hughes), **Retro. Supp. I:** 204

"Poor Bustard, The" (Corso), **Supp. XII:** 134

"Poor but Happy" (Mamet), **Supp. XIV:**252, 253

Poore, Charles, **III:** 364

Poor Fool (Caldwell), **I:** 291, 292, 308

Poorhouse Fair, The (Updike), **IV:** 214, 228–229, 232; **Retro. Supp. I:** 317, 320

"Poor Joanna" (Jewett), **II:** 394

"Poor Man's Pudding and Rich Man's Crumbs" (Melville), **III:** 89–90

"Poor Richard" (James), **II:** 322

Poor Richard's Almanac (undated) (Franklin), **II:** 112

Poor Richard's Almanac for 1733 (Franklin), **II:** 108, 110

Poor Richard's Almanac for 1739 (Franklin), **II:** 112

Poor Richard's Almanac for 1758 (Franklin), **II:** 101

Poor White (Anderson), **I:** 110–111

"Poor Working Girl" (Z. Fitzgerald), **Supp. IX:** 71

Popa, Vasko, **Supp. VIII:** 272

Pope, Alexander, **I:** 198, 204; **II:** 17, 114; **III:** 263, 267, 288, 517; **IV:** 145; **Retro. Supp. I:** 335; **Supp. I Part 1:** 150, 152, 310; **Supp. I Part 2:** 407, 422, 516, 714; **Supp. II Part 1:** 70, 71; **Supp. X:** 32, 36; **Supp. XII:** 260; **Supp. XV:** 258

Pope-Hennessy, James, **Supp. XIV:**348

"Pope's Penis, The" (Olds), **Supp. X:** 207

"Poplar, Sycamore" (Wilbur), **Supp. III Part 2:** 549

Popo and Fifina (Hughes and Bontemps), **Retro. Supp. I:** 203

"Poppies" (Oliver), **Supp. VII:** 240

"Poppies in July" (Plath), **Supp. I Part 2:** 544

"Poppies in October" (Plath), **Supp. I Part 2:** 544

"Poppycock" (Francis), **Supp. IX:** 87

"Poppy Seed" (Lowell), **II:** 523

Popular Culture (Goldbarth), **Supp. XII:** 186

Popular History of the United States (Gay), **Supp. I Part 1:** 158

"Popular Songs" (Ashbery), **Supp. III Part 1:** 6

"Populist Manifesto" (Ferlinghetti), **Supp. VIII:** 290

"Porcelain Bowl" (Glück), **Supp. V:** 83

Porcher, Frances, **Retro. Supp. II:** 71

"Porcupine, The" (Kinnell), **Supp. III Part 1:** 244

Porcupine's Kiss, The (Dobyns), **Supp. XIII:** 89–90

Porgy and Bess (film), **Supp. I Part 1:** 66

Porgy and Bess (play), **Supp. IV Part 1:** 6

"Porphyria's Lover" (Browning), **II:** 522

Portable Beat Reader, The (Charters, ed.), **Supp. XIV:**152

Portable Blake, The (Kazin, ed.), **Supp. VIII:** 103

Portable Faulkner, The (Cowley, ed.), **II:** 57, 59; **Retro. Supp. I:** 73

Portable Paul and Jane Bowles, The (Dillon), **Supp. IV Part 1:** 95

Portable Veblen, The (Veblen), **Supp. I Part 2:** 630, 650

"Porte-Cochere" (Taylor), **Supp. V:** 320

"Porter" (Hughes), **Supp. I Part 1:** 327

Porter, Bern, **III:** 171

Porter, Cole, **Supp. IX:** 189

Porter, Eliot, **Supp. IV Part 2:** 599

Porter, Fairfield, **Supp. XV:** 178

Porter, Herman W., **Supp. I Part 1:** 49

Porter, Horace, **Retro. Supp. II:** 4, 127

Porter, Jacob, **Supp. I Part 1:** 153

Porter, Katherine Anne, **I:** 97, 385; **II:** 194, 606; **III:** 433–455, 482; **IV:** 26, 138, 246, 261, 279, 280, 282; **Retro. Supp. I:** 354; **Retro. Supp. II:** 233, 235; **Supp. IV Part 1:** 31, 310; **Supp. V:** 225; **Supp. VIII:** 156, 157; **Supp. IX:** 93, 94, 95, 98, 128; **Supp. X:** 50; **Supp. XIII:** 294; **Supp. XIV:**3; **Supp. XV:** 338

Porter, Noah, **Supp. I Part 2:** 640

Porter, William Sydney. *See* Henry, O.

Porteus, Beilby, **Supp. I Part 1:** 150

"Portland Going Out, The" (Merwin), **Supp. III Part 1:** 345

Portnoy's Complaint (Roth), **Retro. Supp. II:** 282–286, 291; **Supp. III Part 2:** 401, 404, 405, 407, 412–414, 426; **Supp. V:** 119, 122; **Supp. XI:** 140

Port of Saints (Burroughs), **Supp. III Part 1:** 106

"Portrait" (Dixon), **Supp. XII:** 154

"Portrait, A" (Parker), **Supp. IX:** 192–193

"Portrait, The" (Kunitz), **Supp. III Part 1:** 263

"Portrait, The" (Wharton), **Retro. Supp. I:** 364

"Portrait d'une Femme" (Pound), **Retro. Supp. I:** 288

Portrait in Brownstone (Auchincloss), **Supp. IV Part 1:** 21, 23, 27, 31

"Portrait in Georgia" (Toomer), **Supp. IX:** 314

"Portrait in Greys, A" (W. C. Williams), **Retro. Supp. I:** 416

"Portrait of a Girl in Glass" (T. Williams), **IV:** 383

"Portrait of a Jewelry Drummer" (Untermeyer), **Supp. XV:** 299–300

"Portrait of a Lady" (Eliot), **I:** 569, 570, 571, 584; **III:** 4; **Retro. Supp. I:** 55, 56, 62

Portrait of a Lady, The (James), **I:** 10, 258, 461–462, 464; **II:** 323, 325, 327, 328–329, 334; **Retro. Supp. I:** 215, 216, 217, 219, 220, 223, 224–225, 232, 233, 381

"Portrait of an Artist" (Roth), **Supp. III Part 2:** 412

Portrait of an Eye: Three Novels (Acker), **Supp. XII:** 6, 7–9

"Portrait of an Invisible Man" (Auster), **Supp. XII:** 21

"Portrait of a Supreme Court Judge" (Untermeyer), **Supp. XV:** 299

Portrait of Bascom Hawkes, A (Wolfe), **IV:** 451–452, 456

Portrait of Edith Wharton (Lubbock), **Retro. Supp. I:** 366

Portrait of Logan Pearsall Smith, Drawn from His Letters and Diaries, A (Russell, ed.), **Supp. XIV:**349

Portrait of Picasso as a Young Man (Mailer), **Retro. Supp. II:** 213

"Portrait of the Artist as an Old Man, A" (Humphrey), **Supp. IX:** 109

Portrait of the Artist as a Young Man, A (Joyce), **I:** 475–476; **III:** 471, 561; **Retro. Supp. I:** 127; **Retro. Supp. II:** 4, 331; **Supp. IX:** 236; **Supp. XIII:** 53, 95

"Portrait of the Artist with Hart Crane" (Wright), **Supp. V:** 342

"Portrait of the Intellectual as a Yale Man" (McCarthy), **II:** 563, 564–565

"Portrait of the Self . . . , A" (Sobin), **Supp. XVI:**288

Portraits and Elegies (Schnackenberg), **Supp. XV:** 249, 253–256

"Port Town" (Hughes), **Retro. Supp. I:** 199

Portuguese Voyages to America in the Fifteenth Century (Morison), **Supp. I Part 2:** 488

"Po' Sandy" (Chesnutt), **Supp. XIV:**60

Poseidon Adventure, The (film), **Supp. XII:** 321

Poseidon Adventure, The (Gallico), **Supp. XVI:**238

"Poseidon and Company" (Carver), **Supp. III Part 1:** 137

"Positive Obsession" (O. Butler), **Supp. XIII:** 70

Poss, Stanley, **Supp. XIV:**166

"Possessions" (H. Crane), **I:** 392–393; **Retro. Supp. II:** 78

Possible World, A (Koch), **Supp. XV:** 184

Postal Inspector (film), **Supp. XIII:** 166

Postcards (Proulx), **Supp. VII:** 249, 256–258, 262

"Postcolonial Tale, A" (Harjo), **Supp. XII:** 227

"Posthumous Letter to Gilbert White" (Auden), **Supp. II Part 1:** 26

"Post-Larkin Triste" (Karr), **Supp. XI:** 242–243

Postlethwaite, Diana, **Supp. XII:** 317–318; **Supp. XVI:**176

"Postlude" (W. C. Williams), **Retro. Supp. I:** 415

Postman, Neil, **Supp. XI:** 275

Postman Always Rings Twice, The (Cain), **Supp. XIII:** 165–166

Postman Always Rings Twice, The (film), **Supp. XIV:**241

"Postmortem Guide, A" (Dunn), **Supp. XI:** 155

Postrel, Virginia, **Supp. XIV:**298, 311

"Postscript" (Du Bois), **Supp. II Part 1:** 173

"Postscript" (Nye), **Supp. XIII:** 287

"Potato" (Wilbur), **Supp. III Part 2:** 545

"Potatoes' Dance, The" (Lindsay), **Supp. I Part 2:** 394

Pot of Earth, The (MacLeish), **III:** 5, 6–8, 10, 12, 18

"Pot Roast" (Strand), **Supp. IV Part 2:** 629

Pot Shots at Poetry (Francis), **Supp. IX:** 83–84

Potter, Beatrix, **Supp. I Part 2:** 656; **Supp. XVI:**100

Potter, Stephen, **IV:** 430

Potter's House, The (Stegner), **Supp. IV Part 2:** 598, 606

Poulenc, Francis, **Supp. IV Part 1:** 81

Poulin, Al, Jr., **Supp. IX:** 272; **Supp. XI:** 259

Pound, Ezra, **I:** 49, 58, 60, 66, 68, 69, 105, 236, 243, 256, 384, 403, 428, 429, 475, 476, 482, 487, 521, 578; **II:** 26, 55, 168, 263, 316, 371, 376, 513, 517, 520, 526, 528, 529, 530; **III:** 2, 5, 8, 9, 13–14, 17, 174, 194, 196, 278, 430, 453, 456–479, 492, 504, 511, 523, 524, 527, 575–576, 586, 590; **IV:** 27, 28, 407, 415, 416, 433, 446; **Retro. Supp. I:** 51, 52, 55, 58, 59, 63, 82, 89, 127, 140, 171, 177, 178, 198, 216, 283–294, 298, 299, 359, 411, 412, 413, 414, 417, 418, 419, 420, 423, 426, 427, 430, 431; **Retro. Supp. II:** 178, 183, 189, 326; **Supp. I Part 1:** 253, 255–258, 261–268, 272, 274; **Supp. I Part 2:** 387, 721; **Supp. II Part 1:** 1, 8, 20, 30, 91, 136; **Supp. III Part 1:** 48, 63, 64, 73, 105, 146, 225, 271; **Supp. III Part 2:** 542, 609–617, 619, 620, 622, 625, 626, 628, 631; **Supp. IV Part 1:** 153, 314; **Supp. V:** 331, 338, 340, 343, 345; **Supp. VIII:** 39, 105, 195, 205, 271, 290, 291, 292, 303; **Supp. IX:** 291; **Supp. X:** 24, 36, 112, 120, 122; **Supp. XII:** 97; **Supp. XIV:**11, 55, 83, 272, 284, 286, 287, 347; **Supp. XV:** 20, 42, 43, 51, 93, 161, 181, 297, 298, 299, 301, 302, 306; **Supp. XVI:**47, 282

Pound, Louise, **Retro. Supp. I:** 4; **Supp. XV:** 137

Pound, T. S., **I:** 428

"Pound Reweighed" (Cowley), **Supp. II Part 1:** 143

Powell, Betty, **Retro. Supp. II:** 140

Powell, Dawn, **Supp. IV Part 2:** 678, 682

Powell, Dick, **Supp. IX:** 250

Powell, John Wesley, **Supp. IV Part 2:** 598, 604, 611

Powell, Lawrence Clark, **III:** 189

Powell, William, **Supp. IV Part 1:** 355

"Power" (Corso), **Supp. XII:** 117, 126, 127, 128

"Power" (Emerson), **II:** 2, 3

"Power" (Rich), **Supp. I Part 2:** 569

"Power and Light" (Dickey), **Supp. IV Part 1:** 182

Power and the Glory, The (Greene), **III:** 556

"Powerhouse" (Welty), **Retro. Supp. I:** 343, 346

"Power Never Dominion" (Rukeyser), **Supp. VI:** 281

"Power of Fancy, The" (Freneau), **Supp. II Part 1:** 255

Power of Myth, The (Campbell), **Supp. IX:** 245

"Power of Prayer, The" (Lanier), **Supp. I Part 1:** 357

"Power of Stories, The" (Sanders), **Supp. XVI:**278

"Power of Suggestion" (Auchincloss), **Supp. IV Part 1:** 33

Power of Sympathy, The (Brown), **Supp. II Part 1:** 74

Power Politics (Atwood), **Supp. XIII:** 20, 33–34, 35

Powers, J. F., **Supp. V:** 319

Powers, Kim, **Supp. VIII:** 329, 340

Powers, Richard, **Supp. IX:** 207–225

Powers of Attorney (Auchincloss), **Supp. IV Part 1:** 31, 32, 33

"Powers of Darkness" (Wharton), **Retro. Supp. I:** 379

Powys, John Cowper, **Supp. I Part 2:** 454, 476; **Supp. IX:** 135

Poynton, Jerome, **Supp. XIV:**147, 150

Practical Agitation (Chapman), **Supp. XIV:**41

Practical Criticism: A Study of Literary Judgment (Richards), **Supp. XIV:**3, 16

Practical Magic (film), **Supp. X:** 80

Practical Magic (Hoffman), **Supp. X:** 78, 82, 88–89

"Practical Methods of Meditation, The" (Dawson), **IV:** 151

Practical Navigator, The (Bowditch), **Supp. I Part 2:** 482

Practice of Perspective, The (Dubreuil), **Supp. IV Part 2:** 425

Practice of Reading, The (Donoghue), **Supp. VIII:** 189

Pragmatism: A New Name for Some Old Ways of Thinking (James), **II:** 352

"Pragmatism's Conception of Truth" (James), **Supp. XIV:**40

Prague Orgy, The (Roth), **Retro. Supp. II:** 280

"Praire, The" (Clampitt), **Supp. IX:** 42

"Prairie" (Sandburg), **III:** 583, 584

Prairie, The (Cooper), **I:** 339, 342

"Prairie Birthday" (Leopold), **Supp. XIV:**185

Prairie Home Companion, A (Keillor, radio program), **Supp. XIII:** 274; **Supp. XVI:**169–171, 173–178

Prairie Home Morning Show, A (Keillor, radio program), **Supp. XVI:**171

"Prairie Life, A Citizen Speaks" (Dunn), **Supp. XI:** 145

"Prairies, The" (Bryant), **Supp. I Part 1:** 157, 162, 163, 166

Praise (Hass), **Supp. VI:** 104–105, 106
"Praise for an Urn" (Crane), **I:** 388
"Praise for Sick Women" (Snyder), **Supp. VIII:** 294
"Praise in Summer" (Wilbur), **Supp. III Part 2:** 546–548, 560, 562
"Praise of a Palmtree" (Levertov), **Supp. III Part 1:** 284
"Praise of the Committee" (Rukeyser), **Supp. VI:** 278
"Praises, The" (Goldbarth), **Supp. XII:** 185
"Praises, The" (Olson), **Supp. II Part 2:** 558, 560, 563, 564
Praises and Dispraises (Des Pres), **Supp. X:** 120
Praisesong for the Widow (Marshall), **Supp. IV Part 1:** 14; **Supp. XI:** 18, 276, 278, 284–286, 287
"Praise to the End!" (Roethke), **III:** 529, 532, 539
Prajadhipok, King of Siam, **I:** 522
Prater Violet (Isherwood), **Supp. XIV:**164–166, 169–170, 171
Pratt, Anna (Anna Alcott), **Supp. I Part 1:** 33
Pratt, Louis H., **Retro. Supp. II:** 6
Pratt, Mary Louise, **Retro. Supp. II:** 48
Pratt, Parley, **Supp. IV Part 2:** 603
"Prattler" (newspaper column), **I:** 207
"Prattler, The" (Bierce), **I:** 196
"Prayer" (Gioia), **Supp. XV:** 117
"Prayer" (Olds), **Supp. X:** 204
"Prayer" (Toomer), **Supp. IX:** 318
"Prayer, A" (Kushner), **Supp. IX:** 134
"Prayer for Columbus" (Whitman), **IV:** 348
"Prayer for My Daughter" (Yeats), **II:** 598
"Prayer for My Grandfather to Our Lady, A" (Lowell), **II:** 541–542
"Prayer for my Son" (C. Frost), **Supp. XV:** 98–99
Prayer for Owen Meany, A (Irving), **Supp. VI:** 164, 165, 166, 175–176
"PRAYER FOR SAVING" (Baraka), **Supp. II Part 1:** 52–53
"Prayer in Spring, A" (Frost), **II:** 153, 164
"Prayer on All Saint's Day" (Cowley), **Supp. II Part 1:** 138, 153
Prayers for Dark People (Du Bois), **Supp. II Part 1:** 186
"Prayer to Hermes" (Creeley), **Supp. IV Part 1:** 156, 157
"Prayer to Masks" (Senghor), **Supp. IV Part 1:** 16
"Prayer to the Child of Prague" (Salinas), **Supp. XIII:** 327

"Prayer to the Good Poet" (Wright), **Supp. III Part 2:** 603
"Prayer to the Pacific" (Silko), **Supp. IV Part 2:** 560
"Pray without Ceasing" (Emerson), **II:** 9–10
Praz, Mario, **IV:** 430
"Preacher, The" (Whittier), **Supp. I Part 2:** 698–699
Preacher and the Slave, The (Stegner), **Supp. IV Part 2:** 599, 608, 609
Precaution (Cooper), **I:** 337, 339
"Preconceptions of Economic Science, The" (Veblen), **Supp. I Part 2:** 634
Predecessors, Et Cetera (Clampitt), **Supp. IX:** 37
"Predicament, A" (Poe), **Retro. Supp. II:** 273
Predilections (Moore), **III:** 194
Prefaces and Prejudices (Mencken), **III:** 99, 104, 106, 119
Preface to a Twenty Volume Suicide Note. . . . (Baraka), **Supp. II Part 1:** 31, 33–34, 51, 61
"Preference" (Wylie), **Supp. I Part 2:** 713
"Prejudice against the Past, The" (Moore), **IV:** 91
Prejudices (Mencken), **Supp. I Part 2:** 630
Prejudices: A Selection (Farrell, ed.), **III:** 116
Prejudices: First Series (Mencken), **III:** 105
"Preliminary Remarks on the Poetry in the First Person" (Wright), **Supp. XV:** 339
Prelude, A: Landscapes, Characters and Conversations from the Earlier Years of My Life (Wilson), **IV:** 426, 427, 430, 434, 445
Prelude, The (Wordsworth), **III:** 528; **IV:** 331, 343; **Supp. I Part 2:** 416, 676; **Supp. XI:** 248
Prelude and Liebestod (McNally), **Supp. XIII:** 201
"Preludes" (Eliot), **I:** 573, 576, 577; **Retro. Supp. I:** 55; **Supp. IV Part 2:** 436
Preludes for Memnon (Aiken), **I:** 59, 65
Preludes from Memnon (Aiken), **Supp. X:** 50
"Prelude to an Evening" (Ransom), **III:** 491, 492–493
Prelude to Darkness (Salinas), **Supp. XIII:** 311, 318–319, 320
"Prelude to the Present" (Mumford), **Supp. II Part 2:** 471
"Premature Burial, The" (Poe), **III:**

415, 416, 418; **Retro. Supp. II:** 270
Preminger, Otto, **Supp. IX:** 3, 9
"Premonition" (Hay), **Supp. XIV:**122
"Premonitions of the Bread Line" (Komunyakaa), **Supp. XIII:** 114, 115
Prenshaw, Peggy Whitman, **Supp. X:** 229
"Preparations" (Silko), **Supp. IV Part 2:** 560
Preparatory Meditations (Taylor), **IV:** 145, 148, 149, 150, 152, 153, 154–155, 164, 165
"Prepare" (Carruth), **Supp. XVI:**59
Prepositions: The Collected Critical Essays of Louis Zukofsky (Zukofsky), **Supp. III Part 2:** 630
Prescott, Anne, **Supp. IV Part 1:** 299
Prescott, Orville, **Supp. IV Part 2:** 680; **Supp. XI:** 340
Prescott, Peter, **Supp. X:** 83
Prescott, Peter S., **Supp. XVI:**212
Prescott, William, **Retro. Supp. I:** 123
Prescott, William Hickling, **II:** 9, 310, 313–314; **IV:** 309; **Supp. I Part 2:** 414, 479, 493, 494
"Prescription of Painful Ends" (Jeffers), **Supp. II Part 2:** 424
"Presence, The" (Gordon), **II:** 199, 200
"Presence, The" (Kumin), **Supp. IV Part 2:** 445, 455
Presence and Desire: Essays on Gender, Sexuality, Performance (Dolan), **Supp. XV:** 327
"Presence of Others, The" (Kenyon), **Supp. VII:** 164
Presences (Taylor), **Supp. V:** 325
"Present Age, The" (Emerson), **II:** 11–12
Present Danger, The: Do We Have the Will to Reverse the Decline of American Power? (Podhoretz), **Supp. VIII:** 241
Present for Young Ladies, A (Rowson), **Supp. XV:** 245
"Present Hour" (Sandburg), **III:** 593–594
Present Philosophical Tendencies (Perry), **I:** 224
"Present State of Ethical Philosophy, The" (Emerson), **II:** 9
"Present State of Poetry, The" (Schwartz), **Supp. II Part 2:** 666
"Preservation of Innocence" (Baldwin), **Supp. I Part 1:** 51
"Preserving Wildness" (Berry), **Supp. X:** 28, 29, 32
"President and Other Intellectuals, The" (Kazin), **Supp. VIII:** 104
Presidential Papers, The (Mailer), **III:**

35, 37–38, 42, 45; **Retro. Supp. II:** 203, 204, 206

"Presidents" (Merwin), **Supp. III Part 1:** 351

Presnell, Robert, Sr., **Supp. XIII:** 166

"PRES SPOKE IN A LANGUAGE" (Baraka), **Supp. II Part 1:** 60

"Pretext, The" (Wharton), **Retro. Supp. I:** 371

Pretty Boy Floyd (McMurtry), **Supp. V:** 231

"Pretty Girl, The" (Dubus), **Supp. VII:** 87–88

"Pretty Mouth and Green My Eyes" (Salinger), **III:** 560

"Previous Condition" (Baldwin), **Supp. I Part 1:** 51, 55, 63

"Previous Tenant, The" (Simpson), **Supp. IX:** 278–279

Priaulx, Allan, **Supp. XI:** 228

Price, Alan, **Retro. Supp. I:** 377

Price, Reynolds, **Supp. VI:** 253–270; **Supp. IX:** 256, 257

Price, Richard, **II:** 9; **Supp. I Part 2:** 522

Price, The (A. Miller), **III:** 165–166

"Price of the Harness, The" (Crane), **I:** 414

Pricksongs & Descants; Fictions (Coover), **Supp. V:** 39, 42, 43, 49, 50

"Pride" (Hughes), **Supp. I Part 1:** 331

Pride and Prejudice (Austen), **II:** 290

Prideaux, Tom, **Supp. IV Part 2:** 574, 590

"Priesthood, The" (Winters), **Supp. II Part 2:** 786

Priestly, Joseph, **Supp. I Part 2:** 522

Primary Colors, The (A. Theroux), **Supp. VIII:** 312

"Primary Ground, A" (Rich), **Supp. I Part 2:** 563

"Prime" (Auden), **Supp. II Part 1:** 22

"Primer Class" (Bishop), **Retro. Supp. II:** 38, 51

Primer for Blacks (Brooks), **Supp. III Part 1:** 85

"Primer for the Nuclear Age" (Dove), **Supp. IV Part 1:** 246

Primer of Ignorance, A (Blackmur), **Supp. II Part 1:** 91

Primitive, The (C. Himes), **Supp. XVI:**139, 141–142

"Primitive Black Man, The" (Du Bois), **Supp. II Part 1:** 176

"Primitive Like an Orb, A" (Stevens), **IV:** 89; **Retro. Supp. I:** 309

Primitive People (Prose), **Supp. XVI:**255, 256, 257

"Primitive Singing" (Lindsay), **Supp. I**

Part 2: 389–390

Primitivism and Decadence (Winters), **Supp. II Part 2:** 786, 803–807, 812

Prince, Richard, **Supp. XII:** 4

"Prince, The" (Jarrell), **II:** 379

"Prince, The" (Winters), **Supp. II Part 2:** 802

Prince and the Pauper, The (Twain), **IV:** 200–201, 206

Prince Hagen (Sinclair), **Supp. V:** 280

Prince of a Fellow, A (Hearon), **Supp. VIII:** 58, 62–63

Princess, The (Tennyson), **Supp. I Part 2:** 410

Princess and the Goblins, The (Macdonald), **Supp. XIII:** 75

Princess Casamassima, The (James), **II:** 276, 291; **IV:** 202; **Retro. Supp. I:** 216, 221, 222, 225, 226–227

"Princess Casamassima, The" (Trilling), **Supp. III Part 2:** 502, 503

Princess of Arcady, A (Henry), **Retro. Supp. II:** 97

"Principles" (Du Bois), **Supp. II Part 1:** 172

Principles of Literary Criticism (Richards), **I:** 274; **Supp. I Part 1:** 264; **Supp. XIV:**3

Principles of Psychology, The (James), **II:** 321, 350–352, 353, 354, 357, 362, 363–364; **IV:** 28, 29, 32, 37

Principles of Zoölogy (Agassiz), **Supp. I Part 1:** 312

Prior, Matthew, **II:** 111; **III:** 521

Prior, Sir James, **II:** 315

"Prison, The" (Malamud), **Supp. I Part 2:** 431, 437

Prisoner of Second Avenue, The (Simon), **Supp. IV Part 2:** 583, 584

Prisoner of Sex, The (Mailer), **III:** 46; **Retro. Supp. II:** 206

Prisoner of Zenda, The (film), **Supp. I Part 2:** 615

Prisoner's Dilemma (Powers), **Supp. IX:** 212, 214–216, 221

Pritchard, William, **Supp. XVI:**71

Pritchard, William H., **Retro. Supp. I:** 131, 141; **Supp. IV Part 1:** 285; **Supp. IV Part 2:** 642; **Supp. XI:** 326

Pritchett, V. S., **II:** 587; **Supp. II Part 1:** 143; **Supp. VIII:** 171; **Supp. XIII:** 168

"Privatation and Publication" (Cowley), **Supp. II Part 1:** 149

Private Contentment (Price), **Supp. VI:** 263

"Private History of a Campaign That Failed" (Twain), **IV:** 195

Private Life of Axie Reed, The (Knowles), **Supp. XII:** 249

"Private Man Confronts His Vulgarities at Dawn, A" (Dunn), **Supp. XI:** 146

Private Memoirs and Confessions of a Justified Sinner, The (Hogg), **Supp. IX:** 276

"Private Property and the Common Wealth" (Berry), **Supp. X:** 25

Private Snafu series (Geisel), **Supp. XVI:**102

"Private Theatricals" (Howells), **II:** 280

Privilege, The (Kumin), **Supp. IV Part 2:** 442–444, 451

Prize Stories 1918 : The O. Henry Awards, **Supp. XVI:**16

"Probing the Dark" (Komunyakaa), **Supp. XIII:** 131

"Problem from Milton, A" (Wilbur), **Supp. III Part 2:** 550

"Problem of Anxiety, The" (Koch), **Supp. XV:** 183

"Problem of Being, The" (James), **II:** 360

Problem of Classification in the Theory of Value, The (Locke), **Supp. XIV:**199

"Problem of Housing the Negro, The" (Du Bois), **Supp. II Part 1:** 168

"Problem of the Religious Novel, The" (Isherwood), **Supp. XIV:**172

Problems and Other Stories (Updike), **Retro. Supp. I:** 322, 329

"Problem Solving" (Goldbarth), **Supp. XII:** 185

Procedures for Underground (Atwood), **Supp. XIII:** 33

"Procedures for Underground" (Atwood), **Supp. XIII:** 33

Processional (Lawson), **I:** 479

"Procession at Candlemas, A" (Clampitt), **Supp. IX:** 41

Proclus, **Retro. Supp. I:** 247

"Prodigal" (Ammons), **Supp. VII:** 29

"Prodigal, The" (Bishop), **Supp. I Part 1:** 90, 92

Prodigal Parents, The (Lewis), **II:** 454–455

"Prodigy" (Simic), **Supp. VIII:** 278

"Proem" (Crane), **I:** 397

"Proem, The: By the Carpenter" (O. Henry), **Supp. II Part 1:** 409

"Professions for Women" (Woolf), **Supp. XIII:** 305

"Professor" (Hughes), **Supp. I Part 1:** 330

"Professor, The" (Bourne), **I:** 223

Professor at the Breakfast Table, The

(Holmes), **Supp. I Part 1:** 313, 316
"Professor Clark's Economics" (Veblen), **Supp. I Part 2:** 634
Professor of Desire, The (Roth), **Retro. Supp. II:** 288; **Supp. III Part 2:** 403, 418–420
Professor's House, The (Cather), **I:** 325–336; **Retro. Supp. I:** 16
"Professor Veblen" (Mencken), **Supp. I Part 2:** 630
Proffer, Carl R., **Supp. VIII:** 22
Profits of Religion, The (Sinclair), **Supp. V:** 276
"Prognosis" (Warren), **IV:** 245
"Progress Report" (Simic), **Supp. VIII:** 278
"Project for a Trip to China" (Sontag), **Supp. II Part 2:** 454, 469
"Project for *The Ambassadors*" (James), **Retro. Supp. I:** 229
"Projection" (Nemerov), **III:** 275
"Projective Verse" (Olson), **Supp. III Part 1:** 30; **Supp. III Part 2:** 555, 556, 557, 624; **Supp. IV Part 1:** 139, 153; **Supp. VIII:** 290
"Projector, The" (Baker), **Supp. XIII:** 53, 55
Prokofiev, Sergey Sergeyevich, **Supp. IV Part 1:** 81
"Prolegomena, Section 1" (Pound), **Supp. III Part 2:** 615–616
"Prolegomena, Section 2" (Pound), **Supp. III Part 2:** 616
"Prolegomenon to a Biography of Mailer" (Lucid), **Retro. Supp. II:** 195
Proletarian Literature in the United States (Hicks), **Supp. I Part 2:** 609–610
"Prologue" (MacLeish), **III:** 8, 14
"Prologue to Our Time" (Mumford), **Supp. III Part 2:** 473
"Prometheus" (Longfellow), **II:** 494
Prometheus Bound (Lowell), **II:** 543, 544, 545, 555
Promise, The (Buck), **Supp. II Part 1:** 124
"Promise, The" (Olds), **Supp. X:** 213
Promised Land, The (M. Antin), **Supp. IX:** 227; **Supp. XVI:**148, 149
Promised Land, The (Porter), **III:** 447
Promised Lands (Sontag), **Supp. III Part 2:** 452
Promise of American Life, The (Croly), **I:** 229
"Promise of Blue Horses, The" (Harjo), **Supp. XII:** 228
Promise of Rest, The (Price), **Supp. VI:** 262, 266
Promises (Warren), **Supp. XIV:**15

Promises: Poems 1954–1956 (Warren), **IV:** 244–245, 249, 252
Promises, Promises (musical), **Supp. IV Part 2:** 575
"Promise This When You Be Dying" (Dickinson), **Retro. Supp. I:** 44, 46
Proof, The (Winters), **Supp. II Part 2:** 786, 791, 792–794
Proofs and Theories: Essays on Poetry (Glück), **Supp. V:** 77, 79, 92; **Supp. XIV:**269
"Propaganda of History, The" (Du Bois), **Supp. II Part 1:** 182
Propertius, Sextus, **III:** 467; **Retro. Supp. II:** 187; **Supp. XII:** 2
Property Of: A Novel (Hoffman), **Supp. X:** 77, 79, 80–82
"Prophecy of Samuel Sewall, The" (Whittier), **Supp. I Part 2:** 699
"Prophetic Pictures, The" (Hawthorne), **II:** 227
"Proportion" (Lowell), **II:** 525
"Proposal" (Carver), **Supp. III Part 1:** 149
Proposals Relating to the Education of Youth in Pensilvania (Franklin), **II:** 113
"Proposed New Version of the Bible" (Franklin), **II:** 110
Prose, Francine, **Supp. XII:** 333; **Supp. XVI:**249–264
"Prose for Departure" (Merrill), **Supp. III Part 1:** 336
Prose Pieces (Bynner), **Supp. XV:** 52
"Prose Poem as an Evolving Form, The" (R. Bly), **Supp. IV Part 1:** 64
"Proserpina and the Devil" (Wilder), **IV:** 358
"Prosody" (Shapiro), **Supp. II Part 2:** 710
Prospect before Us, The (Dos Passos), **I:** 491
"Prospective Immigrants Please Note" (Rich), **Supp. I Part 2:** 555
Prospect of Peace, The (Barlow), **Supp. II Part 1:** 67, 68, 75
Prospects of Literature, The (L. P. Smith), **Supp. XIV:**343
Prospects on the Rubicon (Paine), **Supp. I Part 2:** 510–511
Prospectus of a National Institution, to Be Established in the United States (Barlow), **Supp. II Part 1:** 80, 82
Prospice (Browning), **IV:** 366
"Protestant Easter" (Sexton), **Supp. II Part 2:** 684
"Prothalamion" (Schwartz), **Supp. II Part 2:** 649, 652
"Prothalamion" (Spenser), **Retro. Supp. I:** 62

Proud, Robert, **Supp. I Part 1:** 125
"Proud Farmer, The" (Lindsay), **Supp. I Part 2:** 381
Proud Flesh (Humphrey), **Supp. IX:** 94, 95, 96, 102–103, 104, 105, 109
"Proud Flesh" (Warren), **IV:** 243
"Proud Lady" (Wylie), **Supp. I Part 2:** 711–712
Proulx, Annie, **Supp. VII:** 249–267
Proust, Marcel, **I:** 89, 319, 327, 377, 461; **II:** 377, 514, 606; **III:** 174, 181, 184, 244–245, 259, 471; **IV:** 32, 201, 237, 301, 312, 328, 359, 428, 431, 434, 439, 443, 466, 467; **Retro. Supp. I:** 75, 89, 169, 335; **Supp. III Part 1:** 10, 12, 14, 15; **Supp. IV Part 2:** 600; **Supp. VIII:** 103; **Supp. IX:** 211; **Supp. X:** 193, 194; **Supp. XII:** 289; **Supp. XIV:**24, 83, 95; **Supp. XVI:**295
Proverbs, **Supp. X:** 45
"Providence" (Komunyakaa), **Supp. XIII:** 132
"Provincia deserta" (Pound), **Retro. Supp. I:** 289
"Provisional Remarks on Being / A Poet / of Arkansas" (Wright), **Supp. XV:** 337
Pruette, Lorine, **Supp. IV Part 2:** 522
Prufrock and Other Observations (Eliot), **I:** 569–570, 571, 573, 574, 576–577, 583, 584, 585; **Retro. Supp. I:** 59, 62
"Prufrock's Perivigilium" (Eliot), **Retro. Supp. I:** 57
Pryor, Richard, **Supp. XIII:** 343
Pryse, Marjorie, **Retro. Supp. II:** 139, 146
"Psalm" (Ginsberg), **Supp. II Part 1:** 312
"Psalm" (Simic), **Supp. VIII:** 282
"Psalm: Our Fathers" (Merwin), **Supp. III Part 1:** 350
"Psalm and Lament" (Justice), **Supp. VII:** 116, 117–118, 120–122, 124
"Psalm of Life, A" (Longfellow), **II:** 489, 496; **Retro. Supp. II:** 164, 168, 169; **Supp. I Part 2:** 409
"Psalm of the West" (Lanier), **Supp. I Part 1:** 362, 364
Psalms (biblical book), **I:** 83; **II:** 168, 232; **Retro. Supp. I:** 62; **Supp. I Part 1:** 125
Psalms, Hymns, and Spiritual Songs of the Rev. Isaac Watts, The (Worcester, ed.), **I:** 458
Psychiatric Novels of Oliver Wendell Holmes, The (Oberndorf), **Supp. I Part 1:** 315
Psychology: Briefer Course (James),

II: 351–352

"Psychology and Form" (Burke), **I:** 270

Psychology of Art (Malraux), **IV:** 434

Psychology of Insanity, The (Hart), **I:** 241–242, 248–250

Psychopathia Sexualis (Shanley), **Supp. XIV:** 316, 329

Psychophysiks (Fechner), **II:** 358

"Publication is the Auction" (Dickinson), **Retro. Supp. I:** 31

"Public Bath, The" (Snyder), **Supp. VIII:** 298

Public Burning, The (Coover), **Supp. IV Part 1:** 388; **Supp. V:** 44, 45, 46–47, 48, 51, 52

"Public Burning of Julius and Ethel Rosenberg, The: An Historical Romance" (Coover), **Supp. V:** 44

"Public Figure" (Hay), **Supp. XIV:** 124

"Public Garden, The" (Lowell), **II:** 550

Public Good (Paine), **Supp. I Part 2:** 509–510

Public Poetry of Robert Lowell, The (Cosgrave), **Retro. Supp. II:** 185

Public Speech: Poems (MacLeish), **III:** 15–16

Public Spirit (Savage), **II:** 111

"Puck" (Monette), **Supp. X:** 157–158

Pudd'nhead Wilson (Twain), **I:** 197

"Pudd'nhead Wilson's Calendar" (Twain), **I:** 197

"Pueblo Revolt, The" (Sando), **Supp. IV Part 2:** 510

Puella (Dickey), **Supp. IV Part 1:** 178, 185

Pulitzer, Alfred, **Retro. Supp. I:** 257

Pull Down Vanity (Fiedler), **Supp. XIII:** 103

Pullman, George, **Supp. I Part 1:** 9

"Pullman Car Hiawatha" (Wilder), **IV:** 365–366

Pull My Daisy (film), **Supp. XII:** 126–127

"Pulpit and the Pew, The" (Holmes), **Supp. I Part 1:** 302

"Pulse-Beats and Pen-Strokes" (Sandburg), **III:** 579

"Pump, The" (Humphrey), **Supp. IX:** 101

Pump House Gang, The (Wolfe), **Supp. III Part 2:** 575, 578, 580, 581

Punch, Brothers, Punch and Other Sketches (Twain), **IV:** 200

Punch: The Immortal Liar, Documents in His History (Aiken), **I:** 57, 61

Punishment Without Vengeance (Vega; Merwin, trans.), **Supp. III Part 1:** 341, 347

"Pupil" (F. Barthelme), **Supp. XI:** 26

"Pupil, The" (James), **II:** 331; **Retro. Supp. I:** 217, 219, 228

"Purchase" (Banks), **Supp. V:** 6

"Purchase of Some Golf Clubs, A" (O'Hara), **III:** 369

"Purdah" (Plath), **Supp. I Part 2:** 602

Purdy, Charles, **Supp. VIII:** 330

Purdy, James, **Supp. VII:** 269–285

Purdy, Theodore, **Supp. VIII:** 153

Pure (C. Frost), **Supp. XV:** 93, 101–102, 104, 106

"Pure" (C. Frost), **Supp. XV:** 101–102

"Pure and the Good, The: On Baseball and Backpaking" (Maclean), **Supp. XIV:** 222

"Pure Good of Theory, The" (Stevens), **Retro. Supp. I:** 310

Purgatorio (Dante), **III:** 182

Puritan Family (Morgan), **Supp. I Part 1:** 101

"Puritanical Pleasures" (Hardwick), **Supp. III Part 1:** 213–214

Puritan Origins of the American Self, The (Bercovitch), **Supp. I Part 1:** 99

Puritan Pronaos, The: Studies in the Intellectual Life of New England in the Seventeenth Century (Morison), **Supp. I Part 2:** 485

Puritans, The (P. Miller), **Supp. VIII:** 101

"Puritan's Ballad, The" (Wylie), **Supp. I Part 2:** 723

"Purloined Letter, The" (Poe), **Retro. Supp. II:** 271, 272

Purple Cane Road (Burke), **Supp. XIV:** 32, 33

Purple Decades, The (Wolfe), **Supp. III Part 2:** 584

"Purple Hat, The" (Welty), **IV:** 264

Purple Rose of Cairo, The (film; Allen), **Supp. XV:** 1, 9–10, 12, 14

Purser, John T., **Supp. XIV:** 4

"Pursuit of Happiness" (Simpson), **Supp. IX:** 279

"Pursuit of Happiness, The" (Ashbery), **Supp. III Part 1:** 23

Pursuit of the Prodigal, The (Auchincloss), **Supp. IV Part 1:** 25

Pushcart at the Curb, A (Dos Passos), **I:** 478, 479

"Pushcart Man" (Hughes), **Supp. I Part 1:** 330

Pushcart Prize, XIII, The (Ford), **Supp. V:** 58

"Pushing 100" (Mora), **Supp. XIII:** 215

Pushkin, Aleksander, **III:** 246, 261, 262; **Retro. Supp. I:** 266, 269; **Supp. XVI:** 188

Pussy, King of the Pirates (Acker), **Supp. XII:** 6–7

"Pussycat and the Expert Plumber Who Was a Man, The" (A. Miller), **III:** 146–147

Pussycat Fever (Acker), **Supp. XII:** 6

Putnam, George P., **II:** 314

Putnam, Phelps, **I:** 288

Putnam, Samuel, **II:** 26; **III:** 479; **Supp. III Part 2:** 615

"Put Off the Wedding Five Times and Nobody Comes to It" (Sandburg), **III:** 586–587

Puttenham, George, **Supp. I Part 1:** 113

Puttermesser Papers, The (Ozick), **Supp. V:** 269

"Putting on *Visit to a Small Planet*" (Vidal), **Supp. IV Part 2:** 683

Put Yourself in My Shoes (Carver), **Supp. III Part 1:** 139

"Put Yourself in My Shoes" (Carver), **Supp. III Part 1:** 139, 141

Putzi, Jennifer, **Supp. XV:** 284

Puzo, Mario, **Supp. IV Part 1:** 390

"Puzzle of Modern Society, The" (Kazin), **Supp. VIII:** 103

Pygmalion (Shaw), **Supp. XII:** 14

Pyle, Ernie, **III:** 148; **Supp. V:** 240

Pylon (Faulkner), **II:** 64–65, 73; **Retro. Supp. I:** 84, 85

Pynchon, Thomas, **III:** 258; **Retro. Supp. I:** 278; **Retro. Supp. II:** 279, 324; **Supp. II Part 2:** 557, 617–638; **Supp. III Part 1:** 217; **Supp. IV Part 1:** 53, 279; **Supp. IV Part 2:** 570; **Supp. V:** 40, 44, 52; **Supp. VIII:** 14; **Supp. IX:** 207, 208, 212; **Supp. X:** 260, 301, 302; **Supp. XI:** 103; **Supp. XII:** 289; **Supp. XIV:** 49, 53, 54, 96; **Supp. XVI:** 123, 128

Pyrah, Gill, **Supp. V:** 126

"Pyramid Club, The" (Doctorow), **Supp. IV Part 1:** 234

"Pyrography" (Ashbery), **Supp. III Part 1:** 18

Pythagoras, **I:** 332

Pythagorean Silence (Howe), **Supp. IV Part 2:** 426, 428–429

Q

"Qebehseneuf" (Goldbarth), **Supp. XII:** 186

"Quai d'Orléans" (Bishop), **Supp. I Part 1:** 89

"Quail for Mr. Forester" (Humphrey), **Supp. IX:** 94

"Quail in Autumn" (W. J. Smith), **Supp. XIII:** 334–335, 339

"Quaker Graveyard in Nantucket, The"

(Lowell), **II:** 54, 550; **Retro. Supp. II:** 178, 186–187

"Quake Theory" (Olds), **Supp. X:** 203

Qualey, Carlton C., **Supp. I Part 2:** 650

Quality of Hurt, The (C. Himes), **Supp. XVI:**137, 145

"Quality of Wine" (Carruth), **Supp. XVI:**59

"Quality Time" (Kingsolver), **Supp. VII:** 203

Quang-Ngau-chè, **III:** 473

Quarles, Francis, **I:** 178, 179

Quarry, The (Chesnutt), **Supp. XIV:**76

"Quarry, The" (Nemerov), **III:** 272

Quarry, The: New Poems (Eberhart), **I:** 532, 539

Quartermain, Peter, **Supp. IV Part 2:** 423, 434

"Quaternions, The" (Bradstreet), **Supp. I Part 1:** 104–106, 114, 122

"Quatrains for Ishi" (Komunyakaa), **Supp. XIII:** 129

"Queen of the Blues" (Brooks), **Supp. III Part 1:** 75

Queen of the Damned, The (Rice), **Supp. VII:** 290, 292–293, 297, 299

Queen of the Mob (film), **Supp. XIII:** 170

"Queens of France" (Wilder), **IV:** 365

"Queen's Twin, The" (Jewett), **Retro. Supp. II:** 138

Queen's Twin, The, and Other Stories (Jewett), **Retro. Supp. II:** 140

Queen Victoria (Strachey), **Supp. I Part 2:** 485, 494; **Supp. XIV:**342

Queer (Burroughs), **Supp. III Part 1:** 93–102

"Queer Beer" (Hansberry), **Supp. IV Part 1:** 374

"Quelques considérations sur la méthode subjective" (James), **II:** 345–346

"Question" (Swenson), **Supp. IV Part 2:** 640

"Question and Answer" (Hughes), **Retro. Supp. I:** 211

"Questioning Faces" (Frost), **Retro. Supp. I:** 141

"Question Mark in the Circle, The" (Stegner), **Supp. IV Part 2:** 597

"Questionnaire, The" (Snodgrass), **Supp. VI:** 318

"Question of Fidelity, A" (Beauvoir), **Supp. IX:** 4

"Question of Our Speech, The" (Ozick), **Supp. V:** 272

"Question of Simone de Beauvoir, The" (Algren), **Supp. IX:** 4

"Questions of Geography" (Hollander),

Supp. I Part 1: 96

Questions of Travel (Bishop), **Retro. Supp. II:** 46–48; **Supp. I Part 1:** 72, 83, 92, 94

"Questions of Travel" (Bishop), **Retro. Supp. II:** 47

"Questions to Tourists Stopped by a Pineapple Field" (Merwin), **Supp. III Part 1:** 355

"Questions without Answers" (T. Williams), **IV:** 384

"Quest of the Purple-Fringed, The" (Frost), **Retro. Supp. I:** 139

Quest of the Silver Fleece, The (Du Bois), **Supp. II Part 1:** 176–178

Quevedo y Villegas, Francisco Gómez, **Retro. Supp. I:** 423

Quickly: A Column for Slow Readers (Mailer), **Retro. Supp. II:** 202

"Quies," (Pound), **Retro. Supp. I:** 413

Quiet Days in Clichy (H. Miller), **III:** 170, 178, 183–184, 187

"Quiet Desperation" (Simpson), **Supp. IX:** 277–278

"Quiet of the Mind" (Nye), **Supp. XIII:** 284

Quindlen, Anna, **Supp. XVI:**108

Quinlan, Kathleen, **Supp. X:** 80

Quinn, John, **III:** 471

Quinn, Paul, **Supp. V:** 71

Quinn, Sister M. Bernetta, **III:** 479; **IV:** 421

Quinn, Vincent, **I:** 386, 401, 402; **Supp. I Part 1:** 270

"Quinnapoxet" (Kunitz), **Supp. III Part 1:** 263

Quinn's Book (W. Kennedy), **Supp. VII:** 133, 148–150, 153

Quintero, José, **III:** 403

Quintilian, **IV:** 123

Quinzaine for This Yule, A (Pound), **Retro. Supp. I:** 285

Quite Contrary: The Mary and Newt Story (Dixon), **Supp. XII:** 144, 153

Quod Erat Demonstrandum (Stein), **IV:** 34

Quo Vadis? (Sienkiewicz), **Supp. IV Part 2:** 518; **Supp. XVI:**182

R

Raab, Max, **Supp. XI:** 309

"Rabbi, The" (Hayden), **Supp. II Part 1:** 363, 369

Rabbit, Run (Updike), **IV:** 214, 223, 230–234; **Retro. Supp. I:** 320, 325, 326, 327, 331, 333, 335; **Supp. XI:** 140; **Supp. XII:** 298; **Supp. XVI:**220

"Rabbit, The" (Barnes), **Supp. III Part 1:** 34

Rabbit at Rest (Updike), **Retro. Supp. I:** 334

Rabbit Is Rich (Updike), **Retro. Supp. I:** 334

Rabbit novels (Updike), **Supp. V:** 269

Rabbit Redux (Updike), **IV:** 214; **Retro. Supp. I:** 332, 333

Rabbit's Umbrella, The (Plimpton), **Supp. XVI:**244

"Rabbits Who Caused All the Trouble, The" (Thurber), **Supp. I Part 2:** 610

Rabelais, and His World (Bakhtin), **Retro. Supp. II:** 273

Rabelais, François, **I:** 130; **II:** 111, 112, 302, 535; **III:** 77, 78, 174, 182; **IV:** 68; **Supp. I Part 2:** 461

Rabelais and His World (Bakhtin), **Supp. X:** 120

Rabinbach, Anson, **Supp. XII:** 166

Rabinowitz, Paula, **Supp. V:** 161

"Race" (Emerson), **II:** 6

"Race Contacts and Inter-Racial Relations" (Locke), **Supp. XIV:**211

"Race Contacts and Inter-Racial Relations: A Study in the Theory and Practice of Race" (lectures, Locke), **Supp. XIV:**199, 209

Race Contacts and Interracial Relations: Lectures on the Theory and Practice of Race (Locke, Stewart, ed.), **Supp. XIV:**196, 209–210

"'RACE LINE' IS A PRODUCT OF CAPITALISM, THE" (Baraka), **Supp. II Part 1:** 61

"Race of Life, The" (Thurber), **Supp. I Part 2:** 614

"Race Problems and Modern Society" (Toomer), **Supp. III Part 2:** 486

Race Questions, Provincialism, and Other American Problems (Royce), **Supp. XIV:**199

"Race Riot, Tulsa, 1921" (Olds), **Supp. X:** 205

Race Rock (Matthiessen), **Supp. V:** 201

"Races, The" (Lowell), **II:** 554

Rachel Carson: Witness for Nature (Lear), **Supp. IX:** 19

Rachel River (film, Smolan), **Supp. XVI:**36

"Racial Progress and Race Adjustment" (Locke), **Supp. XIV:**210

Racine, Jean Baptiste, **II:** 543, 573; **III:** 145, 151, 152, 160; **IV:** 317, 368, 370; **Supp. I Part 2:** 716

"Radical" (Moore), **III:** 211

"Radical Chic" (Wolfe), **Supp. III Part 2:** 577–578, 584, 585

Radical Chic & Mau-mauing the Flak Catchers (Wolfe), **Supp. III Part 2:** 577–578

Radical Empiricism of William James, The (Wild), **II:** 362, 363–364

Radicalism in America, The (Lasch), **I:** 259

"Radical Jewish Humanism: The Vision of E. L. Doctorow" (Clayton), **Supp. IV Part 1:** 238

"Radically Condensed History of Postindustrial Life, A" (Wallace), **Supp. X:** 309

Radinovsky, Lisa, **Supp. XV:** 284, 285

"Radio" (O'Hara), **III:** 369

Radio Days (film; Allen), **Supp. XV:** 9

"Radio Pope" (Goldbarth), **Supp. XII:** 188, 192

Raditzer (Matthiessen), **Supp. V:** 201

Radkin, Paul, **Supp. I Part 2:** 539

"Rafaela Who Drinks Coconut & Papaya Juice on Tuesdays" (Cisneros), **Supp. VII:** 63

Rafelson, Bob, **Supp. XIV:**241

Raffalovich, Marc-André, **Supp. XIV:**335

"Raft, The" (Lindsay), **Supp. I Part 2:** 393

Rag and Bone Shop of the Heart, The: Poems for Men (Bly, Hillman, and Meade, eds.), **Supp. IV Part 1:** 67

Rage in Harlem (C. Himes). See *For Love of Imabelle* (C. Himes)

Rage to Live, A (O'Hara), **III:** 361

Raglan, Lord, **I:** 135

Rago, Henry, **Supp. III Part 2:** 624, 628, 629

Ragtime (Doctorow), **Retro. Supp. II:** 108; **Supp. IV Part 1:** 217, 222–224, 231, 232, 233, 234, 237, 238; **Supp. V:** 45

"Ragtime" (Doctorow), **Supp. IV Part 1:** 234

Ragtime (film), **Supp. IV Part 1:** 236

Ragtime (musical, McNally), **Supp. XIII:** 207

Rahv, Philip, **Retro. Supp. I:** 112; **Supp. II Part 1:** 136; **Supp. VIII:** 96; **Supp. IX:** 8; **Supp. XIV:**3; **Supp. XV:** 140

"Raid" (Hughes), **Retro. Supp. I:** 208

Raids on the Unspeakable (Merton), **Supp. VIII:** 201, 208

Rail, DeWayne, **Supp. XIII:** 312

"Rain and the Rhinoceros" (Merton), **Supp. VIII:** 201

Rainbow, The (Lawrence), **III:** 27

"Rainbows" (Marquand), **III:** 56

Rainbow Tulip, The (Mora), **Supp. XIII:** 221

"Rain Country" (Haines), **Supp. XII:** 210

"Rain-Dream, A" (Bryant), **Supp. I**

Part 1: 164

Raine, Kathleen, **I:** 522, 527

"Rain Falling Now, The" (Dunn), **Supp. XI:** 147

"Rain in the Heart" (Taylor), **Supp. V:** 317, 319

Rain in the Trees, The (Merwin), **Supp. III Part 1:** 340, 342, 345, 349, 354–356

"Rainmaker, The" (Humphrey), **Supp. IX:** 101

Rainwater, Catherine, **Supp. V:** 272

"Rainy Day" (Longfellow), **II:** 498

"Rainy Day, The" (Buck), **Supp. II Part 1:** 127

"Rainy Mountain Cemetery" (Momaday), **Supp. IV Part 2:** 486

Rainy Mountain Christmas Doll (painting) (Momaday), **Supp. IV Part 2:** 493

"Rainy Season: Sub-Tropics" (Bishop), **Supp. I Part 1:** 93

"Raise High the Roof Beam, Carpenters" (Salinger), **III:** 567–569, 571

Raise High the Roof Beam, Carpenters; and Seymour: An Introduction (Salinger), **III:** 552, 567–571, 572

Raise Race Rays Raze: Essays Since 1965 (Baraka), **Supp. II Part 1:** 47, 52, 55

Raisin (musical), **Supp. IV Part 1:** 374

Raising Demons (Jackson), **Supp. IX:** 125–126

Raisin in the Sun, A (film: Columbia Pictures), **Supp. IV Part 1:** 360, 367

Raisin in the Sun, A (Hansberry), **Supp. IV Part 1:** 359, 360, 361, 362–364; **Supp. VIII:** 343

Raisin in the Sun, A (television film: American Playhouse), **Supp. IV Part 1:** 367, 374

Raisin in the Sun, A (unproduced screenplay) (Hansberry), **Supp. IV Part 1:** 360

Rajan, R., **I:** 390

"Rake, The" (Mamet), **Supp. XIV:**240

Rake's Progress, The (opera), **Supp. II Part 1:** 24

Rakosi, Carl, **Supp. III Part 2:** 614, 615, 616, 617, 618, 621, 629; **Supp. XIV:**286, 287

Ralegh, Sir Walter, **Supp. I Part 1:** 98

Raleigh, John Henry, **IV:** 366

Ramakrishna, Sri, **III:** 567

Ramakrishna and His Disciples (Isherwood), **Supp. XIV:**164

Ramazani, Jahan, **Supp. IV Part 2:** 450

"Ramble of Aphasia, A" (O. Henry),

Supp. II Part 1: 410

Ramey, Phillip, **Supp. IV Part 1:** 94

Rampersad, Arnold, **Retro. Supp. I:** 196, 200, 201, 204; **Supp. IV Part 1:** 244, 250

Rampling, Anne, **Supp. VII:** 201. *See also* Rice, Anne

Rampling, Charlotte, **Supp. IX:** 253

Ramsey, Priscilla R., **Supp. IV Part 1:** 15

Ramsey, Roger, **Supp. XVI:**69

Ramus, Petrus, **Supp. I Part 1:** 104

Rand, Ayn, **Supp. I Part 1:** 294; **Supp. IV Part 2:** 517–535

Randall, Jarrell, 1914–1965 (Lowell, Taylor, and Warren, eds.), **II:** 368, 385

Randall, John H., **III:** 605

Randolph, John, **I:** 5–6

"Range-Finding" (Frost), **Retro. Supp. I:** 131

Rangoon (F. Barthelme), **Supp. XI:** 25

Rank, Otto, **I:** 135; **Supp. IX:** 105; **Supp. X:** 183, 185, 193

Ranke, Leopold von, **Supp. I Part 2:** 492

Rankin, Daniel, **Retro. Supp. II:** 57, 72; **Supp. I Part 1:** 200, 203, 225

Ransohoff, Martin, **Supp. XI:** 305, 306

Ransom, John Crowe, **I:** 265, 301; **II:** 34, 367, 385, 389, 536–537, 542; **III:** 454, 480–502, 549; **IV:** 121, 122, 123, 124, 125, 127, 134, 140, 141, 236, 237, 433; **Retro. Supp. I:** 90; **Retro. Supp. II:** 176, 177, 178, 183, 220, 228, 246; **Supp. I Part 1:** 80, 361; **Supp. I Part 2:** 423; **Supp. II Part 1:** 90, 91, 136, 137, 139, 318; **Supp. II Part 2:** 639; **Supp. III Part 1:** 318; **Supp. III Part 2:** 542, 591; **Supp. IV Part 1:** 217; **Supp. V:** 315, 331, 337; **Supp. X:** 25, 56, 58; **Supp. XIV:**1

"Rape" (Coleman), **Supp. XI:** 89–90

"Rape, The" (Baraka), **Supp. II Part 1:** 40

Rape of Bunny Stuntz, The (Gurney), **Supp. V:** 109

"Rape of Philomel, The" (Shapiro), **Supp. II Part 2:** 720

"Rape of the Lock, The" (Pope), **Supp. XIV:**8

Raphael, **I:** 15; **III:** 505, 521, 524; **Supp. I Part 1:** 363

"Rapist" (Dunn), **Supp. XI:** 144

Rap on Race, A (Baldwin and Mead), **Supp. I Part 1:** 66

"Rappaccini's Daughter" (Hawthorne), **II:** 229

"Rapunzel" (Sexton), **Supp. II Part 2:** 691

Rare & Endangered Species: A Novella & Short Stories (Bausch), **Supp. VII:** 51, 54

"Raree Show" (MacLeish), **III:** 9

Rascoe, Burton, **III:** 106, 115

Raskin, Jonah, **Supp. XV:** 116

"Raskolnikov" (Simic), **Supp. VIII:** 282

Rasmussen, Douglas, **Supp. IV Part 2:** 528, 530

Rasselas (Johnson), **Supp. XI:** 209

Rathmann, Andrew, **Supp. XV:** 34

"Ration" (Baraka), **Supp. II Part 1:** 50

"Rationale of Verse, The" (Poe), **III:** 427–428; **Retro. Supp. II:** 266

Ratner, Rochelle, **Supp. XV:** 105

Ratner's Star (DeLillo), **Supp. VI:** 1, 2, 3, 4, 10, 12, 14

"Rat of Faith, The" (Levine), **Supp. V:** 192

Rattigan, Terence, **III:** 152

Raugh, Joseph, **Supp. I Part 1:** 286

Rauschenberg, Robert, **Supp. XV:** 187

Rauschenbusch, Walter, **III:** 293; **Supp. I Part 1:** 7

Ravelstein (Bellow), **Retro. Supp. II:** 19, 33–34

Raven, Simon, **Supp. XII:** 241

"Raven, The" (Poe), **III:** 413, 421–422, 426; **Retro. Supp. II:** 265, 266–267

Raven, The, and Other Poems (Poe), **III:** 413

Ravenal, Shannon, **Supp. IV Part 1:** 93

"Raven Days, The" (Lanier), **Supp. I Part 1:** 351

Ravenna, Michael. *See* Welty, Eudora

Raven's Road (Gunn Allen), **Supp. IV Part 1:** 330, 335

"Ravine, The" (Carruth), **Supp. XVI:**53

Rawlings, Marjorie Kinnan, **Supp. X:** 219–237

Ray, David, **Supp. IV Part 1:** 61

Ray, Jeanne Wilkinson, **Supp. XII:** 308, 310

Ray, John, **II:** 111, 112

Ray, Man, **IV:** 404; **Retro. Supp. I:** 416; **Supp. XII:** 124

Ray Bradbury Theatre, The (television show), **Supp. IV Part 1:** 103

"Razor's Edge, The" (Wasserstein), **Supp. XV:** 328

Reactionary Essays on Poetry and Ideas (Tate), **Supp. II Part 1:** 106, 146

Read, Deborah, **II:** 122

Read, Forrest, **III:** 478

Read, Herbert, **I:** 523; **II:** 372–373, 377–378; **Retro. Supp. I:** 54; **Supp. III Part 1:** 273; **Supp. III Part 2:** 624, 626

Read, William A., **Supp. XIV:**4

Reade, Charles, **Supp. I Part 2:** 580

Reader, Constant. *See* Parker, Dorothy

Reader, Dennis J., **Supp. I Part 2:** 454

Reader's Encyclopedia, The: An Encyclopedia of World Literature and the Arts (W. Benét), **Supp. XI:** 44

Reader's Guide to William Gaddis's The Recognitions, A (Moore), **Supp. IV Part 1:** 283

Reader's Map of Arkansas (Wright), **Supp. XV:** 348

"Reader's Tale, A" (Doty), **Supp. XI:** 119, 120, 128, 129

"Reading" (Auden), **Supp. VIII:** 155

"Reading Group Guide," **Supp. XI:** 244–245

"Reading Lao Tzu Again in the New Year" (Wright), **Supp. V:** 343

"Reading Late of the Death of Keats" (Kenyon), **Supp. VII:** 169

"Reading Myself" (Lowell), **II:** 555

Reading Myself and Others (Roth), **Retro. Supp. II:** 282; **Supp. V:** 45

"Reading *Ode to the West Wind* 25 Years Later" (McCarriston), **Supp. XIV:**271–272

"Reading of the Psalm, The" (Francis), **Supp. IX:** 79

"Reading Philosophy at Night" (Simic), **Supp. VIII:** 272

Reading Rilke: Reflections on the Problems of Translation (Gass), **Supp. VI:** 92, 93–94

"Reading Rorty and Paul Celan One Morning in Early June" (Wright), **Supp. V:** 343

"Reading Sarcophagi: An Essay" (Sobin), **Supp. XVI:**290

"Readings of History" (Rich), **Supp. I Part 2:** 554

"Reading the Signs, Empowering the Eye" (Bambara), **Supp. XI:** 17–18

Reading the Spirit (Eberhart), **I:** 525, 527, 530

"Ready Or Not" (Baraka), **Supp. II Part 1:** 50

Reagan, Ronald, **Supp. IV Part 1:** 224–225

"Real Class" (Vidal), **Supp. IV Part 1:** 35

Real Cool Killers, The (C. Himes), **Supp. XVI:**143

Real Dope, The (Lardner), **II:** 422–423

"Real Estate" (Moore), **Supp. X:** 178

"Real Gone Guy, A" (McGrath), **Supp. X:** 117

"Real Horatio Alger Story, The" (Cowley), **Supp. II Part 1:** 143

"Realities" (MacLeish), **III:** 4

"Reality in America" (Trilling), **Supp. III Part 2:** 495, 502

"Reality! Reality! What Is It?" (Eberhart), **I:** 536

Reality Sandwiches, 1953–60 (Ginsberg), **Supp. II Part 1:** 315, 320

Real Life of Sebastian Knight, The (Nabokov), **III:** 246; **Retro. Supp. I:** 266, 269, 270, 274

"Really Good Jazz Piano, A" (Yates), **Supp. XI:** 342

Real Presence: A Novel (Bausch), **Supp. VII:** 42–43, 50

"Real Revolution Is Love, The" (Harjo), **Supp. XII:** 224, 225–226

"Real Thing, The" (H. James), **Retro. Supp. I:** 228; **Retro. Supp. II:** 223

"Real Two-Party System" (Vidal), **Supp. IV Part 2:** 679

Real West Marginal Way, The (Hugo), **Supp. VI:** 132, 134

"Real World around Us, The" (Carson), **Supp. IX:** 21

Reaper Essays, The (Jarman and McDowell), **Supp. IX:** 270

"Reapers" (Toomer), **Supp. III Part 2:** 481; **Supp. IX:** 312

"Reason and Race: A Review of the Literature of the Negro for 1946" (Locke), **Supp. XIV:**206

"Reason for Moving, A" (Strand), **Supp. IV Part 2:** 624

"Reason for Stories, The: Toward a Moral Fiction" (Stone), **Supp. V:** 298, 300

Reasons for Moving (Strand), **Supp. IV Part 2:** 624–626, 626

"Reasons for Music" (MacLeish), **III:** 19

"Reasons of the Body" (Sanders), **Supp. XVI:**274

Rebecca, or, The Fille de Chambre (Rowson), **Supp. XV:** 229, 235–236, 238

Rebecca Harding Davis Reader, A (Pfaelzer, ed.), **Supp. XVI:**88, 90

Rebel Angels: 25 Poets of the New Formalism (Jarman and Mason, eds.), **Supp. XV:** 251

"Rebellion" (Lowell), **Retro. Supp. II:** 187

Rebel Powers (Bausch), **Supp. VII:** 41, 45–46, 49–51

Rebel without a Cause (film), **Supp. XII:** 9

"Rebirth of God and the Death of Man, The " (Fiedler), **Supp. XIII:** 108

Rebolledo, Tey Diana, **Supp. XIII:** 214

Recapitulation (Stegner), **Supp. IV Part 2:** 598, 600, 612–613

"Recapitulation, The" (Eberhart), **I:** 522

"Recapitulations" (Shapiro), **Supp. II Part 2:** 701, 702, 708, 710–711

"Recencies in Poetry" (Zukofsky), **Supp. III Part 2:** 615

Recent Killing, A (Baraka), **Supp. II Part 1:** 55

"Recent Negro Fiction" (Ellison), **Supp. II Part 1:** 233, 235

"Recital, The" (Ashbery), **Supp. III Part 1:** 14

"Recitative" (H. Crane), **I:** 390; **Retro. Supp. II:** 78

Reckless Eyeballing (Reed), **Supp. X:** 241

Recognitions, The (Gaddis), **Supp. IV Part 1:** 279, 280–285, 286, 287, 288, 289, 291, 292, 294

Recollections (R. H. Stoddard), **Supp. XV:** 271

Recollections of Logan Pearsall Smith: The Story of a Friendship (Gathorne-Hardy), **Supp. XIV:**344

"Reconciliation" (Whitman), **IV:** 347

"Reconstructed but Unregenerate" (Ransom), **III:** 496

"Reconstruction and Its Benefits" (Du Bois), **Supp. II Part 1:** 171

Recovering (Sarton), **Supp. VIII:** 264

Recovering the U.S. Hispanic Literary Heritage (Paredes), **Supp. XIII:** 320

"Recovery" (Dove), **Supp. IV Part 1:** 248

Rector of Justin, The (Auchincloss), **Supp. IV Part 1:** 21, 23, 27–30, 36

"RED AUTUMN" (Baraka), **Supp. II Part 1:** 55

Red Badge of Courage, The (Crane), **I:** 201, 207, 212, 405, 406, 407, 408, 412–416, 419, 421, 422, 423, 477, 506; **II:** 264; **III:** 317; **IV:** 350; **Retro. Supp. II:** 108; **Supp. IV Part 1:** 380; **Supp. XIV:**51

"Redbirds" (C. Frost), **Supp. XV:** 99

"Redbreast in Tampa" (Lanier), **Supp. I Part 1:** 364

"Red Brocade" (Nye), **Supp. XIII:** 288

Redburn: His First Voyage (Melville), **III:** 79–80, 84; **Retro. Supp. I:** 245, 247–248, 249

"Red Carpet for Shelley, A" (Wylie), **Supp. I Part 2:** 724

Red Channels (Harnett), **Supp. XV:** 198

"Red Clowns" (Cisneros), **Supp. VII:** 63

Red Coal, The (Stern), **Supp. IX:** 291–292

Red Coat, The (Shanley), **Supp. XIV:**316–317

"Red Cross" (Hughes), **Retro. Supp. I:** 205

Red Cross (Shepard), **Supp. III Part 2:** 440, 446

Red Death, A (Mosley), **Supp. XIII:** 237, 239, 240

"Red Deer" (C. Frost), **Supp. XV:** 101

Redding, Saunders, **Supp. I Part 1:** 332, 333

Reddings, J. Saunders, **Supp. IV Part 1:** 164

Red Dust (Levine), **Supp. V:** 178, 183–184, 188

"Red Dust" (Levine), **Supp. V:** 184

"Redemption" (Gardner), **Supp. VI:** 72

"Redeployment" (Nemerov), **III:** 267, 272

Redfield, Robert, **IV:** 475

Redford, Robert, **Supp. IX:** 253, 259; **Supp. XIII:** 267; **Supp. XIV:**223

Redgrave, Lynn, **Supp. V:** 107

Red Harvest (Hammett), **Supp. IV Part 1:** 346–348, 348; **Supp. IV Part 2:** 468

Red-Headed Woman (film), **Retro. Supp. I:** 110; **Supp. XVI:**191

"Red Horse Wind over Albuquerque" (Harjo), **Supp. XII:** 219

Red Hot Vacuum, The (Solotaroff), **Retro. Supp. II:** 281

"Red Leaves" (Faulkner), **II:** 72

"Red Meat: What Difference Did Stesichoros Make?" (Carson), **Supp. XII:** 107

"Red Pawn" (Rand), **Supp. IV Part 2:** 520

Red Pony, The (Steinbeck), **IV:** 50, 51, 58, 70

Redrawing the Boundaries (Fisher), **Retro. Supp. I:** 39

Red Robins, The (Koch), **Supp. XV:** 185–186, 187

Red Roses for Bronze (Doolittle), **Supp. I Part 1:** 253, 268, 271

Red Rover, The (Cooper), **I:** 342–343, 355

"Red Silk Stockings" (Hughes), **Retro. Supp. I:** 200

Redskins, The (Cooper), **I:** 351, 353

"Red Star, Winter Orbit" (W. Gibson and B. Sterling), **Supp. XVI:**123

Red Suitcase (Nye), **Supp. XIII:** 277, 278, 287

"Red Wheelbarrow, The" (W. C. Williams), **IV:** 411–412; **Retro. Supp. I:** 419, 430

"Red Wind" (Chandler), **Supp. IV Part 1:** 122

"Redwings" (Wright), **Supp. III Part 2:** 603

Reed, Edward Bliss, **Supp. XV:** 297, 298, 300

Reed, Ishmael, **Retro. Supp. II:** 111, 324–325; **Supp. II Part 1:** 34; **Supp. X:** 239–257, 331; **Supp. XIII:** 181, 182; **Supp. XVI:**143

Reed, J. D., **Supp. XVI:**174

Reed, John, **I:** 48, 476, 483; **Supp. X:** 136; **Supp. XV:** 295, 299

Reed, Lou, **Retro. Supp. II:** 266

"Reedbeds of the Hackensack, The" (Clampitt), **Supp. IX:** 41

"Reed of Pan, A" (McCullers), **II:** 585

Reedy, Billy, **Retro. Supp. II:** 65, 67, 71, 73

Reedy, William Marion, **Supp. I Part 2:** 456, 461, 465

Reef, The (Wharton), **IV:** 317–318, 322; **Retro. Supp. I:** 372, 373–374

Reena and Other Stories (Marshall), **Supp. XI:** 275, 277, 278

Reeve, F. D., **Supp. XV:** 344, 349

Reeve's Tale (Chaucer), **I:** 131

"Reflection from Anita Loos" (Empson), **Supp. XVI:**190

"Reflections" (Carruth), **Supp. XVI:**54

"Reflections" (Komunyakaa), **Supp. XIII:** 117

Reflections: Thinking Part I (Arendt), **Supp. I Part 2:** 570

Reflections at Fifty and Other Essays (Farrell), **II:** 49

"Reflections by a Fire" (Sarton), **Supp. VIII:** 259

Reflections in a Golden Eye (McCullers), **II:** 586, 588, 593–596, 604; **IV:** 384, 396

Reflections of a Jacobite (Auchincloss), **Supp. IV Part 1:** 31

Reflections on a Gift of Watermelon Pickle (Dunning), **Supp. XIV:**126

Reflections on Poetry and Poetics (Nemerov), **III:** 269

"Reflections on the Constitution of Nature" (Freneau), **Supp. II Part 1:** 274

"Reflections on the Death of the Reader" (Morris), **III:** 237

Reflections on the End of an Era (Niebuhr), **III:** 297–298

"Reflections on the Life and Death of

Lord Clive" (Paine), **Supp. I Part 2:** 505

Reflections on the Revolution in France (Burke), **Supp. I Part 2:** 511, 512

"Reflex Action and Theism" (James), **II:** 345, 363

"Refrains/Remains/Reminders" (Goldbarth), **Supp. XII:** 180–181, 181

"Refuge" (Kingsolver), **Supp. VII:** 208

"Refuge, A" (Goldbarth), **Supp. XII:** 190

Refugee Children: Theory, Research, and Services (Ahearn and Athey, eds.), **Supp. XI:** 184

"Refugees, The" (Jarrell), **II:** 371

"Refusal" (C. Frost), **Supp. XV:** 102

Regarding Wave (Snyder), **Supp. VIII:** 299–300

Regina (Epstein), **Supp. XII:** 170–171

"Regional Literature of the South" (Rawlings), **Supp. X:** 228

"Regional Writer, The" (O'Connor), **Retro. Supp. II:** 223, 225

Régnier, Henri de, **II:** 528–529

Regulators, The (King), **Supp. V:** 141

Rehder, Robert, **Supp. IV Part 1:** 69

Reichel, Hans, **III:** 183

Reichl, Ruth, **Supp. X:** 79, 85

Reich,Tova, **Supp. XVI:**158

Reid, B. L., **II:** 41, 47

Reid, Thomas, **II:** 9; **Supp. I Part 1:** 151

Reign of Wonder, The (Tanner), **I:** 260

Rein, Yevgeny, **Supp. VIII:** 22

Reinagle, Alexander, **Supp. XV:** 238, 240

"Reincarnation" (Dickey), **Supp. IV Part 1:** 181–182

Reine des pommes, La (C. Himes). See *For Love of Imabelle* (C. Himes)

Reiner, Carl, **Supp. IV Part 2:** 591

Reinfeld, Linda, **Supp. IV Part 2:** 421

Reinhardt, Max, **Supp. XV:** 307

Reinventing the Enemy's Language: Contemporary Native Women's Writing of North America (Bird and Harjo, eds.), **Supp. XII:** 216, 217

Reisman, Jerry, **Supp. III Part 2:** 618

Reitlinger, Gerald, **Supp. XII:** 161

Reivers, The: A Reminiscence (Faulkner), **I:** 305; **II:** 57, 73; **Retro. Supp. I:** 74, 82, 91

"Rejoicings" (Stern), **Supp. IX:** 289–290

Rejoicings: Selected Poems, 1966–1972 (Stern), **Supp. IX:** 289–290

Relation of My Imprisonment, The (Banks), **Supp. V:** 8, 12–13

"Relations between Poetry and Painting, The" (Stevens), **Retro. Supp. I:** 312

Relations of the Alabama-Georgia Dialect to the Provincial Dialects of Great Britain, The (Brooks), **Supp. XIV:**3

"Relativity of Beauty, The" (Rawlings), **Supp. X:** 226

Relearning the Alphabet (Levertov), **Supp. III Part 1:** 280, 281

"Release, The" (MacLeish), **III:** 16

Reles, Abe ("Kid Twist"), **Supp. IV Part 1:** 382

"Relevance of an Impossible Ethical Ideal, The" (Niebuhr), **III:** 298

"Religion" (Dunbar), **Supp. II Part 1:** 199

"Religion" (Emerson), **II:** 6

Religion of Nature Delineated, The (Wollaston), **II:** 108

Religious Rebel, A: The Letters of "H. W. S." (Mrs. Pearsall Smith) (L. P. Smith), **Supp. XIV:**349

"Reluctance" (Frost), **II:** 153

Reluctantly: Autobiographical Essays (Carruth), **Supp. XVI:**45–46, 50

Remains (Snodgrass), **Supp. VI:** 311, 313–314

"Remains, The" (Strand), **Supp. IV Part 2:** 627

"Remarks on Color" (Wright), **Supp. XV:** 346

"Remarks on Spencer's *Definition of Mind as Correspondence*" (James), **II:** 345

Remarque, Erich Maria, **Retro. Supp. I:** 113; **Supp. IV Part 1:** 380

Rembrandt, **II:** 536; **IV:** 310; **Supp. IV Part 1:** 390, 391

"Rembrandt, The" (Wharton), **IV:** 310

"Rembrandt's Hat" (Malamud), **Supp. I Part 2:** 435, 437

Rembrandt Takes a Walk (Strand), **Supp. IV Part 2:** 631

"Rembrandt to Rembrandt" (Robinson), **III:** 521–522

Remembered Earth, The: An Anthology of Contemporary Native American Literature (Hobson, ed.), **Supp. IV Part 1:** 321

Remembered Yesterdays (Johnson), **Supp. IX:** 184

"Remembering" (Angelou), **Supp. IV Part 1:** 15

"Remembering Allen Tate" (Cowley), **Supp. II Part 1:** 153

"Remembering Barthes" (Sontag), **Supp. III Part 2:** 451, 471

"Remembering Guston" (Kunitz), **Supp. III Part 1:** 257

"Remembering James Laughlin" (Karr), **Supp. XI:** 242

Remembering Laughter (Stegner), **Supp. IV Part 2:** 598, 606, 607, 608, 611, 614

"Remembering Lobo" (Mora), **Supp. XIII:** 220, 227

"Remembering My Father" (Berry), **Supp. X:** 23

"Remembering that Island" (McGrath), **Supp. X:** 116

"Remembering the Children of Auschwitz" (McGrath), **Supp. X:** 127

"Remembering the Lost World" (Jarrell), **II:** 388

"Remembering the Sixties" (Simpson), **Supp. IX:** 279

Remember Me to Tom (T. Williams), **IV:** 379–380

"Remember the Moon Survives" (Kingsolver), **Supp. VII:** 209

Remember to Remember (H. Miller), **III:** 186

"Remembrance, A" (Gioia), **Supp. XV:** 112

Remembrance of Things Past (Proust), **Supp. IV Part 2:** 600; **Supp. XII:** 9; **Supp. XIII:** 44

Remembrance Rock (Sandburg), **III:** 590

Reminiscence, A (Ashbery), **Supp. III Part 1:** 2

Remnick, David, **Supp. XVI:**246

"Remora" (Merrill), **Supp. III Part 1:** 326

"Removal" (White), **Supp. I Part 2:** 664–665

"Removal, The" (Merwin), **Supp. III Part 1:** 350, 351

Removed from Time (Matthews and Feeney), **Supp. IX:** 154

Remsen, Ira, **Supp. I Part 1:** 369

"Rémy de Gourmont, A Distinction" (Pound), **III:** 467

"Renaissance" (Carruth), **Supp. XVI:**56

Renaissance in the South (Bradbury), **I:** 288–289

"Renaming the Kings" (Levine), **Supp. V:** 184

Renan, Joseph Ernest, **II:** 86; **IV:** 440, 444

Renard, Jules, **IV:** 79

"Renascence" (Millay), **III:** 123, 125–126, 128; **Supp. XV:** 42

Renault, Mary, **Supp. IV Part 2:** 685

"Rendezvous, The" (Kumin), **Supp. IV Part 2:** 455

René, Norman, **Supp. X:** 146, 152

Renée (anonymous author), **Supp.**

XVI:64, 66

"Renegade, The" (Jackson), **Supp. IX:** 120

Renewal of Life series (Mumford), **Supp. II Part 2:** 476, 479, 481, 482, 485, 495, 497

Renoir, Jean, **Supp. XII:** 259

Renouvrier, Charles, **II:** 344–345, 346

"Renunciation" (Banks), **Supp. V:** 10

Renza, Louis A., **Retro. Supp. II:** 142

"Repeating Dream" (Gander), **Supp. XV:** 340

Repent in Haste (Marquand), **III:** 59

Reperusals and Re-Collections (L. P. Smith), **Supp. XIV:**346–347

"Repetitive Heart, The: Eleven Poems in Imitation of the Fugue Form" (Schwartz), **Supp. II Part 2:** 645–646

"Replacing Regionalism" (Murphy), **Retro. Supp. II:** 143

Replansky, Naomi, **Supp. X:** 119

"Reply to Mr. Wordsworth" (MacLeish), **III:** 19

"Report from a Forest Logged by the Weyhaeuser Company" (Wagoner), **Supp. IX:** 328

"Report from North Vietnam" (Paley), **Supp. VI:** 227

Report from Part One (Brooks), **Supp. III Part 1:** 70, 72, 80, 82–85

Report from Part Two (Brooks), **Supp. III Part 1:** 87

Report on a Game Survey of the North Central States (Leopold), **Supp. XIV:**182

"Report on the Barnhouse Effect" (Vonnegut), **Supp. II Part 2:** 756

"Report to Crazy Horse" (Stafford), **Supp. XI:** 324–325

"Repose of Rivers" (H. Crane), **I:** 393; **Retro. Supp. II:** 78, 81

"Repossession of a Heritage, The" (Zagarell), **Supp. XV:** 270, 281

"Representation and the War for Reality" (Gass), **Supp. VI:** 88

Representative Men (Emerson), **II:** 1, 5–6, 8

"Representing Far Places" (Stafford), **Supp. XI:** 321

"REPRISE OF ONE OF A. G.'S BEST POEMS" (Baraka), **Supp. II Part 1:** 59

"Reproducing Ourselves Is All Very Well" (E. Hoffman), **Supp. XVI:**155

Republic (Plato), **I:** 485

"Republican Manifesto, A" (Paine), **Supp. I Part 2:** 511

Republic of Love, The (Shields), **Supp. VII:** 323–324, 326, 327

"Requa" (Olsen), **Supp. XIII:** 294, 302–303, 304

Requa, Kenneth A., **Supp. I Part 1:** 107

"Requa I" (Olsen). See "Requa" (Olsen)

"Request for Offering" (Eberhart), **I:** 526

"Requiem" (Akhmatova), **Supp. VIII:** 20

"Requiem" (LaBastille), **Supp. X:** 105

Requiem for a Nun (Faulkner), **II:** 57, 72–73

Requiem for Harlem (H. Roth), **Supp. IX:** 235, 236, 240–242

"Rescue, The" (Updike), **IV:** 214

Rescued Year, The (Stafford), **Supp. XI:** 321–322

"Rescued Year, The" (Stafford), **Supp. XI:** 322, 323

"Rescue with Yul Brynner" (Moore), **III:** 215

"Resemblance" (Bishop), **Supp. I Part 1:** 86

"Resemblance between a Violin Case and a Coffin, A" (T. Williams), **IV:** 378–379

"Reservations" (Taylor), **Supp. V:** 323

"Reserved Memorials" (Mather), **Supp. II Part 2:** 446, 449

"Resistance to Civil Government" (Thoreau), **Supp. X:** 27, 28

Resist Much, Obey Little (Berry), **Supp. XIII:** 2

"Resolution and Independence" (Wordsworth), **Supp. XV:** 346

Resources of Hope (R. Williams), **Supp. IX:** 146

"Respectable Place, A" (O'Hara), **III:** 369

"Respectable Woman, A" (Chopin), **Retro. Supp. II:** 66

Responses (Wilbur), **Supp. III Part 2:** 541

"Response to a Rumor that the Oldest Whorehouse in Wheeling, West Virginia, Has Been Condemned" (Wright), **Supp. III Part 2:** 602

Restif de La Bretonne, Nicolas, **III:** 175

"Rest of Life, The" (Gordon), **Supp. IV Part 1:** 311

Rest of Life, The: Three Novellas (Gordon), **Supp. IV Part 1:** 310–312

Rest of the Way, The (McClatchy), **Supp. XII:** 255, 258–259

Restoration comedy, **Supp. I Part 2:** 617

"Restraint" (F. Barthelme), **Supp. XI:** 26

"Result" (Emerson), **II:** 6

"Résumé" (Parker), **Supp. IX:** 189

Resurrection (Della Francesca), **Supp. XV:** 262

"Resurrection" (Harjo), **Supp. XII:** 224

Resurrection, The (Gardner), **Supp. VI:** 61, 63, 64–65, 68, 69, 73, 74

"Retort" (Hay), **Supp. XIV:**133

Retour amont (Char; Sobin, trans.), **Supp. XVI:**282

Retrieval System, The (Kumin), **Supp. IV Part 2:** 449, 451, 452

"Retrievers in Translation" (Doty), **Supp. XI:** 132

"Retroduction to American History" (Tate), **IV:** 129

"Retrospects and Prospects" (Lanier), **Supp. I Part 1:** 352

"Return" (Corso), **Supp. XII:** 135

"Return" (Creeley), **Supp. IV Part 1:** 141, 145

"Return" (MacLeish), **III:** 12

"Return: An Elegy, The" (Warren), **IV:** 239

"Return: Buffalo" (Hogan), **Supp. IV Part 1:** 411

"Return, The" (Bidart), **Supp. XV:** 32–33

"Return, The" (Pound), **Retro. Supp. I:** 288

"Return, The" (Roethke), **III:** 533

"Return, The: Orihuela, 1965" (Levine), **Supp. V:** 194

"Returning" (Komunyakaa), **Supp. XIII:** 122

"Returning a Lost Child" (Glück), **Supp. V:** 81

"Returning from the Enemy" (Harjo), **Supp. XII:** 229–230

"Returning the Borrowed Road" (Komunyakaa), **Supp. XIII:** 113, 133

"Return of Alcibiade, The" (Chopin), **Retro. Supp. II:** 58, 64

Return of Ansel Gibbs, The (Buechner), **III:** 310; **Supp. XII:** 48

"Return of Spring" (Winters), **Supp. II Part 2:** 791

Return of the Native, The (Hardy), **II:** 184–185, 186

Return of the Vanishing American, The (Fiedler), **Supp. XIII:** 103

Return to a Place Lit by a Glass of Milk (Simic), **Supp. VIII:** 274, 276, 283

"Return to Lavinia" (Caldwell), **I:** 310

Reuben (Wideman), **Supp. X:** 320

Reuben and Rachel; or, Tales of Old

Times (Rowson), **Supp. XV:** 240–241

Reunion (Mamet), **Supp. XIV:**240, 247, 254

"Reunion in Brooklyn" (H. Miller), **III:** 175, 184

Reuther brothers, **I:** 493

"Rev. Freemont Deadman" (Masters), **Supp. I Part 2:** 463

"Reveille" (Kingsolver), **Supp. VII:** 208

"Reveille" (Untermeyer), **Supp. XV:** 300

"Reveille, The" (Harte), **Supp. II Part 1:** 342–343

Revelation (biblical book), **II:** 541; **IV:** 104, 153, 154; **Supp. I Part 1:** 105, 273

"Revelation" (O'Connor), **III:** 349, 353–354; **Retro. Supp. II:** 237

"Revelation" (Warren), **III:** 490

Revenge (Harrison), **Supp. VIII:** 39, 45

"Revenge of Hamish, The" (Lanier), **Supp. I Part 1:** 365

"Revenge of Hannah Kemhuff, The" (Walker), **Supp. III Part 2:** 521

"Revenge of Rain-in-the-Face, The" (Longfellow), **Retro. Supp. II:** 170

Reverberator, The (James), **Retro. Supp. I:** 227

"Reverdure" (Berry), **Supp. X:** 22

Reverdy, Pierre, **Supp. XV:** 178, 182

"Reverend Father Gilhooley" (Farrell), **II:** 45

Reverse Transcription (Kushner), **Supp. IX:** 138

Reviewer's ABC, A (Aiken), **I:** 58

"Revolt, against the Crepuscular Spirit in Modern Poetry" (Pound), **Retro. Supp. I:** 286

Revolutionary Petunias (Walker), **Supp. III Part 2:** 520, 522, 530

Revolutionary Road (Yates), **Supp. XI:** 334, 335–340

"Revolutionary Symbolism in America" (Burke), **I:** 272

"Revolutionary Theatre, The" (Baraka), **Supp. II Part 1:** 42

Revolution in Taste, A: Studies of Dylan Thomas, Allen Ginsberg, Sylvia Plath, and Robert Lowell (Simpson), **Supp. IX:** 276

"Revolution in the Revolution in the Revolution" (Snyder), **Supp. VIII:** 300

Revon, Marcel, **II:** 525

"Rewaking, The" (W. C. Williams), **Retro. Supp. I:** 430

"Rewrite" (Dunn), **Supp. XI:** 147

Rexroth, Kenneth, **II:** 526; **Supp. II Part 1:** 307; **Supp. II Part 2:** 436; **Supp. III Part 2:** 625, 626; **Supp. IV Part 1:** 145–146; **Supp. VIII:** 289; **Supp. XIII:** 75; **Supp. XIV:**287; **Supp. XV:** 140, 141, 146

Reynolds, Ann (pseudo.). See Bly, Carol

Reynolds, Clay, **Supp. XI:** 254

Reynolds, David, **Supp. XV:** 269

Reynolds, Quentin, **IV:** 286

Reynolds, Sir Joshua, **Supp. I Part 2:** 716

Reznikoff, Charles, **IV:** 415; **Retro. Supp. I:** 422; **Supp. III Part 2:** 615, 616, 617, 628; **Supp. XIV:**277–296

"Rhapsodist, The" (Brown), **Supp. I Part 1:** 125–126

"Rhapsody on a Windy Night" (Eliot), **Retro. Supp. I:** 55

Rhetoric of Motives, A (Burke), **I:** 272, 275, 278, 279

Rhetoric of Religion, The (Burke), **I:** 275, 279

"Rhobert" (Toomer), **Supp. IX:** 316–317

"Rhododendrons" (Levis), **Supp. XI:** 260, 263

Rhubarb Show, The (radio, Keillor), **Supp. XVI:**178

"Rhyme of Sir Christopher, The" (Longfellow), **II:** 501

Rhymes to Be Traded for Bread (Lindsay), **Supp. I Part 2:** 380, 381–382

Rhys, Ernest, **III:** 458

Rhys, Jean, **Supp. III Part 1:** 42, 43

"Rhythm & Blues" (Baraka), **Supp. II Part 1:** 37–38

Rhythms (Reznikoff), **Supp. XIV:**279, 282, 283

Rhythms II (Reznikoff), **Supp. XIV:**282, 283, 284

Ribalow, Harold, **Supp. IX:** 236

Ribbentrop, Joachim von, **IV:** 249

Ribicoff, Abraham, **Supp. IX:** 33

Ricardo, David, **Supp. I Part 2:** 628, 634

Rice, Allen Thorndike, **Retro. Supp. I:** 362

Rice, Anne, **Supp. VII:** 287–306

Rice, Elmer, **I:** 479; **III:** 145, 160–161

Rice, Mrs. Grantland, **II:** 435

Rice, Philip Blair, **IV:** 141

Rice, Stan, **Supp. XII:** 2

Rice, Tom, **Supp. XIV:**125

Rich, Adrienne, **Retro. Supp. I:** 8, 36, 42, 47, 404; **Retro. Supp. II:** 43, 191, 245; **Supp. I Part 2:** 546–547,

550–578; **Supp. III Part 1:** 84, 354; **Supp. III Part 2:** 541, 599; **Supp. IV Part 1:** 257, 325; **Supp. V:** 82; **Supp. VIII:** 272; **Supp. XII:** 217, 229, 255; **Supp. XIII:** 294; **Supp. XIV:**126, 129; **Supp. XV:** 176, 252

Rich, Arnold, **Supp. I Part 2:** 552

Rich, Frank, **Supp. IV Part 2:** 585, 586; **Supp. V:** 106

Richard Cory (Gurney), **Supp. V:** 99–100, 105

"Richard Hunt's 'Arachne'" (Hayden), **Supp. II Part 1:** 374

Richard III (Shakespeare), **Supp. I Part 2:** 422

Richards, David, **Supp. IV Part 2:** 576

Richards, Grant, **I:** 515

Richards, I. A., **I:** 26, 273–274, 279, 522; **III:** 498; **IV:** 92; **Supp. I Part 1:** 264, 265; **Supp. I Part 2:** 647

Richards, Ivor Armonstrong, **Supp. XIV:**2–3, 16

Richards, Laura E., **II:** 396; **III:** 505–506, 507

Richards, Leonard, **Supp. XIV:**48

Richards, Lloyd, **Supp. IV Part 1:** 362; **Supp. VIII:** 331

Richards, Rosalind, **III:** 506

Richardson, Alan, **III:** 295

Richardson, Dorothy, **I:** 53; **II:** 320; **Supp. III Part 1:** 65

Richardson, Helen Patges, **Retro. Supp. II:** 95

Richardson, Henry Hobson, **I:** 3, 10

Richardson, Maurice, **Supp. XII:** 241

Richardson, Samuel, **I:** 134; **II:** 104, 111, 322; **Supp. V:** 127; **Supp. IX:** 128; **Supp. XV:** 232

Richardson, Tony, **Supp. XI:** 305, 306

"Richard Wright and Recent Negro Fiction" (Ellison), **Retro. Supp. II:** 116

"Richard Wright's Blues" (Ellison), **Retro. Supp. II:** 117, 124

"Richard Yates: A Requiem" (Lawrence), **Supp. XI:** 335

"Rich Boy, The" (Fitzgerald), **II:** 94; **Retro. Supp. I:** 98, 108

"Riches" (Bausch), **Supp. VII:** 54

Richler, Mordecai, **Supp. XI:** 294, 297

Richman, Robert, **Supp. XI:** 249; **Supp. XV:** 120–121, 251

Richmond (Masters), **Supp. I Part 2:** 471

Richter, Conrad, **Supp. X:** 103

Richter, Jean Paul, **II:** 489, 492; **Supp. XVI:**182

Rick Bass (Weltzien), **Supp. XVI:**20

Rickman, Clio, **Supp. I Part 2:** 519

Ricks, Christopher, **Retro. Supp. I:** 56

Riddel, Joseph N., **IV:** 95

"Riddle, The" (Hay), **Supp. XIV:**130

"Riders to the Blood-Red Wrath" (Brooks), **Supp. III Part 1:** 82–83

Riders to the Sea (Synge), **III:** 157

Ridge, Lola, **Supp. IX:** 308; **Supp. XV:** 307

Riding, Alan, **Supp. XVI:**294

Riding, Laura, **I:** 437

"Riding Out at Evening" (McCarriston), **Supp. XIV:**262–263

Riding the Iron Rooster: By Train through China (Theroux), **Supp. VIII:** 324

Riesenberg, Felix, **I:** 360, 361

Riesman, David, **Supp. I Part 2:** 649, 650

"Rif, to Music, The" (Bowles), **Supp. IV Part 1:** 89

Riffs & Reciprocities (Dunn), **Supp. XI:** 154–155

Riggs, Marlon, **Supp. XI:** 19

Right Madness on Skye, The (Hugo), **Supp. VI:** 145–147

Rights of Man (Paine), **Supp. I Part 2:** 508, 511, 512–514, 516, 519, 523

"Rights of Woman" (Rowson), **Supp. XV:** 243

"Rights of Women, The" (Brown). *See Alcuin: A Dialogue* (Brown)

Right Stuff, The (Wolfe), **Supp. III Part 2:** 581–584

Right Thoughts in Sad Hours (Mather), **IV:** 144

Rigney, Barbara Hill, **Supp. VIII:** 215

"Rigorists" (Moore), **III:** 198

Riis, Jacob A., **I:** 293; **Supp. I Part 1:** 13

Riley, James Whitcomb, **I:** 205; **Supp. II Part 1:** 192, 193, 196, 197

Rilke, Rainer Maria, **I:** 445, 523; **II:** 367, 381, 382–383, 389, 543, 544; **III:** 552, 558, 563, 571, 572; **IV:** 380, 443; **Retro. Supp. II:** 20, 187; **Supp. I Part 1:** 264; **Supp. I Part 2:** 573; **Supp. III Part 1:** 239, 242, 246, 283, 319–320; **Supp. IV Part 1:** 284; **Supp. V:** 208, 343; **Supp. VIII:** 30, 40; **Supp. X:** 164; **Supp. XI:** 126; **Supp. XIII:** 74, 88; **Supp. XV:** 93, 212, 222,**Supp. XV:** 223, 225; **Supp. XVI:**292

Rilke on Love and Other Difficulties (Rilke), **Supp. X:** 164

"Rilke's Growth as a Poet" (Dobyns), **Supp. XIII:** 77

"Rimbaud" (Kerouac), **Supp. III Part 1:** 232

Rimbaud, Arthur, **I:** 381, 383, 389, 391, 526; **II:** 528, 543, 545; **III:** 23, 174, 189; **IV:** 286, 380, 443; **Retro. Supp. I:** 56; **Retro. Supp. II:** 187, 326; **Supp. III Part 1:** 14, 195; **Supp. IV Part 2:** 624; **Supp. VIII:** 39, 40; **Supp. XII:** 1, 16, 128, 255; **Supp. XIII:** 284; **Supp. XIV:**338

Rinehart, Stanley, **III:** 36

Ring, Frances Kroll, **Supp. IX:** 63, 64

Ring and the Book, The (Browning), **Supp. I Part 2:** 416, 468

Ring cycle (Wagner), **Supp. IV Part 1:** 392

Ringe, Donald, **I:** 339, 343; **Retro. Supp. II:** 270

"Ringing the Bells" (Sexton), **Supp. II Part 2:** 672, 687

Ringle, Ken, **Supp. X:** 15

Ring of Heaven: Poems (Hongo), **Supp. X:** 292

Rink, The (musical, McNally), **Supp. XIII:** 207

Rio Lobo (film), **Supp. XVI:**246

Ríos, Alberto Alvaro, **Supp. IV Part 2:** 537–556

"Riot" (Brooks), **Supp. III Part 1:** 71, 84–85

Ripley, Ezra, **II:** 8; **IV:** 172

Rip-off Red, Girl Detective (Acker), **Supp. XII:** 3–4

Ripostes (Pound), **Retro. Supp. I:** 287–288, 413

Ripostes of Ezra Pound, The, Whereunto Are Appended the Complete Poetical Works of T. E. Hulme, with Prefatory Note (Pound), **III:** 458, 464, 465

Riprap (Snyder), **Supp. VIII:** 292–294, 295

"Riprap" (Snyder), **Supp. VIII:** 293–294

"Rip Van Winkle" (Irving), **II:** 304–306; **Supp. I Part 1:** 185

Risco-Lozado, Eliezar, **Supp. XIII:** 313

Rise of David Levinsky, The (Cahan), **Supp. IX:** 227; **Supp. XIII:** 106

Rise of Silas Lapham, The (Howells), **II:** 275, 279, 283–285; **IV:** 202; **Retro. Supp. II:** 93, 101

"Rise of the Middle Class" (Banks), **Supp. V:** 10

Rising and Falling (Matthews), **Supp. IX:** 154, 160

"Rising Daughter, The" (Olds), **Supp. X:** 204

Rising from the Plains (McPhee), **Supp. III Part 1:** 309–310

Rising Glory of America, The (Brackenridge and Freneau), **Supp.**

I Part 1: 124; **Supp. II Part 1:** 67, 253, 256, 263

"Rising of the Storm, The" (Dunbar), **Supp. II Part 1:** 199

Rising Sun in the Pacific, The (Morison), **Supp. I Part 2:** 490

Risk Pool, The (Russo), **Supp. XII:** 328–331

Ristovic, Aleksandar, **Supp. VIII:** 272

"Rita Dove: Identity Markers" (Vendler), **Supp. IV Part 1:** 247, 257

Ritchey, John, **Supp. XIV:**122

"Rite of Passage" (Olds), **Supp. X:** 206

"Rites and Ceremonies" (Hecht), **Supp. X:** 61

"Rites of Spring, The" (Morris), **III:** 223

Ritivoi, Andreea Deciu, **Supp. XVI:**148

Ritschl, Albrecht, **III:** 309, 604

Ritsos, Yannis, **Supp. X:** 112

"Ritsos and the Metaphysical Moment" (Dobyns), **Supp. XIII:** 78

Rittenhouse, David, **Supp. I Part 2:** 507

Rittenhouse, Jessie, **Supp. XV:** 295

"Ritual and Renewal: Keres Traditions in the Short Fiction of Leslie Silko" (Ruoff), **Supp. IV Part 2:** 559

Ritz, The (film), **Supp. XIII:** 206

Ritz, The (McNally), **Supp. XIII:** 198

"Rival, The" (Plath), **Retro. Supp. II:** 254

Riven Rock (Boyle), **Supp. VIII:** 5–6

"River" (Ammons), **Supp. VII:** 28

"River, The" (O'Connor), **III:** 344, 352, 353, 354, 356; **Retro. Supp. II:** 229, 231–232

Rivera, Tomás, **Supp. XIII:** 216, 221

Riverbed (Wagoner), **Supp. IX:** 327–328

"River Driftwood" (Jewett), **Retro. Supp. II:** 132, 133, 147

"River Jordan, The" (DeLillo), **Supp. VI:** 3, 4

River King, The (Hoffman), **Supp. X:** 78, 85, 90, 91–92

"River Merchant's Wife: A Letter, The" (Pound), **III:** 463

"River Now, The" (Hugo), **Supp. VI:** 144

"River of Rivers in Connecticut, The" (Stevens), **Retro. Supp. I:** 313

River of the Mother of God and Other Essays by Aldo Leopold, The (Leopold), **Supp. XIV:**180

"River Profile" (Auden), **Supp. II Part 1:** 26

"River Road" (Kunitz), **Supp. III Part 1:** 260

"River Runs Through It, A" (Maclean), **Supp. XIV:**222–223, 223–229, 233, 234, 235; **Supp. XVI:**98

River Runs Through It and Other Stories, A (Maclean), **Supp. XIV:**221, 223

Rivers, Larry, **Supp. III Part 1:** 3; **Supp. XV:** 177, 178, 186

Rivers and Mountains (Ashbery), **Supp. III Part 1:** 10, 26

Riverside Drive (Simpson), **Supp. IX:** 275–276

Rivers to the Sea (Teasdale), **Supp. XV:** 295

River Styx, Ohio, and Other Poems, The (Oliver), **Supp. VII:** 231, 232

"River That Is East, The" (Kinnell), **Supp. III Part 1:** 241–242

"River Towns" (Masters), **Supp. I Part 2:** 473

Rives, Amélie, **II:** 194

Rivière, Jacques, **Retro. Supp. I:** 63

"Rivington's Last Will and Testament" (Freneau), **Supp. II Part 1:** 261

"Rivulet, The" (Bryant), **Supp. I Part 1:** 155, 162

Rix, Alice, **I:** 199

RL's Dream (Mosley), **Supp. XIII:** 234, 244–245, 249

Roach, Max, **Supp. X:** 239

"Road, Roadsides, and the Disparate Frames of a Sequence" (Sobin), **Supp. XVI:**288

Road Between, The (Farrell), **II:** 29, 38, 39–40

"Road Between Here and There, The" (Kinnell), **Supp. III Part 1:** 254

"Road Home, The" (Hammett), **Supp. IV Part 1:** 343

Road Home, The (Harrison), **Supp. VIII:** 37, 45, 48, 49–50, 53

Roadless Yaak, The: Reflections and Observations about One of Our Last Great Wild Places (Bass, ed.), **Supp. XVI:**23

"Road Not Taken, The" (R. Frost), **II:** 154; **Retro. Supp. I:** 131; **Supp. XI:** 150; **Supp. XV:** 127

Roadside Poems for Summer Travellers (Larcom, ed.), **Supp. XIII:** 142

Roads of Destiny (O. Henry), **Supp. II Part 1:** 410

Road through the Wall, The (Jackson), **Supp. IX:** 115, 118, 120, 123–124

"Road to Avignon, The" (Lowell), **II:** 516

"Road to Hell, The" (Fante), **Supp. XI:** 160

Road to Los Angeles, The (Fante), **Supp. XI:** 160, 166, 167, 168, 172

Road to Many a Wonder, The (Wagoner), **Supp. IX:** 327, 336

Road to the Temple, The (Glaspell), **Supp. III Part 1:** 175, 182, 186

Road to Wellville, The (Boyle), **Supp. VIII:** 6–8

Road to Xanadu, The (Lowes), **IV:** 453

"Roan Stallion" (Jeffers), **Supp. II Part 2:** 428–429

"Roast-beef" (Stein), **IV:** 43

Roast Leviatham (Untermeyer), **Supp. XV:** 307

"Roast Possum" (Dove), **Supp. IV Part 1:** 247, 248

Robards, Jason, Jr., **III:** 163, 403

Robb, Christina, **Supp. XV:** 251

Robbe-Grillet, Alain, **I:** 123; **IV:** 95; **Supp. IV Part 1:** 42; **Supp. V:** 47, 48

Robber Bride, The (Atwood), **Supp. XIII:** 30–31

Robber Bridegroom, The (Welty), **IV:** 261, 266–268, 271, 274; **Retro. Supp. I:** 347

Robbins, Harold, **Supp. XII:** 6

Robbins, Henry, **Supp. IV Part 1:** 198, 201, 210, 211

Robbins, Katherine Robinson, **Supp. X:** 264

Robbins, Thomas, **Supp. XV:** 271

Robbins, Tom, **Supp. IV Part 1:** 227; **Supp. VIII:** 14; **Supp. X:** 259–288; **Supp. XIII:** 11

"Robe, The" (Douglas), **IV:** 434

"Robert Bly" (Davis), **Supp. IV Part 1:** 70

Robert Bly (Sugg), **Supp. IV Part 1:** 68

Robert Bly: An Introduction to the Poetry (Nelson), **Supp. IV Part 1:** 66

Robert Bly: The Poet and His Critics (Davis), **Supp. IV Part 1:** 63

"Robert Bly and the Trouble with America" (Mitchell), **Supp. IV Part 1:** 70

Robert Coover: The Universal Fiction-making Process (Gordon), **Supp. V:** 46

Robert Creeley (Ford), **Supp. IV Part 1:** 140

Robert Creeley and the Genius of the American Common Place (Clark), **Supp. IV Part 1:** 140

Robert Creeley's Poetry: A Critical Introduction (Edelberg), **Supp. IV Part 1:** 155

Robert Frost (Meyers), **Retro. Supp. I:** 138

Robert Lowell (Meyers), **Retro. Supp. II:** 191

Robert Lowell: The First Twenty years (Staples), **Retro. Supp. II:** 187

Robert Lowell and the Sublime (Hart), **Retro. Supp. II:** 187

Robert Lowell's Shifting Colors (Doreski), **Retro. Supp. II:** 185

Roberts, Diane, **Supp. X:** 15

Roberts, J. M., **IV:** 454

Roberts, Leo, **II:** 449

Roberts, Margaret, **II:** 449; **IV:** 453, 454

Roberts, Matthew, **Retro. Supp. II:** 324

Roberts, Meade, **IV:** 383

Roberts, Michael, **I:** 527, 536

Roberts, Richard, **III:** 297

Roberts, Wally, **Supp. XI:** 119, 120, 126

Roberts, William, **Supp. XI:** 343

Roberts Brothers, **Retro. Supp. I:** 31, 35

Robertson, D. B., **III:** 311

Robertson, David, **Supp. VIII:** 305

Robertson, Nan, **Supp. IV Part 1:** 300

Robertson, William, **II:** 8

Robert the Devil (Merwin, trans.), **Supp. III Part 1:** 341, 346

Robeson, Paul, **III:** 392; **Supp. IV Part 1:** 360, 361; **Supp. X:** 137

Robespierre, Maximilien, **Supp. I Part 2:** 514, 515, 517

"Robinson" (Kees), **Supp. XV:** 143–144

Robinson, Christopher L., **Supp. XII:** 13, 14

Robinson, Dean, **III:** 506

Robinson, Edward, **III:** 505

Robinson, Edward G., **Supp. XI:** 306

Robinson, Edwin Arlington, **I:** 480; **II:** 388, 391, 529, 542; **III:** 5, 503–526, 576; **Supp. I Part 2:** 699; **Supp. II Part 1:** 191; **Supp. III Part 1:** 63, 75; **Supp. III Part 2:** 592, 593; **Supp. IX:** 77, 266, 276, 308; **Supp. XV:** 256, 299, 300, 301, 306

Robinson, Forrest G., **Supp. IV Part 2:** 597, 601, 604

Robinson, H. M., **IV:** 369, 370

Robinson, Herman, **III:** 506–507

Robinson, Jackie, **Supp. I Part 1:** 338

Robinson, James Harvey, **I:** 214; **Supp. I Part 2:** 492

Robinson, James K., **Supp. IX:** 328

Robinson, Margaret G., **Supp. IV Part 2:** 597, 601, 604

Robinson, Mary, **Supp. XI:** 26

Robinson, Sugar Ray, **Supp. IV Part 1:** 167

Robinson, Ted, **Supp. XIII:** 166

Robinson Crusoe (Defoe), **II:** 159; **III:** 113, 423; **IV:** 369; **Retro. Supp. II:** 274; **Supp. I Part 2:** 714; **Supp. IV Part 2:** 502

Robison, Mary, **Supp. V:** 22

Roblès, Emmanuel, **Supp. I Part 1:** 283

"Robstown" (Salinas), **Supp. XIII:** 315

Rochefort, Christina, **Supp. XVI:**143

Rochefoucauld, Louis Alexandre, **Supp. I Part 2:** 510

"Rock" (Nye), **Supp. XIII:** 287

Rock (Wagoner), **Supp. IX:** 324, 334, 335

Rock, Catherine, **Supp. XII:** 17

Rock, The (Eliot), **Retro. Supp. I:** 65

Rock, The (Stevens), **Retro. Supp. I:** 309, 312

"Rock, The" (Stevens), **Retro. Supp. I:** 312

Rockaway (Shanley), **Supp. XIV:**315

"Rock Climbers, The" (Francis), **Supp. IX:** 82

Rock-Drill (Pound), **Retro. Supp. I:** 293

Rockefeller, John D., **I:** 273; **III:** 580; **Supp. I Part 2:** 486; **Supp. V:** 286

Rockefeller, Nelson, **III:** 14, 15

Rocket to the Moon (Odets), **Supp. II Part 2:** 541–543, 544

Rock Garden, The (Shepard), **Supp. III Part 2:** 432, 447

"Rocking Horse Winner, The" (Lawrence), **Supp. I Part 1:** 329

Rocking the Boat (Vidal), **Supp. IV Part 2:** 683

"Rockpile, The" (Baldwin), **Supp. I Part 1:** 63

Rock Springs (Ford), **Supp. V:** 57, 58–59, 68–69

Rocky Mountains, The: or, Scenes, Incidents, and Adventures in the Far West; Digested from the Journal of Captain E. L. E Bonneville, of the Army of the United States, and Illustrated from Various Other Sources (Irving), **II:** 312

Rodden, John, **Supp. XVI:**63, 69, 72

Roderick, David, **Supp. XV:** 223

Roderick Hudson (James), **II:** 284, 290, 324, 326, 328; **Retro. Supp. I:** 219, 220–221, 221, 226; **Supp. IX:** 142

Rodgers, Richard, **III:** 361

Rodgers, Ronald, **Supp. IV Part 2:** 503

Rodker, John, **III:** 470

Rodman, Selden, **Supp. I Part 1:** 83;

Supp. X: 115

"Rodrigo Returns to the Land and Linen Celebrates" (Cisneros), **Supp. VII:** 68

Rodriguez, Randy A., **Supp. XIV:**312

Rodriguez, Richard, **Supp. XIV:**297–313

Roethke, Charles, **III:** 531

Roethke, Theodore, **I:** 167, 171–172, 183, 254, 285, 521; **III:** 273, 527–550; **IV:** 138, 402; **Retro. Supp. II:** 178, 181, 246; **Supp. I Part 2:** 539; **Supp. III Part 1:** 47, 54, 56, 239, 253, 260–261, 350; **Supp. IV Part 2:** 626; **Supp. IX:** 323; **Supp. XV:** 140, 145, 212

"Roger Malvin's Burial" (Hawthorne), **II:** 243; **Retro. Supp. I:** 153

Rogers, Michael, **Supp. X:** 265, 266

Rogers, Samuel, **II:** 303; **Supp. I Part 1:** 157

Rogers, Will, **I:** 261; **IV:** 388

Roger's Version (Updike), **Retro. Supp. I:** 325, 327, 330

Roget, Peter Mark, **Supp. I Part 1:** 312

"Rogue River Jet-Board Trip, Gold Beach, Oregon, July 4, 1977" (Carver), **Supp. III Part 1:** 140

"Rogue's Gallery" (McCarthy), **II:** 563

Roland de La Platière, Jean Marie, **II:** 554

Rôle du Nègre dans la culture des Amériques, La (Locke), **Supp. XIV:**202

"Role of Society in the Artist, The" (Ammons), **Supp. VII:** 34

Rolfe, Alfred, **IV:** 427

"Roll, Jordan, Roll" (spiritual), **Supp. IV Part 1:** 16

"Roll Call" (Komunyakaa), **Supp. XIII:** 123

Rolle, Esther, **Supp. IV Part 1:** 367

Rollin, Charles, **II:** 113

Rolling Stones (O. Henry), **Supp. II Part 1:** 410

Rolling Thunder Logbook (Shepard), **Supp. III Part 2:** 433

"Rolling Up" (Simpson), **Supp. IX:** 265, 274, 280

Rollins, Howard E., Jr., **Supp. IV Part 1:** 236

Rollins, Hyder E., **Supp. IV Part 1:** 168

Rollins, Sonny, **Supp. V:** 195

"Rollo" tales (Abbott), **Supp. I Part 1:** 38

"Roma I" (Wright), **Supp. V:** 338

"Roma II" (Wright), **Supp. V:** 338

Romains, Jules, **I:** 227

Román, David, **Supp. XIII:** 208

"Romance and a Reading List" (Fitzgerald), **Retro. Supp. I:** 101

Romance of a Plain Man, The (Glasgow), **II:** 175, 180–181

"Romance of Certain Old Clothes, The" (James), **II:** 322; **Retro. Supp. I:** 218

"Roman Elegies" (Brodsky), **Supp. VIII:** 29

"Roman Fever" (Wharton), **Retro. Supp. I:** 382

"Roman Fountain" (Bogan), **Supp. III Part 1:** 56

"*Romanitas* of Gore Vidal, The" (Tatum), **Supp. IV Part 2:** 684

Romaniuk, Zbigniew, **Supp. XVI:**154

Romano, John, **Supp. XV:** 253

"Roman Sarcophagus, A" (Lowell), **II:** 544

Roman Spring of Mrs. Stone, The (T. Williams), **IV:** 383, 385

"Romantic, The" (Bogan), **Supp. III Part 1:** 50

Romantic Comedians, The (Glasgow), **II:** 175, 186, 190, 194

Romantic Egoists, The (Auchincloss), **Supp. IV Part 1:** 25

Romantic Egotist, The (Fitzgerald), **II:** 82

"Romantic Egotist, The" (Fitzgerald), **Retro. Supp. I:** 100

"Romanticism and Classicism" (Hulme), **III:** 196

"Romanticism Comes Home" (Shapiro), **Supp. II Part 2:** 713

Romantic Manifesto, The: A Philosophy of Literature (Rand), **Supp. IV Part 2:** 521, 523, 527, 529–530

"Romantic Regionalism of Harper Lee, The" (Erisman), **Supp. VIII:** 126

"Rome" (W. C. Williams), **Retro. Supp. I:** 420

Rome Brothers, **Retro. Supp. I:** 393

Romeo and Juliet (Shakespeare), **Supp. V:** 252; **Supp. VIII:** 223

Romola (Eliot), **II:** 291; **IV:** 311

Romulus: A New Comedy (Vidal), **Supp. IV Part 2:** 683

Romulus der Grosse (Dürrenmatt), **Supp. IV Part 2:** 683

Ronald, Ann, **Supp. XIII:** 4, 5, 6, 7, 9, 11

"Rondel for a September Day" (White), **Supp. I Part 2:** 676

"Ron Narrative Reconstructions, The" (Coleman), **Supp. XI:** 83

Ronsard, Pierre de, **Supp. X:** 65; **Supp. XV:** 165

Rood, John, **IV:** 261

"Roof, the Steeple, and the People, The" (Ellison), **Retro. Supp. II:** 118, 126; **Supp. II Part 1:** 248

"Room" (Levertov), **Supp. III Part 1:** 282

"Room at the Heart of Things, A" (Merrill), **Supp. III Part 1:** 337

Room Called Remember, A: Uncollected Pieces (Buechner), **Supp. XII:** 53

"Roomful of Hovings, A" (McPhee), **Supp. III Part 1:** 291, 294

Room of One's Own, A (Woolf), **Supp. V:** 127; **Supp. IX:** 19; **Supp. XIII:** 305

Room Rented by a Single Woman (Wright), **Supp. XV:** 340–341

Room Temperature (Baker), **Supp. XIII:** 41, 43–45, 48, 50

Room to Swing (Lacy), **Supp. XV:** 202, 203, 205, 207

"Room Upstairs, The" (Gioia), **Supp. XV:** 120–121, 124

Roosevelt, Eleanor, **IV:** 371; **Supp. IV Part 2:** 679

Roosevelt, Franklin, **Supp. V:** 290

Roosevelt, Franklin Delano, **I:** 482, 485, 490; **II:** 553, 575; **III:** 2, 18, 69, 110, 297, 321, 376, 476, 580, 581; **Supp. I Part 2:** 488, 489, 490, 491, 645, 654, 655

Roosevelt, Kermit, **III:** 508

Roosevelt, Theodore, **I:** 14, 62; **II:** 130; **III:** 508; **IV:** 321; **Retro. Supp. I:** 377; **Supp. I Part 1:** 1, 21; **Supp. I Part 2:** 455, 456, 502, 707; **Supp. V:** 280, 282; **Supp. IX:** 184

Roosevelt After Inauguration And Other Atrocities (Burroughs), **Supp. III Part 1:** 98

"Roosters" (Bishop), **Retro. Supp. II:** 39, 43, 250; **Supp. I Part 1:** 89

Root, Abiah, **I:** 456

Root, Elihu, **Supp. IV Part 1:** 33

Root, Simeon, **I:** 548

Root, Timothy, **I:** 548

Rootabaga Stories (Sandburg), **III:** 583, 587

"Rootedness: The Ancestor as Foundation" (Morrison), **Supp. III Part 1:** 361

Roots in the Soil (film), **Supp. IV Part 1:** 83

"Rope" (Porter), **III:** 451

Rope, The (O'Neill), **III:** 388

Ropemakers of Plymouth, The (Morison), **Supp. I Part 2:** 494

"Ropes" (Nye), **Supp. XIII:** 276

"Rope's End, The" (Nemerov), **III:** 282

Roquelaure, A. N., **Supp. VII:** 301. *See also* Rice, Anne

Rorem, Ned, **Supp. IV Part 1:** 79, 84

"Rosa" (Ozick), **Supp. V:** 271

Rosa, Rodrigo Rey, **Supp. IV Part 1:** 92

Rosaldo, Renato, **Supp. IV Part 2:** 544

"Rosalia" (Simic), **Supp. VIII:** 278

Roscoe, Will, **Supp. IV Part 1:** 330

"Rose" (Dubus), **Supp. VII:** 88

Rose (L.-Y. Lee), **Supp. XV:** 211, 212–215, 218

Rose, Alice, Sister, **III:** 348

Rose, Mickey, **Supp. XV:** 3

Rose, Philip, **Supp. IV Part 1:** 362

"Rose, The" (Roethke), **III:** 537

"Rose, The" (W. C. Williams), **Retro. Supp. I:** 419

Rose, Where Did You Get That Red?: Teaching Great Poetry to Children (Koch), **Supp. XV:** 189

"Rose for Emily, A" (Faulkner), **II:** 72; **Supp. IX:** 96

Rose in Bloom (Alcott), **Supp. I Part 1:** 42

"Rose-Johnny" (Kingsolver), **Supp. VII:** 203

Rose Madder (King), **Supp. V:** 141, 148, 150, 152

"Rose-Morals" (Lanier), **Supp. I Part 1:** 364

Rosen, Kenneth, **Supp. IV Part 2:** 499, 505, 513

Rosenbaum, Alissa Zinovievna. *See* Rand, Ayn

Rosenberg, Bernard, **Supp. I Part 2:** 650

Rosenberg, Harold, **Supp. XV:** 143

Rosenberg, Julius and Ethel, **Supp. I Part 1:** 295; **Supp. I Part 2:** 532; **Supp. V:** 45

Rosenberg, Liz, **Supp. XV:** 251

Rosenbloom, Joel, **Supp. IV Part 2:** 527

Rosenfeld, Alvin H., **Supp. I Part 1:** 120

Rosenfeld, Isaac, **Supp. XII:** 160

Rosenfeld, Paul, **I:** 116, 117, 231, 245

Rosenfelt, Deborah, **Supp. XIII:** 296, 304

Rosenfield, Isaac, **IV:** 3

Rosenthal, Ira, **Supp. XIV:** 146–147

Rosenthal, Lois, **Supp. VIII:** 258

Rosenthal, M. L., **II:** 550; **III:** 276, 479; **Supp. V:** 333

"Rose Pogonias" (Frost), **Retro. Supp. I:** 127

"Rose Red and Snow White" (Grimms), **Supp. X:** 82

"Roses" (Conroy), **Supp. XVI:** 72

"Roses" (Dove), **Supp. IV Part 1:** 246

"Roses and Skulls" (Goldbarth), **Supp. XII:** 192

"Roses for Lubbock" (Nye), **Supp. XIII:** 281

"Roses Only" (Moore), **III:** 195, 198, 200, 202, 215

Rose Tattoo, The (T. Williams), **IV:** 382, 383, 387, 388, 389, 392–393, 394, 397, 398

"Rosewood, Ohio" (Matthews), **Supp. IX:** 160

Rosinante to the Road Again (Dos Passos), **I:** 478

Roskolenko, Harry, **Supp. XV:** 179

Rosmersholm (Ibsen), **III:** 152

Rosmond, Babette, **II:** 432

Ross, Eleanor. *See* Taylor, Eleanor Ross

Ross, Harold, **Supp. I Part 1:** 174; **Supp. I Part 2:** 607, 617, 653, 654, 655, 660; **Supp. VIII:** 151, 170; **Supp. IX:** 190

Ross, Herbert, **Supp. XV:** 2

Ross, John F., **II:** 110

Ross, Lillilan, **Retro. Supp. II:** 198

Ross, Mitchell S., **Supp. IV Part 2:** 692; **Supp. X:** 260

Rossen, Robert, **Supp. XI:** 306

Rosset, Barney, **III:** 171

Rossetti, Christina, **Supp. XIV:** 128

Rossetti, Dante Gabriel, **I:** 433; **II:** 323; **Retro. Supp. I:** 128, 286; **Supp. I Part 2:** 552

Rossetti, William Michael, **Retro. Supp. I:** 407

Rosskam, Edwin, **IV:** 477

Ross Macdonald (Bruccoli), **Supp. IV Part 2:** 468, 470

Rostand, Edmond, **II:** 515; **Supp. IV Part 2:** 518

Rosy Crucifixion, The (H. Miller), **III:** 170, 187, 188–189, 190

Roth, Henry, **Supp. IV Part 1:** 314; **Supp. VIII:** 233; **Supp. IX:** 227–243; **Supp. XIII:** 106

Roth, Philip, **I:** 144, 161; **II:** 591; **Retro. Supp. II:** 22, 279–297; **Supp. I Part 1:** 186, 192; **Supp. I Part 2:** 431, 441, 443; **Supp. II Part 1:** 99; **Supp. III Part 2:** 401–429; **Supp. IV Part 1:** 236, 379, 388; **Supp. V:** 45, 119, 122, 257, 258; **Supp. VIII:** 88, 236, 245; **Supp. IX:** 227; **Supp. XI:** 64, 68, 99, 140; **Supp. XII:** 190, 310; **Supp. XIV:** 79, 93, 111, 112; **Supp. XVI:** 206

Roth, Rita, **Supp. XVI:** 112

Roth, William, **Supp. XV:** 142

Rothenberg, Jerome, **Supp. VIII:** 292; **Supp. XII:** 3

Rothermere, Lady Mary, **Retro. Supp. I:** 63

Rothko, Mark, **Supp. XV:** 144

Rothstein, Mervyn, **Supp. VIII:** 142

"Rouge High" (Hughes), **Supp. I Part 1:** 330

Rougemont, Denis de, **II:** 586; **IV:** 216; **Retro. Supp. I:** 328, 329, 330, 331

Roughing It (Twain), **II:** 312; **IV:** 195, 197, 198

Roughing It in the Bush (Shields), **Supp. VII:** 313

"Rough Outline" (Simic), **Supp. VIII:** 276

Rougon-Macquart, Les (Zola), **II:** 175–176

Roumain, Jacques, **Retro. Supp. I:** 202; **Supp. IV Part 1:** 360, 367

"Round, The" (Kunitz), **Supp. III Part 1:** 268

"Round Trip" (Dunn), **Supp. XI:** 148–149

Round Up (Lardner), **II:** 426, 430, 431

Rourke, Constance, **I:** 258; **IV:** 339, 352

Rourke, Milton, **Retro. Supp. II:** 89

Rousseau, Jean-Jacques, **I:** 226; **II:** 8, 343; **III:** 170, 178, 259; **IV:** 80, 173, 440; **Supp. I Part 1:** 126; **Supp. I Part 2:** 637, 659; **Supp. IV Part 1:** 171; **Supp. XI:** 245; **Supp. XVI:**292

Roussel, Raymond, **Supp. III Part 1:** 6, 7, 10, 15, 16, 21; **Supp. XV:** 182

"Routes" (Everwine), **Supp. XV:** 82

"Route Six" (Kunitz), **Supp. III Part 1:** 258

Route Two (Erdrich and Dorris), **Supp. IV Part 1:** 260

"Routine Things Around the House, The" (Dunn), **Supp. XI:** 148

Rover Boys (Winfield), **III:** 146

Rovit, Earl, **IV:** 102

Rowan, Carl T., **Supp. XIV:**306

Rowe, Anne E., **Supp. X:** 223

Rowe, John Carlos, **Retro. Supp. I:** 216

"Rowing" (Sexton), **Supp. II Part 2:** 696

"Rowing Endeth, The" (Sexton), **Supp. II Part 2:** 696

Rowlandson, Mary, **Supp. IV Part 2:** 430, 431

"Rows of Cold Trees, The" (Winters), **Supp. II Part 2:** 790–791, 800

Rowson, Susanna, **Supp. I Part 1:** 128; **Supp. XV:** 229–248

Roxanna Slade (Price), **Supp. VI:** 267

Roxie Hart (Watkins), **Supp. XVI:**188

"Royal Palm" (Crane), **I:** 401

Royce, Josiah, **I:** 443; **III:** 303, 600; **IV:** 26; **Retro. Supp. I:** 57; **Supp. XIV:**197, 199

Royster, Sarah Elmira, **III:** 410, 429

Royte, Elizabeth, **Supp. XV:** 59

Rózewicz, Tadeusz, **Supp. X:** 60

Ruas, Charles, **Supp. IV Part 1:** 383

Rubáiyát (Khayyám), **I:** 568

Rubáiyát of Omar Khayyam (Fitzgerald), **Supp. I Part 2:** 416; **Supp. III Part 2:** 610; **Supp. XV:** 156

"Rubber Life" (Prose), **Supp. XVI:**256

Rub from Snub, A (Swanwick), **Supp. XV:** 237

Rubin, Louis, **Supp. I Part 2:** 672, 673, 679; **Supp. X:** 42

Rubin, Louis D., Jr., **IV:** 116, 462–463

Rubin, Stan, **Supp. XIV:**307, 310

Rubin, Stan Sanvel, **Supp. IV Part 1:** 242, 245, 252

"Ruby Brown" (Hughes), **Supp. I Part 1:** 327

"Ruby Daggett" (Eberhart), **I:** 539

Rucker, Rudy, **Supp. X:** 302

Rudd, Hughes, **Supp. XII:** 141

"Rude Awakening, A" (Chopin), **Retro. Supp. II:** 64

Rudens (Plautus), **Supp. III Part 2:** 630

Ruderman, Judith, **Supp. IV Part 1:** 380

Rudge, Olga, **Supp. V:** 338

Rudikoff, Sonya, **Supp. XIV:**113

Rueckert, William, **I:** 264

Ruesch, Jurgen, **Supp. XV:** 147

Rugby Chapel (Arnold), **Supp. I Part 2:** 416

"Rugby Road" (Garrett), **Supp. VII:** 100

Ruining the New Road (Matthews), **Supp. IX:** 154, 155–157

"Ruins of Italica, The" (Bryant, trans.), **Supp. I Part 1:** 166

Rukeyser, Muriel, **Retro. Supp. II:** 48; **Supp. VI:** 271–289; **Supp. XV:** 349

"Rule of Phase Applied to History, The" (Adams), **I:** 19

Rule of the Bone (Banks), **Supp. V:** 16

"Rules by Which a Great Empire May Be Reduced to a Small One" (Franklin), **II:** 120

Rules For the Dance: A Handbook for Reading and Writing Metrical Verse (Oliver), **Supp. VII:** 229, 247

Rules of the Game, The (film), **Supp. XII:** 259

Rulfo, Juan, **Supp. IV Part 2:** 549

Rumbaut, Rubén, **Supp. XI:** 184

Rumens, Carol, **Supp. XI:** 14; **Supp. XVI:**212

Rumkowski, Chaim, **Supp. XII:** 168

Rummel, Mary Kay, **Supp. XIII:** 280

"Rumor and a Ladder" (Bowles), **Supp. IV Part 1:** 93

Rumors (Simon), **Supp. IV Part 2:** 582–583, 591

Rumpelstiltskin (Gardner), **Supp. VI:** 72

"Rumpelstiltskin" (Grimm), **IV:** 266

"Rumpelstiltskin" (Sexton), **Supp. II Part 2:** 690

"Runagate Runagate" (Hayden), **Supp. II Part 1:** 377

"Runes" (Nemerov), **III:** 267, 277–278

Run Man Run (C. Himes), **Supp. XVI:**142, 143

"Running" (Wilbur), **Supp. III Part 2:** 558–559

Running Dog (DeLillo), **Supp. VI:** 3, 6, 8, 14

"Running the Table" Conroy), **Supp. XVI:**75

"Run of Bad Luck, A" (Proulx), **Supp. VII:** 253–254

Run of Jacks, A (Hugo), **Supp. VI:** 131, 133, 134, 135, 136

Run River (Didion), **Supp. IV Part 1:** 197, 199–200, 201

Ruoff, A. LaVonne Brown, **Supp. IV Part 1:** 324, 327; **Supp. IV Part 2:** 559

Rupert, Jim, **Supp. XII:** 215

Ruppert, James, **Supp. IV Part 1:** 321

Rural Hours (Cooper), **Supp. XIII:** 152

"Rural Route" (Wright), **Supp. V:** 340

"Rural South, The" (Du Bois), **Supp. II Part 1:** 174

Rush, Benjamin, **Supp. I Part 2:** 505, 507

Rushdie, Salman, **Supp. IV Part 1:** 234, 297

Rushdy, Ashraf, **Supp. X:** 250

Rushing, Jimmy, **Retro. Supp. II:** 113

Rusk, Dean, **II:** 579

Ruskin, John, **II:** 323, 338; **IV:** 349; **Retro. Supp. I:** 56, 360; **Supp. I Part 1:** 2, 10, 87, 349; **Supp. I Part 2:** 410

Russell, Ada Dwyer, **II:** 513, 527

Russell, Bertrand, **II:** 27; **III:** 605, 606; **Retro. Supp. I:** 57, 58, 59, 60; **Supp. I Part 2:** 522; **Supp. V:** 290; **Supp. XII:** 45; **Supp. XIV:**337

Russell, Diarmuid, **Retro. Supp. I:** 342, 345, 346–347, 349–350

Russell, George, **Retro. Supp. I:** 342

Russell, Herb, **Supp. I Part 2:** 465–466

Russell, John, **Supp. XIV:**344, 347, 348

Russell, Peter, **III:** 479

Russell, Richard, **Supp. XI:** 102

Russell, Sue, **Supp. IV Part 2:** 653

Russert, Tim, **Supp. XII:** 272

Russia at War (Caldwell), **I:** 296

Russian Journal, A (Steinbeck), **IV:** 52, 63

Russo, Richard, **Supp. XI:** 349; **Supp. XII:** 325–344

"Rusty Autumn" (Swenson), **Supp. IV Part 2:** 640

Rutabaga-Roo: I've Got a Song and It's for You (Nye, album), **Supp. XIII:** 274

Ruth (biblical book), **Supp. I Part 2:** 516

Ruth, George Herman ("Babe"), **II:** 423; **Supp. I Part 2:** 438, 440

Ruth Hall (Fern), **Supp. V:** 122

Rutledge, Ann, **III:** 588; **Supp. I Part 2:** 471

Ruwe, Donelle R., **Supp. XII:** 215

Ryder (Barnes), **Supp. III Part 1:** 31, 36–38, 42, 43

"Ryder" (Rukeyser), **Supp. VI:** 273, 283

Rymer, Thomas, **IV:** 122

S

S-1 (Baraka), **Supp. II Part 1:** 55, 57

S. (Updike), **Retro. Supp. I:** 330, 331, 332, 333

Saadi, **II:** 19

Saar, Doreen Alvarez, **Supp. XV:** 237

"Sabbath, The" (Stowe), **Supp. I Part 2:** 587

"Sabbath Mom" (White), **Supp. I Part 2:** 671–672

Sabbaths (Berry), **Supp. X:** 31

Sabbath's Theater (Roth), **Retro. Supp. II:** 279, 288

Sabines, Jaime, **Supp. V:** 178

"Sabotage" (Baraka), **Supp. II Part 1:** 49, 53

Sacco, Nicola, **I:** 482, 486, 490, 494; **II:** 38–39, 426; **III:** 139–140; **Supp. I Part 2:** 446; **Supp. V:** 288–289; **Supp. IX:** 199

Sachs, Hanns, **Supp. I Part 1:** 259; **Supp. X:** 186

"Sacks" (Carver), **Supp. III Part 1:** 143–144

Sacks, Peter, **Supp. IV Part 2:** 450

Sackville-West, Vita, **Supp. VIII:** 263

"Sacrament of Divorce, The" (Patchett), **Supp. XII:** 309

"Sacraments" (Dubus), **Supp. VII:** 91

Sacred and Profane Memories (Van Vechten), **Supp. II Part 2:** 735, 749

"Sacred Chant for the Return of Black Spirit and Power" (Baraka), **Supp. II Part 1:** 51

"Sacred Factory, The" (Toomer), **Supp. IX:** 320

Sacred Fount, The (James), **II:** 332–333; **Retro. Supp. I:** 219, 228, 232

"Sacred Hoop, The: A Contemporary Perspective" (Gunn Allen), **Supp. IV Part 1:** 324

Sacred Hoop, The: Recovering the Feminine in American Indian Traditions (Gunn Allen), **Supp. IV Part 1:** 319, 320, 322, 324, 325, 328–330, 331, 333, 334

Sacred Journey, The (Buechner), **Supp. XII:** 42, 53

Sacred Wood, The (Eliot), **IV:** 431; **Retro. Supp. I:** 59, 60; **Supp. I Part 1:** 268; **Supp. II Part 1:** 136, 146

Sacrifice, The (Bidart), **Supp. XV:** 22, 27–30, 35

"Sacrifice, The" (Bidart), **Supp. XV:** 29

"Sacrifice, The" (Oates), **Supp. II Part 2:** 523

Sacrilege of Alan Kent, The (Caldwell), **I:** 291–292

"Sad Brazil" (Hardwick), **Supp. III Part 1:** 210

"Sad Dust Glories" (Ginsberg), **Supp. II Part 1:** 376

Sad Dust Glories: Poems Written Work Summer in Sierra Woods (Ginsberg), **Supp. II Part 1:** 326

Sade, Marquis de, **III:** 259; **IV:** 437, 442; **Supp. XII:** 1, 14–15

Sad Flower in the Sand, A (film), **Supp. XI:** 173

Sad Heart at the Supermarket, A (Jarrell), **II:** 386

"Sadie" (Matthiessen), **Supp. V:** 201

Sadness and Happiness (Pinsky), **Supp. VI:** 235, 237–241

"Sadness of Brothers, The" (Kinnell), **Supp. III Part 1:** 237, 251

"Sadness of Days, The" (Salinas), **Supp. XIII:** 325

Sadness of Days, The: Selected and New Poems (Salinas), **Supp. XIII:** 311, 324–326

"Sadness of Lemons, The" (Levine), **Supp. V:** 184

"Sad Rite" (Karr), **Supp. XI:** 243

"Sad Strains of a Gay Waltz" (Stevens), **Retro. Supp. I:** 302

"Safe" (Gordon), **Supp. IV Part 1:** 299, 306

"Safe in their Alabaster Chambers" (Dickinson), **Retro. Supp. I:** 30

"Safe Subjects" (Komunyakaa), **Supp. XIII:** 118

"Safeway" (F. Barthelme), **Supp. XI:** 26, 27, 36

Saffin, John, **Supp. I Part 1:** 115

Saffy, Edna, **Supp. X:** 227

"Saga of Arturo Bandini" (Fante), **Supp. XI:** 159, 166–169

"Saga of King Olaf, The" (Longfellow), **II:** 489, 505; **Retro. Supp. II:** 154, 155, 164

"Sage of Stupidity and Wonder, The" (Goldbarth), **Supp. XII:** 191

Sahl, Mort, **II:** 435–436

"Said" (Dixon), **Supp. XII:** 149–150

"Sailing after Lunch" (Stevens), **IV:** 73

"Sailing Home from Rapallo" (Lowell), **Retro. Supp. II:** 189

Sailing through China (Theroux), **Supp. VIII:** 323

"Sailing to Byzantium" (Yeats), **III:** 263; **Supp. VIII:** 30; **Supp. X:** 74; **Supp. XI:** 281

"Sail Made of Rags, The" (Nye), **Supp. XIII:** 277

"Sailors Lost at Sea" (Shields), **Supp. VII:** 318

"St. Augustine and the Bullfights" (Porter), **III:** 454

St. Elmo (Wilson), **Retro. Supp. I:** 351–352

"St. Francis Einstein of the Daffodils" (W. C. Williams), **IV:** 409–411

"St. George, the Dragon, and the Virgin" (R. Bly), **Supp. IV Part 1:** 73

St. George and the Godfather (Mailer), **III:** 46; **Retro. Supp. II:** 206, 208

St. John, David, **Supp. V:** 180; **Supp. XI:** 270, 272; **Supp. XIII:** 312

St. John, Edward B., **Supp. IV Part 2:** 490

St. John, James Hector. *See* Crèvecoeur, Michel-Guillaume Jean de

St. Louis Woman (Bontemps and Cullen), **Supp. IV Part 1:** 170

St. Mawr (Lawrence), **II:** 595

St. Petersburg (Biely), **Supp. XII:** 13

"St. Roach" (Rukeyser), **Supp. VI:** 286

"St. Thomas Aquinas" (Simic), **Supp. VIII:** 281

"*St Anne*/Santa Ana" (Mora), **Supp. XIII:** 229

"*Saint Anthony of Padua*/San Antonio de Padua" (Mora), **Supp. XIII:** 228

Sainte-Beuve, Charles Augustin, **IV:** 432

"Saint Emmanuel the Good, Martyr" (Unamuno; Everwine, trans.), **Supp. XV:** 79

Sainte Vierge, La (Picabia), **Retro. Supp. II:** 331

Saint-Exupéry, Antoine de, **Supp. IX:** 247

Saint-Gaudens, Augustus, **I:** 18, 228; **II:** 551

Saint-Gaudens, Homer, **Supp. XV:** 41

Saint Jack (Theroux), **Supp. VIII:** 319

"Saint John and the Back-Ache" (Stevens), **Retro. Supp. I:** 310

Saint Judas (Wright), **Supp. III Part 2:** 595–599

"Saint Judas" (Wright), **Supp. III Part 2:** 598–599

Saint Maybe (Tyler), **Supp. IV Part 2:** 670–671

"Saint Nicholas" (Moore), **III:** 215

Saint-Phalle, Niki de, **Supp. XV:** 187

"Saint Robert" (Dacey), **Supp. IV Part 1:** 70

Saintsbury, George, **IV:** 440; **Supp. XV:** 181

Saints' Everlasting Rest, The (Baxter), **III:** 199; **IV:** 151, 153

Saint-Simon, Claude Henri, **Supp. I Part 2:** 648

Saks, Gene, **Supp. IV Part 2:** 577, 588

Salamun, Tomaz, **Supp. VIII:** 272

Salazar, Dixie, **Supp. V:** 180; **Supp. XV:** 73

Saldívar, José David, **Supp. IV Part 2:** 544, 545

Sale, Richard, **Supp. IV Part 1:** 379

Sale, Roger, **Supp. V:** 244

Saleh, Dennis, **Supp. V:** 182, 186

"Salem" (Lowell), **II:** 550

Salemi, Joseph, **Supp. IV Part 1:** 284

Salem's Lot (King), **Supp. V:** 139, 144, 146, 151

"Sale of the Hessians, The" (Franklin), **II:** 120

Salinas, Luis Omar, **Supp. IV Part 2:** 545; **Supp. V:** 180; **Supp. XIII:** 311–330; **Supp. XV:** 73

"Salinas Is on His Way" (Salinas), **Supp. XIII:** 317

"Salinas Sends Messengers to the Stars" (Salinas), **Supp. XIII:** 317

"Salinas Summering at the Caspian and Thinking of Hamlet" (Salinas), **Supp. XIII:** 320

"Salinas Wakes Early and Goes to the Park to Lecture Sparrows" (Salinas), **Supp. XIII:** 320

Salinger, Doris, **III:** 551

Salinger, J. D., **II:** 255; **III:** 551–574; **IV:** 190, 216, 217; **Retro. Supp. I:**

102, 116, 335; **Supp. IV Part 2:** 502; **Supp. V:** 23, 119; **Supp. VIII:** 151; **Supp. XI:** 2, 66; **Supp. XIV:**93

Salisbury, Harrison, **Supp. I Part 2:** 664

Salle, David, **Supp. XII:** 4

Salley, Columbus, **Supp. XIV:**195

"Sally" (Cisneros), **Supp. VII:** 63

"Sally's Choice" (E. Stoddard), **Supp. XV:** 282

Salmagundi; or, The Whim-Whams and Opinions of Launcelot Langstaff Esq., and Others (Irving), **II:** 299, 300, 304

Salome (Strauss), **IV:** 316

Salon (online magazine), **Supp. VIII:** 310; **Supp. X:** 202

Salt Eaters, The (Bambara), **Supp. XI:** 1, 12–14

Salt Ecstasies, The (White), **Supp. XI:** 123

Salter, James, **Supp. IX:** 245–263; **Supp. XVI:**237, 247

Salter, Mary Jo, **Supp. IV Part 2:** 653; **Supp. IX:** 37, 292; **Supp. XV:** 251, 253

Salt Garden, The (Nemerov), **III:** 269, 272–275, 277

"Salt Garden, The" (Nemerov), **III:** 267–268

Salting the Ocean (Nye, ed.), **Supp. XIII:** 280

Salt Lesson, The (C. Frost), **Supp. XV:** 92, 96

"Salt Lesson, The" (C. Frost), **Supp. XV:** 99

"Salts and Oils" (Levine), **Supp. V:** 190

Saltzman, Arthur, **Supp. XIII:** 48

Saltzman, Harry, **Supp. XI:** 307

"Salut au Monde!" (Whitman), **Retro. Supp. I:** 387, 396, 400

"Salute" (MacLeish), **III:** 13

"Salute to Mister Yates, A" (Dubus), **Supp. XI:** 347, 349

Salvador (Didion), **Supp. IV Part 1:** 198, 207–208, 210

"Salvage" (Clampitt), **Supp. IX:** 41

Samain, Albert, **II:** 528

Same Door, The (Updike), **IV:** 214, 219, 226; **Retro. Supp. I:** 320

"Same in Blues" (Hughes), **Retro. Supp. I:** 208

Sam Lawson's Oldtown Fireside Stories (Stowe), **Supp. I Part 2:** 587, 596, 598–599

"Sa'm Pèdi" (Bell), **Supp. X:** 17

"Sampler, A" (MacLeish), **III:** 4

Sampoli, Maria, **Supp. V:** 338

Sampson, Edward, **Supp. I Part 2:** 664, 673

Sampson, Martin, **Supp. I Part 2:** 652

Sam's Legacy (Neugeboren), **Supp. XVI:**221, 222

Samson Agonistes (Milton), **III:** 274

"Samson and Delilah" (Masters), **Supp. I Part 2:** 459

Samuel de Champlain: Father of New France (Morison), **Supp. I Part 2:** 496–497

Samuels, Charles Thomas, **Retro. Supp. I:** 334

"Samuel Sewall" (Hecht), **Supp. X:** 58

Sanborn, Franklin B., **IV:** 171, 172, 178

Sanborn, Kate, **Supp. XIII:** 152

Sanborn, Sara, **Supp. XIV:**113

Sanchez, Carol Anne, **Supp. IV Part 1:** 335

Sanchez, Carol Lee, **Supp. IV Part 2:** 499, 557

Sanchez, Sonia, **Supp. II Part 1:** 34

Sanctified Church, The (Hurston), **Supp. VI:** 150

"Sanction of the Victims, The" (Rand), **Supp. IV Part 2:** 528

Sanctuary (Faulkner), **II:** 57, 61–63, 72, 73, 74, 174; **Retro. Supp. I:** 73, 84, 86–87, 87; **Supp. I Part 2:** 614; **Supp. XII:** 16

Sanctuary (Wharton), **IV:** 311

"Sanctuary" (Wylie), **Supp. I Part 2:** 711

"Sanctuary, The" (Nemerov), **III:** 272, 274

Sand, George, **II:** 322; **Retro. Supp. I:** 235, 372; **Supp. XV:** 275

"Sandalphon" (Longfellow), **II:** 498

Sandbox, The (Albee), **I:** 74–75, 89

Sandburg, Carl, **I:** 103, 109, 384, 421; **II:** 529; **III:** 3, 20, 575–598; **Retro. Supp. I:** 133, 194; **Supp. I Part 1:** 257, 320; **Supp. I Part 2:** 387, 389, 454, 461, 653; **Supp. III Part 1:** 63, 71, 73, 75; **Supp. IV Part 1:** 169; **Supp. IV Part 2:** 502; **Supp. IX:** 1, 15, 308; **Supp. XIII:** 274, 277; **Supp. XV:** 293, 299, 300, 301, 302, 306

Sandburg, Helga, **III:** 583

Sandburg, Janet, **III:** 583, 584

Sandburg, Margaret, **III:** 583, 584

Sandburg, Mrs. Carl (Lillian Steichen), **III:** 580

Sand County Almanac and Sketches Here and There, A (Leopold), **Supp. XIV:**177, 178, 182–192

"Sand Dabs" (Oliver), **Supp. VII:** 245

"Sand Dunes" (Frost), **Retro. Supp. I:**

137; **Retro. Supp. II:** 41

Sander, August, **Supp. IX:** 211

Sanders, Scott Russell, **Supp. XVI:**265–280

"Sandman, The" (Barthelme), **Supp. IV Part 1:** 47

Sando, Joe S., **Supp. IV Part 2:** 510

Sandoe, James, **Supp. IV Part 1:** 131; **Supp. IV Part 2:** 470

Sandoz, Mari, **Supp. XV:** 141

Sandperl, Ira, **Supp. VIII:** 200

"Sand-Quarry and Moving Figures" (Rukeyser), **Supp. VI:** 271, 278

Sand Rivers (Matthiessen), **Supp. V:** 203

"Sand Roses, The" (Hogan), **Supp. IV Part 1:** 401

Sands, Diana, **Supp. IV Part 1:** 362

Sands, Robert, **Supp. I Part 1:** 156, 157

"Sands at Seventy" (Whitman), **IV:** 348

"Sandstone Farmhouse, A" (Updike), **Retro. Supp. I:** 318

Sandy Bottom Orchestra, The (Keillor and Nilsson), **Supp. XVI:**177

Sanford, John, **IV:** 286, 287

San Francisco (film), **Supp. XVI:**181, 192

"San Francisco Blues" (Kerouac), **Supp. III Part 1:** 225

Sangamon County Peace Advocate, The (Lindsay), **Supp. I Part 2:** 379

Sanger, Margaret, **Supp. I Part 1:** 19

Sansom, William, **IV:** 279

Sans Soleil (film), **Supp. IV Part 2:** 436

"Santa" (Sexton), **Supp. II Part 2:** 693

Santa Claus: A Morality (Cummings), **I:** 430, 441

"Santa Fé Trail, The" (Lindsay), **Supp. I Part 2:** 389

"Santa Lucia" (Hass), **Supp. VI:** 105–106

"Santa Lucia II" (Hass), **Supp. VI:** 105–106

Santayana, George, **I:** 222, 224, 236, 243, 253, 460; **II:** 20, 542; **III:** 64, 599–622; **IV:** 26, 339, 351, 353, 441; **Retro. Supp. I:** 55, 57, 67, 295; **Retro. Supp. II:** 179; **Supp. I Part 2:** 428; **Supp. II Part 1:** 107; **Supp. X:** 58; **Supp. XIV:**199, 335, 340, 342; **Supp. XVI:**189

Santiago, Esmeralda, **Supp. XI:** 177

"Santorini: Stopping the Leak" (Merrill), **Supp. III Part 1:** 336

Santos, John Phillip, **Supp. XIII:** 274

Santos, Sherod, **Supp. VIII:** 270

Sapir, Edward, **Supp. VIII:** 295; **Supp. XVI:**283

Sapphira and the Slave Girl (Cather), **I:** 331; **Retro. Supp. I:** 2, 19–20

Sappho, **II:** 544; **III:** 142; **Supp. I Part 1:** 261, 269; **Supp. I Part 2:** 458; **Supp. XII:** 98, 99

"Sappho" (Wright), **Supp. III Part 2:** 595, 604

"Sarah" (Schwartz), **Supp. II Part 2:** 663

Sarah; or, The Exemplary Wife (Rowson), **Supp. XV:** 242

"Saratoga" mysteries (Dobyns), **Supp. XIII:** 79–80

Sargent, John Singer, **II:** 337, 338

Saroyan, Aram, **Supp. XV:** 182

Saroyan, William, **III:** 146–147; **IV:** 393; **Supp. I Part 2:** 679; **Supp. IV Part 1:** 83; **Supp. IV Part 2:** 502; **Supp. XIII:** 280

Sarris, Greg, **Supp. IV Part 1:** 329, 330

Sarton, George, **Supp. VIII:** 249

Sarton, May, **Supp. III Part 1:** 62, 63; **Supp. VIII:** 249–268; **Supp. XIII:** 296

Sartoris (Faulkner), **II:** 55, 56–57, 58, 62; **Retro. Supp. I:** 77, 81, 82, 83, 88

Sartor Resartus (Carlyle), **II:** 26; **III:** 82

Sartre, Jean-Paul, **I:** 82, 494; **II:** 57, 244; **III:** 51, 204, 292, 453, 619; **IV:** 6, 223, 236, 477, 487, 493; **Retro. Supp. I:** 73; **Supp. I Part 1:** 51; **Supp. IV Part 1:** 42, 84; **Supp. VIII:** 11; **Supp. IX:** 4; **Supp. XIII:** 74, 171; **Supp. XIV:**24

Sassone, Ralph, **Supp. X:** 171

Sassoon, Siegfried, **II:** 367; **Supp. XV:** 308

Satan in Goray (Singer), **IV:** 1, 6–7, 12; **Retro. Supp. II:** 303, 304–305

Satan Says (Olds), **Supp. X:** 201, 202, 202–204, 215

"Satan Says" (Olds), **Supp. X:** 202

Satanstoe (Cooper), **I:** 351–352, 355

"Sather Gate Illumination" (Ginsberg), **Supp. II Part 1:** 329

"Satire as a Way of Seeing" (Dos Passos), **III:** 172

Satires of Persius, The (Merwin, trans.), **Supp. III Part 1:** 347

Satirical Rogue on Poetry, The (Francis). *See Pot Shots at Poetry* (Francis)

Satori in Paris (Kerouac), **Supp. III Part 1:** 231

"Saturday" (Salinas), **Supp. XIII:** 315

Saturday Night at the War (Shanley), **Supp. XIV:**315

"Saturday Rain" (Kees), **Supp. XV:** 136

"Saturday Route, The" (Wolfe), **Supp. III Part 2:** 580

Satyagraha (Gandhi), **IV:** 185

Saunders, Richard, **II:** 110

Savage, Augusta, **Retro. Supp. II:** 115

Savage, James, **II:** 111

Savage Holiday (Wright), **IV:** 478, 488

Savage in Limbo: A Concert Play (Shanley), **Supp. XIV:**315, 319–321, 323, 324

Savage Love (Shepard and Chaikin), **Supp. III Part 2:** 433

Savage Wilds (Reed), **Supp. X:** 241

Save Me, Joe Louis (Bell), **Supp. X:** 7, 10, 11–12

Save Me the Waltz (Z. Fitzgerald), **II:** 95; **Retro. Supp. I:** 110; **Supp. IX:** 58, 59, 65, 66–68

Savers, Michael, **Supp. XI:** 307

Saving Lives (Goldbarth), **Supp. XII:** 192

Saving Private Ryan (film), **Supp. V:** 249; **Supp. XI:** 234

Savings (Hogan), **Supp. IV Part 1:** 397, 404, 405, 406, 410

Savo, Jimmy, **I:** 440

Savran, David, **Supp. IX:** 145; **Supp. XIII:** 209; **Supp. XV:** 321

Sawyer-Lauçanno, Christopher, **Supp. IV Part 1:** 95

Saxon, Lyle, **Retro. Supp. I:** 80

Saye and Sele, Lord, **Supp. I Part 1:** 98

Sayer, Mandy, **Supp. XIII:** 118

Sayers, Dorothy, **Supp. IV Part 1:** 341; **Supp. IV Part 2:** 464

Sayers, Valerie, **Supp. XI:** 253

"Sayings/For Luck" (Goldbarth), **Supp. XII:** 176

Say! Is This the U.S.A.? (Caldwell), **I:** 293, 294–295, 304, 309, 310

Saylor, Bruce, **Supp. XII:** 253

Sayre, Joel, **Supp. XIII:** 166

Sayre, Nora, **Supp. XII:** 119

Sayre, Zelda, **Retro. Supp. I:** 101, 102–103, 104, 105, 108, 109, 110, 113, 114. *See also* Fitzgerald, Zelda (Zelda Sayre)

"Say Yes" (Wolff), **Supp. VII:** 344

"Scales of the Eyes, The" (Nemerov), **III:** 272, 273, 277

Scalpel (McCoy), **Supp. XIII:** 174–175

Scalpel (screen treatment, McCoy), **Supp. XIII:** 174

Scandalabra (Zelda Fitzgerald), **Supp. IX:** 60, 61, 65, 67, 68–70

"Scandal Detectives, The" (Fitzgerald), **II:** 80–81; **Retro. Supp. I:** 99

Scarberry-García, Susan, **Supp. IV Part 2:** 486

"Scarecrow, The" (Farrell), **II:** 45

"Scarf, A" (Shields), **Supp. VII:** 328

Scarlet Letter, The (Hawthorne), **II:** 63, 223, 224, 231, 233, 239–240, 241, 243, 244, 255, 264, 286, 290, 291, 550; **Retro. Supp. I:** 63, 145, 147, 152, 157–159, 160, 163, 165, 220, 248, 330, 335; **Retro. Supp. II:** 100; **Supp. I Part 1:** 38; **Supp. II Part 1:** 386; **Supp. VIII:** 108, 198; **Supp. XII:** 11

Scarlet Plague, The (London), **II:** 467

Scar Lover (Crews), **Supp. XI:** 103, 107, 114–115

"Scarred Girl, The" (Dickey), **Supp. IV Part 1:** 180

Scates, Maxine, **Supp. XIV:**264, 265, 274

"Scenario" (H. Miller), **III:** 184

"Scene" (Howells), **II:** 274

"Scene in Jerusalem, A" (Stowe), **Supp. I Part 2:** 587

"Scenes" (Shields), **Supp. VII:** 318

Scènes d'Anabase (chamber music) (Bowles), **Supp. IV Part 1:** 82

Scenes from American Life (Gurney), **Supp. V:** 95, 96, 105, 108

Scenes from Another Life (McClatchy), **Supp. XII:** 255–256

"Scenes of Childhood" (Merrill), **Supp. III Part 1:** 322, 323, 327

"Scented Herbage of My Breast" (Whitman), **IV:** 342–343

"Scent of a Woman's Ink" (Prose), **Supp. XVI:**259

"Scent of Unbought Flowers, The" (Ríos), **Supp. IV Part 2:** 547

Scepticisms (Aiken), **I:** 58

Scève, Maurice, **Supp. III Part 1:** 11

Schad, Christian, **Supp. IV Part 1:** 247

Schafer, Benjamin G., **Supp. XIV:**144

Schaller, George, **Supp. V:** 208, 210–211

Schapiro, Meyer, **II:** 30

Scharmann, Hermann Balthazar, **Supp. XII:** 41

Schary, Dore, **Supp. IV Part 1:** 365; **Supp. XIII:** 163

Schaumbergh, Count de, **II:** 120

Scheele, Roy, **Supp. XVI:**54

Scheffauer, G. H., **I:** 199

"Scheherazade" (Ashbery), **Supp. III Part 1:** 18

Scheick, William, **Supp. V:** 272

Scheler, Max, **I:** 58

Schelling, Friedrich, **Supp. I Part 2:** 422

Schenck, Joseph, **Supp. XVI:**186

Schenk, Margaret, **I:** 199

Scheponik, Peter, **Supp. X:** 210

Scherer, Loline, **Supp. XIII:** 161

Schevill, James, **I:** 116

Schickel, Richard, **Supp. XV:** 1

Schilder, Paul, **Supp. I Part 2:** 622

Schiller, Andrew, **II:** 20

Schiller, Frederick, **Supp. V:** 290

Schiller, Johann Christoph Friedrich von, **I:** 224; **Supp. IV Part 2:** 519; **Supp. XVI:**292

Schiller, Lawrence, **Retro. Supp. II:** 208, 212, 214

Schimmel, Harold, **Supp. V:** 336

Schlegel, Augustus Wilhelm, **III:** 422, 424

Schlegell, David von, **Supp. IV Part 2:** 423

Schleiermacher, Friedrich, **III:** 290–291, 309

Schlesinger, Arthur, Jr., **III:** 291, 297–298, 309

Schmidt, Jon Zlotnik, **Supp. IV Part 1:** 2

Schmidt, Kaspar. *See* Stirner, Max

Schmidt, Michael, **Supp. X:** 55

Schmitt, Carl, **I:** 386–387

Schmitz, Neil, **Supp. X:** 243

Schnackenberg, Gjertrud, **Supp. XV:** 249–268

Schneider, Alan, **I:** 87

Schneider, Louis, **Supp. I Part 2:** 650

Schneider, Romy, **Supp. IV Part 2:** 549

Schneider, Steven, **Supp. IX:** 271, 274

Schnellock, Emil, **III:** 177

Schneour, Zalman, **IV:** 11

Schnitzler, Arthur, **Supp. XV:** 307; **Supp. XVI:**187

"Scholar Gypsy, The" (Arnold), **II:** 541

"Scholastic and Bedside Teaching" (Holmes), **Supp. I Part 1:** 305

Schöler, Bo, **Supp. IV Part 1:** 399, 400, 403, 407, 409; **Supp. IV Part 2:** 499

Scholes, Robert, **Supp. V:** 40, 42

Schomburg, Arthur, **Supp. X:** 134

Schoolboy Howlers (Abingdon), **Supp. XVI:**99

Schoolcraft, Henry Rowe, **II:** 503; **Retro. Supp. II:** 160

"School Daze" (Bambara), **Supp. XI:** 19

School Daze (film), **Supp. XI:** 19, 20

"Schoolhouse" (Levis), **Supp. XI:** 258

"School of Giorgione, The" (Pater), **I:** 51

"School Play, The" (Merrill), **Supp. III Part 1:** 336

"Schooner Fairchild's Class" (Benét), **Supp. XI:** 55

Schopenhauer, Arthur, **III:** 600, 604; **IV:** 7; **Retro. Supp. I:** 256; **Retro. Supp. II:** 94; **Supp. I Part 1:** 320; **Supp. I Part 2:** 457; **Supp. X:** 187; **Supp. XVI:**184

Schorer, Mark, **II:** 28; **III:** 71; **Retro. Supp. I:** 115; **Supp. IV Part 1:** 197, 203, 211; **Supp. XVI:**206

Schott, Webster, **Supp. IX:** 257

Schotts, Jeffrey, **Supp. XII:** 193

Schrader, Mary von. *See* Jarrell, Mrs. Randall (Mary von Schrader)

Schreiner, Olive, **I:** 419; **Supp. XI:** 203

Schroeder, Eric James, **Supp. V:** 238, 244

Schubert, Franz Peter, **Supp. I Part 1:** 363

Schubnell, Matthias, **Supp. IV Part 2:** 486

Schulberg, Budd, **II:** 98; **Retro. Supp. I:** 113; **Supp. XIII:** 170; **Supp. XV:** 194

Schulz, Bruno, **Supp. IV Part 2:** 623

Schuman, William, **Supp. XII:** 253

Schumann, Dr. Alanson Tucker, **III:** 505

Schuster, Edgar H., **Supp. VIII:** 126

Schuyler, George S., **III:** 110; **Supp. XVI:**142

Schuyler, James, **Supp. XV:** 177, 178

Schuyler, William, **Supp. I Part 1:** 211

Schwartz, Delmore, **I:** 67, 168, 188, 288; **IV:** 128, 129, 437; **Retro. Supp. II:** 29, 178; **Supp. II Part 1:** 102, 109; **Supp. II Part 2:** 639–668; **Supp. VIII:** 98; **Supp. IX:** 299; **Supp. XIII:** 320; **Supp. XIV:**3; **Supp. XV:** 184

Schwartz, Leonard, **Supp. XVI:**289

Schwartz, Lloyd, **Supp. I Part 1:** 81

Schwartz, Marilyn, **Supp. XII:** 126, 128, 130, 132

Schwartz, Richard B., **Supp. XIV:**23, 27

Schweitzer, Albert, **Supp. IV Part 1:** 373

Schweitzer, Harold, **Supp. X:** 210

Schwerdt, Lisa M., **Supp. XIV:**155, 171

Schwitters, Kurt, **III:** 197; **Retro. Supp. II:** 322, 331, 336; **Supp. IV Part 1:** 79

"Science" (Jeffers), **Supp. II Part 2:** 426

Science and Health with Key to the Scriptures (Eddy), **I:** 383

"Science Favorable to Virtue" (Freneau), **Supp. II Part 1:** 274

Science of English Verse, The (Lanier), **Supp. I Part 1:** 368, 369

"Science of the Night, The" (Kunitz), **Supp. III Part 1:** 258, 265

Sciolino, Martina, **Supp. XII:** 9

Scopes, John T., **III:** 105, 495

"Scorched Face, The" (Hammett), **Supp. IV Part 1:** 344

"Scorn" (C. Frost), **Supp. XV:** 105

"Scorpion, The" (Bowles), **Supp. IV Part 1:** 84, 86

Scorsese, Martin, **Supp. IV Part 1:** 356

Scott, A. O., **Supp. X:** 301, 302; **Supp. XII:** 343

Scott, Anne Firor, **Supp. I Part 1:** 19

Scott, Evelyn, **Retro. Supp. I:** 73

Scott, George C., **III:** 165–166; **Supp. XI:** 304

Scott, George Lewis, **Supp. I Part 2:** 503, 504

Scott, Herbert, **Supp. V:** 180

Scott, Howard, **Supp. I Part 2:** 645

Scott, Lizabeth, **Supp. IV Part 2:** 524

Scott, Lynn Orilla, **Retro. Supp. II:** 12

Scott, Mark, **Retro. Supp. I:** 127

Scott, Nathan A., Jr., **II:** 27

Scott, Paul, **Supp. IV Part 2:** 690

Scott, Ridley, **Supp. XIII:** 268

Scott, Sir Walter, **I:** 204, 339, 341, 343, 354; **II:** 8, 17, 18, 217, 296, 301, 303, 304, 308; **III:** 415, 482; **IV:** 204, 453; **Retro. Supp. I:** 99; **Supp. I Part 2:** 579, 580, 685, 692; **Supp. IV Part 2:** 690; **Supp. IX:** 175; **Supp. X:** 51, 114

Scott, Walter, **Supp. XVI:**7, 13

Scott, Winfield Townley, **II:** 512; **Supp. I Part 2:** 705; **Supp. XV:** 51

Scottsboro boys, **I:** 505; **Supp. I Part 1:** 330

Scottsboro Limited (Hughes), **Retro. Supp. I:** 203; **Supp. I Part 1:** 328, 330–331, 332

Scoundrel Time (Hellman), **Supp. I Part 1:** 294–297; **Supp. IV Part 1:** 12; **Supp. VIII:** 243

Scrambled Eggs Super! (Geisel), **Supp. XVI:**105

Scrambled Eggs & Whiskey: Poems, 1991–1995 (Carruth), **Supp. XVI:**47

Scratch (MacLeish), **III:** 22–23

"Scratch Music" (Wright), **Supp. XV:** 343

"Scream, The" (Lowell), **II:** 550

"Screamer, The" (Coleman), **Supp. XI:** 92–93

"Screamers, The" (Baraka), **Supp. II Part 1:** 38

"Screen Guide for Americans" (Rand), **Supp. IV Part 2:** 524

"Screeno" (Schwartz), **Supp. II Part 2:** 660

Screens, The (Genet), **Supp. XII:** 12

Scripts for the Pageant (Merrill), **Supp. III Part 1:** 332, 333, 335

Scrolls from the Dead Sea, The (Wilson), **IV:** 429

Scruggs, Earl, **Supp. V:** 335

Scudder, Horace Elisha, **II:** 400, 401; **Retro. Supp. II:** 67; **Supp. I Part 1:** 220; **Supp. I Part 2:** 410, 414

Scully, James, **Supp. XII:** 131

"Sculpting the Whistle" (Ríos), **Supp. IV Part 2:** 549

"Sculptor" (Plath), **Supp. I Part 2:** 538

"Sculptor's Funeral, The" (Cather), **I:** 315–316; **Retro. Supp. I:** 5, 6; **Supp. XV:** 40

Scum (Singer), **Retro. Supp. II:** 316–317

Scupoli, Lorenzo, **IV:** 156

"Scythe Song" (Lang), **Retro. Supp. I:** 128

"*Se:* Hegel's Absolute and Heidegger's *Ereignis*" (Agamben), **Supp. XVI:**289

Sea and the Mirror, The: A Commentary on Shakespeare's "The Tempest" (Auden), **Supp. II Part 1:** 2, 18

Sea around Us, The (Carson), **Supp. IX:** 19, 23–25

Sea around Us, The (film), **Supp. IX:** 25

Sea Birds Are Still Alive, The (Bambara), **Supp. XI:** 1, 4, 7–12

"Sea Birds Are Still Alive, The" (Bambara), **Supp. XI:** 8

"Sea-Blue and Blood-Red" (Lowell), **II:** 524

Seabrook, John, **Supp. VIII:** 157

"Sea Burial from the Cruiser Reve" (Eberhart), **I:** 532–533

Seabury, David, **Supp. I Part 2:** 608

"Sea Calm" (Hughes), **Retro. Supp. I:** 199

"Sea Chanty" (Corso), **Supp. XII:** 118

"Sea Dream, A" (Whitter), **Supp. I Part 2:** 699

"Seafarer, The" (Pound, trans.), **Retro. Supp. I:** 287

Seagall, Harry, **Supp. XIII:** 166

Sea Garden (Doolittle), **Supp. I Part 1:** 257, 259, 266, 269, 272

Seager, Allan, **IV:** 305

"Seagulls and Children" (C. Frost), **Supp. XV:** 95

"Sea Lily" (Doolittle), **Supp. I Part 1:** 266

Sea Lions, The (Cooper), **I:** 354, 355

Sealts, Merton M., Jr., **Retro. Supp. I:** 257

Seaman, Donna, **Supp. VIII:** 86; **Supp. X:** 1, 4, 12, 16, 213; **Supp. XV:** 65

"Séance, The" (Singer), **IV:** 20

Séance and Other Stories, The (Singer), **IV:** 19–21

Sea of Cortez (Steinbeck), **IV:** 52, 54, 62, 69

"Sea Pieces" (Melville), **III:** 93

Searches and Seizures (Elkin), **Supp. VI:** 49

"Search for Southern Identity, The" (Woodward), **Retro. Supp. I:** 75

Search for the King, A: A Twelfth-Century Legend (Vidal), **Supp. IV Part 2:** 681

Searching for Caleb (Tyler), **Supp. IV Part 2:** 663–665, 671

"Searching for Poetry: Real *vs.* Fake" (B. Miller), **Supp. IV Part 1:** 67

Searching for Survivors (Banks), **Supp. V:** 7

"Searching for Survivors (I)" (Banks), **Supp. V:** 8

"Searching for Survivors (II)" (Banks), **Supp. V:** 7, 8

Searching for the Ox (Simpson), **Supp. IX:** 266, 274–275

"Searching for the Ox" (Simpson), **Supp. IX:** 275, 280

"Searching in the Britannia Tavern" (Wagoner), **Supp. IX:** 327

Searching Wing, The, (Hellman), **Supp. I Part 1:** 277, 278, 281–282, 283, 292, 297

"Search Party, The" (Matthews), **Supp. IX:** 156

Searle, Ronald, **Supp. I Part 2:** 604, 605

Sea Road to the Indies (Hart), **Supp. XIV:**97

"Seascape" (Bishop), **Retro. Supp. II:** 42–43

"Sea's Green Sameness, The" (Updike), **IV:** 217

Seaside and the Fireside, The (Longfellow), **II:** 489; **Retro. Supp. II:** 159, 168

Season in Hell, A (Rimbaud), **III:** 189

Seasons, The (Thomson), **II:** 304; **Supp. I Part 1:** 151

Seasons' Difference, The (Buechner), **Supp. XII:** 47

Seasons of Celebration (Merton), **Supp. VIII:** 199, 208

Seasons of the Heart: In Quest of Faith (Kinard, comp.), **Supp. XIV:**127

"Seasons of the Soul" (Tate), **IV:** 136–140

Seasons on Earth (Koch), **Supp. XV:** 183–184

"Sea Surface Full of Clouds" (Stevens), **IV:** 82

"Sea Unicorns and Land Unicorns" (Moore), **III:** 202–203

Seaver, Richard, **Supp. XI:** 301

"Seaweed" (Longfellow), **II:** 498

Sea-Wolf, The (London), **II:** 264, 466, 472–473

Sebald, W. G., **Supp. XIV:**96

Seckler, David, **Supp. I Part 2:** 650

Second American Revolution and Other Essays (1976–1982), The (Vidal), **Supp. IV Part 2:** 679, 687, 688

Secondary Colors, The (A. Theroux), **Supp. VIII:** 312

Second Chance (Auchincloss), **Supp. IV Part 1:** 33

"Second Chances" (Hugo), **Supp. VI:** 144, 145

Second Coming, The (Percy), **Supp. III Part 1:** 383, 384, 387, 388, 396–397

"Second Coming, The" (Yeats), **III:** 294; **Retro. Supp. I:** 290, 311; **Supp. VIII:** 24; **Supp. XVI:**159

Second Decade, The. See Stephen King, The Second Decade: "Danse Macabre" to "The Dark Half" (Magistrale)

Second Dune, The (Hearon), **Supp. VIII:** 58, 59–60

Second Flowering, A: Works and Days of the Lost Generation (Cowley), **Retro. Supp. II:** 77; **Supp. II Part 1:** 135, 141, 143, 144, 147, 149

Second Growth (Stegner), **Supp. IV Part 2:** 599, 608

"Second Hour of the Night, The" (Bidart), **Supp. XV:** 32, 33–34

Second Marriage (F. Barthelme), **Supp. XI:** 32, 33

"Second Marriage" (McCarriston), **Supp. XIV:**262

Second Nature (Hoffman), **Supp. X:** 88, 89

"2nd Air Force" (Jarrell), **II:** 375

Second Set, The (Komunyakaa and Feinstein, eds.), **Supp. XIII:** 125

Second Sex, The (Beauvoir), **Supp. IV Part 1:** 360

Second Stone, The (Fiedler), **Supp. XIII:** 102

"Second Swimming, The" (Boyle), **Supp. VIII:** 13, 14

Second Tree from the Corner (White), **Supp. I Part 2:** 654

"Second Tree from the Corner" (White), **Supp. I Part 2:** 651

Second Twenty Years at Hull-House, The: September 1909 to September 1929, with a Record of a Growing World Consciousness (Addams), **Supp. I Part 1:** 24–25

Second Voyage of Columbus, The (Morison), **Supp. I Part 2:** 488

Second Words, (Atwood), **Supp. XIII:** 35

Second World, The (Blackmur), **Supp. II Part 1:** 91

Secret, The (E. Hoffman), **Supp. XVI:**151, 155–158, 161

"Secret, The" (Levine), **Supp. V:** 195

Secret Agent, The (Conrad), **Supp. IV Part 1:** 341

Secret Agent X-9 (Hammett), **Supp. IV Part 1:** 355

"Secret Courts of Men's Hearts, The: Code and Law in Harper Lee's *To Kill a Mockingbird*" (Johnson), **Supp. VIII:** 126

"Secret Dog, The" (Cameron), **Supp. XII:** 83–84

Secret Garden, The (Burnett), **Supp. I Part 1:** 44

"Secret Gladness, A" (C. Frost), **Supp. XV:** 91

Secret Historie (J. Smith), **I:** 131

Secret History of the Dividing Line (Howe), **Supp. IV Part 2:** 424, 425–426

"Secret Integration, The" (Pynchon), **Supp. II Part 2:** 624

"Secret Life of Musical Instruments, The" (Wright), **Supp. XV:** 343

"Secret Life of Walter Mitty, The" (Thurber), **Supp. I Part 2:** 623; **Supp. XVI:**233

"Secret Lion, The" (Ríos), **Supp. IV Part 2:** 543, 544

"Secret of the Russian Ballet, The" (Van Vechten), **Supp. II Part 2:** 732

"Secret Prune" (Ríos), **Supp. IV Part 2:** 549

Secret River, The (Rawlings), **Supp. X:** 233

Secrets and Surprises (Beattie), **Supp. V:** 23, 27, 29

Secrets from the Center of the World (Harjo), **Supp. XII:** 223–224

"Secret Sharer, The" (Conrad), **Supp. IX:** 105

"Secret Sharer, The" (J. Conrad), **Supp. XVI:**158

"Secret Society, A" (Nemerov), **III:** 282

Secrets of the Universe: Scenes from the Journey Home (Sanders), **Supp. XVI:**273–274

Secular Journal of Thomas Merton, The, **Supp. VIII:** 206

"Security" (Stafford), **Supp. XI:** 329

Sedges, John (pseudonym). *See* Buck, Pearl S.

Sedgwick, Catherine Maria, **I:** 341; **Supp. I Part 1:** 155, 157

Sedgwick, Christina. *See* Marquand, Mrs. John P. (Christina Sedgwick)

Sedgwick, Ellery, **I:** 217, 229, 231; **III:** 54–55

Sedgwick, Henry, **Supp. I Part 1:** 156

Sedgwick, Robert, **Supp. I Part 1:** 156

Sedore, Timothy, **Supp. XIV:**312

"Seduction and Betrayal" (Hardwick), **Supp. III Part 1:** 207

Seduction and Betrayal: Women and Literature (Hardwick), **Supp. III Part 1:** 194, 204, 206–208, 212, 213; **Supp. XIV:**89

Seed, David, **Supp. IV Part 1:** 391

"Seed Eaters, The" (Francis), **Supp. IX:** 82

"Seed Leaves" (Wilbur), **Supp. III Part 2:** 558

"Seeds" (Anderson), **I:** 106, 114

Seeds of Contemplation (Merton), **Supp. VIII:** 199, 200, 207, 208

Seeds of Destruction (Merton), **Supp. VIII:** 202, 203, 204, 208

"See(k)ing the Self: Mirrors and Mirroring in Bicultural Texts" (Oster), **Supp. XVI:**151

Seeing through the Sun (Hogan), **Supp. IV Part 1:** 397, 400, 401–402, 402, 413

"See in the Midst of Fair Leaves" (Moore), **III:** 215

"Seekers, The" (McGrath), **Supp. X:** 117

"Seeking a Vision of Truth, Guided by a Higher Power" (Burke), **Supp. XIV:**21, 23

"Seele im Raum" (Jarrell), **II:** 382–383

"Seele im Raum" (Rilke), **II:** 382–383

"See Naples and Die" (Hecht), **Supp. X:** 69, 70

"Seen from the 'L'" (Barnes), **Supp. III Part 1:** 33

"See the Moon?" (Barthelme), **Supp. IV Part 1:** 42, 49–50, 50

Segal, D. (pseudonym). *See* Singer, Isaac Bashevis

Segal, George, **Supp. XI:** 343

Segal, Lore, **Supp. XVI:**203

Segregation: The Inner Conflict in the South (Warren), **IV:** 237, 238, 246, 252

Seidel, Frederick, **I:** 185

Seize the Day (Bellow), **I:** 144, 147, 148, 150, 151, 152, 153, 155, 158, 162; **Retro. Supp. II:** 19, 23–24, 27, 32, 34; **Supp. I Part 2:** 428

Selby, Hubert, **Supp. III Part 1:** 125

Selby, John, **Retro. Supp. II:** 221, 222

Selden, John, **Supp. XIV:**344

Seldes, Gilbert, **II:** 437, 445; **Retro. Supp. I:** 108

Selected Criticism: Prose, Poetry (Bogan), **Supp. III Part 1:** 64

Selected Essays (Eliot), **I:** 572

Selected Essays and Reviews (Carruth), **Supp. XVI:**46

Selected Journals and Other Writings (Audubon), **Supp. XVI:**10, 12, 13

Selected Letters (Bynner), **Supp. XV:** 52

Selected Letters (W. C. Williams), **Retro. Supp. I:** 430

Selected Letters, 1940–1956 (Kerouac), **Supp. XIV:**137, 144

Selected Letters of Robert Frost (Thompson, ed.), **Retro. Supp. I:** 125

Selected Levis, The (Levis), **Supp. XI:** 257, 272

Selected Poems (Aiken), **I:** 69

Selected Poems (Ashbery), **Supp. III Part 1:** 25–26

Selected Poems (Brodsky), **Supp. VIII:** 22

Selected Poems (Brooks), **Supp. III Part 1:** 82–83

Selected Poems (Bynner), **Supp. XV:** 51, 52

Selected Poems (Corso), **Supp. XII:** 129

Selected Poems (Dove), **Supp. IV Part 1:** 241, 243, 250

Selected Poems (Frost), **Retro. Supp. I:** 133, 136

Selected Poems (Guillevic; Levertov, trans.), **Supp. III Part 1:** 283

Selected Poems (Hayden), **Supp. II Part 1:** 363, 364, 367

Selected Poems (Hughes), **Retro. Supp. I:** 202; **Supp. I Part 1:** 341, 345, 346

Selected Poems (Hugo), **Supp. VI:** 143

Selected Poems (Jarrell), **II:** 367, 370, 371, 374, 377, 379, 380, 381, 382, 384

Selected Poems (Justice), **Supp. VII:** 115

Selected Poems (Kinnell), **Supp. III Part 1:** 235, 253

Selected Poems (Levine, 1984), **Supp. V:** 178, 179

Selected Poems (Lowell), **II:** 512, 516; **Retro. Supp. II:** 184, 186, 188, 190

Selected Poems (Merton), **Supp. VIII:** 207, 208

Selected Poems (Moore), **III:** 193, 194, 205–206, 208, 215

Selected Poems (Pound), **Retro. Supp. I:** 289, 291

Selected Poems (Ransom), **III:** 490, 492

Selected Poems (Reznikoff), **Supp. XIV:**288

Selected Poems (Rukeyser), **Supp. VI:** 274

Selected Poems (R. Bly), **Supp. IV Part 1:** 60, 62, 65, 66, 68, 69–71

Selected Poems (Sexton), **Supp. IV Part 2:** 449

Selected Poems (Strand), **Supp. IV Part 2:** 630

Selected Poems 1936–1965 (Eberhart), **I:** 541

Selected Poems 1965–1975 (Atwood), **Supp. XIII:** 32–34

Selected Poems, 1923–1943 (Warren), **IV:** 241–242, 243

Selected Poems, 1928–1958 (Kunitz), **Supp. III Part 1:** 261, 263–265

Selected Poems, 1938–1988 (McGrath), **Supp. X:** 127

Selected Poems: 1957–1987 (Snodgrass), **Supp. VI:** 314–315, 323, 324

Selected Poems, 1963–1983 (Simic), **Supp. VIII:** 275

Selected Poems II: Poems Selected and New, 1976–1986 (Atwood), **Supp. XIII:** 20, 34–35

Selected Poems of Ezra Pound (Pound), **Supp. V:** 336

Selected Poems of Gabriela Mistral (Hughes, trans.), **Supp. I Part 1:** 345

Selected Poetry of Amiri Baraka/LeRoi Jones (Baraka), **Supp. II Part 1:** 58

Selected Poetry of Hayden Carruth, The (Carruth), **Supp. XVI:**53

Selected Stories (Dubus), **Supp. VII:** 88–89

Selected Stories of Richard Bausch, The (Bausch), **Supp. VII:** 42

Selected Translations (Snodgrass), **Supp. VI:** 318, 324, 325–326

Selected Verse of Margaret Haskins Durber, The (Keillor), **Supp. XVI:**171

Selected Witter Bynner, The, **Supp. XV:** 52

Selected Works of Djuna Barnes, The (Barnes), **Supp. III Part 1:** 44

Selected Writings 1950–1990 (Howe), **Supp. VI:** 116–117, 118, 120

Selected Writings of John Jay Chapman, The (Barzun), **Supp. XIV:**54

Select Epigrams from the Greek Anthology (Mackail), **Supp. I Part 2:** 461

"Selene Afterwards" (MacLeish), **III:** 8

"Self" (James), **II:** 351

Self and the Dramas of History, The (Niebuhr), **III:** 308

Self-Consciousness (Updike), **Retro. Supp. I:** 318, 319, 320, 322, 323, 324

"Self-Exposed, The" (X. J. Kennedy), **Supp. XV:** 159

Self-Help: Stories (Moore), **Supp. X:** 163, 166, 167–169, 174, 175

Self-Interviews (Dickey), **Supp. IV Part 1:** 179

"Self-Made Man, A" (Crane), **I:** 420

"Self Pity" (C. Frost), **Supp. XV:** 93, 94, 101, 102, 104

"Self-Portrait" (Creeley), **Supp. IV Part 1:** 156

"Self-Portrait" (Mumford), **Supp. II Part 2:** 471

"Self-Portrait" (Wylie), **Supp. I Part 2:** 729

Self-Portrait: Ceaselessly into the Past (Millar, ed. Sipper), **Supp. IV Part 2:** 464, 469, 472, 475

"Self-Portrait in a Convex Mirror" (Ashbery), **Supp. III Part 1:** 5, 7, 9, 16–19, 22, 24, 26

"Self-Reliance" (Emerson), **II:** 7, 15, 17; **Retro. Supp. I:** 159; **Retro. Supp. II:** 155; **Supp. X:** 42, 45

Sélincourt, Ernest de, **Supp. I Part 2:** 676

Selinger, Eric, **Supp. XVI:**47

Selinger, Eric Murphy, **Supp. XI:** 248

Sell, Henry, **Supp. XVI:**188

Sellers, Isaiah, **IV:** 194–195

Sellers, Peter, **Supp. XI:** 301, 304, 306, 307, 309

Sellers, William, **IV:** 208

Seltzer, Mark, **Retro. Supp. I:** 227

Selznick, David O., **Retro. Supp. I:** 105, 113; **Supp. IV Part 1:** 353

"Semi-Lunatics of Kilmuir, The"

(Hugo), **Supp. VI:** 145

"Semiotics/The Doctor's Doll" (Goldbarth), **Supp. XII:** 183–184

Semmelweiss, Ignaz, **Supp. I Part 1:** 304

Senancour, Étienne Divert de, **I:** 241

Sendak, Maurice, **Supp. IX:** 207, 208, 213, 214; **Supp. XVI:**110

Seneca, **II:** 14–15; **III:** 77

Senghor, Leopold Sédar, **Supp. IV Part 1:** 16; **Supp. X:** 132, 139

Senier, Siobhan, **Supp. IV Part 1:** 330

"Senility" (Anderson), **I:** 114

"Senior Partner's Ethics, The" (Auchincloss), **Supp. IV Part 1:** 33

Senlin: A Biography (Aiken), **I:** 48, 49, 50, 52, 56, 57, 64

Sennett, Dorothy, **Supp. XVI:**43

Sennett, Mack, **III:** 442

"Señora X No More" (Mora), **Supp. XIII:** 218

"Señor Ong and Señor Ha" (Bowles), **Supp. IV Part 1:** 87

Sense of Beauty, The (Santayana), **III:** 600

Sense of Life in the Modern Novel, The (Mizener), **IV:** 132

"Sense of Shelter, A" (Updike), **Retro. Supp. I:** 318

"Sense of the Meeting, The" (Conroy), **Supp. XVI:**72

Sense of the Past, The (James), **II:** 337–338

"Sense of the Past, The" (Trilling), **Supp. III Part 2:** 503

"Sense of the Present, The" (Hardwick), **Supp. III Part 1:** 210

"Sense of the Sleight-of-Hand Man, The" (Stevens), **IV:** 93

"Sense of Where You Are, A" (McPhee), **Supp. III Part 1:** 291, 296–298

"Sensibility! O La!" (Roethke), **III:** 536

"Sensible Emptiness, A" (Kramer), **Supp. IV Part 1:** 61, 66

"Sensuality Plunging Barefoot Into Thorns" (Cisneros), **Supp. VII:** 68

"Sentence" (Barthelme), **Supp. IV Part 1:** 47

Sent for You Yesterday (Wideman), **Supp. X:** 320, 321

"Sentimental Education, A" (Banks), **Supp. V:** 10

"Sentimental Journey" (Oates), **Supp. II Part 2:** 522, 523

"Sentimental Journey, A" (Anderson), **I:** 114

Sentimental Journey, A (Sterne), **Supp. I Part 2:** 714

"Sentimental Journeys" (Didion), **Supp. IV Part 1:** 211

Sentimental Journey through France and Italy, A (Sterne), **Supp. XV:** 232

"Sentiment of Rationality, The" (James), **II:** 346–347

Separate Flights (Dubus), **Supp. VII:** 78–83

"Separate Flights" (Dubus), **Supp. VII:** 83

Separate Peace, A (Knowles), **Supp. IV Part 2:** 679; **Supp. XII:** 241–249

Separate Way (Reznikoff), **Supp. XIV:**280

"Separating" (Updike), **Retro. Supp. I:** 321

"Separation, The" (Kunitz), **Supp. III Part 1:** 263

"Sepia High Stepper" (Hayden), **Supp. II Part 1:** 379

September (film; Allen), **Supp. XV:** 11

"September" (Komunyakaa), **Supp. XIII:** 130

"September 1, 1939" (Auden), **Supp. II Part 1:** 13; **Supp. IV Part 1:** 225; **Supp. VIII:** 30, 32; **Supp. XV:** 117–118

September 11, 2001: American Writers Respond (Heyen), **Supp. XIII:** 285

September Song (Humphrey), **Supp. IX:** 101, 102, 108–109

"September Twelfth, 2001" (X. J. Kennedy), **Supp. XV:** 171

"Sept Vieillards, Les" (Millay, trans.), **III:** 142

Sequel to Drum-Taps (Whitman), **Retro. Supp. I:** 406

"Sequence, Sometimes Metaphysical" (Roethke), **III:** 547, 548

Sequence of Seven Plays with a Drawing by Ron Slaughter, A (Nemerov), **III:** 269

Sequoya, Jana, **Supp. IV Part 1:** 334

Seraglio, The (Merrill), **Supp. III Part 1:** 331

Seraphita (Balzac), **I:** 499

Seraph on the Suwanee (Hurston), **Supp. VI:** 149, 159–160

Serenissima: A Novel of Venice (Jong). *See Shylock's Daughter: A Novel of Love in Venice (Serenissima)* (Jong)

Sergeant, Elizabeth Shepley, **I:** 231, 236, 312, 319, 323, 328

Sergeant Bilko (television show), **Supp. IV Part 2:** 575

"Serious Talk, A" (Carver), **Supp. III Part 1:** 138, 144

Serly, Tibor, **Supp. III Part 2:** 617, 619

"Sermon by Doctor Pep" (Bellow), **I:** 151

Sermones (Horace), **II:** 154

"Sermon for Our Maturity" (Baraka), **Supp. II Part 1:** 53

Sermons and Soda Water (O'Hara), **III:** 362, 364, 371–373, 382

"Sermons on the Warpland" (Brooks), **Supp. III Part 1:** 84

"Serpent in the Wilderness, The" (Masters), **Supp. I Part 2:** 458

Servant of the Bones (Rice), **Supp. VII:** 298, 302

"Servant to Servants, A" (Frost), **Retro. Supp. I:** 125, 128; **Supp. X:** 66

Seshachari, Neila, **Supp. V:** 22

"Session, The" (Adams), **I:** 5

"Sestina" (Bishop), **Supp. I Part 1:** 73, 88

Set-angya, **Supp. IV Part 2:** 493

Seth's Brother's Wife (Frederic), **II:** 131–132, 137, 144

Set This House on Fire (Styron), **IV:** 98, 99, 105, 107–113, 114, 115, 117

Setting Free the Bears (Irving), **Supp. VI:** 163, 166–167, 169–170

Setting the Tone (Rorem), **Supp. IV Part 1:** 79

Settle, Mary Lee, **Supp. IX:** 96

Settlement Horizon, The: A National Estimate (Woods and Kennedy), **Supp. I Part 1:** 19

"Settling the Colonel's Hash" (McCarthy), **II:** 559, 562

Setzer, Helen, **Supp. IV Part 1:** 217

"Seurat's Sunday Afternoon along the Seine" (Schwartz), **Supp. II Part 2:** 663–665

Seven against Thebes (Aeschylus; Bacon and Hecht, trans.), **Supp. X:** 57

Seven Ages of Man, The (Wilder), **IV:** 357, 374–375

Seven Deadly Sins, The (Wilder), **IV:** 357, 374–375

Seven Descents of Myrtle, The (T. Williams), **IV:** 382

Seven Guitars (Wilson), **Supp. VIII:** 331, 348–351

Seven Lady Godivas, The (Geisel), **Supp. XVI:**100, 103

Seven-League Crutches, The (Jarrell), **II:** 367, 372, 381, 382, 383–384, 389

Seven Mountains of Thomas Merton, The (Mott), **Supp. VIII:** 208

Seven-Ounce Man, The (Harrison), **Supp. VIII:** 51

"Seven Places of the Mind" (Didion), **Supp. IV Part 1:** 200, 210

Seven Plays (Shepard), **Supp. III Part 2:** 434

"Seven Stanzas at Easter" (Updike), **IV:** 215

Seven Storey Mountain, The (Merton), **Supp. VIII:** 193, 195, 198, 200, 207, 208

Seventh Heaven (Hoffman), **Supp. X:** 87, 89

"Seventh of March" (Webster), **Supp. I Part 2:** 687

"7000 Romaine, Los Angeles 38" (Didion), **Supp. IV Part 1:** 200

"Seventh Street" (Toomer), **Supp. IX:** 316

Seven Types of Ambiguity (Empson), **II:** 536; **IV:** 431

77 Dream Songs (Berryman), **I:** 168, 169, 170, 171, 174, 175, 183–188

73 Poems (Cummings), **I:** 430, 431, 446, 447, 448

7 Years from Somehwere (Levine), **Supp. V:** 178, 181, 188–189

Sevier, Jack, **IV:** 378

Sévigné, Madame de, **IV:** 361

Sewall, Richard, **Retro. Supp. I:** 25

Sewall, Samuel, **IV:** 145, 146, 147, 149, 154, 164; **Supp. I Part 1:** 100, 110

Sewell, Elizabeth, **Supp. XIII:** 344

"Sex" (Carruth), **Supp. XVI:**58

Sex, Economy, Freedom and Community (Berry), **Supp. X:** 30, 36

"Sex Camp" (Mamet), **Supp. XIV:**240

Sex Castle, The (Lacy), **Supp. XV:** 206

Sex & Character (Weininger), **Retro. Supp. I:** 416

"Sext" (Auden), **Supp. II Part 1:** 22

Sexton, Anne, **Retro. Supp. II:** 245; **Supp. I Part 2:** 538, 543, 546; **Supp. II Part 2:** 669–700; **Supp. III Part 2:** 599; **Supp. IV Part 1:** 245; **Supp. IV Part 2:** 439, 440–441, 442, 444, 447, 449, 451, 620; **Supp. V:** 113, 118, 124; **Supp. X:** 201, 202, 213; **Supp. XI:** 146, 240, 317; **Supp. XII:** 217, 253, 254, 256, 260, 261; **Supp. XIII:** 35, 76, 294, 312; **Supp. XIV:**125, 126, 132, 269; **Supp. XV:** 123, 252, 340

Sexual Behavior in the American Male (Kinsey), **Supp. XIII:** 96–97

Sexual Perversity in Chicago (Mamet), **Supp. XIV:**239, 240, 246–247, 249

"Sexual Revolution, The" (Dunn), **Supp. XI:** 142

Sexus (H. Miller), **III:** 170, 171, 184, 187, 188

"Sex Without Love" (Olds), **Supp. X:** 206

Seyersted, Per E., **Retro. Supp. II:** 65; **Supp. I Part 1:** 201, 204, 211, 216, 225; **Supp. IV Part 2:** 558

Seyfried, Robin, **Supp. IX:** 324

"Seymour: An Introduction" (Salinger), **III:** 569–571, 572

Seymour, Miranda, **Supp. VIII:** 167

Shacochis, Bob, **Supp. VIII:** 80

"Shadow" (Creeley), **Supp. IV Part 1:** 158

"Shadow, The" (Lowell), **II:** 522

Shadow and Act (Ellison), **Retro. Supp. II:** 119; **Supp. II Part 1:** 245–246

"Shadow and Shade" (Tate), **IV:** 128

"Shadow and the Flesh, The" (London), **II:** 475

"Shadow A Parable" (Poe), **III:** 417–418

Shadow Country (Gunn Allen), **Supp. IV Part 1:** 322, 324, 325–326

Shadow Man, The (Gordon), **Supp. IV Part 1:** 297, 298, 299, 312–314, 315

Shadow of a Dream, The, a Story (Howells), **II:** 285, 286, 290

"Shadow of the Crime, The: A Word from the Author" (Mailer), **Retro. Supp. II:** 214

Shadow on the Dial, The (Bierce), **I:** 208, 209

"Shadow Passing" (Merwin), **Supp. III Part 1:** 355

Shadows (Gardner), **Supp. VI:** 74

Shadows and Fog (film; Allen), **Supp. XV:** 11

Shadows by the Hudson (Singer), **IV:** 1

Shadows of Africa (Matthiessen), **Supp. V:** 203

Shadows on the Hudson (Singer), **Retro. Supp. II:** 311–313

Shadows on the Rock (Cather), **I:** 314, 330–331, 332; **Retro. Supp. I:** 18

Shadow Train (Ashbery), **Supp. III Part 1:** 23–24, 26

"Shad-Time" (Wilbur), **Supp. III Part 2:** 563

Shaffer, Thomas L., **Supp. VIII:** 127, 128

Shaft (Parks; film), **Supp. XI:** 17

Shaftesbury, Earl of, **I:** 559

Shahn, Ben, **Supp. X:** 24

Shakedown for Murder (Lacy), **Supp. XV:** 203

Shakelford, Dean, **Supp. VIII:** 129

Shaker, Why Don't You Sing? (Angelou), **Supp. IV Part 1:** 16

Shakespear, Mrs. Olivia, **III:** 457;

Supp. I Part 1: 257

"Shakespeare" (Emerson), **II:** 6

Shakespeare, William, **I:** 103, 271, 272, 284–285, 358, 378, 433, 441, 458, 461, 573, 585, 586; **II:** 5, 8, 11, 18, 72, 273, 297, 302, 309, 320, 411, 494, 577, 590; **III:** 3, 11, 12, 82, 83, 91, 124, 130, 134, 145, 153, 159, 183, 210, 263, 286, 468, 473, 492, 503, 511, 567, 575–576, 577, 610, 612, 613, 615; **IV:** 11, 50, 66, 127, 132, 156, 309, 313, 362, 368, 370, 373, 453; **Retro. Supp. I:** 43, 64, 91, 248; **Retro. Supp. II:** 114, 299; **Supp. I Part 1:** 79, 150, 262, 310, 356, 363, 365, 368, 369, 370; **Supp. I Part 2:** 397, 421, 422, 470, 494, 622, 716, 720; **Supp. II Part 2:** 624, 626; **Supp. IV Part 1:** 31, 83, 87, 243; **Supp. IV Part 2:** 430, 463, 519, 688; **Supp. V:** 252, 280, 303; **Supp. VIII:** 160, 164; **Supp. IX:** 14, 133; **Supp. X:** 42, 62, 65, 78; **Supp. XII:** 54–57, 277, 281; **Supp. XIII:** 111, 115, 233; **Supp. XIV:**97, 120, 225, 245, 306; **Supp. XV:** 92

Shakespeare and His Forerunners (Lanier), **Supp. I Part 1:** 369

Shakespeare in Harlem (Hughes), **Retro. Supp. I:** 194, 202, 205, 206, 207, 208; **Supp. I Part 1:** 333, 334, 345

Shalit, Gene, **Supp. VIII:** 73

Shall We Gather at the River (Wright), **Supp. III Part 2:** 601–602

"Shame" (Oates), **Supp. II Part 2:** 520

"Shame" (Wilbur), **Supp. III Part 2:** 556

"Shameful Affair, A" (Chopin), **Retro. Supp. II:** 61

Shamela (Fielding), **Supp. V:** 127

"Shampoo, The" (Bishop), **Retro. Supp. II:** 46; **Supp. I Part 1:** 92

Shange, Ntozake, **Supp. VIII:** 214

Shank, Randy, **Supp. X:** 252

Shankaracharya, **III:** 567

Shanley, John Patrick, **Supp. XIV:**315–332

Shannon, Sandra, **Supp. VIII:** 333, 348

"Shape of Flesh and Bone, The" (MacLeish), **III:** 18–19

Shape of Me and Other Stuff, The (Geisel), **Supp. XVI:**111

Shape of the Journey, The (Harrison), **Supp. VIII:** 53

Shapes of Clay (Bierce), **I:** 208, 209

Shaping Joy, A: Studies in the Writer's Craft (Brooks), **Supp. XIV:**13

Shapiro, David, **Supp. XII:** 175, 185

Shapiro, Dorothy, **IV:** 380

Shapiro, Karl, **I:** 430, 521; **II:** 350; **III:** 527; **Supp. II Part 2:** 701–724; **Supp. III Part 2:** 623; **Supp. IV Part 2:** 645; **Supp. X:** 116; **Supp. XI:** 315

Shapiro, Laura, **Supp. IX:** 120

Sharif, Omar, **Supp. IX:** 253

"Shark Meat" (Snyder), **Supp. VIII:** 300

Shatayev, Elvira, **Supp. I Part 2:** 570

Shaviro, Steven, **Supp. VIII:** 189

Shaw, Colonel Robert Gould, **II:** 551

Shaw, Elizabeth. *See* Melville, Mrs. Herman (Elizabeth Shaw)

Shaw, George Bernard, **I:** 226; **II:** 82, 271, 276, 581; **III:** 69, 102, 113, 145, 155, 161, 162, 163, 373, 409; **IV:** 27, 64, 397, 432, 440; **Retro. Supp. I:** 100, 228; **Supp. IV Part 1:** 36; **Supp. IV Part 2:** 585, 683; **Supp. V:** 243–244, 290; **Supp. IX:** 68, 308; **Supp. XI:** 202; **Supp. XII:** 94; **Supp. XIV:**343

Shaw, Irwin, **IV:** 381; **Supp. IV Part 1:** 383; **Supp. IX:** 251; **Supp. XI:** 221, 229, 231

Shaw, Joseph Thompson ("Cap"), **Supp. IV Part 1:** 121, 345, 351; **Supp. XIII:** 161

Shaw, Judge Lemuel, **III:** 77, 88, 91

Shaw, Peter, **Supp. XVI:**70

Shaw, Sarah Bryant, **Supp. I Part 1:** 169

Shaw, Wilbur, Jr., **Supp. XIII:** 162

Shawl, The (Mamet), **Supp. XIV:**245

Shawl, The (Ozick), **Supp. V:** 257, 260, 271

"Shawl, The" (Ozick), **Supp. V:** 271–272

Shawl and Prarie du Chien, The: Two Plays (Mamet), **Supp. XIV:**243–244

Shawn, William, **Supp. VIII:** 151, 170

"Shawshank Redemption, The" (King), **Supp. V:** 148

She (Haggard), **III:** 189

Shearer, Flora, **I:** 199

"Sheaves, The" (Robinson), **III:** 510, 524

"She Came and Went" (Lowell), **Supp. I Part 2:** 409

Sheed, Wilfrid, **IV:** 230; **Supp. XI:** 233

Sheeler, Charles, **IV:** 409; **Retro. Supp. I:** 430

Sheeper (Rosenthal), **Supp. XIV:**147

Sheffer, Jonathan, **Supp. IV Part 1:** 95

She Had Some Horses (Harjo), **Supp. XII:** 220–223, 231

"She Had Some Horses" (Harjo), **Supp. XII:** 215, 222

"Shell, The" (Humphrey), **Supp. IX:** 94

Shelley, Percy Bysshe, **I:** 18, 68, 381, 476, 522, 577; **II:** 331, 516, 535, 540; **III:** 412, 426, 469; **IV:** 139; **Retro. Supp. I:** 308, 360; **Supp. I Part 1:** 79, 311, 349; **Supp. I Part 2:** 709, 718, 719, 720, 721, 722, 724, 728; **Supp. IV Part 1:** 235; **Supp. V:** 258, 280; **Supp. IX:** 51; **Supp. XII:** 117, 132, 136–137, 263; **Supp. XIV:**271–272; **Supp. XV:** 92, 175, 182

Shellow, Sadie Myers, **Supp. I Part 2:** 608

"Shelter" (Doty), **Supp. XI:** 132

Sheltered Life, The (Glasgow), **II:** 174, 175, 179, 186, 187–188

Sheltering Sky, The (Bowles), **Supp. IV Part 1:** 82, 84, 85–86, 87

Sheltering Sky, The (film), **Supp. IV Part 1:** 94, 95

Shelton, Frank, **Supp. IV Part 2:** 658

Shelton, Mrs. Sarah. *See* Royster, Sarah Elmira

Shelton, Richard, **Supp. XI:** 133; **Supp. XIII:** 7

Shenandoah (Schwartz), **Supp. II Part 2:** 640, 651–652

"Shenandoah" (Shapiro), **Supp. II Part 2:** 704

Shepard, Alice, **IV:** 287

Shepard, Odell, **II:** 508; **Supp. I Part 2:** 418

Shepard, Sam, **Supp. III Part 2:** 431–450

Shepard, Thomas, **I:** 554; **IV:** 158

"Shepherd of Resumed Desire, The" (Wright), **Supp. XV:** 349

Sheppard Lee (Bird), **III:** 423

"She Remembers the Future" (Harjo), **Supp. XII:** 222

Sheridan, Richard Brinsley, **Retro. Supp. I:** 127

Sherlock, William, **IV:** 152

Sherman, Sarah Way, **Retro. Supp. II:** 145

Sherman, Stuart Pratt, **I:** 222, 246–247; **Supp. I Part 2:** 423

Sherman, Susan, **Supp. VIII:** 265

Sherman, Tom, **IV:** 446

Sherman, William T., **IV:** 445, 446

Sherwood, Robert, **II:** 435; **Supp. IX:** 190

Sherwood Anderson & Other Famous Creoles (Faulkner), **I:** 117; **II:** 56

Sherwood Anderson Reader, The (Anderson), **I:** 114, 116

Sherwood Anderson's Memoirs (Anderson), **I:** 98, 101, 102, 103, 108, 112, 116

Sherwood Anderson's Notebook (Anderson), **I:** 108, 115, 117

She Stoops to Conquer (Goldsmith), **II:** 514

Shestov, Lev, **Supp. VIII:** 20, 24

Shetley, Vernon, **Supp. IX:** 292; **Supp. XI:** 123

"She Wept, She Railed" (Kunitz), **Supp. III Part 1:** 265

"Shiddah and Kuziba" (Singer), **IV:** 13, 15

Shield of Achilles, The (Auden), **Supp. II Part 1:** 21

"Shield of Achilles, The" (Auden), **Supp. II Part 1:** 21, 25

Shields, Carol, **Supp. VII:** 307–330

Shifting Landscape: A Composite, 1925–1987 (H. Roth), **Supp. IX:** 233–235

Shifts of Being (Eberhart), **I:** 525

Shigematsu, Soiko, **Supp. III Part 1:** 353

Shihab, Aziz, **Supp. XIII:** 273

Shih-hsiang Chen, **Supp. VIII:** 303

Shiksa Goddess; or, How I Spent My Forties (Wasserstein), **Supp. XV:** 319, 320, 325, 332, 333

"Shiloh" (Mason), **Supp. VIII:** 140

Shiloh and Other Stories (Mason), **Supp. VIII:** 133, 139–141, 143, 145

Shilts, Randy, **Supp. X:** 145

Shining, The (King), **Supp. V:** 139, 140, 141, 143–144, 146, 149, 151, 152

Shinn, Everett, **Retro. Supp. II:** 103

"Ship of Death" (Lawrence), **Supp. I Part 2:** 728

Ship of Fools (Porter), **III:** 433, 447, 453, 454; **IV:** 138

Shipping News, The (Proulx), **Supp. VII:** 249, 258–259

"Ships" (O. Henry), **Supp. II Part 1:** 409

Ships Going into the Blue: Essays and Notes on Poetry (Simpson), **Supp. IX:** 275

Ship to America, A (Singer), **IV:** 1

"Shipwreck, The" (Merwin), **Supp. III Part 1:** 346

Shirley, John, **Supp. XVI:**123, 128

"Shirt" (Pinsky), **Supp. VI:** 236–237, 239, 240, 241, 245, 247

"Shirt Poem, The" (Stern), **Supp. IX:** 292

"Shiva and Parvati Hiding in the Rain"

(Pinsky), **Supp. VI:** 244

Shively, Charley, **Retro. Supp. I:** 391; **Supp. XII:** 181, 182

Shock of Recognition, The (Wilson), **II:** 530

Shock of the New, The (Hughes), **Supp. X:** 73

Shoe Bird, The (Welty), **IV:** 261; **Retro. Supp. I:** 353

Shoemaker of Dreams (Ferragammo), **Supp. XVI:**192

"Shoes" (O. Henry), **Supp. II Part 1:** 409

"Shoes of Wandering, The" (Kinnell), **Supp. III Part 1:** 248

"Shooters, Inc." (Didion), **Supp. IV Part 1:** 207, 211

"Shooting, The" (Dubus), **Supp. VII:** 84, 85

"Shooting Niagara; and After?" (Carlyle), **Retro. Supp. I:** 408

"Shooting Script" (Rich), **Supp. I Part 2:** 558; **Supp. IV Part 1:** 257

Shooting Star, A (Stegner), **Supp. IV Part 2:** 599, 608–609

"Shooting Whales" (Strand), **Supp. IV Part 2:** 630

"Shopgirls" (F. Barthelme), **Supp. XI:** 26, 27, 33, 36

Shop Talk (Roth), **Retro. Supp. II:** 282

Shoptaw, John, **Supp. IV Part 1:** 247

Shore Acres (Herne), **Supp. II Part 1:** 198

Shorebirds of North America, The (Matthiessen), **Supp. V:** 204

"Shore House, The" (Jewett), **II:** 397

Shore Leave (Wakeman), **Supp. IX:** 247

"Shoreline Horses" (Ríos), **Supp. IV Part 2:** 553

Shores of Light, The: A Literary Chronicle of the Twenties and Thirties (Wilson), **IV:** 432, 433

Shorey, Paul, **III:** 606

Short Cuts (film), **Supp. IX:** 143

"Short End, The" (Hecht), **Supp. X:** 65

"Shorter View, The" (X. J. Kennedy), **Supp. XV:** 160, 168

Short Fiction of Norman Mailer, The (Mailer), **Retro. Supp. II:** 205

Short Friday and Other Stories (Singer), **IV:** 14–16

"Short Happy Life of Francis Macomber, The" (Hemingway), **II:** 250, 263–264; **Retro. Supp. I:** 182; **Supp. IV Part 1:** 48; **Supp. IX:** 106

Short Night, The (Turner), **Supp. XV:** 201

Short Novels of Thomas Wolfe, The

(Wolfe), **IV:** 456

Short Poems (Berryman), **I:** 170

"SHORT SPEECH TO MY FRIENDS" (Baraka), **Supp. II Part 1:** 35

Short Stories (Rawlings), **Supp. X:** 224

"Short Story, The" (Welty), **IV:** 279

Short Story Masterpieces, **Supp. IX:** 4

Short Studies of American Authors (Higginson), **I:** 455

"Short-timer's Calendar" (Komunyakaa), **Supp. XIII:** 125

Shosha (Singer), **Retro. Supp. II:** 313–314

Shostakovich, Dimitri, **IV:** 75; **Supp. VIII:** 21

"Shots" (Ozick), **Supp. V:** 268

Shotts, Jeffrey, **Supp. XV:** 103, 104

"Should Wizard Hit Mommy?" (Updike), **IV:** 221, 222, 224; **Retro. Supp. I:** 335

Shoup, Barbara, **Supp. XV:** 55, 59, 62, 69

"Shovel Man, The" (Sandburg), **III:** 553

Showalter, Elaine, **Retro. Supp. I:** 368; **Supp. IV Part 2:** 440, 441, 444; **Supp. X:** 97; **Supp. XVI:**80, 92

"Shower of Gold" (Welty), **IV:** 271–272

"Shrike and the Chipmunks, The" (Thurber), **Supp. I Part 2:** 617

Shrimp Girl (Hogarth), **Supp. XII:** 44

"Shriveled Meditation" (X. J. Kennedy), **Supp. XV:** 170

Shropshire Lad, A (Housman), **Supp. XV:** 41

"Shrouded Stranger, The" (Ginsberg), **Supp. II Part 1:** 312

"Shroud of Color, The" (Cullen), **Supp. IV Part 1:** 166, 168, 170, 171

Shtetl (film; Marzynski), **Supp. XVI:**153

Shtetl: The Life and Death of a Small Town and the World of Polish Jews (E. Hoffman), **Supp. XVI:**152, 153–155

Shuffle (L. Michaels), **Supp. XVI:**202, 203, 213

Shuffle Along (musical), **Supp. I Part 1:** 322; **Supp. X:** 136

Shultz, George, **Supp. IV Part 1:** 234

Shurr, William, **Retro. Supp. I:** 43

Shuster, Joel, **Supp. XI:** 67

Shusterman, Richard, **Retro. Supp. I:** 53

"Shut a Final Door" (Capote), **Supp. III Part 1:** 117, 120, 124

Shut Up, He Explained (Lardner), **II:** 432

Shylock's Daughter: A Novel of Love in Venice (Serenissima) (Jong), **Supp. V:** 115, 127, 128–129

Siberian Village, The (Dove), **Supp. IV Part 1:** 255, 256

Sibley, Mulford Q., **Supp. I Part 2:** 524

"Sibling Mysteries" (Rich), **Supp. I Part 2:** 574

Sibon, Marcelle, **IV:** 288

"Sicilian Emigrant's Song" (W. C. Williams), **Retro. Supp. I:** 413

Sicilian Miniatures (Sobin), **Supp. XVI:**288

"Sick Wife, The" (Kenyon), **Supp. VII:** 173, 174

"'Sic transit gloria mundi'" (Dickinson), **Retro. Supp. I:** 30

Sid Caesar Show (television show), **Supp. IV Part 2:** 575

Siddons, Sarah, **II:** 298

Side Effects (Allen), **Supp. XV:** 3, 14, 15–16

Side of Paradise, This (Fitgerald), **Supp. IX:** 56

Sidnee Poet Heroical, The (Baraka), **Supp. II Part 1:** 55

Sidney, Algernon, **II:** 114

Sidney, Mary, **Supp. I Part 1:** 98

Sidney, Philip, **II:** 470; **Supp. I Part 1:** 98, 111, 117–118, 122; **Supp. I Part 2:** 658; **Supp. II Part 1:** 104–105; **Supp. V:** 250; **Supp. XII:** 264; **Supp. XIV:**128

Sidney, Sylvia, **Supp. I Part 1:** 67

Sidney Lanier: A Bibliographical and Critical Study (Starke), **Supp. I Part 1:** 371

Sidney Lanier: A Biographical and Critical Study (Starke), **Supp. I Part 1:** 371

Siegel, Barry, **Supp. XIV:**82

Siegel, Catherine, **Supp. XII:** 126

Siegel, Jerry, **Supp. XI:** 67

"Siege of London, The" (James), **Retro. Supp. I:** 227

Siegle, Robert, **Supp. XII:** 8

Sienkiewicz, Henryk, **Supp. IV Part 2:** 518; **Supp. XVI:**182

"Sierra Kid" (Levine), **Supp. V:** 180–181

Sigg, Eric, **Retro. Supp. I:** 53

"Sight" (Merwin), **Supp. III Part 1:** 356

"Sight in Camp in the Daybreak Gray and Dim, A" (Whitman), **II:** 373

Sights and Spectacles (McCarthy), **II:** 562

"Sights from a Steeple" (Hawthorne), **Retro. Supp. I:** 62

Sights Unseen (Gibbons), **Supp. X:** 49–50

"Signals" (Carver), **Supp. III Part 1:** 143

"Signature for Tempo" (MacLeish), **III:** 8–9

"Signed Confession of Crimes against the State" (Merton), **Supp. VIII:** 201

Signifying Monkey, The (Gates), **Supp. X:** 243

Signifying Monkey, The (Hughes), **Retro. Supp. I:** 195

"Signing, The (Dixon), **Supp. XII:** 146

Sign in Sidney Brustein's Window, The (Hansberry), **Supp. IV Part 1:** 359, 365, 369, 370–372

Sign of Jonas, The (Merton), **Supp. VIII:** 194–195, 195, 197, 200, 206, 207

"Sign of Saturn, The" (Olds), **Supp. X:** 206

Sigourney, Lydia, **Supp. I Part 2:** 684

Sikora, Malgorzata, **Retro. Supp. II:** 324

Silas Marner (Eliot), **II:** 26

Silberg, Richard, **Supp. XV:** 116

"Silence" (Moore), **III:** 212

"Silence" (Poe), **III:** 416

"Silence" (Sanders), **Supp. XVI:**278

"Silence, A" (Clampitt), **Supp. IX:** 53

"Silence—A Fable" (Poe), **III:** 416

"Silence Before Harvest, The" (Merwin), **Supp. III Part 1:** 352

Silence Dogood Papers, The (Franklin), **II:** 106–107

Silence in the Snowy Fields (R. Bly), **Supp. IV Part 1:** 60–61, 62, 63, 65, 66, 72

Silence of History, The (Farrell), **II:** 46–47

Silence Opens, A (Clampitt), **Supp. IX:** 53

Silences (Olsen), **Supp. XIII:** 293, 294, 295, 296, 304–306

"Silences: When Writers Don't Write" (Olsen), **Supp. XIII:** 294

Silencing the Past: Power and the Production of History (Trouillot), **Supp. X:** 14

"Silent in America" (Levine), **Supp. V:** 183

Silent Life, The (Merton), **Supp. VIII:** 208

Silent Partner, The (Odets), **Supp. II Part 2:** 539

"Silent Poem" (Francis), **Supp. IX:** 86

"Silent Slain, The" (MacLeish), **III:** 9

"Silent Snow, Secret Snow" (Aiken), **I:** 52

Silent Spring (Carson), **Supp. V:** 202; **Supp. IX:** 19, 24, 31–34; **Supp. XIV:**177; **Supp. XVI:**36

Silhouettes of American Life (Davis), **Supp. XVI:**85

"Silken Tent, The" (Frost), **Retro. Supp. I:** 138–139; **Supp. IV Part 2:** 448

Silko, Leslie Marmon, **Supp. IV Part 1:** 274, 319, 325, 333–334, 335, 404; **Supp. IV Part 2:** 499, 505, 557–572; **Supp. V:** 169; **Supp. XI:** 18; **Supp. XII:** 217

Silliman, Ron, **Supp. IV Part 2:** 426; **Supp. XV:** 344

Silman, Roberta, **Supp. X:** 6

Silverblatt, Michael, **Supp. XV:** 224

"Silver Crown, The" (Malamud), **Supp. I Part 2:** 434–435, 437; **Supp. V:** 266

"Silver Dish, The" (Bellow), **Retro. Supp. II:** 30

"Silver Filigree" (Wylie), **Supp. I Part 2:** 707

Silvers, Phil, **Supp. IV Part 2:** 574

Silverthorne, Elizabeth, **Supp. X:** 220, 221, 222, 226, 234

"Silver To Have and to Hurl" (Didion), **Supp. IV Part 1:** 197

Simic, Charles, **Supp. V:** 5, 332; **Supp. VIII:** 39, 269–287; **Supp. XI:** 317; **Supp. XV:** 179, 185

"Similar Cases" (Gilman), **Supp. XI:** 200, 202

Similitudes, from the Ocean and Prairie (Larcom), **Supp. XIII:** 141

Simmel, Georg, **Supp. I Part 2:** 644

Simmons, Charles, **Supp. XI:** 230

Simmons, Maggie, **Retro. Supp. II:** 21

Simms, Michael, **Supp. XII:** 184

Simms, William Gilmore, **I:** 211

Simon, John, **Supp. IV Part 2:** 691

Simon, Neil, **Supp. IV Part 2:** 573–594

"Simon Gerty" (Wylie), **Supp. I Part 2:** 713

Simonides, **Supp. XII:** 110–111

"Simon Ortiz" (Gingerich), **Supp. IV Part 2:** 510

Simon Ortiz (Wiget), **Supp. IV Part 2:** 509

Simonson, Lee, **III:** 396

"Simple Art of Murder, The" (Chandler), **Supp. IV Part 1:** 121, 341

"Simple Autumnal" (Bogan), **Supp. III Part 1:** 52–53

Simple Heart (Flaubert), **I:** 504

Simple Speaks his Mind (Hughes), **Retro. Supp. I:** 209; **Supp. I Part 1:** 337

Simple Stakes a Claim (Hughes), **Retro. Supp. I:** 209; **Supp. I Part 1:** 337

Simple's Uncle Sam (Hughes), **Retro. Supp. I:** 209; **Supp. I Part 1:** 337

Simple Takes a Wife (Hughes), **Retro. Supp. I:** 209; **Supp. I Part 1:** 337

Simple Truth, The (Hardwick), **Supp. III Part 1:** 199, 200, 208

Simple Truth, The (Levine), **Supp. V:** 178, 179, 193–194

"Simplicity" (Sanders), **Supp. XVI:**276

Simply Heavenly (Hughes), **Retro. Supp. I:** 209; **Supp. I Part 1:** 338, 339

Simpson, Louis, **Supp. III Part 2:** 541; **Supp. IV Part 2:** 448, 621; **Supp. VIII:** 39, 279; **Supp. IX:** 265–283, 290; **Supp. XI:** 317; **Supp. XII:** 130; **Supp. XIII:** 337

Simpson, Mona, **Supp. XVI:**206

"Sin" (C. Frost), **Supp. XV:** 96

Sinatra, Frank, **Supp. IX:** 3; **Supp. X:** 119; **Supp. XI:** 213

Sincere Convert, The (Shepard), **IV:** 158

Sincerely, Willis Wayde (Marquand), **III:** 61, 63, 66, 67–68, 69

Sincerity (Rowson), **Supp. XV:** 242

Sincerity and Authenticity (Trilling), **Supp. III Part 2:** 510–512

"Sincerity and Objectification: With Special Reference to the Work of Charles Reznikoff" (Zukofsky), **Supp. XIV:**286

Sinclair, Mary Craig (Mary Craig Kimbrough), **Supp. V:** 275, 286, 287

Sinclair, Upton, **II:** 34, 440, 444, 451; **III:** 580; **Retro. Supp. II:** 95; **Supp. V:** 275–293; **Supp. VIII:** 11

Sinclair Lewis: An American Life (Schorer), **II:** 459

"Singapore" (Oliver), **Supp. VII:** 239, 240

Singer, Bennett L., **Supp. IV Part 1:** 330

Singer, Beth, **Supp. XIV:**203

Singer, Isaac Bashevis, **I:** 144; **IV:** 1–24; **Retro. Supp. II:** 22, 299–320; **Supp. IX:** 114

Singer, Israel Joshua, **IV:** 2, 16, 17; **Retro. Supp. II:** 302

Singer, Joshua, **IV:** 4

Singer, Rabbi Pinchos Menachem, **IV:** 16

Singin' and Swingin' and Gettin'

Merry Like Christmas (Angelou), **Supp. IV Part 1:** 2, 5, 6–7, 9, 13, 14

"Singing & Doubling Together" (Ammons), **Supp. VII:** 34–35

Singing Jailbirds (Sinclair), **Supp. V:** 277

"Singing the Black Mother" (Lupton), **Supp. IV Part 1:** 7

Single Hound, The (Sarton), **Supp. VIII:** 251, 265

Single Hound, The: Poems of a Lifetime (Dickinson; Bianchi, ed.), **Retro. Supp. I:** 35

Single Man, A (Isherwood), **Supp. XIV:** 157, 164, 169–170, 171

"Single Sonnet" (Bogan), **Supp. III Part 1:** 56–58

Singley, Carol, **Retro. Supp. I:** 373

Singular Family, A: Rosacoke and Her Kin (Price), **Supp. VI:** 258–259, 260

"Singular First Person, The" (Sanders), **Supp. XVI:** 274

Singularities (Howe), **Supp. IV Part 2:** 431

Sin in Their Blood (Lacy), **Supp. XV:** 200

"Sinister Adolescents, The" (Dos Passos), **I:** 493

Sinister Street (Mackenzie), **II:** 82

Sinners in the Hands of an Angry God (Edwards), **I:** 546, 552–553, 559, 562

Sinning with Annie, and Other Stories (Theroux), **Supp. VIII:** 318

"Sins of Kalamazoo, The" (Sandburg), **III:** 586

Sintram and His Companions (La Motte-Fouqué), **III:** 78

"Siope" (Poe), **III:** 411

"Sipapu: A Cultural Perspective" (Gunn Allen), **Supp. IV Part 1:** 323

Sipchen, Bob, **Supp. X:** 145

Sipper, Ralph B., **Supp. IV Part 2:** 475

"Sire" (Cisneros), **Supp. VII:** 62–63, 64

"Siren and Signal" (Zukofsky), **Supp. III Part 2:** 611, 612

Sirens of Titan, The (Vonnegut), **Supp. II Part 2:** 757, 758, 760, 765–767

"Sir Galahad" (Tennyson), **Supp. I Part 2:** 410

Sirin, V. (pseudonym), **Retro. Supp. I:** 266. *see also* Nabokov, Vladimir

Sir Vadia's Shadow: A Friendship across Five Continents (Theroux), **Supp. VIII:** 309, 314, 321, 325

"Sis" (F. Barthelme), **Supp. XI:** 26

Sisley, Alfred, **I:** 478

Sissman, L. E., **Supp. X:** 69

"Sister" (Hughes), **Retro. Supp. I:** 208

Sister Carrie (Dreiser), **I:** 482, 497, 499, 500, 501–502, 503–504, 505, 506, 515, 519; **III:** 327; **IV:** 208; **Retro. Supp. I:** 376; **Retro. Supp. II:** 93, 96–99

"Sister of the Minotaur" (Stevens), **IV:** 89; **Supp. IX:** 332

"Sisters, The" (Whittier), **Supp. I Part 2:** 696

Sister's Choice (Showalter), **Retro. Supp. I:** 368

Sisters Rosensweig, The (Wasserstein), **Supp. XV:** 320, 328–330

"Sisyphus" (Kumin), **Supp. IV Part 2:** 443, 444, 451

"Sitalkas" (Doolittle), **Supp. I Part 1:** 266

Sitney, P. Adams, **Supp. XII:** 2

Sitting In: Selected Writings on Jazz, Blues, and Related Topics (Carruth), **Supp. XVI:** 46

"Sitting in a Rocking Chair Going Blind" (Komunyakaa), **Supp. XIII:** 114

Sitti's Secrets (Nye), **Supp. XIII:** 278

Situation Normal (A. Miller), **III:** 148, 149, 156, 164

Situation of Poetry, The: Contemporary Poetry and Its Traditions (Pinsky), **Supp. VI:** 237–238, 239, 241, 242

Sitwell, Edith, **IV:** 77; **Supp. I Part 1:** 271

"Six Brothers" (Cisneros), **Supp. VII:** 67

Six Characters in Search of an Author (Pirandello), **Supp. IV Part 2:** 576

"Six Days: Some Rememberings" (Paley), **Supp. VI:** 226

"65290" (Leopold), **Supp. XIV:** 184–185

Six French Poets (Lowell), **II:** 528–529

"Six Persons" (Baraka), **Supp. II Part 1:** 53

Six Sections from Mountains and Rivers without End (Snyder), **Supp. VIII:** 305

"Sixteen Months" (Sandburg), **III:** 584

1601, or Conversation as It Was by the Fireside in the Time of the Tudors (Twain), **IV:** 201

"Sixth-Month Song in the Foothills" (Snyder), **Supp. VIII:** 297

Sixties, The (magazine) (R. Bly), **Supp. IV Part 1:** 60; **Supp. IX:** 271

"Sixty" (Dunn), **Supp. XI:** 155

"Sixty Acres" (Carver), **Supp. III Part 1:** 141

"69 Hidebound Opinions, Propositions, and Several Asides from a Manila Folder concerning the Stuff of Poetry" (Wright), **Supp. XV:** 344–345

Sixty Stories (Barthelme), **Supp. IV Part 1:** 41, 42, 44, 47, 49, 50

63: Dream Palace (Purdy), **Supp. VII:** 270–271

"Six Variations" (Levertov), **Supp. III Part 1:** 277–278

"Six-Year-Old Boy" (Olds), **Supp. X:** 206

"Six Years Later" (Brodsky), **Supp. VIII:** 26, 28

"Size and Sheer Will" (Olds), **Supp. X:** 206

Size of Thoughts, The: Essays and Other Lumber (Baker), **Supp. XIII:** 52–53, 55, 56

Sizwe Bansi Is Dead (Fugard), **Supp. VIII:** 330

"Skagway" (Haines), **Supp. XII:** 206

"Skaters, The" (Ashbery), **Supp. III Part 1:** 10, 12, 13, 18, 25

"Skaters, The" (Jarrell), **II:** 368–369

Skau, Michael, **Supp. XII:** 129, 130, 132, 134

Skeeters Kirby (Masters), **Supp. I Part 2:** 459, 470, 471

Skeleton Crew (King), **Supp. V:** 144

"Skeleton in Armor, The" (Longfellow), **Retro. Supp. II:** 168

"Skeleton's Cave, The" (Bryant), **Supp. I Part 1:** 157

Skelton, John, **III:** 521

Skepticisms (Aiken), **Supp. XV:** 298, 302

Sketch Book of Geoffrey Crayon, Gent., The (Irving), **II:** 295, 303, 304–308, 309, 311, 491; **Supp. I Part 1:** 155

Sketches of Art (Jameson), **Retro. Supp. II:** 58

Sketches of Eighteenth Century America (Crèvecoeur), **Supp. I Part 1:** 233, 240–241, 250, 251

"Sketches of Female Biography" (Rowson), **Supp. XV:** 245

Sketches of Switzerland (Cooper), **I:** 346

Sketches Old and New (Twain), **IV:** 198

"Sketch for a Job-Application Blank" (Harrison), **Supp. VIII:** 38

Sketch of Old England, by a New England Man (Paulding), **I:** 344

"Skier and the Mountain, The" (Eberhart), **I:** 528–529

Skinker, Mary Scott, **Supp. IX:** 20

Skinny Island (Auchincloss), **Supp. IV Part 1:** 33

Skinny Legs and All (Robbins), **Supp. X:** 267, 273, 276–279

Skin of Our Teeth, The (Wilder), **IV:** 357, 358, 369–372; **Supp. IV Part 2:** 586

"Skins" (Wright), **Supp. V:** 340

Skins and Bones: Poems 1979–1987 (Gunn Allen), **Supp. IV Part 1:** 321, 331

"Skipper Ireson's Ride" (Whittier), **Supp. I Part 2:** 691, 693–694

"Skirmish at Sartoris" (Faulkner), **II:** 67

Skow, John, **Supp. V:** 213; **Supp. XVI:**174

"Skunk Cabbage" (Oliver), **Supp. VII:** 235, 236

"Skunk Hour" (Lowell), **II:** 548–550; **Retro. Supp. II:** 188, 189; **Supp. XIV:**269

Sky, The Stars, The Wilderness, The (Bass), **Supp. XVI:**19, 20

"Sky Dance" (Leopold), **Supp. XIV:**186

"Sky Line" (Taylor), **Supp. V:** 316

"Sky Line, The" (Mumford), **Supp. II Part 2:** 475

"Skyscraper" (Sandburg), **III:** 581–582

Sky's the Limit, The: A Defense of the Earth (Nichols), **Supp. XIII:** 268

"Sky Valley Rider" (Wright), **Supp. V:** 335, 340

Sky-Walk; or the Man Unknown to Himself (Brown), **Supp. I Part 1:** 127–128

"Slang in America" (Whitman), **IV:** 348

Slapstick (Vonnegut), **Supp. II Part 2:** 753, 754, 778

Slapstick Tragedy (T. Williams), **IV:** 382, 393

Slate, Lane, **Supp. IX:** 251, 253

Slattery, Mary Grace. *See* Miller, Mrs. Arthur (Mary Grace Slattery)

"Slaughterer, The" (Singer), **IV:** 19

Slaughterhouse-Five (Vonnegut), **Supp. II Part 2:** 755, 758–759, 760, 770, 772–776; **Supp. V:** 41, 244

Slave, The (Baraka), **Supp. II Part 1:** 42, 44, 56

Slave, The: A Novel (Singer), **IV:** 13; **Retro. Supp. II:** 305–307

"Slave Coffle" (Angelou), **Supp. IV Part 1:** 16

"Slave on the Block" (Hughes), **Supp. I Part 1:** 329

Slave Power, The: The Free North and Southern Domination, 1780–1860

(Richards), **Supp. XIV:**48

"Slave Quarters" (Dickey), **Supp. IV Part 1:** 181

"Slave's Dream, The" (Longfellow), **Supp. I Part 2:** 409

Slave Ship: A Historical Pageant (Baraka), **Supp. II Part 1:** 47–49, 53, 56–57

"Slave-Ships, The" (Whittier), **Supp. I Part 2:** 687–688

Slaves in Algiers; or, A Struggle for Freedom (Rowson), **Supp. XV:** 236–237

Slavs! Thinking about the Longstanding Problems of Virtue and Happiness (Kushner), **Supp. IX:** 146

Sledge, Eugene, **Supp. V:** 250

Sleek for the Long Flight (Matthews), **Supp. IX:** 154, 155, 157–158

Sleep (Dixon), **Supp. XII:** 154

"Sleep, The" (Strand), **Supp. IV Part 2:** 627

Sleeper (film; Allen), **Supp. XV:** 5

"Sleeper, The" (Poe), **III:** 411

"Sleeper 1, The" (Hay), **Supp. XIV:**132–133

"Sleeper 2, The" (Hay), **Supp. XIV:**132–133

"Sleepers, The" (Whitman), **IV:** 336

"Sleepers in Jaipur" (Kenyon), **Supp. VII:** 172

Sleepers in Moon-Crowned Valleys (Purdy), **Supp. VII:** 274, 275

"Sleepers Joining Hands" (R. Bly), **Supp. IV Part 1:** 63, 73

Sleeping Beauty (Macdonald), **Supp. IV Part 2:** 474, 475

Sleeping Beauty, The (Carruth), **Supp. XVI:**53, 57–58

"Sleeping Beauty Syndrome, The: The New Agony of Single Men" (Wasserstein), **Supp. XV:** 328

"Sleeping Fury, The" (Bogan), **Supp. III Part 1:** 58

Sleeping Fury, The: Poems (Bogan), **Supp. III Part 1:** 55–58

Sleeping Gypsy and Other Poems, The (Garrett), **Supp. VII:** 96–98

Sleeping in the Forest (Oliver), **Supp. VII:** 233

"Sleeping in the Forest" (Oliver), **Supp. VII:** 233–234

Sleeping in the Woods (Wagoner), **Supp. IX:** 328

Sleeping on Fists (Ríos), **Supp. IV Part 2:** 540

Sleeping on the Wing: An Anthology of Modern Poetry (Koch and Farrell, eds.), **Supp. XV:** 187–188

"Sleeping Standing Up" (Bishop),

Supp. I Part 1: 85, 89, 93

"Sleeping with Animals" (Kumin), **Supp. IV Part 2:** 454

Sleeping with One Eye Open (Strand), **Supp. IV Part 2:** 621–624, 623, 628

Sleep in Thunder (Lacy), **Supp. XV:** 206

"Sleepless, The" (L.-Y. Lee), **Supp. XV:** 224

"Sleepless at Crown Point" (Wilbur), **Supp. III Part 2:** 561

Sleepless Nights (Hardwick), **Supp. III Part 1:** 193, 208–211

Sleight, Ken, **Supp. XIII:** 12

Slick, Sam (pseudonym). *See* Haliburton, Thomas Chandler

"Slick Gonna Learn" (Ellison), **Retro. Supp. II:** 116; **Supp. II Part 1:** 237–238

"Slight Rebellion off Madison" (Salinger), **III:** 553

"Slight Sound at Evening, A" (White), **Supp. I Part 2:** 672

"Slim Graves Show, The" (Keillor), **Supp. XVI:**172

"Slim Greer" series (Hayden), **Supp. II Part 1:** 369

"Slim in Hell" (Hayden), **Supp. II Part 1:** 369

"Slim Man Canyon" (Silko), **Supp. IV Part 2:** 560

"Slippery Fingers" (Hammett), **Supp. IV Part 1:** 343

Slipping-Down Life, A (Tyler), **Supp. IV Part 2:** 660–661

Sloan, Jacob, **IV:** 3, 6

Sloan, John, **I:** 254; **IV:** 411; **Retro. Supp. II:** 103

Sloane, John, **Supp. XV:** 295

"Slob" (Farrell), **II:** 25, 28, 31

Slocum, Joshua, **Supp. I Part 2:** 497

Slonim, Véra. *See* Nabokov, Véra

Slouching towards Bethlehem (Didion), **Supp. IV Part 1:** 196, 197, 200–201, 202, 206, 210

Slovic, Scott, **Supp. XVI:**277

"Slow Child with a Book of Birds" (Levis), **Supp. XI:** 268

"Slow Down for Poetry" (Strand), **Supp. IV Part 2:** 620

"Slow Pacific Swell, The" (Winters), **Supp. II Part 2:** 790, 793, 795, 796, 799

Slow Parade (Kees), **Supp. XV:** 137

"Slumgullions" (Olsen), **Supp. IV Part 1:** 54

Slumgullion Stew: An Edward Abbey Reader (Abbey), **Supp. XIII:** 4

"S & M" (Komunyakaa), **Supp. XIII:** 114

"Small" (C. Frost), **Supp. XV:** 102

Small, Albion, **Supp. I Part 1:** 5

"Small, Good Thing, A" (Carver), **Supp. III Part 1:** 145, 147

Small, Miriam Rossiter, **Supp. I Part 1:** 319

Small Boy and Others, A (James), **II:** 337, 547; **Retro. Supp. I:** 235

"Small but Urgent Request to the Unknowable" (Karr), **Supp. XI:** 243

Small Ceremonies (Shields), **Supp. VII:** 312–315, 320

Small Craft Warnings (T. Williams), **IV:** 382, 383, 384, 385, 386, 387, 392, 393, 396, 398

Small Place, A (Kincaid), **Supp. VII:** 186–187, 188, 191

"Small Rain, The" (Pynchon), **Supp. II Part 2:** 620

Small Room, The (Sarton), **Supp. VIII:** 252, 255–256

Smalls, Bob, **II:** 128

Small Time Crooks (film; Allen), **Supp. XV:** 11

Small Town, A (Hearon), **Supp. VIII:** 65–66

"Small Vases from Hebron, The" (Nye), **Supp. XIII:** 283

"Small Vision, The" (Goldbarth), **Supp. XII:** 180

"Small Voice from the Wings" (Everwine), **Supp. XV:** 76

"Small Wire" (Sexton), **Supp. II Part 2:** 696

Smardz, Zofia, **Supp. XVI:**155

Smart, Christopher, **III:** 534; **Supp. I Part 2:** 539; **Supp. IV Part 2:** 626

Smart, Joyce H., **Supp. XI:** 169

"Smart Cookie, A" (Cisneros), **Supp. VII:** 64

"Smashup" (Thurber), **Supp. I Part 2:** 616

Smedly, Agnes, **Supp. XIII:** 295

"Smelt Fishing" (Hayden), **Supp. II Part 1:** 367

"Smile of the Bathers, The" (Kees), **Supp. XV:** 145

"Smiles" (Dunn), **Supp. XI:** 151

Smiles, Samuel, **Supp. X:** 167

Smiley, Jane, **Supp. VI:** 291–309; **Supp. XII:** 73, 297; **Supp. XIII:** 127

Smith, Adam, **II:** 9; **Supp. I Part 2:** 633, 634, 639

Smith, Annick, **Supp. XIV:**223

Smith, Benjamin, **IV:** 148

Smith, Bernard, **I:** 260

Smith, Bessie, **Retro. Supp. I:** 343; **Supp. VIII:** 330

Smith, Charlie, **Supp. X:** 177

Smith, Dale, **Supp. XV:** 136, 138, 139

Smith, Dave, **Supp. V:** 333; **Supp. XI:** 152; **Supp. XII:** 178, 198

Smith, David, **Supp. XIII:** 246, 247

Smith, David Nichol, **Supp. XIV:**2

Smith, Dinitia, **Supp. VIII:** 74, 82, 83

Smith, Elihu Hubbard, **Supp. I Part 1:** 126, 127, 130

Smith, George Adam, **III:** 199

Smith, Hannah Whitall, **Supp. XIV:**333, 334, 338

Smith, Harrison, **II:** 61

Smith, Henry Nash, **IV:** 210; **Supp. I Part 1:** 233

Smith, Herbert F., **Supp. I Part 2:** 423

Smith, James, **II:** 111

Smith, Jedediah Strong, **Supp. IV Part 2:** 602

Smith, Jerome, **Supp. IV Part 1:** 369

Smith, Joe, **Supp. IV Part 2:** 584

Smith, John, **I:** 4, 131; **II:** 296

Smith, John Allyn, **I:** 168

Smith, Johnston (pseudonym). *See* Crane, Stephen

Smith, Kellogg, **Supp. I Part 2:** 660

Smith, Lamar, **II:** 585

Smith, Lee, **Supp. XII:** 311

Smith, Logan Pearsall, **Supp. XIV:**333–351

Smith, Lula Carson. *See* McCullers, Carson

Smith, Martha Nell, **Retro. Supp. I:** 33, 43, 46, 47

Smith, Mary Rozet, **Supp. I Part 1:** 5, 22

Smith, Mrs. Lamar (Marguerite Walters), **II:** 585, 587

Smith, Oliver, **II:** 586

Smith, Patricia Clark, **Supp. IV Part 1:** 397, 398, 402, 406, 408, 410; **Supp. IV Part 2:** 509; **Supp. XII:** 218

Smith, Patrick, **Supp. VIII:** 40, 41

Smith, Patti, **Supp. XII:** 136; **Supp. XIV:**151

Smith, Porter, **III:** 572

Smith, Red, **II:** 417, 424

Smith, Robert McClure, **Supp. XV:** 270

Smith, Robert Pearsall, **Supp. XIV:**333

Smith, Seba, **Supp. I Part 2:** 411

Smith, Sidonie Ann, **Supp. IV Part 1:** 11

Smith, Stevie, **Supp. V:** 84

Smith, Sydney, **II:** 295; **Supp. XIV:**112

Smith, Thorne, **Supp. IX:** 194

Smith, Wendy, **Supp. XII:** 330, 335

Smith, Wilford Bascom "Pitchfork," **Supp. XIII:** 168

Smith, William, **II:** 114

Smith, William Gardner, **Supp. XVI:**142–143

Smith, William Jay, **Supp. XIII:** 331–350

Smoke (film), **Supp. XII:** 21

Smoke and Steel (Sandburg), **III:** 585–587, 592

"Smokers" (Wolff), **Supp. VII:** 340–341

"Smoking My Prayers" (Ortiz), **Supp. IV Part 2:** 503

"Smoking Room, The" (Jackson), **Supp. IX:** 116

"Smoky Gold" (Leopold), **Supp. XIV:**186

Smolan, Sandy, **Supp. XVI:**36

Smollett, Tobias G., **I:** 134, 339, 343; **II:** 304–305; **III:** 61

Smuggler's Bible, A (McElroy), **Supp. IV Part 1:** 285

Smuggler's Handbook, The (Goldbarth), **Supp. XII:** 181, 183

Smugglers of Lost Soul's Rock, The (Gardner), **Supp. VI:** 70

Smyth, Albert Henry, **II:** 123

"Snack Firm Maps New Chip Push" (Keillor), **Supp. XVI:**168, 169

"Snail, The" (Hay), **Supp. XIV:**124

"Snake, The" (Berry), **Supp. X:** 31

"Snake, The" (Crane), **I:** 420

"Snakecharmer" (Plath), **Supp. I Part 2:** 538

"Snakes, Mongooses" (Moore), **III:** 207

"Snakes of September, The" (Kunitz), **Supp. III Part 1:** 258

"Snapshot of 15th S.W., A" (Hugo), **Supp. VI:** 141

"Snapshot Rediscovered, A" (X. J. Kennedy), **Supp. XV:** 170

"Snapshots of a Daughter-in-Law" (Rich), **Supp. I Part 2:** 553–554

Snapshots of a Daughter-in-Law: Poems, 1954–1962 (Rich), **Supp. I Part 2:** 550–551, 553–554; **Supp. XII:** 255

Sneetches and Other Stories, The (Geisel), **Supp. XVI:**109

"Sneeze, The" (Chekhov), **Supp. IV Part 2:** 585

Snell, Ebenezer, **Supp. I Part 1:** 151

Snell, Thomas, **Supp. I Part 1:** 153

"Snob, The" (Shapiro), **Supp. II Part 2:** 705

Snobbery: The America Version (Epstein), **Supp. XIV:**102, 114–115

Snodgrass, Kathleen, **Supp. XVI:**42

Snodgrass, W. D., **I:** 400; **Retro. Supp. II:** 179; **Supp. III Part 2:** 541; **Supp. V:** 337; **Supp. VI:** 311–328;

Supp. XI: 141, 315; **Supp. XIII:** 312; **Supp. XV:** 92, 153
"Snow" (Frost), **Retro. Supp. I:** 133
"Snow" (Haines), **Supp. XII:** 212
"Snow" (Sexton), **Supp. II Part 2:** 696
Snow, C. P., **Supp. I Part 2:** 536
Snow, Hank, **Supp. V:** 335
Snow: Meditations of a Cautious Man in Winter (Banks), **Supp. V:** 6
Snow Ball, The (Gurney), **Supp. V:** 99
"Snow-Bound" (Whittier), **Supp. I Part 2:** 700–703
"Snow Bound at Eagle's" (Harte), **Supp. II Part 1:** 356
"Snowflakes" (Longfellow), **II:** 498
"Snow Goose, The" (Gallico), **Supp. XVI:**238
Snow-Image and Other Twice Told Tales, The (Hawthorne), **II:** 237; **Retro. Supp. I:** 160
"Snowing in Greenwich Village" (Updike), **IV:** 226; **Retro. Supp. I:** 321
"Snow in New York" (Swenson), **Supp. IV Part 2:** 644
Snow Leopard, The (Matthiessen), **Supp. V:** 199, 207–211
"Snow Man, The" (Stevens), **IV:** 82–83; **Retro. Supp. I:** 299, 300, 302, 306, 307, 312
"Snowmass Cycle, The" (Dunn), **Supp. XI:** 152
Snow Poems, The (Ammons), **Supp. VII:** 32–34
"Snows of Kilimanjaro, The" (Hemingway), **II:** 78, 257, 263, 264; **Retro. Supp. I:** 98, 182; **Supp. XII:** 249
"Snows of Studiofiftyfour, The" (Plimpton), **Supp. XVI:**245
"Snow Songs" (Snodgrass), **Supp. VI:** 324
"Snowstorm, The" (Oates), **Supp. II Part 2:** 523
"Snowstorm as It Affects the American Farmer, A" (Crèvecoeur), **Supp. I Part 1:** 251
Snow White (Barthelme), **Supp. IV Part 1:** 40, 47, 48–49, 50, 52; **Supp. V:** 39
"Snowy Mountain Song, A" (Ortiz), **Supp. IV Part 2:** 506
Snyder, Gary, **Supp. III Part 1:** 350; **Supp. IV Part 2:** 502; **Supp. V:** 168–169; **Supp. VIII:** 39, 289–307; **Supp. XVI:**283
Snyder, Mike, **Supp. XIV:**36
"So-and-So Reclining on Her Couch" (Stevens), **IV:** 90

"Soapland" (Thurber), **Supp. I Part 2:** 619
Soares, Lota de Macedo, **Retro. Supp. II:** 44; **Supp. I Part 1:** 89, 94
"Sobbin' Women, The" (Benét), **Supp. XI:** 47
Sobin, Gustaf, **Supp. XVI:**281–298
Social Ethics (Gilman), **Supp. XI:** 207
"Socialism and the Negro" (McKay), **Supp. X:** 135
"Socialism of the Skin, A (Liberation, Honey!)" (Kushner), **Supp. IX:** 135
Social Thought in America: The Revolt against Formalism (White), **Supp. I Part 2:** 648, 650
"Society, Morality, and the Novel" (Ellison), **Retro. Supp. II:** 118, 123–124
"Sociological Habit Patterns in Linguistic Transmogrification" (Cowley), **Supp. II Part 1:** 143
"Sociological Poet, A" (Bourne), **I:** 228
Socrates, **I:** 136, 265; **II:** 8–9, 105, 106; **III:** 281, 419, 606; **Supp. I Part 2:** 458; **Supp. XII:** 98
Socrates Fortlow stories (Mosley), **Supp. XIII:** 242–243
So Forth (Brodsky), **Supp. VIII:** 32–33
"So Forth" (Brodsky), **Supp. VIII:** 33
Soft Machine, The (Burroughs), **Supp. III Part 1:** 93, 103, 104
"Soft Mask" (Karr), **Supp. XI:** 243
Soft Side, The (James), **II:** 335; **Retro. Supp. I:** 229
"Soft Spring Night in Shillington, A" (Updike), **Retro. Supp. I:** 318, 319
"Soft Wood" (Lowell), **II:** 550–551
"So Help Me" (Algren), **Supp. IX:** 2
Soil and Survival: Land Stewardship and the Future of American Agriculture (C. Bly, J. Paddock and N. Paddock), **Supp. XVI:**36–37
"Soirée in Hollywood" (H. Miller), **III:** 186
Sojourner, The (Rawlings), **Supp. X:** 233–234
"Sojourn in a Whale" (Moore), **III:** 211, 213
"Sojourns" (Didion), **Supp. IV Part 1:** 205
Solanus, Jane, **Supp. XVI:**293
Solar Storms (Hogan), **Supp. IV Part 1:** 397, 410, 414–415
"Soldier, The" (Frost), **II:** 155
"Soldier Asleep at the Tomb" (Schnackenberg), **Supp. XV:** 262–263
Soldier Blue (film), **Supp. X:** 124

"Soldier of Fortune" (Wright), **Supp. XV:** 341
"Soldier's Home" (Hemingway), **Retro. Supp. I:** 189
Soldier's Joy (Bell), **Supp. X:** 7, 7–8, 10, 11
Soldiers of the Storm (film), **Supp. XIII:** 163
Soldiers' Pay (Faulkner), **I:** 117; **II:** 56, 68; **Retro. Supp. I:** 80, 81
"Soldier's Testament, The" (Mumford), **Supp. II Part 2:** 473
"Soliloquy: Man Talking to a Mirror" (Komunyakaa), **Supp. XIII:** 116–117
"Solitary Confinement" (X. J. Kennedy), **Supp. XV:** 157
"Solitary Pond, The" (Updike), **Retro. Supp. I:** 323
So Little Time (Marquand), **III:** 55, 59, 65, 67, 69
"Solitude" (Maupassant), **Supp. I Part 1:** 223
Solo Faces (Salter), **Supp. IX:** 259–260
Solomon, Andy, **Supp. X:** 11
Solomon, Carl, **Supp. XIV:**143, 150
Solomon, Charles, **Supp. VIII:** 82
Solomon, Henry, Jr., **Supp. I Part 2:** 490
Solomons, Leon, **IV:** 26
So Long, See You Tomorrow (Maxwell), **Supp. VIII:** 156, 160, 162, 167–169
"So Long Ago" (Bausch), **Supp. VII:** 41–42
Solotaroff, Robert, **Retro. Supp. II:** 203
Solotaroff, Theodore, **III:** 452–453; **Retro. Supp. II:** 281; **Supp. I Part 2:** 440, 445; **Supp. X:** 79; **Supp. XI:** 340; **Supp. XII:** 291
"Solstice" (Jeffers), **Supp. II Part 2:** 433, 435
"Solstice, The" (Merwin), **Supp. III Part 1:** 356
"Solus Rex" (Nabokov), **Retro. Supp. I:** 274
"Solutions" (McCarthy), **II:** 578
"Solving the Puzzle" (Dunn), **Supp. XI:** 152
Solzhenitsyn, Alexandr, **Retro. Supp. I:** 278; **Supp. VIII:** 241
"Some Afternoon" (Creeley), **Supp. IV Part 1:** 150–151
Some American People (Caldwell), **I:** 292, 294, 295, 296, 304, 309
"Some Ashes Drifting above Piedra, California" (Levis), **Supp. XI:** 264–265
"Some Aspects of the Grotesque in

Southern Fiction" (O'Connor), **Retro. Supp. II:** 223, 224

"Somebody Always Grabs the Purple" (H. Roth), **Supp. IX:** 234

Somebody in Boots (Algren), **Supp. IX:** 3, 5–7, 12

Somebody's Darling (McMurtry), **Supp. V:** 225

Some Came Running (film), **Supp. XI:** 213

Some Came Running (Jones), **Supp. XI:** 214, 215, 220, 222–223, 226, 227, 232

Some Can Whistle (McMurtry), **Supp. V:** 229

"Some Children of the Goddess" (Mailer), **Retro. Supp. II:** 204

Someday, Maybe (Stafford), **Supp. XI:** 323–325; **Supp. XIII:** 281

"Some Dreamers of the Golden Dream" (Didion), **Supp. IV Part 1:** 200

"Some Foreign Letters" (Sexton), **Supp. II Part 2:** 674

"Some General Instructions" (Koch), **Supp. XV:** 182

"Some Good News" (Olson), **Supp. II Part 2:** 575, 576, 577

"Some Grass along a Ditch Bank" (Levis), **Supp. XI:** 266

"Some Greek Writings" (Corso), **Supp. XII:** 130

Some Honorable Men: Political Conventions, 1960–1972 (Mailer), **Retro. Supp. II:** 208

Some Imagist Poets (Lowell), **III:** 511, 518, 520; **Supp. I Part 1:** 257, 261

"Some keep the Sabbath going to Church" (Dickinson), **Retro. Supp. I:** 30

"Some Laughed" (L. Michaels), **Supp. XVI:** 207

"Some Like Indians Endure" (Gunn Allen), **Supp. IV Part 1:** 330

"Some Like Them Cold" (Lardner), **II:** 427–428, 430, 431; **Supp. IX:** 202

"Some Lines from Whitman" (Jarrell), **IV:** 352

"Some Matters Concerning the Occupant" (Keillor), **Supp. XVI:** 167

"Some Negatives: X. at the Chateau" (Merrill), **Supp. III Part 1:** 322

"Some Neglected Points in the Theory of Socialism" (Veblen), **Supp. I Part 2:** 635

"Some Notes for an Autobiographical Lecture" (Trilling), **Supp. III Part 2:** 493, 497, 500

"Some Notes on French Poetry" (R. Bly), **Supp. IV Part 1:** 61

"Some Notes on Miss L." (West), **IV:** 290–291, 295; **Retro. Supp. II:** 322

"Some Notes on Organic Form" (Levertov), **Supp. III Part 1:** 272, 279

"Some Notes on Teaching: Probably Spoken" (Paley), **Supp. VI:** 225

"Some Notes on the Gazer Within" (Levis), **Supp. XI:** 270

"Some Notes on Violence" (West), **IV:** 304; **Retro. Supp. II:** 322, 323

"Some Observations Now" (Conroy), **Supp. XVI:** 75

Some of the Dharma (Kerouac), **Supp. III Part 1:** 225

"Someone Is Buried" (Salinas), **Supp. XIII:** 324

"Someone Puts a Pineapple Together" (Stevens), **IV:** 90–91

"Someone's Blood" (Dove), **Supp. IV Part 1:** 245

"Someone Talking" (Harjo), **Supp. XII:** 219–220

"Someone Talking to Himself" (Wilbur), **Supp. III Part 2:** 557

"Someone to Watch Over Me" (Stern), **Supp. IX:** 300

Someone to Watch Over Me: Stories (Bausch), **Supp. VII:** 53

Some People, Places, & Things That Will Not Appear in My Next Novel (Cheever), **Supp. I Part 1:** 184–185

"Some Poets' Criticism and the Age" (Yenser), **Supp. XV:** 113–114

Some Problems of Philosophy: A Beginning of an Introduction to Philosophy (James), **II:** 360–361

"Some Questions You Might Ask" (Oliver), **Supp. VII:** 238–239

"Some Remarks on Humor" (White), **Supp. I Part 2:** 672

"Some Remarks on Rhythm" (Roethke), **III:** 548–549

Somers, Fred, **I:** 196

Somerville, Jane, **Supp. IX:** 289, 296–297

"Some Secrets" (Stern), **Supp. IX:** 286, 287, 288, 289, 295

Some Sort of Epic Grandeur (Bruccoli), **Retro. Supp. I:** 115, 359

"Something" (Oliver), **Supp. VII:** 236

Something Happened (Heller), **Supp. IV Part 1:** 383, 386–388, 389, 392

"*Something Happened:* The Imaginary, the Symbolic, and the Discourse of the Family" (Mellard), **Supp. IV Part 1:** 387

Something in Common (Hughes), **Supp. I Part 1:** 329–330

Something Inside: Conversations with

Gay Fiction Writers (Gambone), **Supp. XII:** 81

"Something New" (Stern), **Supp. IX:** 290

"Something's Going to Happen" (Zinberg), **Supp. XV:** 196

"Something Spurious from the Mindinao Deep" (Stegner), **Supp. IV Part 2:** 605

Something to Declare (Alvarez), **Supp. VII:** 1, 2, 11, 17–19

Something to Remember Me By (Bellow), **Retro. Supp. II:** 32

"Something to Remember Me By" (Bellow), **Retro. Supp. II:** 32

Something Wicked This Way Comes (Bradbury), **Supp. IV Part 1:** 101, 110–111

"Something Wild . . ." (T. Williams), **IV:** 381

"Some Thoughts" (McNally), **Supp. XIII:** 207

"Some Thoughts on the Line" (Oliver), **Supp. VII:** 238

"Sometimes, Reading" (Stafford), **Supp. XI:** 314

"Sometimes I Wonder" (Hughes), **Supp. I Part 1:** 337

Sometimes Mysteriously (Salinas), **Supp. XIII:** 311, 326–328

"Sometimes Mysteriously" (Salinas), **Supp. XIII:** 328

Some Trees (Ashbery), **Supp. III Part 1:** 3–7, 12

"Some Trees" (Ashbery), **Supp. III Part 1:** 2

"Some Views on the Reading and Writing of Short Stories" (Welty), **Retro. Supp. I:** 351

"Somewhere" (Nemerov), **III:** 279–280

"Somewhere Else" (Paley), **Supp. VI:** 227

"Somewhere in Africa" (Sexton), **Supp. II Part 2:** 684–685

"Somewhere Is Such a Kingdom" (Ransom), **III:** 492

"Somewhere near Phu Bai: (Komunyakaa), **Supp. XIII:** 123–124

"Some Words with a Mummy" (Poe), **III:** 425

"Some Yips and Barks in the Dark" (Snyder), **Supp. VIII:** 291

Sommers, Michael, **Supp. IV Part 2:** 581

Sommers, William, **I:** 387, 388

"Somnambulisma" (Stevens), **Retro. Supp. I:** 310

"So Much Summer" (Dickinson),

Retro. **Supp. I:** 26, 44, 45
"So Much the Worse for Boston" (Lindsay), **Supp. I Part 2:** 398
"So Much Water So Close to Home" (Carver), **Supp. III Part 1:** 143, 146
Son, Cathy, **Supp. X:** 292
"Son, The" (Dove), **Supp. IV Part 1:** 245
"Sonata" (Schnackenberg), **Supp. XV:** 259
"Sonata for the Invisible" (Harjo), **Supp. XII:** 228
Sonata for Two Pianos (Bowles), **Supp. IV Part 1:** 83
Son at the Front, A (Wharton), **II:** 183; **IV:** 320; **Retro. Supp. I:** 378
Sondheim, Stephen, **Supp. XII:** 260; **Supp. XVI:**194
Son Excellence Eugène Rougon (Zola), **III:** 322
"Song" (Bogan), **Supp. III Part 1:** 57
"Song" (Bryant). *See* "Hunter of the West, The"
"Song" (Dunbar), **Supp. II Part 1:** 199
"Song" (Ginsberg), **Supp. II Part 1:** 317
"Song" (Kenyon), **Supp. VII:** 169
"Song" (Rich), **Supp. I Part 2:** 560
"Song" (Wylie), **Supp. I Part 2:** 729
"Song, A" (Creeley), **Supp. IV Part 1:** 145
"Song: Enlightenment" (X. J. Kennedy), **Supp. XV:** 169
"Song: Love in Whose Rich Honor" (Rukeyser), **Supp. VI:** 285
"Song: Now That She Is Here" (Carruth), **Supp. XVI:**59
"Song: 'Rough Winds Do Shake the Darling Buds of May'" (Simpson), **Supp. IX:** 268
"Song, The" (Gioia), **Supp. XV:** 117
Song and Idea (Eberhart), **I:** 526, 529, 533, 539
"Song for Myself and the Deer to Return On" (Harjo), **Supp. XII:** 225
"Song for My Sixtieth Year" (Carruth), **Supp. XVI:**54
"Song for Occupations, A" (Whitman), **Retro. Supp. I:** 394
"Song for Simeon, A" (Eliot), **Retro. Supp. I:** 64
"Song for the Coming of Smallpox" (Wagoner), **Supp. IX:** 329, 330
"Song for the End of Time" (Gioia), **Supp. XV:** 126–127
"Song for the First People" (Wagoner), **Supp. IX:** 328
"Song for the Last Act" (Bogan), **Supp. III Part 1:** 64
"Song for the Middle of the Night, A"

(Wright), **Supp. III Part 2:** 594
"Song for the Rainy Season" (Bishop), **Supp. I Part 1:** 93–94, 96
"Song for the Romeos, A" (Stern), **Supp. IX:** 296
"Song from a Courtyard Window" (Gioia), **Supp. XV:** 119
"Songline of Dawn" (Harjo), **Supp. XII:** 229
"Song of Advent, A" (Winters), **Supp. II Part 2:** 789
"Song of a Man Who Rushed at the Enemy" (Wagoner), **Supp. IX:** 329, 330
"Song of Courage, A" (Masters), **Supp. I Part 2:** 458
Song of God, The: Bhagavad-Gita (Isherwood and Prabhavananda, trans.), **Supp. XIV:**156, 157, 164
Song of Hiawatha, The (Longfellow), **II:** 501, 503–504; **Retro. Supp. II:** 155, 159–161, 162, 163
"Song of Innocence, A" (Ellison), **Retro. Supp. II:** 126; **Supp. II Part 1:** 248
"Song of My Fiftieth Birthday, The" (Lindsay), **Supp. I Part 2:** 399
"Song of Myself" (Whitman), **II:** 544; **III:** 572, 584, 595; **IV:** 333, 334, 337–339, 340, 341, 342, 344, 348, 349, 351, 405; **Retro. Supp. I:** 388, 389, 395–399, 400; **Supp. V:** 122; **Supp. IX:** 131, 136, 143, 328, 331; **Supp. XIV:**139
Song of Russia (film), **Supp. I Part 1:** 281, 294
"Song of Self" (Huncke), **Supp. XIV:**138–139, 145
Song of Solomon (biblical book), **III:** 118; **IV:** 150
Song of Solomon (Morrison), **Supp. III Part 1:** 364, 368, 369, 372, 379
Song of Songs (biblical book), **II:** 538; **IV:** 153–154; **Supp. XV:** 221
"Song of the Answerer" (Whitman), **Retro. Supp. I:** 393, 399
"Song of the Chattahoochee, The" (Lanier), **Supp. I Part 1:** 365, 368
"Song of the Degrees, A" (Pound), **III:** 466
"Song of the Exposition" (Whitman), **IV:** 332
"Song of the Gavilan" (Leopold), **Supp. XIV:**189
"Song of the Gourd" (Wright), **Supp. XV:** 348–349
"Song of the Greek Amazon" (Bryant), **Supp. I Part 1:** 168
Song of the Lark, The (Cather), **I:** 312, 319–321, 323; **Retro. Supp. I:** 1, 3,

7, 9–11, 13, 19, 20
"Song of the Open Road" (McGrath), **Supp. X:** 127
"Song of the Open Road" (Whitman), **IV:** 340–341; **Retro. Supp. I:** 400; **Supp. IX:** 265
"Song of the Redwood Tree" (Whitman), **IV:** 348
"Song of the Scullery" (McCarriston), **Supp. XIV:**272
"Song of the Sky Loom" (traditional Tewa poem), **Supp. IV Part 1:** 325
"Song of the Son" (Toomer), **Supp. III Part 2:** 482–483; **Supp. IX:** 313
"Song of the Sower, The" (Bryant), **Supp. I Part 1:** 169
"Song of the Stars" (Bryant), **Supp. I Part 1:** 163
"Song of the Swamp-Robin, The" (Frederic), **II:** 138
"Song of the Vermonters, The" (Whittier), **Supp. I Part 2:** 692
"Song of Three Smiles" (Merwin), **Supp. III Part 1:** 344
"Song of Wandering Aengus, The" (Yeats), **IV:** 271; **Retro. Supp. I:** 342, 350
"Song of Welcome" (Brodsky), **Supp. VIII:** 32
"Song on Captain Barney's Victory" (Freneau), **Supp. II Part 1:** 261
"Song/Poetry and Language-Expression and Perception" (Ortiz), **Supp. IV Part 2:** 500, 508
Songs and Satires (Masters), **Supp. I Part 2:** 465–466
Songs and Sonnets (L. P. Smith), **Supp. XIV:**341
Songs and Sonnets (Masters), **Supp. I Part 2:** 455, 459, 461, 466
"Songs for a Colored Singer" (Bishop), **Supp. I Part 1:** 80, 85
Songs for a Summer's Day (A Sonnet Cycle) (MacLeish), **III:** 3
Songs for Eve (MacLeish), **III:** 3, 19
"Songs for Eve" (MacLeish), **III:** 19
"Songs for My Father" (Komunyakaa), **Supp. XIII:** 128
"Songs for Two Seasons" (C. Frost), **Supp. XV:** 95–96
Songs from This Earth on Turtle's Back: Contemporary American Indian Poetry (Bruchac, ed.), **Supp. IV Part 1:** 320, 328
"Songs of a Housewife" (Rawlings), **Supp. X:** 221–222
"Songs of Billy Bathgate, The" (Doctorow), **Supp. IV Part 1:** 230
Songs of Innocence (Blake), **Supp. I Part 2:** 708

Songs of Jamaica (McKay), **Supp. X:** 131, 133

"Songs of Maximus, The" (Olson), **Supp. II Part 2:** 567

"Songs of Parting" (Whitman), **IV:** 348

Songs of the Sierras (J. Miller), **I:** 459

Songs of Three Centuries (Whittier and Larcom, eds.), **Supp. XIII:** 142

"Song to David" (Smart), **III:** 534

"Song to No Music, A" (Brodsky), **Supp. VIII:** 26

Sonneschein, Rosa, **Retro. Supp. II:** 65

"Sonnet" (Rukeyser), **Supp. VI:** 284

"Sonnets" (Carruth), **Supp. XVI:**56

"Sonnets at Christmas" (Tate), **IV:** 135

Sonnets to Orpheus (Rilke), **Supp. XV:** 222

"Sonnet-To Zante" (Poe), **III:** 421

"Sonny's Blues" (Baldwin), **Retro. Supp. II:** 7, 8, 10, 14; **Supp. I Part 1:** 58–59, 63, 67; **Supp. XI:** 288

Son of Laughter, The: A Novel (Buechner), **Supp. XII:** 54

Son of Perdition, The (Cozzens), **I:** 359–360, 377, 378, 379

Son of the Circus, A (Irving), **Supp. VI:** 165, 166, 176–179

"Son of the Gods, A" (Bierce), **I:** 202

Son of the Morning (Oates), **Supp. II Part 2:** 518, 519, 520–522

Son of the Morning Star: Custer and the Little Bighorn (Connell), **Supp. XIV:**80, 82, 97

"Son of the Romanovs, A" (Simpson), **Supp. IX:** 273–274

Son of the Wolf, The (London), **II:** 465, 469

"Son of the Wolfman" (Chabon), **Supp. XI:** 76

"Sonrisas" (Mora), **Supp. XIII:** 216, 219

Sons (Buck), **Supp. II Part 1:** 117–118

Sons and Lovers (Lawrence), **III:** 27

Sontag, Kate, **Supp. XV:** 104

Sontag, Susan, **IV:** 13, 14; **Retro. Supp. II:** 279; **Supp. I Part 2:** 423; **Supp. III Part 2:** 451–473; **Supp. VIII:** 75; **Supp. XIV:**14, 15, 95–96, 167; **Supp. XVI:**201, 204, 206

"Soonest Mended" (Ashbery), **Supp. III Part 1:** 1, 13

"Sootfall and Fallout" (White), **Supp. I Part 2:** 671

Sophocles, **I:** 274; **II:** 291, 385, 577; **III:** 145, 151, 152, 153, 159, 398, 476, 478, 609, 613; **IV:** 291, 363, 368, 370; **Supp. I Part 1:** 153, 284; **Supp. I Part 2:** 491; **Supp. V:** 97;

Supp. VIII: 332; **Supp. XV:** 265, 266

"Sophronsiba" (Bourne), **I:** 221

Sorcerer's Apprentice, The: Tales and Conjurations (Johnson), **Supp. VI:** 192–193, 194

"Sorcerer's Eye, The" (Nemerov), **III:** 283

Sordello (Browning), **III:** 467, 469, 470

"Sordid? Good God!" (Williams), **Retro. Supp. II:** 334

"Sorghum" (Mason), **Supp. VIII:** 146

Sorokin, Pitirim, **Supp. I Part 2:** 679

Sorrentino, Gilbert, **Retro. Supp. I:** 426; **Supp. IV Part 1:** 286; **Supp. XII:** 139

"Sorrow" (Komunyakaa), **Supp. XIII:** 119

Sorrow Dance, The (Levertov), **Supp. III Part 1:** 279–280, 283

"Sorrowful Guest, A" (Jewett), **Retro. Supp. II:** 137

Sorrows of Fat City, The: A Selection of Literary Essays and Reviews (Garrett), **Supp. VII:** 111

Sorrows of Young Werther, The (Goethe), **Supp. XI:** 169

Sorrows of Young Werther, The (Goethe; Bogan and Mayer, trans.), **Supp. III Part 1:** 63

"Sorting Facts; or, Nineteen Ways of Looking at Marker" (Howe), **Supp. IV Part 2:** 434, 436

"S O S" (Baraka), **Supp. II Part 1:** 50

"So Sassafras" (Olson), **Supp. II Part 2:** 574

"So There" (Creeley), **Supp. IV Part 1:** 157

Sotirov, Vasil, **Supp. IX:** 152

Soto, Gary, **Supp. IV Part 2:** 545; **Supp. V:** 180; **Supp. XI:** 270; **Supp. XIII:** 313, 315, 316, 320, 323; **Supp. XV:** 73

"Soto Thinking of the Ocean" (Salinas), **Supp. XIII:** 321

"Sotto Voce" (Kunitz), **Supp. III Part 1:** 265

Sot-Weed Factor, The (Barth), **I:** 122, 123, 125, 129, 130, 131–134, 135

Soul, The (Brooks), **I:** 244

Soul and Body of John Brown, The (Rukeyser), **Supp. VI:** 273

Soul Clap Hands and Sing (Marshall), **Supp. XI:** 276, 278, 280–282

SOUL EXPEDITIONS (SINGER). *SEE* SHOSHA

(SINGER)

Soul Gone Home (Hughes), **Retro. Supp. I:** 203; **Supp. I Part 1:** 328

"Soul inside the Sentence, The" (Gass), **Supp. VI:** 88

Soul Is Here for Its Own Joy, The (Bly, ed.), **Supp. IV Part 1:** 74

Soul of Man under Socialism, The (Wilde), **Supp. IX:** 134–135

Soul of the Far East, The (Lowell), **II:** 513

Soul on Ice (Cleaver), **Retro. Supp. II:** 12, 13

"Souls Belated" (Wharton), **Retro. Supp. I:** 364

"Soul selects her own Society, The" (Dickinson), **Retro. Supp. I:** 37

Souls of Black Folk, The (Du Bois), **Supp. II Part 1:** 33, 40, 160, 168–170, 176, 183; **Supp. IV Part 1:** 164; **Supp. IX:** 305, 306; **Supp. X:** 133; **Supp. XIII:** 185, 238, 243

"Sound, The" (Olds), **Supp. X:** 214

"Sound and Fury" (O. Henry), **Supp. II Part 1:** 402

Sound and the Fury, The (Faulkner), **I:** 480; **II:** 55, 57, 58–60, 73; **III:** 237; **IV:** 100, 101, 104; **Retro. Supp. I:** 73, 75, 77, 82, 83–84, 86, 88, 89, 90, 91, 92; **Supp. VIII:** 215; **Supp. IX:** 103; **Supp. X:** 44; **Supp. XII:** 33; **Supp. XIV:**12

"Sound Bites" (Alvarez), **Supp. VII:** 11

Sound I Listened For, The (Francis), **Supp. IX:** 78–79, 87

"Sound Mind, Sound Body" (Lowell), **II:** 554

"Sound of Distant Thunder, A" (Elkin), **Supp. VI:** 42–43, 44

"Sound of Light, The" (Merwin), **Supp. III Part 1:** 356

Sound of Mountain Water, The (Stegner), **Supp. IV Part 2:** 595, 596, 598, 600, 608

"Sound of Talking" (Purdy), **Supp. VII:** 270

Sounds of Poetry, The (Pinsky), **Supp. VI:** 236, 247, 248

Soupault, Philippe, **IV:** 288, 404; **Retro. Supp. II:** 85, 321, 324

Source (Doty), **Supp. XI:** 121, 134–137

"Source" (Doty), **Supp. XI:** 136

"Source, The" (Olds), **Supp. X:** 211

"Source, The" (Porter), **III:** 443

Source of Light, The (Price), **Supp. VI:** 262, 266

"Sources of Soviet Conduct, The" (Kennan), **Supp. VIII:** 241

Sour Grapes (W. C. Williams), **Retro. Supp. I:** 418

"South" (Levis), **Supp. XI:** 266

"South, The" (Hughes), **Supp. I Part 1:** 321

"Southbound on the Freeway" (Swenson), **Supp. IV Part 2:** 643

Southern, Terry, **Supp. IV Part 1:** 379; **Supp. V:** 40, 201; **Supp. XI:** 293–310; **Supp. XVI:**230

Southern Cross, The (Wright), **Supp. V:** 332, 342

"Southern Cross, The" (Wright), **Supp. V:** 338

"Southerner's Problem, The" (Du Bois), **Supp. II Part 1:** 168

"Southern Girl" (Zelda Fitzgerald), **Supp. IX:** 71

"Southern Mode of the Imagination, A" (Tate), **IV:** 120

"Southern Romantic, A" (Tate), **Supp. I Part 1:** 373

Southern Terry, **Supp. XIV:**82

Southey, Robert, **II:** 304, 502; **Supp. I Part 1:** 154

South Moon Under (Rawlings), **Supp. X:** 225–226, 229, 233

South Pacific Affair (Lacy), **Supp. XV:** 206

Southpaw, The (Harris), **II:** 424–425

"South Sangamon" (Cisneros), **Supp. VII:** 66

Southwell, Robert, **IV:** 151

Southwick, Marcia, **Supp. XI:** 259

Southworth, E. D. E. N, **Retro. Supp. I:** 246

Souvenir of the Ancient World, Selected Poems of Carlos Drummond de Andrade (Strand, trans.), **Supp. IV Part 2:** 630

"Sow" (Plath), **Supp. I Part 2:** 537

Space between Our Footsteps, The: Poems and Paintings from the Middle East (Nye, ed.), **Supp. XIII:** 280

"Space Quale, The" (James), **II:** 349

"Spaces Between, The" (Kingsolver), **Supp. VII:** 209

Spackman, Peter, **Supp. XVI:**221

Spacks, Patricia, **Supp. XVI:**251

"Spain" (Auden), **Supp. II Part 1:** 12–13, 14

"Spain in Fifty-Ninth Street" (White), **Supp. I Part 2:** 677

"Spanish-American War Play" (Crane), **I:** 422

Spanish Ballads (Merwin, trans.), **Supp. III Part 1:** 347

Spanish Bayonet (Benét), **Supp. XI:** 45, 47

Spanish Earth, The (film), **Retro. Supp. I:** 184

Spanish Papers and Other Miscellanies (Irving), **II:** 314

"Spanish Revolution, The" (Bryant), **Supp. I Part 1:** 153, 168

Spanish Student, The (Longfellow), **II:** 489, 506; **Retro. Supp. II:** 165

Spanking the Maid (Coover), **Supp. V:** 47, 48, 49, 52

Spargo, John, **Supp. I Part 1:** 13

"Spark, The" (Wharton), **Retro. Supp. I:** 381

"Sparkles from the Wheel" (Whitman), **IV:** 348

Sparks, Debra, **Supp. X:** 177

Sparks, Jared, **Supp. I Part 1:** 156

"Sparrow" (Berry), **Supp. X:** 31

Sparrow, Henry, **III:** 587

Sparrow, Mrs. Henry, **III:** 587

Spaulding, William, **Supp. XVI:**106

"Spawning Run, The" (Humphrey), **Supp. IX:** 95

"Speak, Gay Memory" (Kirp), **Supp. XI:** 129

Speak, Memory (Nabokov), **III:** 247–250, 252; **Retro. Supp. I:** 264, 265, 266, 267, 268, 277; **Supp. XVI:**148

Speaking and Language (Shapiro), **Supp. II Part 2:** 721

Speaking for Nature: How Literary Naturalists from Henry Thoreau to Rachel Carson Have Shaped America (Brooks), **Supp. IX:** 31

Speaking for Ourselves: American Ethnic Writing (Faderman and Bradshaw, eds.), **Supp. XIII:** 313

Speaking of Accidents (Everwine), **Supp. XV:** 75, 88

"Speaking of Accidents" (Everwine), **Supp. XV:** 88–89

"Speaking of Counterweights" (White), **Supp. I Part 2:** 669

Speaking of Literature and Society (Trilling), **Supp. III Part 2:** 494, 496, 499

"Speaking of Love" (Gioia), **Supp. XV:** 124–125

Speaking on Stage (Kolin and Kullman, eds.), **Supp. IX:** 145

Speaking on Stage: Interviews with Contemporary American Playwrights (Balakian), **Supp. XV:** 327

"Speaking Passions" (Kitchen), **Supp. XV:** 215

Speak What We Feel (Not What We Ought to Say): Reflections on Literature and Faith (Buechner), **Supp. XII:** 57

Spear, Roberta, **Supp. V:** 180; **Supp. XV:** 73

"Special Kind of Fantasy, A: James Dickey on the Razor's Edge" (Niflis), **Supp. IV Part 1:** 175

"Special Pleading" (Lanier), **Supp. I Part 1:** 364

"Special Problems in Teaching Leslie Marmon Silko's *Ceremony*" (Gunn Allen), **Supp. IV Part 1:** 333

Special Providence, A (Yates), **Supp. XI:** 342, 344–345

"Special Time, a Special School, A" (Knowles), **Supp. XII:** 236

Special View of History, The (Olson), **Supp. II Part 2:** 566, 569, 572

Specimen Days (Whitman), **IV:** 338, 347, 348, 350; **Retro. Supp. I:** 408

Specimens of the American Poets, **Supp. I Part 1:** 155

"Spectacles, The" (Poe), **III:** 425

Spectator Bird, The (Stegner), **Supp. IV Part 2:** 599, 604, 606, 611–612

Spector, Robert, **Supp. XIII:** 87

Spectra: A Book of Poetic Experiments (Bynner and Ficke), **Supp. XV:** 43

"Spectre Bridegroom, The" (Irving), **II:** 304

"Spectre Pig, The" (Holmes), **Supp. I Part 1:** 302

"Speculating Woman" (X. J. Kennedy), **Supp. XV:** 168

"Speech Sounds" (O. Butler), **Supp. XIII:** 61, 70

"Speech to a Crowd" (MacLeish), **III:** 16

"Speech to the Detractors" (MacLeish), **III:** 16

"Speech to the Young" (Brooks), **Supp. III Part 1:** 79, 86

"Speech to Those Who Say Comrade" (MacLeish), **III:** 16

Speedboat (Adler), **Supp. X:** 171

Speed of Darkness, The (Rukeyser), **Supp. VI:** 274, 281

Speed-the-Plow (Mamet), **Supp. XIV:**241, 246, 249, 250, 251

Speilberg, Steven, **Supp. XI:** 234

"Spell" (Francis), **Supp. IX:** 87

Spelling Dictionary, A (Rowson), **Supp. XV:** 244

Spence, Thomas, **Supp. I Part 2:** 518

Spence + Lila (Mason), **Supp. VIII:** 133, 143–145

Spencer, Edward, **Supp. I Part 1:** 357, 360

Spencer, Herbert, **I:** 515; **II:** 345, 462–463, 480, 483, 536; **III:** 102, 315; **IV:** 135; **Retro. Supp. II:** 60, 65, 93, 98; **Supp. I Part 1:** 368; **Supp.**

I **Part 2:** 635

Spencer, Sharon, **Supp. X:** 185, 186, 195, 196

Spencer, Theodore, **I:** 433; **Supp. III Part 1:** 2

Spender, Natasha, **Supp. IV Part 1:** 119, 127, 134

Spender, Stephen, **II:** 371; **III:** 504, 527; **Retro. Supp. I:** 216; **Retro. Supp. II:** 243, 244; **Supp. I Part 2:** 536; **Supp. II Part 1:** 11; **Supp. IV Part 1:** 82, 134; **Supp. IV Part 2:** 440; **Supp. X:** 116

Spengler, Oswald, **I:** 255, 270; **II:** 7, 577; **III:** 172, 176; **Retro. Supp. II:** 324; **Supp. I Part 2:** 647

Spens, Sir Patrick, **Supp. I Part 2:** 404

Spenser, Edmund, **I:** 62; **III:** 77, 78, 89; **IV:** 155, 453; **Retro. Supp. I:** 62; **Supp. I Part 1:** 98, 152, 369; **Supp. I Part 2:** 422, 719

"Spenser's Ireland" (Moore), **III:** 211, 212

Sperry, Margaret, **Supp. IV Part 1:** 169

Sphere: The Form of a Motion (Ammons), **Supp. VII:** 24, 32, 33, 35, 36

"Sphinx" (Hayden), **Supp. II Part 1:** 373

"Spiced Plums" (Ríos), **Supp. IV Part 2:** 553

"Spider and the Ghost of the Fly, The" (Lindsay), **Supp. I Part 2:** 375

Spider Bay (Van Vechten), **Supp. II Part 2:** 746

"Spiders" (Schwartz), **Supp. II Part 2:** 665

Spider's House, The (Bowles), **Supp. IV Part 1:** 87–89, 90, 91

Spider Woman's Granddaughters: Traditional Tales and Contemporary Writing by Native American Women (Gunn Allen, ed.), **Supp. IV Part 1:** 320, 326, 332–333; **Supp. IV Part 2:** 567

Spiegelman, Willard, **Supp. XI:** 126

Spillane, Mickey, **Supp. IV Part 2:** 469, 472; **Supp. XV:** 200

Spiller, Robert E., **I:** 241; **Supp. I Part 1:** 104

Spillway (Barnes), **Supp. III Part 1:** 44

Spingarn, Amy, **Supp. I Part 1:** 325, 326

Spingarn, Joel, **I:** 266; **Supp. I Part 1:** 325

Spinoza, Baruch, **I:** 493; **II:** 590, 593; **III:** 600; **IV:** 5, 7, 11, 12, 17; **Retro. Supp. II:** 300; **Supp. I Part 1:** 274;

Supp. I Part 2: 643; **Supp. XVI:**184

"Spinoza of Market Street, The" (Singer), **IV:** 12–13; **Retro. Supp. II:** 307

"Spinster" (Plath), **Supp. I Part 2:** 536

"Spinster's Tale, A" (Taylor), **Supp. V:** 314–315, 316–317, 319, 323

Spiral of Memory, The: Interviews (Coltelli, ed.), **Supp. XII:** 215

Spires, Elizabeth, **Supp. X:** 8

"Spire Song" (Bowles), **Supp. IV Part 1:** 80

Spirit and the Flesh, The: Sexual Diversity in American Indian Culture (W. L. Williams), **Supp. IV Part 1:** 330

"Spirit Birth" (Cullen), **Supp. IV Part 1:** 168

Spirit in Man, The (Jung), **Supp. IV Part 1:** 68

Spirit of Culver (West), **IV:** 287

Spirit of Romance, The (Pound), **III:** 470; **Retro. Supp. I:** 286

Spirit of Youth and the City Streets, The (Addams), **Supp. I Part 1:** 6–7, 12–13, 16, 17, 19

"Spirits" (Bausch), **Supp. VII:** 46–47

Spirits, and Other Stories (Bausch), **Supp. VII:** 46–47, 54

"Spirit Says, You Are Nothing, The" (Levis), **Supp. XI:** 265–266

Spiritual Conflict, The (Scupoli), **IV:** 156

Spiritual Exercises, The (Loyola), **IV:** 151; **Supp. XI:** 162

"Spiritual Manifestation, A" (Whittier), **Supp. I Part 2:** 699

"Spirituals and Neo-Spirituals" (Hurston), **Supp. VI:** 152–153

Spits, Ellen Handler, **Supp. XII:** 166

"Spitzbergen Tales" (Crane), **I:** 409, 415, 423

Spitzer, Philip, **Supp. XIV:**21

"Spleen" (Eliot), **I:** 569, 573–574

Spleen de Paris, Le (Baudelaire), **Supp. XIV:**337

Splendid Drunken Twenties, The (Van Vechten), **Supp. II Part 2:** 739–744

"Splittings" (Rich), **Supp. I Part 2:** 570–571

"Splitting Wood at Six Above" (Kumin), **Supp. IV Part 2:** 449

Spofford, Harriet Prescott, **Supp. XIII:** 143

Spoils of Poynton, The (James), **I:** 463; **Retro. Supp. I:** 229–230

Spoken Page, The (Nye), **Supp. XIII:** 274

"Spokes" (Auster), **Supp. XII:** 23

Spokesmen (Whipple), **II:** 456

Spook Sonata, The (Strindberg), **III:** 387, 392

Spooky Art, The: A Book about Writing (Mailer), **Retro. Supp. II:** 214

"Spoon, The" (Simic), **Supp. VIII:** 275

Spoon River Anthology (Masters), **I:** 106; **III:** 579; **Supp. I Part 2:** 454, 455, 456, 460–465, 466, 467, 471, 472, 473, 476; **Supp. IX:** 306; **Supp. XIV:**282–283

Sport and a Pastime, A (Salter), **Supp. IX:** 254–257; **Supp. XVI:**237

Sporting Club, The (McGuane), **Supp. VIII:** 43

Sport of the Gods, The (Dunbar), **Supp. II Part 1:** 193, 200, 207, 214–217

"Sportsman Born and Bred, A" (Plimpton), **Supp. XVI:**241

Sportsman's Sketches, A (Turgenev), **I:** 106; **IV:** 277

Sportswriter, The (Ford), **Supp. V:** 57, 58, 62–67

"Spotted Horses" (Faulkner), **IV:** 260

Sprague, Morteza, **Retro. Supp. II:** 115

Spratling, William, **II:** 56; **Retro. Supp. I:** 80

Sprawl trilogy (W. Gibson), **Supp. XVI:**117, 122, 124

"Spray Paint King, The" (Dove), **Supp. IV Part 1:** 252–253

Spreading Fires (Knowles), **Supp. XII:** 249

Sprigge, Elizabeth, **IV:** 31

"Spring" (Millay), **III:** 126

"Spring" (Mora), **Supp. XIII:** 217

"Spring 1967" (Carruth), **Supp. XVI:**55

Spring and All (W. C. Williams), **Retro. Supp. I:** 412, 418, 418–420, 427, 430, 431

"Spring and All" (W. C. Williams), **Retro. Supp. I:** 419

"Spring Break-Up" (Carruth), **Supp. XVI:**56

"Spring Bulletin" (Allen), **Supp. XV:** 15

"Spring Evening" (Farrell), **II:** 45

"Spring Evening" (Kenyon), **Supp. VII:** 173

"Springfield Magical" (Lindsay), **Supp. I Part 2:** 379

Spring in New Hampshire and Other Poems (McKay), **Supp. X:** 131, 135

"Spring Notes from Robin Hill" (Carruth), **Supp. XVI:**48

"Spring Pastoral" (Wylie), **Supp. I Part 2:** 707

"Spring Pools" (Frost), **II:** 155; **Retro.**

Supp. I: 137

"Spring Snow" (Matthews), **Supp. IX:** 160

"SPRING SONG" (Baraka), **Supp. II Part 1:** 60

Springsteen, Bruce, **Supp. VIII:** 143

"Spring Strains" (W. C. Williams), **Retro. Supp. I:** 416

Spring Tides (Morison), **Supp. I Part 2:** 494

Springtime and Harvest (Sinclair), **Supp. V:** 280

Spruance, Raymond, **Supp. I Part 2:** 479, 491

"Spruce Has No Taproot, The" (Clampitt), **Supp. IX:** 41–42

"Spunk" (Hurston), **Supp. VI:** 150, 151–152

Spunk: The Selected Stories (Hurston), **Supp. VI:** 150

Spurr, David, **Supp. XV:** 183

Spy, The (Cooper), **I:** 335, 336, 337, 339, 340; **Supp. I Part 1:** 155

"Spy, The" (Francis), **Supp. IX:** 81

Spy, The (Freneau), **Supp. II Part 1:** 260

Spy in the House of Love, A (Nin), **Supp. X:** 186

Squanto, **Supp. I Part 2:** 486

"Square Business" (Baraka), **Supp. II Part 1:** 49

Square Root of Wonderful, The (McCullers), **II:** 587–588

"Squash in Blossom" (Francis), **Supp. IX:** 81

"Squatter on Company Land, The" (Hugo), **Supp. VI:** 133

"Squatter's Children" (Bishop), **Retro. Supp. II:** 47

Squeeze Play (Auster), **Supp. XII:** 21

Squires, Radcliffe, **IV:** 127; **Supp. XV:** 118

Squirrels (Mamet), **Supp. XIV:**240

S.S. Gliencairn (O'Neill), **III:** 387, 388, 405

S.S. San Pedro (Cozzens), **I:** 360–362, 370, 378, 379

"Ssshh" (Olds), **Supp. X:** 215

St. John, David, **Supp. XV:** 73, 253

"Stacking the Straw" (Clampitt), **Supp. IX:** 41

Stade, George, **Supp. IV Part 1:** 286

Staël, Madame de, **II:** 298

"Staff of Life, The" (H. Miller), **III:** 187

Stafford, Jean, **II:** 537; **Retro. Supp. II:** 177; **Supp. V:** 316

Stafford, William, **Supp. IV Part 1:** 72; **Supp. IV Part 2:** 642; **Supp. IX:** 273; **Supp. XI:** 311–332; **Supp.**

XIII: 76, 274, 276, 277, 281, 283; **Supp. XIV:**119, 123

"Stage All Blood, The" (MacLeish), **III:** 18

"Staggerlee Wonders" (Baldwin), **Retro. Supp. II:** 15

Stained White Radiance, A (Burke), **Supp. XIV:**28, 31

Stalin, Joseph, **I:** 261, 490; **II:** 39, 40, 49, 564; **III:** 30, 298; **IV:** 372; **Supp. V:** 290

"Stalking the Billion-Footed Beast: A Literary Manifesto for the New Social Novel" (Wolfe), **Supp. III Part 2:** 586

Stallman, R. W., **I:** 405

Stamberg, Susan, **Supp. IV Part 1:** 201; **Supp. XII:** 193

Stamford, Anne Marie, **Supp. XII:** 162

Stanard, Mrs. Jane, **III:** 410, 413

Stand, The (King), **Supp. V:** 139, 140–141, 144–146, 148, 152

"Standard of Liberty, The" (Rowson), **Supp. XV:** 243

"Standard of Living, The" (Parker), **Supp. IX:** 198–199

Stander, Lionel, **Supp. I Part 1:** 289

Standing by Words (Berry), **Supp. X:** 22, 27, 28, 31, 32, 33, 35

"Standing Halfway Home" (Wagoner), **Supp. IX:** 324

Stand in the Mountains, A (Taylor), **Supp. V:** 324

Standish, Burt L. (pseudonym). *See* Patten, Gilbert

Standish, Miles, **I:** 471; **II:** 502–503

Standley, Fred L., **Retro. Supp. II:** 6

Stand Still Like the Hummingbird (H. Miller), **III:** 184

"Stand Up" (Salinas), **Supp. XIII:** 315

Stand with Me Here (Francis), **Supp. IX:** 76

Stanford, Ann, **Retro. Supp. I:** 41; **Supp. I Part 1:** 99, 100, 102, 103, 106, 108, 109, 113, 117; **Supp. IV Part 2:** 637

Stanford, Donald E., **II:** 217

Stanford, Frank, **Supp. XV:** 338, 339, 341, 342–343, 343, 345, 348, 350

Stanford, Ginny (Crouch), **Supp. XV:** 339

Stanford, Leland, **I:** 196, 198

Stanislavsky, Konstantin, **Supp. XIV:**240, 243

"Stanley Kunitz" (Oliver), **Supp. VII:** 237

Stanton, Frank L., **Supp. II Part 1:** 192

Stanton, Robert J., **Supp. IV Part 2:** 681

"Stanzas from the Grande Chartreuse" (Arnold), **Supp. I Part 2:** 417

Stanzas in Meditation (Stein), **Supp. III Part 1:** 13

Staples, Hugh, **Retro. Supp. II:** 187

Star, Alexander, **Supp. X:** 310

Starbuck, George, **Retro. Supp. II:** 53, 245; **Supp. I Part 2:** 538; **Supp. IV Part 2:** 440; **Supp. XIII:** 76

Star Child (Gunn Allen), **Supp. IV Part 1:** 324

Stardust Memories (film; Allen), **Supp. XV:** 1, 4, 8, 9, 13

"Stare, The" (Updike), **Retro. Supp. I:** 329

"Starfish, The" (R. Bly), **Supp. IV Part 1:** 72

"Staring at the Sea on the Day of the Death of Another" (Swenson), **Supp. IV Part 2:** 652

Star Is Born, A (film), **Supp. IV Part 1:** 198; **Supp. IX:** 198

Stark, David, **Supp. XII:** 202

"Stark Boughs on the Family Tree" (Oliver), **Supp. VII:** 232

Starke, Aubrey Harrison, **Supp. I Part 1:** 350, 352, 356, 360, 362, 365, 370, 371

Starkey, David, **Supp. XII:** 180, 181

"Starlight" (Levine), **Supp. V:** 188

"Starlight Scope Myopia" (Komunyakaa), **Supp. XIII:** 123, 124

"Star of the Nativity" (Brodsky), **Supp. VIII:** 33

Starr, Ellen Gates, **Supp. I Part 1:** 4, 5, 11

Starr, Jean. *See* Untermeyer, Jean Starr

Starr, Ringo, **Supp. XI:** 309

Star Rover, The (London), **II:** 467

"Starry Night, The" (Sexton), **Supp. II Part 2:** 681

"Stars" (Frost), **II:** 153

Stars, the Snow, the Fire, The: Twenty-five Years in the Northern Wilderness (Haines), **Supp. XII:** 199–201, 206, 209

Star Shines over Mt. Morris Park, A (H. Roth), **Supp. IX:** 227, 236, 236–237

"Stars of the Summer Night" (Longfellow), **II:** 493

"Stars over Harlem" (Hughes), **Retro. Supp. I:** 207

"Star-Spangled" (García), **Supp. XI:** 177, 178

Star-Spangled Girl, The (Simon), **Supp. IV Part 2:** 579

"Star-Splitter, The" (Frost), **Retro. Supp. I:** 123, 133

Stars Principal (McClatchy), **Supp. XII:** 256–258

"Starting from Paumanok" (Whitman), **IV:** 333

Starting Out in the Thirties (Kazin), **Supp. VIII:** 95–97

"Starved Lovers" (MacLeish), **III:** 19

Starved Rock (Masters), **Supp. I Part 2:** 465

"Starving Again" (Moore), **Supp. X:** 163, 172, 175

"State, The" (Bourne), **I:** 233

State and Main (Mamet), **Supp. XIV:**241

"Statement: Phillipa Allen" (Rukeyser), **Supp. VI:** 283–284

"Statement of Principles" (Ransom), **III:** 496

"Statements on Poetics" (Snyder), **Supp. VIII:** 291, 292

"Statement with Rhymes" (Kees), **Supp. XV:** 139

"State of the Art, The" (Elkin), **Supp. VI:** 52

"State of the Arts, The" (Wasserstein), **Supp. XV:** 332

State of the Nation (Dos Passos), **I:** 489

"State of the Union" (Vidal), **Supp. IV Part 2:** 678

Static Element, The: Selected Poems of Natan Zach (Everwine, trans.), **Supp. XV:** 73, 75, 85–88

"Statue, The" (Berryman), **I:** 173

"Statue and Birds" (Bogan), **Supp. III Part 1:** 50

"Statues, The" (Schwartz), **Supp. II Part 2:** 654, 659

"Status Rerum" (Pound), **Supp. I Part 1:** 257

Stavans, Ilan, **Supp. XI:** 190

"Staying Alive" (Levertov), **Supp. III Part 1:** 281

Staying Alive (Wagoner), **Supp. IX:** 324, 326

"Staying at Ed's Place" (Swenson), **Supp. IV Part 2:** 648

Staying Put : Making a Home in a Restless World (Sanders), **Supp. XVI:**274–275

Stayton, Richard, **Supp. IX:** 133

Steadman, Goodman, **IV:** 147

"Steak" (Snyder), **Supp. VIII:** 301

Steal Away: Selected and New Poems (Wright), **Supp. XV:** 337, 340, 348, 350–351

Stealing Beauty (Minot), **Supp. VI:** 205

Stealing Glimpses (McQuade), **Supp. IX:** 151

Stealing the Language: The Emergence of Women's Poetry in America (Ostriker), **Supp. XV:** 251

"Stealing the Thunder: Future Visions for American Indian Women, Tribes, and Literary Studies" (Gunn Allen), **Supp. IV Part 1:** 331

"Steam Shovel Cut" (Masters), **Supp. I Part 2:** 468

Stearns, Harold, **I:** 245

Stedman, Edmund Clarence, **Supp. I Part 1:** 372; **Supp. II Part 1:** 192; **Supp. XV:** 115, 269, 273, 274, 282, 286

Steele, Max, **Supp. XIV:**82

Steele, Sir Richard, **I:** 378; **II:** 105, 107, 300; **III:** 430

Steele, Timothy, **Supp. XV:** 251

Steenburgen, Mary, **Supp. IV Part 1:** 236

Steeple Bush (Frost), **II:** 155; **Retro. Supp. I:** 140; **Retro. Supp. II:** 42

"Steeple-Jack, The" (Moore), **III:** 212, 213, 215

"Steerage" (Goldbarth), **Supp. XII:** 187

Steers, Nina, **Retro. Supp. II:** 25

Steffens, Lincoln, **II:** 577; **III:** 580; **Retro. Supp. I:** 202; **Retro. Supp. II:** 101; **Supp. I Part 1:** 7

Stegner, Page, **IV:** 114, 116; **Supp. IV Part 2:** 599

Stegner, Wallace, **Supp. IV Part 2:** 595–618; **Supp. V:** 220, 224, 296; **Supp. X:** 23, 24; **Supp. XIV:**82, 193, 230, 233

"Stegner's Short Fiction" (Ahearn), **Supp. IV Part 2:** 604

Steichen, Edward, **III:** 580, 594–595

Steichen, Lillian. *See* Sandburg, Mrs. Carl (Lillian Steichen)

Steier, Rod, **Supp. VIII:** 269

Steiger, Rod, **Supp. XI:** 305

Stein, Gertrude, **I:** 103, 105, 476; **II:** 56, 251, 252, 257, 260, 262–263, 264, 289; **III:** 71, 454, 471–472, 600; **IV:** 24–48, 368, 375, 404, 415, 443, 477; **Retro. Supp. I:** 108, 170, 176, 177, 186, 418, 422; **Retro. Supp. II:** 85, 207, 326, 331; **Supp. I Part 1:** 292; **Supp. III Part 1:** 13, 37, 225, 226; **Supp. III Part 2:** 626; **Supp. IV Part 1:** 11, 79, 80, 81, 322; **Supp. IV Part 2:** 468; **Supp. V:** 53; **Supp. IX:** 55, 57, 62, 66; **Supp. XII:** 1, 139; **Supp. XIV:**336; **Supp. XVI:**187

Stein, Jean, **Supp. XVI:**245

Stein, Karen F., **Supp. XIII:** 29, 30

Stein, Leo, **IV:** 26; **Supp. XIV:**336; **Supp. XV:** 298

Stein, Lorin, **Supp. XII:** 254

Steinbeck, John, **I:** 107, 288, 301, 378, 495, 519; **II:** 272; **III:** 382, 453, 454, 589; **IV:** 49–72; **Retro. Supp. II:** 19, 196; **Supp. IV Part 1:** 102, 225; **Supp. IV Part 2:** 502; **Supp. V:** 290, 291; **Supp. VIII:** 10; **Supp. IX:** 33, 171; **Supp. XI:** 169; **Supp. XIII:** 1, 17; **Supp. XIV:**21, 181

Steinbeck, Olive Hamilton, **IV:** 51

Steinberg, Saul, **Supp. VIII:** 272

Steinem, Gloria, **Supp. IV Part 1:** 203

Steiner, George, **Retro. Supp. I:** 327; **Supp. IV Part 1:** 286; **Supp. XVI:**230

Steiner, Nancy, **Supp. I Part 2:** 529

Steiner, Stan, **Supp. IV Part 2:** 505

Steinhoff, Eirik, **Supp. XVI:**290

Steinman, Michael, **Supp. VIII:** 172

Steinmetz, Charles Proteus, **I:** 483

Steinway Quintet Plus Four, The (Epstein), **Supp. XII:** 159, 162–166

Stekel, Wilhelm, **III:** 554

Stella (Goethe), **Supp. IX:** 133, 138

Stella (Kushner), **Supp. IX:** 133

Stella, Joseph, **I:** 387

"Stellaria" (Francis), **Supp. IX:** 83

Stelligery and Other Essays (Wendell), **Supp. I Part 2:** 414

Stendhal, **I:** 316; **III:** 465, 467; **Supp. I Part 1:** 293; **Supp. I Part 2:** 445

Stepanchev, Stephen, **Supp. XI:** 312

Stephen, Leslie, **IV:** 440

Stephen, Saint, **II:** 539; **IV:** 228

Stephen, Sir Leslie, **IV:** 440; **Supp. I Part 1:** 306

Stephen Crane (Berryman), **I:** 169–170, 405

Stephen King: The Art of Darkness (Winter), **Supp. V:** 144

Stephen King, The Second Decade: "Danse Macabre" to "The Dark Half" (Magistrale), **Supp. V:** 138, 146, 151

Stephens, Jack, **Supp. X:** 11, 14, 15, 17

Stephenson, Gregory, **Supp. XII:** 120, 123

"Stepping Out" (Dunn), **Supp. XI:** 140, 141

Steps (Kosinski), **Supp. VII:** 215, 221–222, 225

"Steps" (Nye), **Supp. XIII:** 288

Steps to the Temple (Crashaw), **IV:** 145

"Steps Toward Poverty and Death" (R. Bly), **Supp. IV Part 1:** 60

Stepto, Robert B., **Retro. Supp. II:** 116, 120, 123

Sterile Cuckoo, The (Nichols), **Supp.**

XIII: 258, 259–263, 264
Sterling, Bruce, **Supp. XVI:**118, 121, 123, 124, 128–129
Sterling, George, **I:** 199, 207, 208, 209; **II:** 440; **Supp. V:** 286
Stern, Bernhard J., **Supp. XIV:**202, 213
Stern, Daniel, **Supp. VIII:** 238
Stern, Frederick C., **Supp. X:** 114, 115, 117
Stern, Gerald, **Supp. IX:** 285–303; **Supp. XI:** 139, 267; **Supp. XV:** 211, 212
Stern, Madeleine B., **Supp. I Part 1:** 35
Stern, Maurice, **IV:** 285
Stern, Philip Van Doren, **Supp. XIII:** 164
Stern, Richard, **Retro. Supp. II:** 291
Stern, Richard G., **Retro. Supp. II:** 204
"Sterne" (Schwartz), **Supp. II Part 2:** 663
Sterne, Laurence, **II:** 302, 304–305, 308; **III:** 454; **IV:** 68, 211, 465; **Supp. I Part 2:** 714; **Supp. IV Part 1:** 299; **Supp. V:** 127; **Supp. X:** 324; **Supp. XV:** 232
Sterritt, David, **Supp. IV Part 2:** 574
Stetson, Caleb, **IV:** 178
Stetson, Charles Walter, **Supp. XI:** 195, 196, 197, 202, 204, 209
Stevens, Mrs. Wallace (Elsie Kachel), **IV:** 75
Stevens, Wallace, **I:** 60, 61, 266, 273, 462, 521, 528, 540–541; **II:** 56, 57, 530, 552, 556; **III:** 19, 23, 194, 216, 270–271, 272, 278, 279, 281, 453, 463, 493, 509, 521, 523, 600, 605, 613, 614; **IV:** 73–96, 140, 141, 332, 402, 415; **Retro. Supp. I:** 67, 89, 193, 284, 288, 295–315, 335, 403, 411, 416, 417, 422; **Retro. Supp. II:** 40, 44, 326; **Supp. I Part 1:** 80, 82, 257; **Supp. II Part 1:** 9, 18; **Supp. III Part 1:** 2, 3, 12, 20, 48, 239, 318, 319, 344; **Supp. III Part 2:** 611; **Supp. IV Part 1:** 72, 393; **Supp. IV Part 2:** 619, 620, 621, 634; **Supp. V:** 337; **Supp. VIII:** 21, 102, 195, 271, 292; **Supp. IX:** 41; **Supp. X:** 58; **Supp. XI:** 123, 191, 312; **Supp. XIII:** 44, 45; **Supp. XV:** 39, 41, 92, 115, 250, 261, 298, 302, 306, 307; **Supp. XVI:**64, 158, 202, 210, 288
"Stevens and the Idea of the Hero" (Bromwich), **Retro. Supp. I:** 305
Stevenson, Adlai, **II:** 49; **III:** 581
Stevenson, Anne, **Supp. XV:** 121

Stevenson, Burton E., **Supp. XIV:**120
Stevenson, David, **Supp. XI:** 230
Stevenson, Robert Louis, **I:** 2, 53; **II:** 283, 290, 311, 338; **III:** 328; **IV:** 183–184, 186, 187; **Retro. Supp. I:** 224, 228; **Supp. I Part 1:** 49; **Supp. II Part 1:** 404–405; **Supp. IV Part 1:** 298, 314; **Supp. VIII:** 125; **Supp. XIII:** 75; **Supp. XIV:**40
Stevick, Robert D., **III:** 509
Stewart, Dugald, **II:** 8, 9; **Supp. I Part 1:** 151, 159; **Supp. I Part 2:** 422
Stewart, Jeffrey C., **Supp. XIV:**196, 209, 210
Stewart, Randall, **II:** 244
Stewart, Robert E., **Supp. XI:** 216
Stickeen (Muir), **Supp. IX:** 182
"Sticks and Stones" (L. Michaels), **Supp. XVI:**205
Sticks and Stones (Mumford), **Supp. II Part 2:** 475, 483, 487–488
Sticks & Stones (Matthews), **Supp. IX:** 154, 155, 157, 158
Stieglitz, Alfred, **Retro. Supp. I:** 416; **Retro. Supp. II:** 103; **Supp. VIII:** 98
"Stigmata" (Oates), **Supp. II Part 2:** 520
Stiles, Ezra, **II:** 108, 122; **IV:** 144, 146, 148
Still, William Grant, **Retro. Supp. I:** 203
"Stillborn" (Plath), **Supp. I Part 2:** 544
"Still Here" (Hughes), **Retro. Supp. I:** 211
"Still Just Writing" (Tyler), **Supp. IV Part 2:** 658
"Still Life" (Hecht), **Supp. X:** 68
"Still Life" (Malamud), **Supp. I Part 2:** 450
"Still Life" (Sandburg), **III:** 584
"Still Life: Moonlight Striking up on a Chess-Board" (Lowell), **II:** 528
"Still Life Or" (Creeley), **Supp. IV Part 1:** 141, 150, 158
Still Life with Oysters and Lemon (Doty), **Supp. XI:** 119, 121, 133–134
Still Life with Woodpecker (Robbins), **Supp. X:** 260, 271–274, 282
"Still Moment, A" (Welty), **IV:** 265; **Retro. Supp. I:** 347
Stillness (Gardner), **Supp. VI:** 74
"Stillness in the Air" (Dickinson), **Supp. XV:** 261
"Still Small Voices, The" (Fante), **Supp. XI:** 164
Still Such (Salter), **Supp. IX:** 246
"Still the Place Where Creation Does

Some Work on Itself" (Davis), **Supp. IV Part 1:** 68
Stimpson, Catharine R., **Supp. IV Part 2:** 686
Stimson, Eleanor Kenyon. *See* Brooks, Mrs. Van Wyck
"Stimulants, Poultices, Goads" (Wright), **Supp. XV:** 349
"Stings" (Plath), **Retro. Supp. II:** 255; **Supp. I Part 2:** 541
"Stirling Street September" (Baraka), **Supp. II Part 1:** 51
Stirner, Max, **II:** 27
"Stirrup-Cup, The" (Lanier), **Supp. I Part 1:** 364
Stitt, Peter, **Supp. IV Part 1:** 68; **Supp. IV Part 2:** 628; **Supp. IX:** 152, 163, 291, 299; **Supp. XI:** 311, 317; **Supp. XIII:** 87; **Supp. XV:** 98, 99
Stivers, Valerie, **Supp. X:** 311
Stock, Noel, **III:** 479
Stockton, Frank R., **I:** 201
Stoddard, Charles Warren, **I:** 193, 195, 196; **Supp. II Part 1:** 192, 341, 351
Stoddard, Elizabeth, **II:** 275; **Supp. XV:** 269–291
Stoddard, Richard, **Supp. I Part 1:** 372
Stoddard, Richard Henry, **Supp. XV:** 269, 271, 272, 273, 274, 278, 279, 286
Stoddard, Solomon, **I:** 545, 548; **IV:** 145, 148
Stoic, The (Dreiser), **I:** 497, 502, 508, 516; **Retro. Supp. II:** 95, 96, 101, 108
Stokes, Geoffrey, **Supp. XV:** 256
"Stolen Calf, The" (Dunbar), **Supp. II Part 1:** 196
Stolen Jew, The (Neugeboren), **Supp. XVI:**222–224, 225
Stolen Past, A (Knowles), **Supp. XII:** 249
Stone, Edward, **III:** 479
Stone, I. F., **Supp. XIV:**3
Stone, Irving, **II:** 463, 466, 467
Stone, Oliver, **Supp. XIV:**48, 316
Stone, Phil, **II:** 55
Stone, Richard, **Supp. XIV:**54
Stone, Robert, **Supp. V:** 295–312; **Supp. X:** 1
Stone, Rosetta (pseudo.). *See* Geisel, Theodor Seuss (Dr. Seuss)
Stone, Wilmer, **Supp. I Part 1:** 49
Stone and the Shell, The (Hay), **Supp. XIV:**122, 123, 127, 130
"Stone Bear, The" (Haines), **Supp. XII:** 206–207, 212
"Stone City" (Proulx), **Supp. VII:** 251–253
Stone Country (Sanders), **Supp.**

XVI:271–272

Stone Diaries, The (Shields), **Supp. VII:** 307, 315, 324–326, 327

"Stone Dreams" (Kingsolver), **Supp. VII:** 203

Stone Harp, The (Haines), **Supp. XII:** 204, 205, 206, 207

Stonemason, The (McCarthy), **Supp. VIII:** 175, 187

"Stones" (Kumin), **Supp. IV Part 2:** 447

"Stones, The" (Plath), **Supp. I Part 2:** 535, 539

"Stones in My Passway, Hellhounds on My Trail" (Boyle), **Supp. VIII:** 15

Stones of Florence, The (McCarthy), **II:** 562

"Stone Walls" (Sarton), **Supp. VIII:** 259

"Stop" (Wilbur), **Supp. III Part 2:** 556

"Stop Me If You've Heard This One" (Lardner), **II:** 433

Stopover: Tokyo (Marquand), **III:** 53, 57, 61, 70

Stoppard, Tom, **Retro. Supp. I:** 189

"Stopping by Woods" (Frost), **II:** 154

"Stopping by Woods on a Snowy Evening" (Frost), **Retro. Supp. I:** 129, 133, 134, 135, 139

Stopping Westward (Richards), **II:** 396

"Stop Player. Joke No. 4" (Gaddis), **Supp. IV Part 1:** 280

Stop-Time (Conroy), **Supp. XVI:**63–71, 72, 75, 76–77

Store, The (Stribling), **Supp. VIII:** 126

"*Store* and *Mockingbird:* Two Pulitzer Novels about Alabama" (Going), **Supp. VIII:** 126

Storer, Edward, **Supp. I Part 1:** 261, 262

Stories: Elizabeth Stoddard, **Supp. XV:** 270

Stories, Fables and Other Diversions (Nemerov), **III:** 268–269, 285

Stories for the Sixties (Yates, ed.), **Supp. XI:** 343

Stories from Our Living Past (Prose), **Supp. XVI:**251

Stories from the Italian Poets (Hunt), **Supp. XV:** 175

Stories from the Old Testament Retold (L. P. Smith), **Supp. XIV:**342

Stories from World Literature, **Supp. IX:** 4

"Stories in the Snow" (Leopold), **Supp. XIV:**183

Stories of F. Scott Fitzgerald, The (Cowley, ed.), **Retro. Supp. I:** 115

Stories of F. Scott Fitzgerald, The (Fitzgerald), **II:** 94

Stories of Modern America, **Supp. IX:** 4

Stories of Stephen Dixon, The (Dixon), **Supp. XII:** 152

Stories of the Spanish Civil War (Hemingway), **II:** 258

Stories Revived (James), **II:** 322

Stories that Could Be True (Stafford), **Supp. XI:** 325–327

Storm, The (Buechner), **Supp. XII:** 54–57

"Storm, The" (Chopin), **Retro. Supp. II:** 60, 68; **Supp. I Part 1:** 218, 224

"Storm Fear" (Frost), **II:** 153; **Retro. Supp. I:** 127

"Storm Ship, The" (Irving), **II:** 309

"Storm Warnings" (Kingsolver), **Supp. VII:** 207–208

"Stormy Weather" (Ellison), **Supp. II Part 1:** 233

"Story" (Everwine), **Supp. XV:** 89

"Story, A" (Jarrell), **II:** 371

Story, Richard David, **Supp. IV Part 2:** 575, 588

"Story about Chicken Soup, A" (Simpson), **Supp. IX:** 272–273

"Story about the Anteater, The" (Benét), **Supp. XI:** 53

"Story About the Body, A" (Hass), **Supp. VI:** 107–108

"Story Hearer, The" (Paley), **Supp. VI:** 230, 231

"Story Hour" (Hay), **Supp. XIV:**124

Story Hour: A Second Look at Cinderella, Bluebeard, and Company (Hay), **Supp. XIV:**119, 124, 125, 132, 133

Story of a Country Town, The (Howe), **I:** 106

"Story of an Hour, The" (Chopin), **Retro. Supp. II:** 72; **Supp. I Part 1:** 212–213, 216

Story of a Novel, The (Wolfe), **IV:** 456, 458

"Story of a Proverb, The" (Lanier), **Supp. I Part 1:** 365

"Story of a Proverb, The: A Fairy Tale for Grown People" (Lanier), **Supp. I Part 1:** 365

Story of a Story and Other Stories, The: A Novel (Dixon), **Supp. XII:** 155

Story of a Wonder Man, The (Lardner), **II:** 433–434

"Story of a Year, The" (James), **Retro. Supp. I:** 218

"Story of Gus, The" (A. Miller), **III:** 147–148

"Story of How a Wall Stands, A" (Ortiz), **Supp. IV Part 2:** 499, 507

Story of Mount Desert Island, Maine, The (Morison), **Supp. I Part 2:** 494

Story of My Boyhood and Youth, The (Muir), **Supp. IX:** 172–174, 176

Story of My Father, The: A Memoir (Miller), **Supp. XII:** 301

Story of O, The (Réage), **Supp. XII:** 9, 10

Story of Our Lives, The (Strand), **Supp. IV Part 2:** 620, 628–629, 629

Story of the Normans, The, Told Chiefly in Relation to Their Conquest of England (Jewett), **II:** 406

"Story of Toby, The" (Melville), **III:** 76

"Story of To-day, A" (Davis), **Supp. XVI:**88, 89. See also *Margret Howth*

Story of Utopias, The (Mumford), **Supp. II Part 2:** 475, 483–486, 495

Story on Page One, The (Odets), **Supp. II Part 2:** 546

Storyteller (Silko), **Supp. IV Part 2:** 558, 559, 560, 561, 566–570

"Storyteller" (Silko), **Supp. IV Part 2:** 569

"*Storyteller:* Grandmother Spider's Web" (Danielson), **Supp. IV Part 2:** 569

"Storyteller's Notebook, A" (Carver), **Supp. III Part 1:** 142–143

Story Teller's Story, A: The Tale of an American Writer's Journey through His Own Imaginative World and through the World of Facts . . . (Anderson), **I:** 98, 101, 114, 117

"Story That Could Be True, A" (Stafford), **Supp. XI:** 326

"Stout Gentleman, The" (Irving), **II:** 309

Stover at Yale (Johnson), **III:** 321

Stowe, Calvin, **IV:** 445; **Supp. I Part 2:** 587, 588, 590, 596, 597

Stowe, Charles, **Supp. I Part 2:** 581, 582

Stowe, Eliza, **Supp. I Part 2:** 587

Stowe, Harriet Beecher, **II:** 274, 399, 403, 541; **Retro. Supp. I:** 34, 246; **Retro. Supp. II:** 4, 138, 156; **Supp. I Part 1:** 30, 206, 301; **Supp. I Part 2:** 579–601; **Supp. III Part 1:** 154, 168, 171; **Supp. IX:** 33; **Supp. X:** 223, 246, 249, 250; **Supp. XI:** 193; **Supp. XIII:** 141, 295; **Supp. XV:** 278; **Supp. XVI:**82, 85

Stowe, Samuel Charles, **Supp. I Part 2:** 587

Stowe, William, **Supp. IV Part 1:** 129

Strachey, Lytton, **I:** 5; **IV:** 436; **Retro.**

Supp. I: 59; Supp. I Part 2: 485, 494; Supp. XIV:342; Supp. XVI:191

Straight Cut (Bell), Supp. X: 5, 6–7, 10

Straight Man (Russo), Supp. XII: 335–339, 340

Straits: Poems (Koch), Supp. XV: 184

Strand, Mark, Supp. IV Part 2: 619–636; Supp. V: 92, 332, 337, 338, 343; Supp. IX: 155; Supp. XI: 139, 145; Supp. XII: 254; Supp. XIII: 76; Supp. XV: 74

Strand, Paul, Supp. VIII: 272

Strandberg, Victor, Supp. V: 273

Strange Case of Dr. Jekyll and Mr. Hyde, The (Stevenson), II: 290

Strange Children, The (Gordon), II: 196, 197, 199, 211–213

"Strange Fruit" (Harjo), Supp. XII: 224, 225

"Strange Fruit" (song), Supp. I Part 1: 80

Strange Interlude (O'Neill), III: 391, 397–398; IV: 61

Stranger, The (Camus), I: 53, 292; Supp. VIII: 11; Supp. XV: 352

"Stranger, The" (Rich), Supp. I Part 2: 555, 560

"Stranger, The" (Salinger), III: 552–553

"Stranger in My Own Life, A: Alienation in American Indian Poetry and Prose" (Gunn Allen), Supp. IV Part 1: 322

"Stranger in the Village" (Baldwin), Retro. Supp. II: 3; Supp. I Part 1: 54; Supp. IV Part 1: 10

"Stranger in Town" (Hughes), Supp. I Part 1: 334

"Strangers" (Howe), Supp. VI: 120

Strangers and Wayfarers (Jewett), Retro. Supp. II: 138

"Strangers from the Horizon" (Merwin), Supp. III Part 1: 356

Strangers on a Train (Highsmith), Supp. IV Part 1: 132

"Strange Story, A" (Taylor), Supp. V: 323

"Strange Story, A" (Wylie), Supp. I Part 2: 723

Strange Things (Atwood), Supp. XIII: 35

"Strato in Plaster" (Merrill), Supp. III Part 1: 328

Straus, Ralph, Supp. XIII: 168

Straus, Roger, Supp. VIII: 82; Supp. XV: 59

Strauss, Harold, Supp. XV: 137

Strauss, Johann, I: 66

Strauss, Richard, IV: 316

Strauss, Robert, Supp. XI: 141, 142

Stravinsky (De Schloezer), III: 474

Stravinsky, Igor, Retro. Supp. I: 378; Supp. IV Part 1: 81; Supp. XI: 133; Supp. XV: 265

"Stravinsky's Three Pieces 'Grotesques,' for String Quartet" (Lowell), II: 523

Straw, The (O'Neill), III: 390

"Stray Document, A" (Pound), II: 517

Streaks of the Tulip, The: Selected Criticism (W. J. Smith), Supp. XIII: 333, 334, 344, 347–348

Streamline Your Mind (Mursell), Supp. I Part 2: 608

"Street, Cloud" (Ríos), Supp. IV Part 2: 549

Streetcar Named Desire, A (T. Williams), IV: 382, 383, 385, 386, 387, 389–390, 395, 398; Supp. IV Part 1: 359

Street in Bronzeville, A (Brooks), Retro. Supp. I: 208; Supp. III Part 1: 74–78

"Street Moths" (X. J. Kennedy), Supp. XV: 170

"Street Musicians" (Ashbery), Supp. III Part 1: 18

"Street off Sunset, A" (Jarrell), II: 387

"Streets" (Dixon), Supp. XII: 145–146

Streets in the Moon (MacLeish), III: 5, 8–11, 15, 19

Streets of Laredo (McMurtry), Supp. V: 230

"Streets of Laredo" (screenplay) (McMurtry and Ossana), Supp. V: 226, 230

Streets of Night (Dos Passos), I: 478, 479–480, 481, 488

Streitfeld, David, Supp. XIII: 234; Supp. XVI:63

Strength of Fields, The (Dickey), Supp. IV Part 1: 178

"Strength of Fields, The" (Dickey), Supp. IV Part 1: 176, 184–185

"Strength of Gideon, The" (Dunbar), Supp. II Part 1: 212

Strength of Gideon and Other Stories, The (Dunbar), Supp. II Part 1: 211, 212

"Strenuous Artistry" (Zagarell), Supp. XV: 281

Strether, Lambert, II: 313

Stribling, T. S., Supp. VIII: 126

Strickland, Joe (pseudonym). *See* Arnold, George W.

"Strictly Bucolic" (Simic), Supp. VIII: 278

Strictly Business (O. Henry), Supp. II Part 1: 410

"Strike, The" (Olsen), Supp. XIII: 292, 297

"Strikers" (Untermeyer), Supp. XV: 296

Strindberg, August, I: 78; III: 145, 165, 387, 390, 391, 392, 393; IV: 17

"String, The" (Dickey), Supp. IV Part 1: 179

String Light (Wright), Supp. XV: 345–346

"Strivings of the Negro People" (Du Bois), Supp. II Part 1: 167

Stroby, W. C., Supp. XIV:26

Strohbach, Hermann, Supp. XI: 242

"Stroke of Good Fortune, A" (O'Connor), III: 344; Retro. Supp. II: 229, 232

Strom, Stephen, Supp. XII: 223

Strong, George Templeton, IV: 321

Strong, Josiah, Supp. XIV:64

"Strong Draughts of Their Refreshing Minds" (Dickinson), Retro. Supp. I: 46

Strong Opinions (Nabokov), Retro. Supp. I: 263, 266, 270, 276

"Strong Women" (Dorman), Supp. XI: 240

Strout, Elizabeth, Supp. X: 86

Structure of Nations and Empires, The (Niebuhr), III: 292, 308

"Structure of Rime, The" (Duncan), Supp. XVI:287

Struggle, The (film; Griffith), Supp. XVI:191

"Strumpet Song" (Plath), Retro. Supp. II: 246; Supp. I Part 2: 536

Strunk, William, Supp. I Part 2: 652, 662, 670, 671, 672

Strunsky, Anna, II: 465

"Strut for Roethke, A" (Berryman), I: 188

Strychacz, Thomas F., Supp. XVI:69–70

Stuart, Gilbert, I: 16

Stuart, J. E. B., III: 56

Stuart, Michael, Supp. XV: 140

Stuart Little (White), Supp. I Part 2: 655–658

"Student, The" (Moore), III: 212, 215

"Student of Salmanaca, The" (Irving), II: 309

"Student's Wife, The" (Carver), Supp. III Part 1: 141

Studies in American Indian Literature: Critical Essays and Course Designs (Gunn Allen), Supp. IV Part 1: 324, 333

Studies in Classic American Literature (Lawrence), **II:** 102; **III:** 33; **IV:** 333; **Retro. Supp. I:** 421

Studies in Short Fiction (Malin), **Supp. XVI:**71

"Studs" (Farrell), **II:** 25, 28, 31

Studs Lonigan: A Trilogy (Farrell), **II:** 25, 26, 27, 31–34, 37, 38, 41–42

"Study of Images" (Stevens), **IV:** 79

"Study of Lanier's Poems, A" (Kent), **Supp. I Part 1:** 373

Study of Milton's Prosody (Bridges), **II:** 537

"Study of the Negro Problems, The" (Du Bois), **Supp. II Part 1:** 165

Stuewe, Paul, **Supp. IV Part 1:** 68

Stuhlmann, Gunther, **Supp. X:** 182, 184, 185, 187

Stultifera Navis (Brant), **III:** 447

Sturak, John Thomas, **Supp. XIII:** 162, 163, 165, 168

Sturgis, George, **III:** 600

Sturgis, Howard, **IV:** 319; **Retro. Supp. I:** 367, 373

Sturgis, Susan, **III:** 600

Sturm, Margaret. *See* Millar, Margaret

Stuttaford,Genevieve, **Supp. IX:** 279

Stuyvesant, Peter, **II:** 301

"Style" (Nemerov), **III:** 275

Styles of Radical Will (Sontag), **Supp. III Part 2:** 451, 459, 460–463

Styne, Jule, **Supp. XVI:**193

Styron, William, **III:** 40; **IV:** 4, 97–119, 216; **Supp. V:** 201; **Supp. IX:** 208; **Supp. X:** 15–16, 250; **Supp. XI:** 229, 231, 343; **Supp. XIV:**82; **Supp. XVI:**235–236

Suares, J. C., **Supp. IV Part 1:** 234

Suarez, Ernest, **Supp. IV Part 1:** 175; **Supp. V:** 180

"Sub, The" (Dixon), **Supp. XII:** 146

Subjection of Women, The (Mill), **Supp. XI:** 196, 203

"Subjective Necessity for Social Settlements" (Addams), **Supp. I Part 1:** 4

"Subject of Childhood, A" (Paley), **Supp. VI:** 221

"Submarginalia" (Howe), **Supp. IV Part 2:** 422

Substance and Shadow (James), **II:** 344

Subterraneans, The (Kerouac), **Supp. III Part 1:** 225, 227–231

"Subtitle" (Kees), **Supp. XV:** 139

Subtreasury of American Humor, A (White and White), **Supp. I Part 2:** 668

"Suburban Culture, Imaginative Wonder: The Fiction of Frederick Bar-

thelme" (Brinkmeyer), **Supp. XI:** 38

Suburban Sketches (Howells), **II:** 274, 277

"Subverted Flower, The" (Frost), **Retro. Supp. I:** 139

"Subway, The" (Tate), **IV:** 128

"Subway Singer, The" (Clampitt), **Supp. IX:** 45

"Success" (Mora), **Supp. XIII:** 217

Successful Love and Other Stories (Schwartz), **Supp. II Part 2:** 661, 665

Succession, The: A Novel of Elizabeth and James (Garrett), **Supp. VII:** 104–107, 108

"Success is counted sweetest" (Dickinson), **Retro. Supp. I:** 30, 31–32, 38; **Supp. XV:** 126

Success Stories (Banks), **Supp. V:** 14–15

"Success Story" (Banks), **Supp. V:** 15

"Such Counsels You Gave to Me" (Jeffers), **Supp. II Part 2:** 433

Such Silence (Milburn), **Supp. XI:** 242

"Such Things Happen Only in Books" (Wilder), **IV:** 365

Suddenly, Last Summer (film) (Vidal), **Supp. IV Part 2:** 683

Suddenly Last Summer (T. Williams), **I:** 73; **IV:** 382, 383, 385, 386, 387, 389, 390, 391, 392, 395–396, 397, 398

Sudermann, Hermann, **I:** 66

Sugg, Richard P., **Supp. IV Part 1:** 68

"Suggestion from a Friend" (Kenyon), **Supp. VII:** 171

"Suicide" (Barnes), **Supp. III Part 1:** 33

"Suicide off Egg Rock" (Plath), **Supp. I Part 2:** 529, 538

Suicides and Jazzers (Carruth), **Supp. XVI:**46

"Suicide's Note" (Hughes), **Retro. Supp. I:** 199

"Suitable Surroundings, The" (Bierce), **I:** 203

"Suitcase, The" (Ozick), **Supp. V:** 262, 264

"Suite for Augustus, A" (Dove), **Supp. IV Part 1:** 245

"Suite for Lord Timothy Dexter" (Rukeyser), **Supp. VI:** 283, 285

"Suite from the Firebird" (Stravinsky), **Supp. XI:** 133

"Suitor, The" (Kenyon), **Supp. VII:** 164–165

Sukarno, **IV:** 490

Sukenick, Ronald, **Supp. V:** 39, 44, 46; **Supp. XII:** 139

Sula (Morrison), **Supp. III Part 1:** 362, 364, 367, 368, 379; **Supp. VIII:** 219

Sullivan, Andrew, **Supp. IX:** 135

Sullivan, Frank, **Supp. IX:** 201

Sullivan, Harry Stack, **I:** 59

Sullivan, Jack, **Supp. X:** 86; **Supp. XII:** 331

Sullivan, Noel, **Retro. Supp. I:** 202; **Supp. I Part 1:** 329, 333

Sullivan, Richard, **Supp. VIII:** 124

Sullivan, Walter, **Supp. VIII:** 168

"Sullivan County Sketches" (Crane), **I:** 407, 421

"Sumach and Goldenrod: An American Idyll" (Mumford), **Supp. II Part 2:** 475

Suma Genji (Play), **III:** 466

Sumerian Vistas (Ammons), **Supp. VII:** 34, 35

"Summer" (Emerson), **II:** 10

Summer (Gioia), **Supp. XV:** 117

"Summer" (Lowell), **II:** 554

Summer (Wharton), **IV:** 317; **Retro. Supp. I:** 360, 367, 374, 378–379, 382

Summer, Bob, **Supp. X:** 1, 5, 6, 42

"Summer: West Side" (Updike), **Retro. Supp. I:** 320

Summer and Smoke (T. Williams), **IV:** 382, 384, 385, 386, 387, 395, 397, 398; **Supp. IV Part 1:** 84

Summer Anniversaries, The (Justice), **Supp. VII:** 115, 117

"Summer Commentary, A" (Winters), **Supp. II Part 2:** 808

"Summer Day" (O'Hara), **III:** 369

"Summer Days, The" (Oliver), **Supp. VII:** 239

"Summer Night" (Hughes), **Supp. I Part 1:** 325

"Summer Night, A" (Auden), **Supp. II Part 1:** 8

"Summer Night—Broadway" (Untermeyer), **Supp. XV:** 296

"Summer Noon: 1941" (Winters), **Supp. II Part 2:** 811

"Summer of '82" (Merwin), **Supp. III Part 1:** 355–356

Summer on the Lakes in 1843 (Fuller), **Supp. II Part 1:** 279, 295–296

"Summer People" (Hemingway), **II:** 258–259

"Summer People, The" (Jackson), **Supp. IX:** 120

"Summer People, The" (Merrill), **Supp. III Part 1:** 325–326

"Summer Ramble, A" (Bryant), **Supp. I Part 1:** 162, 164

Summers, Claude J., **Supp. IV Part 2:**

680–681; **Supp. XIV:**161, 169
Summers, Robert, **Supp. IX:** 289
"Summer Solstice, New York City" (Olds), **Supp. X:** 207
"Summer's Reading, A" (Malamud), **Supp. I Part 2:** 430–431, 442
"Summer Storm" (Gioia), **Supp. XV:** 127
"Summer Storm" (Simpson), **Supp. IX:** 268
"'Summertime and the Living . . .'" (Hayden), **Supp. II Part 1:** 363, 366
Summertime Island (Caldwell), **I:** 307–308
"Summer with Tu Fu, A" (Carruth), **Supp. XVI:**55, 58
"Summit Beach, 1921" (Dove), **Supp. IV Part 1:** 249
Summoning of Stones, A (Hecht), **Supp. X:** 57, 58, 58–59
"Summons" (Untermeyer), **Supp. XV:** 296
Summons to Memphis, A (Taylor), **Supp. V:** 313, 314, 327
Summons to the Free, A (Benét), **Supp. XI:** 47
Sumner, Charles, **I:** 3, 15; **Supp. I Part 2:** 685, 687
Sumner, John, **Retro. Supp. II:** 95
Sumner, John B., **I:** 511
Sumner, William Graham, **III:** 102, 108; **Supp. I Part 2:** 640
"Sumptuous Destination" (Wilbur), **Supp. III Part 2:** 553
"Sun" (Moore), **III:** 215
"Sun" (Swenson), **Supp. IV Part 2:** 640
"Sun, Sea, and Sand" (Marquand), **III:** 60
Sun Also Rises, The (Hemingway), **I:** 107; **II:** 68, 90, 249, 251–252, 260, 600; **III:** 36; **IV:** 35, 297; **Retro. Supp. I:** 171, 177–180, 181, 189; **Supp. I Part 2:** 614; **Supp. XIII:** 263
"Sun and Moon" (Kenyon), **Supp. VII:** 168
"Sun and the Still-born Stars, The" (Southern), **Supp. XI:** 295
Sun at Midnight (Soseki; Merwin and Shigematsu, trans.), **Supp. III Part 1:** 353
"Sun Crosses Heaven from West to East Bringing Samson Back to the Womb, The" (R. Bly), **Supp. IV Part 1:** 73
"Sun Dance Shield" (Momaday), **Supp. IV Part 2:** 491
Sunday, Billy, **II:** 449
"Sunday Afternoons" (Komunyakaa),

Supp. XIII: 127
Sunday after the War (H. Miller), **III:** 184
"Sunday at Home" (Hawthorne), **II:** 231–232
"Sunday Morning" (Stevens), **II:** 552; **III:** 278, 463, 509; **IV:** 92–93; **Retro. Supp. I:** 296, 300, 301, 304, 307, 313; **Supp. XV:** 120; **Supp. XVI:**210
"Sunday Morning Apples" (Crane), **I:** 387
"Sunday Morning Prophecy" (Hughes), **Supp. I Part 1:** 334
"Sundays" (Salter), **Supp. IX:** 257
"Sundays, They Sleep Late" (Rukeyser), **Supp. VI:** 278
"Sundays of Satin-Legs Smith, The" (Brooks), **Supp. III Part 1:** 74, 75
"Sundays Visiting" (Ríos), **Supp. IV Part 2:** 541
Sundial, The (Jackson), **Supp. IX:** 126–127
Sundog (Harrison), **Supp. VIII:** 46–48
Sun Dogs (R. O. Butler), **Supp. XII:** 64–65
Sun Do Move, The (Hughes), **Supp. I Part 1:** 339
Sundquist, Eric, **Supp. XIV:**66, 71
"Sunfish" (C. Frost), **Supp. XV:** 100–101, 102
"Sunflower Sutra" (Ginsberg), **Supp. II Part 1:** 317, 321; **Supp. XV:** 215
Sunlight Dialogues, The (Gardner), **Supp. VI:** 63, 68, 69, 70
"Sunlight Is Imagination" (Wilbur), **Supp. III Part 2:** 549
Sun Out: Selected Poems, 1952–1954 (Koch), **Supp. XV:** 179
"Sunrise" (Lanier), **Supp. I Part 1:** 370
"Sunrise runs for Both, The" (Dickinson), **Retro. Supp. I:** 45
Sunrise with Seamonsters: Travels and Discoveries, 1964–1984 (Theroux), **Supp. VIII:** 311, 313, 323, 325
"Sun Rising" (Donne), **Supp. VIII:** 164
"Sunset" (Ransom), **III:** 484
"Sunset from Omaha Hotel Window" (Sandburg), **III:** 584
Sunset Gun (Parker), **Supp. IX:** 192
Sunset Limited (Burke), **Supp. XIV:**32, 33
Sunset Limited (Harrison), **Supp. VIII:** 51
"Sunset Maker, The" (Justice), **Supp. VII:** 123
Sunset Maker, The: Poems, Stories, a Memoir (Justice), **Supp. VII:** 116,

118, 119, 123–124
Sunshine Boys, The (film), **Supp. IV Part 2:** 589
Sunshine Boys, The (Simon), **Supp. IV Part 2:** 575, 584–585
"Sunthin' in the Pastoral Line" (Lowell), **Supp. I Part 2:** 415–416
Sun to Sun (Hurston), **Supp. VI:** 154
Sun Tracks (Ortiz), **Supp. IV Part 2:** 499, 500
Sun Under Wood (Hass), **Supp. VI:** 103, 108–109
"Superb Lily, The" (Pinsky), **Supp. VI:** 250
"Superman Comes to the Supermarket" (Mailer), **Retro. Supp. II:** 204
"Supermarket in California, A" (Ginsberg), **Supp. XI:** 135
"Supernatural Love" (Schnackenberg), **Supp. XV:** 257, 259–260
Supernatural Love: Poems 1976–1992 (Schnackenberg), **Supp. XV:** 253, 256, 260, 263
Suplee, Curt, **Supp. XVI:**202
"Supper After the Last, The" (Kinnell), **Supp. III Part 1:** 239
"Supposedly Fun Thing I'll Never Do Again, A" (Wallace), **Supp. X:** 315
Supposedly Fun Thing I'll Never Do Again, A: Essays and Arguments (Wallace), **Supp. X:** 314–316
Suppressed Desires (Glaspell), **Supp. III Part 1:** 178
Suppression of the African Slave Trade to the United States of America, 1638–1870 (Du Bois), **Supp. II Part 1:** 157, 162
Supreme Fiction, The (Stevens), **Supp. XVI:**158
Sure Hand of God, The (Caldwell), **I:** 297, 302
"Surety and Fidelity Claims" (Stevens), **Retro. Supp. I:** 296, 309
Surface of Earth, The (Price), **Supp. VI:** 261–262
"Surfaces" (Ammons), **Supp. VII:** 36
Surfacing (Atwood), **Supp. XIII:** 20, 21, 22–23, 24, 33, 35
"Surgeon at 2 A.M." (Plath), **Supp. I Part 2:** 545
Surmmer Knowledge (Schwartz), **Supp. II Part 2:** 662, 665
"Surprise" (Kenyon), **Supp. VII:** 173
Surprised by Sin: The Reader in Paradise Lost (Fish), **Supp. XIV:**15
"Surround, The Imagining Herself as the Environment,/She Speaks to James Wright at Sundow" (Dickey), **Supp. IV Part 1:** 185

"Survey of Literature" (Ransom), **III:** 480

"Surveyor, The" (H. Roth), **Supp. IX:** 233, 234

Survival (Atwood), **Supp. XIII:** 20, 22, 35

"Survival as Tao, Beginning at 5:00 A.M." (Carruth), **Supp. XVI:**56

Survival of the Bark Canoe, The (McPhee), **Supp. III Part 1:** 301, 302, 308, 313

Survival This Way: Interviews with American Indian Poets (Bruchac), **Supp. IV Part 2:** 506

"Surviving Love" (Berryman), **I:** 173

Survivor (O. Butler), **Supp. XIII:** 62, 63

Susan and God (film; Cukor), **Supp. XVI:**192

Susanna Moodie: Voice and Vision (Shields), **Supp. VII:** 313

Suspect in Poetry, The (Dickey), **Supp. IV Part 1:** 177

"Sustained by Fiction" (Hoffman), **Supp. X:** 90, 92

"Susto" (Ríos), **Supp. IV Part 2:** 553

Sutherland, Donald, **IV:** 38, 44; **Supp. IX:** 254

Sutherland, Efua, **Supp. IV Part 1:** 9, 16

Sutherland-Smith, James, **Supp. X:** 211, 212

Sut Lovingood's Yarns (Harris), **II:** 70

Sutton, Roger, **Supp. X:** 266

Sutton, Walter, **III:** 479

Suttree (McCarthy), **Supp. VIII:** 178–180, 189

Suvero, Mark di, **Supp. IX:** 251

Svevo, Italo, **Supp. XIV:**112

Swados, Harvey, **Supp. XI:** 222

Swallow, Alan, **Supp. X:** 112, 115, 116, 120, 123

Swallow Barn (J. P. Kennedy), **II:** 313

"Swamp Boy" (Bass), **Supp. XVI:**20

Swan, Barbara, **Supp. IV Part 2:** 447

Swan, Jon, **Supp. IV Part 1:** 176

Swan Lake (Tchaikovsky), **Supp. IX:** 51

"Swan Legs" (Stern), **Supp. IX:** 299

Swann (Shields), **Supp. VII:** 315, 318–323, 326

Swann, Brian, **Supp. IV Part 2:** 500

Swanson, Gloria, **II:** 429

Swanson, Stevenson, **Supp. XIV:**111

Swanton, John Reed, **Supp. VIII:** 295

Swanwick, John, **Supp. XV:** 237

Swanwick, Michael, **Supp. XVI:**128

"Swarm, The" (Plath), **Retro. Supp. II:** 255

"Sway" (Simpson), **Supp. IX:** 276

Sweat (Hurston), **Supp. VI:** 152

Swedenborg, Emanuel, **II:** 5, 10, 321, 342, 343–344, 396

Sweeney Agonistes (Eliot), **I:** 580; **Retro. Supp. I:** 64, 65; **Retro. Supp. II:** 247

"Sweeney Among the Nightingales" (Eliot), **III:** 4

Sweet, Blanche, **Supp. I Part 2:** 391

Sweet, Timothy, **Supp. IV Part 1:** 330

Sweet and Lowdown (film; Allen), **Supp. XV:** 11

Sweet and Sour (O'Hara), **III:** 361

Sweet Bird of Youth (T. Williams), **IV:** 382, 383, 385, 386, 387, 388, 389, 390, 391, 392, 395, 396, 398; **Supp. IV Part 1:** 84, 89

Sweet Charity (musical), **Supp. IV Part 2:** 575

Sweet Flypaper of Life, The (Hughes), **Supp. I Part 1:** 335–336

"Sweetheart of the Song Tra Bong, The" (O'Brien), **Supp. V:** 243, 249

"Sweethearts" (Ford), **Supp. V:** 69

Sweet Hereafter, The (Banks), **Supp. V:** 15–16

Sweet Machine (Doty), **Supp. XI:** 121, 131–132, 135

Sweet Sue (Gurney), **Supp. V:** 105, 107–108

Sweet Sweetback's Baadasss Song (Peebles; film), **Supp. XI:** 17

Sweet Thursday (Steinbeck), **IV:** 50, 52, 64–65

Sweet Will (Levine), **Supp. V:** 178, 187, 189, 190

"Sweet Will" (Levine), **Supp. V:** 190

"Sweet Words on Race" (Hughes), **Retro. Supp. I:** 211

Sweezy, Paul, **Supp. I Part 2:** 645

"Swell-Looking Girl, A" (Caldwell), **I:** 310

Swenson, May, **Retro. Supp. II:** 44; **Supp. IV Part 2:** 637–655

"Swift" (Schwartz), **Supp. II Part 2:** 663

Swift, Jonathan, **I:** 125, 194, 209, 441; **II:** 110, 302, 304–305, 577; **III:** 113; **IV:** 68; **Retro. Supp. I:** 66; **Supp. I Part 2:** 406, 523, 603, 656, 665, 708, 714; **Supp. IV Part 1:** 51; **Supp. IV Part 2:** 692; **Supp. XI:** 105, 209; **Supp. XII:** 276; **Supp. XV:** 258; **Supp. XVI:**110

"Swimmer" (Francis), **Supp. IX:** 82

"Swimmer, The" (Cheever), **Supp. I Part 1:** 185, 187

"Swimmer, The" (Glück), **Supp. V:** 82

"Swimmers" (Untermeyer), **Supp. XV:** 300

"Swimmers, The" (Fitzgerald), **Retro. Supp. I:** 110, 111

"Swimmers, The" (Tate), **IV:** 136

"Swimming" (Harjo), **Supp. XII:** 218

Swinburne, Algernon C., **I:** 50, 384, 568; **II:** 3, 4, 129, 400, 524; **IV:** 135; **Retro. Supp. I:** 100; **Supp. I Part 1:** 79; **Supp. I Part 2:** 422, 552; **Supp. XIV:**120, 344

"Swinburne as Poet" (Eliot), **I:** 576

Swinger of Birches, A: A Portrait of Robert Frost (Cox), **Retro. Supp. I:** 132

"Swinging on a Birch-Tree" (Larcom), **Supp. XIII:** 147

Switch, The (Dixon), **Supp. XII:** 141

Swope, D. B., **Supp. IX:** 95

Sword Blades and Poppy Seed (Lowell), **II:** 518, 520, 522, 532

Sybil (Auchincloss), **Supp. IV Part 1:** 25

"Sycamore" (Stern), **Supp. IX:** 294

"Sycamore, The" (Moore), **III:** 216

"Sycamores, The" (Whittier), **Supp. I Part 2:** 699

Sylvester, Johnny, **Supp. I Part 2:** 438

Sylvester, Joshua, **I:** 178, 179; **II:** 18; **III:** 157; **Supp. I Part 1:** 98, 104, 114, 116

Sylvia (Gurney), **Supp. V:** 105

"Sylvia" (Larcom), **Supp. XIII:** 144

"Sylvia" (L. Michaels), **Supp. XVI:**202, 213

"Sylvia" (Stern), **Supp. IX:** 297

Sylvia: A Fictional Memoir (L. Michaels), **Supp. XVI:**202, 213

Sylvia Plath: Method and Madness (Butscher), **Supp. I Part 2:** 526

Sylvia Plath: Poetry and Existence (Holbrook), **Supp. I Part 2:** 526–527

"Sylvia's Death" (Sexton), **Supp. II Part 2:** 671, 684, 685

"Symbol and Image in the Shorter Poems of Herman Melville" (Dickey), **Supp. IV Part 1:** 176

Symbolist Movement in Literature, The (Symons), **I:** 50, 569; **Retro. Supp. I:** 55

Symonds, John Addington, **I:** 241, 242, 251, 259; **IV:** 334; **Supp. XIV:**329, 335

Symons, Arthur, **I:** 50, 569; **Retro. Supp. I:** 55

Symons, Julian, **Supp. IV Part 1:** 343, 351

"Sympathy" (Dunbar), **Supp. IV Part 1:** 15

Sympathy of Souls, A (Goldbarth), **Supp. XII:** 175, 176, 186–187

"Symphony, The" (Lanier), **Supp. I Part 1:** 352, 360–361, 364; **Supp. I Part 2:** 416

Symposium (Plato), **Retro. Supp. II:** 31; **Supp. IV Part 1:** 391

Symposium: To Kill a Mockingbird (Alabama Law Review), **Supp. VIII:** 127, 128

Symptoms of Being 35 (Lardner), **II:** 434

Synge, John Millington, **I:** 434; **III:** 591–592; **Supp. III Part 1:** 34; **Supp. VIII:** 155

Synthetic Philosophy (Spencer), **II:** 462–463

"Syringa" (Ashbery), **Supp. III Part 1:** 19–21, 25

"Syrinx" (Clampitt), **Supp. IX:** 53

"Syrinx" (Merrill), **Supp. III Part 1:** 328

Syrkin, Marie, **Supp. XIV:**279, 288, 291

"System, The" (Ashbery), **Supp. III Part 1:** 14, 15, 18, 21–22

System of Dante's Hell, The (Baraka), **Supp. II Part 1:** 39–41, 55

"System of Dante's Inferno, The" (Baraka), **Supp. II Part 1:** 40

"System of Doctor Tarr and Professor Fether, The" (Poe), **III:** 419, 425

System of General Geography, A (Brown), **Supp. I Part 1:** 146

Sze, Mai-mai, **Supp. X:** 291

Szentgyorgyi, Tom, **Supp. IX:** 135, 136, 140, 141–142

Szulc, Tad, **Supp. XVI:**154

Szymborka, Wislawa, **Supp. XI:** 267

T

T. S. Eliot and American Philosophy (Jain), **Retro. Supp. I:** 58

T. S. Eliot's Silent Voices (Mayer), **Retro. Supp. I:** 58

Tabios, Eileen, **Supp. XV:** 214, 225, 226

"Table of Delectable Contents, The" (Simic), **Supp. VIII:** 276

Tabloid Dreams (R. O. Butler), **Supp. XII:** 70–72, 74

Tacitus, Cornelius, **I:** 485; **II:** 113

Tadic, Novica, **Supp. VIII:** 272

Taft (Patchett), **Supp. XII:** 307, 312, 314–317

"Tag" (Hughes), **Supp. I Part 1:** 341

Taggard, Genevieve, **IV:** 436

Taggart, John, **Supp. IV Part 2:** 421

Tagore, Rabindranath, **I:** 383

"Taibele and Her Demon" (Singer), **Retro. Supp. II:** 307

Taibl, Erika, **Supp. XV:** 255

"Tailor Shop, The" (H. Miller), **III:** 175

"Tails" (Dixon), **Supp. XII:** 154

Taine, Hippolyte, **I:** 503; **II:** 271; **III:** 323; **IV:** 440, 444

"Tain't So" (Hughes), **Supp. I Part 1:** 330

Takasago (play), **III:** 466

Take Away the Darkness (Bynner), **Supp. XV:** 51

Take Me Back: A Novel (Bausch), **Supp. VII:** 41, 43–45, 46, 49

"Take My Saddle from the Wall: A Valediction" (McMurtry), **Supp. V:** 219

"'Take No for an Answer'" (Didion), **Supp. IV Part 1:** 203

"Take Pity" (Malamud), **Supp. I Part 2:** 427, 428, 435, 436, 437

"Takers, The" (Olds), **Supp. X:** 205

"Take the I Out" (Olds), **Supp. X:** 213

Take the Money and Run (film; Allen), **Supp. XV:** 3–4, 6

"Taking Away the Name of a Nephew" (Ríos), **Supp. IV Part 2:** 545–546

Taking Care of Mrs. Carroll (Monette), **Supp. X:** 153

"Taking of Captain Ball, The" (Jewett), **Retro. Supp. II:** 134

"Taking Out the Lawn Chairs" (Karr), **Supp. XI:** 241

"Taking the Bypass" (Epstein), **Supp. XIV:**110

"Taking the Bypass" (J. Epstein), **Supp. XVI:**230

"Taking the Forest" (Howe), **Supp. IV Part 2:** 433

"Taking the Lambs to Market" (Kumin), **Supp. IV Part 2:** 455

"Tale, A" (Bogan), **Supp. III Part 1:** 50, 51

Taleb-Khyar, Mohamed, **Supp. IV Part 1:** 242, 243, 244, 247, 257

"Tale of Jerusalem, A" (Poe), **III:** 411

Tale of Possessors Self-Dispossessed, A (O'Neill), **III:** 404

Tale of the Body Thief, The (Rice), **Supp. VII:** 290, 293–294, 297

Tale of Two Cities, A (film), **Supp. I Part 1:** 67

"Tale of Two Liars, A" (Singer), **IV:** 12

Tales (Baraka), **Supp. II Part 1:** 39, 55

Tales (Poe), **III:** 413

Tales and Stories for Black Folks (Bambara, ed.), **Supp. XI:** 1

Tales before Midnight (Benét), **Supp. XI:** 46, 53, 57

Talese, Gay, **Supp. XVI:**273

Tales of a Traveller (Irving), **II:** 309–310

Tales of a Wayside Inn (Longfellow), **II:** 489, 490, 501, 502, 504–505; **Retro. Supp. II:** 154, 162–165

Tales of Glauber-Spa (Bryant, ed.), **Supp. I Part 1:** 157

Tales of Manhattan (Auchincloss), **Supp. IV Part 1:** 23

Tales of Men and Ghosts (Wharton), **IV:** 315; **Retro. Supp. I:** 372

Tales of Rhoda, The (Rice), **Supp. VII:** 288

Tales of Soldiers and Civilians (Bierce), **I:** 200–203, 204, 206, 208, 212

Tales of the Argonauts (Harte), **Supp. II Part 1:** 337, 348, 351

Tales of the Fish Patrol (London), **II:** 465

Tales of the Grotesque and Arabesque (Poe), **II:** 273; **III:** 412, 415; **Retro. Supp. II:** 270

Tales of the Jazz Age (Fitzgerald), **II:** 88; **Retro. Supp. I:** 105; **Supp. IX:** 57

"Talisman, A" (Moore), **III:** 195–196

Talisman, The (King), **Supp. V:** 140, 144, 152

"Talkin Bout Sonny" (Bambara), **Supp. XI:** 6–7

"Talking" (Merwin), **Supp. III Part 1:** 354

Talking All Morning (R. Bly), **Supp. IV Part 1:** 59, 60, 61, 62, 64, 65

Talking Dirty to the Gods (Komunyakaa), **Supp. XIII:** 130–131

"Talking Horse" (Malamud), **Supp. I Part 2:** 435

Talking Soft Dutch (McCarriston), **Supp. XIV:**260–263, 266, 270, 271

"Talking to Barr Creek" (Wagoner), **Supp. IX:** 328

"Talking to Sheep" (Sexton), **Supp. II Part 2:** 695

Talking to the Sun: An Illustrated Anthology of Poems for Young People (Koch and Farrell, eds.), **Supp. XV:** 188

"Talk of Heroes" (C. Bly), **Supp. XVI:**34

"Talk of the Town" (*The New Yorker* column), **IV:** 215; **Supp. IV Part 1:** 53, 54

"Talk with the Yellow Kid, A" (Bellow), **I:** 151

Tallent, Elizabeth, **Supp. IV Part 2:** 570

Tallman, Warren, **Supp. IV Part 1:** 154

TallMountain, Mary, **Supp. IV Part 1:** 324–325

Talma, Louise, **IV:** 357

Talmadge, Constance, **Supp. XVI:**186, 187, 196

Talmadge, Norma, **Supp. XVI:**186, 187, 196

Talmadge Girls, The (Loos), **Supp. XVI:**186, 196

Talmey, Allene, **Supp. IV Part 1:** 197; **Supp. XIII:** 172

Talmud, **IV:** 8, 17

Taltos: Lives of the Mayfair Witches (Rice), **Supp. VII:** 299–300

"Tamar" (Jeffers), **Supp. II Part 2:** 427–428, 436

Tamar and Other Poems (Jeffers), **Supp. II Part 2:** 416, 419

Tambourines to Glory (Hughes), **Supp. I Part 1:** 338–339

"Tame Indians" (Jewett), **Retro. Supp. II:** 141

"Tamerlane" (Poe), **III:** 426

Tamerlane and Other Poems (Poe), **III:** 410

"Tam O'Shanter" (Burns), **II:** 306

Tan, Amy, **Supp. X:** 289–300

Tangential Views (Bierce), **I:** 209

"Tangier 1975" (Bowles), **Supp. IV Part 1:** 94

"Tankas" (McClatchy), **Supp. XII:** 266

Tanner, Laura E., **Supp. X:** 209

Tanner, Tony, **I:** 260, 261; **Retro. Supp. II:** 205; **Supp. IV Part 1:** 285; **Supp. XVI:**65, 69

Tannhäuser (Wagner), **I:** 315

"Tan Ta Ra, Cries Mars...," (Wagoner), **Supp. IX:** 325

Tao of Physics, The (Capra), **Supp. X:** 261

Tao Teh Ching (Bynner, trans.), **Supp. XV:** 46, 47

Tapahonso, Luci, **Supp. IV Part 1:** 404; **Supp. IV Part 2:** 499, 508

Tape for the Turn of the Year (Ammons), **Supp. VII:** 31–33, 35

"Tapestry" (Ashbery), **Supp. III Part 1:** 22–23

"Tapiama" (Bowles), **Supp. IV Part 1:** 89–90

"Tapiola" (W. C. Williams), **Retro. Supp. I:** 429

Tappan, Arthur, **Supp. I Part 2:** 588

Taps at Reveille (Fitzgerald), **II:** 94, 96; **Retro. Supp. I:** 113

Tar: A Midwest Childhood (Anderson), **I:** 98, 115; **II:** 27

Tarantino, Quentin, **Supp. IV Part 1:** 356

Tar Baby (Morrison), **Supp. III Part 1:** 364, 369–372, 379; **Supp. IV Part 1:** 13

Tarbell, Ida, **III:** 322, 580; **Retro. Supp. II:** 101

"Target Study" (Baraka), **Supp. II Part 1:** 49–50, 54

Tarkington, Booth, **II:** 444; **III:** 70; **Retro. Supp. I:** 100; **Supp. XV:** 41

Tarpon (film), **Supp. VIII:** 42

Tarr, Rodger L., **Supp. X:** 222, 224, 226

Tartuffe (Molière; Wilbur, trans.), **Supp. III Part 2:** 560

Tarumba, Selected Poems of Jaime Sabines (Levine and Trejo, trans.), **Supp. V:** 178

"Tarzan Is an Expatriate" (Theroux), **Supp. VIII:** 313

Task, The (Cowper), **II:** 304

Tasso, Torquato, **I:** 276

Taste of Palestine, A: Menus and Memories (Shihab), **Supp. XIII:** 273

Tate, Alan, **Supp. XV:** 141

Tate, Allen, **I:** 48, 49, 50, 67, 69, 381, 382, 386, 390, 396, 397, 399, 402, 441, 468; **II:** 197–198, 367, 536, 537, 542, 551, 554; **III:** 424, 428, 454, 482, 483, 485, 493, 495, 496, 497, 499, 500, 517; **IV:** 120–143, 236, 237, 433; **Retro. Supp. I:** 37, 41, 90; **Retro. Supp. II:** 77, 79, 82, 83, 89, 176, 178, 179; **Supp. I Part 1:** 364, 371; **Supp. I Part 2:** 423; **Supp. II Part 1:** 90–91, 96, 98, 103–104, 136, 139, 144, 150, 151, 318; **Supp. II Part 2:** 643; **Supp. III Part 2:** 542; **Supp. V:** 315, 331; **Supp. X:** 1, 52; **Supp. XIV:**2

Tate, Benjamin Lewis Bogan, **IV:** 127

Tate, Greg, **Supp. XIII:** 233, 237

Tate, James, **Supp. V:** 92, 338; **Supp. VIII:** 39, 279; **Supp. XV:** 250

Tate, John Allen, **IV:** 127

Tate, Michael Paul, **IV:** 127

Tate, Mrs. Allen (Caroline Gordon). *See* Gordon, Caroline

Tate, Mrs. Allen (Helen Heinz), **IV:** 127

Tate, Mrs. Allen (Isabella Gardner), **IV:** 127

Tate, Nancy, **II:** 197

Tattooed Countess, The (Van Vechten), **I:** 295; **Supp. II Part 2:** 726–728, 738, 742

Tattooed Feet (Nye), **Supp. XIII:** 274

"Tattoos" (McClatchy), **Supp. XII:**

266–267, 268

"Tattoos" (Wright), **Supp. V:** 335, 340

Tatum, Anna, **I:** 516

Tatum, James, **Supp. IV Part 2:** 684

Taupin, René, **II:** 528, 529; **Supp. III Part 2:** 614, 615, 617, 621

Tawney, Richard Henry, **Supp. I Part 2:** 481

Taylor, Bayard, **II:** 275; **Supp. I Part 1:** 350, 361, 362, 365, 366, 372; **Supp. XV:** 269

Taylor, Cora. *See* Howarth, Cora

Taylor, Deems, **III:** 138

Taylor, Edward, **III:** 493; **IV:** 144–166; **Supp. I Part 1:** 98; **Supp. I Part 2:** 375, 386, 546

Taylor, Eleanor Ross, **Supp. V:** 317, 318

Taylor, Elizabeth, **II:** 588

Taylor, Frank, **III:** 81

Taylor, Frederick Winslow, **Supp. I Part 2:** 644

Taylor, Graham, **Supp. I Part 1:** 5

Taylor, Henry, **Retro. Supp. I:** 212; **Supp. XI:** 317; **Supp. XIII:** 333

Taylor, Henry W., **IV:** 144

Taylor, Jeremy, **II:** 11; **III:** 487; **Supp. I Part 1:** 349; **Supp. XII:** 45; **Supp. XIV:**344, 345

Taylor, John, **IV:** 149

Taylor, Katherine, **Supp. VIII:** 251

Taylor, Kezia, **IV:** 148

Taylor, Mrs. Edward (Elizabeth Fitch), **IV:** 147, 165

Taylor, Mrs. Edward (Ruth Wyllys), **IV:** 148

Taylor, Nathaniel W., **Supp. I Part 2:** 580

Taylor, Paul, **I:** 293

Taylor, Peter, **Retro. Supp. II:** 179; **Supp. V:** 313–329; **Supp. XIV:**3

Taylor, Raynor, **Supp. XV:** 238

Taylor, Richard, **IV:** 146

Taylor, Robert, **Supp. I Part 1:** 294; **Supp. XV:** 135, 138; **Supp. XVI:**277

Taylor, Stephan, **Supp. XVI:**203

Taylor, Thomas, **II:** 10

Taylor, William, **IV:** 145–146

Taylor, Zachary, **I:** 3; **II:** 433–434

Tchelitchew, Peter, **II:** 586

Tea and Sympathy (Anderson), **Supp. I Part 1:** 277; **Supp. V:** 108

"Tea at the Palaz of Hoon" (Stevens), **Retro. Supp. I:** 300, 302, 306

"Teacher's Pet" (Thurber), **Supp. I Part 2:** 605–606

"Teaching and Story Telling" (Maclean), **Supp. XIV:**234

Teaching a Stone to Talk: Expeditions

and Encounters (Dillard), **Supp. VI:** 23, 26, 28, 32, 33, 34–35

Teachings of Don B., The (Barthelme), **Supp. IV Part 1:** 53

Teale, Edwin Way, **Supp. XIII:** 7

Teall, Dorothy, **I:** 221

Team Team Team (film), **Supp. IX:** 251

"Tea on the Mountain" (Bowles), **Supp. IV Part 1:** 90

"Tea Party, The" (MacLeish), **III:** 11

"Tears, Idle Tears" (Lord Tennyson), **Supp. XIV:**8

"Tears of the Pilgrims, The" (McClatchy), **Supp. XII:** 256

Teasdale, Sara, **Retro. Supp. I:** 133; **Supp. I Part 2:** 393, 707; **Supp. XIV:**127; **Supp. XV:** 295, 297, 301, 305, 307, 308

Tebeaux, Elizabeth, **Supp. IX:** 109

Technics and Civilization (Mumford), **Supp. I Part 2:** 638; **Supp. II Part 2:** 479, 493, 497

Technics and Human Development (Mumford), **Supp. I Part 2:** 638; **Supp. II Part 2:** 497

"Teddy" (Salinger), **III:** 561–563, 571

"Te Deum" (Reznikoff), **Supp. XIV:**281

Tedlock, Dennis, **Supp. IV Part 2:** 509

"Teeth Mother Naked at Last, The" (R. Bly), **Supp. IV Part 1:** 63, 68, 73

Teggart, Richard, **Supp. I Part 2:** 650

Tegnér, Esaias, **Retro. Supp. II:** 155

Teilhard de Chardin, Pierre, **Supp. I Part 1:** 314

Telephone, The (film), **Supp. XI:** 309

"Telephone Call, A" (Parker), **Supp. IX:** 202–203

"Telephone Number of the Muse, The" (Justice), **Supp. VII:** 124–125

Telephone Poles and Other Poems (Updike), **IV:** 214, 215

"Television" (Beattie), **Supp. V:** 33

Teller, Edward, **I:** 137

"Telling" (Ortiz), **Supp. IV Part 2:** 509

"Telling It in Black and White: The Importance of the Africanist Presence in *To Kill a Mockingbird*" (Baecker), **Supp. VIII:** 128

Telling Secrets (Buechner), **Supp. XII:** 53–54

Telling Stories (Didion), **Supp. IV Part 1:** 197

"Telling Stories" (Didion), **Supp. IV Part 1:** 197

"Telling the Bees" (Whittier), **Supp. I Part 2:** 694–695

Telling the Truth: The Gospel as Tragedy, Comedy, and Fairy Tale

(Buechner), **Supp. XII:** 53

"Tell Me" (Hughes), **Supp. VIII:** 213

Tell Me, Tell Me (Moore), **III:** 215

Tell Me Again How the White Heron Rises and Flies across the Nacreous River at Twilight toward the Distant Islands (Carruth), **Supp. XVI:**56

Tell Me a Riddle (film), **Supp. XIII:** 295

Tell Me a Riddle (Olsen), **Supp. XIII:** 294, 296, 298–302, 303, 305

"Tell Me a Riddle" (Olsen), **Supp. XIII:** 294, 297, 298, 300–302, 305

Tell Me How Long the Train's Been Gone (Baldwin), **Retro. Supp. II:** 9, 11–12, 14; **Supp. I Part 1:** 48, 52, 63–65, 67

"Tell Me My Fortune" (Epstein), **Supp. XII:** 163

Tell Me Your Answer True (Sexton), **Supp. II Part 2:** 683

Tell My Horse (Hurston), **Supp. VI:** 149, 156, 158

"Tell-Tale Heart, The" (Poe), **III:** 413, 414–415, 416; **Retro. Supp. II:** 267, 269, 270

"Tell the Women We're Going" (Carver), **Supp. III Part 1:** 138, 144

"Telluride Blues—A Hatchet Job" (Abbey), **Supp. XIII:** 10

Telushkin, Dvorah, **Retro. Supp. II:** 317

Temblor (Howe), **Supp. IV Part 2:** 431

"Temper of Steel, The" (Jones), **Supp. XI:** 218

Tempers, The (W. C. Williams), **Retro. Supp. I:** 413–414, 415, 416, 424

Tempest, The (Shakespeare), **I:** 394; **II:** 12; **III:** 40, 61, 263; **Retro. Supp. I:** 61; **Supp. IV Part 2:** 463; **Supp. V:** 302–303; **Supp. XII:** 54–57; **Supp. XV:** 255, 256

Temple, Minnie, **II:** 323

Temple, The (Herbert), **IV:** 145, 153

Temple, William, **III:** 303

Temple House (E. Stoddard), **Supp. XV:** 273, 284–286

Temple of My Familiar, The (Walker), **Supp. III Part 2:** 521, 527, 529, 535, 537; **Supp. IV Part 1:** 14

"Temple of the Holy Ghost, A" (O'Connor), **III:** 344, 352; **Retro. Supp. II:** 232

Templin, Charlotte, **Supp. V:** 116

Temporary Shelter (Gordon), **Supp. IV Part 1:** 299, 305–307

"Temporary Shelter" (Gordon), **Supp. IV Part 1:** 306

Temptation Game, The (Gardner), **Supp. VI:** 72

"Temptation of St. Anthony, The" (Barthelme), **Supp. IV Part 1:** 47

Temptations, The, **Supp. X:** 242

"Tenancy, A" (Merrill), **Supp. III Part 1:** 322, 323

Tenants, The (Malamud), **Supp. I Part 2:** 448–450

Ten Commandments (McClatchy), **Supp. XII:** 262–265

Ten Days That Shook the World (Reed), **II:** 577; **Supp. X:** 136

Tendencies in Modern American Poetry (Lowell), **II:** 529

"Tender, Hilarious Reminiscences of Life in Mythical Lake Wobegon" (MacDougall), **Supp. XVI:**174

Tender Buttons (G. Stein), **I:** 103, 105; **IV:** 27, 42–43; **Retro. Supp. II:** 331; **Supp. XV:** 347

"Tenderfoot" (Haines), **Supp. XII:** 209

Tender Is the Night (Fitzgerald), **I:** 375; **II:** 79, 84, 91, 95–96, 97, 98, 420; **Retro. Supp. I:** 105, 108, 109, 110–112, 114; **Supp. IX:** 59, 60, 61; **Supp. XV:** 197

"Tenderloin" (Crane), **I:** 408

"Tenderly" (Dobyns), **Supp. XIII:** 86–87

'Tender Man, A" (Bambara), **Supp. XI:** 9–10

"Tenderness" (Dunn), **Supp. XI:** 149, 150

"Tender Offer, The" (Auchincloss), **Supp. IV Part 1:** 34

"Tender Organizations, The" (C. Bly), **Supp. XVI:**40, 42

"Tenebrae" (Komunyakaa), **Supp. XIII:** 132

"Ten Forty-Four" (Kingsolver), **Supp. VII:** 208

Ten Indians (Bell), **Supp. X:** 7, 12

"Ten Neglected American Writers Who Deserve to Be Better Known" (Cantor), **Supp. IV Part 1:** 285

Tennent, Gilbert, **I:** 546

Tennessee Day in St. Louis (Taylor), **Supp. V:** 324

"Tennessee's Partner" (Harte), **Supp. II Part 1:** 345, 348–350

"Tennis" (Pinsky), **Supp. VI:** 241, 242

Tennis Court Oath, The (Ashbery), **Supp. III Part 1:** 7, 9, 12, 14, 26

Ten North Frederick (O'Hara), **III:** 361

Tennyson, Alfred, Lord, **I:** 587–588; **II:** 18, 82, 273, 338, 404, 439, 604; **III:** 5, 409, 469, 485, 511, 521, 523; **Retro. Supp. I:** 100, 325; **Retro. Supp. II:** 135; **Supp. I Part 1:** 349, 356; **Supp. I Part 2:** 410, 416, 552; **Supp. IX:** 19; **Supp. X:** 157; **Supp.**

XIII: 111; **Supp. XIV:**40, 120

Tennyson, Alfred Lord, **Supp. XV:** 275

"Ten O'Clock News" (Ortiz), **Supp. IV Part 2:** 503–504

Ten Poems (Dove), **Supp. IV Part 1:** 244

Ten Poems of Francis Ponge Translated by Robert Bly and Ten Poems of Robert Bly Inspired by the Poems by Francis Ponge (R. Bly), **Supp. IV Part 1:** 71

"Tension in Poetry" (Tate), **IV:** 128, 129, 135

Tenth Muse, The (Bradstreet), **Supp. I Part 1:** 102, 103, 114

"Tent on the Beach, The" (Whittier), **Supp. I Part 2:** 703

"Teodoro Luna Confesses after Years to His Brother, Anselmo the Priest, Who Is Required to Understand, But Who Understands Anyway, More Than People Think" (Ríos), **Supp. IV Part 2:** 552

Teodoro Luna's Two Kisses (Ríos), **Supp. IV Part 2:** 550–552, 553

"Tepeyac" (Cisneros), **Supp. VII:** 69

"Terce" (Auden), **Supp. II Part 1:** 22

Terence, **IV:** 155, 363; **Supp. I Part 2:** 405

Terkel, Studs, **Supp. IV Part 1:** 364

"Term" (Merwin), **Supp. III Part 1:** 356–357

"Terminal Days at Beverly Farms" (Lowell), **Retro. Supp. II:** 189

Terminating, or Sonnet LXXV, or "Lass Meine Schmerzen nicht verloren sein, or Ambivalence" (Kushner), **Supp. IX:** 132

Terminations (James), **Retro. Supp. I:** 229

"Terminus" (Emerson), **II:** 13, 19

"Terminus" (Wharton), **Retro. Supp. I:** 371

"Terms in Which I Think of Reality, The" (Ginsberg), **Supp. II Part 1:** 311

Terms of Endearment (film), **Supp. V:** 226

Terms of Endearment (McMurtry), **Supp. V:** 224–225

"Terrace, The" (Wilbur), **Supp. III Part 2:** 550

Terrarium (Sanders), **Supp. XVI:**270

"Terrence McNally" (Bryer), **Supp. XIII:** 200

"Terrence McNally" (Di Gaetani), **Supp. XIII:** 200

Terrence McNally: A Casebook (Zinman), **Supp. XIII:** 209

"Terrible Peacock, The" (Barnes),

Supp. III Part 1: 33

Terrible Threes, The (Reed), **Supp. X:** 241, 253

Terrible Twos, The (Reed), **Supp. X:** 241, 252–253

"Terrific Mother" (Moore), **Supp. X:** 178

Territory Ahead, The (Morris), **III:** 228–229, 236

Terrorism (Wright), **Supp. XV:** 341, 342

"Terrorism" (Wright), **Supp. XV:** 341

Terry, Edward A., **II:** 128, 129

Terry, Rose, **Supp. I Part 2:** 420

Tertium Organum (Ouspensky), **I:** 383

Tess of the d'Ubervilles (Hardy), **II:** 181; **Retro. Supp. II:** 100

"Testament" (Berry), **Supp. X:** 36

"Testament" (Carruth), **Supp. XVI:**59

"Testament (Or, Homage to Walt Whitman)" (Jong), **Supp. V:** 130

"Testament of Flood" (Warren), **IV:** 253

Testament of François Villon, The (Pound, opera), **Retro. Supp. I:** 287

"Testimonia on the Question of Stesichoros' Blinding by Helen" (Carson), **Supp. XII:** 107

"Testimony" (Komunyakaa), **Supp. XIII:** 129

Testimony: The United States (1885–1890): Recitative (Reznikoff), **Supp. XIV:**279, 280, 281, 285, 289–291

Testimony: The United States (1891–1900): Recitative (Reznikoff), **Supp. XIV:**291

"Testimony of James Apthorp, The" (Kees), **Supp. XV:** 146

"Testing-Tree, The" (Kunitz), **Supp. III Part 1:** 269

Testing-Tree, The (Kunitz), **Supp. III Part 1:** 260, 263, 264, 267, 268

Test of Poetry, A (Zukofsky), **Supp. III Part 2:** 618, 622

"Teutonic Scholar" (X. J. Kennedy), **Supp. XV:** 161

"Texas Moon, and Elsewhere, The" (McMurtry), **Supp. V:** 225

Texas Poets in Concert: A Quartet (Gwynn, ed.), **Supp. XIII:** 277

Texas Summer (Southern), **Supp. XI:** 309

Texasville (McMurtry), **Supp. V:** 228, 233

Thacher, Molly Day, **IV:** 381

Thackeray, William Makepeace, **I:** 194, 354; **II:** 182, 271, 282, 288, 316, 321, 322; **III:** 64, 70; **IV:** 326; **Retro. Supp. I:** 218; **Supp. I Part 1:** 307; **Supp. I Part 2:** 421, 495,

579; **Supp. IV Part 1:** 297; **Supp. IX:** 200; **Supp. XI:** 277; **Supp. XIV:**306

Thaddeus, Janice Farrar, **Supp. IV Part 1:** 299

"Thailand" (Barthelme), **Supp. IV Part 1:** 41

Thalberg, Irving, **Retro. Supp. I:** 109, 110, 114; **Supp. XVI:**191, 192

Thales, **I:** 480–481

Thalia Trilogy (McMurtry), **Supp. V:** 220–223, 234

Tham, Claire, **Supp. VIII:** 79

"Thanatopsis" (Bryant), **Supp. I Part 1:** 150, 154, 155, 170

Thanatos Syndrome, The (Percy), **Supp. III Part 1:** 385, 397–399

"Thanksgiving" (Glück), **Supp. V:** 83

"Thanksgiving, A" (Auden), **Supp. II Part 1:** 26

"Thanksgiving for a Habitat" (Auden), **Supp. II Part 1:** 24

Thanksgivings (Traherne), **Supp. XVI:**288

"Thanksgiving Spirit" (Farrell), **II:** 45

Thanksgiving Visitor, The (Capote), **Supp. III Part 1:** 116, 118, 119

Thank You, Fog (Auden), **Supp. II Part 1:** 24

"Thank You, Lord" (Angelou), **Supp. IV Part 1:** 15

Thank You, Mr. Moto (Marquand), **III:** 57, 58

Thank You and Other Poems (Koch), **Supp. XV:** 180–181

"Thank You in Arabic" (Nye), **Supp. XIII:** 273, 281

"Thar's More in the Man Than Thar Is in the Land" (Lanier), **Supp. I Part 1:** 352–353, 359–360

"That Evening Sun" (Faulkner), **II:** 72; **Retro. Supp. I:** 75, 83

That Horse (Hogan), **Supp. IV Part 1:** 397, 404, 405

"That I Had the Wings" (Ellison), **Supp. II Part 1:** 238

"That's the Place Indians Talk About" (Ortiz), **Supp. IV Part 2:** 511

"That the Soul May Wax Plump" (Swenson), **Supp. IV Part 2:** 650

"That the Universe Is Chrysalid" (Sobin), **Supp. XVI:**284

"That Tree" (Porter), **III:** 434–435, 446, 451

That Was the Week That Was (television program), **Supp. XIV:**125

"That Year" (Olds), **Supp. X:** 203

"Thaw" (C. Frost), **Supp. XV:** 93, 104, 105

Thaxter, Celia, **Retro. Supp. II:** 136,

147; **Supp. XIII:** 143, 153

Thayer, Abbott, **I:** 231

Thayer, Scofield, **I:** 231; **Retro. Supp. I:** 58

Thayer and Eldridge, **Retro. Supp. I:** 403

"Theater" (Toomer), **Supp. IX:** 309, 317–318

"Theater Chronicle" (McCarthy), **II:** 562

"Theater Problems? Call Dr. Chekhov" (Wasserstein), **Supp. XV:** 320

Theatricals (James), **Retro. Supp. I:** 228

"Theft" (Porter), **III:** 434, 435

Theft, A (Bellow), **Retro. Supp. II:** 31–32, 34

Their Eyes Were Watching God (Hurston), **Supp. VI:** 149, 152, 156–157

Their Heads Are Green and Their Hands Are Blue: Scenes from the Non-Christian World (Bowles), **Supp. IV Part 1:** 89

"Their Losses" (Taylor), **Supp. V:** 320

Their Wedding Journey (Howells), **II:** 277–278; **Retro. Supp. I:** 334

them (Oates), **Supp. II Part 2:** 503, 511–514

Theme Is Freedom, The (Dos Passos), **I:** 488–489, 492, 494

"Theme with Variations" (Agee), **I:** 27

"Then" (Barthelme), **Supp. IV Part 1:** 48

"Then It All Came Down" (Capote), **Supp. III Part 1:** 125, 131

Theocritus, **II:** 169; **Retro. Supp. I:** 286

"Theodore the Poet" (Masters), **Supp. I Part 2:** 461

Theological Position, A (Coover), **Supp. V:** 44

Theophrastus, **I:** 58

"Theoretical and Scientific Conceptions of Race, The" (Locke), **Supp. XIV:**209

Theory and Practice of Rivers and Other Poems, The (Harrison), **Supp. VIII:** 47, 49

Theory of Business Enterprise, The (Veblen), **Supp. I Part 2:** 638, 641, 644

Theory of Flight (Rukeyser), **Supp. VI:** 272, 275, 277–278, 284

"Theory of Flight" (Rukeyser), **Supp. VI:** 277–278

Theory of Moral Sentiments, The (A. Smith), **Supp. I Part 2:** 634

Theory of the Leisure Class, The (Veblen), **I:** 475–476; **Supp. I Part**

2: 629, 633, 641, 645; **Supp. IV Part 1:** 22

"There" (Taylor), **Supp. V:** 323

"There Are No Such Trees in Alpine California" (Haines), **Supp. XII:** 207

"There Goes (Varoom! Varoom!) That Kandy-Kolored Tangerine-Flake Streamline Baby" (Wolfe), **Supp. III Part 2:** 569–571

"There Is a Lesson" (Olsen), **Supp. XIII:** 292, 297

"There Is Only One of Everything" (Atwood), **Supp. XIII:** 34

There Is Something Out There (McNally). *See And Things That Go Bump in the Night* (McNally)

"There's a certain Slant of light" (Dickinson), **Retro. Supp. I:** 38

There's a Wocket in My Pocket! (Geisel), **Supp. XVI:**111

Thérèse de Lisieux, Saint, **Supp. VIII:** 195

"There She Is She Is Taking Her Bath" (Anderson), **I:** 113, 114

"There Was a Child Went Forth" (Whitman), **IV:** 348

"There Was a Man, There Was a Woman" (Cisneros), **Supp. VII:** 70

"There Was an Old Woman She Had So Many Children She Didn't Know What to Do" (Cisneros), **Supp. VII:** 60

"There Was a Youth Whose Name Was Thomas Granger" (Olson), **Supp. II Part 2:** 558, 560, 563

There Were Giants in the Land (Benét), **Supp. XI:** 50

There You Are (Simpson), **Supp. IX:** 279–280

"There You Are" (Simpson), **Supp. IX:** 279

"Thermopylae" (Clampitt), **Supp. IX:** 43

Theroux, Alexander, **Supp. VIII:** 312

Theroux, Marcel, **Supp. VIII:** 325

Theroux, Paul, **Supp. V:** 122; **Supp. VIII:** 309–327

"These Are My People" (Hayden), **Supp. II Part 1:** 365

"These are the days when Birds come back" (Dickinson), **Retro. Supp. I:** 30

"These Days" (Olds), **Supp. X:** 215

"These Flames and Generosities of the Heart: Emily Dickinson and the Illogic of Sumptuary Values" (Howe), **Supp. IV Part 2:** 431

"These saw Visions" (Dickinson),

Retro. Supp. I: 46

These Thirteen (Faulkner), **II:** 72

These Three (film), **Supp. I Part 1:** 281

These Times (Untermeyer), **Supp. XV:** 299–300, 303

"These Times" (Untermeyer), **Supp. XV:** 300

"Thessalonica: A Roman Story" (Brown), **Supp. I Part 1:** 133

Thévenaz, Paul, **Supp. XV:** 42

Thew, Harvey, **Supp. XIII:** 166

"They Ain't the Men They Used To Be" (Farrell), **II:** 45

"They Burned the Books" (Benét), **Supp. XI:** 46

They Came Like Swallows (Maxwell), **Supp. VIII:** 155–159, 168, 169

"They Can't Turn Back" (Baldwin), **Supp. I Part 1:** 52

They Do Not: The Letters of a Non-Professional Lady Arranged for Public Consumption (Clements), **Supp. XVI:**190

They Feed They Lion (Levine), **Supp. V:** 178, 179, 181, 184–185, 186

"They Feed They Lion" (Levine), **Supp. V:** 188

"They Lion Grow" (Levine), **Supp. V:** 184–185

"They're Not Your Husband" (Carver), **Supp. III Part 1:** 141, 143

They're Playing Our Song (musical), **Supp. IV Part 2:** 589

They Shall Inherit the Laughter (Jones), **Supp. XI:** 217, 218, 232

They Shoot Horses (film), **Supp. XIII:** 159

They Shoot Horses, Don't They? (McCoy), **Supp. XIII:** 159, 164–166, 168, 171, 172, 174

"They Sing, They Sing" (Roethke), **III:** 544

They Stooped to Folly (Glasgow), **II:** 175, 186–187

They Whisper (R. O. Butler), **Supp. XII:** 72–73

Thidwick the Big-Hearted Moose (Geisel), **Supp. XVI:**104

"Thieves" (Yates), **Supp. XI:** 349

Thieves of Paradise (Komunyakaa), **Supp. XIII:** 113, 128–130, 132

"Thimble, The" (Kenyon), **Supp. VII:** 164

"Thing and Its Relations, The" (James), **II:** 357

"Things" (Haines), **Supp. XII:** 207

"Things" (Kenyon), **Supp. VII:** 169

"Things, The" (Kinnell), **Supp. III Part 1:** 246

Things As They Are (Stein), **IV:** 34, 37, 40

"Things Don't Stop" (Nye), **Supp. XIII:** 287

Things Gone and Things Still Here (Bowles), **Supp. IV Part 1:** 91

"Things of August" (Stevens), **Retro. Supp. I:** 309

Things of This World (Wilbur), **Supp. III Part 2:** 552–555

Things Themselves: Essays and Scenes (Price), **Supp. VI:** 261

Things They Carried, The (O'Brien), **Supp. V:** 238, 239, 240, 243, 248–250

"Thing That Killed My Father Off, The" (Carver), **Supp. III Part 1:** 143

"Think about It" (Conroy), **Supp. XVI:**75

Think Back on Us . . . (Cowley), **Supp. II Part 1:** 139, 140, 142

Think Fast, Mr. Moto (Marquand), **III:** 57, 58

"Thinking about Barbara Deming" (Paley), **Supp. VI:** 227

"Thinking about Being Called Simple by a Critic" (Stafford), **Supp. XI:** 328

Thinking about the Longstanding Problems of Virtue and Happiness: Essays, a Play, Two Poems, and a Prayer (Kushner), **Supp. IX:** 131, 134, 135

"Thinking about the Past" (Justice), **Supp. VII:** 123–124

"Thinking about Western Thinking" (Didion), **Supp. IV Part 1:** 204, 206

"'Thinking against Oneself': Reflections on Cioran" (Sontag), **Supp. III Part 2:** 459–460

"Thinking Back Through Our Mothers: Traditions in Canadian Women's Writing" (Shields), **Supp. VII:** 307–308

"Thinking for Berky" (Stafford), **Supp. XI:** 320

"Thinking like a Mountain" (Leopold), **Supp. XIV:**188, 189

"Thinking of the Lost World" (Jarrell), **II:** 338–389

Thin Man, The (film), **Supp. IV Part 1:** 342, 355

Thin Man, The (Hammett), **Supp. IV Part 1:** 354–355

"Thinnest Shadow, The" (Ashbery), **Supp. III Part 1:** 5

"Thin People, The" (Plath), **Supp. I Part 2:** 538, 547

Thin Red Line, The (film; Malick),

Supp. V: 249; **Supp. XV:** 351

Thin Red Line, The (Jones), **Supp. XI:** 219, 224–225, 229, 231, 232, 233, 234

"Thin Strips" (Sandburg), **III:** 587

"Third Avenue in Sunlight" (Hecht), **Supp. X:** 61

"Third Body, A" (R. Bly), **Supp. IV Part 1:** 71

Third Circle, The (Norris), **III:** 327

"Third Expedition, The" (Bradbury), **Supp. IV Part 1:** 103, 106

Third Generation, The (C. Himes), **Supp. XVI:**135, 140–141

Third Life of Grange Copeland, The (Walker), **Supp. III Part 2:** 520, 527–536

Third Mind, The (Burroughs), **Supp. XII:** 3

Third Rose, The (Brinnin), **IV:** 26

"Third Sermon on the Warpland, The" (Brooks), **Supp. III Part 1:** 85

"Third Thing That Killed My Father Off, The" (Carver), **Supp. III Part 1:** 144

Third Violet, The (Crane), **I:** 408, 417–418

Thirlwall, John C., **Retro. Supp. I:** 430

"Thirst: Introduction to Kinds of Water" (Carson), **Supp. XII:** 103

13 by Shanley (Shanley), **Supp. XIV:**316

Thirteen Hands: A Play in Two Acts (Shields), **Supp. VII:** 322–323

Thirteen O'Clock (Benét), **Supp. XI:** 46

Thirteen Other Stories (Purdy), **Supp. VII:** 278

"Thirteenth and Pennsylvania" (Stafford), **Supp. XI:** 324

"Thirteen Ways of Looking at a Blackbird" (Stevens), **IV:** 94; **Supp. IX:** 47

"30. Meditation. 2. Cor. 5.17. He Is a New Creature" (Taylor), **IV:** 144

30: Pieces of a Novel (Dixon), **Supp. XII:** 152, 153–154

30/6 (poetry chapbook), **Supp. V:** 5, 6

"Thirty Bob a Week" (Davidson), **Retro. Supp. I:** 55

"Thirty Delft Tiles" (Doty), **Supp. XI:** 131

"35/10" (Olds), **Supp. X:** 206

"35,000 Feet—The Lanterns" (Goldbarth), **Supp. XII:** 182

31 Letters and 13 Dreams (Hugo), **Supp. VI:** 141–144

Thirty Poems (Bryant), **Supp. I Part 1:** 157, 158

Thirty-Six Poems (Warren), **IV:** 236, 239, 240

"33" (Alvarez), **Supp. VII:** 4

"3275" (Monette), **Supp. X:** 148, 159

Thirty Years (Marquand), **III:** 56, 60–61

Thirty Years of Treason (Bentley), **Supp. I Part 1:** 297

This, My Letter (Hay), **Supp. XIV:**121, 122, 129, 131

"This, That & the Other" (Nemerov), **III:** 269

This Body Is Made of Camphor and Gopherwood (R. Bly), **Supp. IV Part 1:** 63–65, 66, 71

This Boy's Life: A Memoir (T. Wolff), **Supp. VII:** 334–339, 340, 343; **Supp. XI:** 246, 247

"This Bright Dream" (Benét), **Supp. XI:** 55

This Coffin Has No Handles (McGrath), **Supp. X:** 117

"This Configuration" (Ashbery), **Supp. III Part 1:** 22

"This Corruptible" (Wylie), **Supp. I Part 2:** 727, 729

"This Crutch That I Love" (Nye), **Supp. XIII:** 288

"This Gentile World" (H. Miller), **III:** 177

"This Hand" (Wylie), **Supp. I Part 2:** 713

"This Hour" (Olds), **Supp. X:** 212

"This House I Cannot Leave" (Kingsolver), **Supp. VII:** 208

This Hunger (Nin), **Supp. X:** 185

"This Is a Photograph of Me" (Atwood), **Supp. XIII:** 33

"This Is a Poem, Good Afternoon" (Keillor), **Supp. XVI:**167

"This Is It" (Stern), **Supp. IX:** 290

"This Is Just to Say" (W. C. Williams), **Supp. XI:** 328

"This Is My Heart" (Harjo), **Supp. XII:** 230

"This Is Not Who We Are" (Nye), **Supp. XIII:** 285, 286

"This Is What I Said" (Salinas), **Supp. XIII:** 322

This Journey (Wright), **Supp. III Part 2:** 605–606

This Man and This Woman (Farrell), **II:** 42

"This Morning" (Kenyon), **Supp. VII:** 164

"This Morning, This Evening, So Soon" (Baldwin), **Supp. I Part 1:** 63

"This Morning Again It Was in the

Dusty Pines" (Oliver), **Supp. VII:** 240

This Music Crept by Me upon the Waters (MacLeish), **III:** 21

This People Israel: The Meaning of Jewish Existence (Baeck), **Supp. V:** 260

"This Personal Maze Is Not the Prize" (Selinger), **Supp. XI:** 248

"This Place in the Ways" (Rukeyser), **Supp. VI:** 273–274

This Property Is Condemned (T. Williams), **IV:** 378

This Proud Heart (Buck), **Supp. II Part 1:** 119–120

This Same Sky: A Collection of Poems from around the World (Nye, ed.), **Supp. XIII:** 280

"This Sandwich Has No Mayonnaise" (Salinger), **III:** 552–553

This Side of Paradise (Fitzgerald), **I:** 358; **II:** 77, 80, 81, 82–83, 84, 85–87, 88; **Retro. Supp. I:** 99–100, 101–102, 103, 105, 106, 110, 111

This Singing World: An Anthology of Modern Poetry for Young People (Untermeyer, ed.), **Supp. XV:** 306

This Stubborn Self: Texas Autobiographies (Almon), **Supp. XIII:** 288

This Thing Don't Lead to Heaven (Crews), **Supp. XI:** 112

This Time: New and Selected Poems (Stern), **Supp. IX:** 290–291, 299

"Thistle Seed in the Wind" (Francis), **Supp. IX:** 81

"Thistles in Sweden, The" (Maxwell), **Supp. VIII:** 169

"This Tokyo" (Snyder), **Supp. VIII:** 298

This Tree Will Be Here for a Thousand Years (R. Bly), **Supp. IV Part 1:** 65–66, 71, 72

This Tree Will Be Here for a Thousand Years (revised edition) (R. Bly), **Supp. IV Part 1:** 66

This Very Earth (Caldwell), **I:** 297, 302

Thoens, Karen, **Supp. V:** 147

Thomas, Brandon, **II:** 138

Thomas, D. M., **Supp. VIII:** 5

Thomas, Debra, **Supp. XIII:** 114

Thomas, Dylan, **I:** 49, 64, 382, 432, 526, 533; **III:** 21, 521, 528, 532, 534; **IV:** 89, 93, 136; **Supp. I Part 1:** 263; **Supp. III Part 1:** 42, 47; **Supp. V:** 344; **Supp. VIII:** 21; **Supp. IX:** 114; **Supp. X:** 115; **Supp. XV:** 74

Thomas, Edward, **II:** 154; **Retro. Supp. I:** 127, 131, 132; **Supp. I Part 1:** 263; **Supp. II Part 1:** 4

Thomas, J. Parnell, **Supp. I Part 1:** 286; **Supp. XV:** 198

Thomas, James, **Supp. XVI:** 268

Thomas, Lewis, **Retro. Supp. I:** 323

Thomas, William I., **Supp. I Part 2:** 641

Thomas-a-Kempis, **Retro. Supp. I:** 247

Thomas and Beulah (Dove), **Supp. IV Part 1:** 242, 247–248, 249

Thomas Aquinas (Saint), **I:** 13, 14, 265, 267; **III:** 270; **Retro. Supp. II:** 222; **Supp. IV Part 2:** 526

"Thomas at the Wheel" (Dove), **Supp. IV Part 1:** 248

"Thomas McGrath: Words for a Vanished Age" (Vinz), **Supp. X:** 117

Thomas Merton on Peace, **Supp. VIII:** 208

Thomas Merton Studies Center, The, **Supp. VIII:** 208

Thompson, Barbara, **Supp. V:** 322

Thompson, Cy, **I:** 538

Thompson, Dorothy, **II:** 449–450, 451, 453; **Supp. XV:** 307

Thompson, E. P., **Supp. X:** 112, 117

Thompson, Francis, **Retro. Supp. I:** 55

Thompson, Frank, **II:** 20

Thompson, George, **Supp. I Part 2:** 686

Thompson, Hunter S., **Supp. VIII:** 42; **Supp. XI:** 105; **Supp. XIII:** 1, 17

Thompson, James R., **Supp. IV Part 1:** 217

Thompson, John, **Supp. V:** 323

Thompson, Lawrance, **II:** 508

Thompson, Lawrance Roger, **Retro. Supp. I:** 138, 141

Thompson, Morton, **Supp. XIII:** 170

Thompson, Theresa, **Supp. V:** 141

Thompson, William T., **Supp. I Part 2:** 411

Thomson, James, **II:** 304; **Supp. I Part 1:** 150, 151

Thomson, Virgil, **IV:** 45; **Supp. IV Part 1:** 81, 83, 84, 173; **Supp. XVI:** 195

"Thoreau" (Lowell), **Supp. I Part 2:** 420, 422

Thoreau, Henry David, **I:** 98, 104, 228, 236, 257, 258, 261, 305, 433; **II:** 7, 8, 13, 17, 101, 159, 224, 273–274, 295, 312–313, 321, 457–458, 540, 546–547; **III:** 171, 174, 186–187, 189, 208, 214–215, 453, 454, 507, 577; **IV:** 167–189, 191, 341; **Retro. Supp. I:** 51, 62, 122; **Retro. Supp. II:** 13, 96, 142, 158; **Supp. I Part 1:** 29, 34, 116, 188, 299, 358; **Supp.**

I Part 2: 383, 400, 420, 421, 507, 540, 579, 580, 655, 659, 660, 664, 678; **Supp. III Part 1:** 340, 353; **Supp. IV Part 1:** 236, 392, 416; **Supp. IV Part 2:** 420, 430, 433, 439, 447; **Supp. V:** 200, 208; **Supp. VIII:** 40, 42, 103, 105, 198, 201, 204, 205, 292, 303; **Supp. IX:** 25, 90, 171; **Supp. X:** 21, 27, 28–29, 101, 102; **Supp. XI:** 155; **Supp. XIII:** 1, 17; **Supp. XIV:** 40, 54, 106, 177, 181

Thoreau, John, **IV:** 171, 182

Thoreau, Mrs. John, **IV:** 172

"Thorn, The" (Gordon), **Supp. IV Part 1:** 314

Thorne, Francis, **Supp. XII:** 253

"Thorn Merchant, The" (Komunyakaa), **Supp. XIII:** 119–120

Thornton, Billy Bob, **Supp. VIII:** 175

Thornton, Lionel, **III:** 291

"Thorofare" (Minot), **Supp. VI:** 209–210

"Thorow" (Howe), **Supp. IV Part 2:** 419, 420, 421, 431, 433–434

Thorp, Willard, **Supp. XIII:** 101

Thorslev, Peter L., Jr., **I:** 524

Thorstein Veblen (Dowd), **Supp. I Part 2:** 650

Thorstein Veblen (Qualey, ed.), **Supp. I Part 2:** 650

Thorstein Veblen: A Chapter in American Economic Thought (Teggart), **Supp. I Part 2:** 650

Thorstein Veblen: A Critical Interpretation (Riesman), **Supp. I Part 2:** 649, 650

Thorstein Veblen: A Critical Reappraisal (Dowd, ed.), **Supp. I Part 2:** 650

Thorstein Veblen and His America (Dorfman), **Supp. I Part 2:** 631, 650

Thorstein Veblen and the Institutionalists: A Study in the Social Philosophy of Economics (Seckler), **Supp. I Part 2:** 650

"Those before Us" (Lowell), **II:** 550

"Those Being Eaten by America" (R. Bly), **Supp. IV Part 1:** 62

Those Bones Are Not My Child (Bambara), **Supp. XI:** 1, 14, 20–22

Those Extraordinary Twins (Twain), **IV:** 205–206

"Those Graves in Rome" (Levis), **Supp. XI:** 266

"Those of Us Who Think We Know" (Dunn), **Supp. XI:** 146

"Those Times . . ." (Sexton), **Supp. II Part 2:** 670, 684

"Those Various Scalpels" (Moore), **III:** 202

"Those Were the Days" (Levine), **Supp. V:** 190

"Those Who Don't" (Cisneros), **Supp. VII:** 60

"Those Who Thunder" (Hogan), **Supp. IV Part 1:** 406

"Thought, A" (Sarton), **Supp. VIII:** 262

Thought and Character of William James (Perry), **II:** 362

Thoughtbook of Francis Scott Key Fitzgerald (Fitzgerald), **Retro. Supp. I:** 99

"Thoughtful Roisterer Declines the Gambit, The" (Hecht), **Supp. X:** 63

"Thought of Heaven, The" (Stern), **Supp. IX:** 297

"Thoughts after Lambeth" (Eliot), **I:** 587; **Retro. Supp. I:** 324

Thoughts and Reflections (Lord Halifax), **II:** 111

Thoughts in Solitude (Merton), **Supp. VIII:** 207

"Thoughts on Being Bibliographed" (Wilson), **IV:** 435

"Thoughts on the Establishment of a Mint in the United States" (Paine), **Supp. I Part 2:** 512

"Thoughts on the Gifts of Art" (Kenyon), **Supp. VII:** 167

Thousand Acres, A (Smiley), **Supp. VI:** 292, 301–303

"Thousand and Second Night, The" (Merrill), **Supp. III Part 1:** 324

"Thousand Dollar Vagrant, The" (Olsen), **Supp. XIII:** 292, 297

"Thousand Faces of Danny Torrance, The" (Figliola), **Supp. V:** 143

"Thousand Genuflections, A" (McCarriston), **Supp. XIV:**266

Thousand-Mile Walk to the Gulf, A (Muir), **Supp. IX:** 177–178

"Thou Shalt Not Steal" (McClatchy), **Supp. XII:** 264

"Thread, The" (Merwin), **Supp. III Part 1:** 351

Three (film), **Supp. IX:** 253

3-3-8 (Marquand), **III:** 58

"Three Academic Pieces" (Stevens), **IV:** 90

"Three Agee Wards, The" (Morris), **III:** 220–221

"Three American Singers" (Cather), **Retro. Supp. I:** 10

"Three Around the Old Gentleman" (Berryman), **I:** 188

"Three Avilas, The" (Jeffers), **Supp. II Part 2:** 418

Three Books of Song (Longfellow), **II:** 490

"Three Bushes" (Yeats), **Supp. I Part 1:** 80

Three Cantos (Pound), **Retro. Supp. I:** 290

Three Centuries of Harvard (Morison), **Supp. I Part 2:** 485

Three Comrades (Remarque), **Retro. Supp. I:** 113

"Three Corollaries of Cultural Relativism" (Locke), **Supp. XIV:**202

"Three-Day Blow, The" (Hemingway), **II:** 248

Three Essays on America (Brooks), **I:** 246

Three Farmers on Their Way to a Dance (Powers), **Supp. IX:** 211–212, 213–214, 222

"Three Fates, The" (Benét), **Supp. XI:** 48–49, 50

Three Gospels (Price), **Supp. VI:** 267

"Three Kings, The: Hemingway, Faulkner, and Fitzgerald" (Ford), **Supp. V:** 59

Three Lives (Auchincloss), **Supp. IV Part 1:** 25

Three Lives (Stein), **I:** 103; **IV:** 26, 27, 31, 35, 37–41, 42, 45, 46; **Supp. IX:** 306

"THREE MOVEMENTS AND A CODA" (Baraka), **Supp. II Part 1:** 50

Three One Act Plays (Riverside Drive, Old Saybrook, and *Central Park West)* (Allen), **Supp. XV:** 3

Three on the Tower: The Lives and Works of Ezra Pound, T. S. Eliot, and William Carlos Williams (Simpson), **Supp. IX:** 276

Three Papers on Fiction (Welty), **IV:** 261

Three-Penny Opera (Brecht), **I:** 301; **Supp. XIV:**162

Three Philosophical Poets (Santayana), **III:** 610–612

"Three Pigs in Five Days" (Prose), **Supp. XVI:**257, 258

"Three Players of a Summer Game" (T. Williams), **IV:** 383

Three Poems (Ashbery), **Supp. III Part 1:** 2, 3, 14, 15, 18, 24–26

"Three Pokes of a Thistle" (Nye), **Supp. XIII:** 281

Three Roads, The (Macdonald, under Millar), **Supp. IV Part 2:** 466, 467

"Three Silences of Molinos, The" (Longfellow), **Retro. Supp. II:** 169

Three Sisters, The (Chekhov), **Supp. XV:** 323

"Three Sisters, The" (Cisneros), **Supp. VII:** 64

Three Soldiers (Dos Passos), **I:** 477–478, 480, 482, 488, 493–494

"Three Songs at the End of Summer" (Kenyon), **Supp. VII:** 169–170

"Three Steps to the Graveyard" (Wright), **Supp. III Part 2:** 593, 596

Three Stories and Ten Poems (Hemingway), **II:** 68, 263

Three Taverns, The (Robinson), **III:** 510

"Three Taverns, The" (Robinson), **III:** 521, 522

Three Tenant Families (Agee), **I:** 37–38

Three Tenors, One Vehicle: A Book of Songs (X. J. Kennedy, Camp, and Waldrop), **Supp. XV:** 165

"Three Types of Poetry" (Tate), **IV:** 131

"Three Vagabonds of Trinidad" (Harte), **Supp. II Part 1:** 338

"Three Waterfalls, The" (Lanier), **Supp. I Part 1:** 350

"Three-Way Mirror" (Brooks), **Supp. III Part 1:** 69–70

"Three Women" (Plath), **Supp. I Part 2:** 539, 541, 544, 545, 546

Three Young Poets (Swallow, ed.), **Supp. X:** 116

Threnody (Emerson), **Supp. I Part 2:** 416

"Threnody" (Emerson), **II:** 7

"Threnody for a Brown Girl" (Cullen), **Supp. IV Part 1:** 166

"Threshing-Floor, The" (Baldwin), **Supp. I Part 1:** 50

Threshold (film), **Supp. IX:** 254

"Threshold" (Goldbarth), **Supp. XII:** 175

Threshold (Jackson), **Supp. IX:** 117

"Throat" (Goldbarth), **Supp. XII:** 177–178

Throne of Labdacus, The (Schnackenberg), **Supp. XV:** 260, 263–266

Thrones (Pound), **Retro. Supp. I:** 293

Through Dooms of Love (Kumin), **Supp. IV Part 2:** 444

"Through the Black Curtain" (Kingston), **Supp. V:** 169

Through the Forest: New and Selected Poems, 1977–1987 (Wagoner), **Supp. IX:** 330–331

"Through the Hills of Spain" (Salinas), **Supp. XIII:** 315

"Through the Hole in the Mundane Millstone" (West), **Retro. Supp. II:** 321, 322

Through the Ivory Gate (Dove), **Supp. IV Part 1:** 242, 243, 251, 252, 253–254, 254

"Through the Kitchen Window, Chiapas" (Nye), **Supp. XIII:** 277

"Through the Smoke Hole" (Snyder), **Supp. VIII:** 299

Thucydides, **II:** 418; **IV:** 50; **Supp. I Part 2:** 488, 489, 492; **Supp. IV Part 1:** 391; **Supp. XIII:** 233

Thunderbolt and Lightfoot (film), **Supp. X:** 126

"Thunderhead" (MacLeish), **III:** 19

Thurber, James, **I:** 487; **II:** 432; **IV:** 396; **Supp. I Part 2:** 602–627, 653, 654, 668, 672, 673, 679; **Supp. II Part 1:** 143; **Supp. IV Part 1:** 349; **Supp. IX:** 118; **Supp. XIV:**104; **Supp. XVI:**167

Thurber, Mrs. James (Althea Adams), **Supp. I Part 2:** 613, 615, 617

Thurber, Mrs. James (Helen Muriel Wismer), **Supp. I Part 2:** 613, 617, 618

Thurber, Robert, **Supp. I Part 2:** 613, 617

Thurber, Rosemary, **Supp. I Part 2:** 616

Thurber, William, **Supp. I Part 2:** 602

Thurber Album, The (Thurber), **Supp. I Part 2:** 611, 619

Thurber Carnival, The (Thurber), **Supp. I Part 2:** 620; **Supp. XIV:**104

Thurman, Judith, **Supp. IV Part 1:** 309

Thurman, Wallace, **Retro. Supp. I:** 200; **Supp. I Part 1:** 325, 326, 328, 332; **Supp. IV Part 1:** 164; **Supp. X:** 136, 139; **Supp. XVI:**135

"Thursday" (Millay), **III:** 129

"Thurso's Landing" (Jeffers), **Supp. II Part 2:** 433

"Thus Do I Refute Gioia" (Junker), **Supp. XV:** 116

Thus Spake Zarathustra (Nietzsche), **II:** 463; **Supp. IV Part 1:** 110; **Supp. IV Part 2:** 519

Thwaite, Lady Alicia. *See* Rawlings, Marjorie Kinnan

"Tiara" (Doty), **Supp. XI:** 122

"Tibetan Time" (Prose), **Supp. XVI:**255

Ticket for a Seamstitch, A (Harris), **II:** 424–425

Tickets for a Prayer Wheel (Dillard), **Supp. VI:** 22, 34

Ticket That Exploded, The (Burroughs), **Supp. III Part 1:** 93, 103, 104

Tickless Time (Glaspell), **Supp. III Part 1:** 179

Ticknor, George, **II:** 488; **Supp. I Part 1:** 313

"Ti Démon" (Chopin), **Supp. I Part 1:** 225

Tide of Time, The (Masters), **Supp. I Part 2:** 471

"Tide Rises, the Tide Falls, The" (Longfellow), **I:** 498

Tidyman, Ernest, **Supp. V:** 226

Tietjens, Eunice, **Supp. XV:** 47, 297

"Tiger" (Blake), **Supp. I Part 1:** 80; **Supp. VIII:** 26

Tiger (Bynner), **Supp. XV:** 42, 50

"Tiger, The" (Buechner), **Supp. XII:** 48

Tiger in the House, The (Van Vechten), **Supp. II Part 2:** 736

Tiger Joy (Benét), **Supp. XI:** 45

Tiger-Lilies (Lanier), **Supp. I Part 1:** 350–351, 357, 360, 371

Tiger Who Wore White Gloves, The: or, What You Are, You Are (Brooks), **Supp. III Part 1:** 86

Till, Emmett, **Supp. I Part 1:** 61

Tillich, Paul, **II:** 244; **III:** 291, 292, 303, 309; **IV:** 226; **Retro. Supp. I:** 325, 326, 327; **Supp. V:** 267; **Supp. XIII:** 74, 91

Tillie Olsen: A Study of the Short Fiction (Frye), **Supp. XIII:** 292, 296, 298, 299, 302

Tillman, Lynne, **Supp. XII:** 4

Tillotson, John, **II:** 114

Tillstrom, Burr, **Supp. XIV:**125

Till the Day I Die (Odets), **Supp. II Part 2:** 530, 533–536, 552

Tilton, Eleanor, **Supp. I Part 1:** 317

Timaeus (Plato), **II:** 10; **III:** 609

Timber (Jonson), **II:** 16

Timberg, Scott, **Supp. XV:** 116

Timbuktu (Auster), **Supp. XII:** 34, 35–36

"Time" (Matthews), **Supp. IX:** 165–166

"Time" (Merrill), **Supp. III Part 1:** 325

"Time and Again" (Sanders), **Supp. XVI:**269

Time and a Place, A (Humphrey), **Supp. IX:** 95, 98, 100–102

"Time and the Garden" (Winters), **Supp. II Part 2:** 801, 809

"Time and the Liturgy" (Merton), **Supp. VIII:** 199

Time and Tide: A Walk through Nantucket (Conroy), **Supp. XVI:**63, 71, 76–77

Time in the Rock (Aiken), **I:** 65

Time Is Noon, The (Buck), **Supp. II Part 1:** 129, 130–131

Time & Money (Matthews), **Supp. IX:** 155, 165–167

"Time of Friendship, The" (Bowles), **Supp. IV Part 1:** 90–91

"Time of Her Time, The" (Mailer), **III:** 37, 45; **Retro. Supp. II:** 200

Time of Our Time, The (Mailer), **Retro. Supp. II:** 213–214

Time of the Assassins, The: A Study of Rimbaud (H. Miller), **III:** 189

"Time Past" (Morris), **III:** 232

"Time Present" (Morris), **III:** 232

"Times" (Beattie), **Supp. V:** 31

"Times, The" (Emerson), **II:** 11–12

Times Are Never So Bad, The (Dubus), **Supp. VII:** 87–88

Time's Arrow (Amis), **Retro. Supp. I:** 278

"Time Shall Not Die" (Chandler), **Supp. IV Part 1:** 120

Times of Melville and Whitman, The (Brooks), **I:** 257

"Timesweep" (Sandburg), **III:** 595–596

Time to Act, A (MacLeish), **III:** 3

Time to Go (Dixon), **Supp. XII:** 147

Time to Kill (film), **Supp. IV Part 1:** 130

Time to Speak, A (MacLeish), **III:** 3

Time Will Darken It (Maxwell), **Supp. VIII:** 159, 162–164, 169

"Timing of Sin, The" (Dubus), **Supp. VII:** 91

Tim O'Brien (Herzog), **Supp. V:** 239

Timoleon (Melville), **III:** 93; **Retro. Supp. I:** 257

Timothy Dexter Revisited (Marquand), **III:** 55, 62, 63

Tin Can, The (W. J. Smith), **Supp. XIII:** 334, **Supp. XIII:** 336, 337

"Tin Can, The" (W. J. Smith), **Supp. XIII:** 337–339

Tin Can Tree, The (Tyler), **Supp. IV Part 2:** 659–660

Tinguely, Jean, **Supp. XV:** 187

Tinker, Chauncey Brewster, **Supp. XIV:**12

Tintern Abbey (Wordsworth), **Supp. I Part 2:** 673, 675

Tiny Alice (Albee), **I:** 81–86, 87, 88, 94

"Tiny Mummies! The True Story of the Ruler of 43rd Street's Land of the Walking Dead" (Wolfe), **Supp. III Part 2:** 573, 574

"Tip-Top Club, The" (Keillor), **Supp. XVI:**172

"Tired" (Hughes), **Supp. I Part 1:** 331

"Tired and Unhappy, You Think of Houses" (Schwartz), **Supp. II Part 2:** 649

"Tiresias" (Garrett), **Supp. VII:** 96–97
'Tis (McCourt), **Supp. XII:** 271, 279–286
Tisch (Dixon), **Supp. XII:** 141, 155–156
Titan, The (Dreiser), **I:** 497, 501, 507–508, 509, 510; **Retro. Supp. II:** 94, 101, 102
Titian, **Supp. I Part 2:** 397, 714
"Tito's Goodbye" (García), **Supp. XI:** 190
To a Blossoming Pear Tree (Wright), **Supp. III Part 2:** 602–605
"To a Blossoming Pear Tree" (Wright), **Supp. III Part 2:** 604
"To Abolish Children" (Shapiro), **Supp. II Part 2:** 717
To Abolish Children and Other Essays (Shapiro), **Supp. II Part 2:** 703
"To a Caty-Did, the Precursor of Winter" (Freneau), **Supp. II Part 1:** 274–275
"To a Chameleon" (Moore), **III:** 195, 196, 215
"To a Conscript of 1940" (Read), **II:** 372–373, 377–378
"To a Contemporary Bunk Shooter" (Sandburg), **III:** 582
"To a Cough in the Street at Midnight" (Wylie), **Supp. I Part 2:** 727, 729–730
"To a Defeated Savior" (Wright), **Supp. III Part 2:** 593–594, 596
"To a Face in the Crowd" (Warren), **IV:** 239
"To a Fish Head Found on the Beach near Malaga" (Levine), **Supp. V:** 185
"To a Friend" (Nemerov), **III:** 272
"To a Friend Whose Work Has Come to Triumph" (Sexton), **Supp. II Part 2:** 683
To a God Unknown (Steinbeck), **I:** 107; **IV:** 51, 59–60, 67
"To a Greek Marble" (Aldington), **Supp. I Part 1:** 257
"To a Locomotive in Winter" (Whitman), **IV:** 348
"To a Military Rifle" (Winters), **Supp. II Part 2:** 810, 811, 815
"To a Mouse" (Burns), **Supp. IX:** 173
"To a Negro Jazz Band in a Parisian Cabaret" (Hughes), **Supp. I Part 1:** 325
"To an Old Philosopher in Rome" (Stevens), **III:** 605; **Retro. Supp. I:** 312
"To an Old Poet in Peru" (Ginsberg), **Supp. II Part 1:** 322
"To a Now-Type Poet" (X. J. Kennedy), **Supp. XV:** 161
"To Any Would-Be Terrorists" (Nye), **Supp. XIII:** 285, 286
"To a Poet" (Rich), **Supp. I Part 2:** 571
"To a Prize Bird" (Moore), **III:** 215
"To a Republican, with Mr. Paine's Rights of Man" (Freneau), **Supp. II Part 1:** 267
"To a Shade" (Yeats), **III:** 18
"To a Skylark" (Shelley), **Supp. I Part 2:** 720; **Supp. X:** 31
"Toast to Harlem, A" (Hughes), **Supp. I Part 1:** 338
"To Aunt Rose" (Ginsberg), **Supp. II Part 1:** 320
"To Autumn" (Keats), **Supp. IX:** 50
"To a Waterfowl" (Bryant), **Supp. I Part 1:** 154, 155, 162, 171
"To a Young Poet" (X. J. Kennedy), **Supp. XV:** 161
"To a Young Writer" (Stegner), **Supp. X:** 24
Tobacco Road (Caldwell), **I:** 288, 289, 290, 295–296, 297, 298, 302, 307, 309, 310; **IV:** 198
"To Be a Monstrous Clever Fellow" (Fante), **Supp. XI:** 167
To Bedlam and Part Way Back (Sexton), **Retro. Supp. II:** 245; **Supp. II Part 2:** 672–678; **Supp. IV Part 2:** 441; **Supp. XI:** 317
"To Beethoven" (Lanier), **Supp. I Part 1:** 364
Tobey, Mark, **Supp. X:** 264
To Be Young, Gifted, and Black: Lorraine Hansberry in Her Own Words (Nemiroff), **Supp. IV Part 1:** 372, 374
"To Big Mary from an Ex-Catholic" (Mora), **Supp. XIII:** 217, 224, 228
"Tobin's Palm" (O. Henry), **Supp. II Part 1:** 408; **Supp. XV:** 40
Tobit (apocryphal book), **I:** 89
"To Build a Fire" (London), **II:** 468
Toby Tyler: or, Ten Weeks with a Circus (Otis), **III:** 577
"To Change in a Good Way" (Ortiz), **Supp. IV Part 2:** 511
"To Charlotte Cushman" (Lanier), **Supp. I Part 1:** 364
"To Cole, the Painter, Departing for Europe" (Bryant), **Supp. I Part 1:** 157, 161
Tocqueville, Alexis de, **III:** 261; **IV:** 349; **Retro. Supp. I:** 235; **Supp. I Part 1:** 137; **Supp. I Part 2:** 659, 660; **Supp. II Part 1:** 281, 282, 284; **Supp. XIV:** 306, 312
"To Crispin O'Conner" (Freneau),
Supp. II Part 1: 268
"To Da-Duh, In Memoriam" (Marshall), **Supp. XI:** 276
"TODAY" (Baraka), **Supp. II Part 1:** 55
"Today" (Ginsberg), **Supp. II Part 1:** 328
"Today Is a Good Day To Die" (Bell), **Supp. X:** 7
Todd, Mabel Loomis, **I:** 454, 470; **Retro. Supp. I:** 33, 34, 35, 39, 47
"To Death" (Levertov), **Supp. III Part 1:** 274
"To Delmore Schwartz" (Lowell), **II:** 547; **Retro. Supp. II:** 188
"to disembark" (Brooks), **Supp. III Part 1:** 86
"To Dorothy on Her Exclusion from The Guinness Book of Records" (X. J. Kennedy), **Supp. XV:** 166
"To Dr. Thomas Shearer" (Lanier), **Supp. I Part 1:** 370
"To E. T." (Frost), **Retro. Supp. I:** 132
"To Earthward" (Frost), **II:** 154
"To Edwin V. McKenzie" (Winters), **Supp. II Part 2:** 801
"To Eleonora Duse" (Lowell), **II:** 528
"To Elizabeth Ward Perkins" (Lowell), **II:** 516
"To Elsie" (W. C. Williams), **Retro. Supp. I:** 419
"To Emily Dickinson" (H. Crane), **Retro. Supp. II:** 76
To Feel These Things (L. Michaels), **Supp. XVI:**205, 213–214
"To Feel These Things" (L. Michaels), **Supp. XVI:**214
Toffler, Alvin, **Supp. IV Part 2:** 517
"To Fill" (Moore), **Supp. X:** 168, 169
"To Gabriela, a Young Writer" (Mora), **Supp. XIII:** 220
To Have and Have Not (film), **Supp. XV:** 347
To Have and Have Not (Hemingway), **I:** 31; **II:** 253–254, 264; **Retro. Supp. I:** 182, 183, 187
"To Helen" (Poe), **III:** 410, 411, 427; **Retro. Supp. II:** 102
"To Hell With Dying" (Walker), **Supp. III Part 2:** 523
"To His Father" (Jeffers), **Supp. II Part 2:** 415
Toilet, The (Baraka), **Supp. II Part 1:** 37, 40–42
"To James Russell Lowell" (Holmes), **Supp. I Part 1:** 311
To Jerusalem and Back (Bellow), **Retro. Supp. II:** 29
"To Jesus on His Birthday" (Millay), **III:** 136–137

"To John Keats" (Lowell), **II:** 516

"To Judge Faolain, Dead Long Enough: A Summons" (McCarriston), **Supp. XIV:**264–265

"To Justify My Singing" (Wright), **Supp. III Part 2:** 590

"To Kill a Deer" (C. Frost), **Supp. XV:** 102

To Kill a Mockingbird (film), **Supp. VIII:** 128–129

To Kill a Mockingbird (Lee), **Supp. VIII:** 113–129; **Supp. XVI:**259

"*To Kill a Mockingbird:* Harper Lee's Tragic Vision" (Dave), **Supp. VIII:** 126

To Kill a Mockingbird: Threatening Boundaries (Johnson), **Supp. VIII:** 126

Toklas, Alice B., **IV:** 27; **Supp. IV Part 1:** 81, 91; **Supp. XVI:**187

"Tokyo Story" (Wasserstein), **Supp. XV:** 328

"To Light" (Hogan), **Supp. IV Part 1:** 402

"To Live and Diet" (Wasserstein), **Supp. XV:** 328

Tolkien, J. R. R., **Supp. V:** 140

Tolkin, Michael, **Supp. XI:** 160

Toller, Ernst, **I:** 479

"To Lose the Earth" (Sexton), **Supp. II Part 2:** 684, 685

Tolson, Melvin, **Retro. Supp. I:** 208, 209, 210

Tolstoy, Leo, **I:** 6, 7, 58, 103, 312, 376; **II:** 191–192, 205, 271, 272, 275, 276, 281, 285, 286, 320, 407, 542, 559, 570, 579, 606; **III:** 37, 45, 61, 323, 467, 572; **IV:** 17, 21, 170, 285; **Retro. Supp. I:** 91, 225; **Retro. Supp. II:** 299; **Supp. I Part 1:** 2, 3, 6, 20; **Supp. IV Part 1:** 392; **Supp. V:** 277, 323; **Supp. IX:** 246; **Supp. XI:** 68; **Supp. XII:** 310, 322; **Supp. XIV:**87, 97, 98

"To Lu Chi" (Nemerov), **III:** 275

Tom (Cummings), **I:** 430

"Tom" (Oliver), **Supp. VII:** 232

"Tom, Tom, the Piper's Son" (Ransom), **Supp. X:** 58

"To M, with a Rose" (Lanier), **Supp. I Part 1:** 364

To Make a Prairie (Kumin), **Supp. IV Part 2:** 440, 441

"To Make Words Disappear" (Simpson), **Supp. IX:** 265–266

Tomás and the Library Lady (Mora), **Supp. XIII:** 216, 221

"Tomatoes" (Francis), **Supp. IX:** 82

"Tom Brown at Fisk" (Du Bois), **Supp. II Part 1:** 160

Tom Brown's School Days (Hughes), **Supp. I Part 2:** 406

"Tomb Stone" (Dickey), **Supp. IV Part 1:** 185

Tomcat in Love (O'Brien), **Supp. V:** 238, 240, 243, 252–254

"Tomcat's Wife, The" (C. Bly), **Supp. XVI:**40

Tomcat's Wife and Other Stories, The (C. Bly), **Supp. XVI:**40–41

"Tom Fool at Jamaica" (Moore), **III:** 215

To Mix with Time (Swenson), **Supp. IV Part 2:** 637, 643–645, 645

Tom Jones (Fielding), **I:** 131; **Supp. V:** 127

Tomlinson, Charles, **Supp. XVI:**284

Tommy Gallagher's Crusade (Farrell), **II:** 44

Tommyknockers, The (King), **Supp. V:** 139, 144

"Tommy's Burglar" (Henry), **Supp. II Part 1:** 399, 401

Tomo Cheeki (pseudonym). *See* Freneau, Philip

"Tomorrow the Moon" (Dos Passos), **I:** 493

"Tom Outland's Story" (Cather), **I:** 325–326

Tompkins, Jane, **Supp. XVI:**89

Tompson, Benjamin, **Supp. I Part 1:** 110, 111

Tom Sawyer (musical) (Gurney), **Supp. V:** 96

Tom Sawyer (Twain). *See Adventures of Tom Sawyer, The* (Twain)

Tom Sawyer Abroad (Twain), **II:** 482; **IV:** 19, 204

Tom Sawyer Detective (Twain), **IV:** 204

"Tom's Husband" (Jewett), **Retro. Supp. II:** 132, 141

Tom Swift (Stratemeyer), **III:** 146

"Tom Wolfe's Guide to Etiquette" (Wolfe), **Supp. III Part 2:** 578

"To My Brother Killed: Haumont Wood: October, 1918" (Bogan), **Supp. III Part 1:** 58

"To My Class, on Certain Fruits and Flowers Sent Me in Sickness" (Lanier), **Supp. I Part 1:** 370

"To My Father's Ghost" (Everwine), **Supp. XV:** 76

"To My Ghost Reflected in the Auxvasse River" (Levis), **Supp. XI:** 265

"To My Greek" (Merrill), **Supp. III Part 1:** 326

"To My Mother" (Berry), **Supp. X:** 23

"To My Small Son, at the Photographer's" (Hay), **Supp. XIV:**121

"To My Small Son, on Certain Occasions" (Hay), **Supp. XIV:**121

"To Name is to Possess" (Kincaid), **Supp. VII:** 194

Tone, Aileen, **I:** 21–22

"Tongue Is, The" (Komunyakaa), **Supp. XIII:** 113

Tongues (Shepard and Chaikin), **Supp. III Part 2:** 433

Tongues of Angels, The (Price), **Supp. VI:** 265

Tongues Untied (Riggs; film), **Supp. XI:** 19, 20

"Tonight" (Lowell), **II:** 538

Tony Kushner in Conversation (Vorlicky, ed.), **Supp. IX:** 132

"Too Anxious for Rivers" (Frost), **II:** 162

"Too Blue" (Hughes), **Retro. Supp. I:** 207

"Too Damn Close: Thresholds and Their Maintenance in Rick Bass's Work" (Kerridge), **Supp. XVI:**26

"Too Early" (Leopold), **Supp. XIV:**186

"Too Early Spring" (Benét), **Supp. XI:** 53

"Too Far from Home" (Bowles), **Supp. IV Part 1:** 94–95

Too Far from Home: Selected Writings of Paul Bowles (Halpern, ed.), **Supp. IV Part 1:** 94, 95

Too Far to Go: The Maples Stories (Updike), **Retro. Supp. I:** 321

"Too Good To Be True": The Life and Art of Leslie Fiedler (Winchell), **Supp. XIII:** 94, 98, 99, 101

Toohey, John Peter, **Supp. IX:** 190

Toolan, David, **Supp. IV Part 1:** 308

Too Late (Dixon), **Supp. XII:** 143–144

"Too-Late Born, The" (Hemingway), **III:** 9

Toole, John Kennedy, **Supp. XIV:**21

Toomer, Jean, **Retro. Supp. II:** 79; **Supp. I Part 1:** 325, 332; **Supp. III Part 2:** 475–491; **Supp. IV Part 1:** 16, 164, 168; **Supp. IX:** 305–322; **Supp. XIII:** 305

Toomer, Nathan Eugene Pinchback. *See* Toomer, Jean

Too Much Johnson (film), **Supp. IV Part 1:** 83

"To One Who Said Me Nay" (Cullen), **Supp. IV Part 1:** 166

Tooth, The" (Jackson), **Supp. IX:** 122

Tooth of Crime, The (Shepard), **Supp. III Part 2:** 432, 441–445, 447

"Too Young" (O'Hara), **III:** 369

"To P. L., 1916–1937" (Levine), **Supp. V:** 185

"Top Israeli Official Hints at 'Shared'

Jerusalem" (Nye), **Supp. XIII:** 287

"To Please a Shadow" (Brodsky), **Supp. VIII:** 30

"Top of the Hill" (Jewett), **II:** 406

"Topography" (Olds), **Supp. X:** 208

Topper (T. Smith), **Supp. IX:** 194

Torah, **IV:** 19

"Torquemada" (Longfellow), **II:** 505; **Retro. Supp. II:** 164

Torrence, Ridgely, **III:** 507

Torrent and the Night Before, The (Robinson), **III:** 504

Torrents of Spring, The (Hemingway), **I:** 117; **II:** 250–251

Torres, Héctor A., **Supp. XIII:** 225

Torres, Louis, **Supp. IV Part 2:** 529, 530

Torsney, Cheryl, **Retro. Supp. I:** 224

Tortilla Curtain, The (Boyle), **Supp. VIII:** 9–10

Tortilla Flat (Steinbeck), **IV:** 50, 51, 61, 64

Tory Lover, The (Jewett), **II:** 406; **Retro. Supp. II:** 144–145

"Toscana" (Dixon), **Supp. XII:** 154

"To Sir Toby" (Freneau), **Supp. II Part 1:** 269

"To Sophy, Expectant" (Mumford), **Supp. II Part 2:** 475

"To Speak of Woe That Is in Marriage" (Lowell), **II:** 550

"To Statecraft Embalmed" (Moore), **III:** 197

To Stay Alive (Levertov), **Supp. III Part 1:** 280–282

"Total Eclipse" (Dillard), **Supp. VI:** 28

Toth, Emily, **Retro. Supp. II:** 71

Toth, Susan Allan, **Retro. Supp. II:** 138

"To the Americans of the United States" (Freneau), **Supp. II Part 1:** 271

"To the Apennines" (Bryant), **Supp. I Part 1:** 157, 164

"To the Bleeding Hearts Association of American Novelists" (Nemerov), **III:** 281

"To the Botequim & Back" (Bishop), **Retro. Supp. II:** 51

To the Bright and Shining Sun (Burke), **Supp. XIV:**22, 25

"To the Citizens of the United States" (Paine), **Supp. I Part 2:** 519–520

"To the Dandelion" (Lowell), **Supp. I Part 2:** 424

"To the End" (Haines), **Supp. XII:** 212–213

To the Ends of the Earth: The Selected Travels of Paul Theroux, **Supp.**

VIII: 324

To the Finland Station: A Study in the Writing and Acting of History (Wilson), **IV:** 429, 436, 443–444, 446

"To the Governor & Legislature of Massachusetts" (Nemerov), **III:** 287

To the Holy Spirit (Winters), **Supp. II Part 2:** 810

"To the Keeper of the King's Water Works" (Freneau), **Supp. II Part 1:** 269

"To the Lacedemonians" (Tate), **IV:** 134

"To the Laodiceans" (Jarrell), **Retro. Supp. I:** 121, 140

To the Lighthouse (Woolf), **I:** 309; **II:** 600; **Retro. Supp. II:** 337; **Supp. VIII:** 155

"To the Man on Trail" (London), **II:** 466

"To the Memory of the Brave Americans Under General Greene" (Freneau), **Supp. II Part 1:** 262, 274

"To the Muse" (Wright), **Supp. III Part 2:** 601

"To the Nazi Leaders" (Hay), **Supp. XIV:**121

"To the New World" (Jarrell), **II:** 371

"To the One of Fictive Music" (Stevens), **IV:** 89; **Retro. Supp. I:** 297, 300

"To the One Upstairs" (Simic), **Supp. VIII:** 283

"To the Peoples of the World" (Du Bois), **Supp. II Part 1:** 172

"To the Pliocene Skull" (Harte), **Supp. II Part 1:** 343–344

"To the Reader" (Baudelaire), **II:** 544–545

"To the Reader" (Levertov), **Supp. III Part 1:** 277

"To the River Arve" (Bryant), **Supp. I Part 1:** 163

"To the Snake" (Levertov), **Supp. III Part 1:** 277

"To the Stone-Cutters" (Jeffers), **Supp. II Part 2:** 420

"To the Unseeable Animal" (Berry), **Supp. X:** 31

"To the Western World" (Simpson), **Supp. IX:** 269, 270

To the White Sea (Dickey), **Supp. IV Part 1:** 186, 190–191

"To the Young Who Want to Die" (Brooks), **Supp. III Part 1:** 85–86

"To Tlaoc of the Rain" (Everwine), **Supp. XV:** 77

"To Train a Writer" (Bierce), **I:** 199

"Touch, The" (Sexton), **Supp. II Part 2:** 687

"Touching the Tree" (Merwin), **Supp. III Part 1:** 355

Touching the World (Eakin), **Supp. VIII:** 167

Touch of Danger, A (Jones), **Supp. XI:** 226, 228–229

Touch of the Poet, A (O'Neill), **III:** 385, 401, 404

Touchstone, The (Wharton), **Retro. Supp. I:** 365

"Touch-up Man" (Komunyakaa), **Supp. XIII:** 119

Tough Guys Don't Dance (Mailer), **Retro. Supp. II:** 211

Toulet, Paul Jean, **IV:** 79

Tour (McNally), **Supp. XIII:** 197

"Tour 5" (Hayden), **Supp. II Part 1:** 381

To Urania (Brodsky), **Supp. VIII:** 22, 28–29

Tourgée, Albion W., **Supp. XIV:**63

"Tour Guide" (Komunyakaa), **Supp. XIII:** 114

"Tourist Death" (MacLeish), **III:** 12

Tour of Duty (Dos Passos), **I:** 489

Touron the Prairies, A (Irving), **II:** 312–313

Tovey, Donald Francis, **Supp. XIV:**336

To Walk a Crooked Mile (McGrath), **Supp. X:** 117

Toward a New Synthesis (Begiebing), **Retro. Supp. II:** 210

"Toward Nightfall" (Simic), **Supp. VIII:** 277

Towards a Better Life (Burke), **I:** 270

"Towards a Chicano Poetics: The Making of the Chicano Subject, 1969–1982" (Saldívar), **Supp. IV Part 2:** 544

Towards an Enduring Peace (Bourne), **I:** 232

Toward the Blanched Alphabets (Sobin), **Supp. XVI:**290

Toward the Gulf (Masters), **Supp. I Part 2:** 465–466

"Toward the Solstice" (Rich), **Supp. I Part 2:** 575–576

Toward Wholeness in Paule Marshall's Fiction (Pettis), **Supp. XI:** 276

"Tower" (Merwin), **Supp. III Part 1:** 343

"Tower Beyond Tragedy, The" (Jeffers), **Supp. II Part 2:** 429–430

Tower of Ivory (MacLeish), **III:** 3–4

Towers, Robert, **Supp. IX:** 259; **Supp. XVI:**211

"To What Red Hell" (C. Himes), **Supp. XVI:**137

"To Whistler, American" (Pound), **III:** 465–466

"To Wine" (Bogan), **Supp. III Part 1:** 57, 58

Town, The (Faulkner), **II:** 57, 73; **Retro. Supp. I:** 74, 82

Town and the City, The (Kerouac), **Supp. III Part 1:** 222–224; **Supp. XIV:**143

"Town Crier" (Bierce), **I:** 193, 194, 195, 196

"*Town Crier* Exclusive, Confessions of a Princess Manqué: 'How Royals Found Me "Unsuitable" to Marry Their Larry'" (Elkin), **Supp. VI:** 56

Town Down the River, The (Robinson), **III:** 508

"Town Dump, The" (Nemerov), **III:** 272, 275, 281

Towne, Robert, **Supp. XI:** 159, 172, 174

"Townhouse Interior with Cat" (Clampitt), **Supp. IX:** 40

"Townies" (Dubus), **Supp. VII:** 86

"Town of the Sound of a Twig Breaking" (Carson), **Supp. XII:** 102

"Town Poor, The" (Jewett), **Retro. Supp. II:** 138, 139, 143

Townsend, Alison, **Supp. XIII:** 222

Townsend, Ann, **Supp. V:** 77

"Towns in Colour" (Lowell), **II:** 523–524

Townsman, The (Sedges), **Supp. II Part 1:** 124–125

"To World War Two" (Koch), **Supp. XV:** 184

Toys in a Field (Komunyakaa), **Supp. XIII:** 121–122

"Toys in a Field" (Komunyakaa), **Supp. XIII:** 122

Toys in the Attic (Hellman), **Supp. I Part 1:** 289–290

Tracer (F. Barthelme), **Supp. XI:** 31–32, 33

Traces of Thomas Hariot, The (Rukeyser), **Supp. VI:** 273, 274, 283

"Tracing Life with a Finger" (Caldwell), **I:** 291

Tracker (Wagoner), **Supp. IX:** 329, 336–337

"Tracking" (Wagoner), **Supp. IX:** 329

"Track Meet, The" (Schwartz), **Supp. II Part 2:** 665

Tracks (Erdrich), **Supp. IV Part 1:** 259, 262–263, 269, 272, 273–274, 274, 275

"Tract" (W. C. Williams), **Retro. Supp. I:** 414

"Tract against Communism, A"

(Twelve Southerners), **IV:** 125, 237

Tracy, Lee, **IV:** 287, 288

Tracy, Steven, **Retro. Supp. I:** 195

"Trade, The" (Levine), **Supp. V:** 193

Trading Twelves (Callahan and Murray, eds.), **Retro. Supp. II:** 119

"Tradition and Industrialization" (Wright), **IV:** 489–490

"Tradition and Mythology: Signatures of Landscape in Chicana Poetry" (Rebolledo), **Supp. XIII:** 214

"Tradition and the Individual Talent" (Eliot), **I:** 441, 574, 585; **Retro. Supp. I:** 59, 286

Tragedies, Life and Letters of James Gates Percival (Swinburne), **Supp. I Part 2:** 422

Tragedy of Don Ippolito, The (Howells), **II:** 279

"Tragedy of Error, A" (James), **II:** 322; **Retro. Supp. I:** 218

Tragedy of Pudd'nhead Wilson, The (Twain), **IV:** 206–207

Tragic America (Dreiser), **Retro. Supp. II:** 95

"Tragic Dialogue" (Wylie), **Supp. I Part 2:** 724

Tragic Ground (Caldwell), **I:** 297, 306

Tragic Muse, The (James), **Retro. Supp. I:** 227

Traherne, Thomas, **IV:** 151; **Supp. III Part 1:** 14; **Supp. V:** 208; **Supp. XV:** 212; **Supp. XVI:**282, 288, 295

"Trail, The" (W. J. Smith), **Supp. XIII:** 342

Trailerpark (Banks), **Supp. V:** 12

"Trailing Arbutus, The" (Whittier), **Supp. I Part 2:** 691

Trail of the Lonesome Pine, The (Fox), **Supp. XIII:** 166

"Train, The" (O'Connor), **Retro. Supp. II:** 225

"Train Rising Out of the Sea" (Ashbery), **Supp. III Part 1:** 22

"Trains" (Banks), **Supp. V:** 8

"Train Tune" (Bogan), **Supp. III Part 1:** 64

"Traits of Indian Character" (Irving), **II:** 303

Tramp Abroad, A (Twain), **IV:** 200

Tramping With a Poet in the Rockies (S. Graham), **Supp. I Part 2:** 397

Tramp's Excuse, The (Lindsay), **Supp. I Part 2:** 379, 380, 382

"Transatlantic" (Toomer), **Supp. III Part 2:** 486

Transatlantic Sketches (James), **II:** 324; **Retro. Supp. I:** 219

"Transcendental Etude" (Rich), **Supp. I Part 2:** 576

"Transcontinental Highway" (Cowley), **Supp. II Part 1:** 141

"Transducer" (Ammons), **Supp. VII:** 28

"Transfigured Bird" (Merrill), **Supp. III Part 1:** 320–321

"Transformations" (Harjo), **Supp. XII:** 226

Transformations (Sexton), **Supp. II Part 2:** 689–691; **Supp. IV Part 2:** 447; **Supp. XIV:**125

Transforming Madness: New Lives for People Living with Mental Illness (Neugeboren), **Supp. XVI:**229

"Transit" (Conroy), **Supp. XVI:**72

Transit to Narcissus, A (Mailer), **Retro. Supp. II:** 196

"Translation and Transposition" (Carne-Ross), **Supp. I Part 1:** 268–269

"Translation of a Fragment of Simonides" (Bryant), **Supp. I Part 1:** 153, 155

"Translations" (Rich), **Supp. I Part 2:** 563

Translations of Ezra Pound, The (Kenner, ed.), **III:** 463

Translations of the Gospel Back into Tongues (Wright), **Supp. XV:** 342–343, 346

"Trans-National America" (Bourne), **I:** 229, 230

"Transparency" (X. J. Kennedy), **Supp. XV:** 159–160

"Transparent Itineraries: 1983" (Sobin), **Supp. XVI:**287

"Transparent Itineraries: 1984" (Sobin), **Supp. XVI:**287

"Transparent Itineraries: 1992" (Sobin), **Supp. XVI:**289

"Transparent Itineraries" poems (Sobin), **Supp. XVI:**290

Transparent Man, The (Hecht), **Supp. X:** 57, 69–71

"Transparent Man, The" (Hecht), **Supp. X:** 69–70

Transparent Things (Nabokov), **Retro. Supp. I:** 266, 270, 277

"Transport" (Simic), **Supp. VIII:** 282

Transport to Summer (Stevens), **IV:** 76, 93; **Retro. Supp. I:** 309–312

Tranströmer, Thomas, **Supp. IV Part 2:** 648

"Traps for the Unwary" (Bourne), **I:** 235

Trash Trilogy (McMurtry), **Supp. V:** 225–226, 231

Traubel, Horace, **IV:** 350

"Travel: After a Death" (Kenyon), **Supp. VII:** 169

Travel Alarm (Nye), **Supp. XIII:** 277

"Traveler, The" (Haines), **Supp. XII:** 203–204, 210

"Traveler, The" (Stegner), **Supp. IV Part 2:** 605

Traveler at Forty, A (Dreiser), **I:** 515

Traveler from Altruria, a Romance A, (Howells), **II:** 285, 287

Traveler's Tree, The: New and Selected Poems (W. J. Smith), **Supp. XIII:** 332, 347

"Traveling" (Paley), **Supp. VI:** 230

"Traveling Light" (Wagoner), **Supp. IX:** 329

"Traveling Onion, The" (Nye), **Supp. XIII:** 276

Traveling through the Dark (Stafford), **Supp. XI:** 311, 316, 318–321

"Traveling through the Dark" (Stafford), **Supp. XI:** 318–320, 321, 323, 329

Travelling in Amherst: A Poet's Journal, 1931–1954, **Supp. IX:** 88–89

Travels in Alaska (Muir), **Supp. IX:** 182, 185–186

"Travels in Georgia" (McPhee), **Supp. III Part 1:** 293–294

"Travels in North America" (Kees), **Supp. XV:** 133–134

Travels in the Congo (Gide), **III:** 210

"Travels in the South" (Ortiz), **Supp. IV Part 2:** 506

Travels with Charley (Steinbeck), **IV:** 52

"Travel Writing: Why I Bother" (Theroux), **Supp. VIII:** 310

Travis, Merle, **Supp. V:** 335

Travisano, Thomas, **Retro. Supp. II:** 40

Treasure Hunt (Buechner), **Supp. XII:** 52

Treasure Island (Stevenson), **Supp. X:** 230

"Treasure of the Redwoods, A" (Harte), **Supp. II Part 1:** 337

Treasury of Art Masterpieces, A: From the Renaissance to the Present Day (Craven), **Supp. XII:** 44

Treasury of English Aphorisms, A (L. P. Smith), **Supp. XIV:**344

Treasury of English Prose, A (L. P. Smith, ed.), **Supp. XIV:**341

Treasury of the Theatre, A (Gassner), **Supp. I Part 1:** 292

Treasury of Yiddish Stories, A (Howe and Greenberg, eds.), **Supp. I Part 2:** 432

Treat 'Em Rough (Lardner), **II:** 422–423

Treatise Concerning Religious Affec-

tions (Edwards), **I:** 547, 552, 554, 555, 557, 558, 560, 562

Treatise Concerning the Lord's Supper (Doolittle), **IV:** 150

"Treatise on Poetry" (Milosz), **Supp. VIII:** 20

Treatise on Right and Wrong, A (Mencken), **III:** 110, 119

"Treatise on Tales of Horror, A" (Wilson), **IV:** 438

Treatise on the Gods, A (Mencken), **III:** 108–109, 119

"Treatment" (Wright), **Supp. XV:** 343

Trece poetas del mundo azteca (León-Portilla), **Supp. XV:** 77

Tre Croce (Tozzi), **Supp. III Part 2:** 616

"Tree, a Rock, a Cloud, A" (McCullers), **II:** 587

"Tree, The" (Pound), **Retro. Supp. I:** 286; **Supp. I Part 1:** 255

"Tree, the Bird, The" (Roethke), **III:** 548

"Tree at My Window" (Frost), **II:** 155

Tree Grows in Brooklyn, A (film; Kazan), **Supp. XVI:**193

"Tree House at Night, The" (Dickey), **Supp. IV Part 1:** 179

Tree Is Older Than You Are, The (Nye, ed.), **Supp. XIII:** 280

"Tree of Laughing Bells, The" (Lindsay), **Supp. I Part 2:** 376

"Tree of Night, A" (Capote), **Supp. III Part 1:** 114, 120

Tree of Night and Other Stories, A (Capote), **Supp. III Part 1:** 114

"Trees, The" (Rich), **Supp. I Part 2:** 555

"Trees Listening to Bach" (Merrill), **Supp. III Part 1:** 336

Tree Where Man Was Born, The (Matthiessen), **Supp. V:** 199, 203, 204

Trejo, Ernesto, **Supp. V:** 178, 180; **Supp. XIII:** 313, 316; **Supp. XV:** 73

Trelawny, Edward John, **Supp. I Part 2:** 721

"Trellis for R., A" (Swenson), **Supp. IV Part 2:** 647

Tremblay, Bill, **Supp. XIII:** 112

Tremble (Wright), **Supp. XV:** 348–349

"Trespass" (Frost), **Retro. Supp. I:** 139

"Tretitoli, Where the Bomb Group Was" (Hugo), **Supp. VI:** 138

Trevelyan, Robert C., **Supp. XIV:**334

Trevor-Roper, Hugh, **Supp. XIV:**348

Trial, The (Kafka), **IV:** 113; **Retro. Supp. II:** 20

"Trial, The" (Rukeyser), **Supp. VI:** 278

"Trial by Existence, The" (Frost), **II:** 166

Trial of a Poet, The (Shapiro), **Supp. II Part 2:** 710

Trial of the Hawk, The: A Comedy of the Seriousness of Life (Lewis), **II:** 441

Trials of the Human Heart (Rowson), **Supp. XV:** 237, 239

Tribal Secrets: Recovering American Indian Intellectual Traditions (Warrior), **Supp. IV Part 1:** 329

"Tribute (To My Mother)" (Cullen), **Supp. IV Part 1:** 166

"Tribute, A" (Easton), **Supp. IV Part 2:** 461

"Tribute, The" (Doolittle), **Supp. I Part 1:** 267

Tribute to Freud (Doolittle), **Supp. I Part 1:** 253, 254, 258, 259, 260, 268

Tribute to the Angels (Doolittle), **Supp. I Part 1:** 272

"Trick on the World, A" (Ríos), **Supp. IV Part 2:** 553

"Tricks" (Olds), **Supp. X:** 203–204

"Trick Scenery" (F. Barthelme), **Supp. XI:** 26

Trifler, The (Masters), **Supp. I Part 2:** 459–460

Trifles (Glaspell), **Supp. III Part 1:** 175, 178, 179, 182, 186, 187; **Supp. X:** 46

Trifonov, Iurii V., **Retro. Supp. I:** 278

Triggering Town, The: Lectures and Essays on Poetry and Writing (Hugo), **Supp. VI:** 133, 140

Trilling, Diana, **II:** 587, 600; **Supp. I Part 1:** 297; **Supp. XII:** 126

Trilling, Lionel, **I:** 48; **II:** 579; **III:** 308, 310, 319, 327; **IV:** 201, 211; **Retro. Supp. I:** 19, 97, 121, 216, 227; **Supp. III Part 2:** 493–515; **Supp. V:** 259; **Supp. VIII:** 93, 98, 190, 231, 236, 243; **Supp. IX:** 266, 287; **Supp. XIII:** 100–101; **Supp. XIV:**280, 288–289; **Supp. XV:** 20, 140, 152

Trilogy (Doolittle), **Supp. I Part 1:** 271, 272

Trilogy of Desire (Dreiser), **I:** 497, 508; **Retro. Supp. II:** 94, 96, 101–102

Trimmed Lamp, The (O. Henry), **Supp. II Part 1:** 410

"Trinc" (McGrath), **Supp. X:** 127

Trio (Baker), **Supp. I Part 1:** 277

"Trip" (F. Barthelme), **Supp. XI:** 26

Triple Thinkers, The: Ten Essays on

Literature (Wilson), **IV:** 428, 431; **Supp. II Part 1:** 146

"Triplex" (Doolittle), **Supp. I Part 1:** 271

Tripmaster Monkey: His Fake Book (Kingston), **Supp. V:** 157, 158, 169, 170–173

"Trip to Hanoi" (Sontag), **Supp. III Part 2:** 460–462

Trip to Parnassus, A; or, The Judgement of Apollo on Dramatic Authors and Performers (Rowson), **Supp. XV:** 232–233

"Triptych" (Eberhart), **I:** 522, 539

Tristan and Iseult, **Retro. Supp. I:** 328, 329, 330, 331

Tristessa (Kerouac), **Supp. III Part 1:** 225, 227, 229

Tristram (Robinson), **III:** 521, 522, 523

Tristram Shandy (Sterne), **I:** 299; **IV:** 465–466; **Supp. V:** 127

"Triumphal March" (Eliot), **I:** 580; **III:** 17; **Retro. Supp. I:** 64

Triumph of Achilles, The (Glück), **Supp. V:** 79, 84–86, 92

"Triumph of a Modern, The, or, Send for the Lawyer" (Anderson), **I:** 113, 114

"Triumph of the Egg, The" (Anderson), **I:** 113

Triumph of the Egg, The: A Book of Impressions from American Life in Tales and Poems (Anderson), **I:** 112, 114

Triumph of the Spider Monkey, The (Oates), **Supp. II Part 2:** 522

Triumphs of the Reformed Religion in America (Mather), **Supp. II Part 2:** 453

Trivia; or, the Art of Walking the Streets of London (Gay), **Supp. XIV:** 337

Trivia: Printed from the Papers of Anthony Woodhouse, Esq. (L. P. Smith), **Supp. XIV:** 336, 337–340

Trivial Breath (Wylie), **Supp. I Part 2:** 709, 722–724

Trocchi, Alexander, **Supp. XI:** 294, 295, 301

Troilus and Criseyde (Chaucer), **Retro. Supp. I:** 426

Trois contes (Flaubert), **IV:** 31, 37

Trojan Horse, The: A Play (MacLeish), **III:** 21

"Trojan Women, The" (Maxwell), **Supp. VIII:** 169

Troll Garden, The (Cather), **I:** 313, 314–316, 322; **Retro. Supp. I:** 5, 6, 8, 14

"Trolling for Blues" (Wilbur), **Supp. III Part 2:** 563–564

Trollope, Anthony, **I:** 10, 375; **II:** 192, 237; **III:** 51, 70, 281, 382; **Retro. Supp. I:** 361

Trombly, Albert Edmund, **Supp. I Part 2:** 403

"Troop Train" (Shapiro), **Supp. II Part 2:** 707

"Tropes of the Text" (Gass), **Supp. VI:** 88

Tropic of Cancer (H. Miller), **III:** 170, 171, 174, 177, 178–180, 181, 182, 183, 187, 190; **Supp. V:** 119; **Supp. X:** 187

Tropic of Capricorn (H. Miller), **III:** 170, 176–177, 178, 182, 183, 184, 187, 188–189, 190

Trotsky, Leon, **I:** 366; **II:** 562, 564; **IV:** 429

Trotter, W., **I:** 249

Troubled Island (opera; Hughes and Still), **Retro. Supp. I:** 203

Troubled Lovers in History (Goldbarth), **Supp. XII:** 176, 192–193

Trouble Follows Me (Macdonald, under Millar), **Supp. IV Part 2:** 466

Trouble in July (Caldwell), **I:** 297, 304–305, 306, 309

Trouble Island (Hughes), **Supp. I Part 1:** 328

"Trouble of Marcie Flint, The" (Cheever), **Supp. I Part 1:** 186

Trouble with Francis, The: An Autobiography (Francis), **Supp. IX:** 76, 77, 82, 84–85

Trouble with God, The (Francis), **Supp. IX:** 88

"Trouble with the Stars and Stripes" (Nye), **Supp. XIII:** 277

Trouillot, Michel-Rolphe, **Supp. X:** 14–15

Troupe, Quincy, **Retro. Supp. II:** 15, 111; **Supp. X:** 242

"Trout" (Hugo), **Supp. VI:** 135

Trout Fishing in America (Brautigan), **Supp. VIII:** 43

"Trouvée" (Bishop), **Retro. Supp. II:** 49

"Truce of the Bishop, The" (Frederic), **II:** 139–140

"Truck Stop: Minnesota" (Dunn), **Supp. XI:** 145–146

True and False: Heresy and Common Sense for the Actor (Mamet), **Supp. XIV:** 241, 243

Trueblood, Valerie, **Supp. XIII:** 306

True Confessions (Dunne), **Supp. IV Part 1:** 198

True Confessions (film), **Supp. IV Part 1:** 198

True History of the Conquest of New Spain, The (Castillo), **III:** 13

True Intellectual System of the Universe, The (Cuddleworth), **II:** 10

"True Love" (Olds), **Supp. X:** 212

Trueman, Matthew (pseudonym). *See* Lowell, James Russell

"True Morality" (Bell), **Supp. X:** 13

True Stories (Atwood), **Supp. XIII:** 34–35

"True Stories" (Atwood), **Supp. XIII:** 34

"True Stories of Bitches" (Mamet), **Supp. XIV:** 246, 252

"Truest Sport, The: Jousting with Sam and Charlie" (Wolfe), **Supp. III Part 2:** 581–582

"True Vine" (Wylie), **Supp. I Part 2:** 723

True West (Shepard), **Supp. III Part 2:** 433, 441, 445, 447, 448

Truman, Harry, **III:** 3

Truman Capote: In Which Various Friends, Enemies, Acquaintances, and Detractors Recall His Turbulent Career (Plimpton), **Supp. XVI:** 245

Truman Show, The (film), **Supp. XVI:** 271

Trumbo, Dalton, **Supp. I Part 1:** 295; **Supp. XIII:** 6

Trumbull, John, **Supp. II Part 1:** 65, 69, 70, 268

Trump, Donald, **Supp. IV Part 1:** 393

Trumpener, Katie, **Retro. Supp. I:** 380

"Trumpet Player" (Hughes), **Supp. I Part 1:** 333

Trumpet Shall Sound, The (Wilder), **IV:** 356

"Truro Bear, The" (Oliver), **Supp. VII:** 234

Truscott, Lucian K., **Supp. IV Part 2:** 683

Trust (Ozick), **Supp. V:** 257–258, 259, 260–263, 270, 272

Trust Me (Updike), **Retro. Supp. I:** 322

"Trust Yourself" (Emerson), **II:** 10

"Truth" (Emerson), **II:** 6

"Truth, The" (Jarrell), **II:** 381–382

"Truth about God, The" (Carson), **Supp. XII:** 105–106

"Truthful James" (Harte), **IV:** 196

"Truth Is, The" (Hogan), **Supp. IV Part 1:** 401–402

"Truth Is Forced, The" (Swenson), **Supp. IV Part 2:** 652

"Truth of the Matter, The" (Nemerov), **III:** 270

Truth Serum (Cooper), **Supp. XI:** 129

"Truth the Dead Know, The" (Sexton), **Supp. II Part 2:** 681

Trying to Save Piggy Sneed (Irving), **Supp. VI:** 19–165

"Trying to Talk with a Man" (Rich), **Supp. I Part 2:** 559

"Tryptich I" (Bell), **Supp. X:** 7

"Tryst, The" (Wharton), **Retro. Supp. I:** 378

"Try the Girl" (Chandler), **Supp. IV Part 1:** 125

"Ts'ai Chih" (Pound), **III:** 466

Tsvetayeva, Marina, **Supp. VIII:** 30

"T-2 Tanker Blues" (Snyder), **Supp. VIII:** 294

"Tuberoses" (E. Stoddard), **Supp. XV:** 282

Tuckerman, Frederick Goddard, **IV:** 144

"Tuesday, November 5th, 1940" (Benét), **Supp. XI:** 46, 52

"Tuesday April 25th 1966" (Olson), **Supp. II Part 2:** 585

"Tuesday Night at the Savoy Ballroom" (Komunyakaa), **Supp. XIII:** 132

Tuffield, Aviva, **Supp. XVI:**147, 148

"Tuft of Flowers, The" (Frost), **II:** 153; **Retro. Supp. I:** 126, 127

Tufts, James Hayden, **Supp. I Part 2:** 632

Tu Fu, **II:** 526; **Supp. XV:** 47

Tu Fu (Ayscough), **II:** 527

Tugwell, Rexford Guy, **Supp. I Part 2:** 645

"Tulip" (Hammett), **Supp. IV Part 1:** 356

"Tulip Man, The" (McCarriston), **Supp. XIV:**261

"Tulips" (Nye), **Supp. XIII:** 281

"Tulips" (Plath), **Retro. Supp. II:** 252–253; **Supp. I Part 2:** 540, 542, 544

"Tulips" (Snodgrass), **Supp. VI:** 325

Tulips and Chimneys (Cummings), **I:** 436, 437, 440, 445, 447

Tully, Jim, **III:** 103, 109

Tumble Tower (Modarressi and Tyler), **Supp. IV Part 2:** 657

"Tuned in Late One Night" (Stafford), **Supp. XI:** 327–328

Tunnel, The (Gass), **Supp. V:** 44; **Supp. VI:** 89–91, 94

"Tunnel, The" (Strand), **Supp. IV Part 2:** 622

"Tunnels" (Komunyakaa), **Supp. XIII:** 123

Tuqan, Fadwa, **Supp. XIII:** 278

Tura, Cosimo, **III:** 474–475

Turandot and Other Poems (Ashbery), **Supp. III Part 1:** 3

Turco, Lewis, **Supp. XV:** 118

Turgenev, Ivan Sergeevich, **I:** 106; **II:** 263, 271, 275, 280, 281, 288, 319, 320, 324–325, 338, 407; **III:** 461; **IV:** 17, 277; **Retro. Supp. I:** 215, 222; **Supp. VIII:** 167

Turgot, Anne Robert Jacques, **II:** 103; **Supp. I Part 1:** 250

"Turkey and Bones and Eating and We Liked It" (Stein), **IV:** 44

Turman, Glynn, **Supp. IV Part 1:** 362

Turnbull, Dr. George, **II:** 113

Turnbull, Lawrence, **Supp. I Part 1:** 352

"Turned" (Gilman), **Supp. XI:** 207

Turner, Addie, **IV:** 123

Turner, Darwin, **Supp. I Part 1:** 339; **Supp. IV Part 1:** 165

Turner, Frederick Jackson, **Supp. I Part 2:** 480, 481, 632, 640; **Supp. IV Part 2:** 596

Turner, Nat, **IV:** 113–114, 115, 116, 117

Turner, Patricia, **Supp. XIII:** 237

Turner, Russell. See Lacy, Ed

Turner, Victor, **Supp. IV Part 1:** 304

"Turning Away Variations on Estrangement" (Dickey), **Supp. IV Part 1:** 183

Turning Point, The (McCoy), **Supp. XIII:** 175

"Turning Thirty, I Contemplate Students Bicycling Home" (Dove), **Supp. IV Part 1:** 250

Turning Wind, A (Rukeyser), **Supp. VI:** 272–273, 279–280

Turn of the Screw, The (James), **Retro. Supp. I:** 219, 231; **Supp. IV Part 2:** 682

"Turn of the Screw, The" (James), **II:** 331–332; **Retro. Supp. I:** 228, 229, 231, 232

Turns and Movies and Other Tales in Verse (Aiken), **I:** 65

"Turn with the Sun, A" (Knowles), **Supp. XII:** 237–238

Turow, Scott, **Supp. V:** 220

Turrinus, Lucius Mamilius, **IV:** 373

"Turtle" (Hogan), **Supp. IV Part 1:** 401

Turtle, Swan (Doty), **Supp. XI:** 121–122

"Turtle, Swan" (Doty), **Supp. XI:** 121–122

Turtle Island (Snyder), **Supp. VIII:** 300–303

Turtle Moon (Hoffman), **Supp. X:** 77, 87–88, 89

"Turtle Shrine near Chittagong, The" (Nye), **Supp. XIII:** 277

Turturro, John, **Supp. XI:** 174

Tuscan Cities (Howells), **II:** 280

Tuskegee movement, **Supp. II Part 1:** 169, 172

Tuten, Frederic, **Supp. VIII:** 75, 76; **Supp. XIII:** 237, 249

Tuthill, Louisa Cavolne, **Supp. I Part 2:** 684

"Tutored Child, The" (Kunitz), **Supp. III Part 1:** 264

Tuttleton, James W., **Supp. IV Part 1:** 166, 168

"T.V.A." (Agee), **I:** 35

Tvedten, Brother Benet, **Supp. IV Part 2:** 505

"TV Men" (Carson), **Supp. XII:** 105, 112

Twain, Mark, **I:** 57, 103, 107, 109, 190, 192, 193, 195, 197, 203, 209, 245, 246, 247–250, 255, 256, 257, 260, 261, 292, 342, 418, 469, 485; **II:** 70, 140, 259, 262, 266–268, 271, 272, 274–275, 276, 277, 280, 285–286, 287, 288, 289, 301, 304, 306, 307, 312, 415, 432, 434, 436, 446, 457, 467, 475, 476, 482; **III:** 65, 101, 102, 112–113, 114, 220, 347, 357, 409, 453, 454, 504, 507, 554, 558, 572, 575, 576; **IV:** 190–213, 333, 349, 451; **Retro. Supp. I:** 169, 194, 195; **Retro. Supp. II:** 123; **Supp. I Part 1:** 37, 39, 44, 247, 251, 313, 317; **Supp. I Part 2:** 377, 385, 393, 410, 455, 456, 457, 473, 475, 579, 602, 604, 618, 629, 651, 660; **Supp. II Part 1:** 193, 344, 354, 385; **Supp. IV Part 1:** 386, 388; **Supp. IV Part 2:** 463, 468, 603, 607, 693; **Supp. V:** 44, 113, 131; **Supp. VIII:** 40, 189; **Supp. IX:** 14, 171; **Supp. X:** 51, 227; **Supp. XII:** 343; **Supp. XIII:** 1, 17; **Supp. XV:** 41; **Supp. XVI:**66, 208

"Twa Sisters, The" (ballad), **Supp. I Part 2:** 696

Twelfth Night (Shakespeare), **Supp. IV Part 1:** 83; **Supp. IX:** 14

Twelve Men (Dreiser), **Retro. Supp. II:** 94, 104

Twelve Moons (Oliver), **Supp. VII:** 231, 233–236, 238, 240

"12 O'Clock News" (Bishop), **Retro. Supp. II:** 48

Twelve Southerners, **IV:** 125; **Supp. X:** 25

Twelve Years a Slave (Northup), **Supp. XIV:**32

Twentieth Century Authors, **I:** 376, 527

"Twentieth Century Fiction and the Black Mask of Humanity" (Ellison),

Retro. Supp. II: 118

Twentieth Century Pleasures (Hass), **Supp. VI:** 103, 106, 109

"28" (Levine), **Supp. V:** 187, 191

"Twenty-Four Poems" (Schwartz), **Supp. II Part 2:** 646, 649

"2433 Agnes, First Home, Last House in Missoula" (Hugo), **Supp. VI:** 139–140

"Twenty Hill Hollow" (Muir), **Supp. IX:** 178

"Twenty Minutes" (Salter), **Supp. IX:** 260

"Twenty-One Love Poems" (Rich), **Supp. I Part 2:** 572–573

"Twenty-One Poems" (MacLeish), **III:** 19

Twenty Poems (Haines), **Supp. XII:** 204, 205–206

Twenty Poems of Anna Akhmatova (Kenyon), **Supp. VII:** 165–166

Twenty Questions: (Posed by Poems) (McClatchy), **Supp. XII:** 254, 259–262

27 Wagons Full of Cotton and Other One-Act Plays (T. Williams), **IV:** 381, 383

Twenty Thousand Leagues under the Sea (Verne), **I:** 480; **Supp. XI:** 63

"Twenty Years Ago" (Lindsay), **Supp. I Part 2:** 384, 399

Twenty Years at Hull-House (Addams), **Supp. I Part 1:** 3, 4, 11, 16

Twice over Lightly: New York Ten and Now (Hayes and Loos), **Supp. XVI:**195

Twice-Told Tales (Hawthorne), **I:** 354; **II:** 224; **III:** 412, 421; **Retro. Supp. I:** 154–155, 160

Twichell, Chase, **Supp. V:** 16

Twilight (Frost), **II:** 151

"Twilight's Last Gleaming" (Burroughs and Elvins), **Supp. III Part 1:** 93, 94, 101

Twilight Sleep (Wharton), **IV:** 320–322, 324–325, 327, 328; **Retro. Supp. I:** 381

"Twin, The" (Olds), **Supp. X:** 207

"Twin Beds in Rome" (Updike), **Retro. Supp. I:** 332

"Twins of Table Mountain, The" (Harte), **Supp. II Part 1:** 355

"Twist, The" (Olson), **Supp. II Part 2:** 570

Two: Gertrude Stein and Her Brother (Stein), **IV:** 43

Two Admirals, The (Cooper), **I:** 350

Two against One (F. Barthelme), **Supp. XI:** 32, 33, 36

"Two Boys" (Moore), **Supp. X:** 173

"Two Brothers, The" (Jewett), **Retro. Supp. II:** 132

Two-Character Play, The (T. Williams), **IV:** 382, 386, 393, 398

Two Citizens (Wright), **Supp. III Part 2:** 602–604

"Two Deer" (Bass), **Supp. XVI:**24

"Two Domains, The" (Goldbarth), **Supp. XII:** 192

"Two Environments, The" (Trilling), **Supp. III Part 2:** 510

"Two-Fisted Self Pity" (Broyard), **Supp. XI:** 348

Two for Texas (Burke), **Supp. XIV:**25, 34

"Two Friends" (Cather), **I:** 332

"Two Gardens in Linndale" (Robinson), **III:** 508

Two Gentlemen in Bonds (Ransom), **III:** 491–492

"Two Ghosts" (Francis), **Supp. IX:** 87

"Two Hangovers" (Wright), **Supp. III Part 2:** 596

Two-Headed Poems (Atwood), **Supp. XIII:** 34

Two Hot to Handle (Lacy), **Supp. XV:** 206

Two Hours to Doom (Bryant), **Supp. XI:** 302

"Two Ladies in Retirement" (Taylor), **Supp. V:** 320

Two Letters to the Citizens of the United States, and One to General Washington (Barlow), **Supp. II Part 1:** 80

"Two Lives, The" (Hogan), **Supp. IV Part 1:** 400, 402, 403, 406, 411

Two Long Poems (Stern), **Supp. IX:** 296

"Two Lovers and a Beachcomber by the Real Sea" (Plath), **Supp. I Part 2:** 536

Two Men (E. Stoddard), **Supp. XV:** 272, 273, 283–284

"Two Men" (McClatchy)", **Supp. XII:** 269

Two Men of Sandy Bar (Harte), **Supp. II Part 1:** 354

"Two Moods of Love" (Cullen), **Supp. IV Part 1:** 166

"Two Morning Monologues" (Bellow), **I:** 150; **Retro. Supp. II:** 20

Two-Ocean War, The (Morison), **Supp. I Part 2:** 491

"Two of Hearts" (Hogan), **Supp. IV Part 1:** 410

"Two on a Party" (T. Williams), **IV:** 388

"Two Pendants: For the Ears" (W. C. Williams), **Retro. Supp. I:** 423

"Two Poems of Going Home" (Dickey), **Supp. IV Part 1:** 182–183

"Two Portraits" (Chopin), **Supp. I Part 1:** 218

"Two Presences, The" (R. Bly), **Supp. IV Part 1:** 65

"Two Rivers" (Stegner), **Supp. IV Part 2:** 605

Tworkov, Jack, **Supp. XII:** 198

"Two Scenes" (Ashbery), **Supp. III Part 1:** 4

Two Serious Ladies (Jane Bowles), **Supp. IV Part 1:** 82

"Two Silences" (Carruth), **Supp. XVI:**55

"Two Sisters" (Farrell), **II:** 45

Two Sisters: A Memoir in the Form of a Novel (Vidal), **Supp. IV Part 2:** 679

"Two Sisters of Persephone" (Plath), **Retro. Supp. II:** 246

"Two Songs on the Economy of Abundance" (Agee), **I:** 28

"Two Tales of Clumsy" (Schnackenberg), **Supp. XV:** 258

"Two Temples, The" (Melville), **III:** 89–90

Two Thousand Seasons (Armah), **Supp. IV Part 1:** 373

Two Trains Running (Wilson), **Supp. VIII:** 345–348

"Two Tramps in Mudtime" (Frost), **II:** 164; **Retro. Supp. I:** 137; **Supp. IX:** 261

"Two Views of a Cadaver Room" (Plath), **Supp. I Part 2:** 538

"Two Villages" (Paley), **Supp. VI:** 227

"Two Voices in a Meadow" (Wilbur), **Supp. III Part 2:** 555

"Two Witches" (Frost), **Retro. Supp. I:** 135

"Two Words" (Francis), **Supp. IX:** 81

Two Years before the Mast (Dana), **I:** 351

Tyler, Anne, **Supp. IV Part 2:** 657–675; **Supp. V:** 227, 326; **Supp. VIII:** 141; **Supp. X:** 1, 77, 83, 85; **Supp. XII:** 307; **Supp. XVI:**37

Tyler, Royall, **I:** 344; **Retro. Supp. I:** 377

Tymms, Ralph, **Supp. IX:** 105

Tyndale, William, **II:** 15

Tyndall, John, **Retro. Supp. II:** 93

Typee: A Peep at Polynesian Life (Melville), **III:** 75–77, 79, 84; **Retro. Supp. I:** 245–246, 249, 252, 256

Typewriter Town (W. J. Smith), **Supp. XIII:** 332

"Typhus" (Simpson), **Supp. IX:** 277
Tyranny of the Normal (Fiedler), **Supp. XIII:** 107–108
"Tyranny of the Normal" (Fiedler), **Supp. XIII:** 107–108
"Tyrant of Syracuse" (MacLeish), **III:** 20
"Tyrian Businesses" (Olson), **Supp. II Part 2:** 567, 568, 569
Tytell, John, **Supp. XIV:**140
Tzara, Tristan, **Supp. III Part 1:** 104, 105
U
U and I (Baker), **Supp. XIII:** 45–47, 48, 52, 55
Überdie Seelenfrage (Fechner), **II:** 358
Ubu Roi (Jarry), **Supp. XV:** 178, 186
"Ulalume" (Poe), **III:** 427; **Retro. Supp. II:** 264, 266
Ulin, David, **Supp. XIII:** 244; **Supp. XVI:**74
Ullman, Leslie, **Supp. IV Part 2:** 550
Ultimate Good Luck, The (Ford), **Supp. V:** 57, 61–62
Ultima Thule (Longfellow), **II:** 490; **Retro. Supp. II:** 169
"Ultima Thule" (Nabokov), **Retro. Supp. I:** 274
Ultramarine (Carver), **Supp. III Part 1:** 137, 138, 147, 148
Ulysses (Joyce), **I:** 395, 475–476, 478, 479, 481; **II:** 42, 264, 542; **III:** 170, 398; **IV:** 103, 418, 428, 455; **Retro. Supp. I:** 59, 63, 290, 291; **Retro. Supp. II:** 121; **Supp. I Part 1:** 57; **Supp. III Part 2:** 618, 619; **Supp. IV Part 1:** 285; **Supp. IV Part 2:** 424; **Supp. V:** 261; **Supp. IX:** 102; **Supp. X:** 114; **Supp. XIII:** 43, 191; **Supp. XV:** 305
"*Ulysses,* Order and Myth" (Eliot), **Retro. Supp. I:** 63
Unaccountable Worth of the World, The (Price), **Supp. VI:** 267
Unamuno y Jugo, Miguel de, **III:** 310; **Supp. XV:** 79
"Unattached Smile, The" (Crews), **Supp. XI:** 101
"Unbelievable Thing Usually Goes to the Heart of the Story, The: Magic Realism in the Fiction of Rick Bass" (Dwyer), **Supp. XVI:**16
"Unbeliever, The" (Bishop), **Retro. Supp. II:** 43
"Unborn Song" (Rukeyser), **Supp. VI:** 274
Unbought Spirit: A John Jay Chapman Reader (Stone, ed.), **Supp. XIV:**54
Uncalled, The (Dunbar), **Supp. II Part 1:** 200, 211, 212

Uncertain Certainty, The: Interviews, Essays, and Notes on Poetry (Simic), **Supp. VIII:** 270, 273, 274
Uncertainty and Plenitude: Five Contemporary Poets (Stitt), **Supp. IX:** 299
"Uncle" (Levine), **Supp. V:** 186
"Uncle Christmas" (Ríos), **Supp. IV Part 2:** 552
"Uncle Jim's Baptist Revival Hymn" (Lanier and Lanier), **Supp. I Part 1:** 353
"Uncle Lot" (Stowe), **Supp. I Part 2:** 585–586
Uncle Remus Tales (Harris), **Supp. II Part 1:** 201
Uncle Tom's Cabin (Stowe), **II:** 291; **Supp. I Part 1:** 49; **Supp. I Part 2:** 410, 579, 582, 589–592; **Supp. II Part 1:** 170; **Supp. III Part 1:** 154, 171; **Supp. IX:** 19; **Supp. X:** 246, 249, 250; **Supp. XIII:** 95; **Supp. XVI:**82, 85, 88
Uncle Tom's Children (Wright), **IV:** 476, 478, 488; **Supp. II Part 1:** 228, 235
"Uncle Wiggily in Connecticut" (Salinger), **III:** 559–560, 563
"Unclouded Day, The" (Proulx), **Supp. VII:** 254–255
"Uncommon Visage" (Brodsky), **Supp. VIII:** 31
"Uncommon Woman: An Interview with Wendy Wasserstein" (Cohen), **Supp. XV:** 323
Uncommon Women and Others (Wasserstein), **Supp. XV:** 320–321, 322–323
Uncompromising Fictions of Cynthia Ozick (Pinsker), **Supp. V:** 272
"Unconscious Came a Beauty" (Swenson), **Supp. IV Part 2:** 646
"Uncreation, The" (Pinsky), **Supp. VI:** 245
"Undead, The" (Wilbur), **Supp. III Part 2:** 556
"Undefeated, The" (Hemingway), **II:** 250; **Retro. Supp. I:** 180
Under a Glass Bell (Nin), **Supp. X:** 186
"Under Ben Bulben" (Yeats), **Supp. V:** 220
Undercliff: Poems 1946–1953 (Eberhart), **I:** 528, 536–537
Under Cover (Goldbarth), **Supp. XII:** 177, 180, 193
Undercover Doctor (film), **Supp. XIII:** 170
"Under Cygnus" (Wilbur), **Supp. III Part 2:** 558

"Under Forty" (Trilling), **Supp. III Part 2:** 494
Underground Man, The (film), **Supp. IV Part 2:** 474
Underground Man, The (Macdonald), **Supp. IV Part 2:** 474, 475
"Under Libra: Weights and Measures" (Merrill), **Supp. III Part 1:** 328
Under Milk Wood (D. Thomas), **III:** 21
"Undersea" (Carson), **Supp. IX:** 21
Understanding Cynthia Ozick (Friedman), **Supp. V:** 273
Understanding Drama (Brooks and Heilman), **Supp. XIV:**12
Understanding E. L. Doctorow (Fowler), **Supp. IV Part 1:** 226
Understanding Fiction (Brooks and Warren), **IV:** 279; **Supp. XIV:**11
Understanding Flannery O'Connor (Whitt), **Retro. Supp. II:** 226
Understanding Nicholson Baker (Saltzman), **Supp. XIII:** 48
Understanding Poetry: An Anthology for College Students (Brooks and Warren), **IV:** 236; **Retro. Supp. I:** 40, 41; **Supp. XIV:**4–5
Understanding Tim O'Brien (Kaplan), **Supp. V:** 241
Understanding To Kill a Mockingbird: A Student Casebook to Issues, Sources, and Documents (Johnson), **Supp. VIII:** 127
Undertaker's Garland, The (Wilson and Bishop), **IV:** 427
"Under the Cedarcroft Chestnut" (Lanier), **Supp. I Part 1:** 364
"Under the Harbour Bridge" (Komunyakaa), **Supp. XIII:** 125
"Under the Influence" (Sanders), **Supp. XVI:**274, 277
Under the Lilacs (Alcott), **Supp. I Part 1:** 42–43, 44
"Under the Maud Moon" (Kinnell), **Supp. III Part 1:** 246–247
Under the Mountain Wall: A Chronicle of Two Seasons in the Stone Age (Matthiessen), **Supp. V:** 202
"Under the Rose" (Pynchon), **Supp. II Part 2:** 620
Under the Sea-Wind: A Naturalist's Picture of Ocean Life (Carson), **Supp. IX:** 19, 22–23
Under the Sign of Saturn (Sontag), **Supp. III Part 2:** 451, 452, 458, 470–471
"Under the Sign of Saturn" (Sontag), **Supp. III Part 2:** 470
"Under the Sky" (Bowles), **Supp. IV Part 1:** 87

"Under the Willows" (Lowell), **Supp. I Part 2:** 416

Under the Willows and Other Poems (Lowell), **Supp. I Part 2:** 424

Underwood, Wilbur, **Retro. Supp. II:** 79

Underworld (DeLillo), **Supp. VI:** 2, 4–5, 6–7, 8, 9, 10, 11, 13–15; **Supp. XI:** 68

Undine (La Motte-Fouqué), **II:** 212; **III:** 78

Undiscovered Country, The (Howells), **II:** 282

"Undressing, The" (C. Frost), **Supp. XV:** 98

Uneasy Chair, The (Stegner), **Supp. IV Part 2:** 599

"Unemployed, Disabled, and Insane, The" (Haines), **Supp. XII:** 211–212

Unending Blues (Simic), **Supp. VIII:** 278–279

"Unexpressed" (Dunbar), **Supp. II Part 1:** 199

"Unfinished Bronx, The" (Paley), **Supp. VI:** 228

"Unfinished Poems" (Eliot), **I:** 579

"Unfinished Song" (C. Frost), **Supp. XV:** 97

Unfinished Woman, An (Hellman), **Supp. I Part 1:** 292, 293, 294; **Supp. IV Part 1:** 12, 353–354; **Supp. IX:** 196, 200–201

Unforeseen Wilderness, The: An Essay on Kentucky's Red River Gorge (Berry), **Supp. X:** 28, 29, 30, 36

Unforgotten Years (L. P. Smith), **Supp. XIV:**333, 334, 335, 336, 347

"Unfortunate Coincidence" (Parker), **Supp. IX:** 190

Unframed Originals (Merwin), **Supp. III Part 1:** 341

Ungar, Sanford, **Supp. XI:** 228

Ungaretti, Giuseppe, **Supp. V:** 337

Unguided Tour (Sontag), **Supp. III Part 2:** 452

"Unheimliche, Das" (The Uncanny) (Freud), **Supp. XVI:**157–158

"Unidentified Flying Object" (Hayden), **Supp. II Part 1:** 368

"Unifying Principle, The" (Ammons), **Supp. VII:** 28

"Union" (Hughes), **Supp. I Part 1:** 331

"Union Street: San Francisco, Summer 1975" (Carver), **Supp. III Part 1:** 138

United States Army in World War II (Morison), **Supp. I Part 2:** 490

United States Constitution, **I:** 6, 283

United States Essays, 1951–1991

(Vidal), **Supp. IV Part 2:** 678, 687

United States of Poetry, The (television series), **Supp. XIII:** 274

"Unity through Diversity" (Locke), **Supp. XIV:**212, 213

Universal Baseball Asociation, Inc., J. Henry Waugh, Prop., The (Coover), **Supp. V:** 39, 41–42, 44, 46

Universal Passion (Young), **III:** 111

"Universe of Death, The" (H. Miller), **III:** 184

Universe of Time, A (Anderson), **II:** 27, 28, 45, 46, 48, 49

"Universities" (Emerson), **II:** 6

"Universities: A Mirage? " (Mora), **Supp. XIII:** 219

"University" (Shapiro), **Supp. II Part 2:** 704–705, 717

"University Avenue" (Mora), **Supp. XIII:** 216

"University Days" (Thurber), **Supp. I Part 2:** 605

"University Hospital, Boston" (Oliver), **Supp. VII:** 235

"Unknowable, The" (Levine), **Supp. V:** 195

"Unknown Girl in the Maternity Ward" (Sexton), **Supp. II Part 2:** 676

"Unknown Love, The" (Chandler), **Supp. IV Part 1:** 120

"Unknown War, The" (Sandburg), **III:** 594

Unleashed (anthology), **Supp. XI:** 132

"Unlighted Lamps" (Anderson), **I:** 112

Unloved Wife, The (Alcott), **Supp. I Part 1:** 33

Unmarried Woman, An (film), **Supp. IV Part 1:** 303

"Unnatural Mother, The" (Gilman), **Supp. XI:** 207

"Unnatural State of the Unicorn" (Komunyakaa), **Supp. XIII:** 119

"Unparalleled Adventure of One Hans Pfaall, The" (Poe), **III:** 424

Unprecedented Era, The (Goebbels), **III:** 560

"Unprofitable Servant, The" (O. Henry), **Supp. II Part 1:** 403

Unpublished Poems of Emily Dickinson (Bianchi and Hampson, ed.), **Retro. Supp. I:** 35

Unpunished (Gilman), **Supp. XI:** 208

"Unreal City" (Eliot), **Supp. XV:** 218

"Unreasoning Heart" (Untermeyer), **Supp. XV:** 309

"Unsaid" (Gioia), **Supp. XV:** 129

"Unseen, The" (Pinsky), **Supp. VI:** 243–244

"Unseen, The" (Singer), **Retro. Supp. II:** 307

Unseen Hand, The (Shepard), **Supp. III Part 2:** 439, 445–446

Unselected Poems (Levine), **Supp. V:** 179

Unsettling of America, The: Culture and Agriculture (Berry), **Supp. X:** 22, 26, 29, 32, 33, 35; **Supp. XIV:**177, 179

Unspeakable Gentleman, The (Marquand), **III:** 53–54, 60, 63

Unspeakable Practices, Unnatural Acts (Barthelme), **Supp. IV Part 1:** 39

"Unspeakable Things Unspoken: The Afro-American Presence in American Literature" (Morrison), **Supp. III Part 1:** 375, 377–379

"Untelling, The" (Strand), **Supp. IV Part 2:** 629

Unterecker, John, **I:** 386

Untermeyer, Jean Starr, **II:** 530; **Supp. XV:** 294, 295, 303, 307, 308, 310

Untermeyer, Louis, **II:** 516–517, 530, 532; **III:** 268; **Retro. Supp. I:** 124, 133, 136; **Supp. III Part 1:** 2; **Supp. IX:** 76; **Supp. XIV:**119, 123; **Supp. XV:** 293–318

Untimely Papers (Bourne), **I:** 218, 233

"Untitled" (C. Frost), **Supp. XV:** 103

"Untitled Blues" (Komunyakaa), **Supp. XIII:** 117

"Untrustworthy Speaker, The" (Glück), **Supp. V:** 86

"Unused" (Anderson), **I:** 112, 113

Unvanquished, The (Faulkner), **II:** 55, 67–68, 71; **Retro. Supp. I:** 84; **Supp. I Part 2:** 450

"Unvexed Isles, The" (Warren), **IV:** 253

"Unwedded" (Larcom), **Supp. XIII:** 144

"Unweepables, The" (Karr), **Supp. XI:** 243

Unwelcome Words (Bowles), **Supp. IV Part 1:** 93, 94

"Unwelcome Words" (Bowles), **Supp. IV Part 1:** 94, 95

Unwin, T. Fisher, **Supp. XI:** 202

"Unwithered Garland, The" (Kunitz), **Supp. III Part 1:** 265

Unwobbling Pivot, The (Pound, trans.), **III:** 472

"Unwritten, The" (Merwin), **Supp. III Part 1:** 352

"Unwritten Law" (Glück), **Supp. V:** 91

Up (Sukenick), **Supp. V:** 39

Up Above the World (Bowles), **Supp. IV Part 1:** 82, 91, 92

"Up and Down" (Merrill), **Supp. III Part 1:** 328

Upanishads, **IV:** 183

Up Country: Poems of New England (Kumin), **Supp. IV Part 2:** 446, 447–448, 453

"Update" (Dunn), **Supp. XI:** 150–151

Updike, John, **I:** 54; **III:** 572; **IV:** 214–235; **Retro. Supp. I:** 116, 317–338; **Retro. Supp. II:** 213, 279, 280; **Supp. I Part 1:** 186, 196; **Supp. IV Part 2:** 657; **Supp. V:** 23, 43, 95, 119; **Supp. VIII:** 151, 167, 236; **Supp. IX:** 208; **Supp. XI:** 65, 66, 99, 140; **Supp. XII:** 140, 296, 298, 310; **Supp. XIII:** 45–46, 47, 52; **Supp. XIV:**79, 93, 111; **Supp. XVI:**205, 207, 220

Updike, Mrs. Wesley, **IV:** 218, 220

Up from Slavery (Washington), **Supp. II Part 1:** 169; **Supp. IX:** 19

Upham, Thomas Goggswell, **II:** 487

"Upholsterers, The" (Lardner), **II:** 435

"Up in Michigan" (Hemingway), **II:** 263

Upjohn, Richard, **IV:** 312

"Upon a Spider Catching a Fly" (Taylor), **IV:** 161

"Upon a Wasp Child with Cold" (Taylor), **IV:** 161

"Upon Meeting Don L. Lee, in a Dream" (Dove), **Supp. IV Part 1:** 244

"Upon My Dear and Loving Husband His Going into England, Jan. 16, 1661" (Bradstreet), **Supp. I Part 1:** 110

"Upon Returning to the Country Road" (Lindsay), **Supp. I Part 2:** 382

"Upon the Burning of Our House, July 10th, 1666" (Bradstreet), **Supp. I Part 1:** 107–108, 122

"Upon the Sweeping Flood" (Taylor), **IV:** 161

"Upon Wedlock, and Death of Children" (Taylor), **IV:** 144, 147, 161

"Upset, An" (Merrill), **Supp. III Part 1:** 336

Upstairs and Downstairs (Vonnegut), **Supp. II Part 2:** 757

Upstate (Wilson), **IV:** 447

Upton, Lee, **Supp. X:** 209

"Upturned Face" (Crane), **I:** 423

Upward, Allen, **Supp. I Part 1:** 262

Upward, Edward, **Supp. XIV:**159, 160

"Upward Moon and the Downward Moon, The" (R. Bly), **Supp. IV Part 1:** 71

Urania: A Rhymed Lesson (Holmes), **Supp. I Part 1:** 300

"Urban Convalescence, An" (Merrill), **Supp. III Part 1:** 322–324

"Urban Renewal" (Komunyakaa),

Supp. XIII: 113

Urdang, Constance, **Supp. XV:** 74

"Urganda and Fatima" (Rowson), **Supp. XV:** 234

Urial Accosta: A Play (Reznikoff), **Supp. XIV:**282, 288

Urich, Robert, **Supp. V:** 228

"Uriel" (Emerson), **II:** 19

Uris, Leon, **Supp. IV Part 1:** 285, 379

Uroff, Margaret D., **Supp. I Part 2:** 542

"Us" (Sexton), **Supp. II Part 2:** 687

U.S. 1 (Rukeyser), **Supp. VI:** 272, 278, 283, 285

"U.S. Commercial Orchid, The" (Agee), **I:** 35

U.S.A. (Dos Passos), **I:** 379, 475, 478, 482–488, 489, 490, 491, 492, 493, 494, 495; **Retro. Supp. II:** 197; **Supp. I Part 2:** 646; **Supp. III Part 1:** 104, 105; **Supp. XIV:**24

"U.S.A. School of Writing, The" (Bishop), **Retro. Supp. II:** 43

"Used-Boy Raisers, The" (Paley), **Supp. VI:** 218, 228

"Used Cars on Oahu" (Nye), **Supp. XIII:** 282

"Used Side of the Sofa, The" (Ríos), **Supp. IV Part 2:** 551

Use of Fire, The (Price), **Supp. VI:** 265

"Use of Force, The" (W. C. Williams), **Retro. Supp. I:** 424

Use of Poetry and the Use of Criticism, The (Eliot), **Retro. Supp. I:** 65

Uses of Enchantment, The: The Meaning and Importance of Fairy Tales (Bettelheim), **Supp. XIV:**126

Uses of Enchantment, The: The Meaning and Importance of Fairy Tales (Bettleheim), **Supp. X:** 77

"Uses of Hell, The" (E. Hoffman), **Supp. XVI:**154

"Uses of Hell, The: An Exchange"(Novick, Katz, and Szulc), **Supp. XVI:**154

Uses of Literacy, The (Hoggart), **Supp. XIV:**299

"Uses of Poetry, The" (W. C. Williams), **Retro. Supp. I:** 412

"Uses of the Blues, The" (Baldwin), **Retro. Supp. II:** 8

"USFS 1919: The Ranger, the Cook, and a Hole in the Sky" (Maclean), **Supp. XIV:**230, 234

Ushant: An Essay (Aiken), **I:** 49, 54, 55, 56, 57

"Usher 11" (Bradbury), **Supp. I Part 2:** 622

"Using Parrots to Kill Mockingbirds: Yet Another Racial Prosecution and

Wrongful Conviction in Maycomb" (Fair), **Supp. VIII:** 128

Usual Star, The (Doolittle), **Supp. I Part 1:** 270

"Usurpation (Other People's Stories)" (Ozick), **Supp. V:** 268, 271

Utopia 14 (Vonnegut), **Supp. II Part 2:** 757

V

V. (Pynchon), **Supp. II Part 2:** 618, 620–622, 627–630; **Supp. IV Part 1:** 279

V. S. Naipaul: An Introduction to His Work (Theroux), **Supp. VIII:** 314, 318

"V. S. Pritchett's Apprenticeship" (Maxwell), **Supp. VIII:** 172

"V. V." (Alcott), **Supp. I Part 1:** 37

"Vacation" (Stafford), **Supp. XI:** 321, 322

"Vacation Trip" (Stafford), **Supp. XI:** 322

Vachel Lindsay: A Poet in America (Masters), **Supp. I Part 2:** 473, 474

"Vachel Lindsay: The Midwest as Utopia" (Whitney), **Supp. I Part 2:** 403

"Vachel Lindsay Writes to Floyd Dell" (Tanselle), **Supp. I Part 2:** 403

"Vacillation" (Yeats), **Supp. XV:** 253

Vadim, Roger, **Supp. XI:** 293, 307

"Vag" (Dos Passos), **I:** 487–488

Valentine, Jean, **Supp. V:** 92

Valentine, Saint, **IV:** 396

Valentino, Rudolph, **I:** 483

Valéry, Paul, **II:** 543, 544; **III:** 279, 409, 428, 609; **IV:** 79, 91, 92, 428, 443; **Retro. Supp. II:** 187

"Valhalla" (Francis), **Supp. IX:** 77

Valhalla and Other Poems (Francis), **Supp. IX:** 76

Validity in Interpretation (Hirsch), **Supp. XIV:**15

Valitsky, Ken, **Supp. XII:** 7

Vallejo, César, **Supp. V:** 332; **Supp. IX:** 271; **Supp. XIII:** 114, 315, 323

"Valley, The" (Bass), **Supp. XVI:**20, 22

"Valley Between, The" (Marshall), **Supp. XI:** 278

Valley of Decision, The (Wharton), **IV:** 311, 315; **Retro. Supp. I:** 365–367

Valley of the Moon, The (London), **II:** 467, 481

"Valley of Unrest, The" (Poe), **III:** 411

Valli, Alida, **Supp. IV Part 2:** 520

"Valor" (Bausch), **Supp. VII:** 54

Valparaiso (DeLillo), **Supp. VI:** 4, 12

"Value of a Place, The" (Bass), **Supp. XVI:**18

"Values and Fictions" (Toomer), **Supp. III Part 2:** 485–486

"Values and Imperatives" (Locke), **Supp. XIV:**199, 202, 212

Values of Veblen, The: A Critical Appraisal (Rosenberg), **Supp. I Part 2:** 650

"Vampire" (Karr), **Supp. XI:** 241

Vampire Armand, The (Rice), **Supp. VII:** 290, 294–295

Vampire Chronicles, The (Rice), **Supp. VII:** 290

Vampire Lestat, The (Rice), **Supp. VII:** 290–292, 298, 299

Van Buren, Martin, **II:** 134, 312; **III:** 473

Vande Kieft, Ruth M., **IV:** 260

Vanderbilt, Cornelius, **III:** 14

Van Dine, S. S., **Supp. IV Part 1:** 341

Van Doren, Carl, **I:** 252–253, 423; **II:** 103, 111, 112; **Supp. I Part 2:** 474, 486, 707, 709, 717, 718, 727; **Supp. II Part 1:** 395; **Supp. VIII:** 96–97

Van Doren, Mark, **I:** 168; **III:** 4, 23, 589; **Supp. I Part 2:** 604; **Supp. III Part 2:** 626; **Supp. VIII:** 231; **Supp. IX:** 266, 268; **Supp. XV:** 152, 305, 307

Vandover and the Brute (Norris), **III:** 314, 315, 316, 320–322, 328, 333, 334

Van Duyn, Mona, **Supp. IX:** 269

Van Dyke, Annette, **Supp. IV Part 1:** 327

Van Dyke, Henry, **I:** 223; **II:** 456

Van Gogh, Vincent, **I:** 27; **IV:** 290; **Supp. I Part 2:** 451; **Supp. IV Part 1:** 284

Van Gogh's Room at Arles (Elkin), **Supp. VI:** 56

"Vanisher, The" (Whittier), **Supp. I Part 2:** 691

"Vanishing Red, The" (Frost), **Retro. Supp. II:** 47

"Vanity" (B. Diop), **Supp. IV Part 1:** 16

Vanity Fair (Thackeray), **I:** 354; **II:** 91; **III:** 70; **Supp. IX:** 200

"Vanity of All Wordly Things, The" (Bradstreet), **Supp. I Part 1:** 102, 119

Vanity of Duluoz (Kerouac), **Supp. III Part 1:** 221, 222

"Vanity of Existence, The" (Freneau), **Supp. II Part 1:** 262

Van Matre, Lynn, **Supp. V:** 126

Vann, Barbara, **Supp. XV:** 187

Vanquished, The (Faulkner), **I:** 205

Van Rensselaer, Stephen, **I:** 351

Van Vechten, Carl, **I:** 295; **IV:** 76;

Supp. I Part 1: 324, 327, 332; **Supp. I Part 2:** 715; **Supp. II Part 2:** 725–751; **Supp. X:** 247; **Supp. XVI:**135

Vanzetti, Bartolomeo, **I:** 482, 486, 490, 494; **II:** 38–39, 426; **III:** 139–140; **Supp. I Part 2:** 446, 610, 611; **Supp. V:** 288–289; **Supp. IX:** 199

"Vapor Trail Reflected in the Frog Pond" (Kinnell), **Supp. III Part 1:** 242–243

"Vapor Trails" (Snyder), **Supp. VIII:** 298

"Variation: Ode to Fear" (Warren), **IV:** 241

"Variation on a Sentence" (Bogan), **Supp. III Part 1:** 60

"Variation on Gaining a Son" (Dove), **Supp. IV Part 1:** 248

"Variation on Pain" (Dove), **Supp. IV Part 1:** 248

"Variations: The air is sweetest that a thistle guards" (Merrill), **Supp. III Part 1:** 321

"Variations: White Stag, Black Bear" (Merrill), **Supp. III Part 1:** 321

"Varick Street" (Bishop), **Supp. I Part 1:** 90, 92

Varieties of Metaphysical Poetry, The (Eliot), **Retro. Supp. I:** 65

Varieties of Religious Experience, The (William James), **II:** 344, 353, 354, 359–360, 362; **IV:** 28, 291; **Supp. IX:** 19

Variety (film), **Supp. XII:** 7

Variorum (Whitman), **Retro. Supp. I:** 406

Various Miracles (Shields), **Supp. VII:** 318–320, 323, 324

"Various Miracles" (Shields), **Supp. VII:** 318–319, 324

Various Poems (Zach), **Supp. XV:** 86

"Various Tourists" (Connell), **Supp. XIV:**79

"Varmint Question, The" (Leopold), **Supp. XIV:**180–181

Vasari, Giorgio, **Supp. I Part 2:** 450; **Supp. III Part 1:** 5

Vasquez, Robert, **Supp. V:** 180

Vassall Morton (Parkman), **Supp. II Part 2:** 595, 597–598

Vasse, W. W., **III:** 478

Vaudeville for a Princess (Schwartz), **Supp. II Part 2:** 661–662

Vaughan, Henry, **IV:** 151; **Supp. XV:** 251

Vaughn, Robert, **Supp. XI:** 343

Vazirani, Reetika, **Supp. XIII:** 133

Veblen (Hobson), **Supp. I Part 2:** 650

Veblen, Andrew, **Supp. I Part 2:** 640

Veblen, Mrs. Thorstein (Ellen Rolfe), **Supp. I Part 2:** 641

Veblen, Oswald, **Supp. I Part 2:** 640

Veblen, Thorstein, **I:** 104, 283, 475–476, 483, 498, 511; **II:** 27, 272, 276, 287; **Supp. I Part 2:** 628–650; **Supp. IV Part 1:** 22

Veblenism: A New Critique (Dobriansky), **Supp. I Part 2:** 648, 650

"Veblen's Attack on Culture" (Adorno), **Supp. I Part 2:** 650

Vechten, Carl Van, **Retro. Supp. I:** 199

Vedanta for Modern Man (Isherwood, ed.), **Supp. XIV:**164

Vedanta for the Western World (Isherwood, ed.), **Supp. XIV:**164

Vedas, **IV:** 183

Vega, Janine Pommy, **Supp. XIV:**148

Vega, Lope de, **Retro. Supp. I:** 285; **Supp. III Part 1:** 341, 347

Vegetable, The (Fitzgerald), **Retro. Supp. I:** 105; **Supp. IX:** 57

Vegetable, The, or From President to Postman (Fitzgerald), **II:** 91

Veinberg, Jon, **Supp. V:** 180; **Supp. XIII:** 313; **Supp. XV:** 76–77, 86

Vein of Iron (Glasgow), **II:** 175, 186, 188–189, 191, 192, 194

Vein of Riches, A (Knowles), **Supp. XII:** 249

Velie, Alan R., **Supp. IV Part 2:** 486

Velocities: New and Selected Poems, 1966–1992 (Dobyns), **Supp. XIII:** 86–87, 87, 88

"Velorio" (Cisneros), **Supp. VII:** 66

"Velvet Shoes" (Wylie), **Supp. I Part 2:** 711, 714

Venant, Elizabeth, **Supp. XI:** 343

Vencloca, Thomas, **Supp. VIII:** 29

Vendler, Helen H., **Retro. Supp. I:** 297; **Retro. Supp. II:** 184, 191; **Supp. I Part 1:** 77, 78, 92, 95; **Supp. I Part 2:** 565; **Supp. IV Part 1:** 245, 247, 249, 254, 257; **Supp. IV Part 2:** 448; **Supp. V:** 78, 82, 189, 343; **Supp. XII:** 187, 189; **Supp. XV:** 20, 184

"Venetian Blind, The" (Jarrell), **II:** 382–383

Venetian Glass Nephew, The (Wylie), **Supp. I Part 2:** 707, 709, 714, 717–719, 721, 724

Venetian Life (Howells), **II:** 274, 277, 279

Venetian Vespers, The (Hecht), **Supp. X:** 57, 65–69

"Venetian Vespers, The" (Hecht), **Supp. X:** 65, 66–67

Venice Observed (McCarthy), **II:** 562

Ventadorn, Bernard de, **Supp. IV Part 1:** 146

"Ventriloquists' Conversations" (Gentry), **Supp. IV Part 1:** 236

"Venus, Cupid, Folly and Time" (Taylor), **Supp. V:** 322–323

Venus and Adonis (film), **Supp. IV Part 1:** 82

Venus and Don Juan (C. Frost), **Supp. XV:** 93, 102–103, 104, 107

"Venus and Don Juan" (C. Frost), **Supp. XV:** 103

Venus Blue (Sobin), **Supp. XVI:**293–294, 294

Venus in Sparta (Auchincloss), **Supp. IV Part 1:** 25

"Venus's-flytraps" (Komunyakaa), **Supp. XIII:** 126, 127

"Veracruz" (Hayden), **Supp. II Part 1:** 371, 373

Verga, Giovanni, **II:** 271, 275

Verghese, Abraham, **Supp. X:** 160

Verhaeren, Emile, **I:** 476; **II:** 528, 529

Verlaine, Paul, **II:** 529, 543; **III:** 466; **IV:** 79, 80, 86, 286; **Retro. Supp. I:** 56, 62; **Retro. Supp. II:** 326

"Vermeer" (Nemerov), **III:** 275, 278, 280

Vermeer, Jan, **Retro. Supp. I:** 335

"Vermont" (Carruth), **Supp. XVI:**54

Vermont Notebook, The (Ashbery), **Supp. III Part 1:** 1

"Vernal Ague, The" (Freneau), **Supp. II Part 1:** 258

Verne, Jules, **I:** 480; **Retro. Supp. I:** 270; **Supp. XI:** 63

Vernon, John, **Supp. X:** 15

Verplanck, Gulian C., **Supp. I Part 1:** 155, 156, 157, 158

Verrazano, Giovanni da, **Supp. I Part 2:** 496, 497

Verse (Zawacki), **Supp. VIII:** 272

"Verse for Urania" (Merrill), **Supp. III Part 1:** 329, 330

Verses (Wharton), **Retro. Supp. I:** 362

Verses, Printed for Her Friends (Jewett), **II:** 406

"Verses for Children" (Lowell), **II:** 516

"Verses Made at Sea in a Heavy Gale" (Freneau), **Supp. II Part 1:** 262

"Verses on the Death of T. S. Eliot" (Brodsky), **Supp. VIII:** 19

"Version of a Fragment of Simonides" (Bryant), **Supp. I Part 1:** 153, 155

Verulam, Baron. *See* Bacon, Francis

Very, Jones, **III:** 507

"Very Hot Sun in Bermuda, The" (Jackson), **Supp. IX:** 126

Very Old Bones (W. Kennedy), **Supp.**

VII: 133, 148, 150–153

"Very Proper Gander, The" (Thurber), **Supp. I Part 2:** 610

"Very Short Story, A" (Hemingway), **II:** 252; **Retro. Supp. I:** 173

"Vesalius in Zante" (Wharton), **Retro. Supp. I:** 372

Vesey, Denmark, **Supp. I Part 2:** 592

Vesey, Desmond, **Supp. XIV:**162

"Vespers" (Auden), **Supp. II Part 1:** 23

"Vespers" (Glück), **Supp. V:** 88

Vestal Lady on Brattle, The (Corso), **Supp. XII:** 119, 120–121, 134

Vested Interests and the Common Man, The (Veblen), **Supp. I Part 2:** 642

"Vesuvius at Home" (Rich), **Retro. Supp. I:** 42

"Veteran, The" (Crane), **I:** 413

"Veterans' Cemetery" (Gioia), **Supp. XV:** 117

"Veteran Sirens" (Robinson), **III:** 512, 524

"Veterinarian" (X. J. Kennedy), **Supp. XV:** 168

"Vetiver" (Ashbery), **Supp. III Part 1:** 26

"Via Dieppe-Newhaven" (H. Miller), **III:** 183

"Via Negativa" (Salter), **Supp. IX:** 257

Vicar of Wakefeld, The (Goldsmith), **I:** 216

"Vicissitudes of the Avant-Garde, The" (Gass), **Supp. VI:** 91

Victim, The (Bellow), **I:** 144, 145, 147, 149, 150, 151, 152, 153, 155, 156, 158, 159, 164; **IV:** 19; **Retro. Supp. II:** 21, 22, 34

"Victor" (Mumford), **Supp. II Part 2:** 476

Victoria (Rowson), **Supp. XV:** 231

"Victories" (Untermeyer), **Supp. XV:** 300

"Victory at Sea" (television series), **Supp. I Part 2:** 490

"Victory comes late" (Dickinson), **Retro. Supp. I:** 45

"Victory of the Moon, The" (Crane), **I:** 420

Vidal, Gore, **II:** 587; **IV:** 383; **Supp. IV Part 1:** 22, 35, 92, 95, 198; **Supp. IV Part 2:** 677–696; **Supp. IX:** 96; **Supp. X:** 186, 195; **Supp. XIV:**156, 170, 338

Viebahn, Fred, **Supp. IV Part 1:** 248

Viera, Joseph M., **Supp. XI:** 178, 186

Viereck, Peter, **Supp. I Part 2:** 403

Viertel, Berthold, **Supp. XIV:**165

Viertel, Salka, **Supp. XVI:**192

Viet Journal (Jones), **Supp. XI:** 230–231

Vietnam (McCarthy), **II:** 578–579

"Vietnam in Me, The" (O'Brien), **Supp. V:** 241, 252

Vie unanime, La (Romains), **I:** 227

"View, The" (Roussel), **Supp. III Part 1:** 15, 16, 21

View from 80, The (Cowley), **Supp. II Part 1:** 141, 144, 153

View from the Bridge, A (A. Miller), **III:** 147, 148, 156, 158, 159–160

View of My Own, A: Essays in Literature and Society (Hardwick), **Supp. III Part 1:** 194, 200

"View of the Capital from the Library of Congress" (Bishop), **Retro. Supp. II:** 45

View of the Soil and Climate of the United States, A (Brown, trans.), **Supp. I Part 1:** 146

"View of the Woods, A" (O'Connor), **III:** 349, 351, 358; **Retro. Supp. II:** 237

"Views of the Mysterious Hill: The Appearance of Parnassus in American Poetry" (Strand), **Supp. IV Part 2:** 631

"Vigil" (Karr), **Supp. XI:** 241

"Vigil, The" (Dante), **III:** 542

Vigny, Alfred Victor de, **II:** 543

Vildrac, Charles, **Supp. XV:** 50

Vile Bodies (Waugh), **Supp. I Part 2:** 607

Villa, Pancho, **I:** 210; **III:** 584

"Village Blacksmith, The" (Longfellow), **Retro. Supp. II:** 167, 168; **Supp. I Part 2:** 409

Village Hymns, a Supplement to Dr. Watts's Psalms and Hymns (Nettleton), **I:** 458

"Village Improvement Parade, The" (Lindsay), **Supp. I Part 2:** 388, 389

Village Magazine, The (Lindsay), **Supp. I Part 2:** 379–380, 382

Village Virus, The (Lewis), **II:** 440

"Villanelle at Sundown" (Justice), **Supp. VII:** 119, 122–123

"Villanelle of Change" (Robinson), **III:** 524

Villard, Oswald, **Supp. I Part 1:** 332

"Villa Selene" (Simpson), **Supp. IX:** 279

Villon, François, **II:** 544; **III:** 9, 174, 592; **Retro. Supp. I:** 286; **Supp. I Part 1:** 261; **Supp. III Part 1:** 235, 243, 249, 253; **Supp. III Part 2:** 560; **Supp. IX:** 116

"Villonaud for This Yule" (Pound), **Retro. Supp. I:** 286

Vindication of the Rights of Woman (Wollstonecraft), **Supp. I Part 1:** 126; **Supp. XI:** 203

Vines, Lois Davis, **Retro. Supp. II:** 261

"Vintage Thunderbird, A" (Beattie), **Supp. V:** 27

Vinz, Mark, **Supp. X:** 117

Violence (Bausch), **Supp. VII:** 48–49, 54

Violent Bear It Away, The (O'Connor), **III:** 339, 345–348, 350, 351, 354, 355, 356, 357; **Retro. Supp. II:** 233, 234–236

"Violent Vet, The" (O'Brien), **Supp. V:** 238

Violin (Rice), **Supp. VII:** 302

Viorst, Judith, **Supp. X:** 153

Viper Run (Karr), **Supp. XI:** 248–251

Virgil, **I:** 312, 322, 587; **II:** 133, 542; **IV:** 137, 359; **Retro. Supp. I:** 135; **Supp. I Part 1:** 153; **Supp. I Part 2:** 494; **Supp. IV Part 2:** 631

"Virgin and the Dynamo" (Adams), **III:** 396

"Virgin Carrying a Lantern, The" (Stevens), **IV:** 80

Virginia (Glasgow), **II:** 175, 178, 181–182, 193, 194

"Virginia" (Lindsay), **Supp. I Part 2:** 398

"Virginia Britannia" (Moore), **III:** 198, 208–209

"Virginians Are Coming Again, The" (Lindsay), **Supp. I Part 2:** 399

"Virgin Violeta" (Porter), **III:** 454

"Virility" (Ozick), **Supp. V:** 262, 265

Virtual Light (W. Gibson), **Supp. XVI:** 124, 129, 130

Virtue of Selfishness, The: A New Concept of Egoism (Rand), **Supp. IV Part 2:** 527, 530–532

"Virtuoso" (Francis), **Supp. IX:** 82

Virtuous Woman, A (Gibbons), **Supp. X:** 44–45, 46, 50

Visconti, Luchino, **Supp. V:** 51

Visible Saints: The History of a Puritan Idea (Morgan), **IV:** 149

"Vision, A" (Olds), **Supp. X:** 214

"Vision, A" (Winters), **Supp. II Part 2:** 785, 795

"Vision and Prayer" (D. Thomas), **I:** 432

"Visionary, The" (Poe), **III:** 411

Visionary Farms, The (Eberhart), **I:** 537–539

Visioning, The (Glaspell), **Supp. III Part 1:** 175–177, 180, 187, 188

Vision in Spring (Faulkner), **Retro. Supp. I:** 79

Vision of Columbus (Barlow), **Supp. I Part 1:** 124; **Supp. II Part 1:** 67, 68, 70–75, 77, 79

Vision of Sir Launfal, The (Lowell), **Supp. I Part 1:** 311; **Supp. I Part 2:** 406, 409, 410

"Vision of the World, A" (Cheever), **Supp. I Part 1:** 182, 192

Visions of Cody (Kerouac), **Supp. III Part 1:** 225–227

Visions of Gerard (Kerouac), **Supp. III Part 1:** 219–222, 225, 227, 229

"Visions of the Daughters of Albion" (Blake), **III:** 540

"Visit" (Ammons), **Supp. VII:** 28–29

"Visit, The" (Kenyon), **Supp. VII:** 169

"Visitant, The" (Dunn), **Supp. XI:** 147

"*Visitation, The*/La Visitación" (Mora), **Supp. XIII:** 217, 224, 228

"Visit Home, A" (Stafford), **Supp. XI:** 318

Visit in 2001, The (musical, McNally), **Supp. XIII:** 207

"Visiting My Own House in Iowa City" (Stern), **Supp. IX:** 300

"Visit of Charity, A" (Welty), **IV:** 262

"Visitors" (Salinas), **Supp. XIII:** 318

"Visitors, The/Los Visitantes" (Kingsolver), **Supp. VII:** 208

"Visits to St. Elizabeths" (Bishop), **Retro. Supp. II:** 47

"Visit to a Small Planet" (teleplay) (Vidal), **Supp. IV Part 2:** 682

Visit to a Small Planet: A Comedy Akin to Vaudeville (Vidal), **Supp. IV Part 2:** 682–683

"Visit to Avoyelles, A" (Chopin), **Supp. I Part 1:** 213

"Vissi d'Arte" (Moore), **Supp. X:** 173–174

Vistas of History (Morison), **Supp. I Part 2:** 492

"Vita" (Stafford), **Supp. XI:** 330

Vital, David, **Supp. XVI:** 160

Vital Provisions (Price), **Supp. VI:** 262–263

"Vitamins" (Carver), **Supp. III Part 1:** 138

Vita Nova (Glück), **Supp. V:** 90–92

Vitruvius, **Supp. XVI:** 292

Vittorio, the Vampire (Rice), **Supp. VII:** 295–296

Viudas (Dorfman), **Supp. IX:** 138

"Viva Vargas!" (Allen), **Supp. XV:** 15

Viviparous Quadrupeds of North America, The (Audubon and Bachman), **Supp. XVI:** 10

Vizenor, Gerald, **Supp. IV Part 1:** 260, 262, 329, 404; **Supp. IV Part 2:** 502

Vladimir Nabokov: The American Years (Nabokov), **Retro. Supp. I:** 275

Vlag, Piet, **Supp. XV:** 295

"Vlemk, the Box Painter" (Gardner), **Supp. VI:** 73

"V-Letter" (Shapiro), **Supp. II Part 2:** 707

V-Letter and Other Poems (Shapiro), **Supp. II Part 2:** 702, 706

"Vocabulary of Dearness" (Nye), **Supp. XIII:** 284

"Vocation" (Stafford), **Supp. XI:** 312, 321

Vocation and a Voice, A (Chopin), **Retro. Supp. II:** 67, 72

"Vocation and a Voice, A" (Chopin), **Retro. Supp. II:** 72; **Supp. I Part 1:** 200, 220, 224, 225

Vogel, David, **Supp. XV:** 88

Vogel, Speed, **Supp. IV Part 1:** 390

"Voice, The" (Dunn), **Supp. XI:** 152

Voiced Connections of James Dickey, The (Dickey), **Supp. IV Part 1:** 177

"Voice from the Woods, A" (Humphrey), **Supp. IX:** 101

"Voice from Under the Table, A" (Wilbur), **Supp. III Part 2:** 553, 554

Voice of Reason, The: Essays in Objectivist Thought (Rand), **Supp. IV Part 2:** 527, 528, 532

"Voice of Rock, The" (Ginsberg), **Supp. II Part 1:** 313

Voice of the Butterfly, The (Nichols), **Supp. XIII:** 270

Voice of the City, The (O. Henry), **Supp. II Part 1:** 410

"Voice of the Mountain, The" (Crane), **I:** 420

Voice of the Negro (Barber), **Supp. II Part 1:** 168

Voice of the People, The (Glasgow), **II:** 175, 176

Voice of the Turtle: American Indian Literature 1900–1970 (Gunn Allen, ed.), **Supp. IV Part 1:** 332, 334

Voices from the Moon (Dubus), **Supp. VII:** 88–89

"Voices from the Other World" (Merrill), **Supp. III Part 1:** 331

Voices in the House (Sedges), **Supp. II Part 1:** 125

Voices of the Night (Longfellow), **II:** 489, 493; **Retro. Supp. II:** 154, 157, 168

"Voices of Village Square, The" (Wolfe), **Supp. III Part 2:** 571–572

Voice That Is Great within Us, The (Caruth, ed.), **Supp. XIII:** 112

Voigt, Ellen Bryan, **Supp. XIII:** 76

Volkening, Henry, **Retro. Supp. II:** 117; **Supp. XV:** 142

Vollmann, William T., **Supp. XIV:**96

Volney, Constantin François de Chasseboeuf, **Supp. I Part 1:** 146

Voltaire, **I:** 194; **II:** 86, 103, 449; **III:** 420; **IV:** 18; **Retro. Supp. II:** 94; **Supp. I Part 1:** 288–289; **Supp. I Part 2:** 669, 717; **Supp. XV:** 258

Volunteers, The (Rowson and Reinagle), **Supp. XV:** 238

Vonnegut, Kurt, **Retro. Supp. I:** 170; **Supp. II Part 2:** 557, 689, 753–784; **Supp. IV Part 1:** 227, 392; **Supp. V:** 40, 42, 237, 244, 296; **Supp. X:** 260; **Supp. XI:** 104; **Supp. XII:** 139, 141

"Voracities and Verities" (Moore), **III:** 214

Vore, Nellie, **I:** 199

Vorlicky, Robert, **Supp. IX:** 132, 135, 136, 141, 144, 147

"Vorticism" (Pound), **Retro. Supp. I:** 288

Voss, Richard, **I:** 199–200

"Vow, The" (Hecht), **Supp. X:** 64

"Vowels 2" (Baraka), **Supp. II Part 1:** 51

Vow of Conversation, A: Journal, 1964–1965 (Merton), **Supp. VIII:** 206

Vox (Baker), **Supp. XIII:** 47–49, 50, 52, 53

"Voyage" (MacLeish), **III:** 15

"Voyage, The" (Irving), **II:** 304

Voyage, The, and Other Versions of Poems by Baudelaire (Lowell), **Retro. Supp. II:** 187

Voyage dans la Haute Pennsylvanie et dans l'état de New-York (Crèvecoeur), **Supp. I Part 1:** 250–251

Voyage of the Beagle (Darwin), **Supp. IX:** 211

Voyage Out, The (Woolf), **Supp. XV:** 65

"Voyager, The" (Everwine), **Supp. XV:** 75

"Voyages" (H. Crane), **I:** 393–395; **Retro. Supp. II:** 78, 80, 81

"Voyages" (Levine), **Supp. V:** 190

Voyages and Discoveries of the Companions of Columbus (Irving), **II:** 310

Voyage to Pagany, A (W. C. Williams), **IV:** 404; **Retro. Supp. I:** 418–419, 420–421, 423

Voyaging Portraits (Sobin), **Supp. XVI:**282, 287

"Voyeur, The" (Gioia), **Supp. XV:** 125

Voznesensky, Andrei, **II:** 553; **Supp. III Part 1:** 268; **Supp. III Part 2:** 560

Vrbovska, Anca, **Supp. IV Part 2:** 639

"Vulgarity in Literature" (Huxley), **III:** 429–430

"Vultures" (Oliver), **Supp. VII:** 235

W

W (Viva) (Cummings), **I:** 429, 433, 434, 436, 443, 444, 447

"W. D. Sees Himself Animated" (Snodgrass), **Supp. VI:** 327

"W. D. Sits in Kafka's Chair and Is Interrogated Concerning the Assumed Death of Cock Robin" (Snodgrass), **Supp. VI:** 319

"W. D. Tries to Warn Cock Robin" (Snodgrass), **Supp. VI:** 319

Wabash (R. O. Butler), **Supp. XII:** 61, 68–69

Wade, Grace, **I:** 216

"Wading at Wellfleet" (Bishop), **Retro. Supp. II:** 42, 43; **Supp. I Part 1:** 80, 85, 86

Wadsworth, Charles, **I:** 454, 470; **Retro. Supp. I:** 32, 33

Wagenknecht, Edward, **II:** 508; **Supp. I Part 2:** 408, 584; **Supp. IV Part 2:** 681

"Wages of Poetry, The" (Wright), **Supp. XV:** 337

Wagner, Jean, **Supp. I Part 1:** 341, 346; **Supp. IV Part 1:** 165, 167, 171

Wagner, Richard, **I:** 284, 395; **II:** 425; **III:** 396, 507; **Supp. IV Part 1:** 392

Wagner, Robert, **Supp. IX:** 250

"Wagnerians, The" (Auchincloss), **Supp. IV Part 1:** 23

"Wagner Matinee, A" (Cather), **I:** 315–316; **Retro. Supp. I:** 5, 8

Wagoner, David, **Supp. IX:** 323–340; **Supp. XII:** 178

Waid, Candace, **Retro. Supp. I:** 360, 372, 373

Waif, The (Longfellow, ed.), **Retro. Supp. II:** 155

"Waif of the Plains, A" (Harte), **Supp. II Part 1:** 354

Wain, John, **Supp. XIV:**166

"Wait" (Kinnell), **Supp. III Part 1:** 250

"Waiting" (Dubus), **Supp. VII:** 87

"Waiting" (W. C. Williams), **Retro. Supp. I:** 418

"Waiting, The" (L.-Y. Lee), **Supp. XV:** 218

"Waiting, The" (Olds), **Supp. X:** 209

"Waiting between the Trees" (Tan), **Supp. X:** 290

"Waiting by the Gate" (Bryant), **Supp. I Part 1:** 171

Waiting for God (Weil), **I:** 298

Waiting for Godot (Beckett), **I:** 78, 91, 298; **Supp. IV Part 1:** 368–369

Waiting for Lefty (Odets), **Supp. I Part 1:** 277; **Supp. II Part 2:** 529, 530–533, 540; **Supp. V:** 109

Waiting for the End of the World (Bell), **Supp. X:** 4–5, 11

Waiting for the Verdict (Davis), **Supp. XVI:**85, 89, 90

"Waiting in a Rain Forest" (Wagoner), **Supp. IX:** 329

Waiting Room, The (Kees), **Supp. XV:** 133, 148

Waiting to Exhale (McMillan), **Supp. XIII:** 184, 185, 189–190, 191

"Waiting to Freeze" (Banks), **Supp. V:** 5, 6

Waiting to Freeze: Poems (Banks), **Supp. V:** 6, 8

Waits, Tom, **Supp. VIII:** 12

Wait until Spring, Bandini (Fante), **Supp. XI:** 160, 161, 164, 165, 166–167

Wait until Spring, Bandini (film), **Supp. XI:** 173

"Wake, The" (Dove), **Supp. IV Part 1:** 250

"Wakefield" (Hawthorne), **Retro. Supp. I:** 154, 159

Wakefield, Dan, **Supp. VIII:** 43; **Supp. XVI:**220

Wakefield, Richard, **Supp. IX:** 323

"Wake Island" (Rukeyser), **Supp. VI:** 273

Wakeman, Frederic, **Supp. IX:** 247

Wake Up and Live! (Brande), **Supp. I Part 2:** 608

"Waking" (C. Frost), **Supp. XV:** 93

Waking, The (Roethke), **III:** 541

"Waking Early Sunday Morning" (Lowell), **II:** 552; **Retro. Supp. II:** 190

"Waking in the Blue" (Lowell), **II:** 547; **Retro. Supp. II:** 180

"Waking in the Dark" (Rich), **Supp. I Part 2:** 559

"Waking Up the Rake" (Hogan), **Supp. IV Part 1:** 415–416, 416

Wakoski, Diane, **Supp. V:** 79; **Supp. XII:** 184; **Supp. XV:** 252

Walcott, Charles C., **II:** 49

Walcott, Derek, **Supp. VIII:** 28; **Supp. X:** 122, 131; **Supp. XV:** 256

Walcott, Jersey Joe, **Supp. V:** 182

Wald, Alan, **Supp. XV:** 202

Wald, Lillian, **Supp. I Part 1:** 12

Walden (Thoreau), **Supp. XIV:**177,

227; **Supp. XV:** 275

Walden, Daniel, **Supp. IV Part 2:** 584, 591; **Supp. V:** 272

Walden; or, Life in the Woods (Thoreau), **I:** 219, 305; **II:** 8, 142, 159, 312–313, 458; **IV:** 168, 169, 170, 176, 177–178, 179–182, 183, 187; **Retro. Supp. I:** 62; **Supp. I Part 2:** 579, 655, 664, 672; **Supp. VIII:** 296; **Supp. X:** 27, 101; **Supp. XIII:** 152

Waldman, Anne, **Supp. XIV:**150

Waldmeir, Joseph, **III:** 45

Waldmeir, Joseph J., **Supp. I Part 2:** 476

Waldo (Theroux), **Supp. VIII:** 313, 314, 314–315

Waldrop, Keith, **Supp. XV:** 153, 165

Waley, Arthur, **II:** 526; **III:** 466; **Supp. V:** 340

"Walk, A" (Snyder), **Supp. VIII:** 297

"Walk at Sunset, A" (Bryant), **Supp. I Part 1:** 155

"Walk before Mass, A" (Agee), **I:** 28–29

Walker, Alice, **Retro. Supp. I:** 215; **Supp. I Part 2:** 550; **Supp. III Part 2:** 488, 517–540; **Supp. IV Part 1:** 14; **Supp. VIII:** 141, 214; **Supp. IX:** 306, 311; **Supp. X:** 85, 228, 252, 325, 330; **Supp. XIII:** 179, 185, 291, 295; **Supp. XVI:**39

Walker, Cheryl, **Supp. XI:** 145

Walker, David, **Supp. V:** 189

Walker, Franklin D., **III:** 321

Walker, Gue, **Supp. XII:** 207

Walker, Marianne, **Supp. VIII:** 139

Walker, Obadiah, **II:** 113

Walker, Scott, **Supp. XV:** 92

Walker in the City, A (Kazin), **Supp. VIII:** 93–95, 99

Walk Hard (Blum and Hill), **Supp. XV:** 194

Walk Hard-Talk Loud (Zinberg), **Supp. XV:** 194, 202

"Walking" (Hogan), **Supp. IV Part 1:** 416

"Walking" (Thoreau), **Supp. IV Part 1:** 416; **Supp. IX:** 178

"Walking Along in Winter" (Kenyon), **Supp. VII:** 167

"Walking around the Block with a Three-Year-Old" (Wagoner), **Supp. IX:** 331–332

"Walking Backwards into the Future" (R. Williams), **Supp. IX:** 146

Walking Down the Stairs: Selections from Interviews (Kinnell), **Supp. III Part 1:** 235, 249

"Walking Home" (Schnackenberg). See

"Laughing with One Eye" (Schnackenberg)

"Walking Home at Night" (Ginsberg), **Supp. II Part 1:** 313

Walking Light (Dunn), **Supp. XI:** 140, 141, 153

"Walking Man of Rodin, The" (Sandburg), **III:** 583

"Walking Sticks and Paperweights and Water Marks" (Moore), **III:** 215

Walking Tall (Dunn), **Supp. XI:** 140

Walking the Black Cat (Simic), **Supp. VIII:** 280, 282–284

Walking to Sleep (Wilbur), **Supp. III Part 2:** 557–560

"Walking to Sleep" (Wilbur), **Supp. III Part 2:** 544, 557, 559, 561, 562

Walkin' the Dog (Mosley), **Supp. XIII:** 242

"Walk in the Moonlight, A" (Anderson), **I:** 114

Walk on the Wild Side, A (Algren), **Supp. V:** 4; **Supp. IX:** 3, 12–13, 14

"Walks in Rome" (Merrill), **Supp. III Part 1:** 337

Walk with Tom Jefferson, A (Levine), **Supp. V:** 179, 187, 190–191

"Wall, The" (Brooks), **Supp. III Part 1:** 70, 71, 84

Wall, The (Hersey), **IV:** 4

"Wall, The" (Roethke), **III:** 544

"Wall, The" (Sexton), **Supp. II Part 2:** 696

Wallace, David Foster, **Retro. Supp. II:** 279; **Supp. X:** 301–318

Wallace, Henry, **I:** 489; **III:** 111, 475; **Supp. I Part 1:** 286; **Supp. I Part 2:** 645

Wallace, Mike, **Supp. IV Part 1:** 364; **Supp. IV Part 2:** 526

Wallace Stevens (Kermode), **Retro. Supp. I:** 301

Wallace Stevens: The Poems of our Climate (Bloom), **Retro. Supp. I:** 299

Wallace Stevens: Words Chosen out of Desire (Stevens), **Retro. Supp. I:** 297

Wallach, Eli, **III:** 161

Wallant, Edward Lewis, **Supp. XVI:**220

Wallas, Graham, **Supp. I Part 2:** 643

"Walled City" (Oates), **Supp. II Part 2:** 524

Wallenstein, Anna. See Weinstein, Mrs. Max (Anna Wallenstein)

Waller, Edmund, **III:** 463

Waller, Fats, **IV:** 263

Walling, William English, **Supp. I Part**

2: 645; **Supp. XV:** 295

Walls Do Not Fall, The (Doolittle), **Supp. I Part 1:** 271, 272

"Wall Songs" (Hogan), **Supp. IV Part 1:** 413

Wall Writing (Auster), **Supp. XII:** 23–24

Walpole, Horace, **I:** 203; **Supp. I Part 2:** 410, 714

Walpole, Hugh, **Retro. Supp. I:** 231

Walpole, Robert, **IV:** 145

Walsh, David M., **Supp. XV:** 5

Walsh, Ed, **II:** 424

Walsh, George, **Supp. IV Part 2:** 528

Walsh, Raoul, **Supp. XIII:** 174

Walsh, Richard J., **Supp. II Part 1:** 119, 130

Walsh, William, **Supp. IV Part 1:** 242, 243, 246, 248, 252, 254, 257

Walter, Eugene, **Supp. XVI:**230

Walter, Joyce, **Supp. XV:** 121

Walter Benjamin at the Dairy Queen: Reflections at Sixty and Beyond (McMurtry), **Supp. V:** 232

Walters, Barbara, **Supp. XIV:**125

Walters, Marguerite. See Smith, Mrs. Lamar (Marguerite Walters)

"Walter T. Carriman" (O'Hara), **III:** 368

Walton, Izaak, **Supp. I Part 2:** 422

"Walt Whitman" (Masters), **Supp. I Part 2:** 458

"Walt Whitman at Bear Mountain" (Simpson), **Supp. IX:** 265

Walt Whitman Bathing (Wagoner), **Supp. IX:** 331–332

Walt Whitman Handbook (Allen), **IV:** 352

Walt Whitman Reconsidered (Chase), **IV:** 352

"Waltz, The" (Parker), **Supp. IX:** 204

"Waltzer in the House, The" (Kunitz), **Supp. III Part 1:** 258

Walzer, Kevin, **Supp. XII:** 202; **Supp. XV:** 118

Wambaugh, Joseph, **Supp. X:** 5

Wampeters, Foma, & Granfalloons (Vonnegut), **Supp. II Part 2:** 758, 759–760, 776, 779

Wand, David Hsin-fu, **Supp. X:** 292

"Wanderer, The" (W. C. Williams), **Retro. Supp. I:** 414, 421

"Wanderers, The" (Welty), **IV:** 273–274

"Wandering Jew, The" (Robinson), **III:** 505, 516–517

Wanderings of Oisin (Yeats), **Supp. I Part 1:** 79

Wang, Dorothy, **Supp. X:** 289

Wang Wei, **Supp. XV:** 47

Waniek, Marilyn Nelson, **Supp. IV Part 1:** 244

"Wan Lee, the Pagan" (Harte), **Supp. II Part 1:** 351

"Want, The" (Olds), **Supp. X:** 210

Want Bone, The (Pinsky), **Supp. VI:** 236–237, 244–245, 247

"Wanted: An Ontological Critic" (Ransom), **III:** 498

"Wanting to Die" (Sexton), **Supp. II Part 2:** 684, 686; **Supp. XIV:**132

"Wants" (Paley), **Supp. VI:** 219

Waples, Dorothy, **I:** 348

Wapshot Chronicle, The (Cheever), **Supp. I Part 1:** 174, 177–180, 181, 196

Wapshot Scandal, The (Cheever), **Supp. I Part 1:** 180–184, 187, 191, 196

"War" (Kingston), **Supp. V:** 169

"War" (Simic), **Supp. VIII:** 282

"War, Response, and Contradiction" (Burke), **I:** 283

"War and Peace" (Sanders), **Supp. XVI:**277

War and Peace (Tolstoy), **I:** 6, 7; **II:** 191, 205, 291; **IV:** 446; **Supp. V:** 277; **Supp. XI:** 68; **Supp. XIV:**97

War and War (F. Barthelme), **Supp. XI:** 25

"War Between Men and Women, The" (Thurber), **Supp. I Part 2:** 615

War Bulletins (Lindsay), **Supp. I Part 2:** 378–379

Ward, Aileen, **II:** 531

Ward, Artemus (pseudonym). *See* Browne, Charles Farrar

Ward, Douglas Turner, **Supp. IV Part 1:** 362

Ward, Henry, **Supp. I Part 2:** 588

Ward, Leo R., **Supp. VIII:** 124

Ward, Lester F., **Supp. I Part 2:** 640; **Supp. XI:** 202, 203

Ward, Lynn, **I:** 31

Ward, Mrs. Humphry, **II:** 338

Ward, Nathaniel, **Supp. I Part 1:** 99, 102, 111, 116

Ward, Theodora, **I:** 470; **Retro. Supp. I:** 28

Ward, William Hayes, **Supp. I Part 1:** 371

"War Debt, A" (Jewett), **Retro. Supp. II:** 138, 141

"War Diary, A" (Bourne), **I:** 229

War Dispatches of Stephen Crane, The (Crane), **I:** 422

"Ward Line, The" (Morris), **III:** 220

Warfel, Harry R., **Supp. I Part 1:** 366

War Games (Morris), **III:** 238

War in Heaven, The (Shepard and Chaikin), **Supp. III Part 2:** 433

War Is Kind (Crane), **I:** 409; **III:** 585

"War Is Kind" (Crane), **I:** 419

Warlock (Harrison), **Supp. VIII:** 45, 46

Warm as Wool (Sanders), **Supp. XVI:**269

Warner, Charles Dudley, **II:** 405; **IV:** 198

Warner, Jack, **Supp. XII:** 160–161

Warner, John R., **III:** 193

Warner, Oliver, **I:** 548

Warner, Susan, **Retro. Supp. I:** 246; **Supp. XV:** 275

Warner, Sylvia Townsend, **Supp. VIII:** 151, 155, 164, 171

Warner, W. Lloyd, **III:** 60

"Warning" (Hughes), **Supp. I Part 1:** 343

"Warning" (Pound), **III:** 474

"Warning, The" (Creeley), **Supp. IV Part 1:** 150

"Warning, The" (Longfellow), **II:** 498

Warning Hill (Marquand), **III:** 55–56, 60, 68

"War of Eyes, A" (Coleman), **Supp. XI:** 93–94

War of Eyes and Other Stories, A (Coleman), **Supp. XI:** 91–92

War of the Classes (London), **II:** 466

"War of the Wall, The" (Bambara), **Supp. XI:** 15–16

"War of Vaslav Nijinsky, The" (Bidart), **Supp. XV:** 21–22, 27–29

"War Poems" (Sandburg), **III:** 581

Warren, Austin, **I:** 265, 268, 271; **Supp. I Part 2:** 423

Warren, Earl, **III:** 581

Warren, Gabriel, **IV:** 244

Warren, Mercy Otis, **Supp. XV:** 230

Warren, Mrs. Robert Penn (Eleanor Clark), **IV:** 244

Warren, Robert Penn, **I:** 190, 211, 517; **II:** 57, 217, 228, 253; **III:** 134, 310, 382–383, 454, 482, 485, 490, 496, 497; **IV:** 121, 122, 123, 125, 126, 236–259, 261, 262, 279, 340–341, 458; **Retro. Supp. I:** 40, 41, 73, 90; **Retro. Supp. II:** 220, 235; **Supp. I Part 1:** 359, 371; **Supp. I Part 2:** 386, 423; **Supp. II Part 1:** 139; **Supp. III Part 2:** 542; **Supp. V:** 261, 316, 318, 319, 333; **Supp. VIII:** 126, 176; **Supp. IX:** 257; **Supp. X:** 1, 25, 26; **Supp. XI:** 315; **Supp. XII:** 254, 255; **Supp. XIV:**1, 2, 3, 4, 11, 14, 15

Warren, Rosanna, **IV:** 244; **Supp. XV:** 251, 261, 262, 263

Warrington Poems, The (Ríos), **Supp. IV Part 2:** 540

Warrior, Robert Allen, **Supp. IV Part 1:** 329

"Warrior, The" (Gunn Allen), **Supp. IV Part 1:** 326

"Warrior: 5th Grade" (Olds), **Supp. X:** 214

"Warrior Road" (Harjo), **Supp. XII:** 217

Warshavsky, Isaac (pseudonym). *See* Singer, Isaac Bashevis

Warshow, Robert, **Supp. I Part 1:** 51

Wars I Have Seen (Stein), **IV:** 27, 36, 477

Wartime (Fussell), **Supp. V:** 241

"War Widow, The" (Frederic), **II:** 135–136

"Was" (Creeley), **Supp. IV Part 1:** 155

"Was" (Faulkner), **II:** 71

"Wash" (Faulkner), **II:** 72

Wash, Richard, **Supp. XII:** 14

"Washed in the Rain" (Fante), **Supp. XI:** 165

Washington, Booker T., **Supp. I Part 2:** 393; **Supp. II Part 1:** 157, 160, 167, 168, 171, 225; **Supp. XIV:**198, 199, 201

Washington, D.C. (Vidal), **Supp. IV Part 2:** 677, 684, 686–687, 690

Washington, George, **I:** 453; **II:** 313–314; **Supp. I Part 2:** 399, 485, 508, 509, 511, 513, 517, 518, 520, 599

Washington Crossing the Delaware (Rivers), **Supp. XV:** 186

Washington Post Book World (Lesser), **Supp. IV Part 2:** 453; **Supp. VIII:** 80, 84, 241; **Supp. X:** 282

Washington Square (James), **II:** 327, 328; **Retro. Supp. I:** 215, 220, 222–223

"Washington Square, 1946" (Ozick), **Supp. V:** 272

Washington Square Ensemble, The (Bell), **Supp. X:** 1, 3–4

"Was Lowell an Historical Critic?" (Altick), **Supp. I Part 2:** 423

Wasserman, Earl R., **Supp. I Part 2:** 439, 440

Wasserman, Jakob, **Supp. I Part 2:** 669

Wasserstein, Wendy, **Supp. IV Part 1:** 309; **Supp. XV:** 319–336

Wasson, Ben, **Retro. Supp. I:** 79, 83

"Waste Carpet, The" (Matthews), **Supp. IX:** 158–159

Waste Land, The (Eliot), **I:** 107, 266, 298, 395, 396, 482, 570–571, 572, 574–575, 577–578, 580, 581, 584, 585, 586, 587; **III:** 6–8, 12, 196,

277–278, 453, 471, 492, 586; **IV:** 122, 123, 124, 140, 418, 419, 420; **Retro. Supp. I:** 51, 60, 60–62, 63, 64, 66, 210, 290, 291, 299, 311, 420, 427; **Retro. Supp. II:** 85, 121, 190; **Supp. I Part 1:** 272; **Supp. I Part 2:** 439, 455, 614; **Supp. II Part 1:** 4, 5, 11, 96; **Supp. III Part 1:** 9, 10, 41, 63, 105; **Supp. IV Part 1:** 47, 284; **Supp. V:** 338; **Supp. IX:** 158, 305; **Supp. X:** 125; **Supp. XIII:** 341–342, 344, 346; **Supp. XIV:**6, 284; **Supp. XV:** 21, 181, 261, 306; **Supp. XVI:**204

"Waste Land, The": A Facsimile and Transcript of the Original Drafts Including the Annotations of Ezra Pound (Eliot, ed.), **Retro. Supp. I:** 58

Waste Land and Other Poems, The (Eliot), **Supp. XV:** 305

Wat, Alexander, **Supp. XVI:**155, 161

Watch, The (Bass), **Supp. XVI:**16–17

"Watch, The, —" (Bass), **Supp. XVI:**17

Watch and Ward (James), **II:** 323; **Retro. Supp. I:** 218, 219, 220

"Watcher, The" (R. Bly), **Supp. IV Part 1:** 71

"Watcher by the Dead, A" (Bierce), **I:** 203

Watchfires (Auchincloss), **Supp. IV Part 1:** 23

"Watching Crow, Looking toward the Manzano Mountains" (Harjo), **Supp. XII:** 219

"Watching the Sunset" (Coleman), **Supp. XI:** 92

Watch on the Rhine (Hellman), **Supp. I Part 1:** 276, 278, 279–281, 283–284; **Supp. IV Part 1:** 83

"Water" (Emerson), **II:** 19

"Water" (Komunyakaa), **Supp. XIII:** 132

"Water" (Lowell), **II:** 550

"Waterbird" (Swenson), **Supp. IV Part 2:** 651

"Water Borders" (Dillard), **Supp. VI:** 27

"Water Buffalo" (Komunyakaa), **Supp. XIII:** 122

"Watercolor of Grantchester Meadows" (Plath), **Supp. I Part 2:** 537

"Waterfall, The" (Clampitt), **Supp. IX:** 44

"Water Hose Is on Fire, The" (Simic), **Supp. XV:** 185

Waterhouse, Keith, **Supp. VIII:** 124

"Waterlily Fire" (Rukeyser), **Supp. VI:** 285, 286

Waterlily Fire: Poems 1935–1962 (Rukeyser), **Supp. VI:** 274, 283, 285

Watermark (Brodsky), **Supp. VIII:** 29

Water-Method Man, The (Irving), **Supp. VI:** 163, 167–179, 180

Water Music (Boyle), **Supp. VIII:** 1, 3–5, 8, 14

"Water Music for the Progress of Love in a Life-Raft Down the Sammamish Slough" (Wagoner), **Supp. IX:** 326

"Water People" (Burke), **Supp. XIV:**21

"Water Picture" (Swenson), **Supp. IV Part 2:** 641

"Water Rising" (Hogan), **Supp. IV Part 1:** 400

Waters, Ethel, **II:** 587

Waters, Frank, **Supp. X:** 124

Waters, Muddy, **Supp. VIII:** 345

"Watershed" (Kingsolver), **Supp. VII:** 208

"Watershed" (Warren), **IV:** 239

"Watershed, The" (Auden), **Supp. II Part 1:** 5

Waters of Siloe, The (Merton), **Supp. VIII:** 196, 208

Waterston, Sam, **Supp. IX:** 253

Water Street (Merrill), **Supp. III Part 1:** 321–323

"Water Walker" (Wilbur), **Supp. III Part 2:** 548, 560

Water-Witch, The (Cooper), **I:** 342–343

Waterworks, The (Doctorow), **Supp. IV Part 1:** 218, 222, 223, 231–233, 234

"Water Works, The" (Doctorow), **Supp. IV Part 1:** 234

Watkin, E. I., **Retro. Supp. II:** 187

Watkins, Floyd C., **IV:** 452

Watkins, James T., **I:** 193, 194

Watkins, Maureen, **Supp. XVI:**188

Watkins, Mel, **Supp. X:** 330; **Supp. XIII:** 246

Watrous, Peter, **Supp. VIII:** 79

Watson, Burton, **Supp. XV:** 47

Watson, J. B., **II:** 361

Watson, James Sibley, Jr., **I:** 261

Watson, Richard, **Supp. I Part 2:** 516, 517

Watson, William, **II:** 114

Watt, Ian, **Supp. VIII:** 4

Watteau, Jean Antoine, **III:** 275; **IV:** 79

Watts, Emily Stipes, **Supp. I Part 1:** 115

Waugh, Evelyn, **I:** 480; **III:** 281; **Supp. I Part 2:** 607; **Supp. IV Part 2:** 688; **Supp. XI:** 305, 306

"Wave" (Snyder), **Supp. VIII:** 299

Wave, A (Ashbery), **Supp. III Part 1:** 1, 4, 24–26

"Wave, A" (Ashbery), **Supp. III Part 1:** 9, 19, 24–25

"Wave, The" (MacLeish), **III:** 19

"Wave, The" (Untermeyer), **Supp. XV:** 300

"Waxwings" (Francis), **Supp. IX:** 82

Way, The (Steiner and Witt, eds.), **Supp. IV Part 2:** 505

"Way Down, The" (Kunitz), **Supp. III Part 1:** 263

"Way It Is, The" (Ellison), **Supp. II Part 1:** 245

"Way It Is, The" (Jones), **Supp. XI:** 229

Way It Is, The (Stafford), **Supp. XIII:** 274

"Way It Is, The" (Strand), **Supp. IV Part 2:** 627

"Wayland" (Sanders), **Supp. XVI:**275

Wayne, John, **Supp. IV Part 1:** 200

Way of Chuang-Tzu, The (Merton), **Supp. VIII:** 208

"Way of Exchange in James Dickey's Poetry, The" (Weatherby), **Supp. IV Part 1:** 175

Way of Life According to Laotzu, The (Bynner), **Supp. XV:** 46, 48

Way Out, A (Frost), **Retro. Supp. I:** 133

Wayside Motor Inn, The (Gurney), **Supp. V:** 96, 105, 109

Ways of the Hour, The (Cooper), **I:** 354

Ways of White Folks, The (Hughes), **Retro. Supp. I:** 203, 204; **Supp. I Part 1:** 329, 330, 332

Way Some People Die, The (Macdonald), **Supp. IV Part 2:** 470, 471, 472, 474

Way Some People Live, The (Cheever), **Supp. I Part 1:** 175

"Way the Cards Fall, The" (Komunyakaa), **Supp. XIII:** 117

Way to Rainy Mountain, The (Momaday), **Supp. IV Part 2:** 485–486, 487–489, 491, 493

Way to Wealth, The (Franklin), **II:** 101–102, 110

Wayward and the Seeking, The: A Collection of Writings by Jean Toomer (Toomer), **Supp. III Part 2:** 478–481, 484, 487

Wayward Bus, The (Steinbeck), **IV:** 51, 64–65

"Way We Live Now, The" (Sontag), **Supp. III Part 2:** 467–468

"Way You'll Never Be, A" (Hemingway), **II:** 249

Weaks, Mary Louise, **Supp. X:** 5

Weales, Gerald, **II:** 602

"Wealth," from *Conduct of Life, The* (Emerson), **II:** 2, 3–4

"Wealth," from *English Traits* (Emerson), **II:** 6

Wealth of Nations, The (A. Smith), **II:** 109

"We Are Looking at You, Agnes" (Caldwell), **I:** 309

We Are Still Married: Stories and Letters (Keillor), **Supp. XVI:**176, 177

"We Are the Crazy Lady and Other Feisty Feminist Fables" (Ozick), **Supp. V:** 259

Weary Blues, The (Hughes), **Retro. Supp. I:** 195, 197, 198, 199, 200, 203, 205; **Supp. I Part 1:** 325

"Weary Blues, The" (Hughes), **Retro. Supp. I:** 198, 199; **Supp. I Part 1:** 324, 325

"Weary Kingdom" (Irving), **Supp. VI:** 163

Weasels and Wisemen: Ethics and Ethnicity in the Work of David Mamet (Kane), **Supp. XIV:**250

Weatherby, H. L., **Supp. IV Part 1:** 175

"Weathering Out" (Dove), **Supp. IV Part 1:** 248

Weaver, Harriet, **III:** 471

Weaver, Mike, **Retro. Supp. I:** 430

Weaver, Will, **Supp. XVI:**39

"Weaving" (Larcom), **Supp. XIII:** 142, **Supp. XIII:** 144–145, 150, 151

"Web" (Oliver), **Supp. VII:** 236

Web and the Rock, The (Wolfe), **IV:** 451, 455, 457, 459–460, 462, 464, 467, 468

Webb, Beatrice, **Supp. I Part 1:** 5

Webb, Mary, **I:** 226

Webb, Sidney, **Supp. I Part 1:** 5

Webb, W. P., **Supp. V:** 225

Weber, Brom, **I:** 383, 386

Weber, Carl, **Supp. IX:** 133, 138, 141

Weber, Max, **I:** 498; **Supp. I Part 2:** 637, 648

Weber, Sarah, **Supp. I Part 1:** 2

Web of Earth, The (Wolfe), **IV:** 451–452, 456, 458, 464, 465

"Web of Life, The" (Nemerov), **III:** 282

Webster, Brenda, **Supp. XVI:**157, 161

Webster, Daniel, **II:** 5, 9; **Supp. I Part 2:** 659, 687, 689, 690

Webster, John, **I:** 384; **Supp. I Part 2:** 422

Webster, Noah, **Supp. I Part 2:** 660; **Supp. II Part 1:** 77

Wector, Dixon, **II:** 103

"Wedding, The" (Everwine), **Supp. XV:** 83

"Wedding Cake" (Nye), **Supp. XIII:** 283

"Wedding in Brownsville, A" (Singer), **IV:** 15

Wedding in Hell, A (Simic), **Supp. VIII:** 280, 282

"Wedding of the Rose and Lotus, The" (Lindsay), **Supp. I Part 2:** 387

"Wedding Supper, The" (Rowson), **Supp. XV:** 243

"Wedding Toast, A" (Wilbur), **Supp. III Part 2:** 561

Wedekind, Frank, **III:** 398

Wedge, The (W. C. Williams), **Retro. Supp. I:** 424

"Wednesday at the Waldorf" (Swenson), **Supp. IV Part 2:** 647

"We Don't Live Here Anymore" (Dubus), **Supp. VII:** 78–79, 85

"Weed" (McCarriston), **Supp. XIV:**259, 273

"Weed, The" (Bishop), **Supp. I Part 1:** 80, 88–89

"Weeds, The" (McCarthy), **II:** 566

"Weekend" (Beattie), **Supp. V:** 27

Weekend, The (Cameron), **Supp. XII:** 80, 81, 86–88

"Weekend at Ellerslie, A" (Wilson), **IV:** 431

Weekend Edition (National Public Radio), **Supp. IX:** 299

Week on the Concord and Merrimack Rivers, A (Thoreau), **IV:** 168, 169, 177, 182–183; **Supp. I Part 2:** 420; **Supp. XIV:**227

Weeks, Edward, **III:** 64

Weeks, Jerome, **Supp. VIII:** 76

"Weeping Burgher" (Stevens), **IV:** 77

"Weeping Women" (Levertov), **Supp. III Part 1:** 282

We Fly Away (Francis), **Supp. IX:** 79–80, 84

We Have Always Lived in the Castle (Jackson), **Supp. IX:** 121, 126, 127–128

"We Have Our Arts So We Won't Die of Truth" (Bradbury), **Supp. IV Part 1:** 105

Weich, Dave, **Supp. XII:** 321

"Weight" (Wideman), **Supp. X:** 321

Weigl, Bruce, **Supp. VIII:** 269, 274; **Supp. XV:** 342

Weil, Dorothy, **Supp. XV:** 231

Weil, Robert, **Supp. IX:** 236

Weil, Simone, **I:** 298; **Supp. XV:** 259

Weiland (C. B. Brown), **Supp. XIII:** 100

Weinauer, Ellen, **Supp. XV:** 270, 284

Weinberger, Eliot, **Supp. IV Part 1:** 66; **Supp. VIII:** 290, 292; **Supp. XVI:**284

Weininger, Otto, **Retro. Supp. I:** 416

Weinreb, Mindy, **Supp. X:** 24

Weinreich, Regina, **Supp. XIV:**22

Weinstein, Hinda, **IV:** 285

Weinstein, Max, **IV:** 285

Weinstein, Mrs. Max (Anna Wallenstein), **IV:** 285, 287

Weinstein, Nathan. See West, Nathanael

Weisheit, Rabbi, **IV:** 76

Weismuller, Johnny, **Supp. X:** 264

Weiss, David, **Supp. XVI:**55

Weiss, Peter, **IV:** 117

Weiss, Theodore, **Supp. IV Part 2:** 440; **Supp. IX:** 96

Weist, Dianne, **Supp. X:** 80

Weithas, Art, **Supp. XI:** 231

Welch, James, **Supp. IV Part 1:** 404; **Supp. IV Part 2:** 503, 513, 557, 562

Welch, Lew, **Supp. V:** 170; **Supp. VIII:** 303

"Welcome from War" (Rukeyser), **Supp. VI:** 286

"Welcome Morning" (Sexton), **Supp. II Part 2:** 696

"Welcome the Wrath" (Kunitz), **Supp. III Part 1:** 261

Welcome to Hard Times (Doctorow), **Supp. IV Part 1:** 218, 219–220, 222, 224, 230, 238

Welcome to Hard Times (film), **Supp. IV Part 1:** 236

Welcome to Our City (Wolfe), **IV:** 461

Welcome to the Monkey House (Vonnegut), **Supp. II Part 2:** 758

Welcome to the Moon (Shanley), **Supp. XIV:**318

Welcome to the Moon and Other Plays (Shanley), **Supp. XIV:**315, 316–319

Weld, Theodore, **Supp. I Part 2:** 587, 588

Weld, Tuesday, **Supp. XI:** 306

Welded (O'Neill), **III:** 390

"Well, The" (Momaday), **Supp. IV Part 2:** 483

"Well Dressed Man with a Beard, The" (Stevens), **Retro. Supp. I:** 297

Wellek, René, **I:** 253, 261, 282; **II:** 320; **Supp. XIV:**12, 14

Weller, George, **III:** 322

Welles, Gideon, **Supp. I Part 2:** 484

Welles, Orson, **IV:** 476; **Supp. I Part 1:** 67; **Supp. IV Part 1:** 82, 83; **Supp. V:** 251; **Supp. VIII:** 46; **Supp. XI:** 169, 307

"Wellfleet Whale, The" (Kunitz), **Supp. III Part 1:** 263, 269

Wellfleet Whale and Companion Poems, The (Kunitz), **Supp. III Part 1:** 263

Wellman, Flora, **II:** 463–464, 465

"Well Rising, The" (Stafford), **Supp. XI:** 318

Wells, H. G., **I:** 103, 226, 241, 243, 253, 405, 409, 415; **II:** 82, 144, 276, 337, 338, 458; **III:** 456; **IV:** 340, 455; **Retro. Supp. I:** 100, 228, 231; **Supp. XVI:**190

Wellspring, The (Olds), **Supp. X:** 211–212

Well Wrought Urn, The: Studies in the Structure of Poetry (Brooks), **Supp. XIV:**1, 8–9, 14, 15, 16

Welsh, Mary. *See* Hemingway, Mrs. Ernest (Mary Welsh)

Welty, Eudora, **II:** 194, 217, 606; **IV:** 260–284; **Retro. Supp. I:** 339–358; **Retro. Supp. II:** 235; **Supp. IV Part 2:** 474; **Supp. V:** 59, 315, 336; **Supp. VIII:** 94, 151, 171; **Supp. X:** 42, 290; **Supp. XII:** 310, 322; **Supp. XIV:**3; **Supp. XV:** 338

Weltzien, O. Alan, **Supp. XVI:**20–21, 28

"We miss Her, not because We see—" (Dickinson), **Retro. Supp. I:** 46

We Must Dance My Darlings (Trilling), **Supp. I Part 1:** 297

Wendell, Barrett, **III:** 507; **Supp. I Part 2:** 414; **Supp. XIV:**197

Wendell, Sarah. *See* Holmes, Mrs. Abiel (Sarah Wendell)

Wendy Wasserstein: A Casebook (Barnett), **Supp. XV:** 323, 330

"Wendy Wasserstein's Three Sisters: Squandered Privilege" (Brewer), **Supp. XV:** 330

Wept of Wish-ton-Wish, The (Cooper), **I:** 339, 342, 350

Werbe, Peter, **Supp. XIII:** 236

"We Real Cool" (Brooks), **Supp. III Part 1:** 80

We're Back! A Dinosaur's Story (screenplay, Shanley), **Supp. XIV:**316

"We're Friends Again" (O'Hara), **III:** 372–373

"Were the Whole Realm of Nature Mine" (Watts), **I:** 458

Werewolves in Their Youth (Chabon), **Supp. XI:** 66, 76–77

Werlock, Abby, **Supp. XIII:** 293

Werthman, Michael, **Supp. V:** 115

"Wer-Trout, The" (Proulx), **Supp. VII:** 255–256

Wescott, Glenway, **I:** 288; **II:** 85; **III:** 448, 454; **Supp. VIII:** 156; **Supp. XIV:**342; **Supp. XVI:**195

"We Shall All Be Born Again But We Shall Not All Be Saved" (Matthews), **Supp. IX:** 162

West, Anthony, **Supp. IV Part 1:** 284

West, Benjamin, **Supp. I Part 2:** 511

West, Dorothy, **Supp. XIII:** 295

West, James, **II:** 562

West, Nathanael, **I:** 97, 107, 190, 211, 298; **II:** 436; **III:** 357, 425; **IV:** 285–307; **Retro. Supp. II:** 321–341; **Supp. IV Part 1:** 203; **Supp. VIII:** 97; **Supp. XI:** 85, 105, 159, 296; **Supp. XII:** 173, 310; **Supp. XIII:** 106, 170

West, Ray, **Supp. XV:** 142

West, Rebecca, **II:** 412, 445; **Supp. XVI:**152, 153

Westall, Julia Elizabeth. *See* Wolfe, Mrs. William Oliver (Julia Elizabeth Westall)

"We Stand United" (Benét), **Supp. XI:** 46

"West Authentic, The: Willa Cather" (Stegner), **Supp. IV Part 2:** 608

"West Coast, The: Region with a View" (Stegner), **Supp. IV Part 2:** 608–609

Westcott, Edward N., **II:** 102

"Western Association of Writers" (Chopin), **Supp. I Part 1:** 217

"Western Ballad, A" (Ginsberg), **Supp. II Part 1:** 311

Western Borders, The (Howe), **Supp. IV Part 2:** 424–425

Western Canon: The Books and Schools of the Ages (Bloom), **Supp. IX:** 146

Western Lands, The (Burroughs), **Supp. III Part 1:** 106

Western Star (Benét), **Supp. XI:** 46, 47, 57

"West Marginal Way" (Hugo), **Supp. VI:** 131, 135

West of Yesterday, East of Summer: New and Selected Poems, 1973–1993 (Monette), **Supp. X:** 159

West of Your City (Stafford), **Supp. XI:** 316, 317–318, 321, 322

Weston, Jessie L., **II:** 540; **III:** 12; **Supp. I Part 2:** 438

"West Real" (Ríos), **Supp. IV Part 2:** 539, 540

"West-running Brook" (Frost), **II:** 150, 162–164

West-running Brook (Frost), **II:** 155;

Retro. Supp. I: 136, 137

"West Wall" (Merwin), **Supp. III Part 1:** 355

"Westward Beach, A" (Jeffers), **Supp. II Part 2:** 418

Westward Ho (Harrison), **Supp. VIII:** 51, 52

Westward the Course of Empire (Leutze), **Supp. X:** 307

"Westward the Course of Empire Takes Its Way" (Wallace), **Supp. X:** 307–308

"West Wind" (Oliver), **Supp. VII:** 246

West Wind: Poems and Prose Poems (Oliver), **Supp. VII:** 243, 246–248

"West Wind, The" (Bryant), **Supp. I Part 1:** 155

"Wet Casements" (Ashbery), **Supp. III Part 1:** 18–20

We the Living (film), **Supp. IV Part 2:** 520

We the Living (Rand), **Supp. IV Part 2:** 520–521

Wet Parade (Sinclair), **Supp. V:** 289

"We've Adjusted Too Well" (O'Brien), **Supp. V:** 247

Wevill, David, **Retro. Supp. II:** 247, 249

"We Wear the Mask" (Dunbar), **Supp. II Part 1:** 199, 207, 209–210

Weybright, Victor, **Supp. XIII:** 172

Weyden, Rogier van der, **Supp. IV Part 1:** 284

Whalen, Marcella, **Supp. I Part 1:** 49

Whalen, Philip, **Supp. VIII:** 289

Whalen-Bridge, John, **Retro. Supp. II:** 211–212

"Whales off Wales, The" (X. J. Kennedy), **Supp. XV:** 163

Wharton, Edith, **I:** 12, 375; **II:** 96, 180, 183, 186, 189–190, 193, 283, 338, 444, 451; **III:** 69, 175, 576; **IV:** 8, 53, 58, 308–330; **Retro. Supp. I:** 108, 232, 359–385; **Supp. IV Part 1:** 23, 31, 35, 36, 80, 81, 310; **Supp. IX:** 57; **Supp. XII:** 308; **Supp. XIV:**337, 347; **Supp. XVI:**189

Wharton, Edward Robbins, **IV:** 310, 313–314, 319

"What" (Dunn), **Supp. XI:** 144

What a Kingdom It Was (Kinnell), **Supp. III Part 1:** 235, 238, 239

"What America Would Be Like without Blacks" (Ellison), **Retro. Supp. II:** 123

What Are Masterpieces (Stein), **IV:** 30–31

What Are Years (Moore), **III:** 208–209, 210, 215

"What Are Years?" (Moore), **III:** 211, 213

What a Way to Go (Morris), **III:** 230–232

"What a Wonder among the Instruments Is the Walloping Trombone!" (Carruth), **Supp. XVI:**51

"What Became of the Flappers?" (Zelda Fitzgerald), **Supp. IX:** 71

"What Can I Tell My Bones?" (Roethke), **III:** 546, 549

"What Do We Have Here" (Carson), **Supp. XII:** 101

"What Do We See" (Rukeyser), **Supp. VI:** 282

What Do Women Want? Bread Roses Sex Power (Jong), **Supp. V:** 115, 117, 129, 130

"What Do You Do in San Francisco?" (Carver), **Supp. III Part 1:** 143

What D'Ya Know for Sure (Zinberg), **Supp. XV:** 196

Whatever Happened to Gloomy Gus of the Chicago Bears? (Coover), **Supp. V:** 51, 52

Whatever Happened to Jacy Farrow? (Cleveland), **Supp. V:** 222

"What Every Boy Should Know" (Maxwell), **Supp. VIII:** 169

"What Feels Like the World" (Bausch), **Supp. VII:** 46

"What Fort Sumter Did for Me" (E. Stoddard), **Supp. XV:** 282

"What God Is Like to Him I Serve" (Bradstreet), **Supp. I Part 1:** 106–107

"What Happened Here Before" (Snyder), **Supp. VIII:** 302

What Have I Ever Lost by Dying? (R. Bly), **Supp. IV Part 1:** 71–72

What Have You Lost? (Nye, ed.), **Supp. XIII:** 280

"What I Believe" (Mumford), **Supp. II Part 2:** 479

"What I Call What They Call Onanism" (Goldbarth), **Supp. XII:** 175

What I Did Last Summer (Gurney), **Supp. V:** 96, 100, 107, 108

"What if God" (Olds), **Supp. X:** 208

"What I Have to Defend, What I Can't Bear Losing" (Stern), **Supp. IX:** 286, 287, 288, 298

"What I Know about Being a Playwright" (McNally), **Supp. XIII:** 195, 207

"What I Mean" (Ortiz), **Supp. IV Part 2:** 497

"What Is an Emotion" (James), **II:** 350

What Is Art? (Tolstoy), **I:** 58

"What Is Civilization? Africa's Answer" (Du Bois), **Supp. II Part 1:** 176

"What Is College For?" (Bourne), **I:** 216

"What Is Exploitation?" (Bourne), **I:** 216

"What Is It?" (Carver), **Supp. III Part 1:** 139

What Is Man? (Twain), **II:** 434; **IV:** 209

"What Is Poetry" (Ashbery), **Supp. III Part 1:** 19

"What Is Seized" (Moore), **Supp. X:** 164, 168, 169, 172, 175

"What Is the Earth?" (Olds), **Supp. X:** 213

"What Is This Poet" (Stern), **Supp. IX:** 295

"What I Think" (Hogan), **Supp. IV Part 1:** 406

What Maisie Knew (James), **II:** 332; **Retro. Supp. I:** 229, 230

What Makes Sammy Run? (Schulberg), **Supp. XIII:** 170

What Moon Drove Me to This? (Harjo), **Supp. XII:** 218–220

"What Must" (MacLeish), **III:** 18

"What Sally Said" (Cisneros), **Supp. VII:** 63

"What's Happening in America" (Sontag), **Supp. III Part 2:** 460–461

"What's in Alaska?" (Carver), **Supp. III Part 1:** 141, 143

What's New, Pussycat? (film; Allen), **Supp. XI:** 307; **Supp. XV:** 1, 2, 14

"What's New in American and Canadian Poetry" (R. Bly), **Supp. IV Part 1:** 67

What's O'Clock (Lowell), **II:** 511, 527, 528

What's Up, Tiger Lily? (film; Allen), **Supp. XV:** 2, 3

"What the Arts Need Now" (Baraka), **Supp. II Part 1:** 47

"What the Brand New Freeway Won't Go By" (Hugo), **Supp. VI:** 132–133

"What the Gypsies Told My Grandmother While She Was Still a Young Girl" (Simic), **Supp. VIII:** 283

"What the Prose Poem Carries with It" (R. Bly), **Supp. IV Part 1:** 64

"What They Wanted" (Dunn), **Supp. XI:** 151

What Thou Lovest Well (Hugo), **Supp. VI:** 140, 141

"What Thou Lovest Well Remains American" (Hugo), **Supp. VI:** 140, 141

What Time Collects (Farrell), **II:** 46, 47–48

What to Do? (Chernyshevsky), **Retro. Supp. I:** 269

What Use Are Flowers? (Hansberry), **Supp. IV Part 1:** 359, 368–369, 374

What Was Literature? (Fiedler), **Supp. XIII:** 96–97, 105–106

What Was Mine (Beattie), **Supp. V:** 33, 35

What Was the Relationship of the Lone Ranger to the Means of Production? (Baraka), **Supp. II Part 1:** 58

"What We Came Through" (Goldbarth), **Supp. XII:** 179–180

What We Talk About When We Talk About Love (Carver), **Supp. III Part 1:** 142–146

What We Talk about When We Talk about Love (Carver), **Supp. XII:** 139

"What Why When How Who" (Pinsky), **Supp. VI:** 244

What Will Suffice: Contemporary American Poets on the Art of Poetry (Buckley and Young, eds.), **Supp. XIII:** 313

What Work Is (Levine), **Supp. V:** 181, 187, 192–193

"What You Hear from Em" (Taylor), **Supp. V:** 314, 320, 324

"What You Want" (O. Henry), **Supp. II Part 1:** 402

Wheatly, Phyllis, **Supp. XIII:** 111

Wheeler, David, **Supp. XVI:**277

Wheeler, John, **II:** 433

Wheeler, Monroe, **Supp. XV:** 295

Wheelock, John Hall, **IV:** 461; **Supp. IX:** 268; **Supp. XIV:**120; **Supp. XV:** 301

Wheel of Life, The (Glasgow), **II:** 176, 178, 179, 183

Wheelwright, Philip, **Supp. XV:** 20

"When" (Olds), **Supp. X:** 207

When Boyhood Dreams Come True (Farrell), **II:** 45

"When Death Came April Twelve 1945" (Sandburg), **III:** 591, 593

"When Death Comes" (Oliver), **Supp. VII:** 241

"When De Co'n Pone's Hot" (Dunbar), **Supp. II Part 1:** 202–203

"When God First Said" (Zach; Everwine trans.), **Supp. XV:** 87

"When Grandma Died—1942" (Shields), **Supp. VII:** 311

"When Howitzers Began" (Carruth), **Supp. XVI:**55

"When I Buy Pictures" (Moore), **III:** 205

"When I Came from Colchis" (Merwin), **Supp. III Part 1:** 343

"When I Left Business for Literature" (Anderson), **I:** 101

"When in Rome—Apologia" (Komunyakaa), **Supp. XIII:** 120

"When It Comes" (Olds), **Supp. X:** 213

"When I Was Seventeen" (Kincaid), **Supp. VII:** 181

When Knighthood Was in Flower (Major), **III:** 320

"[0]sqb;When[0]sqb; Let by rain" (Taylor), **IV:** 160–161

"When Lilacs Last in the Dooryard Bloom'd" (Whitman), **IV:** 347–348, 351; **Retro. Supp. I:** 406; **Supp. IV Part 1:** 16; **Supp. XV:** 215

"When Malindy Sings" (Dunbar), **Supp. II Part 1:** 200, 204–205

When Peoples Meet: A Study of Race and Culture (Locke and Stern), **Supp. XIV:** 202, 213

When She Was Good (Roth), **Retro. Supp. II:** 282, 283, 284; **Supp. III Part 2:** 403, 405, 410–413

"When Sue Wears Red" (Hughes), **Retro. Supp. I:** 195, 204

"When the Dead Ask My Father about Me" (Olds), **Supp. X:** 210

"When the Frost Is on the Punkin" (Riley), **Supp. II Part 1:** 202

When the Jack Hollers (Hughes), **Retro. Supp. I:** 203; **Supp. I Part 1:** 328

"When the Last Riders" (Zach; Everwine, trans.), **Supp. XV:** 75, 86

"When the Light Gets Green" (Warren), **IV:** 252

"When the Peace Corps Was Young" (Theroux), **Supp. VIII:** 314

When the Sun Tries to Go On (Koch), **Supp. XV:** 185

"When the Sun Tries to Go On" (Koch), **Supp. XV:** 179, 180

"When the World Ended as We Knew It" (Harjo), **Supp. XII:** 231

When Time Was Born (Farrell), **II:** 46, 47

"When We Dead Awaken: Writing as Re-Vision" (Rich), **Supp. I Part 2:** 552–553, 560

"When We Gonna Rise" (Baraka), **Supp. II Part 1:** 48

"When We Have To" (Salinas), **Supp. XIII:** 322–323

"WHEN WE'LL WORSHIP JESUS" (Baraka), **Supp. II Part 1:** 54

"When Women Throw Down Bundles: Strong Women Make Strong Na-

tions" (Gunn Allen), **Supp. IV Part 1:** 328

"'When You Finally See Them': The Unconquered Eye in *To Kill a Mockingbird*" (Champion), **Supp. VIII:** 128

"When You Lie Down, the Sea Stands Up" (Swenson), **Supp. IV Part 2:** 643

Where Does One Go When There's No Place Left to Go? (Crews), **Supp. XI:** 103

"Where I Come from Is Like This" (Gunn Allen), **Supp. IV Part 1:** 319

"Where I'm Calling From" (Carver), **Supp. III Part 1:** 145

Where I'm Calling From: New and Selected Stories (Carver), **Supp. III Part 1:** 138, 148

"Where I Ought to Be" (Erdrich), **Supp. IV Part 1:** 265

Where Is My Wandering Boy Tonight? (Wagoner), **Supp. IX:** 335–336

"Where Is the Island?" (Francis), **Supp. IX:** 78

"Where Is the Voice Coming From?" (Welty), **IV:** 280; **Retro. Supp. I:** 355

Where Joy Resides (Isherwood), **Supp. XIV:** 156

"Where Knock Is Open Wide" (Roethke), **III:** 533–535

"Where My Sympathy Lies" (H. Roth), **Supp. IX:** 234

Where's My Money? (Shanley), **Supp. XIV:** 316, 328, 330–331

Where the Bluebird Sings to the Lemonade Springs (Stegner), **Supp. IV Part 2:** 596, 597, 598, 600, 604, 606, 613

Where the Cross Is Made (O'Neill), **III:** 388, 391

Where the Sea Used to Be (Bass), **Supp. XVI:** 21

"Where the Sea Used to Be" (Bass), **Supp. XVI:** 20, 21

"*Where the Sea Used to Be:* Rick Bass and the Novel of Ecological Education" (Dixon), **Supp. XVI:** 21

"Where the Soft Air Lives" (Nye), **Supp. XIII:** 275

Where the Twilight Never Ends (Haines), **Supp. XII:** 211

Where the Wild Things Are (Sendak), **Supp. IX:** 207

"Wherever Home Is" (Wright), **Supp. III Part 2:** 605, 606

Where Water Comes Together With Other Water (Carver), **Supp. III Part 1:** 147, 148

"Where We Crashed" (Hugo), **Supp. VI:** 138

"Where You Are" (Doty), **Supp. XI:** 131

Where You'll Find Me, and Other Stories (Beattie), **Supp. V:** 30–31

Whicher, Stephen, **II:** 20

"Which Is More Than I Can Say for Some People" (Moore), **Supp. X:** 177, 178

Which Ones Are the Enemy? (Garrett), **Supp. VII:** 98

"Which Theatre Is the Absurd One?" (Albee), **I:** 71

"Which Way to the Future?" (Rehder), **Supp. IV Part 1:** 69

While I Was Gone (Miller), **Supp. XII:** 290, 301–303

"While Seated in a Plane" (Swenson), **Supp. IV Part 2:** 645

Whilomville Stories (Crane), **I:** 414

"Whip, The" (Robinson), **III:** 513

Whipple, Thomas K., **II:** 456, 458; **IV:** 427

"Whippoorwill, The" (Francis), **Supp. IX:** 90

"Whip-poor-will, The" (Thurber), **Supp. I Part 2:** 616

"Whispering Gallery, The" (Komunyakaa), **Supp. XIII:** 132

"Whispering Leaves" (Glasgow), **II:** 190

Whispering to Fool the Wind (Ríos), **Supp. IV Part 2:** 540–541, 544, 545

"Whispers in the Next Room" (Simic), **Supp. VIII:** 278

"Whispers of Heavenly Death" (Whitman), **IV:** 348

"Whispers of Immortality" (Eliot), **Supp. XI:** 242

Whistle (Jones), **Supp. XI:** 219, 224, 231–234

"Whistle, The" (Franklin), **II:** 121

"Whistle, The" (Komunyakaa), **Supp. XIII:** 111, 126

"Whistle, The" (Welty), **IV:** 262

Whistler, James, **I:** 484; **III:** 461, 465, 466; **IV:** 77, 369

Whistler, James Abbott McNeill, **Supp. XIV:** 335–336

"Whistling Dick's Christmas Stocking" (O. Henry), **Supp. II Part 1:** 390, 392

Whistling in the Dark (Garrett), **Supp. VII:** 111

Whistling in the Dark: True Stories and Other Fables (Garrett), **Supp. VII:** 95

Whitcher, Frances Miriam Berry, **Supp. XIII:** 152

"White" (Simic), **Supp. VIII:** 275–276
White, Barbara, **Retro. Supp. I:** 379
White, E. B., **Retro. Supp. I:** 335; **Supp. I Part 2:** 602, 607, 608, 612, 619, 620, 651–681; **Supp. II Part 1:** 143; **Supp. VIII:** 171; **Supp. IX:** 20, 32; **Supp. XVI:** 167
White, Elizabeth Wade, **Supp. I Part 1:** 100, 103, 111
White, Henry Kirke, **Supp. I Part 1:** 150
White, James L., **Supp. XI:** 123
White, Joel, **Supp. I Part 2:** 654, 678
White, Katharine. (Katharine Sergeant Angell), **Supp. I Part 2:** 610, 653, 655, 656, 669; **Supp. VIII:** 151, 171
White, Lillian, **Supp. I Part 2:** 651
White, Lucia, **I:** 258
White, Maria. *See* Lowell, Mrs. James Russell (Maria White)
White, Morton, **I:** 258; **Supp. I Part 2:** 647, 648, 650
White, Roberta, **Supp. XII:** 293
White, Stanford, **Supp. IV Part 1:** 223
White, Stanley, **Supp. I Part 2:** 651, 655
White, T. H., **III:** 522
White, T. W., **III:** 411, 415
White, Walter, **Supp. I Part 1:** 345
White, William, **Retro. Supp. II:** 326
White, William A., **I:** 252
White Album, The (Didion), **Supp. IV Part 1:** 198, 202, 205–207, 210
"White Album, The" (Didion), **Supp. IV Part 1:** 205, 206
"White Angel" (Cunningham), **Supp. XV:** 59
White Buildings (H. Crane), **I:** 385, 386, 390–395, 400; **Retro. Supp. II:** 77–78, 80–81, 82, 83, 85
White Butterfly (Mosley), **Supp. XIII:** 237, 238, 240
White Center (Hugo), **Supp. VI:** 144–145
"White Center" (Hugo), **Supp. VI:** 144, 146
Whited, Stephen, **Supp. XI:** 135
White Deer, The (Thurber), **Supp. I Part 2:** 606
White Doves at Morning (Burke), **Supp. XIV:** 22–23, 32, 35–36
"White Eagle, The" (Chopin), **Retro. Supp. II:** 72
White Fang (London), **II:** 471–472, 481
Whitefield, George, **I:** 546
White-Footed Deer and Other Poems (Bryant), **Supp. I Part 1:** 157
White Goddess, The (Graves), **Supp.**

IV Part 1: 280
White-Haired Lover (Shapiro), **Supp. II Part 2:** 703, 717
Whitehead, Alfred North, **III:** 605, 619, 620; **IV:** 88; **Supp. I Part 2:** 554, 647
Whitehead, Colson, **Supp. XIII:** 233, 241
Whitehead, James, **Supp. XV:** 339
Whitehead, Margaret, **IV:** 114, 115, 116
Whitehead, Mrs. Catherine, **IV:** 116
White Heat (Walsh), **Supp. XIII:** 174
"White Heron, A" (Jewett), **II:** 409; **Retro. Supp. II:** 17
White Heron and Other Stories, A (Jewett), **II:** 396
White Horses (Hoffman), **Supp. X:** 83–85, 90, 92
White House Diary, A (Lady Bird Johnson), **Supp. IV Part 1:** 22
White Jacket; or, The World in a Man-of-War (Melville), **III:** 80, 81, 84, 94; *Retro* **Supp. I:** 248, 249, 254
White Lantern, The (Connell), **Supp. XIV:** 97
"White Lights, The" (Robinson), **III:** 524
"White Lilies, The" (Glück), **Supp. V:** 88
White Man, Listen! (Wright), **IV:** 478, 488, 489, 494
"White Mulberry Tree, The" (Cather), **I:** 319; **Retro. Supp. I:** 7, 9, 17
White Mule (W. C. Williams), **Retro. Supp. I:** 423
"White Negro, The" (Mailer), **III:** 36–37; **Retro. Supp. II:** 202
"Whiteness of the Whale, The" (Melville), **III:** 84, 86
"White Night" (Oliver), **Supp. VII:** 236
"White Nights" (Auster), **Supp. XII:** 23–24
White Noise (DeLillo), **Supp. VI:** 1, 3–4, 5–7, 10, 11–12, 16
White Oxen and Other Stories, The (Burke), **I:** 269, 271
White Paper on Contemporary American Poetry (McClatchy), **Supp. XII:** 253, 259–260
"White Pine" (Oliver), **Supp. VII:** 244
White Pine: Poems and Prose Poems (Oliver), **Supp. VII:** 243–246
"White Silence, The" (London), **II:** 468
"White Silk" (Nye), **Supp. XIII:** 275
"White Snake, The" (Sexton), **Supp. II Part 2:** 691
"White Spot" (Anderson), **I:** 116

"White-Tailed Hornet, The" (Frost), **Retro. Supp. I:** 138
Whitfield, Raoul, **Supp. IV Part 1:** 345
Whitlock, Brand, **II:** 276
Whitman (Masters), **Supp. I Part 2:** 473, 475, 476
Whitman, George, **IV:** 346, 350
Whitman, Sarah Wyman, **Retro. Supp. II:** 136
"Whitman: The Poet and the Mask" (Cowley), **Supp. II Part 1:** 143
Whitman, Walt, **I:** 61, 68, 98, 103, 104, 109, 219, 220, 227, 228, 242, 246, 250, 251, 260, 261, 285, 381, 384, 386, 396, 397, 398, 402, 419, 430, 459, 460, 483, 485, 486, 577; **II:** 7, 8, 18, 127, 140, 273–274, 275, 289, 295, 301, 320, 321, 373, 445, 446, 451, 457, 494, 529, 530, 552; **III:** 171, 175, 177, 181–182, 189, 203, 234, 260, 426, 430, 453, 454, 461, 505, 507–508, 511, 528, 548, 552, 555, 559, 567, 572, 576, 577, 579, 584, 585, 595, 606, 609; **IV:** 74, 169, 191, 192, 202, 331–354, 405, 409, 416, 444, 450–451, 457, 463, 464, 469, 470, 471; **Retro. Supp. I:** 8, 52, 194, 254, 283, 284, 333, 387–410, 412, 417, 427; **Retro. Supp. II:** 40, 76, 93, 99, 155, 156, 158, 170, 262; **Supp. I Part 1:** 6, 79, 167, 311, 314, 325, 365, 368, 372; **Supp. I Part 2:** 374, 384, 385, 387, 389, 391, 393, 399, 416, 436, 455, 456, 458, 473, 474, 475, 525, 540, 579, 580, 582, 682, 691; **Supp. III Part 1:** 6, 20, 156, 239–241, 253, 340; **Supp. III Part 2:** 596; **Supp. IV Part 1:** 16, 169, 325; **Supp. IV Part 2:** 597, 625; **Supp. V:** 113, 118, 122, 130, 170, 178, 183, 277, 279, 332; **Supp. VIII:** 42, 95, 105, 126, 198, 202, 269; **Supp. IX:** 8, 9, 15, 38, 41, 44, 48, 53, 131, 292, 298, 299, 308, 320; **Supp. X:** 36, 112, 203, 204; **Supp. XI:** 83, 123, 132, 135, 203, 321; **Supp. XII:** 132, 185, 190, 256; **Supp. XIII:** 1, 77, 115, 153, 221, 304, 335; **Supp. XIV:** 89, 312, 334, 335, 338; **Supp. XV:** 41, 93, 181, 183, 212, 213, 218, 250, 275, 301, 302, 303, 309, 352; **Supp. XVI:** 209
Whitmarsh, Jason, **Supp. VIII:** 283
Whitmer, Peter, **Supp. X:** 264, 265
Whitney, Blair, **Supp. I Part 2:** 403
Whitney, Josiah, **Supp. IX:** 180, 181
Whitt, Margaret Earley, **Retro. Supp. II:** 226

Whittemore, Reed, **III:** 268; **Supp. XI:** 315

Whittier, Elizabeth, **Supp. I Part 2:** 700, 701, 703; **Supp. XIII:** 141, 142

Whittier, John Greenleaf, **I:** 216; **II:** 275; **III:** 52; **Retro. Supp. I:** 54; **Retro. Supp. II:** 155, 163, 169; **Supp. I Part 1:** 168, 299, 313, 317, 372; **Supp. I Part 2:** 420, 602, 682–707; **Supp. VIII:** 202, 204; **Supp. XI:** 50; **Supp. XIII:** 140, 145; **Supp. XV:** 246

Whittier, Mary, **Supp. I Part 2:** 683

"Whittier Birthday Speech" (Twain), **Supp. I Part 1:** 313

"Who" (Kenyon), **Supp. VII:** 174

"Who" (Sobin), **Supp. XVI:**284–285

"Who Am I—Who I Am" (Corso), **Supp. XII:** 134

"Who Be Kind To" (Ginsberg), **Supp. II Part 1:** 323

"Whoever Was Using This Bed" (Carver), **Supp. III Part 1:** 148

"Whoever You Are Holding Me Now in Hand" (Whitman), **IV:** 342; **Retro. Supp. I:** 52

Who Gathered and Whispered behind Me (Goldbarth), **Supp. XII:** 181, 182

"Who in One Lifetime" (Rukeyser), **Supp. VI:** 276, 279

Who Is Witter Bynner? (Kraft), **Supp. XV:** 40, 52

"Who Is Your Mother? Red Roots of White Feminism" (Gunn Allen), **Supp. IV Part 1:** 329

Whole Hog (Wagoner), **Supp. IX:** 337–338

"Whole Mess...Almost, The" (Corso), **Supp. XII:** 135

"Whole Moisty Night, The" (R. Bly), **Supp. IV Part 1:** 69

Whole New Life, A (Price), **Supp. VI:** 265, 266, 267

"Whole Self, The" (Nye), **Supp. XIII:** 275

"Whole Soul, The" (Levine), **Supp. V:** 192

"Whole Story, The" (Strand), **Supp. IV Part 2:** 622

Whole Town's Talking, The (Loos), **Supp. XVI:**187

"Whole World Knows, The" (Welty), **IV:** 272; **Retro. Supp. I:** 343

Who'll Stop the Rain (film), **Supp. V:** 301

Who Lost an American? (Algren), **Supp. IX:** 15–16

Who Owns America? (symposium), **Supp. XIV:**4

"Who Puts Together" (Hogan), **Supp. IV Part 1:** 403, 405, 412–413

"Whore of Mensa, The" (Allen), **Supp. XV:** 15

Whorf, Benjamin Lee, **Supp. XVI:**283

Who's Afraid of Virginia Woolf? (Albee), **I:** 71, 77–81, 83, 85, 86, 87, 94; **IV:** 230

Who Shall Be the Sun? Poems Based on the Lore, Legends, and Myths of the Northwest Coast and Plateau Indians (Wagoner), **Supp. IX:** 328, 329–330, 337

"Whosis Kid, The" (Hammett), **Supp. IV Part 1:** 344

"Who Sit Watch in Daylight" (Wright), **Supp. XV:** 342

"Who's Passing for Who?" (Hughes), **Supp. I Part 1:** 330

"Who Speak on the Page?" (Sanders), **Supp. XVI:**278

Who Will Run the Frog Hospital?: A Novel (Moore), **Supp. X:** 163, 165, 169, 175–177

Why Are We in Vietnam? (Mailer), **III:** 27, 29, 30, 33, 34–35, 39, 42, 44; **Retro. Supp. II:** 205–206

"Why Did the Balinese Chicken Cross the Road?" (Walker), **Supp. III Part 2:** 527

"Why Do the Heathens Rage?" (O'Connor), **III:** 351

"Why Do You Write About Russia?" (Simpson), **Supp. IX:** 277

"Why I Am a Danger to the Public" (Kingsolver), **Supp. VII:** 204

Why I Am Not a Christian (Russell), **Supp. I Part 2:** 522

"Why I Entered the Gurdjieff Work" (Toomer), **Supp. III Part 2:** 481

"Why I Like Laurel" (Patchett), **Supp. XII:** 309

"Why I Live at the P.O." (Welty), **IV:** 262; **Retro. Supp. I:** 345

"Why Is Economics Not an Evolutionary Science?" (Veblen), **Supp. I Part 2:** 634

"Why I Write" (Didion), **Supp. IV Part 1:** 201, 203

Why Johnny Can't Read: And What You Can Do About It (Flesch), **Supp. XVI:**105

"Why Negro Women Leave Home" (Brooks), **Supp. III Part 1:** 75

"Why the Little Frenchman Wears His Hand in a Sling" (Poe), **III:** 425

Why We Behave Like Microbe Hunters (Thurber), **Supp. I Part 2:** 606

Why We Were in Vietnam (Podhoretz), **Supp. VIII:** 241

"Why Write?" (Updike), **Retro. Supp. I:** 317

"Wichita Vortex Sutra" (Ginsberg), **Supp. II Part 1:** 319, 321, 323–325, 327

Wickes, George, **Supp. XIV:**165

Wickford Point (Marquand), **III:** 50, 58, 64–65, 69

Wicks, Robert Russell, **Supp. XII:** 49

Wide, Wide World, The (Warner), **Supp. XV:** 275

"Wide Empty Landscape with a Death in the Foreground" (Momaday), **Supp. IV Part 2:** 492

Wideman, John Edgar, **Retro. Supp. II:** 123; **Supp. X:** 239, 250, 319–336; **Supp. XI:** 245; **Supp. XIII:** 247

"Wide Net, The" (Welty), **IV:** 266

Wide Net and Other Stories, The (Welty), **IV:** 261, 264–266, 271; **Retro. Supp. I:** 347–349, 352, 355

Widening Spell of the Leaves, The (Levis), **Supp. XI:** 258, 259, 261, 268–269, 271

"Wide Prospect, The" (Jarrell), **II:** 376–377

Widow for One Year, A (Irving), **Supp. VI:** 165, 179–181

Widows of Thornton, The (Taylor), **Supp. V:** 320, 321

Wieland; or, The Transformation. An American Tale (Brown), **Supp. I Part 1:** 128–132, 133, 137, 140

Wiene, Robert, **Retro. Supp. I:** 268

Wiener, John, **Supp. IV Part 1:** 153

Wieners, John, **Supp. II Part 1:** 32

Wiest, Dianne, **Supp. XV:** 12

"Wife, Forty-five, Remembers Love, A" (Shields), **Supp. VII:** 310

"Wifebeater, The" (Sexton), **Supp. II Part 2:** 693

"Wife for Dino Rossi, A" (Fante), **Supp. XI:** 165

"Wife of His Youth, The" (Chesnutt), **Supp. XIV:**63–66

Wife of His Youth and Other Stories of the Color Line, The (Chesnutt), **Supp. XIV:**62, 63

"Wife of Jesus Speaks, The" (Karr), **Supp. XI:** 250–251

"Wife of Nashville, A" (Taylor), **Supp. V:** 320

"Wife's Story, The" (Davis), **Supp. XVI:**85, 91, 92–93

Wife's Story, The (Shields), **Supp. VII:** 316. *See also* Happenstance

"Wife-Wooing" (Updike), **IV:** 226

Wigan, Gareth, **Supp. XI:** 306

Wiget, Andrew, **Supp. IV Part 2:** 509

Wigglesworth, Michael, **IV:** 147, 156; **Supp. I Part 1:** 110, 111
Wilbur, Richard, **III:** 527; **Retro. Supp. II:** 50; **Supp. III Part 1:** 64; **Supp. III Part 2:** 541–565; **Supp. IV Part 2:** 626, 634, 642; **Supp. V:** 337; **Supp. VIII:** 28; **Supp. X:** 58, 120; **Supp. XII:** 258; **Supp. XIII:** 76, 336; **Supp. XV:** 51, 251, 256
Wilcocks, Alexander, **Supp. I Part 1:** 125
Wilcox, Ella Wheeler, **Supp. II Part 1:** 197
Wild 90 (film) (Mailer), **Retro. Supp. II:** 205
Wild, John, **II:** 362, 363–364
Wild, Peter, **Supp. V:** 5
Wild, Robert, **IV:** 155
"Wild, The" (Berry), **Supp. X:** 30
Wild and Woolly (film), **Supp. XVI:**185
Wild Boy of Aveyron, The (Itard). *See* De l'éducation d'un homme sauvage
Wild Boys, The: A Book of the Dead (Burroughs), **Supp. III Part 1:** 106–107
Wilde, Oscar, **I:** 50, 66, 381, 384; **II:** 515; **IV:** 77, 350; **Retro. Supp. I:** 56, 102, 227; **Retro. Supp. II:** 76, 326; **Supp. IV Part 2:** 578, 679, 683; **Supp. V:** 106, 283; **Supp. IX:** 65, 66, 68, 189, 192; **Supp. X:** 148, 151, 188–189; **Supp. XIV:**324, 334; **Supp. XV:** 350
Wilder, Amos Parker, **IV:** 356
Wilder, Billy, **Supp. IV Part 1:** 130; **Supp. XI:** 307
Wilder, Isabel, **IV:** 357, 366, 375
Wilder, Mrs. Amos Parker (Isabella Thornton Niven), **IV:** 356
Wilder, Thornton, **I:** 360, 482; **IV:** 355–377, 431; **Retro. Supp. I:** 109, 359; **Supp. I Part 2:** 609; **Supp. IV Part 2:** 586; **Supp. V:** 105; **Supp. IX:** 140; **Supp. XII:** 236–237
"Wilderness" (Leopold), **Supp. XIV:**190
"Wilderness" (Sandburg), **III:** 584, 595
Wilderness (Warren), **IV:** 256
"Wilderness, The" (Merwin), **Supp. III Part 1:** 340, 345
"Wilderness, The" (Robinson), **III:** 524
Wilderness of Vision, The: On the Poetry of John Haines (Bezner and Walzer, eds.), **Supp. XII:** 202
Wilderness Plots: Tales about the Settlement of the American Land (Sanders), **Supp. XVI:**267–268, 269
Wilderness World of Anne LaBastille, The (LaBastille), **Supp. X:** 105, 106

Wild Flag, The (White), **Supp. I Part 2:** 654
"Wildflower, The" (W. C. Williams), **Retro. Supp. I:** 420
"Wild Flowers" (Caldwell), **I:** 310
"Wildflowers" (Minot), **Supp. VI:** 208
"Wild Geese" (Oliver), **Supp. VII:** 237
"Wild Honey Suckle, The" (Freneau), **Supp. II Part 1:** 253, 264, 266
Wild in the Country (Odets), **Supp. II Part 2:** 546
Wild Iris, The (Glück), **Supp. V:** 79, 87–89, 91
Wildlife (Ford), **Supp. V:** 57, 69–71
Wildlife in America (Matthiessen), **Supp. V:** 199, 201, 204
"Wildlife in American Culture" (Leopold), **Supp. XIV:**190, 191
"Wildness" (Sanders), **Supp. XVI:**276
Wild Old Wicked Man, The (MacLeish), **III:** 3, 20
Wild Palms, The (Faulkner), **II:** 68–69; **Retro. Supp. I:** 85
"Wild Palms, The" (Faulkner), **II:** 68
"Wild Peaches" (Wylie), **Supp. I Part 2:** 707, 712
Wild Roses of Cape Ann and Other Poems (Larcom), **Supp. XIII:** 142, 147
Wild Seed (O. Butler), **Supp. XIII:** 62, 63
"Wild Swans at Coole, The " (W. B. Yeats), **Supp. XVI:**48
"Wild Swans at Norfolk, The" (Carruth), **Supp. XVI:**48
Wild to the Heart (Bass), **Supp. XVI:**16
"Wildwest" (MacLeish), **III:** 14
Wiley, Craig, **Supp. VIII:** 313
Wilhelm Meister (Goethe), **II:** 291
Wilkes, John, **Supp. I Part 2:** 503, 519, 522
Wilkie, Curtis, **Supp. V:** 11
Wilkins, Roy, **Supp. I Part 1:** 345
Wilkinson, Alec, **Supp. VIII:** 164, 168, 171
Wilkinson, Max, **Supp. IX:** 251
Willard, Samuel, **IV:** 150
Willard Gibbs (Rukeyser), **Supp. VI:** 273, 283, 284
Willett, Ralph, **Supp. XIV:**27
Willey, Basil, **Retro. Supp. II:** 243
William Carlos Williams (Koch), **Retro. Supp. I:** 428
William Carlos Williams: An American Artist (Breslin), **Retro. Supp. I:** 430
William Carlos Williams: The American Background (Weaver), **Retro. Supp. I:** 430
William Carlos Williams and Alterity

(Ahearn), **Retro. Supp. I:** 415
William Carlos Williams and the Meanings of Measure (Cushman), **Retro. Supp. I:** 430
William Faulkner: A Critical Study (Howe), **Supp. VI:** 119–120, 125
William Faulkner: Early Prose and Poetry (Faulkner), **Retro. Supp. I:** 80
William Faulkner: First Encounters (Brooks), **Supp. XIV:**13
"William Faulkner: The Stillness of Light in August" (Kazin), **Supp. VIII:** 104
William Faulkner: The Yoknapatawpha Country (Brooks), **Supp. XIV:**12–13, 16
William Faulkner: Toward Yoknapatawpha and Beyond (Brooks), **Supp. XIV:**13
"William Faulkner's Legend of the South" (Cowley), **Supp. II Part 1:** 143
"William Humphrey, 73, Writer of Novels about Rural Texas" (Gussow), **Supp. IX:** 93
William Humphrey. Boise State University Western Writers Series (Winchell), **Supp. IX:** 109
William Humphrey, Destroyer of Myths (Almon), **Supp. IX:** 93
William Humphrey. Southwestern Series (Lee), **Supp. IX:** 109
"William Humphrey Remembered" (Masters), **Supp. IX:** 96
"William Ireland's Confession" (A. Miller), **III:** 147–148
William James and Phenomenology: A Study of the "Principles of Psychology" (Wilshire), **II:** 362
William Lloyd Garrison (Chapman), **Supp. XIV:**46–51, 52, 53, 55
Williams, Annie Laurie, **Supp. IX:** 93
Williams, C. K., **Supp. XIII:** 114
Williams, Cecil, **II:** 508
Williams, Charles, **Supp. II Part 1:** 15, 16
Williams, Dakin, **IV:** 379
Williams, David Reichard, **Supp. XIII:** 162
Williams, Edward, **IV:** 404
Williams, Edwina Dakin, **IV:** 379
Williams, Esther, **Supp. XII:** 165
Williams, Fannie Barrier, **Supp. XIV:**201
Williams, George, **Supp. V:** 220
Williams, Horace, **IV:** 453
Williams, Joan, **Supp. IX:** 95
Williams, John A., **Supp. XVI:**143
Williams, John Sharp, **IV:** 378
Williams, Lyle, **Supp. XIV:**22

Williams, Michael, **Supp. V:** 286

Williams, Miller, **Supp. XIV:**126; **Supp. XV:** 339

Williams, Mrs. William Carlos (Florence Herman), **IV:** 404

Williams, Paul, **IV:** 404

Williams, Raymond, **Supp. IX:** 146

Williams, Roger, **Supp. I Part 2:** 699

Williams, Rose, **IV:** 379

Williams, Sherley Anne, **Supp. V:** 180

Williams, Solomon, **I:** 549

Williams, Stanley T., **II:** 301, 316; **Supp. I Part 1:** 251

Williams, Stephen, **IV:** 148

Williams, Ted, **IV:** 216; **Supp. IX:** 162

Williams, Tennessee, **I:** 73, 81, 113, 211; **II:** 190, 194; **III:** 145, 147; **IV:** 4, 378–401; **Supp. I Part 1:** 290, 291; **Supp. IV Part 1:** 79, 83, 84, 359; **Supp. IV Part 2:** 574, 682; **Supp. IX:** 133; **Supp. XI:** 103; **Supp. XIII:** 331; **Supp. XIV:**250, 315; **Supp. XVI:**194

Williams, Terry Tempest, **Supp. XIII:** 16

Williams, Walter L., **Supp. IV Part 1:** 330, 331

Williams, William, **IV:** 404, 405

Williams, William Carlos, **I:** 61, 62, 229, 255, 256, 261, 285, 428, 438, 446, 539; **II:** 133, 536, 542, 543, 544, 545; **III:** 194, 196, 198, 214, 269, 409, 453, 457, 458, 464, 465, 591; **IV:** 30, 74, 75, 76, 94, 95, 286, 287, 402–425; **Retro. Supp. I:** 51, 52, 62, 209, 284, 285, 288, 296, 298, 411–433; **Retro. Supp. II:** 178, 181, 189, 250, 321, 322, 326, 327, 328, 334, 335; **Supp. I Part 1:** 254, 255, 259, 266; **Supp. II Part 1:** 9, 30, 308, 318; **Supp. II Part 2:** 421, 443; **Supp. III Part 1:** 9, 147, 239, 271, 275, 276, 278, 350; **Supp. III Part 2:** 542, 610, 613, 614, 615, 616, 617, 621, 622, 626, 628; **Supp. IV Part 1:** 151, 153, 246, 325; **Supp. V:** 180, 337; **Supp. VIII:** 195, 269, 272, 277, 292; **Supp. IX:** 38, 268, 291; **Supp. X:** 112, 120, 204; **Supp. XI:** 311, 328; **Supp. XII:** 198; **Supp. XIII:** 77, 90, 335; **Supp. XIV:**280, 284, 285, 293; **Supp. XV:** 42, 51, 182, 250, 306, 307; **Supp. XVI:**48, 282

Williams, Wirt, **Supp. XIV:**24

Williamson, Alan, **Retro. Supp. II:** 185

William Styron's Nat Turner: Ten Black Writers Respond (Clarke, ed.), **IV:** 115

Williams-Walsh, Mary Ellen, **Supp. IV Part 2:** 611

William the Conqueror, **Supp. I Part 2:** 507

William Wetmore Story and His Friends (James), **Retro. Supp. I:** 235

William Wilson (Gardner), **Supp. VI:** 72

"William Wilson" (Poe), **II:** 475; **III:** 410, 412; **Retro. Supp. II:** 269; **Supp. IX:** 105

"Willie" (Angelou), **Supp. IV Part 1:** 15

Willie Masters' Lonesome Wife (Gass), **Supp. VI:** 77, 84–85, 86–87

"Willing" (Moore), **Supp. X:** 178

Willis, Bruce, **Supp. IV Part 1:** 236

Willis, Gordon, **Supp. XV:** 7

Willis, Mary Hard, **Supp. V:** 290–291

Willis, Nathaniel Parker, **II:** 313; **Supp. I Part 2:** 405

Williwaw (Vidal), **Supp. IV Part 2:** 677, 680, 681

"Willow Woman" (Francis), **Supp. IX:** 78

Wills, Garry, **Supp. I Part 1:** 294; **Supp. IV Part 2:** 355

Wills, Ridley, **IV:** 122

Wills, Ross B., **Supp. XI:** 169

"Will to Believe, The" (James), **II:** 352; **Supp. XIV:**50

Will to Believe, The, and Other Essays in Popular Philosophy (James), **II:** 356; **IV:** 28

Will to Change, The: Poems, 1968–1970 (Rich), **Supp. I Part 2:** 551, 557–559

"Will We Plug Chips into Our Brains?" (W. Gibson), **Supp. XVI:**117–118

"Will You Please Be Quiet, Please?" (Carver), **Supp. III Part 1:** 137, 141

Will You Please Be Quiet, Please? (Carver), **Supp. III Part 1:** 138, 140, 144

"Will You Tell Me?" (Barthelme), **Supp. IV Part 1:** 42, 47

Wilsdorf, Anne, **Supp. XVI:**177

Wilshire, Bruce, **II:** 362, 364

Wilshire, Gaylord, **Supp. V:** 280

Wilson, Adrian, **Supp. XV:** 147

Wilson, Alexander, **Supp. XVI:**4, 6

Wilson, Angus, **IV:** 430, 435

Wilson, August, **Supp. VIII:** 329–353

Wilson, Augusta Jane Evans, **Retro. Supp. I:** 351

Wilson, E. O., **Supp. X:** 35

Wilson, Earl, **Supp. X:** 264

Wilson, Edmund, **I:** 67, 185, 236, 247, 260, 434, 482; **II:** 79, 80, 81, 86, 87, 91, 97, 98, 146, 276, 430, 530, 562, 587; **III:** 588; **IV:** 308, 310, 426–449; **Retro. Supp. I:** 1, 97, 100, 101, 103, 104, 105, 115, 274; **Retro. Supp. II:** 321, 327, 329; **Supp. I Part 1:** 372; **Supp. I Part 2:** 407, 646, 678, 709; **Supp. II Part 1:** 19, 90, 106, 136, 137, 143; **Supp. III Part 2:** 612; **Supp. IV Part 2:** 693; **Supp. VIII:** 93, 95, 96, 97, 98–99, 100, 100, 101, 103, 105, 162; **Supp. IX:** 55, 65, 190; **Supp. X:** 186; **Supp. XI:** 160; **Supp. XIII:** 170; **Supp. XIV:**338; **Supp. XV:** 142, 308; **Supp. XVI:**194

Wilson, Edmund (father), **IV:** 441

Wilson, Henry, **Supp. XIV:**48

Wilson, Reuel, **II:** 562

Wilson, Robert, **Supp. XI:** 144

Wilson, Sloan, **Supp. IV Part 1:** 387

Wilson, Thomas, **IV:** 153

Wilson, Victoria, **Supp. X:** 166

Wilson, Woodrow, **I:** 245, 246, 490; **II:** 183, 253; **III:** 105, 581; **Supp. I Part 1:** 21; **Supp. I Part 2:** 474, 643; **Supp. V:** 288

Wilton, David, **IV:** 147

Wiman, Christian, **Supp. XV:** 251, 253, 264

Wimberly, Lowry, **Supp. XV:** 136, 137

Wimsatt, William K., **Supp. XIV:**12

Winchell, Mark, **Supp. VIII:** 176, 189

Winchell, Mark Royden, **Supp. VIII:** 241; **Supp. IX:** 97, 98, 109; **Supp. XIII:** 94, 98, 99, 101; **Supp. XIV:**103, 106, 111

Winckelmann, Johann Joachim, **Supp. XII:** 178

Wind, Sand, and Stars (Saint-Exupéry), **Supp. IX:** 247

Wind Chrysalid's Rattle (Sobin), **Supp. XVI:**283

Windham, Donald, **IV:** 382

"Windhover" (Hopkins), **I:** 397; **II:** 539; **Supp. IX:** 43

Winding Stair and Other Poems, The (Yeats), **Supp. XV:** 253

"Winding Street, The" (Petry), **Supp. XI:** 6

"Window" (Pinsky), **Supp. VI:** 237, 247

Windows (Creeley), **Supp. IV Part 1:** 157, 158

"Windows" (Jarrell), **II:** 388, 389

"Window Seat, A" (Goldbarth), **Supp. XII:** 185

Wind Remains, The (opera) (Bowles), **Supp. IV Part 1:** 83

"Winds, The" (Welty), **IV:** 265; **Retro. Supp. I:** 348, 350

"Wind up Sushi" (Goldbarth), **Supp.**

XII: 186–187
"Windy Day at the Reservoir, A" (Beattie), **Supp. V:** 33
Windy McPherson's Son (Anderson), **I:** 101, 102–103, 105, 111
"Wine" (Carver), **Supp. III Part 1:** 138
"Wine Menagerie, The" (H. Crane), **I:** 389, 391; **Retro. Supp. II:** 82
Wine of the Puritans, The: A Study of Present-Day America (Brooks), **I:** 240
"Wine of Wizardry, A" (Sterling), **I:** 208
Winer, Linda, **Supp. IV Part 2:** 580; **Supp. XV:** 332
Winesburg, Ohio: A Group of Tales of Ohio Small Town Life (Anderson), **I:** 97, 102, 103, 104, 105–108; **III:** 112, 113, 114, 116, 224, 579; **Supp. V:** 12; **Supp. IX:** 306, 308; **Supp. XI:** 164; **Supp. XVI:**17
Wing-and-Wing, The (Cooper), **I:** 350, 355
Winged Seed, The: A Remembrance (L.-Y. Lee), **Supp. XV:** 211, 220–223
Winged Words: American Indian Writers Speak (Coltelli), **Supp. IV Part 2:** 493, 497
"Wingfield" (Wolff), **Supp. VII:** 341–342
"Wings, The" (Doty), **Supp. XI:** 124
Wings of the Dove, The (James), **I:** 436; **II:** 320, 323, 333, 334–335; **Retro. Supp. I:** 215, 216, 217, 232, 233–234; **Supp. II Part 1:** 94–95; **Supp. IV Part 1:** 349
Winner Take Nothing (Hemingway), **II:** 249; **Retro. Supp. I:** 170, 175, 176, 181
"Winnie" (Brooks), **Supp. III Part 1:** 86
Winokur, Maxine. *See* Kumin, Maxine
Winslow, Devereux, **II:** 547
Winslow, Harriet, **II:** 552–553
Winslow, Ola Elizabeth, **I:** 547
Winslow, Warren, **II:** 540
Winston, Andrew, **Supp. XII:** 189
Winston, Michael R., **Supp. XIV:**197
Winter, Douglas, **Supp. V:** 144
Winter, Johnny and Edgar, **Supp. V:** 334
Winter, Kate, **Supp. X:** 104
Winter: Notes from Montana (Bass), **Supp. XVI:**17–18
"Winter Branch, A" (Irving), **Supp. VI:** 163
"Winter Burial, A" (Clampitt), **Supp. IX:** 48

Winter Carnival (film), **Retro. Supp. I:** 113
"Winter Daybreak at Vence, A" (Wright), **Supp. III Part 1:** 249–250
Winter Diary, A (Van Doren), **I:** 168
"Winter Dreams" (Fitzgerald), **II:** 80, 94; **Retro. Supp. I:** 108
"Winter Drive, A" (Jewett), **Retro. Supp. II:** 147
"Winter Eden, A" (Frost), **Retro. Supp. I:** 137
"Winter Father, The" (Dubus), **Supp. VII:** 83, 87
Winter Hours: Prose, Prose Poems, and Poems (Oliver), **Supp. VII:** 230, 247
"Winter in Dunbarton" (Lowell), **II:** 547; **Retro. Supp. II:** 187
"Wintering" (Plath), **Retro. Supp. II:** 255
Winter Insomnia (Carver), **Supp. III Part 1:** 138
Winter in the Blood (Welch), **Supp. IV Part 2:** 562
"Winter Landscape" (Berryman), **I:** 174; **Retro. Supp. I:** 430
Winter Lightning (Nemerov), **III:** 269
Winter News (Haines), **Supp. XII:** 199, 201–204, 207–208, 208
Winternitz, Mary. *See* Cheever, Mrs. John (Mary Winternitz)
Winter of Our Discontent, The (Steinbeck), **IV:** 52, 65–66, 68
"Winter on Earth" (Toomer), **Supp. III Part 2:** 486
"Winter Piece, A" (Bryant), **Supp. I Part 1:** 150, 155
"Winter Rains, Cataluña" (Levine), **Supp. V:** 182
"Winter Remembered" (Ransom), **III:** 492–493
Winterrowd, Prudence, **I:** 217, 224
Winters, Jonathan, **Supp. XI:** 305
Winters, Yvor, **I:** 59, 63, 386, 393, 397, 398, 402, 471; **III:** 194, 498; **IV:** 153; **Retro. Supp. II:** 76, 77, 78, 82, 83, 85, 89; **Supp. I Part 1:** 268; **Supp. II Part 2:** 416, 666, 785–816; **Supp. IV Part 2:** 480; **Supp. V:** 180, 191–192; **Supp. XIV:**287; **Supp. XV:** 74, 341
"Winter Scenes" (Bryant). *See* "Winter Piece, A"
Winterset (Anderson), **III:** 159
"Winter Sleep" (Wylie), **Supp. I Part 2:** 711, 729
Winter's Tale, The (Shakespeare), **Supp. XIII:** 219

Winter Stars (Levis), **Supp. XI:** 259, 266–268
"Winter Stars" (Levis), **Supp. XI:** 267–268
"Winter Stop-Over" (Everwine), **Supp. XV:** 76
Winter Stop-Over (Everwine), **Supp. XV:** 74, 76
"Winter Swan" (Bogan), **Supp. III Part 1:** 52
Winter Thunder (X. J. Kennedy), **Supp. XV:** 167
"Winter Thunder" (X. J. Kennedy), **Supp. XV:** 169
Winter Trees (Plath), **Retro. Supp. II:** 257; **Supp. I Part 2:** 526, 539, 541
"Winter Weather Advisory" (Ashbery), **Supp. III Part 1:** 26
"Winter without Snow, The" (C. Frost), **Supp. XV:** 96, 105–106
"Winter Words" (Levine), **Supp. V:** 192
Winthrop, John, **Supp. I Part 1:** 99, 100, 101, 102, 105; **Supp. I Part 2:** 484, 485
Winthrop Covenant, The (Auchincloss), **Supp. IV Part 1:** 23
Wirt, William, **I:** 232
Wirth, Louis, **IV:** 475
"Wisdom Cometh with the Years" (Cullen), **Supp. IV Part 1:** 166
Wisdom of the Desert, The: Sayings from the Desert Fathers of the Fourth Century (Merton), **Supp. VIII:** 201
Wisdom of the Heart, The (H. Miller), **III:** 178, 184
Wise Blood (O'Connor), **III:** 337, 338, 339–343, 344, 345, 346, 350, 354, 356, 357; **Retro. Supp. II:** 219, 221, 222, 223, 225–228
Wise Men, The (Price), **Supp. VI:** 254
"Wiser Than a God" (Chopin), **Retro. Supp. II:** 61; **Supp. I Part 1:** 208
Wishes, Lies, and Dreams: Teaching Children to Write Poetry (Koch), **Supp. XV:** 176, 189
"Wish for a Young Wife" (Roethke), **III:** 548
Wishful Thinking: A Theological ABC (Buechner), **Supp. XII:** 53
Wishing Tree, The: Christopher Isherwood on Mystical Religion (Adjemian, ed.), **Supp. XIV:**164, 173
Wismer, Helen Muriel. *See* Thurber, Mrs. James (Helen Muriel Wismer)
Wisse, Ruth, **Supp. XII:** 167, 168
Wister, Owen, **I:** 62; **Retro. Supp. II:** 72; **Supp. XIV:**39

"Witchbird" (Bambara), **Supp. XI:** 11

"Witch Burning" (Plath), **Supp. I Part 2:** 539

Witchcraft of Salem Village, The (Jackson), **Supp. IX:** 121

"Witch Doctor" (Hayden), **Supp. II Part 1:** 368, 380

Witches of Eastwick, The (Updike), **Retro. Supp. I:** 330, 331

Witching Hour, The (Rice), **Supp. VII:** 299–300

"Witch of Coös, The" (Frost), **II:** 154–155; **Retro. Supp. I:** 135; **Retro. Supp. II:** 42

"Witch of Owl Mountain Springs, The: An Account of Her Remarkable Powers" (Taylor), **Supp. V:** 328

"Witch of Wenham, The" (Whittier), **Supp. I Part 2:** 694, 696

"With a Little Help from My Friends" (Kushner), **Supp. IX:** 131

"With Che at Kitty Hawk" (Banks), **Supp. V:** 6

"With Che at the Plaza" (Banks), **Supp. V:** 7

"With Che in New Hampshire" (Banks), **Supp. V:** 6

"Withdrawal Symptoms" (Mora), **Supp. XIII:** 216

"Withered Skins of Berries" (Toomer), **Supp. III Part 2:** 485; **Supp. IX:** 320

Withers, Harry Clay, **Supp. XIII:** 161

Witherspoon, John, **Supp. I Part 2:** 504

With Eyes at the Back of Our Heads (Levertov), **Supp. III Part 1:** 276–277

With Her in Ourland (Gilman), **Supp. XI:** 208–209

With His Pistol in His Hand (Paredes), **Supp. XIII:** 225

"Within the Words: An Apprenticeship" (Haines), **Supp. XII:** 197

"With Kit, Age 7, at the Beach" (Stafford), **Supp. XI:** 323

"With Mercy for the Greedy" (Sexton), **Supp. II Part 2:** 680

With My Trousers Rolled (Epstein), **Supp. XIV:**101, 105

Without a Hero (Boyle), **Supp. VIII:** 16

Without Feathers (Allen), **Supp. XV:** 3, 14, 15

Without Stopping (Bowles), **Supp. IV Part 1:** 79, 81, 85, 90, 91, 92

"Without Tradition and within Reason: Judge Horton and Atticus Finch in Court" (Johnson), **Supp. VIII:** 127

With Shuddering Fall (Oates), **Supp. II Part 2:** 504–506

"With the Dog at Sunrise" (Kenyon), **Supp. VII:** 170

With the Empress Dowager of China (Carl), **III:** 475

"With the Horse in the Winter Pasture" (McCarriston), **Supp. XIV:**262

With the Old Breed: At Peleliu and Okinawa (Sledge), **Supp. V:** 249–250

"With the Violin" (Chopin), **Retro. Supp. II:** 61

"Witness" (Clampitt), **Supp. IX:** 42–43, 45, 46

"Witness" (Dubus), **Supp. VII:** 89

"Witness" (Harjo), **Supp. XII:** 227–228

Witness (McNally), **Supp. XIII:** 197

"Witness, The" (Porter), **III:** 443–444

"Witness for Poetry, A" (Stafford), **Supp. XI:** 324

"Witness for the Defense" (Hay), **Supp. XIV:**124

"Witnessing My Father's Will" (Karr), **Supp. XI:** 241

"Witnessing to a Shared World" (Sanders), **Supp. XVI:**278

Witness to the Times! (McGrath), **Supp. X:** 118

Witness Tree, A (Frost), **II:** 155; **Retro. Supp. I:** 122, 137, 139

Wit's End: Days and Nights of the Algonquin Round Table (Gaines), **Supp. IX:** 190

Wits Recreations (Mennes and Smith), **II:** 111

Witt, Shirley Hill, **Supp. IV Part 2:** 505

Wittels, Anne F., **Supp. XV:** 59

Wittenberg, Judith Bryant, **Retro. Supp. II:** 146

Wittgenstein, Ludwig, **Retro. Supp. I:** 53; **Supp. III Part 2:** 626–627; **Supp. X:** 304; **Supp. XII:** 21; **Supp. XV:** 344, 346

Wittliff, William, **Supp. V:** 227

"Witty War, A" (Simpson), **Supp. IX:** 268

"Wives and Mistresses" (Hardwick), **Supp. III Part 1:** 211–212

Wizard of Loneliness, The (Nichols), **Supp. XIII:** 259, 263, 264

Wizard of Oz, The (Baum), **Supp. IV Part 1:** 113

Wizard of Oz, The (film), **Supp. X:** 172, 214

Wizard's Tide, The: A Story (Buechner), **Supp. XII:** 54

"WLT (The Edgar Era)" (Keillor), **Supp. XVI:**172

WLT: A Radio Romance (Keillor), **Supp. XVI:**176

Wobegon Boy (Keillor), **Supp. XVI:**177

Wodehouse, P. G., **Supp. IX:** 195

Woiwode, Larry, **Supp. VIII:** 151; **Supp. XVI:**206

Wojahn, David, **Supp. IX:** 161, 292, 293

Wolcott, James, **Supp. IX:** 259

Wolf: A False Memoir (Harrison), **Supp. VIII:** 40, 41–42, 45

Wolf, Christa, **Supp. IV Part 1:** 310, 314

Wolf, Daniel, **Retro. Supp. II:** 202

Wolfe, Ben, **IV:** 454

Wolfe, Gregory, **Supp. XIV:**307

Wolfe, James, **Supp. I Part 2:** 498

Wolfe, Linnie, **Supp. IX:** 176

Wolfe, Mabel, **IV:** 454

Wolfe, Mrs. William Oliver (Julia Elizabeth Westall), **IV:** 454

Wolfe, Thomas, **I:** 288, 289, 374, 478, 495; **II:** 457; **III:** 40, 108, 278, 334, 482; **IV:** 52, 97, 357, 450–473; **Retro. Supp. I:** 382; **Supp. I Part 1:** 29; **Supp. IV Part 1:** 101; **Supp. IX:** 229; **Supp. X:** 225; **Supp. XI:** 213, 216, 217, 218; **Supp. XIII:** 17; **Supp. XIV:**122

Wolfe, Tom, **Supp. III Part 2:** 567–588; **Supp. IV Part 1:** 35, 198; **Supp. V:** 296; **Supp. X:** 264; **Supp. XI:** 239; **Supp. XV:** 143

Wolfe, William Oliver, **IV:** 454

"Wolfe Homo Scribens" (Cowley), **Supp. II Part 1:** 144

Wolfert's Roost (Irving), **II:** 314

Wolff, Cynthia Griffin, **Retro. Supp. I:** 379; **Supp. IV Part 1:** 203

Wolff, Donald, **Supp. XIII:** 316, 317, 326

Wolff, Geoffrey, **Supp. II Part 1:** 97; **Supp. XI:** 239, 245, 246

Wolff, Tobias, **Retro. Supp. I:** 190; **Supp. V:** 22; **Supp. VII:** 331–346; **Supp. X:** 1; **Supp. XI:** 26, 239, 245, 246, 247; **Supp. XV:** 223; **Supp. XVI:**39, 41, 63, 70, 77

Wolfson, P. J., **Supp. XIII:** 172

"Wolf Town" (Carson), **Supp. XII:** 102

Wolf Willow: A History, a Story, and a Memory of the Last Plains Frontier (Stegner), **Supp. IV Part 2:** 595, 596, 597, 598, 599, 600, 601, 604, 606, 611, 613, 614

Wolitzer, Hilma, **Supp. XV:** 55

Wolitzer, Meg, **Supp. XV:** 65

Wollaston, William, **II:** 108

Wollstonecraft, Mary, **Supp. I Part 1:**

126; **Supp. I Part 2:** 512, 554

"Woman" (Bogan), **Supp. X:** 102

"Woman, I Got the Blues" (Komunyakaa), **Supp. XIII:** 117

"Woman, Why Are You Weeping?" (Kenyon), **Supp. VII:** 174–175

"Woman, Young and Old, A" (Paley), **Supp. VI:** 222, 225

Woman Aroused, The (Lacy), **Supp. XV:** 199–200

Woman at the Washington Zoo, The (Jarrell), **II:** 367, 386, 387, 389

"Woman Dead in Her Forties, A" (Rich), **Supp. I Part 2:** 574–575

"Woman Hanging from the Thirteenth Floor Window, The" (Harjo), **Supp. XII:** 216, 221

"Woman Hollering Creek" (Cisneros), **Supp. VII:** 70

Woman Hollering Creek and Other Stories (Cisneros), **Supp. VII:** 58, 68–70

"Womanhood" (Brooks), **Supp. III Part 1:** 77

"Woman in Rain" (X. J. Kennedy), **Supp. XV:** 168

Woman in the Dark (Hammett), **Supp. IV Part 1:** 343

"Woman in the House, A" (Caldwell), **I:** 310

Woman in the Nineteenth Century (Fuller), **Retro. Supp. I:** 156; **Supp. II Part 1:** 279, 292, 294–296; **Supp. XI:** 197, 203

Woman in White, The (Collins), **Supp. I Part 1:** 35, 36

"Womanizer, The" (Ford), **Supp. V:** 71, 72

"Woman Like Yourself, A" (C. Frost), **Supp. XV:** 107

Woman Lit by Fireflies, The (Harrison), **Supp. VIII:** 50–51

"Woman Loses Cookie Bake-Off, Sets Self on Fire" (R. O. Butler), **Supp. XII:** 72

Woman of Andros, The (Wilder), **IV:** 356, 363–364, 367, 368, 374

Woman of Means, A (Taylor), **Supp. V:** 319–320

Woman on the Edge of Time (Piercy), **Supp. XIII:** 29

Woman on the Porch, The (Gordon), **II:** 199, 209–211

"Woman on the Stair, The" (MacLeish), **III:** 15–16

"Woman's Dream, A" (E. Stoddard), **Supp. XV:** 278

"Woman's Heartlessness" (Thaxter), **Retro. Supp. II:** 147

Woman's Honor (Glaspell), **Supp. III Part 1:** 179

"Woman Singing" (Ortiz), **Supp. IV Part 2:** 513

Woman's Share in Primitive Culture (Mason), **Supp. I Part 1:** 18

"Woman Struck by Car Turns into Nymphomaniac" (R. O. Butler), **Supp. XII:** 72

"Woman's Work" (Alvarez), **Supp. VII:** 4

"Woman Uses Glass Eye to Spy on Philandering Husband" (R. O. Butler), **Supp. XII:** 70, 72

Woman Warrior (Kingston), **Supp. IV Part 1:** 12; **Supp. V:** 157, 158, 159, 160–164, 166, 169; **Supp. X:** 291–292; **Supp. XIV:** 162

Woman Warrior, The (Kingston), **Supp. XV:** 220

Woman Who Fell from the Sky, The (Harjo), **Supp. XII:** 226–228

"Woman Who Fell From the Sky, The" (Iroquois creation story), **Supp. IV Part 1:** 327

Woman Who Owned the Shadows, The (Gunn Allen), **Supp. IV Part 1:** 320, 322, 326, 327–328

Woman Within, The (Glasgow), **II:** 183, 190–191

"Womanwork" (Gunn Allen), **Supp. IV Part 1:** 326

Women (Bukowski), **Supp. XI:** 172

"Women" (Didion), **Supp. IV Part 1:** 205

"Women" (Swenson), **Supp. IV Part 2:** 647

Women, The (film), **Retro. Supp. I:** 113

Women, The (film; Cukor), **Supp. XVI:** 181, 192

"Women and Children First" (Prose), **Supp. XVI:** 254

Women and Children First: Stories (Prose), **Supp. XVI:** 254

Women and Economics (Gilman), **Supp. I Part 2:** 637; **Supp. V:** 284; **Supp. XI:** 200, 203–204, 206

Women and Thomas Harrow (Marquand), **III:** 50, 61, 62, 66, 68, 69–70, 71

Women and Wilderness (LaBastille), **Supp. X:** 97, 102–104

"Women as They Are" (Rowson), **Supp. XV:** 243

Women at Point Sur, The (Jeffers), **Supp. II Part 2:** 430–431

Women in Love (Lawrence), **III:** 27, 34

Women of Brewster Place, The: A Novel in Seven Stories (Naylor),

Supp. VIII: 213, 214–218

Women of Manhattan: An Upper West Side Story (Shanley), **Supp. XIV:** 315, 326–327

"Women of My Color" (Coleman), **Supp. XI:** 88–89

Women of Trachis (Pound, trans.), **III:** 476

Women on the Wall, The (Stegner), **Supp. IV Part 2:** 599, 605, 606

Women Poets in English (Stanford, ed.), **Retro. Supp. I:** 41

"Women Reformers and American Culture, 1870–1930" (Conway), **Supp. I Part 1:** 19

"Women's Movement, The" (Didion), **Supp. IV Part 1:** 206

"Women Waiting" (Shields), **Supp. VII:** 320

"Women We Love Whom We Never See Again" (R. Bly), **Supp. IV Part 1:** 66

"Women We Never See Again" (R. Bly), **Supp. IV Part 1:** 66

Women with Men (Ford), **Supp. V:** 57, 71–72

"Wonder" (Olds), **Supp. X:** 210

Wonder Boys (Chabon), **Supp. XI:** 67, 73–75, **Supp. XI:** 78; **Supp. XVI:** 259

Wonder Boys (film), **Supp. XI:** 67

Wonderful O, The (Thurber), **Supp. I Part 2:** 612

"Wonderful Old Gentleman, The" (Parker), **Supp. IX:** 197

"Wonderful Pen, The" (Swenson), **Supp. IV Part 2:** 650

Wonderful Words, Silent Truth: Essays on Poetry and a Memoir (Simic), **Supp. VIII:** 270

Wonderland (Oates), **Supp. II Part 2:** 511, 512, 514–515

Wonders Hidden (Sanders), **Supp. XVI:** 269

Wonders of the Invisible World, The (Mather), **Supp. II Part 2:** 456–459, 460, 467

Wonder-Working Providence (Johnson), **IV:** 157

Wong, Hertha, **Supp. IV Part 1:** 275

Wong, Jade Snow, **Supp. X:** 291

Wong, Shawn, **Supp. XV:** 221

"Wood" (Nye), **Supp. XIII:** 276

Wood, Audrey, **IV:** 381

Wood, Charles Erskine Scott, **Supp. XV:** 301

Wood, Clement, **Supp. XV:** 298

Wood, Clement Biddle, **Supp. XI:** 307

Wood, James, **Supp. XIV:** 95–96

Wood, Mabel, **I:** 199

Wood, Michael, **Supp. IV Part 2:** 691

Wood, Mrs. Henry, **Supp. I Part 1:** 35

Wood, Norman Barton, **Supp. XIV:**201

Wood, Susan, **Supp. XVI:**123

Woodard, Calvin, **Supp. VIII:** 128

Woodard, Charles L., **Supp. IV Part 2:** 484, 493

Woodard, Deborah, **Supp. XIII:** 114

Woodberry, George Edward, **III:** 508

Woodbridge, Frederick, **I:** 217, 224

Woodbridge, John, **Supp. I Part 1:** 101, 102, 114

"Wood-Choppers, The" (Chopin), **Retro. Supp. II:** 72

Woodcock, George, **Supp. XIII:** 33

"Wood Dove at Sandy Spring, The" (MacLeish), **III:** 19

"Wooden Spring" (Rukeyser), **Supp. VI:** 285

"Wooden Umbrella, The" (Porter), **IV:** 26

"Woodnotes" (Emerson), **II:** 7, 19

"Wood-Pile, The" (Frost), **Retro. Supp. I:** 128; **Supp. IV Part 2:** 445

Woodrow, James, **Supp. I Part 1:** 349, 366

"Woods, Books, and Truant Officers, The" (Maclean), **Supp. XIV:**221, 225

Woods, Robert A., **Supp. I Part 1:** 19

Woods, The (Mamet), **Supp. XIV:**241, 254–255

Woodswoman (LaBastille), **Supp. X:** 95, 96–99, 108

Woodswoman **III:** Book Three of the Woodswoman's Adventures (LaBastille), **Supp. X:** 95, 106–107

"Wood Thrush" (Kenyon), **Supp. VII:** 172

Woodward, C. Vann, **IV:** 114, 470–471; **Retro. Supp. I:** 75, 76

"Wooing the Inanimate" (Brodsky), **Supp. VIII:** 32

Woolcott, Alexander, **Supp. IX:** 197

Wooley, Bryan, **Supp. V:** 225

Woolf, Leonard, **Supp. IX:** 95

Woolf, Virginia, **I:** 53, 79, 112, 309; **II:** 320, 415; **IV:** 59; **Retro. Supp. I:** 59, 75, 170, 215, 291, 359; **Supp. I Part 2:** 553, 714, 718; **Supp. IV Part 1:** 299; **Supp. V:** 127; **Supp. VIII:** 5, 155, 251, 252, 263, 265; **Supp. IX:** 66, 109; **Supp. XI:** 134, 193; **Supp. XII:** 81, 98, 289; **Supp. XIII:** 305; **Supp. XIV:**341–342, 342, 343, 346, 348; **Supp. XV:** 55, 65

Woollcott, Alexander, **IV:** 432; **Retro. Supp. II:** 327; **Supp. I Part 2:** 664; **Supp. IX:** 190, 194

Woollstonecraft, Mary, **Supp. XVI:**184

"Woolly Mammoth" (X. J. Kennedy), **Supp. XV:** 163–164

Woolman, John, **Supp. VIII:** 202, 204, 205

Woolson, Constance Fenimore, **Retro. Supp. I:** 224, 228

Worcester, Samuel, **I:** 458

Word and Idioms: Studies in the English Language (L. P. Smith), **Supp. XIV:**343

Word of God and the Word of Man, The (Barth), **Retro. Supp. I:** 327

"Word out of the Sea, A" (Whitman), **IV:** 344

Words (Creeley), **Supp. IV Part 1:** 139, 150–153, 154, 155, 158

"Words" (Creeley), **Supp. IV Part 1:** 152

"Words" (Gioia), **Supp. XV:** 125

"Words" (Merwin), **Supp. III Part 1:** 352

"Words" (Plath), **Supp. I Part 2:** 547

"Words" (Shields), **Supp. VII:** 323

"Words, The" (Wagoner), **Supp. IX:** 326

"Words above a Narrow Entrance" (Wagoner), **Supp. IX:** 325

"Words for a Bike-Racing, Osprey-Chasing Wine-Drunk Squaw Man" (Gunn Allen), **Supp. IV Part 1:** 325

Words for Dr. Y (Sexton), **Supp. II Part 2:** 698

"Words for Hart Crane" (Lowell), **I:** 381; **II:** 547; **Retro. Supp. II:** 188

"Words for Maria" (Merrill), **Supp. III Part 1:** 327

"Words for the Unknown Makers" (Kunitz), **Supp. III Part 1:** 264

Words for the Wind (Roethke), **III:** 529, 533, 541, 543, 545

"Words for the Wind" (Roethke), **III:** 542–543

Words in the Mourning Time (Hayden), **Supp. II Part 1:** 361, 366, 367

"Words in the Mourning Time" (Hayden), **Supp. II Part 1:** 370–371

"Words into Fiction" (Welty), **IV:** 279

"Words Like Freedom" (Hughes), **Retro. Supp. I:** 207

"Words of a Young Girl" (Lowell), **II:** 554

Words under the Words: Selected Poems (Nye), **Supp. XIII:** 277

Wordsworth, Dorothy, **Supp. IX:** 38

Wordsworth, William, **I:** 283, 522, 524, 525, 588; **II:** 7, 11, 17, 18, 97, 169, 273, 303, 304, 532, 549, 552; **III:** 219, 263, 277, 278, 511, 521, 523, 528, 583; **IV:** 120, 331, 343, 453, 465; **Retro. Supp. I:** 121, 196; **Supp. I Part 1:** 150, 151, 154, 161, 163, 312, 313, 349, 365; **Supp. I Part 2:** 375, 409, 416, 422, 607, 621, 622, 673, 674, 675, 676, 677, 710–711, 729; **Supp. II Part 1:** 4; **Supp. III Part 1:** 12, 15, 73, 279; **Supp. IV Part 2:** 597, 601; **Supp. V:** 258; **Supp. VIII:** 273; **Supp. IX:** 38, 41, 265, 274; **Supp. X:** 22, 23, 65, 120; **Supp. XI:** 248, 251, 312; **Supp. XIII:** 214; **Supp. XIV:**184; **Supp. XV:** 93, 250

Work (Alcott), **Supp. I Part 1:** 32–33, 42

Work (Dixon), **Supp. XII:** 141, 143

"Work" (Oliver), **Supp. VII:** 243

Work and Love (Dunn), **Supp. XI:** 147–148

"Worker" (Coleman), **Supp. XI:** 89

Working Class Movement in America, The (E. Marx and E. Aveling), **Supp. XVI:**85

Working Papers: Selected Essays and Reviews (Carruth), **Supp. XVI:**46

"Working the Landscape" (Dunn), **Supp. XI:** 151

Workin' on the Chain Gang: Shaking Off the Dead Hand of History (Mosley), **Supp. XIII:** 247, 248

"Work Notes '66" (Baraka), **Supp. II Part 1:** 47

Work of Art (Lewis), **II:** 453–454

"Work of Shading, The" (Simic), **Supp. VIII:** 277–278

Work of Stephen Crane, The (Follett, ed.), **I:** 405

"Work on Red Mountain, The" (Harte), **Supp. II Part 1:** 339

Works of Love, The (Morris), **III:** 223–224, 225, 233

Works of Witter Bynner, The (Kraft, ed.), **Supp. XV:** 52

"World, The" (Simic), **Supp. VIII:** 282

World According to Garp, The (Irving), **Supp. VI:** 163, 164, 170–173, 181

World and Africa, The: An Inquiry into the Part Which Africa Has Played in World History (Du Bois), **Supp. II Part 1:** 184–185

"World and All Its Teeth, The" (Nye), **Supp. XIII:** 282

"World and the Door, The" (O. Henry), **Supp. II Part 1:** 402

"World and the Jug, The" (Ellison), **Retro. Supp. II:** 112, 119, 123

"World as We Know It, The" (Barresi), **Supp. XV:** 100

World Authors 1950–1970, **Supp. XIII:** 102

World Below, The (Miller), **Supp. XII:** 303–304

World Below the Window, The: Poems 1937–1997 (W. J. Smith), **Supp. XIII:** 332, 340, 345

World Doesn't End, The (Simic), **Supp. VIII:** 272, 279–280

World Elsewhere, A: The Place of Style in American Literature (Poirier), **I:** 239

"World Ends Here, The" (Harjo), **Supp. XII:** 227–228

World Enough and Time (Warren), **IV:** 243, 253–254

"World I Live In, The" (T. Williams), **IV:** 388

World I Never Made, A (Farrell), **II:** 34, 35, 424

World in the Attic, The (Morris), **III:** 222–223, 224

World in the Evening, The (Isherwood), **Supp. XIV:**157, 164, 165, 166–167, 170

World Is a Wedding, The (Schwartz), **Supp. II Part 2:** 643, 654–660

"World Is a Wedding, The" (Schwartz), **Supp. II Part 2:** 655–656, 657

"World Is Too Much with Us, The" (Wordsworth), **Supp. I Part 1:** 312

Worldly Hopes (Ammons), **Supp. VII:** 34

Worldly Philosophers, The (Heilbroner), **Supp. I Part 2:** 644, 650

World of Apples, The (Cheever), **Supp. I Part 1:** 191, 193

World of David Wagoner, The (McFarland), **Supp. IX:** 323

"World of Easy Rawlins, The" (Mosley), **Supp. XIII:** 234, 236

World of Gwendolyn Brooks, The (Brooks), **Supp. III Part 1:** 83, 84

World of H. G. Wells, The (Brooks), **I:** 240, 241, 242

World of Light, A: Portraits and Celebrations (Sarton), **Supp. III Part 1:** 62; **Supp. VIII:** 249, 253, 262

World of Our Fathers: The Journey of the Eastern European Jews to America and the Life They Found and Made (Howe), **Supp. VI:** 113, 114, 116, 118, 119, 120–125; **Supp. XIV:**104

"World of Pure Experience, A" (James), **II:** 356–357

World of Raymond Chandler, The (Spender), **Supp. IV Part 1:** 119

World of Sex, The (H. Miller), **III:** 170, 178, 187

"World of the Perfect Tear, The" (McGrath), **Supp. X:** 116, 118

World of the Ten Thousand Things, The: Selected Poems (Wright), **Supp. V:** 333

"World of Tomorrow, The" (White), **Supp. I Part 2:** 663

World of Washington Irving, The (Brooks), **I:** 256–257

World Over, The (Wharton), **Retro. Supp. I:** 382

"Worlds" (Goldbarth), **Supp. XII:** 183, 189

World's Body, The (Ransom), **III:** 497, 499; **Supp. II Part 1:** 146

World's End (Boyle), **Supp. VIII:** 11–12

World's End and Other Stories (Theroux), **Supp. VIII:** 322

"World's Fair" (Berryman), **I:** 173

World's Fair (Doctorow), **Supp. IV Part 1:** 217, 224, 227–229, 234, 236–237

World's Fair, The (Fitzgerald), **II:** 93

Worlds of Color (Du Bois), **Supp. II Part 1:** 185–186

"Worlds of Color" (Du Bois), **Supp. II Part 1:** 175

World So Wide (Lewis), **II:** 456

"World's Worst Boyfriends, The" (Wasserstein), **Supp. XV:** 328

"World-Telegram" (Berryman), **I:** 173

World View on Race and Democracy: A Study Guide in Human Group Relations (Locke), **Supp. XIV:**205, 206

World within the Word, The (Gass), **Supp. VI:** 77

"World Without Objects Is a Sensible Place, A" (Wilbur), **Supp. III Part 2:** 550

"World Without Rodrigo, The" (Cisneros), **Supp. VII:** 68

"Worm Moon" (Oliver), **Supp. VII:** 234

"Worn Path, A" (Welty), **IV:** 262; **Retro. Supp. I:** 345–346

"Worsening Situation" (Ashbery), **Supp. III Part 1:** 17–18

"Worship" (Emerson), **II:** 2, 4–5

"Worship and Church Bells" (Paine), **Supp. I Part 2:** 521

Worster, Donald, **Supp. IX:** 19

Worthington, Marjorie, **Supp. XII:** 13

Wouldn't Take Nothing for My Journey Now (Angelou), **Supp. IV Part 1:** 10, 12, 14, 15, 16

Wound and the Bow, The: Seven Studies in Literature (Wilson), **IV:** 429

Wounds in the Rain (Crane), **I:** 409, 414, 423

Woven Stone (Ortiz), **Supp. IV Part 2:** 501, 514

Woven Stories (Ortiz), **Supp. IV Part 2:** 503

"Wraith, The" (Roethke), **III:** 542

"Wrath of God, The" (Fante), **Supp. XI:** 160, 164

"Wreath for a Bridal" (Plath), **Supp. I Part 2:** 537

Wreath for Garibaldi and Other Stories, A (Garrett), **Supp. VII:** 99–101

"Wreath of Women" (Rukeyser), **Supp. VI:** 280

Wreckage of Agathon, The (Gardner), **Supp. VI:** 63, 65–66

Wrecking Crew (Levis), **Supp. XI:** 259–260

"Wreck of Rivermouth, The" (Whittier), **Supp. I Part 2:** 694, 696–697

"Wreck of the Deutschland" (Hopkins), **Supp. X:** 61

"Wreck of the Hesperus, The" (Longfellow), **Retro. Supp. II:** 168, 169

Wrestler's Cruel Study, The (Dobyns), **Supp. XIII:** 82–83

"Wrestler with Sharks, A" (Yates), **Supp. XI:** 341

Wright, Bernie, **I:** 191, 193

Wright, C. D. (Carolyn Doris), **Supp. XV:** 337–355

Wright, Charles, **Supp. V:** 92, 331–346; **Supp. VIII:** 272; **Supp. XIII:** 114

Wright, Chauncey, **II:** 344

Wright, Frank Lloyd, **I:** 104, 483

Wright, George, **III:** 479

Wright, Harold Bell, **II:** 467–468

Wright, Holly, **Supp. VIII:** 272

Wright, James, **I:** 291; **Supp. III Part 1:** 249; **Supp. III Part 2:** 541, 589–607; **Supp. IV Part 1:** 60, 72; **Supp. IV Part 2:** 557, 558, 561, 566, 571, 623; **Supp. V:** 332; **Supp. IX:** 152, 155, 159, 265, 271, 290, 293, 296; **Supp. X:** 69, 127; **Supp. XI:** 150; **Supp. XII:** 217; **Supp. XIII:** 76; **Supp. XV:** 79, 93, 212

Wright, Mrs. Richard (Ellen Poplar), **IV:** 476

Wright, Nathalia, **IV:** 155

Wright, Philip Green, **III:** 578, 579, 580

Wright, Richard, **II:** 586; **IV:** 40, 474–497; **Retro. Supp. II:** 4, 111, 116, 120; **Supp. I Part 1:** 51, 52, 64, 332, 337; **Supp. II Part 1:** 17, 40, 221, 228, 235, 250; **Supp. IV Part 1:** 1, 11, 84, 374; **Supp. VIII:** 88;

Supp. IX: 316; **Supp. X:** 131, 245, 254; **Supp. XI:** 85; **Supp. XII:** 316; **Supp. XIII:** 46, 233; **Supp. XIV:**73; **Supp. XVI:**135, 139, 141, 143

Wright, Sarah, **Supp. IV Part 1:** 8; **Supp. XIII:** 295

Wright, William, **Retro. Supp. II:** 76, 77

"Writer" (Sanders), **Supp. XVI:**277

"Writer, The" (Wilbur), **Supp. III Part 2:** 561, 562

"Writer as Alaskan, The" (Haines), **Supp. XII:** 199

Writer in America, The (Brooks), **I:** 253, 254, 257

Writer in America, The (Stegner), **Supp. IV Part 2:** 597, 599, 607

"Writers" (Lowell), **II:** 554

Writer's Almanac, The (Keillor, radio program), **Supp. XIII:** 274; **Supp. XVI:**178

Writer's America, A: Landscape in Literature (Kazin), **Supp. VIII:** 106

Writer's Capital, A (Auchincloss), **Supp. IV Part 1:** 21, 23, 24, 31

"Writer's Credo, A" (Abbey), **Supp. XIII:** 1, 17

Writer's Eye, A: Collected Book Reviews (Welty), **Retro. Supp. I:** 339, 354, 356

Writers in Revolt (Southern, Seaver, and Trocchi, eds.), **Supp. XI:** 301

Writer's Notebook, A (Maugham), **Supp. X:** 58

Writers on America (U.S. Department of State, ed.), **Supp. XIII:** 288

Writers on the Left (Aaron), **IV:** 429; **Supp. II Part 1:** 137

Writers on Writing (Prose), **Supp. XVI:**259

"Writer's Prologue to a Play in Verse" (W. C. Williams), **Retro. Supp. I:** 424

"Writer's Quest for a Parnassus, A" (T. Williams), **IV:** 392

Writers' Workshop (University of Iowa), **Supp. V:** 42

"Writers Workshop, The" (Conroy), **Supp. XVI:**76

"Writing" (Nemerov), **III:** 275

"Writing About the Universe" (Mosley), **Supp. XIII:** 247

"Writing American Fiction" (Roth), **Retro. Supp. II:** 279; **Supp. I Part 1:** 192; **Supp. I Part 2:** 431; **Supp. III Part 2:** 414, 420, 421; **Supp. V:** 45

"Writing and a Life Lived Well" (Patchett), **Supp. XII:** 308

Writing a Woman's Life (Heilbrun),

Supp. IX: 66

Writing Chicago: Modernism, Ethnography, and the Novel (Cappetti), **Supp. IX:** 4, 8

Writing from the Center (Sanders), **Supp. XVI:**266, 275–276

"Writing from the Inside Out: Style Is Not the Frosting; It's the Cake" (Robbins), **Supp. X:** 266

"Writing here last autumn of my hopes of seeing a hoopoe" (Updike), **Retro. Supp. I:** 335

Writing in Restaurants (Mamet), **Supp. XIV:**246

"Writing Lesson, The" (Gordon), **Supp. IV Part 1:** 306

Writing Life, The (Dillard), **Supp. VI:** 23, 31

"Writing of Apollinaire, The" (Zukofsky), **Supp. III Part 2:** 616, 617

"Writing of *Fearless Jones*, The" (Mosley), **Supp. XIII:** 242

Writing on the Wall, The, and Literary Essays (McCarthy), **II:** 579

Writings to an Unfinished Accompaniment (Merwin), **Supp. III Part 1:** 352

"Writing the Universe-Mind" (Tabios), **Supp. XV:** 225

Writing the World (Stafford), **Supp. XI:** 314

"Writing to Save Our Lives" (Milligan), **Supp. XIII:** 274

Writin' Is Fightin' (Reed), **Supp. X:** 241

"Writ on the Eve of My 32nd Birthday" (Corso), **Supp. XII:** 129–130

"Written History as an Act of Faith" (Beard), **Supp. I Part 2:** 492

"Wrong Notes" (S. Kauffmann), **Supp. XVI:**74

"Wrought Figure" (McCarriston), **Supp. XIV:**272

"Wunderkind" (McCullers), **II:** 585

Wunderlich, Mark, **Supp. XI:** 119, 132

Wundt, Wilhelm, **II:** 345

Wurster, William Wilson, **Supp. IV Part 1:** 197

WUSA (film), **Supp. V:** 301

Wuthering Heights (E. Brontë), **Supp. V:** 305; **Supp. X:** 89

WWII (Jones), **Supp. XI:** 219, 231

Wyandotté (Cooper), **I:** 350, 355

Wyatt, Robert B., **Supp. V:** 14

Wyatt, Thomas, **Supp. I Part 1:** 369

Wycherly Woman, The (Macdonald), **Supp. IV Part 2:** 473

Wydra, Ewa. *See* Hoffman, Eva

Wyler, William, **Supp. XV:** 195

Wylie, Elinor, **IV:** 436; **Supp. I Part 2:** 707–730; **Supp. III Part 1:** 2, 63, 318–319; **Supp. XI:** 44; **Supp. XIV:**127; **Supp. XV:** 307

Wylie, Horace, **Supp. I Part 2:** 708, 709

Wylie, Philip, **III:** 223

Wyllys, Ruth. *See* Taylor, Mrs. Edward (Ruth Wyllys)

"Wyoming Valley Tales" (Crane), **I:** 409

Wyzewa, Théodore de, **Supp. XIV:**336

X

Xaipe (Cummings), **I:** 430, 432–433, 447

Xenogenesis trilogy (O. Butler), **Supp. XIII:** 63–66, 69

Xenophon, **II:** 105

X Factor, The: A Quest for Excellence (Plimpton), **Supp. XVI:**241

X Files (television series), **Supp. XVI:**125

Xiaojing, Zhou, **Supp. XV:** 214

Xingu and Other Stories (Wharton), **IV:** 314, 320; **Retro. Supp. I:** 378

Xionia (Wright), **Supp. V:** 333

XLI Poems (Cummings), **I:** 429, 432, 440, 443

Y

Yacoubi, Ahmed, **Supp. IV Part 1:** 88, 92, 93

Yage Letters, The (Burroughs), **Supp. III Part 1:** 94, 98, 100

Yagoda, Ben, **Supp. VIII:** 151

Yamamoto, Isoroku, **Supp. I Part 2:** 491

Yankee City (Warner), **III:** 60

Yankee Clipper (ballet) (Kirstein), **Supp. IV Part 1:** 82

Yankee in Canada, A (Thoreau), **IV:** 188

Yankey in London (Tyler), **I:** 344

"Yánnina" (Merrill), **Supp. III Part 1:** 329

"Yanosz Korczak's Last Walk" (Markowick-Olczakova), **Supp. X:** 70

Yarboro, Chelsea Quinn, **Supp. V:** 147

Yardley, Jonathan, **Supp. V:** 326; **Supp. XI:** 67

"Yard Sale" (Kenyon), **Supp. VII:** 169

Yates, Richard, **Supp. XI:** 333–350

"Year, The" (Sandburg), **III:** 584

"Year Between, The" (Neugeboren), **Supp. XVI:**226

Year in Provence, A (Mayle), **Supp. XVI:**295

Yearling, The (Rawlings), **Supp. X:** 219, 230–231, 233, 234

Year of Happy, A (Goldbarth), **Supp. XII:** 180

"Year of Mourning, The" (Jeffers), **Supp. II Part 2:** 415

Year of Silence, The (Bell), **Supp. X:** 1, 5–6, 7

"Year of the Double Spring, The" (Swenson), **Supp. IV Part 2:** 647

Year's Best Science Fiction, The (Merril, ed.), **Supp. XVI:**123

Year's Life, A (Lowell), **Supp. I Part 2:** 405

"Years of Birth" (Cowley), **Supp. II Part 1:** 149

Years of My Youth (Howells), **II:** 276

"Years of Wonder" (White), **Supp. I Part 2:** 652, 653

Years With Ross, The (Thurber), **Supp. I Part 2:** 619

Yeats, Jack, **Supp. XVI:**190

Yeats, John Butler, **III:** 458

Yeats, William Butler, **I:** 69, 172, 384, 389, 403, 434, 478, 494, 532; **II:** 168–169, 566, 598; **III:** 4, 5, 8, 18, 19, 20, 23, 29, 40, 205, 249, 269, 270–271, 272, 278, 279, 294, 347, 409, 457, 458–460, 472, 473, 476–477, 521, 523, 524, 527, 528, 533, 540, 541, 542, 543–544, 591–592; **IV:** 89, 93, 121, 126, 136, 140, 271, 394, 404; **Retro. Supp. I:** 59, 66, 127, 141, 270, 283, 285, 286, 288, 290, 311, 342, 350, 378, 413; **Retro. Supp. II:** 185, 331; **Supp. I Part 1:** 79, 80, 254, 257, 262; **Supp. I Part 2:** 388, 389; **Supp. II Part 1:** 1, 4, 9, 20, 26, 361; **Supp. III Part 1:** 59, 63, 236, 238, 253; **Supp. IV Part 1:** 81; **Supp. IV Part 2:** 634; **Supp. V:** 220; **Supp. VIII:** 19, 21, 30, 155, 156, 190, 239, 262, 292; **Supp. IX:** 43, 119; **Supp. X:** 35, 58, 119, 120; **Supp. XI:** 140; **Supp. XII:** 132, 198, 217, 266; **Supp. XIII:** 77, **Supp. XIII:** 87; **Supp. XIV:**7; **Supp. XV:** 36, 41, 181, 186; **Supp. XVI:**47–48, 159

Yellin, Jean Fagan, **Supp. XVI:**88, 89

Yellow Back Radio Broke-Down (Reed), **Supp. X:** 240, 242, 243–245

"Yellow Dog Café" (Komunyakaa), **Supp. XIII:** 126

"Yellow Girl" (Caldwell), **I:** 310

Yellow Glove (Nye), **Supp. XIII:** 275, 276–277

"Yellow Glove" (Nye), **Supp. XIII:** 276

"Yellow Gown, The" (Anderson), **I:** 114

Yellow House on the Corner, The (Dove), **Supp. IV Part 1:** 244, 245, 246, 254

"Yellow Raft, The" (Connell), **Supp. XIV:**85–86

"Yellow River" (Tate), **IV:** 141

"Yellow Violet, The" (Bryant), **Supp. I Part 1:** 154, 155

"Yellow Wallpaper, The" (Gilman), **Supp. XI:** 198–199, 207; **Supp. XVI:**84

"Yellow Woman" (Keres stories), **Supp. IV Part 1:** 327

"Yellow Woman" (Silko), **Supp. IV Part 2:** 567–568

Yelverton, Theresa, **Supp. IX:** 181

Yenser, Stephen, **Supp. X:** 207, 208; **Supp. XV:** 113–114

"Yentl the Yeshiva Boy" (Singer), **IV:** 15, 20

Yerkes, Charles E., **I:** 507, 512

Yerma (opera) (Bowles), **Supp. IV Part 1:** 89

Yertle the Turtle and Other Stories (Geisel), **Supp. XVI:**109

"Yes" (Stafford), **Supp. XI:** 329

Yes, Mrs. Williams (W. C. Williams), **Retro. Supp. I:** 423

Yes, Yes, No, No (Kushner), **Supp. IX:** 133

"Yes and It's Hopeless" (Ginsberg), **Supp. II Part 1:** 326

Yesenin, Sergey, **Supp. VIII:** 40

"Yes! No!" (Oliver), **Supp. VII:** 243–244

Yesterday and Today: A Comparative Anthology of Poetry (Untermeyer, ed.), **Supp. XV:** 309

Yesterday's Self: Nostalgia and the Immigrant Identity (Ritivoi), **Supp. XVI:**148

Yesterday Will Make You Cry (C. Himes), **Supp. XVI:**137

"Yet Another Example of the Porousness of Certain Borders" (Wallace), **Supp. X:** 309

"Yet Do I Marvel" (Cullen), **Supp. IV Part 1:** 165, 169

Yet Other Waters (Farrell), **II:** 29, 38, 39, 40

Yevtushenko, Yevgeny, **Supp. III Part 1:** 268

Yezzi, David, **Supp. XII:** 193

Yizkor Book, **Supp. XVI:**154

Y no se lo trago la tierra (And the Earth Did Not Cover Him) (Rivera), **Supp. XIII:** 216

¡Yo! (Alvarez), **Supp. VII:** 1, 15–17

Yohannan, J. D., **II:** 20

"Yoke, The" (Bidart), **Supp. XV:** 33

Yonge, Charlotte, **II:** 174

"Yonnondio" (Whitman), **Supp. XIII:** 304

Yonnondio: From the Thirties (Olsen), **Supp. XIII:** 295, 295, **Supp. XIII:** 292, 296, 303–304, 305

"Yore" (Nemerov), **III:** 283

"York Beach" (Toomer), **Supp. III Part 2:** 486

Yorke, Dorothy, **Supp. I Part 1:** 258

Yorke, Henry Vincent. *See* Green, Henry

"York Garrison, 1640" (Jewett), **Retro. Supp. II:** 141

Yosemite, The (Muir), **Supp. IX:** 185

"Yosemite Glaciers: Ice Streams of the Great Valley" (Muir), **Supp. IX:** 181

Yoshe Kalb (Singer), **IV:** 2

"You, Andrew Marvell" (MacLeish), **III:** 12–13

"You, Dr. Martin" (Sexton), **Supp. II Part 2:** 673

You, Emperors, and Others: Poems 1957–1960 (Warren), **IV:** 245

"You, Genoese Mariner" (Merwin), **Supp. III Part 1:** 343

"You All Know the Story of the Other Woman" (Sexton), **Supp. II Part 2:** 688

You Are Happy (Atwood), **Supp. XIII:** 34

"You Are Happy" (Atwood), **Supp. XIII:** 34

"You Are in Bear Country" (Kumin), **Supp. IV Part 2:** 453, 455

"You Are Not I" (Bowles), **Supp. IV Part 1:** 87

"You Begin" (Atwood), **Supp. XIII:** 34

"You Bring Out the Mexican in Me" (Cisneros), **Supp. VII:** 71

You Came Along (film), **Supp. IV Part 2:** 524

"You Can Go Home Again" (TallMountain), **Supp. IV Part 1:** 324–325

"You Can Have It" (Levine), **Supp. V:** 188–189

You Can't Go Home Again (Wolfe), **IV:** 450, 451, 454, 456, 460, 462, 468, 469, 470

You Can't Keep a Good Woman Down (Walker), **Supp. III Part 2:** 520, 525, 531

You Can't Take It with You (Kaufman and Hart), **Supp. XIV:**327

"You Can't Tell a Man by the Song He Sings" (Roth), **Supp. III Part 2:** 406

"You Don't Know What Love Is" (Carver), **Supp. III Part 1:** 147

"You Have Left Your Lotus Pods on the Bus" (Bowles), **Supp. IV Part 1:** 91

You Have Seen Their Faces (Caldwell), **I:** 290, 293–294, 295, 304, 309

You Know Me, Al: A Busher's Letters (Lardner), **Supp. XVI:**189

You Know Me Al (comic strip), **II:** 423

You Know Me Al (Lardner), **II:** 26, 415, 419, 422, 431

"You Know What" (Beattie), **Supp. V:** 33

"You Know Who You Are" (Nye), **Supp. XIII:** 275

You Might As Well Live: The Life and Times of Dorothy Parker (Keats), **Supp. IX:** 190

You Must Revise Your Life (Stafford), **Supp. XI:** 312–313, 313–314, 315

"Young" (Sexton), **Supp. II Part 2:** 680

Young, Al, **Supp. X:** 240

Young, Art, **IV:** 436

Young, Brigham, **Supp. IV Part 2:** 603

Young, Edward, **II:** 111; **III:** 415, 503

Young, Gary, **Supp. XV:** 88

Young, Mary, **Supp. XIII:** 236, 238, 239, 240

Young, Philip, **II:** 306; **Retro. Supp. I:** 172

Young Adventure (Benét), **Supp. XI:** 44

"Young America" (Brooks), **Supp. XV:** 298

"Young Child and His Pregnant Mother, A" (Schwartz), **Supp. II Part 2:** 650

Young Christian, The (Abbott), **Supp. I Part 1:** 38

"Young Dr. Gosse" (Chopin), **Supp. I Part 1:** 211, 216

Younger Choir, The (anthology), **Supp. XV:** 294

Younger Quire, The (Untermeyer), **Supp. XV:** 294, 297

"Young Folks, The" (Salinger), **III:** 551

Young Folk's Cyclopaedia of Persons and Places (Champlin), **III:** 577

"Young Goodman Brown" (Hawthorne), **II:** 229; **Retro. Supp. I:** 151–152, 153, 154; **Supp. XI:** 51; **Supp. XIV:**48, 50

Young Harvard: First Poems of Witter Bynner (Bynner), **Supp. XV:** 41

Young Hearts Crying (Yates), **Supp. XI:** 348

"Young Housewife, The" (W. C. Williams), **Retro. Supp. I:** 415

Young Immigrants, The (Lardner), **II:** 426

"Young Lady's Friend, The: Verses, Addressed to a Young Lady, on Her Leaving School" (Rowson), **Supp. XV:** 234

Young Lonigan: A Boyhood in Chicago Streets (Farrell), **II:** 31, 41

Young Manhood of Studs Lonigan, The (Farrell), **II:** 31, 34

Young Men and Fire (Maclean), **Supp. XIV:**221, 231–233

Young People's Pride (Benét), **Supp. XI:** 44

Young Poet's Primer (Brooks), **Supp. III Part 1:** 86

Youngren, J. Alan, **Supp. XVI:**174

"Young Sammy's First Wild Oats" (Santayana), **III:** 607, 615

"Young Sor Juana, The" (Mora), **Supp. XIII:** 218

"Your Death" (Dove), **Supp. IV Part 1:** 250

You're Only Old Once! (Geisel), **Supp. XVI:**111

"You're Ugly, Too" (Moore), **Supp. X:** 171

"Your Face on the Dog's Neck" (Sexton), **Supp. II Part 2:** 686

Your Job in Germany (film, Capra), **Supp. XVI:**102

Your Job in Japan (film, Capra), **Supp. XVI:**102

"Your Life" (Stafford), **Supp. XI:** 329

"Your Mother's Eyes" (Kingsolver), **Supp. VII:** 209

"You Take a Train through a Foreign Country" (Dobyns), **Supp. XIII:** 90

"Youth" (Hughes), **Supp. I Part 1:** 321

"Youth" (Huncke), **Supp. XIV:**145

Youth and Life (Bourne), **I:** 217–222, 232

Youth and the Bright Medusa (Cather), **I:** 322; **Retro. Supp. I:** 14

"Youthful Religious Experiences" (Corso), **Supp. XII:** 117

Youth of Parnassus, and Other Stories, The (L. P. Smith), **Supp. XIV:**336

Youth's First Steps in Geography (Rowson), **Supp. XV:** 243

You Touched Me! (Williams and Windham), **IV:** 382, 385, 387, 390, 392–393

"You Touch Me" (X. J. Kennedy), **Supp. XV:** 166

Yurka, Blanche, **Supp. I Part 1:** 67

Yutang, Adet, **Supp. X:** 291

Yutang, Anor, **Supp. X:** 291

Yutang, Lin, **Supp. X:** 291; **Supp. XVI:**190

Yutang, Mei-mei, **Supp. X:** 291

Yvernelle: A Legend of Feudal France (Norris), **III:** 314

Y & X (Olson), **Supp. II Part 2:** 556

Z

Zabel, Morton Dauwen, **II:** 431; **III:** 194, 215; **Supp. I Part 2:** 721

Zach, Natan, **Supp. XV:** 75, 82, 85

Zagarell, Sandra, **Supp. XV:** 269, 270, 278, 281, 282

Zagarell, Sandra A., **Retro. Supp. II:** 140, 143

"Zagrowsky Tells" (Paley), **Supp. VI:** 229

Zakrzewska, Marie, **Retro. Supp. II:** 146

Zaleski, Jeff, **Supp. XI:** 143

Zall, Paul, **Supp. XIV:**156

Zaltzberg, Charlotte, **Supp. IV Part 1:** 374

"Zambesi and Ranee" (Swenson), **Supp. IV Part 2:** 647

Zamir, Israel, **Retro. Supp. II:** 303, 317

Zamora, Bernice, **Supp. IV Part 2:** 545

Zamoyski, Adam, **Supp. XV:** 257

Zangwill, Israel, **I:** 229

Zanita: A Tale of the Yosemite (Yelverton), **Supp. IX:** 181

Zanuck, Darryl F., **Supp. XI:** 170; **Supp. XII:** 165

Zapata, Emiliano, **Supp. XIII:** 324

"Zapatos" (Boyle), **Supp. VIII:** 15

Zapruder, Matthew, **Supp. XVI:**55

Zarathustra, **III:** 602

Zawacki, Andrew, **Supp. VIII:** 272

"Zaydee" (Levine), **Supp. V:** 186

Zebra-Striped Hearse, The (Macdonald), **Supp. IV Part 2:** 473

Zechariah (biblical book), **IV:** 152

Zeidner, Lisa, **Supp. IV Part 2:** 453

"Zeitl and Rickel" (Singer), **IV:** 20

Zeke and Ned (McMurtry and Ossana), **Supp. V:** 232

Zeke Proctor, Cherokee Outlaw (Conley), **Supp. V:** 232

Zelda: A Biography (Milford), **Supp. IX:** 60

"Zelda and Scott: The Beautiful and Damned" (National Portrait Gallery exhibit), **Supp. IX:** 65

Zelig (film; Allen), **Supp. XV:** 4, 6, 8–9

Zen and the Birds of Appetite (Merton), **Supp. VIII:** 205–206, 208

Zend-Avesta (Fechner), **II:** 358

Zeno, **Retro. Supp. I:** 247

Zero db and Other Stories (Bell), **Supp. X:** 1, 5, 6

"Zeus over Redeye" (Hayden), **Supp. II Part 1:** 380

Zevi, Sabbatai, **IV:** 6

Ziegfeld, Florenz, **II:** 427–428

Zigrosser, Carl, **I:** 226, 228, 231

Zimmerman, Paul D., **Supp. IV Part 2:** 583, 589, 590

Zinberg, Leonard S. See Lacy, Ed

Zinman, Toby Silverman, **Supp. XIII:** 207–208, 209

Zinn, Howard, **Supp. V:** 289

Zinsser, Hans, **I:** 251, 385

Zipes, Jack, **Supp. XIV:**126

"Zipper, The" (L. Michaels), **Supp. XVI:**214

"Zizi's Lament" (Corso), **Supp. XII:** 123

Zodiac, The (Dickey), **Supp. IV Part 1:** 178, 183–184, 185

Zola, Émile, **I:** 211, 411, 474, 500, 502, 518; **II:** 174, 175–176, 182, 194, 275, 276, 281, 282, 319, 325, 337, 338; **III:** 315, 316, 317–318, 319–320, 321, 322, 323, 393, 511, 583; **IV:** 326; **Retro. Supp. I:** 226, 235; **Retro. Supp. II:** 93; **Supp. I Part 1:** 207; **Supp. II Part 1:** 117

Zolotow, Maurice, **III:** 161

"Zone" (Bogan), **Supp. III Part 1:** 60–61

Zone Journals (Wright), **Supp. V:** 332–333, 342–343

"Zooey" (Salinger), **III:** 564–565, 566, 567, 569, 572

"Zoo Revisited" (White), **Supp. I Part 2:** 654

Zoo Story, The (Albee), **I:** 71, 72–74, 75, 77, 84, 93, 94; **III:** 281

Zorach, William, **I:** 260

Zuccotti, Susan, **Supp. XVI:**154

Zuckerman Bound: A Trilogy and Epilogue (Roth), **Supp. III Part 2:** 423

Zuckerman Unbound (Roth), **Retro. Supp. II:** 283; **Supp. III Part 2:** 421–422

Zueblin, Charles, **Supp. I Part 1:** 5

Zuger, Abigail, **Supp. X:** 160

Zukofsky, Celia (Mrs. Louis), **Supp. III Part 2:** 619–621, 623, 625, 626–629, 631

Zukofsky, Louis, **IV:** 415; **Retro. Supp. I:** 422; **Supp. III Part 2:** 619–636; **Supp. IV Part 1:** 154; **Supp. XIV:**279, 282, 285, 286–287

Zukofsky, Paul, **Supp. III Part 2:** 622, 623–626, 627, 628

Zuleika Dobson (Beerbohm), **Supp. I Part 2:** 714

Zverev, Aleksei, **Retro. Supp. I:** 278

Zwinger, Ann, **Supp. X:** 29

Zyda, Joan, **Retro. Supp. II:** 52

A Complete Listing of Authors in
American Writers

Abbey, Edward   Supp. XIII
Acker, Kathy   Supp. XII
Adams, Henry   Vol. I
Addams, Jane   Supp. I
Agee, James   Vol. I
Aiken, Conrad   Vol. I
Albee, Edward   Vol. I
Alcott, Louisa May   Supp. I
Algren, Nelson   Supp. IX
Allen, Woody   Supp. XV
Alvarez, Julia   Supp. VII
Ammons, A. R.   Supp. VII
Anderson, Sherwood   Vol. I
Angelou, Maya   Supp. IV
Ashbery, John   Supp. III
Atwood, Margaret   Supp. XIII
Auchincloss, Louis   Supp. IV
Auden, W. H.   Supp. II
Audubon, John James   Supp. XVI
Auster, Paul   Supp. XII
Baker, Nicholson   Supp. XIII
Baldwin, James   Supp. I
Baldwin, James   Retro. Supp. II
Bambara, Toni Cade   Supp. XI
Banks, Russell   Supp. V
Baraka, Amiri   Supp. II
Barlow, Joel   Supp. II
Barnes, Djuna   Supp. III
Barth, John   Vol. I
Barthelme, Donald   Supp. IV
Barthelme, Frederick   Supp. XI
Bass, Rick   Supp. XVI
Bausch, Richard   Supp. VII
Beattie, Ann   Supp. V
Bell, Madison Smartt   Supp. X
Bellow, Saul   Vol. I
Bellow, Saul   Retro. Supp. II

Benét, Stephen Vincent   Supp. XI
Berry, Wendell   Supp. X
Berryman, John   Vol. I
Bidart, Frank   Supp. XV
Bierce, Ambrose   Vol. I
Bishop, Elizabeth   Supp. I
Bishop, Elizabeth   Retro. Supp. II
Blackmur, R. P.   Supp. II
Bly, Carol   Supp. XVI
Bly, Robert   Supp. IV
Bogan, Louise   Supp. III
Bourne, Randolph   Vol. I
Bowles, Paul   Supp. IV
Boyle, T. C.   Supp. VIII
Bradbury, Ray   Supp. IV
Bradstreet, Anne   Supp. I
Brodsky, Joseph   Supp. VIII
Brooks, Cleanth   Supp. XIV
Brooks, Gwendolyn   Supp. III
Brooks, Van Wyck   Vol. I
Brown, Charles Brockden   Supp. I
Bryant, William Cullen   Supp. I
Buck, Pearl S.   Supp. II
Buechner, Frederick   Supp. XII
Burke, James Lee   Supp. XIV
Burke, Kenneth   Vol. I
Burroughs, William S.   Supp. III
Butler, Octavia   Supp. XIII
Butler, Robert Olen   Supp. XII
Bynner, Witter   Supp. XV
Caldwell, Erskine   Vol. I
Cameron, Peter   Supp. XII
Capote, Truman   Supp. III
Carruth, Hayden   Supp. XVI
Carson, Anne   Supp. XII
Carson, Rachel   Supp. IX
Carver, Raymond   Supp. III

Cather, Willa   Vol. I
Cather, Willa   Retro. Supp. I
Chabon, Michael   Supp. XI
Chandler, Raymond   Supp. IV
Chapman, John Jay   Supp. XIV
Cheever, John   Supp. I
Chesnutt, Charles W.   Supp. XIV
Chopin, Kate   Supp. I
Chopin, Kate   Retro. Supp. II
Cisneros, Sandra   Supp. VII
Clampitt, Amy   Supp. IX
Coleman, Wanda   Supp. XI
Connell, Evan S.   Supp. XIV
Conroy, Frank   Supp. XVI
Cooper, James Fenimore   Vol. I
Coover, Robert   Supp. V
Corso, Gregory   Supp. XII
Cowley, Malcolm   Supp. II
Cozzens, James Gould   Vol. I
Crane, Hart   Vol. I
Crane, Hart   Retro. Supp. II
Crane, Stephen   Vol. I
Creeley, Robert   Supp. IV
Crèvecoeur, Michel-Guillaume Jean de
    Supp. I
Crews, Harry   Supp. XI
Cullen, Countee   Supp. IV
Cummings, E. E.   Vol. I
Cunningham, Michael   Supp. XV
Davis, Rebecca Harding   Supp. XVI
DeLillo, Don   Supp. VI
Dickey, James   Supp. IV
Dickinson, Emily   Vol. I
Dickinson, Emily   Retro. Supp. I
Didion, Joan   Supp. IV
Dillard, Annie   Supp. VI
Dixon, Stephen   Supp. XII
Dobyns, Stephen   Supp. XIII
Doctorow, E. L.   Supp. IV
Doolittle, Hilda (H.D.)   Supp. I
Dos Passos, John   Vol. I
Doty, Mark   Supp. XI
Douglass, Frederick   Supp. III
Dove, Rita   Supp. IV

Dreiser, Theodore   Vol. I
Dreiser, Theodore   Retro. Supp. II
Du Bois, W. E. B.   Supp. II
Dubus, Andre   Supp. VII
Dunbar, Paul Laurence   Supp. II
Dunn, Stephen   Supp. XI
Eberhart, Richard   Vol. I
Edwards, Jonathan   Vol. I
Eliot, T. S.   Vol. I
Eliot, T. S.   Retro. Supp. I
Elkin, Stanley   Supp. VI
Ellison, Ralph   Supp. II
Ellison, Ralph   Retro. Supp. II
Emerson, Ralph Waldo   Vol. II
Epstein, Joseph   Supp. XIV
Epstein, Leslie   Supp. XII
Erdrich, Louise   Supp. IV
Everwine, Peter   Supp. XV
Fante, John   Supp. XI
Farrell, James T.   Vol. II
Faulkner, William   Vol. II
Faulkner, William   Retro. Supp. I
Fiedler, Leslie   Supp. XIII
Fitzgerald, F. Scott   Vol. II
Fitzgerald, F. Scott   Retro. Supp. I
Fitzgerald, Zelda   Supp. IX
Ford, Richard   Supp. V
Francis, Robert   Supp. IX
Franklin, Benjamin   Vol. II
Frederic, Harold   Vol. II
Freneau, Philip   Supp. II
Frost, Carol   Supp. XV
Frost, Robert   Vol. II
Frost, Robert   Retro. Supp. I
Fuller, Margaret   Supp. II
Gaddis, William   Supp. IV
García, Cristina   Supp. XI
Gardner, John   Supp. VI
Garrett, George   Supp. VII
Gass, William   Supp. VI
Geisel, Theodor Seuss   Supp. XVI
Gibbons, Kaye   Supp. X
Gibson, William   Supp. XVI
Gilman, Charlotte Perkins   Supp. XI

Ginsberg, Allen   Supp. II
Gioia, Dana   Supp. XV
Glasgow, Ellen   Vol. II
Glaspell, Susan   Supp. III
Goldbarth, Albert   Supp. XII
Glück, Louise   Supp. V
Gordon, Caroline   Vol. II
Gordon, Mary   Supp. IV
Gunn Allen, Paula   Supp. IV
Gurney, A. R.   Supp. V
Haines, John   Supp. XII
Hammett, Dashiell   Supp. IV
Hansberry, Lorraine   Supp. IV
Hardwick, Elizabeth   Supp. III
Harjo, Joy   Supp. XII
Harrison, Jim   Supp. VIII
Harte, Bret   Supp. II
Hass, Robert   Supp. VI
Hawthorne, Nathaniel   Vol. II
Hawthorne, Nathaniel   Retro. Supp. I
Hay, Sara Henderson   Supp. XIV
Hayden, Robert   Supp. II
Hearon, Shelby   Supp. VIII
Hecht, Anthony   Supp. X
Heller, Joseph   Supp. IV
Hellman, Lillian   Supp. I
Hemingway, Ernest   Vol. II
Hemingway, Ernest   Retro. Supp. I
Henry, O.   Supp. II
Hijuelos, Oscar   Supp. VIII
Himes, Chester Bomar   Supp. XVI
Hoffman, Alice   Supp. X
Hoffman, Eva   Supp. XVI
Hogan, Linda   Supp. IV
Holmes, Oliver Wendell   Supp. I
Howe, Irving   Supp. VI
Howe, Susan   Supp. IV
Howells, William Dean   Vol. II
Hughes, Langston   Supp. I
Hughes, Langston   Retro. Supp. I
Hugo, Richard   Supp. VI
Humphrey, William   Supp. IX
Huncke, Herbert   Supp. XIV
Hurston, Zora Neale   Supp. VI

Irving, John   Supp. VI
Irving, Washington   Vol. II
Isherwood, Christopher   Supp. XIV
Jackson, Shirley   Supp. IX
James, Henry   Vol. II
James, Henry   Retro. Supp. I
James, William   Vol. II
Jarrell, Randall   Vol. II
Jeffers, Robinson   Supp. II
Jewett, Sarah Orne   Vol. II
Jewett, Sarah Orne   Retro. Supp. II
Johnson, Charles   Supp. VI
Jones, James   Supp. XI
Jong, Erica   Supp. V
Justice, Donald   Supp. VII
Karr, Mary   Supp. XI
Kazin, Alfred   Supp. VIII
Kees, Weldon   Supp. XV
Keillor, Garrison   Supp. XVI
Kennedy, William   Supp. VII
Kennedy, X. J.   Supp. XV
Kenyon, Jane   Supp. VII
Kerouac, Jack   Supp. III
Kincaid, Jamaica   Supp. VII
King, Stephen   Supp. V
Kingsolver, Barbara   Supp. VII
Kingston, Maxine Hong   Supp. V
Kinnell, Galway   Supp. III
Knowles, John   Supp. XII
Koch, Kenneth   Supp. XV
Komunyakaa, Yusef   Supp. XIII
Kosinski, Jerzy   Supp. VII
Kumin, Maxine   Supp. IV
Kunitz, Stanley   Supp. III
Kushner, Tony   Supp. IX
LaBastille, Anne   Supp. X
Lacy, Ed   Supp. XV
Lanier, Sidney   Supp. I
Larcom, Lucy   Supp. XIII
Lardner, Ring   Vol. II
Lee, Harper   Supp. VIII
Lee, Li-Young   Supp. XV
Leopold, Aldo   Supp. XIV
Levertov, Denise   Supp. III

Levine, Philip   Supp. V
Levis, Larry   Supp. XI
Lewis, Sinclair   Vol. II
Lindsay, Vachel   Supp. I
Locke, Alain   Supp. XIV
London, Jack   Vol. II
Longfellow, Henry Wadsworth   Vol. II
Longfellow, Henry Wadsworth
    Retro. Supp. II
Loos, Anita   Supp. XVI
Lowell, Amy   Vol. II
Lowell, James Russell   Supp. I
Lowell, Robert   Vol. II
Lowell, Robert   Retro. Supp. II
McCarriston, Linda   Supp. XIV
McCarthy, Cormac   Supp. VIII
McCarthy, Mary   Vol. II
McClatchy, J. D.   Supp. XII
McCourt, Frank   Supp. XII
McCoy, Horace   Supp. XIII
McCullers, Carson   Vol. II
Macdonald, Ross   Supp. IV
McGrath, Thomas   Supp. X
McKay, Claude   Supp. X
Maclean, Norman   Supp. XIV
MacLeish, Archibald   Vol. III
McMillan, Terry   Supp. XIII
McMurty, Larry   Supp. V
McNally, Terrence   Supp. XIII
McPhee, John   Supp. III
Mailer, Norman   Vol. III
Mailer, Norman   Retro. Supp. II
Malamud, Bernard   Supp. I
Mamet, David   Supp. XIV
Marquand, John P.   Vol. III
Marshall, Paule   Supp. XI
Mason, Bobbie Ann   Supp. VIII
Masters, Edgar Lee   Supp. I
Mather, Cotton   Supp. II
Matthews, William   Supp. IX
Matthiessen, Peter   Supp. V
Maxwell, William   Supp. VIII
Melville, Herman   Vol. III
Melville, Herman   Retro. Supp. I

Mencken, H. L.   Vol. III
Merrill, James   Supp. III
Merton, Thomas   Supp. VIII
Merwin, W. S.   Supp. III
Michaels, Leonard   Supp. XVI
Millay, Edna St. Vincent   Vol. III
Miller, Arthur   Vol. III
Miller, Henry   Vol. III
Miller, Sue   Supp. XII
Minot, Susan   Supp. VI
Momaday, N. Scott   Supp. IV
Monette, Paul   Supp. X
Moore, Lorrie   Supp. X
Moore, Marianne   Vol. III
Mora, Pat   Supp. XIII
Morison, Samuel Eliot   Supp. I
Morris, Wright   Vol. III
Morrison, Toni   Supp. III
Mosley, Walter   Supp. XIII
Muir, John   Supp. IX
Mumford, Lewis   Supp. III
Nabokov, Vladimir   Vol. III
Nabokov, Vladimir   Retro. Supp. I
Naylor, Gloria   Supp. VIII
Nemerov, Howard   Vol. III
Neugeboren, Jay   Supp. XVI
Nichols, John   Supp. XIII
Niebuhr, Reinhold   Vol. III
Nin, Anaïs   Supp. X
Norris, Frank   Vol. III
Nye, Naomi Shihab   Supp. XIII
Oates, Joyce Carol   Supp. II
O'Brien, Tim   Supp. V
O'Connor, Flannery   Vol. III
O'Connor, Flannery   Retro. Supp. II
Odets, Clifford   Supp. II
O'Hara, John   Vol. III
Olds, Sharon   Supp. X
Oliver, Mary   Supp. VII
Olsen, Tillie   Supp. XIII
Olson, Charles   Supp. II
O'Neill, Eugene   Vol. III
Ortiz, Simon J.   Supp. IV
Ozick, Cynthia   Supp. V

Paine, Thomas   Supp. I
Paley, Grace   Supp. VI
Parker, Dorothy   Supp. IX
Parkman, Francis   Supp. II
Patchett, Ann   Supp. XII
Percy, Walker   Supp. III
Pinsky, Robert   Supp. VI
Plath, Sylvia   Supp. I
Plath, Sylvia   Retro. Supp. II
Plimpton, George   Supp. XVI
Podhoretz, Norman   Supp. VIII
Poe, Edgar Allan   Vol. III
Poe, Edgar Allan   Retro. Supp. II
Porter, Katherine Anne   Vol. III
Pound, Ezra   Vol. III
Pound, Ezra   Retro. Supp. I
Powers, Richard   Supp. IX
Price, Reynolds   Supp. VI
Prose, Francine   Supp. XVI
Proulx, Annie   Supp. VII
Purdy, James   Supp. VII
Pynchon, Thomas   Supp. II
Rand, Ayn   Supp. IV
Ransom, John Crowe   Vol. III
Rawlings, Marjorie Kinnan   Supp. X
Reed, Ishmael   Supp. X
Reznikoff, Charles   Supp. XIV
Rice, Anne   Supp. VII
Rich, Adrienne   Supp. I
Rich, Adrienne   Retro. Supp. II
Ríos, Alberto Álvaro   Supp. IV
Robbins, Tom   Supp. X
Robinson, Edwin Arlington   Vol. III
Rodriguez, Richard   Supp. XIV
Roethke, Theodore   Vol. III
Roth, Henry   Supp. IX
Roth, Philip   Supp. III
Roth, Philip   Retro. Supp. II
Rowson, Susanna   Supp. XV
Rukeyser, Muriel   Supp. VI
Russo, Richard   Supp. XII
Salinas, Luis Omar   Supp. XIII
Salinger, J. D.   Vol. III
Salter, James   Supp. IX

Sandburg, Carl   Vol. III
Sanders, Scott Russell   Supp. XVI
Santayana, George   Vol. III
Sarton, May   Supp. VIII
Schnackenberg, Gjertrud   Supp. XV
Schwartz, Delmore   Supp. II
Sexton, Anne   Supp. II
Shanley, John Patrick   Supp. XIV
Shapiro, Karl   Supp. II
Shepard, Sam   Supp. III
Shields, Carol   Supp. VII
Silko, Leslie Marmon   Supp. IV
Simic, Charles   Supp. VIII
Simon, Neil   Supp. IV
Simpson, Louis   Supp. IX
Sinclair, Upton   Supp. V
Singer, Isaac Bashevis   Vol. IV
Singer, Isaac Bashevis   Retro. Supp. II
Smiley, Jane   Supp. VI
Smith, Logan Pearsall   Supp. XIV
Smith, William Jay   Supp. XIII
Snodgrass, W. D.   Supp. VI
Snyder, Gary   Supp. VIII
Sobin, Gustaf   Supp. XVI
Sontag, Susan   Supp. III
Southern, Terry   Supp. XI
Stafford, William   Supp. XI
Stegner, Wallace   Supp. IV
Stein, Gertrude   Vol. IV
Steinbeck, John   Vol. IV
Stern, Gerald   Supp. IX
Stevens, Wallace   Vol. IV
Stevens, Wallace   Retro. Supp. I
Stoddard, Elizabeth   Supp. XV
Stone, Robert   Supp. V
Stowe, Harriet Beecher   Supp. I
Strand, Mark   Supp. IV
Styron, William   Vol. IV
Swenson, May   Supp. IV
Tan, Amy   Supp. X
Tate, Allen   Vol. IV
Taylor, Edward   Vol. IV
Taylor, Peter   Supp. V
Theroux, Paul   Supp. VIII

Thoreau, Henry David   Vol. IV
Thurber, James   Supp. I
Toomer, Jean   Supp. IX
Trilling, Lionel   Supp. III
Twain, Mark   Vol. IV
Tyler, Anne   Supp. IV
Untermeyer, Louis   Supp. XV
Updike, John   Vol. IV
Updike, John   Retro. Supp. I
Van Vechten, Carl   Supp. II
Veblen, Thorstein   Supp. I
Vidal, Gore   Supp. IV
Vonnegut, Kurt   Supp. II
Wagoner, David   Supp. IX
Walker, Alice   Supp. III
Wallace, David Foster   Supp. X
Warren, Robert Penn   Vol. IV
Wasserstein, Wendy   Supp. XV
Welty, Eudora   Vol. IV
Welty, Eudora   Retro. Supp. I
West, Nathanael   Vol. IV
West, Nathanael   Retro. Supp. II
Wharton, Edith   Vol. IV
Wharton, Edith   Retro. Supp. I

White, E. B.   Supp. I
Whitman, Walt   Vol. IV
Whitman, Walt   Retro. Supp. I
Whittier, John Greenleaf   Supp. I
Wilbur, Richard   Supp. III
Wideman, John Edgar   Supp. X
Wilder, Thornton   Vol. IV
Williams, Tennessee   Vol. IV
Williams, William Carlos   Vol. IV
Williams, William Carlos   Retro. Supp. I
Wilson, August   Supp. VIII
Wilson, Edmund   Vol. IV
Winters, Yvor   Supp. II
Wolfe, Thomas   Vol. IV
Wolfe, Tom   Supp. III
Wolff, Tobias   Supp. VII
Wright, C. D.   Supp. XV
Wright, Charles   Supp. V
Wright, James   Supp. III
Wright, Richard   Vol. IV
Wylie, Elinor   Supp. I
Yates, Richard   Supp. XI
Zukofsky, Louis   Supp. III